Urban
Education

URBAN EDUCATION

A Comprehensive Guide for Educators, Parents, and Teachers

Edited by
Joe L. Kincheloe
kecia hayes
Karel Rose
Philip M. Anderson

Rowman & Littlefield Education
Lanham, Maryland • Toronto • Plymouth, UK
2007

Published in the United States of America
by Rowman & Littlefield Education
A Division of Rowman & Littlefield Publishers, Inc.
A wholly owned subsidary of The Rowman & Littlefield Publishing Group, Inc.
4501 Forbes Boulevard, Suite 200, Lanham, Maryland 20706
www.rowmaneducation.com

Estover Road
Plymouth PL6 7PY
United Kingdom

British Library Cataloguing in Publication Information Available

Library of Congress Cataloging-in-Publication Data

Urban education : a comprehensive guide for educators, parents, and teachers / edited
by Joe L. Kincheloe . . . [et al.].
     p. cm.
Rev. ed. of: The Praeger handbook of urban education. 2006
Includes bibliographical references and index.
ISBN-13: 978-1-57886-616-8 (pbk.)
ISBN-10: 1-57886-616-2 (pbk. : alk. paper)
1. Education, Urban—United States—Handbooks, manuals, etc. I. Kincheloe, Joe L.
II. Praeger handbook of urban education.

LC5131.P7   2007
370.9173'2—dc22

2007015531

∞™ The paper used in this publication meets the minimum requirements
    of American National Standard for Information Sciences—Permanence of
Paper for Printed Library Materials, ANSI/NISO Z39.48-1992. Manufactured in
the United States of America.

Contents

Preface

Joe L. Kincheloe, kecia hayes, Karel Rose, and Philip M. Anderson

One of the most compelling concerns of our era is the question of what to do about the neglect of our urban schools. Thirty-one percent of U.S. elementary and secondary students go to school in 226 large urban districts. There are nearly 16,000 school districts in the United States and almost one-third of all students attend 1.5 percent of them (Fuhrman, 2002). In the urban context one finds "the emergent U.S. culture." The ways in which urban educators shape urban pedagogy in the coming years is central to the way people in this country reinvent the nation (Anderson and Summerfield, 2004). With this in mind the United States faces an uncertain future, because in the schools in these 226 urban districts, observers encounter a wide diversity of problems and successes.

Urban education is always in crisis—yesterday, today, and certainly in the near future. Teacher shortages force many urban school administrators to scramble madly during the first weeks of school to fill classroom vacancies. Inadequate funds cause cutbacks in essential services in the middle of the school year. In contemporary U.S. society the use of the term "urban" has become in many quarters a signifier for poverty, nonwhite violence, narcotics, bad neighborhoods, an absence of family values, crumbling housing, and failing schools. Over the past several decades, educational researchers have been collecting data confirming the deficits of urban youth while sensationalized media produce images of urban youth running wild and out of control. In this context, many urban school leaders attempt to hide the problems undermining education at their particular schools (NWREL, 1999; Ciani, 2002; Kozleski, 2002). The problems—the crises—besiege many of us who work in urban systems. We have come to realize that without significant structural changes, even increased funding will merely prop up pathological systems and provide little help for students and teachers.

In the eye of the perpetual crisis, teachers keep on teaching and many students keep on learning. Indeed, there are urban teachers who perform good work in a context in which impediments are many and resources are few. Even if resources were provided and equal funding of urban school systems were mandated, there would still be inadequate monies. Poor urban schools are so in need of financial help that equal funding would have to be supplemented by additional infusions of resources just to get to where they might be able to visualize the equality of resources on the distant horizon. Reform efforts proliferate in this context. Overwhelmed by these disparities and the crisis atmosphere surrounding them, urban policy makers have sought to replace huge, bureaucratic systems overseen by boards of education with new smaller, locally operated organizations.

There is nothing simple about urban education. *Urban Education: A Comprehensive Guide for Educators, Parents, and Teachers* highlights the interaction between the challenges and opportunities found within the diverse educational spaces of our urban contexts. Throughout the handbook this dialectic will assert itself in every topic addressed. Indeed, the central watchword of this work is *complexity*. Just when we think that we've made a definitive statement about the uniqueness of the category, up pops a contradiction that subverts our confident pronouncement. What passes as urban education involves a wide range of circumstances (Willard-Holt, 2000). Keeping in mind the complexity and contradictions of urban education, the handbook asks whether there are unique features of urban education. After careful study of the question we believe that the following characteristics apply:

- Schools operate in areas with high population density.
- Schools are bigger and school districts serve more students.
- Schools function in areas marked by profound economic disparity.
- Urban areas and urban schools have a higher rate of ethnic, racial, and religious diversity.
- Urban schools experience factionalized infighting on school boards over issues concerning resources and influence.
- Urban school systems are undermined by ineffective business operations.
- Poor urban students are more likely to experience health problems.
- Urban schools experience higher student, teacher, and administrator mobility.
- Urban schools serve higher immigrant populations.
- Urban schools are characterized by linguistic diversity.
- Urban schools experience unique transportation problems.

- Teachers working in poor urban schools are less likely to live in the communities neighboring the schools than are teachers in suburban and rural systems.

With these rationales in mind, the editors and authors of *Urban Education* have created a diverse body of work that speaks directly to the needs of urban educators and the teacher-educators who teach them. Although attempting to develop a vision of what urban education can become, we are profoundly concerned with providing material that urban educators can use in their professional lives. We have organized this book into thematic sections. In the section on Context, we highlight the need for a rigorous, inter-/multidisciplinary understanding of urban education that draws on several disciplines and transdisciplines, including history, cognitive studies, sociology, anthropology, cultural studies, philosophy, political science, economics, and geography to help teachers and educators understand the complex space in which urban education takes place. In this way teachers and educators gain unique and powerful insights into research on educational policy, pedagogy, and the lives of children living in densely populated urban settings. Understanding the effects of such forces, however, must not lapse into a deterministic view of how such contextual forces inexorably shape the schooling process and student performance. Understanding the impact of political and economic factors and the cultural mismatches between home and school culture does not mean students, teachers, and parents *cannot* overcome these contextual impediments.

The sections on Race and Ethnicity, Power, and Language address the many ways in which the different social constructions of culture, and the demonstrations of those social constructions, reflect hierarchical power distinctions and privileges that shape an individual's position within the society. "In an ideal world, every child born would have the same opportunity to realize his or her potential. In the real world, this is not the case. Socially constructed differences in race, class, and gender turn out to be very costly for some and very profitable for others. . . . They impact directly on the life chances of everyone, and they reflect and perpetuate the cycle of racism, sexism, and class inequality that constitutes both their cause and their effect" (Rothenberg in *Race, Class, and Gender in the United States*, p. 188). As the primary social institution responsible for the socialization of youth into the society, schools rest at the dynamic intersection of race, ethnicity, class, and gender. Essentially, schools become the sites where, on one end of the spectrum, we reproduce the hegemonic tendencies inherent in our socially constructed notions of race, ethnicity, class, and gender. On the other end of the spectrum, we engage in acts of criticality to challenge and reconstruct these conceptualizations to create new relations of power within the web of reality. In these sections, we are especially interested in the impact of the current power blocs on children and adults and their efforts to enter into the processes of teaching and learning. Contributors also study the means by which the intersections of race, ethnicity, class, and gender within school systems (i.e., public schools, independent schools, and alternative schools including charter schools) can be challenged and altered to provide a more egalitarian experience of education for children and adults.

In the section on Social Justice, we challenge teachers and educational leaders to confront their relationship with some long-term historical trends rarely discussed in the contemporary public conversation and in urban teacher education. Indeed, everyone in the contemporary United States is shaped by this knowledge in some way, whether they are conscious of it or not. We cannot erase the fact that European colonialism dominated the world from the late fifteenth century until the twentieth century, when it mutated into a neocolonialism grounded on economic and cultural dynamics led primarily by the United States. The knowledges of teacher education coming from both colleges of education and colleges of liberal arts and sciences are too often based on an acceptance of the status quo in urban education. When teacher education and schools fall into this monological trap, they are telling urban students from diverse backgrounds that their knowledges, values, and ways of living are not important. Schools are here to provide them with the correct ways of being—the proper ways of seeing that come from the dominant white upper-middle-class culture. Such insights force us to rethink knowledge production, curriculum development, and the core of urban educational practice. In this context we begin to see urban education not as a means of socially controlling the poor and nonwhite but as a means of liberating and cultivating the intellect while providing the tools for socioeconomic mobility. A critical urban pedagogy studies the context of education for the purpose of enhancing human agency—the capacity to act in transformative ways—not to minimize it.

The focus of the section on Teaching and Pedagogy is on the many different ways in which teachers experience the urban classroom. Too often these teachers leave the profession without ever learning diverse ways of working with and motivating urban students. As we know, many times these young urban teachers come from socioeconomic locales very different than those of their lower socioeconomic class students. These are the teachers who are sometimes the most vulnerable to the social representations of urban poverty and poor urban students. Living lives so culturally distant from their students, these teachers and teacher-education students need to understand both the communities in which poor urban students live and the nature of their daily lives. They need to have field experiences during their teacher education in urban schools so they won't experience culture shock when they assume teaching positions. These are also teachers and teacher-education students who—moving to the other end of the spectrum—sometimes develop an unhealthy desire to "save" or "rescue" poor Latino/-a or African-American students. In this mode such teachers see the cultural capital of white middle-class lifestyles as the antidote to "urban-ness." These rescuers are missionaries who bring salvation through "proper ways of being."

In the section on Research, our goal is to highlight the scholarly work that grants insight into working in the everyday world of urban schools and other educational locales. Producing literature and research on urban education in the contemporary sociopolitical climate is difficult in that it must address the dominant representations of the urban poor and poor urban students as "the undeserving poor" rather than the "underserved poor." In the contemporary climate of the No Child Left Behind act, the methodological influence on educational research has been one of socially decontextualized cause-effect and of a hypothetical-deductive system of reasoning. Our goal is to push the margins of this constrictive mode of research conceptualization such that we can begin to understand all of the nuances of a child's experiences in the urban classroom. This means that we must embrace notions of the teacher-researcher and the student-researcher in order to generate research that is representative and truly informative.

Authors who contributed to the section on Aesthetics understand that the urban environment provides a remarkable opportunity for the educator to explore philosophic, pedagogic, and aesthetic principles. Our cities are characterized by people of increasing diversity, and educators as social architects can help make it possible for urban areas to become rich, caring, beautiful places to work and live. We recognize that young people within these urban centers have been significantly affected by such forces and often find no sanctioned spaces in which to voice reactions to the ways they experience urban life. Consequently, urban youth have constructed aesthetic forms within youth culture that facilitate expression of their lived experiences. However, there is a disconnection between the expression constructed by youth and the expression valued and legitimated by schools. In the Aesthetics section, we explore how students and teachers can feel greater empowerment in the urban environment through an appreciation of its rich aesthetic opportunities for learning. The aesthetic experience, whether it happens on the streets, in the schools, or in the cultural institutions of the city, can help learners of all ages recognize that cities have long been the centers of world culture.

In the section on Policy, we acknowledge that the current framework of our educational system reinforces the idea that because of asymmetrical representation, urban educational policy rarely reflects the interests and needs of its clients. Politicians are becoming more unilaterally responsible for schooling that changes the nature, rather than the reality, of the politicization of schools. With such unilateralism, those who are routinely engaged with the experiences of schooling do not have any control over their experiences. Educational bureaucracies have historically operated to diminish the self-direction of participants in the system. Authors writing in this domain assess the extent to which the constituent groups of students, parents, and educators gain and lose power within new, but not necessarily different, political dynamics. We also explore the extent to which urban educators can create a politically restructured system in which all clients, especially new social actors seeking access to the discourse, can participate. Such actions position participants in ways that release them from the control of the bureaucracies that shape the policy frameworks of schooling and the discourses of reform according to their own limited understandings and interests.

Susan Fuhrman (2002) argues that in the contemporary era there are endless attempts at urban school reform with little improvement to show for the efforts. She is correct, and one of the most important reasons for these failures at reform involves the lack of a sense of educational purpose. Without this key ingredient most educational reforms amount to little more than taking an aspirin to ease the pain of a kidney stone. The urban education promoted herein demands a fundamental rethinking, a deep reconceptualization of what human beings are capable of achieving—the role of the social, cultural, and political in shaping human identity, the relationship between community and schooling, and ways that power operates to create purposes for schooling that are not necessarily in the best interests of the children who attend them.

Introduction: The Power of Hope in the Trenches

Joe L. Kincheloe, kecia hayes, Karel Rose, and Philip M. Anderson

Karel Rose writes:

The first day of school in September is the best time to be driving through Brooklyn. Fathers, mothers and grandparents clutch the hands of their young treasures as they walk them to what each child hopes will be the best day of his or her life. All parents send to school the best they have and most share their children's great expectations. In an urban area, children of all races and ethnicities proudly stride toward the schoolhouse: their braided pigtails with colorful ribbons, their shiny backpacks, and their bright socks, a testimony to their optimism. Sometimes, their dreams are realized; too often, urban schools fail these children and their teachers.

The New Yorker March 7, 2005, cover: A naked and frightened Adam and Eve are running across the Brooklyn Bridge fleeing New York City. We see the pointed finger of God throwing them out of New York City, the unaffordable Eden. Where will they go? Many of our cities have become increasingly unaffordable—hospitable only to those with power and means. As a result, any urban schools bedeviled by bureaucratic demands too often replicate this dismissal of poor populations. Despite high-sounding rhetoric and claims of higher test scores, the disregard for public schooling in many urban areas is apparent. Although there is real reason for gloom, the contributors to this handbook speak eloquently and hold out enormous hope that community workers, parents, artists, and educators are finding new ways to change the ethos of urban schooling. Our writers' suggestions and experiences are multifaceted and their optimism is not grounded in a facile naïveté that raises expectations disconnected from reality. All are practitioners and they write about the reality of their experiences. Imelda Castañeda-Emenaker and Lionel Brown address the complexities of city living by suggesting six different types of alternative education. Hollyce C. Giles directs her attention to approaches to community organizing as a means for reforming the schools. The richness of community cultures is echoed by Korina M. Jocson as not only a source of knowledge but also as a teaching resource. Gene Díaz describes teachers as urban gypsies who travel among us leaving their creative work as a gift to fractured and fragile communities. In their distinctive styles, each author highlights liberatory educational practices that foster the personal and social powers of students and teachers in urban areas. The arts are the vehicle of choice for many of our writers.

Each semester, I begin my philosophy of education class by asking the students to provide adjectives that describe their notions of "a good education." Here are some of the words that I get: *inspiring, joyful, bottomless, challenging, messy, hopeful, fun, concerned, multifaceted, complex, compelling, caring passionate, liberating.* I know that because these students in my class are future teachers, this is the kind of education they want to provide for their students. We continue the exercise and I ask them about their notions of "a good city." The words they offer are *grand, sophisticated, nurturing, protective, multiethnic, noisy, challenging, center of civilization, tempestuous, changing, exciting, multifaceted, available, alive, communal.*

I am continually struck by the parallels between a good education and a good city. My students' voices and the voices in this book continually suggest that cities can contribute in very positive ways to the lives of teachers as well as students. For those of us who are teacher-educators, the responsibility is to assist our students to ask their own questions about the relationship between urban education and urban life. City teachers face the same dilemmas as their students. Neither geography nor personal and professional lives remain discrete entities.

THE IMAGINATION TO BUILD A MULTICULTURAL DEMOCRACY

Many urban teachers live in the city where they teach and their everyday life pulsates with urban rhythms. The chapters in this handbook suggest in many ways that teachers need not only to understand but also to transform for their students those responsibilities and strategies that are specific to the urban scene. The assumptions of many of our writers reflect August Heckscher's concept that democracy is the pursuit of public happiness as

well as John Dewey's perspective that the classroom is the microcosm of the world and schools are where students learn the meaning of democracy.

What follows are some of our writers' assumptions for teachers and students about urban life and urban education:

- Every voice is worthwhile.
- Each voice needs to be supported by other voices in order to be heard.
- Schools and cities should serve concepts of equality and build a multicultural democracy.
- Schools and cities are in a constant state of flux and have renaissances because of the people who inhabit them.
- Private and public responsibility is set in motion by citizens trained and committed to taking ownership of their schools and cities.
- Long-range planning is essential for the health of schools and cities.
- Muses are all over the city, but not all of them are at black tie affairs.
- Muses are all over the schools and many of them are the students.
- Teachers are invaluable community resources and support systems.
- Communities and neighborhoods are critical to the success of urban schools.

TOWARD THE EMPOWERMENT OF IMAGINATION

We begin with an epistemology that honors the imagination. Immanuel Kant tells us that imagination is the catalyst for the intellect. Imagine a city and school that are nurturing, safe, economically viable, respectful of diversity, and are providers of appropriate social services. There is pleasing architecture all around, open spaces, appropriate places for silence and conversation, and many opportunities for cultural events. There are celebrations, festivals, and pageants honoring different cultures. Beauty abounds in the eyes of the beholder and there is an ethic that dignifies individual imagination. Therefore, the teachers, students, and civic leaders dare to imagine a better world and are prepared to transform and bring new forms, new ideas, and new ways of being into existence. Artful teachers are high functioning transformers. With the perspective that a school, a community, and a city are all laboratories, living museums, and generative studios, teachers can link their efforts and provide direction as to how one transforms.

URBAN EDUCATION AND THE ARTS

I chose to solicit and edit chapters to *Urban Education: A Comprehensive Guide for Educators, Parents, and Teachers* on the arts. This domain represents to me the hope in the trenches that all of the editors wished to convey in this undertaking. The teaching behaviors of those who wrote chapters about the arts in urban education are grounded in the larger concepts that they want their readers to take seriously. They may share similar beliefs but develop them quite differently. What follows are some of the very exciting pedagogical perspectives embedded in the authors' chapters:

- Make sense of the visual languages in the culture (the architecture, the imaginative appeals, the power thrusts, the diversity, the consumerism).
- Sift through the cacophony of information and try to understand its intentionality.
- Theorize from all the messages and evolve some workable concepts.
- Make the familiar strange by finding similarities in differences.
- Cautiously embrace, but do embrace, the new.
- Extend boundaries by tearing down fences and unpacking your suitcase.
- Recognize that teaching and learning, like life and art, are improvisational.
- Plug into interest, energy, and passion.

When we honor urban schools, urban society, people of all colors and backgrounds, art in museums and on apartment house walls, immigrants and citizens, children and adults, differing political and religious perspectives, we begin to acknowledge the new reality of our flat world and the importance of a holistic view. Holistic education, Ron Miller (1997) tells us, is not merely a romantic, New Age fantasy but a coherent and significant, theoretical perspective. At a time of crisis in our cities and schools, Jane Jacobs (2004)—not a romantic by any definition but a highly respected and influential gadfly who tackles the plight of U.S. cities with imagination and thoughtfulness—looks to higher education and self-policing by the learned professions as the great hope against racism and the growing gap between rich and poor. As educators, we are charged with the responsibility of finding the pedagogy and theories that will lift the gloom. Despite what this writer or those of us involved with this project see as enlightened views on urban issues, the most salient perspective is to recognize that education is all about the self-exploration of endless possibilities girded by hope, celebration, and the belief that educators and schooling make a difference.

I am probably older than most of the contributors to this handbook, but I cherish and try to sustain that part of me that is continually surprised, open, and ready to change. Authentic engagement with students and colleagues and frequent encounters with the imaginations of others facilitates my efforts. Philosophically, urban education presents an enormous challenge to our imaginations and suggests that we have a moral responsibility not only to transform but also to be hopeful about the possibility for transformation. Hope becomes an ethic and a guide for behavior.

Philip M. Anderson writes:

The city is the teacher of the man. (Simonides c. 556–468 BC)

Urban education is about possibilities. The city is complex, vibrant—full of people and events. In the city lie the treasures of the civilization. The city is an archeological record of the past and the place where the future is being shaped. If a person is to be educated, he or she needs to make a trip to town.

The myth of the people of the United States has always been centered on the small town and people of the frontier. The last generation of citizens who began the movement back into the center of cities were called "urban pioneers." Those myths were dealt with handily by Sinclair Lewis in his novels *Main Street* and *Babbitt* in the 1920s, but the rural myth returns regularly as an "alternative" to the city. The rural is natural, the city is artificial (or even artifice), goes the story. But, cities, of course, are just as "natural" as rural living, since both are human constructions. And, there is also nature in the middle of the city, whether contained in arboretums, laid out in parks, or maintained as a legacy by all manner of wild creatures.

James Bryant Conant tried to unravel the rural myth when he consolidated high schools in the 1960s; the rural model was not up to the demands of post-World War II life, he argued quite persuasively. Today we are trying to deconsolidate the high schools and make them into "small schools," which are really like the old-time rural schools. It all seems like nostalgia for a time that, even if it ever existed, is now gone.

It might be worth a moment to dispel the rural myth further. The United States was essentially urban by the 1870s, and by 1905 the superintendent of the Winnebago County schools in northern Illinois was publishing a book on the need to focus on the educational needs of the remaining rural populations. Most of the proposals in the book are about consolidation of the existing schools and more emphasis on the practical and scientific that will be possible in the larger, expanded mission schools. The consolidation was about modernization, not just efficiency. The older local schools were basic education mills, whereas the new schools would serve the new scientific needs of the citizen. Conant had to have read this book.

Returning to the Simonides quotation from the ancient word, the city has always been the center of human culture. And we are more urban as a culture than we have ever been. If education in the postmodern sense is to be about identity construction, then education needs to draw on the resources of the urban way of living. The urban way of living requires negotiation, tolerance, communication, and a host of other skills not needed by hermits. None of these virtues are antithetical to the goals of a humanistic education in any of the great state universities situated in their rural settings. (Although it must be noted that the No. 1 major in those rural settings is business administration.)

Increasingly, the urban landscape is populated with artists and cultural workers who are interested in educational matters. The great museums themselves have invested in education divisions and hired specialists in curriculum and pedagogy. Although the museums were originally constructed with an educational mission, that is, they were sources of knowledge and experience otherwise unavailable in time or place, the new museum sees that work as a more formal part of its mission. The museum lecture is still a mainstay of these institutions' work, but now there are programs for children and outreach to the schools themselves. Even teacher preparation is now part of the mission of these cultural institutions.

Some critics complain that the richness of the artistic and cultural resources in some urban areas is used as an excuse to limit art education, for example, in the public schools. It seems that the schools are richer for the contact with the museums and arts organizations. But, clearly, the museums cannot serve all the children in large urban areas and the schools must work in concert with the resources in the community. It is this connection between the schools and the other cultural institutions in the city that provides some of the richest opportunity.

Cultural institutions and organizations in the city are not limited to museums, of course. There are theaters, groups of writers, musicians, and a wide and fascinating array of performers and performances within the city's cultural walls. Children and adolescents (as well as the adults they become) are inundated with possibilities for cultural experience and educational opportunities. The life outside of school (and the life outside of school sanctioned by the school) is a complex and rich environment that refines the idea of formal schooling itself.

However, seeing the potential in the urban educational landscape is to invite complexity. The standardization and mechanization moment that has dogged urban schooling for the past century or so still has adherents. The current chancellor of the largest urban school district in the United States appears to have as his goal the reduction of the curriculum, the standardization of student performance, and supervision of every move of the teacher in the classroom. The city outside the school looks nothing like that—how is this model of school preparing these students for "life" in the city? The vision here is from Terry Gilliam's film *Brazil*—those who wish to control the city end up controlling the city dwellers. The city is a living organism (a natural image, to be sure) and cannot grow by constant pruning.

Diversity is also the mark of the city. The city is a rich bazaar that needs to be explored and sampled. There are many true stories of students on Long Island who have never been to Manhattan; there are also true stories of kids from Brooklyn who have never been to Manhattan. How could responsible school authorities let that happen? Shouldn't the cultural institutions of the great cities be "required" as much as mathematics and school lunch?

In the diversity of the city one finds all the possibilities that one's local community denies. As anyone who has grown up in a homogeneous community knows, experience outside of the community tends to promote tolerance as well as reflection. Growing up in a heterogeneous community *requires* tolerance and reflection. The urban school is a social experiment necessary to the global community in which we now find ourselves. The urban way of life is the way to international communication and community.

The most common complaint about urban education, and urbanism in general, is that it is "too big." But the scale of urban life is part of its magic: the scale of buildings, the diversity of the population, the richness of opportunity, all made possible by the size of the city. There is literally something for everyone.

And yet, the myth of the little red schoolhouse is still invoked. "Could we just make schools smaller" to solve the "crisis" of urban education? The cities get bigger, the buildings grow larger, budgets and taxes increase, but the "solution" to urban schooling's problems is "smallness." The smallness of schools is just another way of recreating localness, an attempt to resist the diversifying demands of urban life. One sometimes thinks of the hilltop towns in Italy whose citizens built the defensive towers for family homes—the skyscrapers in the city can serve the same purpose.

The "crisis" in urban education that everyone appears to be trying to solve is its heterogeneity—the situation looks more and more like a simple resistance to tolerance and diversity. Big schools mean that the population of the school will be more diverse. A complex curriculum means that diversity and complexity will be encouraged, a situation that works against tight control (of both money and ideology). The richness of the city is only for the rich when the schools offer only the most meager of curricula.

If the city is the teacher, then we really need to look to the city for answers to our educational questions. The urban curriculum needs to be urban in direction and shaped by the tenets of urbanism. Dreaming about olive gardens and teaching about the "natural" virtues isn't going to cut it. The city is big—our ideas about education ought to be big. The world will not get smaller in this century—the problems of human life will not get any simpler. The success of the city is the success of human life. The schools are necessary to that urban life and must construct themselves as part of that urban life.

Joe L. Kincheloe writes:

As my coeditors Karel Rose and Philip M. Anderson make crystal clear in their pieces in this Introduction, the city is complex and full of possibilities. And in that complexity and possibility resides great hope. Hope in the trenches is the central theme of *Urban Education.* And as I will argue in the remainder of this Introduction, the hope articulated by Karel and Phil is not a blind hope but an informed, mature hope grounded on a stark understanding of the vicious fight ahead. In the following pages I want to lay out a vision of urban education replete with all of the obstacles that operate to subvert, even mock, such a socioeducational dream. Despite the images that circulate through our collective consciousness in the twenty-first century, the dream is alive. It is nurtured and sustained on a daily basis by an amazing corps of urban teachers who fight—despite the lack of respect and material reward—to make the vision a reality.

DOWN AND DIRTY: MAKING SURE WE KNOW WHAT WE'RE GETTING INTO

A quick picture of urban education from far above helps us understand what we're up against. We see an urban school district in need of thousands of faculty members encircled by suburbs and villages in which every teaching position draws hundreds of applications. Martin Haberman (2002) maintains that based on his research,

about three of every twenty new teachers are willing to apply to urban districts. Of this group, about only one in ten, he concludes, has the disposition to stay in urban education long enough to become good city teachers. Obviously, most people interested in a career in education are not drawn to the conditions we are addressing in this book. There are many reasons, of course, for such choices. One explanation involves the difficulty many find in working with individuals who are culturally different from them. Because of the diversity of urban education, teachers who come from white middle- and upper-middle class backgrounds often find themselves culturally displaced by contact with very poor, nonwhite people who speak English as a second or third language. Given the representations of such people in the media and other knowledge sources over the last few decades, some teachers may experience fear in such circumstances.

A critical urban pedagogy encourages teachers to analyze such fear and the ways that such representations of "otherness" may have shaped their vision of themselves and the world. The perpetuation of such fear plays a powerful role in oppressing poor and nonwhite urban dwellers while ensuring that little is done to help improve their circumstances. In addition to this socially constructed fear of difference, many teachers are unwilling to put up with the divergent ways teachers are treated in more upscale suburban as opposed to poor urban schools. In many—but certainly not all—well-to-do schools teachers are treated more like professionals with qualifications and perspectives on the accomplishment of the task at hand. In many poor urban schools—certainly not all—teachers are treated as temporary bureaucratic functionaries as they enter the building for the first time. After a few hours of fingerprinting and other forms of systemic processing, a first-year teacher hardly possesses the heady confidence that she is off to a happy start on her life's professional journey.

This depersonalizing and deprofessionalizing dimension of urban education catalyzed the teacher union movements. To insulate urban teachers from a barrage of indignities, teacher unions organized to regulate the workplace. Union organizers recognized that the only way that urban teachers were treated as professionals is that they were paid for their labor. Unlike doctors, lawyers, architects, journalists, and other professionals, teachers did not devise the goals and objectives of their practice, the subject matter of their profession, the number of clients (students) with whom they would work, the nature and organization of the schools in which they would operate, or the terms of their own and their students' evaluation. The advent of teacher unions has not solved these issues, however. Indeed, with legislation such as No Child Left Behind, the twenty-first century is rechallenging teacher professionalism.

In the last half of the first decade of the twenty-first century, teachers in all locales—urban teachers, especially—are losing many professional prerogatives. In the contemporary era, one is hard-pressed to walk into an urban school without seeing specific curriculum packages and methods forced upon teachers. Chillingly, one routinely watches teachers teach from scripted lessons. No pretense of teacher professionalism is offered in these circumstances. If professionalism has to do with the possession of special expertise, an ability to conduct research and produce relevant knowledge about professional practice, and control the terms of one's labor, then urban teachers too often work in a deprofessionalized educational cosmos. Our pedagogy challenges this scourge of deprofessionalization and, in the process, promotes and respects teachers who can critically analyze the multiple contexts in which they operate, work for democratic action, and challenge the unjust realities that face urban students and urban communities (Kincheloe, 1995; Weiner, 1999; Carvan, Nolen, & Yinger, 2002; Haberman, 2002).

FUNDAMENTAL PREMISES OF A CRITICAL URBAN PEDAGOGY

Our concept of urban teaching finds its philosophical foundation in the notions of empowered, professionalized teachers working to cultivate the intellect and enhance the socioeconomic mobility of marginalized urban students. Teachers in a critical urban pedagogy conduct research into social and educational problems. They design curricula around multiple macro-knowledges of education and the contexts in which they operate and the micro-situations in the communities and schools in which their students find themselves. Such teachers build coalitions of scholars in urban education and other related areas, teachers, parents, students, community members, and sociopolitical organizations. In this context teachers who enact a transformative urban pedagogy are serious students of education who apply their insights to promote new educational psychologies and learning theories, new cultural studies of urban communities and the young people who live in them, and subjugated knowledges derived from organic intellectuals who live and operate in urban neighborhoods. Such teachers are motivated by the power of ideas to reshape the world in which they operate, the notion that human beings can become far more than they presently are, and the belief that ultimately the fate of humanity is related to these ideas.

DEVELOPING A SENSE OF PURPOSE

Advocates of a critical urban pedagogy maintain that they must use these fundamental premises to build a clear, pragmatic, and transformative sense of purpose. What should we be attempting to accomplish in urban education? As the cities deteriorated in the middle of the twentieth century, urban schools lost their sense of direction. With few shared values and little discussion of larger goals, urban educators retreated to their private hells. In the midst of such fragmentation, deliberation about the intellectual, social, and political goals of urban education never took place. School reforms came and went without ever answering the questions:

- What are the intellectual goals of urban education—what does it mean to be an educated person?
- What are the social goals of urban education—what social changes in the domains of race, class, language, and power need to take place so that urban education can be improved?
- What are the political goals of urban education—how do urban educators and their allies build coalitions that are strong enough to circumvent the obstacles to systematic reform in city schools?

Advocates of this contextualized, multidimensional urban pedagogy must develop ways of answering these questions that help school leaders, community members, teachers, parents, and students articulate a powerful multilogical (informed by numerous perspectives and concerns) conception of urban school purpose (Bamburg, 1994; Peterson, 1994; Hill & Celio, 1998; MDRC, 2002). In the spirit of valuing the power of different perspectives, therefore, critical teachers not only seek new knowledges but also search for ways of seeing that provide new vantage points on a particular phenomenon. As opposed to the work of many mainstream urban educators, a critical urban pedagogy values the voices of the subjugated and marginalized that are too often banished from the conversation about the goals of urban education. Thus, the idea of subjugated knowledge is central to our teaching. With this idea in mind, critical urban educators do not assume that experts in the disciplines possess the final word on a domain of study.

Sometimes what such experts report needs to be reanalyzed in light of the insights of those operating outside the framework of dominant power. As a scholar of education I have often observed how some of the most compelling insights concerning pedagogy come from those individuals living and operating outside the boundaries of educational scholarship. Sometimes such individuals are not formal scholars at all but individuals who have suffered at the hands of educational institutions. Such experiences provided them a vantage point and set of experiences profoundly different from those of more privileged scholars. This phenomenon is not unique to the study of urban education but can be viewed in a variety of domains (O'Sullivan, 1999; Pickering, 1999; Thayer-Bacon, 2000, 2003; Malewski, 2001).

Because of the absurdly high turnover rate in urban school leadership, this critical pedagogical effort to use diverse stakeholder insights to help build visionary, long-term coalitions takes on profound importance. As the parade of urban school leaders passes through designed office spaces, the plans that Chancellor Levy promoted were discarded when Chancellor Klein took the reins of the city's schools. When Chancellor Klein leaves the post the erasure of everything past will begin again. In such situations little is learned, few strides are made to improve urban schools, and learning communities have the longevity of a mayfly. A distributed community of learners and policy makers drawing upon and producing a wide variety of perspectives is the only alternative to these periodic purges of the reigning urban education politburo. Critical communities of diverse stakeholders understand that there are no shortcuts to the reform of urban education. Permanent but flexible reform strategies must be devised, which are supported by a wide range of groups and individuals. Efforts to reform urban education cannot go back to the beginning each time a new regime enters the superintendent's office.

Armed with their literacy of power—with its understanding of the insidious ways dominant power blocs operate to promote the interests of the privileged, their commitment to democratic and socially just goals, and the worth of investing social resources to cultivate the intellect of urban students—proponents of a critical pedagogy push ahead. They have good times—they have bad times. They get depressed—they get over it. Such educators know they have to work hard every day with the understanding that all improvements in urban education require long-term efforts. Not only do they require continuing labor but such reforms also necessitate a form of restructuring that gets beyond merely rearranging the furniture of urban education.

Too many of the reforms of the last decade have done little more than create new regulations that serve to weaken schools. Overwhelmed by trivial rules, school administrators and teachers lose their sense of control over what happens to students at school. This orgy of micromanagement has disempowered educators as it fragments the curriculum and strips it of meaning. One dimension of education becomes so isolated from others that individuals operating in different domains of education find it difficult to talk to one another. Curriculum development, fiscal policy, building maintenance, teacher education, community relations, and personnel policies exist in separate universes. Without a larger sense of intellectual, social, and political purpose urban education becomes a latter-day Tower of Babel where no one understands anyone else (Bamburg, 1994; Hill & Celio, 1998; Fuhrman, 2002).

CONSTRUCTING A VISION: SELF AND SOCIAL TRANSFORMATION

To begin, a critical urban pedagogy works to make sure that schools in the poorest and most marginalized urban communities operate simply to *not* retard the intellectual growth of their students. It may seem silly to make such an assertion, but I believe that a detailed, experiential knowledge of many urban schools in poor communities—despite the efforts of brave, talented, and committed educators—often works to impede students' personal and cognitive development. This pedagogy of poverty (Haberman, 2004) or insidious deficitism is supported by the structures we have previously analyzed. A poverty-stricken pedagogy has a familiar look and smell no matter where we encounter it. As a student who attended poor schools in rural southern Appalachia, I watched a hillbilly version of it operate throughout my early life. In the poverty curriculum, teaching is routinely separated from connection to the lived world.

Ritual acts are established that emphasize form and compliance over substance. Here information is distributed for later recitation, the ability to follow directions (orders) takes precedence over making meaning, and convergent, one-right-answer questions on tests take on an exaggerated importance. Students in such a pedagogy become unbearably bored, as they see little connection between the pedagogy of poverty and their immediate daily concerns—not to mention the improvement of their lives. They want to scream and flail their arms in the air just to break the deadening monotony of it all. Such students are insulted by the dumbed-down content they are expected to know and spit back on tests. Such procedures position them as dolts who are biologically incapable of engaging with mature information and the cognitive sophistication it demands (Kincheloe, Steinberg, & Gresson, 1996).

Our understanding of the urban pedagogy of poverty confronts us head-on with the larger philosophical question: What are schools in contemporary society attempting to do—train "compliant workers" or educate discerning, empowered citizens?

In my observations of far too many high-poverty urban schools, I conclude the answer to this question has little to do with graduating smart citizens for a democratic society. In this context our conception of urban teaching and learning is very clear about its intentions. A democratic society demands empowered citizens who can work to make sure it does not continue to subvert egalitarian and democratic principles. In an era unfriendly to both political and economic notions of democracy, the future of our political institutions depends on the success of this venture. In addition it is necessary for individual students to develop through their schooling the power, confidence, creativity, and deportment to forge their own way in the cosmos. This is why our urban pedagogy is based on a commitment to social and personal transformation.

Such a commitment means that a critical form of urban education embraces a new vision of what it means to be an educated person. In a context where marginalization by race, class, gender, or religion is the norm, an educated person understands that things must change, that he or she must comprehend and work to overcome the impediments to personal and social progress. Like their teachers, marginalized students must join with larger groups that can help make these dreams realities. Social and personal transformation are inseparable (USSR, 1998; Cuello, 1999; Hurley, 2003; Rose, 2005). Thus, our urban curriculum begins this transformative process by ensuring that school is never separate from the lived world, from the personal experience of students. Although this is important in the larger quest to make education meaningful and useful—more than an empty ritual of compliance—it is also important for other reasons. When academic activity is connected to the world and the lived experience of students, it is, simply put, more damned interesting.

Indeed, it is very important for students (and teachers) to find pleasure in academic work. No matter how long right-wing commentators proclaim that students must be disciplined to learn boring lessons, I will argue that all great teachers must find ways to make becoming a scholar interesting. In my own life as a scholar I had to search for a way to make rigorous scholarship interesting. I had to frame it as a pleasurable activity. I had watched too many would-be scholars fail to become the researchers they wanted to be because they could not make the process interesting for themselves. The same is even more germane for elementary and secondary students from high-poverty and racially marginalized backgrounds. We operate in a media-driven, hyper-real world that has successfully represented academic work as intrinsically boring and irrelevant. A critical urban pedagogy refuses to accept such constructions and works to make intellectual labor a source of personal satisfaction. Social and personal transformation is not possible without this important step.

In this affective context, it is not inappropriate for advocates of a transformative urban pedagogy to devote much time and energy to developing education for enjoyment and personal satisfaction (Cuello, 1999). Neither is it out of place to engage urban students in conversations about what it might mean to be a scholar in their own sociohistorical context. The urban pedagogy supported here promotes a redefinition of the role of the intellectual for marginalized urban students. Indeed, I talk unabashedly with students about a demilitarized, gender-inclusive notion of a warrior intellectual. Such a concept situates the quest for personal and social transformation in the mean streets of our cities. Warrior intellectuals are tough young men and women who:

- Develop the ability to think critically and analytically.
- Cultivate their intellects.
- Understand the world as *it is* in relation to what *it could be.*

- Interpret and make sense of the world around them by understanding the invisible forces at work in shaping particular situations.
- Employ their creative ability to get beyond ritualized but failed practices in school and society.
- Use their imagination to transcend the trap of traditional gender, racial, sexual, and class-based stereotypes and the harm they can cause in individual lives and the larger society.
- Reconceptualize the role of "good citizen" in a way that speaks and acts in relation to dominant power and how it oppresses those around them.
- Develop the ability to teach themselves what they need to know to take on a particular task.
- Cultivate a humility that allows them to be both good leaders and good members of diverse learning communities.
- Devote themselves to never-ending, lifelong growth as citizens, parents, workers, teachers, scholars, researchers, and lovers.

THE POWER OF CONTEXTUAL UNDERSTANDINGS IN URBAN EDUCATION

Teaching and learning, as well as the study of teaching and learning, have to do with exploring the context in which they take place. And this context, advocates of a critical urban pedagogy maintain, is always complex and multidimensional. Insight into the context allows researchers and educators a clearer view into the complicated processes that operate to shape urban education. Take, for example, historical processes. In an emancipatory education, it is believed that teachers are ill-equipped to teach in urban schools without a profound understanding of the history of urban education, the history of urbanization and the evolution of urban areas, the history of social policies in relation to urban life, the history of racism and class bias in various societies, the history of urban youth culture, and so on.

These historical dynamics constantly shape what goes on in schools and in the lives of urban students. In the grotesquely unequal socioeconomic conditions that exist in most urban areas, poor students confront realities that undermine their readiness for learning (USSR, 1998). If urban educators are not aware of how these processes work, they are unprepared to deal with the lived realities they produce. When educators fail to understand these processes, they often resort to easy attributions of individual blame. Juan and Jasmine don't do well in school, such teachers tell their colleagues, because they are so lazy. Such an explanation is oblivious to the social forces shaping these students' fatigue in the teacher's class. Juan and Jasmine may be up all night taking care of younger brothers and sisters while their single mother works the graveyard shift at the local factory. I have seen ways that urban students spend their nights that are even more exhausting than babysitting. For many students, a full night of babysitting may look like a good option.

Understanding Juan and Jasmine's nighttime activities may make a dramatic difference in how a particular teacher views these students as human beings or interprets their academic performance. Advocates of critical teaching understand the larger concept at work in such a context: Knowledge of anything in the world is contingent on the context in which we view it (Harding, 1998). Knowing takes place in particular microsituations, cultural contexts, and moments in history. Change the situation, context, or moment, and the knowledge produced and the meaning ascribed it will be forever modified. Such an understanding is a key element of higher orders of cognition—a critical urban pedagogy in this context perpetually seeks to move practitioner thinking to more rigorous and complex domains.

Thus, those of us attempting to implement a transformative curriculum always work to understand urban classrooms as part of a larger system. We cannot think of our purpose as urban educators outside of this set of connections. Thus, in the most generic pedagogical sense, critical urban educators never teach anything without considering the context in which they and their students are operating. Teaching academic skills in the context of developing higher-order thinking abilities in relation to problems important to the everyday lives of urban students is quite different from learning fragments of information by rote (Weil, 2001). The former reflects the spirit of our contextualized pedagogy; the latter replicates the logic of rational irrationality found in such so-called educational reforms as Success for All and No Child Left Behind.

Implementing a critical urban education is a complex cognitive activity that well-educated, experienced teachers are quite capable of enacting in their professional lives. Armed with historical, social, cultural, economic, political, philosophical, and pedagogical insight, critical urban teachers observe, reflect on their experiences, connect these observations and reflections to their contextual and subject matter knowledges, and act accordingly. These are high expectations for professionals so demeaned by politicians, academicians, and many others—but they are not unrealistic. The public has yet to comprehend the complexity and multidimensionality of urban education reform. Thus, an important dimension of our urban pedagogy involves engaging the public in the complexity of the urban educational context. This means helping lay people understand the great strengths that urban teachers bring to their teaching, and what is needed to improve urban education.

A TRANSFORMATIVE URBAN PEDAGOGY, POSTFORMALISM, AND CONTEXTUALIZATION

In work published elsewhere, I have injected this power of contextualizing into a larger cognitive theory called postformalism (Kincheloe & Steinberg, 1993; Kincheloe, Steinberg, & Hinchey, 1999; Kincheloe, Steinberg, & Villaverde, 1999). Postformal contextualization is a key dimension of a critical articulation of urban education. Contextualization in the postformal sense involves understanding that knowledge can never stand alone or be complete in and of itself. In the act of abstraction—as in the abstract individual of Cartesianism—an analyst takes something out of its context. Of course, this cannot be avoided in everyday life because of the bombardment of information humans have to deal with in the process of living. In this context if an object of thinking cannot be abstracted, it will be lost in a larger pattern. While the postformal thinker must be adept at such abstraction, it must take place without a concurrent loss of sight of the larger conceptual field—the context that provides separate entities with meaning. This is a tricky act that complex critical thinkers must learn to perform adeptly. Postformalists place great importance on the notion of context and the act of contextualization in every aspect of their lives. When urban teachers who are postformal thinkers encounter problems in their work lives, they connect the difficulty to a wider frame of reference with a wide array of possible causes.

When pedagogical problems fail to meet the criteria of an archetype, postformalists explore unused sources and employ the information acquired to develop a larger understanding of the interaction of the various contexts surrounding an issue. When teachers, for example, fail to perform such an act of contextualization, students get hurt. When educational leaders are unequipped to contextualize, they tend to isolate various dimensions of a larger socioeducational circumstance and call each a separate problem. Thus, they tinker with components of the problems but never approach the macrocontext of which such complications are mere parts. In this context postformal advocates of criticality understand that data derive their meanings only in the context created by other data. Context, thus, may be more important than content. These insights change the way researchers, urban educational professionals, policy analysts, and practitioners of all varieties conduct their work.

As Ray Horn (2000) contends, postformalism is profoundly concerned with creating dialogues about power and context. Thus, postformalist urban teachers examine curriculum and instruction in light of the urban community and the forces that affect it. Here urban teachers employing the power of contextualization study media representations of urban education, urban youth culture, and the socioeconomic forces that help shape these dynamics. In a postformal context, therefore, learning cannot be separated from an individual's identity, her personal history in her lived material environments (Hanrahan, 1998). All teaching in this postformal formulation is an act of connecting the act of learning to the learner and her context(s). When urban educators apply these ideas to curriculum development, educational policy, and classroom teaching, the world of urban education changes forever.

RIGHT-WING EDUCATION RESISTS OUR CRITICAL URBAN PEDAGOGY'S EFFORTS TO CONTEXTUALIZE

In the numerous educational reforms promoted by right-wing politicos, the importance of context is quashed. Such reforms create an urban education in which connections to city neighborhoods and the urban political economy are irrelevant. The desire of many urban high school students to make these contextual connections part of the curriculum falls on regressive deaf ears in the right-wing cosmos. Such a stance often induces urban students to assert that such educational and political leaders don't give a damn about them (Miron, 2004). Viewing many of these economically poor and racially

marginalized students as abstract individuals who are "weak students" with a propensity for crime, many right-wing politicos maintain that such students are not worth the public's financial investment. They argue that monies devoted to their education should be diverted to the cognitively able; to the gifted, and talented who score high on IQ and other standardized tests (Herrnstein & Murray, 1994; Kincheloe et al., 1996).

Such ways of seeing urban students emerge from particular constructions of culture. In this formulation culture is assumed to be a monolithic concept, a homogenous set of conventions and practices, not a multilogical domain of difference, interconnections, and power. Attention here is diverted from the multiple subcultures and ways of being in a contemporary nation-state. Indeed, only one variety of a national culture (e.g., that of the United States) is validated as a legitimate social identity (Apple, 1993, 1999; Steinberg, 2001; McLaren, 2002; Rose & Kincheloe, 2003). Even though there is a constant synthesis of diverse cultural characteristics from diverse social locations in contemporary electronic societies, within the right-wing construction of culture the national culture is superior and must be protected from these pollutants. Thus, the school curriculum takes on a fetishistic importance in the larger effort to defend the dominant civilization. As Philip Anderson and Judith Summerfield (2004) contend, urban areas of the United States, with their "multiethnic, multiracial, multireligious, multiclass, multigendered, multinational, multidimensional" (pp. 38–39) emergent culture are always positioned as a threat to monological notions of U.S./Western homogeneity. Such pervasive right-wing ways of seeing dramatically change the ways advocates of a critical urban education approach their jobs.

In this cultural context the politics of knowledge becomes profoundly important in urban education. Here the standardization of curriculum movements we find in many societies and the ideological control of textbooks become markers of the larger effort to perpetuate the dominance of "mainstream" culture—white supremacy, Christian ascendancy, patriarchal hegemony, class elitism, heteronormativity, and so on. Because in the decontextualized right-wing pedagogical framework learning is an individual activity, none of these social dimensions are relevant in the educational conversation. Indeed, in the conservative construction talk about such social, cultural, political, and economic factors is merely a left-wing way of politicizing what should be a nonpolitical, relatively simplistic dialogue about inculcating human beings' greatest insights on the true, the beautiful, and the good into the minds of our students. Those individuals who possess inherited intellectual capacity—high IQs—will learn these truths; those who don't, won't.

Thus, in the decontextualized right-wing educational cosmos we (representatives of dominant power) need to simply get on with the task of identifying the crème de la crème and separating them from the urban whey. In our just meritocratic system such activity represents the hand of a benevolent Calvinist God benignly intervening in human affairs. To hell with multilogicality, multiculturalism, and multidimensionality, we know the truth, who's talented, and whose culture is of the most worth. Those minority kids from poor urban neighborhoods will have to accept their level of competence and find commensurate social/vocational positions. If we can keep contextual understandings of the social construction of competence, truth, and curriculum out of the mix, we can protect the privileged position of those from dominant cultural and class backgrounds. If we can use only one-dimensional notions of intelligence that exclude contextual insights about the test taker's linguistic, socioeconomic class,

racial/cultural milieu, then we can justify diverting educational monies to the gifted and talented few.

In this decontextualized mode of urban education a standardized curriculum is constructed that effectively works to keep practitioners of a critical pedagogy from forging a course of study reflective of student cultural concerns and what is meaningful for them in the context of their lived experiences. Thus, urban education becomes less timely, less flexible, and less connected to the dispositions and the immediate and long-term needs of its most marginalized students. Local community needs are irrelevant and evaluation becomes something imposed on schools, not an important learning process directed by schools (Elmore, 1997; Norris, 1998). Looking only at decontextualized data about the low levels of urban teacher and student performance on standardized evaluation instruments, right-wing analysts can paint a picture of hopelessness that justifies abandoning the effort to provide an empowering education for city kids. Advocates of a liberatory urban pedagogy refuse to allow this decontextualized, elitist, and nihilistic way of representing urban education, urban teachers, and urban students carry the day. We believe that the struggle for a rigorous, pragmatic, empowering, transformational urban education can be won.

DISEMPOWERING URBAN CONTEXTS: OVERCOMING MARGINALIZATION, ASSERTING AGENCY

The sociopolitical, cultural dynamics that frame urban education, to say the least, are not conducive to personal and social transformation. Indeed, it is not a stretch to maintain that such dynamics operate to undermine the life chances of marginalized students. This is the stark reality that faces all urban educators. As previously maintained, we can with great commitment and effort overcome its effects with individual students in specific classrooms, but there is nothing simple and easy about the process. When the success of right-wing political alliances over the last 25 years is added to this sobering mix, efforts for just, democratic reform of urban education become even more difficult. The goals of the right-wing coalition—maintaining dominant power relations, enhancing international competition, increasing corporate profit margins, and strengthening the social regulation of the "dangerous" poor and non-white—do not provide more hope for poor urban students.

Activists in urban communities can help teachers in city schools connect their curricula to such ideological understandings. For students to grasp these concepts, interpretive frameworks must be constructed in close relationship with their collective lifeworlds and a community-based historical consciousness. Such a relationship creates an ideological zone of proximal development (ZPD) where new meanings emerge in dialogue with stories from the community. These interpretive frameworks and new meanings constitute a much needed ideological shield against the assault on learning poverty unleashes on urban students. Boys and girls from poor urban neighborhoods need this ideological shield to fight off poverty- and racism-induced

- Anger that works to subvert efforts to socially survive in school
- Low expectation to succeed in school
- Hopelessness concerning life expectations
- Resentment of the middle class that makes it impossible to cooperate with many teachers
- Rejection of the possibility that education may be worth pursuing
- Equation of getting an education with "selling out" one's friends and neighbors (Apple, 1993, 1996, 1999; Henke, 2000; Carvan et al., 2002)

When many sociologists characterize inner-city schools as being populated by those left behind, ensnared in hopelessness by their economic unimportance (Bartlet, quoted in Wang & Kovach, 1996), then time has come for a dramatic change. In less than sixty years these urban schools have moved from white, middle class bastions with a broad tax base to low-income, minority systems with an ever-shrinking share of economic resources and political power. In what many call the metropolitan problem, well-to-do urban and suburban districts have not been willing to help those caught in this urban briar patch with shared resources and financial aid (Halford, 1996). In the electronic hyper-reality of the last three or so decades racial inscriptions ideologically frame discussions of urban issues such as these (Leonardo, 2004).

In the right-wing cultural logic that shapes our ideological landscape residents of well-to-do urban and suburban districts are often not willing to help people in poor neighborhoods because they are black or Latino/-a. In the racial ideology of our contemporary era such peoples are often represented as bringing on themselves the problems that they face. The normalizing impulses found in many educational and developmental psychology departments relegate these students to the dustbin of incompetence. Using middle-class and upper-middle class, white, first-language English-speaking children as the norm, such psychologists pathologize those who are culturally different (Kincheloe et al., 1999; Haberman, 2002). The individualizing, decontextualizing impulse of contemporary right-wing ways of seeing again rears its unsightly head.

Community has been shattered in these domains and self-efficacy has been assaulted by decontextualized and "objective" psychological pronouncements that play the deficit game. In such a displaced culture our critical urban pedagogy's curriculum of place seems apropos, as it attempts to create a sense of belongingness in a world that rejects those very urban students we admire so much and care about so deeply. Urban dwellers in poor neighborhoods are alienated and isolated in a plethora of ways. Poor African Americans and Latinos/-as, for example, are purposefully secluded by city planning and are districted politically to minimize their political influence (Ng, 2003). Advocates of criticality understand that urban students and their families desperately need a sense of community. One of the roles of urban schools in poor settings, therefore, is to create this community consciousness wherever and when the opportunity arises in the classroom, in out-of-school activities, in personal relationships, in community organizations, and so forth.

Critical urban educators understand that their students who are marginalized by race and class are alienated individuals. To be isolated from other humans, to be cast aside as worthless is to be cursed in contemporary society. Right-wing, ethnocentric Western values thrive on such alienation and the creation of human detritus. Positivist academics stand ready with their standardized tests and personality profiles to validate such inhumane actions with the imprimatur of science. All of this is justified in the hypermasculinity of rugged individualism. To conceptualize the world in cooperative rather than competitive modalities, to fight rather than passively accept alienation is to be unmanly, a wimp in the patriarchal discourse of right-wing hypermasculinity.

The fear of such epithets moves many young urban (and other) men to reject humanistic values and critical ways of being. Critical urban teachers make it a point to understand these dynamics as they play out in the processes of marginalization and the assertion of agency and empowerment. With such understanding at the forefront of their consciousness, they understand that a wide variety of factors will shape students' relationship to the critical urban curriculum. Divergent students will react totally differently to different curricular experiences for a vari-

ety of reasons. Once again the ante of urban educational complexity increases. A critical urban education engages students in analyses of these complex reactions to its goals and purposes. Indeed, this is a key aspect of the critical curriculum.

MOTIVATION IN URBAN EDUCATION

In technical models of urban education and the right-wing reforms being promoted in the twenty-first century, advocates of a critical urban pedagogy witness an abject failure to motivate urban students from marginalized backgrounds. Far too often such students fail, in my opinion quite understandably, to discern any connection between the curriculum they encounter and their lives. Much of the learning in which they engage in this fragmented context seems to them an empty exercise devoid of intrinsic value. Once urban teachers gain a contextual, multiperspectival understanding of the purposes, the ideological dynamics, and many contexts that frame urban schooling, they are ready to engage in one of the toughest educational tasks imaginable—developing a pedagogy that engages marginalized urban students in academic work that is life transforming and is connected to larger social problems and issues. I am amazed by those brilliant urban teachers who accomplish this task month after month, year after year.

In the spirit of critical teaching that promotes social and personal transformation, these brilliant urban teachers are able to make sure that students find academic learning instantly gratifying. As John Dewey (1916) put it time and time again, education is not for the future but is for the present. We become smarter, more socially adept, better citizens in relation to our present lives—not for some imagined life far from our present circumstances. Our motivation comes from felt needs in the present. Few teachers have been successful who attempt to inspire their students with the assertion that they will need this knowledge in a couple of decades. Advocates of a transformative pedagogy attempt to balance motivation between the dialectic of social and personal transformation. They understand that no education for personal transformation is complete without a commitment to social transformation and vice versa.

In this context critical urban teachers work to cultivate the intellectual ability to acquire, analyze, and produce both self-knowledge and social knowledge. Grounded in such knowledge and scholarly facility, individuals would be equipped to participate in the democratic process as committed and informed citizens. A basic assumption in this civic context involves the belief that, in terms of a critical vision of a democratic social order and education, Western societies in the twenty-first century are in great trouble. As previously mentioned, corporations and other power wielders have gained increasing control over the production and flow of information. Here, public consciousness is aligned in a complex and never completely successful interactive process with the interests of power. I have found throughout my teaching career that students once alerted to these power dynamics tend to become extremely interested in understanding them in more detail and discerning their effects on their own lives.

In this context critical urban teachers understand that one of the most important goals of public life over the last few decades has been the cultivation of more and more social obedience and less democracy. The effort to win the consent of the public (hegemony) via appeals to both logic and affect, for privatization projects that may not be in the public's best interests, has been frighteningly successful. Of course, what makes this privatization impulse so messy and complex is that public urban schooling driven by many of the same forces has failed to pro-mote a rigorous, democratic education. Operating in the shadow of Frankfurt School critical social theorist Theodor Adorno, critical educators reference his notion of "half-education," which describes how mainstream education perpetuates students' alienation from knowledge of the social and the self.

In this process, agency is undermined in a sea of social confusion (Sunker, 1994). To confront this alienation, critical teachers must provide specific examples of formal and informal educational programs that promote a progressive curriculum that fights such alienation. Understanding the affective dimensions of these programs, critical urban educators analyze why students and other individuals are emotionally invested in specific programs, why energy is produced and absorbed by participants, and why the disposition to imagine and create new projects is cultivated in some programs and not in others. This is where advocates of critical frameworks formulate and deploy their reconceptualization of the prevailing notions of what it means to be an intellectual. There is absolutely no reason that a scholar who studies hard and learns how to produce knowledge about social and personal transformation can't become a positive model for marginalized urban students.

As we consider the above-mentioned alienation in urban educational context, urban teachers know that there is a crisis of academic motivation within contemporary Western societies. The larger society has represented academic work as a form of mental drudgery that should be avoided at all costs. The joys of developing disciplined forms of thinking, reading, and writing are not a part of the twenty-first century cultural landscape. Most psychologists—not to mention most educators and parents—have not understood that learning always involves a change in identity. I understood that before I became a writer, I had to change the person I was as a human being. I had to actually become a writer, one who loved the process and was willing to sacrifice particular dimensions of my life in order to claim this "persona." To become what I wanted to become, I had to learn to like to write: to gain pleasure from turning a good phrase, set goals for publication, understand how I would integrate writing into my life, and appreciate the relationship between my personal transformation into a writer and larger issues of social transformation.

Critical urban teachers challenge their students to change their lives as learners. They help urban students construct conceptual frameworks tied to personal and social goals that create a taste for academic work. This dispositional dimension of learning is far more important that educational psychologists have ever understood. Advocates of a critical pedagogy appreciate the dispositional domain and always consider it when engaging in curriculum development, constructing pedagogical methods, and evaluating their students' work. Being lucky enough to grow up in a marginalized subculture—the southern Appalachian Mountains—I have always been able to empathize with many of my marginalized urban students in regard to their feelings about intellectuals. Often times these scholarly types were exactly the ones who looked down on us for being stupid hillbillies with funny accents.

I could often see my African-American and Latino/-a, as well as my Russian and other recently immigrated, urban students reacting the same way to such condescension as my hillbilly friends and I did—we all "played dumb" for the elitists. We would exaggerate our accents and stupidity and *play hillbilly*. Hell, I still find myself in adulthood doing just that when someone talks down to me because of my low-status Tennessee mountain accent. I always knew what Thurgood Marshall—the first African-American member of the U.S. Supreme Court—meant when asked

about his favorite pastime. He would say something like, "I like to jive white people." Thus, for Justice Marshall and myself—not that I should compare myself to a man of such great accomplishment—part of our passion to become scholars involved transforming ourselves into learned men who always remembered where we came from and pursued a humble, not an elitist, conception of intellectualism.

Thus, when we act on our understanding of the connection between learning and identity, we pay serious attention to understanding our students' identities. We take the knowledges they bring to class very seriously, always exploring how to acknowledge such data while building on and expanding them. In this context we uncover as many entry points to learning as possible, creating portals through which students can develop their own personal relationship to scholarship and the skills it demands. Such an approach poses an omnipresent question to urban students: How can I find both my individual and communitarian role as a learner? This all-pervading question is followed by two more queries: How can I imagine my life changing, as I become this learner? How does the learning with which I'm now involved relate to my larger efforts to create my new learner persona?

Critical urban educators keep these ideas in mind as they construct their learning communities. One way of thinking about a learning community is as a cultural location where individuals engage in activities where they learn to become particular types of people. In the interrelationships and the connections made in these learning communities individuals come to see themselves in new ways as they learn new skills and insights. Nothing could be more relevant to our lives than such learning. Nothing could be grounded on a more different view of the right-wing fragmented, individualized, abstracted, pedagogical act than such a sociocognitive conception (Cuello, 1999; Carvan et al., 2002; Morrell, 2003). Thus, a critical urban education is inseparable from a vision of social and individual transformation.

A CRITICAL URBAN EDUCATIONAL PSYCHOLOGY: RELATIONALISM AND LEARNING

In a cognitive theoretical context understanding the relationship between human learning and identity fundamentally undermines the mechanistic learning theories used for decades by mainstream educators. In the contextualized cognitive theory we begin to make distinctions between "learning *about*" and "learning *to be*." Thus, learning is as much an ontological (concerned with being in the world) act as it is an epistemological act. Most school learning in a decontextualized framework involves committing to memory preexisting knowledge domains—the truth of scientifically based disciplines. In learning to be, individuals become members of communities of practice in the process constructing a new relational identity (Hung, Bopry, Looi, & Koh, 2005; Kinnucan-Welsch, 2005).

Understanding this relational identity is central to a critical urban pedagogy. Such an identity plays a key role in shaping what it is that a student learns. We can see this ontological dynamic play out in schools on a daily basis as students who enter particular youth subcultures where the changes in their identities profoundly shape not only what they know about the world but also how they see both the world and themselves. This is a profound learning experience. Thus, we cannot see *learning* and *being* apart from the contexts in which we operate. Thus, we are not self and world in the way coffee is in a can. The self is the world and the world is the self in a critical ontology (Kincheloe, 2003). The very concept of human *being* cannot be understood outside of sociopo-

litical context. This is a subtle proposition. As Hung et al. (2005) remind us, "although being can be phenomenologically perceived separately from the world, being exists or takes meaning only in relation to the world."

In this context the absurdity of the way IQ tests have been developed and used comes into clear focus. Constructed as measures of the individual's ability, their failure to account for the connection between the individual and the contexts of which she is a part renders them useless. If the individual and her cognitive orientations are shaped by this being-in-the-world, psychological tests miss the origins and causes of why individuals display particular cognitive characteristics. They attribute to nature what is a manifestation of a particular set of social, political, economic, cultural, and historical relationships. Thus, the cognitive theoretical base (postformalism; see Kincheloe & Steinberg, 1993; Kincheloe et al., 1999) of our pedagogy views the self, the development of selfhood, and cognitive ability in new and exciting ways. These dynamics create a dramatic rupture with the past. Our relational ontological perspectives provide us with a new means of understanding the way individuals relate to and learn about the world around them (Taylor, 2005).

This notion of the relational self is central to our conception of urban education—all learning theories and pedagogies are directly connected to how we view the nature of selfhood. Obviously, selfhood is a profoundly complex concept. Advocates of a critical urban pedagogy operating in light of this complexity understand that the distinction between the social and the individual is not as clear as traditional sociologists and psychologists assumed it to be. While retaining the notion of individuality and the agency of the individual, critical urban educators appreciate the instability of selfhood and the limits of rational regulation of one's intellectual activity. The notion of a fixed, unitary self has been subverted by psychoanalytic, situated cognitive, and enactivist insights. When we examine a critical pedagogy's concern with context from this psychological perspective, we begin to understand in even more detail its importance.

Context is not simply the "box" in which an abstract individual operates. Instead, context is a web of reality made up of human actions, cultural practices, linguistic dynamics, and matrices of human consciousness all working to construct selfhood. Here we come to understand that context influences not only the types of experiences in which humans engage, but that it also shapes the ways individuals make sense of and act in response to such involvements. Thus, meaning and context are difficult to separate—learning is situated, knowledge is inseparable from the context in which it is produced and comprehended. Theories of knowledge and pedagogy that see information simply as some "thing" that one carries around in her head until she needs it again miss the significance of this contextualism. With this understanding in mind we can more clearly discern the ways our social location, our power/status relations in particular settings shape our learning and how we are perceived as learners.

Thus, advocates of transformative urban education possess a process-oriented view of the self. With components both inside the individual and in the context around her, selfhood is always *in process*, meaning that it is an ever-evolving interaction between individual and setting. In such a process we can rethink our relationship to the world, we can reconnect to the natural order from which Western modernity has alienated us. In this construction people are no longer alone in their own minds. Instead they are unfinished entities always reaching out to other selves in diverse contexts. Indeed, the self is ongoing and as such cannot be "measured" by primitive instruments such as the IQ test.

If, as individuals, we are active in our own self construction, then an IQ is but a mere photograph of where we were at a particular moment in time in relation to a task imposed on us by outsiders from a different context. There are insights we might gain from the test, but it tells us little about the capability of the self in some "natural state." As long as abstracted, decontextualized views of selfhood are accepted and IQ and other standardized tests are viewed as scientifically valid, objective statements of one's biological intelligence, marginalized urban students will be unlikely to be perceived as high performing scholars.

What are critical urban teachers to do with this knowledge of the relational, contextualized, process-oriented self? How does such insight help them teach urban students oppressed by race, class, and gender forces? This is where my notion of critical ontology returns to a critical urban pedagogy. In this context teachers engage their students in the exploration of the construction of the self by power structures and other contextual forces. In addition students study the production of their own selfhood in particular. As students come to understand these productive dynamics, teachers constantly work to engage them in creating narratives that explain their role(s) in the society, the political state, the city, the neighborhood, the school, the peer group, and the family. In these narratives students attempt to articulate a positive role for themselves.

This process must be directly connected to the academic curriculum. As a student of history, what are the possible roles a student can play in the metahistorical themes playing out in the world and in our lives? Am I able to position myself as a young, African-American male, for example, to construct a story for myself in the as yet unfinished anticolonial movement that swept through all parts of the world in the twentieth century? Am I able to situate myself as a young Moroccan woman who wants to be a writer in relation to the stories of Zora Neale Hurston? As I read them, do I gain insights into how I might tell my stories in my own unique way? In my own life as a wannabe rock 'n' roll musician, I constantly create narratives of myself as a singer and piano and organ player in relation to particular songs I study. How does knowing the work of great bluesman Howlin' Wolf help me play better, sing better, cultivate my own style, write better music, and understand the concept of soul in a deeper manner? I cannot listen to the Wolf and not think of my own "musical narrative."

Thus, in this context our emancipatory pedagogy teaches a rigorous academic curriculum that is always connected to the production of the self—human beings' selfhood in general and the student's in particular. Such a cognitive orientation enhances our efforts at social and personal transformation. As teachers and students study the self as a historical construction, they learn why they see themselves and the world as they do. With such knowledge students have a much better opportunity to transform the self from what it now is to what they would like for it to be. This is not some New Age, touchy-feely process—it is a rigorous academic act. It is not a narcissistic turning inward but an engagement with the world, with knowledge production and its uses. It is an engagement with the contemporary *Zeitgeist*, the prevailing social (un)consciousness. Indeed, it is a serious analysis of our relational selves—in particular, of what they are operating in relation to. In this process of critical transformation students become more and more adept at negotiating and traversing the ideological and discursive landscapes that position them in the world, in school, in the labor market, and in their communities.

Such a pedagogy enables students to evaluate their agency—to assess their ability to do what they want to do and become what their narratives portended. Because it is a critical pedagogy the forces and structures that impede their agency are named and addressed. Such a process transcends antiquated beliefs that view learning as the process of acquiring and filing information, as it moves into a far more complex and pragmatic territory. Thus, we are formulating a pedagogy of becoming—a dispositional, ethical, intellectual mode of teaching and learning that consciously changes teachers and students into something greater than they now are (Madison, 1988; May, 1993; Bruner, 1996; Bodeau, 1999; Pickering, 1999; Fenwick, 2000; Kincheloe, 2005b).

A TRANSFORMATIVE URBAN PEDAGOGY AND PSYCHOLOGY: AGENCY AND INTELLIGENCE ARE LEARNABLE

Agency involves human beings' ability to instigate and carry out our actions in a way that accomplishes our larger goals. Such agency is closely aligned with selfhood, the relational self, and intelligence, as individuals and groups develop a consciousness of "agentive encounters with the world" (Bruner, 1996, p. 36). These individual and group memories are interpreted and projected into the future, into considerations of what could be, in light of what is and what has been. Intelligence has something to do with a learning community's and/or an individual's ability to engage in such projections into possibility. How can our extrapolations in math help us in our efforts to rebuild the racing car we bought? How can our political understandings facilitate our work in organizing the community to fight the toxic dumping by local corporations? Again, in these contexts individuals are creating narratives for themselves concerning their participation in the world. Such an act provides a more specific element to the critical notion of empowerment. Empowerment here is not some vague concept but a concrete one with very pragmatic outcomes.

Such empowerment provides us with an autobiography—a life story that is inseparable from other individuals and meso- and macrocontexts. Critical agency does not merely provide us with an abstracted autobiography free from contextual influences but one that understands our situatedness, the construction and reconstruction of selfhood in relation to larger structures, forces, and processes. Students (or anyone, for that matter) who are able to describe themselves and their construction in this way have moved to a new cognitive and scholarly domain. They have gained an ability to engage in the hermeneutic circle, where they look at the specific (their individual lives) in relation to the general (the larger contexts and processes in which they operate). In this circle they begin to discern connections and relationships that have operated to shape who they are. In such a context they are better able to imagine compelling narratives of where they might go and what they might do.

Dominant power can be quite brutal in its evaluation of the worth of our narratives. In the case of marginalized urban students, the narratives they imagine for themselves as agents of social change and ideological resisters of oppressive dominant cultural practices may be deemed unacceptable. Students must be ready for such condemnation and develop pragmatic strategies to deal with it. Dominant culture, for example, often denigrates marginalized urban students' abilities to negotiate and survive life on tough streets. The types of skills needed in this struggle are, by nature, sophisticated and nuanced. The idea that such savvy students who have not had the opportunity to learn basic literacy skills would be judged as cognitively incapable of doing academic work because of low standardized test scores is incomprehensible to me. Yet, this is the reality such students face. Critical urban teachers use these insights in their pedagogical work with these students in their efforts to tie academic concerns to the narratives the students create about themselves in the world.

These sociopsychological dimensions of our pedagogy are grounded in the understanding that intelligence and agency are linked and both are teachable and learnable. This simple statement in an era of right-wing reform and mechanistic educational psychology is a radical assertion. As I examine contemporary educational and cognitive practice, I am convinced that many political and educational leaders and psychological scholars do not believe that marginalized urban students can learn (Norris, 1998; Nations, 2005). Producers of standardized tests, despite overwhelming evidence to the contrary, maintain that nothing can be done to improve standardized test scores. Don't bother with test coaching, the Educational Testing Service (ETS) tells potential test takers, it won't help. The assumption here is that intelligence is a genetic, fixed, intransigent entity and there is nothing one can do to increase it (Owen & Doerr, 1999). The fact that test coaching consistently works to help raise test scores must be suppressed—the implications of such knowledge are dangerous.

Such danger not only threatens the testing industry and its explosive profits in the era of No Child Left Behind, but it actually shakes the foundation of the meritocratic house of cards on which contemporary education precariously rests. If we reveal the intelligence myth, the corresponding fable that assures us we live in a just society and the people who succeed in it do so because of their cognitive and moral superiority crumbles in its wake. Hurricanes and lightning, heavy metal thunder—here the cracks in the foundations of dominant power are revealed. Yet for those of us not wedded to the protection of an unjust status quo, the news here is good and quite electrifying: Most human beings without severe brain damage or physiological impairments can become much smarter, they can learn new forms of agency that help them realize their dreams and contribute to the larger social good. The key to using this knowledge in education involves our concern with context. By understanding the contexts, processes, and matrices in which people operate, we begin to develop a network-oriented, not a brain-centered view of intelligence. Stated differently, we begin to see intelligence as a social as well as an individual dynamic (Perkins, 1995; Lepani, 1998).

Psychometrics embraces a brain-centered view of intelligence where abstract individuals ply their inherited abilities in isolated situations. Our social distributed notion of intelligence understands that thinking is always shaped by the:

- Artifacts we use
- Individuals/communities with whom we come into contact
- Symbol systems we employ
- Nature of our interactions with our sociopolitical contexts and the dispositions toward particular types of learning they produce
- Knowledges to which we have or do not have access
- Our relationship with dominant forms of power, and so forth.

This critical cognitive theory—elsewhere I refer to it as postformalism—maintains that resources not located inside the brain affect what we refer to as intelligence.

Once individuals understand this distributed dimension of intelligence, they can begin to rearrange their lives as learners. If I want to be a great critical scholar, I need to build a community of critical scholars in which I can participate. I need to make use of their expertise to help me construct new narratives about my present and future role in the world, in particular my role as a critical scholar. If I am aware of these sociocognitive dynamics as a teacher, I can create situations in which I facilitate students' efforts to build these communities, to gain access to helpful artifacts and tools, to monitor their dis-

positions in relation to issues of power and inclusion, and to explore their self-narratives in relation to these distributed forces. Thus, the relational individual is taught in a relation-based pedagogy.

The nature of students' and teachers' social interactions with both one another and in general becomes profoundly important in our critical urban pedagogy (Morrell, 2003; Quartz, Olsen, & Duncan-Andrade, 2003). Transmission of information in this context is decentered as the basic form of instruction to a more situated location where it is used only in particular contexts and when the pedagogical timing is right. Pedagogical expertise in this context often revolves around connecting students to particular contexts and integrating them into specific learning communities. A central task of a critical urban teacher involves creating diverse learning communities. Such a charge involves bringing particular people together, creating affective and emotional climates that are warm, nurturing, inclusive, and inviting to students who have often experienced rejection, tutoring particular groups and/or individuals as to the dynamics of learning hidden in their everyday activities, naming the tacit knowledges and skills employed in particular contexts, and so on. This is how teachers and students become more intelligent and enhance their agency to make a difference in the world.

CREATING A SENSE OF BELONGING FOR URBAN STUDENTS IN CRITICAL LEARNING COMMUNITIES

Urban students marginalized by poverty and racism will rarely succeed in school until they gain a sense of belongingness in particular classrooms and learning communities. A central dimension of our pedagogy involves making sure that these students can find safe places where they belong. As critical urban teachers are working on this goal, they must also make sure that they themselves have safe places in school where they too can belong. Too often, young teachers dedicated to the principles of a critical urban education find themselves alone and isolated in their schools. It will be difficult to create a sense of belongingness for students if teachers do not have their own support structures. Urban schools in poor neighborhoods can be alienated, anonymous venues that consume those who walk into them without social and emotional sustenance. It is important for teachers in such settings to remember that there are other teachers who may feel as lonely as they do. Building networks of teachers and then connecting those associations to students are necessary dimensions of critical urban teaching.

In this context many urban teachers make particular assignments directly for the purpose of building learning communities and solidarity among their students. No teacher ever constructed a classroom that was too safe, too inclusive, or too interconnected. In addition to making students feel better about school and setting up the type of learning communities needed to engage in the curriculum of social and self-transformation, the construction of classrooms in which students feel like they belong does more than any other single action to create a well-managed classroom. A teacher can attend 37 workshops on classroom discipline or work individually with the five-thousand-dollar-a-day consultant who devised the program "Ready, Set, Discipline" (RSD) and not find a better form of classroom management. Connecting classroom management with the larger goal of social and personal transformation via learning communities in which students create their self-narratives is a holistic, integrated approach to constructing classrooms that works.

Of course, there are no sure-fire, no-miss strategies when it comes to classroom management in urban schools—especially if the teacher wants to control the behavior of her students to *make* them do what she wants. In urban settings where students' life experiences can come so quickly and intensely, teachers who want to make students act in a particular way typically don't last too long. "With all the things we have to worry about," students often conclude, "we don't need that teacher telling us how to sit in our chairs." Thus, critical teachers articulate their macroexpectations (social and personal transformation) and their microexpectations (a climate of mutual respect, belongingness, cooperation, and safety in the classroom). I have always let my students know as quickly as possible by both words and deeds that I would stand up for them—even when it was not in my own self-interest. They knew that I would tell them the truth and not defend school policies or actions that were unfair.

When I was a young high school teacher in the 1970s, for example, I had a group of students who had long hair, embraced radical politics, loved rock music, and wore funky and unusual used clothing. It was still a time that the word "hippie" was used and that's what many of my colleagues on the faculty called them—those "goddamn hippie kids." I loved these students. They were highly motivated and flourished in my American history and cultural geography courses. They worked with me on special projects during their study hall breaks and after school. We wrote songs about what we were studying and played them on our guitars and keyboards for other students. They trusted me and I trusted them. One afternoon while I was sitting at my cubicle reading in the teachers' lounge, I overheard two other social studies teachers talking about how much they hated these students and how they wished they could remove them from the school.

As they mentioned particular names of my beloved students and what they would like to do to them, my stomach churned with anger. At that point in the conversation one teacher told the other, "I know those hippies are selling dope here in the school—especially Wavy [pseudonym]. I wish we could catch him and kick him out of school." Thinking for a second the other teacher said: " I think that can be arranged. My son can get me some pot. We'll put some in his locker between classes and call the cops. We'll make sure that little bastard, Wavy, is expelled." I didn't hesitate for a second. Making sure the teachers didn't see me, I sneaked out of the lounge. I happened to know where Wavy was at that moment and ran down to his classroom. I knocked on the door and told his teacher that I needed to talk to him for a few minutes. I told Wavy what I had just heard. He was shocked, he told me, but not surprised. Understanding the gravity of the situation, he agreed to check his locker after every class to see if the evidence had been planted. We never did find anything in his locker but Wavy knew I could be trusted. This kind of relationship with students in marginalized urban settings is necessary in a transformative curriculum. I don't believe such a personal approach to teaching and learning can work without it.

Thus, knowing students well, understanding what they are dealing with outside of school, appreciating the problems their parents are facing, and gaining an awareness of what is happening at home that might undermine their ability to concentrate on academic work are the ways critical teachers operationalize a sense of belonging among their students. There is no doubt that urban schools located in poor neighborhoods can be violent places. But most of the time violence is rare in classrooms where students feel like they belong, work is meaningful and connected to the world, and teachers are viewed by students as individuals who can be trusted to stand up for them when needed. Also, when teachers attempt to understand rather than condemn the behaviors many students adopt to survive the violent streets on which they live, the threat of classroom violence is lessened.

The tough demeanors, self-protective bearings, and aggressive postures many urban students employ for their public persona seem to me quite logical given the circumstances they all have to face. If one doesn't understand this dynamic, a few late night rides on the B Train through Brooklyn may help get the point across. On poor urban streets one's effort to stay healthy is not enhanced by broadcasting signals of weakness. Should I be surprised when a student who has to deal with these everyday circumstances shows a little resistance, a toughness on the first day of class when I ask him to stop picking on the student in the seat next to him? I'm not surprised by such behavior and instead of vilifying the student, I reflect on how I would probably react in a similar context. When I think of a student's behavior/demeanor in such a way, I find that the chance that I will ultimately connect with him or her is profoundly increased.

In a critical urban pedagogy teachers who treat students with respect and attempt to create a sense of belongingness in their classrooms do not feel morally superior to other practitioners because of such conduct. They know that once such feelings of arrogance seep in to their consciousness, they are setting themselves up for trouble. In schools as troubled as many are in poor urban areas with racially, linguistically, and culturally diverse students operating in economically trying circumstances, teachers should not be surprised when their actions are not received and interpreted by students in the way they intended them. In this context they must not feel that such students are betraying them because of the anger they show in such circumstances. I have watched too many urban teachers who say after an unpleasant encounter with a student: "to hell with her—I treat her better than any other teacher in this school and she acts like that toward me." Because of the difference in the webs of reality of middle-class teachers and students living in poverty, particular actions will sometimes be viewed differently by divergent groups. Thus, there will be misunderstandings. The more students feel a sense of belongingness and safety in one's classroom, the less the impact of such misunderstandings.

Most new urban teachers are nervous about these issues of classroom management. Many white, middle-class, first-year teachers are fearful of poor students of color and the neighborhoods in which they live. Such feelings are not odd, given the media portrayal of poor urban schools. Just as examples, "The Substitute" series—"The Substitute," "The Substitute II: School's Out," and "The Substitute III: Winner Takes All"—grant us a look at the way the public sees urban schools and urban students. One learns from watching all three movies that the only answer to the problem presented by violent, animalistic urban high school students of color is the *final solution*: Kill them before they kill us. If such images permeate the social unconsciousness, wouldn't anyone be scared to walk into such pits of violence and crime? The alternative to such dystopian, nihilistic views of marginalized urban students rests with the contextualization, dignity, understanding, ideological insights, and respect for all students promoted by critical forms of urban education.

Certainly there are unprovoked attacks on great urban teachers, and this is always a horrific tragedy whenever it occurs. So many of the violent incidents that I've witnessed in schools, however, have been perpetrated by overstressed students confronted by teachers, administrators, or other personnel who showed them no respect or empathy. For example, too many times I watched an assistant principal keep pushing a student until she finally exploded, committing a violent act that got her expelled or incarcerated. As I watched such incidents, I thought to myself, how easily this entire scene could have been avoided. Learning from such observations, I always asked myself as a teacher: Are the actions I'm requiring of the students necessary to their social and intellectual development? Could such goals be accomplished without the mandated behaviors? Do the students feel a greater sense of belongingness as a result of the classroom requirements?

Many times, classroom conflicts can be avoided if we simply think of rules and regulations in these larger frameworks. If we are going to ask students to give up their survival-mode street stare—their tough demeanors, self-protective bearings, and aggressive postures—then we have to make sure that they feel safe and have a strong sense of being a valued participant in our classrooms. The best way to accomplish this goal is to know what we're doing (Kincheloe, 1995, 2005a; Weiner, 1999). When students know that their teacher can help them and their families in a variety of important ways including overcoming problems that interfere with their academic work, constructing lessons that change their lives in positive ways, building communities where they are respected and valued, they will work hard to assist teachers in creating loving, vibrant, and happy classrooms.

There is no reason that critical urban educators can't take the sense of community and belonging they construct in their classrooms and extend it to the creation of broader learning communities that connect in-school and out-of-school experience. A key dimension of a liberatory pedagogy in this context involves making connections with community organizations and service agencies in the neighborhoods surrounding the school. The work begun in critical classrooms can be enhanced and extended by these organizations and agencies, and synergistic partnerships can be established that connect academic learning to social change projects in the neighborhood.

Critical urban teachers are dedicated to taking advantage of the resources urban life provides and establishing connections with these groups is a central way of doing this. Through such community organizations urban teachers could, for example, hold "parents night" meetings in a Dominican Community Center employing numerous Spanish-English interpreters. Such a move would work to make many parents who were not first-language English speakers feel more comfortable in their interactions with teachers. Also, it would help dispel the perception and too often the reality that schools are created for middle-class, white, English-speaking students. Critical urban teachers work hard to make sure that such disparities are openly addressed and overcome (Wang & Kovich, 1996; McDermott & Rothenberg, 2000; Carvan et al., 2002).

The complexity of the problems of urban education can often times be represented in such a way that all parties involved with the domain develop a sense of paralysis. kecia hayes, Philip Anderson, Karel Rose, and I promote an urban pedagogy that works to overcome this inaction not by ignoring the social, cultural, political, and economic forces that undermine our efforts to improve urban schools but by facing such impediments head-on. Advocates of a critical urban pedagogy understand better than anyone the difficulty of the task at hand, but plow on in the face of such adversity with an iron resolve to construct critical learning communities both within the school and with the larger urban community. With our irrepressible belief in the power of human agency even in the face of potent oppressive forces and structures, advocates of a transformative approach to teaching and learning maintain that urban schools can, despite the odds, accomplish great things for the benefit of students. Even in these dark times, the hope that Karel and Philip write about in the beginning of this introduction can be kept alive and progress can be made in public urban schools.

Urban
Education

The Context of Urban Education

NO CHILD LEFT BEHIND AND URBAN EDUCATION: THE PURPOSE AND FUNDING OF PUBLIC EDUCATION

Thomas Brignall III

This chapter generates a discourse surrounding two major issues in national urban education. The first is whether there is a commonly accepted accord as to the purpose of education. A dialectical approach will help bring out the dynamic interconnectedness and the conflicts that exist among the various theoretical perspectives on public education. In recent elections, one of the top issues has been the improvement of public education. Yet, from the nation's president to local PTAs, public education is regularly criticized for failing to do a good job. However, before trying to address any specific education issues, it is reasonable to first identify the purpose of public education. Arguably, the only effective way to evaluate whether public education is a success is to delineate its goals.

The second issue is to assess the often-cited need for increased funding for public schools. Government officials and others who propose changes to the public education system often try to give a well-defined purpose of education. However, when an initiative is announced, the mechanisms for such reforms are often absent altogether or added as an after-

thought. Kozol contends that many public school systems are struggling to scrape up enough funds to pay their heating bills, buy enough textbooks, and provide Internet connections.[1]

I will analyze various theoretical purposes of education and the goals of the No Child Left Behind bill, as well as the current funding methods of public education and the need for further funding of schools that fail to meet federal standards. Following these two takes, I will offer some suggestions to help address the funding dilemma faced by public education.

DEFINING THE PURPOSE OF PUBLIC EDUCATION

For the sake of brevity, I will assume that the majority of citizens views public education as necessary and important, and accepts that it will continue to be publicly funded by taxes. Instead of engaging in a historiographical debate, I will attempt to identify the purposes of the public school (or what it should be), and whom the public school serves (or should serve).

Four theoretical models would seem to be relevant in this pursuit: (1) functionalist,

(2) class-cultural reproductive, (3) integrative-reproductive, and (4) neofunctionalist assimilationist. I provide a brief example of each theoretical model, rather than an exhaustive overview.

Functionalist

Some functionalists contend that public education is a structure for positive social change. For example, according to Button and Provenzo, Thomas Jefferson intended public education to exist for the purpose of training individuals to be good citizens.[2] Beyond basic instruction in reading, writing, and arithmetic, each individual would be provided a general background of the concept of democracy. The second phase of Jefferson's program was composed of schools for those who wished to pay the necessary tuition (with a few scholarships for the most talented boys). This second phase would be training for politicians, doctors, and other professional positions. Button and Provenzo contend that Jefferson believed the purpose of education was assimilationist in nature, to acculturate individuals into becoming good Americans.[3]

The assimilationist position is one of the oldest functionalist positions regarding public education. Shaping new immigrants into good citizens has been a goal of many previous educators. James G. Carter maintained that the poor and ignorant did not seek education. Unless properly educated, they posed a serious revolutionary threat to the integrity of the republic.[4] Tozer, Violas, and Senese contend that Calvin Stowe believed foreigners who settle on American soil should cease to be Europeans and become Americans.[5] Pluralism and multiculturalism were seen as being un-American, and a potential threat to the political stability of the nation. For Tozer, Violas, and Senese, the early public schools were structures that could help prevent revolution, build a nationalistic spirit, and instill values defined in accordance with the Protestant ideology.

Horace Mann believed that public education could be used to provide individuals with egalitarian opportunities.[6] He argued that public education would facilitate development of liberal and human values of rationality and tolerance, as well as equality of opportunity. Mann contended that public education would eventually solve all social issues and problems by producing educated citizens.

Class-Cultural Reproductive

Class-cultural reproductive theorists claim that the educational system is primarily shaped by the struggle among different social classes. Each social class has access to distinct educational structures, and individuals use education to ameliorate their own status within the social stratification system. One of the consequences of a stratified education system is that the educational credentials and qualifications students earn have no necessary technical and economic function. Instead, credentials simply reflect the ability of certain groups to exclude those without such credentials or similar status characteristics.

Bowles and Gintis, for example, argue that educational institutions in capitalist societies do not serve the interests of society as a whole.[7] Instead, the primary purpose of public education is to correspond with the needs of the production system and the interests of the bourgeoisie. For Bowles and Gintis, public schooling is imposed on the poor to help shape them into content producers and consumers of commodities. Indeed, Bowles and Gintis deny that the development of public education has created equality of opportunity. For them, public education is not about emancipation, it is about the continuation of bourgeoisie exploitation.

Collins' historical analysis effectively demonstrates his claim that the enormous expansion of education since the mid-nineteenth century has had no impact at all on increased social mobility.[8] Instead, Collins argues that the reason most students are in school is that they want a decent job.[9] School becomes a forum to procure a level of status credential in order to be able to struggle for various levels of status and access to economic goals.

Pierre Bourdieu also asserts that public education contributes to the reproduction of the structure of power and symbolic relationships between classes, by contributing to the reproduction of the structure of the distribution of cultural capital among classes.[10] In his view, the object of education is the production of habitus, the reinforcement of the system of dispositions that act as a mediation between structures and practice. He argues that education creates symbolic wealth that legitimizes culture and the status level that a given element of culture has.

Bourdieu criticizes ideas of equity that might be achievable. In theory, if a poor family sent their child to a higher-status school, and the child received a degree, the child would be likely to join the elite. Bourdieu makes the case that, outside the specifically academic market, the value of a diploma depends on the economic and social values of the person who possesses it. Education is for everyone, but only the elites who get the proper diplomas will be allowed by other elites to participate in the creation and reward of cultural capital and career and social success.

Integrative-Reproductive

Integrative-reproductive theorists argue that there is an inevitable subjective-objective split in social theory as to the purpose of schooling that cannot ultimately be resolved.[11] Consequently, integrative-reproductive theorists argue that educational reproduction and change can only be understood by focusing on the state as the mediating point through which various economic, class, and technical factors are regulated to create social order. When certain transformative-resistance conditions occur, individuals and collective subjects become mobilized as part of

counter-hegemonic trends. Group members need to break the bonds and control of cultural capital by an acceptance of multiple perspectives, and by either creating new acceptable forms of cultural capital or devaluing those that currently exist.

Freire contends simply that there is no neutral education. Education is either for domestication or for freedom—an initial choice is required of the educator.[12] For Freire, the teacher must abandon the banking method of education. The banking method of teaching is when the teacher knows everything and students know nothing; the teacher thinks and the students are thought about; the teacher acts and the students have the illusion of acting through the actions of the teacher; and the teacher is the subject of the learning process, while the pupils are mere objects.

Freire argues that the current banking concept of teaching attempts to control thinking and action, leads women and men to adjust to the world, and inhibits their creative power. The students must not be docile listeners, but critical co-investigators with the teacher. In this attempt individuals will gain respect not only for their own knowledge but for the knowledge of others. The dominant elite consider the remedy for the problems of education to be more domination and repression carried out in the name of freedom, order, and social peace.

Neofunctionalist Assimilationists

Neofunctionalist assimilationists argue for a back-to-basics approach to solve the problems in education. Education must instill the values of hard work and obedience, proper aspects of morality, and concepts of right and wrong. To reverse the failures of the current education system, new programs such as cultural literacy, curriculum redesign, standardized tests to measure success, and professionalization of curricula are not only important but necessary. Thus, the purpose of education reverts back to the ideas of Jefferson and Mann. According to Nash, by creating equity for those individuals who wish to work hard at the American dream, the education system is still working (although damaged).[13] Therefore, the solutions to current education problems are a return to morality, equality, and truth.

William Bennett argues for the necessity of a national effort to help form the moral character of the young and to aid them in achieving moral literacy.[14] Bennett proposes a core curriculum that would provide the same basic liberal arts education to all students. Bennett believes a person who is morally literate will be immeasurably better equipped than a morally illiterate person to reach a reasoned and ethnically defensible position on these tough issues.[15]

Hirsch advocates that schools should follow the ideas of Jefferson as to how curricula should be developed. Jefferson encouraged devising a common curriculum in order that the great mass of people be taught not just the elements of reading, writing, and arithmetic, but also that their minds be filled with the most useful facts from Greek, Roman, European, and American history, as well as the first elements of morality.[16] Newcomers to a country who are not immersed in its frames of reference often remain outsiders.

Finally, Bloom mourns the modern loss of faith in natural rights, essential being, and religion whereby people once found a fundamental basis of unity and sameness.[17] Bloom argues that it is human nature for all children everywhere, regardless of class, ethnicity, race, or gender, to want to know the truth and to lead a morally good life. He stresses the importance in Western cultural heritage embodying this universal truth, and the responsibility of the public schools to transmit this truth to all children.

THE PURPOSE OF PUBLIC EDUCATION: A COMMON THREAD

There does appear to be a common thread running through the several perspectives on public education: the means by which education instills in citizens cultural traits and values. The functionalists and the neofunctionalist assimilationists would certainly agree that an approach stressing accountability, morals, and a common cultural identity is critical to a successful education system. Bowles and Gintis would also seem to agree, albeit they believe the current education system is already conveying the goals of the bourgeoisie in particular.[18] This is consistent with Collins and Bourdieu, who argue that public education ultimately promotes the aspirations of those in power. These views are in contrast to the integrative-reproductive theorists who believe that education should be used to promote multicultural worldviews, economic equality, justice, global value systems, and the rejection of monoculture. Nevertheless, this contrast points to a common thread among all four of the theoretical models: cultural indoctrination of citizens. However, it does not appear as though an accord will soon be reached regarding which cultural ideas should be promoted, or by which process these cultural ideas should be disseminated.

Even the integrative-reproductive theorists such as Freire, who argue that such cultural conditioning would bankrupt the country with mindless automatons, are proposing a form of cultural conditioning—one that calls for emancipating individuals from the current cultural conditioning. If individuals are free and encouraged to acquire independent conclusions about the world around them, surely there will be some students who support the current political and economic system and others who will oppose it. In either case, this is a form of cultural conditioning, and it is a fundamental purpose of public education.

Bowles and Gintis, Collins, and Bourdieu all take a critical perspective in arguing that public education creates an oppressive structure where students are indoctrinated into accepting a stratified system. Regardless of whether their perspectives are completely accurate, it would seem logically obvious that students need to learn how to function socially, politically, economically, and spiritually in society in order to survive and prosper. I am not proposing that everyone should accept the capitalist model. Nevertheless, students do need job and life skills, regardless of whether they are going to be rock singers, factory workers, or teachers. Students need to develop analytic thinking skills to navigate the various problems they will encounter.

A second common thread linking the perspectives on public education could be the development of students who think critically and are culturally aware. Although this is a form of emancipation, it is not a rejection of everything traditional, current, or beloved. In this view, students are emancipated from the notions that oppress them—from ideas that privilege only certain forms of knowledge or hold them back from achieving their goals. Instead, students learn multiple perspectives on life—spiritual, economic, and philosophical. Basic skills such as reading, writing, and mathematics are still a priority. However, these priorities do not come at the expense of creative, critical, or cooperative learning.

This view provides multiple approaches to public education, each allowing students to pick a path that is most comfortable for them. Students could choose college, a job, or an artistic or hybrid education path. For students who do not wish to pursue higher education, high schools could train students to pursue jobs directly out of high school. If business and industry assume some of the burden of job training, educators could focus on the basic skills students need to function in society, such as reading, writing, and communications skills. Public education could focus on life skills instead of on direct job training. This way, as jobs and technology change, students would have the critical learning skills they need to quickly adapt to new social and economic environments.

FUNDING PUBLIC EDUCATION

The ubiquity and pace of social and technological change underscore one of the most difficult problems of public education funding. According to St. John, the total revenue for public education in 2001 was \$401 billion.[19] Federal sources of funding accounted for 7.3 percent, local and intermediate sources accounted for 43.1percent, and the remaining 49.7 percent came from state resources. Although most of these monies appear to come from property tax collections, the exact amounts derived from taxes or other revenue sources frequently cannot be determined from state education agency accounting records.[20]

The National Governors Association has argued that most state governments have been experiencing their worst fiscal crisis since the Second World War.[21] Because of the budget crisis of 2001–04, many states have had to close substantial budget gaps. Of the 47 states responding to a National Conference of State Legislatures (NCSL) survey, all but five states projected 2004 budget deficits.[22] There are limited options available to most states when cutting budgets. Over the last few years, most states have depleted their extra funds, enacted cuts in spending, raised taxes, and sometimes resorted to borrowing. Because of the size of most budgets for public education, these became obvious targets for spending cuts. According to Reschovsky, 35 states cut their 2002–04 education budgets when measured by expenditures per pupil in public education.[23]

Researchers like Orfield and Lee,[24] Ravitch,[25] and Wilson contend that there is a strong correlation between poverty and race with regard to both access to and quality of public education.[26] This correlation is particularly important in the nation's urban school systems. Ravitch contends that while urban schools enroll only 24 percent of all public school students in the United States, they enroll 35 percent of poor students, and 43 percent of minority students. The odds are against poor students in urban public schools.[27] Ravitch reports only 23 percent of fourth graders meet minimal standards. Poor children in city schools are far less likely to meet the basic achievement level on National Assessment of Educational Progress (NAEP) tests than are poor children who do not live in cities. Poverty is highly correlated to poor health, inadequate housing, high crime rates, single-parent families, and substance abuse. All these conditions create an environment in which heroic efforts are necessary to sustain aspirations for the future and a willingness to work hard for delayed benefits.[28]

Although Collins believes that education fails most individuals who want to rise in class standings,[29] Wilson argues that immigrants have used public education for hundreds of years as an effective mechanism of upward social mobility.[30] He maintains that many blacks moved out of the agricultural South to urban areas in the North, East, and Midwest. Because of access to quality public education in those places, blacks could compete for and get jobs, mostly in manufacturing and then later in professional occupations. According to Wilson, there is today a well-established black middle class that owes its very existence to public education.

So why is it that many urban education districts are so poorly funded and have so many students who are struggling? According to Greenberg, localities raise revenues for public education primarily through property values and local tax rates.[31] Funding disparities occur because tax bases among school districts vary widely. School districts with low property values tend to raise less local revenue per pupil, even with higher tax rates. In those urban areas whose industries and busi-

nesses have moved out to the suburbs or out of the country completely, and where the majority of citizens have low incomes, there are few significant tax resources and schools are poorly funded. Greenberg contends that these poor students risk academic failure simply because their communities lack the resources to adequately prepare them.[32]

According to the National Center for Education, the difference in earnings between a high school graduate and a college graduate is significant. In 2002, the unemployment rate for high school dropouts was 7.3 percent, while for people with a bachelor's degree it was only 2.3 percent. Similarly, median annual earnings for high school dropouts aged 25–34 were only $19,225 for males and $11,583 for females. In contrast, males with a high school diploma or equivalent earned $26,399, and females earned $16,573. Most strikingly, however, the median annual earnings for males with a bachelor's degree were $56,334 and for females $40,415.[33]

The majority of respondents to recent Gallop, Roper, Zogby, and Harris polls perceive education as a top issue. Many citizens see public education as a crucial element directly related to opportunities for social mobility. In addition to national defense and public health, education is one of the few easily perceived universal government benefits. If the majority of the public perceives education as a citizen's benefit, it therefore behooves the federal government, along with state and local governments, to financially support public education.

In a recent *Education Week* report, the performance of African-American and non-Hispanic white students on the 2003 administration of the National Assessment of Educational Progress in fourth-grade reading and eighth-grade mathematics were problematic. Sixty-one percent of African Americans and 26 percent of whites scored below basic proficiency levels in reading, and 61 percent of African Americans and 21 percent of whites scored below basic proficiency in mathematics.[34] Hendrie contends that the racial and ethnic achievement gap has become a top issue among policymakers. Eliminating disparities between blacks and Hispanics, on the one hand, and whites and Asian Americans on the other, is a primary goal of the No Child Left Behind Act.[35]

NO CHILD LEFT BEHIND

President George W. Bush proposed the No Child Left Behind (NCLB) Act to tackle the problems of reduced access to quality education among the poor and minorities.[36] According to Orfield, the bill is an 1,100-page research document calling for impossible achievements that have yet to be accomplished anywhere; requiring the use of fifty different sets of standards; and incorporating very rigid sanctions.[37] Although he is pessimistic about NCLB, Orfield contends that there are some good things about the act: more money for poor schools, a new reading program, and money to improve existing reading programs.

However, Orfield also points out that standardized testing has led to increased drop-out rates, especially among disadvantaged children. To this point, schools have been able to get credit for raising test scores by getting rid of their low-achieving students.[38] The primary problem Orfield sees with the act is that it requires 90 percent of the children of all racial groups to be at or above the higher achievement level within a period of only 12 years.

Orfield, Kim, and Sunderman believe the act radically alters the role of federal and state governments while imposing unprecedented responsibilities and accountability for test-score gains. The requirements have no common meaning across state lines, with sanctions falling especially hard on minority and integrated schools, and ask-

ing for much less progress from affluent suburban schools.[39] In effect, if states cannot comply with federal demands, they stand to lose federal funds for other state programs. Thus, the federal government is demanding regulatory power without providing the funding necessary to implement the program demands. Indeed, by June of 2003, only 11 states had accountability plans that were fully approved by the U.S. Department of Education.[40]

The research of Holmes and Wolman finds that funding provided by NCLB fell short by more than $32 billion in 2003.[41] Holmes and Wolman believe that federal funding on top of federal regulation is crucial, because states and local governments already contribute 90 percent of the total funding for education and are currently struggling with budgets. Van Harken notes that many school districts in need of funding are cutting school programs that are not perceived as part of test preparation for improved accountability test scores.[42] An unintended consequence of the Act is that art, music, gym, science, and social studies are frequently cut or compromised to make the budget focus more on the core curriculum.

One provision of the No Child Left Behind Act provides for students whose schools are not meeting federal education standards. They can ask to attend another school of their choice. However, relatively few seem to be making this choice. Although thousands of students were eligible to transfer, fewer than 3 percent requested to change schools.[43] Students—especially poor and minority students—have problems transferring to new schools, such as difficulty arranging transportation, lack of additional resources to participate in extracurricular programs of more upscale schools, and the absence of peers at the new school.

A criticism common to many recent educational reforms is the inconsistency of standards from state to state, county to county, city to city, neighborhood to neighborhood.

Maybe it is time for the federal government to hold public schools accountable, since states and local school districts seem unable to achieve consistency of standards. Indeed, it is time for a modified form of No Child Left Behind. However, if the federal government is going to hold states and school districts accountable for raising the achievement of all students to strict proficiency standards, should not the federal government be accountable for fully funding the programs designed to support that effort?

The fight for education opportunity has been largely about money since *Brown v. Board of Education*.[44] However, it is not enough to provide equal funding. Equal funding can easily be manipulated. Adequate funding for the provision of minimum standards is more important. Kozol notes that some of the poorest schools are forced to spend immense portions of their budgets on heating and building maintenance alone.[45] Even when their basic infrastructures are sound, schools do not have appropriate student: teacher ratios, enough books and equipment, or library resources. They do not have adequate staff or security, and extracurricular activities are minimal. These situations are problems that adequate funding could solve. The question is, Where will the money come from?

CONCLUSION

This chapter began with two express purposes: to identify the fundamental purpose of public education, and to assess the need for increased funding for public education. It is apparent from all major theoretical perspectives that the fundamental purpose of public education is the cultural indoctrination of citizens, carried out in one fashion or another. Although there are (and historically have been) many declared purposes and goals of the U.S. public education system, cultural indoctrination seems universal.

Given the goal of acculturation of its citizens, it is therefore consistent that the government should fund public education. If this is the case, it can be strongly argued that federal, state, and local governments should share the cost of public education—with the greatest burden carried by state and local governments. However, the variety of standards across the country and the clear lack of equal access to quality education within certain sectors of the population make it obvious that increased levels of federal support are necessary. This has become particularly apparent with implementation of the No Child Left Behind Act. Because the federal government has mandated and is enforcing the application of federal standards, it is reasonable to assert that the federal government should increase its share of the costs of public education.

In these days of trillion-dollar federal budgets, moving from the current level of only 7 percent (or about $30 billion) of education funding to 10 or 12 percent ($40–50 billion) would seem both economically and politically feasible. Such increases would certainly be modest, compared to the cost of maintaining the nation's military, and it would seem that the goal of providing equal access to quality education is worthwhile.

NOTES

1. Kozol, J. (1991). *Savage inequalities: Children in America's schools.* New York: Crown Publishers.

2. Button, W., & Provenzo, E. Jr. (1989). *History of education & culture in America.* Englewood Cliffs, NJ: Prentice Hall.

3. Button & Provenzo (1989).

4. Button & Provenzo (1989).

5. Tozer, S., Violas, P., and Senese, G. (1989). *School and society: Historical and contemporary perspectives* (Rev. ed.). Boston: McGraw-Hill.

6. Mann, H. (1969). *Lectures on education.* New York: Ayer Press.

7. Bowles, H., & Gintis, S. (1976). *Schooling in capitalist America: Education reform and the contradictions of economic life.* New York: Basic Books Inc.

8. Collins, R. (1979). *The credential society: A historical sociology of education and stratification.* p. 182. New York: Academic Press.

9. Collins (1979).

10. Bourdieu, P. (1973). Cultural reproduction and social reproduction. In R. Brown (Ed.). *Knowledge, education, and cultural change,* pp. 71–112. London: Tavistock.

11. Morrow, R., & Torres, C. (1995). *Social theory and education: A critique of theories of social and cultural reproduction,* p. 38. Albany: State University Press.

12. Freire, P. (1997). *Pedagogy of the oppressed, p. VI.* (Rev. ed.) (M. Ramos, Trans.). New York: Continuum.

13. Nash, R. (1997). *Answering the virtuecrats: A moral conversation on character education.* New York: Teachers College Press.

14. Bennett, W. (1992). *The de-valuing of America: The fight for our culture and our children.* New York: Simon & Schuster.

15. Bennett, W. (1988). *Our children & our country,* p. 84. New York: Simon & Schuster.

16. Hirsch, E. (1987). *Cultural literacy: What every American needs to know,* p. 17. New York: Houghton Mifflin.

17. Bloom, A. (1987). *The closing of the American mind,* p. 17. New York: Simon & Schuster.

18. Bowles, H., & Gintis, S. (1976). *Schooling in capitalist America: Education reform and the contradictions of economic life.* New York: Basic Books Inc.

19. St. John, E. Revenues and expenditures for public elementary and secondary education: school year 2000-01, from http://nces.ed.gov/.

20. U.S. Census Bureau. Public education finances 2001, from http://www.census.gov/govs/www/school01.html.

21. National Governors Association. State budget outlook remains bleak, from http://www.nga.org/nga/newsRoom/1,1169,C_PRESS_RELEASE^D_4693,00.html9.

22. National Conference of State Legislatures. State budget update: February 2003, from http://www.ncsl.org/programs/fiscal/budget.htm.

23. Reschovsky, A. The impact of state government fiscal crises on local governments and schools, from http://www.lafollette.wisc.edu/publications/otherpublications.html.

24. Orfield, G., & Lee, C. *Brown* at 50: King's dream or Plessy's nightmare? from www.civilrightsproject.harvard.ed.

25. Ravitch, D. A new era in urban education? Policy Brief #35, from http://www.brookings.edu/comm/PolicyBriefs/pb035/pb35.htm.

26. Wilson, W. (1990). *The truly disadvantaged: The inner city, the underclass, and public policy.* Chicago: University of Chicago Press.

27. Ravitch, D. A new era in urban education? Policy Brief #35, from http://www.brookings.edu/comm/PolicyBriefs/pb035/pb35.htm.

28. Ravitch, Policy Brief #35.

29. Collins (1979).

30. Wilson, W. (1980). *The declining significance of race: Blacks and changing American institutions.* Chicago: University of Chicago Press.

31. Greenberg, C. Public school funding in Massachusetts: How does the commonwealth compare to the rest of the nation? from http://www.massbudget.org/list .php?content=all.

32. Greenberg, Public school funding in Massachusetts.

33. National Center for Education Statistics. (2002). Digest of education statistics 2002, from http://nces.ed.gov/edstats/.

34. The achievement gap. *Education Week,* from http://www.edweek.org.

35. Hendrie, C. In U.S. schools, race still counts, *Education Week,* from www.edweek.org/sreports/.

36. United States Department of Education. Introduction: No child left behind, from http://www.ed.gov/nclb/overview/intro/index.html.

37. Orfield, G. No child left behind? A faculty response to President Bush's education bill, from http://www.gse.harvard.edu/.

38. Orfield. No child left behind?

39. Orfield, G., Kim, J. & Sunderman, G. No child left behind: A federal, state, and district level look at the first year, from http://www.gse.harvard.edu/.

40. Orfield, G., & Lee, C. *Brown* at 50.

41. Holmes, D., & Wolman, P. No child left behind? The funding gap in ESEA and other federal education programs, from http://www.nea.org/esea/fundinggap.html.

42. Van Harken, J. Budget cut student experience, from http://www.cnn.com/2003/EDUCATION/ 08/13/sprj.sch.cuts/.

43. Orfield, G., Kim, J. & Sunderman, G. No child left behind: A federal, state, and district level look at the first year, from http://www.gse.harvard.edu/.

44. Winter, G. 50 years after *Brown*, the issue is often money, from http://www.nytimes.com.

45. Kozol, J. (1991). *Savage inequalities: Children in America's schools*. New York: Crown Publishers.

THE MILITARIZED ZONE

Ronnie Casella

With federal support, school administrators, police departments, and security professionals have established what could be described as militarized zones in middle schools and high schools in urban areas. In some cases, the militarized zone is a select sector of the school composed of those in Junior Reserve Officers' Training Corps (JROTC) programs, those who are steered to military recruiters (often by school counselors), and those submitted to the most stringent aspects of security enforcement (often youths in the lower tracks of schools, specifically African-American, Native American, and Latino/-a youths). In other cases, the militarized zone encompasses entire schools, as in the case of the Valley Forge Military Academy, a 7–12 boarding school, and the Chicago Military Academy and Carver Military High School, both public high schools in Chicago.[1] The militarized zone accustoms youths to military-like thinking and discipline and facilitates their recruitment into branches of the military. In addition to the overt recruitment of youths, militarized zones are recognizable by the military-like tactics and equipment that school police, security officers, and guards use to "combat" violence, which creates in schools (just when youths are forming their ideas about society) not only a security regime resembling soldiers (who end up replacing teachers and school administrators as disciplinarians), but also the expectation that life is a military state where police, surveillance cameras, checkpoints, and military tactics are ever present

and taken for granted. The military is especially interested in urban areas, where its major enticements—education, a salary, and a career—resonate with young people with limited opportunities but much motivation, many of whom are African American and Latino/-a. Democrats as well as Republicans within the federal government have supported the training of these mostly poor and lower-middle-class teenagers for military service, recognizing that global capitalism will need a steady stream of police, guards, security consultants, and military personnel for protection, to oversee new colonies, to monopolize scarce resources, and to repress dissent abroad and in the United States.

MILITARY TACTICS AND TECHNOLOGIES

The adoption of military-like security tactics by schools (including raids, sweeps, random searches, detainment, and checkpoints) along with new security technologies (from surveillance to biometrics) has occurred as concerns about violence have increased but also as advanced security technologies and funding to install the equipment and hire police and guards have become more readily available to schools by the federal government. Through various funding sources, including Community-Oriented Policing Service (COPS) grants and the Safe and Drug-Free Schools Act, police departments have been able to expand their links to schools at the same time that they have expanded their links to the military, especially through police training sessions that teach military tactics and the use of new military equipment.[2] New urban police gear and uniforms borrow heavily from military stock, including helmets, "body bunkers," combat boots, padding and vests, and shoulder microphones. At the federal level, the U.S. Department of Defense (DoD) and National Institute of Justice conduct joint conferences and training sessions on security, and the Defense Advanced Research Projects Agency (DARPA) develops technologies for both military and criminal justice applications. The DoD, National Institute of Justice, U.S. Department of Education, and the Secret Service have begun collaborative research and training projects together, as well.

In a militarized zone, there is sometimes a blurring among police, private security, and military divisions—sometimes the difference between a police officer, school resource officer, a guardsman, military enlistee, and private security officer is little more than the organizations paying their salaries. They not only look similar and use similar tactics, and receive training from similar governmental and professional groups, but one profession is often training for another. It is typical for police officers to have served in the military, or for retired police officers to work for security firms, or for students directed toward the military through JROTC to one day have a job in a security firm or police department, perhaps working in a school. The military is a pathway for many youths to enter the police profession and, more recently, an entryway into the security profession. It is not a coincidence that a U.S. military Web site in 2004 featured a very professional African American whose biography appears in their "life story" section: From high school he joined the Army and then became founder and CEO of a private security firm. Another life story highlights a young white boy who claims that he wants to become a police officer after his military service.[3]

The establishment of militarized zones has meant a windfall of money for security businesses as well. According to common knowledge, the installation of security technologies in schools is an outcome of unprecedented school violence in the 1990s and terrorism threats in the early twenty-first century. But school administrators have also been supported by federal and state authorities, and often prodded by the public, to buy into the techno-security buildup, and the security industry has nursed the public school sector, turning it into one of the most lucrative new markets of the twenty-first century.[4] Whether in the form of radios, upright and handheld metal detectors, scanners, closed-circuit televisions (CCTVs), access control equipment, face or iris recognition systems, or other forms of biometrics, school security is a rapidly growing niche for the security industry, which itself is a growing international organization composed of security businesses with contracting links to the military, schools, prisons, and government offices, as well as technology labs and computer companies that aid in the development of the equipment and architectural and engineering firms that help with their installation and design. Many security items, including those sold by companies with household names (such as Honeywell, G.E., and Sony), were developed for military purposes. Created by military scientists, microchip technologies (aiding in the development of computers); geographical information, positioning, and mapping technologies; digital messaging; and laser technologies have all been indispensable for the development of surveillance, tracking, metal detection, and information-gathering devices used in schools and elsewhere.[5]

Education policy also supports the production and use of school security equipment. The federal Secure Our Schools matching grant program (reauthorized in 2003) provides schools with funding to purchase security equipment, conduct security assessments and training of personnel, and coordinate with police. The National Institute of Justice has provided funds to schools to install security devices, and the 2002 No Child Left Behind law has provided money to Sandia National Laboratories in Albuquerque, New Mexico, where scientists are working to develop advanced security technology for use by the military, police, prisons, and schools.[6] Sandia National Laboratories was established in 1941 as part of the U.S. Department of Energy to aid in the development of atomic and nuclear weapons for the United States. The Security Technologies and Research Division of Sandia is in charge of the research, design, development, and testing of security technologies for government offices, prisons, and schools; its School Security Technology and Resource Center distributes information about school security specifically.

Although the use of new security technologies is still relatively modest, with support from military, police, school, and federal sectors, the number of schools relying on security equipment is increasing. According to a National Center for Education Statistics study conducted in 1996–97, about 4 percent of public schools conducted random metal detector checks on students, and 1 percent of schools required that students pass through an upright metal detector each morning.[7] In a study conducted in 1999–2000, the use of random metal detector checks doubled, occurring in nearly 8 percent of schools, and the daily use of upright metal detectors increased to 1.7 percent of public schools.[8] In the 1996–97 study, the use of video surveillance was not included, but in the 1999–2000 study, the category was included, and 15 percent of public schools reported that they used surveillance cameras in their buildings. The later study also included the pres-

ence of police in schools: Nearly one in four schools reported that they used police or guards in their schools. According to the 1999–2000 study, the random use of metal detectors is about three times higher in urban schools (about 14% of urban schools) than in suburban and rural schools, and the daily use of upright metal detectors is nearly five times higher in urban schools (about 5% of all urban public schools). However, the use of video surveillance is relatively the same in urban (15.5%), suburban (15%), and rural schools (14.1%), which demonstrates how individuals across a large swath of demographics have become accustomed to random surveillance, creating what some have called a "surveillance society."[9]

The earlier 1996–97 study included two categories related to security equipment (two categories about metal detectors) and the rest of the categories related to actions or rules: "visitors must sign in," "closed campus for most students during lunch," "controlled access to school buildings," "controlled access to school grounds," and "one or more drug sweeps." In the 1999–2000 study, there are three categories related to security equipment ("video surveillance" was added) and another related to the presence of school police or guards. It is possible that future reports will continue a trend that began with these two reports, replacing old categories having to do with actions and rules with more categories relating to policing and equipment. In other words, it is likely that categories such as "visitors must sign in" and "closed campus for most students during lunch" (which are in the 1999–2000 study) will be replaced with categories relating to the use of palm and iris scanners and facial recognition technology such as those used in schools in Philadelphia, Arizona, New Jersey, and elsewhere.[10]

The use of such technologies is not a natural outgrowth or logical response to school shootings. It is an effort by federal and state officials, business people, and school administrators to fortify schools—without much evidence that the school will actually be safer—because it benefits those individuals involved in the fortification efforts. The corporate sector obviously prospers as the public school market is laid open to private companies. The federal government benefits because it can support the military economy at the same time that it "earns extra points" for developing school and police security devices (since all these devices are so similar). The federal government, in conjunction with Sandia National Laboratories and security corporations, can also try out their products, using schools as testing grounds for the newest technologies. States and the public school sector benefit from federal funding and welcome the fortification of schools as an easy way of controlling students. School districts also benefit from lower insurance premiums as a result of security installation; a reduction in mischief, vandalism, and crime (although research demonstrates mixed results regarding the effectiveness of security equipment); and the award of various perks (in the form of funding as well as public approval) when they install the equipment. The military benefits when young people are conditioned to accept the militarization of public schools, when they learn to submit to authority and surveillance, and when they begin to see all sorts of military tactics and technologies as part of normal life. There are many ways of dealing with crime and violence. That the United States has turned to a mainly technological method that relies on devices that need to be continually redesigned and run by trained guards, security personnel, and police is not a commonsense response. It is made to be commonsense through these many efforts to promulgate the naturalness of mass security for the benefit of a select but powerful sector of U.S. society.

JROTC PROGRAMS AND MILITARY RECRUITMENT

Installing security equipment in schools accustoms youths to a militarized society, where police resemble military personnel; security is big business; and surveillance, bodily detections, and scans are a part of life not to be questioned or even thought about, for, we are led to believe, our authorities know what they are doing. Under these circumstances, military training in school seems logical and even desirable. This has been the case in high schools in the United States since early in the twentieth century, when the National Defense Act of 1916 established the JROTC during World War I. This authorized the use of military equipment by schools and assigned active duty military personnel to instruct students in military strategy and history. In 1964, during the Kennedy Administration and the Vietnam War, the ROTC Revitalization Act (Public Law 88–647) expanded the JROTC program to other military services (which in 2004 included the army, navy, air force, and marines) and replaced many of the military men teaching the program with military retirees. It also mandated that costs of the program be paid for, in part, by school districts. By the late 1990s, JROTC programs had been established in about 3,000 schools in the United States and included about 400,000 student cadets and nearly 4,000 instructors. By the late 1990s the DoD was spending about $166 million on JROTC.[11] For those students involved in the program—who take military classes, run maneuvers in the courtyard or sport fields of their schools, wear JROTC uniforms, and participate in city and school marches—public high school is one step short of military school.

Like the military itself, JROTC is increasingly focused on youths of color. According to a 1999 report, *JROTC: Contributing to America's Communities*, African Americans made up 33 percent of all participants nationwide during the 1996–97 school year, up from 26 percent in 1994–95. Hispanics composed 10 percent of those in JROTC programs during the 1996–97 school year, up slightly from 9 percent in 1994–95. White students composed 41 percent of JROTC students during 1996–97—*down* from 50 percent in 1994–95.[12]

Proponents view the JROTC program as a stepping-stone for youths coming from poor communities, giving direction to those who may not be attending college or may be close to dropping out of school, and providing solid discipline for youths who lack family structure—all of which are clear references to city youths. George H. W. Bush's Operation Capital initiative was an effort to double the size of JROTC by targeting inner-city youths in Washington, DC, and other cities. Speaking to students at Lincoln Technical Institute in 1992, Bush said, "JROTC is a great program that boosts high school completion rates, reduces drug use, raises self-esteem, and gets kids firmly on the right track."[13] Similarly, then Secretary of State General Colin Powell issued a memorandum to the Bush administration stating that JROTC should be focused on areas "where drugs, gangs, and juvenile delinquency flourish."[14] In addition, JROTC advertisements hail the powers of the program to help youths graduate from high school and be successful: As its Web site states, JROTC "is a stimulus for promoting graduation from high school, and it provides instruction and rewarding opportunities that will benefit the student, community, and nation."[15]

Title 10 of the U.S. Military Code states that "it is a purpose of the [JROTC] to instill in students in United States secondary educational institutions the values of citizenship, service to the United States, and personal responsibility and a sense of accomplishment." It also requires that "the institution provide a course of military instruction of not less than three academic years' duration, as prescribed by

the Secretary of the military department concerned." Given the fact that cadets must receive "not less than three academic years" of military instruction, youths need to be identified and recommended for JROTC by ninth grade. To some extent, the JROTC program is another education track, a military track that sometimes blends with the lower and vocational education tracks, to which students are assigned based on middle school records and the behavior and abilities they demonstrate (usually by test scores) when they are as young as 13 or 14 years old.

That JROTC is a mechanism for the recruitment of especially urban youths is clear. Although there is no compensation for being in the program (as in the college-level program), students who enter the military from JROTC do so at a higher pay scale than those not in the program. Louis Caldera, secretary of the army during the Clinton Administration, stated in a report that JROTC "may inform young Americans about the opportunities available in the military while providing a positive influence during the high school years," and Colonel Carlos Glover, JROTC director at the time, stated that the point of JROTC is to "Recruit quality prospects, retain quality cadets to commission, and sustain the force."[16] At the school level, counselors will suggest that particular students enter JROTC, and these same students are the first to be notified when recruiters are in the building. In some schools, JROTC cadets are required or strongly urged to greet military recruiters when they are in the building. Given all these prods and perks, about 47 percent of students in JROTC do enter the military.[17]

The recruitment of high school students has met with sometimes-successful resistance by opponents, even in cities.[18] But the military is one of the most diverse organizations in the United States, partly because of the great number of youths of color from urban areas who are attracted to military careers. Many students are enticed by the educational opportunities ("hottest civilian jobs") and pay that the military provides, and military advertisements stress these points:[19]

- The U.S. Military operates a world-class job-training network, which includes over 300 schools teaching over 10,000 vocational and technical courses. The military created it because the Services need and train people constantly for hundreds of jobs. Some of them equate to the hottest civilian jobs, such as computer programming, medical technician, and health-care worker. Nearly every civilian job has a military equivalent (journalist, radio broadcaster, photographer, surveyor, driver, and so on)—but in the military, your training is free: Enlisted Training; Army; Navy; Air Force; Marine Corps; and Coast Guard. In 2003, new recruits start at about $1000 per month, which automatically increases to about $1239 per month after four months. By the time your first enlistment is up—say, at four years—you should be making approximately $1680 per month base pay, a nearly 59 percent increase from when you started. If you have some college education or completed JROTC in high school, some Services will start you as an E-3—at $1300 per month.
- Fact: Raises generally come faster and more reliably than in civilian life. In the military, you earn pay raises every two years simply for serving, and most people are promoted at least three times during their first four-year enlistment. Now that's something to add to your "pros" list.
- Base pay is just that—it's where your total compensation begins. Your total financial package also includes the value of your free housing and meals, and remember that, in the military, your money goes much farther than in the civilian world, thanks to military perks like low-cost life insurance, everyday shopping discounts, and so on.

The military also administers the Armed Services Vocational Aptitude Battery (ASVAB) Career Exploration Program, developed by the DoD and used in about 14,000 high schools. It includes an aptitude test, an interest inventory, and various career-planning surveys meant to introduce youths to possible careers. The test also includes a Military Careers Score that can be used with the guide *Military Careers*, which describes about 140 military careers available to youths. High school students also receive a Military Entrance Score—or Armed Forces Qualification Test (AFQT) score—that determines whether a student has met the entrance requirements for military service.

If this career planner—along with JROTC and military advertisements—is not enough, recruiters can go right to the source. Since the enactment of the No Child Left Behind (NCLB) law, military recruiters are allowed access to students' contact information. Previously, the Family Educational Rights and Privacy Act (FERPA) required written permission from parents before student records could be released to third parties. Since adoption of NCLB, recruiters can access student contact information unless a parent states in writing that the information should *not be* released. Hence, instead of opting in, parents must opt out. This was accomplished by amending FERPA "directory information" protocols. Schools are allowed to designate some information as public information, such as information about a student's participation in sports or information about a student's award: This is directory information. Under Section 9528 of NCLB—Armed Forces Recruiter Access to Students and Student Recruiting Information, a title that is clear about the intensions of the mandate—a student's name and contact information are now directory information for military recruiters.[20] Prior to passage of NCLB, a school board could have contested the release of information even when an appropriate FERPA request had been issued. However, with NCLB school administrators no longer have this option; they must release student contact information. Exceptions are made in the following cases: (1) a private school shows a documented history demonstrating a religious objection to the military; and (2) the governing body of a school votes in favor of barring military recruiters. As with the original FERPA legislation, schools that do not comply risk losing funds through Title I of the Elementary and Secondary Education Act.

School and military policies that promote recruitment, JROTC, aggressive school policing, and the use of military-like security tactics and technologies suit the needs of political elites who must train new generations of security forces to protect national interests (which are often the same as the economic interests of U.S. businesses) and to be the foot soldiers (the security guards and attendants, police, soldiers, special forces, etc.) for global capitalism. Hence, political elites must educate young people not only to accept greater militarization within the United States and abroad, but also to be part of it—to do the grunt work to sustain it.[21] And because recruitment has been in a slump for nearly two decades, the military has had to go right to the source of fresh men and women—to the schools.

THE MILITARY FUNCTION OF URBAN SCHOOLS UNDER GLOBAL CAPITALISM

As occurred in Chicago and elsewhere, an urban school district in Connecticut proposed in 2003 to use money from a U.S. Department of Homeland Security grant to build a separate public high school that would train students for careers in national security (including military service, and jobs as correction officers, police, and security guards). The school was proposed as an alternative school and a way to deal with troublesome youths. It would benefit the school district by providing a place to house their at-risk students. But the school would also be training the students to someday watch over other troublesome individuals in the United States or overseas—a scheme that would benefit those

in the higher echelons of society with investments in countries outside the United States. That such individuals benefit is not new, although the stakes have changed. In industrial society, these young people would have been placed in an alternative school to be taught manual or factory labor. In postindustrial society, we teach them to oversee unruly masses and protect the assets of global barons.

Schools have always served an economic function, and some would argue that schools are primarily a function of the state, which uses them to sort students, maintain control of youths, and provide bodies and brains for various national needs: military needs, professional needs, intellectual needs, political needs, and especially economic needs. Although a number of authors have made the point, Bowles and Gintis provided one of the first explanations of the schools' role in capitalist society, where students' access to knowledge is limited and circumscribed by disciplines, divisions of labor are established, schoolwork entails menial and repetitive chores, respect for authority is instilled, and the status quo is continually reproduced.[22] In this way, rule-abiding and semi-docile workers are formed, and elites assert their authority and maintain economic and social dominance over others. In industrial society, schools functioned to socialize youths for the needs of industrial society (for vocational training and consumption), for the way factories were structured, and for the development of a work ethic that was conducive to labor-intensive jobs. In postindustrial society, cities have lost their manufacturing base due to economic globalization, and those youths who would have been prepared for blue-collar work have become what some refer to as a "superfluous population"—a population that is no longer needed.[23]

In our society of instant communication, advanced technology, transnational conglomerates, and free-trade agreements, jobs in manual labor have been mostly replaced by work in the service industries and professional occupations (white collar, mid-level salary, or temp workers); work is often more temporal and spatially dispersed (people can work from their homes for businesses that are hundreds of miles away; people are quick to change jobs); technology has made work more efficient (hence fewer workers are needed); and corporations are less devoted to particular places. They now operate in a more international world that stretches jobs across continents.[24] Once organized around centers of commerce (a port, industrial center, or downtown business area), cities are now organized around entertainment districts, the creation of which has entailed gentrification, revitalization of "choice" neighborhoods, and subsequent displacement and isolation of those who cannot benefit the new economy and who are a detriment to the plans of developers.[25]

These changes have virtually cut off whole segments of mostly poor African–Americans, Latinos, and disenfranchised whites who lack professional backgrounds, were often moved out of neighborhoods to make way for gentrification or suburban sprawl, and were never educated to succeed in an information-technology world. They are therefore directed to confinement in either segregated neighborhoods or in prisons.[26] For those students who want to avoid pitfalls that so easily lead to prison but do not have what it takes, for whatever reason, to get into an affordable college yet want to get out of their poor neighborhoods where there is little work, the military is a likely option. To some extent, the induction of youths into the military is a way of tracking students to a career in a world that no longer needs factory workers but does need soldiers to provide the backbone that political, corporate, and military elites need to maintain dominance in a postindustrial, global economy. Because of socioeconomic and demographic realities, urban areas have become

prime recruitment grounds for the new types of masses that are needed today.

Economic globalization relies on controlling increasingly limited resources, sometimes through military might. And because economic globalization depends on some level of shared interest among political elites, good relations between military, political, and corporate interests must be maintained within the United States and with elites abroad. This is often done through international organizations, such as the World Bank, Organization for Economic Cooperation and Development, United Nations, the G8, World Trade Organization, and other international and especially economic groups (which are often dominated by the United States and its allies). When power becomes concentrated in these organizations, the power brokers wielding the greatest influence within them must protect their power and dominance to ensure that their own interests are met. Although there are vast differences and good intentions among the international groups, each is composed of individuals who make worldwide economic decisions that sometimes sustain vast divisions between rich and poor and developed and underdeveloped lands.

The militarized zone is established to prepare new generations of youths for a more militarized society where wars will be fought over access to resources, and oppressed and newly decolonized countries will try to establish their own power and gain access to the resources now controlled by mostly European and U.S. global barons and their international organizations. When such resistance and power grabbing become evident, troops will be sent in. This is a system of governance that does the bidding of the market, not the people, and veils economic wars in the discourse of democracy and liberation. It is a military system, economic system, and school system wrapped into one effort, which the United States pays for dearly. The military budget for the United States in 2003 (not including money to fund the Iraq invasion) was $379 billion, an increase of $48 billion from the previous year.[27] Just the $48 billion increase was more than the entire military budget of every other country in the world. (The United Kingdom had the second largest military budget, estimated at $35 billion.) A country that spends this much on the military cannot help but become a militarized society—a nation in perpetual preparation for war.

The increased uses of school policing and security devices, combined with stepped-up efforts to recruit high school students and expand JROTC, are ways of addressing school violence. But so are peer mediation programs, conflict resolution programs, and violence prevention programs, mentoring efforts, restorative justice, peace education, and hundreds of other programs, pedagogies, and strategies that guide, prod, urge, and teach youths how to behave and how to deal with conflict. In spite of some efforts and federal support, conflict resolution is becoming a passing phenomenon of the 1990s, often overshadowed by character education, Drug Abuse Resistance Education (DARE), and especially school militarization and security enforcement. But school militarization is not a logical response to school violence; it is a response that is subsidized by benefactors who make logic coincide with the reality that best suits their interests. There has always been the expectation that schools prepare youths for the real world. In this real world of the early twenty-first century, though, military and quasi-military forces will have to be trained and continually deployed. And those deployed will range mostly from lower-middle-class to poor, will come from urban (and poor rural) areas, and will be Latino/-a and African American. These youths will be the protectors of a mostly white and Christian U.S. aristocracy with Ivy League educations and dynasty-like connections.

The author wishes to thank Jack Gilroy and John Amidon for invaluable help on this chapter.

NOTES

1. Lipman, P. (2003). Cracking down: Chicago school policy and the regulation of black and Latino youth. In K. Saltman & D. Gabbard (Eds.), *Education as enforcement: The militarization and corporatization of schools* (pp. 81–102). New York: RoutledgeFalmer.

2. Nunn, S. (2001). Police technology in cities: Changes and challenges. *Technology in Society, 23,* 11–27.

3. U.S. military Web site. *Today's military—Life stories.* www.todaysmilitary.com.

4. Casella, R. (2003). The false allure of security technologies. *Social Justice, 30,* 82–93.

5. Lyon, D., & Zureik, E. (1996). *Computers, surveillance, and privacy.* Minneapolis: University of Minnesota Press; Monmonier, M. (2002). *Spying with maps: Surveillance technologies and the future of privacy.* Chicago: University of Chicago Press.

6. Green, M. (1999). *The appropriate and effective use of security technologies in U.S. schools.* Washington, DC: National Institute of Justice & Sandia National Laboratories.

7. National Center for Education Statistics, U.S. Department of Education, Fast Response Survey System. (1997). Principal/school disciplinary survey on school violence. *FRSS, 63.*

8. National Center for Education Statistics, U.S. Department of Education, Schools and Staffing Survey (SASS). (1999–2000). *Public and public charter school surveys.*

9. Lyon, D. (1994). *The electronic eye: The rise of surveillance society.* Minneapolis: University of Minnesota Press.

10. Eisenberg, E., & Steinhardt, B. (2003). *ACLU asks Arizona school district to reject face-recognition checkpoints.* Retrieved from the American Civil Liberties Union Web site: www.aclu.org; Wagman, J. (2002, October 24). District will use eye scanning. *The Philadelphia Inquirer,* www.philly.com.

11. Taylor, W. (1999). *JROTC: Contributing to America's communities, final report of the CSIS political-military studies project on the JROTC.* Washington, DC: Center for Strategic and International Studies.

12. Taylor (1999).

13. Berlowitz, M., & Long, N. (2003). The proliferation of JROTC: Education reform or militarization. In K. Saltman & D. Gabbard (Eds.), *Education as enforcement: The militarization and corporatization of schools* (pp. 163–176). New York: RoutledgeFalmer.

14. Berlowitz & Long (2003).

15. JROTC. (2005). *JROTC academy.* www.jrotc. org.

16. Berlowitz, M., & Long, N. (2003).

17. Saltman, K. (2003). Introduction. In K. Saltman & D. Gabbard (Eds.), *Education as enforcement: The militarization and corporatization of schools* (pp. 1–24). New York: RoutledgeFalmer.

18. Amidon, J. (2001). *Community opposition sends marine JROTC unit into retreat.* Retrieved from the Veterans for Peace Web site: www.veterans forpeace.org; Brune, A. (2003, October 9). No child left alone. *The Hartford Advocate*, p. 12.

19. U.S. military Web site. *My future—Military opportunities.* www.myfuture.com.

20. Daggett, L. (2002). FERPA update 2002: The two new Supreme Court FERPA cases, and post 9/11 congressional balancing of student privacy and safety interests. In *Balancing rights: Education law in a brave new world.* Education Law Association, Conference Papers, pp. 255–269, Nov. 14–16, 2002; Doyle, S. (2002). FERPA: What exactly is an educational record?" In *Balancing rights: Education law in a brave new world.* Education Law Association, Conference Papers, pp. 271–278, Nov. 14–16, 2002.

21. Gilroy, J. (1999, November 12). Time for academics to teach U.S. youth to wage peace.

National Catholic Reporter, p. 12; Harris, I., & Morrison, M. (2003). *Peace education.* Jefferson, North Carolina: McFarland & Company.

22. Bowles, S., & Gintis, H. (1976). *Schooling in capitalist America.* New York: Basic Books.

23. Duncan, G. (2000). Urban pedagogies and the celling of adolescents of color. *Social Justice, 27,* 29–42.

24. Brown, P., & Lauder, H. (1996). Education, globalization, and economic development. *Journal of Education Policy, 11,* 1–25; Casella, R. (2002). Globalization, child welfare policy, and the economics of social uplift. *Educational Foundations, 16,* 5–24; Torres, C. (2002). Globalization, education, and citizenship: Solidarity versus markets? *American Educational Research Journal, 39,* 363–378.

25. Anyon, J. (1997). *Ghetto schooling: A political economy of urban educational reform.* New York: Teachers College Press; Lipman, P. (2002). Making the global city, making inequality: The political economy and cultural politics of Chicago school policy. *American Educational Research Journal, 39,* 379–422.

26. Brown, J. (2003). *Derailed: The school to jailhouse track.* Washington, DC: The Advancement Project; Dunbar, C. (2001). From alternative school to incarceration. *Qualitative Inquiry, 7,* 158–170; Ferguson, A. (2000). *Bad boys: Public schools in the making of black masculinity.* Ann Arbor: University of Michigan Press.

27. Arenas, A. (2003). In defense of good work: Jobs, violence, and the ethical dimension. *Social Justice, 30,* 94–107.

BIG CITIES, SMALL SCHOOLS: REDEFINING EDUCATIONAL SPACES IN THE URBAN CONTEXT

Rebecca Sánchez and Mostafa Mouhie Eddine

The struggle is to make the tensions and issues of teaching and learning public so that the critique of a de facto school system is commonly understood and can become the basis for restructuring a school system. The small schools are models of how things can be—not perfect, not a panacea—but a series of real, working pictures.[1]

Standardized tests, super-sized schools, and prescriptive (canned) curricula have created a pedagogy of regimentation in many urban schools. It is troubling although not surprising when kids, especially poor and minority kids, opt out of education. Impersonal schooling, lack of proximal mentors, and mass-produced curriculum make educational success difficult for many. As educators it is imperative to understand the inequity, loneliness, and disconnectedness that many youth face in large, impersonal urban schools. How can we infuse just practices into our educational system? How can we redesign and restructure schools so kids don't fall out of the system? What can we do as educators and community members to commit to and connect with our youth?

Educational reform must occur at more than one level in order to make a lasting and consequential impact on students. The focus on pedagogical practice, professional development, and policy analysis and creation address the breadth of educational reforms necessary in our diverse society. In his book *Empowering Education*, Ira Shor describes democratic and libratory pedagogical practices that occur at the classroom level.[2] Classroom level changes can enhance and contribute to more meaningful educational opportunities; however, the interconnectedness of policy and practice must also be addressed. In *The Right to Learn* Darling-Hammond states, "Progressive education requires more than committed teachers striving for classroom-level reform."[3] She then describes systemic hindrances to change: "But it is the system's deeply ingrained mechanisms for organizing schooling that have thus far prevented the enactment of widespread change."[4]

The *Small Schools Movement* is a grassroots effort to redefine, redesign, and reform public schools to better serve a diverse student population. The goal of this movement is to move away from large *factory-model schools* and create small, community schools in an effort to increase student success. Factory-model schools have been criticized for their impersonal structures, fragmented curricula, segregated and unequal program options, and inability to respond effectively to various students needs.[5]

The Small Schools Movement is one example of how educators are working to redefine educational possibilities for students. The movement is also encouraging to critical educators because it provides hopeful examples of communities, educators, and students actively working and engaging in systemic, curricular, and pedagogical change. Beyer and Apple state,

Meaningful curriculum reform must occur within those social institutions, and by those people, most intimately connected to the lives of students: teachers, administrators, students, and community members whose work in schools aids the process of genuinely transforming educational practice.[6]

The Small Schools Movement demonstrates this type of collaborative educational endeavor.

This chapter has two purposes. The first is to identify some of the historical, social, curricular, cultural, and educational possibilities and implications for small schools, especially in relation to furthering social justice. The emphasis on this overview section will be to analyze how small schools impact schooling for diverse populations within the urban context. The second purpose is to describe the organizational efforts of two urban communities to develop small schools as an option for educational reform.

A BRIEF LOOK BACK

Small schools have been the norm for a significant portion of our nation's educational history. However, during the latter part of the last century, schools moved from being small, intimate learning places, to being large factory-model schools. Even schools with few students, began to follow the large school model of education. In her reflection on multicultural educational practices, bell hooks describes how for many of us, education has been frighteningly similar:

Let's face it; most of us were taught in classrooms where styles of teachings reflected the notion of a single norm of thought and experience, which we were encouraged to believe was universal.[7]

Such universality and mechanized education came about with the value shift of the industrial revolution.

Hampel identifies five major beliefs about education that influenced educational systems to abandon small school models in favor of large ones. The first belief was that larger schools would allow for the separation of students by grade and also by ability within a grade. This was seen as an institutional solution to dealing with varied ability. A second belief was that students would benefit from a larger facility. More programs could be offered in a larger school, and this was an appealing prospect for educators. The third belief was that large schools had better teachers and leadership. However, because of their size it was scientific management techniques that became the norm.[8] The fourth belief was that larger schools could perpetuate a more sophisticated value system. Small schools were more common in small, rural communities. Large schools therefore had the possibility to further urban values and the ideas of science and progress. Finally, the author identifies that the size of individual classes was believed to be the more conclusive indicator of better achievement but the school size itself was not examined.[9] These arguments in favor of large schools are still used today. A primary argument in favor of small schools is that these large schools have been unsuccessful for many students, especially at the high school level.

Graduation rates are dismal for many school districts, and many urban areas report that minority students are less likely than white students to graduate from high school.[10] Drop-out rates are estimated to range from between 40 percent to 70 percent in some communities.[11] The problem is not only with the size of the high school, but also with the educational model that is used, such as the length of the periods, ability and age tracking, lack of connectedness among classes and disciplines, and selection of books and materials that make cooperation difficult.[12] This ties back to the factory model of education with its emphasis on conformity, uniformity, and tracking for efficiency. These difficult learning constraints are exacerbated by the emotional disconnectedness and effects of overcrowding that must be dealt with on a daily basis by students.[13] "Besides anonymity and distrust, bigness leads the way to ever-increasing bureaucratization—and loss of local power."[14] Utilizing the small-schools concept in education can lessen the negative effects of large, overcrowded schools, and power can be reinfused into the hands of community members.

BENEFITS OF SMALL SCHOOLS

Educators, students, and community members in areas where small schools are providing alternative public education are documenting the benefits of this educational model. This section describes the benefits of small schools to demonstrate the educational, social, and emotional motivations for moving into this educational model. After describing the failings of large high schools, the promising data of small high schools, which are small by choice, can be used to illuminate the educational possibilities and alternative spaces that are created for learners who do not fit into the large factory model high schools.

In his article on small (by choice) high schools, Ark describes a litany of benefits that occur because of reorganization. Graduation rates are higher, college attendance is higher, smaller schools are more cost-effective, school violence is decreased, student involvement increases, and collegiality among teachers and students increases.[15] A comparative study of high school students in Chicago found that

compared with students in host schools, students in schools-within-schools attended up to five more days of school per semester, dropped out at one-third to one-half the rate, had up to 0.22 higher grade-point averages, and improved reading scores by the equivalent of almost half a year.[16]

This is but one example of positive correlations between achievement and small-school attendance.

In an era where test score data and numerical measures of success are over-emphasized, social and emotional development are often overlooked. Anonymity is a major problem for our youth. As Deborah Meier describes, "By the time youngsters reach their late teens they know barely any adults outside of their families well, and they see relatively little of even these."[17] Small schools have the potential to reduce anonymity and disenfranchisement among students in several ways. First, they can offer unique programs based on student interests.[18] Second, the size itself deters anonymity because students are more likely to feel like part of a community in a smaller group. Teachers are also better suited to look out for and monitor their students in a smaller setting.[19] Darling-Hammond, in her description of the importance of relationships, says, "Students' trust in their teachers helps them develop the commitment and motivation needed to tackle challenging learning tasks."[20] Furthermore, small schools are more capable of nurturing the multitude of relationships necessary to cultivate a sense of belonging. One study asserts that "strong relationships between and among students and faculty were central to participants'

success."[21] Because teachers in small schools have significantly smaller caseloads than teachers in traditional large schools, they can better get to know individual students. The focus on strong interpersonal relationships is in and of itself a compelling merit of small schools.

Parental and family involvement is encouraged and expected in small schools; therefore, the amount of parental involvement is high compared to parental involvement in large high schools. The second part of the chapter describes the parental and community efforts to create small schools in their communities. This active role often continues after the small school has been established. Participation in PTA meetings, classroom volunteering, attendance at parent conferences, and attendance at school planning meetings are some of the ways that parental involvement can occur.[22] One small school in Wisconsin has extended its critical analysis of curriculum and pedagogy to parental involvement. The school has continually redefined how parents can get involved. They have used innovative strategies to encourage participation.

We paid 15 parents to participate in a six-week evening workshop in which they discussed school issues and wrote about their children. Parents who didn't usually participate in school activities were encouraged to participate.[23]

This school also conducted parent discussion groups to educate and sensitize parents to the different lifestyles and family situations that exist among the school's families. Because of the size, parental involvement can evolve and change to continually meet the needs of the school community. Parental involvement must be meaningful. To that end, Peterson describes how parents who can "exercise genuine power in decisions that directly affect the future of the school and their children's lives" will participate at increased rates.[24]

Design Features of Small Schools

Small schools by choice come in many different forms. Provided is a brief overview of some of the successful models of small schools to demonstrate the variety and potential that exist within this movement. Individual difference is paramount in the Small Schools Movement.

Small schools share some of the same design characteristics, yet other characteristics are unique to each school. Small schools are small by choice, and they are designed by the community.[25] The community is encouraged to participate in curricular, leadership, and instructional issues related to the school. Small schools also depend on teacher participation and the facilitation of relationships. As Michael Klonsky, a leader in the Small Schools Movement, describes, "The two key ingredients must be: (1) teachers working together in a professional community, and (2) staying together with a group of students long enough to get to know them well."[26] This sentiment emphasizes the importance of human relationships in the educational context. Failure to develop meaningful relationships has been a major problem in large schools.

The leadership in small schools varies by school. However, many small schools operate on a shared leadership model in which teachers, parents, students, and the principal share in the major decision-making of the school.[27] Some small schools shy away from the hierarchical model of schooling altogether and function without a designated principal. These schools use collective thinking, action, decision-making, and delegation to manage the school.

Small schools provide a plethora of curricular opportunities for educators and students. In the diverse society we live in, a responsive and meaningful curriculum must include elements that reflect the lived experience of the student participants in the school community. This section reviews some of the curricular possibilities that can be developed within the small-schools context. Because of the small size and the encouragement of staff collaboration and team teaching, small schools are able to implement innovative curricula. Furthermore, the instructional approaches can facilitate critical learning, and factory-like assignments such as memorization and rote learning can be avoided. In a review of small schools, Darling-Hammond describes how

most of the assignments that we reviewed required the production of analytic work— research papers and projects, demonstrations and discussions of problems, experiments and data collection organized to answer open-ended questions. Worksheets and fill-in-the-blank tasks were rare. Extensive reading and writing were expected in all schools.[28]

Aside from emphasizing analytic and problem-solving skills across the curricula, many small schools implement curricula that have been defined and chosen by the community. Some of the curricular foci being used at different schools include world languages, Mexican folk art, medical technology, science and math, visual and performing arts, and dual languages.[29] Drawing on diverse areas of emphasis is a powerful way to help students find meaning in their work.

SOCIAL JUSTICE AND SMALL SCHOOLS

Many small schools choose social justice as a pedagogical and curricular emphasis. Social justice also factors into small schools because when students, teachers, and community members come together and democratically construct education, socially just education can result. This section describes what other authors have noticed about social justice, small schools, and education.

A promising feature of small schools has to do with their dedication to provide quality education to all students, regardless of their background. Education that promotes social justice must occur at several levels simultaneously in order for lasting improvement to be achieved. Michelle Fine has identified four *lenses* that can be utilized to examine educational practices for justice. They are:

The social relations within and around the school . . . A curriculum and pedagogy for social justice . . . A schoolwide dedication to high expectations for all and the dramatic narrowing of historic achievement gaps . . . An insistence upon systemwide educational justice.[30]

These four lenses offer a powerful way to scrutinize schools for justice. Small schools are often set up to address these four areas. Because of their size, it becomes easier to build strong relationships. Students are seen as humans with a complex set of emotional needs and concerns.[31] There is an inherent sense of value in what they know and offer to the learning community. Teachers, families, and community members also have the opportunity to develop curriculum and pedagogical practices that emphasize social justice. At Berkley High, for example, students in a freshman course explore issues of fairness in literature, art, and history.[32] Analyzing text for justice issues prepares students to apply that same analytical framework to other curricular areas. Small schools are often created with a group of teachers and staff who are committed to working toward building equitable learning opportunities for all students. This commitment furthers justice because students are not tracked and separated. The same-quality program is available to all students.[33] The fourth lens that Fine identifies for social justice is also included in the Small Schools Movement. Transforming education to be more inclusive and meaningful is the movement's goal. The move to small is a way to combat the multitude of inequities and problems that students face in large schools.[34]

The ability to rethink power in the educational setting is also linked to social justice.

In small schools the power is dispersed more equitably. Students have a hand in the power structure of the school. Teachers, parents, and community members also have a hand in the power structure of the school. Shared power can encourage democratic practices that increase participation of all stakeholders.[35]

As described throughout, small schools by choice are individual. Organization, curricula, and instruction vary by school. Also unique to small schools is the manner in which they are created and developed. The impetus for creating the schools demonstrates the desire in some urban communities for meaningful educational reform. One school in the making, and the target student population it will serve, is described to demonstrate the unique ability of small schools to serve diverse urban populations.

THE FIGHT FOR EQUITY AND JUSTICE IN ONE URBAN COMMUNITY

In a Midwestern urban center, members of one Mexican-American community were frustrated because their section of town did not have a proximal high school to serve the students of their community. Some of the families in this area were recent immigrants, while many others were predominantly established, working class, Mexican-American families. Five elementary schools served this neighborhood, but the students were bussed to adjacent communities for high school. The families of this community grew tired of sending their children away for high school. For many years the elected officials and the school board had promised the citizens of this community that a new high school would be built in their community. However, there was little to no action on the project for many years. Members of the community had organized for many years to get the new high school constructed in their community. They were promised funds for the school, and site preparation had begun. However, without word or explanation from the district the project was stopped.

Disturbed by the discontinuation of the project, community members demanded a meeting with school officials. Unhappy with the continued excuses made by the board and the district leadership, the women of the community began a 19-day hunger strike to demand construction of a high school. The community members were fighting for a large high school because they wanted a school that would accommodate all of the high school-bound students in their community. Second, they wanted a facility as elaborate and well-equipped as those found in the higher-income sections of the city. In a qualitative interview conducted in the community, one mother and community activist described how "the hunger strike came about a few days after the meeting. We were asking for the world. They had to make restitution to our kids. We wanted a big school so all of our kids could stay in the area." The community members were equating bigger schools with better schools. Big high schools have a century-long history of appeal. For this community, a large, expensive building with all the extras was a requisite to bring a form of justice to their community. After several weeks, the hunger strike mobilized enough support and pressure that the school district agreed to build the most expensive high school facility in the city.

After community members began visiting schools around the city and the country, they realized the value of small schools. At this point they decided to create four, autonomous small schools within their one building facility. These four schools would emphasize different curricular areas and they would utilize some of the other design features of small schools, such as intense curriculum integration, multiage grouping, small class sizes, and mentorship opportunities.

Parental and community activism did not end with the agreement to construct the small-schools high school. Rather, empowered by the ability to participate meaningfully, the community members divided into separate committees to provide leadership, knowledge, and input into the other important decisions for the school. For example, a team of parents served on the architectural planning committee. Many of their design ideas were incorporated into the blueprints that will be used for the school facility. Other parents and community members served on the curriculum committee. This committee set out to identify and develop the school's four curricular emphasis areas based on student and family interest. Although the four small schools will have their own emphasis areas, the individual schools will still meet and exceed state curricular standards and benchmarks for high schools. The big difference for students will be in the choices offered by the small schools.

Information for this story was collected as part of a qualitative research project examining motivation for the development of a small-schools high school. At the time of this writing, the school was under construction. This small-schools high school serves as a positive example of committed parents and community members organizing for systemic educational change. It also illustrates how power structures can be rearranged to encourage community participation. By creating small schools, this community will also have the opportunity to design alternative curricular and instructional strategies to better serve the student population.

FINAL REFLECTIONS

Bob Peterson describes how small schools are not going to transform education or society alone. Broader societal issues must be addressed simultaneously to improve student leaning and participation.

"Large class sizes, lack of teacher planning time, and the broader problems of poverty, child abuse, and unemployment all reflect the triumph of private profit over human need."[36] However, small schools are one way to address some of the problems and challenges of an outdated educational system that fails to satisfy the needs of a diverse student population. Small schools are valuable as an alternative—an educational choice that can define new educational spaces for students who are unsuccessful in the factory-model schools that dominate in this country.

Diversity of background and diversity of need can be respected and promoted if individuals have the opportunity to develop communities. Small schools are stepping up to the challenge "to teach in a manner that respects and cares for the souls of our students."[37] Furthermore, as the Midwestern example illustrates, parents and community members are willing to organize and mobilize support for a new kind of learning environment for their children. Although small schools may not be the singular force to redefine society, they are one positive example of how devoted citizens can work together to create democratic and meaningful educational spaces for students.

NOTES

1. Lyon, G. (2000). When Jamas is enough: Creating a school for a community. In W. Ayers, M. Klonsky & G. Lyon (Eds.), *A simple justice: The challenge of small schools* (pp. 125–136). New York: Teachers College Press.

2. Shor, I. (1992). *Empowering education*. Chicago: University of Chicago Press.

3. Darling-Hammond, L. (1997). *The right to learn* (p. 34). San Francisco: Jossey-Bass.

4. Darling-Hammond (1997).

5. Darling-Hammond, L., Ancess, J., & Ort, J. (2002). Reinventing high school: Outcomes of the Coalition Campus Schools Project. *American Educational Research Journal, 39* (3), 639–673.

6. Beyer, L., & Apple, M. (1998). *The curriculum: Problems, politics, and possibilities*. Albany: State University of New York Press.

7. hooks, b. (1994). *Teaching to transgress.* New York: Routledge.

8. Hampel, R. (2002). Historical perspectives on small schools. *Phi Delta Kappan, 83,* 357–363.

9. Hampel (2002).

10. Ark, L. (2002). The case for small high schools. *Educational Leadership, 59* (3), 55–59.

11. Stern, D. (2000). Practicing social justice in the high school classroom. In W. Ayers, M. Klonsky & G. Lyon (Eds.), *A simple justice: The challenge of small schools* (pp. 110–124). New York: Teachers College Press.

12. Ark (2002).

13. Stern (2000).

14. Meier, D. (2000). The crisis of relationships. In W. Ayers, M. Klonsky & G. Lyon (Eds.), *A simple justice: The challenge of small schools* (pp. 33–37). New York: Teachers College Press.

15. Ark (2002).

16. Wasley, P., & Lear, R. (2001). Small schools, read gains. *Educational Leadership, 58* (6), 22–27.

17. Meier (2000).

18. Klonsky, S., & Klonsky, M. (1999). In Chicago: Countering anonymity through small schools. *Educational Leadership, 57,* 38–41.

19. Klonsky & Klonsky (1999).

20. Klonsky & Klonsky (1999).

21. Darling-Hammond, Ancess, & Ort (2002).

22. Meier, D. (2002). The genesis of a small public school, *Educational Leadership, 59* (5), 76–79.

23. Peterson, B. (1995). La escuela frantney: A journey toward democracy. In M. Apple & J. Beane (Eds.), *Democratic schools* (pp. 58–82). Alexandria: Association for Supervision and Curriculum Development.

24. Peterson (1995).

25. Ark (2002).

26. Klonsky, M. (2000). Grounded insights. In W. Ayers, M. Klonsky & G. Lyon (Eds.), *A simple justice: The challenge of small schools* (pp. 19–22). New York: Teachers College Press.

27. Hess, A. (2000). Who leads small schools? Teacher leadership in the midst of democratic governance. In W. Ayers, M. Klonsky & G. Lyon (Eds.), *A simple justice: The challenge of small schools* (pp. 38–52). New York: Teachers College Press.

28. Darling-Hammond, Ancess, & Ort (2002).

29. Lyon (2000).

30. Fine, M. (2000). A small price to pay for justice. In W. Ayers, M. Klonsky & G. Lyon (Eds.),

A simple justice: The challenge of small schools (pp. 168–179). New York: Teachers College Press.

31. Ayers, W. (2000). Simple justice: Thinking about teaching, learning, equity and the fight for small schools. In W. Ayers, M. Klonsky & G. Lyon (Eds.), *A simple justice: The challenge of small schools* (pp. 1–8). New York: Teachers College Press.

32. Ayers (2000).

33. Klonsky (2000).

34. Fine (2000).

35. Schubert, W. (2000). John Dewey as a philosophical basis for small schools. In W. Ayers, M. Klonsky & G. Lyon (Eds.), *A simple justice: The challenge of small schools* (pp. 53–66). New York: Teachers College Press.

36. Peterson (1995).

37. hooks (1994).

THE SIGNIFICANCE OF URBAN STREET VENDORS

Marina Karides

Street vendors, traders, and hawkers have reemerged as a focus of study in sociology.[1] Street vendors are gaining recognition as central urban actors rather than as remnants of traditional premodern social structures or as an outcome of failed development policies.[2] This developing body of literature brings forth the economic, political, and social significance of street vendors for understanding the urban condition.

Yet street vendors have not garnered enough theoretical attention in urban sociology. Even as the field turns toward the examination of urban consumption patterns and tourism, street vendors—who often provide consumers the opportunities to purchase low-cost, tourist, or popular goods—should receive more direct consideration. With few exceptions, such as that shown by Mitch Duneier's *Sidewalk*,[3] street vendors have been primarily the purview of the sociology of development rather than of urban sociology. Indeed, it is possible to complete a university course in urban studies and scarcely consider street vendors' role in the construction of cities. For three reasons, this is problematic for urban education. First, consider the visibility and large presence of street vendors in cities throughout the world. Students often come to urban education seeking a greater understanding of the context in which they live. Yet often the most visible city dwellers, street vendors, are overlooked or not thoroughly discussed. Particularly when students visit Third World cities, they inevitably become aware of the large number of persons selling items on the street. Urban education needs to present students with an understanding of the global and national factors that lead to such large vending populations in postcolonial urban centers. However, the agency of street vendors also must be articulated so that students recognize how vendors create employment and shape the urban environment. The second reason street vendors are an important focus of urban education is their impact on the organization of urban space. Certainly urban design and politics play a large role in the organization of a city and influence social relations. Yet through their resistance to laws that render street vending illegal and interfere with their ability to practice their trade, street vendors help to define city space and the identity of various neighborhoods. In addition, street vendors' businesses are in many instances central to the economic survival of postcolonial cities.[4]

Finally, the perpetuation of street vending as a major sector of employment in many postcolonial countries suggests that the formal sector is incapable of employing all workers.[5] The vending population consists mostly of workers who are either marginalized from the formal sector or who found the marginal positions in the formal sector less lucrative than street vending.[6] Street or pavement vending indicates global, national, and urban systems of race, class, and gender inequality. Women, ethnic, or indigenous minorities are more likely to be drawn to street vending out of choice or necessity.[7] Urban education has an important role to play in teaching students to appreciate the intricacies of the lives of these ever-present urban informal workers.

The first part of the chapter provides some parameters of the urban street vending population and briefly presents a historical framing of the conceptions of street vendors in the sociological literature. The second half of the chapter uses three studies of street vendors in three different national contexts to demonstrate the economic, political, or social influences of urban street vendors and offers suggestions on how street vendors could be integrated into urban education.

THE CONDITIONS OF URBAN STREET VENDING

The experiences of street vendors around the globe are linked by the daily prospect of arrest for working in the street trade. Recent studies on street vendors document the various tactics street vendors employ to conduct business on high-traffic city streets.[8] Whether they engage in political activism or a system of paying off police offers to turn a blind eye, or simply scatter when police patrols arrive, street vendors regularly must contend with harassment, fines, or arrests.

In more rural settings, vendors may benefit from a designated set of stalls where they can conduct their business. In many instances, these stalls have been an established vending location for decades and sometimes centuries.[9] However, the urban environment, and capital cities in particu-

lar, represent a nation's modernization efforts and are less likely to maintain traditional vending stalls. If the contemporary urban vendor has access to stalls or an officially recognized vending location, often these venues are not centrally located or the rental payment is not worthwhile or is beyond the means of many vendors.

The portion of a nation's population most likely to engage in vending are those marginalized from the formal labor force—including women, immigrants, and minority ethnic or racial groups. These groups face discrimination in the formal sector that limits their employment opportunities. Women in particular have turned to street vending and other forms of informal self-employment not only because of the lack of formal job opportunities but also because of the types of formal jobs available to them. In many instances, women prefer the autonomous conditions of street vending to the low wages and restrictive supervision of formal sector jobs available to them. Research conducted in Tanzania, Mexico, and Peru suggests that marginalized groups participate in informal self-employment as an alternative to poorly paying formal sector employment.[10]

Although some workers engage in street vending to supplement formal sector income, street vendors usually work full-time. Various studies also indicate that vendors operate on a regular schedule in terms of both days and hours.[11] Rather than an arena of exploitation, the expansion of street vending represents the agency of marginalized workers.

The presence, agency, and regularity of street vendors in cities make them an important pursuit for broadening urban education. As public and often illegal figures in urban centers, street vendors can have tremendous insight into the social, political, and economic conditions of a nation. Usually aware that it is their social status—whether defined by age, race or ethnicity, or gender—that limits their formal job opportunities, they create alternative employment options and attempt to circumvent social hierarchies that interfere with their ability to earn a livelihood. Because they must negotiate the legal system to earn a livelihood they participate in city politics to advocate for their economic survival. Therefore, street vendors can be especially informed of a city's political dynamics and the government that they must address. Urban education has an important role to play in teaching students to appreciate the agency of these ever-present urban informal workers and how race, class, and gender shape the street trader's livelihood.

ACADEMIC PERCEPTIONS OF STREET VENDORS

Originally, both Marxist and conservative scholars and practitioners of economic development evaluated street vendors as holdovers from traditional society who interfered with the development process.[12] As Geertz explains in his ethnographic study of culture and economic development in Indonesia,

The trader is perpetually looking for a chance to make a smaller or larger killing, not attempting to build up a clientele or a steadily growing business. . . . It [informal trade] has the disadvantage that it turns even the established businessman away from an interest in reducing costs and developing markets and toward petty speculation and short-run opportunism.[13]

Overall, Western scholars held a negative evaluation of Third World street vendors and suggested that street vendors hindered development.[14] It was assumed that industrialization eventually would subsume all workers and street vending would eventually diminish.[15] Modernization scholars' analyses of postcolonial economies suggested that labor markets were divided into a traditional sector, consisting of informally self-employed workers who produced to meet consumption needs, and a capitalist sector, primarily interested in the generation of profits that created the basis for development and the expansion of employment.[16] The capitalist sector would initially make large gains because of the low wages employers could pay workers; yet these wages provided greater earning than traditional or informal work.[17] These profits would enable the capitalist sector to create more jobs, and eventually the majority of workers would be absorbed into the capitalist sector. The turning point for the economic advancement of postcolonial nations would occur when labor scarcity drove up wages in the formal labor force.[18]

Instead the "development" of the Third World has been characterized by overurbanization or the limited formal employment opportunities for urban workers as well as the inability of urban infrastructure to accommodate the increasing number of persons arriving in cities.[19] Migrating from underdeveloped rural areas, workers arrive in cities seeking employment opportunities. Yet the number of rural immigrants seeking formal and industrial employment far exceeds the formal job opportunities available, driving most of these migrants into the low-waged informal sector. Rather than investing and increasing employment opportunities in rural areas to deter the number of migrating workers, expansive cities are built to aid the accumulation of capital and serve the needs of the local elite.[20] In addition, Third World nations, trapped into attracting foreign capital to sustain economic growth, place their resources in urban development projects that facilitate and expedite the international movement of capital.[21] Interested only in increasing profitability, the spatial arrangement of global capitalist production favors urban concentration. Workers are attracted from various regions of a nation to one localized space.[22]

Scholars focused on the rapid expansion of Third World urbanization have helped to clarify the expansion of self-employed informal workers. Street vendors, although not formally employed by a capitalist enterprise, may vend mass-produced goods at almost no cost to capital.[23] Street vendors also sell items to formal sector workers at a lower cost than formal enterprises, thus reducing the cost of reproducing the formal labor force.[24] As an alternative means of employment, an extensive informal sector not only provides a cheap source of labor and means of distributing goods, but can also decrease wages of the formal sector and the strength of unions.[25] Generally street vendors maintain capitalist accumulation by providing cheap labor and inexpensively distributing goods.[26]

The expansion of the informal sector and of undocumented and unregulated work and employment conditions was highlighted in the sociology of development throughout the 1980s.[27] Traditional urban sociology took less of an interest in street vendors as principle actors of the urban environment. Even new urban sociology, which brought forth a Marxist analysis of urban development, primarily focused on macroeconomic structures. Yet, the examination of street vendors' roles in urban systems is useful for exploring various urban theoretical traditions.

In the next section I demonstrate the economic, political, and social significance of street vendors for urban education. I rely on the research of Hernando de Soto conducted in Lima, Peru, to examine the powerful economic contributions of street vending.[28] Next, I highlight the research of John Cross on street vendors and the state in Mexico City to consider street vendors' influence on the political urban landscape.[29] Last, I turn to my own research on street vending in Port of Spain, Trinidad, which investigates how street vendors' resistance to capitalist development strategies and government policies contributes to the organization of city space.

Street Vendors and Economic Development

Hernando de Soto, a Peruvian economist, has been instrumental in the recent appreciation of the urban informal sector as an alternative route for national economic growth. Studying informal sector operations in Peru, de Soto concluded that marginalized workers independent of the state and development agencies were able to create a market economy in which they earn income, provide essential services, and serve as the backbone of the nation's economy.[30] To make his case, de Soto considers the informal housing market, informal transportation, and street trade. De Soto and his followers argue that governments and development agencies have neglected the resourcefulness and vitality of the urban poor. The state interferes with the development of small enterprises by heeding only the needs of larger domestic firms.[31] State regulations lead to an impoverished informal sector because small and incipient enterprises do not have the financial resources needed to meet the regulations and requirements imposed by the state.[32] Yet, de Soto overlooks the precarious nature of small enterprises; workers in this sector also lack the benefits of government social programs such as unemployment insurance, social security benefits, and sick leave.

Arguing that the informal and formal sectors are not economically linked, de Soto sees the two sectors in competition— the informal is pitted against the formal, the latter having the advantage of economic power and state support.[33] For instance, police raids of vendors occur because the vendors compete with formal capitalist enterprises. State laws and policies impede the growth of microenterprises to maintain the status quo.[34] However, the links between the informal and formal sectors have been articulated, where the former subsidizes the latter by providing affordable goods for low paid formal workers.

Referring to the expanding informal sector as "the other path of development," de Soto argues that this sector represents an entrepreneurial response to an overregulatory state. In his volume, *The Other Path of Development*, de Soto catalogs various types of vendors—for example, itinerant vendors, persons who walk around selling small items or prepared foods, or fixed location vendors, people who occupy a permanent although illegal location.[35] Through a series of surveys, de Soto establishes the size of the vending population in Lima as close to one hundred thousand persons who operate independently, maintain a specialized area of sales, and consist of the age group of the economically active population. His figures further establish that, between dependents and suppliers, more than three hundred thousand people rely on street vending. He also estimates that gross sales of vendors is $322.2 million per year and that vendors earn 38 percent more per month than the minimum wage. De Soto is arguing that the informal trade system established by vendors supersedes the formal system and is the most important economic force in Lima's development.

If we take de Soto's premise seriously, then the street vendors become central to any course on urbanization, particularly any discussion of Third World urbanization. Although street vendors and other informal sector workers do receive some attention, particularly in discussions on the overurbanization of Third World cities, they are less noted for their economic significance and impact on the urban economy. Fresh approaches to urban education that consider the agency of street vendors, rather than repeating previous assumptions that informal sector workers are total subjects of the global economy, would provoke students to challenge and alter widely held stereotypes of the Third World. More so, discovering the economic innovativeness, entrepreneurialism, and planning of what is still often

perceived and presented as day-to-day living would contribute to the broadening of student understanding of the urbanization process.

De Soto's research was an important instigator to the current worldwide reevaluation of informal microenterprises. Professionals in development agencies and multinational agencies have begun to appreciate street vendors and other informal sector workers as nascent entrepreneurs who, with assistance, could develop larger businesses. Yet the rhetoric of microenterprise development does not take seriously the accumulated skills and experiences of the vending community, nor does it address the illegal conditions under which they must perform their trade and the political participation required of vendors to secure a semiformal business location.[36]

Street Vendors and the State

John C. Cross brings the political activism of street vendors to the forefront of informal sector studies.[37] Cross demonstrates the political influence of Mexico City's street vendors in the implementation of state policies that affect them. Because the Mexican state is not well integrated, city officials have leeway in choosing when and where to implement state policies—especially the murky policies that apply to the informal sector. Street vendors are an attractive constituency to politicians because the autonomy and flexibility of vending allows for impromptu participation at political protests and events. Cross suggests that in gaining political access, vendors have the advantage over other marginalized groups such as formal workers and peasants because of vendors' visibility, flexibility, and the necessity for perpetual engagement with the state to secure a place to sell and earn a living. Cross's research demonstrates that although marginalized, informal sector workers shape Mexico's political landscape. By focusing on the political opportunity structure or the ways interest groups or social movements might infiltrate the state, Cross shows how street vendor organizations gain tolerances—the informal permission or official "blind eye" from state actors to vend in city streets (an illegal act). In case after case, Cross demonstrates how leaders of street vendors' organizations negotiate with low-level political officials who in most situations agree to tolerate street vending in exchange for their political patronage.

Cross's analysis of Mexico City's street vendors' political organizations is geared toward addressing debates in social movement theory. However, his findings also make important contributions to theoretical issues within urban sociology. The focus on the political participation of street vendors could be a vehicle for introducing students to the relationship among urban politics, urban development, and social class. His research presents a well-described example of how marginalized groups inform state policies and challenge assumptions that urban development is determined only by elite forces.

The Spatial Resistance of Street Vendors

The study of urban education is often students' first introduction to studies of spatiality. In gaining an understanding of the urbanization process, students begin to consider efforts of urban planning and the organization and social construction of city space. Most recently, postmodern analyses of urban space have infused urban literature with an architectural focus of spatiality.[38] These studies primarily take account of the dissonance of urban architecture and the state of disorientation they establish. Marxist analyses of urban space, which generally predate postmodernism, have effectively articulated the production of space for the expansion of capitalism.[39] In particular, the work of Henri Lefebvre demonstrates how urbanization or the capitalist control of spatial production penetrates and organizes our daily practices and sense of being.[40] Although critical of class oppression, Marxists' critiques of urbanization give limited attention to the gendered and racial organization of urban space and to how this also serves capitalist expansion. In addition, they fail to theorize how local resistance to urban planning can subvert and alter urban development strategies.

The multiracial context of Trinidad brings forth the stratification of urban space by race and gender. In Port of Spain, Trinidad, most vendors are African-Caribbean women. Although young men have started to sell on the city streets due to shrinking job opportunities, in this nation street vending is perceived as a feminine occupation. As in most urban centers, street vending is an illegal activity and vendors are subject to fines and arrests. Similar to the descriptions of the vending populations above, Port of Spain's street vendors consist of the active labor force population and they work regular and steady hours. For the majority of these self-employed informal workers, vending is a long-term employment strategy.

These vendors carry out their trade in contested space. In Port of Spain, police patrols harass vendors on a daily basis; yet as soon as the patrols depart, street vendors reemerge and, in effect, control the streets. City planners and local businesses are eager to remove street vendors from the downtown streets of the nation's capital. Government leaders, seeking to establish Port of Spain as the foremost modern business center of the Caribbean, view vendors as a hindrance to developing this status. Many local capitalists, with business locations in downtown Port of Spain, also suggest that street vendors inhibit their success and advocate their removal.

Focus on the political and economic efforts of street vendors suggests that vendors structure city space by creating their business locations contrary to the plans of the state and large capital. The vendors and the products they sell in different locations establish the identity of certain streets in Port of Spain. For instance, one avenue might be dedicated to vendors who trade in produce whereas another street may be known for the series of vendors selling shoes. Through their resistance to capital and government policies, African-Caribbean women street vendors not only influence the organization of downtown Port of Spain but also determine its dominant race and gender. The struggle for control over the downtown streets of Port of Spain, Trinidad, has been ongoing for more than thirty years.

Too much emphasis in the postmodern literature is placed on the power of urban structures to determine a city's orientation. Marxist analyses tend to overdesignate control of urban planning to macroeconomic variables. By centering on the street vendor, urban education can demonstrate how local urban actors modify capitalist penetration of urban space. Courses on Third World urbanization successfully articulate the negative impact of foreign capital penetration. Urban poverty and unemployment, increased inequality, and the expansion of the informal sector are easily connected to the neoliberal form of globalization. Yet urban education that investigates the lives and strategies of street vendors will also reveal cities as spaces of resistance to the infiltration of global capital.

CONCLUSION

The studies described herein overlap in their emphasis on street vendors as economic and political agents. Together they challenge previously held assumptions of street vending as casual and irregular work that is a temporary or immediate means of earning cash. All three studies clearly establish that street vending is a long-term employment strategy requiring regular business practices. In demonstrating the economic, political, and spatial impact of street vendors on the urban environment, these studies demonstrate

the significance of street vendors to urban education pursuits.

Although these studies agree on the agency of street vendors, they differ in their explanations for the vast informal sector that characterizes the Caribbean and Latin America. De Soto argues that local capitalists who feel threatened by vendors whom they see as their competition drive government policies that deter or challenge street vending.[41] As local elites they are able to create government policies that favor their business endeavors and maintain the informality of street vendors' ventures. Cross also emphasizes national factors as guiding policy toward Mexico City's street vendors.[42] He argues that government structure and state precedence explain the system of street vending. My research considers national concerns as important for understanding the increase of street vendors, but also purports that the global economy plays a large role in shaping urban development strategies. In particular, the postcolonial nations of Latin American and the Caribbean are pressed by the Unites States and transnational capital to implement neoliberal policies, open their economies, and remove regulated labor conditions.

Courses in urban education, especially those focused on Third World urbanization, will benefit by debating the factors that contribute to the postmodern increase of street vendors. Urban theoretical traditions such as new urban sociology, the world cities' perspective, and postmodern perspectives can all be introduced and compared and contrasted in considering the factors that lead to the conditions of street vending. However, the primary emphasis of this chapter is to showcase the agency of street vendors and how they shape the urban environment. Centering on marginalized sectors of the urban population offers a method of articulating economic and political systems that overcomes the oversight of the daily urban experience and the collective influence of marginalized groups that occurs with macrolevel analysis of urbanization.

Urban education also can help to reorient traditional perceptions of street vendors. Contemporary street vendors are not remnants of a nation's traditional past but reflect the economic strategies of urban workers. To the extent that urban education courses become informed by recent sociological studies that incorporate the street vendor as a central figure, they will gain a richer evaluation of urban life.

NOTES

1. Duneier, M. (1999). *Sidewalk.* New York: Farrar, Straus, & Giroux.; Cross, J. (1998). *Informal politics: Street vendors and the state in Mexico City.* Stanford, CA: Stanford University Press.

2. Itzigohn, J. (2000). *Developing, poverty: The state, labor market deregulation, and the informal economy in Costa Rica and the Dominican Republic.* University Park: University of Pennsylvania Press; Rakowski, C. (1994). *Contrapunto: The informal sector debate in Latin American perspectives.* New York: State University Press of New York; De Soto, H. (1989). *The other path of development: The invisible revolution in the third world.* New York: Harper and Row; Tripp, A. (1997). *Changing the rules: The politics of liberalization and the urban informal economy in Tanzania.* Berkeley, Los Angeles, & London: University of California Press; Reddock, R. (1994). *Women, labor, and politics in Trinidad and Tobago.* London: Zed Books.

3. Duneier (1999).

4. De Soto (1989); Tripp (1997).

5. De Soto (1989); Tripp (1997).

6. De Soto (1989); Tripp (1997).

7. Reddock (1994); Harrison, F. (1991). Women in Jamaica's urban informal economy. In C. Mohanty, A. Russo, & L. Torres (Eds.), *Third world women and the politics of feminism* (pp. 173–196). Bloomington: Indiana University Press.

8. Duneier (1999); Cross (1998).

9. Babb, F. (1989). *Between the field and the cooking pot: The political economy of marketwomen in Peru.* Austin: University of Texas Press.

10. Cross (1998); De Soto (1989); Tripp (1997).

11. Itzigohn (2000).

12. Cross (1998); Geertz, C. (1963). *Peddlers and princes, social change and economic modernization in two Indonesian towns.* Chicago: University of Chicago Press; Sanyal, B. (1991). Organizing the self-employed: The politics of the urban informal sector. *International Labor Review, 130,* 39–56.

13. Geertz (1963), p. 35.

14. Rakowski (1994).

15. Malaki, A. (1996). *Development patterns in the Commonwealth Caribbean: Jamaica and Trinidad and Tobago.* Stockholm, Sweden: Stockholm University, Institute of Latin American Studies; Lewis, A. (1954, May). Economic development with unlimited supplies of labour. *The Manchester School of Economics and Social Studies.*

16. Malaki (1996); Lewis (1954, May).

17. Lewis (1954, May).

18. Malaki (1996); Lewis (1954, May).

19. Evans, P., & Timberlake, M. (1980). Dependence, inequality, and the growth of tertiary: A comparative analysis of less developed countries. *American Sociological Review, 45,* 532–552.

20. London, B., & Smith, D. (1988). Urban bias, dependence, and economic stagnation in noncore nations. *American Sociological Review, 53,* 454–463.

21. Smith, D. (1996). *Third world cities in global perspective: The political economy of uneven urbanization.* Boulder, CO: Westview Press.

22. Smith (1996).

23. Harrison (1991); Portes, A., Castells, M., & Benton, L. (1989). *The informal economy: Studies in advanced and less developed countries.* Baltimore: Johns Hopkins University Press.

24. Portes, Castells, & Benton (1989).

25. Evans & Timberlake (1980).

26. Harrison (1991).

27. Rakowski (1994); Portes, Castells, & Benton (1989).

28. De Soto (1989).

29. Cross (1998).

30. De Soto (1989).

31. Rakowski (1994); De Soto (1989).

32. De Soto (1989).

33. Rakowski (1994).

34. Cross (1998); De Soto (1989); Safa, H. (1995). Economic restructuring and gender subordination. In M. Smith & J. Feagin (Eds.), *The capitalist city: Global restructuring and com-*

munity politics (pp. 252–274). New York: Basil Blackwell Ltd.

35. De Soto (1989).
36. Karides, M. (2005). Whose solution is it anyway? Gender and the work of micro-entrepreneurs in Caribbean context. *International Sociology and Social Policy.*
37. Cross (1998).

38. Soja, E. (1989). *Postmodern geographies.* London & New York: Verso.
39. Soja (1989); Lefebvre, H. (2003). *The urban revolution.* Minneapolis & London: University of Minnesota Press.
40. Lefebvre (2003).
41. De Soto (1989).
42. Cross (1998).

WHY SHOULD URBAN EDUCATORS CARE ABOUT COMMUNITY ORGANIZING TO REFORM SCHOOLS?

Hollyce C. Giles

A gang was recruiting girls at my daughter's school, and I was a teacher at another school. I remember sitting at a coffee shop with Jim Keddy, an organizer from my church's Oakland Community Organizations committee; that's the organizing group my church was a member of;[1] he asked me what I care about, what's important to me. I told him that I was worried about my daughter, and that I was angry and frustrated about things at the neighborhood middle school. I'll never forget that meeting. He says to me, "You want power!" And I thought oh my God, how did he ever get the idea that I wanted power? I said, "Oh no, no, you totally misunderstood me. That's not why I'm doing this; that's not what I'm about at all." He says, "You want power." I go, "No I don't; I just want to help the kids." He's like, "You want power." Finally I said, "Why do you keep saying this to me?" And he says, "Tell me what you want." And I said, "I want to change Roosevelt Middle School. I want Roosevelt Middle School to be the safest place in the neighborhood, not the most dangerous place in the neighborhood." He says to me, "Do you think you can do that without being powerful?" I go, "Oh, OK; you're right, I want power." But that was this aha for me; I always thought power was bad.[2]

—Liz Sullivan
Oakland Community Organizations

Liz Sullivan's feelings of frustration and anger about the conditions in the public school in her neighborhood are not unusual; urban educators across the United States are deeply concerned about the problems in their schools:[3] overcrowded classrooms, outdated textbooks, tense and distant relations with each other and with parents, and rigid top-down mandates for their curricula, to name but a few of the troubling issues interfering with their efforts to educate students. What *is* unusual is the opportunity Sullivan had as a teacher, and as a parent, to have a conversation in which she was pushed to the surprising realization that *she wanted the power to make the school better.*

Concerns regarding inequities in education among groups from different social classes, races, and ethnicities have fueled the community organizing movement as a means to reform schools.[4] In this rapidly growing movement, local community organizations around the country are engaging teachers, parents, youth, and neighborhood residents in conversations similar to the one between Liz Sullivan and Jim Keddy, in which they identify issues that interfere with teaching and learning in their schools, and realize that together they have the power to take action to address these issues. Organizing initiatives engage ordinary people both to improve schools *and* to address larger issues and public policies related to jobs, housing, and poverty that negatively impact the lives of children, youth, and their families. Although the movement has yielded significant positive change in urban schools and communities across the United States, offering hope for improving the lives of children in poor and working-class schools and communities, and enhancing the richness and quality of educators' work with each other, most educators are not even aware that such initiatives exist. When they do become aware of organizing initiatives, educators sometimes are skeptical about the benefits of community action for them and their schools and are reluctant to participate.

In this chapter, I provide an overview of community organizing for school reform, and offer evidence why it is in educators' self-interest to seek out and collaborate with groups engaged in organizing approaches to transforming urban schools; put simply, why urban educators should "care" about community organizing. I also explore reasons for educators' resistance to participating in organizing efforts, drawing from my research and consultation with organizing initiatives, the research literature, and my experience teaching organizing to graduate students, many who are teachers, in a school of education in an urban public university.

WHAT IS COMMUNITY ORGANIZING TO REFORM SCHOOLS?

In organizing approaches to improve schools, a local community organization brings together parents, members of congregations, community residents, youth, and educators, for the purpose of identifying and taking action on issues that interfere with teaching and learning in their schools. Cortes captures the basic logic of the approach, in his description of the role that institutions such as civic associations, public schools, churches, and synagogues play in the organizing effort:

These institutions provide the public space where people of different backgrounds connect with one another, to listen to each other's stories, to share concerns, to argue, debate, and deliberate. . . . In the context of these public relationships, parents and community members can initiate conversations around their core concerns and values. Through these conversations, people develop the trust and consensus needed for action.[5]

Through these relationships of greater trust, people also develop the *power*, or "ability to act" together to transform their schools and communities, and often, their sense as individuals that "they count" in their neighborhoods and workplaces.

Although the community organizing movement to improve schools is in a relatively early stage of development, its impact on urban education has been significant, including: smaller class sizes and smaller schools; innovative, high-quality professional development driven by the specific needs of teachers and the principal in a school; new schools and improved facilities in overcrowded districts; increased school safety; access for low-income students to rigorous academic programs and bilingual instruction; a greater presence of parents in schools; and productive, mutually respectful collaborations between parents and educators of different races and class backgrounds.[6]

Community organizing groups traditionally have focused on helping low-income and working-class communities to gain the power to improve their housing and employment, and to address environmental issues in their neighborhoods, such as pollution, sanitation and sewer conditions and services, and the condition of local parks and recreation areas. Although groups of citizens in the United States have tackled the complex and thorny issues involved in obtaining a quality public education for their children since the beginning of free public schools,[7] in the past 15 years, a growing movement of community organizing to reform schools has taken shape. With philosophical and strategic roots in the American labor organizing and civil rights movements, the more recent movement has benefited from the interest and support of education research and advocacy nonprofit groups,[8] and funding by major private foundations such as Ford, Rockefeller, and Mott.[9]

Recent national studies have documented over 200 locally based groups involved in community organizing to reform schools, some affiliated with national community organizing networks,[10] some independent, and others associated with local groups that offer community services as well. Most of the groups address multiple issues that affect the lives of people in their communities, such as housing, environmental justice, and obtaining a fair wage, in addition to education, while a smaller number of the groups focus solely on improving public schools. Some groups work to address macroeconomic regional and federal public policies that contribute to joblessness, poverty, and other problems that can undermine the benefits of reformed schools. All of the organizing groups are composed of members who have an interest in improving their community; some groups seek out individual members, while others are made up of member institutions, such as religious congregations, civic associations, labor unions, and schools. Most of the organizations

engage adults in their initiatives to improve schools, although a growing number of groups organize youth to address issues in their schools and districts, and a smaller number engage in intergenerational organizing that brings together adults and youth. The groups' funding consists of a combination of membership dues, and foundation and government grants, and the majority of the groups have annual budgets that range from $100,000 to $500,000.[11]

It is important here to make two points about what community organizing for school reform is *not*. First, community organizing groups are not part of local political machines. They are independent, established organizations whose members identify the issues that are important to them to address at a particular time. The organizations have "no permanent friends, and no permanent enemies." That is, they seek the support of local public officials on specific issues, but do not "exchange favors" with local politicians, or engage in patronage.[12]

Second, community organizing to reform schools is not standard "parent involvement." Whereas traditional parent involvement tends to engage parents as "consumers" of education for their individual children, community organizing brings together parents in the role of "citizens" to improve the quality of education for *all* of the children in a school.[13] Also, although parents engaged in community organizing to improve schools often collaborate with educators, they have a base of institutional support that is independent of the school in the community organizing group. This independent base allows the group to bring its power to address important educational issues that the local school, district, or city educational system may resist addressing at a particular time. On the other hand, the primary vehicle of traditional parent involvement, the Parent Teacher Association or the Parent Association, lies within the control of the local education system, and as such, often faces obstacles to addressing issues in a school or district that local officials are reluctant to deal with, but which parents—and in some cases, the principal and teachers as well—view as essential to improving the quality of education for their children.

As a consequence of their participation in community organizing, parents often become more involved in the traditional types of parent involvement as defined by Epstein: parenting, communicating, volunteering, learning at home, decision making, and collaborating with the community to bring services and resources to the school.[14] As parents become more knowledgeable about their children's education through their participation in community organizing initiatives, they feel more confident and authorized to have a role in their education both at home and at school.[15]

HOW DO COMMUNITY ORGANIZING GROUPS REFORM SCHOOLS?

Although there are various starting places for a community organizing initiative to improve schools, an organizer hired by a local community group typically holds individual conversations with parents, community residents, youth, and educators to learn what issues concern them about their schools. The organizer then meets with participants in "house meetings," small groups in which people identify the issues that they want to address together. In a variation of the house meeting, some communities have "breakfast meetings" where they bring together individuals to dialogue about their concerns and identify issues they want to take action on together. Another important strategy is a community walk, in which parents, students, teachers, and administrators gather at their school and then go out in small teams to visit parents at home; the purpose is to engage families in conversation about their concerns for

the school and community, and to build relationships with them.

Organizers encourage participants to identify "winnable issues," to give the group confidence and energy to take on larger issues later on. Typical initial issues groups have addressed include concerns about school safety, and such problems with the physical plant of the school as unsanitary and unsafe bathrooms, and inadequate classroom space. After groups identify an issue, they do "research actions" to gather information about the issue. Typically, members of a group interview "experts" on the topic, and may also draw on the research of nonprofit education advocacy and research groups. The group then decides on the actions they will take to address the issue. In preparation for their action, participants often do a "power analysis" to identify people and groups that have power over education in their community. Actions often include parent, youth, or community leaders meeting with the officials who have power to create positive change around the issue that the group is addressing, to propose or demand a particular approach to resolving the issue.

Although the philosophy and strategies of community organizing originally were highly confrontational (heavily influenced by Saul Alinsky, the legendary organizer based in Chicago from the 1940s through the early 1970s), groups involved in education organizing have learned through trial and error that their efforts to improve schools and education systems are more effective when they work from a collaborative, relational model with educators, where possible.[16] Community organizing initiatives depend on the goodwill and collaboration of educators "inside" the education system, both to provide information about issues that need to be addressed in the school and to implement changes to improve the quality of education there. However, in instances where educators are not open to community organizing efforts or to collaboration, organizing groups may turn to more confrontational strategies, such as mobilizing a large number of their members to seek support from a public official for a particular issue, or holding a press conference to engage the media to raise the visibility of an issue the group is working to address. Once they have the attention of power-holders, the education organizing groups can then shift to a more collaborative stance. The aim of the groups is to develop productive and collaborative relationships with powerful public officials, not to alienate them.

To build the capacity of parents, youth, and educators to participate in organizing initiatives, community organizing groups offer a significant amount of training. The training includes extensive leadership development, as well as workshops on topics relevant to public education, such as school safety, approaches to school governance, and innovative curricula and pedagogy. A central tenet of community organizing that undergirds the groups' training and strategies is commonly known as the "iron rule": "Never do for another person what they can do for themselves." This rule reflects the priority given to parents, youth, and educators developing their own capacities and strength to create positive change in the institutions that affect their lives, rather than relying on experts or authorities to do it for them.

TWO EXAMPLES OF COMMUNITY ORGANIZING INITIATIVES TO REFORM SCHOOLS

A description of two education organizing initiatives will help make concrete the benefits of the strategies described above. In early 2000, Austin Interfaith, a local affiliate of the Industrial Areas Foundation, began organizing teachers and parents of students at Johnston High School in Austin, Texas, to improve the quality of education in the school. After their first

two years' effort—which included obtaining $140,000 in grant funding for staff development, parent training, and after-school programs; running a job readiness training program that placed more than 100 students in summer jobs with the city of Austin; and engaging more than 600 parent and community participants in the initiative—the school district removed Johnston High from the city's list of failing schools. Students' math scores increased significantly, and the dropout rate fell.

Following these victories, the initiative focused on developing a more rigorous curriculum and keeping honors scholars and athletes who live in the neighborhood at their high school. The Austin school district recently had decided to move the magnet academy located at the high school to a school in another part of the city. Students in the magnet academy were mostly white and high-performing. Students in the "host school" were 80 percent Latino, and 15 percent African American. Also, many of the honors scholars and athletes from the host school were being recruited by schools on the affluent side of town as part of a "diversity choice" policy. Through their organizing, the initiative's core team fought to: (1) obtain substantial funding for training for teachers to offer Advanced Placement and honors courses; (2) assure that parents and teachers would be involved in future major decisions about programs at the school; (3) have a buffer from staff cuts at the school for three years; and (4) begin to coordinate the academic program with feeder elementary and middle schools.

Doug Greco, a teacher on Johnston High School's core organizing team, told me that the school's partnership with Austin Interfaith had outlasted five principals in its first two years, and that the partnership is what kept him at the school. He shared with me that several teachers, including teachers in the magnet program, had felt so discouraged by the constant turnover of principals and the loss of talented neighborhood students to other schools through open enrollment, that they felt like leaving teaching. As a result of their participation in the organizing initiative with Austin Interfaith, these teachers remained in their profession, and stayed on at the school.[17]

Another example of a community organizing initiative, one focused on reforming several schools in a district, is the Community Collaborative to Improve District 9 Schools (CC9) in the South Bronx in New York City.[18] This initiative, started in 2001, involves the collaboration of six South Bronx community-based organizations,[19] NYU's Institute for Education and Social Policy, and the city teachers' union, the United Federation of Teachers (UFT). The parent and teacher leaders of CC9 negotiated with the New York City Department of Education to obtain $1.6 million for a "Lead Teacher" program in which a lead teacher position is being established in every grade in the ten CC9 schools. The lead teacher opens "his/her classroom as a laboratory for other teachers to visit and learn from best practices and also lead[s] professional development activities to support the other teachers in their grade," and is "half-time in the classroom and half-time providing leadership support to the other teachers." CC9 developed this campaign to "strengthen and stabilize the teaching force within each of these schools" based on the research they conducted that showed that teachers in the South Bronx are less experienced and less stable than teachers in higher-performing districts. Their research indicated that 35–40 percent of new teachers in New York City, and 50 percent of teachers in schools in the South Bronx leave teaching during their first five years.[20]

CC9 also organized tours of the neighborhoods of their schools for more than 300 of the schools' teachers—most of whom live outside the community—to help them see the strengths of the neighborhood and become more comfortable and familiar there, and to encourage the teachers to patronize local businesses—a trend that would strengthen the community's economic base.

Through their participation in these and other community organizing initiatives, educators, parents, and youth have experienced the power of their ideas and actions in the context of education bureaucracies that often induce feelings of powerlessness. Educators, parents, and youth have seen that what they think counts, and that they can make a difference in their schools and communities. The following section will explore in greater detail the benefits to educators of "caring" about and participating in organizing initiatives.

WHY URBAN EDUCATORS SHOULD CARE ABOUT COMMUNITY ORGANIZING TO REFORM SCHOOLS

As described earlier, one of the key strategies of community organizing groups is engaging in conversations with people, individually and in small groups, to get to know them and to find out what they *care* about and what their core values are. By finding out what people care about, the groups learn what motivates them, and what they are likely to be willing to spend their time and energy on. What people care about is known in organizing circles as "self-interest." Self-interest is not selfishness. It is people's deepest concerns, which emerge out of their relationships with their families, friends, neighbors, and coworkers. For example, Liz Sullivan was concerned that gangs were recruiting at her daughter's school; it was in her self-interest to end gang activity at the school. This section explores ways in which community organizing to reform schools is in the self-interest of urban educators, that is, why they should care about it.

The first and most obvious way in which community organizing approaches to reforming schools is in the self-interest of educators is that it results in improvements that enhance the quality of their professional lives in schools. For example, Oakland Community Organizations (OCO) developed the grassroots power that won the policy change resulting in Oakland's new small-school reform strategy.[21] Several groups have obtained city and state funds to improve school buildings, reduce class size, and develop innovative, rigorous professional development such as the Lead Teacher program in the South Bronx and training in teaching Advanced Placement and honors courses in Austin, Texas, described earlier. Groups also have increased parent involvement in their children's education, and have developed relationships of mutual respect and collaboration among parents and educators through their work together on these initiatives.[22]

A second, perhaps more important, reason that educators should care about community organizing is that participating in organizing reform initiatives often gives educators a sense of their own power to create positive change in their schools. Even though teachers in many large urban school districts belong to labor unions that protect their jobs, the unions do not protect teachers from feelings of powerlessness when faced with conditions in their schools that negatively impact their ability to teach, and over which they typically have little say. These conditions include "drive-by" professional development that offers little ongoing mentoring or help in applying the content of workshops to actual teaching; highly scripted curricula selected and mandated by the education bureaucracy that leave little room for teachers to adapt to the needs of their students; and decisions to change programs, or even close entire schools, with little input from the educators at the school.

In my own practice as a professor of students in the graduate school of education in an urban public university, I have become deeply familiar with urban educators' feelings of powerlessness. My students, many of whom are relatively new teachers in New York City schools, frequently have told me that they feel like "cogs in the machinery" of the city's education bureaucracy, and that what they think matters little in the decisions made about their classrooms or their schools. Many of them report that the only time they feel they have any power is "behind the closed doors of their classrooms." They often feel they have little possibility of "owning," or controlling, or of putting their "selves"—their thinking and creativity—into their teaching. Their presentation of their experience evokes the impression that they labor in the enterprise of educating students for the "boss"—the Department of Education.

Community organizing initiatives offer an antidote to educators' sense of powerlessness and alienation through their strategy of creating a relational culture—as opposed to a bureaucratic culture—in the public schools in which they are involved. Through their individual and small-group meetings with educators, parents, youth, and community leaders, these organizations both seek participants' ideas about their schools, and build relationships of trust and reciprocity among participants, which they eventually can draw upon to make positive changes in their schools. This process was evident in the organizing reform initiative in Austin, described earlier, in which the principal, teachers, and parents met frequently about the district's decision to move the magnet academy, and to decide how they would negotiate with the district to address their concerns and strengthen the school. Without the work of the organizing group, the teachers who felt like leaving teaching, in all likelihood would have left when the magnet academy moved to the affluent side of town. Teachers' sense of alienation was replaced by hope for what they could accomplish together to rebuild the school, and a sense of their collective power to make these positive changes.

A third way that education organizing is in the self-interest of urban educators is that organizers not only ask participants—including educators—what they think about their local schools, but they also develop their capacity as *critical* thinkers with an understanding of the broad context and political dynamics that shape public education. Participants engage in conversation about the historical, political, and economic factors that impact the quality of education in their schools, and the pros and cons of different strategies, pedagogies, curricula, and forms of governance that might be used to improve the schools.

It is important here to describe the educational background of many teachers, counselors, and administrators in public schools in low-income urban neighborhoods to fully understand the benefit to educators—and ultimately to their K–12 students—of community organizing approaches. Many urban educators attended the underfunded, overcrowded public schools in the same communities in which they now teach. Often, they attended underfunded city colleges and universities to prepare to become teachers in the same or nearby communities, as well. Although it is not monolithic, this cycle of education *typically* does not develop critical thinking or high-level analytical skills, but emphasizes rote learning, responsible work habits, and obedience to authority figures—the kind of education Anyon observed in schools in working-class neighborhoods.[23] The current focus by education policy makers on improving "teacher quality" typically addresses this cycle with initiatives that recruit "better qualified" teachers from other (i.e., more middle-class, better educated, often more white) communities to replace the teachers educated in schools in working-class and low-income communities.

On the other hand, community organizing approaches to reform tend to address the need to improve teacher quality quite differently—in a way that is more in the self-interest of urban educators. First, as touched upon earlier, organizing groups teach critical thinking and analytical skills through the process of organizing. The groups challenge educators to think about their own work, to understand the political and social factors shaping it, and to identify and take action on issues interfering with their ability to offer a better-education to students in their schools. Essentially the groups teach participants how to use critical thinking to solve the new and different problems they face in their work as educators, as opposed to either unthinking compliance or rebellion in response to the demands and dilemmas facing them.

The power analysis is a key strategy community organizing groups use to teach participants to think critically about education. The analysis helps educators see how it is in their self-interest to understand the social and political context in which they teach. In the "Schools and Communities " course I teach to graduate students in education, my students and I construct a power analysis of the individuals and groups in New York City who have power over public education. We apply our analysis to the inequities in schooling in the South Bronx, graphically and poignantly described by Kozol.[24] The power analysis includes a description of the political structure in which public education is embedded, as well as the salaries of public officials, including the mayor, chancellor of schools, superintendents, and others in the state and local political and education systems. The response of one of my colleagues, observing my teaching on the day of the power analysis, is revealing of the usually implicit expectations for the thinking of urban educators. My colleague told me that my students, who are preparing to be school counselors, do not need to know this information, as it will only upset them. My colleague's comment suggests an assumption that urban educators cannot make a difference in the political factors that shape the quality of education in their schools, so they should not even know or think about them. Such thinking contributes to educators' perceptions of themselves as passive, with little agency or power in their own workplaces.

My students, most of whom attended public schools in New York City, actually find the power analysis upsetting, but they also find it fascinating. The analysis stirs many of the students to look at the contexts of their own education and teaching in a new way, considering the social and political factors that impact them, their teaching, and their students. Paradoxically, even though many of my students have been educated in and have taught in schools similar to those in the South Bronx described by Kozol, they are almost always surprised and deeply disturbed by the inequities Kozol highlights. Their surprise suggests that they have not been invited to look critically at their own education and work contexts in a systemic and informed way. The important question here is, if educators are not accustomed to thinking critically, then how can they teach the skills of critical thinking to their students?

A second way that community organizing groups address the issue of teacher quality is by innovative professional development and teacher education, such as the Lead Teacher program created by CC9, and the field-based teacher education program at the University of Texas at El Paso (UTEP), associated with El Paso Inter-Religious Sponsoring Organization (EPISO), part of the Texas IAF network. UTEP's students are

65 percent Mexican Americans and 8 percent Mexican nationals. Most students are from El Paso County (85%) and intend to stay there . . . most were educated by teachers who were graduates of UTEP, creating a "continuous loop" in which students and teachers share common roots.[25]

These programs do not rely primarily on recruiting educators from outside the communities of the low-performing schools to improve teacher quality. Because they value educators' knowledge of the communities in which they teach, they develop strategies for increasing their capacity as educators. Grounded in the principles and pedagogies of adult education, the programs assume that adults can learn to be better teachers.

Teachers in urban schools who were raised and educated in more middle-class communities also benefit from participating in the training and professional development associated with community organizing initiatives. They learn ways of relating to students and their parents that are mutually respectful and focus on families' strengths and knowledge, not on their deficits and not on "saving" them.[26]

To summarize, I am suggesting that three important ways in which community organizing to reform schools is in the self-interest of urban educators are in approaches that: (1) improve the concrete conditions in which they educate their students; (2) help them develop a sense of their own power to create change; and (3) expand their capacity as critical thinkers and the quality of their teaching. Despite these potential benefits, educators sometimes resist participating in organizing initiatives. The following section offers some hypotheses about the source of educators' resistance, as well as approaches to engage them to move beyond it.

REASONS EDUCATORS MAY RESIST COMMUNITY ORGANIZING TO REFORM SCHOOLS

Drawing on my work with educators and organizing initiatives, and on the small but growing literature on the role of educators in community organizing to reform schools, four areas of concern emerge that may deter educators from participating in organizing initiatives: (1) concerns related to their professional role and identity; (2) fear that participating may jeopardize their jobs; (3) concerns about the motives and legitimacy of community-based organizations; and (4) concerns about the separation between church and state. I briefly will describe each area of concern.

Concerns related to educators' role and identity as professionals appear to stem for the most part from a conception of being professional that involves putting distance between themselves and members of the community, or "laypersons." Initiatives in which parents, youth, and community members address issues related to school governance, curriculum, and pedagogy violate some educators' sense of the boundary between layperson and professional, and may threaten their identity as professionals. In a related concern, teachers who have participated in organizing initiatives occasionally have expressed concerns about whether they should be involved in organizing activities that are not directly related to academics and their classroom teaching.[27] Also, a lack of confidence in developing productive relationships with parents, particularly among new teachers, may lead educators to keep their distance from community initiatives as well.[28]

The most effective response to these concerns has been field-based professional development and teacher education that helps to build teachers' confidence working with families, and which demonstrates a conception of being a professional that includes working closely with communities and valuing the knowledge that families offer about their children. For example, in my "Schools and Communities" course, half of our class sessions take place at an innovative small high school, the Bushwick School for Social Justice (BSSJ).[29] Among other activities, the students participate in an informative and moving neighborhood tour led by youth organizers from one of the school's partners, the community organizing group, Make the Road by Walking (MTRBW). They also go on a community walk with teachers and staff from MTRBW

to meet with parents in their homes. During these meetings, they ask about parents' hopes, concerns, and ideas for their children's education, and share their own hopes and ideas about BSSJ and their lives and vocations.

Another issue that may lead to educators' resistance to organizing initiatives is educators' fear that their jobs will be jeopardized if they collaborate with community organizing groups to try to change policies and practices put in place by the local department of education, their employer. Actually, it is relatively rare for educators to experience a threat to their jobs because of their participation in efforts to improve teaching and learning. In fact, following successful organizing initiatives, some school districts have promoted teachers into administrative positions. In situations where they have experienced tension around their participation, some educators have ceased their public, visible role in an initiative, and let the community organizing group continue to put external pressure on the education system to take action to improve the school.

Another source of educators' resistance to organizing initiatives comes from their concerns about the motives of community-based organizations. Because some community groups have used their organizations primarily to enrich the leaders or to expand the power of local politicians or community activists, educators may be reluctant to believe that a particular community organizing group is genuinely working to improve public schools. Educators can seek information about the legitimacy of an organization by finding out about its accomplishments in public education, and its affiliations either with national organizing networks, or with local coalitions of groups working to improve schools.

One final issue raised by educators in my courses, and documented in the research literature as being on the minds of other educators as well, concerns whether faith-based community organizing groups violate the legal separation of church and state by their efforts to improve public schools.[30] Shirley reports that an IAF group consulted with lawyers about this issue and learned that as long as the organizing groups were not teaching religious doctrine in schools (which they do not), they were not violating the doctrine of the separation of church and state.[31]

A better understanding of educators' resistance to organizing initiatives, including the four concerns identified in this section—issues related to their professional role and identity; to job security; to the legitimacy of community organizing groups; and to the separation of church and state—will allow the creation of more effective approaches to reducing the resistance, and ultimately, to closer collaboration among educators and communities to improve the quality of education in their schools.

CONCLUSION

Liz Sullivan, the urban teacher whose words began this chapter, eventually claimed the power she originally denied she wanted; she accepted the organizer's invitation to join with other educators, parents, and neighborhood residents in a community organizing initiative that ended the gang's activity at her daughter's school. She also went on to participate in other campaigns by the organization to improve local public schools in her city, later becoming an organizer herself.

This chapter proposes that community organizing approaches to reforming schools address the deepest concerns of urban educators, including their perhaps inchoate desire for the power to improve their schools. I argue that it is in educators' self-interest to seek out and collaborate with education organizing groups. Only as educators are able to address their concerns about the concrete conditions in which they teach, and about the quality of their relationships with each other, with their students, and their communities, can they address that which is of utmost importance—the intellectual and emotional development of their students.

NOTES

1. Oakland Community Organizations (OCO) is a community organizing group in Oakland, California, affiliated with the Pacific Institute of Community Organizing (PICO), one of the national organizing networks in the United States.

2. Interview with Liz Sullivan, July 2003.

3. "Educators" refers to teachers, counselors, principals, superintendents, and other professionals who contribute to the education of students in a school or district.

4. An article by Glenn Loury, "Why should we care about group inequality?" *Social Philosophy & Policy,* 5, no. 1 (1987), pp. 249–271, inspired the title of this chapter.

5. Cortes, E. (1996). Engaging the community in education reform. *School Voices,* 5 (2), 27–32.

6. Gold, E., Simon, E., & Brown, C. (2002). *Strong neighborhoods, strong schools: The indicators project on education organizing.* Chicago: Cross City Campaign for Urban School Reform & Research for Action; Mediratta, K., Fruchter, N., & Lewis, A. (2002). *Organizing for school reform: How communities are finding their voices and reclaiming their public schools.* New York: Institute for Education and Social Policy, New York University.

7. Cutler, W. (2000). *Parents and schools: The 150-year struggle for control in American education.* Chicago: The University of Chicago Press.

8. These nonprofit groups include the Institute for Education and Social Policy at New York University, the National Center for Schools and Communities at Fordham University, the Center for Public Policy at Temple University, the Cross City Campaign for Urban School Reform, and Research for Action.

9. Shirley, D. (1997). *Community organizing for urban school reform.* Austin: University of Texas Press; Williams, M. (1989). *Neighborhood organizing for urban school reform.* New York: Teachers College Press.

10. The major national organizing networks include the Industrial Areas Foundation (IAF), the Association of Community Organizations for Reform Now (ACORN), the Gamaliel Foundation, the Pacific Institute of Commu-

nity Organizing (PICO), and the Direct Action Research and Training Center (DART).

11. Gold, Simon, & Brown (2002); Mediratta, Fruchter, & Lewis (2002).

12. Shirley (1997).

13. Giles, H. (1998). *ERIC digest: Parent engagement as a school reform strategy.* New York: ERIC Clearinghouse on Urban Education.

14. Epstein, J. (1995). School/family/community partnerships: Caring for the children we share. *Phi Delta Kappan, 76* (9), 701–707.

15. Giles (1998).

16. Shirley (1997).

17. Interview with Doug Greco, May 28, 2002.

18. Dingerson, L., & Levner, A. (2005). A true Bronx tale: How parents and teachers joined forces to improve teacher quality. In *Philanthropy's role in fostering partnerships: Collaborating with unions, school districts and communities.* New York City: Grantmakers for Education; NYU Institute for Education and Social Policy. (2002). Parents and teachers partner in the South Bronx. *NYC Schoolwatch.* New York: NYU Institute for Education and Social Policy.

19. The organizations are ACORN, Citizens Advice Bureau, Highbridge Community Life Center, Mid-Bronx Council, New Settlement Apartments, and Northwest Bronx Community and Clergy Coalition.

20. NYU Institute for Education and Social Policy, Handout. (n.d.). *CC9 Community Collaborative to Improve District 9 Schools.* New York: NYU Institute for Education and Social Policy.

21. Gold, Simon & Brown (2002).

22. Shirley (1997).

23. Anyon, J. (1981). Social class and school knowledge. *Curriculum Inquiry, 11,* 3–42.

24. Kozol, J. (1991). The savage inequalities of public education in New York. In *Savage inequalities: Children in America's schools* (pp. 83–132). New York: Harper.

25. Harvard Family Research Project. (2001). Program spotlight, featured program: Field-based program, University of Texas, El Paso . FINE Forum-e-Newsletter, Issue 2. Cambridge, MA: President and Fellows of Harvard College, Summer/Fall, 2001. Retrieved July 1, 2004 from www.gse.harvard.edu/hfrp/projects/fine/fineforum/forum2/spotlight.html.

26. Giles, H. (2005). Three narratives of parent-educator relationships: Toward counselor repertoires for bridging the urban parent-school divide. *Professional School Counseling Journal, 8* (3), 228–235.

27. Quezada, T. (2003). Faith-based organizing for school improvement in the Texas borderlands: A case study of the alliance school initiative. Research Digest. Cambridge, MA: Harvard Family Research Project. Retrieved July 1, 2004 from www.gse.harvard.edu/hfrp/projectsfine/resources/digest/tasi.html.

28. Harvard Family Research Project, Program spotlight.

29. Giles, H. (in press). The birth of a movement school in a public education bureaucracy: The Bushwick School for Social Justice. In C. Payne & C. Strickland (Eds.), *Teach freedom: The African-American tradition of education for liberation.*

30. Quezada, T. Faith-based organizing for school improvement.

31. Shirley (1997).

Race/Ethnicity and Urban Education

A SOCIOLOGICAL CRITIQUE OF *MEANINGFUL DIFFERENCES*: A FUNCTIONAL APPROACH TO THE PARENTING STYLE OF LOW-INCOME AFRICAN-AMERICAN FAMILIES

Linda B. Benbow

Meaningful Differences in the Everyday Experience of Young American Children is a meticulously designed observation study of language development of children based on their early childhood environment.[1] In this study, an excerpt of which was recently published in *American Educator*, Hart and Risley conducted an analysis of the qualities of parenting that make a difference in the language development of children.[2] Using economic deprivation and comparative deficit approaches, they compared the parenting styles of upper-class and welfare families and found that upper-class parents socialize their children in an environment that significantly increases their children's vocabulary growth and IQ scores. In contrast, they found that parenting in welfare families significantly prohibited their children's vocabulary growth and subsequently diminished their IQ scores.

This paper will begin with a summary of the methodology and findings of *Meaningful Differences*. A critique of the study,

which begins with a discussion of Hart and Risley's use of an economic deprivation approach to the understanding of academic achievement among children in welfare families, will follow. It will also examine the efficacy of Hart and Risley's dismissal of race as a factor affecting both the amount of talking and parental styles found in the homes of African-American welfare families, which is both methodologically and theoretically problematic. The position taken here is that any intervention designed to eradicate aspects of a culture that are not beneficial in mainstream society, must first address why aspects of that cultural phenomenon are functional within the particular subcultural group. In an effort to do so, this paper offers a speculative approach to the experiences of African Americans, which facilitated and continues to make necessary a culture of silence. This discussion will utilize the concept of a culture of silence and try to show that it is imperative for any intervention that aims to improve the language development of disadvantaged African-American children to include parental and community involvement.

SUMMARY

Meaningful Differences began as an investigation into the failure of the 1960s War on Poverty Head Start programs, which were designed and funded to give children isolated in poverty (African Americans, Native Americans, Latinos, and poor whites) the social and cognitive experiences that contribute to the academic success of advantaged children. According to the researchers, the failure of Head Start was evident: Achievement scores in the 1970s were similar to those before the War on Poverty; American children enter school ill-prepared to benefit from education and drop out in large numbers, leading to welfare and unemployment. The intent of the study, the accumulation of more than twenty years' research, is to improve the educational and developmental experiences of impoverished children.

The researchers, who were clinical language intervention specialists during the early stage of the study, joined a team of experts in Turner House, a community-based research program in an impoverished African-American community. Instead of focusing on a theory-based curriculum, they designed an intervention program that focused on the everyday language the children were using. Believing that spontaneous speech is the best indicator of cognitive functioning, they looked for improvements in how the children functioned in their daily activities in preschool. Over time, they became uncertain about what language skills should be improved; when they listened to Turner House children talk during free play, they seemed able to explain and elaborate on topics typical of preschoolers. They decided to compare the spontaneous speech of advantaged children (white professors' children) to those of Turner House children (all African American) in terms of grammar and content. When the researchers projected the developmental growth curves of the two groups, they found an ever-widening vocabulary resource gap, which "seemed to foreshadow the findings from other studies that in high school many children from families in poverty lack the vocabulary used in advanced textbooks."[3]

Hart and Risley used vocabulary growth as a measure of accumulated experience, which they believe is strongly associated with cognitive growth. This led them to conclude that the goal of intervention for disadvantaged children needs to be changing their developmental trajectory. Rather than yield to biological determinism as an explanation, they questioned whether vocabulary growth rates were related to the gulf in amount and richness of the daily experiences separating advantaged and disadvantaged children. Believing that there was a relationship between academic achievement and the home environment, they wanted to understand how and when the developmental gaps they observed began. The researchers determined that they needed to find out what was happening to children at home during the early stages of the development of vocabulary growth and wanted to know specifically what parents were doing, which made a lasting difference in how fast their children's vocabulary grows. Rather than depend on self-reports, the researchers observed 42 families for hour-long monthly observations for a period of two-and-one-half years. During these visits they counted all verbal and nonverbal gestures made by significant family members and the children involved.

Hart and Risley found that families differ immensely in the amount of language experience and interaction they provide their children and that these differences were strongly linked to language development among children. The largest and most consistent differences in how much familics talked to their children, however, were found between upper socioeconomic status (racially mixed) and welfare families (all African Americans). The utterances of upper-class parents were not only greater than those of welfare parents but also richer in certain quality features. Another difference associated with social strata was in the amount of prohibitions parents gave their children. As well, the researchers concluded that the frequency and tone of interaction in welfare families limited the number of words and meanings children heard. The differences in amount of talking, interaction, and prohibitions found in households of different social strata reflect different cultural priorities that parents transmit to their children. They suggest that intervention programs for children raised in poverty would need to provide them with experiences with language richer in quality features than the language they heard at home. Further, they conclude that intervention should begin during the early stage of language development, before age three, when "children are uniquely susceptible to the culture of adults, before interaction with peers and the social standards of schools become important influences on what children learn."[4] Hart and Risley's central concern in the later stage of their research asked whether welfare children hear a language so impoverished that intervention would be needed to provide them with language richer in quality than the language they learn at home.[5]

AN ECONOMIC DEPRIVATION APPROACH

Utilizing an economic deprivation model "places heavy weight on the economic circumstances (family income, assets, and housing quality) in which a child is nurtured and suggests that poverty and economic deprivation causes low levels of academic achievement."[6] Abstractly,

Hart and Risley's findings related to language development reconfirm what has already been confirmed. According to Chall and Jacobs,

Administration of reading tests by National Assessment of Educational Progress (NAEP) have since 1971 confirmed . . . Children from more economically advantaged families score significantly higher than the less advantaged at all ages tested . . . and the gap becomes greater with increasing age.[7]

This idea is closely associated with the work of Kohn, who also investigated social class variations in parenting styles. He found that due to the character of the parents' occupational experience and the transmission of these values, childrearing practices perpetuate the existing class order. He found that the characteristics that lower-class parents desired most in their children are good manners, neatness, politeness, obedience, honesty, and being a good student.[8] Hart and Risley's research found similar parental goals among African-American welfare families, which they state are:

To teach socially acceptable behavior, language rich in nouns and modifiers was not called for . . . Rather than attempting to prepare their children with the knowledge and skills required in a technological world with which the parents had little experience, parents seemed to be preparing their children for jobs . . . in which success and advancement would be determined by attitude, how well the children presented themselves, and whether they could prove themselves through performance.[9]

Hart and Risley, unlike earlier researchers, avoid using a language of disorganization or pathology to describe the parenting style found in the welfare families they studied.[10] In fact, they describe the welfare mothers as nurturing and affectionate, despite their high levels of social isolation.[11] However, they found that African-American welfare mothers "make few efforts to engage the child in conversation or prompt the child to practice. She does not redirect or elaborate the child's initiatives; most of the feedback she gives is corrective or critical."[12] The central concern of their study is the implications this parenting style has on language development. The premise of their research is that low economic status, regardless of race, leads to a certain kind of parenting style that has a negative impact on the academic achievement of children reared in poverty. They suggest, "Children in welfare families received less than half the language experience of working-class children in each hour of their lives, due more to the lesser amount of talking in the family than because their parents' utterances were somewhat less rich in quality features."[13]

A COMPARATIVE DEFICIT MODEL

In consideration of the issue of race and racism in society, Hart and Risley's position that "race [is] a central issue only in designing strategies to preserve cultural identity within mainstream society" is a serious theoretical oversight.[14] Although it is fair to suggest that the researchers are neoliberal and try not to resort to a culture of poverty hypothesis, there is, however, an undercurrent of a cultural deficiency model. According to Peters, this kind of comparative deficit approach is problematic because "black mothers [are] compared to white mothers indirectly and by assumption."[15] The concept of race is also problematic for several other reasons related to using a combination of economic deprivation and comparative deficit models.

In *Meaningful Differences*, Hart and Risley dismissed race as a significant variable in their study. They state that they observed "a demographic range of African American families" and "quickly" eliminated the influence of race on amount of talking and socializing.[16] It may be extremely difficult to quantify the effects of race on parenting style, or the later academic achievement of children in

a quantitative study that utilizes the combined effect of earnings and education as the causal variables; however, this does not dismiss our need to incorporate these important determinants of the socialization process and life chances of American families and children. In fact it is imperative to do so because any intervention program designed to equalize the early experiences of children raised in poverty has to be appropriate for black, Latino, and Native American children who are disproportionately poor and disproportionately subject to academic failure.

Another problematic aspect of Hart and Risley's dismissal of race as a significant variable in *Meaningful Differences* is that all six of the welfare families they used to generalize about the parenting style of impoverished families were African American. Under more ideal circumstances, an intervention that aims to "interrupt the cycle of poverty,"[17] should be more inclusive; the welfare group was the only group in their study that was not racially mixed. It is extremely problematic to model remediation programs based upon conclusions drawn from a sample of one racial group because, as the theorists suggest, "poverty is differentially prevalent among minorities."[18] As well, the children of poor whites would also benefit from an equalization of early childhood experiences, but it does not necessarily follow that the parenting style found in these homes and the remediation effort for these children should be the same as one proposed for African-American welfare families. The value of whiteness in our society combined with the fact that poor whites are not isolated in inner-city ghetto communities, as are impoverished African-American families, may contribute to a qualitative difference in their poverty experience and educational attainment. It follows that what should be done to equalize the experiences of all American children remains an enigma.

THE SIGNIFICANCE OF CULTURE

One thing is clear. American children should have the opportunity to thrive, and most parents, regardless of income, have aspirations for their children to do so. However, the remedial program espoused in *Meaningful Differences* would be problematic because the researchers believe, if a national program concerned with early childhood is not formulated, children should spend long hours in state-funded day care centers prior to age three so that they can be guarded from the culture that is transmitted to them via their parents. The central concern in Hart and Risley's study is intervention. They state:

Our data showed that the magnitude of children's accomplishments depends less on the material and educational advantages available in the home and more on the amount of experience children accumulate with parenting that provides language diversity, affirmative feedback, symbolic emphasis, gentle guidance, and responsiveness . . . If children [could] be given better parenting, intervention might be unnecessary.[19]

From the functionalist perspective formulated by Parsons,[20] which fundamentally views society as made up of interrelated parts whose task is to sustain the life of the whole, the remediation that Hart and Risley propose is one in which the state takes over fundamental aspects of the socialization role of "parents." This would be most problematic for families and children because the family is the most significant means by which children develop self-identity. According to Jackson, McCullough, and Gurin,

The intrafamilial socialization of group and personal identity has considerable bearing upon personal functioning in a society that cultivates negative conceptions of minority group members through direct interaction, the media, and institutional barriers.[21]

Considering the unique socialization experience of minorities, the kind of intervention proposed in *Meaningful Differences* could be potentially disastrous for African-American children reared in poverty.

Hart and Risley are aware of the significance of culture as a way of life. They state, "The early experience of children in other cultures is likely to differ, as are the skills needed for success; in Navajo culture, for example, talking a great deal may not be considered socially appropriate."[22] However, because they do not take race into consideration as an important variable, they fail to consider the unique historical experience of African Americans. This experience may contribute to the manner and amount of talking that goes on, as well as to other parent–child interaction patterns they observed. Although the researchers point out that the skills needed for success among Native Americans and African Americans are different (that is, vis-à-vis the larger society), they do not consider that "children are socialized into a particular subculture, not into a culture as a whole. This means that initially children learn not the ways of their society, but the ways of a particular segment of it."[23] Second, they fail to consider the ways in which the historical mistreatment that both Native Americans and African Americans experienced and continue to experience in the United States— the direct result of race and racism—and how these factors, despite what it takes to thrive in the larger society, may contribute to the parenting styles evident in both groups.

In addition, it is important to consider that cultural patterns are not easily changed and that, furthermore, there is great resistance to change when the change is externally imposed and when the behaviors derived in response to environmental exigencies are still functional for the group or subculture. This suggests that the parenting style may be functional, given the unique sociohistoric experiences of the group. Thus, this chapter suggests that the most effective approach to the eradication or amelioration of aspects of a subculture that are not functional in the larger society is to know from whence the subculture came and why it is still so stable. This is imperative because the "low levels of achievement among black children spring from the same roots as do many other social problems of black children—poverty, powerlessness, ignorance, and most of all racism."[24] In effect, a functional approach such as the one espoused in this paper will enable us to better understand parenting styles found in these communities in order to create intervention programs that will be pertinent to the experiences of African-American welfare families.

A CULTURE OF SILENCE: AFRICAN-AMERICAN WELFARE FAMILIES

A culture of silence is the utilization of taciturnity or code restriction, consciously or unconsciously, among groups and individuals.[25] Although it is often used as a protective device among disadvantaged racial–ethnic minorities, it should not be thought of as a characteristic of a culture of poverty, as defined by Oscar Lewis.[26] Rather, a culture of silence is conceptualized as the consistent use of nonverbal communication techniques or the use of curt phrases rather than complete sentences. The use of these communication techniques can be situational, as found among ethnic females from low socioeconomic status who are trying to negotiate the demands of graduate school where their professors are middle-aged and older, white, male, and very conservative.[27] A culture of silence is not confined to racial and ethnic groups but is more broadly noted among groups and individuals who find themselves in long-term or temporary circumstances where the verbalization of one's thoughts is perceived as more problematic than silence. Thus, it is utilized among people who are involved in armed conflict as well as among college professors, self included, who often look on in silence when

approached by disgruntled students. Both are protective devices. However, a culture of silence is conceptualized as a way of life when the behaviors associated with it are characteristic of large numbers of individuals in a particular group and when the behaviors are passed from one generation to another. This operationalization of the concept of a culture of silence is the way I conceptualized it in an unpublished critique of *Meaningful Differences* that I wrote in 1996 while taking a Social, Human, and Cultural Capital graduate course with Paul Attewell at City University Graduate Center at City University of New York.

As utilized in the African-American community, a culture of silence stems from, but is an adaptation of, the African-based oral tradition. According to Smitherman, the core of the oral tradition is the high value placed on the spoken word. "The force, responsibility, and commitment of the word (the concept of Nommo) and the awareness that the word alone alters the world,"[28] are part of the cultural baggage that Africans brought to America. Under the conditions of slavery, Jim Crow segregation, and oppression, the power of the spoken word became ever more important among African Americans. Smitherman points out that through verbal gymnastics, "black folk are acculturated—initiated—into the black value system where talk is a functional dynamic that is simultaneously a mechanism for learning about life and the world, and a vehicle for achieving group approval and recognition."[29] Thus, the importance of the spoken word contributes to a culture of silence among blacks where there is tendency toward taciturnity—as though less is more—when using spoken words in specific social settings. It is a testament to both the significance and the power of the word because it is believed, consciously and unconsciously, that the word, as other sources of power, can be dangerous. A culture of silence is derived from the collective experiences of African Americans, but it is not a race-based phenomenon. All oppressed groups exhibit some degree of a culture of silence, although it varies by socioeconomic status.

An examination of the behavioral style of African-American parents from a functional perspective will begin with the early stages of the development of African-American culture, which originate from the conditions of chattel slavery. Because cultural patterns of behavior, values, and beliefs are often products of the distant past, the conditions of slavery may have relevance for childrearing behavior among low-income African Americans in the contemporary society. Although there are very few studies of parenting styles among slaves, a brief examination of the literature about the experiences of slave children—who were "silent and invisible"— can identify the rudimentary elements of the parenting style now found among low-income African-American families.[30] On plantations, youngsters went to nurseries to be cared for by slaves too old, too young, or too infirm to work elsewhere; thus parents did not spend a great deal of time with their offspring.[31] However, they valued the time they spent with their children, and parents and others played a significant role in teaching behavior, such as courteousness, that was appropriate for slave children. Many slave parents, according to King:

[D]emanded obedience from their children, but they were not sadistic. Their basic goal was to protect their children from harm at the hands of malicious whites . . . Parents demanded obedience, respect, and unity from children to achieve that result . . . Application of the axiom "Children are to be seen and not heard" served as a protective armor against children who talked too much. Parents could not tolerate "enemies within their own families."[32]

It is apparent that childrearing practices had some implication for the tendency of low-income African-American families to demand obedience from their children, and for the culture of silence Hart and Risley observed, however, limited our knowledge. Nevertheless, we know more about language development among slaves than we do about actual parenting styles.

One aspect of the development of language among slaves that has a direct impact on the culture of silence and the amount of talking that takes place in African-American welfare families relates to the importance of nonverbal communication. The basic components and functions of many nonverbal gestures among African Americans "can no longer be ignored or overlooked in any comprehensive theory involving language and its relation to culture, learning, and psychology."[33] Cooke's work is basically a catalog of many different nonverbal gestures that African Americans commonly use. He explains that this mode of communication is cultural and plays an integral "part in the African American communication system."[34] Cooke's work offers no explanation for the origin of the nonverbal communication style or its cultural relevance. However, it does imply that an effort to change language patterns among African-American welfare children must begin with an understanding of the importance and relevance of nonverbal communication among members of the group, which varies by social class. Under the circumstances of slavery, it can be speculated that nonverbal communication was quite functional.

A significant portion of the slaves brought to the Americas during the transatlantic slave trade did not speak the language of their captors, which made nonverbal communication essential. Nonverbal communication was also necessary because "a divide-and-rule principle [was] built into the slave system [that in part] involved the separation of slaves from the same region of origin in order to forestall any attempts to plot revolts or insurrections."[35] The result of these factors is that

African slaves developed the ability to understand the slave owners and each other primarily through nonverbal communication. Nonverbal communication and silence offered some degree of protection during the slave era, and part of the folklore that came out of slavery attests to the importance of silence. For example, there are several variations of a story that involves a slave who told his master on several occasions that there was a ghost down by the river. When the master finally accompanied the slave to the river but did not find a ghost, he killed the slave for lying. The moral of the story is not: Do not tell a lie. Rather it is: Do not let your mouth put your life on the line. There are, in fact, a myriad of such sayings still commonly used in the African-American community, indicative of their continued importance, which will be discussed shortly.

Nonverbal communication was as important after slavery—when African Americans lost the protections of having "belonged" to a slave owner—as it was during slavery. It remained functional for the group because it was a way of sharing knowledge under extremely dangerous circumstances. The Reconstruction and Jim Crow eras both demanded a kind of racial etiquette; the foundation of which was essentially silence. It was imperative that African Americans mask their feelings and show deference to, and mince words in the presence of, whites. The reign of terror to which the Ku Klux Klan subjected African Americans during the turn of the last century made a culture of silence imperative; the lives of African Americans depended upon it. Although the majority of black men and women were powerless, dependent on whites, and limited in avenues available for self-expression, socioeconomic variations did exist. Those African Americans who lacked educational and economic opportunities (i.e., the working class and the poor) were most vulnerable and thus,

more guarded with the use of the spoken word. Recognizing this culture of silence among poor blacks does not suggest that they do not speak. Rather, it suggests that depending on the audience, their conscious and unconscious concern for the implications of what they say contributes to taciturnity.

The tendency toward guarded speech among poor African Americans—already culturally derived—became vital to their way of life as they became more involved in and connected to social institutions. For example, from the Freedmen's Bureau to the New Deal legislation and Aid to Dependent Children (ADC) that came out of it, these were unofficially and later officially means-tested programs at federal and state levels;[36] eligibility requirements and visits from social workers necessitated a culture of silence. In the presence of government officials, who were in most cases white, African-American women had to strike a balance between making sure they neither said nor did anything to contribute to a loss of aid, while giving the appearance, by any means necessary, of providing a home that was suitable for children. Their children dare not say anything in the presence of these officials. For those African-American women who worked as domestic servants where there was an "intense relationship between mistress and maid, and the inevitable intrusion of temperamental factors into that relationship,"[37] a significant amount of silent resistance among servants resulted. The tendency toward taciturnity was not confined to work in domestic settings. From the turn of the last century through World War II, those African-American men and women who avoided domestic work "toiled silently" in factories as appendages of machines.[38]

A culture of silence had a threefold function, individually and collectively; it was utilized as acceptance of one's fate, as an act of resistance, and as a protective device from uncertain and harsh circumstances. A culture of silence is deeply ingrained in cultural patterns found in the homes and communities of working-class and poor African-American families. Adults in these families talk a great deal to children when they are preverbal; clearly they know the importance of verbal communication for the development of communication skills. However, as children grow older, the amount of everyday parent–child talking tends to diminish. Narrative speech and the storytelling tradition, on the part of parents, become more prominent in their interactions with their children as the children grow older and everyday speech decreases. The goal of these tales, fictional or not, is to teach children life lessons, particularly those related to managing the self. This supports Hart and Risley's findings. They note, "After children learned to talk and had all the skills needed to talk more than the family, they did not; the amount they talked stopped increasing as soon as they began to talk the amount typical of the family."[39] Wilson speculates that, "the lower-class parent's childrearing behavior does not exist in a vacuum; it is intimately connected with the parent's . . . experience in the larger society."[40] What is that experience in the modern society?

Welfare families have minimal experience with the use of elaborated codes in their daily lives. The exception may be watching television. As noted in Hart and Risley, the most intimate friends that welfare mothers may have are the characters in soap operas.[41] Otherwise, the actual experience these mothers have with elaborated codes occurs in the context of their experiences with white and black middle-class bureaucrats—police, teachers, social workers, legal and social service officials—whose task it is to inform them of prescriptive and proscriptive behaviors expected of them by this or that agency.[42] As is typical in hierarchical bureaus, these parents are not viewed as parents as much as they are viewed as "clients." They are not asked

what would be feasible, reasonable, or convenient for them; rather they are told what they must and must not do in many aspects of their lives. Wilson makes an interesting point when he says, "What is demanded of the parents in the larger social context is what the parents demanded of their children within the family context."[43] From this perspective, what is demanded from the parent is silence, and this is exactly what the parent demands of the child.

From informal observations of African-American poor and working-class adults, it is apparent that they believe, consciously and unconsciously, that there can be consequences for saying too much in the presence of bureaucrats. This manifests in their childrearing practices, historically. In contemporary society, these parents fundamentally believe that it is disrespectful for a child to interrupt or involve themselves in adult conversations or to speak when they are not spoken to. As well, they believe it is not desirable to have children who say more than that which the family members feel is desirable or necessary to say on any given topic. As well, it is considered inappropriate for children to ask too many questions. All of the above varies according to the experiences of the adults, but most do not have a great deal of patience with talkative children who they consider "testing" the limits. This is also consistent with Hart and Risley's observations. They mentioned that children who attended Head Start programs in the 1960s showed improvements in performance, which they carried over into the home. "Although parents did not necessarily appreciate the changes in their children's behavior, they accepted the increases in activity and curiosity that resulted from the enriched experiences."[44] The problem with their interpretation is that the degree to which parents "accept" an increase in activity and curiosity among children is not the same as accepting the use of elaborate code among children because a great deal of effort is used to control the amount of conversing that goes on between young children and adults in working-class and welfare African-American families. Thus, as Hart and Risley observed, neither parents nor adults who visited the homes of welfare families engaged in a great deal of conversation with children.[45]

The culture of silence is not a family-based phenomenon in the sense that it is confined to mothers' ideas about appropriate parenting techniques and expectations of their children's behavior. Rather it is both communal and intergenerational. These mothers, as many do, rely on information from family and friends to help them manage their childrearing responsibilities. Thus, their ideals about what is appropriate behavior for children are not exclusive, but in many important respects are based on the expectations of the community. When these mothers, for example, do not appear to control the behavior and verbal gestures of their children, they are sanctioned by members of the community, who say: "You don't know who is the mother and who is the child," or "You need to show that child who is boss." The motto in these families is: "If you don't tolerate it [unruly behavior among children] from the start, you won't have a problem with it later."

Another motto deeply ingrained in the African-American community is: "Silence is golden." Due to the nature of the black experience in the United States, and most evident among those groups who are trapped in intergenerational poverty, they do not value the spoken word in the manner that it is embraced in the larger society. Among low-income African Americans, there is a tendency to not trust the spoken word and to be leery of it. Thus, it is very common for low-income African-American adults to make the following kinds of comments: "You can't trust what people say, only what they do." "I'd rather be thought a fool than to open my mouth and

remove all doubt." "You never know when you have said too much, until you have said too much." "You cannot listen if you don't stop talking." "Talking too much can get you in trouble." Thus, Hart and Risley may be correct to assume that children who are placed in developmental centers for eight to ten hours a day, as they propose, will learn to use elaborated codes. However, without the involvement of the family and community, this may have a deleterious effect on the social–psychological development of these children who may, in the course of acculturation into the larger society, become alienated from their families, community, and in effect, from their culture.

From a middle-class perspective, it is easy to identify the many ways in which a culture of silence may be dysfunctional; however, silence offers all kinds of protections that opening one's mouth and uttering a (right or wrong) gesture does not. For this reason, although it may not appear to be functional in our technologically advanced and communication-oriented society, a culture of silence is functional among low-income African Americans and among other racial–ethnic minorities who are also interinstitutionally disadvantaged—that is, in the schools, the labor market, and in other institutions in society. The culture of silence is so deeply ingrained in the culture of low-income African Americans that even when someone raised in this environment attains educational opportunities and learns to use elaborated code and middle-class jargon, it requires a breaking away from fundamental aspects of one's culture. First, one must learn to be empowered by and comfortable with hearing one's own voice, an opportunity taken for granted by white and middle-class members of society. Second, one must learn to deal with the "gaze"[46] of those—middle-class whites—who believe without a doubt that African Americans are inferior, even when faced with evidence to the contrary. Still, there is a desire or need to belong to one's families and communities; thus, one must learn to manage the former hurdles and deal with yet another: Those who venture from a low-income to a middle-class lifestyle must be able to switch codes more than resort to the exclusive use of elaborated codes in order to belong to, or at least manage, two different communities with different speech and behavioral expectations.

CONCLUSION AND IMPLICATIONS

The importance of Hart and Risley's study is that it shows the importance of environmental impact (parenting styles) on language development of children. Their research is well documented and supported by other research that shows a relationship between social class and parenting styles. The most significant weakness of *Meaningful Differences* is that the researchers fail to take into account the effect of race on the amount of talking and socializing they observed in welfare families. This is problematic because all members of the welfare group were African-American; ideally research that attempts to address a problem should include a representative sample. Because the welfare families in Hart and Risley's study were all African Americans, it is not far-fetched to suggest that the researchers embrace Wilson's view that "black children must learn to handle Standard English as competently as any white middle class child."[47] However, as Peters suggests, due to racial oppression in our society, African-American children must learn to use Standard English that is complemented by racial competence, which they learn within the context of their racial group.[48] This is inevitably why the type of intervention proposed in *Meaningful Differences*, where impoverished African-American children are separated from their families for many hours each day from ten months old until they attend school, would be

problematic. There are "harmful effects" of all subcultural socialization processes vis-à-vis the larger society, but there are also functional aspects of the process, which cannot be hastily overlooked.

The foregoing discussion has shown that the culture of silence developed out of the historical experiences of African Americans and is still functional for low-income members of the group. Although the effect of this parenting style may not be functional in the larger society, the purpose of it is to teach children how to protect themselves by not saying more than necessary and, at the same time, teach them something they must know in order to survive: They must know that the world owes them nothing; they must learn to accept "No" for an answer; and that responding to racist, arrogant, or demeaning comments from racist whites. In effect, these children, from slavery to the present, are taught the value of invisibility in a racist society, which manifests in a culture of silence among members of the subcultural group.

The most effective way to do away with the parenting style that contributes to a culture of silence is to eradicate the conditions that create and sustain the culture. This chapter suggests that in the interim, urban educators, whether in preschool programs or public schools, have an obligation to consider the important fact that the children they teach are not isolated entities but part of a subcultural community. Instead of devising policies to "save" them from their culture by separating them from their families for long periods of the day, beginning at ten months old, it would be more cost-effective, monetarily and socially, to create policies that will help children increase their vocabulary growth rate within the confines of their communities. This would require that urban educators understand the function of nonverbal communication, or the culture of silence, that operates in impoverished African-American communities.

The Milwaukee intervention program, which included a child intervention component and a parent education program, showed that early intervention programs for impoverished children that include their parents contributed to impressive gains in their cognitive and language development.[49] However, even without these kinds of fiscal expenditures, we can do a great deal to help disadvantaged children and their families. Urban educators already have curriculum materials designed to increase children's vocabulary. However, there is very little emphasis on actually getting children to use the vocabulary words they learn beyond the lesson of the week. In schools, it is too often the case that children learn vocabulary words by learning to spell them and then writing a sentence that helps them understand what the word means. Curriculum development in urban communities should emphasize encouraging children to use the vocabulary words they learn in school in the classroom and at home on a continuous basis, not just within the confines of a particular lesson. Learning new words increases vocabulary growth, but rate of growth, it is clear from Hart and Risley's study, can be significantly accelerated if children use the words they learn. Urban educators must also take into consideration that there are low levels of talking taking place in the home and should include parents in the children's learning process.

In order to include parents (who are representative of the community) in the vocabulary learning process, urban educators should develop the kinds of learning activities that involve parents. Impoverished parents' vocabulary is limited due to the poor quality of education they received, but this does not negate the fact that they want their children to do well in school. However, they were reared in the same culture of silence they rear their children in and, while they may subconsciously know that it is important for their children to learn words, they may not know the significant role that talking plays in this process. Thus, parents must be included in the learning process so they are not alienated from their children and so their children are not alienated from them. There are ways this can be achieved. Urban educators can include parents in the process of children learning words if they create the kinds of homework projects that include children working with their parents. Public service campaigns in school systems in urban communities that emphasize the importance of reading books can also be utilized to let parents know the important role that talking plays in language development and, in the long run, in the educational attainment of their children.

NOTES

1. Hart, B., & Risley, T. (1995). *Meaningful differences in the everyday experience of young American children*. Baltimore: Paul H. Brookes Publishing Co.

2. Hart, B., & Risley, T. (Spring 2003). The early catastrophe: The 30 million-word gap. *American Educator*, pp. 4–9.

3. Hart & Risley (Spring 2003), p. 4.

4. Hart & Risley (1995), p. 180.

5. Hart & Risley (1995), p. 120.

6. Haveman, R., & Wolfe, B. (1994). *Succeeding generations: On the effects of investments in children*. New York: Russell Sage Foundation.

7. Chall, J., & Jacobs, V. (Spring 2003). The classic study on poor children's fourth-grade slump. *American Educator*, pp. 14–15.

8. Kohn, M. (1977). *Class and conformity: A study in values* (2nd ed.). Chicago: University of Chicago Press.

9. Hart & Risley (1995), p. 134.

10. Frazier, E. (1948). *The Negro family in the United States*. Chicago: Chicago University Press; Moynihan, D. (1965). *The Negro family: A case for national action*. Washington, DC: Government Printing Office.

11. Hart & Risley (1995), p. 69.

12. Hart & Risley (1995), p. 187.

13. Hart & Risley (1995), p. 127.

14. Hart & Risley (1995), p. 1.

15. Peters, M. (1988). Parenting in black families with young children. In H. McAdoo (Ed.), *Black families* (p. 231). Newbury: Sage Publications.

16. Hart & Risley (1995), p. 1.

17. Hart & Risley (1995), p. 1.

18. Hart & Risley (1995), p. 1.

19. Hart & Risley (1995), p. 210.

20. Parsons, T. (1951). *The social system*. New York: Free Press.

21. Jackson, J., McCullough, W., & Gurin, G. (1988). Family, socialization environment, and identity development in black Americans. In H. McAdoo (Ed.), *Black families* (2nd ed., p. 244). Newbury: Sage Publications.

22. Hart & Risley (1995), p. 195.

23. Elkin, F., & Handel, G. (1989). *The child and society: The process of socialization* (5th ed., p. 82). New York: McGraw-Hill, Inc.

24. Wilson, A. (1987). *The developmental psychology of the black child* (6th ed., p. 172). New York: Africana Research Publications.

25. Bernstein, B. (1972). Social class, language and socialization. In P. Giglioli (Ed.), *Language and social context: Selected readings*. Harmondsworth, England: Penguin Books.

26. Lewis, O. (1968). The culture of poverty. In D. Moynihan (Ed.), *On understanding poverty: Perspectives from the social sciences*. New York: Basic Books.

27. Margolis, E., & Romero, M. (1998). "The department is very male, very white, very old, and very conservative": The functioning of the hidden curriculum in graduate school sociology departments. *Harvard Educational Review, 68* (1), 1.

28. Smitherman, G. (1977). *Talkin' and testifyin': The language of black America* (p. 78). Detroit: Wayne State University Press.

29. Smitherman (1977), p. 80.

30. King, W. (1977). *Stolen childhood: Slave youth in nineteenth-century America* (p. xviii). Bloomington: Indiana University Press.

31. King (1977), p. 13.

32. King (1977), p. 69.

33. Cooke, B. (1980). Nonverbal communication among Afro-Americans: An initial classification. In R. Jones (Ed.), *Black psychology* (p. 139). New York: Harper and Row Publishers.

34. Cooke (1980).

35. Thompson, V. (1987). *The making of the African diaspora in the Americas*, 1441–1900 (p. 162). New York: Longman, Inc.

36. Jones, J. (1985). *Labor of love, labor of sorrow: Black women, work, and the family from slavery to the present*. New York: Vintage Books.

37. Jones (1985), p. 133.

38. Jones (1985), p. 133.

39. Hart & Risley (1995), p. 59.

40. Wilson (1987), p. 166.

41. Hart & Risley (1995), p. 69.

42. Bernstein (1972).

43. Wilson (1987), p. 166.

44. Hart & Risley (1995), p. 4.

45. Hart & Risley (1995).

46. hooks, b. (1994). *Teaching to transgress: Education as the practice of freedom*. New York: Routledge.

47. Wilson (1987), p. 157.

48. Peters, M. (2002). Racial socialization of young black children. In H. McAdoo (Ed.), *Black children* (2nd ed.). Thousand Oaks: Sage Publications.

49. Wasik, B. (1994). Off to a good start: Effects of birth-to-three interventions on early school success. In Slavin, Karweit, & Wasik (Eds.), *Preventing early school failure: Research, policy, and practice*. Boston: Allyn and Bacon.

BLACK WOMEN ACTIVISTS, LEADERS, AND EDUCATORS: TRANSFORMING URBAN EDUCATIONAL PRACTICE

Gaetane Jean-Marie, Channelle James, and Shirley Bynum

Many black professionals have dedicated their lives to ensuring that urban youths are successful academically and socially. They take on this work because of the similarities in their own personal experiences and the experiences of the children they serve. As a result, these women have had to develop unconventional ways to act as advocates for themselves and those in their community. Through activism, leadership, and spirituality, these women have been able to negotiate the injustices inflicted upon them.

Even today, educational systems fail to provide black women with the resources needed to adequately meet the challenges they face in a changing global society. Black women still remain marginalized and voiceless in their communities and in educational institutions. President Bush's educational reform, No Child Left Behind, may further exacerbate these problems by redirecting needed resources to initiatives that do not adequately consider the circumstances of how diverse communities live their lives. Bush's reform fails to take a holistic approach to education, and thereby promotes segregation, and alienation of black and/or minority children.

In this chapter, the authors highlight alternative ways to enhance educational frameworks and theoretical practices through black women's epistemologies. Theory alone is not as important here as is the opportunity to derive theory from untraditional (academic and nonacademic) sources, herald this theory as academically legitimate, and return its yield to the communities that need it most. This exercise is important if we are ever to approach educational reforms from a more humanistic, pluralistic perspective. We believe that high-quality, equitable education addresses the needs of the whole child. As a foundation, we will focus on black women who are active in their community and the educational system.

THEORETICAL FRAMEWORK
Focus of Urban Education

Fifty years after *Brown v. Board of Education*, urban education and the research that supports its efforts seem to remain enormous and ambiguous. The growing interest in assessment measures and accountability has interfered with the focus on urban education and issues of equity. As a result, those who should most benefit from equity-in-education legislation are least likely to receive the effective teaching, cutting-edge curriculum, and adequate technology that would make a difference in their learning experience. One of the most important steps that educators can take is to make justice and equity a central part of education policy.

An important question for research on urban education is to ask why urban education is still a difficult topic to grapple. We know that children who live in urban areas confront multiple hurdles to their academic success. Those who live in urban, as opposed to suburban, areas are more likely to struggle economically. "Studies have shown that children benefit when their parents support and encourage their education."[1] Students need economic and parental support to supplement the education they receive in schools, and working-class families in urban areas are least likely to have the resources to provide this supplemental support. As more individuals face decreasing amounts of real economic power, investment in education becomes impossible. Helping families maneuver the economic aspects of education should be a key part of urban education. As the country's economic situation becomes more complicated, so do the responsibilities associated with urban education.

Another difficulty of urban education is associated with the identity of educators. As a result of the desegregation policies in this country, a whole generation of black educators of the 1950s and 1960s were lost in the confusion of unethical school employment plans. These plans required that black educators be released from their jobs because of the chance that they may be responsible for the education of white children. When those educators lost their jobs, important traditions in black education were also lost. Black educators who saw the importance of connecting the community and its institutions to the curriculum slowly disappeared. Although we have many black educators today, the ideals of a past generation have almost been forgotten.

Last, we know that urban education has been linked to affirmative action and other equal opportunity issues. The 1980s and 1990s and the new century have seen a backlash to mandates calling for equal treatment in many institutions. Education has not been spared in this backlash; many use the term "urban education" to explain multiple issues of difference without considering issues of equity and power. It is on these important issues that we focus our attention regarding urban education to bring equity to students who have been ignored in the educational process.

Black Women as a Force in Urban Education

One way of exploring what can be done to enhance urban education is to look back at historical positions of black women and their roles as teachers, activists, and leaders. When communities were segregated by race, these women took on the responsibility of ensuring that black children had the tools they needed to be successful in a world that would deny them an appropriate quality of life. When school systems provided inferior equipment and inadequate facilities, black women stepped in to make up the difference. They used their creativity and knowledge of the world—both inside and outside of formal education processes—to show youth in their communities that they could be successful, educated, and respected. The children not only learned the standard curriculum, but were also taught community ethics, racial pride, and how to protect themselves from the brutality that awaited them in a white-dominated world.

In the days before desegregation, it was standard practice for schools, families, churches, and other civic organizations to cross bureaucratic boundaries, to allow for effective utilization of community resources. With the church as a guide, black women affirmed their commitment to unity among neighbors and friends. As a result, religious ethics was an important motivator in community involvement. The success of one child was seen as an advancement of the community. How did black women have such a powerful impact on the success of black children? Their religious beliefs provided them with the main ingredients to be advocates for the liberation and empowerment of their communities.

Commitment to Excellence through Leadership

Many Southern black women leaders, educators, and community activists view their vocations as a way of serving both God and humankind. These women are actively involved in policy decision making that affects the education of urban youth, and are committed to supporting personal and academic success within their community. As suggested by Bakhtin,[2] black women leaders exercise responsibility as community elders. The women become organic intellectuals of and for the community.[3]

Foster's critical perspective offers the lens through which to examine the kind of leadership that supports and promotes urban education.[4] This leadership fosters a democratic process that calls for political activism that connects to social justice, and the economic development of communities. Be it in formal or informal roles, the women in this chapter are leaders in school (public and higher education), church, and community, whose primary concern is to improve social conditions, empower others, and support democratic participation in their roles.

Interdependence of the Community

The development of communities has long been a part of the social fabric of American society. For many reasons, including as means of survival, individuals have come together as families and friends to provide support in dealing with social, civic, and economic issues. For those in minority communities, racial bias and seg-regation required that they rely on the sup-port of their respective communities. Shirley Heath writes:

Despite the untenable conditions of slavery and racial divisions, strong coalitions of com-munity evolved across regions and in the face of hostile opposition. These came first through the underground railroad and later through religion and political affiliations—often covertly and always from a sense of criti-cal need.[5]

African Americans, who have been sub-jected to social and economic oppression, found that close community relationships provided them with the emotional and physical support that was sorely needed as their personal dignity was stripped away in mainstream society. Black Americans have a long history of creating their own institutions, including churches, schools, businesses, and civic/social organizations, to support their way of life. These institu-tions symbolize a sense of hope and place of refuge for blacks, particularly in urban neighborhoods. They have been pivotal in revolutionary movements for the intellec-tual, social, and economic development of the black community.

Black Prophetic Religious Tradition

For more than 430 years, blacks have relied on a religious tradition for suste-nance in the struggle for liberation, equal-ity, and meaningful existence, but this religious tradition is vanishing. Many fac-ets of the black church enable people to interpret their lives in ways that make them feel capable. Cornel West argued, "The major black cultural response to the temptation of despair has been the black Christian [prophetic religious] tradition."[6] Historically, the black prophetic religious tradition has been the agent for social activism. Three of the largest areas of socialization for the black community have been family, school, and church.

A prophetic religious tradition has pro-vided African Americans with answers to questions on black existence and black cri-sis. Existential questions that focus on the here, the now, and roles in the future, such as "What is the truth?" "Who is the I?" and "What is the quality of the I?" are answered through faith in a prophetic reli-gion with transcendent powers. African Americans found peace, acceptance, equal-ity, and answers in a prophetic religion, and it became the foundation of their strength to resist the chains of bondage and struggle for freedom and justice—if not in this world, then in God's home.

African-American women have under-stood the importance of education in the success of community growth, and dedi-cated their lives to the uplift of the race by reaching back to pull up the children. In today's society, we find the religious tradi-tion that sustained the spiritual black woman for more than 430 years and was the source that protected her and her com-munity, to be a missing component in urban education.

Black Women's Self-Definition

Our position in this research is that black women have a belief system that has a posi-tive impact on the education of urban youth. To better define these beliefs, we look to the work of black women theorists as a founda-tion. Black women believe that in order to understand their lives, they must examine the intersecting positions of their oppres-sion.[7] Through the examination of the reality of their lives, the women created ways to resist oppression. This resistance was the apparatus through which the women sur-vived the circumstances of everyday lives. In that sense, black women understand that urban education is about more than under-standing racial, ethnic, gender, and class dif-ferences; it is also about survival of those who compose the urban community.

During the fight for civil rights, black women questioned the sexism in institutionalized systems. Disenchantment with the white-dominated feminist movement and with black male scholars' exclusive concern with racial issues[8] heightened black women's interest in liberation. Finding no place in the existing movement and wanting to respond to the racism of white feminists and the sexism of black men, black women formed separate black feminist groups.[9] They sought to create new knowledge about African-American women to "formulate and rearticulate the distinctive, self-defined standpoint of African American women."[10] They also sought to change the one-dimensional perspectives of women's reality.[11]

As African-American women continue the fight to make gains in educational attainment and inroads into professions and occupations previously dominated by Euro-American women,[12] they will likely impact the representation of African-American women of all echelons:

As more Black women earn advanced degrees, the range of Black feminist scholarships is expanding. Increasing numbers of African-American women scholars are explicitly choosing to ground their work in Black women's experiences, and by doing so, many implicitly adhere to an Afrocentric feminist epistemology.[13]

Through these efforts, African-American women have positioned themselves to engage in critical analysis by articulating their "voices to express a collective, self-defined black women's standpoint."[14] Voice defines these women, interprets what their experiences are, and analyzes their coping mechanisms for survival. Consequently, African-American women develop a double consciousness that empowers them to move in and out of diverse spaces (work, community, academia, and so on).[15]

ANALYSIS AND DISCUSSION

In analyzing the three studies on African-American women administrators, educators, and community activists, three overarching themes dominate the discourse on

urban education and its implications for the African-American community: (1) the fabric of excellence: preparation, confidence, and connection; (2) strong communities as a resource in urban education; and (3) the diminishing role of a black prophetic religious tradition.

The Fabric of Excellence: Preparation, Confidence, and Connection

Because research on African-American communities often centers on examining pathologies, it is hard for the larger society to imagine that academic excellence is a central part of African-American discourses. In *Teaching to Transgress: Education as the Practice of Freedom*, bell hooks[16] writes of her experience with African-American teachers, in which teachers "were committed to nurturing intellect so that we could become scholars, thinkers, and cultural workers—black folks who used our 'minds'."[17] Annie, a participant in the study on black women educators, spoke about the positive influence her teachers had on her:

I had wonderful teachers who taught me not just facts and figures, but culture and poise. We just had a totally complete, well-rounded education. So they dealt with everything—from manners to how you sit with legs crossed at the ankles, your back erect and the whole bit. They had very high expectations for us; taught us how to behave as young women.

All of our participants purport to have been academically successful and socially prepared to enter society. They often contribute their love of learning to the expectations that their teachers had for them. Education was exulted as a way to overcome the oppressive conditions in which most of the participants lived.

Across the three studies, the participants talked about their life experiences. The majority of them were reared during the period of officially sanctioned segregation, and they also experienced the turbulence of desegregation. In the first study—on black women administrators—Dr. Gwendolyn Smith described the support she received from home and school:

We went to a three-room schoolhouse with teachers who had nothing but our future at point. Everything they did was in the vein of telling us we have to make it. You cannot live the way we have lived and these are things that you have to do to make it. They took the old books that the school system gave us and taught us like you would never believe.

Similarly, in the second study—on black women community activists—we hear in Mrs. Carol Johnson's reflection on her grandfather that the supportive structures of an extended family were in place for her:

He was a very strong, influential, take-charge, and serious person. With a second-grade education but who could read and write, he was very attuned to serious values about living and life, strong in his conviction about very basic things in life (e.g., study hard, work ethic were important things to him).

In the third study—on black spiritual women as resources in the education of poor children—participant Mrs. Annie Burroughs tells how she grew up during an era when segregation was prevalent. The love and support she received from her family and community were instrumental in her growth as a loving and caring person. Annie understood that "there was definitely a dividing line between black and white." She explained how she grew up in a "village where people cared about me, who kept their eyes on me and their hands on me when it was necessary and helped to shape and mold my life." This ideology of reaching back to pick up the other grew out of an African worldview that derives from the struggles of an enslaved people for justice, liberation, and a sense of purpose in a world immersed in racism, injustice, and inequality.

As expressed by the participants in all the studies, the importance of education was demonstrated by the support, commitment, and affirmation their teachers displayed. The dominant message communicated to the women from their families and communities was, "Education is a given!"

To best characterize the communities of support (family and school) that have shaped the educational experience of the participants across the three studies, one must consider the interpretive traditions that are indicative of their life experiences and how they translate into these women's commitment to uplift the urban community through education initiatives in public and higher education and in the community.

Interpretive tradition refers to vocabulary, metaphors, accepted wisdom, and norms used by persons with similar experiences.[18] These experiences form a common location in which members of the group become interpretive communities whose ways of being reflect their connectedness. The participants across the three studies represent an African-American interpretive tradition of community building that extends beyond the family structure to schools, churches, and community organizations. Despite the shared historical locations (e.g., segregation and desegregation) the majority of the women come from, their pursuit of excellence in education helped shaped their lives. They have maintained a level of excellence throughout their personal and professional lives. In so doing, they continually have sought ways to improve the educational experiences of urban youths who often are not provided the quality of education offered to others in the public sphere. Recognizing the inequalities and injustices experienced by urban youths in public and higher education, the participants became a collective spokesperson to demand equity in education, transform existing conditions that deter African Americans from pursuing excellence in education, and mentor young men and women to become socially responsible.

Whether in the classroom, at board meetings, or while reaching out to parents, advocacy on the part of the participants has been a central aspect of their promotion of academic excellence. They have taken on the social responsibility and remained attentive to the issues that impact the community. As Carol Johnson stated, "I was a member of a generation where you didn't do it for yourself. You did it because it was for everybody." Holding firm to their commitment to social responsibility, the participants across the studies brought those interpretive traditions to their present work. They have critically examined urban education and engaged in discourses on how to develop and elevate the next generation.

While the focus on excellence is on academic achievement, it is also defined in the context of school as community. Too often, the challenge facing many urban youth in public education is their disconnection from school. In *Other People's Children*, Lisa Delpit[19] addresses the cultural divide between black children and white teachers. Similarly, Dr. Rosalyn Giddens, a former administrator and professor, critiques why integration has been a failure for the black community:

We get the teachers who don't know how to teach the students and are afraid to teach black students. They are going to tell my race of children that they can't learn their own English language. If we don't train the teachers that we are teaching now, we are going to be a lost generation.

Relating this discussion to her educational experience, Dr. Giddens reflected on her former black teachers who understood the significance of providing a high-quality education to black children. For participants across the three studies, being connected to their schools and teachers occurred because many were taught by predominantly black teachers who not only lived in their neighborhoods, but also were visible in church and community organizations.

The importance of community cannot be undermined in examining the narratives of African-American women. All the women in our research stressed how the communities they grew up in had a significant impact on their development and success. These communities cannot be described with conformity, but as a mosaic or quilt where a diversity of shapes forms to make a strong and intricate masterpiece.[20] Central to this sense of community is the idea that children belong to everyone in the community and that their success is everyone's responsibility. According to Michelle Foster:

When students and teachers share a common cultural background and are able to engage in productive interactions, it is possible that they might develop attachments to education that they otherwise might not.[21]

Many of the women articulate that their teachers lived in their neighborhoods, which meant that their teachers could easily make connections between the women's personal lives and the experiences they faced at school. Instead of the territorial lines that exist between schools and families today, schools and teachers then were an extension of what occurred in the home and in the neighborhood.[22] The participants' teachers were genuinely interested in them and developed a personal relationship with them and their parents. So when Annie became an educator, she modeled what many of her teachers practiced:

I've always been actively involved in the community with children and not just going there when they're misbehaving . . . going to the games of the children and stopping by sometimes to say, "Your child was good in school today."

In higher education, Dean Frazier and Dr. Smith recognize that a number of African-American students are first-generation college students who require additional support to excel. Modeling their own teachers, who'd made countless sacrifices for them, they have committed themselves to prepare future generations for a better tomorrow not only by advocating in meetings on their behalf and impacting policy decisions, but also by availing themselves to students. Dr. Smith vowed, "I want to make sure that I in no way make students feel they can't succeed."

As these women have alluded to, they are constantly analyzing the quality of education being delivered to students and consider its implications by applying the educative and ethical component of Foster's model to examine the past and present conditions of American education.[23] They remain in constant inquiry of how to transform practices that hinder students from obtaining equal access to education. The ethic of care and support of students that they demonstrate embodies Foster's critical perspective of leadership, borne of an urgency to not let the past be repeated. They remember what it was like to be the first to integrate public schools, uncertain of the consequences, or be looked down upon by college professors who thought they had no place in higher education. In their present roles as administrators, educators, and community activists, they have committed themselves to taking high-achieving and marginalized students to a level of academic and personal success, which has a trickle-down effect on the development of strong communities.

Strong Communities as a Resource in Urban Education

Those responsible for instituting historic black institutions articulated a social responsibility to develop young women and men to become productive members of the black community and of the larger one. Their political engagement and conscious efforts to transform the educational conditions of black students speak to the nature of what Gramsci identifies as the organic intellectual concerned with ideologies and activities in developing specific groups or communities.[24] bell hooks also sees this commitment in black women as they make their intellectual presence in the academy and in the wider community.[25] In addition, Cornel West's insurgency model for black intellectual activity emphasizes this commitment, as he challenges blacks to be organically linked with Afro-American cultural life.[26]

As we move into a new century, however, we can see that the sense of community once available to African Americans may be slipping away. The promise of all Americans being able to live a middle-class lifestyle, no matter their economic and social standing, has encouraged many African Americans to neglect their responsibility to support the community institutions that may have mentored them. This lack of community understanding has had a profound effect on how youth in urban communities receive the support they need. Schools may fail to provide access to equal education to inner-city youth, but their communities are ill-equipped to provide a substitute. It is important that we identify why the concept of community has become difficult to maintain in black urban communities and find ways to remedy this problem. According to Cornel West, "the crisis in black leadership can be remedied only if we candidly confront its existence."[27] West argues that we once had a social structure—the black church—that was a nurturer of many prominent leaders, including Martin Luther King, Jr. In today's society, we do not even have anyone grooming to take Dr. King's place, and there is a lack of prophetic tradition in some churches. We must look at what is here in the black community right now, and try to figure out what is fundamentally different.

The Diminishing Role of a Black Prophetic Religious Tradition

Have we as African Americans forsaken our prophetic religious tradition? West argues African Americans are not living as the black religious tradition dictates.[28] According to him, things that are manifesting in black society are morally and spiritually corrupt, and African Americans are forsaking a religious tradition that dictates an outreach ministry to *the least, the lost, and the lame*, and our poor black students are suffering.

Poor black students are having difficulty identifying with school, and this lack of identity results in low self-esteem and fear of failure. The social glue that holds the community and school together is missing. Claude Steele notes:

Students who cannot identify with school *disidentify* with school and become alienated [italics added]. "American blacks may find it harder to assimilate. For them, the offer for acceptance in return for assimilation carries a primal insult: It asks them to join in something that has made them invisible."[29]

So many students choose to *disidentify* with school and develop a noncaring attitude. One of the participants, Dr. Keenya Royster, a university professor, has this to say about the students she sees at her university:

These young people have tremendous potential; but they don't have the same resources available to them . . . I want them to come into our institution and take these "diamonds in the rough" and want them to "shine" with brilliance when they leave. I want them to have confidence that they can do it!

She does not rely on solitary efforts to accomplish this undertaking. Instead, she becomes involved in student affairs, challenges her staff, and partners with other community constituents to move the university forward for the benefit of the students.

Strong communities can be tools for bridging the gap of inequality for urban children. This idea has long been appreciated by African Americans, whose families are in many cases composed in forms different from "the norm." Among African Americans, the term "community" has a specific meaning linked throughout a tumultuous history. The black community acted as an extended family, an idea stemming from African roots. The idea of community is conceptualized around the idea that the members believe and have faith in each other. The members of the community believe that they have common goals and collective identities, and are willing to pull together their resources for the advancement of the whole.[30]

When the urban educational system reaches a stage of social awareness in which "schools become places concerned with the meaning of citizenship and democracy rather than test scores and success,"[31] the escalating dropout rates for poor students, especially young black men, will decrease. The number of black men in the court system outweighs the number of black men in universities. The social disconnection from a system that does not value all of its people results in increased numbers of families receiving Temporary Assistance for Needy Families (TANF), and the "community" of addicts continues to grow. Some people have chosen to disconnect from society and have taken to the streets as a result of the limited connection to family, community, and church. The rate of black-on-black crime is increasing and yet the connection to the church is diminishing. Too many children are being allowed to sleep in on Sunday mornings, and some of the children who do make it to church are being dropped off by their parents.

If a culture of connectedness and empowerment is endorsed, West asserts the issues must first be addressed among African Americans.[32] If African Americans are turning away from the church—the one place that sustains the future struggle for social justice—how will this affect the future for African Americans? Just as our African ancestors used the black religious tradition to sustain them through cruel and inhumane treatment, African Americans today need to embrace a religious tradition to find solutions and answers to today's injustices. The religious tradition that sustained the spiritual black woman—the source that protected her and her community—is a component missing from the urban educational environment.

CONCLUSION AND IMPLICATIONS FOR PRACTICE

This chapter illuminates three qualitative research studies that examined the lives of black women from different walks of life who committed themselves to transformative and empowering education. The analysis addresses the work of African-American women who are concerned with issues of justice and equity in promoting the vision of urban education. The women interviewed articulated their political engagements and efforts to improve educational conditions of African-American students and communities affected by a new century of social, political, and cultural challenges.

From exploring the narratives of activists, administrators, and teachers across the three studies, there emerge two important implications for urban education. The first suggests that teachers, activists, administrators, and schools understand that they and their students are part of the same community. In practice, this means that a teacher's success is based not only on fulfilling state mandates, but also on contributing to the welfare of children in the community. If the educational system reaches this stage of school-community connection, dropout rates for poor students will decrease and the disconnection so prevalent in society will diminish. The more we create an environment for students to grow, mature, and blossom—both internally and externally—the more meaning, direction, and personal empowerment they will have.

An important aspect of the first implication is Ladson-Billings's concept of "culturally relevant teaching."[33] Ladson-Billings

urges teachers to remember the strong culture of African-American children. She asserts that teachers should be aware that "they are teaching children who are heirs to a great tradition of art, music, dance, science, invention, oratory."[34] To help students' dreams become reality, Ladson-Billings offers these suggestions:

1. Recruit teacher candidates who have expressed an interest and desire to work with African-American students.
2. Provide educational experiences that help teachers understand the central role of culture.
3. Provide teacher candidates with opportunities to critique the system in ways that will help them choose a role as either agent of change or defender of the status quo.
4. Conduct student teaching over a longer period of time and in a more controlled environment.
5. Honor and respect the students' home culture.

In implementing these practices, a more humanizing school curriculum results, in which students' connection to home further extends into school with teachers and school providers.

The second implication of the three narrative studies is that educators should walk in the spirit of a religious tradition, which is a discourse of love, community, humility, trust, and horizontal relationships. We are not advocating that every teacher have the religious tradition that African Americans have used in our struggle for survival. What we are promoting is the "power of intense connectedness [relationships] that is informed by truths, armed with tools of resistance, and moved by faith in justice, and struggles without end."[35] We recognize the strength of a prophetic religious tradition and find it to meet all the criteria of which Collins speaks. We saw it move in the life histories of our narrators as they moved from the brink of personal disaster to an outreach ministry to the downtrodden (in schools and community).

We were privy to the importance of their relationships within the community and with teachers, family members, and the spirit of God, guiding and directing their lives. If the power of supportive, loving, and unselfish relationships could bring the enslaved out of bondage, and bring our narrators from paths of destruction, then surely it is worth investigating as a means of saving the future for our urban students, God's children.

It is our hope that the life stories of our African-American narrators will move education toward a connected curriculum, with teachers who value the significance of caring relationships. We express this hope by recognizing and giving voice to urban students' struggles for meaning and understanding, while recognizing limitations and inequities. May our research for this chapter promote relationships that lead to a critical consciousness to nurture and love, against all odds.

NOTES

1. Hidalgo, N., Siu, S., Bright, J., Swap, S., & Epstein, J. (2003). Research on families, schools, and communities: A multicultural perspective. In J. Banks (Ed.), *Handbook of research on multicultural education* (p. 499). San Francisco: Jossey-Bass.

2. Bakhtin, M. (1981). *The dialogic imagination* (M. Holquist, ed., C. Emerson & M. Holquist, trans.). Austin: University of Texas Press.

3. Forgacs, D. (Ed.). (2000). *The Gramsci reader: Selected writings 1916–1935.* New York: New York University Press.

4. Foster, W. (1989). Toward a critical practice of leadership. In J. Smyth (Ed.), *Critical perspectives on educational leadership.* New York: Falmer Press; Foster, W. (1986). *Paradigms and promises: New approaches to educational administration.* New York: Prometheus Books.

5. Heath, S. (2001). Ethnography in communities: Learning the everyday life of America's subordinated youth. In J. Banks (Ed.), *Handbook of research on multicultural education* (p. 115). San Francisco: Jossey-Bass.

6. West, C. (1999). *The Cornel West reader* (p. 112). New York: Basic Civitas Books.

7. Collins, P. (2000). *Black feminist thought: Knowledge, consciousness, and the politics of empowerment.* New York: Routledge.

8. Schiller, N. (2000). A short history of Black feminist scholars. *Journal of Blacks in Higher Education, 29,* 119–124.

9. hooks, b. (1981). *Talking back: Thinking feminist, thinking black.* Boston: South End.

10. Collins, P. (1996). The social construction of Black feminist thought. In A. Garry & M. Pearsall (Eds.), *Women, knowledge and reality: Explorations in feminist philosophy* (p. 225). New York: Routledge.

11. hooks, b. (2000). *All about love.* New York: William Morrow and Company, Inc.

12. Mullings, L. (1997). *On our terms: Race, class and gender in the lives of African American women.* New York: Routledge.

13. Collins (1996), p. 239.

14. Collins (2000), p. 99.

15. Collins (2000).

16. hooks, b. (1994). *Teaching to transgress: Education as the practice of freedom.* New York: Routledge.

17. hooks (1994), p. 2.

18. Jean-Marie, G. (2002). Educational leaders as transformative intellectuals: Examining leadership discourses of African American women administrators in historically Black colleges and universities (Doctoral dissertation, University of North Carolina at Greensboro, 2002). *Dissertation Abstracts International, 63,* 1206.

19. Delpit, L. (1995). *Other people's children: Cultural conflict in the classroom.* New York: New York Press.

20. Collins, P. (1998). *Fighting words: Black women and the search for justice.* Minneapolis: University of Minnesota Press.

21. Foster, M. (2001). African American teachers and cultural relevant pedagogy. In James and Cherry Banks (Eds.), *Handbook of research on multicultural education* (p. 575). San Francisco: Jossey-Bass.

22. Ladson-Billings, G. (1994). *The dreamkeepers: Successful teachers of African American children.* San Francisco: Jossey-Bass.

23. Foster (1989); Foster (1986).

24. Gramsci, A. (1968). The formation of intellectuals. In *The modern prince & other writings.* New York: International Publishers.

25. hooks, b. (1981). Keeping close to home: Class and education. In b. hooks (Ed.), *Talking back: Thinking feminist, thinking black.* Boston: South End.

26. West, C. (1991). The dilemma of the black intellectual. In b. hooks & C. West (Eds.), *Breaking bread: insurgent black intellectual life*. Boston: South End.

27. West, C. (1994). *Race matters* (p. 69). Philadelphia: The Westminster Press.

28. West (1994).

29. Steele, C. (1992). Race and the schooling of Black Americans. *Atlantic Monthly, 67,* 269–272.

30. Guinier, L., & Torres, G. (2002). *The miner's canary.* Cambridge, MA: Harvard University Press.

31. Shapiro, S. (1995). Public school reform: The mismeasure of education. *Tikkun Magazine, 13* (1), 54.

32. West (1994).

33. Ladson-Billings (1994).

34. Ladson-Billings (1994).

35. Collins (1998).

DILEMMAS CONFRONTING URBAN PRINCIPALS IN THE POST-CIVIL RIGHTS ERA

Tondra L. Loder

Fifty years after the landmark *Brown v. Board of Education of Topeka, Kansas* Supreme Court case declared legalized racial segregation in public education unconstitutional, African-American principals in urban schools confront leadership dilemmas unlike any others they have faced in United States history. As student bodies become increasingly ethnically and economically diverse, and as social and technological changes render the principal's role more complex, urban principals today confront problems and crises that did not exist for principals fifty years ago.[1] It is ironic to note that as desegregation policies opened doors for African Americans to become principals, African-American principals in the post-civil rights era find themselves at the helm of extremely troubled urban schools.[2] Since *Brown,* urban school districts across the nation have experienced severe economic, fiscal, and social problems caused largely by the loss of middle-class white and African-American students and families who were formerly invested in urban schools, coupled with a rise in the enrollment of students who are socially and economically disenfranchised, shrinking financial commitments from state and federal governments, and the bombardment of negative press coverage of the so-called urban school crisis.[3]

Today—especially in light of events commemorating the fiftieth anniversary of *Brown*—scholars, policy makers, politicians, and citizens alike have been weighing the gains and losses of African-American educators in the wake of school desegregation. Some scholars contend that *Brown* has had both positive and negative impacts on the livelihood of African-American educators. They cite the most significant gains having occurred among those educators "who were 'ready' to participate, contribute, and play leadership roles in the more-open society wrought by the civil rights movement that followed the 1954 decision."[4] On the other hand, many African-American educators fared poorly due to the loss of jobs, status, and socioemotional ties to communities with which they closely identified. Some scholars contend that the long-term effects of school desegregation have been to divorce African-American principals and teachers from African-American students,[5] and to drain a talented pool of African-American educators from public schools.[6] According to Wesson, the loss of African-American principals "created a leadership vacuum in [African-American] communities that has not since been recovered."[7]

Hugh Scott's analysis of problems encountered by African-American urban school superintendents in the post-civil rights era foreshadowed the problems that African-American principals would encounter in ensuing decades.[8] Echoing the sentiments of the scholars aforementioned, Scott suggested that African-American superintendents were better off professionally prior to the touted gains of the civil rights struggles. Preceding their rise to leadership in integrated urban school districts between the late 1960s and early 1970s, African-American superintendents, like most principals at the time, held positions primarily in very small and predominantly rural school systems in the South and Southwest. According to Scott, these segregated rural school systems offered African-American superintendents more promotional opportunities than did integrated urban school systems. By inference, Scott suggested that African-American superintendents had the advantage of garnering community support within the smaller, rural, cohesive communities in their traditional geographical stronghold of the South.

Forecasting an increasingly racially and ethnically diverse and poor student population, declines in reading and math achievement test scores, lack of financial and material resources, coupled with tenuous political clout, Scott concluded that African-American superintendents in the post-Civil Rights era would confront the conundrum of being viewed either as messiahs by African Americans or as scapegoats by white political and business stakeholders—as well as by some African Americans. He surmised that on the one hand, they would be viewed as messiahs because African Americans in the local school community would hold unrealistic expectations and unusually high hopes that significant improvements in public education could be gained solely through the empowerment of African-American school leaders and teachers. Scott contended that on the other hand, African-American superintendents would be distrusted by African Americans who would perceive them as official representatives of white middle-class-dominated school districts. In turn, Scott charged that white politicians and members of the business community would berate urban school leaders for failing schools and blame urban schools for proliferating societal ills. His prediction is underscored by authors Henig, Hula, Orr, and Pedescleaux, who noted that the advent of African-American leadership in urban schools was met with declining corporate-sector interest in public schools. As these authors concluded, "the white business community . . . psychologically disengaged from the public school system once it became perceived as the responsibility of the black elected elite."[9]

In this chapter, I discuss the dilemmas that urban principals confront in the post-civil rights era. As a framework for this discussion, I identify and examine a tension in the educational leadership scholarship between two competing portrayals of African-American principals. Each is bound within a distinct historical context that lies on opposite sides of the civil rights era. One portrayal, associated with the pre-Civil Rights era of segregated schooling, is of African-American principals as *messiahs*. They are presented as indigenous leaders willing to cast off their professional obligations to white-controlled school systems for the good of African-American children and rural communities. A contrasting portrayal, which has emerged in more recent discussions of urban school reform, is of African-American principals as *scapegoats* who are viewed as exogenous to the local school community and as roadblocks to democratic reform. Reflecting on a 1988 Chicago Public School (CPS) reform experiment, I consider the implications of these two contrasting portrayals in relation to grassroots efforts to empower the local school community to govern urban schools.

AFRICAN-AMERICAN PRINCIPALS PRE- AND POST-CIVIL RIGHTS: MESSIAHS OR SCAPEGOATS?

Two competing portrayals of African-American principals tend to dominate the still-too-sparse scholarship on African-American principals. One portrayal, which situates African-American principals in the era of segregated schooling prior to *Brown*, presents these leaders as *messiahs*—folk heroes who are indigenous to the local school community and willing to sacrifice their professional security (albeit tenuous) within white-controlled school systems for the good of African-American children and community members. This portrayal emphasizes historical continuities between the activist mission and leadership orientation of contemporary African-American principals and their counterparts in the pre-civil rights era.[10] In contrast, an alternative portrayal emerges from the scholarship on urban school reform. Decontextualized from the tradition of activist leadership, in this portrayal African-American principals are criticized for their "autocratic" style of leadership, which some reformers contend undermines the principles and goals of democratic school governance.[11] While other African-American scholars attempt to ameliorate this critique, acknowledging that what reformers perceive as an autocratic leadership style may be deemed legitimate by members of the local school community, their portrayal of urban principals is a notable departure from the harmonious African-American principal–community relationship characterized in the former portrayal.[12]

African-American Principals as Messiahs

The leadership orientation of African-American principals has historically been rooted in their relationship to the African-American community.[13] Prior to *Brown*, segregated school systems helped produce and nurture African-American educators who figured as an important segment of the African-American community and composed a significant proportion of its middle class.[14] Principals were looked upon to provide leadership beyond the walls of the school; in many respects, teaching and leading became forms of social activism. Principals and teachers of segregated African-American schools attempted to create institutions for African-American children that intentionally countered their negative caste group status.[15] One scholar has described the African-American principal as a Renaissance man who filled the multiple roles of superintendent, supervisor, family counselor, financial advisor, community leader, employer, and politician:

The man who headed this important community structure, "the principal," was the man who ran the school and, in many cases, the black community. His influence in community affairs was, almost without exception, great. He was, therefore, central in community life and was indeed more knowledgeable about what was going on than anyone else.[16]

Education historian Vanessa Siddle Walker has done some of the most extensive work examining the prominent role of the African-American principal in the rural, segregated, pre-Civil Rights South.[17] The principal—typically an African-American man—served as the middleman through whom the needs of the school were translated to the local community. He was a liaison and power broker between the school and the white-dominated school board; therefore, he walked a fine line in interpreting the needs of the local community to the school and vice versa. Siddle Walker portrayed a principal who moved easily between the seamless boundaries of the school and the community. Members of the local African-American community used the term "professor" or "'fessor" to refer to the principal, signaling the high respect and decorum reserved for those in this position. Principals strategically participated in activities that would directly benefit the larger community (e.g., serving on boards on which they could lobby for benefits for the elderly and building houses to help raise African Americans' living standards). The African-American principal became adept at "leapfrogging" (i.e., finding creative ways to undermine the authority of racist members of the white school district, garnering resources for the school, and still managing to hold onto his job).[18]

Siddle Walker's portrayal of African-American principals of a bygone era, while sensitive to historical context and a welcome counterpoint to recent negative portrayals, falls short in helping us understand the dilemmas facing today's African-American urban principals. In response, some scholars have presented more contemporary portrayals of African-American principals in urban schools, while highlighting the continuity between their experiences and those of their predecessors in the rural, segregated, pre-civil rights era.[19] These scholars portray principals who are deeply committed to the education of African-American children and who believe it is critical to their success as leaders to stay attuned to African-American community concerns. In contrast, historian Vincent P. Franklin has charged that contemporary African-American educators have dropped the ball by failing to continue the tradition of activism begun by their predecessors in the nineteenth and early twentieth centuries. Franklin suggests that the recent failure in urban schools has not been met with the kind of resistance and activist efforts traditionally attributed to African-American educators.[20] A more apologetic view is that African-American principals (and teachers) have historically borne unrealistic expectations for

changing social conditions and educating African-American children.[21]

African-American Urban Principals as Scapegoats: Reflections on Chicago School Reform

In contrast to some scholars' positive portrayal of African-American principals' relationship with the local school community, a competing portrayal has emerged in recent scholarship on urban school leadership. This portrayal focuses on a contentious relationship between African-American principals and members of the local school community. Hence, those African-American principals whom authors Hudson and Holmes suggested were "ready" for desegregation have witnessed their historic home and power bases in the local school community become transformed into hotbeds of urban school reform politics. As Henig and his colleagues have noted, public institutions led by African Americans in the post-civil rights era are characterized by the same political conflict and inefficacious governance that has traditionally plagued white-led cities. Hence, rather than coalescing in the name of racial solidarity, black-led urban public institutions are often fragmented along the lines of neighborhood and class.[22]

I turn briefly to the movement for urban school reform governance in Chicago as a lens for examining the portrayal of African-American principals as scapegoats. I chose to highlight this particular reform because of Chicago's long history of grassroots activism to effect change in urban education, particularly with regard to increasing the representation of African Americans in CPS principalships.[23]

Grassroots efforts to increase African-American representation in the principalship began to intensify in the late 1960s and early 1970s, during which time the CPS was charged with being too heavily dominated by white male principals. As a result of these efforts, the CPS witnessed a significant increase in the number of African-American principals between 1967 and 1977. More recently, adoption of the Chicago School Reform Act of 1988 led to a groundswell in the number of African Americans certified for the principalship.[24] In 2000, African Americans made up the majority of principals (54%).[25] This increase can be attributed partly to reform efforts and demographic changes that resulted in significant decreases in the white population simultaneous with increases in the black population between 1970 and 1990.[26]

The most novel of the 1988 act's provisions was the creation of local school councils (LSCs) comprising parent, community, and school representatives (including the principal). The LSCs were granted authority to share governance with principals and to hire and fire them. Principals lost tenure and were required to work under four-year contracts that were subject to renewal by the LSCs. Although there has been much debate about whether this reform has truly leveled the playing field between principals and parents and community members—especially in light of subsequent reforms that have recentralized control into the hands of the mayor[27]—the 1988 act is arguably the single most revolutionary school governance reform in recent U.S. history.[28]

Whereas many members of the local school community viewed Chicago school reform as an effort to increase African-American representation in the principalship, and thereby give voice to the concerns of the African-American community, some reformers viewed it as an opportunity to dismantle what they considered to be an undemocratic approach to urban school leadership. A few investigators have argued that the autocratic leadership style of some urban principals—likened to paternal and maternal leaders of school "families"—does not facilitate collaborative leadership in urban schools because it consolidates power in the hands of the principal.[29] One scholar has observed that some autocratic styles of

governance may be viewed as legitimate by local community members in schools that are well-run, yet urban schools "see the harsher side of autocracy far more than the softer face."[30] Other scholars have pointed out that the urban social context has worsened since the emergence of citizen empowerment efforts in the 1960s and 1970s, suggesting that the relationships and resources necessary for local school communities to enact these reforms may be very limited in some places, leaving schools vulnerable to the consolidation of power within the principalship.[31]

The CPS urban governance reform movement has had a transforming effect—at least in principle—on the relationship between African-American principals and the local school community, particularly with its direct challenge to the historic authority African-American principals have had to make decisions about African-American children's schooling.[32] Notably, the movement for community control of schools in Chicago was sparked by long-standing distrust and resentment harbored by African Americans who believed they were unfairly represented in CPS leadership. It is ironic to note that by granting parents the authority to hire and fire principals and to play a central role in urban school governance, the CPS reform movement increased African-American representation in the principalship while simultaneously setting the stage for power struggles between newly appointed principals and members of the local school community. Emerging evidence suggests that African-American women principals who came of age and began working in schools prior to and during the civil rights era are not experiencing the harmonious authoritarian relationships with their local school communities that have been portrayed in previous literature.[33] On the contrary, African-American principals whose leadership orientation falls within the activist tradition of their pre-civil rights era predecessors are finding themselves increasingly vulnerable to power struggles with recently empowered parents who are younger, poorer, and generationally distant from those they encountered during earlier decades of their career.

CONCLUSION

The role of the urban principal has become increasingly complex, especially for principals who work in inner-city schools. As education scholars in the early 1980s warned, urban school governance presents unique dilemmas for African-American principals in the twenty-first century, especially with regard to their relationship with the local school community. In an apparent effort to counteract the negative images of urban schools presented in the national and local media and in scholarly literature, some have portrayed an idyllic image of African-American principals that situates them within the bygone era of legally segregated public education. Despite these efforts, this idyllic portrayal has been eclipsed by a more condemning portrayal of African-American principals that blames them for urban school failure and views them as roadblocks to reform. Dramatic urban social changes and the arrival of reforms that challenge traditional urban school governance have complicated relationships between African-American principals and the local school community in the post-civil rights era.[34] The Chicago School Reform Act of 1988 is a case in point, as it changed the rules of urban school governance just at the moment African Americans were making inroads to the principalship. However, in spite of an ever-changing U.S. urban social context—most notably, the decidedly conservative political climate of high-stakes assessment and accountability—the portrayal of contemporary African-American principals in the education literature remains sparse,[35] and in some instances dated and one-dimensional with regard to describing their relationship with the local school community. In light of the issues raised in this review, scholars are challenged to examine the urban principalship from perspectives that are more nuanced, complex, and contemporary.

NOTES

1. Goldring, E., & Rallis, S. (1993). *Principals of dynamic schools: Taking charge of change.* Newbury Park, CA: Corwin.

2. Miklos, E. (1988). Administrator selection, career patterns, succession, and socialization. In N. Boyan (Ed.), *Handbook of research on educational administration* (pp. 53–76). New York: Longman; Scott, H. (1980). *The Black school superintendent: Messiah or scapegoat?* Washington, DC: Howard University.

3. Miron, L. (1996). *The social construction of urban schooling.* Cresskill, NJ: Hampton; Orfield, G., & Eaton, S. (1996). *Dismantling desegregation: The quiet reversal of Brown v. Board of Education.* New York: The New Press.

4. Hudson, M., & Holmes, B. (1994). Missing teachers, impaired communities: The unanticipated consequences of Brown vs. Board of Education on the African American teaching force at the precollegiate level. *Journal of Negro Education, 63,* 388–393. Quote from p. 392.

5. Foster, M. (1990). The politics of race: Through the eyes of African-American teachers. *Journal of Education, 172,* 123–141; Foster, M. (1993). Self-portraits of Black teachers: Narratives of individual and collective struggle against racism. In D. McLaughlin & W. Tierney (Eds.), *Naming silenced lives: Personal narratives & processes of educational change* (pp. 155–176). New York: Routledge; Foster, M. (1997). *Black teachers on teaching.* New York: Norton; Hudson & Holmes (1994); Siddle Walker, V. (2000). Valued segregated schools for African American children in the South, 1935–1969: A review of common themes and characteristics. *Review of Educational Research, 70,* 253–285.

6. Coffin, G. (1972). The black school administrator and how he's being pushed to extinction. *American School Board Journal, 159* (11), 33–36; Weinberg, M. (1977). *A chance to learn: The history of race and education in the United States.* Cambridge, MA: Cambridge University Press.

7. Wesson, L. (1995). Equity issues for women and minorities in educational administration. In

B. Irby & G. Brown (Eds.), *Women as school executives: Voices and visions* (pp. 149–157). Austin: Texas Association of School Administrators. Quote from p. 152.

8. See Scott (1980).

9. Henig, J., Hula, R., Orr, M., & Pedescleaux, D. (1999). *The color of school reform: Race, politics, and the challenge of urban education.* Princeton, NJ: Princeton University Press. Quote from p. 51.

10. Franklin, V. (1990). They rose and fell together: African American educators and community leadership, 1795–1954. *Journal of Education, 72,* 39–64; Pollard, D. (1997). Race, gender, and educational leadership: Perspectives from African American principals. *Educational Policy, 11,* 353–374.

11. Bryk, A., Sebring, P., Kerbow, D., Rollow, S., & Easton, J. (1998). *Charting Chicago school reform: Democratic localism as a lever for change.* Boulder, CO: Westview; Rollow, S., & Bennett, M. (1996). *Parents' participation and Chicago school reform: Issues of race, class and expectations.* Retrieved May 1, 2002 from ERIC database (ED412635).

12. Payne, C. (1997). *I don't want your nasty pot of gold: Urban school climate and public policy.* Retrieved May 1, 2002 from ERIC database (ED412313); Payne, C., & Kaba, M. (2001). *So much reform, so little change: Building-level obstacles to urban school reform.* Unpublished manuscript.

13. Anderson, J. (1988). *The education of Blacks in the South, 1860–1935.* Chapel Hill: University of North Carolina; Fairclough, A. (2001). *Teaching equality: Black schools in the age of Jim Crow.* Athens: University of Georgia Press; Perkins, L. (1989). The history of Blacks in teaching. In D. Warren (Ed.), *American teachers: Histories of a profession at work* (pp. 344–369). New York: MacMillan; Siddle Walker, V. (1996). *Their highest potential: An African American school community in the segregated South.* Chapel Hill: University of North Carolina Press; Siddle Walker (2000); Siddle Walker, V. (2003). The architects of Black schooling in the segregated South: The case of one principal leader. *Journal of Curriculum and Supervision, 19* (1), 54–72.

14. Anderson (1988); Henig, Hula, Orr, & Pedescleaux (1999); Perkins (1999).

15. Perry, T. (2003). Achieving in post-civil rights America. In T. Perry, C. Steele, & A. Hilliard III (Eds.), *Young, gifted, and Black* (pp. 87–108). Boston, MA: Beacon.

16. Rodgers, R. (1975). *The Black high school and its community.* Lexington, MA: Lexington. Quote from p. 16.

17. Siddle Walker (1996); Siddle Walker (2000); Siddle Walker (2003).

18. Siddle Walker (2003), p. 65.

19. Lomotey, K. (1987). Black principals for Black students: Some preliminary observations. *Urban Education, 22* (2), 173–181; Lomotey, K. (1989). *African-American principals: School leadership and success.* Westport, CT: Greenwood; Lomotey, K. (1993). African-American principals: Bureaucrat/administrators & ethnohumanists. *Urban Education, 27* (4), 395–412; Morris, J. (1999). A pillar of strength: An African American school's communal bonds with families and community since 'Brown'. *Urban Education, 33* (5), 584–605; Pollard, D. Race, gender, and educational leadership.

20. Franklin (1990).

21. Fultz, M. (1995). African American teachers in the South, 1890–1940: Powerlessness and the ironies of expectations of protest. *History of Education Quarterly, 35* (4), 401–422.

22. Henig, Hula, Orr, & Pedescleaux (1999).

23. Crowson, R. (1982). The desegregation of school administrators: Reactions and adjustments of transferred principals. In G. Noblit & B. Johnson (Eds.), *The school principal and desegregation* (pp. 96–112). Springfield, IL: Charles C. Thomas; Lewis, L. (1997). The history of principal hiring in Chicago. *Catalyst.* Retrieved October 31, 2001 from www.catalyst-chicago.org.

24. Consortium on Chicago School Research. (1992). *Charting reform: The principal's perspective.* Chicago: Consortium on Chicago School Research; Consortium on Chicago School Research. (1997). *Charting reform: LSC's–Local leadership at work.* Chicago: Consortium on Chicago School Research.

25. Chicago Public Schools. (2000). [Data file].

26. London, R., & Puntenney, D. (1993). *A profile of Chicago's poverty and related conditions.* Evanston, IL: Center for Urban Affairs and Policy Research, Northwestern University.

27. Cuban, L., & Usdan, M. (2003). *Powerful reforms with shallow roots: Improving America's urban schools.* New York: Teachers College; Duffrin, E. (2004, March). Where councils lost ground. *Catalyst.* Retrieved on May 17, 2004 at http://catalyst-chicago.org/03-04/0304mainprint.htm; Hendrie, C. (1999, May

5). Battle over principals in Chicago: Administration vs. local councils. *Education Week on the Web*. Retrieved May 15, 2003 from www.edweek.org.

28. Katz, M. (1995). *Improving poor people: The welfare state, the "underclass," and urban schools as history*. Princeton, NJ: Princeton University Press.

29. Bryk, Sebring, Kerbow, Rollow, & Easton (1998); Rollow & Bennett (1996).

30. Payne (1997), p. 21.

31. Rollow & Bennett (1996).

32. See Loder, T. (2005). African American women principals' reflections on social change, community othermothering, and Chicago Public School reform. *Urban Education, 40* (3), 298–320.

33. Loder (1995).

34. See Wilson, W. (1987). *The truly disadvantaged: The inner city, the underclass, and public policy*. Chicago: The University of Chicago Press.

35. Recent contributions to the scholarship on African American principals by Linda Tillman and her colleagues are noteworthy. See Tillman, L. (2004). African American principals and the legacy of Brown. *Review of Research in Education, 28*, 101–146; and a special issue on African-American principals in the *Educational Administration Quarterly* (2005) *41* (4).

BRING IN DA NOISE, BRING IN DU BOIS: INFUSING AN AFRICAN-AMERICAN EDUCATIONAL IDEOLOGY INTO THE URBAN EDUCATION DISCOURSE

kecia hayes

The education of African Americans historically has been defined and structured by the social prerogatives of those who rule the political and economic spheres of American society rather than by the community itself.[1] To facilitate their enslavement and grow America's slave-based economy, African Americans were initially denied an education. Later, they were minimally educated for the lowest positions in the labor market of the country's emergent industrialized economy. African Americans were not systematically educated to develop to their full potential or acquire the knowledges and skills that ultimately could be leveraged to effect appreciable change within civil society. Despite this reality, the African-American community did challenge and resist the dominant culture's imposition of an oppressive educational ideology.

In his 1906 address to the Second Annual Meeting of the Niagara Conference, William Edward Burghardt Du Bois articulated a framework for the education of African Americans that defied the conventional wisdom of the ruling elite:

And when we call for education, we mean real education. We believe in work. We ourselves are workers, but work is not necessarily education. Education is the development of power and ideal. We want our children trained as intelligent human beings should be, and we will fight for all time against any proposal to educate black boys and girls simply as servants and underlings, or simply for the use of other people. They have a right to know, to think, to aspire.[2]

As American society settles into the twenty-first century and we examine the educational experiences and outcomes of urban youth of color, it is unmistakable that far too many black boys and girls are still not being educated to know, to think, and to aspire as intelligent human beings should be. According to *The State of America's Children 2004* report by the Children's Defense Fund (CDF), children of color are far more likely to attend overcrowded schools with larger class sizes and to have teachers with less academic attainment than students in high-income, low-minority schools. The CDF specifically notes that a black child has a one-in-three chance of attending a school that has a ninety percent minority enrollment, is forty percent more likely to be a student in a class with an out-of-field teacher, and is half as likely as a white student to be placed in gifted and talented classes with advanced, college-track curricula.[3] The Campaign for Fiscal Equity (CFE) demonstrates that the state of education for children of color within the urban context of New York City reflects the national landscape as documented by the CDF.

Summarizing data from the *New York State Education Department's 2003 State of Learning* report, CFE notes that 69 percent of New York State's 1.3 million minority children are enrolled in the public schools of New York City. Characterized as a district plagued with high student needs and high local costs, New York City had a per-pupil expenditure of $11,474, compared to the state average of $11,584 and a downstate suburb average of $13,680. While 87 percent of New York State's teachers have either permanent or provisional certification, only 71 percent of the teachers in New York City public schools possess such credentials. The turnover rate among New York City's teachers is 22 percent, which exceeds the 13 percent average turnover for the state. In terms of class size, New York City's elementary and secondary public schools contained, on average, four to seven more students per class than schools in the state's other districts. Not surprisingly, the dropout rate for New York City's students was 11.2 percent while the statewide rate was only 5.7 percent; only 53 percent of New York City's students—significantly fewer than the state average of 75 percent—received their high school diploma on time, and only 71 percent of New York City's students graduate to college, compared with the state average of 93 percent.[4]

Despite the promises of numerous educational reform efforts, including the recent No Child Left Behind (NCLB) Act,

to improve the educational outcomes of all children, urban youth of color remain tragically left behind. The consequences have been both distressing and debilitating. In 2000, there were almost 791,600 African-American men in our nation's prisons and only 603,032 enrolled in institutions of higher education.[5] Unemployment and underemployment rates for blacks also have been staggering. Blacks are twice as likely as whites to be unemployed, and black males tend to earn seventy percent of the compensation of their white counterparts.[6] Within the contemporary milieu, a black boy has a 1-in-6 chance of receiving a bachelor's degree, a 1-in-9,900 chance of obtaining a PhD in math or computer science, but a 1-in-13 chance of going to prison by the age of twenty.[7] It would be naïve to ignore the fact that the consistent underresourcing of urban education significantly contributes to these negative outcomes. However, we would be remiss to not look beyond the fiscal constraints to ask ourselves what purposes have we imbued in the current educational structures that engage urban youth of color, especially when the data suggest that black children are being educated simply to be servants and underlings in America's new social order.

There is an opportunity for those engaged in the urban education discourse to reconsider and reconstruct the idea of *a sound basic education*.[8] In this discussion, I want to begin to cultivate a *crisis of democracy* within the contemporary urban education discourse by invoking the *noise* of Du Bois's rhetoric as a relevant and culturally indigenous framework for providing African Americans with *a sound basic education*. By *crisis of democracy*, I am referring to that moment when the masses attempt to reposition themselves as active, rather than passive, participants within the political, economic, and social arenas, and the ruling elites react to subdue resistance to their authority.[9] Urban communities of color must be repositioned as active participants in the educational systems and discourses that structure the lives of their children. Du Bois articulated a critical pedagogy to empower racially marginalized people to effectively engage in the social, economic, and political realms of American society without sacrificing their cultured selves. His articulation represents the *noise* needed to substantively and constructively interrupt the rhetoric of those who now reign over the policies and practices of our urban schools.

To understand how Du Bois's ideology is relevant to our current urban education discourse, it is important to examine the historical context and evolution of his educational philosophy. In addition to situating Du Bois, the controversy between W.E.B. Du Bois and Booker Taliaferro Washington best reflects the dichotomy within the range of responses generated by the community as they grappled with the historically quintessential question about the education of African Americans: Should black people be educated to *challenge* or to *accommodate* the oppressive Southern political economy?[10] Although both men saw the purpose of education as a means to achieve social uplift for their socially marginalized community, they significantly differed in how to define social uplift and how to conceptualize an appropriate educational process to achieve uplift.

Washington was mentored by Samuel Chapman Armstrong, creator of the Hampton model of industrial education and one of the major white architects of black education. In 1868, Armstrong established Hampton Institute, a coed industrial education school, where black students "learned such basic trade skills as laundry work and domestic service for the girls and proper farming techniques for the boys."[11] The Hampton model dominated the educational landscape, and its proliferation was facilitated by funding from Northern philanthropists like William H. Baldwin, who believed that blacks

were economic capital to be appropriately refitted for the nation's new industrial order. The problem with the Hampton model rested not in its specific focus on farming, but rather in its sole reliance on teaching the technique of farming as opposed to the science of agriculture and the technique of domestic service as opposed to the business of the hospitality industry. Blacks were being schooled exclusively to become laborers and not owners within the new economic order. According to Watkins (2001),

The Hampton idea was about much more than education. It was about nation building. It was about carefully situating the newly freed Black in a new sociopolitical and economic order. It was about (re)shaping delicate race relations. Finally and most important, it was about forging a social order rooted in apartheid, economic exploitation, oppression, and inequality.[12]

Washington, the founder and principal of Tuskegee Institute, embraced the Hampton model and advocated the idea that African Americans were fundamentally responsible for pulling themselves up by their own bootstraps.[13] He believed that blacks, through racialized compromise with white labor and capital, would realize economic mobility within America's hegemonic social order, and that eventually they would be granted uncontested political enfranchisement. Within his framework, vocational and agricultural training programs were the means by which economic mobility would be achieved. Washington's concept of social uplift had at its foundation the idea of socioeconomic mobility, even if such mobility lacked parity with whites and if there wasn't simultaneous sociopolitical mobility. For Washington, the purpose of education for the black community was more about accommodating the existing social order with the hope that eventually sociopolitical change would occur rather than cultivating a direct challenge and resistance to the racialized status quo.

Du Bois understood that the framework endorsed by Washington disregarded the prerogative of individual African Americans to decide for themselves how they would participate in the labor force of America's new industrial order, and strangled their ability to realize sustainable mobility across all social spectra. Du Bois believed that Washington's program would enhance

the economic status of the Negro, but on the other hand, and just as surely, it did not show a way out because it fastened the chains of exploitation on Negro labor and increased labor antagonism in the laboring classes. This was particularly shown in the new development in the South where white labor used its political and social influence to replace black labor and eliminate the so-called Negro jobs.[14]

The dominant culture steadfastly remained the gatekeepers of black socioeconomic mobility, which was counterproductive to the community's efforts toward social uplift. Du Bois's opposition to industrial education should not be interpreted as an abandonment of the idea that blacks needed vocational training. For him, vocational training was necessary but not sufficient for social uplift.

In *The Philadelphia Negro*, Du Bois clearly expressed his understanding and support of the idea that economic survival was essential for freedmen, and he advocated for their vocational training. However, in *Black Reconstruction in America 1860–1880* and in subsequent works, he sociopolitically contextualizes his perspective of the economic survival and development of the African-American community, which places him in stark contrast to Washington. Du Bois stressed the idea that social uplift had to consist of not only the socioeconomic mobility that can result from vocational training, but also simultaneously had to incorporate efforts toward sociopolitical advancement if the uplift was to substantively benefit the individual and the community.

Social uplift cannot be essentialized in socioeconomic terms, but has to be more broadly conceptualized in terms of empowerment across economic, political, and social domains, allowing marginalized people to not only effectively transform their status within the American hegemony, but to deconstruct hegemonic structures altogether. This perspective is especially relevant to today's discourse on urban education because of the need to move beyond the idea that we are simply educating young people for employment in a globalized economy. Urban youth of color, in particular, need a sound basic education that empowers them to exercise the full extent of their civic agency across the economic, political, and social domains of society. Achieving a particular level of income is not a sufficient condition for uplift, especially since this can be accomplished through participation in illegal economies, which ultimately are destructive to the self and the community. Furthermore, when it occurs in the absence of an understanding and control of the sociopolitical dynamics of wealth accumulation, the socioeconomic mobility can be incredibly transient, and an uplift unilaterally linked to it would be just as fleeting.

Education for empowerment requires the development of economic capital in its broadest sense. Du Bois believed that industrial schools failed to effectively link their vocational curricula to the political economy of society's new industrial reality. He understood that a solitary program of industrial education hindered the community's ability to acquire the necessary economic capital for empowered and sustained social uplift. Du Bois problematized the pedagogical philosophy and practices of industrial schools because he understood that the lack of accumulated wealth and the poverty within the community was related, in part, to how black laborers were restricted in their labor market participation in capitalist America. "In this new organization of business the colored man meets two difficulties: first, he is not trained to take part in it; and secondly, if he gets training, he finds it almost impossible to gain a foothold."[15]

The industrial schools were inattentive in design and practice to the impact of societal prejudice and capitalist industrialization—two important intersecting social dynamics of the time that significantly influenced African Americans' social position. Through their industrial education programs, schools such as Hampton and Tuskegee effectively prepared blacks to be laborers in America's new industrial order. However, their failure to educate blacks about the sociopolitical contexts of labor in the new industrial order stymied their potential to socially advance in any substantive and sustainable way. Du Bois leveled this critique not only against the industrial schools, but also against the Negro colleges and universities because they, too, were failing to provide students any understanding of how to engage the political economy of the industrializing and hegemonically racialized nation.

Acquiring as we do in college no guidance to a broad economic comprehension and a sure industrial foundation, and simultaneously a tendency to live beyond our means, and spend for show, we are graduating young men and women with an intense and overwhelming appetite for wealth and no reasonable way of gratifying it, no philosophy for counteracting it.[16]

African Americans were not thoroughly knowledgeable about the power relationships and interconnectivities among labor, capitalists, and consumers such that they were able to avoid their own exploitation as laborers and consumers. For instance, through study of the nation's industrial history and labor movements in the white and black communities, African Americans would gain insight into the sociopolitical dynamics of their economic oppression within a racialized American capitalist system, and into the ways in which to resist such oppression. Without this knowledge, the impetus and vision for activism to transform the sociopolitical realities of the nation's economic structure would be lost.

Today, we continue to graduate young men and women of color who have an overwhelming appetite for immediate wealth, no reasonable way of gratifying it, and no understanding of how to counteract it. Contemporary educational policies and practices of schools serving urban youth of color fail to integrate any pedagogical focus on their development of economic capital. Our failure to acknowledge and fulfill this responsibility is fundamentally problematic because young people are not sufficiently equipped to accumulate, manage, or leverage wealth to achieve sustainable uplift in all domains of civil society. Furthermore, they lack the ability to critically assess the local social impact of today's global political economy on their lives, including the fact that black workers in urban areas are more likely than their white counterparts to be isolated from employment opportunities, contributing to blacks and Latinos being twice as likely to be among the working poor as are whites.[17]

Urban youth of color must be empowered to critically think about the dynamics of our political economy and its impact on the communities from which they come. They also need to be able to expand their considerations to a global context, and critically examine the many ways in which the world's economic elites oppress others through organized structures such as the International Monetary Fund that control the global political economy. Within a Du Boisian framework, urban youth of color would be educated to critically comprehend the functions of the global and local political economies. They would understand how they and other marginalized peoples across the globe are connected in their situatedness within the political economy—as labor, as capitalists, and as consumers—and begin to participate strategically and deliberately within it.

An example of the impact of their lack of such economic capital is the contemporary commodification and commercialization of the musical forms of America's urban youth of color, most notably including hip-hop and rap music. Within this context, urban youth of color are alienated workers—in a Marxist sense—and naïve consumers who are easily victimized by a corporatism that exploits their cultural art forms for enormous profits that filter down to neither the artist nor the community. "Black Americans, while still driving the artistic engine of rap music, are not necessarily the chief beneficiaries of Hip Hop's economic boom."[18] Urban youth of color not only passively produce and consume the commodity of popularized hip-hop and rap, but fail to grasp how export of this commodity exponentially increases the industry's profit and mediates how the world negatively imagines and engages them. The ways in which urban youth of color participate in the commodification and commercialization of the musical forms suggest that they are not critically aware of their multifaceted exploitation by the entertainment industry. Despite the wealth that they have created for an industry and those who control it, they are powerless to use that accumulated wealth and economic capital to transform the hegemonic realities of the local and global political economies that challenge racialized communities at home and abroad. An education that develops a Du Boisian sense of economic capital makes young people aware of the dynamics of the political economy so that they can critically engage it as they seek social uplift.

Du Bois also advocated the acquisition of cultural capital. Like economic capital, represented by monetary and property holdings, cultural capital can be leveraged for wealth accumulation and social mobility. It is best understood as a set of cultural competencies around language, customs, traditions, and beliefs. Whereas the government validates economic capital, institutions of education and the arts validate cultural capital. By virtue of their control over such institutions, the ruling elite ultimately structures the legitimization of economic and cultural capital. In *The Philadelphia Negro*, Du Bois outlined five axiomatic propositions including, "It is the duty of the Negro to raise himself by every effort to the standards of modern civilization and not to lower those standards in any degree."[19] Immersion in classical curricula would move the African American toward those standards where the culture and knowledges of Western civilization were privileged. Du Bois was pragmatic about his insistence on the value of a classical education. In responding to the principal of a state school who was forced to stop teaching Latin to black students, he noted that "as long as the leading Northern colleges require Latin in their entrance examinations, our schools must meet that requirement or our children will be refused admission."[20]

Although the classical curriculum would prepare students for college through its academic alignment with higher education and inculcation of mental discipline, Du Bois understood that it represented the imposition of an arbitrary knowledge. The problem with such an imposition, in terms of the development of appropriate cultural capital, was not its inclusion of Western knowledges, but its intentional exclusion and subjugation of other knowledges, particularly those indigenous to marginalized communities. A pedagogy that privileges Western knowledge "otherizes" students who are culturally different. The knowledge and the process by which it is disseminated and measured in schools reflect the culture of those who dominate the system. It is their power, not any objective criteria, that justifies their ability to inculcate others with the knowledges emanating from their cultural perspectives.

Through decisions on which knowledge is acceptable, desirable, and respected, teachers (as the guardians and pawns) of educational structures regulate how the world enters into students as well as how students enter the world. Logically, dominant group educational structures are not overly concerned with empowering the dominated.[21]

Despite these consequences, the pragmatic Du Bois was resolute in his belief that African Americans had to successfully acquire knowledges propagandized by the dominant culture through its educational institutions.

Most often, Du Bois's rhetoric about the development of cultural capital is discussed and critiqued in terms of the racialized elitism of the *Talented Tenth*. "It is generally known that Du Bois—at least in his early years—embraced an elitist program for Afro-American racial strategy."[22] The *Talented Tenth*, a framework that is often incorrectly credited to Du Bois, represented the group of black elites who would transform society by orchestrating and leading the liberation of the African-American community. The concept originated in 1896 among Northern white liberals of the American Baptist Home Missionary Society, which established Southern black colleges to educate Negro elites. Henry Morehouse coined the term *Talented Tenth* to distinguish his liberal arts education programs and students from the vocational education programs and students associated with Booker T. Washington.[23] It is important to remember that during the late 1800s, many in the newly freed African-American community were intensely focused on the creation of a cadre of African-American leaders who would guide the community toward uplift through societal agitation. They embraced the *Talented Tenth* framework as a means to leverage the community's greatest intellectual assets to generate African-American leadership and ensure that the struggle for collective uplift would not be defined or co-opted by white leaders whose agenda may not benefit the community.

Du Bois readily conceded that his conceptualization of a leadership vehicle for African Americans limited the democratic process within the community, but he believed that the sacrifice was required. Ultimately, he became disillusioned with the *Talented Tenth* cadre because they failed to construct and implement an agenda for empowerment that was directly connected to the needs of the masses. Their immersion in the classical curricula and dominant culture facilitated their deradicalization through an "otherization" of their culturally indigenous knowledges and experiences. "In their haste to become Americans, their desire not to be peculiar or segregated in mind or body, they try to escape their cultural heritage and the body of experience which they themselves have built up."[24]

With this disappointment and a deeper understanding of Marxist thought, Du Bois reconsidered his dogmatic conceptualizations of black leadership and democratized his concept of race leaders. In his 1948 address at Wilberforce State University, Du Bois acknowledged that "Americanization" nurtured the alienation of the *Talented Tenth* from its racialized self. He expressed deep frustration with this unintended consequence and articulated a directive for a *New Tenth*.

This deradicalization process, according to Du Bois, occurs when more privileged African Americans (re)align themselves to function as a middle class interested in individual group gain rather than race leadership for mass development. Asserting that the New Tenth must remain connected to the mass, he highlights a new leadership in conflict with an assimilated or assimilating African-American elite.[25]

Related to this dilemma was Du Bois's conceptualization of *double consciousness*:

The Negro is a sort of seventh son, born with a veil, and gifted with second-sight in this American world—a world which yields him no true self-consciousness, but only lets him see himself through the revelation of the other world. It is a peculiar sensation, this double-consciousness, this sense of always looking at one's self through the eyes of others, of measuring one's soul by the tape of a world that looks on in amused contempt and pity. One ever feels his two-ness—an American, a Negro; two souls, two thoughts, two unreconciled strivings; two warring ideals in one dark body, whose dogged strength alone keeps it from being torn asunder.[26]

The double consciousness framework was essential to Du Bois's critical theory of education in highlighting the multiplicity and complexity of the ontology of the oppressed.

Double consciousness emerges from the unhappy symbiosis between three modes of thinking, being, and seeing. The first is racially particularistic, the second nationalistic in that it derives from the nation state in which the ex-slaves but not-yet-citizens find themselves, rather than from their aspiration towards a nation state of their own. The third is diasporic or hemispheric, sometimes global and occasionally universalist.[27]

Within the educational paradigm that embraced the notion of double consciousness, African Americans had to be trained in a manner that would nurture a balance of the ontological tensions of their multifarious sociocultural identity. It is only through management of the tension, as opposed to the eradication of it, that the community can gain the cultural capital to transform—not accommodate—the hegemonic society. Eradication of the socially subjugated component of one's double consciousness results in conformity to society's hegemonic oppression because it conceals the natural contradictions between one's lived experiences and knowledges, and the traditions and knowledges promulgated by society through the schools. It prevents students from critically reading the world, and from understanding the reasons and linkages behind what are presented as facts through manipulation of the indigenous consciousness of experience and knowledge.

Indeed, the interests of the oppressors lie in "changing the consciousness of the oppressed, not the situation which oppresses them" for the more the oppressed can be led to adapt to that situation, the more easily they can be dominated. To achieve this end, the oppressors use the banking concept of education.[28]

As such, an educational process that includes a more balanced representation of the cultural plurality of the individual is necessary.

This is further evident in Du Bois's discussion of culture, defined as knowledge of the historicity from which the group emerges, and which must be known by the community so that its members can understand how they are situated within the world. Du Bois's perspective, especially as it relates to education, was made more explicit in his admonition that "Negroes must know the history of the Negro race in America . . . They ought to study intelligently, and from their own point of view, the slave trade, slavery, emancipation, Reconstruction, and present economic development."[29] In this respect, he was advocating not the simplistic embrace of an Afrocentric pedagogical approach, but rather, the need to use the cultural position of the students as a point of entry to interrogate and examine the subject matter of the various academic disciplines. Consequently, the knowledges of the community are integrated, rather than sacrificed, into the context of learning within a framework of critical pedagogy where students come to understand the society in which they live and the meaning of their cultured experiences in that society.

Du Bois understood that education for empowerment would allow African Americans to know their fully embodied ontological, or essential, selves. In discussing school integration, Du Bois focused on the inclusion of black history, as opposed to black bodies, in the schools. He noted,

There are going to be schools which do not discriminate against colored people and the number is going to increase slowly in the present, but rapidly in the future until long before the year 2000, there will be no school segregation on the basis of race. The deficiency in knowledge of Negro history and culture, however, will remain and this danger must be met or else American Negroes will disappear. Their history and culture will be lost.[30]

With comprehensive ontological knowledge, individuals can better engage in transformative social activism to support community empowerment. The alternative is cultural capital predicated on the basis of privileging the cultural knowledges of society's ruling elite at the sacrifice of one's own.

Exclusive curricular focus on Western knowledges, at the exclusion of culturally indigenous knowledges, is currently pervasive in our schools, and has negatively impacted urban students of color. For instance, academic success within prevailing school structures is equated with the loss or appropriation of one's cultural self by the dominant culture. Academic achievement is viewed as becoming the *other*, or achieving racelessness. Fordham notes, "Most of these students view success in school as embodying the construction of Otherness, and they associate such success with an inevitable degree of Self-alienation."[31] Because successful engagement with school has covert implications for one's authentic cultural self, youth of color must devise strategies to "survive" schooling, and must reconcile the conflict that results in conformity with or resistance to the curricula and pedagogy that *otherize* one's cultured self.

Capital [High School] students who attempt to resist Self-appropriation often unwittingly reinforce rather than transform the existing social imaging of the Black Other. . . . It is not surprising, therefore, that among the underachieving students at Capital High, schooling is generally constructed as a kind of warfare, an emboldened attempt to reclaim the appropriated Black Self, to avoid being constructed as (an) Other. Unlike the high-achieving students who

resist dominant claims of Black people's intellectual inadequacy by consciously conforming to school norms and expectations, underachieving students resist through avoidance."[32]

Urban youth of color are exceedingly aware of this conflict as evidenced in their music:

> I tried to pay attention but they classes
>   wasn't interesting
> They seemed to only glorify the Europeans
> Claimin' Africans were only three-fifths
>   a human being
> They schools can't teach us shit
> Tellin' me white man lies straight bullshit
> So school don't even relate to us.[33]

A raceless curriculum breeds alienation and resentment among those who are excluded from the canon of knowledges. The resultant frustration is clear in the music of urban youth of color, but it also manifests in the ways students engage in the educational process. If nothing else, urban schools must prevent students' estrangement from the learning process, which must be a lifelong endeavor. Unfortunately, schools are inviting exactly this estrangement by facilitating the development of a cultural capital among urban youth of color that negates their cultured selves. Through an embrace of Du Bois's comprehensive notion of cultural capital, the integration of culturally indigenous knowledges of marginalized communities into the structures of schooling can foster students' ability to better connect with the learning process, and allow them to critically examine the juxtapositions of subjugated and dominant knowledges. Such a pedagogical approach can yield the necessary cultural capital for sustained and substantively empowered uplift.

Du Bois's educational ideology also focused on the development of political capital, the power and ability to influence public policy. He believed that the *personal is political*, and that political capital therefore exists within the sphere of the masses, and not in an elite cadre of race leaders.

All individuals have the capacity of agency, actualized or potential, to democratize political life and transform society. Du Bois always saw education as inextricably linked to the ability of individuals to effectively exercise their political agency. In his judgment, "No civilized state should have citizens too ignorant to participate in government," which was but a step from the observation that "no state is civilized which has citizens too ignorant to help rule it." In other words, "education is not a prerequisite to political control— political control is the cause of popular education."[34] In *The Philadelphia Negro*, Du Bois acknowledged that the enfranchisement of America's ex-slaves provided them with an important means of defense against a society that was not particularly interested in their full civic empowerment and participation.

Although access to the ballot did afford African Americans some political power and control, the potency of their suffrage was diminished because they lacked an understanding of the breadth and depth of the American political sphere.

It became clearer and clearer, as the plan of political power to emancipate the American Negro was followed, that something was lacking; that the poverty and inexperience of the Negro made it impossible for him to exercise his political power in full.[35]

Suffrage, in the hands of a politically inexperienced community, was easily exploited and corrupted through bribery as well as by indirect compensation and influence. The community needed more than just the ballot to attain empowerment. It also needed to understand the democratization process and the dynamics of power within a hegemonic society. Without such training, the community would be unable to convert its political capital into influence over social policies impacting its uplift and societal transformation. African Americans had to think critically about developing their own sociopolitical agenda and about how

the political agenda of those who sought elected office supported or hindered their own agenda.

Du Bois's focus on the development of political capital that extended beyond access to the ballot intensified as he became more steeped in Marxist philosophies of politicized labor movements. He began to articulate with more nuance how power is deployed and manipulated by the nation's capitalists to prevent the full conversion of political control by labor, both black and white.

Nevertheless, industry took pains to protect itself wherever possible. It excluded illiterate foreign voters from the ballot and advocated a reservoir of nonvoting common labor; and it stood ready at any time by direct bribery or the use of its power to hire and discharge labor, to manipulate the labor vote.[36]

In this way, the industrialists were able to reign over the socioeconomic and sociopolitical lives of the masses. Du Bois understood that the only way for laborers to break free of such control was through a coalition of workers exerting the full influence of their collective political capital. Without understanding these power dynamics and their political realities, it would be impossible to build an informed and empowered labor coalition. Unfortunately, the racist policies of the nation's mainstream labor movement excluded African Americans, to labor's overall detriment but to the benefit of the industrialists who saw it as an opportunity to maintain the political dilution of labor.

Individuals must acquire the requisite political capital to understand how to deploy power to achieve change within the social sphere. Political power emanates in part from the recognition of one's own agency to engage in acts of transformation and resistance. Education can help to inform and structure one's agency into strategic sociopolitical resistance rather than oppositional confrontation. Political capital can be leveraged to move the self, the community, and the society toward radical change. Without educational opportunities to effectively politicize their participation in the democracy, African Americans would be rendered civically irrelevant within America's racialized, classed, and gendered hegemony. Considering the extent to which urban youth of color are disconnected from the political process, it is clear that their political capital remains profoundly undernourished.

When educational programs focus on the development of political capital, only two dimensions—general knowledge of the law and the development of civic virtues— are emphasized.[37] Urban youth of color need to understand the political context that structures their lives, the need for an egalitarian redistribution of power, and how to build local as well as global coalitions to transform social, economic, and political hindrances. They must be nurtured for consistent engagement in the political process, understand the possibilities of a redistribution of power, become connected to the development of policies and practices of our democracy, acquire knowledge of the issues of power and elements of informal democratic learning, and know the history and impact of social movements and public policies that have played a role in the democratization of our society by empowering marginalized people.[38] Education is the means by which this can happen. With appropriately designed education, urban youth of color could be prepared to exercise their agency to advocate for equal funding for their schools, to join the struggle against felon disenfranchisement, and to address a host of other sociopolitical issues.

Within Du Bois's educational framework, the development of political capital would necessarily include a Pan-Africanist perspective. "Pan-Africa means intellectual understanding and co-operation among all groups of Negro descent in order to bring about at the earliest possible time the industrial and spiritual emancipation of the Negro peoples."[39] He cautioned that blacks would first have to rid themselves of preconceived ideas, promulgated by white media, in order to build a Pan-Africanist movement to collectively address their common problems resulting from their colonialization and oppression. It is essential that urban youth of color acquire this Pan-Africanist knowledge, which can push them outside of the particularities of their oppression in America and connect them with oppressed youth around the world. As they understand their sociopolitical positioning within the Diaspora of oppressed people as well as the political machinery of American society and the global ruling elites, urban youth of color can help create strategies to transform such ills as the ethnic genocides in Rwanda and the Sudan and the AIDS epidemic in Africa, rather than be sociopolitically complicit in the occurrence of these phenomena because of ignorance or apathy. This represents the type of uplift that can only be achieved with the full development of urban youth's political capital.

Du Bois noted that

unless we develop our full capabilities, we cannot survive. If we are to be trained grudgingly and suspiciously; trained not with reference to what we can be, but with sole reference to what somebody wants us to be; if instead of following the methods pointed out by the accumulated wisdom of the world for the development of full human power, we simply are trying to follow the line of least resistance and teach black men only such things and by such methods as are momentarily popular, then my fellow teachers, we are going to fail and fail ignominiously in our attempt to raise the black race to its full humanity and with that failure falls the fairest and fullest dream of a great united humanity.[40]

His educational ideology is critical to our contemporary discourse on urban education because he advocated for the development of economic, cultural, and political knowledges and skills as a means to empower one of our most marginalized communities without negating their culturally indigenous knowledges and skills. This perspective needs to enter our contemporary urban education discourse because far too few urban youth of color are being uplifted, much less empowered.

Our conceptualization of a *sound basic education* must be informed by the idea that

there is no such thing as a *neutral* educational process. Education either functions as an instrument that is used to facilitate the integration of the younger generation into the logic of the present system and bring about conformity to it, *or* it becomes "the practice of freedom," the means by which men and women deal critically and creatively with reality and discover how to participate in the transformation of their world.[41]

Du Bois's educational ideology was fundamentally about the practice of freedom. Freedom equips individuals with the skills to critically read and strategically challenge the economic, cultural, and political realities of our hegemonic society. Our efforts to provide a *sound basic education* to urban students of color must be guided by more than a unilateral quest for culturally arbitrary standards or prescribed employability in a student's future. We must design education that is fundamentally grounded in a culturally relevant critical educational ideology that empowers urban youth to substantively know, think, and aspire as they engage in the economic, cultural, and political domains of our postmodern global society.

NOTES

This chapter is dedicated to my parents, who first exposed me to a racialized critical ideology of education, and to my brother, Changamire Semakokiro, who provided insightful feedback on earlier drafts. Much love, peace, and thanks to you.

1. Anderson, J. (1988). *The education of blacks in the south, 1860–1935*. North Carolina: University of North Carolina Press; Watkins, W. (2001). *The white architects of black education: Ideology and power in America, 1865–1954*. New York: Teachers College Press.

2. Du Bois, W. (2002). *Dusk of dawn: An essay toward an autobiography of a race concept* (p. 92). New Jersey: Transaction Publishers.

3. Children's Defense Fund. (2004). *The state of America's children 2004* (pp. 87–107).

4. Campaign for Fiscal Equity (CFE). The state of learning. In *New York: An annual snapshot with comparisons of select counties around the state*. Retrieved November 2004, from www.cfe.org.

5. Justice Policy Institute. *Cellblocks or classrooms?: The funding of higher education and corrections and its impact on African American men*. Retrieved November 2004, from www.justice policy.org.

6. National Urban League. *The state of black America 2004*. Retrieved November, 2004, from www.nul.org.

7. Children's Defense Fund. *The state of America's children 2004*, p. xxiv.

8. Campaign for Fiscal Equity (CFE). *Summary of the decision by the Court of Appeals in Campaign for Fiscal Equity, Inc. v. State of New York*. Retrieved November, 2004, from http://www.cfequity.org/CrtofAppeals2003.PDF.

9. Chomsky, N. (2000). *Chomsky on miseducation*. New York: Rowman & Littlefield Publisher, Inc.

10. Anderson (1988).

11. Moore, J. (2003). *Booker T. Washington, W.E.B. Du Bois, and the struggle for racial uplift* (p. 22). Delaware: Scholarly Resources Inc.

12. Watkins (2001), p. 43.

13. Moore (2003).

14. Lester, J. (1971). *The seventh son: The thought and writings of W.E.B. Du Bois* (Vol. II, p. 428). New York: Vintage Books.

15. Du Bois, W. (1973). *The education of black people: ten critiques, 1906–1960* (p. 71). New York: Monthly Review Press.

16. Du Bois (1973), p. 67.

17. Children's Defense Fund. *The state of America's children 2005*.

18. Bynoe, Y. (2004). *Stand & deliver: Political activism, leadership, and hip hop culture* (p. 158). New York: Soft Skull Press.

19. Du Bois, W. (1996). *The Philadelphia Negro* (p. 388). Pennsylvania: University of Pennsylvania Press.

20. Du Bois, W. (1920). Latin. *Crisis Magazine*, *20* (3), 120.

21. Jones, R. (2001, Jan./Apr.). *The liberatory education of the talented tenth: Critical consciousness and the continuing black humanization project. The Negro Educational Review, 52* (1/2), 3–18.

22. Reed Jr., A. (1997). *W.E.B. Du Bois and American political thought* (p. 53). New York: Oxford University Press.

23. James, J. (1997). *Transcending the talented tenth: Black leaders and American intellectuals.* New York: Routledge.

24. Du Bois (1973), p. 144.

25. James (1997), p. 24.

26. Du Bois, W. (1986). *The souls of black folk.* New York: First Vintage Books/The Library of America Edition, p. 8.

27. Gilroy, P. (1993). *The black Atlantic: Modernity and double consciousness* (p. 127). Cambridge, MA: Harvard University Press.

28. Freire, P. (1996). *Pedagogy of the oppressed* (p. 55). New York: The Continuum Publishing Company.

29. Lester (1971), p. 415.

30. Du Bois (1973), p. 152.

31. Fordham, S. (1996). *Blacked out: Dilemmas of race, identity, and success at capital high* (p. 283). Illinois: University of Chicago Press.

32. Fordham (1996), p. 282.

33. Dead Prez. (2000). they schools. *lets get free.* Loud Records. © Walk Like a Warrior (BMI)/ The War of Art Music (BMI). Courtesy of The Royalty Network, Inc., 2000.

34. James (1997), p. 127.

35. Lester, J. *The seventh son*, p. 424.

36. Du Bois, W. (1992). *Black reconstruction in America 1860–1880* (p. 184). New York: The Free Press.

37. Schugurensky, D. (2000). *Citizenship learning and democratic engagement: Political capital revisited.* Retrieved November, 2004, from http://www.edst.educ.ubc.ca/aerc/2000/schugurenskyd1-final.PDF.

38. Schugurensky (2000).

39. Lester (1971), p. 208.

40. Du Bois (1973), p. 9.

41. Shaull, R. (1996). In P. Freire, *Pedagogy of the oppressed* (p. 16). New York: The Continuum Publishing Company.

RACE, CLASS, AND GENDER IN URBAN EDUCATION: EXPLORING THE CRITICAL RESEARCH ON URBAN PEDAGOGY AND SCHOOL REFORM

Marvin Lynn, A. Dee Williams, Grace Benigno, Colleen Mitchell, and Gloria Park

In an article published by the Institute for Urban and Minority Education at Columbia University, Flaxman, Schwartz, Weiler, and Lahey[1] provide an extensive overview of the literature in urban education. They argue that two topics dominate the urban education research landscape: multicultural education and school reform. While they briefly discuss multicultural approaches to teaching in urban schools, the authors devote much of the article to describing the multitude of urban school change efforts that have been written about over the years. In doing so, Flaxman and his colleagues focus narrowly on "practice and local policy . . . rather than theory."[2]

After conducting a preliminary content analysis of recent articles published in leading journals that focus on issues in urban education, we found that studies rarely employed theory. In particular, we noticed an absence of theories that address the relationship between urban schools and the larger social context in which they exist. In reviewing the literature, we observed that many of the articles on urban education center almost exclusively on classroom practice or school change efforts while giving little attention to theory or examining the broader social structures in which teaching and school change occur. In particular, the articles examined frequently addressed topics such as immigration, teacher attitudes and beliefs, professional development, parental involvement, and high-stakes testing. For example, articles published in 2002 concentrate on school violence, pre-service teacher education, school–community relations, desegregation, and charter schools. We noted, however, that a few articles did not reflect these general characteristics. One investigation addressed theory on "social change" within the context of urban schools[3] while another study utilized critical theory as a lens to critique existing frameworks typically employed in urban education research.[4] Despite these few exceptions, the majority of the articles we reviewed did not engage theory—or more specifically, critical theory—in a substantive way. We argue that this presents a serious epistemological problem for urban educators in search of ways to improve their schools.

The purpose of this chapter is to highlight specific research in urban education that collectively attempts to incorporate critical theory as a frame to understand and draw relationships between urban education and the larger social and political contexts in which urban schools exist. In our discussion, we will argue that research that utilizes critical theory as a lens for examining and understanding the complexities of urban schools provides a conceptual and epistemological grounding for changing the direction of future research in urban education. We conclude by proposing that a "critical theory of urban education" can lead educators and researchers toward significant insights that can help improve the present condition of urban schools.

UNEARTHING CRITICAL THEORIES

Before critical theory emerged as a major contender in the sea of studies in urban education, that is, before significant numbers of researchers began to draw from sociological theories to define, analyze, and explain schools and schooling processes, cultural deficit theories dominated the urban education landscape.[5] Much of the theorizing about the plight of urban schools resulted from the need of public officials—many of whom were given federal mandates to "fix" ailing urban schools in the 1960s—to explain the outcomes in urban education. The Moynihan Report,[6] for example, boldly put forth the notion that families had the greatest impact on the achievement of students in urban schools. Moynihan's research claimed that black families in inner-city communities in particular had a negative effect on the learning process for black children. This manifested itself in higher than average dropout rates and other social/psychological problems experienced by students in urban schools. About the same time, another national study,[7] under the guise of investigating the "equality of educational opportunity" in urban schools, also argued that family background was the strongest predictor of school success or failure for urban minority students. Moreover, Coleman and his colleagues suggested among other things that an increase in education spending would prove fruitless so long as there were daunting economic disparities between the urban poor and the suburban middle class.

This research gave rise to the development of theories that supported the idea that urban school students, their families, and their communities were primarily responsible for their own academic failure. Expounding on this notion, Lewis,[8] who became a key proponent of the notion we identify as the *cultural deficit framework*, suggested that success or failure in urban schools depended largely on one's personal attitudes and behaviors. According to Lewis, schooling for most urban and poor minority students was a series of reactions to and against forms of social disenfranchisement. Oppositional disposition thus emerged as a belief that school failure reflected "both an adaptation and a reaction of the poor to their marginal position in a class-stratified, highly individuated, capitalistic society."[9]

More recently, anthropologists have adopted the notion of linking academic failure to characteristics of particular children and their families by focusing attention on the relationship between the home and school.[10] Ogbu asserts that students in urban schools tend to develop an oppositional social identity, which begets negative attitudes and behaviors that are inconsistent with school norms. Fordham[11] suggests that minority students in urban schools do not succeed academically because for them, success in school is equated with "acting white." The proliferation of deficit-based theories, however, eventually gave rise to critical theories of education. These alternative perspectives challenged the practice of focusing analyses of the conditions of urban education primarily on the relationship between individuals and their schooling outcomes. Instead critical theories examine schooling outcomes within the context of larger social structures.

Gordon[12] defines critical theory in clear and succinct terms:

Critical theory seeks to understand the origins and operation of repressive social structures. Critical theory is the critique of domination. It seeks to focus on a world becoming less free, to cast doubt on claims of technological scientific rationality, and then to imply that present configurations do not have to be as they are.[13]

Not only do critical theorists attempt to discover why oppressive structures exist and offer criticisms of their effects, they also explore the ways in which we can transform our society. In this sense, critical theory is not simply a critique of social structures; it is an analysis of power relations. In other words, such questions as "What constitutes power?" "Who holds it?," and "In what ways is it utilized to benefit those already in power?" are pursued and investigated. While critical theory is often described as an area of study that emanated from Western Europe,[14] Gordon argues that African Americans established a strong critical theoretical tradition in the United States long before critical European philosophy and thought were popular in the United States.[15] She further states that African-American thinkers like W.E.B. Du Bois, Ida B. Wells, Anna Julia Cooper, and Carter G. Woodson led principled scholarly struggles against the systematic dehumanization of African Americans. As a result, they theorized about the nature of the conditions for people who were racially and culturally subjugated. To that extent, analyses of class and gender, as well as race and culture, become part of the framework we call critical theory. To be specific, we argue that critical frameworks include but are not limited to:

- Marxism/neo-Marxism, which is an approach to examining the impact of capitalism on cultural, social, and political structures including schools
- Critical race theory (CRT), which affords an analytical perspective from which to study race and racism in the law, society, and schools
- Critical feminist theory and black feminist theory, which, unlike traditional feminism, offer a critique of gender domination and articulate a pedagogical approach to transforming gender relations[16]

A critical theory that incorporates analyses of race, class, and gender oppression can be an important tool for framing, analyzing, and calling attention to unjust conditions in urban schools. According to Popkewitz, a critical theory of education could be described as "a broad band of disciplined questioning of the ways in which power works through the discursive practices and performances of schooling." The various modes of critical inquiry are to understand, for example, how the marginalization of people is constructed and in what forms power operates. Furthermore, critical theory also entails "self-reflectivity about the implications of intellectual work as political projects."[17]

Marxist theorists examine the ways in which urban public schools are connected to larger economic forces in society. Social reproduction theory is the study of how society maintains its economic structure.[18] From a social reproduction perspective, schools serve as training mechanisms through which society reproduces itself. Dance suggests that social reproduction theory has a distinct continuum on which the philosophies that draw upon it are organized:[19] the economic determinist and the cultural autonomist.[20] The economic determinist perspective claims that capitalist structures dictate how schools function as social stratifiers.[21] For example, Bowles and Gintis (1976) argue that schools simply "reproduce reserve armies of skilled labor, legitimating the technocratic-meritocratic perspective, reinforcing the fragmentation of groups of workers into stratified status groups, and accustoming youth to the social relationships of dominance and subordinacy in the economic system."[22] Thus, the economic determinist framework can be used to understand how and why schools in urban areas strike a remarkable resemblance to both penal institutions and factories. The cultural autonomist perspective takes a slightly different approach. For example, Willis's study of "counter-school culture" among working-class boys found that students exert a remarkable degree of control over their learning.[23] Similarly, MacLeod believes that students' "insight into the nature of capitalism has the potential to catalyze class solidarity and collective action."[24] Employing a cultural autonomist lens to understand the conditions of urban schooling thus makes possible Freire's ideas of praxis and hope; that is, engaging in critical reflection to empower.[25] More

generally, Marxist theory in urban education focuses on how economic structures perpetuate inequitable schooling outcomes for students. Thus, other forms of difference are not explored. Critical race theory (CRT) in education, however, brings race and racism to the forefront of research on urban schools.

Delgado describes the history of CRT as a legal discourse that identifies race as the central factor in which the inequities of society can be explained.[26] Although race serves as a core issue to be examined, CRT also acknowledges and analyzes the intersections of race, class, and gender. For example, CRT scholars are interested in how race and gender intersect to form a unique set of experiences for black women, who are doubly oppressed.[27] Education scholars have turned to CRT as a means to better understand the nature, form, and function of race and racism in schools. Researchers in education recognize that CRT provides a new, more analytic approach to understanding the persistence of racism in schools and society. Critical race theory explores multiple facets of education, including: (1) policy and practice; (2) educational leadership; (3) curriculum and instruction; and (4) student perspective. In addition, Ladson-Billings applies a CRT framework to understand the purposes, procedures, and effects of teacher education programs.[28] Solorzano and Delgado Bernal also utilize CRT to explain that some forms of resistance to school can have transformative underpinnings.[29] Lynn employs CRT as an approach to analyzing and typifying the work of critical African-American teachers.[30] To summarize, CRT integrates multiple perspectives on law, society, schooling, and inequality in order to frame an analysis that sheds light on the racial dimensions of schooling and schooling practices. We believe that, like other critical theories, CRT can provide substantive insight into the role that urban schools play in helping to maintain current race relations in society. In particular, CRT enables researchers to investigate questions such as: (1) How do urban schools—most of which are deeply embedded within poor communities of color—promote a racial caste system in the United States that is determined by race and class; and (2) In what ways are current policy and practice in urban schools governed by a racial code of ethics that frames urban schools as culturally dysfunctional in ways commonly associated with communities of color?

Although CRT does address patriarchy as a social system, it rarely discusses how gender inequality is advanced in urban public schools in the United States. Weedon argues that there are different interpretations of patriarchy within feminism and that these varying interpretations result in different forms of feminist politics.[31] Liberal feminism, for example, recognizes the effects of patriarchy and strives for full equality for women. Socialist feminists see gender domination as intimately tied to all forms of oppression. They argue that authentic liberation can only occur with the radical reconstruction of societal social structures. Weis contends that educational research, with its conservative tradition, has had to answer feminists' calls for equity in pedagogy and school curricula.[32]

Black feminist and womanist theorists offer a critique of social inequality that is multidimensional in focus because it stresses the importance of understanding the relationship between interconnected forms of oppression, such as racism, sexism, and elitism. Womanist theory has been described as the perspective of women of African origin who are "committed to the survival and wholeness of an entire people, male and female."[33] The black feminist position embraces a position that is grounded in the history and struggles of black women.[34] The black feminist and womanist paradigms compel us to think more deeply about connecting critical

analyses of schooling to a wider discourse on how the institution of schooling maintains racial, class, and gender configurations in the United States.[35] For example, the following question can be examined through a black feminist and womanist lens: "In what ways do urban schools promote a white, middle-class masculine norm that furthers patriarchy?" In addition, feminist and black feminist traditions can enable us to explore the extent to which the "de-skilling" of teachers' work and the subsequent "proletarianization" of teaching might constitute another form of patriarchy where white men—who still control urban schools—exert external control over how teaching is defined and ultimately framed in the urban context.[36]

These frameworks, extending from the field of sociology, offer an alternative approach to understanding race, class, and gender in urban education in that they challenge atheoretical, apolitical, heavily positivist, and supposedly value-neutral research and theory, which maintain that schools are not bound by ideology.[37] To that end, employing critical theory in the study of urban education can examine class-, race-, and gender-based power relations through what appear to be normal, everyday practices in urban schools. Even more important, a critical theory perspective on urban education can provide us with the tools to not only examine inequalities and their root causes, but also work toward the development of "projects" aimed at transforming existing inequalities.[38] Employing a *"new* sociology of education" or "critical theory of education" provides a number of different opportunities for scholars to study long-standing problems in urban education with the fervent hope of moving toward some resolution.[39] In the next section, we provide a more detailed description of the literature in urban education that utilizes critical theory in its variegated forms to either expose existing inequalities or propose actions for change wherein individuals and/or institutions can work toward creating more socially just urban schools.

CRITICAL RESEARCH ON TEACHING IN URBAN CONTEXTS AND SCHOOL REFORM

Critical theory helps illuminate the ways in which the current "crisis" in education extends from social, political, and economic factors that are largely beyond the control of schools. Critical researchers who focus on the work of urban schoolteachers argue that, whereas the social context greatly shapes the capacity of urban schools to provide their students with the resources needed for survival in a credentials-based society,[40] the failure of urban schools also depends, in part, on what happens in classrooms. In other words, these scholars not only situate classrooms within the broader social and political context of a system of structured inequalities, they also explore the role of teaching in either promoting or transforming race, class, and gender inequalities. Classroom teaching practices in urban schools, and insight into inequalities that permeate broader social institutions, are therefore key areas of concentration for critical urban education scholars.

Based on our review, the literature on urban education that utilizes critical theory can be divided into three main areas. The first identifies aspects of classroom teaching practice or teachers' work that fail to promote the academic or personal well-being of urban school students. The second area of literature outlines the characteristics and practices of teachers who work to enhance the academic ability as well as the political awareness of their students. The third area of literature utilizes critical theory to understand urban education by examining the relationship between broader social institutions, school reform efforts, and urban classroom teaching practices. These particular studies attempt to reconcile the complex nature and interaction between these systems of practice.

To start, much of the critical theory-based research that examines urban classroom teaching practices focuses on the injustices poor and minority students experience in this context. In particular, an examination has emerged of traditional classroom practices that further marginalize already disenfranchised students. Furthermore, Anyon and Rist, in their analysis of practices in urban classrooms, argue that a pervasive sense of despair among students and teachers persists in these schools.[41]

The sense of hopelessness in urban classrooms is evidenced in how children in these schools are taught. Anyon found that teachers in poor and working-class schools in New Jersey with majority African-American populations tended to teach students in ways that promulgated the idea of a factory-like life in schools. Furthermore, children were systematically mistreated and not encouraged to engage in critical or reflective thinking, nor were they allowed to work in groups. The experiences of poor and minority students in urban classrooms present a sharp contrast to those of suburban middle- and upper-middle-class students who are often treated with respect and encouraged to work cooperatively to solve problems that promote higher-level thinking.[42] In a classic study of an urban kindergarten classroom, Rist observed similar findings. He found that teachers often relegated the poorest children in the class to the margins of classroom life. For example, the teacher in the study perceived poorer children to be academically weak and thus based their instructional experiences on this belief. This contributed to a lack of self-efficacy among the poorer students that eventually translated into academic failure. That is, negative teacher expectations of poor students contributed to overall negative outcomes for students.[43] This constitutes the self-fulfilling prophecy Rist describes in the study. Because urban schools are most often under-staffed and under-resourced, these conditions are widespread in urban contexts, resulting in teachers meeting the needs and promoting the academic success of only a select few.[44]

The sense of despair in urban education also appears in how teaching and learning are" to refer to teaching practices that neither encourage understanding nor value children's life experiences.[45] Similarly, Freire refers to the notion of "banking education," where students' minds are perceived as empty vessels to be filled with information given by the teacher.[46] Thus, for both Haberman and Freire, teaching in urban schools is the practice of merely disseminating information. In the practice of banking education, culture, race, class, ethnicity, and gender identity are devalued. Consequently, school becomes an oppressive and dehumanizing experience for nondominant students. Leisytna maintains that the pervasiveness of these pedagogies of despair are "culturally homogenizing . . . [and] fundamentally anti-multicultural and anti-democratic."[47] In response, critical theorists have put forth a liberating pedagogy that is not only more sensitive to the needs of disempowered students, but also challenges teachers to empower themselves and their students. We refer to this group of theoretically rich studies of urban teaching as *critical urban pedagogies of hope*.

Critical urban pedagogies of hope characterize the second group of literature we reviewed, which employs critical theory to understand and reconceptualize urban education. These pedagogies of hope include, but are not limited to, critical Marxist pedagogy, often simply referred to as critical pedagogy,[48] critical feminist/womanist pedagogy,[49] and critical race pedagogy, within which we include culturally relevant and responsive teaching.[50] We will explain briefly how we define each of these approaches.

McLaren explains,

Critical pedagogy is a way to bring into the arena of schooling practices insurgent, resistant, and insurrectional modes of interpretation which set out to imperil the familiar, to contest the legitimating norms of mainstream social life and to render problematic the common discursive frames and regimes within which "proper" behavior comportment, social interactions are premised.[51]

Furthermore, McLaren suggests that teachers must reject the commonly accepted modes of instruction and instead critically reflect on their teaching and embrace a philosophy that consciously works toward creating a classroom climate that encourages social and cultural criticism. In the same vein, Aronowitz and Giroux summarize critical pedagogy in the urban classroom as a practice of creating "transformative intellectuals" through active intervention and struggle.[52] They argue that in order for teachers to truly enact a critical pedagogy they must: (1) validate students' prior experiences; (2) engage them in a critical evaluation of these experiences; and (3) encourage the implementation of an "emancipatory curriculum."[53] Kanpol studies the work of critical educators and finds that while their classroom practices are consistent with the major aspects of critical pedagogy, they also strive to "resist" structures in urban schools that fail to enhance the lives of their students.[54] In this sense, critical pedagogues: (1) critique social injustice; (2) reflect on their own work and lives; and (3) encourage critical thought and democratic social action by their students. These ideas serve as a wellspring for a host of other ways of describing teaching methods that embody democratic principles.

Stemming from the work of critical pedagogues, critical feminists have articulated a vision of classroom practice that empowers women and girls in urban classrooms. Critical feminist pedagogues fully embrace the tenets of critical pedagogy; however, they view society as being stratified primarily through gender.[55] Feminist pedagogy seeks social transformation for both students and teachers, and works to break down pre-existing hierarchical structures in society through expanded teaching and learning that empower students to rebel against sexism in urban schools.[56] Black feminist or womanist pedagogy embraces similar themes, except this pedagogy specifically focuses on the unique experiences of black women. Black feminist pedagogues are called to "lift up" the race through the practice of a caring pedagogy.[57] In demonstrating the inextricable link between race and gender, black feminist pedagogy reflects ideas employed by research that utilizes race as a frame to examine pedagogy in urban contexts.

Critical race pedagogy, unlike critical feminist pedagogy and critical pedagogy, focuses specifically on race and racism in urban classrooms, students' identification with their own culture, and the interactions between race, class, and gender in schools.[58] In other words, critical race pedagogy focuses on the ways in which race and racism shape classroom practices. It emphasizes how teachers can resist and break down racist structures.[59] Culturally relevant or responsive teaching shares qualities similar to critical race pedagogy. Culturally relevant teaching, with roots in both the culture-centered and Marxist approaches, requires teachers to empower students to become "creative thinkers, decision makers, and transformers of their current life situations."[60] Urban schoolteachers who apply culturally relevant pedagogy believe that they are responsible for understanding students' cultural background and therefore must adapt their teaching to children's needs to promote full participation and the meaningful construction of knowledge among all students.[61] In Lipman's case study of three African-American urban schoolteachers, she argues that culturally relevant pedagogy is "the kind of teaching that uses the student's culture to help them achieve success."[62] The inclusion of student voice also becomes a venue in which culture becomes active in the classroom. Not only do teachers allow students to utilize their language in the classroom, they also make use of students' particular ways of knowing in order to build curriculum.[63]

To summarize, critical pedagogy, feminist pedagogy, and critical race- and culture-relevant pedagogy help advance teaching practices that recognize the existence of inequalities in the classroom and in the larger world. These pedagogies help us envision how we might deconstruct broader social inequities to promote a socially just education for all students. Recent research in urban education reform, with its focus on the relationship between schools and the larger social context, helps explicate how schools might move even further toward a more equitable and just society.

The third area of literature that utilizes a critical theory lens to understand urban education examines the relationship between broader social institutions, urban school reform efforts, and classroom teaching practices. These studies attempt to reconcile the complex nature and interaction between these systems of practice. Anyon, in *Ghetto Schooling: A Political Economy of Urban Educational Reform*,[64] analyzes the present condition of Marcy school, a K–8 school in central Newark, New Jersey, by situating it within the economic and political circumstances endured by Marcy school since the mid-1800s. This history, she argues, contributed to the increasingly significant social and educational inequalities that characterize current student experiences in inner-city New Jersey. According to Anyon, "urban educational and social reforms are symbiotic."[65] School restructuring therefore cannot occur unless political and economic systems are transformed. Anyon contends that a comprehensive approach is required to enact change in teaching practices in urban classrooms. Elements of this approach include collaboration with other community-based organizations and services, re-examination of state control of failing school systems, leadership development within schools, professional development focusing on improved teaching and learning, teacher education development, school and community programs that address the special needs of students in poor urban schools, and adequate funding to support school reform efforts.

Lipman applies a critical perspective to the investigation of reform initiatives in Chicago, and urges researchers to consider the extent to which efforts to reform urban schools may "exacerbate existing race and class inequalities and create new ones."[66] Lipman calls for researchers to examine whether and how urban classroom practices based on reform initiatives may inadvertently perpetuate social inequalities. Her 2002 study finds that reform policies in Chicago Public Schools were based on a strict "highly regulatory regime centered on high stakes tests, standards and remediation."[67] She further contends that the intense media coverage on test scores in the beleaguered school district detracted from a deeper examination of the ideological underpinnings of these reform teaching practices, and detracted from examining the political and economic implications of these policies for poor students and their families. Lipman suggests that little research has focused on how reforms based on a remediation model perpetuate social inequality by endorsing classroom practices that lock poor students into consistent and persistent patterns of underachievement. She concludes with concrete proposals to move marginalizing urban classroom teaching toward practices that afford increased success and social equity to poor students. In particular, Lipman calls for urban school reform to be considered alongside "goals of rich literacy, cultural and social relevance, and critical approaches to knowledge."[68]

Deschenes, Cuban, and Tyack argue that the standards reform movement can be successful if efforts focus specifically on reexamining and restructuring the institution of schools.[69] Changing the existing structure and culture of schools to reflect socially just schooling practices may help schools more effectively meet the needs of a diverse student population. They offer three policies, given the current standards reform movement: (1) fit the school and the school system to the student; (2) examine broad social inequalities; and (3) undertake comprehensive change.

Orr, Stone, and Stumbo[70] argue in their analysis of reform efforts in Baltimore City Public Schools that policy makers must seriously consider the role of poverty in conceptualizing initiatives for school change. They contend that "specialization" and formulaic approaches applied in Baltimore have been largely unsuccessful because of their failure to attend to the economic context of Baltimore schools, inarguably among the poorest in the country. Orr et al. found that school reform efforts in Baltimore City paid little attention to the magnitude of poverty in the city and its effects on overall school performance. They argue that failure to understand urban schools within the broader context of social and economic conditions leads to the development of remedies that are not likely to have a significant impact on students and their families. In order to make strides in school improvement, the authors promote a holistic approach to community development, with the goal of transforming low-income neighborhoods into places where change is possible.[71]

CONCLUSION: TOWARD A CRITICAL THEORY OF URBAN EDUCATION

In an article that explores the utility of sociological theory for understanding the black–white achievement gap, Hallinan suggests that (critical) theory explaining the social, political, and economic conditions under which minorities and the poor live provides us with a better overall understanding of schooling conditions for these groups.[72] Likewise, we argue that before we can come to an adequate understanding of urban education, we must first begin the process of making sense of the social context in which these schools are embedded. We contend that critical theories of education provide the lens through which to begin the process of deepening our understanding of broader social institutions and the relationship these have with the current condition of urban schools.

Critical research in urban education mainly focuses on classroom teaching practices in urban schools.[73] We found that this literature can be divided into three groups. One group provides a critical analysis of the practices of urban schoolteachers that promote teachers as *agents of an oppressive system* of structured inequalities.[74] A second body of research outlines teaching practices that *humanize* or empower students in urban schools through culturally responsive and politically imbued teaching methods.[75] The final group of literature uses critical theory to examine the relationship between broader social institutions, urban school reform efforts, and classroom teaching practices.[76]

In describing the literature that incorporates critical theories as a lens to deepen our understanding of urban education, we observed a number of compelling arguments and proposals for change that engender hope for the creation of socially just urban schools. For example, critical pedagogy attempts to intertwine gender, race, and culture to describe a method of teaching for social justice and equality. Within a practice of critical pedagogy, teachers engage in transformative teaching in order to prepare their students for an ever-changing society while encouraging students to realize that they have choices, they can make a difference, and they are in control of their lives. As we have shown, much of the critical literature on urban schools offers promising conceptions for the transformation of urban education. In these frameworks, critical and relevant teaching practice can and does enhance the lives of students by openly addressing issues of race, culture, and gender. Critical research on urban education moves us from a place of despair to a place where we can begin to have conversations about how to promote effective teaching practices in urban schools that will develop

creative, critical thinkers who will help foster this country's democratic mission. Finally, in the section on urban school reform, we discussed literature that proposes why reforms succeed or fail, and we demonstrated how research attempts to reconcile the complex interaction among social institutions, urban school reform efforts, and classroom teaching practices.[77] To that end, research on race, class, and gender in urban education not only offers a critique of forms of social inequality that are maintained and supported by urban schools, but also provides some direction about the way forward. The critical urban school reform literature admonishes us to be mindful of the larger context in which reforms are undertaken. In that sense, while we do want to attend to classroom teaching practices, we must also attend to the relationship between the teaching practices in urban schools and the larger systems and institutions that embody the context of urban education.

In their totality, the frameworks that shaped the analysis of the research we reviewed, we believe, can be understood collectively as "a critical theory of urban education" that seeks not only to report on what is happening or not happening in urban schools, but seeks to draw important connections between theory and teaching practice. More importantly, these studies do the important work of situating history, teaching, and school change efforts within the context of social, political, and economic realities. In this way, critical theories of race, class, and gender are wedded to and used as ways in which to explain the everyday functions of urban schools. This is especially needed as urban schools become increasingly diverse and complex organizations.

Cities and urban areas in the United States continue to offer some hope of the possibility of freedom from economic despair for thousands of thousands of new immigrants from Africa, Latin America, the Caribbean, and Asia. In addition, urban schools remain as places where a majority of American-born minorities such as African Americans and

Latinos/as are educated. An apolitical, atheoretical, "business-as-usual" approach to studying urban education where there is little or no discussion of class, race, and gender inequalities in schools and society, will ultimately fail to meet the needs of any of these populations. For this reason, it is crucial that we begin and continue conversations around a critical theory of urban education.

NOTES

We would like to thank Emily Meny and Sara McQueen for their contributions to earlier drafts of this chapter.

1. Flaxman, E., Schwartz, W., Weiler, J., & Lahey, M. (1998). *Trends and issues in urban education.* New York: Columbia University Institute for Urban and Minority Education. http://eric-web.tc.columbia.edu/.

2. Flaxman et al. (1998), p. 1.

3. Chizhik, S., & Chizhik, A. (2002). A path to social change: Examining students' responsibility, opportunity, and emotion toward social justice. *Education and Urban Society, 34* (3), 233–297.

4. Dantley, M. (2002). Uprooting and replacing positivism, the melting pot, multiculturalism, and other impotent notions in educational leadership through an African American perspective. *Education and Urban Society, 34* (3), 334–352.

5. Weiner, L. (1993). *Preparing teachers for urban schools: Lessons from thirty years of school reform.* New York: Teachers College Press.

6. Hallinan, M. (2001). Sociological perspectives on black–white inequalities in American schooling. *Sociology of Education* Extra Issue, 50–70; referencing Coleman (1966).

7. Hallinan (2001).

8. Lewis, O. (1968). The culture of poverty. In D. Moynihan (Ed.), *On understanding poverty: Perspectives from the social sciences* (pp. 187–199). New York: Basic Books.

9. Lewis (1968), p. 188.

10. Ogbu, J. (1992). Understanding cultural diversity and learning. *Educational Researcher, 21* (8), 5–14.

11. Fordham, S. (1996). *Blacked out: Dilemmas of race, identity, and success at Capital High.* Chicago: The University of Chicago Press.

12. Gordon, B. (1995). Knowledge construction, competing critical theories, and education. In J. Banks and C. McGee (Eds.), *Handbook of research on multicultural education* (pp. 184–199). New York: Macmillan Publishers.

13. Gordon (1995), p. 190.

14. McLaren, P. (1998). *Life in schools: An introduction to critical pedagogy in the foundations of education* (3rd ed.). New York: Longman; Popkewitz, T. (1998). The sociology of knowledge and the sociology of education: Michel Foucault and the critical traditions. In C. Torres and T. Mitchell (Eds.), *Sociology of education: Emerging perspectives* (pp. 47–90). Albany: State University of New York Press.

15. Gordon (1995).

16. Weedon, C. (1997). *Feminist practice & poststructuralist theory* (2nd ed.). Cambridge, MA: Blackwell Publishers.

17. Popkewitz (1998), p. 48.

18. Morrow, R., & Torres, C. (1995). *Social theory and education: A critique of theories of social and cultural reproduction.* Albany: State University of New York Press.

19. Dance, L. (2002). *Tough fronts: The impact of street culture on schooling.* New York: Routledge Falmer Press.

20. Bowles, S., & Gintis, H. (1976). *Schooling in capitalist America: Educational reform and the contradictions of economic life.* New York: Basic Books; Giroux, H. (1983). *Theory and resistance in education: A pedagogy for the opposition.* Westport, CT: Greenwood Publishing Group Incorporated; Willis, P. (1977). *Learning to labor.* New York: Columbia University Press.

21. Bowles & Gintis (1976).

22. Bowles & Gintis (1976), p. 76.

23. Willis (1977).

24. MacLeod, J. (1987). *Ain't no making it: Aspirations and attainment in a low-income neighborhood* (p. 19). Boulder, CO: Westview Press.

25. Freire, P. (2002). *Pedagogy of the oppressed.* New York: Continuum International Publishing Group Inc.

26. Delgado, R. (1995). *The Rodrigo chronicles: Conversations about race in America.* New York: New York University Press.

27. Crenshaw, K. (1995). *Critical race theory: The key writings that formed the movement.* New York: W.W. Norton & Co.

28. Ladson-Billings, G. (1998). Preparing teachers for diverse student populations: A critical race theory perspective. *Review of Research in Education, 24,* 211–247.

29. Solorzano, D., & Delgado Bernal, D. (2001). Examining transformational resistance through a critical race and Latcrit theory framework: Chicana and Chicano students in an urban context. *Urban Education, 36* (3), 308–342.

30. Lynn, M. (1999). Toward a critical race pedagogy: A research note. *Urban Education, 33* (5), 606–626.

31. Weedon (1997).

32. Weis, L. (1988). *Class, race, and gender in American education.* Albany: State University of New York Press.

33. Walker, A. (1983). *In search of mother's gardens* (p. xi). San Diego, CA: Harcourt, Brace, Jovanovich.

34. Collins, P. (1991). *Black feminist thought: Knowledge, consciousness, and the politics of empowerment: Perspectives on gender* (Volume 2). New York: Routledge.

35. Lynn (1999), p. 609.

36. Giroux, H. (1988). *Teachers as intellectuals.* New York: Bergin and Garvey.

37. McLaren (1998).

38. Popkewitz (1998).

39. McLaren (1998), p. 163

40. Collins, R. (1979). *The credential society.* New York: Academic Press.

41. Anyon, J. (1995). Race, social class and educational reform in an inner-city school. *Teachers College Record, 97* (1), 69–94; Anyon, J. (1997). *Ghetto schooling: A political economy of urban educational reform.* New York: Teachers College Press; Rist, R. (1970). Student social class and teacher expectations: The self-fulfilling prophecy in ghetto education. *Harvard Educational Review, 40* (3), 70–110.

42. Anyon (1997).

43. Rist (1970), pp. 71–72.

44. Darling-Hammond, L. (2004). What happens to a dream deferred? The continuing quest for equal educational opportunity. In J. Banks and C. McGee (Eds.), *Handbook of research on multicultural education* (pp. 607–630). New York: Macmillan Publishers.

45. Haberman, M. (1996). The pedagogy of poverty versus good teaching. In W. Ayers and P. Ford (Ed.), *City kids city teachers: Reports from the front row* (pp. 118–130). New York: The New Press.

46. Friere (2002).

47. Leistyna, P. (1999). *Presence of mind: Education and the politics of deception.* Boulder, CO: Westview Press.

48. Giroux, H. (1981). *Ideology, culture, and the process of schooling.* Philadelphia: Temple University Press; Giroux (1988); McLaren, P. (1995). *Critical pedagogy and predatory culture: Oppositional politics in a postmodern era.* New York: Routledge.

49. Beauboeuf-Lafontant, T. (2002). A womanist experience of caring: Understanding the pedagogy of exemplary black women teachers. *Urban Review, 34* (1), 71–86; Weiler, K. (1988). *Women teaching for change: Gender, class & power.* New York: Bergin & Gavey Publishers; Lynn (1999).

50. Gay, G. (2000). Culturally responsive teaching: Theory, research and practice. New York: Teachers College Press; Ladson-Billings, G. (1994). *The dreamkeepers: Successful teachers of African American children.* San Francisco: Jossey-Bass Publishers.

51. McLaren (1995), p. 231.

52. Aronowitz, S., & Giroux, H. (1993). *Education still under siege.* Westport, CT: Bergin & Garvey.

53. Aronowitz & Giroux (1993), p. 231.

54. Kanpol, B. (1998). Teacher work tasks as forms of resistance and accommodation to structural factors of schooling. *Urban Education, 23* (2), 173–87; Kanpol, B. (1993). *Towards a theory and practice of teacher cultural politics: Continuing the postmodern debate.* New York: Ablex Publishing Corporation.

55. Weiler (1998).

56. Jackson, S. (1997). Crossing borders and changing pedagogies: From Giroux and Freire to feminist theories of education. *Gender and Education, 9* (4), 457–467.

57. Henry, A. (1998). *Taking back control: African Canadian women teachers' lives and practice.* Albany: State University of New York Press.

58. Lynn (1999).

59. Kanpol (1993).

60. Ball, A. (2000). Empowering pedagogies that enhance the learning of multicultural students. *Teachers College Record, 102* (6), 1006–1034. *See* p. 1007.

61. Gay (2000).

62. Lipman, P. (1996). The missing voice of culturally relevant teachers in school restructuring. *The Urban Review, 28* (1), 41–62. *See* p. 50.

63. Ball (2000); Darder, A. (1993). How does the culture of the teacher shape the classroom experience of Latino students?: The unexamined question in critical pedagogy. In S. Rothstein (Ed.), *Handbook of schooling in urban America* (pp. 195–222). Westport, CT: Greenwood Press; Lipman (1996).

64. Anyon (1997).

65. Lipman (1996), p. 167.

66. Lipman, P. (2002). Making the global city, making inequality: The political economy and cultural politics of Chicago school policy. *American Educational Research Journal, 39* (2), 379–419. See p. 379.

67. Lipman (2002), p. 381.

68. Lipman (2002), p. 411.

69. Deschenes, S., Cuban, L., & Tyack, D. (2001). Mismatch: Historical perspectives on schools and students who don't fit them. *Teachers College Record, 103* (4), 525–547.

70. Orr, M., Stone, C., & Stumbo, C. (2002). *Concentrated poverty and educational achievement: Politics and possibility in the Baltimore region.* http://www.bsos.umd.edu/gvpt/stone/baltimore. html.

71. Orr, Stone, & Stumbo (2002).

72. Hallinan, M. (2001). Sociological perspectives on black–white inequalities in American schooling. *Sociology of Education* Extra Issue, 50–70.

73. Ball (2000); Gay (2000); Lipman (1996); Weisman, E. (2001). Bicultural identity and language attitudes: Perspectives of four Latina teachers. *Urban Education, 36* (2), 203–225.

74. Anyon (1997); Rist (1970).

75. Gay (2000).

76. Ayers, W., & Ford, P. (1996). *City kids. City teachers: Reports from the front row.* New York: The New Press; Dance (2002); Valenzuela, A. (1999). *Subtractive schooling: U.S.–Mexican youth and the politics of caring.* Albany: State University of New York.

77. Anyon (1997); Boyd, W. (1991). What makes ghetto schools succeed or fail?, *Teachers College Record, 92* (3), 331–362; Lipman (2002); Orr, M. (1999). *Black social capital: The politics of school reform in Baltimore, 1986–1998.* Lawrence: University of Kansas Press.

WHITENESS IN TEACHER EDUCATION

Patricia Burdell

So then going into it I was like really nervous so, oh my goodness, what's going to happen to me—and I'm talking to you know my sister who I live with, and she's, like, you know, "I can't believe they're going to make you go there" (laughter) "—and I'm like, "I know, I can't believe this, what if my car, you know—". . . because I have a pretty brand new car that I just got which I love, and so I was really scared and stuff.

The above quotation is representative of remarks made by my white preservice teacher education students in the course of interviews I did for a study on how they experience their whiteness in a field experience in a school that was 99.9 percent African American. I worked long and hard to do my personal and professional best to engage my students in an urban teaching context like the one I worked in and loved for 19 years. Getting them out of the car and into the building was not easy, nor was any other part of it easy. But for seven-plus years that I taught this class, I turned often to theory to help make sense of what I was trying to do. Much has been written categorizing various approaches to multicultural education,[1] and several specialized areas of educational theory focus on providing guidance to teacher educators regarding how to construct curricula that will prepare preservice teachers for contemporary diverse settings. The theoretical approach I am at home with is that of critical pedagogy, or in this instance, critical multicultural perspectives,[2] which is the subject of this chapter, a discourse on whiteness pedagogy.

From this perspective it is argued that a key aspect of the preparation of white students for multicultural environments is understanding how schools are affected by racism and difference. An important aspect of this approach is an understanding of how systems of racial domination and subordination position everyone racially, and impact teaching, learning, and achievement. From this perspective whiteness becomes racialized, meaning that white teachers are encouraged to problematize their shared experiences (and unearned privilege) to actively form alliances with people of color as part of a larger politics of inclusion and diversity. I open this chapter with a discussion of the diversity dilemma that teacher education faces, and then situate whiteness pedagogy as a specific strategy of critical multicultural education. Next I discuss student resistance to this pedagogy, how these resistances are viewed, and some of the classroom teaching experiences studied by educators utilizing this approach. Finally, I consider the effectiveness of whiteness pedagogy in informing how teacher educators engage preservice and in-service teachers with race.

THE DIVERSITY DILEMMA IN TEACHER EDUCATION

The diversity dilemma in teacher education is by no means new to many professionals in the field of teacher education research and policy. To some degree this insight is filtering into the popular press, which publicly comments on the fact that many urban districts are having difficulty hiring and retaining teachers. For example, one of CNN's Web page headlines announced, "White teachers fleeing black schools!" The story focused on the findings of three Georgia State University professors that Georgia's white elementary school teachers were more likely to quit schools with higher proportions of black students and that race was a factor. The story explained,

After the 1999–2000 school year, 31 percent of white teachers quit their jobs at schools where the student population was more than 70 percent black, and those who changed jobs went to schools that served lower proportions of black and poor pupils.

The story stated that other studies have shown "white teacher flight" in California, New York, Texas, and North Carolina The story cited lack of familiarity with black student culture, fear of poor neighborhoods, and the need to show improvement on assessments as reasons for this "white exodus."[3]

Public discussion on this issue often implicates the lack of appropriate preparation of new teachers. In the above mentioned CNN story a principal was quoted as saying, "[S]ome of the blame rests on university education schools. Because they don't train teachers for diverse classrooms, some young white teachers are bewildered by black schools."[4] Many, myself included, would argue that the best way to deal with the problem of enhancing the fit between teachers just out of teacher education programs and high-need urban districts would be to recruit more minority teacher candidates. In a survey by Urban Teacher Collaborative—made up of Recruiting New Teachers, Inc., the Council of the Great City Schools, and the Council of the Great City Colleges of Education—72.5 percent of the largest urban districts indicate they have an immediate need for teachers of color and have under way special recruitment efforts. However, as Hodgkinson states in *The Journal of Teacher Education,*

[T]he teaching force is actually becoming increasingly White, due mainly to the striking decline in Black, Hispanic and Asian enrollments in teacher education programs since 1990, with a proportional increase in minority business majors.[5]

Far from ignoring the need to prepare teachers for diverse teaching environments, there has been a profusion of educational literature addressing diversity within teacher education programs over the last decade. In fact, the National Council for Accreditation of Teacher Education (NCATE) standards, which govern teacher education in 48 states, directly require accredited programs to design, implement, and evaluate curricula and students so it can be documented that "candidates gain knowledge, skills, and dispositions necessary to help all students learn."[6] To this end, in order to be accredited, teacher education programs are required to submit documentation that their students have experience working with diverse higher education and school faculty, diverse candidates, and diverse students in K–12 schools.[7] In general, it can be argued that teacher educators are all too aware that students of color are the majority in 70 of the 130 largest districts in the United States and that a pool of new teachers must be prepared to teach in these schools.[8] They are just as aware that these districts are the least favored places to seek jobs by the majority of their preservice students. However, the NCATE standards for exposing students to diversity require that programs prepare all students in a "standard" fashion, meaning that all students must gain the knowledge, skills, and disposition to teach in all social contexts. This means teacher educators must devise curricula that guide student learning about multiple teaching contexts and provide them with the knowledge and skills to work in urban or other diverse environments—regardless of whether students themselves view this as their own personal career goal.

As Gay and Howard put it,

Coupled with the growing 'demographic divide' among students and teachers there are some troubling attitudes toward racial and ethnic diversity, such as . . . fear of teaching students of color and resistance to dealing directly with race and racism in teacher preparation and classroom practices.[9]

Although I agree with Christine Sleeter that it is inadequate to address racism in education by attempting to educate white teachers as opposed to promoting a more varied pool of teacher candidates, the reality of the institutions I inhabit daily is of a mass of students who are, as Ken Zeichner points out, overwhelmingly white and monolingual, and from rural or suburban communities with little direct intercultural experience.[10] The pragmatic question then becomes, how should we provide this varied group of predominately white students with opportunities to begin to understand diversity in contemporary educational settings and to become competent and professionally articulate concerning contemporary practice in multicultural social contexts.

CRITICAL PEDAGOGY OF WHITENESS

If multicultural curriculum is to help ameliorate the problem of cultural insularity in teacher education, it must provide teachers with knowledge, skills, and dispositions that will enable them to effectively teach ethnically, racially, socially, and linguistically diverse students. At its most basic, one of the established principals of multicultural education has been the need for teachers to become more consciously aware of and articulate about how culture influences development and how they are themselves both culturally the same as and different from their students. Gay and Howard argue,

Unless European-American teachers seriously analyze and change their cultural biases and ethnic prejudices (toward self and others) they are not likely to be very diligent and effective in helping students do likewise.[11]

A prerequisite for this kind of understanding is that students gain perspective on the connection between schools and society and how the everyday practices of schooling work to perpetuate existing social inequalities. Because college students most often come to professional education classes with naïve understandings of social structure, the foundational work of multicultural education becomes that of challenging students to question taken-for-granted assumptions about the social processes of schooling. In order to contextualize the discussion and situate these concepts in students' lived experiences, instructors facing classes that are 80–90 percent white begin to focus on encouraging students to understand how and why their experiences as white students are specific and limited as opposed to universal. As Alice McIntyre puts it, the practice of

examining the system of whiteness and the myriad ways that maintain and sustain educational and societal inequities is a way to disrupt the "dysconscious racism" that many white students bring to their academic environments.[12]

Teacher educators involved in constructing programs and courses from the perspective of critical multiculturalism are informed by a vast body of literature that is situated in interdisciplinary educational theory and draws from social theory, curriculum theory, cultural studies, and feminism. Practitioners informed by these theoretical approaches to multiculturalism attempt to bridge the fissure between academic theory and everyday practice in teacher education classrooms. One of the distinctions between this and other academic approaches to multiculturalism is that it has been informed by theoretical discussion of how and why, as opposed to focusing on the "otherness" of nonwhite people; the idea of being white must be interrogated as reifying or essentialist in multicultural teaching. As Leslie Roman explains in "White Is a Color!," "[T]he phrase 'people of color' still implies that white culture is the *hidden norm* against which all other racially subordinate groups' so-called differences are measured."[13]

Viewing whites as having a racial identity and examining the mechanisms of it's privileging has been considered key to interrupting the business as usual of racism. As Frankenberg states, "Naming 'whiteness' displaces it from the unmarked, unnamed status that is itself an effect of its dominance."[14] According to Joe Kincheloe and Shirley Steinberg, "[C]ritical advocates of pedagogy of whiteness examine the various ways that social forces, including language, knowledge, and ideology, shape white identity and positionality in contemporary American life."[15] For example, in a polemical article in the *Harvard Educational Review* titled "Rewriting the Discourse of Racial Identity: Towards a Pedagogy and Politics of Whiteness," Henry Giroux argues,

Whiteness must be theorized and discussed in a manner that recognizes the potential for criticism as well as the possibility for white students to recognize their own agency and legitimate place within the struggle for social change and an antiracist society.[16]

He goes on to say,

By positioning Whiteness within a notion of cultural citizenship that politically, culturally, and socially affirms difference, students can take notice of how their Whiteness functions as racial identity . . . White students can construct narratives of Whiteness that both challenge and, hopefully provide a basis for transforming the dominant relationship between racial identities and citizenship.[17]

Along the same lines, in an article appearing the same year, "Unthinking Whiteness, Rethinking Democracy: Or Farewell to the Blonde Beast; Toward a Revolutionary Multiculturalism," Peter McLaren states, "My message is that we must create a new public sphere where the practice of whiteness is not only identified and analyzed but also contested and destroyed." McLaren calls for *revolutionary multiculturalism*, which he argues,

is not limited to transforming attitudinal discrimination, but is dedicated to reconstituting the deep structures of political economy, culture, and power in social arrangements . . . The challenge is to create at the level of everyday life a commitment to solidarity with the oppressed and an identification with past and present struggles.[18]

Ideally, the goal of this kind of critical pedagogy is to lay a foundation that enables white students to understand their white privilege and to move forward as effective and confident professionals who can acknowledge their own racial identity in a way that makes it possible for them to understand and connect with the developmental needs of all children—regardless of race, ethnicity, language, and so forth. The goal should be to enable teachers to see multiple possibilities and consider multiple explanations for classroom occurrences. It is in nurturing this kind of thinking that Critical Pedagogy should excel. In outlining their approach to a pedagogy of whiteness, Kinchloe and Steinberg define it as a form of teaching that requires students to think about the implications of membership in a racial group. This includes the three tasks of: (1) understanding the positionality of whiteness, (2) identifying and abandoning the practice of white racism, and (3) developing a critical and progressive white identity. They argue, "The specifics of white cultural identity are still very fuzzy for many whites, and their ability to speak of the way their whiteness shapes their views of self and world is quite limited."[19] In their view, a critical pedagogy of whiteness must engage students in discussion in a nonthreatening atmosphere; or as Giroux states,

Analyzing the historical legacy of Whiteness as an oppressive racial force requires that students engage in a critical form of memory work, while fostering less a sullen silence or paralyzing guilt and more a sense of outrage at historical oppression and desire for racial justice in the present.[20]

STUDENT RESISTANCE

Despite calls for creating a nonthreatening atmosphere and fostering a healthy sense of outrage (at oppression) as opposed to sullen silence, the discussion of whiteness pedagogy has been accompanied at every step by discussion of distress at the instructional difficulties encountered by white student outrage *at* such pedagogies. The act of introducing the topic of race results in antagonistic student responses and dismissal of the topic on the part of some students, which in turn tends to shut down other students.[21] As a way of justifying refusal to discuss race as a factor in learning, many students argue that discussion of race and consciousness of race are in and of themselves the *cause* of racism. For many white students, race is a taboo topic that they are socialized to avoid.[22] Further, many students claim any discussion of race is divisive and itself racist. Kinchloe and Steinberg comment,

Faced with teachers who are reluctant to speak of whiteness and whose conceptual mapping of multiculturalism induces them to see no value in such a pedagogy, critical multiculturalists have a terrific task in front of them.[23]

This conflict between teacher and student has been described, lamented, and studied in multicultural scholarship. For example, in her study of white student teachers, McIntyre describes "white talk," or speech tactics her students used to resist conceptualizing racism in terms of power and privilege, such as evading questions, withdrawing from the discussion, remaining silent, and so forth. One of the strengths of critical approaches to education is that they provide a structural framework from which to understand how ideological values are embedded in structures of social power and how this works discursively to construct consciousness and subjectivity. Recent forays into identity politics, as discussed below, have resulted in considerable scholarship, especially in cultural studies, providing shape to the ideological landscape of white resistance to antiracist pedagogy and affirmative action programs.[24]

Perhaps the most disturbing aspect of this white resistance is the ideological construction of the "white victim." For example, in a well-known study of white university students, "White Reconstruction in the University," Charles Gallagher writes that white students "see themselves as victims of the multicultural, PC [politically correct], feminist onslaught."[25] He claims that many white students have interpreted academic requirements for multiculturalism as a form of "academic punishment" and charge that such curricula are biased. Many white students now perceive their whiteness as a liability rather than a privilege, and feel not only that they are not allowed to "be white," but that nonwhites somehow have more opportunity because of affirmative action and other policies designed to lessen discrimination. According to Gallagher, the enduring belief that the United States is a colorblind and egalitarian society with equal opportunities for all has provoked an angry and defensive posture by many white youth who no longer see themselves as racially invisible and now feel "branded" by their whiteness."[26]

Citing other studies, Ruth Frankenberg states that an underlying theme among white interviewees in several studies of the construction of whiteness is "the conviction that racial formation was, at this time in history, unfair to people like themselves." She states,

Time and again papers detailed white interviewees' sense that while "history" had perhaps dealt an unfair hand to racial and ethnic "minorities". . . history [is] over, and if people of color continued to fare badly, this was possibly thanks to their own lack of effort.[27]

Describing this sense of white victimization among education students, Sleeter observes:

In this era of the post-Civil Rights movement we are witnessing the turning back of the clock, as white people increasingly believe that not only was racism remedied during the 1960s and 1970s, but also that people of color now have systematic advantages over whites. . . . I hear more and more from students, "When are we going to talk about how I am now at a disadvantage because I'm white? When will we do something about reverse discrimination?"[28]

Howard Winant asserts that the representation of whiteness as disadvantage has few precedents in U.S. racial history. He states, "[T]his imaginary white disadvantage—for which there is almost no evidence at the empirical level—has achieved widespread popular credence, and provides the cultural and political 'glue' that holds together a wide variety of reactionary racial politics."[29] Winant argues that since the 1960s, racial discourse has been forced into new articulations—interpretations of the meaning of race and of the necessity of whiteness. The resulting "white racial dualism" is a division in white racial identities born of inheriting the legacy of both white supremacy and its privilege, and the civil rights movement's compelling moral and political challenges to white supremacy. As part of this process, "white identities are now contradictory, as well as confused and anxiety-ridden, to an unprecedented extent."[30]

The imaginary exclusion and denial of the importance of difference and of the advantages of whiteness expressed by the white middle class is understood by Cameron McCarthy as part of the politics of white middle-class resentment. McCarthy (1998) defines resentment as "the process of defining one's identity through the negation of the other [Nietzche, 1967] in popular culture and in education."[31] Resentment is a historically determined and culturally bound emotion that, according to Robert Solomon, is identified by its connection with power. Solomon states that the modern age is virtually defined by bourgeois resentment and the current climate is emotionally charged with resentment's impotent self-righteousness.

Resentment elaborates an ideology of combative complacency, a "leveling" effect that declares society to be "classless" even while maintaining powerful class structures of differences. It is also the pretense of a self-imposed helplessness . . .

active moralism and spirit of condemnation—toward the world.[32]

According to Solomon, resentment is not the same kind of feeling as self-pity, nor is it a burning anger or feeling of outrage in the face of injustice; it is rather an emotion that is obsessive and smoldering or seething, or fuming. Wendy Brown states that *ressentiment* is not a reactionary identity in the sense of being a reaction to an insurgent from below.[33] It is rather an embodiment of a nonclass identity injured and excluded from its own ideal. As Brown puts it, it is the result of ". . . the wounded character of politicized identity's desire."[34] In other words, the white middle class suffers *ressentiment* at being denied (as an entitlement), "an imagined idyllic, unfettered, and uncorrupted historical moment (implicitly located around 1955) when life was good—housing was affordable, men supported families on single incomes, drugs were confined to urban ghettos."[35] In this way the middle class become the (imaginary) excluded. Brown argues that *ressentiment* can be expressed as neoconservative antistatism, racism, with charges of reverse racism, and so forth discussed above.[36]

In the United States, the discourses above obscure how each of us is positioned differently and unequally within overlapping relations of power and privilege. The idea that individuals are self-made and self-sufficient ignores the historical and cultural construction of "difference." The goal of critical whiteness pedagogy is to move beyond simply allowing students to voice their racial politics. It is difficult to get beyond conversations essentializing whiteness, which are an effect of what Linda Brodkey labels "White Noise"—the idea that students cannot hear and respond to "multicultural voices" because they are distracted by White Noise, the "din of common sense . . . which cynically denies that difference matters, by dismissing it as superficial or

maligning it as divisive."[37] In addition, as Cynthia Lavin-Rasky points out, the focus on whiteness easily becomes entangled in internal tensions, in part because the reference to skin color can easily be understood as a concrete signification as opposed to an abstract political one, and reference to it "tempts an unsophisticated definition of racialized categories, including that of whiteness."[38] The pedagogical question that remains is how to open the range of subject positions available to white students in the midst of such misunderstanding, and how to enable students to think in terms of various social locations.

RESPONSES TO STUDENT RESISTANCE

In 1997 Giroux commented that there is an absence of work on whiteness regarding "how students might examine critically the construction of their own identities in order to rethink Whiteness as a discourse of both critique and possibility."[39] In the ensuing years there has been a considerable amount of investigation of the practice of what has become known as critical whiteness pedagogy, especially on the part of practitioners in teacher education as they investigate their own practices. The analyses below demonstrate the increasingly sophisticated theoretical vantage points authors use to understand the nature of student resistance and the implications for teaching future teachers. One approach is to view student resistance as a positive indication of the presence of critical pedagogy. Giroux states:

White students will offer enormous resistance to analyzing critically the normative-residual space of White cultural practice . . . Pedagogically, this suggests allowing students to air their positions on Whiteness and race regardless of how messy or politically incorrect such positions might be . . . [However,] [r]ather than arguing that students simply be allowed to voice their racial politics, I am suggesting they be offered space for dialogue and critique in which such positions can be engaged, challenged, and rearticulated through an ongoing analysis of the material realities and social relations of racism.[40]

Giroux and McLaren conceptualized their ideas of representational pedagogy and border pedagogy as a counterhegemonic political project in which teacher education becomes redefined so that the curriculum takes on the form of cultural politics. From their perspective, teachers are to engage in political struggles in their classrooms, schools, and communities.[41] This casts the problem of student resistance as a political problem, not an academic or curricular one.[42] Several studies of counterhegemonic teaching (or teaching directly informed by a political project) have appeared recently.[43] These studies reveal the texture of what goes on in classrooms and how instructors think about their work and its problems. The underlying assumption is that the resistance, although unpleasant and disturbing, is a necessary effect of counterhegemonic pedagogy.

For example, in a study in *Education and Urban Society*, Estella Chizhk reflects on her use of the social reconstructionist model of Grant and Sleeter, which she turned to as an African-American assistant professor teaching multicultural education to mainly white women students at a conservative Christian, suburban college. In order to understand student resistance—especially student comments on her teaching evaluations—and to help her think about changes in her teaching strategies, Chizhk reflected on the work of several theorists including Sleeter, McLaren, Tatum, and Helms. In the end, Chizhk was able to best understand white student resistance, in large part, as an aspect of "the culture of power,"[44] Lisa Delpit's term describing the relative lack of power teachers of color have over educational policy or theory. She felt it possible that students perceived her, a teacher of color, as having few valuable contributions to make to education in this

situation where her students were predominantly white and middle class. In the end she states, "[B]y engaging in reflective practices about my teaching and about behaviors of my students, I was able to modify the course to minimize (not eradicate) preservice teachers' resistance."[45]

In another study, Carol Schick investigated her classroom attempts at *oppositional pedagogy*. In this study she employed a poststructuralist discourse analysis to investigate "the radicalization of 18 white preservice teachers and the implications of this radicalization on their perception of antiracist pedagogy."[46] Schick makes the point that her interest is in the discursive processes available to these students as they reproduce themselves as dominant white preservice teachers. As a means of emphasizing this focus, she chose to interview only students who declared themselves to be sympathetic to teaching students of another race, in this case, Aboriginal children. Her purpose remained focused on the involuntary aspect of the discursive processes, such as student discussion of the naturalness of their decision to become teachers. Schick concludes her study by calling for "supporting resistance and trauma," that is, recognizing that resistance to oppositional pedagogy can be strong and discouraging and at times seem almost anti-educational, going against the idea of certain knowledge. However, Schick argues, the desire for certainty is what is problematic. Schick states:

Responsible disillusionment is a possibility for coping with the "messy contingency" of knowing that people in dominant positions doing oppositional pedagogy are not going to change the world, but neither should we stop trying to do what is necessary to try, including no longer telling victory narratives without (dominant) selves at the center. It is necessary to accept the challenge that Elizabeth Ellsworth (1997) describes: "to leave the field or point out the contradiction." [47]

The general form the studies above take is of reflection on the nature of white student resistance, followed by eventual resolve to accept the challenge as an inevitable result of transformative work. In the first case, Chizhk left the impression that she would not be permanently teaching multicultural education. At the very least, she felt unprepared for the assignment in the beginning. Her frank portrayal of the students' negative comments and the mismatch in student expectations of course content are extremely representative of the experiences of faculty dealing with multicultural education. While voicing the need to accept the resistance and, in effect, to reduce her expectations for social change, she remained detached. Chizhk points out that theorists like Sleeter argue that the purpose of multicultural education should be to promote teachers' social action. She states, "To achieve such goals, the qualifications of persons to teach to that objective should be based on more than simply the ethnicity of the instructor."[48] In Chizk's view this would be someone who knows the issues and has the strategies to cope with the resistance. In another paper, Schick gives a more skeptical or poststructural interpretation of the transformative possibilities of critical multiculturalism. The study of the resistance becomes a sort of end in itself—an occasion to observe the inevitable indeterminacy or lack of closure involved in critical work. The pedagogy stands as an interruption of hegemonic discourse, which renders it in and of itself a political act.

A second approach to understanding student resistance is provided by Nancy Lesko and Leslie Bloom. Their approach understands student resistance to multicultural pedagogy in relation to epistemology—or as they express it, from the perspective of theories of knowing and learning.[49] As opposed to viewing student resistance as an inevitable result of critical politicized pedagogy, Lesko and Bloom view it as a symptom of modernist assumptions underlying their pedagogy and slippage into positivist and rationalist discourse regarding the overcoming of racism, sexism, and other systems of oppression. Lesko and Bloom examined how the *pedagogical encounters* they had with their students limited the kinds of knowledge that could be constructed in the classroom. Through their discourse analysis and a process of reflection, Lesko and Bloom became aware that their pedagogical approach to multiculturalism seemed "to promote a new orthodoxy, a new authoritative knowledge of life in schools in which prejudice, racism and sexism are due to the lack of knowledge, or error in thinking."[50] However, considering recent feminist work on the construction of subjectivity reminded them that ". . . ignorance is an effect of a particular knowledge, not the absence of it." They began to see their concept of multicultural education as "grounded, if not in a science-fiction plot, at least in a fantasy one in which its main character, the teacher, is engaged in a heroic and solitary act."[51]

Although not abandoning the politicized content of their project—but rather, changing its pedagogical form—Bloom and Lesko, citing Bakhtin, call for "a strategy that emphasizes the production of interpretation as a means of focusing student attention at the multiple nature of truth." They say

One approach to breaking out of this crippling epistemology of positivist opposition may be to define and employ a dialogical theory of knowledge, in which any idea, concept, or utterance is interrogated for the necessary presence of other ideas, forming a chain of connotative associations. Dialogism might be employed as a form of classroom pedagogy to interrogate students' and teachers' utterances so that they might begin to understand the historical, cultural and sociological assumptions.[52]

Bloom and Lesko offer as an example assigning students to write two interpretations of a multicultural text, a conventional one and a critical one. In comparing the two texts, it is possible to see differences in language choice and the presence or absence of race, class, gender, and other power evasions. Because interpretations imply actions with moral dimensions, it is necessary to interrogate particular interpretations for how they would likely affect teachers' relationships with students, parents, and administrators. This emphasis on the dialogic character of knowing—with an emphasis on the production of interpretations that are always in relation to other interpretations—involves sharing the process of thinking about the nature of knowing with students.

CONCLUSIONS

As pointed out in the introduction, I have often turned to theory to help make sense of teaching preservice teachers how to think about urban classrooms. Has this been informative, and in what ways? To sum up my reading of the research and discussion above, the answer is Yes. This line of scholarship has been informative, especially in raising important issues and in interrogating the contradictions embedded within this work. The increasingly sophisticated approaches to the study of the resistance of teacher education students to a critical pedagogy of whiteness offer perspective, a foundation for reflection, and most important, a collegial and affirming conversation about how to blend theory and practice.

In terms of the goal of providing guidance to teacher educators regarding how to construct curricula that will prepare preservice teachers to teach in contemporary diverse settings, I think critical whiteness scholarship demonstrates that it is necessary to interrupt the misconceptions students often bring to teacher education and to foster critical thinking from multiple perspectives and about multiple ways of understanding students and the social contexts of teaching.[53] The work above makes us aware of areas that require special care and consideration to avoid slippage into the debris that can result from the storms and floods of racial discourse. Such slippage can accompany three major tendencies indicated in the work discussed above. The first is the tendency for slippage into combative metaphors and conflicts with students. This conflict casts them in the role of representatives of hegemonic power structures—allowing us as teachers to act out the role of transformative intellectual. As we can learn from Lesko and Bloom, it is more productive to flush out indications of ready-made scripts and to focus instead on the production of interpretations. By focusing on how students are conceptualizing and by explicitly teaching students the process of interpretation and critique, we can build student skill in conceptualizing difference.

The second tendency is for critical whiteness pedagogy to get tripped up in the internal tensions created by reference to skin color in a way that, as Lavin-Rasky puts it, "tempts" racial categorization in "unsophisticated" ways. The term unsophisticated in itself indicates the degree of conceptual complexity required for making the shift from skin color to structural location. As teachers, we know complexity tends to require time, and in this case it also requires knowledge of basic academic sociological concepts that most teacher students do not possess when they enter teacher education programs. This means that programs must be constructed so that prerequisite knowledge is present so that the distinctions of critical whiteness pedagogy can be clearly made. Absent these rational building blocks, classroom conversation is mired in vacuous opinion and emotion. This leads to the third tendency for slippage—the ever present and necessary emotional nature of the discussion. As the work on *ressentiment* above demonstrates, the emotional states are historic and are active in constructing ideology and resistance. To a considerable degree, emotion has been cast as an obstruction to thinking and has been devalued or silenced. Much more work is needed on this mechanism and on classroom implications of this dynamic.

Perhaps most important, scholarship of critical whiteness pedagogy reinforces awareness that the first priority of educators involved in preparing new teachers for urban teaching is to expand the variety of voices in teacher education programs. If educators genuinely want to extend the range and social power of discourse available to new teachers, it is essential, as Zeichner suggests, to find ways to recruit and retain a genuinely diverse body of new teachers.

NOTES

1. See discussions on the various approaches in Sleeter, C., & Grant, C. (1999). *Making choices for multicultural education: Five approaches to race, class, and gender* (3rd ed.). New York: John Wiley & Sons, Inc.; Kincheloe, J., & Steinberg, S. (1998). Addressing the crisis of whiteness: Reconfiguring white identity in pedagogy of whiteness. In J. Kincheloe, S. Steinberg, N. Rodriguez, & R. Chennault (Eds.), *White reign: Deploying whiteness in America* (pp. 3–20). New York: St. Martin's Griffin; and Mahalingam, R., & McCarthy, C. (2000). *Multicultural curriculum: New directions for social theory, practice and policy.* New York: Routledge.

2. Kincheloe, J., & Steinberg, S. (1997). *Changing multiculturalism.* Buckingham, UK: Open University Press; Sleeter, C., & McLaren, P. (2000). *Multicultural education, critical pedagogy, and the politics of difference.* Albany: State University of New York Press; and Sleeter, C. (1996) *Multicultural education as social activism.* Albany: State University of New York Press.

3. Associated Press. (2003, January 13). White teachers fleeing black schools! Retrieved July 7, 2004, from www.CNN.com/education.

4. Associated Press (2003, January 13).

5. Hodgkinson, H. (2002). Demographics in teacher education: An overview. *Journal of Teacher Education, 53* (2), 104.

6. "'All students' includes students with exceptionalities, and of different ethnic, racial, gender, language, religious, socioeconomic, and regional/geographic origins." National Council for Accreditation of Teacher Education. (2002). *Professional standards for the accredi-*

tation of schools, colleges and departments of education (footnote, p. 10). Washington DC: Author.

7. National Council for Accreditation of Teacher Education (2002).

8. Gay, G., & Howard, T. (2000). Multicultural teacher education for the 21st century. *The Teacher Educator, 36* (1), 1–16.

9. Gay & Howard (2000), p. 2.

10. Sleeter, C. (1993). How white teachers construct race. In C. McCarthy & W. Crinchlow (Eds.), *Race, identity and representation in education.* New York: Routledge; Zeichner, K. (1996). Implementing opportunity to learn, standards and assessment. In B. Williams (Ed.), *Closing the achievement gap: A vision for changing beliefs and practices* (pp. 138–153). Alexandria, VA: Association for Supervision and Curriculum Development.

11. Gay & Howard (2000), p. 5.

12. McIntyre, A. (1997). *Making meaning of whiteness: Exploring racial identity with white teachers* (p. 31). Albany: State University of New York Press.

13. Roman, L. (1993) White is a color! White defensiveness, postmodernism, and anti-racist pedagogy. In C. McCarthy & W. Crinchlow (Eds.), *Race, identity, and representation in education* (p. 71). New York: Routledge.

14. Frankenberg, R. (1993). *White women, race matters: The social construction of whiteness* (p. 6). Minneapolis: University of Minnesota Press.

15. Kincheloe & Steinberg (1997), p. 4.

16. Giroux, H. (1997). Rewriting the discourse of racial identity: Towards a pedagogy and politics of whiteness. *Harvard Educational Review, 67* (2), 285.

17. Giroux (1997), p. 299.

18. McLaren, P. (1997). Unthinking whiteness, rethinking democracy: Or farewell to the blonde beast; Towards a revolutionary multiculturalism. *Educational Foundations, 11* (2), 34.

19. Kincheloe & Steinberg (1997), p. 217.

20. Giroux (1997), p. 313.

21. See McIntyre, A. *Making meaning of whiteness*; and Lesko, N., & Bloom, L. (2000). The haunting of multicultural epistemology and pedagogy. In Malingham and McCarthy (Eds.), *Multicultural curriculum* (pp. 242–260).

22. Sleeter, C. How white teachers construct race; and Tatum, B. (1997). *"Why are all the black kids sitting together in the cafeteria?" and other conversations about race.* New York: Basic Books.

23. Kincheloe & Steinberg (1997), p. 219.

24. McIntyre (1997).

25. Gallagher, C. (1995). White reconstruction in the university. *Socialist Review, 94* (1–2), 169.

26. Gallagher (1995).

27. Frankenberg (1993), p. 89.

28. Sleeter. In McIntyre (1993), p. ix.

29. Winant, H. (1997). Whiteness and contemporary U.S. racial politics. In M. Fine, L. Weis, L. Powell & L. Wong (Eds.), *Off white: Readings on race, power, and society* (p. 42). New York: Routledge.

30. Winant. In Fine, Weis, Powell & Wong (1997).

31. McCarthy, C. (1998). Living with anxiety: Race and the renarration of public life. In J. Kinchloe, S. Steinberg, N. Rodriguez & R. Chennault (Eds.), *White Reign* (p. 330). New York: St. Martin's Griffin.

32. Soloman, R. (1990). Nietzsche, postmodernism, and resentment. In C. Koelb (Ed.), *Nietzsche as a postmodernist: Essays pro and contra* (p. 278). Albany: State University of New York Press.

33. Brown, W. (1995). *States of injury: Power and freedom in late modernity* (p. 55). Princeton, NJ: Princeton University Press; Nietzsche, 1918; Scheler. (1961). *Ressentiment* (W. Holdheim, Trans.). New York: Schocken Books. Brown, Nietzsche, and Scheler use the French word *ressentiment*. Solomon and McCarthy convert the word to the English spelling.

34. Brown (1995), p. 55.

35. Brown (1995), p. 60.

36. Brown (1995), p. 67.

37. McCoy, K. (1997). White noise—the sound of epidemic: Reading/writing a climate of intelligibility around the "crisis" of difference. *Qualitative Studies in Education, 10* (3), pp. 335–336.

38. Lavine-Rasky, C. (2000). Framing whiteness: Working through the tensions in introducing whiteness to educators. *Race, Ethnicity and Education, 3* (3), 273.

39. Giroux (1997), p. 314.

40. Giroux (1997), p. 312.

41. Giroux, H., & McLaren, P. (1986). Teacher education and the politics of engagement: The case for democratic schooling. *Harvard Educational Review, 56* (2), 213–238.

42. Morrow, R., & Torres, C. (1995). *Social theory and education: A critique of theories of social and cultural reproduction*. Albany: State University of New York Press.

43. See Aveling, N. (2002). Student teachers' resistance to exploring racism: Reflections on 'doing' border pedagogy. *Asia-Pacific Journal of Teacher Education, 30* (2) 119–130; Johnson, 2002; and McIntyre, 1997.

44. Delpit, L. (1988). The silenced dialogue: Power and pedagogy in educating other people's children. *Harvard Educational Review, 58* (3), 280–298.

45. Chizhik, E. (2003). Reflecting on the challenges of preparing suburban teachers for urban schools. *Education and Urban Society, 35* (4), 459.

46. Schick, C. (2000). By 'virtue of being white': Resistance in anti-racist pedagogy. *Race, Ethnicity, and Education, 3* (1), p. 85.

47. Schick (2000), p. 100.

48. Chizhik (2003), p. 457.

49. Lesko, N., & Bloom, L. (1998). Close encounters: Truth, experience and interpretation. *Curriculum Studies, 30* (4), 375–395.

50. Lesko & Bloom (1998), p. 381.

51. Lesko & Bloom (1998), p. 388.

52. Lesko & Bloom (1998), p. 389.

53. King, J. (1994). Dysconscious racism: Ideology, identity, and the miseducation of teachers. In L. Stone (Ed.), *The Education Feminism Reader* (pp. 336–348). New York: Routledge.

SHOULD THE HOLOCAUST BE TAUGHT IN URBAN SCHOOLS?

Tibbi Duboys

In recent years, the state of New York added to its education law mandates to teach the Holocaust, the Irish potato famine, the underground railroad, and the slaughter of Armenians. The degree to which this is enforced, however, is not widely documented, and is uneven at best. It becomes increasingly important to teach children about these travesties earlier than they are currently taught, so as to offer time and practice in examining the injustices embedded in them, and, it is hoped, to develop strategies to live peaceably with others. Teachers need greater dominion over curriculum, and these ideas are important ones to bring into urban classrooms.

The issues of the Holocaust mandate questions about personhood—one's own and others'. Looking at the Holocaust entails confronting ourselves, perhaps to visit a place within us we haven't been to previously. Children and youth in urban schools tend to be poor, to be of color, and often to be English language learners.[1] It seems especially important to know about others outside of the boundaries of one's daily life.[2] "What would I do if I went home after school, and my parents didn't come home?" "What would I do if it was no longer safe for me to go to school?"[3] "What would I do if my school said I and people of my *race* were responsible for all of the evils that exist in this country?" "What would I do if the school didn't let me return?"[4]

Many urban youth are members of groups that are and have been discriminated against, and are more likely to be seen as "the problem" in our society, so it would seem they are familiar with the language of discrimination and with that which is unfair. "What would I do if none of the friends I had were allowed to be seen speaking with me?"[5] Few events we address in schools are as contemporary as the Holocaust. There are living witnesses to the events mentioned above—events of the Holocaust—which is quite unlike other studies in which we engage.[6]

Diversity in urban settings should most naturally lead us to curiosity about others. Sometimes we find we have stereotypic notions of "them" that need to be confronted. All of us have histories that are

legacies of a past that cannot be redressed. But we can, in schools, focus on the need to include others, if for no other reason than that we, ourselves, would not want to be excluded from society.

Studying the Holocaust represents, in some respects, the quintessential stereotyping. All Jews were lumped together because they were Jews. There was even an elaborate system of labeling people dependent upon the number of Jewish grandparents they had.[7] Although some Jews converted to Christianity in the hope they would thus be more accepted in the society that was determined to reject them, they found their conversions didn't matter if they hadn't taken place prior to a certain date, and that date got earlier and earlier.

A focus on Jews is related to urban children and youth in general, who sometimes feel despised and excluded from this society. They do not fit the norm of what is considered beautiful, or smart, or admired. And there is a further connection in the fact that for Jews, during the Holocaust, what they were, what they did, and how they behaved was of no moment. The intent was to rid all Europe of Jews. Ultimately, two-thirds of European Jewry was murdered. Among those killed were artists, poets, actors, scientists, doctors, teachers, lawyers, postal workers, clerks, as well as thieves and drunkards.[8] They were targets merely because they were Jews. Never before in human history has there been the intention to murder an entire group of people, and never in recorded human history had children and youth been a particular target of such aggression, humiliation, and murder.[9] It was thought that if children were killed, there would be no one to bear witness. It is therefore a tiny step—not a quantum leap—to substitute any of the groups that compose urban landscapes and to substitute the words *my group* for the word *Jew*.

In a more perfect world, we would truly find value in the diversity that is everywhere around us in urban settings. The Holocaust is an example of the opposite of that which we educators strive to achieve. It speaks not of inclusion, but of the ultimate exclusion and the genocide so readily born of the lies and hate that preceded it.[10]

Another reason to teach the Holocaust has to do with those who are members of minority groups. Each *minority* is quite isolated, so that even if we live in neighborhoods where many of the people are *like* us, in the larger scheme we are only loosely connected to others, even those of our own ethnic group in more distant places. We do not have a central leader, confederation, or strong lobbying force to press for our needs. We are, each of us individually, ripe for scapegoating, since the *majority* are not likely to concern themselves with the injustices to which *we* are subjected. As educators, we can teach children and youth that when we do join with others, we increase the power of our individual voices as well as our presence, and thus become a more visible force that can't as readily be ignored.

As I write, snow swirls outside, although it is April. I'm reminded of the bone-chilling cold in April, 1993, when the Holocaust Memorial Museum in Washington first opened. As I waited in line to enter the area where the dedication was to take place, someone remarked that I looked cold. (It might have been my hunched-up posture and chattering teeth that gave me away.) "Compared to Auschwitz?" I asked. The speaker, who had an accent, decided I had a point. No complaints from me, as each time I think I'm cold, I'm reminded of malnourished people in thin clothing, covering the holes in their shoes with rags or paper, walking great distances to quotidian labors. And nowhere, in any of the memoirs I've read, do people speak of having had a cold. They have memories of hunger, of filth, of infected—and in the absence of medicines, unhealed—wounds, but never of the symptoms of colds or flu. Yet when

we suffer from those maladies, we often remove ourselves from our daily routines because of our weakened state and discomfort. Our sense of well-being and discomfort seem relative to the experiences of others, and therein lies another reason to consider teaching about the Holocaust.

It seems especially clear in urban settings that, as we consider those around us, diversity is everywhere in evidence. We're accustomed to seeing those who look different from ourselves. We urban folk are less likely, as Israel Zangweill thought, to "have the dislike of the unlike." We can imagine what it might be like to be a member of a group other than our own. We have seen Asians, Africans, Latinos/-as, even if we're not members of any of the cultures that emanate from Asia, Africa, or Latin America. We need but to stretch, to learn about the cultures of others, and if well taught, to introject the lessons of their past, in the process of understanding. In order to truly understand others, we need to make them real, to identify with their stories, and to take unto ourselves their plight, ever mindful that we know only part of what they have experienced.

In working with students who are preparing to become teachers, or when working with in-service teachers, I do not permit them to compare one group with another. The issues embedded in the Holocaust, unique to Jews, are now part of world history and should not be compared with any of the other abuses we human beings are so practiced in inflicting upon others. The Irish potato famine, the colonization of Puerto Rico, the slaughter of Armenians, and the history of slavery in America are but some examples of damaging and dreadful experiences of various groups of people. But they are each incomparable. To compare them is to trivialize each saga, each life lost, each act of resistance by victims of oppression. The question is not, "Who suffered most?" Rather we might consider how we can do better. As educators, shouldn't we teach about the insidious way in which hate has been, too often in human history, connected to violence? Are we not responsible to teach that the frequency of violence—the bombardment of it in history and in the media—should be repugnant to us? Are we not also obligated to know we cannot reclaim the past, although we can point to a more benevolent future if we eschew some of the actions that have taken place in the world we have been bequeathed. I do not mean this in the sense that knowing about the past will prevent its recurrence.[11] Rather, I mean *how* we learn it—the questions we ask ourselves and the choices we make in response to them—impel us to see events of the past with different eyes. In learning about stories of oppression, we might also consider their relationship to us. That people have acted toward others in particular ways does not insulate us from similar or even worse treatment in a future in which we have become so savvy that there are bombs that can kill people and leave buildings intact. Rather, one hopes teachers will raise questions and offer choices, so students will refuse to act in ways that are damaging and oppressive to others. One hopes our students will find oppression so vile that they will refuse to be perpetrators or bystanders in quite the same way they would refuse to be victims.[12]

Perhaps Elie Wiesel is right in his suggestion that the opposite of love is not hate, but indifference. What processes must take place in order to introject the lessons of history, to lay claim to them within ourselves? In what ways do those events seem familiar in my own experiences? Even very young children understand the importance of families. They also understand the joy of their friendships and their pain when a good friend turns away from them, refuses to be with them, and chooses someone else. That was, of course, the experience of many Jewish children whose Christian friends rejected them after the Nazis rose to power.[13]

While urban settings are particularly violent, the violence that took place in the Holocaust was better organized than any in previous history. Never before had there been participation by all agencies of government and in all strata of society. It involved fire companies, standing by watching while synagogues and Jewish-owned businesses burned to the ground on Nov. 9, 1938. It involved the indifference of police, who observed Nazi youth attack and beat Jews on the streets of cities throughout Germany. It involved the courts, whose judges were—it has been proven—responsible for tens of thousands of deaths of Jews, communists, and trade unionists.[14] It involved the civil service, who did not protest the expulsion of Jews from government work.[15] It points to the complicity of physicians and lawyers who did not publicly protest the Nuremberg laws that militated against their Jewish colleagues. It involved the culpability of the academy, whose professors were silent about the dismissal of Jewish colleagues and the disappearance of Jewish students.[16] It involved the entire society—one in which books by Jews and by non-Jews whose work was deemed decadent, were burned. Heine's warning seems prescient, "Where they burn books, they will also burn human beings."

While the population of Holocaust survivors grows smaller with each passing day, there are witnesses to those events who are resources for our understanding of that time. In classes I have taught, students are confronted with a great deal of material to read. The story is not one with a happy ending, and they are confronted—bombarded even—with unrelenting ugliness and horror. Most students seem to think the high point of the courses has been the presence of a speaker, a survivor of the Holocaust who makes his experiences real to them. It points to the importance of videotaping survivors and their narratives, so that we, who are relatively removed from that time, may make a connection with survivor's stories and our own lives. It helps one realize the survivors were also children who went to school, who celebrated holidays and rites of passage with families, friends, neighbors.[17] It helps to provide context to stories that might otherwise be removed from our own direct experiences, because it's always difficult to imagine the world before we were born.

Talented teachers focus on the overarching concepts that become bases for the kinds of thinking one hopes students will ponder. Many naturalized citizens whose children are born in their adopted nations may be particularly devoted to laws that govern their lives in their new country. At the urban public university where I teach, students are invited to consider what would happen to them if their citizenship were rescinded. The Third Reich provided this very precedent. Victims of the Reich's revocation of citizenship found their countries of origin would not allow them back. Without a passport, they were held hostage, as it were, in a nation that neither wanted them, nor would permit them to leave. It is often said the frustration of Henryk Grynspan, the son of Polish Jews who immigrated to Germany, led to Kristallnacht. The 17-year-old was in Paris to study. Enraged by his parents' statelessness, he shot Ernst Von Rath, an attaché in the German embassy there. When the diplomat died two days later, organized chaos erupted in Germany in response to the shooting. Here, too, is an important concept to teach students:[18] Hostile and violent actions by perpetrators often exaggerate an initial action, for which its victims are punished. The stimulus for punishment may be evil retribution for an initial act. Thus, the death of one person resulted in what is now called Kristallnacht. It entailed the destruction of synagogues and Jewish-owned businesses throughout Germany, in massive arrests, and in the deaths of several hundred Jews. The victims were then blamed for the destruction, forced to pay for the damage, and made to clean the mess created around them. This phenomenon occurred repeatedly. Early on, before the war began in 1939, people were rounded up and sent to Dachau, the first of the concentration camps in which crematoria were installed. Although some internees were released after several weeks, many were killed there and then cremated. A messenger of the Reich would visit the family with a box of ashes and tell the family their loved one had died of a heart attack. In time, such boxes came through the mail, with an enclosed note telling families they had to pay the charges for shipping and handling.

Teaching about the Holocaust, which is unique in human history, should impel us to challenge some widely held assumptions, in addition to forcing us to examine some of our own beliefs. I'm reminded of a Jewish friend from a Hungarian family that emigrated here between 1890 and 1907. He thought Jews should have left Europe at the first sign of discrimination after Hitler came to power. Although he was a brilliant thinker in his own academic discipline, he neglected to raise questions that might have made his comments more understanding of what it meant to be Jewish in Europe. There have been many instances throughout Jewish history of great repression. There were ups and downs of life under Czars. There was the Pale of Settlement, which confined Jews to a specific area. There were pogroms, usually close to Easter, because Jews were thought to be Christ-killers. In various centuries, Jews had been expelled from England, France, Spain, Portugal, and Germany. There were ghettoes in cities to which Jews were confined. The last to be disbanded was in Italy, a country with its own tortured history, but one in which 85 percent of Jews survived despite its early commitment to Mussolini's Fascism.[19] Early in the

Third Reich, Jews, who had historically faced great oppression, believed that the Nuremberg Laws would pass as had other restrictive laws that affected Jews. As we learned after the war, few people believed destruction of such magnitude would be possible, and it was not widely envisioned. My friend not only missed the historical context, he did not consider reasons why individual families did not leave when escape was still possible. In some families, people refused to leave an elderly or ill relative who could not have withstood travel. Some were too poor to muster the resources necessary to pay for transportation. Families whose religious observance was central to their lives would not leave the graves of their loved ones. They could not have known how many cemeteries would be stripped of monuments—ground up for hastily paved roads for the advance of the German military. They also thought, as did much of the world, that a nation as cultured as Germany could not be a place in which such destruction could be planned and implemented.

Jews were, throughout their history, accustomed to being thought of as outsiders. Thus, a German Jew was thought of not as German, but as a Jew. The only nation in Europe whose Jewish citizens were considered equal to all others was Denmark. I'm reminded of a recent experience on a train from Los Angeles to San Diego. Somewhere in Orange County, two teenagers boarded the train. They had never been on a train before and had difficulty in finding the ladies' room. As they sat opposite me, they talked about their school—a fundamentalist Christian one—and about their friends, social activities, and so forth. One asked what nationality I am. I told her "I'm American." She asked again. I said, "America is the nation of my birth, and where we're born is our nationality, so were you really asking something else? Did you mean what religion am I?" Yes, that was it. When I told her, "I'm Jewish," she remarked that I am really not American, since I'm Jewish. Clearly, neither her school nor her family had helped to dispel this young woman's concepts about others. The notion of the "hyphenated American" was incomprehensible to her. Finally, I asked if she were more Pentecostal or more American. She assured me she is both. Whether she was able to make the leap necessary to understand this aspect of the personal identity of others, I cannot say, because our trip was coming to an end.

When we concern ourselves with overarching concepts and probing questions, as teachers we're faced with trying to dispel popularly held notions that limit and distort the past. We often hear that Jews went to their deaths "like lambs to the slaughter," thus raising questions about blaming victims for their own misfortune.[20] We ask how likely people are to resist if restriction of their rights is part of their history. One asks how informed decisions can be made in the absence of information, in the presence of blatant and direct lies, and in the reality of sustained malnutrition? At this point, we're accustomed to the phrase "resettlement in the East" and wonder how people could have been naive enough to believe it.[21] Here again, it is important to understand context—the history of victimization, and the unprecedented organization of mass murder. Thus, as teachers, we raise questions about the conditions in place that allow for scapegoating to thrive and flourish. One has only to examine events in most of Europe in order to understand that the magnitude of Nazi hate and destruction could not have been so pervasive without the complicity of people in almost every nation. We examine the thoughts and beliefs just below the surface that will, under certain conditions, help impel action. We raise questions about empowering a charismatic leader.[22] And we should not lose sight of our willingness to dispense with our own personal liberties and give them up to the governance of others. When we see films of a shouting, podium-slapping Hitler, many people laugh and suggest that he ranted and raved like a madman. This won't do, for educators. If we say someone is crazy, that ends the conversation, since there isn't much more to be said and little to be examined. Rather we need to point to the agenda of the "crazy" one, and to his followers.[23] They were not, as is sometimes said, stupid. Those who constructed The Third Reich were often educated people, some of whom held doctorates and some of whom came from old and noble families where anti-Semitism had a long history. We need to remember that gas chambers were designed by professionally educated engineers, and their success in completing their tasks was applauded. We raise questions about the connection between belonging and independence. And we also raise questions about when we take action against a regime. When does one comply? How do we respond to threats to ourselves and our families? It is one thing to say we would aid victims, but another to know we would receive the same treatment as the victims, were we found to be giving aid. One strategy of Nazi oppression was to prove a point by making public examples of those who disobeyed. The sadism, the unprecedented cruelty of perpetrators who forced parents to witness the murder of their children before they were killed, needs to be studied and focused upon. And we must ask ourselves the fundamental question, "Under what circumstances could we, ourselves, kill another person?" Where did such sadistic and murderous impulses come from? How can we examine our own darker side?[24]

The Holocaust forces to us consider teaching some aspects of religious practice that are not usually addressed in urban public schools. Although urban youth might readily identify as Jews children who attend yeshiva because they dress differently than public school youth, one cannot generally identify Jews by their appearance. One might have to teach about the practices of observant Jews, who consid-

ered modesty in great detail. While images of the body were far less public in the 1930s than is currently the case, married Jewish women were expected to cover the parts of the body thought to be sexually provocative. Their hair had to be covered in public, as did their arms, knees, and shoulders. At the time of their imprisonment in camps, people were forced to march naked before the Nazis who would determine whether they would live or die. In a number of memoirs, survivors record the shock and shame of being naked in the company of others, especially members of the opposite sex. Women sometimes wrote that even they had never before seen their mothers naked.[25] This provides insight into yet another aspect of oppression. It is always the intention of oppressors to humiliate and demoralize their victims. Most often, more than one way is found to achieve those aims, and the history of many peoples is replete with such examples.

It is sometimes useful to be able to identify with stories of others' experience. In Poland, for example, the Nazis counted upon and received help from many Poles and Ukrainians. Approximately 3 million Jews lived in Poland prior to the war. Nearly one-third of Warsaw, Poland's capital, was inhabited by Jews. Germany invaded Poland on September 1, 1939, and in the ensuing five years, Nazis were able to murder millions of Polish Jews. They were helped in identifying them by Polish people, who had lived in close proximity to Jews for hundreds of years. That is not to say that Poles didn't also offer to aid Jews, although in the main, they did not. Poles were also victimized by the Nazis, who considered Slavs just one step above Jews. Sociologist Nechama Tec interviewed Poles who rescued Jews. These were people who used their own resources to provide shelter and support, as opposed to the helpers, paid by those Jews who could afford it to offer assistance. She found only a few hundred Poles who admitted they had been rescuers. A small number did what they did because they were on the margins of society. In a nation as homogeneous as Poland, where most people attended a Catholic church at a given time on Sunday, these were people not likely to attend and who were considered by others to be alienated from the society of the majority. She found another small group who explained their actions as "the right thing to do." They saw an injustice to their fellow human beings and did their best to combat the evil they witnessed. But the overwhelming majority in Tec's sample said they'd hated Jews prior to the war and during the war, and many years later, at the time of the interviews, they still hated them. Their country was under siege by an enemy; as Polish patriots, they hated Germans even more than they hated Jews. Thus they took pride not in helping others, but in helping to thwart the aims of their enemies.[26]

The Holocaust was a time when fear was a constant companion of Jews. People could not make informed decisions because they had limited information. They didn't fully know whom they could trust, and who lived in the service of the hate filled times. My uncle told the following story: When the Lvov ghetto was liquidated, trucks came to take people away. People were forced into a large open area and boarded the trucks in the most crude manner possible. Children, for example, who could not mount the trucks themselves, were picked up by the overseers and hurled onto them. Often, they did not survive. My uncle's neighbor, a middle-aged woman who covered her hair with a scarf, was climbing aboard one of the trucks when another neighbor—someone with whom the first woman had always had close relations—rushed up, pulled the scarf from her head, and said, "You won't need this where you're going." On the other hand, a man I know whose family had a very old and valuable violin entrusted it to a neighbor when they were forced into the

ghetto in Radom. Over the course of time, the man not only took care of it, but also learned to tune and repair violins, which gave him great pleasure. Many years after the war, my friend went to Poland and found the man who'd kept his instrument. The man brought it to him, and showed him the fine shape it was in. My friend couldn't believe his good fortune, since he knew not all Jews had their property returned by people to whom they entrusted valuable belongings. The man wouldn't hear of payment, and waved away thanks. He explained he'd learned new skills that gave him an income and provided great pleasure, and for that he felt grateful to my friend, whose instrument provided the impetus for him to achieve what he did.[27] Embedded in this story is another reality frequently experienced during the Holocaust. This family had to part with the prized instrument because they were going into the ghetto—a change that represented a huge loss, because from the ghettos, should people survive the near-starvation and epidemiological illnesses, they went to concentration camps. There, some would work as slave laborers, whereas others would be put to death soon after they arrived. All who went to camps were forced to leave the possessions with which they had arrived. They were told to strip so they could shower, and that their belongings would be returned to them afterward. This was never the case, however. Those sent to gas chambers had no further need of earthly possessions, and those who did in fact stand briefly under running water were issued uniforms. Every intention was made to further humiliate the new arrivals, such as by issuing to a short person the uniform for a tall person, and making the tall one look ludicrous in the uniform of someone short. This left victims to scramble among themselves to trade with someone for something more suitable to wear. This proved to be a great joke to their Nazi captors and their helpers.[28]

Some final thoughts as to why the Holocaust should be taught in urban schools include basic realities of an urban existence. Urban children and youth clearly live with the dangers that are prevalent in cities. Many children are not permitted to play in the streets near their homes because their parents are afraid of ever-present gangs, drugs, and guns. Many children should thus identify with the children of the Holocaust and with their constant fear. They too were forbidden to play on the streets where they were in hiding. A woman I know spent the time between her eighth and tenth years in the hayloft of a barn, where she was lucky enough to be hidden with her family. When they were finally liberated, she found she was unable to speak above a whisper, since she'd been forbidden to do so for nearly two years. She did not regain her normal voice until a long time after liberation.

We might caution children about the trappings of authority. In Germany, for example, in order to show Aryans' "racial superiority," teachers often dressed in white lab coats and used calipers to measure the circumference of the heads of their students. They took other measurements as well, with great apparent authority. Their students, seeing the certainty and confidence with which these acts were carried out, believed them. Those students chose to have faith in that which made them feel better about themselves, and ultimately, entitled to the privileges of superiority. Also appearing to carry great weight and authority were the shiny boots of marchers and the camp guards' warm woolen coats, which were symbols of the authority wielded over the victims of concentration camps.

In addition, we might teach students about the danger and the personal cost of striving to belong to the majority. In some sense, trying to belong to the majority is a giving up of one's self, the burial of personal thoughts and beliefs for slogans, and a political agenda that may not truly reflect one's own beliefs. The minority status of youth in our society, paired with the plight of urban youth in particular, give pause with respect to the lengths to which one might go in order to belong.

For Jews, the Holocaust represents what had never previously happened in their history. In other nations and at other times, they had the option of converting to Christianity or of going into exile. During the Holocaust, there was no option for Jews. They were victims destined to be eliminated no matter what their peacetime lives had been. Some of those murdered were religiously observant, whereas others were not. Some were politically active, others not. Some were from wealthy, upper–class, educated, and professional families; others were poor and barely literate.[29] Not social class, degree of observance, nor status in the society mattered. In short, there was no way to escape the ever-increasing threat to their lives.

One has only to visit an urban school lunchroom to see the contiguity of our current existence. One sees African Americans sitting with African Americans, Korean Americans with other Korean Americans, Caribbeans with others from the same area, and Latinos/-as grouped according to national origin, for example, Mexicans seated apart from Dominicans. Let's hope this century is one in which we learn to demystify others. If we can't truly call them brothers and sisters, we can at least offer them the respect that is due each person.

Finally, teaching about the Holocaust enables us get past the mystique with which we regard each other. One hopes we will help students see that we are truly involved with each others' suffering. Therein lies great hope for humanity.

NOTES

With thanks to Jerry Weisfogel, who was first to see the possibilities.

1. McNeil, L. (2000). Creating new inequalities: Contradictions of reform. *Phi Delta Kap-*

pan, 729–734; Kozol, J. (1991). *Savage inequalities: Children in America's schools.* New York: Crown.

2. Soto, L. (2001). Silenced lives. In J. Kincheloe & D. Weil (Eds.), *Standards and schooling in the United States: An encyclopedia* (pp. 169–181). Santa Barbara, CA: ABC Clio.

3. David, K. (1989). *A child's war: World War II through the eyes of children.* New York: Four Walls Eight Windows.

4. Appelman-Jurman, A. (1988). *Alicia, my story.* New York: Bantam.

5. Cretzmeyer, S. (1994). *Your name is Renee.* Brunswick, ME: Biddle Publishing.

6. Kovaly, H. (1989). *Under a cruel star.* New York: Penguin Books; Baer, E. (1980). *A frost in the morning.* New York: Schocken.

7. Koehn, I. (1977, 1990). *Michling, second degree: My childhood in Nazi Germany.* New York: Puffin.

8. Roskies, D. (1984). *Against the apocalypse: Responses to catastrophe in modern Jewish culture.* Cambridge: Harvard University Press.

9. Lifton, B. (1988). *The king of children.* New York: Farrar, Straus & Giroux.

10. McKale, D. (2002). *Hitler's shadow war/the Holocaust and World War II.* New York: Cooper Square Press.

11. Dwork D., & van Pelt, R. (2002). *Holocaust: A history.* New York: W.W. Norton.

12. Levi, P. (1973). *Survival in Auschwitz.* New York: Collier Macmillan.

13. Zyskind, S. (1983). *Stolen years.* New York: Signet.

14. Barkai, A. (1989). *From boycott to annihilation.* Hanover, NH: University Press of New England for Brandeis University Press.

15. Richter, H. (1970, 1987). *Friedrich.* New York: Puffin.

16. Taylor, T. (1992). *The anatomy of the Nuremberg Trials.* New York: Knopf.

17. Eliach, Y. (Ed.). (1990). *We were children just like you.* Brooklyn, New York: Center for Holocaust Studies Documentation and Research.

18. Read, A., & Fisher, D. (1989). *Kristallnacht.* New York: Random House.

19. Zuccotti, S. (1987). *The Italians and the Holocaust.* Lincoln, NE: University of Nebraska Press.

20. Kaplan, C. (1965). *Scroll of agony: The Warsaw diary of Chiam A. Kaplan.* New York: Macmillan.

21. Lewin, A. (1988). *A cup of tears.* Oxford: Basil Blackwell.

22. Johnson, E. (2000). *Nazi terror.* New York: Basic Books.

23. Laquer, W. (1996). *Fascism/past, present and future.* New York: Oxford University Press.

24. Frister, R. (1993, 1999). *The cap: The price of a life.* New York: Grove Press.

25. Jackson, L. (1980). *Elli: Coming of age in the Holocaust.* New York: Times Books.

26. Tec, N. (1986). *When light pierced the darkness.* New York: Oxford.

27. Gotfryd, B. (2001). *Anton the dove fancier and other tales of the Holocaust.* Baltimore: Johns Hopkins.

28. Bartoszewski, W. (1987). *The Warsaw ghetto: A Christian's testimony.* Boston: Beacon Press.

29. Ringelblum, E. (1974). *Notes from the Warsaw ghetto.* New York: Schocken.

RETHINKING THE *WHITE MAN'S BURDEN*: IDENTITY AND PEDAGOGY FOR AN INNER-CITY STUDENT TEACHER

John Pascarella and Marie Gironda

ACKNOWLEDGING THE BURDEN: MARIE'S STORY

Since I have been teaching for 31 years to an audience consisting primarily of African-American students, I have sublimi-nally incorporated many of the cultural theories that John (John Pascarella, student teacher who recently completed an internship in an inner-city high school in northern New Jersey) has been research-ing and studying without consciously realizing my own interpretations of the *White Man's Burden* concept. When John came to my classroom, he was primarily concerned with the cultural composition of the student body and his desire to apply the cultural theories he had studied to teaching inner city students. When John began his teaching internship, I did not fully comprehend this aspect of his concentration because all of my efforts were placed in developing his English Literature knowledge base and his pedagogical skills while attempting to maintain the pre-college academic level and pacing that previously existed in my classroom. As John and I discussed his struggle to combine theory and practice, he became more aware of the need to make the transition to viewing himself as an English teacher as I became more knowledgeable of the cultural theories embedded in my teaching style. As a result, I have begun to further examine and evaluate my pedagogical style and curricular choices, while I believe John has begun to understand the ways in which he can subtly blend cultural studies with the teaching of literature, regardless of the cultural origins of that literature.

IDENTIFYING THE BURDEN: JOHN'S STORY

From the moment I realized as an undergrad that I wanted to teach, I began a journey down a path that forced me to examine the components of my identity and my assumptions about those components. Grappling with the elements that constituted the multicultural pedagogy presented to me in my teacher preparation program, breaking down the world around me, circumventing the perspectives of research I was immersed in, and attending academic conferences aided a self-proclaimed mission to become a critical pedagogue. As I crossed borders and realities, leaving home and driving from a predominantly white, upper-middle-class suburb in northern New Jersey to a non-white, lower-class, inner-city community just ten minutes away, I began to negotiate the detours of identity. These detours led to reinventing my *whiteness*, or white identity, and developing pedagogical and social connections with students who happen to be mostly black and of ranging economic and cultural backgrounds.[1]

My path and the recognitions that I experienced should not be read as the answer to how to be a white teacher with students who are from various racial backgrounds; that is, this isn't a guide to understanding how to be white around students who are not. I urge you to engage in the following discussion and pose your own answers to the questions that are raised about identity and critical pedagogy in this unique conversation between me and my former cooperating teacher and mentor, Marie Gironda. In doing so, both authors hope that you will raise your own questions as you begin your journey to becoming a teacher. Gilroy notes:

We live in a world where identity matters. It matters both as a concept, theoretically, and as contested fact of contemporary life. The word itself has acquired a huge contemporary resonance, inside and outside the academic world. It offers much more than an obvious, common-sense way of talking about individuality and community. Principally, identity provides a way of understanding the interplay between our subjective experience of the world and the cultural and historical settings in which that fragile subjectivity is formed.[2]

The dialogue that follows took place during the summer after I finished student teaching, prior to my first days as a teacher with my own classroom students. Marie had just completed her 31st year of teaching. Both of us looked forward to taking the opportunity to reflect back on what had shaped us into the teachers we are.

WHERE DOES AN URBAN EDUCATION BEGIN?

John: When you were completing your initial interviewing process for the inner-city school district where you now teach, you were asked a question that stuck with you; what was that question?

Marie: The question the interviewer posed was, "How would you feel if you were faced with a class of black students?" My response was, "Do they need to learn English?" And his answer was, "Yes." My next question was, "So, what's the difference?" The interviewer was completely stunned; he didn't know what to say. That was the only question he asked me after he had looked at all of my credentials—my resume, portfolio, transcripts, and recommendations.

J: So in retrospect, if asked the question today, would you still give the same answer? Do you think there is a difference now?

M: Looking back, I would have given the same response, because I believe that every student can learn, and I'm more interested in the students' eyes than in the color of their skin. Since I am more knowledgeable now about the community, about the environment, and about the difference in the support systems with which they are provided at home, I would have to say that I've changed my methodology to a great extent during the past 31 years. Perhaps if I were teaching in a school that was upper-middle class, containing more economically privileged students, I might be teaching differently. What I mean by that statement is not that I would change my lessons, because I believe that I maintain a challenging level of instruction in my classroom. The skills level wouldn't change. Although I would still be concerned about the skills the students brought with them, I probably would not be as concerned with the students' cultural origins as I am in my current teaching situation. I think I would be lying to myself to say that there is no difference.

J: Do you think that you were lying to yourself when you first started teaching?

M: No, I don't think I was lying to myself; I think I was simply unaware. I think now I would be lying to myself. I had been raised in a "closed-box" environment in my hometown. I had never even been in the particular urban area in which I was hired, so I entered the halls of a large, comprehensive, inner-city high school in north New Jersey with no preconceived ideas about the students or about the school. So, coming in cold, all I wanted to do was teach. That's all I ever wanted to do; that's still all I want to do. When I consider your questions about culture, I think about my being raised in a home in which we were never allowed to mock any culture, and reply, "Well, if they need to learn English, I will teach them."

J: I think it's important to establish who and what we are before ever entering the classroom. Everybody comes to school carrying the luggage (or baggage, in some cases) that defines that individual's personhood. I had a unique upbringing, attending 15 different public schools before entering college, being raised by a single parent, and living on military installations. Although I didn't understand it at the time, I held a kind of anomic identity, one that often could not relate to many of my peers who grew up with more stable circumstances. But in retrospect, it was and continues to be this anomie that has connected me to many lifelong acquaintances (most of whom lived in one place all their lives) who have felt little sense of any cohesive identity and a profound sense of social disorientation. Giroux describes this as a postmodern youth identity, a definition of self that cannot belong to any one or thing, living in and out of cultural and social spaces, shifting and merging; that is, youth embody a kind of performative anomaly.[3]

Giroux's notion alludes to a greater postmodern condition and is contiguous with the belief that to disengage from identities innately political—be they of race, gender, sexuality, physicality, ethnicity, worldliness, locale, and so on—is an act of empowering a true self, if we can suppose that a self can survive independent of those identities. Perhaps it is a survival measured by one's ability to critically deconstruct the systemic, to embrace the cultures that the true self tours, and to continually engage in the discourse analysis of every production, transmission, and exchange of media and communication. For many, this is a feat conjuring great disillusionment and a compromising of one's presumed primal instincts, constantly questioning one's own sense of familiarity. The notion of a true self is enigmatic, an un-identity. It is a self actualized by a slightly tinted lens that removes the hegemonic glare so one sees and is then able to choose all possible paths of understanding experiences and intelligences of those in and out of the worlds and cultures that surround one, whether or not one hold membership in such worlds or cultures.

Teaching in the inner city is an evolving moment. My journey as a teacher began as a researcher in black studies at the University of Central Florida as an undergraduate student, long before I ever considered teaching high school English. There I attended cultural events in nearby Eatonville, known as the first organized African-American municipality in the United States. Through my involvement, studies, and research, I began to consider notions of cultural and racial selves, blackness, whiteness, and the ideological implications of Americanism. I graduated with a BA—a major in English and a minor in African-American Studies.

In the two years of graduate study at Montclair that followed, I joined many professors in classes, forums, conferences, and in writing publications, contributing to what I believe the mission of cultural studies to be and struggling to implement concrete applications in pedagogical settings. Although I studied the black Diaspora and argued among peers and colleagues its relevance and poignancy as essential components of American life, history, and society, as a white college student I had never been immersed in black culture.

During my student teacher semester, all of that changed. Not only was I entering the inner city, I was entering a "black space"—that is, a black community, teaching in a predominantly black school. It is important to mention at this point that I also realized that the inner city is not necessarily a "black space," but is composed of all races, classes, and backgrounds.

I came to your school, Marie, not knowing whether I wanted to teach because I felt the system and its institutions were deceptive. Opening history books and literature left out of any curriculum that had been implemented in my 15 public schools opened my eyes and horizons to the notion that in the United States, schools are white institutions serving the white middle and upper classes. This means that even nonwhite, non-middle-class, non-upper-class schools still serve to maintain benefit to the white middle and upper classes. If I participated in this system by joining its institution and process as a white teacher in a nonwhite school, what difference or change could I possibly make? And could I handle the responsibility, if change were possible?

Becoming an inner-city teacher meant checking off one of the boxes in response to a questionnaire provided in my teacher preparation program. When I read the "Where do you want to teach?" question, I immediately checked "inner-city." My intentions in becoming a teacher were social, political, and historical reasons that I developed as a college student and researcher. With my academic background, I did not feel that teaching black students would make any difference due to my de facto whiteness; that is, the luggage I carried into their classroom included being young, straight, white, Christian-reared, middle class, and a graduate degree-holding male. But I also did not think I could be compassionate to white students in a middle-class school setting, learning what I had learned.

By acknowledging a true self, a self separate from the labels attached to me, I was forced to negotiate these imposed identities, or the luggage and my assumptions about those impositions—both in and out of the classroom, inner city or not. My decision to break down the components of my identity was the result of developing a critical consciousness of how power works to privilege some and oppress others based on personal characteristics that are ascribed; that is, given at birth without one's personal choice or control. My driving force to become a teacher was a decision to become an inner-city teacher, a decision driven by the impetus of discovering whether I could change the lives of those I thought needed to be saved from the system—that is, the *white system*. This was my white man's burden. But it turned out that the only person I needed to save from the system was I.

Studying black culture as an undergrad gave me the context for a career path where one had been missing and, purposefully or not, left out before I entered the preservice teacher graduate studies program. So before walking into your classroom, Marie, the question had always been, for the 18 months preceding graduate study, "Why do I want to become an inner-city teacher?" However, when I arrived in your classroom, the question transformed into, "Why do I want to be an English teacher?"

If we compare our motives as first-year teachers, we seem to have come to the inner city with completely opposite intentions because as you described earlier, all you wanted to do was teach English; that's all that mattered to you. For me, to arrive in your classroom last October was to arrive in a transformative space, a space where learning poetry and literature was the primary objective, and your pedagogy was the aspect that was transforming your learners. It wasn't until I began asking myself repeatedly why I wanted to be in your role, an English teacher, that I began to catch myself tripping up on my own displacement of racial and cultural identities, both mine and those of my students, in the attempt to practice a curriculum and teach skills that we can agree are essential to any curriculum in language, literacy, and literature. It was frustrating to me—someone who had researched and published studies on culture, class, race, and education—to enter the classroom

and not bridge the practice to the theories in which I had grounded myself. To realize these theories in practice then became a question of identifying key strategies that acknowledge race, culture, gender, religion, sexuality, and so forth in ways that concomitantly acknowledge the system of power and privilege that those constructs (or identities) operate within and without.

FROM REALIZING THEORY TO REALIZING PRACTICE

Marie: I guess the best response to this extremely intricate question is democratic process and individualization of instruction. Once again, the race, culture, gender, religion, and sexuality of the student (or the teacher) are less a consideration for me than the skills and knowledge brought to the classroom and the motivation and desire to develop new skills and assimilate new information for application, synthesis, and evaluation techniques in the future. When I met you, I was not thinking, "Oh, here's another white college student who thinks he is going to 'save' the black kids." My whole thought pattern was based on, "Great! Here is an intelligent young man with 'heart' who will become a great teacher, and I can't wait to share my knowledge and skills with him!" This same reaction is in my mind when my new students arrive each year. I could not tell you how many of my students are black, Hispanic, white, or Asian, but I can tell you which students have the most highly developed analytical skills, and which students demonstrate the best writing skills. Specifically, the pedagogy of ensuring that every student learns—regardless of gender, race, religion, culture, or sexuality—has been the foundation of my teaching method.

If a controversial issue arises, I act as mediator, helping the students to understand that we are all different in some ways, but we must learn to accept each other's dissimilarities in order to function as a respectful unit. These parameters must be set from the first day of school. Sometimes individual conferences with the student and/or parents are necessary, but once a situation of mutual respect is established, the classroom environment will be conducive to most students contributing to the discussion without fear of repercussion or animosity. During many years of teaching, I have worked diligently to share my own beliefs but not impose them, and to help students feel comfortable and accepted in my classroom. Until a student thanks you for helping him or her get into college or you have held in your arms a student who has been abused multiple times, knowing that by holding this child, you are making a difference—those kinds of bridges are difficult to realize.

J: Isn't that a universal experience across all different schools and areas in the country?

M: It might be universal, but in my experience, the school becomes a second home in the inner city due to the economic needs of families. Many of my students stay at school as long as they possibly can because their parents are working extra hours to support their families and they do not want their children to stay at home alone. Teachers have written grant proposals to provide computer lab and library availability after school hours because students might not have sufficient study aids at home. I'm not saying that this experience is necessarily unique to the inner city, but teaching in the inner city is definitely a two-way street. An inner-city teacher must be willing to make an emotional investment in the classroom, and that teacher will receive emotional fulfillment in return.

One of the primary differences can be discovered just by listening to the conversations of teachers from different school systems; I have met hundreds of teachers by attending workshops throughout the state. The major contrast I consistently notice is that I talk about the kids and they talk about the administration, the pay, and maybe the subject matter once in a while, but not about the kids. When you're teaching in the inner city, you will never connect with these students if you can't get into the "inner kid." I don't mean what the kid looks like, I mean getting inside the

kid's mind. I don't mean getting to know the kid's whole tragic life, but looking into that kid's eyes and knowing today's not a good day. We must understand that as teachers, we do not interrupt our lesson because of the student's distress, but simply say, "I know you're having a rough day. If you need me, I'm here." They will come if you say that.

Another aspect I need to add is the anger factor. There's a great deal of anger and animosity in their lives. They are aware that everybody in the state and in the country knows that their city is listed as one of the top worst cities in the nation in which to live. Since they already have this knowledge, shouldn't they be able to go somewhere where somebody is happy with them? If you can't create a welcoming environment in your classroom, then all you've done is add to the angst they constantly experience. When I refer back to this notion of the white man's burden in relation to white literature, white canon, or white curriculum, I never really thought about the connection. I had studied the concept as a component of history, but I never thought about its application in this context until we started having our conversations.

J: You said that your pedagogy is now based on skills development rather than digestion of the white canon. What are some other modifications you made in your strategies and lesson plans?

M: In the beginning, I was a lecturer. I lectured, and the kids all took notes in the 1970s. They threw the information back at me with no problem. I wish I still had those kids. They were amazing kids, and they are probably all successful. However, I didn't realize what I was propagating while I taught: the white canon, the white interpretations, and the stultifying process of having them memorize quotes from the text. I had them memorize who wrote what, and I had them memorize the whole canon. And then all of sudden, a series of turning points began.

The first turning point was when students started to ask me if I knew anything else besides literature by white people. I said, "I do." And they responded, "So why don't you teach us that?" Since I had studied many literary works by African Americans, such as *The Autobiography of Malcolm X* and *Native Son*, I was familiar with selections outside the canon. I believed that I had to familiarize the students with the material in the canon they would never be exposed to, assuming that they were already reading black literature on their own. However, I discovered that they didn't know the black literature either. They didn't know *Native Son*, *Invisible Man*, or *Black Boy*, and they didn't know the poetry of Paul Laurence Dunbar or Langston Hughes. So then I said, "Hmm . . . This is very interesting." That was the first turning point.

The second turning point was realizing that I was not a college professor, and that my job was to have students read and be able to survive on their own, not repeat my words. So I changed my whole pedagogy into emphasizing the process of learning instead of the content.

The third turning point occurred about ten years ago when the school was receiving austere criticism from the students and community because there was no black literature in the curriculum at the time. I realized how strongly the kids must have felt to have pursued the dangerous process of walking out and possibly getting expelled from a magnet school—because the subject meant that much to them. At that point, I started realizing, again, that it isn't so much what you study; it's being able to study. I began making as many connections as I could to the African American, and to all genres, cultures, and experiences.

J: How do you define your whiteness or your white identity in a predominantly nonwhite educative setting?

M: I have difficulty with this question. In my classroom, my students often tell me, "Mrs. Gironda, you are not white! You are Italian!" or "Mrs. Gironda, you are too cool to be white!" Soon, it became obvious that my students have

their own definitions of *white* that have little to do with aspects delineated by anthropologists.

J: Do you see this "too cool to be white" identity as part of you, part of your self-concept, and/or part of your teaching?

M: I define myself as a woman first and a teacher second. I've never defined myself as a white woman or as a white teacher.

J: How do you feel society has defined you as— a white woman or as a white teacher?

M: Society would probably define me as a white, Italian-American woman who keeps a clean house, who can cook spaghetti sauce, who nurtures her children, who can hold a good conversation, who likes to dance, and, you know, that kind of stereotypical description: a sociable, Italian Catholic, white woman.

J: What about how you dress?

M: I dress conservatively, and I feel that this fact is important to the teacher identity. Walking into my first teaching job as a 21-year-old, wearing short skirts and tight clothes, I began to get comments from students that made me reconsider this question: "Should I be maintaining a certain image, a professional look that I want to convey and that is important to my "get the job done" approach? Did I want the students to concentrate on my appearance or on my instructional skills?" Obviously, I opted to change my style so the emphasis shifted to my intellectual capacity, away from my physical presentation.

J: This image, I believe, can also be conveyed as a specifically "white image," that the signifiers of your identity are signifiers of whiteness, signifiers of an autonomous minority status as an Italian woman, signifiers of a specific lifestyle and cultural values and decisions.[4] And while these values are those that may be expressed in the semiotics of your hidden curriculum, I think it's important that we as teachers and researchers examine what exactly the implications are, once students of involuntary minority status are sitting in your classroom and translating the hidden curriculum (or implied set of values) under the guise of your teacher/communicator's white identity. So I guess what I want to know from you, my mentor and cooperating teacher, is, can I step out of my coat of signifiers as a young, straight, white, male, well-educated, well-employed, alcohol-free, drug-free, generally conservatively dressed identity, and be critical of all those signifiers and able to take a counterhegemonic position, such as that of feminist or critical multiculturalist?

M: I think your question clearly states one of the major challenges teachers must face in the inner city, and I have worked diligently to overcome this obstacle throughout the years. Just today, I was teaching the Socratic method. I began the lesson by telling them that the reason I taught the way I did all year is because I never want them to view any concept from one side, ever. I looked at them, and they all looked at me, and I asked, "Did you understand my purpose during the year?" A couple of them spoke up and said, "Yeah, I got that. I got it a couple of times when you made us look at things in a different way throughout the year. You got mad, played devil's advocate and said, 'No, I don't think it means that,' or 'I don't think that all people think that way.'" Back in the beginning of the school year what you would see is a student like Michael (pseudonym) from my fourth-period senior Honors English class, who would say, "Women are supposed to stay home and take care of the kids." At that moment, all of the female students would begin to confront him. Using the democratic process, I would say, "No, we can't all argue or fight with this student. This is a deep, core belief that this young man has. We may think he's completely wrong because maybe we're in the 'feminist zone,' but this is his deep core belief." Hopefully, from his classmates and this discussion, he might learn to reconsider his opinions. As critically minded teachers, we must teach students not to condemn or belittle others. I won't allow anyone to say, "He's wrong." The students' comments should be revamped and redirected, to improve respect for each individual in the classroom. I believe the same technique should be applied in discussions about cultural issues.

J: How do you feel that your behaviors and your strategies and your whole persona contribute to your students' construction and perception of your whiteness?

M: I think the students are willing to trust me because I am willing to "let it go." I never talk about what I own, how much money I have, or what car I drive, but I will tell them I was raised in a four-room apartment and that I have been paying for all my own possessions since I was 15. So, maybe that honesty is part

of the connection. When the students compose personal statements, their writing really opens them up to me. I have that privilege that most teachers don't have. I assure them that I will not share their thoughts with anyone. Maybe it's the trust; maybe it's because I didn't come from the upper class; maybe it's the fact that I consistently tell them that I don't care what I own because it doesn't matter . . . I'm not part of that whole materialistic pursuit. It's interesting because it's been happening to me since my fourth or fifth year as a teacher in the inner city. I remember writing on the board, "Dear Mom, I'm not white," and asking them, "What does that mean?" You saw this relationship when I held the party for you; me throwing off my jacket and dancing to Michael Jackson music, and them huddling around me—what does that mean? I couldn't even explain that moment if I tried, but there's obviously a trust, you know?

J: Let's shift the conversation from your students to how your other colleagues perceive you, your whiteness, and your pedagogy.

M: My close relationship with the students helps me in my work with them in the classroom. My colleagues come to me for advice as you saw when you were here. Are they suspicious? Yes. Do they think I am unconventional? Probably. In my beginning years, the administration sometimes reprimanded me because they said I got too close. They told me to back off, and I told them, "I can't. I can't teach any other way." I think my colleagues are sometimes alienated by my personal relationships with the students, which affect even my relationships with my student teachers. I am not certain whether "whiteness" is an element of this situation.

J: Do you feel that student teachers entering schools need to confront their own identities in any critical way before confronting those of their students?

M: Emphatically, yes! They should consider their racial, cultural, economic, and ethnic identities; absolutely. I even suggested, while discussing my involvement in the initial field experience for student teachers as a contributing faculty member for the new Teaching Academy here, that I should probably include a piece on teacher identity, which I haven't done in the past. I do believe that teachers come to inner-city schools to fulfill their own emotional/intellectual/spiritual needs, as well as to foster academic interests in the students. If the new teacher is going to be successful in the inner-city school, he or she should definitely ask some challenging questions: "Why do I want to teach here?" "How much personal time/emotion/effort am I willing to invest?" "Am I flexible enough to address the individual struggles these students encounter every day of their lives?" "Am I willing to teach them as though they are equal to any other student in the world, or have I already decided that they are 'slower,' 'less capable,' or 'disadvantaged'?" I think this situation becomes a question of "What are you willing to set aside?" or "What are you willing to sacrifice?"

J: When you say, "set aside," what do you mean? Are you saying their white identity? Are you saying their way of life? What are you saying? My question is, "What are you willing to dive into?" "Are you willing to face your own identity?" "Are you willing to look at yourself and ask, 'Wait a second; does everything that I am represent all of these other things that I have to consider?'"

M: I guess I don't mean putting it aside as much as I mean growing out of it. Teachers never actually forget their identity, but if they concentrate fully on the intellectual and skills development of the students, the identity issue will become less troublesome. If trust and respect have been developed within the classroom, the teacher can allow the cultural identities in the group to mesh into one learning environment.

J: Are you really saying that what we need to put aside is all the ignorance and fear, and the biases that go along with them?

M: Yes! For example, I don't listen to the news in the morning, and many people ask why. I say, "Because there's so much negativity." Invariably, I am going to hear about a black person committing a crime, or I am going to hear about the problems in the inner city. If I read *The Star Ledger*, I would see negative images of inner-city people, and I just can't let that information enter my mind, because I know that for every one who is a problem, there are a thousand who are great and are never noticed.

J: For me, it was a process that began as an observer in my initial field experience before I entered your classroom as a student teacher. I found a medium of critical self-reflection

through writing and poetry, the result was creating a collection of poems dedicated "from myself to my whiteself." Here's an example of some work that was published:

before the first day

before the first day
kids won't give a shit whetha youV been
    told or not all your life
the powers & privileges of bein' white
youV been livin'em, haven'tchu

before the first day
it will be about you
all   about   you
but will *you* get it

before the first day
will you finally see
that *these kids* see straight though your
    dominantideology
that *these kids* are oppressed, self-hated,
    systemicallymanipulatedhistorically

before the first day
i wonder, per se,
will you have the balls to say
"I'm colorblind; it's okay."

before the first day
will there be a revolution
will revelation be found in a constitution
will you be the next cultural worker in an
    American institution

before the first day
will you forget all you have learned
will you learn all you have shunned
will you see all you have ignored

before the first day
can you find it in you, a love to bring
do you have it for them, a praxis that sings
will you dig deeper, reachN through a skin
    so thin
or will you give up, everything but your
    privilege
before the first day[5]

M: The one concept that strikes me in this poem is the colorblindness. I think that this term is a fallacy. The color is different; it's there. It has nothing to do with not seeing the color; it has to do with the fact that when I see their eyes, they're the same color as mine. I just think that it has nothing to do with wanting to get into their skin, wanting to understand what it means to be black. You can't; you never will; get over it.

Regarding this statement made by some new teachers, "I'm going to read as much as I can and know as much as I can about black culture." Well, you could read about black culture for the rest of your life, but still fail in the classroom. When I first started teaching, many students asked why I was trying to make them "talk white," and I would spend a great deal of time and effort explaining that many dialects exist among people in America who are black or white, but if they wanted to be able to read and write in the formal English of the universities, I could help them succeed. I have never experienced resentment from the students after I offer this explanation. What you're really talking about is connecting with a person, not connecting with a black person. Now, should you have knowledge of the black experience if most of your students are black? Yes. Should you have an understanding of your own identity, the culture of the school, the culture of the community, and the culture of the home? Yes. Should you take a ride around the entire city in which you work and really see it? Yes. Should you be involved in community projects and services? Absolutely. However, your primary focus should still be placed on the intellectual development of the student's mind, regardless of the student's skills.

J: To me, colorblindness is first a blindness to your own identity as belonging to a socially defined dominant status and second, an inability to recognize your students who are negotiating a socially defined minority status,[6] be that of any identity or an identity considered "less than" in a social paradigm incorporating power, dominance, oppression, and resistance.[7] It is my rebuttal to your initial statement above that if we are all immersed in whiteness, in a society that benefits mainly white middle- and upper-class people, no matter our actual assigned racial identity, that we all must take a period of our lives and make it our prime objective to study the lived and historical experiences of those who, although they are immersed in whiteness, do not have the invisible powers and privileges of having a white identity; that is, to study the history, absorb the literature, taste the music and art and food generated out of the expression of those carrying the weight of white oppression.

Reflecting on your response, Marie, and considering my different conception of col-orblindness, it is clear that you did have a period in which you studied black literature and that you do consider those identity factors in your pedagogy, ultimately privileging transformative power rather than reproductive power in your classroom. To a student teacher, being colorblind is never to fully or critically acknowledge those considerations in the first place, never to understand any other experience than that of being white or part of the majority status, and merely, by default, to say, "I just happen to be a white person teaching in a nonwhite setting."

SOME FINAL THOUGHTS

John

There is a spectrum to consider when it comes to teaching skills and gauging your pedagogy and lesson plans, incorporating outside resources, content, and ancillaries—things essential to framing the connection you desire to make with your students on a daily basis. Whether we choose to acknowledge it or not, the whiteness is still there, the blackness is still there, the Puerto Rican-ness is still there—whatever "it" is, it's there. To me, if we're not willing to acknowledge "it" in even the most subliminal ways before we ever enter the classroom, we're selling our kids short, long before our first day as a teacher. Once in the classroom, whether it's overtly making a cultural reference, bringing to the table a piece of noncanonical literature, or demonstrating an engaging openness and willingness as a teacher to dissolve your attachment to a dominant identity or status while working to transform the powers of control and privilege among students of cultures outside *or inside* the dominant majority, to embrace identity as something that is valid and worthwhile to the discussion and learning to all of those involved is crucial to the foundation of a critical and democratic classroom, before and while the content reaches the class discussion and learning activities.

Marie

Whether white teachers view their experiences in the classroom as the white man's burden" or not, they definitely should be aware of the cultural diversity of their students and strive to incorporate this understanding while thoroughly committing themselves to the intellectual stimulation and development of their students through the Socratic method and democratic process. Any teacher who conducts any lesson should be willing to accept the burden of academically improving his or her students, but the inner-city teacher must also be prepared to offer additional advice, nurturing, encouragement, and flexibility, while taking the risk of becoming emotionally and spiritually involved with the students. Before a student teacher like John accepts a permanent teaching position in the inner city, as he already has, that teacher must fully examine his or her own ability to see the color line, and then see beyond, into the gray matter of the students. A student teacher's understanding of cultural theories will enhance his or her teaching only if the primary concern is the individual development of each student's intellectual abilities. As a result of John's internship in my classroom, I have also learned to be even more vigilant in my attempts to realize the cultural implications of my pedagogy, and to be more cognizant of the preconceived notions that student teachers bring with them when they enter student teaching.

NOTES

1. Gilroy, P. (1997). Diaspora and the detours of identity. In K. Woodward (Ed.), *Identity and difference: Culture, media, and identities*. London: Open University Press.
2. Gilroy (1997), p. 301.
3. Giroux, H. (1994). Doing cultural studies: Youth and the challenge of pedagogy. *Harvard Educational Review, 64* (3), 278–307.
4. Ogbu, J. (1992). Understanding cultural diversity and learning. *Educational Research, 21,* 5–14.
5. Pascarella, J. (in press). Deviation: A preservice teacher in the inner city. *Cultural Studies ↔ Critical Methodologies, 7* (1).
6. Ogbu (1992).
7. Apple, M. (2002). *Power, meaning, and identity.* New York: Peter Lang.

AFRICAN-AMERICAN TEACHERS: THE DYING GROUP

Deidre Ann Tyler

According to recent statistics, of the 2.7 million elementary and secondary U.S. public school teachers, only 7.3 percent are African Americans.[1] The question becomes, why are there so few African-American teachers today? This chapter discusses the historical decline in the number of African-American teachers in the context of such issues as low teacher pay, higher state certification requirements, increased violence against teachers, and alternative occupational choices. Also, several creative solutions to encourage African Americans to become teachers will be discussed.

HISTORY OF AFRICAN AMERICANS AS TEACHERS

Before the landmark *Brown v. Board of Education* decision, one of the few leadership roles and occupations open to African Americans was that of public school teacher. Teaching was a high-status position, because teachers were imparting knowledge, hope, and determination to African-American children.

Before integration, many African-American teachers would openly comment to their students, "You'd better learn your lesson or you will be working on the garbage truck." Such a statement, though offensive if coming from a white person, was simply the voice of reality from a black person. Furthermore, black individuals could teach important lessons that could be imparted only from someone with the experience of being black. Louis Harlan has noted that, between 1932 and 1948, the number of African-American teachers doubled, most of them assigned to teach in elementary schools. Later African-American teachers were assigned to teach in black schools only. African-American teachers were restricted from teaching white students because of the belief that African-American teachers were inferior to white teachers.[2]

The black community was divided over integration because they knew many black teachers would lose their jobs. A famous black female educator, Anna Julia Cooper, said she was not in favor of school desegregation because she feared that black children would not be taught racial pride.[3] In essence, the *Brown* decision was quietly saying to many that black teachers were not as good as white teachers.

It is true that black teachers essentially paid a price after the desegregation of schools. That price was a decrease in their numbers. More than 30,000 black teachers lost their jobs after *Brown v. Board of Education.*[4] Today, as noted above, only 7.3 percent of the nation's K–12 teachers are black. The historical effects of *Brown* alone cannot account for such a long-lasting effect. What are other reasons for this low number?

REASONS FOR THE DECLINE IN AFRICAN-AMERICAN TEACHERS

First, current salaries for teachers are a major reason for a decrease in the number of African-American teachers, a demotivation that they share with their white counterparts. According to the American Federation of Teachers, the average salary for teachers in the United States is $43,250.[5] Many African Americans do not feel a dedication to teaching sufficient to overcome this very real economic barrier. This problem, though real, is not a sufficient explanation, since Zinsmeister and Leher have documented that teachers receive higher pay than workers in other occupations requiring similar and higher levels of education.[6]

A second barrier for many African Americans is the increasingly higher standards for teachers. For instance, New Jersey's State Board of Education requires that all new public school teachers have a college grade point average of 2.7.[7] Many African Americans complete their college degrees in education but fail to pass the state certification examinations, and fewer still pass the National Board Certification. Phaedra Brotherton reported that, in 2000–01, only 148 (30%) out of the 491 African-American teachers who graduated from historically black colleges and universities (HBCUs) who applied for certification were certified.[8]

Another reason why African Americans may seek careers other than in education is the recent upsurge in violent acts by students against teachers. According to a 1993 Metropolitan Life Insurance survey, 11 percent of teachers nationwide reported that a student or students had assaulted them at school that year. African Americans, who have historically been targets of violence, may feel themselves particularly susceptible in volatile situations, and hence may be unwilling to enter a profession that carries with it an increasing risk of physical harm.[9]

Furthermore, African-American college students have many other options, unlike during the pre-*Brown* period. The social pressures that restricted African-American college graduates to such occupations as social work, nursing, teaching, and government work have relaxed. Now, African Americans are able to pursue careers in engineering, computer programming, chemistry, and many other occupations that were traditionally closed to them. Teachers and parents are actively encouraging high school and college students to prepare for nontraditional occupations, while relatively few are encouraging them to enter teaching.

The shift in status that has accompanied the breakdown of these barriers is also a factor. In the past African-American teachers were well respected in the African-American community. People regarded an African-American teacher as a member of an elite group. Endless stories exist of a beloved teacher who worked tirelessly to develop the talents of African-American students, made second-mile efforts to ensure learning, and maintained strong interpersonal mentoring relationships that sometimes spanned two generations. Many paid for school supplies out of their own pockets,[10] intervened with parents, and advocated for their students with police and judges. They were not teaching for a paycheck only. But as the need for such extreme devotion waned, so have its manifestations.

POSSIBLE SOLUTIONS

If this downward trend continues, it is not fanciful to foresee a time when no African Americans will appear in public schools except as parents and pupils. It is urgent to reverse this trend. Here are two creative programs whose purpose is to increase the pool of African-American men available in the nation's classrooms.

- The Marygrove College Program, Detroit, Michigan. This program encourages African-American men to enter teaching and especially appeals to those who are seeking career changes from such professions as lawyer, police officer, and so forth. It allows African-American enrollees to continue their current employment while taking classes toward a teacher's certificate in intensive sessions Friday nights and Saturdays.[11]
- Call Me MISTER, South Carolina. In 2002 Clemson University partnered with Claflin University, Benedict College, and Morris College to recruit 200 African-American men into the field of elementary education to become South Carolina teachers. This program provides tuition assistance and job placement assistance upon graduation and certification.[12]

SUMMARY

One of the ironies of the disappearance of African-American teachers is the implication that life for African Americans may have been better in some respects before *Brown* than afterward. And one of the most frequently cited pieces of evidence is the large number of African-American teachers who were dedicated to uplifting African-American students in pre-*Brown* days. Can we rebuild the link that is missing for the next generation? Some programs are in place to increase the pool of African-American teachers in the United States. It is now up to the participants and the community to turn those possibilities into a reality.

NOTES

1. Yasin, S. (2000). The supply and demand of elementary and secondary teachers in the United States. Retrieved June, 2004 from http://www.ericdigests.org/2000-3/demand.htm.

2. Harlan, L. (1968). *Separate and unequal: Public school campaigns and racism in the southern states 1901–1915.* New York: Atheneum.

3. Hine, D., Brown, E., & Terborg-Penn, R. (1993). *Black women in America: An historical encyclopedia* (p. 7). Bloomington: University Press of Indiana.

4. Ethridge, S. (1979). Impact of 1954 *Brown v. Topeka Board of Education* decision on black educators. *Negro Educational Review, 30* (4), 217–232.

5. American Federation of Teachers. (2002, May). *Annual survey of state departments of education: Early estimates of public elementary and secondary education statistics, 2000–2001.*

Retrieved June, 2004 from U.S. Department of Education Web site: http://www.nces.ed.gov/pubsearch/pubnfo.asp?pubid=2001331.

6. Zinsmeister, K., & Lehrer, E. (2003, Oct.–Nov.). Are teachers underpaid? *American Enterprise, 14* (7), 15.

7. Blair, J. (2003, May 7). Blacks apply, but unlikely to win certification. *Education Week, 22* (5).

8. Brotherton, P. (2002, May 23). Helping teachers make the grade: NBPTS, HBCUs partner to prepare African American teachers for national certification. *Black Issues in Higher Education, 19* (14).

9. Porter, J. (1995, July 7). The target of attacks by students, teachers turn to courts for relief. *Education Week,* 1–2.

10. Wilson, A., & Segall, W. (2001)."*Oh, Do I Remember*": *Experiences of teachers during the desegregation of Austin's schools, 1964–1971* (p. 33). Albany, New York: State University of New York Press.

11. Garsten, E. (1998, October). Detroit college promotes African-American men as educators. Retrieved June, 2004 from cnn.com: http://www.cnn.com/US/9810/13/teacher.shortage.

12. Smiles, R. (2002, Oct. 10). Calling all potential misters: South Carolina's teacher training program, "Call Me Mister," seeks to put black males at the front of the class. *Black Issues in Higher Education, 19* (17), 26.

Social Justice

PARTICIPATORY DEMOCRATIC EDUCATION: IS THE UTOPIA POSSIBLE? PORTO ALEGRE'S CITIZEN SCHOOL PROJECT

Luis Armando Gandin and Gustavo E. Fischman

> Education either functions as an instrument which is used to facilitate the integration of generations into the logic of the present system and bring about conformity to it, or it becomes "the practice of freedom," the means by which men and women deal critically and creatively with reality and discover how to participate in the transformation of their world.
>
> —*P. Freire*
> *Pedagogy of the Oppressed*[1]

This chapter explores the implications of the Citizen School Project (*Escola Cidadã*), an urban education reform project that started in 1989 in the city of Porto Alegre, Brazil. The Citizen School Project is among the most innovative urban educational reform projects implemented during the last two decades, not only because it is successfully educating children and the citizenry of Porto Alegre, but also because it was done under severe economic constraints. Most significantly, the Citizen School Project's pedagogical orientations truly incorporated the voices and needs of a population historically neglected by the state and the educational system. The Citizen School Project was initially considered by many an educational utopia because it was—and continues to be—based on two main principles: (1) the Freirean ideal of simultaneously reading the word and the world; and (2) the interdependence of the political dimensions of urban schooling and the pedagogical dimensions of political participation in the urban landscape. We see both of these foundational assumptions reflected in this statement by the coordinators of the Citizen School Project; as former teachers and union leaders based in the Municipal Secretariat of Education (SMED), they argue that in order to address the serious educational and social problems of Porto Alegre:

It is not possible to change the schools through isolated methodological techniques, restricted to the actions and strategies of teaching in the classrooms. The school only changes when it is articulated to . . . a global political project that includes a democratic educational policy, aimed at social inclusion and emancipation of impoverished people.[2]

One of the core principles of the Citizen School Project is that truly inclusive schooling will not result from simply changing pedagogy. Rather, new teaching methods must also be coupled with a global political project as well as an effort to enact more democratic power relationships. Thus, the Citizen School Project combines pedagogical innovation with a shift in the type of relationships cultivated within the school setting and the type of knowledge being taught.

To implement this transformation, the coordinators in the SMED knew that they would have to incorporate many students (mostly the children of migrant families living in the poorest areas of the city) who had been excluded from the educational system; in short, they would have to build new schools. In 1989, the municipal school system of Porto Alegre provided educational services to only 17,000 students and had a drop-out rate of almost 10 percent. By 2002 the system had increased the coverage to more than 70,000 students, and the drop-out rate decreased to less than 1 percent. In the Brazilian educational system, both the states and the cities maintain public schools, and in Porto Alegre there are many students who attend state public schools; thus, the large number of students in the municipal schools. Nevertheless, the illiteracy rate has decreased from 6 percent to 2.9 percent, and according to Brazilian student achievement measures, the students graduating from the Citizen School Project performed well academically. Other indicators of the quality of this reform project are the outstanding levels of job satisfaction among teachers; changes in curriculum and organizational structures that address the needs of a diverse urban population; the high levels of community participation in the life of the schools; and the key role that schools play in the lives of local communities.

These are impressive results for a Brazilian school district surrounded and pressured by other educational models that run counter to the goals of the Citizen School Project. Furthermore, these results were obtained by adhering to the core values of empowerment; collective work; respect for differences; solidarity; knowledge as a historical experience; and citizenship aimed at democratizing access to school, knowledge, and governance. Given those values, since its conception and initial implementation in 1989, the Citizen School Project has been explicitly designed to radically change both the municipal schools and the relationship among communities, the state, and the educational system. This set of goals and the efforts to implement them are constitutive parts of a clear and explicit project aimed at constructing not only better schooling for the excluded, but also a larger project of radical democracy. After 15 years, the reforms in Porto Alegre are still in progress, but in this chapter we argue that the initial results of the Citizen School Project have crucial implications for how we might think about the politics of education policy and its dialectical role in social transformation not only in Brazil but worldwide. The global implications are even clearer when we consider the fact that both the World Social Forum and the World Education Forum are held in Porto Alegre, not by coincidence but because of the municipality's original contribution to the creation of real social and educational alternatives.

SITUATING THE PROJECT

Located in the south end of Brazil, Porto Alegre is the largest urban district and the capital of the state of Rio Grande do Sul. The city has a population of 1,300,000 distributed in 85 neighborhoods. Since 1989, it has been governed by a coalition of leftist parties under the general leadership of the Workers' Party. The educational project of the municipal government is not an isolated initiative. It is part of a larger program of radical transformation of the relationship between the state (in this case, the municipal state) and civil society, introduced by the government of the Workers' Party, in the city of Porto Alegre. Since its first term, the municipal administration adopted a system of participatory decision making to deliberate on the municipality's budget. This program aims at including the population in the discussion and elaboration of the city's annual Investment Plan. The school reform effort is intimately related to and complements the larger participatory budget decision-making process, yet they are separate endeavors. Given the importance of the city's Planning and Participatory Budget for the implementation of this innovative educational reform effort, we provide a brief summary of its main points.

CITIZEN SCHOOL AND THE OP

The Participatory Budgeting (*Orçamento Participativo* or OP) is credited with the reallocation of resources to the impoverished neighborhoods. The OP is a mechanism that guarantees active popular participation and deliberation in the allocation of resources for investment in the city. In Santos's words,

The participatory budget promoted by the Prefeitura of Porto Alegre is a form of public government that tries to break away from the authoritarian and patrimonialist tradition of public policies, resorting to the direct participation of the population in the different phases of budget preparation and implementation, with special concern for the definition of priorities for the distribution of investment resources.[3]

A few key points raised by Santos are worth elaborating on. Politics in Brazil has been historically characterized by *patrimo-*

nialism and *clientelism*. The government of the Popular Administration was able to break with this tradition, and active popular participation in the construction of policy and allocation of resources has been a key component of its success. The OP is at the core of the project to transform the city of Porto Alegre and incorporate a historically excluded impoverished population into the processes of decision making. As a number of researchers have shown (Baiocchi, 1999; Santos, 1998; Abbers, 1998; Avritzer, 1999), not only have the material conditions of the impoverished population changed, but the OP has also generated an educative process that has forged new social organizations and associations in neighborhoods.

Through the process of constructing organizations that enable full participation in the OP, the citizenry of Porto Alegre has been engaged in an extensive pedagogic project involving their own empowerment. In essence, the OP can be considered a school of democracy. Moreover, the learning acquired within the OP is transferred to other spheres of social life.[4] Yet there may also be an even more significant educational aspect of the OP: Through the OP, government agencies themselves are engaged in a process of "reeducation." Popular participation "teaches" the state to better serve the population. This is a crucial point that is often forgotten in our discussion of the role of democracy in state policy formation and in bureaucratic institutions. Finally, it is important to note that many of the schools built in Porto Alegre in the last 15 years were located in particular neighborhoods because schooling was defined as a priority by their communities in meetings held by the OP.

We believe that the OP illustrates the political will and political resolve necessary to combat the type of corporatist colonization of politics and of schooling associated with neoliberal educational reform agendas, which provide ballast for a process of globalization from above.

THE CITIZEN SCHOOL ORGANIZATION

The Citizen School Project was developed and established in Porto Alegre in the Popular Administration's first term. During the last 15 years, educators, students, parents, community organizations, and individuals have had the opportunity to participate in decisions about the role that schools should play in the larger society, and to reflect upon the type of social, political, and educational practices they would like to see in operation in the municipality's schools. This process of educational reform expresses the articulation of democratic ideals, community experiences, the legacy of the popular education movement, and a firm commitment to create a new model of schooling even amid a dramatic financial and economic crisis.

The educational policies implemented by four different administrations of the Secretary of Education of the City of Porto Alegre have attempted to infuse a radical democratic spirit into the educational sphere by supporting the direct and active participation of students, teachers, administrators, staff, parents, and the community at large in the formulation, administration, and control of the public policies for the municipality.

The *Escola Cidadã* operates from the fundamental premise that democratizing schools requires a collective effort to create an educational project that is open and flexible in its structures while maintaining its goals of radically democratizing school practices. Within such a project, schools are transformed into laboratories for the practice of individual and social rights. For example, at the center of the program are the following ideals: developing autonomous, critical, and creative individuals; developing citizens who support the daily practices of solidarity, justice, freedom, human respect, and equal relationships between men and women; and informing all curriculum practices with a commitment to the development of a less exploitative relationship with the environment. José Clóvis de Azevedo, former secretary of education of Porto Alegre, states that to achieve such ambitious goals it is necessary to recover the sense of schools as laboratories of democracy, a notion that directly counters technocratic attempts to turn schools into markets:

We reaffirm our commitment to expand the humanist character of public schools and we oppose the submission of education to the values of the market and neoliberal reforms in education. The market's main concern is to form consumers and customers, to turn education into merchandise submitted to profit-seeking rationales, naturalizing individualism, conformity, unfair competition, indifference and, consequently, the exclusion of those deemed a priori unsuited to compete.[5]

The results of this program are highly impressive, especially when compared to education in other Latin American countries, and particularly when one considers that the *Escola Cidadã* serves the most impoverished population in the city of Porto Alegre.[6]

A recent report, *SMED 2000*, illustrates some of the most important advances of this endeavor.[7] In 1989, there were 37 municipal schools; by 1999, this number had increased to 89. Accompanying these changes, new programs were created and existing programs were expanded. It is worth noting that among these new programs were the amplification of services for students with special needs; special programs to reach the educational needs of street children; SEJA (*Serviços Educativos para Jovens e Adultos*), an educational program for youth and adults; and MOVA (*Movimento de Alfabetização*), a program of literacy and popular education.

In 1993, *Escola Cidadã* implemented a series of regional meetings to create the School Constituent Congress, a collective structure open to participation by all segments of the school community. The goal of the School Constituent Congress was to establish the guiding principles that would orient the construction of an inclusionary, democratic, and emancipatory school. The regional meetings and the School Constituent Congress were attended by elected delegates, guaranteeing the participation of parents, students, teachers, and staff. The discussion was organized around four thematic axes: Curriculum and Knowledge, Administration, Evaluation, and Norms of Coexistence.

After the School Constituent Congress was established, its participants reaffirmed the goals of *Escola Cidadã* for the democratization of schooling in three primary areas: access to schools, administration, and access to knowledge.

DEMOCRATIZATION OF ACCESS TO SCHOOLS

The democratization of access to schools is connected to the needs of the most impoverished neighborhoods of Porto Alegre where the municipal schools are situated. For the Popular Administration, guaranteeing access to the schools is the first step to the promotion of social justice for communities historically excluded from social goods. The first reform instituted to address the terrible exclusion of students from Brazilian education was the abolition of the grade structure and establishment of three educational cycles, each three years long, at each educational level (elementary, middle, high), totaling nine years of education. Education by cycles is an attempt to eliminate the mechanisms in schools that perpetuate the exclusion of students through failure and dropping out. The students progress from one year to another within one cycle, and the notion of "failure" is eliminated; the cycles model is meant to reframe the conception of failure present in the traditional school, which blames the students for their problems without examining the role of the school in creating students' failure. But this elimination of the mecha-

nisms of exclusion is not enough. The Citizen School also created progression groups and learning laboratories to guarantee the reinclusion of students who had previously been excluded from the school system. In progression, groups of students who come into the municipal schools from other school systems (state schools, for example) and who have experienced multiple failures receive close attention with the goal of integrating them into the cycle at the appropriate level. Learning laboratories are not only a space where students with special difficulties are helped, but also a place where teachers conduct research in order to improve the quality of the regular classes. The emphasis of these policies is the transformation of the school structure in order to address the exclusion problem. Finally, the material conditions of the schools are excellent, especially when compared to other public schools in Brazil: The schools are very well kept, with good libraries and adequate facilities.

DEMOCRATIZATION OF ADMINISTRATION

One of the first actions of *Escola Cidadã* was to establish mechanisms for the direct election of principals and assistant principals in the schools of Porto Alegre. This step was taken to redefine the power relationships inside schools rather than to link the democratization of schools to the election of the administrative and pedagogical leadership. In order to be elected, aspiring principals and assistants are required to present prospective programs for the administration of schools. Successful proposals need the support of staff, teachers, students, and parents, and must be technically and financially responsible. Thus the goals, procedures, and norms for administrative and pedagogic relationships that are developed inside a given school require the consent of teachers, students, educational authorities, and parents.

Another vital mechanism developed to democratize the exercise of power inside schools was the creation of school councils. The school council consists of elected representatives (parents, students, employees, and teachers); is the supreme organ of the school; and exercises considerable influence over administrative, financial, and pedagogic matters. The council defines the more global aspects of the school, the basic lines of administration, and resource allocation and application. The principal, who is part of the council, is responsible for offering political direction to the project.[8]

The administrative structures cannot be democratized without the implementation of the program for Planning and Participatory Budget in Schools. The objective of this program is to democratize decision making at each school site; to provide financial autonomy in the management of expenses, materials, and services; and to develop annual plans for improving educational services.

DEMOCRATIZATION OF ACCESS TO KNOWLEDGE

Curriculum transformation is a crucial part of Porto Alegre's project to build real democracy. The curriculum implemented in the Citizen School Project goes beyond the incorporation of new knowledge within the margins of an intact core of humankind's wisdom. It is a radical transformation aimed at constructing a new epistemological understanding of what knowledge *is*, what must be present for learning to occur, and what changes such learning must bring about. Thus, the Citizen School Project goes beyond the mere episodic mentioning of the structural and cultural manifestations of class, racial, sexual, and gender-based oppression. It includes these themes as an essential part of the process of constructing what counts as knowledge. To achieve this aim, the district of Porto Alegre implemented participatory research strategies to develop school curricula.

One of the most effective tools for resolving the frequent disconnection between the cultural and social frameworks of communities and schools is the use of educational thematic units built around a central concern for the community. Teachers develop these units after conducting a social-anthropological diagnostic evaluation within their school communities. These thematic units become a locally-based and locally-owned instrument designed to construct and distribute knowledge that is socially relevant for the communities served by each school. The critical incorporation of elements deemed relevant for the school community, complemented with pedagogical practices developed to strengthen the concept of radical democracy within *Escola Cidadã*, have given a new meaning to teaching and learning in Porto Alegre.

Perhaps no other example illustrates this better than the role of the educator as defined by the School Constituent Congress, principle number 40:

The educator's role is to be next to the student, challenging the real and imaginary worlds brought to school by students, contributing to the life-world of the students in such a way that the "world" can be understood and reinvented by the student. The educator should also grow, learn, and experience together with the students the conflicts, inventions, curiosity, and desires, respecting each student as a being who thinks differently, respecting each student's individuality.[9]

This program helps consolidate the mutual responsibility and obligations of the state and civil society—and of teachers, communities, and students—by reinventing the proverbial concept of "schools for citizenship" where achievement for all is only the first step toward creating more democratic spaces in education. As Tarso Genro (former mayor of Porto Alegre and current Brazilian minister of education) states:

The truth *about* Escola Cidadã is that fundamentally, it is a rational and undetermined space. In it citizens—teachers and learners—are connecting with the values and legacies of the enlightenment, tolerance, respect for human diversity and cultural pluralism, in dialogical coexistence, sharing experiences and knowledge and identifying history as open future.[10]

PARTICIPATORY DEMOCRATIC EDUCATION: IS THE UTOPIA POSSIBLE?

Supporting and extending real and workable democratic reforms in schools such as the ones created by Escola Cidadã requires that controversial positions be debated fairly within political and social institutions as well as educational systems. The example of Escola Cidadã points to the urgent need for greater understanding of the sociopolitical conditions facing many aggrieved communities within the social order, and to the manifold challenges entailed in cultivating civic responsibility to ensure that public institutions embody community decisions with socially acceptable outcomes.

In short, the case of Escola Cidadã indicates one road leading toward the horizon of possibility charted out by Freire's ideas. The utopian hope inscribed in this educational experiment is present in its promise to implement democratic experiments within schools. These experiments are happening on a large scale in Porto Alegre and on a smaller scale in many more cities around the world.

Whereas the dominant trend in educational reform worldwide includes testing, accountability, and—ultimately—blaming the victims, Porto Alegre has demonstrated that it is possible to create an alternative space where new pedagogical articulations can be forged and where new common sense about education can be created: It is possible to create a space where all children and their communities feel connected to the schools and feel that the schools serve them. Democratizing access,

knowledge, and relationships in the current context of global capitalism is not easy. The fact that Escola Cidadã is still operating after 15 years of structural adjustment in Brazil—and has expanded its service to an increasing proportion of the impoverished communities of greater Porto Alegre—reflects the power of community organizing in the struggle for democracy.

NOTES

1. Freire, P. (1993). *Pedagogy of the oppressed* (rev. 20th anniversary edition, p. 15). New York: Continuum.

2. Azevedo, J. (1999). *Escola Cidadã: Construção coletiva e participação popular* (p. 14). Paper presented at The Comparative and International Education Society, Toronto.

3. Santos, B. (1998). Participatory budgeting in Porto Alegre: Toward a distributive democracy. *Politics and Society, 26* (4), 467.

4. Baiocchi, G. (1999). *Participation, activism, and politics: The Porto Alegre experiment and deliberative democratic theory.* Unpublished manuscript. Bowles, S., & Gintis, H. (1986). *Democracy and capitalism.* New York: Basic Books.

5. Azevedo (1999).

6. Fischman, G., Ball, S., & Gvirtz, S. (Eds.). (2004). *Crisis and hope: The educational hopscotch of Latin America.* New York: Routledge.

7. SMED (Municipal Secretariat of Education). (2000). *Boletim Informativo–Informações Educacionais.* Year 3, no. 7.

8. Azevedo, J. (1999). A democratização do estado: A experiencia de Porto Alegre. In Heron da Silva Lui (Ed.), *Escola Cidadã: Teoria e práctica.* Petrópolis: Vozes Editora.

9. SMED (Municipal Secretariat of Education). (1999). Ciclos de formação–Proposta político-pedagógica da Escola Cidadã. *Cadernos Pedagogicos, 9* (1), 57.

10. Genro, T. (1999). Cidadania, emancipação e cidade. In L. Silva (Ed.), *Escola Cidadã: Teoria e prática* (pp. 7–11). Petrópolis, Brazil: Vozes.

Teaching and Pedagogy

IDENTITY AS DIALECTIC: RE/MAKING SELF IN URBAN SCHOOLING

Wolff-Michael Roth

My game is the game of life. And in the game of life I use my tactics to get what I want, to do what I need to want to do. Which is what I need is what I want and what I want is what I need. If I want to need to do something then I do it.

> —*Shameer,*
> *African-American, twelfth-grade*
> *student in an urban school*

Good teachers know their students, for to prepare an appropriate curriculum, they have to address their emotional, motivational, and cognitive needs. Knowing students—for example, Shameer, the author of the introductory quote—poses questions. "Who are our students?" "How can we find out about them and what their needs are?" "How do students understand themselves today as compared to yesterday and tomorrow?" To understand her students, Joanne, a white, middle-class woman attending a teacher preparation program in a large U.S. city, interviews students during a yearlong internship in an urban school serving a largely poor neighborhood. Among other things, Joanne is interested in the differences between African-American and white experiences of schools and schooling.

Joanne: Do you think there's equal opportunity between blacks and whites?

Shameer: No. 'cause, I have experienced that when I lived in New Jersey. I lived in Linden Hill, New Jersey. I went to a school that was 99 percent white. It was like I would just get B's all the time. I would I know the work, and I was just like, I was young and in my state of mind I was like "Oh, they don't like me." I had a few white friends and you know, we was cool, they didn't see the color thing. It was like, it seemed like the teachers—I remember one time, I was in sixth grade and the teacher, he had put us into groups. It was three black people in the classroom and the rest was white. So, all right, he said we could pick the people we want to work with and there was four people to a group. I had picked—it was me, my friend Richard, Mike, and a girl named Kristen. We always worked together good. And the teacher said no. He put me in the group with the other black kids. That wasn't no problem. I didn't really see that as a problem. But as I got older I began to see that that wasn't right.

In this situation, Shameer talks about himself in a school context where there were predominantly whites. In his account, color was not an issue for his white friends, but in his experience, it had been an issue for the teacher, who has segregated them by color. Shameer says that at the time he did not recognize the segregation as a problem, but he now realizes it as lying at the roots of different social opportunities for white and African-American students. Here, who Shameer is, who he can relate to in school tasks, and the opportunities he has now and in the future, are accounted for in terms of color (race) differences. Not only is he an African-American student, recognizable by his skin color, but his biographical narrative also articulates and reifies these differences as part of and influencing his life trajectory.

There is more to the episode. Shameer has agreed to be interviewed, has shown up on time at the arranged meeting place, and has sincerely answered Joanne's questions. Agreeing, showing up, and answering questions are actions that have specific outcomes. In acting, however, Shameer does more than achieve these outcomes: He also produces himself as a particular kind of student—an African-American urban kid amenable to a white teacher's request, collaborating so that she can complete a university course assignment, and participating willingly, which facilitates Joanne's task tremendously. In these actions, Shameer also re/produces himself, who he is with respect to others—here his teacher, and perhaps through her, also his school. That is, he re/produces identity, an aspect of human life that has received too little attention in the scholarly literature, to the detriment of our being able to understand what knowing, learning, and schooling are all about.

IDENTITY

Identity (from Lat. *idem*, same)—who we are for ourselves and who we are in relation to others—is a mysterious phenomenon for at least two reasons. First, Shameer can point to a picture and say, "This is me when I was five, and the street I lived on—but don't nobody be on there but the drug dealers." In this case, although there are substantial differences between Shameer and the child in the picture with respect to the physique and particulars of the body, including size, hair color, and so on, he is making an assertion about the sameness of whomever is depicted and he indexically refers to that child as "I." He makes this assertion despite recognizing that he was more aggressive at some time in his life, continuously fighting with other kids, and that "[He] ha[s] mellowed in [his] later years." Thus, who he is and was is part of a biography—a narrative featuring the same person (character) with both constant and changing character traits in the course of his life (a plot).

Second, as he is moving from situation to situation in his daily life, he is someone different with respect to the others surrounding him. In the episode, he is a student amenable to his teacher's request for doing an interview. He accedes to her wish and, in a sense, contributes to supporting her development as an urban teacher. But only a few months after the interview, Shameer is involved in an altercation with his chemistry teacher, which escalates to the point that he risks being suspended or even expelled. Shameer's actions and the rules of his school culture seem to be incompatible. That is, Shameer is a different person in a different situation. Who he is with respect to teachers and school is inherently frail so that a stable identity in interaction with others is the outcome of continuous reproduction.

Shameer: When I'm in the house, I curse. An' I curse, and when I'm outside I curse more. An I'm more, when I'm outside I'm more, aw'right—Like aw'right, I don't got to speak to nobody when I'm outside. But I speak to my boys, like "wha'a up" give em a handshake. When I see my friend parents, I say aw'right, "How ya doin' Ms. Debbie. What's up Mr. Earl." Like when I speak to the lady, I say "how ya doin'?" but to the man, "What's up"? See the difference. I curse in school, just not around the teachers. Or when I do curse and it is around teachers, it's probably cursin' with them. . . . Like when I'm cursin' when the teacher hear me, it's probably like helping the teacher out. . . . The teacher probably say, "Thank you," or he say, "Don't curse, but thank you."

There are therefore at least two aspects to identity. On the one hand, a person appears to have a core identity, which undergoes developments that are articulated in autobiographical narratives of self. In this perspective, events in our lives may provide us with resources to understand ourselves differently, leading to changes in our biographies. This aspect has been articulated in terms of the narrative construction and reconstruction of self, which is a function of the particular collective with which we identify. Second, in contrast to the contention of identity as a (relatively) stable phenomenon that is constructed in biographical narratives, the experience of the different ways in which we relate to others in the varying contexts of everyday life has led postmodern scholars to conceive of self in society as something frail, brittle, fractured, and fragmented.[1] We have to ask, how can our identities simultaneously be continuous and discontinuous, context-independent and situated, stable and frail, or adaptive and brittle? Why are there differences between the self in narratives and in ongoing, concrete daily life?

By drawing on documentary materials from research in urban schools, identity here is articulated as a dialectic phenomenon and concept. As in all dialectical units, there is an inner contradiction, which expresses itself in antinomies and logical contradictions, such as the ones articulated here. This dialectical perspective on identity leads to an understanding better than

other theoretical perspectives on the opportunities and constraints that students from poor African-American families face in the schools of a predominantly white society. In this perspective, two elements that do not exist or hardly exist in other approaches take central roles: (1) Human beings have physical bodies that mediate between private and public lives; and (2) the individual and collective (society, culture) stand in a mutually constitutive (dialectical) relation.

The two forms of identity articulated above, despite their radical difference, nevertheless share one aspect: Both are the consequence of actions—*telling* an autobiographical narrative and *doing* interviews or *telling* off a teacher. This makes it appealing to construct a theoretical account that centrally focuses on actions, in which distinct forms of identity are the *effects* of different forms of actions.

IDENTITY AS DIALECTIC

The question of identity can be articulated in terms of the contrast between two contrasts: (1) between "same" and "other," and (2) between the "material body" (flesh) and the "person" as a whole (Figure 1). The relationship between the different contrasts leads to different sets of dialectical relations articulated within different research traditions.

The first contrast articulates the difference between a being caught up in and *practically understanding* the world, from which it is not distinguished ("same"), and a being that experiences itself as different,

same   material body

⇕   ⇔   ⇕

other   person

Figure 1.
Different dialectical relations emerge from the contrast of same and other, on the one hand; and material body and person, on the other—both in cultural (phylogenetic) and individual (ontogenetic) development.

"other" than the world and its objects that are the targets of their intentional and explanatory actions.[2] It is a being that does not reflect on its own relation with the world, a being that simply relates to other things and other people without objectifying them. When Shameer in the heat of the moment says to a teacher, "See man this is why I don't like y'all, I don't like y'all teachers or y'all school," he relates to the teacher in an unmediated way. Upon reflection, which objectifies the situation and its participants, he might regret having made the comment or understands it in context and knows that he would not make it with the principal present. When Shameer is mad at his chemistry teacher and walks out of the classroom after hearing he scored 65 on his test, Shameer is simply relating to his world, including the teacher. When he later says to the teacher, "I just got mad [at you] because it wasn't my paper that you read off your sheet," he is in a mediated relationship to the foregone events and situation. He conceives of the teacher as another person, who became the object of his anger. When anger, grade, and teacher are conscious entities, the relationship to the world is no longer direct but mediated, explicated, and objectified.[3]

The second contrast opposes the material body of a human being with its personhood. Through the materiality of the human body comes the continuity in, and accumulation of, our experience. The human body continuously changes, both as the result of the actions that it brings about and as the recipient of the actions of others. It is because Shameer has a body that others on the street can make him a target of their violence ("Like, yo, these bunch of dudes tried to roll on us, they'd be like how many of them was there and what size was they?") and teachers can "screw him" ("I always get screwed by the teachers."). It is this body that is adorned, coiffed, and put in relief by means of special clothing. The body, carrier of emotions, is central to identity, aspirations,

and identification of the youth. This body is so important, because it is the "mediator between the self and a world which is itself taken in accordance with its variable degrees of practicability and so of foreignness."[4] The body is not merely the seat of knowledge—"wet ware" in computer-speak—but importantly the central structure that gives shape to what and how we know.[5] At the same time, human beings are more than their bodies: They are persons who relate intentionally to other things and beings, who see in others reflections of themselves; that is, beings who have intentions and experience themselves as persons.

When the dimension of *same* is applied to the material body–person contrast (Figure 1), we arrive at the dialectic of *sameness* (material body of the human subject) and *selfhood* (human being as a person). Thus, Shameer's experience of his continuity through time (e.g., his pointing to a childhood picture) is a consequence of sameness, whereas his changing selfhood is apparent when he asserts being different (e.g., in different relations, through time). When the concept of *other* is applied to the material body–person contrast (Figure 1), we arrive at the *otherness* of things (material objects, signs) and persons (human beings). It is because they have bodies that are different from our own that we can both understand others and yet be different from them. It allows Shameer to both understand his teachers ("I was givin' [the teachers] reasons, I was givin' them more and more reasons to make 'em do make 'em suspend me and that's probably what they wanted.") and be different from them.

The experience of the otherness of things and people is neither innate nor does it come by itself: It requires social mediation, as research with very young and older deaf-blind children has shown.[6] That is, the human capacity for communication and reflection is founded on otherness: Both the signs (language) used in communication and the things signs denote are different from (other than) the persons expressing and *explaining* themselves. Applied to the material (body), the same–other distinction leads us to a dialect of the acting subject, distinct from the object of its actions. Applied to the person, the same distinction leads to selfhood and otherhood (otherness of other people), which is at the heart of the dialectical relation between individual and collective (community).

Different traditions use different elements from this overdetermined collection of relations as the starting point for their reflections. In hermeneutic phenomenology,[7] the foundational dialectics required in theorizing identity are selfhood I sameness, selfhood I otherness, and understanding I explaining—where I use "I" to create new, dialectical concepts that are better suited to describe the complexities of life.[8] In cultural historical activity theory, the foundational dialectics required in understanding human activity are subject I object, individual I collective, and unconscious I conscious; the three dialectics arose together with the division of labor and the associated societal mediation of activity, each dialectic presupposing the other two dialectics.[9] So, too, the three dialectics arise in individual development, when children discover themselves and the otherness of their parents, the otherness and permanence of objects surrounding them, and cause and effect relationships (explaining), which already require their practical understanding of how the world works. Common to both approaches is that any of these relations can only be pondered in relation to concrete material actions and activities. To understand actions, a closer look at the agency I structure dialectic is required.

CONTINUOUS RE/PRODUCTION OF IDENTITY AS CONSEQUENCE OF AN AGENCY|STRUCTURE DIALECTIC

Fundamental to recent sociocultural theories is the dialectical relationship that makes agency and structure two mutually constitutive aspects of the *same* unit of action.[10] Concrete actions, such as *uttering* "I was young and in my state of mind I was like 'Oh, they don't like me'" as part *telling* of a biographical narrative or *saying* "eff off" and *showing* the middle finger as a way of "*dissing*" (disrespecting) a teacher, require structures. Without a body, there are no vocal cords to produce utterances and no middle fingers that can be pointed upward. These material (bodily) structures are *resources* that enable actions. Other resources for action are social structures, such as those between teachers and students, which, in the case of "dissing," have not been reproduced in their standard form. There are embodied structures (*schemas*) as well, for without them, sentences and signs could neither be produced as part of social action nor recognized as the social actions of others. What the relevant sociomaterial resources are and which embodied schemas are enacted in a specific situation cannot be known in advance, but are after-the-fact empirical matters. Thus, although Shameer, as an "A" student, may have the intention to follow (school) rules, whether he does can be established only *a posteriori*. Although Shameer only wants to ask his chemistry teacher why he has received a "D" despite answering all the questions, he in fact starts an altercation. That is, he does not merely *ask a question*, but this same action *is starting an altercation*.

Social structure provides resources to action, and therefore resources to the re/production of identity. Whether Shameer will utter a particular phrase takes into account the resources he finds in a situation, such as the institutional position of the other person. Shameer would not say to his principal, "See man, this is why I don't like y'all, I don't like y'all teachers or y'all school," but he "might say that to a teacher." Whether he actually says it to the principal or a particular teacher is again an empirical matter:

Shameer: [With] certain teachers I do certain things—you can't play the same game with all the teachers, 'cause it not the same teacher. So it's certain games you gotta play. If you wanna play—it's like goin' to, it's like goin' on to a basketball court, there certain ways you gotta play with certain teams.

For human beings, schema and sociomaterial resources historically coemerge in and as a result of activity. Thus, early in life, a person does not recognize an action as a social action—Shameer did not perceive his teacher's request to join other African-American students as an act that was *reproducing* racial segregation and social inequalities. It is only now, after appropriate schemas have developed as a result of participating in the world, that he *perceives* racial segregation and the production of inequality when they occur. He has learned to perceive and respond to actions that re/produce particular forms of social structure while participating in various forms of activity, including schooling. That is, participating in various forms of sociomaterial life has formed his body and therefore aspects of his identity such that he can now perceive what he previously was unable to perceive. In addition to bringing about intended results, actions form and are inscribed in human bodies as traces.

Human beings can be the recipients of the actions of others, such as when Shameer became the target of "a bunch of dudes that tried to roll on [him]." But in such situations, human beings are not just recipients ("patients") of the actions of others; rather, the results of actions are codetermined by subsequent actions. Whether the dudes roll on him or whether they just tried depends on Shameer's own actions. Or, to take another example, the institutional relation between an elementary teacher and African-American student were reproduced when Shameer and the three other black students arranged to work together in the new group. Shameer's actions thereby contributed to stabilizing rather than questioning, disrespecting,

and disrupting the traditional authority-based teacher–student relation. In the instance with his chemistry teacher, where he questions the cause of his "D" grade, his actions question not only teacher authority but also school rules, with the result that he was almost suspended or expelled. A suspension or expulsion, in turn, would have contributed to the reproduction of lower attendance rates of urban students.

It is important to note that the same student action can actually achieve two different outcomes. For example, with the action of uttering "See man, this is why I don't like y'all, I don't like y'all teachers or y'all school," Shameer not only produces disrespect for the teacher, but also produces (and gains) respect among his peers. What is the source of these opposite but simultaneously produced meanings? Some social theories distinguish actions that realize the goals of human subjects (individual or group) from activities that pursue collectively (society) formulated motives.[11] Activity and actions, however, mutually constitute one another: They are dialectically related. One the one hand, it takes concrete human actions to bring off an activity—the activity is constituted by an appropriately sequenced series of specific actions. On the other hand, an action is produced in the service of a specific activity. It is only in relation to a specific activity that an action obtains its sense. In the present situation, Shameer is participating in two different forms of activity, pursuing two different motives: *schooling*, with the articulated motive of producing student learning (cultural capital), and *relating to peers*, with the motive of generating social capital.

Most social and psychological theories consider emotions and motivation separately from cognition (e.g., intentional actions). However, both emotion and motivation function as valuations of actions and plans with respect to their potential of increasing individual agency: They are integral to cognition and practical action. Emotions and motivations are not merely aspects of personal identity, something individuals experience just like that and by themselves. They are inherently socially mediated experiences, which human beings learn in the course of their upbringing and therefore have both bodily (momentary, accumulated) experiential and cultural characteristics. Emotions are therefore integral not only to the subject | object dialectic, but also to the individual | collective dialectic, constituting emotional possibilities at the collective level, always concretely realized, produced, and reproduced in particular form at the individual level. Thus, the action of "dissing" the teacher is inherently related to Shameer's personal emotional state and motivation, which are themselves constitutive of and reproducing collective (peer group) emotion, motivation, and solidarity. It is only from the perspectives of school and teacher that Shameer may appear unmotivated and his actions understandable without considering individual and collective emotions. Both motivation and emotion, again, are integral aspects of identity that require a material body.

THE RIDDLE OF SELF: NARRATIVE IDENTITY AND DIS/IDENTIFICATION

One of the fundamental riddles of identity is the continuity and stability of self in the face of the material and personal changes we undergo from situation to situation in and across different periods of our lives. Thus, although the narrator Shameer is no longer the same as the protagonist self-reflectively denoted as "I" in the following account, and although the protagonist has changed even within this account, Shameer and the different "I's" are also held to be the same.

Shameer: I used to get in trouble. I was the biggest problem. I was the teachers' nightmare.

Like when it came down to it, I did do the work but I had a temper and a behavior problem. This was in elementary school. Me and my friend called Sabee used to beat people up. We used to roll on people. Then when me and my bul separated from beating people up, I retired.

When I moved to New Jersey, I was what they wanted. They wanted to get me mad. I was in a school with all Caucasians and there was prejudice. I was a fool cause I was like playin' they game. I would feel like I was getting mistreated different from another student and instead of going to the teacher and talkin' to 'em, I would just get mad and throw stuff, which mean I'd get suspended and I'd get pink slips and all that. I don't know why I got back to Philly. I was like that and then I just changed soon as I got to seventh grade. I just changed. I started getting good grades. I was on honor roll and stuff and it just went from there ever since.

Here, the continuity is re/produced by means of language and the narrative format, associating a character ("I") with a changing personality and a plot (from behavior problem to fool of Caucasians and ultimately honor student). It is through such narratives, which require language as a tool, that the continuous and constant aspects of self are (consciously) produced (which allows for change) and reproduced (which allows for stability and continuity) in the face of change.[12] The narratives have as their main elements a character and a plot, which are the tools for constructing continuity (character) in the face of an unfolding plot.[13] Others can understand Shameer's autobiographical narrative, because of the general nature of the genre. Language and narrative format of autobiographies are the crucial resources for bridging the time, from past to present and future. These resources provide us with a sense of continuity and stability in the face of continuously changing worlds and selves. Without language, humans would not be able to have the particular experiences that make them distinct from other beings. These narratives, therefore, do not describe self as such, but always self in relation to other things and people. Who we are, therefore, is the result of interactions with otherness (things, people) constructed and reified in autobiographical narratives, with which we consciously identify. Generally, these narrative identities are continuously augmented by accounts of new experiences; but, sometimes, new experiences can also lead to a reconfiguration of previous narratives. Thus, Shameer would have told different narratives of self at an earlier time—for example, he now tells what happened to him in the New Jersey school in terms of the color differences between him and his peers, and racism among the teachers, whereas the color differences were not an aspect of his identity earlier in his life.

In acting (saying, manipulating), we not only do something to the world, but also re/produce who we are with respect to others. Thus, when Shameer "disses" his teacher, he also gains respect in his peer community, where others recognize his actions as something familiar, something they themselves might do and recognize as basic emotion that they also experience. In recognizing Shameer's action as part of their action possibilities, Shameer's peers inherently constitute themselves as members of a collective with which they, upon reflection, may also consciously identify. As part of an activity system, individual and collective are always dialectically related. However, individuals may identify or not identify with the collective motive of the activity. Identification and disidentification (as it is commonly called in organizational studies) and emotional tonality (positive, neutral, negative) are correlates— positive and negative emotions in interactions with others are associated with identification (solidarity) and disidentification, respectively. Identification and disidentification are not only the consequences of structural relations between individual and collective, but are also: (1) the outcomes of reflective processes that relate self and collective; and (2) re/produced through shared (solidarity) symbols. It is

at this point where an antinomy can appear between structural identification, based on the re/production of institutional practices (e.g., through their actions, students contribute to reproducing schools and schooling), and personal disidentification, which is the result of emotional and motivational alignment with a different activity.

When Shameer says to his teacher in the presence of peers, "See man, this is why I don't like y'all, I don't like y'all teachers or y'all school," his utterance (action) articulates and expresses an emotional stance which many of his peers unconsciously sense and with which they can (consciously) identify, an emotional stance that they coproduce, for example, by shouting "Yeah!" In the first instance, Shameer's actions re/produce particular structural relations characteristic of urban schools, including resistance to being instructed in a way that normally works for white middle-class students. Much like "taking part in an ethnic riot is not simply a way of acting out a preexisting ethnic identity, but a way of strengthening it, re-creating or even creating it,"[14] taking part in resistance to instruction acts out, strengthens, recreates, and creates (ethnic) identity among the students. Depending on the emotional toning, students consciously dis/identify with the current activity. Thus, within the activity of schooling, Shameer disidentifies with the collective motive, which is articulated and expressed in his utterance. At the same time, he identifies with his peer groups, within which the same utterance is associated with a positive emotional toning.

In this situation, Shameer and his fellow students re/produce *themselves* and their peer community while participating in the re/production of a (shared) *emotional tonality*, which, in its positive incarnation, constitutes their solidarity, and in its negative incarnation, expresses the relation to the (oppressive) school system and its representative, the teacher. Their actions are inherently motivated in this way, although they may not appear so within the activity system defined by schooling and school. However, Shameer and classmates also re/produce themselves as members of their peer group through the public and private identification with symbols, which, when they are shared, characterize solidarity within and of a group. Shameer begins a PowerPoint presentation about his school life ("Life and Times of Shameer") with a title page containing a collage of photographs featuring championship wrestlers, rap artists, and professional athletes (football, basketball players). Several photographs feature persons showing one or both middle fingers and testy facial expressions; in his presentation, Shameer also highlights the strength and attitude of several idols.

In presenting these images, he not only makes statements about himself, who he identifies with, articulating shared symbols of power, attitude, and aptitude, but his statements are recognized and identified with by his peers. In making the statements, he publicly re/produces shared symbols and, in this, also re/produces his own membership in the peer group. Such conscious identification infiltrates articulations of self with respect to school subjects. In the following conversation, Shameer talks about his answer to a question another researcher had asked him about "science and I."

Shameer: It was science is everything, no, science is everything and I'm science. The world and everything in it is science. And I'm science so the world is mine. It's LL Cool J.

Interviewer: Really? Does he say science?

Shameer: No, he say, he say, "Hip-hop the streets and I'm hip-hop, so the streets is mine."

In this episode, two different relations are integrated. Shameer directly relates to the interviewer, and both collaborate to produce a narrative that constitutes him as a particular student. He relates to the interviewer, but the production of this social re-

lation, and therefore the production of his identity, is not thematic in the interview transcript. More so, Shameer does not just say something about his relation to science, but coarticulates identification with the rapper LL Cool J.

Among students, the body plays a central role with respect to identification. Many of Shameer's peers donned cornrows in the style of basketball star Allan Iverson. Here, haircut and hairstyle are symbols leading to and being the result of solidarity, and therefore symbols of individual and collective identification. They play an additional role as a symbol of group solidarity through individual I collective identification with a sports figure, who thereby becomes an emblem for other individuals who have seen this person as the focal center of a collective ritual. Hoods are also symbols of solidarity: Wearing hoods and engaging teachers in a game of putting the hood over the head and being asked to take it off increases the solidarity among students, not in the least because "hood" sounds the same as "'hood," short for neighborhood, the way these urban students refer to where they live. Whereas the teacher instruction "Take your hood off!" may lead a student to take off the hood, the interaction itself leads to a reproduction of his identification with the "'hood." Hairstyle and adornments therefore serve as additional symbols that both create solidarity among students and define the boundaries that exclude teachers and school administrators: "Sometimes you get the evil stares, like 'Oh, he's bad, got graffiti on his jacket and a big 'fro' or if I had braids, 'Oh he bad news, he a gangster or somethin'.'"

IDENTITY, EMOTIONS, AND SCHOOLING

There are both continuous and discontinuous aspects to the human experience of identity, both intimately related to the experience of self with respect to the other and the result of mediational processes. The dialectical nature of identity, integrally related to emotional toning, pre-supposes the human body as the producing and experiencing agent. Although experience is inscribed in the body, which at any moment is the result of all prior experiences, it requires reflection and language as a mediational tool to construct and experience the constant and continuous aspects of identity. Emotional toning and solidarity, available in shared actions (practices) and symbols, allow and constitute dis/identification. Identity and emotions are not stable or personal features of human existence but are continuously re/produced, individually and collectively. Dis/identification and associated motivations are the outcome of underlying dialectic processes rather than constituting internal contradictions. The degree of identification is a function of the relationship between the contribution to the ongoing collective activity and the contribution to enhancing individual possibilities and the individual's capacity to understand this relationship. The identity of the "unmotivated" urban student is re/produced in the lack of a relationship between working for school and getting ahead, or the failure to recognize that doing well can lead to getting ahead despite all odds associated with being an urban kid.

It may be surmised that teachers in urban schools often do not know their students, which mediates the preparation of appropriate curriculum. These teachers neither experience nor participate in producing solidarity, which inherently creates barriers to producing positive emotions and conscious identification with schools and schooling. The values embodied in the students' root culture are different from those embodied in the white, middle-class culture that characterizes schooling. This affects the re/production of emotional toning, interactions in the native and school cultures, and publicly and personally sustained identification through shared symbols (cultural icons). As a re-sult, school culture is not only anathema to the students' home culture, but the difference is continuously reproduced as such.

Change will require processes that allow students and teachers to develop solidarity, which can only come about through mutual focus, collective action, and shared emotionality. Our work in urban schools gave rise to a praxis that has exactly these features: cogenerative dialoguing.[15] In co-generative dialoguing, students, teachers, and administrators (if applicable) get together to talk about and theorize events at the school in order to better understand them and bring about changes together. All members of the newly formed collective contribute, are heard, and enact responsibility for the present and future events. In all participants, this gives rise to a sense of being in the situation together and a positive emotional toning, which are associated with the experience of solidarity. It had been through such a cogenerative dialogue involving Shameer, his chemistry teacher, a preservice teacher, a postdoctoral fellow who knew him well, and two researchers that the main protagonists of the altercation over a grade were able to come to a common understanding of the situation and of the other—which had the consequence that Shameer was not suspended.

CODA

Most discussions in schools and universities uncouple cognitive issues (what is the curriculum to be like) from the emotional and motivational, as if students were computers in which to put information. Identity ought to be more central in considerations of knowing and learning—including emotion and motivation as core elements—without which cognition cannot be understood. Identity, emotion, and motivation are both cultural (collective) and personal (individual), so that they cannot be understood unless we take into account the dialectical relation between collective and individual.

NOTES

I am grateful to Ken Tobin for accepting me into his research group, for the support he provided in my own data collection, and for allowing me to access existing data.

1. Giddens, A. (1991). *Modernity and self-identity: Self and society in the late modern age*. Stanford, CA: Stanford University Press.
2. Buber, M. (1970). *I and thou*. New York: Touchstone.
3. Heidegger, M. (1977). *Sein und zeit*. Tübingen, Germany: Max Niemeyer Verlag.
4. Ricœur, P. (1992). *Oneself as another* (p. 318). Chicago: University of Chicago Press.
5. Merleau-Ponty, M. (1945). *Phénoménologie de la perception*. Paris: Gallimard.
6. Mikhailov, F. (1980). *The riddle of self*. Moscow: Progress.
7. Ricoeur (1992).
8. The Sheffer stroke " | " is a logic combination representing "not and" or (NAND). We use it to create concepts from mutually exclusive terms to describe inherently contradictory phenomena more appropriate. See, for example, Roth, W., Hwang, S., Lee, Y., & Goulart, M. (2005). *Participation, learning, and identity: Dialectical perspectives*. Berlin: Lehmanns Media.
9. Holzkamp, K. (1983). *Grundlagen der psychologie*. Frankfurt/M.: Suhrkamp Verlag.
10. Sewell, W. (1992). A theory of structure: Duality, agency and transformation. *American Journal of Sociology, 98* (1), 1–29.
11. Leont'ev, A. (1978). *Activity, consciousness, and personality*. Englewood Cliffs, NJ: Prentice Hall.
12. Ricœur, P. (1988). *Time and narrative* (vol. 3). Chicago: University of Chicago Press.
13. Roth, W. (In press). Fundamentalist and scientific discourse: Beyond the war metaphors and rhetoric. In L. Jones and M. Reiss (Eds.), *Teaching about scientific origins: Taking account of creationism*. New York: Peter Lang.
14. Collins, R. (2004). *Interaction ritual chains* (pp. 82–83). Princeton, NJ: Princeton University Press.
15. Roth, W., Tobin, K., Elmesky, R., Carambo, C., McKnight, Y., & Beers, J. (2004). Re/making identities in the praxis of urban schooling: A cultural historical perspective. *Mind, Culture, & Activity, 11* (1), 48–69.

THE PROFESSIONAL DEVELOPMENT OF TEACHERS OF SCIENCE IN URBAN SCHOOLS: ISSUES AND CHALLENGES

Mary M. Atwater and Malcolm B. Butler

The most recent reform movement in science education began when the American Association for the Advancement of Science (AAAS) in its Project 2061 asked what science knowledge high school graduates should possess by the year 2061, when Halley's Comet returns. In its publication of *Science for All Americans*, AAAS outlined the "understandings and habits of mind [that] are essential for all citizens in a scientifically literate society."[1] The publication of *Science for All Americans* was the first phase of Project 2061 in its efforts to improve science literacy in the United States. Mathematicians, engineers, natural scientists, and social scientists were asked to define the knowledge, skills, and attitudes *all* students should possess upon high school graduation. However, there was an outcry from the science education community that science and mathematics educators were not involved in the first phase of Project 2061. Hence, AAAS in its second phase of

Project 2061 included these groups in conceptualizing "how students should progress toward science literacy, recommending what they should know and be able to do by the time they reach certain grade levels" in *Benchmarks for Science Literacy*.[2] Now science teachers had guidelines about what concepts and theories should be taught during four grade spans: K–2, 3–5, 6–8, and 9–12. However, the National Research Council decided to expand the works of AAAS by developing standards not only for science content, but science teaching standards, standards for the professional development for teachers of science, standards for assessment in science education, standards for science education programs, and standards for science education systems.[3]

In order for major science curriculum changes to occur in U.S. schools, stakeholders became concerned about how teachers of science (K–12) would enhance their knowledge and skills to implement the new curricula. That began a plethora of National Science Foundation initiatives to enhance school systems to be able to provide quality science to *all* of their students. Thus, large grant initiatives were made available. These include the statewide systemic initiatives, the urban systemic initiatives, the rural systemic initiatives, and the local systemic initiatives. In 1993, the National Science Foundation identified 25 urban school systems that were eligible for funding under the urban systemic initiative (USI) program. Here was the opportunity for some urban schools to change *what* science they taught and *how* science was taught. Many lessons are being learned from these urban science projects. Other private foundations began to fund standards-based systemic reform efforts. Many of these funding sources required a team of a school system and a university or college to submit a grant for funding considerations. However, the U.S. Department of Education had received funding for the professional development of mathematics and science teachers through the Dwight D. Eisenhower Professional Development Program established under Title II of the Elementary and Secondary Education Act of 1965 and amended in 1984.[4] This program funded professional development activities for teachers of mathematics and science through federal activities, state and local activities, and through demonstration projects. The state and local professional development activities were funded by money given to state education agencies, school systems, and state higher education agencies. These funds were targeted for the enhancement of science content based on standards, teaching based on research findings, and the teaching of students from marginalized groups in science.[5] It was now possible for school systems and others to design and implement professional development programs that extended over several years. In addition, school systems had the flexibility to focus on areas that they believed were their greatest need areas: elementary and middle school teachers who teach science.[6]

Since the 1989 publication of *Science for All Americans*, the political climate had changed in the United States so many stakeholders of public education were now concerned about *all* students receiving a quality education in all subject areas. Some of these concerns were implemented in the No Child Left Behind act. The term *all* has been spelled out in this act. Hence, assessment, evaluation, and teacher quality are covered in the No Child Left Behind act.

With all of these legislative events, a variety of professional development efforts have begun. This chapter will discuss some of the issues and identify some of the challenges associated with the professional development of urban teachers of science. The authors will explore the strengths and weaknesses of the various professional development efforts to enhance science teacher quality and discuss implications and recommendations for the professional development of urban teachers of science.

PROFESSIONAL DEVELOPMENT OF URBAN TEACHERS OF SCIENCE

Science learning is influenced by the curriculum, the teacher, the classroom environment, and assessment and evaluation.[7] Much research has been conducted on preservice science teacher education.[8] Less has been done on inservice science teacher education or the professional development of teachers of science after initial certification; yet, in the last few years more research has been done in the area of professional development of beginning teachers.[9] Hence, the professional development of K–12 science teachers has targeted their science content knowledge, teaching methods along with science content, and their abilities and skills related to assessment and evaluation.

When educational reform efforts are under way, stakeholders try to determine what factors influence student performance. In the most recent science education reform efforts, teacher quality has been identified as one of the variables influencing student learning and performance.[10] Teacher effectiveness in science classrooms is influenced by the subject matter knowledge of teachers,[11] knowledge of teaching and learning, teaching experience, and certification status.[12] Since the professional development of teachers of science usually focuses on the changing factors, it makes sense that the professional development of K–12 urban science teachers would include enhancing: (1) the science knowledge of teachers since scientists are making new discoveries each year; and (2) their knowledge of science teaching and learning. Science teaching and learning knowledge would include the new ideas about assessment and evaluation. If the goal is to change the actions of

less successful urban science teachers, then professional development should include opportunities for teachers to try their ideas in the classroom. Hence, one-session workshops do not provide the opportunity for science teachers to discuss with others and evaluate their new teaching efforts in their classrooms. Ongoing, continuous professional development is becoming the new norm.

PROFESSIONAL DEVELOPMENT AND TEACHER QUALITY

Teaching in ways that will realize enhanced goals for diverse students requires a great deal of teachers. They must know their subjects more deeply. They must become students of their students' thinking and learn how to connect new learning to the knowledge their students bring. They [teachers] are also students of their students' cultural backgrounds, examining their own biases, recognizing students' strengths, and reaching diverse learners with a relevant and rigorous curriculum. Teachers need to become designers of learning environments that are sufficiently flexible to accommodate varying needs of learners, with the full array of tools currently available and access to others as new tools emerge.[13]

In the above quote, the authors identify many of the challenges urban teachers of science face as they prepare students to succeed in science in ways that afford their students opportunities for careers in the sciences, while maintaining students' cultural capital and sense of community. When considering the myriad approaches that have been utilized to enhance the knowledge, skills, and attitudes of urban teachers of science, these approaches focus on three areas: teachers' content knowledge, teachers' pedagogical knowledge, and teachers' understanding of the assessment and evaluation of students. These areas can serve as vertices around which to connect the many national, regional, and local attempts to improve the quality of urban teachers of science through professional development. Concomitantly, these areas resonate with the commonly held belief that the classroom teacher has the most potential to improve student performance.[14] As mentioned previously, improved student performance in science is a common theme throughout these teacher learning opportunities.

Teacher's Content Knowledge

The issue of content knowledge has been particularly nettlesome for urban elementary teachers, who typically lack a sound background in the various science content areas, especially in the physical and earth sciences. This issue is much less of a concern in secondary schools. However, for urban schools with large numbers of teachers teaching out of field, it is not unusual to find urban high school science teachers who have very limited science backgrounds.[15]

Many urban professional development programs have included components that attempt to increase the science knowledge of practicing teachers, especially elementary teachers. These programs typically involve professional scientists and science educators implementing inquiry activities that have embedded in them the scientific background necessary to carry out the inquiries. Any increase in the teachers' science content understanding is typically assessed via pre/post assessments.

The Elementary Science Partnership Program (ESEP) is an example of a program with an emphasis on improving the content background of elementary teachers (grades K–5).[16] This program's goal was to effect systemic change in science education over a five-year period. The changes were expected to take place throughout the entire school district. Numerous partners were involved in this project, including the Atlanta Public Schools and seven area institutions of higher education. The content knowledge of the participating elementary teachers was enhanced via summer workshops

with lead teachers who had been taught inquiry approaches to teaching science, as well as the science needed to teach the science kits that were to be used in the teachers' classrooms. During the school year, volunteer faculty scientists from the participating colleges and universities mentored the teachers, focusing specifically on the accuracy of the science being taught by the teachers. The teachers had an undergraduate science major, a "science partner," in their classrooms. These college students were able to assist with numerous aspects of teaching children science, with an emphasis on the science being current and correct. The ESEP is but one example of professional development programs designed to address the science content background needs of urban teachers.

Teacher's Pedagogical Knowledge

There are many issues related to urban teachers of science and their pedagogical skills. Many of these teachers have not been prepared to work with students who have a cultural orientation and lived experiences that are very different from the teachers.[17] How then does one gain the knowledge and skills necessary to teach in ways that will increase the academic performance of students who have traditionally performed poorly on standardized assessment measures? We must help teachers to instruct students in science in ways that build upon students' cultural capital and affords them the opportunity to connect "school science" with the science of their everyday lives, while also preparing students for the world of science beyond high school should those students desire to pursue science, mathematics, engineering and technology (SMET) careers. Consequently, professional development programs for urban teachers of science have focused on topics such as culturally relevant pedagogy and culturally responsive pedagogy.[18]

Two well-respected precollegiate programs that have as one of their outcomes improved science instruction are the Mathematics, Engineering and Science Achievement program (MESA) and the Science, Engineering, Communications and Mathematics Enrichment program (SECME). While the major goal of MESA and SECME is to increase the number of high school students of color who pursue mathematics and science-related majors in college,[19] both programs provide professional development opportunities for the teachers of their student participants. The major component of the professional development takes place during the summer via workshops and institutes. The school year finds MESA and SECME teachers involved with their students on projects and activities learned during the summer. These interactions may require new skills of the teachers, some of which have been learned over the summer. MESA and SECME have had urban communities as their target audiences since their inceptions.

In addition to these two areas of knowledge, a relatively new area of teacher knowledge has emerged in science education—that of pedagogical content knowledge.[20] Pedagogical content knowledge (PCK) is an amalgam of content knowledge and pedagogical knowledge, in which teachers exhibit an understanding of what makes specific concepts difficult or easy to learn, an awareness of the fundamental concepts in a particular discipline, and knowledge of ways of presenting and creating an environment that is conducive and accessible to learners. Since being introduced less than twenty years ago by Shulman,[21] PCK has become an integral component of professional development designs for urban teachers of science.

Assessment and Evaluation

As mentioned earlier, a major emphasis of the reform movement in science education has been the identification of more effective methods of assessing student learning. The primary reason for the push in changes in assessment is because of the disconnect between curriculum, instruction, and assessment. Ideally, the science curriculum should be hands-on and minds-on. Instruction should include inquiry and inquiry-based activities. The assessment, whether formative or summative, should also be reflective of such curriculum and instruction. For urban teachers of science, this sort of assessment is not commonplace for multiple reasons. For example, low student expectations, lack of effective classroom and materials management skills, and inability to link science assessments to students' lives[22] are reasons for lack of attention to student assessment. Professional developers have attempted to address this aspect of teacher quality in multiple ways. A common professional development design includes involving teachers in critically examining current state science standards. Once a sound understanding of the standards is achieved, teachers are then challenged to write and identify effective ways of instructing to meet the new standards. The next logical step is to then have teachers consider how they might assess the standards. Indeed, some states are having teachers submit their assessment ideas so they can be linked to the state standards via the Internet (e.g., see Georgia's new standards, the Georgia Performance Standards, www.doe.k12.ga.us.). When teachers are asked to develop assessments that meet the needs of their students, the needs of the teacher, and the needs of the school district or state, one could expect a certain level of angst. However, the reality for urban teachers of science is indeed one that necessitates they be adept at meeting multiple needs quickly and efficiently. Effective professional development programs afford teachers the time to explore these assessment issues in an intensive manner. As with other professional development programs with systemic expectations, there is a workshop during the summer (when school is not in session), with follow-up during the school year once implementation is under way.

A program organized by the Council of Chief State School Officers (CCSSO) is attempting to address the issue of quality assessment items. The Science Education Assessment Project is part of a larger CCSSO assessment initiative, the State Collaborative on Assessment and Student Standards (SCASS), which began over ten years ago to assist states with assessment issues.[23] Now in its fourth phase, the Science Education Assessment Project has resulted in a CD-ROM that contains over 1,300 science assessment items. The CCSSO staff conducts workshops to assist teachers with the use of these items with their students. Five states are currently involved in this program. Although the current level of involvement is minimal, this initiative does seem to merit watching, especially as more states become involved and look to the program to assist in meeting the needs of urban teachers of science.

Student assessment assistance such as the aforementioned CCSSO initiative has the potential to provide the support urban teachers of science need to better assess and evaluate their students at the confluence of school science and lived science. Multiple assessments give teachers a holistic view of what students know about and are able to do in science. Evaluation can improve if the assessments are multiple, appropriate, and consistent with the curriculum and instruction.

The authors have not attempted to identify an exhaustive list of all the professional development needs of urban teachers of science. The three areas delineated and discussed here seem to be common in most teacher learning activities. We strongly suggest that interested readers delve deeply into the resources at the end of this chapter for much richer discussions of these issues. Many of these writings are the work of people who live with the daily reality of teachers who have a desire to make their science teaching come alive for their students. Their commitment to professional development that improves

teacher quality, and in turn affects student achievement, is quite evident.

IMPLICATIONS AND RECOMMENDATIONS

The overview of professional development for urban teachers of science revealed some highlights as well as areas of concern. It is with these thoughts in mind that some implications and recommendations are offered. It is hoped that the elucidation of these science education-related issues might become a larger part of the conversation of improving urban schools.

One of the most important issues that must be addressed is the lack of attention to the documentation of the professional development of urban teachers of science. While there is a dearth of reports on the professional development of elementary teachers of science, the problem becomes even more acute for the professional development of high school science teachers. The lack of documentation leaves many gaps in the way professional development activities for urban teachers of science are planned, implemented, and evaluated. For example, there are few research findings that are available on successful and systemic professional development efforts for urban K–12 science teachers.[24] School systems, private organizations, and researchers should begin to make available to others their results related to the professional development of K–12 science teachers. These results can be shared through journal publications, paper presentations, books, and postings on Web sites. In addition, more research is needed on the factors affecting the professional development science activities such as science standards, student characteristics, student learning needs, current and proposed teacher practices, and organizational structures and leadership.[25] It is extremely important to identify successful systemic models for the professional development of urban teachers of science. Even though models may need to be altered to be useful in other urban settings, at least professional developers can begin their work in an informed manner.

The selection process for professional development participants should be conducted just as carefully as choosing those teachers who will teach in urban schools.[26] We must continue to study and share what we know and learn about working with urban classroom teachers as they attempt to become better educators for their students.

It is important that stakeholders in science education understand the influence of teacher quality on students' performance in science. Professional development activities can aid developers and researchers in discerning what knowledge and skills should be updated. What professional development activities are needed with beginning K–12 urban science teachers so that fewer and fewer of these teachers leave the profession before the completion of their fifth year of teaching? What professional development efforts are needed to aid K–12 teachers who are teaching students whose backgrounds are different from their own? Unfortunately, most K–12 urban science teachers are monolingual; do we need professional development to help these teachers become literate in a second language that is spoken in their schools? How might these efforts differ for a teacher of science? Such professional development workshops have been implemented; however, one study recommended that more is needed.[27]

The notion of accountability must be a part of any conversation regarding how professional development can serve to improve student performance in science. While urban teachers of science and their professional developers should focus their energies on improving student performance, knowing that improved student performance must be reflected in improved student achievement on statewide assessments will allow teachers to meet the needs of their students and well as the expectations of policy makers.[28]

Technology will continue to play a large role in urban professional development, as a conduit for reaching large numbers with information. However, it should not be seen as a panacea, but rather as a tool that can be used to facilitate change in teacher knowledge and actions so that the performance of urban science students will improve.

Lifelong learning has found support in the academic setting; hence, the professional development of K–12 urban teachers needs to be viewed as one facet of lifelong learning opportunities for teachers. How do school systems fund the professional development of all of their K–12 science teachers? The "lead teacher" approach has been used with elementary urban teachers of science. However, this approach is not effective if "lead teachers" do not have reduced teaching loads to help teachers implement their new knowledge and skills. Funding and time become barriers. Maybe contractual agreements with teachers need to change so that they are paid for professional development activities and implementations.

These are a few implications and recommendations for the professional development of K–12 science teachers. However, it is apparent that if these issues are considered holistically, the expected improvements in teachers' content knowledge, pedagogical knowledge, pedagogical content knowledge, and student assessment and evaluation understanding will be witnessed. As stakeholders learn more about systemic and successful professional development of urban teachers of science, student performance in science will improve so that by year 2061, *all* students in urban schools will be scientifically literate.

NOTES

1. American Association for the Advancement of Science. (1989). *Science for all Americans*. Washington, DC: American Association for the Advancement of Science, Inc., p. 30.

2. American Association for the Advancement of Science. (1993). *Benchmarks for science literacy.* New York: Oxford University Press, p. xi.

3. National Research Council. (1995). *National science education standards.* Washington, DC: National Academy Press.

4. Dauchess, A. *Funding opportunities at the department of education.* http://www.learner.org/theguide.

5. Dauchess, A. *Funding opportunities at the department of education.*

6. Florida Department of Education. *Letter to district school superintendents.* http://www.firn.edu/doe/cefo/archivedmemos/dpbm_memo/dpbm01.

7. Gowin, D. (1981). *Educating.* New York: Cornell University Press; Novak, J. (1977). *A theory of education.* Ithaca, NY: Cornell University Press.

8. Anderson, R., & Mitchner, C. (1994). Research on science teacher education. In D. Gabel (Ed.), *Handbook of research on science teaching and learning* (pp. 3–44). New York: McMillan Publishing Company.

9. Anderson & Mitchener (1994); Wiggins, J. (1993). *Roles, interactions, and mentoring styles of teacher support members in a middle grade science teacher induction program.* Unpublished dissertation, University of Georgia, Athens.

10. Darling-Hammond, L. *Teacher quality and student achievement: A review of state policy evidence.* http://epaa.asu.edu/epaa/v8n/.

11. Druva, C., & Anderson, R. (1983). Science characteristics by teacher behavior and by student outcome: A meta-analysis of research. *Journal of Research in Science Teaching Review, 20* (5), 467–479; Monk, D., & King, J. (1994). Multilevel teacher resource effects in pupil performance in secondary mathematics and science: The case of teacher subject matter preparation. In R. Ehrenberg (Ed.), *Choices and consequences: Contemporary policy issues in education.* New York: ILR Press.

12. Darling-Hammond, *Teacher quality and student achievement: A review of state policy evidence.*

13. Loucks-Horsley, S., Love, N., Stiles, K., Mundry, S., & Hewson, P. (1992). *Designing professional development for teachers of science and mathematics.* California: Corwin Press.

14. Ascher, C., & Fruchter, N. (2001). Teacher quality and student performance in New York City's low-performing schools. *Journal of Education for Students Placed at Risk, 6* (3), 199–214;

Cross, C., & Rigden, D. (2002). Improving teacher quality. *American School Board Journal, 189* (4), 24–27; National Commission on Mathematics and Science Teaching for the 21st Century. (2000). *Before it's too late: A report to the nation from the National Commission on Mathematics and Science Teaching for the 21st Century.* Washington, DC: U.S. Department of Education.

15. National Commission on Mathematics and Science Teaching for the 21st Century (2000).

16. Blackmon, A. (2003). *The influence of science education professional development on African American science teachers' conceptual change and practice.* Unpublished dissertation. Emory University, Atlanta, GA.

17. Seiler, G. (2001). Reversing the "standard" direction: Science emerging from the lives of African American students. *Journal of Research in Science Teaching, 38* (9), 1000–14; Seiler, G., Tobin, K., & Sokolic, J. (2003). Reply: Reconstituting resistance in urban science education. *Journal of Research in Science Teaching Review, 40* (1), 101–103; Tobin, K. (2000). Becoming an urban science educator. *Research in Science Education Review, 30* (1), 89–106.

18. Foster, M. (1995). African American teachers and culturally relevant pedagogy. in J. Banks (Ed.), *Handbook of research on multicultural education* (pp. 570–581). New York: Macmillan Publishing; Nelson-Barber, S., Trumbull, E., & Wenn, R. (2000). *The coconut wireless project: Sharing culturally responsive pedagogy through the world wide web.* Hawaii: WestEd. (ERIC Document Reproduction Services No. Ed465370).

19. Somerton, W. (1994). *The MESA way: A success story of nurturing minorities for math/science-based careers.* California: Caddo Gap Press.

20. Barnett, J., & Hodson, D. (2001). Pedagogical context knowledge: Toward a fuller understanding of what good science teachers know. *Science Education, 85* (4), 426–53; Lederman, N., & and Gess-Newsome, J. (1992). Do subject matter knowledge and pedagogical content knowledge constitute the ideal gas law of science teaching. *Journal of Science Teacher Education, 3* (1), 16–20; Shulman, L. (1986). Those who understand: Knowledge growth in teaching. *Educational Researcher Review, 15* (2), 4–14; van Driel, J., Verloop, N., & DeVos, W. (1998a). Developing science teachers' pedagogical knowledge. *Journal of Teacher of Education, 41,* 3–11; van Driel, J., Verloop, N., & DeVos, W.

(1990b). Developing science teachers' pedagogical content knowledge. *Journal of Research in Science Teaching, 35* (6), 673–695.

21. Shulman (1986).

22. Seiler (2001); Aaronsohn, E. (195). Preparing monocultural teachers for a multicultural world: Attitudes toward inner-city school. *Equity & Excellence in Education, 28* (1), 5–9; Turner, C. (1993, November). *Teachers' perceptions of effective classroom management within an inner-city middle school.* Paper presented at the Annual Meeting of the Mid-South Education Research Association, New Orleans, LA.

23. Halbrook, A. (2003). Science SCASS. *The SCASS Exchange, 4.*

24. Kim, J., Crasco, L., Blank, R., & Smithson, J. (2001). *Survey results of urban school classroom practices in mathematics and science: Using the survey of enacted curriculum conducted during eight USI site visits. How reform works: An evaluative study of National Science Foundation's urban systemic initiatives* (Study Monograph No. 3). Washington, DC: National Science Foundation; and David, J., & Shields, P. (2001). When theory hits reality: Standards-based reform in urban school districts: Final narrative report. Philadelphia, PA: Pew

Charitable Trusts; Lightbody, M., & Jones, L. (1998). *A comparison of the efficacy of different models of technology instruction for inservice teachers.* Paper presented at the annual meeting of the National Association for Research in Science Teaching, San Diego, CA. National Network of Eisenhower Regional Consortia and Clearinghouse (The Eisenhower Network). http://www.math sciencenetwork. org.

25. Loucks-Horsley, Love, Stiles, Mundry, & Hewson (1992).

26. Haberman, M. (1987). *Recruiting and selecting teachers for urban schools.* New York: ERIC Clearinghouse on Urban Education. (ERIC Document Reproduction Services No. ED292942).

27. Burney, T., & Cantalupo, D. (1990). *Staff development workshops for high school science teachers of limited English proficient students 1988–1989.* New York: New York Board of Education. (ERIC Document Reproduction Services No. ED 319611).

28. Powers, J. (2003). An analysis of performance-based accountability: Factors shaping school performance in two urban school districts. *Educational Policy, 17* (5), 558–585.

CONTEMPLATIVE URBAN EDUCATION

David Forbes

AN EMERGING FIELD

Contemplative urban education is a Zen koan: How can one be calm, meditative, and present in an urban school? Such sites are most often typified by overworked, impatient activity governed by the pressured demand to meet preestablished goals: The past determines the present for the sake of a future that never arrives. The reverse is also true: Urban schools tend to be places marked by mind-numbing boredom and dead time; for many, the future (the bell, summer, retirement) cannot arrive soon enough. In all cases urban schools appear to be the antithesis of the contemplative realm, the ability to be fully present, right here, right now.

A contemplative stance, gained through mindfulness meditation, is characterized by uncertainty and open-endedness, a state of awareness in which one is receptive to whatever is occurring in the present. As such it cannot be captured by rubrics, reduced to objectives, or translated into empirical, measurable observations. A contemplative perspective considers education to be more than just academic achievement and economic success. It envisions the cultivation of wisdom and compassion in us and in all our students. There is an urgent need for the contemplative in all levels of education to the extent they share traits similar to Stephen C. Rockefeller's description of undergraduate education as "too head-centered as distinct from heart-centered, more interested in information than appreciation, more concerned about the knowledge which is power than wisdom and ethical values, more oriented toward I-it than I-thou, more skilled at striving for future ends than living a fulfilling life in the present."[1]

The study and practice of contemplative approaches in urban education is an emerging field. Higher education courses that teach a contemplative perspective exist across the United States and Canada, ranging from law and medicine to psychology and the arts.[2] Courses on contemplative approaches to education per se are taught at Columbia, Naropa University, the University of Toronto, and Brooklyn College, among other schools. Linda Lantieri's Project Renewal, which addressed the post-9-11 trauma of New York City students and educators, has developed a contemplative-infused curriculum for urban public schools.[3] Even public school administrators have begun to express an interest in spiritual development as part of educational leadership.[4]

THE FINGER IS NOT THE MOON

Educators tend to seek solutions outside themselves, such as more training or skills, and to seek certainty in the learning process.[5] Yet certainty, knowing the answer or objective in advance, diminishes learning and growth. The field of education favors whatever can be categorized, labeled, observed, and measured, and tends to neglect the realm of conscious development and higher awareness. Educators who become more concerned about test scores, rubrics, and measurement instruments than the experience and process of learning confuse the constructs with the thing itself,

akin to Whitehead's fallacy of misplaced concreteness. To borrow a metaphor from Zen, they are mistaking the finger pointing at the moon with the direct experience of seeing the moon itself.

The social complexities of urban education are considerable. To survive and thrive in such a world, the cultivation of higher consciousness beyond empirical reductionism becomes a universal imperative. Steinberg and colleagues' postformal cognitive theory argues that the way to do so is to contextualize urban education within social, cultural, political, economic, historical, and ideological categories.[6] It also calls for the meaning of personal identity to be seen within broader, socially constructed realms of race, ethnicity, class, gender, and sexuality.

Contextualizing of this sort through social constructions is necessary; yet even such a process may not be sufficient for the enormous task at hand. Contemplative urban education takes this project a step further: it places *all* social and ideological contexts *themselves* within an all-encompassing context. It does so by employing mindfulness meditation, a tool of the contemplative tradition, within everyday urban life. Mindfulness meditation subjects every socially constructed category, identity, and thought to nonconceptual, nondual awareness. To rest one's mind in this infinite, spacious context is to transform the moment and to see things as they are. Social constructs are useful, but they are not ultimately descriptive of the interdependent and unified nature of reality. Over time a meditative practice leads to the experience of wholeness and equanimity, the capacity for compassion and understanding toward all people, and the ability to create a life inseparable from everything in the universe.

Contemplative urban education enables educators to be open to the present and to see the transformative, everyday possibilities that are hidden by socially defined categories. Contemplative practicco extend beyond students' construction of their social identity to the level of spiritual meaning and purpose. This is an interior realm, one with which many educators are unfamiliar and uncomfortable; yet exploring it can lead to higher levels of awareness and growth. In a case study, high school student athletes were able to refer to the experience of the zone as a metaphor for higher states of experience that transcended socially constructed categories such as ethnicity.[7] The zone is a state of higher awareness that can occur when the athlete is playing in the present and can be reached through persistent meditation.

An urban environment is an added challenge. The external distractions and challenges of city life are greater than in a small town or suburb and can match the ones our own minds conjure up. Yet from the standpoint of contemplative traditions themselves, the urban school setting is precisely the place in which to practice mindfulness. Contemplative traditions encourage practitioners to take every distraction not as an obstacle but as an opportunity to get to know one's mind better, to see how it operates, and to bring it to peaceful awareness. Situations that produce disruptions and that lead to disappointments, frustrations, tensions, and difficulties are tremendous opportunities to observe the nature of one's mind. At heart, the urban school evidences the very things that the contemplative vision perceives from a higher perspective: the interdependence of everyone, the necessity for all of us to get along, the appreciation of difference, and the realization of underlying similarities.

Contemplative urban education occurs from time to time within the spaces of everyday urban school life. When a teacher and a class are in sync, silently reflecting on a significant question the answer to which no one knows; when a poem that has been read aloud touches everyone deeply and stuns them into silence; when a genuine dialogue occurs after a painful conflict that opens up the participants to realms of uncharted awareness; when a teacher creates a few moments of meditation to still the mind from frenzied, unreflective thought, and everyone in the room catches a glimpse of peacefulness: that is when a profound, nonconceptual experience occurs that cannot be captured by language. Many educators are startled by such moments and consider them to be serendipitous, inchoate events that are churned back into ordinary classroom experience and forgotten. Contemplative urban educators, however, are mindful of those moments and consciously seek to rescue and nurture them. They propose that the awareness that characterizes these experiences is what education is all about. While bearing in mind that any theory is not the practice itself, contemplative practices that enhance such moments deserve to be legitimated as a higher order educational approach. The contemplative thrives in everyday spaces wherever urban educators and students become mindful of this reality. It is a realm accessible to everyone. Once it is pointed out, it can be practiced, cultivated, discussed, and theorized about. Many of its practical effects can be measured as well.

ROOTS OF CONTEMPLATIVE PRACTICE IN EDUCATION

A significant source of contemplative urban education is the holistic education movement.[8] Holistic educators consider education as a spiritual endeavor that must involve the whole child and his or her interconnectedness with the world. Education in a holistic sense acknowledges the human condition and seeks to promote each individual's search for higher meaning rather than socially determined notions of success and happiness.[9] It transcends the reductionist view that regards education primarily as a means to enhance society's economic efficiency, competition, and domination. Holistic education can include contemplative practices such as being open to and attending to the present, taking care, and seeing in each present moment the opportunity for transformation.[10] It includes both inner development and meaningful social community. Parker Palmer appealed to educators to be faithful to both the inward teacher and the community of truth, and to hold to thinking that allows for both/and, not either/or, experience.[11] David Purpel invoked a prophetic education in which educators promote social justice and oppose violence and exploitation and places these values in a moral and spiritual vision and tradition.[12] Linda Lantieri noted that spiritual aspects such as the capacity for creativity, love, meaning, and purpose cannot be taught, but in schools they can be "uncovered, evoked, found, and recovered."[13]

The contemplative dimensions that give life meaning and purpose have been at the heart of liberal education since its inception, according to physics professor Arthur Zajonc.[14] The contemplative is a method and a realm that is related to truth and is not reduced to religious faith, and can be included in teaching and research.[15] Contemplative practice, along with empirical and rational ways of knowing, leads to the ability to look more deeply at the nature of things within any discipline. Zajonc has described how contemplative practices in science and music courses heighten awareness, attentive listening, and concentration along with traditional analytic approaches.[16] Contemplative practice then is not anti-intellectual, nor does it seek a return to prerational, intuitive levels that celebrate myth or magical thinking; rather, it incorporates and transcends empirical and rational knowledge.[17]

MEDITATION IN SCHOOLS

Mindfulness meditation has measurable benefits that can be applied to education.[18] Meditation is a significant means of contemplation. Through meditation one deliberately creates time for cultivating peace or stillness. The only purpose is to be fully present in the moment. This is a challenging task, as we often spend much if not most of our mental energy thinking about the past or worrying or planning for the future, including fantasizing about what we do not have right now. Thich Nhat Hanh, a Vietnamese Buddhist peace activist and educator, says:

We tend to be alive in the future, not now. We say, wait until I finish school and get my PhD degree, and then I will be really alive. When we have it, and it's not easy to get, we say to ourselves I have to wait until I have a job in order to be really alive.[19]

Peacefulness falls into this category of being a vague goal in some distant future. For Nhat Hanh, however, there is no path to peace; peace is the path. Being peaceful now is what is required. The means must be the ends; a mindful, meditative approach is both a means and an end.

Meditation is the contemplation of one's own mind, beginning by attending to one's breathing as a way to keep bringing the restless mind back into the present. According to Jon Kabat-Zinn:

When you sit, you are not allowing your impulses to translate into action. For the time being, at least you are just watching them. Looking at them, you quickly see that all impulses in the mind arise and pass away, that they have a life of their own, that they are not you but just thinking, and that you do not have to be ruled by them. Not feeding or reacting to impulses, you come to understand their nature as thoughts directly. This process actually burns up destructive impulses in the fires of concentration and equanimity and non-doing. At the same time, creative insights and creative impulses are no longer squeezed out so much by the more turbulent, destructive ones. They are nourished as they are perceived and held in awareness. Mindfulness can thereby refashion links in the chain of actions and consequences, and in doing so it unchains us, frees us, and opens up new directions for us through the moments we call life.[20]

DEVELOPMENTAL ASPECTS OF CONTEMPLATIVE URBAN EDUCATION

The contemplative is a means to uncover and evoke spiritual experience as part of the whole development of the child. Children are natural contemplatives.[21] However, their contemplative capacities are not full blown and need to be cultivated with respect to developmental levels. Contemplative practices in school classrooms can include deep listening, body focusing, and journaling.[22] The contemplative approach assists in different aspects of development including the following.

Cognitive Development

Insight meditation (*vipassana*) may be a valuable tool for cognitive development. It can promote the practice of metacognition, the ability to think about thinking and to further categorize one's thoughts from a higher perspective. The higher stages for developmentalists like Kegan and Loevinger involve the ability to reflect on one's own reflective categories, to make thinking itself an object of higher order thought.[23] Meditation also can help a teen gain insight into the self, by examining thoughts and feelings and tracing them back to broader categories of thoughts that in turn can be examined and attended to with compassion. It provides a method and practice to let go of the attachment to anger and oppositional thinking that often accompanies critical consciousness. Some research suggests that meditation improves cognitive development as measured by Loevinger's sentence completion test.[24]

Gender Identity Development

Both young men and young women experience the strain of maintaining conventional gender identities. Male youth feel their identity must be constantly tested as to whether it is ever masculine enough. Girls feel pressured to be popular and gain approval of boys, often losing their sense of self by taking the perspective of the other.[25] Through meditation young men can become less attached to identifying with constructs of conventional masculinity: acting tough, not expressing nurturing feelings. This provides a way out of the dilemma of either giving up all power or clinging to pressured expectations of manhood, and allows them to develop a broader definition of self. Girls learn to listen to their inner voices and invoke and identify their higher sense of self, one based on nonjudgmental compassion. They watch thoughts and feelings come and go rather than succumbing to conventional pressures and losing their authenticity.

Emotional Development

Meditation helps one become attentive to bodily sensations and emotional feelings. This may be especially beneficial for male youth.[26] Part of the gender role of conventional masculinity is that men are not taught how to recognize their feelings. When boys are asked how they feel, they often do not know how to answer.[27] Ronald Levant presented data that suggested that most boys display low-level alexithymia, being emotionally shut off.[28] Meditation helps all children open up to feeling states and sensations through attending to what they are experiencing. It creates the space for one to notice the changing nature of feelings such as anger or boredom, to trace their origins, and to be mindful enough so that authentic responses to what is going on become possible. Contemplative approaches to music, art, and journal and poetry writing are similar in this regard.

Social Development

The contemplative appreciation of difference can lead to higher development.[29] Relationships are changed through commitment to openness and a tolerance for uncertainty without preconceptions. Through meditation one is more open to and understanding of the other, and learns to see the other as ultimately inseparable from oneself. Multicultural and contemplative awareness complement each other as development occurs in both inner and outer terms.[30] In multicultural settings meditation can diminish anxiety, frustration, and judgmental reactions. Rather than relying on cultural-specific knowledge, people are more understanding of others when they assume a contemplative approach: Detach from one's own experience, observe one's and others' behaviors and reactions, refrain from prejudging, and relax enough to gain an understanding of why differences are disturbing.[31] A contemplative approach can be used in peer mediation and conflict resolution programs in schools. The practice of mindful social engagement as part of a curriculum cultivates compassion for others.[32]

Wellness

Urban adolescents undergo considerable stress. With respect to health and behavior, adolescent students had lower blood pressure from practicing meditation as well as better concentration and fewer attendance and behavior problems in school.[33] In one college level study relaxation meditation improved the memory of African-American college students.[34] James Garbarino has shown that meditation offers a middle way between acting out and repressing one's feelings, and can provide a spiritual grounding for interventions that seek to reduce some effects of early trauma.[35]

As a contemplative practice yoga has physical and emotional benefits for children and has become popular in some schools.[36] Yoga curricula that avoid language that can be construed as religious have been successfully implemented in schools.[37]

Students, especially in urban schools, need a sacred time and space to center themselves and feel a sense of peace. A structured, protected time for meditation and visualization provides some students with the only quiet moment of the day during which they can connect with a deeper part of themselves and the world.[38]

Teachers

Urban teachers themselves undergo considerable stress. They are often exhausted, experience time pressures, and have little time to reflect; some realize they impose some of these pressures on themselves, and often express interest in finding a more balanced life that includes time and space for reflection on what is really important in their lives.

The educator Parker Palmer speaks of the courage to teach, and says that the best teachers are those who teach on the basis of who they are.[39] He has encouraged educators to cease being divided from themselves, to live a whole, full life, and to evoke the voice of the teacher within through contemplative practices before trying to create this kind of community for others.[40] In using Tibetan meditation in teacher education Richard Brown refers to the importance of making friends with one's mind through the direct experience of meditation and compassion.[41] Sam Crowell, a professor of education, suggests that teachers conduct "a genuine investigation into ourselves as part of the process of teaching authentically. . . . When we respond to knowing with our whole being, it not only changes us and our circumstances, but it also transforms the nature of what is known."[42] Rachael Kessler refers to the teaching presence as a necessary quality of good teaching.[43] This requires being present, open to perceiving what is happening and being responsive to the present moment, being able to let go of a particular approach, and clearing our minds and hearts before class; these are contemplative ways of being.[44] A mindful educator practices letting go of being attached to one's ego and is able to take things less personally. Tobin Hart[45] describes how members of his department are committed to an empathic, contemplative approach, which he refers to as *beholding*. Beholding means the open possibility for creative problem solving, discovery, and openness to each other through mindful awareness in which one sees things in less rigid categories, so that the possibility for the unexpected can increase.

After-School Athletic Programs

David Forbes led a meditation/discussion program with an urban high school football team.[46] The young men were motivated to practice meditation as a way to increase their chance of playing in the zone, a state of higher awareness. They worked on noticing and letting go of judgments, worry, irritation, doubts, anger, and other distractions that got in the way of attending to what the moment calls for. Some of the students were able to become more mindful, which allowed them to play in the present, and they applied these skills in other everyday situations with their peers. Athletics and other after-school programs that provide both sufficient motivation and interest to students are potential sites in which educators can cultivate and disseminate contemplative practices within the school.

Whole School

Within the school itself a mindful approach can generate more advocacy and collaboration. Deborah Rozman suggested that teachers also can refer to meditation as awareness training, concentration, centering, and relaxation, among other alternative terms, when bringing a program to members of the school community.[47]

She and other educators have discovered that meditation or some contemplative time at the start of the day creates a more calm, relaxed, and respectful classroom that promotes learning. Mindful classes are linked with good group counseling skills: noticing the stress level in the room, the body language, the energy and participation of the students, and the commitment to cultivating compassionate, open, and wise qualities. Contemplative educators acknowledge difference without becoming overly attached to one's own ethnic, gender, and class identities and the fixed perception of them in others. A meditative approach can contribute to a climate for emotional safety that promotes higher development for all school community members. A contemplative urban educator considers the well-being of the entire school community and is committed to making it a caring, emotionally and physically safe place or sanctuary.[48]

BEING IN THE PRESENT: THE TEACHABLE MOMENT

Urban schools face considerable challenges. There is little in urban education that encourages contemplative practices or provides the space for mindful reflection and awareness of the present that can lead to genuine knowledge. What is more often found is indifference and mindlessness, the lack of presence. Yet bits of awareness are there everyday; what is needed is the sharpening of the contemplative eye to focus the vision. There may be no more pressing need than mindfulness as a means to sanctify and transform the everyday in urban schools. To bear witness with presence and compassion to the pain, humiliation, violence, and hurt feelings; to behold the joys, rhythms, humor, and epiphanies all in the mind's eye is to engage in the life processes of learning, healing, and growth. To contemplate the contemplative within the everyday urban school, a microcosm of the world in all its mad glory, may be a higher awareness still.

NOTES

1. Rockefeller, S. (1994) Meditation, social change, and undergraduate education. Meeting of the Working Group of the Academic Program, Center for Contemplative Mind in Society, September 29–October 2, 1994, Pocantico, NY. Retrieved November 12, 2005 from the Center for Contemplative Mind in Society Web site: www.contemplativemind.org/programs/academic/rockefeller.

2. Retrieved November 12, 2005 from the Center for Contemplative Mind in Society Website: http://www.contemplativemind. org/programs/academic/about/html. Retrieved November 12, 2005.

3. Lantieri, L., with Namblar, M. (2004). Sustaining the soul that serves: Healing from within. *Reclaiming Children and Youth, 3* (4), 120–124.

4. See Spirituality in Leadership issue of the *School Administrator* (2002, September). Retrieved November 13, 2005 from the American Association of School Administrators Web site: http:// www.aasa.org/publications/saissuedetail.cfm ?ItemNumber=1785&snItemNumber=950 &tn ItemNumber=951.

5. Sparks, D. (2003). Interview with Peter Block: The answer to "when?" is "now." Retrieved November 13, 2005 from the National Staff Development Council Web site: http:// www.nsdc.org/library/publications/jsd/ block242.cfm.

6. Steinberg, S., Kincheloe, J., & Hinchey, P. (1999). *The post-formal reader: Cognition and education.* New York: Falmer.

7. Forbes, D. (2004). *Boyz 2 Buddhas: Counseling urban high school male athletes in the zone.* New York: Peter Lang.

8. Miller, R. (1997). *What are schools for? Holistic education in American culture.* Brandon, VT: Holistic Education; Miller, J., Karsten, S., Denton, D., Orr, D., & Kates, I. (Eds.). (2005). *Holistic learning and spirituality in education: Breaking new ground.* Albany, NY: SUNY Press.

9. Krishnamurti, J. (2000). *On education.* Chennai, India: Krishnamurti Foundation.

10. Glazer, S. (1999). Conclusion: The heart of learning. In S. Glazer (Ed.), *The heart of learning: Spirituality in education.* New York: Tarcher.

11. Palmer, P. (1998). *The courage to teach: Exploring the inner landscape of a teacher's life.* San Francisco, CA: Jossey-Bass.

12. Purpel, D. (1989). *The moral and spiritual crisis in education: A curriculum for justice and compassion in education.* Granby, MA: Bergin & Garvey.

13. Lantieri, L. (2001). A vision of schools with spirit. In L. Lantieri (Ed.), *Schools with spirit: Nurturing the inner lives of children and teachers.* Boston, MA: Beacon.

14. Zajonc, A. (2003, Winter). Spirituality in higher education: Overcoming the divide. *Liberal Education,* pp. 50–58.

15. Wilber, K. (1998). *The marriage of sense and soul: Integrating science and religion.* New York:

Broadway; Wilber, K. (2000). *Integral psychology: Consciousness, spirit, psychology, therapy.* Boston: Shambhala.

16. Zajonc (2003, Winter). See Burack, C. (1999, September). Returning meditation to education. *Tikkun* (14), pp. 41–46. Retrieved November 13, 2005, from the *Tikkun* Web site: http:// 72.14.207.104/search?q=cache:4Pt6BqOysiIJ: tikkun.org/magazine/index.cfm/action/ tikkun/issue/tik9909/article/990914a. html+charles+burack+returning+meditation+ to+education+tikkun&hl=en.

17. Wilber (1998).

18. Hart, T. (2004). Opening the contemplative mind in the classroom. *Journal of Transformative Education, 2* (1), 28–46. Retrieved November 13, 2005, from the Mindfulness in Education Network Web site: http://www.mindfuled.org/files/tobin. doc and http://72.14.207.104/search?q=cache: U23Yc-qO9HgJ:66.160.135.235/acrobat/hart_ proofs.pdf+tobin+hart+opening+the+contemplative+mind&hl=en; Miller, J. (1994). *The contemplative practitioner: Meditation in education and the professions.* Westport, CT: Bergin & Garvey; Goleman, D. (2004). *Destructive emotions: How can we overcome them? A scientific dialogue with the Dalai Lama.* New York: Bantam.

19. Kessler, R. (n.d.). The teaching presence. Retrieved November 13, 2005, from the Passage-Ways Institute Web site: www.passageways.org. (Resources, then pdf file, "Teaching Presence")

20. Kabat-Zinn, J. (1994). *Wherever you go there you are: Mindfulness meditation in everyday life* (p. 21). New York: Hyperion.

21. Hart, T. (2003). *The secret spiritual world of children.* Makawao, Maui, HI: Inner Ocean.

22. Hart (2004).

23. Kegan, R. (1994). *In over our heads: The mental demands of modern life.* Cambridge, MA: Harvard; Loevinger, J., & Wessler, R. (1970). *Measuring ego development* (Vols. 1 & 2). San Francisco, CA: Jossey-Bass.

24. Alexander, C., & Langer, E. (Eds.). (1990). *Higher stages of human development: Perspectives on adult growth.* New York: Oxford.

25. Pipher, M. (1994). *Reviving Ophelia: Saving the selves of adolescent girls.* New York: Grosset/ Putnam.

26. Forbes (2004).

27. Kindlon, D., & Thompson, M. (2000). *Raising Cain: Protecting the emotional life of boys.* New York: Ballantine.

28. Levant, R. (1995). Toward the reconstruction of masculinity. In R. Levant & W. Pollack (Eds.), *A new psychology of man* (pp. 229–251). New York: Basic Books.

29. Simmer-Brown, J. (1999). Commitment and openness: A contemplative approach to pluralism. In S. Glazer (Ed.), *The heart of learning: Spirituality in education* (pp. 97–112). New York: Tarcher.

30. Fukuyama, M., & Sevig, T. (1999). *Integrating spirituality into multicultural counseling.* Thousand Oaks, CA: Sage.

31. Fukuyama & Sevig (1999).

32. Arguelles, L. (2002). How do we live, learn and die: A teacher and some of her students meditate and walk on an engaged Buddhist path. In J. Miller & Y. Nakagawa (Eds.), *Nurturing our wholeness: Perspectives on spirituality in education* (pp. 285–303). Brandon, VT: Foundation for Educational Renewal.

33. Barnes, V., Bauza, L., & Treiber, F. (2003). Impact of stress reduction on negative school behavior in adolescents. *Health Quality Life Outcomes*, 1–10. Web reprint retrieved November 13, 2005, from the National Institutes of Health digital archive of biomedical and life sciences journal literature at http://www.pubmedcentral.nih.gov/articlerender.fcgi? artid=155630; Busch, C. (2003, July/August). It's cool to be grounded. *Yoga Journal*, pp. 94–99, 154–156; Fischer, N. (1998, Fall). Teaching meditation to young people. *Turning Wheel: Journal of the Buddhist Peace Fellowship*, pp. 29–31; Fontana, D., & Slack, I. (1997). *Teaching meditation to children: Simple steps to relaxation and well-being.* London: Thorsons/HarperCollins.

34. Hall, P. (1999). The effects of meditation on the academic performance of African American college students. *Journal of Black Studies, 29* (3), 408–415.

35. Getz, A., & Gordhamer, S. Interview with Dr. James Garbarino on mindfulness and violent youth. Retrieved November 13, 2005, from Youth Horizons Web site: http://www.youthhorizons.org/interview/James/html; See Garbarino, J. (2000). *Lost boys: Why our sons turn violent and how we can save them.* New York: Anchor.

36. Brown, P. (2002, March 24). Latest way to cut grade school stress: Yoga. *New York Times*, p. 33.; DeChillo, S. (2002, December 14). Stretch. Pose. Rest. It's kindergarten yoga. *New York Times*, p. B1.

37. Sink, M. (2003, February 8). Yoga in Aspen public schools draws opposition. *New York Times*, p. 36.

38. Glickman, C. (2003). *Holding sacred ground: Courageous leadership for democratic schools.* San Francisco, CA: Jossey-Bass; Kessler, R. (2000). *The soul of education: Helping students find connection, compassion, and character at school.* Alexandria, VA: Association for Supervision and Curriculum Development (ASCD).

39. Palmer, P. (1998). *The courage to teach: Exploring the inner landscape of a teacher's life.* San Francisco, CA: Jossey-Bass; See Intrator, S. (2002). *Stories of the courage to teach: Honoring the teacher's heart.* San Francisco, CA: Jossey-Bass.

40. Sparks, D. (2003, Summer). Honor the human heart: Schools have a responsibility to nurture those who work in them. Interview with Parker Palmer. Retrieved November 13, 2005, from the National Staff Development Council Web site: http://www.nsdc.org/library/publications/jsd/palmer243.cfm.

41. Brown, R. (2002). Taming our emotions: Tibetan Buddhism and teacher education. In J. Miller & Y. Nakagawa (Eds.), *Nurturing our wholeness: Perspectives on spirituality in education* (pp. 3–12). Brandon, VT: Foundation for Educational Renewal.

42. Case studies (2002). Center for Contemplative Mind in Society. Retrieved November 13, 2005, from Center for Contemplative Mind in Society Web site: http://www.contemplativemind.org/publications. "Case Studies" pdf file.

43. Kessler (2000).

44. Arrien, A. (2000). The way of the teacher: Principles of deep engagement. In L. Lantieri (Ed.), *Schools with spirit: Nurturing the inner lives of children and teachers* (pp. 148–157). Boston: Beacon; O'Reilley, M. (1998). *Radical presence: Teaching as contemplative practice.* Portsmouth, NH: Boynton-Cook/Heinemann.

45. Case Studies (2002). Center for Contemplative Mind in Society. Retrieved November 13, 2005, from Center for Contemplative Mind in Society Web site: http://www.contemplativemind.org/publications. "Case Studies" pdf file.

46. Forbes (2004).

47. Rozman, D. (1994). *Meditating with children: The art of concentration and centering.* Boulder Creek, CA: Planetary.

48. Bloom, S. (1997). *Creating sanctuary: Toward the evolution of sane societies.* New York: Routledge.; Noddings, N. (2005). *The challenge to care in schools: An alternative approach to education* (2nd ed.). New York: Teachers College; See Forbes, D. (2004). What

is the role of counseling in urban schools? In S. Steinberg & J. Kincheloe (Eds.), *Nineteen urban ques-* *tions: Teaching in the city* (pp. 69–83). New York: Peter Lang.

CONFLICT RESOLUTION STRATEGIES FOR INNER-CITY YOUTH

Meridith Gould and Anthony Tadduni

Arming youth with relevant violence prevention and conflict resolution strategies is just one example of community-focused approaches to neighborhood transformation. Those of us concerned with the future vitality of all U.S. communities must understand the connections between conflicts that arise on personal, communal, and societal levels. Some thinkers and policy makers have perpetuated the gap between the "inner-city" and the middle- and upper-middle-class communities in the United States. They make the assumption that what affects youth in the lower socioeconomic neighborhoods is not a concern for individuals who live outside of those communities. If we are to build America into a place where all individuals are valued, respected, and treated with equity, we need to take a systemic look at how we create social policies and limit funding to those communities that are most in need. Exemplary groups and individuals have begun to discover creative ways to build bridges across barriers of race, class, and ethnicity—and across generations—through community-focused programming. Instead of drawing lines between communities we need to start teaching community.

THE INNER CITY: A MULTIMODAL SKETCH

It is important to define what is meant by *inner city,* because recent social and economic trends have been altering the landscape of urban centers. It would be problematic to talk about inner-city neighborhoods without also noticing that pockets of affluence have been growing inside cities, which are changing the way that cities look. U.S. suburbanites, fed up with long commutes and high property taxes, are increasingly foraying back into central city neighborhoods, taking advantage of depressed real estate values or just seeking the more fashionable cosmopolitan identity that urban living bespeaks. As a result, checkerboard patterns have emerged within urban neighborhoods and centers; "urban renewal" developers as well as new urban dwellers speak of "good blocks" and "bad blocks," "good neighborhoods" and "bad neighborhoods," coding both class- and race-based stereotypes in these seemingly innocuous classifications. Inner-city neighborhoods are currently being displaced and often exist on the fringes of cities and further away from resources and services. Although cities are changing, inner-city life—defined as economically disadvantaged, isolated, and underresourced—is not; and, in fact, the trend of gentrification just contributes to the list of psychological, social, and economic perils that inner-city residents endure.

Historical, Demographic, and Economic Factors of Inner-City Life

From a historical perspective, gentrification is just the latest movement that is shaping the inner city. During the middle part of the century, suburban migration exploded due to a combination of factors. The G.I. Bill allowed World War II veterans to purchase homes, and many opted for the quiet, wholesome, family-friendly living environment that the suburbs promised. As U.S. cities became overcrowded due to successive waves of immigration and Southern-Northern migration, those who could afford cars and homes often chose the suburbs, seeking to improve their quality of life.

It is important to notice how race played into this history. Despite entrenched enclaves of affluent African Americans in northern cities, many African Americans at the time were recent migrants and, due in part to the inequalities of the public education system, unskilled workers. Suburban migration was therefore not always an option for this segment of the population. The racial isolation that the suburbs offered was no doubt an incentive that influenced suburban migration as well. The 1975 *Milliken v. Bradley* Supreme Court decision, which stated that busing students to the suburbs to integrate inner-city Detroit's mostly African-American student population was not supported by the Constitution or Court precedents, exemplified the notion of building a wall of white privilege around most suburbs.

As the popularity of suburban living increased, demographics in urban centers changed, joblessness expanded, and a majority population of recent immigrants and people of color developed in many American cities. As suburbs expanded, so did public housing projects in inner cities. In the 1932 Museum of Modern Art exhibition of the avant-garde European modernism of Ludwig Mies van der Rohe and Le Corbusier, tall cement buildings—boxes with neat rows of windows punched out— inspired designs for public housing in limited space.[1] In the wake of international economic changes in the 1960s and 1970s, manufacturing jobs, particularly in Northeastern and Midwestern cities, began to disappear. After World War II, most blacks and Hispanics who could follow manufacturing jobs to the suburbs did so, leaving behind the poorest and most unemployable.[2]

The movement of some jobs to the suburbs compounded issues for the urban poor, who often did not have access to automobiles or adequate public transportation available to make urban-suburban commuting feasible. The concentrated poverty of inner-city neighborhoods eroded the tax base of many urban centers during the 1960s and 1970s, and this limited the funding available for public education, law enforcement, and other community services and agencies. In *Inner City Poverty in the United States*,[3] sociologists Laurence Lynn and Michael McGeary note that the suburbs' share of jobs continued to grow in the 1970s, especially in metropolitan areas in which inner-city poverty was increasing the fastest. This suggests that the migration of employment opportunities to the suburbs was related to lower employment rates in inner-city areas. By the 1980s and 1990s, typical poor-neighborhood companies, which provided some of the only employment opportunities available for inner-city residents, intermittently employed workers in nonunion, low-skill, low-wage, and high-risk jobs.[4]

Although it may seem logical, it is not always helpful to make direct connections between joblessness and poverty in inner-city neighborhoods. Poverty and joblessness are often bedfellows, but they are alternately affected by other factors such as racial segregation, access to resources and jobs, social welfare programming, and psychological and social factors. Not only with respect to suburban living, but also within cities, the poor are often priced out of gentrifying neighborhoods due to increasing property taxes and rents, which puts them further away from potential growth sectors of urban economies. William Julius Wilson also argues that inner-city residents in Chicago are subjected to "application profiling"—that is, on the basis of where they live, potential employers often discriminate against them. Employers often assume that if someone has an address that lies within what is considered an inner-city neighborhood, they will most likely lack customer service skills, an appropriate speaking voice to represent the company to the public, and consistent and reliable transportation to the job site.[5] Although these all seem to be reasonable criteria for employment, choosing applicants on the basis of addresses or zip codes often also means discriminating on the basis of class and race.

To gain a clearer picture of the current state of the inner city, it is helpful to look at demographics. People of color and immigrants dominate inner cities. Lynn and McGeary observe that poor blacks are much more concentrated within inner cities than nonblacks.[6] Single-parent families, although also a growing trend for the nation as a whole, have also been increasing in inner cities. The number of female-headed households in inner cities increased 84 percent between 1970 and 1980 in the fifty largest American cities.[7] According to the 1990 census, single-parent families in the five boroughs of New York City represented 38 percent of all families, more than double the percentage in each of three suburban quadrants around New York City. Poverty is also more concentrated in inner cities than in other areas. According the 2000 census, the poverty rate was 31 percent in inner cities compared to 11.3 percent for the rest of the country.[8] Recent increases in homelessness and hunger in U.S. cities, also an indicator of poverty, were one focus of the U.S. Conference of Mayors in 2002.[9]

Inner-City Youth and the Psychological and Cultural Fabric of Communities

For inner-city youth who live outside of mainstream or middle-class culture and, due in part to economic stresses, often lack traditional family structure, gangs often provide a sense of identity, association, pride, and also potential income with respect to drug trafficking. In their review of writings on the subject of inner-city youth violence and drug dealing, Nathan L. Centers and Mark D. Weist argue that many inner-city youth perceive the informal drug trade to offer their most lucrative income opportunities in the face of limited options.[10] The identity, pride, and association that often accompany gang membership come at a price—they involve securing and protecting turf—which often leads to gang violence both in neighborhoods and in schools.

There is a major epidemic of violence in the inner city. Although inner-city violence is often overemphasized in the media and popular culture, it is still a tangible reality for inner-city residents. Interestingly, Mike A. Males has asserted in his book, *Framing Youth*,[11] that white adult crime in the United States, although also on the rise, is seldom discussed. This does not negate the dire consequences of violence in inner cities, particularly for youth. In a sample of 337 New York City high school students, 62 percent had experienced an average of 3.41 of the following 6 types of violence: violence against family, violence against friends, violence against strangers, shot or stabbed, raped, and beaten up or jumped. Just under 30 percent of this same group had seen friends shot or stabbed.[12]

Through one lens, the conflict between community affiliation and violence can be understood through the interplay of middle-class or "dominant" cultural capital and local or "street" cultural capital within the inner city. Cultural capital can be defined as "cultural knowledge, dispositions, and skills that are passed on from one generation to the next."[13] In their analysis of the inner-city Chicago street gang Black Knights Nation (BK), Venkatesh and Levitt show that BK members took cues from images of corrupt capitalists in popular culture in fashioning their personae as major players in Chicago's crack cocaine trade. Although the BK members seem to openly reject white corporate culture and middle-class cultural capital as definitively unattainable to underresourced black men, and although part of their "lit," or mission statement, implies the need for conscious community solidarity, they begin to become more individualist and ambitious for a "respectable" class status as their stakes and prospects in the crack trade become greater. The authors surmise that the brotherhood aspect of the BK, the mentoring to younger kids that had been central to the gang, began to vanish and that "a self-interested preference for illicit earnings was prevalent . . . as a vision [it was] fully compliant with dominant corporate-based ideologies of individual self-worth and identity."[14] In Brian J. Smith's article on a school for juvenile parolees in a large southwestern city,[15] he also highlights the conflict between local cultural capital and dominant cultural capital. Here Smith surmises that it was the school that tried to impart the dominant cultural capital, which emphasizes individual work and achievement, while criticizing and attempting to erase local and gang affiliations. This attempt was unsuccessful, however, because students were entrenched in local cultural capital, which privileged loyalty to gangs and families above all else.[16] Although sanctioning gang presence is not necessarily the answer, it behooves educators and others who are vested in improving inner-city life to investigate and utilize local cultural capital to create more sustainable programming.

Dominant or middle-class cultural capital is reproduced, often unquestionably and without analysis, in schools, at job sites, and in other institutions within the inner city, often compelling inner-city residents to abandon their local cultural capital or risk losing access to resources. One group of sociologists attribute the mutual discomfort between teachers and parents in inner-city schools and the resulting

alienation that ensues to a lack of communication and understanding about cultural differences.[17] Lack of communication and understanding about cultural differences may also limit the relevance and effectiveness of school curricula for inner-city youth. In some local cultures within the inner city, for instance, violence may be considered a normal and even "honorable" response to provocation. This would be important to know when designing violence prevention or conflict resolution curricula for inner-city youth.[18] Educators should investigate and engage with local cultural capital to understand both the challenges and the opportunities that it presents.

Inner-City Communities: Our Communities

Although identifying the challenges of inner-city life is often a reflex for outside observers, it is also important to acknowledge and understand how inner-city neighborhoods have done well in the face of those challenges:

Ethnic minority neighborhoods are not a cultural wasteland. Voluntary spatial concentration can have important social and cultural benefits to ethnic communities and persistent residential segregation is not necessarily associated with labor market exclusion. In addition, many poor neighborhoods possess rich networks of personal and informal relationships that help residents coping with social marginality, the lack of opportunities and resources, and a socio-political climate that deems their lifestyles pathological.[19]

The assumptions that educators make about the inner-city neighborhoods that they work in may either cloud their vision and stifle their effectiveness or present them, and the children and communities that they serve, with a plethora of new ideas and fresh opportunities for holistic engagement.

In the face of many difficult personal, familial, and community issues, inner-city youth—the nurturing of their psychological fortitude and cultural pride—are intrinsic to the endurance and transformation of inner-city neighborhoods, and consequently the health of the country as a whole. Richard Curtis, in his study of neighborhoods in the northeast corner of Brooklyn,[18] which were major trafficking centers for the crack cocaine trade in the 1980s, praised the resilience of local youth. Curtis argues that in the 1990s young people in Bushwick consciously responded to the multiple threats that endangered them—from street-level drug markets, to out-of-control violence, to hard drugs—by altering their own lives.[20] These changes occurred in a neighborhood that was still relatively isolated, poor, and underresourced, proving that being disadvantaged does not necessitate despair.

Much press had been given to the decline in urban crime that has occurred over the last decade. The resulting veneer of "safety" has boded well for proponents of "urban renewal," but the question remains: Who are cities now safer for? Although many American cities have boasted decreases in various types of crime in recent years, approval ratings for some urban police departments have also shown decreases among inner-city residents. This is because crime reduction has in some cases come at the expense of increased targeting and harassment of inner-city residents. The Boston Police Department and a few other urban police departments, however, have taken a community-based approach to crime fighting—engaging with African-American church leaders to help curtail drug trafficking and violence in inner-city communities.[21] Another example of community-minded programming from William Upski Wimsatt's book *No More Prisons* is Barrios Unidos, "a nationwide Latino gang-truce organization with ties to hip-hop," which "takes young gang members to sweat lodges for coming-of-age ceremonies which stimulate the intensity of gang initiations without the violence."[22] This systemic and transformative thinking recognizes the social functions that gangs provide for these youth and manages to curtail violence without stifling community. If educators can understand the importance of conflict resolution and the interconnectedness of personal, communal, and societal issues, then they can factor this understanding into their lessons and policies. Modeling this understanding consistently in the classroom will arm youth with the tools to transform their own communities, and might in turn improve the quality of life in all communities and for all Americans.

CONFLICT RESOLUTION THEORY: AN EDUCATOR'S FRAMEWORK

Conflict Is Constructive

The word "conflict" may be used to refer to a physical confrontation such as a fight, battle, or struggle or used more broadly to mean a disagreement or opposition of interests or ideas. "Conflict," says John Burton, "describes a relationship in which each party perceives the other's goals, values, interests or behavior as antithetical to its own."[23] Conflict is not necessarily negative. Morton Deutsch notes that "conflict is an inevitable feature of all social relations. Conflict can take a constructive or destructive course; it can take the form of enlivening controversy or deadly quarrel."[24] The Chinese pictogram for crisis or conflict has two distinct elements—one meaning danger, but the other meaning opportunity. Conflict resolution is not just about averting danger, or fixing things up, it is about finding and building on the opportunity that is inherent in the event.

Understanding that conflicts arise and are inevitable is an important first step to building peace in our lives. Conflict can be healthy as long as you are choosing effective ways to eliminate the negative consequences of the conflict. Young people are bombarded with conflicts everyday. The objective in using conflict resolution techniques is to move individuals away from a perception of the situation as "us versus them" and to work together to solve the problem. The idea of "win-lose," with one party winning and the other party losing, is replaced by the idea of "win-win": A solution can be found to meet both parties' needs. These techniques, which give people strategies for working together to find win-win solutions to their own problems, can be applied across a wide range of situations in the classroom. Working through small disputes, or even a role play, provides practice in developing the skills and attitudes that will be needed to deal with larger and more difficult conflicts.

Conflict Resolution and Violence Prevention Programming: A "Big Picture" and "Long-Term" Approach

There are many great programs that specialize in creating "safer" schools. They focus on combating bullying, reducing crime, and removing guns from schools. They bring in law enforcement agencies and drug abuse organizations to teach the students why engaging in these behaviors is "bad." What these programs fail to address are the root causes of these important issues. They fail to ask the students, on an individual level, what they think about violence, conflict, and living in their communities. They neglect to ask these inner-city students how they feel about themselves and why they get angry. These programs are reactionary and are usually administered and implemented after a violent act or conflict has taken place. The goal is to create programs that are proactive. Students need the tools to make decisions that are informed and effective before a conflict arises. They need to know how they feel about themselves and how they feel about the world they live in.

Programs that inner-city youth will benefit most from should focus on self, family, and community. They need to promote self-esteem, anger management, alternatives to violence, communication skills, values and ethics, and community and team building. There are many types and levels of violence prevention, conflict resolution, and peace building programming that engage students in meaningful ways. Some of these may already be in place in schools providing opportunities to engage students. Youth need to know who they are and what they value before they are taught how to reduce violence and resolve conflicts. It is important for students to know how they feel about their life situation and what beliefs and behaviors they think are appropriate and ethical. Educators can ensure that school programming is more effective by incorporating conflict resolution principles into the curriculum to work with students on developing these skills.

Conflict resolution strategies and programs for inner-city youth need to be interpersonally and communally focused. Conflict resolution programs created and implemented for schools should not scare educators, parents, or students about violence, but rather make students smarter about the relevant issues. They need to communicate what violence is and how it affects communities.

Students need to understand the violence that exists in their community and learn productive strategies for combating it. It is important to understand that violence is not only defined by isolated incidents, but also embedded in structures that exist in the community. The more students understand about violence and conflict, its causes, and its effects, the more they can do to keep it from growing in their community, their school, and in their own life. Conflict resolution skills do not only focus on violence prevention and creative ways to solve conflicts. The heart of conflict resolution theory is empowering individuals to build peace at an interpersonal, communal, and global level. Teaching students about anger management, diversity, self-esteem, empowerment, effective communication, and team building will enable them to make healthy choices and become change agents in their personal lives and empower others in the communities they live in.

What Students Should Learn from Conflict Resolution and Violence Prevention Programming

Williams and Guerra have identified five core competencies that are important for healthy social and emotional development.[25] If students learn these following tools they will be less likely to engage in violence and conflict situations: positive identity, personal agency, self-regulation, social relationship skills, and a system of belief. Youth need a positive self-concept, hopefulness, and future goals. They need to have self-efficacy and effective coping skills. They should have problem-solving skills, empathy, and peace-making skills. They also need to have norms, values, and moral engagement. When youth lack these skills they engage in violence for many different reasons. Youth associate violence with negative identity, hostile bias, poor impulse control, lack of empathy, and problem-solving skills, aggressive norms, and moral disengagement. An approach to violence prevention and conflict resolution that highlights core competencies emphasizes understanding and addresses the needs of inner-city youth. Introducing these skills alone does not reduce violence and resolve conflicts in the schools. Easy access to firearms and relaxed legislation on firearms makes it easier for inner-city youth to engage in violence behavior. An integrated approach should build on youth development but also acknowledge that there are many social, political, and economic factors that need to be addressed.[26]

In addition to teaching core competency skills students need to learn and feel comfortable expressing their feelings. Youth need to be asked how they are feeling. They need to know that their teachers want to hear what they have to say. Evocative approaches, which empower students to give their perspectives in an environ-ment of shared communication, aid teachers in understanding the root causes of the conflicts their students are experiencing. Creating parameters and team agreements in the classroom allows this evocative process to work very effectively, because it promotes community in the classroom.

Creating experiential activities is very effective in the classroom and can easily incorporate conflict resolution strategies and skills. Students will learn more about the root causes of conflicts and how they handle conflict if you provide them with an experiential lesson. Creating real-life scenarios is also an effective and creative way to get the students interested and involved. Having students analyze and learn about a conflict situation in their community and creating a list of possible resolutions will enable the students to practice for conflicts outside of school. Allowing students to utilize examples of situations similar to those that exist in their community and enabling them to develop their own experience, as a change agent working toward resolving the issue, is fundamentally important.

CONCLUSION

Young people have the opportunity to combat the violence and hateful attitudes that persist in U.S. society. Look around the world today and you will find evidence of violence nearly everywhere. You will see it in the newspaper, at the local movie theater, in the lyrics of the hottest new song on the music charts, and in schools across the country. If violence is this widespread today, think about what it could be like in the future. Youth need to feel that they are important. They need to be able to see change occur. Youth need to be given the skills to learn how to take healthy action so that they can make changes in their own lives and the world they live in. Teaching students to make responsible choices is essential. Having students think about arguments and fights that occur in their school and neighborhood is important so that they can understand that incidents of violence are interconnected. Most young adults have not learned strategies for managing anger and conflicts. They may not even understand what makes them angry, even if the triggers are obvious to people around them.

Students need to feel a sense of accomplishment. Feeling a lack of accomplishment can make them lose respect for themselves and others. When that happens it is easy to forget how to think logically about their choices. Students will be empowered by the freedom to make personal choices and helping them meet this need by choosing their friends and activities. Provide students with the tools to feel a sense of achievement. Encourage students to do well in school, help others, and spend time with their family and off the streets.

APPENDIX: SUGGESTED CONFLICT RESOLUTION LESSONS

Anger Management

The instinctive, natural way to express anger is to respond aggressively. Anger is a natural, adaptive response to threats. It inspires powerful, often aggressive, feelings and behaviors that allow us to fight and to defend ourselves when we are attacked. Anger also can be suppressed and then converted or redirected. Unexpressed anger can create other problems. It can lead to pathological expressions of anger, such as passive-aggressive behavior (getting back at people indirectly—without telling them why, rather than confronting them head on) or a personality that seems perpetually cynical and hostile. People who are constantly putting others down, criticizing everything, and making cynical comments have not learned how to express their anger constructively. The goal of anger management is to reduce both your emotional feelings and the psycho-logical arousal that anger causes. You cannot get rid of, or avoid, the things or the people that enrage you, nor can you change them, but you can learn to control your reactions.

This activity is designed to teach anger management through the "I-message" communication technique and other group activities to help students see that conflict can become a positive situation. It will help students widen their vocabularies with reference to emotions, enable students to describe anger and its effects on them, transition students from inappropriate action when angry to more constructive behavior, give students options with which they can cope with their anger, as well as give students communication tools to aid them in relationships.

Begin the lesson by working with the class to compile a list of feelings: negative in one column, positive in another. You will be referring to this list later. Explain that today the topic will be what happens when people get angry and what they do as well as not do. Ask the class to reflect on the last time that they were angry. Ask them to focus on where that anger came from. Do the angry feelings have synonyms, such as frustration, rage, disappointment, and so on? Ask them to share, as best they can, what happens to them when they got angry. Examples: went to sleep, yelled at their dog, confronted someone, cried, or punched a wall.

Pair the students up and ask them now to share what they felt like when someone was angry at or with them. How did they know the other person was angry? What did they do in reaction to the other person's anger? Have each pair give a brief summary to the group. Record the main ideas on the blackboard. Ask each pair to join with another pair. Ask the new foursomes to discuss if there's any one correct way to handle anger. Report back to the class and record on the blackboard. This is a good time to talk about inappropriate venues of venting anger, such as physical fighting and punching walls. Keep in mind that a physical fight is often honorable with certain peer groups, and often youth are instructed by their parents and peers to only take so much before standing up for themselves physically. Listen and divert to more positive options, rather than challenging the method. Punching a wall and other physical manifestations of anger, if repeated constantly, are mental health issues. The actual physical pain is a catharsis for the internal pain that the student has no idea how to handle. Explain that this lesson is to help students have more options available to them when they feel trapped by their anger.

Self-Respect

The objective here is to illustrate the importance of self-respect and to empower students into believing that only when one respects one's self will they be able to respect others. The first class session will be directed toward preparation for the following session. In session one, each student will be given a brown bag that they will be instructed to decorate with their name and hobbies or interests. Next, the instructor will begin a discussion about positive qualities. Students are encouraged to contribute. Instructor and students should create a list. Examples of qualities include the following: fun, energetic, caring, clever, creative, good friend, polite, loyal, and so on. Following this discussion the instructor will tell each student to pick 15 of their favorite qualities and write them on a piece of paper. The students will then cut each word separate from the others. Each student will place his or her decorated paper bag somewhere around the classroom, taped to the wall. The students will be instructed to place one of each of the pieces of paper into other students' paper bags.

Sheet 1: How I See Myself (using the list of adjectives students are asked to assess themselves using a maximum of ten words). Sheet 2: How I Think Other People See Me. Questions may be provided on these sheets in a true/false setup or the instructor can ask the student to simply write down ten words from the list of adjectives or other words (some may use negative adjectives). Each student will receive the two mentioned sheets. They will be instructed to fill them out honestly. Upon completion of these sheets the instructor will collect them and each student will retrieve his or her paper bag from around the room. Each student will empty out their bag and list the words that other students used to describe them. Follow up the lesson with a discussion.

NOTES

1. Kaslow, A. (1997, August 19). Chronicling the evolution of America's public housing. *Christian Science Monitor, 89* (185), 13.

2. Bernstein, A., Palmeri, C., & Crockett, R. (2003, October 27). An inner-city renaissance. *Business Week* (3855), pp. 64–67.

3. Lynn, L., & McGeary, M. (1990). *Inner city poverty in the United States.* Washington, DC: National Academy Press.

4. Curtis, R. (1998). The impossible transformation of inner-city neighborhoods: Crime, violence, drugs, and youth in the 1990s. *Journal of Criminal Law and Criminology, 88* (4), 1233–1276.

5. Wilson, W. (1999). When work disappears: New implications for race and urban poverty in the global economy. *Ethnic and Racial Studies, 22* (3), 479–499.

6. Lynn & McGeary (1990).

7. Lynn & McGeary (1990).

8. Bernstein, Palmeri, & Crockett (2003).

9. Lowe, E., Slater, A., Welfley, J., & Hardie, D. (December 2002). *A status report on hunger and homelessness in America's cities 2002,* prepared by the U.S. Conference of Mayors. Retrieved from http://www.usmayors.org and http://search.atomz.com/search/?sp-q=Homelessness&sp-a=00061c07-sp00000001&sp-k=Full+Search&sp-advanced=1&sp-p=all&sp-w-control=1& sp-w=alike.

10. Centers, N., & Weist, M. (1998). Inner city youth and drug dealing: A review of the Problem. *Journal of Youth and Adolescence, 27* (3), 395–411.

11. Males, M. (1999). *Framing youth: 10 myths about the next generation*. Monroe, ME: Common Courage Press.

12. Moses, A. (1999). Exposure to violence and hostility in a sample of inner city high school youth. *Journal of Adolescence, 22* (1), 21–32.

13. MacLeod, J. (1995). *Ain't no makin' it*. Boulder, CO: Westview Press.

14. Venkatesh, S., & Levitt, S. (2000). Are we a family or a business? History and disjuncture in the urban American street gang. *Theory and Society, 29* (4), 427–462.

15. Smith, B. (2003). Cultural curriculum and marginalized youth: An analysis of conflict at a school for juvenile parolees. *The Urban Review, 35* (4), 253–280.

16. Smith (2003).

17. Stone, C., et al. (1999). Schools and disadvantaged neighborhoods: The community development challenge. In R. Ferguson & W. Dickens (Eds.), *Urban problems and community development* (pp. 340–360). Washington, DC: Brookings Institute Press.

18. Peacock, M., McClure, F., & Agars,M. (2003). Predictors of delinquent behavior among Latino youth. *Urban Review, 35* (1), 59–72.

19. Boland, J. (2002). Neighborhood effects and cultural exclusion. *Urban Studies, 39* (1), 85–93.

20. Curtis (1998).

21. Winship, C., & Berrien, J. (1999). Boston cops and black churches. *Public Interest, 136*, 52–68.

22. Wimsatt, W. (1999). *No more prisons: Urban life, home schooling, hip-hop leadership, the cool rich kids movement, a hitchhiker's guide to community organizing, and why philanthropy is the greatest art form of the 21st century*. Brooklyn, NY: Soft Skull Press.

23. Burton, J. (1988). *Conflict resolution as a political system, working paper 1*. George Mason University: Center for Conflict Analysis and Resolution, Fairfax, VA.

24. Deutsch, M. (1991). *Educating for a peaceful world*. Presidential Address to the Division of Peace Psychology, Annual Meeting of the American Psychological Association, August 18, 1991. San Francisco, CA.

25. Williams, K., & Guerra, N. (1996). *Supporting youth by strengthening communities*. Boulder, CO: Center for the Study and Prevention of Violence.

26. Williams & Guerra (1996).

ONE DAY AT A TIME: SUBSTITUTE TEACHING IN URBAN SCHOOLS

Frances Helyar

Two seventh-grade girls switch names for a double period, giggling when one is praised in the other's name for her good work. A teacher's lesson plan on a desk in the room to the left at the end of the hall is disconcertingly sketchy; meanwhile, on a desk in the room to the left at the end of the other hall is a detailed outline of the day's activities, carefully placed to greet the substitute's arrival. All the chairs around the teachers' table in the lunchroom are full, and the only available chair is at the empty table in the corner. An eighth-grader says, "Why the hell should I show you my homework?" A 6-year-old, his face wrinkled in frustration, cries, "You're not doing it right! You're messing up!"

A third-grade student proudly explains to his seatmate the difference between a one-third and a one-tenth slice of pizza. Children in a fifth-grade music class enthusiastically follow instructions to play a new song in unison on their recorders. A group of eighth-grade girls greet a returning substitute by name with hugs. A teacher expresses gratitude to the substitute who will take his class during his upcoming absence. A principal offers a permanent teaching position. A fourth-grader says "Thank you for being our teacher" as he goes out the door at the end of the day.

Why would any reasonable human being decide to become a substitute teacher in an urban school? Substitutes enjoy little job security, low wages, and scarce benefits; and the expectations placed on them are frequently unrealistic and often unachievable. Substitutes labor under conditions including scant information, little planning or preparation time, no continuity, the experience of only superficial relationships in the work environment, and at the same time, full legal liability for what happens in the classroom.[1] They're subject to ridicule and worse from students and the public.

Yet for some teachers, the gypsy-like existence of the substitute is appealing. It provides the opportunity to experience a variety of teaching situations and to learn, both positively and negatively, from other educators. It can offer newly trained teachers an improved sense of their own strengths and weaknesses, likes and dislikes, and personal teaching styles. For others, it provides flexibility in working conditions when most needed. It can bring the joy of the teachable moment, the elation of expectations met and exceeded, and the opportunity to be the one to create a meaningful educational connection with a child when few others could.

BAD PRESS FOR SUBSTITUTES

Substitute Teachers in Popular Culture

Films, television programs, and books about substitute teachers generally focus on transforming relationships between the students and the substitute, and the character of the latter may be anything from parental, as in an episode of *The Simpsons*,[2] to threatening, as in the film *The Substitute*.[3] Most portrayals, unless they represent an episode in a continuing series with a school setting, offer scant information about the absent teacher and instead examine the way the substitute and students react and respond to each other. If the set-

ting is urban, the tone is more likely to be dramatic, as in the films *Gryphon* or *Music of the Heart*.[4] Comedies tend to have suburban settings, as in the book *Miss Nelson Is Missing*[5] or the television show *South Park*,[6] although humor is sometimes found in cities, as in the films *Mr. Jealousy* and *School of Rock*.[7] The characterization of the students ranges from the heroic of television's *Buffy the Vampire Slayer* to the criminal of *The Substitute*.[8] In contrast, whether hero or villain, the substitute teacher is consistently an outsider, different from other teachers or adults (*School of Rock*; *The Simpsons*; *South Park*). Thus is reinforced the notion of the substitute as separate from the permanent teacher.

Substitute Teachers in the News Media

Substitutes are rarely mentioned in the mainstream media except when one is accused of wrongdoing.[9] The individual who has managed to slip through the screening process for substitutes or who commits a criminal act while employed becomes an exemplar of all substitute teachers. The World Wide Web produces nearly 12,000 results from a search limited to the terms *substitute teacher* and *charged*. In addition, discussion of the cost of paying substitute teachers perpetuates the assumption that wages for substitute teachers are an unnecessary burden to the taxpayers.[10]

A DAY IN THE LIFE OF A SUBSTITUTE TEACHER

Unless a substitute secures a long-term assignment, the only predictable aspect of daily life is its unpredictability. The call to work may come from a principal or vice-principal, a district or county central dispatcher, or even a private agency. If the teacher is lucky, the call comes the night before the assignment, but more often the phone rings early in the morning. The substitute may have the luxury of refusal, or may be compelled to accept the job. Once the teacher arrives in a school, any number of variables could affect the day's success: Does an administrator or office staff welcome the teacher? Can the teacher find the room and gain entry? Has the absent teacher left a plan with sufficient materials to carry it out? Is information about emergency procedures, class and school rules, seating plans, attendance rolls and procedures, daily schedule and other pertinent documentation readily available? Are other teachers supportive? Are the students clear about what is expected of them, both in terms of behavior and academics, when a substitute is in charge? Even the location of the nearest toilet becomes an important but overlooked piece of information for a substitute teacher in a new school.

Once the day has begun, the substitute teacher's challenges continue. Does the teacher stay in the same room, or face a new group of students in a new classroom with each change of period? Is the subject matter different throughout the day, or will there be a repetition of lessons? What about grade levels? Have any unplanned activities or interruptions appeared on the day's schedule, and how should they be dealt with?

A day's assignment may end with the substitute teacher writing a note to the absent teacher outlining the day's events, although some use the day plan as a checklist, simply indicating which activities were or were not completed. While many teachers appreciate substitutes who mark student work, the absent teacher's marking scheme is not always clear; an acceptable answer to the substitute may not be the same to the absent teacher. One last visit to the office to finalize administrative matters such as payment is not always possible, particularly if the office closes before the substitute leaves the school.

THE DISCOURSE OF
TEACHER ABSENCE

Inherent in any discussion of substitute teachers is the issue of teacher absence. It's a topic that regularly surfaces in the media. For example, a Massachusetts-based newspaper exposé studies the number of sick days allowed in the teachers' union contracts, and unfavorably compares them to the quantity of sick days permitted workers in other, unrelated fields.[11] The importance of educating children is thus undermined by the assumption that teaching is a job, not a profession.

During an era of increased scrutiny of education costs, the reason for the regular teacher's absence is closely examined. But the focus is rarely the nature of the teachers' illness, nor the working conditions or other circumstances that lead to illness, nor an analysis of the societal conditions that necessitate a teacher's absence. Attention is drawn instead to the number of teachers who abuse sick-day benefits by using them as mental health days, to extend a vacation, or to supplement maternity leave. Also included in the litany of abusers is the teacher who claims the day to care for an ill child or an elderly parent. At the same time, the National Center for Educational Statistics cites teacher absenteeism not as a consequence of health issues, but simply as "an indicator of morale," and as "more of a problem in urban schools than in suburban or rural schools, and in urban high poverty schools compared with rural high poverty schools."[12]

SUBSTITUTE TEACHING AS A
CAREER CHOICE

No typical substitute teacher exists. A visit to any public school shows that women predominate in the profession, but the reasons for anyone to choose to work as a substitute are varied. Some are first-time teachers fresh out of colleges of education; some have taken a break, pursued other nonteaching employment after graduation, and are now returning to the profession. Many have left permanent, full-time employment for family reasons and choose substituting as a way of gaining reentry. Others have no desire for permanent work, whether because of family responsibilities or for other reasons, and they prefer the flexibility of substituting. Increasingly, in an era of teacher shortages many are retired teachers seeking to supplement their pensions, while others are high school graduates who are able to take advantage of the minimal qualifications required by some jurisdictions.

Of all the personnel found in an urban school on a given day, the substitute teacher may be the person least familiar to others in the workplace. With half-time assignments, the substitute employed in a large district can spend time in more schools than there are days in the week. The ephemeral nature of the employment means that unless a substitute secures a long-term position or has the chance to work at a school on a regular but not continuous basis, that teacher may find daily work, but in a different school each day. As such, every day is the equivalent of the first day of school. Getting to know the routines, other personnel, and the students are all challenges to be met. With chronic teacher shortages in urban schools drawing talented teachers from the roster of substitutes, at most the substitute is likely to lack training in the subject area of the absent teacher; at least, the substitute is untrained as an educator and lacking any postsecondary studies.

But even when the substitutes are fully trained and experienced educators, they are expected to maintain continuity of instruction, rendering the students' experience as if the permanent teacher were never absent. These expectations, as well as the practice of discarding work done in the permanent teacher's absence, further reinforce the substitute teacher's invisibility.[13]

In spite of the reality of varying backgrounds and reasons for teaching, substitute teachers still labor under fundamental assumptions made by others about their job. The first is that the substitutes would rather be permanent classroom teachers.

Statistics confirm that substitute teaching is a proven way to secure a full-time teaching job.[14] But the dearth of research and statistical analysis about substitute teachers makes it difficult to draw a fully realized picture of the profession and the individuals who take on the role.

RELATIONSHIPS

Administrators

While recruitment, training, and retention of substitute teachers are, in theory, major issues for administrators, the recruitment, training, and retention of permanent teachers take precedence, again making the substitute teacher invisible. Even when statistical analyses of schools and teachers are undertaken, substitutes are minimally considered.[15] Whatever a district's stated policy, the expectations placed on substitute teachers by school principals and other administrators vary. Some define an effective substitute as one who refers no students to the office for disciplining. Others prefer a quiet classroom as an indicator. For these school officials, the substitute is little more than a babysitter. Even school principals with higher expectations do not express uniform definitions of a good substitute. These range from the fulfillment of the goals of the lesson plans, to taking advantage of a teachable moment or bringing something new and different to the class, regardless of the absent teacher's planning.[16] The challenge for the substitute teacher is to determine which of the different expectations are prevalent for any single assignment and meet those expectations while remaining true to one's own teaching style and self-expectations.

TEACHERS

Substitute teachers have two distinct relationships with their permanent counterparts: The first is with the absent teacher, largely a written one consisting of notes and messages often scribbled in haste by each. The second is with other teachers in the school, and while this relationship can be more personal, for a variety of reasons it can also be non-existent, depending upon how willing and able the classroom teachers are to take the time to make contact. Sometimes school policy dictates that a teacher in a room nearby should offer assistance to the substitute, but school policy is not always followed. Other staff may also be aloof, as in lunchroom behavior where substitutes are ignored or subtly encouraged to sit at a remote table. Teachers frequently undermine the substitute's authority by stepping in and dealing with a perceived "situation," whether one exists or not. At issue are differing definitions of what are acceptable and normal practices in a school setting and who has the power to determine which definition is dominant. Rare is the substitute teacher who achieves that power.

STUDENTS

The stereotype of students' responses to substitute teachers is rife with images of paper airplanes flying and a general atmosphere of chaos. In reality, students are quick to respond to a substitute's tentative understanding of school routines and to take advantage of that tentativeness. Some school administrations offset this effect in a number of ways. First, school policy can be clear about expected treatment of guests in the building and the consequences of treating such guests inappropriately. Second, where possible, the students can be informed ahead of time that a substitute will be in the class, or at least provided with a general sense of the expectations should a substitute appear in the future. Third, in leaving a lesson plan the absent teacher can indicate not only the work to be covered (page references, materials, and the like) but also some mention of pedagogical and methodological background of the lesson. Fourth, work left for a substitute to present to a class can have some academic

value. Otherwise, the students' experience of busywork reinforces the attitude that substitutes are less than real teachers.

The personality of a substitute teacher might sometimes be enough to create a meaningful connection with the students. This is particularly the case when the substitute's style is a welcome change and a more comfortable fit for the group than is the permanent teacher's. For example, the students who fear their regular teacher may respond more positively to a less authoritarian presence in the classroom. The substitute teacher who shares the same background as the students may be a novelty, particularly since urban teachers tend to be from non-urban backgrounds.[17]

PARENTS

If teachers, students, administrators, and parents are the fundamental partners of education, a substitute has contact with all but one partner. Substitute teachers rarely have the chance to meet the parents. Unless they hold long-term positions, substitutes are not included in "Meet the Teacher" nights, concerts, presentations, or other events outside of regular school hours, nor would they expect nor even desire to be included. The consequence, however, is that parental perceptions of the substitute teacher are developed at least second- if not third-hand. This lack of direct contact is an overlooked element of substitute teaching and contributes to the public perception of substitutes as lesser participants in the education system.

ISSUES IN SUBSTITUTE TEACHING

A number of work-related concerns surface regularly in the literature by and about substitute teachers. The average pay in city schools for 180 days worked amounts to about $16,000, far less than a beginning teacher's salary.[18] Bargaining rights are sporadic,[19] and health and dental benefits are usually not offered. Overall, the existence can be a lonely one without job security or the collegiality experienced by teachers regularly assigned to a school. The discourse overlooks the fact that just as the majority of classroom teachers in America are women, so are the substitute teachers. The difference is that the substitute's position is insecure and with working conditions even more typical of a gendered profession than those experienced by permanent teachers.[20]

The requirements for individuals to qualify as substitute teachers in the United States amount to a hodgepodge of certificates, licenses, and background checks. Seventy-six percent of respondents to a 1998–1999 survey reported no licensing requirements for substitute teachers in their state.[21] In some jurisdictions the minimum statewide requirement is a high school diploma; in others, the standards vary from district to district or county to county.[22] In times of a national teacher shortage, a corresponding shortage of trained substitutes results, as does the debate about the quality of educators. The subjective nature of the term *quality* is evident in the debate over its definition. Teachers' unions and faculties of education insist that training in methodology, pedagogy, and classroom management is the hallmark of an effective educator, whereas scientists, mathematicians, and historians remain mystified that a teacher can educate young minds without even a post-secondary minor in their subject area. This phenomenon of out-of-field teaching is a direct consequence of a teacher shortage; although it happens to full-time classroom teachers frequently, it is part of the everyday experience of many substitute teachers.[23]

EFFECTIVE SUBSTITUTE TEACHING

Training and Support

Conventional wisdom opines that the substitute teacher should have achieved, at the minimum, a post-secondary education. This notion belies the fact that a bright student can be a more effective purveyor of knowledge than a substitute teacher when the subject is a complex one and the substitute has had no opportunity to prepare. In addition, the nature of the post-secondary degree can be controversial. On one hand is the assumption that only a trained teacher can help students to achieve their academic goals; on the other hand is the belief that a trained subject specialist is the only one who can pass on to children the knowledge needed to succeed. The definition of success is equally controversial: The ultimate goal, whether stated or not, may be simply to help the students score well on standardized tests.

The substitute who wants more education than a high school graduation diploma, but for whom enrollment in part-time college courses or shorter training sessions are not practical, can take advantage of online courses. Offerings range from the suspiciously simplistic, comprising only six lessons,[24] to more comprehensive programs provided at the district or county level, or through colleges such as the Utah State University Substitute Teaching Institute.[25]

Support for substitute teachers is offered in some states or districts through unions, and the National Education Association has a Substitute Teacher Caucus. In other states, advocacy groups have primacy. An Internet search using the term *substitute teacher* yields 164,000 results with sponsors as diverse as the National Substitute Teachers Alliance, the mission of which is "to promote dignity and respect for substitute teachers who provide educational continuity for our nation's students"[26] and a site maintained by a self-proclaimed experienced practitioner advising his readers, "As a Substitute Teacher, You Are the Captain of the Ship."[27]

PREPAREDNESS

Once on the accredited list, the substitute teacher in an urban school can make general preparations for the job ahead of time. First, familiarity with the location of schools removes one element of uncertainty when a call comes in. Finding the best route and actually traveling it beforehand may be a luxury of time and expense, but the journey on the day of the job is consequently less stressful. Having a sense of the school population is important, but not in order to create assumptions about the school. Rather, knowing the size of the school, the catchment area, and other details beforehand frees the teacher to devote time upon arrival to the details of the teaching day. (For example, if students come to school by public transit or school bus, the substitute may need to be sensitive to external reasons for lateness.) Becoming familiar with the person who dispatches the calls to substitutes, keeping a pen and paper next to the phone to record assignments, and preparing clothing and a lunch the night before all help to make the call, especially the last-minute one, less disruptive. Arrival at the school a minimum of thirty minutes before the students generally enables the substitute to meet with administrators, find the classroom and determine the day's proposed lesson plans. Sometimes thirty minutes is not enough, so the conscientious substitute adjusts with experience.

Most substitute teachers bring a package of materials with them to supplement those in the classroom. Among the items for a kit, in no particular order: whistle; pen worn around the neck; extra pens for students who forget theirs; blank grids for class lists; index cards for making quick flashcards, games or other lists; puzzle books; spare paper; all-purpose wipes; commercially prepared flash cards; stopwatch; snack; lunch. Many successful substitutes use *tools of engagement*. The phrase, although used to different purpose in other contexts, refers here to something that creates an air of enthusiastic expectancy, engages the class, makes the experi-

ence memorable, and is often used as a reward for a period of on-task work. These include: guitar or other musical instrument; storytelling preparation; juggling tools; art supplies; hand-held tape recorder; a store of simple games, riddles or mystery stories. The creative substitute can use such tools to extend a lesson, relate the lesson to students' experiences, and create a sense of connection with the substitute, with the world, and with each other.

CLASSROOM MANAGEMENT AND DISCIPLINE

No amount of training can prepare the substitute for the variety of classrooms and classroom behaviors to be encountered. Even with classroom rules posted on the door, the substitute usually has to adapt the guidelines to make them specific to the situation, keeping in mind that, like most human beings, students resist and sometimes react strongly and negatively to change. Among the simplest methods to clarify expectations and create a positive atmosphere are: using the time before class to write the substitute's name and simple instructions on the board (for example, you need a pencil and your notebook during this class); greeting students at the door, positioned with a view of the classroom interior and the hallway, if practical; learning the students' names as soon as possible by using seating charts, mnemonics, word associations, or other strategies. (This practice is effective even if only a few names can be learned. The students who may provide the greatest challenge respond when the teacher names them, as do the students who may offer the most assistance. Of course, students frequently offer the names of others as their own.)

In the event of disruptive behavior, the substitute teacher has a variety of classroom management techniques at hand, and more than the permanent teacher must be capable of changing techniques at short notice as the teaching situation unfolds. Model techniques include everything from the militaristic—with a goal of strict adherence to a narrow set of behavioral guidelines—to constructivist, with choices, consequences, and positive rewards rather than negative punishments. Each substitute teacher finds a style that provides a personal fit; the skill comes when the substitute can quickly adapt and adjust that personal style to the needs of different classrooms and the students in those classes. Sometimes the greatest challenge is suppressing a personal style and philosophy of education in order to more closely match that of the absent teacher, because it is the only approach to which the students respond.

Instances occur in which no amount of education, experience, or wisdom can make a classroom situation a positive one. It happens to permanent teachers, but it happens to substitute teachers more often. The best the substitute teacher can do is to ensure that the safety and dignity of all are preserved as much as possible and to try to learn from the experience.

CONTINUITY OF INSTRUCTION

The favorite statistic of writers about teacher absenteeism and substitute teachers is that fully 10 percent or 5 million of American students on any given day are being taught by a substitute.[28] It's bad news no matter who is delivering it; in educational discourse, continuity of instruction is one of the most important contributors to a student's success in school. The assumption is that learning is a linear process, and any break in the line is disruptive and detrimental to the student's education. But breaks in instruction can just as easily be attributed to numerous other factors in the school apart from the presence of a substitute teacher: announcements, assemblies, class trips and other special events, long weekends and the students' own absences. At the same time, the expectation that a substitute teacher

might achieve continuity is spurious. If the school were a manufacturing plant and the student a widget, one skilled substitute could replace any other teacher and in the end create the same finished product.[29] But schools are not factories, and students are not widgets. Administrators, parents and even students affirm, in the words of the old saw, sometimes a change is as good as a rest.

ORGANIZATIONAL ALTERNATIVES FOR SUBSTITUTE TEACHERS

The negative perception of substitutes leads inevitably to efforts to bring those teachers into a more positive light. Among the more simplistic attempts is the notion that a mere name change would do the trick. Consequently euphemisms like guest, interim, and reserve teacher are recommended and sometimes used.[30] No one is fooled, however, especially not the students.

Many districts attempt to overcome the difficulties associated with substitute teaching in more substantial, creative ways, most notably by assigning substitutes to schools or districts on a full-time permanent basis. They may be called floating or permanent substitutes, building-based educators, or cadres.[31] These substitutes do not become regular classroom teachers; instead, they come to school each day and fill in where needed. On the days when no teachers are absent, the substitute is assigned other teacher-related work in the school. The advantages are numerous: The substitutes become familiar with school procedures and with students, other teachers, administrators, and school staff. They gain a greater sense of employment security, their salary is slightly higher, and health and other benefits are often included. The daily scramble at the school level to find a substitute is avoided. The disadvantages of the system have mostly to do with cost. Jurisdictions where the idea has been tried have sometimes had to cut back in spite of its success simply because the funding was not available.[32]

CONCLUSION

If the many partners in urban education face daily challenges, then substitute teachers in urban schools are the most neglected and forgotten in the struggle. Perhaps because so little is expected of them, whether by administrators, teachers, parents, or students, they are rarely the focus of attention in the general discourse. Their portrayal is unrealistic in popular culture and subject to stereotypes and sensationalism in the news media. Nevertheless, teacher absences ensure that substitute teachers will continue to be an integral part of the educational system in city schools. Whereas any success that substitute teachers experience in positively affecting the lives of their students or colleagues would appear to be against the odds, their role in the education system remains underexamined and thus subject to conjecture instead of direct, serious study.

NOTES

1. Cotton, D.(1995). Liability of educators for the negligence of others (substitutes, aides, student teachers, and new teachers). *Physical Educator, 52* (2), 70–77.

2. Vitti, J. (Writer), & Moore, R. (Director). (1991). Lisa's substitute [Television series episode]. In M. Groenig (Exec. Producer), *The Simpsons.* Century City, CA: Twentieth Century Fox.

3. Eseman, M., & Steele, J. (Producers), & Mandel, R. (Director). (1996). *The substitute* [Motion picture]. United States: Artisan.

4. Haber, C., & Arce, M. (Writers and Producers). (1988). *Gryphon* [Motion picture]. United States: Max Mambru Films; Slotnick, A., Weinstein, B., & Weinstein, H. (Exec. Producers), & Craven, W. (Director). (1999). *Music of the heart* [Motion picture]. United States: Miramax.

5. Allard, H., & Marshall, J. (1977). *Miss Nelson is missing.* Boston: Houghton Mifflin.

6. Parker, T. (Writer/Director). (1998). Tom's rhinoplasty [Television series episode]. In A. Garefino & D. White (Producers), *South Park.* United States: Comedy Central.

7. Castleberg, J. (Producer), & Baumbach, N. (Director). (1997). *Mr. Jealousy* [Motion picture].

United States: Lions Gate Films; Rubin, S. (Producer), & Linklater, R. (Director). (2003). *School of rock* [Motion picture]. United States: Paramount Pictures.

8. Greenwalt, D. (Writer), & Green, B. (Director). (1997). Teacher's pet [Television series episode]. In D. Greenwalt (Producer), *Buffy the vampire slayer.* United States: Twentieth Century Fox.

9. School says substitute teacher allowed children to watch beheading. (2004, May 26). *The Kansas City Star.* Retrieved May 26, 2004, from http://www.kansascity.com/mld/kansascity/news/loca/8760842.htm?1c; Substitute teacher charged with child molestation. (2004, May 6). *The Macon Telegraph.* Retrieved May 27, 2004, from http://www.macon.com/mld/macon/8603123.htm.

10. Joyner, D., & Boburg, S. (2003, June 16). When teacher's out. [Electronic version]. *The Eagle Tribune Publishing Company.* Retrieved April 10, 2004, from http://cltg.org/cltg/educate/03-06-16_Eagle_Tribune_series.htm.

11. Boburg, S. (2003, June 16). Few in work force match sick day benefit [Electronic version]. *The Eagle Tribune Publishing Company.* Retrieved April 10, 2004, from http://cltg.org/cltg/educate/03-06-16_Eagle_Tribune_series.htm.

12. National Center for Educational Statistics [NCES]. (1996). *Urban schools: The challenge of location and poverty. Executive summary,* p. 6. Retrieved April 27, 2004, from http://nces.ed.gov/pubs/web/96184ex.asp.

13. Morrison, M. (1994). Temps in the classroom: A case of hidden identities? In S. Galloway & M. Morrison (Eds.), *The supply story: Professional substitutes in education* (pp. 43–65). London: The Falmer Press.

14. NCES. *Teacher supply in the United States: Sources of newly hired teachers in public and private schools, 1987–88 to 1993–94.* Retrieved April 27, 2004, from http://nces.ed.gov/pubs2000/2000309.pdf.

15. NCES. School District questionnaire. In *Schools and staffing survey 2003–04 school year.* Retrieved April 27, 2004, from http://nces.ed.gov/surveys/SASS/pdf/0304/sass1a.pdf; NCES. Principal questionnaire. In *Schools and staffing survey 2003–04 school year* retrieved April 27, 2004, from http://nces.ed.gov/surveys/SASS/pdf/0304/sass2a.pdf; NCES. Teacher questionnaire. In *Schools and staffing survey 2003–04 school year.* Retrieved April 27,

2004, from http://nces.ed.gov/surveys/SASS/pdf/0304/sass4a.pdf.

16. Newton, M. (1994). From where I stand: A head teacher's account. In S. Galloway and M. Morrison (Eds.), *The supply story: Professional substitutes in education* (pp. 68–81). London: The Falmer Press.

17. Stoddart, T. (1993). Who is prepared to teach in urban schools? *Education and Urban Society, 26* (1), 29–48.

18. American Federation of Teachers. (2001). Survey and analysis of teacher salary trends 2001. IV. Teacher salaries in school districts serving the nation's 100 largest cities. Retrieved May 27, 2004, from http://www.aft.org/salary/2001/download/salarysurvey01.pdf.

19. National Education Association [NEA]. Substitutes: A national overview. Retrieved May 27, 2004, from http://www.nea.org/substitutes/survey.html.

20. Galloway, S., & Morrison, M. (1994). Teacher substitution: A focal point for multiple perspectives. In S. Galloway & M. Morrison (Eds.), *The Supply story: Professional substitutes in education* (pp. 1–13). London: The Falmer Press.

21. NEA. Substitutes: A National Overview. Retrieved May 27, 2004, from http://www.nea.org/substitutes/survey.html.

22. Utah State University. *State by state substitute requirements*. Retrieved April 20, 2004, from http://subed.usu.edu/sma/documents/subrequirements.pdf.

23. Ingersoll, R. (1999). Understanding the problem of teacher quality in American schools [Electronic version]. *Education Statistics Quarterly* 1(1). Retrieved November 10, 2005, from http://nces.ed.gov/programs/quarterly/vol_1/1_1/2-esq11-c.asp.

24. Universal Class. How to become a substitute teacher. Retrieved April 20, 2004, from http://class.universalclass.com/chash/s/u/b/subteacher.htm.

25. Utah State University Substitute Teaching Institute. Retrieved April 20, 2004, from http://subed.usu.edu.

26. National Substitute Teachers Alliance Web site. Retrieved April 20, 2004, from http://www.nstasubs.org/.

27. Substitute Teaching—Tricks of the Trade. Retrieved November 10, 2005, from http://www.av.qnet.com/~rsturgn/.

28. Ban, J. (1990). Help substitute teachers manage student behavior. *The Executive Educator, 12* (2), 24–25; Brace, D. (1990). Establishing a support system for substitute teachers. *NASSP Bulletin, 74* (576), 73–77; Elizabeth, J. (2001, January 7). A substitute for education: When the teacher's away [Electronic version]. *The Pittsburgh Post–Gazette*, retrieved April 10, 2004, from http://www.post-gazette.com/headlines/20010107subs2.asp; Jones, K., & Hawkins, A. (2000, August). Substitute solutions. *American School Board Journal, 187* (8), 34–37.

29. Moses, J. (1989). Adventures in Subland. *Teacher Educator, 24* (4), 2–7.

30. Ferrara, P., & Ferrara, M. (1993, November). Where's our real teacher? Making the substitute experience mean something. *Schools in the Middle, 3* (2), 11–15; GuestTeacher.com Web site, retrieved March 17, 2004, from http://www.guest-teacher.com/; Lassmann, M. (2000). Defining the role of the substitute teacher. *Education, 121* (3), 625–626.

31. Ferrara & Ferrara; Fortier, M. (2003, June 16). No substitute [Electronic version]. *The Eagle Tribune Publishing Company*. Retrieved June 16, 2003, from http://cltg.org/cltg/educate/03-06-16_ Eagle_Tribune_series.htm; Grace, S. (2000). The floating substitute: A novel solution for an old problem. Principal, *79* (5) 42–43; Moses (1989).

32. Fortier. http://cltg.org/cltg/educate/03-06-16_Eagle_Tribune_series.htm.

DEVELOPING SCHOLAR–PRACTITIONER LEADERS IN THE URBAN EDUCATION IN CRISIS

Raymond A. Horn, Jr.

Education in the urban environment continues to be a unique challenge for all educational stakeholders—whether school administrators, teachers, students, parents, and other community members. Urban education has been historically challenging because of high population density, large schools, economic disparity, higher rates of ethnic, racial, and religious diversity, higher immigrant populations, and unique transportation problems.[1] Additional challenges include educational issues such as shortages of educators, teacher mobility, and student achievement. Also, the current standards and accountability reform movement adds to this crisis by imposing technical standards and draconian accountability measures that are grounded in high-stakes standardized testing. One outcome of this reliance on standardized testing as the sole measure of student achievement and school and educator effectiveness is that urban educators are increasingly reduced to the status of technicians whose sole purpose is the implementation of a decontextualized curriculum that is irrelevant to the needs of the urban environment. State takeovers of urban schools, privatization of schools, inequitable funding, and school choice initiatives further diminish the power of urban educators to effectively and equitably meet the needs of children in the urban context.

In this chapter, I present the argument that the challenges of urban education can be best met through the development of school administrators and teachers as scholar-practitioner leaders. First, the development of scholar-practitioner leaders for the urban context will be presented by exploring the scholar-practitioner leader concept and the preparation of school administrators and teachers as scholar-practitioner leaders. This will be followed by a discussion concerning the building and sustaining of urban educational communities through scholar-practitioner leadership. The chapter will conclude with remarks about the authentic education that can occur in the urban context as a result of scholar-practitioner leadership.

SCHOLAR-PRACTITIONER LEADERS IN THE URBAN CONTEXT

Why scholar-practitioner leaders in the urban context? Many well-intended educational reforms either harmlessly fail or exacerbate existing problems because they are externally imposed reforms constructed by individuals who are detached from the local urban context. A foundational assumption about the need for the development of scholar-practitioner leaders is that those who are closest to the urban educational environment are best positioned to provide leadership in the resolution of the problems that assail urban education. In this scenario, urban educators need to acquire the knowledge, skills, and attitudes that will facilitate their urban praxis. Only through the empowerment of local urban educators can the capacity for effective and equitable urban education be built.

DEVELOPING SCHOLAR-PRACTITIONER LEADERSHIP FOR THE URBAN CONTEXT

To understand scholar-practitioner leadership in the urban context requires a familiarity with the scholar-practitioner concept and how school administrators and teachers can become scholar-practitioners.

The Scholar-Practitioner Leader

Understanding the multidimensionality of scholar-practitioner leaders requires an investigation of their knowledge, inquiry methodology, critical disposition, systems orientation, postmodern awareness, understanding and critical pragmatic use of conversation, disposition to be critically reflective and reflexive educators, and recognition of spirituality and an ethic of caring as vital components of the educational environment. The scholar-practitioner concept involves a recognition of and commitment to their understanding and critical use of these dimensions.

Scholar-practitioner leaders value scholarly, professional, practitioner, and locally contextualized knowledge. They understand that all knowledges are equally important in understanding the complexity of urban education and that all knowledge bases mutually inform and mediate each other. In addition, they understand the necessity of knowledge within disciplinary frameworks, but deeply understand that the interdisciplinary nature of all knowledge bases must be recognized if the inherent complexity of urban education is to be effectively and equitably dealt with.

Scholar-practitioner leaders have the disposition and the ability to acquire and effectively use a diversity of inquiry methodologies in their acquisition and evaluation of diverse knowledge bases. They are adept in mixing methodologies without allowing any research paradigm to colonize another. To lead effectively, scholar-practitioner leaders need to function as bricoleurs (i.e., individuals who are adept in the use of multiple and diverse inquiry methodologies) in the sense that they have acquired the knowledge and skill to utilize a diversity of knowledge bases and research methodologies in their engagement with their educational work and community issues. Richard Shavelson positions this need for methodological diversity in the understanding that there is a science of confirmation and a science of discovery. Both sciences raise different questions that require different methods of inquiry.[2] Shavelson maintains that questions that require confirmation tend to be answered through quantitative methods, and questions of discovery require qualitative methods. To engage both types of questions, scholar-practitioners must be critically adept in the utilization of mixed methodologies. To engage the full context of a social phenomenon, scholar-practitioners use a variety of inquiry methods, such as self-reflection, self-criticism, deconstruction, literary criticism, critical hermeneutics, semiotic analysis, case studies, phenomenological studies, historical analysis, postformal analysis, and cultural studies.

Through the use of diverse knowledge bases and inquiry methods, scholar-practitioner leaders are able to pursue their understanding in places that are off limits to traditional inquiry methods that have well-established boundaries. For instance, through the employment of cultural studies, in tandem with other research methods and paradigms, an understanding can be acquired of how popular culture, media representations of education and educational stakeholders, and fields such as business that appear to be unrelated to educational problems are actually very important influences on the educational environment through the hidden curriculum that they promote.[3] This deeper and broader understanding of urban education greatly increases the potential of constructing effective and equitable educational practice and organizational structures.

An integral part of the inquiry process of scholar-practitioner leaders is the on-going and rigorous assessment of the knowledge that is uncovered. Inquiry and assessment attain a synergetic effect through critical reflection and reflexion.[4] Subjecting to critical scrutiny what one has learned, the processes that were utilized, and how one's own beliefs were impacted by the knowledge and inquiry process requires scholar-practitioners to continuously return to their critical beliefs that drive their activity. As reflective and reflexive bricoleurs, scholar-practitioners are postformal inquirers in that they are attentive to the multiple and ever changing contexts of their environment, have a historical understanding of the origins of a phenomenon, and discern the deep and hidden patterns in which the phenomenon is embedded.[5]

Scholar-practitioner leaders are fundamentally critical in that the promotion of social justice, an ethic of caring, and democratic participation is central to their professional and personal activity. Their critical foundation is mediated by the post-structural and postmodern realization that these concepts do not contain fixed essentialized definitions but are critical projects that are under continuous construction. They continuously attempt to personally attain and facilitate in others the development of a critical *awareness* through critical *literacy* that is employed in the critical *interrogation* of educational and social phenomena.[6] They represent a critical pragmatic orientation that recognizes the necessity to be forward-looking and anticipatory in relation to the potential consequences of one's individual and collective actions.[7] They are also aware that a critical pragmatic analysis of consequences and experience needs to contain both critique and inventiveness and innovation. Their propensity for critique, inventiveness, and innovation is based upon their knowledge and use of poststructural and postmodern knowledge and methods. However, they are able to avoid the potential nihilism and enervating relativity of these methods by returning to their evolving critical center and subsequently building egalitarian community by affirming the positive through enabling, encouraging, and augmenting.

Scholar-practitioner leaders are not trapped in the narrow reductionism of the positivist paradigm, but instead are trained to take a systems view of educational and social phenomena. Their development of a systemic view allows them to recognize the interconnectedness of all human activity systems and results in a holistic understanding of the educational and social contexts in which they are embedded.[8] The understandings gained by their systems view are mediated by their acquisition of diverse knowledge, their ability to post-formally inquire, and their critical disposition. Supported by this foundation, their ability to think systemically differs from those who utilize systems thinking as an uncritical problem-solving mechanism designed to merely implement externally imposed policies that lack relevance for the local urban context. Instead, the systems view of the scholar-practitioner leader is an integral component in a process that enhances effective leadership in promoting equitable, caring, and democratic educational and social systems. A critical systems view promotes a commitment that extends scholar-practitioners' critical service from the classroom to the larger educational, local, regional, state, and national communities in which they are nested.[9] Just as scholar-practitioners understand the systemic interconnectivity of social phenomena, they also understand the systemic necessity to coordinate their actions in multiple contexts in order to increase their potential for effective action.

Scholar-practitioner leaders are aware of how the use of different types of conversation mediates and informs human activity. Scholar-practitioner leaders are conversationally literate in the employment of conflictual types of conversation (such as dialectical and discussion) and collegial types (such as dialogue, design, generative, and strategic).[10] They appropriately utilize different types of conversation in their pragmatic critique of social activity and in the promotion of affirmative and enhancing social activity.

Finally, scholar-practitioner leaders recognize that the totality of the human experience is always manifested in all social activity including education. This understanding includes the recognition of how spirituality informs and mediates human activity.[11] Unlike the positivist separation of faith and reason, scholar-practitioner leaders accept the inclusion of spiritual concerns in educational and social activity. Not within a religious context that may attempt to constrain and control relationships but within relationships such as the "I-Thou" of Martin Buber,[12] scholar-practitioner leaders through dialogue and communicative openness attempt to allow individuals to transcend the institutional and formalized frameworks that isolate them.[13] They regard relationships such as these as the essential element "for holding society together, for meeting conditions conducive to cultural creativity and for counteracting the possible stagnating or destructive forces that are endemic in any society."[14] It is the interpersonal relations of the individuals who "are united in a symmetrical bond that maintains their individualities but brings them into living relation with each other."[15] This interpersonal interaction may result in spiritual understandings about each other, but decidedly uncovers individual values and in doing so creates the potential for shared moral action. When schools are characterized by transcendent relationships, "education of this sort means more than teaching the facts and learning the reasons so we can manipulate life toward our ends. It means being drawn into personal responsiveness and accountability to each other and the world of which we are a part."[16] Accountability is not primarily directed toward economic or political interests, but toward truthful relationships with others with whom we are intimately bound. This kind of accountability leads to communities of faithful relationships where the primary bond is not of logic but of love.[17]

Developing Administrators and Teachers as Scholar-Practitioner Leaders

The main goal in the development of scholar-practitioner leaders is to facilitate the development of individuals who will pursue their commitment to fostering social justice through their professional activity in their schools and in the larger community. The achievement of this goal can be facilitated not only in the initial preparation of educators and in the professional development of practicing educators, but also in the promotion of scholar-practitioner activity in the K–12 educational environment. On any of these levels, success in reaching this goal is directly related to the *academic rigor* of the educational program and the use of *authentic* curriculum, instruction, and assessment that is relevant to the needs of the students.

In a general sense, the academic rigor that is necessary to develop scholar-practitioners on any level involves a positive tension between high academic expectations and the willingness of educational programs to support student learning in a positive way.

Specific aspects of this tension in educator preparation programs include:

- A workload that is academically challenging but also is deemed relevant by the students to their professional and personal needs. Also, this workload is characterized by a curricular concern for application to the students' real lives.
- The development of a critical awareness through the concomitant development of a critical literacy that includes the acquisition of a diversity of inquiry methodologies, research epistemologies, and the critical concepts necessary to critically interrogate all knowledges and inquiry processes.
- The development of critical reflection and reflexion skills and the continuous opportunity to employ these skills.
- A continuous scaffolding of all student instructional activity. In this case, scaffolding connotes that all students perceive the coursework and educator feedback and assessment as constructive activity that supports their successful development as scholar-practitioners.
- The use of multiple and authentic assessments in order to capture a holistic view of student growth and to promote the growth of all students instead of the ranking and sorting of students.
- Embedding students within a scholar-practitioner community in order to provide a model of a just and caring community.

Education that is characteristic of scholar-practitioner communities occurs in safe and caring educational environments that are driven by standards and accountability. However, instead of the reductionist technical standards and accountability systems of technical rational educational systems, students in scholar-practitioner communities are guided by standards of complexity that are measured by multiple and authentic assessments.[18] Curriculum that is driven by standards of complexity requires students to develop critical higher-order thinking skills that can be used to interrogate knowledge within the context of lived experience and promotes the development of habits that are the foundation for life-long learning. Standards of complexity require instructional activity such as student participation in their learning, the promotion of a positive integration of emotions and cognition, students actively posing and solving authentic and relevant problems, the incorporation of themes from the students' daily lives, and the facilitation of the development of democratic ideals.

Education within a scholar-practitioner community consistently attempts to lay the foundation for the students' construction and maintenance of their own scholar-practitioner communities. An essential understanding of this goal is that effective critical leadership in a community requires the development of a cadre of leaders who can support each other in their critical praxis. Unlike the hegemonic hierarchical arrangements of leadership found in modernistic organizations, a viable scholar-practitioner community requires all members to assume leadership roles at various times. To lead in this context requires scholar-practitioners to perform a diversity of roles ranging from leader and teacher to follower.[19] Also, scholar-practitioner leaders need to be public intellectuals in the sense that they have or can acquire the scholarly and practitioner knowledge that allows them to take action within their community. With this knowledge and skill they can become cultural workers who understand the dynamics of their culturally diverse communities and can work effectively with these diverse individuals to resolve community problems and social justice inequities.[20]

BUILDING AND SUSTAINING URBAN EDUCATIONAL COMMUNITIES THROUGH SCHOLAR-PRACTITIONER LEADERSHIP

Central to the work of scholar-practitioner leaders is the development of socially just and caring democratic communities. Urban scholar-practitioners understand that the concept of community first entails an awareness that they are part of many and diverse communities. Their systemic view allows them to see the multitude of social systems of which they are a part and to recognize the interdependence and interconnectivity of all of these systems. This systemic awareness requires them to view their critical activity not as action restricted to one subsystem, but as action that can influence the other connected systems. Conversely, action that is restricted to one's classroom or one's school is limited in the positive effect that may occur because of the competing and confounding influences that emanate from the other subsystems. In order to offset that negative influence and to build and sustain one's critical effect, scholar-practitioners must extend their critical activity to those other subsystems.

Secondly, scholar-practitioner leaders understand that their involvement in their community requires them to be a responsive and responsible member of their community. Being responsive implies working with and valuing the knowledge, difference, and culture of the other members of the community. Being responsive further implies a moral obligation to facilitate the empowerment and subsequent autonomy of these individuals, as opposed to imposing another layer of knowledge, beliefs, and values that in turn may further oppress these individuals. Being responsible implies the obligation of using one's critical knowledge and skill to empower others, and to engage in a praxis that fosters the development of socially just and caring democratic communities.

Through their own academic and critical development and that of others, scholar-practitioner leaders work to construct egalitarian communities. They attempt to achieve this goal by working with individuals, but also by constructing support networks with other educators, educational institutions, businesses, and political, cultural, and religious grass roots organizations. Urban scholar-practitioner leaders view this activity as critical urban praxis in that they take informed action, critically reflect upon that action, and take further informed action to achieve their critical goals.

Building and sustaining egalitarian communities are dynamically interrelated and ongoing processes in that the communities are in a state of constant construction, and sustaining them requires an ongoing and innovative reconstruction that is based upon critical and pragmatic reflection and reflexion. These processes require shared ownership by all stakeholders that is fostered through a healthy and productive ownership process that is guided by a shared and critically evolving vision of the school and its place within the urban community.

AUTHENTIC EDUCATION THROUGH A FOCUS ON THE URBAN CONTEXT

Urban scholar-practitioner leaders are guided by certain basic understandings about education within the urban context. In the following urban context as described by Shirley Steinberg and Joe Kincheloe,[21] scholar-practitioner leaders engage their urban context in these ways:

- Scholar-practitioner leaders and those who prepare them are aware that individuals from white backgrounds need to understand how the power of whiteness shapes their perspectives on urban schools and urban students. The critical interrogation of whiteness from an individual and collective perspective is an essential activity in which all scholar-practitioners must engage.

- Urban scholar-practitioner leaders have a rigorous inter/multidisciplinary understanding of urban education. This type of understanding is necessary in order to engage the contextual complexity of urban education. Only through this type of understanding can urban scholar-practitioners become aware of the micro contexts in which their schools are embedded, such as the local communities, family networks, and the emotional and cognitive contexts in which their students live. Additionally on a macro level, urban educators must understand the political, economic, cultural, and social contexts of their region, state, and nation in relation to their effect on the local urban place.

- The urban school led by scholar-practitioners is directly connected to and involved in the local community, especially in facilitating the provision of human services and community development projects. Their systems view recognizes that schools are not isolated institutions, but connected to the larger social systems in which they are embedded.

- Urban scholar-practitioner leaders recognize the centrality of purpose and engage in conversation about purpose and the alignment of the purpose of urban education with reform initiatives. Scholar-practitioners must recognize how the contextual complexity of urban education informs and mediates the purpose of urban education, and how that mediation process impacts urban students and their schools and communities.

- Urban scholar-practitioner leaders embrace a critical multiculturalism "that is concerned with questioning knowledge for the purpose of understanding more critically oneself and one's relation to society, naming and then changing social situations that impeded the development of egalitarian, democratic communities marked by a commitment to economic and social justice."[22] In an urban multicultural curriculum such as this, students learn about cultural differences that revolve around perspectives on race, class, and gender in light of larger questions of pedagogy, justice, and power.[23] In order to critically engage their multicultural environment, urban scholar-practitioner leaders employ a diversity of pedagogical technlques and utilize curricular flexibility in order to facilitate their students' understanding of how power, identity, and knowledge intersect.

CONCLUSION

Urban education is in crisis because too often the normal condition of urban school administrators is one that fosters educational leadership whose potential for critical action is severely constrained by political, business, cultural, and personal views that seek to reproduce an unjust, uncaring, and undemocratic educational environment and urban community. This deleterious condition occurs when the preparation of school administrators is narrowly focused on the development of uncritical managers, when they become professionals who are isolated from other educational stakeholders and the larger community through restrictive role descriptions, when their lack of critical awareness and critical methods blunts their ability to engage in a critical urban praxis, and when their systemic awareness is uncritically restricted. Urban education is also in crisis because of the similar condition of urban teachers—a condition that views them as uncritical and deskilled technicians whose sole purpose is to deliver externally constructed and imposed curriculum, instruction, and assessment.[24]

In this chapter, the argument was presented that the answer to the urban crisis is the empowerment of educators and their students as scholar-practitioner leaders. As scholars, they acquire the academic rigor and skill that allows them to see more deeply and broadly. As practitioners, they apply their knowledge and skill in their urban praxis. As scholar-practitioners, they synergistically merge their scholarship and practice and understand that both mediate and inform each other. Also, as scholar-practitioners, they are critically grounded and utilize their scholarship and practice to promote the development of so-cially just and caring democratic communities. As scholar-practitioner leaders, they work to facilitate the critical growth and development of their colleagues, students, and communities.

NOTES

1. Steinberg, S., & Kincheloe, J. (2004). *19 urban questions: Teaching in the city.* New York: Peter Lang.

2. Shavelson, R. (2004). *Progress and prospects at the Institute of Education Sciences.* Paper presented at the meeting of the American Educational Research Association, San Diego, CA.

3. Dalton, M. (2000). *The Hollywood curriculum: Teachers in the movies.* New York: Peter Lang. Steinberg, S., & Kincheloe, J. (2004). *Kinderculture: The corporate construction of childhood* (2nd ed.). Boulder, CO: Westview Press.

4. Brookfield, S. (1995). *Becoming a critically reflective teacher.* San Francisco: Jossey-Bass. Dewey, J. (1910). *How we think.* Mineloa, NY: Dover Publications. Schön, D. (1983). *The reflective practitioner: How professionals think in action.* New York: Basic Books. Zeichner, K., & Liston, D. (1996). *Reflective teaching: An introduction.* Mahwah, NJ: Erlbaum.

5. Kincheloe J. (Ed.). (1998). *Post-formal thinking defined.* New York: Guilford Press.

6. Kincheloe, J. (1993). *Toward a critical politics of teacher thinking: Mapping the postmodern.* Westport, CT: Bergin & Garvey.

7. Cherryholmes, C. (1999). *Reading pragmatism.* New York: Teachers College Press.

8. Banathy, B. (1992). *A systems view of education: Concepts and principles for effective practice.* Englewood Cliffs, NJ: Educational Technology Publications.

9. Flood, R. (1990). *Liberating systems theory.* New York: Plenum.

10. Horn, R. (2002). Differing perspectives on the magic of dialogue: Implications for a scholar-practitioner leader. *Scholar-Practitioner Quarterly, 1* (2), 83–102. Jenlink, P., & Carr, A. (1996). Conversation as a medium for change in education. *Educational Technology, 36* (1), 31–38.

11. Bentz, V. (2002). The mindful scholar-practitioner (MS-P). *Scholar-Practitioner Quarterly, 1* (1), 7–22. Slattery, P. (1995). *Curriculum development in the postmodern era.* New York: Garland Publishing.

12. Buber, M. (1987). *I and Thou* (Ronald G. Smith, Trans.). New York: Collier Books.

13. Eisenstadt, S. (1992). Introduction: Intersubjectivity, dialogue, discourse, and cultural creativity in the work of Martin Buber. In M. Buber, *On intersubjectivity and cultural creativity* (pp. 1–22). Chicago: University of Chicago Press.

14. Eisenstadt (1992).

15. Buber, M. (1988). *Eclipse of God*. Atlantic Highlands, NJ: Humanities Press Intl.

16. Palmer, P. (1993). *To know as we are known: Education as a spiritual journey* San Francisco: Harper.

17. Palmer (1993).

18. Horn, R. (2004). *Standards primer.* New York: Peter Lang.

19. Sergiovanni, T. (1992). *Moral leadership: Getting to the heart of school reform*. San Francisco, CA: Jossey-Bass.

20. Jenlink, P. (2003). The scholar-practitioner as public intellectual. *Scholar-Practitioner Quarterly 1* (4) 3–8.

21. Steinberg, S., & Kincheloe, J. (2004). 19 Urban Questions.

22. Kincheloe, J., & Steinberg, S. (1997). *Changing multiculturalism: New times, new curriculum.* London: Open University Press.

23. Kincheloe & Steinberg (1997).

24. Horn (2004).

VOICE, ACCESS, AND DEMOCRATIC PARTICIPATION: TOWARD A TRANSFORMATIONAL PARADIGM OF PARENT INVOLVEMENT IN URBAN EDUCATION

Edward M. Olivos and Alberto M. Ochoa

ISSUES IN BICULTURAL PARENT INVOLVEMENT

Despite the fact that education literature and research support the notion that parent participation is beneficial to student success and urban school districts throughout the nation are searching for ways to improve the academic achievement of their historically disenfranchised student groups (i.e., African Americans, Latinos, immigrant students, English Language Learners [ELL], and students from low-income families), educators and policymakers continue to be unsuccessful in establishing an authentic and collaborative relationship with these families.

The "evidence is consistent, positive, and convincing: families have a major influence on their children's achievement in school and through life."[1] Moreover, there is a strong consensus among educators that family and community play a significant role in bicultural student academic performance and social adjustment. Yet, while the research literature on parent involvement emphatically supports their integration into the education system for improved academic achievement, certain key issues emerge that make broad assumptions problematic.[2]

Jordan et al. bring up three important issues in regard to common parent involvement policy and practice that must be considered when working with parents in urban education settings.[3] These are: (1) the "perceptions of appropriate roles of family and community members in connections with the schools"; (2) the "emphasis on school-centered definitions of family and community involvement," in other words, "family and community involvement frequently means helping reach goals defined by the schools (administrators and teachers) that reflect only school values and priorities"; and (3) the "multiple definitions" given to parent involvement—definitions that are at times vague, overlapping, or even contradictory.

The issues raised by Jordan et al. are given another dimension of complexity when the families are from bicultural backgrounds.[4] This is of particular importance in urban education settings in which a higher concentration of ethnic, racial, linguistic, economic, and religious diversity is found,[5] and where failing schools have brought on the urgency of school reform. Thus, a crucial area of attention for parent involvement supporters and advocates is the dynamic nature of how these diverse parent populations relate to their children's schools in particular and the education system in general. Conversely, attention must also be paid to how the school system relates to them. In other words, educators need to begin to understand more clearly how bicultural parents perceive their roles in the education of their children and how school personnel treat and interact with family members who are non-middle-class and nonwhite.

Núñez argues that in order to develop clarity concerning the roles of bicultural parents in the education of their children, two distinct arenas of parent involvement must be explored.[6] The first of these arenas concerns the direct effect that bicultural parents have on their children as their primary source of nurture and socialization; the second concerns their role in the production of education at the school. In regard to the former, research has acknowledged that the home of the bicultural child is a rich sociocultural context of learning and cognition, even if it differs from the dominant culture.[7] In fact, it is acknowledged that even in the poorest of homes, school-like literacy and learning activities are present as well as "alternative conceptualizations of involvement activity,"[8] which are often not recognized by the schools.[9]

In addition to the social, moral, and academic support bicultural families provide their children in the home, it is similarly important to understand the role bicultural parents can play in improving the quality and effectiveness of education at the school site by making it more responsive to their children's needs. Indeed,

several studies [have] found that families of all income and education levels, and from all ethnic and cultural groups, are engaged in supporting their children's learning at home. White, middle-class families, however, tend to be more involved at school. [Thus], supporting more involvement at school from all parents may be an important strategy for addressing the achievement gap.[10]

In short, there is a desperate need to have underrepresented parents in urban communities become vigilant and active participants in school-related matters such as school policy, decision-making, and accountability, particularly if schools are to be transformed to meet the needs of all students and communities.[11]

Notwithstanding the research that supports the positive outcomes of parent involvement in school-related matters, bicultural parents traditionally have not been inclined to participate in their children's schools in large numbers. This has tended to support the assumption among many in public education that bicultural parents simply don't care about the education of their children nor are they interested in participating at the schools, and thus they are ultimately deemed culpable for their children's academic shortcomings. This *deficit perspective* has clearly affected how school personnel involve bicultural parents in the education of their children.

Parent involvement for bicultural parents typically consists of activities that will keep them either busy or contained. Educators' efforts to change bicultural parents, while keeping them at bay, have precluded the development of a meaningful partnership based on respect and mutual responsibility. Furthermore, they have created distrust and indifference, particularly for those bicultural parents who have become cognizant of the fact that their input and participation is not authentically valued, causing them to refuse to attend and participate in meetings in which the decisions have already been made.

These issues suggest that efforts must be made to critically engage ideologies and practices that impede a collaborative and authentic relationship between the public school system and bicultural communities. It further means critiquing policies and practices currently found in the public education system, policies that tend to favor bicultural parent volunteerism and other low-impact participation rather than democratic involvement. Additionally, it means that policymakers and educators must delve deeper into often-unexplored areas of parent involvement, particularly those related to class, race, and language. And finally, it means that parent involvement must be redefined using a paradigm that will provide the space for voice, access, and democratic participation.

RACE, CLASS, AND LANGUAGE IN PARENT INVOLVEMENT

The degree to which bicultural parents become involved in their children's schools depends on a variety of factors. Some factors are linked to personal perceptions of empowerment and self-efficacy,[12] others to the families' socioeconomic class and culture,[13] and still others to the school system's reception and perception about the proper roles of bicultural parents in the education setting.[14]

Factors related to race, class, and language cannot be ignored when working with bicultural parents in urban school settings since for school personnel these features frequently carry specific negative perceptions that tend to discourage an authentic partnership. Fine argues,[15] for ex-

ample, that school personnel are inclined to hold a negative perception of bicultural low-income parents, often viewing them as less than their social equals. In other words, school personnel are likely to attach favorable perceptions to parents who possess dominant social and cultural capital, preferring instead to have bicultural parents, who they often view as incompetent and deficient, defer decisions about teaching, learning, and school policy to teachers and administrators.

The negative perception held by school personnel about bicultural parents develops into a school tension when these parents put into practice newfound knowledge and skills acquired through workshops, trainings, and personal experience, and/or when they become more assertive in demanding their rights from the school—in other words,[16] when they begin to act like high-status parents.[17] This assertiveness is viewed negatively by school personnel who are accustomed to having a compliant bicultural parent population that follows the dictates of the school without question. Ochoa identifies six clusters of tensions that are present in schools with active Latino parents.[18]

Olivos suggests that there are underlying dialectical tensions of knowledge, culture, and power in the relationship between bicultural parents and the school system.[19] He contends that conflicts between Latino parents and the public schools are inevitable and often lie in their differing views and values about education, particularly because these are the most tangible differences. Olivos also suggests that the tense relationship a bicultural (Latino, Asian, African-American, etc.) parent has with the U.S. public school system is compounded by the cultural biases and economic interests inherent within the institution of public education.[20] This is demonstrated through the school system's historic role of using its power to impose the values and wishes of the dominant culture onto bicultural student and parent populations, primarily through Anglo-centric policies that view bicultural parents as deficient.

TRADITIONAL AND ALTERNATIVE PERSPECTIVES ON BICULTURAL PARENT INVOLVEMENT

The absence of a large-scale presence of bicultural parents in the public school system has tended to support the argument among many educators that bicultural parents neither participate nor want to participate in the schooling process of their children, and their absence is often viewed as indifference and/or incompetence.[21] In a general sense, the argument has been that bicultural parents are incapable of effectively participating in the education system due to their inherent weakness, disadvantaged backgrounds, and lack of motivation.[22] Dunn, for example, once argued that Latino parents have been irresponsible in holding up their end of the deal. He stated that "teachers are not miracle workers" and that "Hispanic pupils and their parents have also failed the schools and society, because they have not been motivated and dedicated enough to make the system work for them."[23]

At times, it has also been argued that the educational failure of many Latino and African-American communities rests on the fact that they resist education by developing an oppositional identity and distrust in the education system. That is, they are ambivalent and disillusioned with the education system due to their social and historical experiences with whites.[24] Alternatively, however, one could argue that the absence of these bicultural parents in the schools is more a demonstration of *resistance* (a defense mechanism against oppression and humiliation) than a sign of disinterest. Specifically, the absence of bicultural parents can be interpreted as a rejection of school practices that they find meaningless.

Núñez,[25] for example, writes that "poor [Latino] parent participation is often inter-preted as lack of concern for the education of their children; however, those that do participate often perceive their activity as demeaning and insignificant." This observation is echoed by Jim Cummins,[26] who writes, "Because parents [from culturally diverse backgrounds] fail to show up to meetings designed to teach them 'parenting skills' or other strategies for overcoming their children's 'deficits,' educators have assumed that they are just not interested in their children's education."

Resistance on the part of bicultural parents can take on various forms, not all of which are easily discernable. The simplest and most common form of resistance comes in the form of absence or disengagement as illustrated earlier. In general, bicultural parents simply refuse to attend or participate in school related activities that they believe are useless, particularly in light of other obligations they may have in regard to home or work. Compounding this disengagement, we believe, is the lack of political consciousness among many bicultural parents in regard to how and why the school system frequently functions to their children's disadvantage.

Another form of resistance that is more observable and may occur among more informed bicultural parents is active oppositional behavior, or openly challenging the school system.[27] This oppositional behavior can take on distinct manifestations, however, and is not always transformational in nature. That is, this type of resistance may or may not include an understanding of the social conditions that contribute to the injustices or a focus on social justice whose goal is the permanent transformation of the unjust condition.[28]

According to Solórzano and Delgado Bernal's *Resistance Framework*, resistance runs along two axes.[29] This resistance may or may not include a "critique of social oppression" and/or "an interest of social justice." Ranging from "reactionary resistance" to "transformational resistance," resistance can thus be either self-defeating or transformative. In light of this, we view low bicultural parent participation, while a form of resistance, as self-defeating in nature in that it lacks the critical political consciousness and organization necessary to not only demonstrate dissatisfaction with the unjust conditions at hand, but also the foresight and the commitment to change or transform their root causes. Indeed, the nature of resistance is complex, particularly when it is in response to issues of social injustice. Thus, in order to understand resistance, one must also engage the nature of domination; in particular, the notion that domination is neither absolute nor that it functions unchallenged. Rather, domination is partial and dialectical. Posited within Marx's notion that "history unfolds dialectically," Persell writes, for example:

Since complex totalities are comprised of a number of elements and tendencies, these processes may change at different speeds or in incompatible ways, leading to contradictions within the system and ultimately, perhaps, to the transformation of the system. The notion of contradiction suggests that education does not merely reproduce the social relations of production in an orderly fashion, but also contains potential for change.[30]

Additionally, "models of resistance posit that domination is never as mechanistic as Social and Cultural Reproduction [sic] models would have us assume, and instead is highly contested in the dialectic between ideological and structural constraints and human agency."[31] Within the public education system the dialectical nature of the relationship between the schools and bicultural communities is therefore sometimes played out through submission and acceptance on the part of bicultural parents, and other times through resistance and even conflict.[32] As a result, the struggles of bicultural communities within the public education system should not be considered one of complete despair. To the contrary, particular school policies and practices as well as individual and collective actions on the part of the agents (i.e., parents, students, administrators, and teachers) can promote more democratic schools and opportunities for bicultural communities, particularly when accompanied by political consciousness and organization. This reflects the dynamic, dialectical nature of education and its potential to be empowering instead of oppressive. Indeed, it has been argued that "significant to a dialectical understanding of education is a view of schools as sites of both oppression and empowerment."[33]

BICULTURAL PARENT PERCEPTIONS ABOUT EDUCATION

Whether bicultural parents feel threatened, intimidated, or unwanted, or whether school personnel actively discourage their participation, the issue remains that these parents have not been inclined to visibly participate at their children's schools in large numbers beyond well-defined limits. Therefore, in order to develop an authentic relationship with bicultural parents, it is important to understand how particular groups perceive their interactions with the schools and with school personnel as well as their own personal lived experiences with the public education system.[34]

Lareau and Horvat contend, for example, that African-American parents are quite cognizant of race relations in the school system and often approach the school with distrust, particularly if they are low-income.[35] Lopez argues that Latino parents view themselves as being quite involved in their children's education by supporting their children's educational endeavors through advice and encouragement, though this is not commonly recognized by their children's schools.[36] And certain Asian groups are considered the model minority, and they succeed in school because they are more receptive to the efforts of the school due to their immigrant experience and the value they place on education. That is, they are willing to accept discrimination and prejudice in return for perceived social advancement which, when compared to that offered in their native countries, is quite favorable.[37]

In their study, Riblatt, Beatty, Cronan, and Ochoa surveyed a total of 506 parents of children in San Diego County and came up with similar findings.[38] Factors related to the problem of parental involvement in education were culled from the literature after examining various theoretical models, including Bronfenbrenner's Ecological Model. Items included examining reasons why parents are involved in their children's education as well as why parents are *not* involved in their children's education. Additional items addressed issues directly related to individual parental situations.

The results of the Riblatt, Beatty, Cronan, and Ochoa study allow for certain generalizations that distinct cultural groups interact differently with the school system. For example, they conclude that African-American parents tend to interact with the schools in modes of resistance, given their personal experiences with the system; that Latinos initially give the schools full trust only to find abuse in the relationship; that white parents tend to focus on their children as part of their involvement with the school; and that Asian parents are guided by cultural traditions that give schools the space and authority to educate their children, and thus are open to collaborating with schools at a distance. In other words, Asian parents generally prefer to support their children's academic work at home.

The results also indicated that Latino families felt more confident that the schools were sensitive to their needs, although their responses may have been more related to the cultural lens they used to view education. Specifically, for Latinos, these findings may not tell the full story of their involvement with the schools. The results that point to Latinos having a positive view of the schools' ability to be

sensitive and to express care may in fact be more attributed to a cultural value that places the school/teacher as a coequal with parents in the education of children. In many cases, when the student has a problem, that problem may go uncontested because the schools or teachers are fulfilling their roles as responsible agents. Yet, as Latino parents get more involved with the school system, their level of direct involvement with and concern about the quality of education provided to their daughter or son increases.

African-Americans tended to have more contact with the school, as indicated by the fact that they spent more time on general school issues and on specific issues related to their child, particularly behavioral issues. However, they were also more likely to have been frustrated in some of these contacts, as indicated by their greater feeling of mystification about school matters. Race may play a vital role in their interaction with the school.

Omi and Howard describe how the social construction of race manifests itself in the ways that schools structure inequalities around race.[39] Inequalities then work to determine the limitations placed upon students' opportunities to learn, to have access to the academic curriculum, and to experience educational mobility. For example, students of color may experience lower teacher expectations, differential classroom interactions, inadequate counseling, less access to pertinent information, ability grouping and tracking, disproportionate representation in special education, culturally biased curricular and instructional practices, culturally biased assessment tools, altered discipline methods, and even receive instruction from the least experienced teachers. To counteract these issues Latino and African-American students and parents, as well as other low-income parents, may take an oppositional approach to dealing with school practices.[40] This often places on the parent the task of addressing problems related to their own child. This study also suggests that parents, particularly low-income parents, spent less time than we would like supporting their children's education.

One consideration that likely applies to all families, and thus to every individual family, comes from exchange theory, which posits that individuals' behaviors are driven to gain the maximum profit with minimum costs.[41] The finding that parents are more involved in their individual child's issues than with general school and education issues is congruent with this perspective. Parents who have more than two jobs and are busy providing for their families in a demanding and stressful economic environment focus their efforts and resources to benefit their own children first. Thus, parents prefer to invest their social capital in spending more time doing homework and supervising the educational attainment of their child at home to increase their success in school.[42]

Hoover-Dempsey and Sandler assert that "[P]arents with a higher sense of efficacy for helping the child succeed will tend to see themselves as capable in this domain: Thus, they are likely to believe that their own involvement will make a positive difference for their children."[43] They see quick and direct results when they help with homework, yet may return frustrated from a school board meeting. In order to prevent this feeling of parental frustration, schools need to be transformed into more flexible and democratic systems that are guided by communication, sensitivity to diversity, familiarity with the sociocultural dynamics of the school community, and supportive in engaging parents and the community in the process of education.

Finally, the research of Riblatt, Beatty, Cronan, and Ochoa concludes that there is a need for research that: (1) places attention on the relationship among schools, the wider society, and the conditions that hinder or promote home-school collaboration; (2) focuses on why parents who are marginalized by race, class, and gender are less able to procure high levels of quality educational services for their children and/or access to the college-bound curriculum; (3) examines culturally sensitive approaches to engaging parents in the education of their children and in school governance; and (4) examines how parent involvement can be institutionalized to support schools and facilitate better educational success for low-income children.

A TRANSFORMATIVE PARADIGM OF PARENT INVOLVEMENT

We argue that there is a need to work within a transformative paradigm of parent involvement, one that will work to not only transform the parents' self-awareness and self-efficacy in regard to school-related matters, but will also transform the school system in general. The chronic achievement gap between students of color and middle- and upper-class white students demonstrates the need to improve the education system. We believe that it will be the parents of these low-performing children who will serve as the catalysts that transform the school system to meet the needs of bicultural children.

In a general sense we argue that a transformative paradigm of parent involvement will provide parents and parent advocates the necessary tools to confront the social injustices currently taking place in the public education setting. This will occur by unmasking the contradictions that are found in the current system and by developing a social consciousness among bicultural parents and communities.

Table 1 illustrates a paradigm for analyzing levels of parent involvement in a democratic social and educational context. Democratic education is defined by Pearl and Knight as both a means and an end.[44] The means is informed debate leading to reflective action. The ends are a society where decisions are made on the basis of universal participation in informed action; where the

Table 1.
Parent Involvement Paradigm

Levels	Theoretical/ Social Focus	Olivos's Parental Involvement Models	Solórzano and Delgado Bernal: Resistance Typology	Driving Legal Emphasis	Perception of Parents as Contributors to Schools
I Status quo	Functionalist (Conformity)	Family influence: Change bicultural parents—improve home condition for participants to acquire preferred behaviors/values	Self-defeating resistance	Right to select who meets the preferred social criteria	Connecting parent to school culture (I)
II	Structural functionalist (Social control and harmony)	Cooperative systems: Parents participate within the school culture to assimilate to school practices and behaviors	Conformist-reformist, resistance	Right to equal access	Parents as collaborators of school culture (II)
III	Conflict theory (Equity and power relations)	Alternative school reform: Parents challenge schools to be more responsive, inclusive, and equitable	Reactionary resistance	Right to equal benefits	Parents as co-participants in the decision-making process (III)
IV Open democratic system	Conflict theory, social constructionist, and interpretivist (Transformational change toward cultural and economic democracy)	Transformational education: Problem-posing that seeks solutions enabling inclusion, voice, and representation in decision making	Transformative resistance	Right to social justice, mobility, and equal encouragement	Cultural democracy, parents as action researchers, agents of transformative change in the school and community (IV)

majority rules only to the extent that specified rights of minorities are respected; and where the decisions made equally encourage all members of the society to fully participate in every facet of the society. Four levels of analyses are suggested.

The paradigm assumes that movement from one system to another is driven by the social commitment and developmental consciousness of its participants and communities. The paradigm provides a progressive and developmental course towards socioeconomic-political consciousness.

The paradigm begins and moves from a functionalist philosophical/ideological perspective (Level I), to structural functionalism (Level II), to conflict theory (Level III), and finally to combined use of conflict theory and interpretivist social-constructionist perspectives to create socioeconomically and politically pluralistic school communities. The paradigm also serves to examine where we have been as a nation and the direction that we need to achieve as we seek socioeconomic and political pluralism in our democracy.

Level I of parent involvement centers on the prominent social belief that the school community conforms to the dominant values of the school's culture or in support of the status quo (functionalist). Feinberg and Soltis define the functionalist perspective as serving to socialize parents and students to adapt to the economic, political, and social institutions of that society. In this perspective, functionalists suggest that we view social institutions as analogous to the parts of the body.[45] Each part functions to serve the needs and purpose of the whole.

Olivos identifies this level of parental characteristics as "family influence."[46] This model of school involvement employs techniques and strategies that work to change the bicultural parents in an effort to assimilate them into the school culture. The underlying assumption of bicultural parents as a hindrance instead of an asset can be seen in the parent education classes that are often offered by the school in which parents are given guidelines, materials, and/or trainings to carry out school-like activities in the home.[47] The overall goal of this model is to "improve" the home condition of the student so that it mirrors that of the school culture.

From the resistance perspective, using Sólorzano and Delgado Bernal's typology, this level of parent involvement is "self-defeating resistance," and refers to parents and students who refuse to participate in school meetings they believe are meaningless. This absence, however, does little to change the school or the school culture, yet demonstrates a critique of social oppression but a lack of motivation for social justice. Specifically, this form of resistance not only lacks the critical political consciousness and organization necessary to demonstrate dissatisfaction with the unjust conditions at hand, but also lacks the fore-sight and commitment to change or transform their root causes. From a legal perspective, the functionalist perspective represents our nation before 1954, based on the principle of "separate but equal." The norm is to view people who are different as needing to demonstrate the "preferred characteristics of the dominant society" in order to be given recognition by those in power positions. Thus, Level I is simply concerned with connecting the parent community to the school culture in order for them to conform to the culture of the school.

Level II of the paradigm of parent involvement is guided by the focus on assimilating the parent community to the dominant values of the school's culture or in support of governing rules (structural functionalist). Under this perspective, schooling is seen as a means of socialization for molding the school community to fit existing social practices and requirements.

Olivos identifies this level of parental characteristics as "cooperative systems." In this second level of parent involvement, it is argued that conditions in the home, school, and community are interrelated. Under the assumption that "cooperation exists between the two institutions," this perspective integrates the parents into various roles. It sees the parent as a "volunteer, paid employee (paraprofessional), teacher at home, audience, decision-maker, adult learner."[48] Thus the parents become "part of the system."

From the resistance perspective, using Sólorzano and Delgado Bernal's typology, this level of parent involvement is "conformist resistance" and refers to oppositional behavior of parents and students in addressing social justice inequities while engaging in traditional activities and behaviors that mirror the same conditions of oppression. While engaged in these traditional behaviors, parents blame themselves, their families, or their culture for the negative personal and social conditions.

From a legal perspective, the structural functionalist perspective represents our nation's struggle to define equal opportunity since 1954 (*Brown v. Board of Education*), based on the principle of equal access. The perspective is to view equity as simply providing the same resources to all participants without concern for its benefits or utility. The only concern in this view is providing comparable resources, and it is the responsibility of the participants to fit the institutions' available resources. Quality, relevance and meaningfulness are not criteria for determining benefit or utility of access. Thus, Level II is simply concerned with working with the parent community to collaborate in support of the school's culture in order to take advantage of its available services.

Level III of the paradigm of parent involvement focuses on addressing social and educational inequities that have been created by the dominant culture and embedded in the practices of the school's culture (conflict theory). Under this perspective, schooling is seen as a social practice supported and utilized by those in power to maintain the culture of dominance in the social order. This perspective questions the inequitable class relations in society and urges social action to stop undue schooling as an instrument of class domination serving to produce the workforce and maintain class relationships.[49]

Olivos identifies this level of parental characteristics as "alternative school reform." In this level of parent involvement, parents may try to change the schools to make them more responsive to their children and to their children's needs.[50] For bicultural parents this is done with the goal of making the school personnel more accountable to their children's needs and under the assumption that their suggestions and input will be accommodated. In other words, the parents begin to "take on" the school.

From a resistance concept perspective, using Sólorzano and Delgado Bernal's typology, this level of parent involvement is "reactionary behavior" that refers to parent and students lacking the awareness or consciousness to identify oppressive conditions and being passive in undertaking action with regard to social justice conditions. From a legal perspective, the conflict theorist perspective represents legal and civil rights legislation that advocates for eradicating past discriminatory practices through social and educational institutions that seek to actualize the principle of equal benefits. This principle is not only concerned with access to resources but also with the quality of services to develop the human condition. The responsibility shifts from the individual to institutional services to fit the needs of participants. Quality, relevance, and meaningfulness become the criteria for assessing benefit or utility of access. Thus, Level III is concerned with the parent community becoming co-participant, in the decision-making process of the school, or "having a piece of the pie."

Level IV of the paradigm combines the equity focus of the conflict theorist perspective—the emphasis of the constructivist perspective in seeking an involvement process that promotes parent and student participants in the construction of knowledge, dialogue, and as agents of creating and recreating meaning in the improvement of the school community— and the interpretivist perspective that sees the social world as made up of purposeful actors who acquire, share, and interpret a set of meanings, rules, and norms that make social interaction possible.[51] The focus is on creating culturally democratic participation in developing and implementing social and educational policy that promotes social responsibility and improves the human condition—socially, cognitively, and politically.

Olivos identifies this level of parental characteristics as "transformational education." In this level of parent involvement, the guiding notion is that knowledge is socially learned and developed between participants, and as such, all are equally responsible and capable of contributing, understanding, and transforming the social and educational process.[52]

From the resistance perspective, using Sólorzano and Delgado Bernal's typology, this level of parent involvement is "transformative resistance" and refers to the understanding and social agency in addressing conditions of oppression and social justice inequities. Participants in this level have a deep understanding and social justice orientation in seeking to act on social injustice. From a legal perspective, the combined perspectives seek to operationalize cultural democracy (equal representation, equal participation, equal access, equal encouragement, and the right to social mobility) while directly addressing practices that eliminate racial and class preference. This perspective also seeks to transform the school community to ensure the cultural democracy values and practices. Thus, Level IV is concerned with creating a school community for the "collective we."

The goal of the Olivos and Ochoa parent involvement paradigm is to reach the fourth level of transformational education that is guided by parental participatory involvement. Such involvement ensures the participation of low-income parents and can be viewed as consisting of three interrelated parts. First, it is initiated through a problem-posing process that forms the basis of our inquiry and work. Second, through this process of inquiry and dialogue, participants learn about the world and about themselves, and thus engage in a transformative educational experience. Third, through personal and individual and collective reflection, action is taken toward resolving the issues that initiated the problem-posing process.[53] It is through the act of questioning and inquiry that a true educational act occurs, and in community with others, knowledge is invented or reinvented. According to Freire, "Education as a practice of freedom—as opposed to education as the practice of domination—denies that [we are] abstract isolated, independent and unattached to the world."[54]

In problem-posing dialogue, participants come to recognize their ability to know and to reflect. Parent involvement is based on empowerment that leads to action and further reflection, which, in turn leads to further questions for inquiry and action research.[55] We see knowledge in its action, practice, and reflection. In the words of Maturana and Varela, "Reflection is the process of knowing how we know. It is [the] only chance we have to discover our blindness and to recognize that the certainties and knowledge of others are, respectively, as overwhelming and tenuous as our own."[56]

This paradigm on parent involvement therefore ultimate seeks to pursue the ideal of cultural democracy. Such ideal exits where the principle of equal encouragement is institutionalized in policies and practices that unmask and eliminate discriminatory racial and class institutional policies and practices. The institution attains cultural democracy when its infrastructure is reflective of the total community at all structural levels of the organization. At this point, multi-racial competency becomes the norm. Cultural democracy recognizes the existence of racial and class tensions as a necessary condition of its existence and for actualizing democracy.[57] The paradigm calls for participatory research as a way for researchers and disempowered people to meet in collaboration to address concrete and specific problems and situations.

The objectives behind this research are to examine the nature and cause of poverty, oppression, and exploitation; to seek action to resolve these problems; to empower the participating communities; and to transform social realities in order to achieve social justice.

NOTES

1. Henderson, A. & Mapp, K. (2002). *A new wave of evidence: The impact of school, family and community connections on student achievement* (p.

7). Austin, TX: Southwest Educational Development Laboratory.

2. Jordan, C., Orozco, E., & Averett, A. (2001). *Emerging issues in school, family, & community connections.* Austin, TX: National Center for Family & Community Connections with Schools; McCaleb, S. (1994). *Building communities of learners.* New York: St. Martin's Press; Valdes, G. (1996). *Con respeto Bridging the distances between culturally diverse families and schools: An ethnographic portrait.* New York: Teachers College Press.

3. Jordan, Orozco, & Averett (2001), p. viii.

4. Boethel, M. (2003). *Diversity: School, family, & community connections.* Austin, TX: National Center for Family & Community Connections with Schools.

5. U.S. Department of Education, National Center for Education Statistics (NCES). (2003). *Characteristics of the 100 largest public elementary and secondary school districts in the United States: 2001–02.* Washington, DC: NCES.

6. Núñez, R. (1994). *Schools, parents, and empowerment: An ethnographic study of Mexican-origin parents' participation in their children's schools.* Unpublished doctoral dissertation, San Diego State University/Claremont Graduate School, San Diego, CA/Claremont, CA.

7. Delgado-Gaitan, C., & Trueba, H. (1991). *Crossing cultural borders: Education for immigrant families in America.* London: Falmer Press.

8. Denny, R., & Dorsey-Gaines, C. (1988). *Growing up literate: Learning from inner-city families.* Portsmouth, NH: Heinemann.

9. Lopez, G. (2001). *On whose terms? Understanding involvement through the eyes of migrant parents.* Paper presented at the annual meeting of the American Educational Research Association (AERA), Seattle, WA, as cited in Henderson & Mapp, p. 138.

10. Henderson & Mapp (2002), p. 7.

11. Sullivan, E. (2003). *Civil society and school accountability: A human rights approach to parent and community participation in NYC schools.* New York: Center for Economic and Social Rights.

12. Ritblatt, S., Beatty, J., Terry, T., & Ochoa, A. (2002). Relationships among perceptions of parent involvement, time allocation, and demographic characteristics: Implications for policy formation. *Journal of Community Psychology, 30* (5), 519–549.

13. Lareau, A. (1989). *Home advantage: Social class and parental intervention in elementary education.* Philadelphia, PA: Falmer Press.

14. Jordan, Orozco, & Averett (2001); Shannon, S. (1996). Minority parental involvement: A Mexican mother's experience and a teacher's interpretation. *Education and Urban Society, 29* (1), 71–84.

15. Fine, M. (1993). [Ap]parent involvement: Reflections on parents, power, and urban public schools. *Teachers College Record, 94* (4), 682–710.

16. Ochoa, A. (1997). Empowering parents to be teachers of their children: The Parent Institute for Quality Education. In *Learning communities narratives: Learning from our differences: Color, culture, and class, Part two, 2* (2). Cleveland, OH: Learning Communities Network.

17. Shannon (1996).

18. Ochoa (1997).

19. Olivos, E. (1999). Power, knowledge, and culture in parent involvement. *The Journal of the Association of Mexican American Educators,* 13–23.

20. Olivos, E. (2003). *Dialectical tensions, contradictions, and resistance: A study of the relationship between Latino parents and the public school system within a socioeconomic "structure of dominance."* Unpublished doctoral dissertation, San Diego State University/Claremont Graduate School, San Diego, CA/Claremont, CA; Olivos, E. (In press). *The power of parents: A critical perspective of bicultural parent involvement in public schools.* New York: Peter Lang Publishers, Inc.

21. Valencia, R., & Black, M. (2002). Mexican Americans don't value education!—On the basis of the myth, mythmaking, and debunking. *Journal of Latinos and Education, 1* (2), 81–103.

22. Valencia, R. (Ed.). (1997). *The evolution of deficit thinking: Educational thought and practice.* London: The Falmer Press.

23. As cited in Cummins, J. (1996). *Negotiating identities: Education for empowerment in a diverse society* (2nd ed.). Ontario, CA: California Association for Bilingual Education (CABE).

24. Ogbu, J., & Matute-Bianchi, M. (1992). Understanding sociocultural factors: Knowledge, identity, and school adjustment. In California Department of Education (Ed.). *Beyond language: Social and cultural factors in schooling language minority students.* Los Angeles: Evaluation, Dissemination, and Assessment Center, UCLA.

25. Núñez (1994), p. 34.

26. Cummins (1996), p. 8.

27. Shannon, S., & Lojero-Latimer, S. (1996). A story of struggle and resistance: Latino parent involvement in the schools. *Journal of Educa-*

tional Issues of Language Minority Students, 16, 301–319; Olivos (2004).

28. Solorzano, D., & Delgado Bernal, D. (2001). Examining transformational resistance through a critical race and LatCrit theory framework: Chicana and Chicano students in an urban context. *Urban Education, 36* (3), 308–342.

29. Solorzano & Delgado Bernal (2001).

30. Persell, C. (1977). *Education and inequality: The roots and results of stratification in America's schools* (p. 8). New York: The Free Press.

31. Covarrubias A., & Tijerina-Revilla, A. (2003). Agencies of transformational resistance. *Florida Law Review, 55* (1), 463.

32. Giroux, H. (2001). *Theory and resistance in education: Towards a pedagogy for the opposition.* Westport, CT: Bergin & Garvey.

33. Darder, A. (1991). *Culture and power in the classroom: A critical foundation for bicultural education* (p. 81). Westport, CT: Bergin & Garvey.

34. Olivos (2003).

35. Lareau, A., & Horvat, E. (1999). Moments of social inclusion and exclusion: Race, class, and cultural capital in family-school relationships. *Sociology of Education, 72* (1), 37–53.

36. Lopez (2001).

37. Ogbu & Matute-Bianchi (1992).

38. Ritblatt, Beatty, Terry, & Ochoa (2002).

39. Omi, M., & Howard, W. (1993). On the theoretical concept of race. In C. McCarthy & W. Crichloe (Eds.), *Race identity and representation in education.* New York: Routledge.

40. Olivos (2004).

41. Sabatelli, M., & Shehan, L. (1993). Exchange and resource theories. In P. Boss, D. Doherty, R. LaRossa, W. Schumm & S. Steinmetz (Eds.). *Sourcebook of family theories and methods: A conceptual approach* (pp. 385–417). New York: Plenum Press.

42. Coleman, J., & Hoffer, T. (1987). *Public and private high schools: The impact of communities.* New York: Basic Books.

43. Hoover-Dempsey, K., & Sandler, H. (1997). Why do parents become involved in the children's education? *Review of Educational Research, 67* (1), 19.

44. Pearl, A. & Knight, T. (1999). *The democratic classroom.* Cressskill, NJ: Hampton Press.

45. Feinberg, W., & Soltis, J. (1992). *School and society.* New York: Teachers College Press.

46. Olivos (1999).

47. Delgado-Gaitán. (1990). *Literacy for empowerment: The role of parents in children's education.* New York: The Falmer Press; McCaleb, S. (1994). *Building communities of learners.* New York: St. Martin's Press.

48. Delgado-Gaitán (1990), p. 54.

49. Feinberg & Soltis (1992).

50. McCaleb (1997).

51. Macedo, D. (1991). *The politics of power: What Americans are not allowed to know.* San Francisco: Westview Press; Feinberg & Soltis (1992).

52. McCaleb (1997).

53. Freire, P. (1985). Dialogue is not a chaste event. In P. Jurmo (Ed.), *Issues in Participatory Research.* Amherst, MA: University of Massachusetts Center for International Education.

54. Freire (1985), p. 69.

55. Ada, A. (1998). Creative readings: A relevant methodology for language minority children. In M. Malwe (Ed.). *NABE '87. Theory, research, and applications: Selected papers* (pp. 97–111). Buffalo, NY: State University of New York Press.

56. Maturana, H., & Varela, F. (1987). *The tree of knowledge* (p. 24). Boston: New Science Library.

57. Lindsey, B., Kikanza, N., Raymond, D., & Terrell, D. (1999). *Cultural proficiency: A manual for school leaders.* New York: Corwin Press.

REWRITING THE CURRICULUM FOR URBAN TEACHER PREPARATION

Cynthia Onore

Linda worried from the start of her teacher education program about how the students she had decided she wanted to teach would react to her. In the rationale for her inquiry project about relationships between students and teachers from different racial, ethnic, and economic backgrounds, Linda wrote, "Urban students might not respond well to a teacher of a different race, from a different background, and from a different place." In spite of these concerns, Linda had chosen to participate in a specially designed urban teacher preparation track within her university's teacher education program. One of the statements in her application that was particularly noteworthy asserted her strong desire to fill a gap in her experience and move beyond what she considered to be the limitations of growing up white and middle class in a monocultural environment. Clearly her desire to teach in an urban setting was stronger than her fears of rejection by her urban students.

Victor, another student in the same program, knew from an early age that he wanted to be a teacher in his home community, one of the largest urban centers in the state. Like Linda, Victor also expressed concerns about how his students might view him. He wondered why the young people he met in urban classrooms always seemed to assume that he was a suburban, middle-class African American, rather than someone just like them. In an essay about why he wanted to teach in his home community, Victor wrote, "I know the embarrassment of knowing that my mother didn't have enough money to pay the light bill and that we would have to go for a few days without lights and hot water." He went on to speculate that, perhaps, the reasons why the young people he met during fieldwork made incorrect assumptions about him was that they may not have known anyone in their families or communities who went to college. He also noted these students were shocked by the seeming contradictions between his speech and dress. While Victor had chosen to dress like his students, he always spoke in what he termed, "a professional manner." Nonetheless, his choices of diction and attire did not have the intended effect. Instead of identifying with him and believing that

they, too, could be successful, students rendered him as "other." Victor was deeply concerned about this reaction and thoroughly confused about what he could do to communicate solidarity with his students and hopefulness about their futures.

Each of these students, in his or her own way, is a highly desirable urban teaching candidate, precisely because of their attention to intersection of their personal histories and the lives of their students. At the same time, they provide insight into how we must rewrite the course of study for urban teacher preparation from recruitment through preparation and retention. In the case of students like Linda, who still constitute the majority of those who enter teaching, the challenge is to identify candidates who, on the surface, may appear ill-suited to urban teaching, but who exhibit attitudes and dispositions that provide them with the potential to succeed. These white, middle-class, suburban, mostly female pre-teaching candidates must be committed to teaching those whom they may not know, but whom they nevertheless neither fear nor wish to save. Candidates like Linda understand their commitment to urban teaching as fulfilling a need in themselves, rather than a need solely to serve others. Since the shortage of urban teachers can never be adequately addressed by recruiting only those whose background and experience match those communities, we must actively seek out and support young women like Linda who demonstrate a willingness to reflect on their privilege, a desire to interrogate the limitations of their experiences, and the capacity to view the inner cities and their residents through the lens of hopefulness and meaningful potential.

Victor is another highly desirable teaching candidate, not solely because of his urban background or his race and socioeconomic status, or even because of his deep commitment to his community, but because of his willingness to struggle with his own and his students' beliefs and assumptions about identity and experience. On the surface, it might seem that Victor is automatically well-suited to the work of urban education and that he poses no significant challenges for an urban teacher preparation program. We might assume that all Victor needs is a solid program in curriculum and methods. But both Victor and Linda struggled with issues of identity—their own, as students growing into becoming teachers, and that of their students from the inner city. Both wondered how they could construct meaningful and productive relationships with their students and both needed to see themselves through the eyes of the young people in order to develop teaching identities that could be effective for those they had chosen to teach.

Whether new teachers come from primarily white, suburban backgrounds, or whether they are, themselves, students from urban schools, the curriculum for educating urban teachers must center on nurturing a candidate's need to teach in hard-to-staff settings, and creating opportunities for them to see themselves anew. It must focus on developing a strong sense of personal efficacy, constructing a deep understanding of the funds of knowledge that reside in urban communities, and supporting a commitment to teaching and learning anti-racism. Such a program must have a strong vision of possibility and structured opportunities for participants to challenge taken-for-granted attitudes and beliefs about themselves and others. These are the elements that a teacher preparation program for urban schools must include.

Although it might seem obvious that teachers who plan to teach in the inner city need preparation different from the preparation for those who plan to teach elsewhere, there are very few teacher preparation programs that have a separate course of study or different track for those who have chosen to teach in urban schools. We know from the current emphasis on national standards for teachers and

students that teaching, learning, and curriculum are presumed to be generic, with little need for variation by context. This is compatible with the prevailing attitude that teacher education, for those who believe in it at all, is also a largely generic enterprise—what teachers need to know and be able to do is the same from sea to shining sea and from the city to the suburb and beyond. In the face of calls for renewal in teacher education that will surely benefit teachers in all teaching environments—attention to teaching diverse learners, more and better-integrated clinical experiences, and deeper subject matter knowledge—the case for a unique course of study for urban educators can be difficult to make. Nonetheless, a considerable body of research strongly suggests that, given the kinds of challenges and the numbers of them faced by inner-city teachers and schools, there should be a special preparation to teach there.[1] In short, if urban centers have distinguishing features, then so should urban teacher preparation.

While the need for well-prepared teachers for inner-city schools grows, resources are more limited than ever. Coupled with all-consuming pressures and constraints on teachers and students from the No Child Left Behind legislation, the challenges faced by teacher education programs to recruit and prepare teachers for urban schools are daunting. At the same time, the population of preservice teachers remains largely white, middle class, and female, while inner-city students are largely not white, poor, and may come from homes where English is not spoken. As a result, programs for the preparation of urban educators must be committed to providing preservice teachers with a different kind of preparation—one that creates opportunities for growth in one's identity as a teacher who is culturally responsive, who sees value and promise in urban centers, and who wishes to connect students' lives at home to learning in school.

REWRITING THE CURRICULUM FOR RECRUITMENT

Who should teach in urban schools? Are there particular knowledge, skills, attitudes and dispositions that correlate with effective teaching and learning for urban youth? Are all of these teachable in a teacher preparation program, or do we need to look for those who are already predisposed toward particular ways of acting and being? No matter whether a teacher preparation program is part of the undergraduate experience, a fifth-year program, a post-baccalaureate certification program, or an accelerated, alternate route, the time spent in it will always be only a small portion of one's life experience. So, it is reasonable to question how effective any program can be in altering a teaching candidate's belief system during such a brief span of time. There is substantial evidence that teacher preparation programs can have, at best, a limited impact on teacher learning.[2] So, it stands to reason that selecting the right candidates for urban teaching is a critical component. But how do we do that? One body of work that has had a powerful influence on how we think about candidate selection is that of Martin Haberman, who argues that we are better off identifying the right candidates than we are trying to change people once they're in our programs.[3] Haberman has developed an interview protocol and a training process for interviewers designed to identify those with the most potential for success. Whether using Haberman's approach or some other means of screening in those candidates who exhibit the attitudes and dispositions that correlate with effective practices in urban education, it is clear that not only must preparation for urban teaching differ from other teaching, but so should the teaching candidates. Novel means need to be employed to uncover candidates' potential for teaching in urban settings.

Recruitment raises some interesting dilemmas, exemplified by the stories of Linda and Victor. If we were to assume that only those raised in an urban community are suited to teach there, then not only do we run the risk of essentializing a candidate's identity, but we also run the risk of excluding candidates like Linda. If, on the other hand, we assume that a teaching candidate who comes from the inner city is automatically a good fit for urban teaching, then we run the risk of including some who may not possess the beliefs, attitudes, and dispositions these young people and their schools need, nor the capacity and desire to develop them.

COMMUNITY KNOWLEDGE AS TEACHER KNOWLEDGE

One very promising direction in teacher education for urban schools is the introduction into the curriculum of community-based experiences. A number of scholars and researchers have made the case for the central importance of first-hand experience in the urban communities where candidates intend to teach.[4] The goals of these experiences are fourfold: (1) they acquaint candidates with an understanding of the riches and realities of urban communities; (2) they allow candidates to interact with children in out-of-classroom contexts where they often display their strengths rather than their limitations; (3) they can provide candidates with a heightened awareness of their own potential to support young peoples' learning through individual interactions; and (4) they can help candidates to understand social justice as a active, participatory, anti-racist commitment that they can make, thus constructing their own identities as teacher-activists committed to social justice and anti-racism. Many courses of study for teacher preparation include a service-learning component in which candidates volunteer to staff a social service agency. Although intended to be reciprocal, often these experiences reinforce a one-way contribution—the volunteer gives her time but does not necessarily see the experience as an opportunity to learn in and from the setting. Too often, although such experiences can help a student to see poverty as a complex, institutionalized condition, they are often not able to develop a strong sense of agency. As a result, these experiences can support rather than challenge participants' *savior* mentality.

Nonetheless, community inquiries and internships can have a transformative potential. Given the opportunity to meet parents, religious and community leaders, and to learn about community-based organizations that provide social services and opportunities to engage in the arts, teacher candidates can discover the deep core of activity and commitment in the inner city. Instead of focusing on community deficits, apathy, and intractable problems, opportunities to investigate what a community has to offer its residents can have a deeply transforming power. Coupled with the chance to work alongside of community residents in after-school programs, summer camps, and other extracurricular activities, teaching candidates can begin to have a deeper understanding of their own and residents' agency.

By limiting their opportunities to observe and interact with urban youth to school settings, teacher candidates' assumptions about these students' challenges and limitations can oftentimes be reinforced rather than challenged. After all, many urban students do not have long and strong histories of school success, and they actively resist learning when their own identities, cultures, and talents are not given expression. But outside of a school setting, candidates can see children and youth playing, creating, and interacting at their best. Similarly, urban parents and caregivers do not always feel welcome or appreciated in schools. Their work lives and other responsibilities frequently cause them to miss what the schools deem important educational events, such as back to school nights and meetings with teachers and other parents. Urban parents and caregivers are, therefore, frequently assumed to lack commitment to their children's educations, and even worse, to be indifferent to their children in general. In contrast to working with urban children only inside of school settings, one experience in an after-school program watching families arrive to pick up their children and one casual conversation with them about their children can do much more than most in-school experiences to affect the attitudes and beliefs of preservice teachers about urban families.

Research on one community based internship program demonstrates that urban teaching candidates can learn about the capabilities and talents of young people even in programs that are poorly run and organized.[5] In this study, one group of students was placed in a chaotic, poorly run literacy camp for their internship. Most impressively, these teacher candidates did not blame the children for what they saw. Instead they reported how impressed they were with the children's resiliency, motivation, and commitment to learning in spite of the surround. And these students left their internship more excited and committed to teaching these students than they were before having this experience.

Breaking through the attitudes that many in our society hold about people in poverty is so crucial to urban education that it is surprising how few programs for teacher preparation attend to this issue in their curricula. Learning about institutionalized racism and its effect on economic and social conditions, however, requires more than learning the facts of discrimination. It involves the lived experience of the courage, struggles, and achievements of urban residents in the face of enormous obstacles. Community-based inquiry projects and internships have the potential to make this experience part of an urban educator's working knowledge; therefore, they should be a required part of the urban education curriculum.

Seeing that one's actions can affect children, trying to improve a setting designed to serve young people, working alongside of those whose everyday actions support others, all of these build into teaching candidates a sense of personal and collective agency.

In the study cited above, another group of student interns collaborated to create a recreation curriculum that the children found very engaging. Community-based experiences like these empower preservice teachers and contribute to their sense of personal efficacy. Since there is strong evidence that teachers' beliefs about their own efficacy correlate highly with their classroom performances, the opportunities that community experiences offer are particularly significant in urban teacher preparation.[6] When teachers believe that they can affect students just as much or more than peers and family, they tend to work harder to help students achieve. When they assume that the choices they make instructionally have an impact on students' motivations to learn, they commit themselves to motivating students. When they believe that they can reach all students, teachers take on responsibility to learn about and experiment with more and different approaches to teaching. Above all, positive efficacy beliefs can have a powerful impact on student achievement.[7]

CULTURALLY RELEVANT AND RESPONSIVE TEACHING FOR URBAN SCHOOLS

As the population of students in public schools across the country becomes increasingly diverse, and as the population of new teachers remains fairly homogeneous, culturally responsive teaching emerges as a critical component for all teacher education.[8] The beliefs that teachers hold about those who are different

from themselves have a powerful impact on their expectations for and attitudes toward students. Transforming the platitude that "all students can learn" into an empowerment agenda for teaching and learning is no small task. Although there is much debate about the relative merits of infusing the teacher preparation curriculum with attention to these issues or creating separate coursework that focuses on teaching for equity and diversity, it would appear that a course of study which both infuses and creates a separate focus on multicultural education is probably the soundest. Although a separate course on diversity can send students the message that diversity is less important than other aspects of their curriculum, and discussion of diversity in all courses often causes teacher candidates to remark that race, racism, and cultural diversity are the sole focus of their programs, teacher education programs need to work with students' resistances and place discussions of diversity at the center of the curriculum.

This implies a reconsideration of the coursework students take in their major disciplines as well. If the task of recognizing and celebrating diversity remains the purview of select courses or programs, multiculturalism will forever be marginalized.[9] A course on African-American history or Hispanic-American literature, for example, reinforces the view that these histories and literatures are *not* American history and American literature. So the task of making curricular revisions should not be the sole responsibility of colleges of education. Collaboration with arts and science faculty to approach coursework in the disciplines differently is essential if teachers are to be adequately prepared to meet the challenges they face in urban classrooms. In order to having a transformative impact on teachers' classroom practices, a curriculum steeped in culturally relevant responsive practices is essential. But these approaches may not be sufficient for adequately preparing urban educators. For without active attention to the ways in which curriculum and teaching are racial at their core and thus must be transformed at the core, it is difficult to imagine a truly equitable education for children in the inner city. Facing these challenges may involve an explicitly anti-racist preparation to teach, that is, a focus on the cultural identities of the teaching candidates with an eye toward engendering in them the courage to resist racist discourse no matter how it evidences itself, in self, others, or institutional regularities. There is much good work to draw on here.[10] From investigations of personal identity development to familiarity with scholarship and research on the structures and effects of personal and institutional racism, there is no dearth of promising practices to inform teacher education. But what distinguishes personal identity development and cultural understanding from practicing anti-racism may be even more challenging for urban teacher preparation. Anti-racism relies upon the willingness to interrogate one's own impulses, an active resistance and confrontation in the face of others' discriminatory words and actions, and a keen eye for school structures and practices that reinforce the power and privilege of the white European cultural surround in schools. An urban teacher should be prepared in a pedagogy of courage and hope so that she might be able to recognize, name, resist, and challenge inequity when she sees it.

I am not trying to argue that learning to be a culturally responsive teacher is only important for urban educators. I am also not suggesting that its more robust version—anti-racist pedagogy—is only important in the inner city. So what, if anything, might be different about what teachers preparing for urban schools need to know about the cultures of the children and communities in which they will work? More than coming to know sets of cultural characteristics, which often essentialize and distort the idea of culture in relation to both individuals and groups, urban educators need to understand how to challenge and change situations that disadvantage students. A curriculum that helps new teachers learn who their students are and why they behave as they do; that confronts the fear that new teachers often have of inner-city children, their families, and communities; that focuses them on what actions they can take; and that encourages them to take action in the face of racism is a curriculum for the urban teacher.

As Lois Weiner has pointed out, there is a paucity of research about "the interplay of characteristics of urban schools as organizations and the successful teaching of a culturally diverse student population they serve."[11] Once we acknowledge that diversity is not a synonym for poor, underserved, and dark skinned, then we may uncover limitations of the one-size-fits-all version of culturally relevant teaching. On the surface, the idea that cultural responsiveness could be anything other than context dependent seems absurd. However, if we don't add to cultural knowledge and value, the effects of school (dis)organization, centralized and bureaucratic intrusion on local decision making, poor quality of life in schools, underresourced classrooms, underprepared teachers as colleagues, poverty and lack of cultural capital in overwhelming proportion in the student body, and an overwhelmingly segregated student body, then the version of culturally relevant teaching we espouse in teacher education will be woefully inadequate in its ability to prepare teachers well for urban schools. All of these are best taught and learned in school settings.

AN ON-SITE CURRICULUM FOR URBAN EDUCATION

Carefully selected and supervised clinical experiences as well as opportunities for collective reflection are critical success factors in learning from field experiences. Too often, school visits result in a reinforcement of stereotypes of urban schooling. So the dilemma is how to ground learning in the realities of schooling while engendering hopefulness. One promising approach lies in site-based coursework where groups of students and university faculty have the opportunity to observe and debrief their experiences together. Holding teacher education on site in urban schools must be constructed as more than a change of venue from the university to the field. Instead, school and university based faculty need to work together to construct learning opportunities that take advantage of the site in which they are held. Visiting classrooms as a group, coupled with the chance to meet with teachers to discuss their observations, has great potential to help preservice teachers understand the realities of the classroom and the school. Rethinking the time-honored tradition of sending preservice teachers into classrooms by themselves is particularly important for preparing urban teachers for whom these school sites are often alien environments that require careful, collective reflection. In-common experiences in urban schools not only render the observations more meaningful, but also create a space for all the observers to interrogate their own and one another's misconceptions and negative assumptions. In this way they can collaborate in constructing positive, hopeful images of urban students and their schools. Holding classes on site also allows students to interview and shadow administrators, teachers, and students to gain multiple perspectives on what they see and learn. In this way, teaching candidates can question what they observe, and get help with challenging their assumptions and looking at the actions and attitudes of those they observe from multiple perspectives. Student teaching, naturally, consumes all of the time and energy of the day. Even when students participate in faculty meetings, professional development, and after-school activities, the student teaching experience

focuses their energies on lesson planning and implementation. The on-site course, then, is essential because it creates a separate space: (1) to learn in and from the school setting; (2) to have in-common experiences with peers and course instructors that provide opportunities for collective reflection; and (3) to develop a complex understanding of the culture of the school.

But not just any site will do. Central to the success of on-site preparation to teach is a strong partnership with the school sites. Teacher preparation programs and public schools must work together to educate a new generation of teachers. To do so effectively requires a shared understanding of teaching and learning, shared values about social justice, and collective beliefs about race, culture and language. An effective urban teacher education program needs trusted school partners to do its work well.

I have argued that teacher education should not be a one-size-fits-all enterprise. Especially in the education of teachers for urban schools, programs need curriculum and practices that are different from those preparing teachers for other school settings. One final element needs noting. It is critically important for programs that prepare teachers for urban schools to broadcast their commitments to equity and social justice. It is not enough to espouse beliefs in democratic practice and platitudes about being committed to teaching all children. Urban education programs must make their positions on social, political, and economic issues resoundingly public, and they must express these positions throughout their practices. In these ways, they will not only attract students who share their beliefs, but they will also be able to engage in continual assessment of the congruence among their beliefs, practices, and policies.

During her teacher education coursework, Linda, with whom I began this discussion, and her cohort were able to meet with groups of inner-city students and talk with them about the issues that were most pressing to them. Concerned about how and whether urban youth would accept her as their teacher, Linda was bold enough to ask a group of high school students about what kinds of teachers they believe can best teach them. During an exchange between a class of teacher education students and urban high school students, one urban student's question to Linda left her unnerved. This student asked, "If you have everything in a suburban area, why are you coming here?" Although Linda didn't have an answer on the spot, another of her peers remarked, "I think you are smart and talented and that your school has a lot to offer." Another student said, "Any teacher can teach us as long as they are familiar with and respectful of our culture." When this group of high school students was then asked how teachers might become familiar with their culture, one young man in the group articulated what much of the research on teaching for equity and diversity suggests. He said, "Don't just drive here and park your car. Take a walk with me and see what I see."

This young man is not just advocating that teachers spend time in the communities in which they will teach. He is eschewing the fear of children and families that new teachers in urban environments often feel and imploring teachers to try to see the world he sees as he sees it. On a deeper level, he is demanding that we build new and different relationships with one another. No program of teacher preparation can show people how to build new relationships, but it can engender the intention to come to see and know ourselves and others differently so that we may build new relationships. A curriculum grounded in democratic practice and committed to social justice will always place inquiry at its center. Because urban classrooms are multilingual and multicultural, it is probably not possible to develop a deep knowl-edge of each language and every culture we will find in our urban classrooms. But it is possible to develop knowledge, skills, and dispositions to place questions—not answers—at the core of learning and teaching; to center the development of new urban educators on democratic practice for social justice; and to make courage and hope the centerpieces of our urban teacher education curricula.

NOTES

1. Kincheloe, J., Burstyn, A., & Steinberg, S. (2004). *Teaching teachers.* New York: Peter Lang; Weiner, L. (1993). *Preparing teachers for urban schools: Lessons from thirty years of school reform.* New York: Teachers College Press; Zeichner, K., & Zelnick, S. (1995). *Teacher education for cultural diversity: Enhancing the capacity of teacher education institutions to address diversity issues.* E. Lansing, MI: National Center for Research on Teacher Learning.

2. Weiner, L. (2000). Research in the '90s: Implications for urban teacher preparation. *Review of Educational Research, 70* (3), 369–406.

3. Haberman, M. (1995). Selecting "star" teachers for children and youth in urban poverty. *Phi Delta Kappan, 76* (10) 569–582.

4. Ladson-Billings, G. (2001). *Crossing over to Canaan: The journey of new teachers in diverse classrooms.* San Francisco: Jossey-Bass; Murrell, P. (2001). *The community teacher: A new framework for effective urban teaching.* New York: Teachers College Press; Weiner, 2000, p. 369.

5. Trachtman, R. (2003). Evaluation of year two of the Urban Teaching Academy. Unpublished manuscript, Montclair State University, Montclair, NJ.

6. Darling-Hammond, L., Chung, R., & Frelow, F. (2001). Variation in teacher preparation: How well do different pathways prepare teachers to teach? *Journal of Teacher Education, 53* (4) 286–302; Gibson, S., & Dembo, M. (1984). Teacher efficacy: A construct validation. *Journal of Educational Psychology, 76* (4) 777–781.

7. Darling-Hammond, Chung, & Frelow (2001), p. 286.

8. Villegas, A., & Lucas, T. (2002). *Educating culturally responsive teachers: A coherent approach.* Albany: State University of New York; Ladson-

Billings, G. (2000) Fighting for our lives: Preparing teachers to teach American students. *Journal of Teacher Education, 51* (3), 206–214; Nieto, S. (2000). Placing equity front and center: Some thoughts on transforming teacher education for a new century. *Journal of Teacher Education, 51* (3), 180–187.

9. Castenell, L., & Pinar, W. (1993). *Understanding curriculum as racial text: Representations of identity and difference in education.* Albany: State University of New York.

10. Cochran Smith, M. (2000). Blind vision: Unlearning racism is teacher education. *Harvard Educational Review, 70* (2), 157–190; Derman-Sparks, L., & Phillips, C. (1997). *Teaching/learning anti-racism: A developmental approach.* New York: Teachers College Press; Tatum, B. (1992). Talking about race; learning about racism: The application of racial identity development theory in the classroom. *Harvard Educational Review, 62* (1), 1–24.

11. Weiner (2000), p. 369.

RETHINKING LEARNING AND MOTIVATION IN URBAN SCHOOLS

Robert Rueda and Myron H. Dembo

RETHINKING THE ROLE OF STUDENTS IN ACHIEVEMENT IN URBAN SCHOOLS: A FOCUS ON LEARNING AND MOTIVATION

Academic underachievement is one of the major problems in urban schools, particularly among African-American and Hispanic students[1] who tend to earn lower grades and drop out more often than do white students.[2] Persistent low achievement and its unequal distribution across different groups in American society is a strong concern among most researchers and practitioners. The ways that it is addressed in practice vary greatly. In the worst-case scenario, low achievement is met with high doses of low-level practice and drill, excessive testing, lowered expectations and standards, or punitive measures.

More theory-based and systematic efforts have emerged from the school reform effort. The dominant approach taken to improve urban schools is often called standards-based reform that includes the following elements: clear academic goals, coherent educational standards, frequent measurement of student achievement, im-proved instructional practices, investment in professional development, strong curricula, improved leadership at the system and school levels, and reform of school finance to support the reform activities.[3] The intent of standards-based reform is to integrate key aspects of policy—curriculum, assessment, teacher education, and professional development—around standards describing what students should know and be able to do.[4] These are clearly important elements of improving student achievement, but a noticeable omission from this list is reference to students themselves and how to improve their learning and motivation. While efforts such as those just described have tried to address achievement differences, they have largely ignored the role of the student except as a relatively passive target of intervention.

In this chapter we suggest that there are limitations in current urban school reform efforts that place students in a minor role, and we will focus in particular on issues of student learning and motivation. More specifically, we will argue that educators need to place as much attention on *how* and *why* students learn as they do on *what* they learn; that is, an approach that takes in to account current understanding of learning and motivation processes. Furthermore, we will suggest in addition to a focus on student learning and motivation, that a focus on students' self-regulation of these processes provides new tools to conceptualizing and addressing issues related to student achievement.

CURRENT PERSPECTIVES ON MOTIVATION AND LEARNING

A full review of current research and theory related to learning and motivation is clearly beyond the limitations of this chapter. However, over the past decade, syntheses of current work have been written and are helpful in gaining a quick overview of learning and motivational processes as well as their close relationship. One useful synthesis is based on work done by the American Psychological Association.[5] Condensing these principles in an overview format should not belie the fact that they are based on extensive empirical work; however, they do provide a useful overview. Alexander and Murphy[6] present the following general principles:

> The Knowledge Base. One's existing knowledge serves as the foundation of all future learning by guiding organization and representations, by serving as a basis of association with new information, and by coloring and filtering all new experiences.
> Strategic Processing or Executive Control. The ability to reflect on and regulate one's thoughts and behaviors is essential to learning and development.
> Motivation and Affect. Motivational or affective factors, such as intrinsic motivation, attributions for learning, and personal goals, along with the motivational characteristics of learning tasks, play a significant role in the learning process.
> Development and Individual Differences. Learning progresses through various common stages of development influenced by both inherited and experiential/environmental factors.

> Situation or Context. Learning is as much a socially shared undertaking as it is an individually constructed enterprise.

An additional recent review by Pintrich specifically on motivation outlined several generalizations or principles based on current research. These include the following:[7]

- Adaptive self-efficacy and competence beliefs motivate students
- Adaptive attributions and control beliefs motivate students
- Higher levels of interest and intrinsic motivation motivate students
- Higher levels of (task) value motivate students
- Goals motivate and direct students

While space does not permit more extensive elaboration of these principles and discussion of the associated design principles, the central point is that the role of a learner's beliefs, values, and goals—rather than internal, stable traits—are the important determinants of motivation and engagement. Importantly, the role of cultural considerations in the application of these principles is paramount, even though it is only recently that these factors have gained increased attention.[8] Some considerations related to these factors are described subsequently.

Motivation, Goals, and Cultural Considerations for Underachieving Students in Urban Schools

One strategy for increasing performance in urban schools characterized by low achievement has been to focus on incentives, competition, and social comparison as the primary motivational tool. For example, Tucker and Codding,[9] in discussing how to build a strong accountability system, place on the list of things to do: "Develop incentive systems (systems of rewards and consequences) that will motivate students to reach the student performance standards. . . . Develop a system of awarding a certificate to every student who meets the standard you've established for student performance in the core subjects in the curriculum." Marsh and Codding believe that an important incentive would be a Certificate of Initial Mastery (CIM) that would certify that students have achieved high standards in core subjects.[10] They suggest that this certificate would signal to students that schools expect more and believe that students would respond appropriately.

There are a number of problems with this approach. First, as Covington notes, this approach relies on a view of motivation as a drive, need, or condition that impels individuals toward action.[11] The notion is that if individuals find the right rewards or threaten punishment or sanctions, they can arouse lazy or bored students to attain higher levels of achievement. However, as noted previously, more recent motivational theories focus on a learner's beliefs, values, and goals as the key factors in motivation.[12]

Another problem with incentive-based approaches that stress competition and social comparison is the belief that arousal is maximized when the rewards are given on a competitive basis. However, Covington argues that this perspective has not been successful at motivating students because there is a scarcity of rewards.[13] That is to say, students who perform the best receive the majority of the rewards. The consequences of this perspective encourage low-achieving students to use strategies to avoid failure rather than attempt to master the content.

Finally, the research in motivation indicates that not all students are driven by incentives such as money, certificates, stars, and other benefits of competition and social comparison. Instead, achievement differences among students and cultural groups are reflected in the various goals to which they aspire, even when they come from poor environments. For example, it has been shown that many poor immigrants from Central America thrived in U.S. schools but were not motivated by incentives or personal gain, but rather by the desire to do well to help their families.[14] There is considerable evidence that many students from different cultural groups are motivated to cooperate and help others in a similar manner.[15]

These factors point out the need to rethink incentive-based approaches that stress competition and comparison and instead to try to understand the factors motivating these students. Currently, there is evidence that there are differences among students, although there is still a great deal that is unknown about cultural factors related to motivation and self-regulation in particular and how these vary among different students in urban school settings. As one example of possible differences, Asian-American students have been found to report lower levels of self-efficacy for academic tasks,[16] and African-American students have been found to display relatively high confidence in their academic competence.[17] Although it is dangerous to make inferences about individual students based on group labels, there do appear to be important differences among students that merit consideration. The critical idea is that not all students are motivated by the same factors.

Given what is known about the important connections between learning and motivation, an additional consideration is research that suggests that students can be taught to monitor and control these processes. This perspective is described in the following section.

A SELF-REGULATION PERSPECTIVE ON LEARNING, MOTIVATION, AND ACHIEVEMENT

As noted earlier, current attempts to improve student achievement often focus on attempts to increase the use of appropriate teaching practices through more effective professional development. As one example, Fuhrman and Odden argue that "a stronger focus on instructional improvement and on appropriate professional development is required for a larger payoff in student achievement."[18] Unfortunately, there is little evidence that high-quality professional development will consistently produce high-quality teaching in classrooms that will, in turn, translate into higher levels of student achievement. Teaching practice may not translate into student achievement gains because of the poor alignment between what is taught and what is tested, the lack of sufficient time for the intervention to have an impact on student achievement, as well as the fact that the types of teaching practices studied may not be the ones that change student achievement.[19]

Although we are not opposed to improving teaching practices, we ask: How can "effective" teaching practices impact academic performance when they are considered in isolation from the fact that many students can't control their attention, don't use effective study strategies, can't manage their time, and don't adequately or strategically prepare for or take exams? For this reason, Dembo has urged educators not to lose sight of the importance of students in educational reform.[20] He argues, " if higher academic standards are to be attained, the most important changes must be made by students, not schools." We propose a refocus that places students themselves in the position of serving as active agents of change. We argue that a focus on students in general, and self-regulation in particular, has the potential to make a significant difference in learning outcomes and achievement.

Self-Regulation

The explanations for underachievement in the educational, psychological, and popular literature range from genetic differences in ability to learn to inadequate curricula, with a host of factors in between. One infrequently considered factor in the school reform literature is what has been termed self-regulation, or the ability of students to control their own behavior. Al-

though there are different theoretical approaches used to explain the dynamics of self-regulation,[21] we will focus on the social cognitive perspective as presented in the work of Zimmerman and his colleagues,[22] who have been interested in learning how students become willing and able to assume responsibility for controlling or self-regulating their academic achievement. One promising outcome of this research is that it indicates that learning self-regulatory skills can lead to greater academic achievement.

What is self-regulation more specifically? In the simplest terms, self-regulation can be defined as the ability of students to control the factors or conditions affecting their learning, including learning-related beliefs that impact motivation and learning processes. Research indicates that these self-regulatory beliefs and processes are highly correlated with academic achievement.[23] In the past, much educational practice has been focused on what to do to students. However, many educational researchers now realize that students themselves can do a great deal to promote their own learning through the use of different learning and motivational strategies, and that these skills can be promoted early on.

Zimmerman presents a conceptual framework of self-regulation that consists of six underlying psychological dimensions that learners can self-regulate by employing specific processes.[24] The psychological dimensions of self-regulation in Zimmerman's model and the underlying issues they relate to include the following:

- Motive (Why?)
- Method of learning (How?)
- Time (When?)
- Control of physical environment (Where?)
- Control of social environment (With whom?)
- Control of performance (What?)

Drawing on the work of Zimmerman and his colleagues and Dembo and his colleagues,[25] we discuss each of these dimensions and how to address them in the curriculum.

Motive

Whereas the popular conception of motivation related to learning is that of a fixed trait that individuals either have or don't have, current psychological views of motivation focus on situation-specific, learning-related beliefs and goals. Motive, for example, addresses the question of why learners choose to learn, that is, their motivation for learning. One of the major differences between successful and less successful individuals in any field is that successful individuals know how to motivate themselves even when they do not feel like performing a task, whereas less successful individuals have difficulty controlling their motivation. As a result, less successful individuals are less likely to complete a task, and more likely to quit or complete a task at a lower level of proficiency. Although successful learners may not feel like completing required tasks, they learn how to motivate themselves to completion in order to maintain progress toward achieving their goals.

A number of important self-regulatory strategies can be used to develop and maintain these important motivational beliefs and behavior. The first is goal setting. Educational research indicates that high achievers report using goal setting more frequently and more consistently than low achievers.[26] Moreover, there is evidence that the most effective goals are those that are specific, proximal, and challenging but attainable.[27] When individuals establish and attempt to attain personal goals, they are more attentive to instruction, expend greater effort, and increase their confidence when they see themselves making progress. It is difficult to be motivated to achieve without having specific goals. Therefore, teachers need to help students set both long-range and intermediate goals for their academic, personal, social, and occupational domains in their lives.

A second self-regulatory strategy for motivation is self-verbalization or self-talk. Some of our speech motivates us to try new tasks and persist in difficult situations; other self-talk is unproductive and inhibits our motivation to succeed. One of the most common forms of self-talk is verbal reinforcement or praise following desired behavior. Students can be taught responses like: "Great! I did it!" or "I'm doing a great job concentrating on my readings!" The power of self-talk to influence performance is well established, and based on the notion that what one says to oneself is an important factor in determining attitudes, feelings, emotions, and behaviors. For years, world-class athletes have been trained to use verbal reinforcement. When necessary, more elaborate self-talk training programs are available to help individuals control anxiety, mood, and other emotional responses.[28]

Another motivational self-regulatory strategy is arranging or imagining rewards or punishments for success or failure at an academic task. Students who control their motivation by giving themselves rewards and punishments outperform students who do not use this control technique.[29]

In summary, to control motivation, students need to set goals; develop positive beliefs about their ability to perform academic tasks; and maintain these beliefs while faced with the many disturbances, distractions, occasional failures, and periodic interpersonal conflicts in their lives. When students realize they are responsible for their own motivation, they may be more willing to initiate strategies to control their motivation.

Method

Method addresses questions relating to *how* learners self-regulate learning. The key underlying process regulating method is the use of learning strategies. Learning strategies are the methods students use to acquire information. Research indicates that higher achieving students use more learning strategies than do lower achieving students.[30]

Weinstein and Mayer identify three different categories of learning strategies that learners must acquire.[31] The first type, rehearsal strategies, can be effective for learning factual material. Copying, taking verbatim notes, and reciting words or definitions are all examples of rehearsal strategies. Their limitation, however, is that they make few connections between new information and the knowledge that is already in long-term memory.

The second type, elaboration strategies, helps retention by linking new information with knowledge already in long-term memory. These strategies are useful for improving the recall of names, categories, sequences, or groups of items. There are several elaboration strategies that have proven effective for the integration and retention of new knowledge: summarization, annotation, outline-formatted notes, higher-level questions, elaborative interrogation, and elaborative rehearsal.[32]

The final general category of learning strategies identified by Weinstein and Mayer is organizational strategies.[33] These strategies help learners remember information by allowing them to structure academic content. Students can learn to structure content through visual representations like diagrams, matrices, sequences, and hierarchies.

Time

The time dimension addresses questions relating to when and for how long to study. Students who use their time efficiently are more likely to learn and/or perform better than students who do not have good time management skills. Self-regulated learners know how to manage their time because they are aware of deadlines, how long it will take to complete each assignment, and their own learning processes. They prioritize learning tasks, differentiating more difficult tasks from easier ones in terms of the time required to complete them. They are aware of the need to evaluate how their study time is spent and to reprioritize as necessary. The greater such awareness is, the better time management skills will be, meaning that more material will be read, reviewed, and elaborated upon.[34] In this way, time management improves achievement.

Time management skills can be learned, and subsequent efforts by students to manage their study time do make a difference academically. As time management skills are refined, more time is spent on task, procrastination decreases, tasks are completed on time, and chances of academic achievement and success improve.

Physical Environment

Physical environment concerns where learners learn and which instructional supports they employ. Zimmerman and Martinez-Pons found that high achievers reported greater use of environmental restructuring than did low-achieving students.[35] Self-regulated learners are proactive in choosing where they will study and will take appropriate steps to ensure that they have regulatory control over their learning environment. They are sensitive to their environment and resourceful in altering it as necessary.

For the most part, environmental restructuring refers to locating places to study that are quiet or not distracting. Although this task may not appear difficult for some students, it poses many problems for students who either initially select inappropriate environments or cannot control the distractions once they occur.

Social Environment

Social environment refers to with whom the learner studies.[36] Active learners who are motivated to achieve tend to seek help when it is needed. Self-regulatory learners, like any other students, often realize that they have difficulty learning or achieving their goals. When these conditions occur, they take charge of their learning by seeking assistance from others to remedy the situation. Self-regulation of the social environment relates to the ability of learners to determine when they need to work alone or with others; or when it is time to seek help from instructors, tutors, peers, or even nonsocial resources (such as reference books).

The decision to seek help is influenced by both personal and environmental factors. Personal factors include students' perceptions of their academic and social competencies, the nature of their achievement goals (i.e., mastery vs. performance), and attitudes (i.e., perceived threats and benefits regarding help seeking).[37] Environmental factors include teacher behaviors and classroom practices.[38]

Students' self-perceptions are important factors in predicting help-seeking behaviors. Students who lack confidence in their social and cognitive abilities are more likely to feel threatened when asking their peers for help, and more likely to avoid seeking help than students who are confident in their social and cognitive abilities. Also, high-achieving students are more likely than low-achieving students to seek help from instructors.[39] The research clearly indicates that students who need help the most are least likely to seek it.[40]

Educators have found that different classroom goals (i.e., mastery and performance) are associated with different achievement-related behaviors such as persistence, effort, and the use of more advanced learning strategies. Students with a mastery orientation are more likely to view help seeking as a useful strategy that can help them learn more successfully. In contrast, students with a performance orientation, who are more concerned with achieving higher than others, are more likely to believe that help seeking may incur negative reactions from others. The important point to consider is that students' attitudes about help seeking are related to the achievement goals they pursue.[41]

Teacher behavior also is an important factor influencing students' help-seeking behavior. For example, students' attitudes and behaviors are shaped by teachers who place a value on help seeking by spending time encouraging questions and providing feedback, demonstrating that question-asking is beneficial, and modeling appropriate ways for students to ask for clues rather than answers.[42]

The classroom environment can provide the structure and support to encourage (or impede) self-regulatory behaviors.[43] Therefore, schools that emphasize competition, social comparison of grades, and ability tracking (i.e., establish performance goal orientations) often unintentionally reinforce the reluctance of many students to seek assistance in class.[44]

Performance

Performance addresses questions relating specifically to overt behavior, or what learners do in pursuit of their learning goals. Self-regulated learners are aware of the learning outcomes they expect (have set for themselves), are sensitive to not having achieved those outcomes (if such is the case), and are able to adjust their behavior accordingly in order to make up for any behavioral deficiency in attaining their learning goals.[45]

If an important goal of education is to produce individuals who are capable of educating themselves, then students must learn to manage their lives by setting their own goals, evaluating their progress, and making the necessary changes to attain these goals. Whether writing a paper, completing a test, or reading a book, students can learn how to use self-regulatory processes to influence the quality of their performance. One of the important functions of a goal is to provide an opportunity for students to detect a discrepancy between it and their present performance. This analysis enables them to make corrections in the learning process. When students learn to monitor their work under different learning conditions (e.g., test taking and studying), they are able to determine what changes are needed in their learning and studying behavior. The fact that successful students tend to be aware of how well they have done on a test, even before getting it back from an instructor, indicates the importance of monitoring performance.[46]

CLARIFICATIONS AND SPECIAL CONSIDERATIONS

There are some factors that merit clarification and discussion regarding the approach we propose, since a focus on self-regulation might be taken to mean lack of concern with other factors that impact the school careers of students in at-risk circumstances. We discuss these in the following paragraphs.

Non-Student Influences on Learning and Achievement

There are abundant data that document the inequities in American education, especially in large urban schools.[47] There are inequities in resources in different schools, variation in teacher quality, differences in teacher expectations for different types of students, and socioeconomic status (SES)-related differences that may impact achievement, such as print access (books for example) and exposure to academic English. These structural and resource-based factors are all issues that require attention. Our focus on self-regulation should not be taken to mean that the factors mentioned are not important and should not be addressed. Every student is entitled to an optimal learning environment. Rather, the argument is that chances for school success will be increased by greater attention to self-regulation of learning and motivation, whatever the external circumstances happen to be.

Learning, Motivation, and Notions of Deficit

As previously noted, there are significant differences on a variety of educational indicators among different subgroups in U.S. society, notably those related to SES, race, and ethnicity. One long-standing explanation for these differences in achievement has been focused on learning ability and motivational problems. However, these are often seen as inborn, fixed characteristics of students and/or their families. In contrast, more recent work has focused on learning strategies, strategic learning behavior, and motivational beliefs as phenomena open to examination, change, and ultimately self-regulation. While we believe that school success is closely tied to learners' regulation of their own learning and motivational processes, we do not support the view that maladaptive motivational beliefs or ineffective learning strategies are a function of race, ethnicity, or any other category. Self-regulation should not be seen as a substitute for IQ nor should it be subject to the same misinterpretations and misuses characterizing that construct.

SUMMARY AND CONCLUSIONS

There are significant issues related to achievement in urban schools. Efforts to address achievement gaps have focused on a variety of factors presumed to underlie low achievement, but have tended to ignore student-related factors such as how effectively students learn and the learning goals they set for themselves. In particular, specific attention to students' self-regulation of learning and motivation has been underemphasized.

We have noted that there are many inequities in opportunity to learn and that certain groups of students are more likely to be in at-risk circumstances. We firmly believe that all students should be provided optimal learning environments and have equal opportunity to learn, and that efforts to address these inequities are important. A focus on student self-regulation of learning and motivation does not minimize these concerns, but it does have the potential to increase the chance for academic success under any learning circumstances. Providing students with self-regulatory skills may be the most important curricular change that can be implemented. Such a change would transform low-achieving students in at-risk situations from passive recipients of poor learning environments and low expectations to active agents in their own learning and academic success. Given the potential for improving achievement and the populations of students most impacted, increased attention is warranted.

NOTES

1. Garibaldi, A. (1993). Creating prescriptions for success in urban schools. Turning the corner on pathological explanations for academic failure. In T. Tomlinson (Ed.), *Motivating students to learn* (pp. 125–138). Berkeley, CA: McCutchan; Meece, J., & Kurtz-Costes, B. (2001). Introduction: The schooling of ethnic minority children and youth. *Educational Psychologist, 36,* 1–7; Singham, M. (1998). The canary in the mine: The achievement gap between blacks and white students. *Phi Delta Kappan, 80* (1), 8–15.

2. Haycock, K. (2001). Closing the achievement gap. *Educational Leadership, 58* (6), 6–11.

3. Fuhrman, S., & Odden, A. (2001). School reform: Introduction. *Phi Delta Kappan, 83,* 59–61.

4. Fuhrman, S. (2001). Introduction. In S. Fuhrman (Ed.), *From the capital to the classroom: Standard-based reform in the states. One hundredth yearbook of the National Society for the Study of Education* (Part II) (pp. 1–12). Chicago: University of Chicago Press.

5. Alexander, A., & Murphy, K. (1998). The research base for APA's learner-centered psychological principles. In N. Lambert and B. McCombs (Eds.), *How students learn: Reforming schools through learner-centered education* (pp. 26–60). Alexandria, VA: Association for Supervision and Curriculum Development; Lambert, N., & McCombs, B. (1998). *How students learn: Reforming schools through learner-centered educa-tion. Alexandria, VA: Association for Supervision and Curriculum Development.

6. Alexander & Murphy (1998).

7. Pintrich, P. (2003). A motivational science perspective on the role of student motivation in learning and teaching contexts. *Journal of Educational Psychology, 95* (4), 667–686.

8. Pintrich (2003); National Research Council, Committee on Increasing High School Students' Engagement and Motivation to Learn. (2004). *Engaging schools: Fostering high school students' motivation to learn.* Washington, DC: The National Academies Press; Bransford, J., Brown, A., & Cocking, R. (1999). *How people learn: Brain, mind, experience, and school.* Washington, DC: National Academy Press; Schonkoff, J., & Phillips, D. (2000). *From neurons to neighborhoods: The science of early childhood development.* Washington, DC: National Academy Press.

9. Tucker, M., & Codding, J. (1998). *Standards for our schools: How to set them, measure them, and reach them.* San Francisco: Jossey-Bass, (pp. 238–239).

10. Marsh, D., & Codding, J. (1999). *The new American high school.* Thousand Oaks, CA: Corwin.

11. Covington, M. (2000). Goal theory, motivation, and school achievement: An integrative review. *Annual Review of Psychology, 51,* 171–200.

12. Pintrich (2003).

13. Covington (2000).

14. Suarez-Orozoco, M. (1989). *Central American refugees and U. S. high schools: A psychosocial study of motivation and achievement.* Stanford, CA: Stanford University Press.

15. Castenell, L. (1983). Achievement motivation: An investigation of adolescents' achievement patterns. *American Educational Research Journal, 20,* 503–510; Castenell, L. (1984). A cross-cultural look at achievement motivation research. *Journal of Negro Education, 53,* 435–443; Ramirez, M., & Price-Williams, D. (1976). Achievement motivation in children of three ethnic groups in the United States. *Journal of Cross-Cultural Psychology, 7,* 49–60.

16. Eaton, M., & Dembo, M. (1997). Differences in the motivational beliefs of Asian American and non-Asian students. *Journal of Educational Psychology, 89,* 433–440.

17. Graham, S. (1994). Motivation in African Americans. *Review of Educational Research, 64,* 55–117.

18. Fuhrman & Odden (2001), p. 61.

19. Supovitz, J. (2001). Translating teaching practice into improved student achievement. In S.

Fuhrman (Ed.), *From the capital to the classroom: Standard-based reform in the states. One hundredth yearbook of the National Society for the Study of Education* (Part II). Chicago: University of Chicago Press.

20. Dembo, M. (2004). Don't lose sight of the students. *Principal Leadership, 4*, 37–42.

21. Zimmerman, B. & Schunk, D. (Eds.). (2001). *Self-regulated learning and academic achievement: Theoretical perspectives* (2nd ed). Hillsdale, NJ: Lawrence Erlbaum Associates.

22. Zimmerman, B. (1998). Developing self-fulfilling cycles of academic regulation: An analysis of exemplary instructional models. In D. Schunk & B. Zimmerman (Eds.), *Self-regulated learning: From teaching to self-reflective practice* (pp. 1–19). New York: The Guilford Press; Zimmerman, B. (1994). Dimensions of academic self-regulation: A conceptual framework for education. In D. Schunk and B. Zimmerman (Eds.), *Self-regulation of learning and performance* (pp. 3–21). Hillsdale, NJ: Lawrence Erlbaum Associates; Zimmerman, B., Bonner, S., & Kovach, R. (1996). *Developing self-regulated learners: Beyond achievement to self-efficacy.* Washington, DC: American Psychological Association; Zimmerman, B., & Risemberg, R. (1997). Self-regulatory dimensions of academic learning and motivation. In G. Phye (Ed.), *Handbook of academic learning: Construction of knowledge* (pp. 105–125). San Diego: Academic Press.

23. Zimmerman & Risemberg (1997); Zimmerman, B., & Martinez-Pons, M. (1990). Student differences in self-regulatory learning: Relating grade, sex, and giftedness to self-efficacy and strategy use. *Journal of Educational Psychology, 82*, 284–290.

24. Zimmerman (1998); Zimmerman (1994).

25. Dembo (2004); Dembo, M. (2004). *Motivation and learning strategies for college success: A self-management approach* (2nd ed.). Mahwah, New Jersey: Erlbaum; Dembo, M., & Eaton, M. (2000). Self-regulation of academic learning in middle-level schools. *Elementary School Journal, 100*, 473–490; Dembo, M., Junge, L., & Lynch, R. (In press). Becoming a self-regulated learner: Implications for Web-based education. In H. O'Neil and R. Perez (Eds.), *Web-based learning: Theory, research, and practice.* Mahway, NJ: Erlbaum.

26. Zimmerman, B., & Martinez-Pons, M. (1986). Development of a structured interview for assessing student use of self-regulated learning. *American Educational Research Journal, 23* (4), 614–628.

27. Locke, E., & Latham, G. (1990). *A theory of goal setting and task performance.* Englewood Cliffs, NJ: Prentice Hall.

28. Butler, P. (1981). *Talking to yourself: Learning the language of self-support.* San Francisco: Harper and Row.; Ottens, A. (1991). *Coping with academic anxiety* (2nd ed.). New York: Rosen.

29. Zimmerman & Martinez-Pons (1986).

30. Zimmerman, B., & Martinez-Pons, M. (1988). Construct validation of a strategy model of student self-regulation. *Journal of Educational Psychology, 80*, 284–290.

31. Weinstein, C., & Mayer, R. (1986). The teaching of learning strategies. In M. Wittrock (Ed.), *Handbook of research on teaching* (3rd ed.) (pp. 315–327). New York: Macmillan Publishing Company.

32. Dembo, Junge, & Lynch (in press).

33. Weinstein & Mayer (1986).

34. Zimmerman & Martinez-Pons (1986); Zimmerman, B., Greenberg, D., & Weinstein, C. (1994). Self-regulating academic study time: A strategy approach. In D. Schunk and B. Zimmerman (Eds.), *Self-regulation of learning and performance* (pp. 181–199). Hillsdale, NJ: Lawrence Erlbaum Associates.

35. Zimmerman & Martinez-Pons (1986).

36. Zimmerman, B. (1998). A social cognitive view of self- regulated academic learning. *Journal of Educational Psychology, 81* (2/3), 329–399.

37. Ryan, A., & and Pintrich, P. (1997). "Should I ask for help?" The role of motivation and attitudes in adolescents' help seeking in math class. *Journal of Educational Psychology, 89,* 329, 341.

38. Newman, R. (1998). Adaptive help seeking: A role of social interaction in self-regulated learning. In S. Karabenick (Ed.), *Strategic help seeking: Implications for learning and teaching* (pp. 13–37). Mahwah, NJ: Erlbaum.

39. Newman, R., & Schwager, M. (1992). Student perceptions and academic help-seeking. In D. Schunk and M. Meece (Eds.), *Student perceptions in the classroom* (pp. 123–146). Hillsdale, NJ: Erlbaum.

40. Zimmerman & Martinez-Pons (1986); Karabenick, S. (1998). Help seeking as a strategic resource. In S. Karabenick (Ed.), *Strategic help seeking: Implications for learning and teaching* (pp. 1–11). Mahway, NJ: Erlbaum.

41. Ryan & Pintrich (1997).

42. Arbreton, A. (1998). Student goal orientation and help-seeking strategy use. In S. Karabenick (Ed.), *Strategic help seeking: Implications*

for learning and teaching (pp. 95–116). Mahwah, NJ: Erlbaum.

43. Deci, E., Vallerand, R., Pelletier, L., & Ryan, R. (1991). Motivation and education: The self-determination perspective. *Educational Psychologist, 26*, 325–346; McCaslin, M., & Good, T. (1996). The informal curriculum. In D. Berliner and R. Calfee (Eds.), *Handbook of educational psy-chology* (pp. 622–670). New York: Simon & Schuster Macmillan.

44. Newman & Schwager (1992).

45. Zimmerman (1998).

46. Zimmerman & Martinez-Pons (1986).

47. Noguera, P. (2003). *City schools and the American dream: Reclaiming the promise of public education*. New York: Teachers College Press.

THE TESTING MOVEMENT AND URBAN EDUCATION

Rupam Saran

In the United States, democracy has always been challenged by diversity of race, culture, ethnicity, religion, nationality, and language. In the face of this challenge, pedagogical leaders have hoped that education would play a unifying role, and maintain equilibrium in U.S. society. In this age of neoliberalism and neoconservatism, the landscape of urban education in the United States has been shaken by high-standards, mandatory high-stakes testing, and by testing-based reform movements. However, based on the ideology of accountability and rigorous standardized testing, the current reform movement has not delivered desired results. Analysis of present conditions reveals a grim future for the education reform movement calling for the standardization of education. The term "standardization" implies centralized control of teaching and learning in urban schools.

The goal of such reform is the development of "standards" and the promotion of high test scores. The appeal for high standards and better academic achievement undermines realities that must be acknowledged to ensure success of the reform movement. This ambitious approach to improve learning and teaching has failed to improve the quality of education and has reduced it to a screening procedure. A comprehensive investigation of the effects of standardization and mandated testing actually contradicts the *myth* that standardization is the only means to improve education. The standardization of curriculum demoralizes the objective of higher academic standards. Instead of providing wider learning opportunities, it in fact hinders children in achieving goals of high standards. Students' test scores on commercial tests determine their mastery of content, grade placement promotion, and ultimately graduation. The accountability issue in education uses students' test scores as the only measurement of students', teachers', administrators', and parents' performance and success.[1] Thus, test passing has replaced the main goal of education: acquisition of knowledge and skills. The true virtue of education has been lost in the hollowness of an education reform that is aligned with a testing movement in which standardized achievement tests are used as absolute norms for evaluating the quality of urban students.

The failing educational reform act, No Child Left Behind (NCLB), is a major step toward the push for higher accountability, higher standards, control of schools, and promotion of business-oriented education policies through mandatory, high-stakes standardized testing. The NCLB claims that high-stakes testing and tougher accountability are the only ways to improve education and that high-stakes testing is the accurate measure of students' academic achievements. The NCLB act requires that states meet adequate yearly milestones. Schools must ensure that all children meet the proficiency level in all core subjects; schools that fail to meet the adequate yearly progress face sanctions. The recent push for standardized testing and accountability goes back to the education reform movement of the Reagan administration that was fueled after publication of the education reform report *A Nation at Risk*. In 1983, National Commission on Excellence in Education reported that U.S. students were far behind in basic skills as compared to other nations. The report declared that America was at academic risk.

Education in the United States has a long history of standard-setting activities, and the current movement for high standards is grounded in a long tradition of efforts to establish what students should know. The Committee of Ten was the first panel to establish the high school curriculum. In 1892, the College Entrance Examination Board established uniform standards for high school graduation. Passing the designated test was set for high school graduation. Charles W. Eliot was the chairman of the National Education Association's Committee of Ten. Being an educational reformer, he believed in uniformity of curriculum and argued that the main purpose of elementary and high school education was to prepare for college. In 1929, the first standardized Scholastic Aptitude Test (SAT) was given to high school students. The high school curriculum was very much influenced by the SAT. A very important year in the history of mandated testing was 1926—the year that the Elementary and Secondary Act mandated required testing in all elementary and secondary schools.

SOCIAL STRATIFICATION THROUGH SOCIAL CONTROL AND PROMOTION OF INEQUALITY

The United States is a stratified society that takes pride in equal opportunities and open education for all citizens. However, the history of U.S. education reform and ed-

ucation policy change reveals a strong relationship with capitalist ideology. The dynamic of U.S. education is driven by ideologies that support economic inequality, class struggle, and social stratification. In theory, U.S. democratic values respect one's abilities, virtues, and ambitions regardless of racial, economic, religious, and ethnic background. Theoretically, standardized curricula and high academic standards are based on the ideology of better opportunities and improved quality of education for all students regardless of their racial, socioeconomic, cultural, and religious status. However, the purpose of democratic education reform is shattered by the underlying idea of social control.[2] Standardization of curricula and standardized testing has created contradictions within the education system. Schools are supposed to educate students but in reality, schools are implementing corporate and bureaucratic control through standardized curricula and testing. Tougher accountability, standardization of curricula, and arguments in favor of mandated testing are a means of silencing concerned voices of educators and administrators who are providing a challenging and just pedagogy. The idea of "raising standards" and "higher achievement and performance" revolves around the notion that centralized testing has the power to control and regulate the entire educational establishment. Standardized testing dictates what should be taught in schools, how it should be taught, and what the outcome of learning should be. Thus, teachers, students, and administrators are controlled by behind-the-scenes political and business forces. The justification for mandated testing is that it would raise standards and regulate the education system to ensure better performance. The irony is that the ideology of "raised standards" and "better performance" is damaging to the fundamental goal of "schooling": learning. Consequently, it has turned schools into highly competitive places that often operate to damage students' self-assurance. Students are pressured to pass the test rather than working to be prepared to face the realities of life. Given the fact that high-stakes tests have the power to decide the fate of individual students, teachers, administrators, and even an entire school, test taking has become the focus of teaching and learning.[3]

High-stakes test scores determine students' placement within the hierarchy of a school. In urban settings, magnet schools are continuing the tradition of elite schooling. Magnet schools select students on the basis of their entrance test scores and their academic histories. Such schools then prepare students for college-bound standardized tests. Many magnet school students belong to wealthy families who provide expensive test preparation courses to help them pass the entrance test. The students of magnet schools have high achievement rates on standardized tests, and they succeed in getting admitted to prestigious colleges. The magnet schools function as trainers and recruiters for college. They provide special programs and comparatively better academic opportunities for students. One of the major characteristics of U.S. society is diversity. This diversity plays an important role in dividing communities. While urban schooling thrives on the ideal of equality, the system of busing and magnet schools contradicts the notion of equality, as it equates diversity with deficiency.

The corporate and professional world depends on colleges to produce and supply their employees. Professional-oriented colleges select their students very carefully on the basis of the test results, students' academic backgrounds, the quality of college preparatory courses students have taken in high school, and parents' educational backgrounds. SAT scores are the most important factor for college admission. Almost all prestigious colleges require "a good character and adequate scholastic preparation." The underlying meaning of "character" is family background, and "scholastic preparation" refers to elite schooling and high SAT scores. Obviously, poor and minority students do not meet the criteria for admission to prestigious colleges. Schools in poor neighborhoods lack resources, are ill funded, do not have highly qualified teachers, are less likely to have advanced-placement or honors classes, and are unable to offer college preparatory courses. Schools in poor, race-segregated neighborhoods with large poor ethnic populations receive less funding than schools with more advantaged students in the same school district. Research in the area of school performance and achievement shows that teachers' high expectations have significant influence on the academic achievement of students. Poor minority students are stereotyped as low-achievers and slow learners. In poor communities, teachers have low expectations for negatively stereotyped students due to the "deficit ideology." Wenglinsky asserts, "the effects of classroom practices, when added to those of other teacher characteristics, are comparable in size to those of student background, suggesting that teachers can contribute as much to student learning as the students themselves."[4]

All classroom practices and positive outcomes are influenced by high expectations. Unfortunately, in poor communities, high expectations are not part of instruction and consequently poor students have low achievement rates in general. Schools in poor neighborhoods are often located in high-crime neighborhoods and are poorly maintained. Consequently, many teachers decline to work there. Thus poor neighborhood schools have underqualified, overworked staff. These ill-funded schools are unable to offer high-quality educational opportunities or challenging school experiences and lead poor minority students to downward mobility.

The majority of poor urban students fail to achieve high scores on standardized tests, and it is these very test scores that are used as a measure for college entrance. Because test scores determine the kind of college to which one is admitted, standardized tests block upward mobility in U.S. society.

In U.S. society, education subscribes to the idea of a meritocracy, thus lending itself to credentialism. The United States is a credentialized society where the minimum credential is a college degree. Thus, modern U.S. curricula are based on the underlying ideas of meritocracy and credentialism, and as such promote social stratification. A meritocracy is the legacy of humanist control over U.S. curricula. The humanists stressed the uniformity of curricula and college entrance requirements. Although developmentalists stressed the natural development of children and child-centered curricula, the leader of the developmentalist movement, G. Stanley Hall, argued for segregated school based on merit. The child-study idea opposed the humanistic position, yet supported the idea of segregation on the basis of merit. Consequently, schools were designed to serve a specific purpose, and curricula were developed to promote the ideal of a meritocracy. High standards and standardized curricula were sold as an effort to promote equality in education, but the paradox is that they have become tracking and screening instruments for college-bound education.

BUSINESS RHETORIC OF EFFICIENCY AND PERFORMANCE STANDARDS

American society strongly believes that there is equality in education and that it opens the gate to economic rewards, social prestige, and upward mobility. The American myth is that education is an instrument of upward mobility. According to Lloyd Warner and Leo Srole, the "straight-line" assimilation theorists, immigrant children of poverty will assimilate and move up in U.S. society once they attain a college degree.[5] This theory developed in the context of Eastern and Western European immigrants, and does not apply to all second-generation immigrant students.

The irony is that schools discourage upward mobility among many dark-skinned domestic and immigrant minorities by using high standards and high performance as a control mechanism. Renowned U.S. sociologist Edward A. Ross advanced the idea of social control, which was key in the social efficiency curriculum movement. The famous educationist William Taylor grounded the idea of scientific management of curriculum on the idea of social control. And the efficiency advocate William Bobbitt developed efficiency model curricula that shaped schools as an instrument to bring order, regulation, and hierarchy in society. The social efficiency curricula developed by Ross, Taylor, and Bobbitt is still alive.

There is great inequality in the contemporary U.S. school system. Instead of encouraging a high level of success, curricula are designed to foster failure and frustration among students of lower socioeconomic backgrounds. The social efficiency movement stressed the idea of "order and regulation" in society and advocated that curricula should prepare a workforce for an industrial society and educate people to take their designated places in society. Contemporary curricula are geared to establish social control and hierarchy in U.S. society. The tracking system of grouping students based on the assessment of their abilities discourages students from performing to their full potential. In the neoconservative era, vocational schools are not a part of public education, yet the contemporary system promotes social control by providing less rigorous and challenging curricula to non-college-bound students of poor, immigrant neighborhoods through technical schools.

For educators of the early twentieth-century efficiency movement, curricula were the "trainers of producers and consumers," and this idea projected schools as a business model or factory. According to the early twentieth-century professional educator Ellwood P. Cubberley, "The specifications for manufacturing come from the demands of twentieth-century civilization, and it is the business of school to build its pupils according to the specification laid down."[6] The schools of today are following this business model of preparing a workforce for the corporate world. Although workplace demands have increased and there is a need for a more academically qualified workforce, basic education requirements remain the same. Workers need to have a high school diploma, a positive attitude toward work, obedience, and the ability to follow direction. High-standards and high-stakes testing with tougher penalties for failure maintain order in the business world by producing a workforce with basic skills and basic literacy for low-paying jobs. At the elite end of the scale, it creates a small cadre of highly qualified professionals with sophisticated knowledge. Public school curricula are still serving the manpower needs of the state and the corporate world. Accordingly, high-stakes testing focuses on reading and math achievement because businesses demand basic skill knowledge.[7] Due to sophisticated technological inventions, most complicated tasks are accomplished by computers and other technologies. Consequently, low-wage earners do not need sophisticated skills or talent. The testing movement positions schools in business mode. The stress on accountability, efficiency, control, and quality assurance is projecting education as a business "commodity" that produces controlled and quantified products.[8] Indeed, the testing is a quality control system that selects specific "talent and virtue" for the corporate world. The idea of rule by an intelligent elite and the existence of a regulated social order is the shadow of standardized testing.

The efficiency model of schooling of the early twentieth century used the testing movement to maintain centralization of control and regulation in urban education. The primary function of urban schools was to keep immigrant populations and African Americans on the lower rungs of the class ladder and to define their status in mainstream society by offering them second-class education. Immigrant children of lower classes had no access to curricula that would enable them to achieve success. Proponents of the efficiency model even changed the definition of democracy. According to Thorndike, "The argument for democracy is not that it gives power to men without distinction, but that it gives greater freedom for ability and character to maintain power."[9] Eugenics advocates Edward Thorndike, Lewis M. Terman, and H.H. Goddard, supported by the corporate world, convinced school administrators to classify and standardize all curricula and equipped them with a tracking system developed around needs of the corporate world.

Eugenicists argued for the existence of genetic differences in intelligence and advocated for the improvement of genetic quality by sterilization and better breeding. According to eugenics, intelligence is inherited, and there is disparity of intelligence among people of different race and nationality. The eugenics movement in the United States propagated that feeblemindedness, intelligence, and many behavior disorders were genetically determined, and that all genetic defects needed to be controlled. They argued that "superior intelligence" should rule the mass population. According to Terman, only people of inherited intelligence succeeded in U.S. society, and inferior individuals failed to achieve economic and academic success. Eugenicists were responsible for a more restricted immigration policy, and a compulsory sterilization law for genetically inferior people. In 1924, U.S. immigration policies drastically restricted immigration from eastern and southern Europe because at that time, eugenicists believed that people of northern and western Europe were superior to people of all other races.

The literature from this period reflects the elite class's fear of the masses. Social order and elite rule were key issues of concern. Tests were designed with the intent to serve the needs of the elite and to discriminate against lower-class ethnic minorities who were considered inferior by mainstream society. The U.S. education system was highly influenced by Thorndike's ideology of education. Thorndike set the framework for teaching and evaluating. He was instrumental in designing and implementing National Intelligence tests.[10] In fact, Thorndike had a profound influence on testing and the tracking system. According to Thorndike, men with superior intellect should have superiority over less talented ones. He strongly believed that a superior intellect inherited a superior character. The determinant of intellect, to Thorndike, was the IQ test. The ideal behind this corporate-influenced world was a meritocracy for the upper-middle-class white population. The testing movement played a vital role in establishing it in U.S. society while using persistence score gaps among students of different socioeconomic, racial, and ethnic backgrounds to establish the hypothesis that poor minority children were intellectually inferior and fit only for the workforce.

Interestingly, the history of the testing movement dates back to the mass testing of 1.7 million people for classification in the army during World War I. The contemporary testing movement is deeply rooted in the progressive philosophy and the scientific management movement that stressed the standards of excellence, and the belief in order and control. Ross advocated the idea of social control through education.[11] In industrial societies, he mentioned, education was the "method of indirect social restraint." The prominent leaders of the testing movement, Charles Davenport, H.H. Laughlin, and Thorndike, viewed education in general and testing in particular through the lens of the eugenics movement. In this context, data obtained by "scientific" testing were used to discriminate against southern Europeans in 1924. Information

from army tests and reports from the Eugenics Record Office that dealt with feeble-minded people and the insane enabled the supporters of scientific tests to declare that the new immigrants from Southern Europe were inferior. After World War I, immigration patterns changed due to more restricted immigration laws that admitted immigrants according to the labor needs of U.S. manufacturers.

While the traditional harsh competition of the corporate world still persisted, a comparatively stronger liberal corporate structure emerged. The liberal corporate structure demanded a mass system of education that would serve their interests by controlling the economic system. Thus corporate businesses established foundations that influenced education policies. World War I was a groundbreaking time for the testing movement. Many foundations, such as the Carnegie Foundation for the Advancement of Teaching, The Common Wealth Fund, and the Graduate Record Office of the Carnegie Foundation, extended their support by funding the testing movement. In 1903, the John D. Rockefeller Education Board, and in 1906, the Carnegie Foundation for the Advancement of Education, played very important roles in shaping urban education policy in the United States.[12] The emerging liberal infrastructure advocated for a social system that would provide equal opportunity and would value "true" merit by the process of screening urban students. Intelligence tests were used to measure this so-called true merit and categorize the workforce. Terman, a central figure in the testing movement, designed the famous Stanford-Binet Intelligence Test, Group Test of Mental Ability, and Stanford Achievement Test. He believed in intellectual and occupational hierarchy, and his test reflected class prejudice and presumption of meritocracy. According to Terman, an intelligence test could predict whether a student's ability would fit him or her for professional class, semi-professional class, common skilled worker, semi-skilled worker, or unskilled laborer. He argued that curricula should be able to meet the needs of all students' capabilities, and that the tracking system was an instrument to identify one's intellectual ability. Both Terman's and Thorndike's tests reflected prejudice: They were based on the euphemisms, homilies, and morals inscribed in *Poor Richard's Almanac*, Noah Webster's *Blue-Back Speller*, and *McGuffey's Readers*.[13] The children of the Anglo-Saxon community were more familiar with the content presented in tests than the newcomer immigrant children, to whom the test presented alien material. At the time of mass immigration of the early twentieth century, the testing movement acted as a discriminating agent. Unfortunately, it continues to function the same way in the twenty-first century. Although Terman and Thorndike were criticized for their class bias, their doctrine of meritocracy remains intact, and all contemporary tests are based on their notion of intelligence.

During the 1930s, eclecticism and social reconstructionism played a major role in curriculum development but unfortunately, in contemporary society, the meliorist ideology has been reduced to only a slogan. Although Americans do not approve of curricula based on elitism, they know that it is the "ticket to college" and the demand of modern industrial society and the social order of the capitalist world.[14] The testing movement that is based on high standards, and mandatory high-stakes testing, is endorsed by politicians, neoliberal intellectuals, and corporate associates in the name of reform for their own benefit. Although reform education policies align with parental concern for a better education for their children, they do not provide remedies for persisting problems in urban U.S. education. The education reform policies are based on the business ethics of efficiency and performance standards, and in reality, the slogan of tougher accountability and improved test scores is incapable of answering the parental concerns and

frustration of failing schools. Standardized testing is justified by the claim that it will bring equality in education, but in reality the recent education policies based on intense testing challenge the democratic purpose of urban education and encourage inequality and racial class polarization.[15]

Although World War I stimulated national testing in the urban U.S. education system, it was the period of World War II that justified the importance of centralized national testing for efficient, systematic manpower distribution and planning for manufacturers. In 1946 and 1947, the Carnegie Foundation for the Advancement of Teaching requested that the American Council on Education consolidate various testing agencies such as the College Entrance Examination Board and Graduate Record Office so as to establish one Educational Testing Service comprising members from foundations, public and private colleges, businesses, and government. In 1965, the Carnegie Foundation proposed the formation of a national testing program, "A National Assessment of Educational Progress." The national assessment was supposed to follow Cubberley's concern for "continuous measurement of production," and the "accountability" notion of the efficiency movement that viewed schools as educational production machinery. The Educational Testing Service (ETS) was established based on the recommendation and funding from Carnegie Foundation. ETS was a nonprofit private organization that evolved into the leading testing service. By 1969, ETS had designed and provided tests for virtually all academic establishments and organizations. The tests for all colleges, universities, and all professional schools are controlled by ETS. The test scores determine the intellectual ability of students and open or close the door for professional schools. The powerful ETS institution is controlled by private organizations. Naturally, it serves the interest of corporations and foundations that provide its funding. It was the Carnegie Foundation of Washington that supported the testing movement that emerged during and after the World Wars, and appreciated the values incorporated by Thorndike and Terman in standardized testing. All the tests designed by Thorndike, Terman, or the ETS serve the interests of businesses and manufacturers by classifying and labeling students for employment, and compare white students to other ethnic and racial groups. The persistence group differences in standardized test scores are used as predictors of the academic achievement of different minority groups. At the same time, the disparity in elementary and high school test scores of many ethnic and racial groups pressures policy makers for greater education reform that would be performance-based and produce better academic gains to benefit not only elite but also average and at-risk students.

LACK OF SENSITIVITY FOR STUDENTS OF LOWER SOCIOECONOMIC STATUS

According to a 1999 Population Survey conducted by the U.S. Census Bureau, 18.9 percent of children under the age of 18 live in poverty. This is a higher percentage than that of the population aged 18–64 or over. In the United States, over 40 percent of children live in inner-city poor neighborhoods. In an affluent and industrialized country like the United States, child poverty is thus an area of major concern. A study conducted by the National Assessment of Educational Progress (NAEP) of students in the fourth, eighth, and twelfth grades reveals a strong and unrelenting relationship between achievement and performance gap "among subgroups defined by socioeconomic status and race/ethnicity" (NCTM 1991).[16] Socioeconomic status is one of the strongest determinants of students' academic achievement. The report presented by the National Council of Teachers of Mathematics concerning students' achievement and their socioeconomic status re-

ported that the mean achievement of poor students was significantly lower than the mean achievement of students of higher economic status. In 2001, American Youth Policy Forum reported that the most influential factor in determining educational achievement is family income. The graduation rate of families with 25 percent of the lowest income is 67 percent, compared to 94 percent of the students of families in the top 25 percent. Thus, children of poor families are doomed for academic failure. According to education scholar Michael Apple, low achievement and other curricular problems are related to poverty and the unjust organization of economic, cultural, and social life.[17] The current education reform policy is not sensitive to the issues of poverty and poverty-related problems that affect students' achievements. Advocates of the mandated standardized tests and high performance standards seem to ignore the fact that poor students come to school without much prior academic knowledge, serious academic deficits, and the need for extra attention. According to the national data, school readiness is strongly affected by socioeconomic status. Children who enter school without the first level of academic proficiency often belong to families living in poverty, with both parents or the mother not having earned a high school diploma or being dependent on welfare programs.

Although high standards provide a framework for curriculum and achievement, they are associated negatively with standardized tests. The idea of reward and sanction for high- or low-scoring schools has consequences. The fear of failure and condemnation is discouraging qualified teachers to work in low-performing schools. In many states, such as New York and Florida, qualified teachers are either taking early retirement or transferring to better school districts. Since the low-performing and low-income school districts are having a difficult time retaining good teachers, they are forced to replace them with less experienced and less qualified ones. Urban students' achievement is based on critical factors involving social class, race, and gender. In 1966, sociologist James Coleman and his colleagues published a report based on research conducted on over half a million students at 4,000 schools nationwide. Findings of the study demonstrated that "the most important criterion for school achievement was socioeconomic status, especially related to a child's home environment." More recent research supports Coleman's findings.[18] Parents' socioeconomic status is determined by their human capital; that is, by their educational attainment, work experiences, and job opportunities. Parents with higher levels of human capital have comparatively higher earnings, possess better know-how of the U.S. education system, have higher expectations for their children, and are better equipped to provide challenging educational opportunities for their children—such as providing a home in a better neighborhood with good schools, and many other material and symbolic resources. Consequently, children from upper- and middle-class families score higher in standardized tests than do poor children. A poor home environment and poor urban schools both contribute to a child's academic failure.[19] Students from low-income, less educated families tend to lag behind their more affluent peers because their environment plays a significant role in shaping their attitudes about school, education, and employment. Children living in inner-city neighborhoods live under the constant cloud of crime, drugs, poor health, and possibly a broken family. It is hard for them to live up to mainstream expectations. Standards-based high-stakes tests align with school or social contexts for poor students, and guarantee high rates of failure. In poor neighborhoods, schools have "hidden curricula," which are the behaviors expected of students. The hidden curricula demand obedience and conformity to bureaucratic authority. The context

of inner-city urban schools transmits the dominant culture and hidden curricula to students.

The urban schools of comparatively wealthier neighborhoods often have sophisticated tracking and segregation systems. Although students of various races might attend the same school, they are grouped on the basis of their alleged ability. Very often, poor Hispanic and black children do not make it to special or talented classes and remain in lower-track classes where they are labeled as low achievers. Labeling in the classroom plays a negative role in a student's life. Negative labeling attaches a stigma and forces children to define themselves as failures, relegated to a nonacademic track. The education system that emerged in the "quest of one, best system" did not stay the "one, best system."[20] The system that was grounded on the basis of equality and fairness to all failed to provide "equal opportunity to all." According to David B. Tyack, in the name of equal opportunity and in spite of good intentions, schools have failed to teach poor children effectively.[21] Urban education was supposed to nurture talent and merit and to prepare students for their future role in society. It is a common belief in the United States that one's success depends on academic success in school. Paradoxically, schools are considered the most important instrument of social placement.

HIGH-STAKES TESTING AND ACCOUNTABILITY IDEOLOGY

The ideas of "accountability," high-stakes testing, and high standards in education argue for higher academic performance for all students and remediation programs such as summer school for failing students at all grade levels. The accountability ideology presumes that holding teachers, students, parents, and schools accountable for higher academic achievement (or failure) will improve educational practices. Thus, the accountability ideology blames individuals for their failure or achievement. High standards and high-stakes testing argue that tests score are accurate determinants of students' knowledge, learning, and teaching practices. The reform policies stress that grade retention and mandatory remedial programs will bridge the achievement gap and improve education for all students. However, a closer look at accountability reveals that it perpetuates test-driven teaching practices and test-focused learning. School administrators, teachers, and students are threatened by the consequences of high-stakes testing. Consequently, teachers concentrate on test preparation and teach students the content to be covered in tests, and pay extra attention to those students who show the potential to do better in tests. Administrators demand that teachers prepare students to pass tests. Thus the testing movement has created a testing culture and test-oriented teaching practices that focus on test-passing skills, not on classroom transmission of knowledge. The scores of standardized tests demonstrate that the accountability and test-driven instructional practices neither improve the quality of education nor help low-scoring students.

According to 2002 New York Regent Data, only 11 to 22 percent of students in high-need districts passed the Regent with scores in the 55–65 range. These scores confirm the belief that high standards and high-stakes testing are not geared to improving the academic performance of low-performing students. Schools in poor neighborhoods with large African-American and Latino/-a populations experience more test preparation anxiety and pressure than high-performing schools in wealthier communities. Therefore, the lowest-performing schools spend extensive amounts of time on test-taking skills and techniques at the cost of rich, interactive instruction. On the other hand, better-performing schools experience less pressure and can afford to provide interactive critical think-ing-oriented instruction. Thus with narrow measures of achievement, high-stakes testing is pushing schools to follow a narrow curriculum and to practice instructional strategies that are based on lower level cognitive skills. Low or high test scores are not always representative of students' learning. According to Linda Darling Hammond, "teaching to the test may be raising scores on the state high-stakes test in ways that do not generalize to other test that examine a broader set of higher order skills; many students are excluded from the state tests to prop up average scores; and the tests have been made easier."[22] Thus, standard-based, high-stakes testing does not provide adequate learning opportunities, and its ideology needs to be corrected.

THE TESTING MOVEMENT AND HIGH STANDARDS PERPETUATE RACE AND CLASS HIERARCHY

The contemporary high-standards and high-stakes testing-based education reform movement in the United States claims that all students can learn and are entitled to the best education. The goal of the reform plan is that all students should achieve high scores on tests and must pass tests to graduate from high school. According to Robert P. Moses, the assumption that all students are capable of learning and the commitment to provide them the best education and opportunities is an ideal that unfortunately implies no concrete action but rather only lip service.[23] The elements of the testing movement are racism, elitism, and nativism. The founding members of the tracking system created this system to strengthen racism covertly. The political goal of educating all by stressing high standards and mandating high-stakes testing is not geared to filling the gap between universal free public education and the universal completion of college prep courses. Rather, it is a political act to maintain white supremacy in the U.S. education system. Although education reform policies stress one standard curriculum for all urban students, in reality there is no standard curriculum. The early curriculum planners Terman, Babbit, and Thorndike planned discriminatory and racially segregated, four-track hierarchical curricula. They rationalized this as a "democratic curriculum" to fulfill the needs of all individuals. This four-tired curriculum consisted of an honors track for the gifted and talented students, a general track and college preparation track for average students, and a special education track for the slow and inferior masses. This tracking system is still guiding educational policies and the empirical data from tests are supporting this system. In U.S. society, the highly paid, challenging professions are dominated by whites. Medicine, engineering, law, and the technical fields are professions of the intelligent white population. All professional schools require high test scores for admission. The prevalent myth is that African Americans, Latinos/-as, and Mexicans are unintelligent slow learners who are fit for the basic skill curriculum. Thus they receive lower-track education. Schooling testing has different meanings for whites and for children of color because their place is predetermined in a white-dominated education system. White educators and the white power structure make policies that force students of color to adapt to white middle-class academic norms. High-stakes testing and high standards are an inherently racialized discourse of deficit ideology. The deficit ideology advocates that people of color have learning deficits; therefore, their academic performance is lower than the performance of white students. In the context of the race and class hierarchy, the testing movement emphasizes centralized control of poor immigrant and African-American students who need to be controlled. John Ogbu argues that the underachievement of the immigrant population and people of color is rooted in historical racism and institutional oppression.[24]

Unfortunately, the testing and high accountability-based reform plan exerts a negative effect on students' academic achievement, their placement, and their opportunity to learn. The inclusion of Latino/-a and African-American students is significantly low in prestigious urban magnet schools because of their low test scores.[25]

In New York, Georgia, Florida, Texas, and Massachusetts, the negative effect of high-stakes testing is visible and the dropout rate is increasing. In these states, low scores are not used to evaluate students' weaknesses and provide valuable opportunities to improve those areas. Rather they are used as a device to label students as failures, holding them back and encouraging them to drop out of school. In this process, poor and working-class African-American and other nonwhite marginalized students suffer the most.[26] Students labeled as failures or who have lower academic ability view themselves as "less worthy" and develop low self-esteem. Consequently, they stop trying to achieve. Academic labeling and the stigma attached to it initiate the self-fulfilling prophecy that leads to negative outcomes such as dropping out of school. Thus, negative labeling fosters low academic achievement rates among African-American, Latino/-a, and Hispanic students, and acts as gatekeeper to higher education. According to Paulo Freire, schools maintain a "pedagogy of oppression."[27] Apple claims that high-stakes testing does not have the capacity to solve deep-rooted educational and social problems through rationing education.[28]

Contemporary high-stakes testing encourages a tracking system that favors the dominant elite and demoralizes the oppressed. The curriculum that is guided by high-stakes testing separates college-bound and non-college-bound students. College-bound students benefit from a more challenging, more rigorous curriculum and better opportunities to excel in courses such as college-level math and science. Urban mathematics education is used as gatekeeper by education reform policy. The traditional role of mathematics has not been changed by the reform. Rather, it has been strengthened by the idea of high-standards, high- stakes testing. Mathematics education was used to find intelligent minds to attend college for training as the professional elite class. Mathematics education was used as gatekeeper for college education. Unfortunately, it is still serving the same function. Advanced mathematics courses such as algebra, calculus, and trigonometry are used as college preparation courses. An enriched mathematics core curriculum is the most important element of college preparation courses. Advanced mathematics courses are used as a weeding-out instrument for college. The traditional role of mathematics has been maintained by education reform. Schools in poor communities do not offer the challenging core mathematics curriculum that is essential to prepare students for standardized tests. According to the recent reform policy, all students are required to pass the Regent exam in order to graduate from high school. The irony is that students in poor school districts are not being prepared for the challenging mathematics Regent exam. A student who is not taught to high standards throughout elementary, middle, and high school is expected to pass this test, but is headed for failure. In contrast, schools in wealthy neighborhoods offer challenging, advanced mathematics curricula and prepare their students for standardized tests. Affluent parents have the resources to pay for coaching services such as the Princeton Review, Kaplan Test Prep, and so on. Unfortunately, poor parents lack resources to provide their children additional academic help, and many parents are not even aware of such courses.

Poor neighborhoods lack qualified mathematics teachers and have difficulty recruiting and retaining them.[29] Teachers in poor communities teach in dangerous neighborhoods and face more challenges than teachers in affluent communities. They teach in neighborhoods with high crime rates and a highly mobile student population with limited English language proficiency. Constant teacher turnover is a major problem in poor communities. The reform movement in the area of mathematics education demands high standards and high achievement regardless of the students' socioeconomic, ethnic, racial, and educational background. The achievement gap in mathematics education is wider than the gap in reading, and this gap is persistent. Although reform policies stress equal opportunities for all, they do not address the need for all. Standards-based, high-stakes testing has become an instrument that widens the achievement gap between students of lower socioeconomic background and students of the affluent class. Education reform is institutionalizing the achievement gap. Social conditions, traditions, and goals influence students' learning and achievement. Students of poverty lack social conditions that motivate learning and higher achievement. Academic failure, high mobility, and lack of motivation are highly correlated with poverty. High-stakes testing does not take into account students' socioeconomic status. According to Lipman, "Tying teaching and learning even more tightly to standardized testing has particularly negative consequences for low-income students and students of color."[30]

Although there are remediation programs for low achievers, in reality, these students are discouraged and given curricula that do not facilitate higher-order critical thinking. Thus, these urban schools have internal segregation that discourages the learning of less advantaged students. Additionally, internal segregation encourages the discriminatory notion that less advantaged students should be denied equal opportunities and stay within their academic and social limitations. Consequently, due to negative labeling, pessimistic attitudes toward academic achievement, and low self-perception, students of color tend to withdraw from school.

WIDENING THE GAP BETWEEN SOCIAL CLASSES AND RACES

The testing movement that promotes the narrow notion of knowledge production and learning through "continuous measurement" and "accountability" holds teachers, students, and parents accountable for academic achievement or failure. Instead of installing confidence and a sense of accomplishment, the test-driven environment of school and the pressure of high-stakes testing promote the idea of mediocrity. Ostensibly, continuous measurement is intended to identify students' needs and schools are intended to provide opportunities for improvement in areas of academic need. However, the process increases chances of grade retention, dropping out, and test-driven teaching. Thus test-driven teaching and high-stakes testing widen the gap between white, educated, middle-class students and poor immigrants and students of color. Underprivileged and marginalized students who have limited access to the "production and processing" of knowledge are weeded out by the process of continuous testing.[31] Unfortunately, most of the weeded-out students never gain economic success, and wind up in the low-paying workforce. For the testing movement, "Whiteness has become the normative structure."[32]

It is evident that high-stakes testing is working to fulfill the demands of the market-driven postindustrial economy that relies on a highly stratified labor force to maintain the class system of capitalistic society. The postindustrial conditions in the United States favor an education system that can supply high-skilled professionals and low-skilled technical workers. The high-stakes test-oriented education system submits itself to business requirements. Simultaneously, it widens the gap between the lower and upper classes by maintaining the social and academic isolation of nonwhite immigrants, Latinos/-as, and African Americans.

HIGH-STAKES TESTING AND LANGUAGE ISSUES

Recently, the SAT added essay writing as a compulsory component of the test. Consequently, essay writing will most likely become crucial for immigrant students with limited English language proficiency. New immigrants such as Latinos, Hispanics, Mexicans, Salvadorians, and Guatemalans struggle in school and in the job market due to their very limited English language proficiencies.[33] Many of these new immigrant students are either enrolled below grade level or drop out of school. The essay-writing component of the SAT will increase the dropout rate and decrease the graduation rate among these students. The test evaluation process does not have a separate assessment procedure for students who are learning English as a second language (ESL) or are bilingual. A large number of new immigrants enter U.S. urban schools at the junior high or high school level. Before they adjust to the new environment or learn English well, they are required to take the test and begin the journey to the low-paying job market. Very often, even before they take tests, they are placed in low-track curricula, and are trained for low-status roles in U.S. society.[34] New immigrant ESL students are deprived of parental guidance concerning school because their parents often do not understand underlying assumptions of the U.S. education system and are unable to obtain accurate information concerning their children's schooling. In this context, students depend on schools for guidance and support. Unfortunately, schools do not provide adequate support systems for ESL students. In the majority of cases, guidance counselors fail to give sound advice to these students and stigmatize them as slow and unmotivated learners.

CONCLUSION

Standardized tests are constructed without taking into account the diversity of literacy, socioeconomic status, or cultural and racial constructs of student populations. Consequently, the tests are biased and the test scores lack validity and accountability. The testing movement has stressed measuring individual students, entire schools, teachers, and principals on a single high-stakes test that is unfair to all individuals involved. The most important aspect of the testing movement is its undermining of the democratic goal of pedagogy. Despite the slogan of equality, the testing movement supports the existing system of quality control and helps only those who survive the "gauntlet of tests" and possess specific literacies and dispositions that business demands.[35] There is a need for additional measures of achievement that take the cultural and socioeconomic factors of student populations into consideration. The testing movement should concentrate on positive gains rather than use subtractive strategies to discriminate against underachievers. The standardized test score should not be considered the single determinant of one's intellectual abilities.

NOTES

1. McNeil, L. (2000). *Contradictions of school reform: Educational costs of standardized testing.* New York: Routledge.

2. Hauser, R. (1999). On ending "social promotion" in Chicago. In D. Moore (Ed.), *Comment on ending social promotion: The first two years* (Attachment B). Chicago: Design on Change.

3. Apple, M. (1999). *Power, meaning, and identity: Essays in critical educational studies.* New York: Peter Lang.

4. Wenglinsky, H. (2002). How schools matter: The link between teacher classroom practices and student academic performance. *Education Policy Analysis Archives, 10* (12), 1–31.

5. Warner, L., & Srole, L (1945). *The social system of American ethnic groups.* New Haven, CT: Yale University Press.

6. Kliebard, M. (1995). *The struggle for the American curriculum: 1893–1958.* New York: Routledge.

7. Lipman, P. (2003). Bush's education plan, globalization, and the politics of race. ERIC Document.

8. Lipman, P. (2002). Making the global city, making inequality: The political economy and cultural politics of Chicago school policy. *American Education Research Journal, 39* (2), 379–419.

9. Karier, J. (1972). Testing for order and control in the corporate liberal state. *Journal of Educational Theory, 22,* 154–177.

10. Karier (1972).

11. Ross, E. (1901). *Social control: A survey of the foundation of order.* New York: Macmillan.

12. Karier (1972).

13. Karier (1972).

14. Karier (1972).

15. Saltman, K. (2000). *Collateral damage: Corporatizing public schools—A threat to democracy.* Lanham, MD: Rowman and Littlefield.

16. National Council of Teachers of Mathematics (NCTM). (1991). *Professional standards for teaching mathematics.* Reston, VA: NCTM.

17. Apple, M. (2001). *Educating the "right" way: Markets, standards, God, inequality.* New York: Routledge.

18. Milligan, C. (1993). Education, society, and the school dropout. *Handbook of Schooling in Urban America* (pp. 317–331). Westport, CT: Greenwood.

19. Ray, C., & Mickelson, R. (1993). Restructuring students for restructured work: Economy, school reform, and non-college-bound youths. *Sociology of Education, 66,* 1–20.

20. Tyack, D. (1974). *The one best system: A history of American urban education.* Cambridge, MA: Harvard University Press.

21. Tyack (1974).

22. Hammond, D. *Standards and assessments: Where we are and what we need.* Stanford University. Retrieved from http://www.tcrecord.

23. Moses, R., & Cobb, C. (2001). *Radical equations: Civil rights from Mississippi to the Algebra Project.* Boston: Beacon Press.

24. Ogbu, J. (1993). Frameworks—Variability in minority school performance: A problem in search of an explanation. In E. Jacob & C. Jordan (Eds.), *Minority education anthropological perspective.* Norwood, NJ: Ablex.

25. Ray & Mickelson (1993).

26. Apple, M. (1990). *Ideology and curriculum.* 2nd ed. New York: Routledge.

27. Freire, P. (1970). *Pedagogy of the oppressed.* Translated by Myra Bergman Ramos. New York: Seabury.

28. Apple (1990).

29. Entwistle, D., & Alexandra, K. (1992). Summer setback: The racial composition of schools and learning; mathematics achievement in the first two years of school. *American Sociological Review, 57,* 72–84.

30. Lipman (2003).

31. Lipman (2003).

32. Apple (1990).

33. Kincheloe, J., & Steinberg, S. (1997). *Changing multiculturalism.* Buckingham: Open University Press.

34. Kincheloe & Steinberg (1997).

35. Lipman (2003).

FORMING A CIRCLE: CREATING A LEARNING COMMUNITY FOR URBAN COMMUTING ADULT STUDENTS IN AN INTERDISCIPLINARY STUDIES PROGRAM

Roslyn Abt Schindler

We do not exist as individuals in isolation. Humankind's survival is dependent on our ability to form community with others.

—*Randee Lipson Lawrence*

PRELUDE AND CONTEXT

Within the vast scope of literature on learning communities, studies abound that focus on the mutually beneficial relationship between learning communities and interdisciplinary studies. A growing number of texts on learning communities focus on the characteristics and needs of adult students; the urban environment; students of diverse racial, ethnic, and cultural backgrounds; and commuting students.[1] Notably missing within the literature is a focus on the latter five as interactive factors within the context of learning communities. The Department of Interdisciplinary Studies (IS) in the College of Urban, Labor, and Metropolitan Affairs (CULMA) at Wayne State University (WSU) in Detroit, Michigan, offers successful bachelor's and master's degree programs for adult students and a learning community characterized by all five factors. Hence, the program provides an excellent case study and contribution to the literature. Specifically, this program's Interdisciplinary Studies Seminar (ISS) is highlighted as a unique example of a gateway course for first-year students within the context of the philosophy and practices of learning communities.

LEARNING COMMUNITIES: THE TIES THAT BIND

Learning communities have a long, rich, and proud history and provide many benefits to students and faculty. One generally accepted definition comes from The Evergreen State College:

In higher education, learning communities are classes that are linked or clustered during an academic term, often around an interdisciplinary theme, and enroll a common cohort of students. A variety of approaches [or models or structures] are used to build these learning communities, with all intended to restructure the students' time, credit, and learning experiences to build community among students, between students and their teachers, and among faculty members and disciplines.[2]

According to the experts at The Evergreen State College and our own experience in IS, benefits abound for both students and faculty. Benefits to students include increased intellectual engagement, motivation, and development; increased student involvement in both academic and non-academic settings (especially true for commuter and urban campuses); stronger ties and increased collaboration between and among students and with their teachers; improved student academic achievement and maturity; increased student satisfaction and, hence, retention; shortened time to degree; and improved course and degree completion rates.[3] Faculty benefit from learning communities in the following ways, maintains Karen Kellogg:

They become re-energized and feel empowered. They feel as if their opinions are valued; and the rich teaching experience allows them to be creative and increases their commitment to the institution. Institutions report that learning communities draw diverse elements together toward a common goal, which improves the overall campus climate. Learning communities have proven to be a practical solution to long-standing, complex educational issues.[4]

Within the context of complexity, Valerie Bystrom offers one of numerous excellent affirmations of the inextricable connection between learning communities and interdisciplinary studies. Bystrom writes:

Learning communities . . . assume that the human construction of knowledge may be vast and complex, a finally independent cathedral with zillions of parts, with vaults, buttresses, and dazzling windows, amazing in its aspects but connected, linked, and, if not available to anyone in its totality, still not itself offerable in several hundred, or million, tidy boxes for easy storage. Interdisciplinary studies courses let the knowledge out of the boxes, so that students set to building connections, buttresses, windows.[5]

The themes of complexity and making connections are ever present in literature about liberal education and interdisciplinary studies as well as learning communities. Two prominent scholars, Carol Geary Schneider and Barbara Leigh Smith, are exemplars for current as well as future visions of these linked topics.[6] They stress the connections that can and should be made within the curriculum and outside the curriculum to promote not only interdisciplinary learning, but also integrative learning (includes service learning, living-learning communities, study travel programs, and other forms of experiential learning). Another strong voice in this conversation is William Cronon. He asks: "How does one recognize liberally educated people?"[7] His answer:

They follow E.M. Forster's injunction from *Howard's End*: "Only Connect." More than anything else, being an educated person means being able to see connections that allow one to make sense of the world and act within it in creative ways. Every one of the qualities I have described here—listening, reading, talking, writing, puzzle solving, truth seeking, seeing through other people's eyes, leading, working in a community—is finally about connecting. A liberal education is about gaining the power and the wisdom, the generosity and the freedom to connect.[8]

Rounding the final base of making connections is the discovery that adult learners and interdisciplinary studies form "a marriage made in heaven."[9] We have learned this experientially at Wayne State, and our longtime experience is confirmed by the scholarly literature of the last 25 years.[10] Both adult learning and interdisciplinary studies emphasize and value "confidence-building; attention to context; practical, problem-solving, even job-related skills; [an] individualized approach to learning; collaborative learning opportunities."[11] And we add liberal education and learning communities, which adult students clearly prize as well.

THE DEPARTMENT OF INTERDISCIPLINARY STUDIES AND ITS PREDECESSORS

Historical Connections

The Department of Interdisciplinary Studies (IS) began in 1973 as the innovative experimental University Studies/ Weekend College Program (US/WCP), founded by the late Dr. Otto Feinstein. The US/WCP, like some of its noteworthy peer experimental programs of the 1960s and 1970s (The Hutchins School of Liberal Studies, Sonoma State University; The University of Wisconsin-Green Bay; The Evergreen State College; and the School of Interdisciplinary Studies—Western College Program—at Miami University of Ohio), had a fierce commitment to breaking new ground and reforming post-secondary education in a visionary manner, even if their curricular programs and teaching strategies differed in kind. The US/WCP was committed to being a change agent, to developing a more holistic, civic-engagement, real-world-application learning model that focused on knowledge, skills, values, responsibility, freedom, and growth. These are core values of liberal education, which are highlighted in the 1998 report by the Boyer Commission on Educating Undergraduates in the Research University as well as in the writings of William Cronon and Carol Geary Schneider.[12]

The US/WCP bachelor's degree program organized its curriculum around theme-driven clustered courses with common readings taken by cohort groups of students around the burning quintessential and universal topics, problems, and issues of human experience and events, often emphasizing urban themes. Both the innovative curricular structure and interdisciplinary content for post-secondary students were part of high-impact educational reform. However, the US/WCP had as its target population adult learners (age 22 and older) as opposed to traditional college-age students (18–22 years old), and,

therefore, set up its delivery modes for busy, involved commuting adult learners. There were telecourses, weekend conferences, directed-study courses, and once-a-week workshops. Field trips (e.g., to a local theater or music performance related to course content) or other student activities (e.g., special lectures or exhibits on campus and elsewhere in the city) were included as well, benefiting from and often focusing on the urban setting. This structure enabled students to earn up to 12 or even 16 credit hours during one semester with minimum contact or seat time. For example, a typical Fall 1976 first-semester student curriculum consisted of a workshop for four credit hours (Introduction to Ethnic Studies), a television course for four credit hours (Culture, Community, and Identity: An Ethnic Perspective), and a three-weekend conference course for four credit hours (Community and Culture in Urban Life).

The US/WCP was well ahead of its time in its use of technology and other resourceful teaching methods to deliver its curriculum to adult learners. The program was a direct descendant of Wayne State's Monteith College and thus, in part, has Monteith to thank for its innovative philosophy and practice. Monteith, however, served the college-age student population with its resourceful, learning community-focused methods to offer its interdisciplinary studies curriculum. While this study is not about Monteith College, discontinued in 1974, it is important to pause to recognize its extraordinary legacy in its large number of proud graduates and in the IS department today.

Interdisciplinary Studies follows US/ WCP's (and, by historical extension, Monteith's) philosophy, mission, and practices in its course structure, interdisciplinary content, and course delivery—even if now modified, expanded, or extended in more contemporary and visionary ways. For example, a current first-semester student curriculum currently consists of the Interdisciplinary Studies Seminar (ISS) for four credit hours and an interdisciplinary written and/or oral communication skills course for four credit hours. In a subsequent semester, students may cluster two science and technology courses, Health Concepts and Strategies for three credit hours and Changing Life on Earth for four credit hours alongside an interdisciplinary computers and society course for four credit hours. Or students may cluster Significant Issues in Cultural Studies for four credit hours and Music and American Culture for three credit hours alongside a critical thinking course for four credit hours. Throughout their degree program, students must complete a set of general education requirements, a junior-level interdisciplinary core seminar as well as a senior writing requirement. Among the choices that our students have to complete their undergraduate degree program are other courses as diverse as One Globe—Many Worlds; The Africans; Bearing Witness: Understanding the Holocaust One Life at a Time; and White Collar Crime. The original US/WCP concepts and practices have also been modernized with current advanced technology, such as online teaching, interactive television, and use of the Internet. The IS curriculum is ever evolving to challenge and excite our students and provide them with the kind of interdisciplinary education that will enable them to deal now and in the future with an ever more complex world.

It is significant that Monteith College—founded in 1959, right at the start of the experimental college fervor—was modeled after Alexander Meiklejohn's Experimental College at the University of Wisconsin in 1927. Meiklejohn is credited as the founder of the concept and practice of learning communities, which has taken on, in its seven-decade history, many structural and substantive forms at over 500 American colleges and universities—at public and private, rural and urban, two-year, community, and four-year institutions of higher learning; for first-year and subsequent-year students; for typical college-age and older students; and so on.[13] In 1996, the Washington Center for Improving the Quality of Undergraduate Education began serving as the national resource for curricular learning community work.

INTERDISCIPLINARY STUDIES STUDENT PROFILE

The Department of Interdisciplinary Studies (IS), one of the oldest and foremost comprehensive interdisciplinary studies programs in the country (W. Newell, personal communication, April 9, 2004), offers the Bachelor of Interdisciplinary Studies (BIS), the Bachelor of Technical and Interdisciplinary Studies (BTIS; for students with technical, professional, or vocational associate's degrees), the Master of Interdisciplinary Studies (MIS), and an undergraduate minor as well as a post-baccalaureate certificate in nonprofit sector studies. The department has a racially, ethnically, and culturally diverse adult commuter-student population whose average age is 38; our students are often the first in their family to go to college. Carol Schneider, president of the Association of American College and Universities, provides us with useful contextual statistics: "Forty-three percent of all college students are age 24 or older"; adult students are "the new majority" on college campuses.[14] Among IS's approximately 750 undergraduate students are women (63%) and men (37%), majority (30%) and minority (70%), blue collar and white collar workers, managers and other professionals, unemployed and underemployed, prepared and underprepared, mothers, fathers, grandparents, sons, daughters, married, divorced, and single.

Our students reflect a panorama of ethnic, racial, and cultural backgrounds and voices, the full gamut of the adult population at-large. They live in Detroit or in the tri-county area and commute to the main campus of Wayne State or to any of its extension sites in and around the metropolitan area. They work day shifts, night shifts, or some of each. They have family and community responsibilities. They take classes mostly in the evenings, sometimes in the mornings, and occasionally on the weekends. The length of classes and meeting times are tailored to their needs; IS classes typically meet once a week for three or four hours, depending upon the credit hours earned. They enroll during the fall and winter semesters as well as during the summer semester to expedite their progress. What is unique about our students is their decision to enter or return to college, the motivation to improve their lives with an education, no matter what the risks, no matter what the obstacles, no matter what the anxieties—and there are many. Our students are motivated both internally and externally "to enroll in college, and their motivations may change as they persist in college . . . [A]dult participation is shaped differently from that of traditional-aged students, primarily because of adult commitments to work, community, and family life that complete and complement the learning process."[15] In keeping with these motivations, our students find that fulfilling a dream to make other dreams possible is what it's all about. Breaking out of heretofore restricted life boundaries energizes, excites, and engages them.

Well more than half of our graduates, once lacking self-confidence about their ability to succeed academically, seek a graduate or professional degree or training within a few years of graduation, if not immediately after graduation. Most of our graduates are well into their 40s or 50s at that stage; some are even in their 60s and a few, in their 70s. They have been inspired— "bitten by the bug." There is no holding them back. Those who choose not to continue with graduate or professional degrees or training use their undergraduate degree to become upwardly mobile in their careers or choose new careers. And still others who may be retired from their careers feel the extraordinary satisfaction of having com-

pleted an undergraduate degree, the dream of their lives—true actually for all of our graduates whose degrees signify singular achievements of which they and the faculty and staff of IS are very proud.

Many of our students have never been to college or have been out of college for ten years or more. They enter or return with high anxiety regarding oral and written communication skills, knowledge of mathematics, critical thinking skills, academic reading, academic savvy, study skills, and more. As adult commuter students with family commitments, jobs or careers, and community responsibilities, they need a special kind of learning community right from the start to enable them to succeed in order to avoid the "revolving door" in which adult students often get caught. These students require special nurturing, confidence building, and challenges to enable them to succeed in their academic endeavors. Most especially, it is challenging for faculty and staff as well as commuting adult students to develop a learning community in which they can thrive. Student and alumni testimony eloquently documents how successful IS has been in this regard. In response to a January, 2004, questionnaire I asked former students to complete (from which I have their kind permission to quote and reveal names), Brenda Doll, 2003 graduate, writes:

My years in the program were nothing short of miraculous. I developed bonds from the beginning with fellow students, and this relationship continued pretty much throughout my time at Wayne State. It was so comforting to count on seeing familiar faces on a weekly basis in my classes . . . The feeling of camaraderie was very strong.

Judy Dolsen, Class of 2002, agrees:

The program presented a viable solution for me to complete my undergraduate degree. I no longer had to swim upstream. The welcoming spirit I received from advisors and faculty prompted me to attend the first session and complete the program. Although I graduated almost two years ago, I still feel connected to faculty and advisors who guided me through the program.

Luann Brennan, class of 2001, proclaims,

[T]he experience was one of the best in my life. I did form bonds early with some of my fellow students that continue to this day, two years after graduation. I also developed bonds with some of the faculty as well that have turned into friendships. The faculty are so supportive and willing to do whatever it takes for their students to succeed.

A final comment in this section comes from a forthcoming graduate, Lynn Farthing:

[In the program,] so much of what had already been "my life" converged, and I was able to become more aware, more conscious of my own thoughts in relation to my life; thus I began the essential task of beginning to understand my own life in relation to the world, and in that I am finding the idea that to make the choice to "connect" is freedom.

We hear echoes of Carol Geary Schneider, Jerry Gaff, and William Cronon, among other voices. But most importantly, these quotations are our own expressive student voices. And the liberating and exhilarating experiences they describe started with their participation in the Interdisciplinary Studies Seminar.

INTERDISCIPLINARY STUDIES: GATEWAY TO ADULT STUDENT LEARNING

Underlying Philosophy and Inspiration

The Interdisciplinary Studies Seminar (ISS) is IS's gateway course that our adult students take during their first semester, along with other courses mentioned previously. This configuration creates a cluster of complementary courses, marking the beginning of the students' participation in a successful learning community. The ISS course incorporates the theoretical concepts and pedagogical practices of interdisciplinary studies, learning communities, and liberal education for our diverse adult students. The ISS introduces or reintroduces our students to academic reading and analytical writing, academic savvy, study and time management skills, critical thinking skills, and interdisciplinary studies. This course creates a special comfort zone for students in which they bond with each other and with their instructor and begin to develop an active learning environment and trust regarding their journey. The bonding process that occurs in the ISS course is essential to students' success throughout the program and beyond. Will MacFarland, Class of 2004, considers his experience with our program to be "very positive . . . particularly the introductory course. It made the transition back into school much easier. It essentially set me up for academic success." Brenda Doll shares her own history:

I was returning to school after a five-year hiatus [most of our students return after 10, 15, or even 20 years]. On the one hand, I was thrilled to have the opportunity to finish my bachelor's degree (a long-held dream of mine). On the other hand, I was nervous because I feared failure. I was feeling rusty regarding all facets of my academic skills. The [ISS course] provided the safe environment of a cozy group on a weekly basis where I could gradually ease back into an academic routine.

Luann Brennan reveals very similar experiences:

My experience with the core seminar was wonderful. I had been out of school for a number of years, and I had some anxiety about what school would be like and whether I would be able to handle the pressures of work, school, and family. The class was tough. There was a lot of reading, writing, and just general preparation work in order to be able to take part in the weekly discussions. I loved it. The nurturing and support I got from the professor enabled me to fit school into my already busy schedule. I felt that my opinions mattered and that I had something to contribute. Not only were my fellow students my peers, the professor made us all feel like her peers as well. Because of that, my fear disappeared. I found myself looking forward to going to class; I couldn't wait for Tuesdays to come around. It was almost like an addiction. I loved the class discussions and the group work. The professor kept us engaged at all times. The analytical and critical thinking skills I acquired from that class are invaluable. I use them in all areas of my life, not just school. I came out of that class with renewed confidence in my reading, writing, and thinking skills.

Both of these former students are now master's students: Brenda in elementary education and Luann in our Master of Interdisciplinary Studies Program. They represent in their statements—and in their lives—an effective synthesis of the important characteristics of a learning community. These include the principles of liberal education, the aspects of education that are important to adult learners (especially those who commute and live or work in an urban environment), and hallmarks of interdisciplinary studies—in effect, the mission, structure, and content of the Department of Interdisciplinary Studies degree program.

Our students take time out of their busy schedules for classes—for most, a considerable sacrifice. In addition, many students, like Luann Brennan, Barbara Flis, and Lynn Farthing (in my ISS course during the 1999–2000 academic year), find time for activities outside the classroom: departmental committees, Student Senate, conference hosting, refreshment sales at our academic weekend conference courses to benefit our Women's Scholarship Fund, and more. Luann Brennan maintains, "I never would have done that if I hadn't felt a strong bond to the department, faculty and their importance to students. I really wanted to be an advocate for the department because I felt so strongly about it." In contrast to what we normally hear about adult students—that they have neither time for nor interest in such activities because they are too busy—these students and many others in our department want to "give back" by participating and collaborating, a testimony to them and to our program and faculty and staff for inspiring such interest and commitment. The concepts of participation and collaboration, embedded in the academic ethos of interdisciplinary studies programs, are alive and well in the extracurricular realm as well. While not the Residential College at the University of Michigan or James Madison College at Michigan State University, the Department of Interdisciplinary Studies comes close to being a living-learning community in that so many of its students are "around," make themselves available—are always "at the ready"—for all kinds of departmental and college activities and events and interact regularly with each other and with faculty and staff. And it is in the ISS course in which all of the characteristics and values of an interdisciplinary studies learning community are introduced.

INTERDISCIPLINARY STUDIES SEMINAR CURRICULUM

The ISS is a 15-week, team-developed, and team-taught course for four credits. There are 13 workshop meetings at different locations, depending upon the section, and two all-day plenary Saturday on the main campus. Typically, there are four or five sections of the course in the fall semester and three or four in the winter semester. Each section meets weekly with a workshop instructor and has reading, writing, and exercise assignments from common texts, *The Townsend Thematic Reader* (TTR) and *The Everyday Writer* (EW), as well as from a team-coordinated course-specific reader.[16] The *TTR* is a stimulating collection of brief, historical to contemporary, gender-, ethnic-, and race-inclusive essays and short stories by authors such as Maya Angelou, Gary Soto, Alex Haley, Jade Snow Wong, and Isaac Asimov. The reading selections are accompanied by thought-provoking oral discussion topics and diverse writing assignments that reflect back on and integrate their own experience with the readings. Students compose essays on various topics, including their philosophy of life, a person who threw them a lifeline when they needed it most, a contrast of two historical periods that interest them with regard to a specific focus (e.g., music, technology, etc.), and problems that face the elderly. The *EW* is an excellent writing and research source book used throughout our writing intensive program; the text includes accessible information on grammar, effective writing strategies, research methods, citation forms, and more. The reader is program-specific and focuses on interdisciplinary studies, academic reading strategies, academic writing, peer editing, critical thinking, and so on. The reading and writing assignments are intended to encourage critical thinking and lively discussion; short essays reflect students' assimilation of the text with their own experiences.

All the sections come together for the two Saturday plenary sessions held on the main campus at roughly one-third intervals during the first nine weeks of the course. At the plenary sessions, there are special lectures and discussions on the course topics: special challenges of and strategies for success in college, effective writing, research methods and cautions (especially with regard to plagiarism), critical reading of texts (print and nonprint), and interdisciplinary studies, among others. The plenary sessions give students further opportunity to interact with and learn from each other and from the various instructors who make presentations. These are long, action-packed days that could tire or even bore students; instead, our students are energetic and enthusiastic, stimulated by their active learning.

One key component, or thread, during the first of the two plenary sessions is the technology connection—an introduction to the ways that technology can benefit adult students. There are three guided, interactive discussions with three seasoned instructors who have expertise in teaching with technology. First among them is on the technology resources at Wayne State University;

second, on how to take an online course; and third, on research methods and cautions. While many of our new or returning students may use computers at work, they may be ill-prepared for, and hence anxious about, learning with technology. Therefore, they require thorough orientation about the use of technology within an academic environment: online courses, should they elect to take one or more; interactive television; Internet research with all of its advantages and pitfalls; and finally the use of e-mail, threaded discussions, or course management systems, like Blackboard, that "facilitate, strengthen, and deepen communication and hence community between and among students and teachers."[17] Students must get used to accessing WSU's Pipeline for special postings, early assessment, and final grades, and the IS Web site for semester course schedules, special events, faculty Web sites (for syllabi, course assignments, and course materials), and so on. In sum, students must become technology-savvy in order to gain access to their future—academically and otherwise—just as they seek to broaden their horizons in other educational settings.

The ISS instructor engages his or her students on a weekly basis to involve them in a learning community, which will continue throughout their degree program. A number of teaching strategies, both face-to-face and online, promote the success of this course. First, the students always sit in a circle and begin the semester by introducing themselves and talking briefly about their lives, personally and professionally, as they feel moved. The instructor begins that process to break the ice. Randee Lipson Lawrence informs us about the history and significance of the circle formation:

The circle has come to be almost synonymous with adult education. Chairs are arranged in a circle to promote free-flowing dialogue and democratic process. The concept of the circle, however, goes much deeper than an arrangement of furniture. Forming a circle is an ancient ritual. Our ancestors gathered in a circle around a fire for warmth and to cook the food that was provided by groups of hunters and gatherers. The circle provides the basis for socialization, decision making, and problem solving.[18]

Bonding, interactive learning, and a mutual sense of responsibility for discussion are key results—the underlying motivations and goals for effective teaching and learning in the ISS classroom.

Second, large group and small group student/teacher activities as well as one-on-one consultations with the instructor are included each week. Collaborative/cooperative learning is encouraged to foster students' learning and interaction, in both written and oral form. With an interdisciplinary focus in mind, students interact with the texts, discuss critically their own and peers' writing and improvement needs, and engage in active class discussion (to emphasize effective, persuasive speaking skills) on important historical to contemporary topics, problems, or issues that emerge from the readings, writings, presentations, and films.

Third, electronic interaction and learning provide an excellent complement to face-to-face instruction for students, easing them into the use of technology in an academic setting. The instructor provides individual attention as needed through e-mail or in-person consultations about progress on all fronts; submission of written work is encouraged online. The instructor guides students toward responsible use of the Internet for research in some of the papers assigned. Early assessment grades and final grades are provided online. Office hours are held both in person and electronically. The instructor also encourages students to interact with each other both in and out of class, and the latter interactions are often maintained electronically. The students meet in other classes as well, so these newly won connections grow and deepen. Students also communicate with their instructor outside of class. Luann Brennan recalls, "I did communicate a lot through e-mail, and that I found to be great. My professors were on-

line at all different times of the day, and if I had a question on a Sunday, I could usually get it answered that same day. This flexibility was indispensable to me." Luann's perspective is shared by most of our students who value the online option as an enhancement to learning and communication.

CONCLUSION

The literature shows that adult students who commute and work off-campus are still able to learn effectively: "[T]heir learning [is] not harmed by the same constraints as younger students," whose learning tends to suffer "when they spend time working and commuting."[19] Adult students are able to maximize opportunities for learning, and that includes instruction with technology as an enhancement to their educational experience. Our ethnically and racially diverse adult students value our interdisciplinary studies program in an urban setting because it provides a nurturing environment for growth and connections, a learning community in structure and content in which they can thrive. Now one of our enthusiastic master's degree students, Luann Brennan states with pride:

The experience was so good for me that I decided to remain in the department for graduate school, which is something I never thought I would ever do. [The program] gave me the confidence to think bigger. I now have the confidence to realize that I can control my future and that the world is full of opportunities. Also, it's never too late to start anew.

This special relationship between and among students and teachers as well as among the courses they take in our undergraduate degree program begins with the Interdisciplinary Studies Seminar.

In memory of Dr. Otto Feinstein and Dr. Alma Harrington Young. And dedicated, with ever deepening appreciation, to our students.

NOTES

1. Gaff, J. (1989). The resurgence of interdisciplinary studies. *National Forum*, 69 (2), 4–5; Bystrom, V. (2002). Teaching on the edge: Interdisciplinary teaching in learning communities. In C. Haynes (Ed.), *Innovations in interdisciplinary teaching* (pp. 67–93). Westport, CT: ACE/Oryx Press; Kilgore, D. (2003). Planning programs for adults. *New directions for student services*, 102, 81–88; Chaves, C. (2003). *Student involvement in the community college setting.* Los Angeles: ERIC Clearinghouse for Community Colleges, University of California; Schroeder, C. (2003). Supporting the new students in higher education today. *Change*, 35 (2), 55–58; Lundberg, C. (2003). The influence of time-limitations, faculty, and peer relationships on adult student learning: A causal model. *The Journal of Higher Education*, 74 (6), 665–688.

2. Retrieved February 15, 2004 from The Evergreen State College Web site: http://www.evergreen.edu.

3. http://www.evergreen.edu.

4. Kellogg, K. (1999). *Learning communities.* Washington, DC: ERIC Clearinghouse on Higher Education, George Washington University.

5. Bystrom, V. (2002). Teaching on the edge: Interdisciplinary teaching in learning communities. In C. Haynes (Ed.), *Innovations in interdisciplinary teaching* (pp. 67–93). Westport, CT: ACE/Oryx Press.

6. Schneider, 2003; Smith, B. (2003). Learning communities and liberal education. *Academe*, 89 (1), 14–18.

7. Cronon, W. (1998–1999, Winter). 'Only connect': The goals of a liberal education. *The Key Reporter*, 64 (1), 2–4.

8. Cronon (1998–1999, Winter).

9. Schindler, R. (2002). Interdisciplinarity and the adult/lifelong learning connection: Lessons from the classroom. In C. Haynes (Ed.), *Innovations in interdisciplinary teaching* (pp. 221–235). Westport, CT: ACE/Oryx Press.

10. Halliburton, D. (1981). Interdisciplinary studies. In A. Chickering (Ed.), *The modern American college* (pp. 453–471) San Francisco: Jossey-Bass; Klein, J. (1995, Fall). Interdisciplinarity and adult learners. *The Journal of Graduate Liberal Studies*, 1 (1), 113–126; Dinmore, I. (1997). Interdisciplinarity and integrative learning: An imperative for adult education. *Education, 117* (3), 452–467.

11. Schindler (2002).

12. Boyer Commission on Educating Undergraduates in the Research University. (1998). *Reinventing undergraduate education: A blueprint for America's research universities.* Stony Brook: State University of New York.

13. Smith (2003); Kellogg, K. (1999). *Learning communities.* Washington, DC: ERIC Clearinghouse on Higher Education, George Washington University.

14. Schneider (2003).

15. Kilgore, D., & Rice, P. (2003, Summer). New directions for inquiry and practice. *New Directions for Student Services*, 102, 89–91.

16. Hayes, C., & McAlexander, P. (Eds.). (2002). *The Townsend thematic reader.* Marlton, NJ: Townsend Press; Lunsford, A. (2005). *The everyday writer.* Boston: Bedford/St. Martin's Press.

17. Retrieved February 15, 2004 from The Evergreen State College Web site: http://www.evergreen.edu.

18. Lawrence, R. (2002, Fall). A small circle of friends: Cohort groups as learning communities. *New directions for adult and continuing education, 95*, 83.

19. Lundberg (2003).

TOLERANCE WITH CHILDREN: A CRITIQUE OF ZERO TOLERANCE IN SCHOOL DISCIPLINE

Jill Rogers

The juvenile justice system exists as a system separate from the adult criminal justice system because, although society is skeptical about the ability of adults to change, many believe that children can change for the better. This belief parallels the belief that drives current school reforms: All children can learn, and no child should be left behind. In spite of the coherence of these beliefs, zero tolerance, which is the form of school discipline that predominates in the public-school systems, is founded on a conflicting belief: that some children are bad apples and that one bad apple can poison the barrel. In order to explore the current state of school discipline, it is important to look at the theories about juveniles' behavior that shape discipline policies. After briefly outlining the historical development of schools, this article will place school disciplinary practices in the context of criminal sentencing theory in order to suggest that schools can increase safety by altering discipline policies to reflect rehabilitative justifications.

THE CURRENT STATE OF SCHOOL DISCIPLINE: ZERO TOLERANCE

Since the 1990s, the prevalent approach to school discipline has been a zero-tolerance approach. Although zero-tolerance policies differ in their exact requirements, the term "'zero tolerance' refers to school policies that provide for strict, predetermined consequences to specified student behavior(s), with little to no discretion on the part of school officials charged with enforcing the policies."[1] Most zero-tolerance policies require the use of suspensions of varying lengths and expulsions to respond to prohibited behavior. Some schools have had zero-tolerance policies since the late 1980s,[2] but most states adopted zero-tolerance policies after the enactment of the Gun-Free Schools Act of 1994, Pub. L. No. 103-382, by the federal government.[3] The Gun-Free Schools Act conditioned federal funding on schools' adoption of policies requiring expulsion of students for at least a year if the student brought a firearm to school "except that such State law shall allow the chief administering officer of a local educational agency to modify such expulsion requirement for a student on a case-by-case basis if such modification is in writing."[4] This

act, although strict, did provide for discretion by the administering officer. State and local school boards sometimes made their zero-tolerance policies even stricter by omitting this administrative discretion.

In addition, states and local school boards that adopted policies to comply with the Gun-Free Schools Act often extended the zero-tolerance punishments to less serious violations.[5] According to a survey of public schools in the 1996–97 school year, at least 90 percent of schools had a zero-tolerance policy for deadly weapons and 88 percent for drugs.[6] Over the years, the application of zero tolerance evolved so that "[t]he term, *zero tolerance,* now often means that the school will automatically suspend or expel a student for a variety of infractions, from knowing possession of drugs or a weapon to childish pranks and simple poor judgment."[7]

A report written by the American Bar Association found that "[p]ublic policy towards children has moved towards treating them more like adults and in ways that increasingly mimic the adult criminal justice system. The most recent version of this movement is so-called 'zero tolerance' in schools, where theories of punishment that were once directed to adult criminals are now applied to first-graders. . . . Zero tolerance has become a one-size-fits-all solution to the [complex] problems that schools confront . . . and has redefined all students as criminals, with unfortunate consequences."[8] This movement toward treating children like adults when they misbehave is in direct opposition to the philosophy that led to the creation of the juvenile justice system, which was built on a philosophy of rehabilitation that dealt with each juvenile "not as a criminal but as a child needing care, education, and protection."[9] In 1825 when the New York House of Refuge was created, it was founded on the idea that juvenile institutions "should be rather schools for instruction than places for punishment like our present State prisons."[10] The American Bar

Association's statement that zero-tolerance policies "redefined all students as criminals,"[11] contrasts sharply with the rehabilitative ideal that even juveniles who have committed crimes should be cared for and educated.

THE HISTORICAL PHILOSOPHIES OF SCHOOL DISCIPLINE

Schools have reflected rehabilitative ideals in some ways and in some ways have undermined them. With the rapid rate of urbanization in the United States between 1820 and 1860,[12] a need emerged for new institutions that could intervene in areas formerly left to families.[13] As with other institutions, the schools had to shift their practices to address the large numbers of urban poor children.

In the early 1800s, schools were primarily one-room school houses, and education was neither required nor available for all children.[14] In the mid-1800s, as the nation became urbanized and industrialized, cities began to set up systems of free, public education.[15] This movement to create a system of standardized schooling was, in part, a response to the growth of the poor, immigrant community.[16] Far from rejecting the idea of rehabilitation altogether, the school system itself was designed to rehabilitate potentially dangerous children.[17] Tyack writes that leaders saw public education as "the most humane form of social control and the safest method of social renewal" and quotes an educator who said in 1882, "If we were to define the public school as an instrument for disintegrating mobs, we would indicate one of its most important purposes."[18] By the end of the 1800s, many states were requiring compulsory education largely to rehabilitate the "deviant minority."[19]

While there was a sense that institutions could reform poor and immigrant youths, there was also a fear that these youths would harm other youths. The board committee in Chicago argued that some "chil-dren were filthy and 'not fitted for the ordinary classroom,' [and urged] that they be segregated in a special classroom or school."[20] The movements to track students and create alternative schools in the early 1900s were solutions that would "rehabilitate wayward youth" while "minimiz[ing] their contaminating effect on normal students in the regular classrooms."[21] Schools, which were under pressure from the outside to educate and socialize all youth, were simultaneously figuring out ways to *protect* the traditional classroom and student body. The view that students need to be educated and rehabilitated is in tension with the view that the "good" children need to be protected from the "bad" children, and this tension persists today. Scholarship regarding theories of criminal sentencing can shed light on the philosophies that currently underlie and the philosophies that should underlie school discipline policies.

THEORIES OF CRIMINAL SENTENCING AND THEIR APPLICATION IN SCHOOLS

The sections that follow will define four justifications for responding to criminal actions and discuss their application to school discipline policies. The four justifications are rehabilitation, retribution, deterrence, and incapacitation.[22]

Rehabilitation

Black's Law Dictionary defines rehabilitation as "[t]he process of seeking to improve a criminal's character and outlook so that he or she can function in society without committing other crimes."[23] This response to crime assumes that people commit crimes in response to need rather than based on their genetics or some inherent criminality.

The distinction between blaming the inherent criminality of the child and blaming circumstances affecting the child is apparent in the academic context. A nineteenth-century researcher, Barbara Joan Finkel stein, wrote, "[E]vidence suggests that teachers in every setting only rarely distinguished between the intellectual and the social aspects of student behavior as they meted out rewards and punishments."[24] Academic failure was seen "not as a reflection [on teachers'] own inabilities as instructors, but as evidence of the students' personal and moral recalcitrance," thus making corporal punishment or humiliation common responses to academic failure.[25] Although students today are often held accountable for their academic failure by being given low grades and even being held back, there are many policies in place that acknowledge the many possible causes for academic failure aside from students' "moral recalcitrance."

The federal No Child Left Behind Act, 20 U.S.C. §§ 6301 *et seq.*, includes in its statement of purpose the goal of "holding schools, local educational agencies, and States accountable for improving the academic achievement of all students, and identifying and turning around low-performing schools that have failed to provide a high-quality education to their students, while providing alternatives to students in such schools to enable the students to receive a high-quality education."[26] In holding *schools* accountable for students' failure to achieve, and providing students in low-performing schools with alternatives, the Act is embracing a rehabilitative attitude toward academic failure. This attitude is also apparent in schools that deal with academic failure through rehabilitative means like rewriting papers, correcting tests or repeating tests, and tutoring.

For students who have not been identified as students with disabilities, there are fewer examples of rehabilitative responses to social misbehavior than there are to academic failure.[27] In the Gun-Free Schools Act of 1994, for example, schools are required to respond to student misbehavior by expulsion rather than by providing the student with services.[28] While schools are still held accountable, they are held accountable for their reactions to student misbehavior rather than the behavior itself.

New York City's public school disciplinary policy provides an example of the peripheral role assigned to rehabilitation even in school discipline policies that provide relatively more discretion. New York City's Discipline Code is not a pure zero-tolerance policy because it offers a range of responses for each category of misbehaviors rather than providing a set consequence.[29] Because it has a minimum-disciplinary response for each infraction, however, it has some of the aspects of a zero-tolerance policy. The Discipline Code states, "It should, however, be recognized that inappropriate behavior or violations of the discipline code may be symptomatic of more serious problems that students are experiencing. It is, therefore, important that school personnel be sensitive to issues that may be impacting upon the behavior of students and respond in a manner that is most supportive of their needs."[30] However, the 13 pages listing the categories of infractions and the possible disciplinary responses list no rehabilitative responses.[31] The first page of infractions and responses lists the lowest level infractions for Kindergarten through fifth grade, and the disciplinary responses for these infractions range from admonishment by the school staff to removal from classroom by teacher. A school policy that was serious about recognizing behavior as "symptomatic of more serious problems" and the importance of responding "in a manner that is most supportive of their needs" as stated in the introduction should list rehabilitative responses in its "range of possible disciplinary responses."

The 18th page of the 26-page Disciplinary Code is titled "Additional Responses and Supports." It lists rehabilitative responses, including intervention by mental health providers, peer mediation, and a mentoring program, all of which "may be used in conjunction with the disciplinary responses for each level of behavior."[32] This page is sandwiched between the list of nonrehabilitative responses and the descriptions of the nonrehabilitative responses.[33] This policy conveys the mandatory nature of removals, suspensions, and expulsions, and states that the listed rehabilitative responses are optional and are not replacements for the mandatory punishments. This nod to rehabilitative responses is not present in most zero-tolerance policies, which provide much less discretion and often more severe penalties for disciplinary infractions.

Retribution

Retribution is embodied in the phrase from the Judeo-Christian tradition, "an eye for an eye, a tooth for a tooth."[34] *Black's Law Dictionary* defines retribution as "[p]unishment imposed as repayment or revenge for the offense committed; requital . . . 2. Something justly deserved; repayment; reward."[35] People who see retribution as the underlying justification for punishment believe that the moral and/or legal wrong committed is inherently deserving of punishment.[36] This theory of punishment focuses on the individual who acted and does not look at the impact of the act or punishment on society as a whole.[37] It is a notion that, whether or not the person will ever commit a crime again, he or she committed a wrong and deserves to suffer in proportion.

One of the most prevalent forms of retributive punishment in schools is corporal punishment. Corporal punishment can act as retribution or deterrence or both depending on the purpose for which it is administered. When the Supreme Court upheld schools' ability to use corporal punishment in *Ingraham v. Wright*, the limiting principle allowed school officials to use "such force as a teacher or administrator 'reasonably believes to be necessary for [the child's] proper control, training, or education.' *Restatement (Second) of Torts* § 147

(2) (1965); see *id.*, § 153 (2)."[38] This principle allows school officials to take into account the behavior and intent of the child who misbehaved, but it does not suggest that school officials can take into consideration the education or control of other students, which would be required for general deterrence. This principle could suggest a justification of specific deterrence (i.e., deterring the child who misbehaved from misbehaving again), and it suggests a retributive justification.

One of the 22 states permitting corporal punishment policies today is Tennessee.[39] Memphis, Tennessee, which is currently reviewing its corporal punishment policy,[40] provides for corporal punishment "in cases meriting such action" and indicates that it should typically only be used after other forms of punishment have failed.[41] The language of Memphis's policy reflects the sense of proportionality inherent in the theoretical underpinnings of retributive justice. Unlike deterrence and incapacitation, retribution focuses on the individual who misbehaved and his or her blameworthiness for that specific act, which relies on an inherent sense that punishments must be proportionate to the wrong. Determining the theoretical justification, however, is difficult because those passing the policy may support one theory of punishment, and those administering it may support another. In practice, "critics say that students [in Memphis schools] have been routinely paddled for whispering in class, playing poorly in an athletic event, and other minor matters,"[42] which indicates that those applying the policy may be trying to deter others rather than punishing to match the level of moral blameworthiness.

In 1977 when *Ingraham v. Wright* was decided, only two states had banned corporal punishment,[43] whereas 28 states have banned corporal punishment today.[44] According to statistics from the federal Department of Education, the number of paddlings of public school students declined from 1.5 million in 1976 to 342,038 in 2000.[45]

Further evidence that corporal punishment is not the predominant form of punishment is present in the statistic that 83 percent of the serious disciplinary actions in the 1999–2000 school year were suspensions lasting at least five days.[46] Even though Memphis has retained its corporal punishment policy, it has a distinct "Safe Schools: Zero-Tolerance" policy, which requires schools to expel students for at least a year if they are found in possession of a firearm or explosive, if they are found in possession of illegal drugs, or if they commit battery against school personnel.[47] The trend in schools is away from punishments justified by theories of retribution and toward zero-tolerance policies, which are justified by theories of deterrence and incapacitation.

Deterrence

Deterrence is defined by *Black's Law Dictionary* as "[t]he act or process of discouraging certain behavior, particularly by fear; esp. as a goal of criminal law, the prevention of criminal behavior by fear of punishment."[48] Deterrence is a justification based on utilitarian principles: It is just to punish people for criminal acts because that will intimidate potential criminal actors and, therefore, reduce crime.[49] Although proportionality is not inherent in deterrence justifications as it is in retribution justifications, many people who support deterrence try to build in proportionality. Some theorists, like Bentham, go as far as to try to calculate the sentences by weighing the costs of punishing someone (both economic and pain and suffering) against the benefits of the resulting deterrence.[50] This economic model for deterrence builds in a retribution-like sense of proportionality where lesser crimes receive lesser punishments. Utilitarians support this result because it discourages more serious crimes: "When people commit crimes . . . it is preferable that they commit lesser rather than greater

ones."[51] This does not mean that the punishment will fit the moral blameworthiness of the crime, however, but rather that the severity of the punishments will descend as the blameworthiness of the crime lessens. This could support, for example, punishment if a student accidentally broke a window as long as the intentional breaking of a window was punished with more severe punishment.

Punishment based on deterrence, although not necessarily disproportionate, has a high likelihood of becoming disproportionate. Society persistently believes that there is too much crime, which pushes institutions to respond with harsher punishments at times.[52] This can be illustrated to some degree with corporal punishment. Corporal punishment, which may be justified as a retributive punishment, often is used in part because of its perceived ability to deter others. While the Court in *Ingraham v. Wright* found "[t]he uncontradicted evidence suggests that corporal punishment in the Dade County schools was, '[w]ith the exception of a few cases . . . unremarkable in physical severity,'"[53] there is evidence from other settings suggesting the common administration of disproportionate corporal punishments. Discussions of proportion will inevitably depend on the frame of reference; however, some punishments are chosen for their ability to deter seemingly because of their disproportionate nature. Tyack writes about corporal punishment in schools in the 1800s:

In the basement of a building in the stockyards, Inspector Todd stumbled over a thirteen-year-old boy who had huddled there, hoping she would not discover him. He wept bitterly when told he would have to go to school, blurting between his sobs that "they hits ye if yer don't learn, and they hits ye if ye whisper, and they hits ye if ye have string in yer pocket, and they hits ye if yer seat squeaks, and they hits ye if ye don't stan' up in time, and they hits ye if yer late, and they hits ye if ye ferget the page." Again and again she heard the same story: 269 children said they preferred factory to school because no one hit them there.[54]

Unless a student is trying intentionally to make his or her seat squeak to provoke the teacher, it is hard to imagine that, even in the context of the 1800s, hitting the student was seen as proportionate to the blameworthiness of the student. Rather, the corporal punishment was seen as a necessary means of scaring the rest of the students so that order would be maintained.

Although corporal punishment, in both its retributive and deterrent forms, has traditionally been a common form of punishment for students,[55] a different form of deterrence, zero tolerance, has been growing in prominence and eclipsing corporal punishment policies.[56] Zero tolerance, which is not based on retributive justice, faces serious problems of disproportional punishments. Zero-tolerance policies "have resulted in persistent incidents of disproportionately harsh punishments,"[57] like a three-week suspension for a second grade student who brought a one-inch-long imitation Swiss Army knife to school.[58] Proportionality is threatened because the moral blameworthiness of the individual is not at issue in punishments based on deterrence.

Because deterrence does not focus on the guilt of the actor as much as it focuses on using the actor as an example of the consequences of breaking rules, zero-tolerance policies, which are based on deterrence, often do not require the individual to have intent or a guilty mind.[59] The facts of *Ratner v. Loundoun Public Schools*,[60] an unpublished Fourth Circuit decision, illustrate two of the problems with school discipline policies that do not require knowledge or intent. An eighth-grade girl told her friend that she was suicidal and had brought a knife to school in her binder.[61] Her friend, Benjamin Ratner, who had known her for two years and who knew about her previous suicide at-

tempts, took the binder from her and placed it in his locker.[62] A school administrator heard about the situation and asked Benjamin to bring the binder to her, and he did.[63] He was suspended for the rest of the term, which was from October 8 to February 1, even though the administrator "acknowledged that she believed Ratner acted in what he saw as the girl's best interest and that at no time did Ratner pose a threat to harm anyone with the knife."[64] The Fourth Circuit held:

However harsh the result in this case, the federal courts are not properly called upon to judge the wisdom of a zero tolerance policy of the sort alleged to be in place . . . or of its application to Ratner. Instead, our inquiry here is limited to whether Ratner's complaint alleges sufficient facts which if proved would show that the implementation of the school's policy in this case failed to comport with the United States Constitution. We conclude that the facts alleged in this case do not so demonstrate.[65]

Although the courts are divided as to whether or not zero-tolerance policies in schools are required to consider the students' knowledge of the act,[66] it is significant that even some courts uphold these policies when most criminal laws require *mens rea*, or a guilty mind.[67]

The first and most obvious problem with policies that punish students like Ratner is that schools are institutions that should be modeling democracy and justice, and should not have policies that knowingly punish innocent students. As the concurrence in *Ratner* states, "Ratner's nearly four-month suspension from middle school is not justifiable. Indeed, it is a calculated overkill when the punishment is considered in light of Ratner's good-faith intentions and his, at best, if at all, technical violation of the school's policy."[68] During adolescence, students are particularly attuned to issues of justice and should be provided with positive models and lessons of justice.[69] The second problem is that policies that blindly apply to all students regardless of intent can actually deter actions that schools should encourage. For instance, if the same situation came up in that school again, the example of Ratner would deter students from confiscating a knife from a friend. While students would be able to go directly to the teachers without taking the knife and would escape punishment, they would be telling the teachers to suspend the suicidal friend, which would be hard for an adult to do, let alone an eighth-grader.

Beyond the fact that deterrent policies can ignore the specific considerations of individual cases, deterrent policies also rely on assumptions about delinquency that conflict with the mission of schools. Because deterrence punishes individuals to prevent all the other potential criminals from acting, it focuses on the student body as a group of potential criminals rather than on the students and their moral development. This focus is reminiscent of some of the racist and xenophobic ideas that were prevalent in schools at the end of the nineteenth century:

Justifying the use of corporal punishment in schools in immigrant wards, a member of the Boston school committee declared in 1889 that "many of these children come from homes of vice and crime. In their blood are generations of iniquity . . . They hate restraint or obedience to law. They know nothing of the feelings which are inherited by those who were born on our shores."[70]

Some of the same fears and prejudices exist today. An assistant principal in Mississippi said that his principal repeatedly admonished him for his reluctance to paddle students with comments such as, "These kids are different, all they understand is the paddle," and a representative of a leading anti-paddling group, Nadine Block, told reporters that "black students are paddled more than twice as often as other students, proportionate to the overall population."[71] Schools should not let fears dictate disciplinary policies that refuse to look at students as individuals.

Furthermore, there is the question of whether deterrence really works. Setting ideas of proportionality aside, someone who favors deterrence would say that sentences should be determined based on their ability to deter others, and this should be determined based on the effect that changes in punishments have on crime rates.[72] Because of the infinite number of variables affecting crime rates, however, research is largely inconclusive as to the deterrent effects of punishments.[73] It is no easier to draw conclusions with any degree of confidence about the impact of zero-tolerance policies, but one of the only studies that looks at the effectiveness of zero-tolerance policies, a study by the National Center for Education Statistics (NCES), indicates that zero tolerance is not effective.[74] The study surveyed principals and found that schools with zero-tolerance policies were less safe than schools without zero-tolerance policies both at the time of the initial survey and four years later.[75] Furthermore, data based on surveys of principals from 1991 to 1997 showed "virtually no changes across either minor misbehavior or more serious infractions" in those years.[76] There is no convincing data finding that zero-tolerance policies are effective in reducing school violence.[77]

Whereas there is little evidence of the effectiveness of zero tolerance on school violence, there are data finding that zero-tolerance policies' overuse of suspensions negatively affects student learning. Deterrence-based policies tend to focus on the impact that punishment has on the population at large, but they tend to ignore the effect the punishment has on the punished, which may undermine the deterrent effect. Long-term suspensions, some of the most common punishments assigned by zero-tolerance policies, negatively affect student learning. During the 1998 school year, an estimated 3.1 million students were suspended and 87,000 expelled.[78] According to North Carolina's Department of

Public Instruction, "[o]ut-of-school suspensions accounted for approximately one million lost instructional days in the 2001–2002 school year."[79] This loss of educational time can cause students to fall behind in class work, which may make them more likely to act out.[80] Poor academic performance may also cause students to be held back, which can alienate the students and make them more hostile to schools and school authorities.[81] Additionally, the lack of supervision and the opportunity to "socialize with deviant peers" may increase the likelihood of behavior problems for some students.[82] These impacts are particularly alarming because data from the Department of Education at the turn of the millennium indicated that African-American children, although only 17 percent of the national public school enrollment, represented 32 percent of out-of-school suspensions.[83]

Furthermore, school suspension is a "moderate to strong predictor of a student's dropping out of school," with sophomores who dropped out in the 1980s being three times more likely than their peers to have been suspended.[84] The 2000 Census indicated that approximately 11 percent of 16- to 19-year-olds did not have a high school diploma or GED and were not enrolled in school.[85] Students who drop out of high school are 72 percent more likely to be unemployed than students who graduate, and 82 percent of all prison inmates dropped out of high school.[86] Although these facts apply to all suspensions and not just suspensions resulting from a zero-tolerance policy, they indicate some of the problematic implications of zero-tolerance policies.

Incapacitation

Incapacitation is the act of restraining individuals.[87] The concept, as Bentham writes, is "firmly laid in school-logic . . . for *a body to act in a place*, it must be there. Keep a man . . . out of Britain, for a given time: he will neither pick a pocket, nor break into a house, nor present a pistol to a passenger, on any spot of British ground within that time."[88] Incapacitation is the underlying justification for prisons and jails.[89] Although people have argued that deterrence is the justification for imprisonment, the incapacitation justification seems to explain why prisons and jails are used rather than other forms of punishments that would deter such as "fines, corporal punishment, loss of privileges," and so forth.[90] People have also tried to justify jails and prisons as sites where rehabilitative services can be provided, which has led to prisons being called "correctional institutions" and "reformatories,"[91] but people promote imprisonment even when prisons clearly lack good rehabilitative programs. Although there are few studies exploring the actual effect of incapacitation on the crime rate,[92] the appealing simplicity of the logic has led to its widespread acceptance. This pervasive justification has seeped into school discipline as well.

Suspensions and expulsions, which are some of the most popular extra-judicial responses to student misbehavior,[93] appeal to schools because of their ability to remove troublemakers from the classroom or the school. These responses are based on the theory of incapacitation. Suspensions are temporary removals from either the classroom or the school. Students with in-school suspensions have to report to school, but are not permitted to go to their regular classes and interact with the other students. They should complete schoolwork during the in-school suspension. Students with out-of-school suspensions do not come to school for the duration of the suspension. Schools should provide the student with schoolwork to complete while suspended. Expulsions are permanent removals from a school. Students who are expelled are sometimes admitted to an alternative school.

According to Troyan, "Students who receive [in-school suspensions] . . . are frequently the students who constantly interrupt the teacher, who use inappropriate language in class, who choose not to follow basic instructions,"[94] but also include students caught "fighting with another student, talking rudely to a teacher, or [being habitually tardy] to class."[95] A student who was disrupting the class, once suspended, can no longer disrupt the class. As with the idea that "each additional prisoner represents more crime prevented as long as it is assumed that offenders will persist in crime unless confined,"[96] the idea in schools is that each student suspended means less classroom disruption if the student would have persisted in disrupting the class. This loses some of its rhetorical power when challenged.

The first challenge to incapacitation is an ethical one. Incapacitation works from what scholar Lewis terms a "victimization perspective" of crime that "treats crime as an experience of citizens rather than as the activity of an offender," which reduces the need to understand the motivations of offenders.[97] Schools should look at students as individuals and try to help them develop rather than categorizing students as offenders and victims. In addition, Max Grünhut describes the science of criminology with the observation, "The incorrigible criminal. . . 'should be incapacitated from crime by imprisonment for life or for an indeterminate period.'"[98] According to this philosophy, criminals who cannot be rehabilitated can at least be incapacitated.[99] In schools this is problematic not only because it leaves some children behind, but also because it may encourage teachers to use stereotypes. To achieve the greatest degree of discipline, school officials would want to predict which students were most likely to misbehave in the future and suspend those students for the longest amount of time,[100] but when school officials are left to judge the character of someone to determine future misbehavior rather than looking at past conduct, their judgment is apt to be strongly influenced by stereotypes. According to Russ Skiba and Reece Peterson, "[S]chools that rely most heavily on suspension and expulsion are also those that show the highest rates of minority overrepresentation in school disciplinary consequences."[101]

The second challenge to incapacitation concerns what happens after incapacitation. Suspending students permanently (i.e., expelling students) is repugnant to the idea of schools and, in addition, schools' authority to expel students is limited in most states. In New York City, for example, it is illegal to expel students who are classified as special education students or are general education students who did not turn 17 before July 1 of the school year.[102] Therefore, schools use suspensions much more often than expulsions, and suspensions vary greatly in duration. In spite of the fact that students will return from suspensions and will return very quickly from short-term suspensions, incapacitation does not purport to affect the behavior of someone after the period of incarceration. Certainly a school should aim higher than just temporarily preventing disruption, but the even more troubling possibility is that temporary suspension may increase a student's potential to disrupt. When a student is suspended, the student's teacher should provide work for the student so that he or she does not fall behind.[103] In practice, however, teachers sometimes do not know that their students were suspended in time to prepare work for them.[104] When teachers do provide work for the suspended students, the assignments still cannot replicate the classroom interactions, and students in suspension typically have to complete the work on their own without help from a teacher.[105] Finally, students may not work during suspension at all.[106] A student who has fallen behind the rest of the class and has no idea what is going on when he or she returns from suspension is as likely or more likely to be disruptive than before. Furthermore, students who have been suspended from school are more likely to drop out and more likely to participate in inappropriate behavior.[107]

These problems with the theoretical underpinnings of incapacitation do not mean that schools should never suspend students. Suspensions differ widely in their implementation and length. A one-day in-school suspension is different from a one-day out-of-school suspension, and there are a range of practices employed with each of those types of suspensions as to whether the student is able to continue learning or not. There are also huge differences in the impact of suspensions depending on whether they are measured in days or weeks or months. Furthermore, suspensions can be carefully considered responses to student behavior, or they can be inflexibly assigned as the result of a zero-tolerance policy. Even though the critiques of incapacitation are general and will apply to different policies differently, it is useful to think through the theoretical foundations of policies in order to develop just and effective school discipline policies.

Conclusion

School districts should rethink their disciplinary policies in light of rehabilitative theories of justice. The prevalence of zero-tolerance policies in schools is problematic both because of the assumptions these policies communicate about children and because these policies negatively impact children in schools. While it is unlikely that schools will completely dismantle zero-tolerance policies in this decade, schools can make aggressive efforts to rework those policies and to introduce additional support for innovative, rehabilitative responses to student misbehavior. Schools may be well-advised to consider deterrence, incapacitation, or retribution in some circumstances, and many responses can be justified on multiple grounds, but examining disciplinary policies for their rehabilitative effects will help schools de-velop policies that are consistent with the best interests of the child.[108]

School violence continues to be an important issue, and schools will continue to face pressure to react strongly. Reactions such as zero-tolerance policies, however, are ineffective and undermine the mission of schools. The justifications of deterrence and incapacitation that underlie zero-tolerance policies focus on the student body as potential criminals and as victims. Although rehabilitation is not the only justification for disciplinary responses that can be appropriate in schools, measuring disciplinary options against the theory of rehabilitation will help schools ensure that their policies treat students as individuals and as children.

NOTES

1. Jenkins, J., & Dayton, J. (2003). Students, weapons, and due process: An analysis of zero-tolerance policies in public schools. *Education Law Reporter, 171*, p. 18.

2. Skiba, R., & Peterson, R. (Jan. 1999). The dark side of zero tolerance: Can punishment lead to safe schools? *Phi Delta Kappan, 80*, p. 372.

3. Jenkins & Dayton (2003), p. 19.

4. Gun-Free Schools Act of 1994, Pub. L. No. 103-382, 108 Stat. 3907 (current version at 20 U.S.C. § 7151 [2004]).

5. Casella, R. (2003). Zero tolerance policy in schools: Rationale, consequences, and alternatives. *Teachers College Record, 105* (5), 872.

6. Cloud, R. (2003). Due process and zero tolerance: An uneasy alliance. *Education law reporter, 178*, p. 9.

7. Cloud (2003), p. 2.

8. American Bar Association. (2001, February 19). Zero tolerance policy report. Submitted to the House of Delegates, San Diego, CA, p. 1. Retrieved November 25, 2005, from http://www.abane.org/crimjust/juvjus/zerotolreport.html.

9. Jacobs, T. (2003-04). *Arizona practice series: Arizona juvenile law and practice, 5*, §1.1(A).

10. Bernard, T. (1992). *The cycle of juvenile justice* (p. 62). New York: Oxford University Press.

11. American Bar Association, 2001, February 19, p. 1.

12. Tyack, D. (1974). *The one best system*. Cambridge, MA: Harvard University Press.

13. Bernard (1992), pp. 59–61.

14. Tyack (1974), pp. 15–16, 28, 56–57.

15. Tyack (1974), p. 29.

16. Tyack (1974), p. 33.

17. Sedlak, M. (1981). Schooling as a response to crime. In Dan A. Lewis (Ed.), *Reactions to crime*. Beverly Hills, CA: Sage Publications.

18. Tyack (1974), p. 74.

19. Tyack (1974), pp. 68, 71.

20. Tyack (1974), p. 70.

21. Sedlak (1981), pp. 206, 213–214.

22. These four justifications are sometimes classified in the two categories of utilitarianism and retribution. Although not all authors discuss all four, this chapter looks at each of the four categories separately.

23. Garner, B. (Ed.). (2000). *Black's law dictionary* (7th ed.) (pp. 1032–1033). St. Paul, MN: West Group.

24. Tyack (1974), p. 55.

25. Tyack (1974), p. 55.

26. No Child Left Behind Act, 20 U.S.C. §§6301(4) (2002).

27. Although there are provisions that hold schools accountable for the behavior of students with disabilities, length limitations for this chapter do not allow a full treatment of these provisions. This discussion is therefore limited to issues pertaining to students who are not identified as students with disabilities.

28. Gun-Free Schools Act of 1994, Pub. L. No. 103-382.

29. New York City Department of Education. (2003). Citywide standards of discipline and intervention measures. (The Discipline Code). Retrieved March 18, 2004, from http://www.nycenet.edu/parents/PDFs/DisciplineCode.pdf.

30. New York City Department of Education (2003), p. 1.

31. New York City Department of Education (2003), pp. 4–16.

32. New York City Department of Education (2003), p. 18.

33. New York City Department of Education (2003), pp. 14–21.

34. See Baird, R., & Rosenbaum, S. (1995). *Punishment and the death penalty*. Amherst, NY: Prometheus Books. (Referring to "the ancient Latin phrase *lex talionis*, 'an eye for an eye'").

35. Garner, B. (Ed.). (2000). *Black's law dictionary* (7th ed.) (p. 1056). St. Paul, MN: West Group.

36. Baird & Rosenbaum (1995), p. 9.

37. Baird & Rosenbaum (1995), p. 9.

38. Ingraham v. Wright, 430 U.S. 651, 661 (1977).

39. Gehring, J. (2004, April 14). Review of corporal punishment hits nerve in Memphis. *Education Week, 23*, p. 17.

40. Gehring (2004, April 14), p. 17.

41. Memphis Board of Education. (1982, August 16 revised). Board Policy #5151.1 Corporal punishment. Retrieved March 18, 2004, from http://www.memphis-schools.k12.tn.us/admin/communications/policies/p5151.1.html.

42. Gehring (2004, April 14), p. 17.

43. Ingraham v. Wright, 430 U.S. 651, 663 (1977).

44. Gehring (2004), p. 17.

45. Dobbs, M. (2004, February 21). U.S. students still getting the paddle. *The Washington Post*, p. A1.

46. DeVoe, J., Peter, K., Kaufman, P., Ruddy, S., Miller, A., Planty, M., et al. (2003). *Indicators of school crime and safety*. Washington, DC: U.S. Departments of Education and Justice.

47. Memphis Board of Education. (2001, June 18, revised). Board Policy # 5152 Safe schools: Zero tolerance. Retrieved March 18, 2004, from http://www.memphis-schools.k12.tn.us/admin/communications/policies/p5152.html.

48. Garner, B. (Ed.). (2000). *Black's law dictionary* (7th ed.) (p. 363). St. Paul, MN: West Group.

49. von Hirsch, A. (1985). *Past or future crimes*. Beverly Hills, CA: Sage Publications.

50. von Hirsch (1985), p. 8.

51. von Hirsch (1985), p. 31–32.

52. Bernard (1992), pp. 3–4. *See also* Skiba & Peterson (1999).

53. Ingraham v. Wright, 430 US 651, (1977), p. 677.

54. Tyack (1974), p. 178.

55. Tyack (1974), p. 55.

56. Garner (2000).

57. Jenkins & Dayton (2003), p. 13.

58. Jenkins & Dayton (2003), p. 14.

59. Pelliccioni, C. (2003). Is intent required? Zero tolerance, scienter, and the substantive due process rights of students. *Case Western Reserve Law Review, 53*, p. 979.

60. Ratner v. Loudoun County Pub. Sch., 16 Fed. Appx. 140, 141 (4th Cir. 2001), *cert. denied*, 534 U.S. 1114 (2002).

61. Ratner v. Loudoun County Pub. Sch. (2002), p. 141.

62. Ratner v. Loudoun County Pub. Sch. (2002).

63. Ratner v. Loudoun County Pub. Sch. (2002).

64. Ratner v. Loudoun County Pub. Sch. (2002), p. 141–42.

65. Ratner v. Loudoun County Pub. Sch. (2002), p. 142.

66. In 2000, the Sixth Circuit was the first federal appellate court to rule that policies "suspending or expelling a student for weapons possession, even if the student did not knowingly possess any weapon" violated substantive due process, but other courts have reached mixed results, including a recent Fourth Circuit decision that upheld zero-tolerance policies that punished without regard to intent. Pelliccioni, 2003, pp. 978–79, *citing* Seal v. Morgan 229 F.3d 567 (6th Cir. 2000).

67. Pelliccioni (2003), pp. 996–97 (distinguishing the few criminal offenses, aside from minor public welfare offenses, that lack a *mens rea* element. The main criminal offense that does not require *mens rea* is statutory rape. Strict liability in statutory rape charges is justified based on the idea that the older person engaging in sexual activity should bear the burden of determining whether the act is legal, which does not apply to zero-tolerance policies).

68. Ratner v. Loudoun County Pub. Sch. (2002), p. 144.

69. Advancement Project & the Civil Rights Project. (2000, June 15–16). *Opportunities suspended: The devastating consequences of zero-tolerance and school discipline policies.* Washington DC: Report from a National Summit on Zero Tolerance.

70. Tyack (1974), p. 75.

71. Dobbs (2004), p. A1.

72. von Hirsch (1985), p. 13.

73. von Hirsch (1985), p. 13.

74. Skiba & Peterson (1999).

75. Skiba & Peterson (1999).

76. Skiba & Peterson (1999).

77. Skiba & Peterson (1999).

78. Advancement Project & the Civil Rights Project (2000), p. 3.

79. State of North Carolina Department of Juvenile Justice and Delinquency Prevention Center for the Prevention of School Violence. *DJJDP—Center's efforts involving suspensions and expulsions.* Retrieved March 18, 2004, from http://www.ncdjjdp.org/cpsv/.

80. Advancement Project & the Civil Rights Project (2000), p. 19.

81. Advancement Project & the Civil Rights Project (2000), p. 13.

82. Advancement Project & the Civil Rights Project (2000), p. 11.

83. Advancement Project & the Civil Rights Project (2000), p. 7.

84. Skiba & Peterson (1999).

85. Aron, L., & Zweig, J. (2003, November). Educational alternatives for vulnerable youth: Student needs, program types, and research directions. *The Urban Institute.* Retrieved March 18, 2004, from http://www.urban.org/UploadedPDF/410898_vulnerable_youth.pdf.

86. Aron & Zweig (2003, November), p. 8.

87. *Black's Law Dictionary* defines "incapacitation" as "[t]he action of disabling or depriving of legal capacity." Garner, B. (Ed.). (2000). *Black's law dictionary* (7th ed.) (p. 610). St. Paul, MN: West Group.

88. Zimring, F., & Hawkins, G. (1995). *Incapacitation.* Oxford: Oxford University Press.

89. Zimring & Hawkins (1995), p. v.

90. Zimring & Hawkins (1995), p. 14.

91. Zimring & Hawkins (1995), p. 6.

92. Zimring & Hawkins (1995), p. v.

93. Troyan, B. (2003). The silent treatment: Perpetual in-school suspension and the education rights of students. *Texas Law Review, 81,* 1637–1670.

94. Troyan (2003), p. 1638.

95. Troyan (2003), p. 1642.

96. Zimring & Hawkins (1995), p. 16.

97. Lewis, D. (1981). *Reactions to crime.* Beverly Hills, CA: Sage Publications.

98. Lewis (1981), p. 22.

99. Lewis (1981), p. 24.

100. von Hirsch (1985), p. 14.

101. Skiba & Peterson (1999).

102. New York City Department of Education (2003), p. 20.

103. Troyan (2003), p. 1656.

104. Troyan (2003), p. 1656.

105. Troyan (2003), p. 1657.

106. Troyan (2003), p. 1657.

107. Shiraldi, V., & Ziedenberg, J. (2001). Self-reported crime and the growing use of suspensions. *Justice Policy Institute.* Retrieved March 18, 2004, from http://www.justicepolicy.org/article.php?id=49.

108. Note: For the good of the child, for the good of society: Using Scotland and Jamaica as models to reform U.S. juvenile justice policy. *Harvard Law Review, 115,* p. 1965.

LITERACY IN URBAN EDUCATION: PROBLEMS AND PROMISES

Anne Dichele and Mordechai Gordon

We have failed. As the rhetoric becomes more emotional, the gap in literacy achievement ever widens. The promises of *Brown vs. Board of Education*, the money behind federally mandated desegregation programs, the countrywide establishment of Chapter One programs and Reading First initiatives, the myriad attempts to close the achievement gap and to make education equitable in the United States: All have failed—over and over again. And urban schools are the continuing battleground.

It seems clearly evident from years of attempted changes to curriculum, and federal mandates of all kinds that if we have learned anything at all from former attempts at improving urban literacy, it is that large-scale grants or national initiatives that carry with them meaningful changes in literacy education have not had any significant effect on literacy achievement overall, and arguably may have contributed to the inequities in urban versus non-urban literacy.

Do we know what truly influences literacy achievement? Yes. Although the research-based techniques of improving reading achievement have been in question since the early twentieth century and even well before mandatory schooling became law in the United States, there are some basic tenets of effective literacy instruction that most literacy educators hold to be true, and that research has borne out. Primarily, we know that there is no one right way to teach literacy and that the quality and ability of the teacher matters more than anything else in improving literacy achievement.

Do we know what makes *urban* literacy different? Does it matter that literacy instruction is being conducted in an urban environment? Perhaps. It is clear that socioeconomic status has an impact on levels of achievement and that poverty, more than the urban environment, is the real issue. It is becoming increasingly clear that urban literacy can be achieved and that we need to consider those programs that have been successful and how such programs have been accommodated to meet the unique challenges of urban teaching.

Finally, and perhaps most importantly, we need to ask ourselves honestly: Do we truly *want* to be successful in closing the achievement gap—in providing high rates of literacy for all our students? What would be the outcome of our successes? Are the economic and social systems of the United States prepared for equitable literacy education? Indeed, what happens if the promises of No Child Left Behind (NCLB) are actually kept? It is the contention of the authors that, without grappling honestly with the actual outcomes of successful equitable education, we will never achieve it.

THE FAILURE OF FEDERAL INITIATIVES

The failure of federal initiatives to improve educational achievement—literacy in particular—is well documented. For the last 35 years, the federal government has specifically attempted to fight illiteracy by initiating various research-based programs, beginning with federally funded educational laboratories of the 1960s. Many of the outcomes of these early programs, which were touted as the ultimate panacea for curing illiteracy—such as the International Teaching Alphabet; the Direct

Instructional System for Teaching Arithmetic and Reading (DISTAR); and the Palo Alto linguistic readers—were ultimately abandoned when reading achievement did not improve with implementation.

In the 1970s, accountability issues became highlighted, and student performance on tests became a critical factor in recognizing student achievement. It was during this time that competency testing became the road to achieving universal literacy and maintaining accountability for ineffective literacy instruction. The "back to basics" movements of the late 1970s slid into the 1980s, with Title One programs (renamed Chapter One during the Reagan Administration) and Head Start programs becoming more and more deeply ingrained as part of our national curriculum.

By the 1990s, the goals of federal programs such as Chapter One and Head Start became more modest than at their outset, particularly since those programs clearly had failed to produce the academic gains they were designed to achieve. As Kaestle and Smith noted in their 1982 review of the role of the federal government in education, "perhaps the most lasting outcomes of Head Start and Title I programs are the permanence of federal involvement in public schools."[1]

While federal curricular mandates continued to fail in their implementation, federal commissions issuing massive reports on the teaching of reading continued. It seemed clear that, although literacy achievement in urban settings had seen some successes in some circumstances, the federal government continued to try to find a generalizable, one-size-fits-all curriculum that would work.

In 1985, the Commission on Reading released the report, *Becoming a Nation of Readers*. In that report, research-based evidence for successful reading instruction was specifically delineated: early phonics instruction (completed before grade 3), interesting texts written in natural language, less emphasis on worksheets, more time spent reading, and more time modeling the reading process. It is noticeable that *Becoming a Nation of Readers* did not recommend specific curriculum programs or methodologies. Rather, the report noted what elements of reading instruction appeared to be critical to improving literacy, regardless of methodology or curriculum.

What is fascinating is that the recent research-based report of the National Reading Panel (NRP)—upon which all of the recommendations for the NCLB instructional mandates for literacy are based—directly contradicts many of the research-based findings of the *Becoming a Nation of Readers* report.[2] For example, *Becoming a Nation of Readers* recommended enthusiastically the practice of Sustained Silent Reading (SSR). The practice of SSR basically entails providing time each day for students to silently read books of their own choosing. The report of the National Academy of Science's *Becoming a Nation of Readers* noted: "Research suggests that the amount of independent silent reading children do in school is significantly related to gains in reading achievement."[3] Compare that research-based finding with the more recent recommendations of the NRP, which indicate that "there is no clear evidence that encouraging children to read more actually improves reading achievement."[4]

Such blatantly discrepant recommendations based on "the research" are explained somewhat by critics of the NRP report such as Stephen Krashen. As Krashen points out:

First, while acknowledging that "literally hundreds of correlational studies" indicate that better readers read more than other readers, the NRP, like the Tobacco Institute, argued that experimental studies were needed to verify the observed effect. But true experimental studies will probably not be done because given the correlational evidence, parents aren't likely to give informed consent for their children to be assigned to a no-reading control group.[5]

What is important is that federal initiatives have not only failed to affect long-term achievement in the area of literacy, but they have failed to provide any consistent or sound research to support their recommendations for instruction. The NRP findings, upon which most of the recommendations for *Reading First* are based, have been continuously questioned about the quality of the research done for the Panel, including the surprising and largely overlooked minority report of Panel member, Joanne Yatvin. Tucked behind the 500-plus pages of the full report, the minority report concludes: "In the end, the work of the NRP is not of poor quality; it is just unbalanced, and to some extent, irrelevant."[6] Yet, it is the findings of the National Reading Panel Report—a report that is clearly flawed—that are the basis for NCLB, the largest federal educational legislation ever passed in U.S. history.

Over the last fifty years, federal initiatives have failed to recognize the wealth of research indicating that, indeed there is no optimal program for effective literacy instruction. A multisite study done by Bond and Dykstra in the 1960s looking at the effectiveness of different reading series on literacy achievement found that there was "no clear evidence of the superiority of any one reading series of any particular approach to teaching reading."[7] In the 1970s, House, et al. spearheaded another multisite study of early education programs, once again looking for a program that was consistently effective. Their findings indicated that none of the intervention curricula, even Direct Instruction, produced consistently superior results.[8] More recently, similar findings from Pogrow pointed to the inconsistent results of programs such as Success For All and Direct Instruction.[9]

Thus, while federal initiatives continue to promote "research-based" curricular models and NCLB implies that if only teachers would implement "research-based" instruction 98 percent of all readers would be reading on grade level, the reality is, as Richard Allington tersely states:

No intervention has raised the achievement of 90 percent of poor readers to the 50th percentile. Moreover, no research suggests that classroom teachers can help 90–95 percent of students acquire grade-level reading proficiencies by learning more about phonology, using a scripted curriculum, teaching systematic phonics, or following some "proven program."[10]

Even though it is clear that federal initiatives to improve literacy have failed miserably and will probably continue this trend, it is likely that the federalization of American reading instruction is here to stay. Indeed, according to Richard Elmore, senior research fellow at the Consortium for Policy Research, the new education bill (NCLB) is "the single most damaging expansion of federal power over the nation's education system in history."[11] So where does this policy of federalization leave urban literacy? First, it should be pointed out that the figures for the literacy crisis are distorted overall. Despite the outcry of decline in American literacy scores, the research in literacy, primarily from National Assessment of Educational Progress (NAEP) data, indicates that reading achievement has remained relatively stable for thirty years and has, in fact, increased steadily since the early 1900s.[12] There is little evidence that overall, American reading achievement has declined.

Still, these distortions hide a more frightening scenario for the urban poor. In fact, the NAEP data provide strong evidence that the discrepancies among achievement for rich and poor students is alarming, evidence that should make us very concerned. Twice as many (58%) fourth-grade students who were poor scored below the Basic proficiency level as did students who were not poor (27%). And far fewer poor students (13%) achieved Proficient level than did their peers from more advantaged families (40%).[13] Although policy makers have asserted that NAEP data show 70 percent of urban fourth-graders fell below the Basic proficiency level, the actual figures in the NAEP report indicate that 47 percent of fourth-grade students in the central cities failed to achieve Basic level. But the NAEP data also show that 60 percent of poor children, children eligible for free lunches, fail to meet the Basic level.[14] Poverty, it would seem, is the greatest indicator of literacy failure, not an urban setting.

In conclusion, the failure of federal initiatives to improve literacy instruction in general and urban literacy achievement specifically is that in searching for a tidy panacea to ameliorate all of our literacy problems, we have ignored important research, misinterpreted and misrepresented findings, and disregarded the social issues, in particular poverty, which have the greatest impact on achievement. Equally troubling is the fact that the major initiatives outlined here assume that literacy acquisition is technical in nature and entails merely learning a set of basic skills in reading, writing, and math. These initiatives display little awareness of the fact that literacy acquisition is actually a series of complex tasks that require students, among other things, "to organize information into meaningful constellations by discerning relationships between ostensibly unrelated data."[15] But given that NCLB is here to stay, is there any way to save the federalization of literacy instruction from the failures of the past? What will work for the poor—and in this particular case, the urban poor—to help overcome the gap in achievement for poverty-level children in urban environments?

THE IMPORTANCE OF THE TEACHER

Perhaps the most important research data to come out of any federal commission has been the finding that overall, "teacher quality accounted for 40 to 60 percent of the variance in NAEP achievement for fourth- and eighth-grade reading and math."[16] Similarly, a study conducted in Texas by Ferguson concluded that "the large disparities between black and white students were almost entirely accounted for by differences in the qualifications of their teachers."[17]

Indeed, we have known for more than ten years that the "achievement gap" between minority and majority students can be ameliorated by enhancing the quality of teachers. But it is the urban environments that suffer most from the lack of qualified teachers. According to *Quality Counts 2003*, the qualified teacher shortage will have the greatest impact on schools serving children of poverty, and the number of individuals willing to commit to teaching in inner-city settings serving minority students is dwindling at the same time as these student populations are growing.[18] In Chicago journalists in an award-winning investigative report found that 55 percent of the teachers at one Chicago inner-city school were not fully certified to teach their students. They went on to report that one in five teachers in Chicago's most needy schools was unqualified to teach.[19]

In New York, similar research found that less than half of the teachers in some New York schools held certification for the subject courses they taught. Furthermore, low-income, low-achieving and non-white students were more likely to have teachers who lacked prior teaching experience, had failed a teacher-licensing exam on the first try, or had attended less selective colleges as undergraduates.[20] The impact of individual teachers on learning is so strong that it has led researchers to refer to the paucity of highly qualified teachers for those who need them most as the *Teacher Gap*, a term that attempts to refocus the issue of the minority achievement gap in literacy to the variable that appears to be most influential—quality teachers.[21]

In light of the research, the mandate of NCLB to require states to ensure that all teachers of the core academic subjects must be highly qualified in every subject they teach by the end of the 2005–06 school year is a laudable if not lofty goal. (Core academic subjects include: English, reading or language arts, mathematics, science, foreign languages, civics and government, economics, history, geography, and the arts). NCLB additionally requires, in response to the dire needs of the poor and the urban poor, that newly hired teachers in schools receiving federal money for their at-risk students must meet the new law's requirements right away, in 2004.[22] But where exactly is this new legislation taking teacher preparation?

Marilyn Cochran-Smith, a teacher-educator and policy analyst, has been very vocal in her concern over the Bush administration's true policy agenda when considering the importance of teacher quality and teacher preparation. She states, "There is . . . a well funded movement to deregulate teacher education by dismantling teacher education institutions and breaking up the 'monopoly' that the profession has, according to its critics, too long enjoyed."[23] The irony is that whereas the NCLB is written to encourage states to have high standards for teacher certification, it includes specific language that cites "alternative routes" as a means of maintaining high standards, thus opening the door for deregulation of teacher education.

Interestingly, the policy to deregulate the preparation of teachers is supported by conservative political foundations like the Heritage Foundation, the Pioneer Institute, and the Abell Foundation. A report by the Abell Foundation, *Teacher Certification Reconsidered* (2001), challenges the research on teacher education in closing the literacy and achievement gap in urban settings, arguing for the deregulation of teacher preparation. Like other policy statements in reports funded by conservative political groups, the agenda is clearly intended to open the doors of education to anyone with a bachelor's degree and provide minimal preparation periods for teachers in training. In order to justify this agenda, the report claims that verbal ability, not teacher training, accounts most for teaching effectiveness.

The rhetoric around the issue of teacher quality and teacher preparation is pervasive and inflammatory. In a public forum on evidence-based research in education, Reid Lyon, Chief of the Child Development and Behavior Brand of the National Institute of Child Health and Human Development, stated that reform efforts in teacher education should begin by "blowing up colleges of education."[24] Secretary of Education Rod Paige stated in a report (*Meeting the Highly Qualified Teachers Challenge: The Secretary's Annual Report on Teacher Quality*) that "there is little evidence that education school course work leads to improved student achievement."[25] Perhaps not so surprisingly, this claim is directly contradicted by a research review commissioned by Secretary Paige's own office.[26]

Why would public policy move towards enhancing teacher quality while promoting methods of teacher preparation that have no research basis? There is an obvious appeal to alternative routes to certification. Given the pressing need for an increased supply of teachers, alternative certification routes are cheaper and quicker than more traditional teacher preparation programs. However, the U.S. public would be horrified if similar suggestions were made as public policy statements for the preparation of other professionals (e.g., let's give *surgeons* a few months training, then just put them in the operating rooms. They will figure it [surgery] out with some mentoring and some initial support by colleagues). And although the damage done by poorly trained teachers is well documented, it is currently being ignored by Washington and the proponents of NCLB. In short, we believe that there is a gross inconsistency between the call for improving teacher quality and the claim that teacher preparation programs do not make a difference in student learning. Such a claim not only makes no sense but also contradicts most of the existing research on the impact of teacher education on teacher effectiveness.[27]

URBAN LITERACY AND QUALIFIED TEACHERS

The italicized text that follows is based on the personal experience of Anne Dichele, coauthor of this chapter. We italicize her account to distinguish it from the more formal style of the rest of the chapter.

In 1977, at the height of forced busing and desegregation of the Boston schools, I was hired for my first job as a reading teacher. I was given a class of ninth- graders whose average reading levels were grade two. These were the students that were placed in shop classes and typing—anything but "real classes." After all, they were virtually non-readers.

My first week with these twelve adolescents, four girls and eight boys, was truly awful. They would enter the classroom quietly, take the same seats each day, and look at me with a mixture of boredom and sympathy. It was as if they were saying,"I feel bad for you, new young teacher. They gave you the idiot class." And at the same time, the looks were telling me "We've been in reading classes for years. Nothing really works for us. We'll sit here because we have to sit here, but that's about all we will do. Why bother?"

They were, all in all, good kids. They were well behaved. The fact that they actually felt bad for me that I had them as students floored me. How deeply had the system convinced them of their lack of ability? So, for the first two weeks, I was Ms. Enthusiasm. I designed lessons with television themes to try to connect with what they knew; I brought in videotapes of books so they could understand what they had missed; I tried to make reading exciting; I shared how much I loved to read. My enthusiasm was met with again, a mixture of boredom and sympathy. They didn't care about reading; they simply didn't care.

Finally after two weeks of trying, I gave up. I walked into class one morning and said simply, "This isn't working." They shifted in their seats. They looked at me, really looked at me, for the first time. "May I ask all of you a question?" I ventured. "If I were any one of you, and I was in ninth grade, and I couldn't read, I would be really, really angry." I continued. "I would be thinking, all this time I've spent in school, and I don't even know how to read!" "Why aren't all of you more mad?"

For a moment, no one spoke. Then Roger, whose legs always seemed to be spilling out into the aisles, and who always crossed his arms and closed his eyes through my class, sat up. "We are not stupid, you know." "They think we're stupid, but we're not." "They don't even want to teach us, they never did." The discussion continued for nearly the entire class, some of it sad, some angry, some laughing about years of poor teachers who "pretended to care." All of the discussion centered on the failure of the system to believe in these students, and the failure of teachers to actually help them. I believe it was the first honest conversation they ever had in school.

With five minutes left in class, and their venting continuing, I quietly asked, "So, what are we going to do?" They responded with jokes, but I pressed on. "I think it is terrible that you are all ninth-graders and can't read very well. But I'm a really good reading teacher, and I know I can help you read better. So this time, if you choose not to work with me, you can't blame the system. If you work with me, you will read better. You can stay angry forever, or you can do something about it and show them they were wrong. I can help you to do that. It's up to you."

In truth, my knees were knocking as I spoke to them. I feared I couldn't live up to the promise, but I did honestly believe that if they were willing to try their best, I could teach them to read better. I was well trained, I did know how to do this in ways that I knew would be effective and that they would enjoy. And I knew they could learn.

The next day, the class was different. Not everyone trusted what I had committed to, but they were young and curious and certainly willing to try, if only to prove me wrong. A few of the students never bought in, and remained distrustful of me and of the system. But overall, nine of the twelve made real progress that year, and I learned the lesson of a lifetime as a teacher: you have to believe in your students' ability to learn; you have to make sure your students understand you believe in them and that you care; and you absolutely have to back up your care and your belief with good, strong effective instruction. All are critical, particularly for teaching literacy in urban settings.

The argument for qualified teachers and their effects on achievement is not simply documented by anecdotal experiences; the research on the need for highly qualified teachers with respect to the teaching of literacy is substantial. The work of Linda Darling-Hammond has been seminal in arguing for the importance of preparing quality teachers, particularly for the critical areas of reading and mathematics. In a quantitative analysis of the data of NAEP, Darling-Hammond found measures of teacher preparation and teacher certification to be the strongest correlates of student achievement in reading and mathematics.[28] Even when controlling for variables related to poverty and language status, the resulting correlation between well-trained teachers and reading and math achievement remained.

The research on teacher efficacy and teacher care is also substantial. Efficacy studies, which look at how teachers' own beliefs in their capacity effect change in their students, clearly indicate that those teachers who are most highly effective are ones who believe that the teaching they do can and does impact student learning.[29] To be sure, efficacy and quality are interrelated. Teachers who have been well trained and who have multiple strategies and myriads of knowledge to employ pedagogically see the effects of their efforts. In this way, each success teachers perceive in their students naturally increases their

sense of efficacy, and thus the circle of effective teaching ever-widens.

Equally compelling research evidence exists about the importance of trusting and caring relationships between students and teachers for student achievement. In extensive interviews during three years with over 400 middle- and high-school students in several Philadelphia urban schools, Corbett and Wilson concluded that good teachers are willing to help students, take the time to get to know them, and explain the content until everyone understands.[30] Thus, the research on the importance of caring as critical to urban teaching in general and urban literacy in particular, is growing.

Given all the evidence that exists about the impact of teacher effectiveness, efficacy, and caring relationships on student learning and achievement, we believe that urban schools would be better served if they were not required to implement a standardized, federally mandated program to improve literacy. Rather, individual districts, schools, and teachers should be encouraged to evaluate various literacy programs in order to find the ones that would best address the specific challenges of their students. Success stories of teachers and schools that have done just that are not hard to come by. Gregory Michie, a first-year teacher working in a vocational school with mostly African-American students on the South Side of Chicago, was assigned to teach five groups of seventh- and eighth-graders who were struggling in reading. Upon questioning his students, Michie discovered that the majority of them disliked, even hated to read. In order to spark the kids' interest in reading, he decided to bring in as many outside sources as he could:

We read excerpts from Malcolm X's autobiography and Claude Brown's *Manchild in the Promised Land.* We read up on African-Americans of note, from Marcus Garvey to Mary McLeod Bethune to Charles Drew. We explicated poems of Gwendolyn Brooks and Langston Hughes alongside rap songs by Boogie Down Productions and A Tribe Called Quest.[31]

Another example of helping urban students develop literacy skills comes from *La Escuela Fraternity*, a public school in Milwaukee that has a unique two-way bilingual program in English and Spanish. Serving a mostly Hispanic community, the school is designed to focus on a number of important components: "Multicultural education, a whole language approach to literacy, cooperative learning, and school-based management." The school is unique in that the students learn from the very outset (kindergarten) two languages and in that both languages are valued equally and receive equal attention. According to Rita Tenorio, one of the teachers in this school:

Language is a vehicle for instruction, not simply an end in itself. I am not "teaching Spanish," but rather teaching kindergarten "in Spanish." In the native Spanish-speakers I see better growth this year in their literacy skills. Their self-esteem is enhanced as they become the language resources for the English speakers. The Spanish-speakers can "read" a Big Book to the whole group. They beam with pride as they stand up to tell a story, or share a book they've written in the writing center.[32]

Examples like these, of individual teachers and schools that have adapted a particular approach that has helped their students develop literacy skills, are fairly common. Such teachers and schools have been successful because they have taken risks and been willing to experiment with something different rather than stick to the norm. They have been successful because their literacy programs are designed with thoughtfulness, creativity, and care and because they are determined to make a difference in their students' education.

CONCLUSION:
KEEPING OUR PROMISES

What would it take to keep our promises to our nation's children? What would it take to close the achievement gap and create the conditions that would ensure high rates of literacy for all students, including ones in disadvantaged urban areas? The above discussion suggests that we believe that large-scale federal initiatives that call for a universal remedy are at best halfhearted attempts to deal with this complex and difficult problem. In our view, there cannot be one solution that can be applied across the board to fix the problem of literacy in general and urban literacy in particular. Rather, in order to address this problem we must look to a variety of local efforts, ones that, following the insights of thinkers such as Vygotsky and Freire, take into account the significance of the social and cultural context of the learners. Unless we consider the environment in which children live and operate, we risk alienating many of them even further from schools.[33] Recognizing the importance of this context enables educators to establish connections with students, and helps students get excited about learning and take responsibility for their own growth and development.

Yet despite the preference that must be given to a variety of local efforts to address the problem of urban literacy, there are a number of main features that most of these efforts have in common. To begin with, is the idea that the standards by which we evaluate students' literacy must be rigorous and complex rather than simple and technical. Practically all of the federal initiatives in the past thirty years, including the NCLB, have assumed that high standards are technical in nature and entail the acquisition of a set of predetermined skills and data in reading and math. However, as Joe Kincheloe argues, technical standards, measured by one's performance on standardized tests, are grossly inadequate in that they remove the crucial meaning-making process from students' learning. "Meaning in this context has already been determined by the curriculum makers and is simply imposed on students as a 'done deal'—there is no room for negotiation about the interpretation of information."[34] Kincheloe's point is not that teachers and students should disregard the information that has been generated by others. It is that schools should place less emphasis on the simple acquisition of a set of predigested facts and much more on the ability to interpret and make sense of ideas and experiences that students encounter. Similarly, learning to read is much more than acquiring a useful technical skill; it is the ability to use this skill to understand and critique various ideas and perspectives.

The second feature shared by successful local programs for improving urban literacy is the recognition that significant reform is not possible unless we provide the disadvantaged schools and students with highly qualified and caring teachers. We know that learning to read is a complex act, and that many children, particularly those from impoverished backgrounds, fail to do so beyond minimal achievement. Indeed, learning to read requires development of phonemic awareness skills, phonics, fluency, vocabulary and comprehension strategies. Similarly, learning to write clearly and coherently as well as to compute abstract mathematical problems are very difficult tasks for many children. Mastering these skills requires a great deal of practice and, above all, a teacher who has the content knowledge and the expertise to guide students through all the steps they need to go through to reach the final goal. The fact that many of the federal initiatives in the last thirty years have resulted in the deskilling of the teaching profession and in its degradation from a scholarly vocation to a technical and tedious act contradicts what we know about good teaching.

In addition to providing disadvantaged urban schools with highly qualified and expert teachers, we need to ensure that these teachers are caring and committed to helping students who are struggling learn and reach their potentials. As the narrative above illustrates, a caring relationship between teachers and students is essential for helping students take responsibility for their own learning and for transforming the culture of the school as a whole to an effective learning community. In focusing so much on students' achievement and test scores, the federal initiatives discussed downplay the role that establishing caring relationships between teachers and students can have for enhancing students' learning and literacy.

Finally, local efforts that have been successful in improving literacy have demonstrated an awareness of Vygotsky's insight that students' ability and achievement are embedded in a larger social and cultural context in which students learn and operate. Such an awareness implies that improving urban literacy will require us to transform not only the quality of teachers who work in urban schools, but also address the grave social problems, like poverty, crime, and drug abuse, that many students experience. Research indicates that when teachers take into account the social context of their students in their planning and instruction, the learning that takes place is much more significant and long lasting. In contrast, the federal initiatives mentioned above have a far too narrow focus: improving students' basic skills and raising test scores. As such, they have little chance of helping those students who are really struggling and who often view schoolwork as a series of isolated tasks that have little connection to their lives and aspirations. Only by addressing the broader social context of the students, their families, and their communities, do we have a realistic chance of adequately responding to the challenges of urban literacy.

NOTES

1. Kaestle, C., & Smith, M. (1982). The federal role in elementary and secondary education, 1940–1980. *Harvard Educational Review, 52*, 384–408.

2. National Reading Panel. (2000). *Teaching children to read: An evidence-based assessment of the scientific research literature on reading and its implications for reading instruction. Reports of the subgroups.* Washington, DC: National Institute of Child Health and Human Development.

3. Anderson, R., Hiebert, E., Scott, J., & Wilinson, I. (1985). In National Academy of Science, Commission on Reading. *Becoming a nation of readers* (p. 76). Washington, DC: National Academy of Science.

4. Garan, E. (2001, March). Beyond smoke and mirrors: A critique of the National Reading Panel report on phonics. *Phi Delta Kappan*, 505.

5. Krashen, S. (2002). More smoke and mirrors: A critique of the National Reading Panel report on fluency. In R. Allington (Ed.), *Big brother and the national reading curriculum* (p. 12). Portsmouth, NH: Heinemann.

6. Yatvin, J. (2002). Babes in the woods: The wanderings of the National Reading Panel. In R. Allington (Ed.), *Big brother and the national reading curriculum* (p. 125). Portsmouth, NH: Heinemann.

7. Bond, G., & Dykstra, R. (1967). The cooperative research program in first-grade reading instruction. *Reading Research Quarterly, 2* (4), 5–142.

8. House, E., Glass, G., McLean, L., & Walker, D. (1978). No simple answers: Critique of the follow-through evaluations. *Harvard Educational Review, 48*, 128–160.

9. Pogrow, S. (2000). Success for all does not produce success for all students. *Phi Delta Kappan, 82* (1), 67–80.

10. Allington, R. (2004). Setting the record straight. *Educational Leadership, 61* (6), 22–25.

11. Elmore, R. (2002). Unwarranted intrusion. *Education Next*, Hoover Institution. Retrieved June, 2003 from www.educationnext.org/20021/30.

12. Berliner, D., & Biddle, D. (1996). *The manufactured crisis: Myths, fraud and the attack on America's public schools.* White Plains, NY: Longman.

13. Donahue, P., Voelkl, K., Campbell, J., & Mazzeo, J. (1999). *NAEP reading 1998: Reading report card for the nation and the states.* Washington, DC: U.S. Department of Education, Office of Educational Research and Improvement.

14. Bracey, G. (2001). The condition of public education. *Phi Delta Kappan, 83*, 157–169.

15. Kincheloe, J. (2001). Hope in the shadows—Reconstructing the debate over educational standards. In Kincheloe, J. & Weil, D. (Eds.), *Standards and schooling in the United States, An encyclopedia* (p. 5). Santa Barbara, CA: ABC-CLIO.

16. Darling-Hammond, L. (1999). *Doing what matters most: Investing in quality teaching.* New York: National Commission on Teaching and America's Future. Retrieved July, 2003 from http://www.nctaf.org/publications/index.html.

17. Ferguson, R. (1991). Paying for public education: New evidence on how and why money matters. *Harvard Journal on Legislation, 28*, 465–491.

18. Hoffman, J. (2004). Achieving the goal of a quality teacher of reading for every classroom: Divest, test or invest? *Reading Research Quarterly, 39* (1), 119–128.

19. Grossman, K., Beaupre, B., & Rossi, R. (2001, September 7). Poorest kids often wind up with the weakest teachers. *Chicago Sun Times*.

20. Olson, L. (2003, January 9). The great divide. *Education Week, 18*, 9–16.

21. Ansell, S., & McCabe, M. (2003, January 9). Off target. *Education Week, 18*, 57–58.

22. United States Department of Education. (2003). *Inside No Child Left Behind.* Retrieved August, 2003 from http://www.ed.gov/legislation/ESEA02/pg2.html#sec1119.

23. Cochran-Smith, M. (2001). Constructing outcomes in teacher education: Policy, practice and pitfalls. *Education Policy Analysis Archives, 9* (11), 5.

24. Lyon, R. (2002, November 18). Rigorous evidence: The key to progress in education. Paper presented at the forum of the Coalition for Evidence-Based Policy, Washington, DC.

25. Wilson, S., Floden, R., & Ferrini-Mundy, J. (2001). *Teacher preparation research: Current knowledge, gaps and recommendations.* Seattle, WA: Center for the Study of Teaching and Policy. Retrieved July, 2003 from http://depts.washington.edu/cptmail/Reports/html#TeacherPrep.

26. Darling-Hammond, L., & Youngs, P. (2002). Defining "highly qualified teachers": What does "scientifically-based research" actually tell us? *Educational Researcher, 31* (9).

27. Darling-Hammond, L. (2000). *Teacher quality and student achievement: A review of state policy evidence.* Seattle: Center for Teaching Policy, University of Washington.

28. Kemis, M., & Warren, R. (1991). *Examination of the relationships between perceived teaching potential, commitment, and efficacy and performance* (Report No. SP033517). Iowa: Midwestern

Research Association. (ERIC Document No. ED3407000)

29. Corbett, D., & Wilson, B. (2002, September). What urban students say about good teaching. *Educational Leadership, 60* (1), 18–22.

30. Michie, G. (1999). *Holler if you hear me: The education of a teacher and his students.* New York: Teachers College Press.

31. Tenorio, R. (1996). A vision in two languages: Reflections on a two-way bilingual program. In W. Ayers & P. Ford (Eds.), *City kids, city teachers* (p. 172). New York: The New Press.

32. Vygotsky, L. (1978). *Mind in society: The development of higher psychological processes.* Cambridge, MA.: Harvard University Press.

33. Vygotsky (1978); Freire, P. (1994). *Pedagogy of the oppressed.* New York: Continuum.

34. Kincheloe (2001), p. 4.

COMPLICATING OUR IDENTITIES AS URBAN TEACHERS: A CO/AUTOETHNOGRAPHY

Monica Taylor and Lesley Coia

Freedom is to be found in action *with* others.[1]

—*M. Greene and M. Griffiths*

This autoethnographic study of teacher identity in the urban context is coauthored, thus making a break with other autoethnographic studies of which we are aware. We insist on a co/autoethnographic model because we believe action must happen with others. The coauthorship of autoethnography suits our purposes and in many ways is a logical extension of the general purpose of autoethnography. In this chapter we tell stories—fragmentary stories, our stories—not because they are intrinsically interesting, but because they are a necessary part of understanding our practice and the first step towards improving it. Our concern is to better understand what it means to be a teacher in an urban setting. We are, therefore, not writing urban education from the outside: We are focusing on the importance of understanding the worlds of those involved with urban education, in this case, the world of educators. A premise from which we work is that *urban education* is a relatively meaningless concept without the rich descriptions of the lives lived within its open boundaries. We cannot talk about urban education as if it means something generic.

Although the chapter is ostensibly about individuals—the stories of two individuals do, after all, take center stage—it eschews the individualism of the classroom and the conceptualization of our work as educators as that of the sovereign individual for the idea of the self as complex and fluid, as made and remade in community. We do not address individualism by rational abstract argument, but by living our research and showing the meaning of an anti-individualist stance by the way we present our work and ourselves. We bypass individualist thinking by starting with the recognition that not only are we at best the co-authors of our own lives,[2] but that work in education—more specifically, urban education—demands collaboration.

Coming to know vitally involves telling our stories, but it is more than this. We are sharing our stories with the purpose of understanding our identities as teachers/individuals/members of multiple communities and our teaching practice.[3] It is through this exchange of stories that, as Stanton writes, "Teachers ask themselves not only what they know, but what the enterprise of education is all about, who they can be as a teacher, who the students are, and how to connect students with knowledge."[4] Stories are part of knowledge construction, and that construction cannot occur in isolation. We have to share our stories in order to push ourselves to think reflectively about our experiences. It is not enough to simply tell the story or write a journal entry; it is the give-and-take dialogue that refocuses the lens.[5] We become transformed when we engage in this type of sharing and discussion.[6] As Dyson and Genishi say:

The storytelling self is a social self, who declares and shapes important relationships through the mediating power of words. Thus, in sharing stories, we have the potential for forging new relationships, including local, classroom "cultures" in which new relationships are interconnected and new "we's" formed.[7]

We both started as teachers in urban public schools. Monica was an alternatively prepared teacher of middle-school Spanish in New York City, and Lesley was a secondary English teacher in London. We met when we were teacher educators at a college on Staten Island. We still prepare teachers to teach in an urban context—Monica in New Jersey and Lesley in Atlanta, Georgia. The stories we tell come from these contexts, but also from before we became teachers. It is a vital part of our argument that who we are as teachers is complex: We did not spring fully formed from any teacher education program. Who we are is informed by who we were. Autobiographies, while ostensibly about the past, are in fact about the present and most importantly about the future. It is this insight that originally motivated us, as teacher educators, to use autobiographical writing with the teachers we are preparing to work in an urban context.[8] To paraphrase Abbs, we saw, and continue to see, these seeds—these reflections on our experience—as the harvest of tomorrow.[9]

It is important to note that the stories we tell are not finished. Spaces have been cre-

ated with a purpose, that of opening and continuing a conversation. In the rest of the chapter we tell stories, share responses and dialogue, and in the process exemplify what we have come to term co/autoethnography. In so doing, we hope to show the vital role this method has to play in helping us understand the issues we face in urban education. As part of the process we highlight key features of co/autoethnography with the hopes that others will replicate it in their own knowledge construction.

We intersperse stories with interpretation by both authors, and intersperse these with reflections on the stories and the analyses. To indicate the change of voice, the interpretations by the story authors are printed in italic or standard typeface.

JUST WHO ARE WE?

So we are a group of teacher educators, teachers, administrators, and humanities and sciences faculty participating in a two-week summer professional development program examining teaching for democracy. We are working on examining our own identities and are asked to first fill in boxes with our race, ethnicity, gender, class, religion, and sexual orientation, highlighting those that are of the dominant culture and that are subordinate. We then do a well-known activity designed to reveal our privilege. We answer a series of basic identity questions and take either a step forward or backward. I find myself at the front of the room with several other colleagues (some whose privilege was unknown to me in the past) and wonder what this says about me and about us. It was an awkward feeling—almost as one of my co-participants said, "What a relief! We are outing ourselves as people of privilege."

And surely this is not bad—the moral questions arise when we are outing others without their consent.

Although I know that the organizers' intentions were positive and I embrace this activity as a means to promote self-awareness and help participants to make visible their invisible privileges, I am not sure if that is enough. I am concerned with the ways in which programs/in-stitutions generically address issues of privilege.

This raises all sorts of questions—we want to out people who are using their privilege and don't know it. I know how difficult it is to get some students to see how they have "invisible" privilege and how other people who don't have it have to live. As one of my students once said, before she and her family go on a long car trip they clean the car, dress nicely and make sure they have all their papers in order because they know they are going to be stopped by the police—something you and I never have to think about.

I am well aware I grew up privileged. I have all of the markers of a privileged person. I did grow up with two parents (but I lived in a single household for four years and watched my mother support two children by herself—before her divorce I watched her being abused by my father). I was able to go to a private university and get a first-rate education (but I never thought of myself as smart or having a voice until I was a graduate student at public university). It is essential that we are aware of how the knowledge we construct is influenced by our upbringing and identity, but is it so static? Having navigated boundaries all my life—youth culture/adult culture, urban/suburban, lower class/middle class/upper class, schooled/un-schooled, of color/white, single/married, parent/child, English/Spanish/Italian/French, American/other—these boxes don't feel right to me. They don't, on their own or as binaries, present who I am and what I know.

Clearly, who we are is determined by how others perceive us, and it seems that the exercise shows this very well. While it reflects who we are to others, you are saying that it was less than successful in capturing the subjective nature of experience, which is invariably experienced as culturally complex. I think what you bring out so well is that these types of exercises deal exclusively with the outside—how we appear. I know both of us would be the first to acknowledge the importance of recognizing, viscerally, that who we are is in

large part determined by others' percep-tions and responses to us—and this is largely determined by cultural factors—but I think what you are saying is that who we are is not totally captured by this external perspective. Who would deny this?

My privileged status is forever in my mind because I believe it is essential that I am aware of my position especially as a teacher. I con-stantly question my agenda with students from that lens, checking to see if I am making choices for students that maintain the status quo and, if so, changing those choices and striving to make pedagogical changes that privilege the voices and knowledge of my students whose voices often go unheard. But does discussing who I am in terms of neat divided categories re-ally represent me fully? Do these labels help others to understand who I am and where I am from? Is it beneficial for me to think of myself in such narrow terms?

This story says so much about the ways in which positivism has infected even those who think they are respecting expe-rience. It made me wonder what people who do this—conduct these exercises—think they are doing. Surely everyone feels as you do. I know when I did the activity, it was like scoring points (except you wanted a negative or low score). It seemed so odd that here we were dealing with numbers again. I wondered who was sur-prised, what was learned—except some kind of reverse unthinking snobbery—some kind of privilege born of being work-ing class (amazing how many middle-class professors categorize themselves as this), but the worst of it is, as you say, the unbe-lievable narrowness of thinking in absolute categories—abstracted from experience in-stead of intersections of experience in-formed by ethnicity, gender, and so on. It leaves out all the interesting questions—what does it mean to be a woman in a home in an upper-class community with a mother who is struggling with divorce and two kids and little money?

It brings up so many issues about who is in charge of our experience. In these situations we are often treated as if we don't know who we are and have to be told.

I know exactly what you mean. Perhaps for some people who have not thought a tremendous amount about identity this is a good starting point, but it becomes much more complex once you have realized these markers and want to delve deeper. I am not dismissing these sorts of reflections or self-examinations. I am calling for a deeper analysis, a stronger foundation whereby we can dismantle hegemonic practice.

Yes, our experience of these categories doesn't matter; we are told what they mean, that is, that we are privileged in this, not privileged in that. We need to find a way to be both individuals and socially constructed.

Writing Autobiography

This is a teacher's story: It is based in the idea of personal knowledge.[10] Like other teacher narratives, it acknowledges the connection between how we come to know, what we come to know, and who we are. In general, teachers' stories of their experiences recognize the role of the personal in knowledge construction and are valuable and powerful[11] because, as Dyson and Genishi write:

Stories help us to construct our *selves*, who used to be one way and are now another; stories help us to make sense of, evaluate, and integrate the tensions inherent in experience: the past with the present, the fictional with the "real," the official with the unofficial, the personal and the professional, the canonical with the different or unexpected.[12]

But there is more to knowledge construction than the telling of stories. Many teachers' stories, while necessarily and often centrally involving others, are written by a single author with analysis of the story by the person writing it.[13] They are important because of the value they place on lived experience and their role as a powerful antidote to the positivism inherent in objective accounts. Although valuable, from our experience of writing autobiographical sketches on our own and

with others,[14] we found that this form of reflection had limits in terms of our own purpose: understanding our teaching in an urban context. For example, we keenly felt the limitations of the *genre* of autobiography. Writing on our own without an audience was more of a release than an analysis and reflection. Apple, while recognizing that writing autobiographically is "compelling and insightful," also notes, "Just as often such writing runs the risk of lapsing into possessive individualism."[15] We realized, through working in an autobiography group, that the power of teachers' stories can be enhanced if instead of being constructed as straight autobiography, with all problems attendant on this, they are constructed—written—as autoethnography with others.

WHERE ARE WE COMING FROM?

Although I have many memories of La Retraite, my first is not of arriving, but of the first night in the dormitory with my new teddy bear, Benji, with his secret compartment in the back, bought with my Grandma from a warehouse in Bristol, lying in my narrow bed next to Rebecca who sucked her thumb, her hand folded around a square of her brother's pajamas. She sniffled and cried. I remember looking down the long dormitory to the space where the nun slept in her bed, just like ours, but at the other end of the long room from mine, with curtains that were drawn at nighttime. I wasn't unhappy, I was just a little disorientated. I felt sorry for the young ones: the seven-year-olds who had trouble unpacking on their own. This was all new, but it didn't feel bad, just a little strange. My head was full of stories of boarding school and concerns about finding the bathrooms in the middle of the night. Apprehensive but not worried, I started my life away from home.

Why do you think you were so resilient? Were you pleased to be at school? What did it mean to you?

It was a surprise to read your reaction. I wasn't expecting to have such a strong and positive reaction. I realized that I am so used to this episode being interpreted by others, specifically those who are close to me. My Mum is so full of guilt we cannot even talk about it. This past Christmas we drove over to Wells where my brother, sister and I went to school together for a while, and as we were driving out of the town she said how she used to cry every time she left us, her face reflecting the sorrow she felt then. Even now there is no room for any of my feelings about school in that conversation. My mother isn't alone in "knowing" this experience for me. During conflicts in my adult relationships, others have blamed my problems on my being sent away to school. Again, there is no room for another interpretation. Your questions, on the other hand, seem open and serious and genuine. When I first read them, they made me think, "Was I resilient?" This is something I never considered.

Resilient! When I first read this, I read "resistant." I read your question in terms of the negative and the "not-hearing" response I suppose I have become used to when telling tales about school (interestingly I hadn't thought of this before this "misreading" occurred). "Resistant" would be more palatable to this way of thinking since it implies I was at fault: I didn't try hard enough, I wasn't friendly enough to make a success of it. But "resilient" makes it sound as if I had stuff about me—that I had a backbone.

It is so interesting to me that both of your examples show that it is others' analyses and critiques that matter. How often we try to explain others' behaviors by their past as if we have some ownership and authority—as if outsiders can have more insight into us without the details or the context. I think that my sort of questioning speaks to our methodology—we don't pry or judge—we want to tease out the self-analysis.

This comment is really the right one to make about this experience. I have never been allowed to have it as my own. Interestingly, given what we are discussing, a great source of discomfort was not the fact that I was not Catholic, but that I was boringly and incorrectly borderline working-/middle-class. Many of the girls came from upper-middle-class and upper-class families and had different lives that I didn't know (except through books). Frances, my best friend, hated the narrow little houses beyond the convent wall for their cramped and small lives. I loved them for the lights in the sitting rooms and the families I imagined inside making their tea and sitting down in front of the telly.

Did you feel as though you were on the border? I did. I had plenty of friends in high school that were from working-class and middle-/upper-class backgrounds. I never felt quite comfortable with either extreme. So where do we sit?

Yes, being on the border, being uncomfortable because we were not the same as the others. That is not to say, as you are careful not to, that we were monstrously different—we weren't of a completely different class, but even within seemingly homogenous groups there are differences that make us uncomfortable. We are defined by others because of various factors— being a girl, coming from Park Avenue, graduate of an Ivy League university and all that— but it doesn't capture the experience; that has to come from us.

So this is what we are trying to do: allow people the space to self-examine in a social context using the categories as scaffolding but then focusing on the spaces in between. It is about opening up spaces to view the ways in which we navigate as insiders/outsiders.

Why Autoethnography?

The notion of autoethnography foregrounds the multiple nature of selfhood and opens up new ways of writing about social life. A dualistic view of the autoethnographer may be better substituted with one stressing multiple, shifting identities.[16]

As we found new ways of writing into each other's lives, we were forced to stop seeing our group as an autobiography group. It no longer seemed that we were writing individually. Lesley, with objections to autobiography, and Monica, with ethnographic methods—we found our-selves discovering autoethnography. Be-cause we came to the method ourselves, we have never found the definitions com-pletely satisfying: They do not singly seem to capture what it is we think we do. Fortu-nately, autoethnography is a fluid concept, a concept that Reed-Danahay describes as:

synthesiz[ing] both a postmodern ethnogra-phy, in which the realist conventions and objective observer position of standard ethnog-raphy have been called into question, and a postmodern autobiography, in which the notion of the coherent, individual self has been similarly called into question. The term has a double sense—referring either to the ethnogra-phy of one's own group or to autobiographical writing that has ethnographic interest. Thus, either a self- (auto-) ethnography or an auto-biographical (auto-) ethnography can be sig-naled by "autoethnography"[17]

We are working primarily with the auto-biographic method and using ethno-graphic methods to analyze our autobiographical writing. We are writing as teachers, public figures in other words, with recognizable role characteristics. We are writing as teachers, but we are not writing—it would after all be impossible—merely or solely as teachers. We are writ-ing from the perspective of concrete per-sons with their own subjectivity. We are interested in our work as teachers, but we start from the subjective by starting with and privileging our autobiographical work. The emphasis on autoethnography means that this is not abstract or isolated. It is in understanding this that we found Pratt's work to be instructive.[18] Our work starts out as private, as a conversation be-tween the two of us; but in making it pub-lic, in reconstructing it to be read by others, we address both ourselves and the wider group of which we are part and yet apart. There is a form of educational discourse that leaves our experience out. In the world in which we work, this discourse is dominant. We see our autoethnographic method as a form of resistance to this. Like

Pratt, we see this resistance as not being heroic or romantic, but as an important way of complicating the categories of per-son and teacher, and in so doing compli-cating the cultural categories that are in danger of being essentialized through seemingly innocent activities such as the diversity story with which we started. In our work, we mix up the categories. By not adopting an objective outsider perspective on our work as teachers, by incorporating elements of our life experiences, we are on the most simple level telling our stories in the context of a larger culture: that of ur-ban education. We see autoethnography as a form of self-representation that compli-cates cultural norms by seeing autobiogra-phy as implicated in larger cultural processes. Our aim is similar to Driessen's, who in his discussion of the autobiogra-phy of Matoub, a popular singer from the Berber-speaking Kabyle minority in Alge-ria, views autobiography as speaking to events larger than personal lives.[19] We can use autoethnography because this method, as Russell says in speaking of autoethnogra-phy in film, focuses the fragments and hy-brid identities to "destabilize the very notion of ethnicity" and other categories by which we are defined and by which we define our-selves.[20]

It is a way to develop understanding of the subtle ways in which hegemonic prac-tices in education shape the compliance of teachers. We need autoethnography be-cause there is not a fit between the experi-ences of those marginalized with the dominant discourses that privilege objec-tivity and the dominant academic dis-course. Autoethnography is dangerous for us, because it blurs the genres; it blurs the disciplines. It draws from literary theory, anthropology and communication studies. It eschews demarcation of the disciplines in the interrogation of subjectivity and in-sists on the importance of such an interro-gation for any human activity.

It is dangerous for another reason as well. In education we are overly impressed sometimes by smart sounding words. Autoethnography already seems to be suffering from this fate. It recently came to Lesley's attention that one of her students just submitted the same autobiographical sketch that she wrote for Lesley as a freshman for her final autoethnography project as a senior in sociology. Although we do not need to pin the concept down in the fashion of a dead butterfly (thus sucking all the life out of it in order to preserve it), we do need to know what we are talking about and to be able to distinguish it from other concepts if it is to function as a means of furthering our understanding.

HOW WE COME TO KNOW

I am so angry. I am standing in front of my second-form class (eighth grade). It has been a difficult unit to teach. It is a large class, and they are being uncooperative. I cannot remember the exact remark that set it off, but I am suddenly into a tirade about the evils of racism. I get it all out of my system, the bell rings, and the class gets up to leave. One of the girls comes up to me and says, "I am sorry, Miss. We didn't mean to upset you. We didn't know you were Pakistani."

My students could never believe that I was white. They would always say, "You're not white, Ms. T., You're Spanish." These issues came up in my doctoral research but because it was a participatory ethnographic study and we didn't have to deal with the constraints and parameters that school usually constructs between students and teachers; we were able to cross boundaries throughout our various interactions.

Without any planning, both of our stories are about how our students didn't see us as white. It seems as if they did not see ethnicity as literally in terms of color, but in terms of attitudes and trustworthiness. It brings to mind what Reed-Danahay says about autoethnography: "One of the main characteristics of an autoethnographic perspective is that [of] the boundary-crosser,

and the role can be characterized as that of a dual identity."[21]

This has bothered me for 20 years. I did not have the skills as a teacher at that point to have asked her why she thought I was. Instead I was struck by how, in the face of all evidence to the contrary, the only way she could make sense of my anger was by making me a member of the ethnic group most commonly discriminated against in this London neighborhood. Instead of engaging in a conversation about this, I told the story to my friends and pondered on the nature of thought. I missed an opportunity to grow professionally because I then—as now—underestimated the importance of the personal story in developing knowledge and understanding.

This makes me think of the conversation I had with a student last fall. She is an urban teacher—a graduate student—who couldn't understand why I, as a white middle-class teacher, wanted to teach in an urban setting. She wondered what I got from it?

In this case, she couldn't get beyond her perception of you as white and what that meant to her.

I was taken aback and left speechless. She said that she would never have taught in an urban environment if she weren't from there. I in no way feel as if I am "the great white hope," and I have always hated when people tell me that I am a saint or noble. I told her that I sincerely believed that promoting social justice and helping students to feel empowered and find their voices was an important goal. This is a question that I have thought about a lot through my career as a teacher. I have often wondered what rights I had to teach in an urban setting and what I had to offer the students.

Can I navigate the boundary, crossing backward and forward? I know that I can boundary surf when I am in the middle of the experience—when I am working with kids in the classroom—but I often question myself when I begin to try to reconcile my experiences with the theories and experiences of others that I have read. Do these critical theories open spaces for discussion? Once we are aware of issues of power and inequity, what do we do with the constant inner turmoil that surfaces from this knowledge? These are the feelings and responses that many of my graduate students have when we discuss the school system and teaching democratically or for social justice. I do not want to feel hopelessness. I want to be a change agent.

WHAT IS CO/AUTOETHNOGRAPHY?

Co/autoethnography involves investigating our own selves and engaging in self-/other-analysis because teaching is a profoundly human activity and cannot be accomplished well without self-awareness in a social context. Otherwise, we are reflecting about our experiences in a vacuum. Our specific contribution lies in the interweaving of our stories: the reliance on the reflection that results from our stories being in dialogue, the role of the other in this dialogue adding validity, but also insight and analysis. Our analysis is derived from the knowledge that we bring to conversation, trying to make explicit our experiences and the theories that inform them and are informed by them; trying, in effect, to reveal the process of coming to know where this does not privilege either the subjective or the objective. The process is about heightening awareness—becoming more knowledgeable about our identity development as teachers/people, something, we are arguing, that can only be done in collaboration.

We avoid the Scylla and Charybis of pure individualism and pure social constructivism: We are finding a place for the individual in a world that is socially constructed—the world of urban education. This form of self-/other- social reflection furthers our sense of agency. The ownership of our knowledge construction fosters a feeling of empowerment.

We are focusing on aspects of our identities and how they affect the ways we see teaching in urban contexts. We accept from the beginning that identity is culturally complex, constructed, dynamic, and multifaceted. We therefore see the sharing of our stories as part of what is means to construct our identities now—together. We are, in an important sense, writing into each other's lives.[22] As we hope our stories show, we are not interpreting each other by rewriting our stories according to some preconceived format of what needs to be included (whether narrative or theoretical). This doesn't mean that we are naïve. We recognize the role of narrative structure, the force of our cultural backgrounds, and how these shape our experience and the way we tell them.

We are not inserting ourselves in a story where we have no business, or making ourselves visible as traditional researchers need to. We are insiders and outsiders: We are talking about our own experiences but they are analyzed from a number of perspectives, including our own from different vantage points, combining the defining features of autobiography with the methods of ethnography.

This method addresses some of the criticisms that have been made of autoethnography. Holt for example, has pointed to the problems of using the self as the source of data.[23] We, however, are saying that when we do this type of reflection with someone else we are able to see the selves—us as a form of data—from multiple perspectives. Our blending of stories pushes the analysis to another level. Similarly our method does not seem open to the criticism that it lends itself to self-indulgence and individualism. We freely admit that it encourages introspection, but not self-indulgent or individualistic introspection precisely because co/autethnography is a joint venture for the purpose of something outside ourselves—the betterment of our teaching practice. We are interested in how we come to know and what we know. It is essentially about knowledge construction, and this involves ourselves—necessarily.[24] Knowledge is social and individual. It has to do with who we are. The knower is important.

We argue that to write individual experience is to write social experience. We hope that as we develop this concept of autoethnography it will further be able to overcome the dualism in autoethnography—the author writing so that the reader understands the Other, or the author writing to better understand her Self—to further develop the sociocultural conception of the self.

We are looking at ourselves from the inside and outside. This is big advantage of co/autoethnography over autobiography—recognizing that there is no one single way to capture experience. The subjective is needed to make sense of human beings, but you need the other perspective (outside) to prevent solipsism, narcissism, and pernicious individualism. We play backward and forward with self and other, interpreting each within the context of teaching and learning. The private voice, the subjective voice is necessary if the distancing and objectification of education is really to be rejected. Co/autoethnography can help us with this work.

NOTES

1. Greene, M., & Griffiths, M. (2003). Feminism, philosophy, and education: Imagining public spaces. In N. Blake, P. Smeyers, R. Smith & P. Standish (Eds.), *The Blackwell guide to the philosophy of education* (p. 83). Malden, MA: Blackwell.

2. MacIntyre, A. (1981). *After Virtue*. London: Duckworth.

3. Bakhtin, M. (1981). Discourse in the novel. In M. Holquist (Ed. & Trans.; & C. Emerson, Trans.), *The dialogic imagination: Four essays by M. M. Bakhtin* (pp. 259–422). Austin, TX: University of Texas Press.

4. Stanton, A. (1996). Reconfiguring teaching and knowing in the college classroom. In N. Goldberger, J. Tarule, B. Clinchy & M. Belenky (Eds.), *Knowledge, difference and power: Essays inspired by women's ways of knowing* (p. 35). New York: Harper Collins Publisher.

5. Manke, M., & Allender, J. (2004). *A framework for self-study theory: Past and future*. Paper presented at the annual meeting of the American Educational Research Association, San Diego, CA.

6. Kincheloe, J., & Steinberg, S. (1995). Introduction. In J. Kincheloe & S. Steinberg (Eds.), *Thirteen questions: Reframing education's conversation*, (2nd Ed., pp. 1–11). New York: Peter Lang.

7. Dyson, A., & Genishi, C. (1994). *The need for story: Cultural diversity in classroom and community* (p. 5). Urbana, IL: National Council for Teachers of English.

8. Taylor, M., & Coia, L. (2001, July). Future perfect: Reflecting through personal narrative. Paper presented at the 37th conference of the United Kingdom Reading Association, Canterbury Christ Church University College.

9. Abbs, P. (1974). *Autobiography in education*. London: Heinemann Educational Books.

10. Clandinin, D. (1985, Winter). Personal practical knowledge: A study of teachers' classroom images. *Curriculum Inquiry, 15*, 361–385.

11. Pagano, J. (1991). Moral fictions: The dilemma of theory and practice. In C. Witherell & N. Noddings (Eds.), *Stories lives tell: Narrative and dialogue in education* (pp. 193–206). New York: Teachers College Press; Witherell C., & Noddings, N. (Eds.). (1991). *Stories lives tell: Narrative and dialogue in education*. New York: Teachers College Press.

12. Dyson, A., & Genishi, C. (1994). *The need for story: Cultural diversity in classroom and community* (p. 243). Urbana, IL: National Council for Teachers of English.

13. Florio-Ruane, S. (2000). *Teacher education and the cultural imagination: Autobiography, conversation, and narrative*. Mahwah, NJ: Erlbaum.

14. Coia, L., & Taylor, M. (2001). Writing in the Self: Teachers Writing Autobiographies as a Social Endeavor. In *National Reading Conference Yearbook, 2001* (pp. 142–153). Oak Creek, WI: National Reading Conference.

15. Apple, M. (1997). Consuming the other: Whiteness, education, and cheap French fries. In M. Fine, L. Weis, C. Powell, L. Wong, and L. Mun (Eds.), *Off white: Readings on race, power, and society* (p. 127). London: Routledge.

16. Reed-Danahay, D. (1997). *Auto/ethnography: Rewriting the self and the social* (p. 3). Oxford, England: Berg.

17. Reed-Danahay (1997), p. 2.

18. Pratt, M. (1999). Arts of the contact zone. In D. Bartholomae & A. Petrosky (Eds.), *Ways of reading: An anthology for writers* (pp. 582–595). Boston: St. Martin's Press.

19. Driessen, H. (1997). Lives writ large: Kabyle self-portraits and the question of identity. In D. Reed-Danahay (Ed.), *Auto/ethnography: Rewriting the self and the social* (p. 108). Oxford, England: Berg.

20. Russell, C. (2001). Autoethnography: Journeys of the self. Retrieved June 6, 2004 from http://www.haussite.net/haus.O/SCRIPT/txt2001/01/russel.HTML, p. 2.

21. Reed-Danahay (1997), p. 3.

22. Coia & Taylor (2001).

23. Holt, N. (2003). Representation, legitimation, and autoethnography: An autoethnographic writing story. *International Journal of Qualitative Methods, 2* (1). Article 2. Retrieved May 15, 2004 from http://www.ualberta.ca/~iiqm2_1/pdf/holt. pdf.

24. Code, L. (1991). What can she know? Feminist theory and the construction of knowledge. Ithaca, NY: Cornell University Press.

DEMOCRATIC URBAN EDUCATION: IMAGINING POSSIBILITIES

Patrick M. Jenlink and Karen Embry Jenlink

At the heart of education in a democratic polity must necessarily exist a commitment to maintaining and expanding democracy itself. In *Democracy and Education*, John Dewey singled out the "widening of the area of shared concerns, and the liberation of greater diversity of personal capacity" as hallmarks of democracy.[1] Relatedly, James Fraser argues that any "lesser goal will ultimately fail to maintain public support for the enterprise of public education or foster a dynamic and self-critical democratic society."[2] Urban centers define, in important ways, the identity of America, as well as many if not most countries around the world. Conceptualizing democratic urban education focuses on the importance of understanding the place of difference (racial, ethnic, linguistic, cultural, political, and social) and the role of voice in animating a democratic urban education. Valuing both difference and voice is central to schooling for active citizenship and to fostering a social creativity necessary to address the complex social issues and problems of urban education. Democratic urban education is necessary for nurturing active, critical, and resilient citizens who are able to renew society.

In this chapter, we argue the need for reconsidering urban education—democratic urban education, and relatedly, democratic schooling—beyond modernist definitions. The importance of schooling that fosters critical democratic citizens, and which contributes to a cultural democracy as a part of democratic education will be examined. The need for a social democratic pedagogy, reflecting the role of dialogue and the importance of a critical lens, will be addressed. We call for a critical examination of the normative, making the argument that cultural structures and practices be redefined and urban education be reconsidered through the lens of cultural democracy; that urban schools become "multiracial and multicultural democracies."[3]

THE URBAN CENTER IN A CHANGING SOCIETY

Historically, a continuous movement toward a greater concentration of people characterizes American society, as well as society in nation-states around the world. And with this continuous concentrating of people, there is a growing complexity of cultural and ideological systems facilitated by modern technology. Urbanicity is a phenomenon of growing population density and concentration of people in and around the city. Population shifts amidst a growing diversity in society contribute to problems of city life. Problems associated with education in large cities have been, historically, viewed as functions of immigration, industrialization, and population density. Ethnic, racial, and low socioeconomic groups, historically clustered in rural areas, are among those groups that have now become concentrated in large cities.[4] Within the urban center, there exists a broadened commonality of contextual encounters from which conflicts and confrontations arise within and across communities of difference. This increased awareness of incongruities and conflicts is further heightened by the "spatial and temporal contiguity of pluralistic elements and the requirements that individuals learn to adjust to varied and rapidly changing milieus."[5]

However, while the characteristics of urban city life have focused on population magnitude and density, what emerges today are those growing concerns surrounding the complexities of a modern technological society. Through the capabilities of mass media and technological advances in communication, urbanicity has become an important dynamic part of most people's experience. Most people within society share—either experientially or vicariously—many of the same experiences that characterize life in the large city.[6] Simply stated, urban education has become a societal concern, especially when the success of a democratic society is determined in large part by its educational system.

The education of urban children has likewise become a highly visible issue, increasingly so as racial and ethnic minorities move in, settle, and saturate the urban areas, especially large cities, and as urban minority children come of age in disproportionately large numbers.[7] As the levels of diversity within the urban centers rise, what also becomes apparent is that many of the parents of these children lack education. In other words, for culturally diverse children, in particular children from poor, immigrant families, "going to school is a daily struggle, and succeeding in school is a daunting task."[8] All too often these children, like their parents, experience hegemony, being culturally marginalized to remain at the bottom of society, never advancing. In response to this, a critical issue facing democratic urban education is that of preparing children to meet the challenges that the dominant society presents; educating children so that they can move beyond their parents' status and become actively participating, fully recognized, citizens of a democracy. Becoming active democratic citizens rests in large part on the education children receive against a backdrop of increasing racial, ethnic, and cultural diversity.

Thus, a new definition of urban education is needed, to explore the dimensions of complexity within the sociocultural context of the urban center. As Gordon explains, a definition of urban education must "encompass the cultural, economic, geographic, political, sociological, and psychological paradoxes of contradiction inherent in urbanicity."[9] The urban environment is contradictory in that it is at the same time liberating and highly inhibiting. In effect, this paradox is exemplified in urban schools, where some schools represent highly advanced systems of learning and others represent highly regressive systems. Polarities in the urban school, in relation to this paradox, are exhibited by concentrations of power and resources,[10] for example, whether programs and practices are used to advantage all students or to advantage some while disadvantaging others.

DEMOCRATIC URBAN EDUCATION

Urban education is constituted by the formal and informal systems that transmit culture, knowledge, dispositions, and skills that are artifacts of a modern city-state society. Situated in the multiple social, cultural, and political contexts of the urban city, educators engage with the concept of urban education, specifically concerned with the concentration of people in relation with resources, sources of stimulation, and conflicts found in urban society. In particular, urban educators are concerned with how these relations form interactions that give way to the greatest possible potential for influencing the social well-being of all individuals against the challenge of preparing a democratic citizenry.

Democratic urban education concerns the conjoining of individuals through communicative action, the sharing of personal voice in the "between" space that forms a public sphere, wherein individuals participate in identifying social issues and share in social action to address the issues identified, thereby breaking down the barriers of class, race, ethnicity, language, and culture. Dewey recognized the necessity of connections between personal voice and public space, understanding the inseparable role of education in a democratic society.[11] Dewey argued that a free, open, critical dialogue among the greatest diversity of groups or points of view possible, in a context of shared commitments that promote the capacity for such dialogue, provides conditions for the possibility of warranted knowledge and participatory democratic life. Such dialogues and forms of association presuppose "a large number of values in common, [so] all the members of the group must have an equable opportunity to receive and to take from others. There must be a large variety of shared undertakings and experiences."[12] Dewey believed that we must create the extension in space in society—a public space such as that of urban schools—for preparing democratic citizens, a space wherein an individual who participates has to refer his or her own action to that of others, and "to consider the action of others to give point and direction to his or her own action." Creating such a space would be "equivalent to the breaking down those barriers of class, race, and national territory, which kept men [sic] from perceiving the full import of their activity."[13] Such space can only be created by education, and would become an associated form of living, a democracy.

Importantly, Dewey stated, "the conception of education as a social process and function has no definite meaning until we define the kind of society we have in mind."[14] When we define society as democratic, socially just, caring, and socially equitable, therein we must conceive of an educational system populated by educators who embody the ideal of democracy instructed by ethics of social justice, caring, and equity. The pedagogical practice of such educators is concerned with teaching in a way that arouses vivid, reflexive, experiential responses that move students to conjoin in serious efforts to understand what democratic citizenship requires, what a socially just society actually means, what being a caring and socially tolerant human being might demand. This means that education, and therein teachers, must work toward arousing a consciousness of active, critical membership in society and a consciousness of creative, imaginative possibilities that works to transform "a society of unfilled promises" into a critical democratic society wherein all individuals enjoy the privileges and responsibilities of a democratic citizenry.[15]

Democratic urban education is concerned with creating and sustaining cultural democracy. Democratic urban education is animated by critical pedagogical practices based on an emancipatory authority, practices that enable teachers and students to use their voices, to engage in critical analysis, and to make choices regarding what interests and knowledge claims are most desirable and morally appropriate for living in democratic society—a socially just, caring, and equitable society. Equally important is the need for teachers to engage students in citizenship-building action in order to understand what social and political constraints exist, and to explore ways to remove those constraints that impact the social well-being of less fortunate individuals.

DEMOCRATIC CULTURE/CULTURAL DEMOCRACY

Democracy implies a process of participation wherein all are considered equal. However, education involves a process whereby the "immature" are brought to identify with the principles and forms of life of the "mature" members of society. Thus, the process of constructing the democratic citizen is a process not only of cultural nurturing but also of articulating principles of pedagogic and democratic socialization in individuals who are neither *tabula rasa* in cognitive or ethical terms, nor fully equipped for the exercise of their democratic rights and obligations.[16] What becomes important, then, to understanding democratic urban education, is how democratic socialization is accomplished. More specifically, the question becomes, how do we advance democratic culture in the urban school or classroom, and at the same time foster a cultural democracy that supports democratic urban education?

Democratic Culture

A democratic culture is one that embodies democracy in its philosophy and in its practice. It is therefore an idea that is considered a way of life by people in a culture—a way of associated living as Dewey explained: "Democracy is more than a form of government; it is primarily a mode of associated living, a conjoint communicated experience."[17] Culture as used here also signifies the particular ways in which a social group lives out and makes sense of its circumstances and conditions of life. In the urban school, a democratic culture is contextualized through cultural diversity, and its members seek out insights and alternatives from myriad groups and their experiences in history. For an urban student in a classroom, democratic culture begins with the recognition that diversity can only be embraced when there is a center to which all feel a positive sense of attachment. This center, an authentic sense of community, cannot be imposed, but rather is negotiated by all students and teacher(s) in a participative and discursive fashion. This center is shared by members of a democratic classroom culture and practiced in their social interactions as they engage in collective decision making on issues that affect and interest them.

Another aspect of democratic culture in the urban school and classroom is intimately connected with the question of how *social relations are structured* within class, gender, and age formations that produce forms of oppression and dependency. Importantly, democratic culture is concerned with how life in the school and classroom is a *form of social reproduction* through which different groups in either their dominant or subordinate social relations define and realize their aspirations through asymmetrical relations of power. A democratic culture works to illuminate and interrogate asymmetrical power relations, facilitating students' development of a critical awareness of these power relations while working to mediate how power is used to place individuals in social positions and shape identities. A democratic culture is viewed as a *field of struggle* in which the particular forms of knowledge and experience are central areas of conflict,[18] and wherein, importantly, the democratic philosophy and practices of the culture recognize the endemic nature of such conflict, and work to provide strategies to position students so as to not disadvantage or devalue any individual or group.

Cultural Democracy

Cultural democracy pertains to specific social structures, arrangements, and institutions that are established and animated by democratic ideas and ideals. These social structures and arrangements provide ongoing opportunities, programs, and resources for learning a democratic way of life; for creating and maintaining societal arrangements that empower members of a culture to competently practice cultural democracy, participate in collective decision making, and build institutions that manifest in their practices the culture of democracy. In its basic tenets, cultural democracy is a philosophical precept, which recognizes that the way a person communicates, relates to others, seeks support and recognition from his or her social and cultural contexts, and reasons and learns is inextricably bound within the value system and native culture and history of the individual.

As James Banks notes, there must exist in cultural democracy a cultural freedom that is akin to political freedom. Such freedom "gives individuals and groups the right to practice their ethnic and community cultures and behaviors as long as they do not conflict with the overarching values and goals of the commonwealth."[19] A cultural democracy also embraces a belief, as Dewey argued, that democracy is belief in freedom, "the basic freedom of mind and of whatever degree of freedom of action and experience is necessary to produce freedom of intelligence."[20]

For students in the urban school, cultural democracy works to transform existing social structures and arrangements, allocating resources and advancing alternative methods of stimulating the mind and working to create cultural, political, and intellectual freedom for all students. Fostering a cultural democracy in the urban school and classroom augments the traditional academic canon and offers an alternative to the normative practices and hierarchical social structures and arrangements that limit participation and select and silence individuals and groups. Urban education sees cultural democracy, in part, as the curriculum of the urban student, and therein the urban school becomes a practicum of cultural democracy where students learn to be responsible citizens by exercising citizenship in the classroom and in school and community-based situations. By experiencing cultural democracy, students are able to develop a critical awareness of power, while simultaneously learning to exercise ever-increasing power where they previously held little or no power. Teachers who construct new and alternative pedagogies for practicing cultural democracy enable students to develop an understanding of citizenship responsibility, and its preparation, by establishing the classroom as a practical setting for exploring government. Importantly, bringing cultural democracy to life within the urban classroom recognizes those inherent conflicts and contradictions that students face daily outside the school, and values the histories and experiences that every student brings to the classroom. Student learning situated through the philosophical tenets of cultural democracy, enables students to experience cultural freedom and at the same time opens possibilities for the freedom of mind, for the development of each student's mind as an intellectual means for changing the larger society.

URBAN SCHOOLS AS MULTIRACIAL, MULTICULTURAL DEMOCRACIES: IMAGINING THE POSSIBILITIES

Urban education within schools that are constructed as multiracial, multicultural democracies requires that we acknowledge that schools are simultaneously local agencies of state and national institutions. As such, urban schools—and more importantly, the educational programs and practices therein—are "informed by the social realities of the communities they serve and [are] representative of the vision of the society in which they exist."[21] Dewey is instructive in his argument that a free, open, critical dialogue among the greatest diversity of groups or points of view possible, in a context of shared commitments that promote the capacity for such dialogue, provides conditions for the possibility of warranted knowledge and participatory democratic life.[22]

Democratic urban education reflects Dewey's thoughts, and recognizes the need for a multivoiced culture premised on collective dialogues and actions. Such dialogues and forms of association presuppose, as Dewey noted, "a large number of values in common, [so] all the members of the group must have an equable opportunity to receive and to take from others. There must be a large variety of shared undertakings and experiences."[23] Importantly, urban schools must be seen and understood as multiracial and multicultural centers, characterized by their diversity and recognized for their collective human potential in a genuinely pluralistic democratic society.

The Urban School as a Multiracial Democracy

Urban education that affirms the multiracial and multiethnic diversity of the children who pass through the doors of urban schools daily, acknowledges in its philosophy and practices a democracy predicated on both intragroup and intergroup racial diversity. Increasingly, racial groups such as White, Black, Hispanic, and Asian reflect intragroup diversity, including diverse cultural, socioeconomic, and linguistic backgrounds. Equally important is the intergroup diversity that comes from mixed-race and mixed-ethnic backgrounds. Children who come from a mixed-race and mixed-ethnic background constitute the majority population within urban schools; the complexity of their overlapping cultural, ethnic, and racial backgrounds presents important considerations for constructing alternative curriculum and pedagogical practices. Teachers who seek to democratize education in the urban school find that it is of particular importance to rethink their teaching practices and design learning experiences that create a cultural freedom for all students, including the children of mixed-race and mixed-ethnic backgrounds who often find themselves in the borderlands of the educational environment. As Banks notes, to "create democratic schools for students from diverse racial, ethnic, and cultural groups," the challenge is for teachers to "examine their cultural assumptions and attitudes, their behaviors, the knowledge and paradigms on which their pedagogy is based, and the subject-matter knowledge they teach."[24]

The Urban School as a Multicultural Democracy

Democratic urban education recognizes the multicultural nature of the urban city, and relatedly of the urban school and classroom and works to create schools as multicultural democracies. The aim of a multicultural democracy is to incorporate socioeconomic and cultural diversity with political diversity, while embracing individual difference, group difference, and political community all at once.[25] The urban school or classroom as a multicultural democracy acknowledges the imperative of preparing children as democratic citizens; recognizing the importance of enabling cultural freedom while at the same time embracing democracy's basic tenet of individual liberty, human dignity, and equality. The urban school as a multicultural democracy acknowledges the pluralism of cultures reflective of the cultural origins of students. The democratic urban school is characterized by its multivoiced culture. Democratic urban education aims to shape schools and classrooms as multicultural democracies that minimize the possible existence of marginalized or socially disadvantaged classes of individuals, instead striving to incorporate the cultural and socioeconomic diversity of students in a way that benefits all students. Holding diversity as a central tenet, a multicultural democracy is concerned with who is and is not participating, why, on whose terms, and what determines the ability to participate, or not. Democratic urban education recognizes that honoring students' cultural diversity is essential to their success as active, critical, democratic citizens.

Considerations for Transforming Curriculum and Pedagogy

Conceptualizing the urban school or classroom as a multiracial, multicultural democracy, and as a public space defined by its racial diversity—intragroup and intergroup—and animated by democratic ideals, enables us to understand more clearly that the idea of curriculum is more than just an introduction of children to particular subject disciplines and pedagogical practices; curriculum serves as an introduction to a particular way of life. When that way of life is defined as a multiracial, multicultural democracy within the urban school, the curriculum must not only examine the conditions of knowledge, but should scrutinize the effects of such knowledge, questioning if it is warranted knowledge that leads to democratic participation and determining the effects of such knowledge as it is lived day-to-day.

For example, within a specified course of study in government, the notion of democratic citizenship implies that citizens act as social agents who actively participate in choosing their representatives and monitoring their performance. These

responsibilities imply not only political functions but also offer considerations for pedagogical practices, since individuals are not by nature themselves ready to participate in politics. In schools, students are educated in democratic politics in a number of ways, including normative grounding, ethical behavior, knowledge of the democratic process, and technical performance. The construction of multiracial, multiethnic, and multicultural pedagogies, which recognize intergroup and intragroup diversity, poses a central conceptual problem while at the same time offering possibility and hope for urban educators.

FINAL REFLECTIONS

Conceptualizing the urban school as a multiracial, multicultural democracy requires that social structures and arrangements encourage participation by all students while inviting cultural perspectives and diverse ideas to be illuminated and interrogated. Within new social structures, organizational and pedagogical practices may provide a reflective component for the careful construction of socially meaningful activities designed to foster democratic spaces defined by democratic discourses and practices. Students must learn to not only reflect, but to reflect on the activities that introduce them to democratic life and living together in association with each, regardless of cultural origin or beliefs. Creating the urban school as a multiracial, multicultural democracy embodies making connections to community life, recognizing that students must learn to function within and across cultural contexts as members of cultural communities. A central problem of democratic urban education is how to develop programs and activities that honor, test, and extend the student's own sense of culture and selfhood, both within and across cultures and communities of difference. A challenge of democratic urban education that works to create multiracial, multicultural democracy is to create a curriculum and activities in which urban children can "understand themselves and their relation to each other in the context of the large, impersonal forces that are at work in the world."[26] This is particularly relevant if urban education is concerned with preparing democratic citizens to mediate the conflicts and social issues posed by an increasingly diverse society whose contradictions in cultural perspectives, values, and beliefs make democracy possible.

NOTES

1. Dewey, J. (1916). *Democracy in education: An introduction to the philosophy of education* (pp. 101–102). New York: Macmillan.

2. Fraser, J. (1997). *Reading, writing, and justice: School reform as if democracy matters* (p. xi). Albany, NY: State University of New York Press.

3. Perry, T., & Fraser, J. (1993). Reconstructing schools as multiracial/multicultural democracies: Toward a theoretical perspective. In T. Perry & J. Fraser (Eds.), *Freedom's plow: Teaching in the multicultural classroom* (pp. 3–24). New York: Routledge.

4. Gordon, E. (2003). Urban education. *Teachers College Record, 105* (2), 189–207.

5. Gordon (2003), p. 191.

6. Gordon (2003), p. 190.

7. Zhou, M. (2003). Urban education: Challenges in educating culturally diverse children. *Teachers College Record, 105* (2), 208–225.

8. Zhou (2003), p. 218.

9. Gordon (2003), p. 203.

10. Gordon (2003), pp.189–207.

11. Dewey (1916), pp. 101–102.

12. Dewey (1916), p. 84.

13. Dewey (1916), p. 87.

14. Dewey (1916), p. 97.

15. Greene, M. (1998). Teaching for social justice. In W. Ayers, J. Hunt, & T. Quinn (Eds.), *Teaching for social justice: A democracy and education reader* (p. xxx). New York: Teachers College Press.

16. Torres, C. (1998). *Democracy, education, and multiculturalism: Dilemmas of citizenship in a global world* (pp. 246–247). Boulder, CO: Rowman & Littlefield Publishers.

17. Dewey (1916), p. 87.

18. Giroux, H., & McLaren, P. (1986). Teacher education and the politics of engagement: The case for democratic schooling. *Harvard Educational Review, 56* (3), 213–238.

19. Banks, J. (1997). *Educating citizens in a multicultural society* (p. 123). New York: Teachers College Press.

20. Dewey, J. (1937). Democracy and educational administration. *School and Society, 45* (1162), 459.

21. Perry & Fraser (1993), p. 16.

22. Dewey (1916).

23. Dewey (1916), p. 84.

24. Banks (1997), p. 99.

25. Parker, W. (1996). Advanced ideas about democracy: Toward a pluralist conception of citizen education. *Teacher College Record, 98* (1), 104–125.

26. Kaplan, A. (1997). Public life: A contribution to democratic education. *Journal of Curriculum Studies, 29* (4), 450.

CRITICAL THEORY, VOICE, AND URBAN EDUCATION

Jen Weiss

In her book, *The Dialectic of Freedom*, Maxine Greene asserts that "freedom ought to be conceived of as an achievement within the concreteness of lived social situations rather than as a primordial or original possession," and that "some kind of critical understanding is an important concomi-tant of the search for freedom."[1] By linking criticality with an existential search for freedom, Greene's claim suggests that any working notion of criticality must include a moral commitment on the part of institutions, scholars, and subjects themselves. It is through a dialectic of freedom that

Greene insists that all forms of democratic education be analyzed and critiqued. Any search for urban education, she believes, must also include a search for ways to shore up a commitment to change, liberation, and freedom.

Greene—like John Dewey, W.E.B. DuBois, Paolo Freire, and bell hooks—understands freedom and education dialogically (i.e., that they occur in conversation with one another). So, too, I argue that to understand urban education (and its social world) is to do so in dialogue with not only freedom but also with, and/or through, the lenses of criticality. By extending Greene's *search for freedom* to include the *search for social justice* (a term employed by community organizers), Patti Lather's dialogic concept of "critical inquiry" aims to "turn critical thought into emancipatory practice" and works to move us toward understanding why criticality must also be in dialogue with emancipation and empowerment. Whereas Lather's concept of critical inquiry "focuses on fundamental contradictions that help dispossessed people see how poorly their 'ideological frozen understandings' serve their interests,"[2] Freire's concept of praxis—action and reflection—moves us toward the important tension of "the dialogical man" who "is critical and knows that although it is within the power of human[s] to create and transform, in a concrete situation of alienation, individuals may be impaired in the use of that power."[3]

In this chapter, I aim to create an organic text—one that is spiraling, improvisational, and accumulative—and that builds upon a basic conception of criticality as multidimensional, dialogic, dialectical, and continuous (as in the Frankfurt school's concept of *negation*, which "involves the continuous criticism and reconstruction of what one thinks one knows").[4] In this sense, I use the term "criticality" not only to refer to a set of already existing critical practices, but also as a hopeful vision of how effective analysis, criticism, and politics may be combined.

Not only does this dual conception of criticality lead to a heightened political consciousness, it also provides tools, methodologies, and frameworks for getting there. As related to inquiry, criticality opens up the possibility for question-making, and then forces other questions about the questions themselves: Why? What for? And for whom? Criticality requires that we question ourselves, our biases and assumptions, our position in what Joe Kincheloe refers to as the "web of reality,"[5] as well as that which surrounds us: the institutions, ideologies, practices.

Similar to how social phenomena, as studied by Mauss, Marx, and Alinsky, "come(s) with many dimensions embedded into one comprehensive whole," criticality can be best felt in tension, among and between, and, like the human experience, "always moving and in process."[6] Without this vision of criticality as a practice and a goal, the world and the mind may appear stultifying, unconscious, unidirectional, reductionist, void of multiplicity, inquiry-free, and silent.

Being multidimensional, my notion of criticality spreads out along four themes: (1) voice/narrative, (2) praxis: action/reflection, (3) community, and (4) spaces/sites. These themes will be addressed individually and in depth later in the chapter. Central to each of them is the role language plays in shaping our world, our everyday lives, our education, and thus, enabling (or preventing) our critical consciousness.

ON METHOD

One learns to talk about the subject, but also learns to talk about the talk.[7]

—*Neil Postman*

The role of language is central to my constructed notion of criticality. In order to understand the social and epistemological dynamics that foreground this notion, the first section of this chapter is devoted to the application of discourse to urban educational policy and practice. I begin with a discussion of how educational policies and practices utilize rhetorical language and embedded ideology.

Thus, to begin, I will describe my approach to criticality through the lens of discourse theory. I want to frame discourse in two ways, the first of which can perhaps be represented by the way language is used to misrepresent or mischaracterize school policy, reform, and practice. I will call this form of discourse restricted, or *closed discourse* (i.e., "talking the talk"). I take this kind of discourse to be that which gets away with appropriating language without attending to what I consider the four basic tenets for criticality: voice, action, community, and liberatory sites/spaces. I argue that forms of this kind of discourse are rooted in positivism, where information, data, and "factual" meanings can be exacted for specific, often implicitly political, purposes—many of which cannot be explained by an appeal to the "facts" that led to the deployment of these political purposes *as practices* in the first place. As such, closed discourse is rhetorical in that although it *appears* to be objective and fact-driven, it is ultimately a platform for motivated ends, unargued assumptions, and so on—as is the case with all discourses. (The problem with closed discourses, I believe, lies in their attempt to hide these assumptions and values underneath an umbrella of "facts.") Thus, instead of enabling action, it precludes it. Although I won't focus on this in depth, it is possible that closed discourse operates in opposition to my four tenets; I believe it ultimately supports silence, inaction, individualism, and unsustainable sites/institutions. Deeper analysis may also show that discourse of this kind functions to ignore the ways that meaning is situated and perceived differently, depending on the lived experiences of subjects.

The second form of discourse I am exploring is that which I will call elastic, or

open discourse (i.e., "taking back the talk"). This form is representative of criticality enacted through language and is not insistent upon one kind of reading or interpretation, but enables and is enabled by a multitude of interpretations, assumptions, beliefs, and opinions. In poetic terms, discourse of this kind is often complicated, metaphoric, in-between, and dialogic. It uses language as its medium, but can also be expressed through silence or whispers, or, for Bakhtin, be manifested through series of "utterances" in which "no living word relates to its object in a singular way: Between the word and its object, between the word and the speaking subject, there exists an elastic environment of other alien words about the same object, the same theme."[8] It is through an understanding of open discourse that my four tenets for criticality can be best articulated. The first, voice/narrative, is necessarily framed by this understanding of discourse, and as such opens up the possibility for the other three to exist.

In addition to discourse, my notion of criticality is informed by Albert Murray's concept of the blues idiom, which follows a basic structure, but enables improvised variations on a theme. (In *The Blue Devils of Nada*,[9] Murray uses the blues idiom to explore how the creative act involves giving shape and meaning to experience, and turns it into aesthetic statement.) Recognizing that language is often too fragile to contain any continuous meaning, my articulations are aimed at approximating connections between theory, pedagogy, and practice, and can be read through the language of jazz—as riffs and improvisations. In other words, as I go forth—in this chapter, as well as in my work in urban education—I am inviting the mess that a critically oriented, postmodern exploration allows. That said, I have made every attempt to designate sections and signify when I am shifting gears and why.

The last section is devoted to elaborating on the four tenets of my notion of criticality. I have put this at the end so that it follows my epistemological constructs and the social dynamics at play.

TALKING THE TALK

Discourse of Power

Men are free to make history, but some men are much freer than others. Such freedom requires access to the means of decisions and of power by which history may now be made.[10]

—*C. Wright Mills*

Before exploring discourse in varied contexts, it is important to define it. For the purposes of this chapter, I am sticking to the broadest possible definition. Thus, I take discourse to mean "that which separates us."[11] While I am interested in discourse about schools, that which separates us also includes discourses that arise *within* schools. Or, as Foucault contends in his work on prisons, "the decisions and regulations which are among its constitutive elements, its means of functioning, along with its strategies, its cover discourses and ruses, ruses which are not ultimately played by any particular person, but which are none the less lived, and assure the permanence and functioning of the institution."[12] Such thinking offers a powerful tool for understanding what happens in schools on a daily basis, and also offers a grammar for articulating the way in which discourses interact with the operations of power. My notion of criticality situates power to its relationship to social epistemology. In order to deploy this notion, we must first understand how power interacts with other social systems, such as discourse, "that construct our consciousness."[13]

Locating power in language is not to ignore the social structures that reproduce inequity that cuts across race, class, gender, and sexuality. Nor am I asserting that the only vehicle for change is through new discourses, a new language. Indeed, Sonia

Nieto reminds us that while "discrimination [is] based on perceptions of superiority," is it also part of "the structure of schools, the curriculum, the education most teachers receive, and the interactions among teachers, students, and the community."[14] However, this chapter explores how discourse functions to affirm master narratives (ideologies), discriminates, and ignores the assumptions and biases that go toward keeping those without power from gaining access to voice, collective action, and sites of criticality.

By foregrounding my notion of criticality in a discussion of discourse, I am also listening to Lisa Delpit, who in *Other People's Children* recognizes that while "power plays a critical role in our society and in our educational system, the answers lie not in a proliferation of new reform programs but in some basic understandings of who we are and how we are connected to and disconnected from one another."[15] The understanding she is seeking, I argue, is located in language. Without it, we participate in a silenced dialogue that affects some more than others. Delpit writes, "If you are not already a participant in the culture of power, being told explicitly the rules of that culture makes acquiring power easier."[16] If our concern as critical thinkers is a commitment to social justice, we cannot be blind participators in a silenced dialogue. My goal at the outset, then, is to explore how we communicate, obscure, and complicate what we mean by what we say—and in how we come to understand who we are and who others are.

Rhetoric of Neutrality

Just as schools and school reforms are historically constructed, so too is the discourse that frames and evaluates them. An example of the pervasiveness of *closed discourse* in educational settings can be found in the rhetoric that consistently asserts that schools are neutral, that the failure of progressive curriculum reforms was pedagogical, and that federal and state-mandated high-stakes testing accurately quantifies student "intelligence." Although study after study refutes these assertions, schools are the battleground and rhetoric is the weapon of choice.

If we conclude that schools are not only not neutral, but instead "serve as powerful agents in the economic and cultural reproduction of class relations," then we must also conclude that the knowledge produced (pedagogy, curriculum, discourse, ideology) in these institution is no more neutral. As Michael Apple contends, "academic performance, differentiation, and stratification [is] based on relatively unexamined presuppositions of what is to be construed as valuable knowledge."[17] And the decision to produce and reproduce a hidden curriculum that is, in fact, functionally harmful to students who cannot decode the ways that schools prejudge and judge them is rooted in an ideology that does not believe that students should be included in the organization of content of the curriculum. As Lisa Delpit makes clear, schools enforce a hidden curriculum aimed at reinforcing schools as neutral spaces when, in fact, they are enacting cultural rules. She writes, "schools often see themselves and are seen by the larger society as the arbitrators of what is proper, correct, and decent."[18] Therein lies the crux of neutrality based on a hidden curriculum—a curriculum that masks an ideological, corporate agenda—for it is "uniquely suited to maintain the ideology hegemony of the most powerful classes in this society."[19]

For our discussion of discourse, it is worth pointing out that in order for the rhetoric of neutrality to survive outside of the scientific community it must also be endorsed by other institutions. Merleau-Ponty reminds us that any curriculum instantiated in urban public schools "makes present a certain absence," or conceals more than it reveals. Urban high schools, in particular, seem to make use of disciplinary and surveillance techniques while the absence of intellectual rigor, or assessment

strategies geared toward student success, remains untouched by policy makers. The tension that arises when the still-dominant ideology that says schools are neutral spaces, coupled with a critical awareness of how the acquisition of linguistic and cultural competencies mimic (and solidify) class inequities, is a tension that challenges how rhetoric becomes ideology.

Ideology as Discourse

By illuminating the historical, epistemological, and ideological assumptions of curriculum reforms whose notions of "official knowledge" often occluded (weren't informed by) poor, working-class, and nonwhite voices, theorists have long applied criticality to pedagogic discourse. But before we can do that, we must understand the ways in which voices have been excluded from dominant discourse. "Critical social inquirers," we are reminded, "are interested in questioning the dominant assumptions."[20] A critical awareness of the master narratives historically embedded within curriculum development also recognizes the absence of voices, perspectives, and multiple narratives. For Michael Apple, the discourse of curriculum development "viewed the social role of the curriculum as that of developing a high degree of normative and cognitive consensus among the elements of society" and generally served conservative interests of homogeneity and social control.[21]

In *The Culture of Education*,[22] Jerome Bruner notes how schools and their discourses often deny multiplicity and culture. He writes: "Schools can never be considered as culturally 'free standing.' What it teaches, what modes of thought and what 'speech registers' it actually cultivates in its pupils, cannot be isolated from how the school is situated in the lives and cultures of its students." So that, although classrooms still hold the promise of radical spaces, their implicit cultural values are "never far removed from considerations of social class, gender, and the prerogatives of social power."[23] The absence, then, of multiple narratives inside the discourse of curriculum development or pedagogy tends to subscribe to already-written policy and practices of that reinforce social inequity. These inequities are exercised implicitly through policies: tracking, high-stakes testing, and discipline; and practices: depoliticized teacher education programs and top-down curriculum structures.

As an example of how closed discourse in schools constructs social identities, it is useful to note how labels (e.g., "troublemaker," "teacher's pet") come to stigmatize students socially. The way these social identities come to be defined by language, or the discourse of disability (e.g., "slow learners," "special ed," etc.), follows the rules of social norms. "Since schooling is one of life's earliest institutional involvements outside the family, it is not surprising that it plays a critical role in the shaping of Self."[24] It is easy to see how schools help in transferring socially constructed ideology onto self-identity.

Exposing the Language of Ideology

Anthropologist James C. Scott calls the form of resistance in which "oppressed groups challenge those in power" the "hidden transcript." As a metaphor, the hidden transcript is especially apt for unearthing the discursive, dialectical, and pedagogical significance of this rhetoric.[25] For this, I will take the concept of "competency" that infiltrates not only the way we talk about school reforms, but also the way we think about them.

What, after all, do we mean by competency, whose meanings are excluded, and what is the epistemological significance of the meaning as it translates into school policy? To begin, any notion of competency must be recognized as operating within contested terrain. Therefore, to come to understand competency as a static, monolithic, value-free, and measur-

able quality is to reduce its complexity to a mere scientific construction—and is bad science, at that. From a position of criticality, however, the contested nature of competence is not simply assumed to be problematic, but its condensed, contradictory controversies—rich in significance and meaning—make it a site for deep engagements in philosophy and practice. At a physical level, the very word "competence" calls up my experiences as both student and educator. As a critical inquirer, I am alerted to its underlying discursive qualities—how its ideology necessitates a culturally relevant discussion of value. As a researcher, I want to know how its role and function connect with (or do not connect with) the performance of individual and collective student-subjects (bodies). I may come to ask, as Joshua Fishman does when he wonders, "What does the country lose when it loses individuals who are comfortable with themselves, cultures that are authentic to themselves, the capacity to pursue sensitivity and some kind of recognition that one has a purpose in life."[26]

Seeing competency and my response to it as multifaceted helps to connect us back to the role of language in education, both as a means for expressing first-order values and as a kind of attic of stored beliefs and values. Paying close attention to the variegated roles of language at many different theoretical levels allows us to see not only how language itself is laden with constructed meanings, but also how, once placed into action within institutions (or hidden away in the mechanics of curricula), it signifies different things in different contexts—culturally, linguistically, symbolically, or otherwise. In this context, Harding reminds us of the familiar fact that cultures have different models, metaphors, and narratives about nature and inquiry. Her concept of borderlands epistemology shares Gramsci's splintered concept of "common sense," which says that a culture's ways of seeing and believing (commonly held conceptions of the world) are transmitted by discourse.[27] Their views on culture and knowledge lead us toward a better understanding of how power or hegemony relates to how knowledge is produced. In Gramsci's terms, hegemony is maintained through language, and although "different cultures (difference itself) can lead us to ask different questions about nature and social relations because of their distinctive locations in the natural world," Harding acknowledges that "power differences in this context become very important."[28] While it serves to ask: What results when the dominant culture's value system is prescribed to measure everyone's competencies, Gramsci's insistence that "hegemony exploits language and the worldview it contains"[29] locates the problem in the very language of school reform. A word like "competence" tends to indict everyone who uses it.

Knowing what we know about the student populations of urban public high schools—that although they serve predominantly low-income youth of color, they increasingly underserve their academic and/or economic interests—the questions I have raised above are not simply exercises in discursive (critical) theory, but are essential if we are to measure the competence of our schools, our students, ourselves. They are even more essential if we are to combat those who suggest that competence is quantifiable.

TAKING BACK THE TALK

Returning to Language and Experience

To return to my understanding of open discourse, I take as my starting point that language and experience are inextricable. Thus, to speak with authority about the neutrality of schools or the competence of students is to have experienced some version of this and to ignore the experience of others. Because the experience of education is social, any notion of open discourse

is an acknowledgment of my experience in relation to others.

Phenomenology calls us back to lived experience by asserting the relationship of language to experience. Indeed, "human experience is only possible because we have language."[30] It is, as Gadamer insists, "the fundamental mode of operation of our being-in-the-world."[31] In other words, language is how we come to absorb and understand what we observe. It also "occupies the space between experience and the word"[32] and is therefore always contested. Any analysis of lived experience requires a rendering in the form of language, be it narrative, symbolic, or otherwise. And it is in trying to decipher meaning inside of experience and language that we confront deconstruction as a tool for analyzing rhetorical patterns and ideologies that show up in educational discourse.

Deconstructing Ideology

To use language to counter injustice is to disable it from one context (take it back) and use it as a tool for critical enlightenment. For Gramsci, as discussed by Villanueva in *Bootstraps*, "language is epistemic; the episteme contains ideology."[33] In his book, *Understanding Curriculum as Phenomenological and Deconstructed Text*, William Pinar makes use of Derrida's definition of deconstruction—"to lay bare the construction of discourse," to argue its usefulness in "showing how [such a] discursive system functions, including what it excludes or denies."[34] To expose the ideology of education, we must attack its language, thereby employing the critical concept of deconstruction.

Because we understand the social world of education through our experiences within it, deconstructing its codes from within and outside its setting is both political and necessary for any related critical project. And before one can navigate through the present state of urban education, one must acknowledge how ideology in the context of education has served to exclude voices that were not part of the dominant discourse. For Merleau-Ponty, "what this ultimately means is that the proper essence of the visible is to have a layer of invisibility in the strict sense, which it makes present as certain absence."[35] As suggested earlier, deconstructing educational discourse provides a portal through which to return, to hear whose voices are excluded. By ignoring the absence (silence) of these voices, I believe we risk absenting the project of criticality from educational practices and policies altogether.

Culture: Spaces of Meaning

As cultural theorists have sought to expose, culture mediates experience and language. It signifies a constructed and situated space that enables meaning. Although, as my discussion of it aims to reveal, one's cultural status can be a determining factor in gaining access to educational equity, there is an important tension that arises when culture is added to the equation. From this vantage point, structuralist inquiry gives us a framework and conceptual tool with which to expose not only the codes of *closed discourse*, but also the ways in which pedagogic practice is linked to structurally determined power relations and class inequities.

In his classic study of code theory, Basil Bernstein seeks to "relate shifts in classification and framing to the evolution of the social division of labor."[36] Unlike scientific thinking, "a thinking which looks on from above,"[37] the nature of Bernstein's project is to "build from the bottom to the top"[38] and help link educational processes to larger structural conditions. His work, and that of Bourdieu, can shed light on how schools produce and reproduce social inequities through curricular discourse as well as through culture. These developments helped spur a number of social reproduction theorists to closely examine what is now referred to as "the hidden curriculum"

embedded within the social structure, culture, and pedagogic practice of schools.

For Bourdieu, culture acts as a mitigating force for hegemonic control within schools; it is also directly related to how educational codes function in relation to social structures. For Bourdieu, "schools are a web of symbolic institutions that do not overtly impose docility and oppression, but reproduce existing power relations more subtly through the production and distribution of a dominant culture that tacitly confirms what it means to be educated."[39] This sentiment echoes Bruner's assessment that "school curricula and classroom 'climates' always reflect inarticulate cultural values as well as explicit plans."[40]

By continuing Bruner's work in *The Culture of Education*, the work of Paul Willis, Lisa Delpit, Michelle Fine, and others attuned to the relevance culture and cultural production helps extend the work of Bernstein and Bourdieu, moving it from structuralist inquiry to theories of human agency and resistance. As historian Robin Kelley points out in *Race Rebels*, "some of the most dynamic struggles take place outside—indeed, sometimes in spite of—established organizations and institutions."[41] Thus, whereas the hidden curriculum was working to maintain the ideology and hegemony of dominant society, cultural production/resistance theorists suggested that it was also producing cultures of resistance and transgression. By attending to the "transformative natures of cultures," Willis believes that we, as producers of counterhegemonic elements, can empower students "not only to think like theorists, but to act like activists."[42] Although Pepi Leistyna is quick to point out that what "many educators fail to realize is that even the most progressive and concerned pedagogue can't empower kids,[43] this important and necessary tension shifted critical theory so that it engaged pedagogy toward the idea of "educat[ing] as a practice of freedom."[44]

CHANGING TUNES
Notions of Criticality:
Voice, Action, Community, Site

As Metaphor for Voice

Writing so as not to die—or perhaps even speaking so as not to die—is a task undoubtedly as old as the word.[45]

—*Foucault*

For this section, it is important to note that I have attempted to do much of the preparatory theoretical work in my earlier discussion of discourse. Therefore, I will move forward describing my tenet of "voice" as an element of criticality that grows out of my understanding of discourse—and is in search of what I have called *open discourse.*

To avoid reducing issues in urban education to either social or economic phenomena, I've come to understand this tenet of my notion of criticality as a metaphor. By this I mean "a point where meaning is produced out of non-meaning."[46] In this sense, to voice is to speak concretely or metaphorically about feelings that may be vague, but are perceived as truths (by one or many). Employing the metaphor of *gaining voice, voicing, naming*, it can perhaps best be understood as the opposite of what it is not: silence. Michelle Fine uses *silencing* as a metaphor "for the structural, ideological, and practical organization of comprehensive high schools."[47] For me, voice represents the necessary tension between open and closed discourses, or narratives.

I link voice with narrative because it connects us back to my discussion of discourse. The narratives of schools can be represented as a closed discourse filled with the rhetoric of neutrality, the hidden construction of curriculum, or the unexplored terrain of "official knowledge." By contrast, open discourse must be situated, or contextualized, in order to lead to action. In "Analyzing Master Narratives and Counter Stories," Sarah Carney suggests

that voices [narratives], like the social dynamics of economics, skin color, and gender, "can be understood only in contexts—they cannot, and do not, stand alone."[48] Because I am concerned with how voice leads to action, I recognize the importance, like Foucault, of how "the archaeology of silence"[49] fails to challenge the status quo. In so doing, this tenet speaks directly to policy and practices that underprivilege or ignore the narratives and voices of those being impacted.

Lisa Delpit insists in *The Skin that We Speak*, "language plays an equally pivotal role in determining who we are."[50] For criticality to succeed or lead us toward action it must, like a metaphor, illuminate the way language can signify that which is not obvious, but opaque, hidden, or excluded. In a critical pedagogical context, enabling voice is not an end in itself. It is a searching. As a search for voice, then, this tenet seeks transformation, and as *conscientization*, it honors unheard, oppressed, or subjugated voices as part of the process of dialogue-making. As such, it has two functions: (1) countering silence, and (2) situating voices dialogically and creatively.

In my earlier discussion, I exposed the way that deconstruction can be used as a tool to disempower closed discourse of its rhetorical and ideological weight, to "take it back." As a means of open discourse, countering silence is best expressed as a method of resistance, a form of human agency. One way of countering silence is to put language back in the hands of those against whom it's been used. In her essay, "The Transformation of Silence into Language and Action," Audre Lorde asserts that that which is most important "must be spoken, made verbal and shared."[51] Although enabling voice, like empowering youth, cannot be done for a student, but must be chosen, we might think about how pedagogical methods can be used to counter silence by opening dialogue that leads to making choices (action). In the case of engaging students in (dominant) language acquisition, teacher

Judith Baker "implanted the idea that learning a formal grammar [is] a choice the student makes; not a choice a teacher makes for a student."[52]

Open discourse not only allows for silence to speak, but creates spaces in which it can do so creatively—through the language of poetry, the rhythm of jazz, the movement of dance. As Bruner reminds us, in order for voice to be meaningful for others, and therefore counter silence, it [narrative] "requires work on our part—reading it, making it, analyzing, understanding its craft, sensing its uses, discussing it."[53] As a creative tool, poetry can be both a means of expression and a work-in-progress, chiseled for meaning making. In her study of student-poets in a large, comprehensive high school, Jennifer McCormick suggests that "poetry opens a space for social commentary . . . It enables the writer to turn around and say "that's not me" without repudiating her feelings."[54] Indeed, for it to be made an instrument toward action, voice must do many things and go through many stages, and must at last be dialogic. It must brave exposure "even at the risk of having it bruised or misunderstood."[55]

As Praxis: Thought and Action

Action cannot take place before one envisions a more desirable state of affairs.[56]

—J. Kincheloe

By insisting, in this section, to focus on action through perception, I am attempting to create a foundation for concrete action that is informed by theory and research. I do not mean to sidestep the importance of necessary structural change. For now, however, I am concerned with exploring enacted knowledge—in the hope that the embodiment of praxis may lead us closer to some idea of enacted revolution.

Because my notion of criticality speaks to social change through action, attention must be paid to how "perception and action are fundamentally inseparable in lived cognition." To forget that the mixture of perception and action operating in schools, in classrooms, and at policy tables is multidimensional and loaded with significance is a blatant denial of democratic education. Situated as we are by our unique experiences cannot deny the experience of others if, as critical educators, we are in search of real freedom. As such, our task requires keen attunement to the notion of perception as it relates to action. I am using "action" here in a very general sense, as in the ability for one to act in her own best interests in any given situation—be they political, intellectual, or other. The key to understanding perception, for Varela, is to study "how the perceiver guides his actions in local situations."[57] So, whereas schools provide shared perceptive experiences that may lead to action, they can and often do deny not only the importance of perception as a shared experience, but also the role perception plays in action.

Yet educators fail every day to enact decisions (through policy and practice) that are even remotely sensitive (perceptive) to the ways in which the contested spaces of schools help determine a student's motivation (action) for "success." Although much research contends that children from disadvantaged economic backgrounds consistently underperform on standardized tests,[58] our society's perception of why this is so is still rooted in unjust and racist ideologies around intelligence. Little if any regard is paid to how school policy undermines student achievement. In Linda McNeil's study of standardized testing reform, she notices the student impact of these reforms: "Many students who pass the reading tests are in fact non-readers"; as well the devastating consequences for individuals caught in the grip of reform: "Teachers are advised not to waste their time on the children who scored far below—those would never pass."[59]

In *Subtractive Schooling*, Angela Valenzuela connects school reform policies to student perception: "Schooling that convinces students that no one cares about them and their education sends the message that students themselves should not care because to conform to a U.S. school is to risk losing one's cultural identity."[60] Due to the hierarchical nature of how our schools are structured, those with more power in any given situation are neglectful of anyone's perception other than their own. Perhaps those most lacking self-reflexivity are those seated furthest from our students and our communities: administrators, politicians and policy makers. Given the economic vulnerability of our country's public school children, our inability to perceive, or our lack of tactfulness, costs a price that students often pay and continue to pay.

This is where Du Bois's notion of "double-consciousness"—the ability to see oneself (and one's actions) through the perception of others—can enable a kind of perception that is attuned to our own situatedness, as well as that of our students. Although his scholarship focused mostly on the legacy of historical racism and oppression on the everyday experiences (actions) of African Americans, employing double-consciousness in our educational institutions in which, many argue, everyone feels oppressed not only illuminates how oppression affects perception of self and others, but can also determine the course of our action. For students like John Devine's "hallwalker" or Michelle Fine's "dropout," actions of resistance are highly attuned, often rightly, to implicit policies (ideologies) that require students to conform to someone else's standards for success. If, as critical educators, we are to reach the students we're losing, whose "very presence in the halls poses the question of whether, like Benjamin's *flaneurs*, then we must also be able to recognize how "they serve as oppositional figures, cultural critics themselves of an unjust and failing system."[61] Indeed, as their resistance continues to tell us, unless we are equally sophisticated perceivers of their behavior, we will lose them altogether.

When a student confronts a teacher by stating that "schools are for white kids," he is honoring his perception of things as they seem. Just as his meaning demands a critical hermeneutics that asks not just what he means, but how he means, this student's perception must call forth our ability to perceive: our *readiness-to-action*. For a teacher who hears this comment and thinks it's directed at her would be ignoring the responsibility to be, in Van Manen's words, "pedagogically tactful." Again, Varela's enactive approach is particularly useful: "In the enactive approach reality is not a given: it is perceiver-dependent, not because the perceiver constructs it as he or she pleases, but because what counts as a relevant world is inseparable from the structure of the perceiver.[62] Thus, for the student who believes that school isn't for him, this approach helps lead the teacher away from her own reality (for a minute), but rather guides her back toward her student with the goal of understanding of how he comes to perceive his reality, and what they, together, can do by way of action. This, of course, is a powerful moment for an educator because it initiates a pause, a moment, an opening through which to teach, and at best, contains the possibility for dialogue. For Freire, this is the ultimate opening: "To speak true word is to transform the world. If it is in speaking their word that people, by naming the world, transform it, dialogue imposes itself as the way by which they achieve significance as human beings. Dialogue is thus an existential necessity."[63]

And nothing is more effective at breaking down dialogue, and therefore action, across differences than our lack of "reflexive awareness."[64] Because any urban population cuts across racial, gender, and sexuality, those involved in pedagogy and policy would do well to be mindful of Deborah Meier's words: "We listen with a more critical ear to what we say to parents, wondering how we would hear it as parents ourselves and about how children may interpret the relationship as well."[65] By acknowledging how our and others' perceptions inscribe space and determine action, we can be more fully aware of how and what to communicate to our students.

As Community

A community of practice is an intrinsic condition for the existence of knowledge.[66]

—Lave and Wenger

Although I will not elaborate at length on this tenet, and will instead highlight a few of its key features, it is necessary to think of community not as some whole, but featuring individuals whose disparate selves may or may not define themselves as a community. Indeed, communities, and their meanings, cannot be essentialized into one unifying category. Lave and Wenger define a community as one of practice that is formed by "a set of relations among persons, activity, and world, over time and in relation with other tangential and overlapping communities of practice."[67] Although individuals make up communities, it is through practice, Lave and Wenger argue, that they become "learners." And, like my concept of open discourse, "a learning curriculum unfolds in opportunities for engagement in practice. It is not specified as a set of dictates for proper practice."[68]As I have explored elsewhere in this chapter, it's important to remember how heavily one's individual and social identity is informed by one's schooling; and how indifferent the school environment is to one's community or culture. The space between voice and community, in this sense, is where individual identity is constructed, tested, challenged, asserted. With this in mind, voice plays a central part in forming, maintaining, and understanding communities. "The importance of narrative is critical to understanding communities."[69] Therefore, creating a community of practice that seeks to develop and interact with a "learner's" entire Self cannot ig-

nore the role that community must play in policy and pedagogy. And yet, as educators, we forget this often and relinquish too easily to what Van Manen calls "the greatest enemy of pedagogic tactfulness"—"the hegemony for control."[70]

While research contends that creating curriculum where students engage in narratives or in knowledge producing has long-term sociocognitive gains, it is the first to be compromised within the hierarchical nature of schools. Although the closed discourse of educational policy and teacher preparation insists that the absence of curriculum that reinforces community is merely pragmatic (neutral), one cannot help but wonder if this pragmatism is aimed at keeping students from collectively voicing and/or gathering in protest. Indeed, as Kincheloe writes, "the struggle against the destruction of personal authority necessitates a struggle against the general authoritarian trends of the industrialized, corporate state. Individuals cannot protect their personal autonomy unless they regain their voice."[71]

Last, as a tenet of my notion of criticality, community must allow for both individuality and dissent. That individuality as "complex personhood" enriches and strengthens one's sense of agency within community means that the "stories people tell about themselves, about their troubles, about their social worlds, and about their society's problems are entangled and weave between what is immediately available as a story and what their imaginations are reaching toward."[72] At best, a community's tolerance for the "complex personhood" of its members can lead to action.

This brings us to the idea of dissent within community and in opposition to societal injustices—both of which motivate dialogue and action. "That conflict among groups of people is inherently and fundamentally bad" is a contradiction that community organizers, inspired by Freire and others, have long recognized. For no coalition seeking change through action is built on agreement alone. Open discourse in which long-ignored voices are equally heard does not strive to eliminate conflict, but rather acknowledges it as an aspect of critical consciousness and as a "basic driving force[] in society."[73]

As Sites/Spaces

As Benjamin (1969) remarked on the Parisian arcades of the nineteenth century, the whole environment seemed designed to induce nirvana rather than critical awareness.[74]

—*David Harvey*

As the quotation above suggests, a necessary tension arises within the contradiction of spaces. Similar to the way dissent informs community, this tension found in space can serve to create sites of criticality in opposition to uncritical institutions. Before going further, it is important to note that my notions of criticality within the dialectical whole of urban education situate after-school education and community inside its paradigm. With that in mind, I have come to understand this tenet as attending to both structural/physical issues and emotional/psychological needs of criticality.

Although I won't explore either in depth, this section is primarily concerned with the latter. In positing after-school programs as sites for criticality, I am suggesting that sites/spaces formed either in opposition to, or even ignorant of, the practices and policies employed by dominant institutions of education are at their best when they counter silence, employ critical inquiry/methodology, and support what Pratt refers to as "contact zones— where cultures meet, clash and grapple with each other."[75] Here, we reconnect with the importance of voice, for although we know "it is presumptuous to claim to possess the ability to bequeath the power of expression," the challenge for radical educators remains: to create "dialogical spaces where lived experiences and worldviews can be heard."[76] By honoring voice

and narrative as essential elements to criticality, we move in the direction of making spaces where unheard voices can be heard. In this way, sites become part of the political project of education, and thus gain political ground among students by openly engaging their opinions and relying on their participation. Whereas sites of this kind can be carved out in the spaces of classrooms, after-school programs, and community-based organizations, the question becomes whether they can be sustained and how to ensure the ongoing participation of students.

Ultimately, policy that forces schools to limit student participation in favor of test preparation cannot be concerned with creating sustainable sites of criticality. And if, as Deborah Meier contends, "we have not been cognizant of the ways in which basic inclinations of human learning turn out to be ill-matched to the agenda of the modern secular schools,"[77] we must begin to turn our critical attention to finding ways of fostering and sustaining student participation—without reproducing the very practices and policies of the dominant institutions we have attempted to improve.

NOTES

1. Greene, M. (1988). *The dialectic of freedom.* New York: Teachers College Press.

2. Lather, P. (1991). *Getting smart: Feminist research and pedagogy with/in the postmodern.* New York: Routledge.

3. Freire, P. (1970). *Pedagogy of the oppressed.* New York: Continuum.

4. Kincheloe, J. (2001). *Getting beyond the facts: Teaching social studies/social science in the twenty-first century* (2nd ed). New York: Peter Lang.

5. Kincheloe (2001).

6. Feagin, J., & Vera, H. (2001). *Liberation sociology.* Boulder, CO: Westview Press.

7. Kincheloe (2001).

8. Merleau-Ponty, M. (1964). *The primacy of perception* (C. Dallery & J. Edie, Trans.). Evanston, IL: Northwestern University Press.

9. Murray, A. (1997). *The blue devils of Nada: A contemporary American approach to aesthetic statement.* New York: Vintage.

10. Feagin & Vera (2001).

11. Pinar, W. (1992). Introduction: Curriculum as text. In W. Pinar & W. Reynolds (Eds.), *Understanding curriculum as phenomenological and deconstructed text* (pp. 1–13). New York: Teachers College Press.

12. Foucault, M. (1980). *Power/knowledge* (C. Gordon, L. Marshall, J. Mepham, & K. Soper, Trans.). New York: Pantheon Books.

13. Kincheloe (2001).

14. Nieto, S. (2000). *Affirming diversity: The sociopolitical context of multicultural education.* New York: Addison Wesley Longman, Inc.

15. Delpit, L. (1995). *Other people's children: Cultural conflict in the classroom.* New York: The New Press.

16. Delpit (1995).

17. Apple, M. (1991). *Ideology and curriculum.* New York: Routledge.

18. Delpit (1995).

19. Apple (1991).

20. Kincheloe (2001).

21. Apple (1991).

22. Bruner, J. (1996). *The culture of education.* Cambridge, MA: Harvard University Press.

23. Bruner (1996).

24. Bruner (1996).

25. Scott, J. (1990). *Domination and the arts of resistance.* New Haven, CT: Yale University Press.

26. Fishman, J. (2002). Language and identity. In L. Delpit & J. Kilgour Dowdy (Eds.), *The skin that we speak: Thoughts on language and culture in the classroom* (pp. 1–18). New York: The New Press.

27. Villanueva, V. (1993). *Bootstraps: From an American academic of color.* Urbana, IL: National Council of Teachers of English.

28. Harding, S. (1998). *Is science multicultural?* Indianapolis: University of Indiana Press.

29. Villanueva (1993).

30. Van Manen, M. (1990). *Researching lived experience.* Ontario: The University of Western Ontario.

31. Madison, G. (1988). *The hermeneutics of postmodernity: Figures and themes.* Bloomington, IN: Indiana University Press.

32. Pinar (1992).

33. Villanueva (1993).

34. Pinar (1992).

35. Merleau-Ponty, M. (1964). *The primacy of perception* (C. Dallery & J. Edie, Trans.). Evanston, IL: Northwestern University Press.

36. Sadovnik, A. (1995). Basil Bernstein's theory of pedagogic practice: A structuralist approach. In A. Sadovnik (Ed.), *Knowledge & pedagogy: The sociology of Basil Bernstein* (pp. 3–31). Norwood, NJ: Ablex Publishing Corp.

37. Merleau-Ponty (1964).

38. Sadovnik (1995).

39. Aronowitz, S., & Giroux, H. (1993). *Education still under siege.* Westport, CT: Bergin & Garvey.

40. Bruner (1996).

41. Kelley, R. (1996). *Racer rebels: Culture, politics, and the black working class.* New York: The Free Press.

42. Aronowitz & Giroux (1993).

43. Leistyna, P. (2003). Facing oppression. In J. Saltman & D. Gabbard (Eds.), *Education as enforcement: The militarization and corporation of schools.* New York: RoutledgeFalmer.

44. hooks, b. (1994). *Teaching to transgress: Education as the practice of freedom.* New York: Routledge.

45. Foucault, M. (1977). *Language, counter-memory, practice* (D. Bouchard & S. Simon, Trans.). Ithaca, NY: Cornell University Press.

46. Pinar (1992).

47. Fine, M. (1991). *Framing dropouts: Notes on the politics of an urban public high school.* New York: SUNY.

48. Carney, S. (2001). Analyzing master narratives and counter stories in legal settings: Cases of maternal failure-to-protect. *International Journal of Critical Psychology* 4, Special issue.

49. Pinar (1992).

50. Delpit, L. (2002). Introduction. In L. Delpit & J. Kilgour Dowdy (Eds.), *The skin that we speak: Thoughts on language and culture in the classroom* (pp. 1–18). New York: The New Press.

51. Lorde, A. (1984). *Sister outsider.* New York: The Crossing Press.

52. Baker, J. (1992). Trilingualism. In L. Delpit & J. Kilgour Dowdy (Eds.), *The skin that we speak: Thoughts on language and culture in the classroom* (pp. 49–62). New York: The New Press.

53. Bruner (1996).

54. McCormick, J. (2000). Aesthetic safety zones: Surveillance and sanctuary in poetry by young women. In L. Weis & M. Fine (Eds.), *Construction sites* (pp. 1180–1195). New York: Teachers College Press.

55. Lorde (1984).

56. Kincheloe (2001).

57. Varela, F. (1992). *Ethical know-how: Action, wisdom, and cognition.* Stanford, CA: Stanford University Press.

58. Wilson, W. (1996). *When work disappears: The world of the new urban poor.* New York: Vintage.

59. McNeil, L. (2000). *Contradictions of school reform: Educational costs of standardized testing.* New York: Routledge.

60. Valenzuela, A. (1999). *Subtractive schooling: U.S.-Mexican youth and the politics of caring.* New York: SUNY.

61. Devine, J. (1996). *Maximum security.* Chicago: The University of Chicago Press.

62. Varela (1992).

63. Freire (1970).

64. Kincheloe (2001).

65. Meier, D. (2000). *The power of their ideas.* New York: Teachers College Press.

66. Lave, J. & Wenger, E. (1991). *Situated learning: Legitimate peripheral participation.* New York: Cambridge University Press.

67. Lave & Wenger (1991).

68. Lave & Wenger (1991).

69. Leistyna (2003).

70. Pinar (1992).

71. Kincheloe (2001).

72. Bruner (1996).

73. Apple (1991).

74. Harvey, D. (2000). *Spaces of hope* (p. 168). Berkeley: University of California.

75. Pratt, M. (1991). *Arts of the contact zone.* New York: MLA.

76. Leistyna (2003).

77. Meier (2000).

THE NEED FOR FREE PLAY IN NATURAL SETTINGS

William Crain

You might remember a childhood that included riding bikes around the neighborhood, observing insects and flowers in a vacant lot, and resting under a large shade tree. Such a childhood is rare in the United States today. A nationwide survey reports that when 6- to 12-year-olds aren't in school, they spend an average of only about 35 minutes a week in unstructured outdoor play.[1] Children do, to be sure, get outdoors more often than this; they average about three hours per week in organized sports such as Little League. But the meager amount of time spent in free outdoor play is striking.

This chapter is specifically concerned about the lack of free play in green or natural settings—settings such as parks, backyards, vacant lots, or community green spaces. A small but growing body of research suggests that spontaneous play and exploration in these settings is vital for the child's cognitive and emotional development. Much of this research, moreover, has been conducted in urban areas. Before turning to this research, however, we might consider some reasons why children's play in natural settings is so minimal today.

WHY IS OUTDOOR PLAY SO RARE?

Part of the explanation is today's educational climate. Under pressure to raise academic standards and standardized test scores, schools are eliminating recess, making school days longer, and requiring a good deal of homework. As a result, children have less time for outdoor play, including time in parks and natural settings.

As Moore points out, another factor is the appeal of the electronic media. Instead of spending free time outdoors, children stay indoors to watch television, play video games, and surf the Internet.[2] Children are, to be sure, still interested in nature, but Nabhan and St. Antoine found that even in the rural Sonora Desert along the U.S./Mexico border, most of the 8- to 14-year-olds in their sample learned more about animals from TV and movies than from direct experience outdoors. Most of the youngsters had never spent a half-hour alone in a wild place or had collected natural treasures such as feathers, rocks, and bones from their desert surroundings.[3]

Children today are also kept indoors because of parents' fears. Moore observes that many parents in the United States, Australia, and the United Kingdom are so worried about automobile accidents and kidnappers that they refuse to allow their children to travel to parks and natural settings on their own.[4] Hillman and Adams found that between 1971 and 1990, British parents became only half as likely to allow their 7- to 10-year-olds to travel to any such leisure places by themselves.[5]

And even when children do wander about outdoors, their opportunities to explore natural settings are diminished by the relentless forces of modernization and real estate development. In suburban and rural areas, bulldozers clear the woods and fields to make way for new housing developments, office buildings, and indoor malls. In urban settings, construction crews remove the weedy waysides, vacant lots, and overgrown gardens children once loved to explore. In their place, developers create buildings with manicured lawns, cement paths, and neat flowerbeds. These pristine arrangements meet modern adult tastes, but informal surveys suggest that when adults look back on their childhoods, they fondly remember the rough-strewn and wilder places, which offered elements of mystique and mystery.[6]

NATURE'S BENEFITS

During most of the twentieth century, only a handful of writers discussed the importance of nature in children's lives. Cobb, Montessori, Pearce, and Wilson are among the pioneers and their writings are primarily speculative.[7] But since the 1970s, empirical research on the topic has grown, and it points to several specific ways in which play and exploration in natural settings might help children's cognitive and emotional development.

Focused Attention

In a trailblazing study conducted between 1971 and 1973, Hart investigated the outdoor behavior of the 4- to 12-year-olds in a rural New England town.[8] Hart interviewed the children, observed their free behavior, and followed them about as they led him to their favorite places. As he had expected, the children engaged in lots of active play—running, jumping, and climbing—and they loved to hike in their natural surroundings. But Hart was surprised by the patience and care with which the children simply observed nature. For example, many children spent long stretches of time quietly watching the fish, frogs, salamanders, and insects in the ponds and brooks. As a result of their observations, the children came to know the water species in remarkable detail.

Adopting a similar methodology in the 1970s, Moore found that the 9- to 12-year-olds in urban sections of England liked to go to the parks and undeveloped, weedy areas to collect things such as rocks and acorns and to simply observe wildlife.[9] With rapt attention, they looked at the birds, flowers, bees, lizards, ladybugs, and other small animals.

Nature's effects on children's perceptions became very clear during a project Moore initiated in the city of Berkeley, California, in 1972. Moore and community members transformed an all-blacktop, 1½-acre elementary schoolyard into a new playground that included a half-acre nature area with ponds, streams, and wooded areas. Five years later, Moore interviewed the fourth-graders who had experienced the change, and their comments speak of a sensory awakening. The children said that whereas the all-blacktop yard was "boring," the nature area was a wonderful place just to sit or to "go on little trips and look at things." They intently observed the subtle and varied life forms in their new surroundings.[10]

The studies by Hart and Moore included some quantitative measures, but they primarily provided descriptive accounts of children's behavior. Beginning in the 1990s, several investigators have used more statistical methods to assess the effects of green spaces on children's concentration. Much of this research has focused on children living in the low-income housing projects in Chicago. The green settings in the projects are not particularly lush—they typically consist of grass and a few trees and plants—but the investigators have examined the possibility that exposure to even modest amounts of greenery, compared to concrete and asphalt, will improve children's attention spans.

In making this prediction, the authors often refer to Kaplan's Attention Restoration Theory.[11] According to Kaplan, much of our attention requires effort, as when we do homework or stay alert while driving a car. This "directed attention" produces fatigue. But another kind of attention, which is stimulated by natural settings, is involuntary, effortless, and restful, and it actually restores our ability to concentrate on other tasks.

In one study, Faber Taylor, Kuo, and Sullivan hypothesized that the Chicago children who had views of green settings from their apartment windows would demonstrate greater performance on measures of concentration, such as the ability to repeat a series of numbers backward. Examining their hypothesis among 7- to 12-year-olds, the authors found strong support for it among the girls; the girls who could see greenery from their apartment windows had higher concentration scores than the girls who could not. But the study did not find this difference among the boys. The authors noted that boys, compared to girls, are generally allowed to roam farther from home and spend less time playing in the

green places immediately adjacent to their buildings. So perhaps it's the opportunity to view green places in which one can *play*—and not green views per se—that restores the capacity to concentrate.[12] Another study by the same authors provided indirect support for this possibility.[13]

Testing the same general hypothesis—that green places rejuvenate the mind and restore the ability to concentrate—Wells studied 7- to 12-year-olds whose families changed housing in Chicago's low-income projects.[14] Some of the children moved to apartments with significantly greater vegetation outside, and these children had the highest ability to concentrate on tasks, as assessed by parent ratings, several months after the move.

Today, attention problems are very common. In fact, 3 to 7 percent of U.S. school children have attention difficulties sufficiently severe to warrant the diagnosis of attention-deficit/hyperactivity disorder (ADHD).[15] It is likely that today's high-tech environment contributes to the problem. Electronic devices such as channel changers and video games invite the child to constantly change or accelerate stimulation. In addition, the absence of play in green spaces may be a factor, and it would be helpful to know if natural settings can have a therapeutic affect among children who have been diagnosed with ADHD. Kuo, Faber Taylor, and Sullivan administered nationwide parent surveys and found that such children's attention did seem to improve during the hour or so after playing in outdoor green settings, such as parks, green backyards, or community green spaces. The parents reported that their children were better able to stay focused on unappealing tasks, listen to directions, and resist distractions. The benefits, moreover, were greater than those following play in "built" outdoor environments, such as parking lots or downtown areas, or after indoor play. The findings were consistent among children between 5 and 18 years of age and for both genders. The findings also held true whether the children lived in cities, suburbs, or rural areas, and whether their families were financially poor or well-off.[16]

The investigators not only surveyed parents of children with ADHD diagnoses through questionnaires, but also examined the effects of play in green settings through parent focus groups. Here, too, the parents generally reported positive outcomes. One mother, who had begun taking her son to a local park 30 minutes before school because they "had some time to kill," said, "I noticed his attitude toward going to school has been better . . . I think it's because spending time in the park is pleasurable, peaceful, quiet, calming."[17]

Overall, the research in the Chicago housing projects and the nationwide surveys suggest that nature has substantial power to improve attention. Additional support comes from studies being carried out by Grahn and his colleagues in Sweden.[18] They are finding that nursery school children who play for long periods in green outdoor settings, compared to those who lack these opportunities, receive higher teacher ratings on the overall ability to concentrate on tasks.

Creativity
Building Activities
In rural New England in the early 1970s, Hart was struck by children's creative building projects. The children built tree houses in the sturdy maple and apple trees; they constructed model towns and highways in the loose dirt beneath the trees; and they built hideouts and shelters under the canopies formed by large bushes and trees. In the late-1980s, Sobel documented extensive shelter-building among 8- to 11-year-old children in Devon, England, and Carriacou in the West Indies.[19] Researchers have not systematically investigated these outdoor construction activities in urban settings, but Kirby did find that 4-year-olds loved to play in the shelters they found under the bushes and trees on a grassy Seattle playground.[20] Hart

(personal communication, 2003) suggests that children today still sometimes build shelters, and do so even in urban surroundings, but they often need to see an adult model the beginning of the process.

Art and Poetry
Nature inspires a great deal of children's art and poetry. Parents and teachers know how commonly the sun, trees, clouds, birds, and grass appear in children's drawings. For more than 30 years, my undergraduates at the City College of New York have obtained 6- to 9-year-olds' spontaneous drawings as part of a course project, and the vast majority of the drawings include elements of nature.

Most adults are less familiar with children's poetry, but nature's inspiration seems very powerful. Two classic anthologies contain poems by children who generally seem to have had rich experience with natural settings. Rogers's 1979 anthology, *Those First Affections*,[21] contains 220 poems by children, many in England, between the ages of 2 and 8 years, and I estimate that 85 percent deal with some aspect of the natural world. Chukovsky's 1925 classic, *From Two to Five*,[22] contains 32 poems composed by Russian children between 2 and 6 years of age, and I would classify 66 percent as dealing with some aspect of nature.

Information on inner-city poems comes from works by two poets, Heard and Koch, who taught poetry in New York City schools.[23] Their volumes include 22 and 74 poems, respectively, by children between the ages of 5 and 8 (excluding the poems that Koch might have influenced). I estimate that 56 percent of the poems in Heard's book and 74 percent of the poems in Koch's volume speak about the natural world. Thus, nature inspires a good deal of urban children's poetry, too. Still, the urban children's poems are often a bit sparser than those in the Rogers and Chukovsky books, and they probably would have been enriched by greater contact with natural settings.

Make-Believe Play

One of the most creative activities of early childhood is make-believe play. Young children use sticks, paper clips, dolls, and other props to invent elaborate dramas. Roughly half of the children between the ages of 2 and 7 years even create imaginary companions.[24] Make-believe play generally reaches its peak between the years of about 2 and 7,[25] and it promotes development in several ways. Through it, children begin using symbols (as when the child uses a stick to represent a horse) and engage in imaginative thought. Children who engage in a good deal of make-believe play at the age of 4 years also do better at many reading and writing tasks in kindergarten and first grade.[26]

Two studies indicate that make-believe play is enhanced by natural settings. In Kirby's study of 4-year-olds on a grassy schoolyard, the children engaged in more make-believe play in the two natural shelters than in a built structure.[27] Apparently, the cozy settings and the leaves, soil, and other natural elements stirred the children's imaginations.

In the second study, Taylor, Wiley, Kuo, and Sullivan examined the amount of play among 3- to 12-year-olds in Chicago housing projects. The authors reported that twice as much play—especially creative pretend play—occurred in the areas with grass and trees, compared to the more barren areas.[28]

In this second study, the investigators also found that the children had greater access to adults in the green areas. More grownups were present to watch out for the children, and the children often talked to the adults. This study, along with others in the Chicago housing projects,[29] suggests that common green spaces bring together people of all ages and promote neighborly feelings. The presence of watchful adults is extremely important today, when parents are afraid to let children outdoors alone. Common green spaces can restore the old-style neighborhoods in which the grown-ups look after all the children, not just their own, giving the children opportunities for safe outdoor play.

Peace and Connection

Earlier, I described how natural settings prompt quiet observation. But nature also creates states of quiet and calm that differ from alert observation. In rural New England, Hart found that the children spent considerable time simply resting in a seemingly introspective manner.[30] At the edge of a pond, a child would often stare into the water in a daydream-like state, aimlessly dabbling dirt or water. The child seemed to feel a fluid connection between herself and the water—a oneness with the world.

Nature's quieting effect is striking in Moore's study of the Berkeley schoolyard.[31] When the yard was entirely asphalt, there was constant fighting and bickering. But in the new nature area, the children played together more harmoniously, and they were much quieter. This was true of both the boys and the girls, who had previously played apart. In the nature area, they commonly joined together in relaxed conversation. The children's comments made it sound as if the nature area was like a mother who brings children into her soothing arms: "It makes me feel at home." "Being alone doesn't bother me now." "It's just a good-natured place." "It seems like one big family there." As Moore said, the nature area gave the children a new sense of belonging.[32]

Childhood feelings of calm and connection also are prominent in Chawla's study of twentieth century adult autobiographies.[33] Those writers who remembered intense experiences with nature as children highlighted feelings of calm and rootedness in the world—feelings that lasted a lifetime. As Chawla noted, an eloquent description of such feelings is found in the autobiography of Howard Thurman,[34] an African-American minister whose ethical philosophy strongly influenced that of Martin Luther King, Jr.

Thurman, who grew up in Daytona, Florida, in the early 1900s, frequently felt lonely as a boy. When he was seven years old, his father died, and his mother was distant. But Thurman felt comforted by the night:

There was something about the night that seemed to cover my spirit like a gentle blanket . . . [At times] I could hear the night think, and feel the night feel. This comforted me and I found myself wishing the night would hurry and come.[35]

Thurman felt a similar relationship with an old oak tree in his yard; leaning against it gave him a feeling of peace and strength. But his most intense experiences came at the seashore. When he walked along the shore at night, and the sea was very still:

I had the sense that all things, the sand, the sea, the stars, the night, and I were one lung through which all life breathed. Not only was I aware of a vast rhythm enveloping all, but I was part of it and it was part of me.[36]

Even the storms seemed to embrace the young Thurman, and his experiences of unity with nature as a boy gave him

a certain overriding immunity against much of the pain with which I would have to deal in the years ahead when the ocean was only a memory. The sense held: I felt rooted in life, in nature, in existence.[37]

Do urban children search for similar experiences—of peace and connection to the larger web of life—in their highly developed environments? There are hints that they might.

Coles shares the thoughts of a 12-year-old girl who was among the first African Americans in Boston to be bused to a formerly all-white school:

I guess I'm doin' all right . . . A lot of time, though, I wish I could walk out of that school and find myself a place where there are no whites, no black folk, no people of any kind! I mean, a place where I'd be able to sit still and get my head together; a place where I could walk and walk, and I'd be walking on grass, not cement, with glass and garbage around; a place where there'd be the sky and the sun,

and then the moon and all those stars. At night, sometimes, when I get feeling real low, I'll climb up the stairs to our roof, and I'll look at the sky, and I'll say, hello there, you moon and all your babies—stars! I'm being silly, I know, but up there, I feel I can stop and think about what's happening to me—it's the only place I can, the only place.[38]

In a similar vein, Kotlowitz opens his 1991 book on inner-city Chicago children with 9-year-old Pharoah's experience on top of a weedy cliff, beside the railroad tracks:

He was lost in his thoughts, thoughts so private and fanciful that he would have had trouble articulating them to others. He didn't want to leave this place, the sweet smell of wildflowers and the diving sparrow. There was a certain tranquility here, a peacefulness that extended into the horizon like the straight, silvery rails.[39]

These children yearn for nature's peace.

IS CHILDHOOD A SENSITIVE PERIOD FOR CONTACT WITH NATURE?

Cobb, Pearce, and Wilson have speculated that there may be a sensitive or critical period during which children are most highly motivated to seek contact with nature. The possibility is inspired by the study of imprinting in nonhuman animals. Goslings, ducklings, lambs, and many other species form strong bonds with parent figures, but the young establish such bonds only during a fairly fixed, early period of life. During this sensitive period, the young desperately seek out a parent to follow. The young of many species also learn songs, food preferences, and other habits during early sensitive periods.[40]

Analogously, some scientists and writers believe we may find sensitive periods in human development as well. In his "biophilia" theory, Wilson proposes that humans develop an affinity to nature during the childhood years. During our long evolutionary history, Wilson notes, a sensitivity to plants and wildlife must have conferred survival value on our species, and it was probably adaptive to develop this sensitivity early in life.[41]

Wilson speculates that the sensitive period for an attachment to nature lasts until adolescence, as does Pearce.[42] Cobb suggested that the sensitive period is narrower, from about 6 to 12 years of age.[43] The available evidence does not permit firm conclusions, but it suggests that children have a particularly strong interest in nature from toddlerhood up to the age of 11 or 12.[44]

The toddler's fascination with nature is quite apparent. Toddlers examine sand at a beach, for example, for hours at a time, and are enthralled by the sight of an animal such as a dog or a bird. Indeed, young children are so captivated by animals that they commonly dream about them. Three- to-five-year-olds dream about animals more than any other subject. Animal dreams are nearly as frequent between the ages of 5 and 7, and after this begin to decline.[45] But other activities, such as shelter building in natural settings, are still prominent between the ages of 8 and 11 years. After this, as children enter adolescence, they generally become less interested in the natural world and more interested in fitting into the social world of peers.[46]

If early adolescence marks the end of a true critical or sensitive period, it will be very difficult for people to develop any feeling for nature after this point. At present, though, we cannot say that there is any hard and fast age limit.

CONCLUSION AND FUTURE DIRECTIONS

I have discussed three ways in which free play in natural settings promotes healthy development: It fosters powers of attention, stimulates creativity, and provides a sense of peace and belonging. Although it's too early to say whether childhood is a sensitive period for developing feelings for nature, children seem to have an especially keen interest in it. Thus, it would be prudent to increase their time in natural settings if we want them to develop the above traits.

As educators and psychologists continue to explore the benefits of contact with nature, they need to give more attention to aggressive behavior. The children's comments on the Berkeley schoolyard suggest that natural settings can be so calming that they reduce fighting, but we need more precise data.

Educators are beginning to capitalize on children's keen interest in nature to motivate academic learning. The students in the Berkeley elementary school enthusiastically engaged in science projects based on their observations in the new nature area.[47] According to Russell, inner-city children will also become enthusiastic about science if we just take them on 10- or 15-minute field trips to examine the plants, trees, insects, and other life forms on their ordinary school grounds.[48] Lieberman and Hoody report that several schools (including urban schools) boosted academic achievement by asking students to do projects based on their first-hand investigations of natural settings.[49] But even though academic learning is obviously important, it shouldn't overshadow the development of the personal traits (e.g., patient observation and creativity) that unstructured play and exploration in green settings promote.

Although I have focused on free play and exploration in natural settings, many educators have tried to bring children into contact with nature through gardening. Gardening undoubtedly benefits children in many emotional and cognitive ways. However, gardening is a more structured activity, in which humans manipulate nature according to their own designs. As Hart, Moore, Francis, and others observe, it's important to make sure children also have contact with what Moore calls "rough ground"—vacant lots, weedy waysides, dirt roads, unpruned trees, and tall grass.[50] Adults prefer neater and more manicured surroundings, but a degree of wildness provides greater diversity and unpredictability. One cannot be sure, for example, what plants, birds, or insects will inhabit a vacant lot, and children therefore have opportunities to make original discoveries in it. Wilder places also allow children to develop feelings for nature as it really is, not as humans have designed it.

In most city parks, landscapers and designers overstructure play areas with built equipment such as prefabricated tree houses. Hart and Moore, in contrast, emphasize the need for "loose parts" such as fallen branches, discarded wood, or cardboard boxes.[51] Loose parts may clutter a setting, but they enable children to do their own building.

An ideal project, Moore says, would be to "rip up some asphalt, surround it with a sturdy enclosure, add some fertile soil and leave it alone . . . Make it a spot for kids and wildlife to colonize together."[52] Few modern adults would have patience with such a project, but ideas for maintaining a degree of wildness in parks and neighborhoods are found in the publications of the Learning through Landscapes Trust.[53]

To increase children's contact with nature, we must address parents' concerns about safety. Playground leaders and other adults can play an essential role by simply keeping an eye on the children. We commonly assume that we must teach or direct children, but just our watchful presence is often most helpful, for it enables children to explore the world on their own.[54]

Many of us may never become involved in children's play activities. But we can still help immensely by defending the natural places in our communities against relentless real estate development.[55] If we can protect natural settings, children will benefit enormously—to say nothing of other species.

NOTES

1. Hofferth, S., & Sandberg, J. (2001). Changes in American children's time, 1981–1997. In T. Owens and S. Hofferth (Eds.), Chil-dren at the millennium: Where have we come from, where are we going. New York: Elsevier Science.

2. Moore, R. (1997). The need for nature: A childhood right. Social Justice, 24 (3), 203–220. See also Cordes, C., Miller, E., Almon, J., and the Alliance for Childhood. (2004). High-tech childhood. Encounter: Education for Meaning and Social Justice, 17 (4), 21–27.

3. Nabhan, G., & St. Antoine, S. (1993). The loss of floral and faunal story: The extinction of experience. In S. Kellert & E. Wilson (Eds.), The biophilia hypothesis (pp. 229–250). Washington, DC: Island Press.

4. Moore (1997).

5. Hillman, M., & Adams, J. (1992). Children's freedom and safety. Children's Environments, 9 (2), 10–22.

6. Francis, M. (1995). Childhood's garden: Memory and meaning of gardens. Children's Environments, 12 (2), 183–191.

7. Cobb, E. (1959). The ecology of imagination in childhood. Daedalus, 88 (3), 537–548; Montessori, M. (1964). The Montessori method (A. George, Trans.). New York: Shocken. (Original work published in 1909.); Pearce, J. (1977). Magical child. New York: Dutton; Wilson, E. (1993). Biophilia and the conservation ethic. In S. Kellert & E. Wilson (Eds.), The biophilia hypothesis (pp. 31–41). Washington, DC: Island Press.

8. Hart, R. (1979). Children's experience of place. New York: Irvington.

9. Moore, R. (1986). Childhood's domain. London: Croom Helm.

10. Moore, R. (1989). Before and after asphalt: Diversity as an ecological measure of quality in children's outdoor environments. In M. Bloch & A. Pellegrini (Eds.), The ecological context of children's play (p. 202). Norwood, NJ: Ablex.

11. Kaplan, S. (1995). The restorative benefits of nature: Toward an integrative framework. Journal of Environmental Psychology, 15, 169–182.

12. Faber Taylor, A., Kuo, F., & Sullivan, W. (2002). Views of nature and self-discipline: Evidence from inner city children. Journal of Environmental Psychology, 22, 49–63.

13. Faber Taylor, A., Kuo, F., & Sullivan, W. (2001). Coping with ADD: The surprising connection to green play settings. Environment and Behavior, 33 (1), 54–77.

14. Wells, N. (2002). At home with nature: Effects of "greenness" on children's cognitive functioning. Environment and Behavior, 32 (6), 775–796.

15. Faber Taylor, Kuo, & Sullivan (2001).

16. Faber Taylor, Kuo, & Sullivan (2001); also Kuo, F. & Faber Taylor, A. (2004). A potential natural treatment for attention-deficit/hyperactivity disorder: Evidence from a national study. *American Journal of Public Health, 94* (9), 1580–1586.

17. Faber Taylor, Kuo, & Sullivan (2001), p. 66.

18. Grahn, P., Martensson, F., Lindblad, B., Nilsson, P., & Ekman, A. (1997). Ute på dagis [Outdoors at daycare]. *Stud och land* [City and country], (145). Hassleholm, Sweden: Norra Skane Offset.

19. Sobel, D. (1993). *Children's special places.* Tucson, AZ: Zephyr.

20. Kirby, M. (1989). Nature as refuge in children's environments. *Children's Environments Quarterly, 6* (1), 7–12.

21. Rogers, T. (1979). *Those first affections: An anthology of poems composed between the ages of two and eight.* London: Routledge & Kegan Paul.

22. Chukovsky, K. (1968). *From two to five.* Berkeley, CA: University of California Press. (Original work published in 1925.)

23. Heard, G. (1989). *For the good of the earth and sun.* Portsmouth, NH: Heinemann; Koch, K. (1970). *Wishes, lies, and dreams.* New York: Perennial Library.

24. Taylor, M. (1999). *Imaginary companions and the children who create them.* New York: Oxford University Press; Taylor, M., Carslon, S., Maring, B., Gerow, L., & Charley, C. (2004). The characteristics and correlates of fantasy in school-aged children: Imaginary companions, impersonation, and social understanding. *Developmental Psychology, 40* (6), 1173–1187.

25. Crain, W. (2003). *Reclaiming childhood: Letting children be children in our achievement-oriented society.* New York: Holt.

26. Berke, L. (2001). *Awakening children's minds* (p. 123). Oxford, UK: Oxford University Press.

27. Kirby (1989).

28. Taylor, A., Wiley, A., Kuo, F., & Sullivan, W. (1998). Growing up in the inner city: Green spaces as places to grow. *Environment and Behavior, 30* (1), 3–28.

29. Kuo, F., & Sullivan, W. (1997). Where does community grow? The social context created by nature in urban public housing. *Environment and Behavior, 29* (4), 468–494; Kuo, F., Sullivan, W., Coley, R., & Brunson, L. (1998). Fertile ground for community: Inner-city neighborhood common spaces. *American Journal of Community Psychology, 26* (6), 823–851.

30. Hart (1979, pp. 171, 205.

31. Moore (1989), pp. 201–203.

32. Moore, R., & Wong, H. (1997). *Natural learning* (p. 182). Berkeley, CA: MIG Communications.

33. Chawla, L. (1990). Ecstatic places. *Children's Environments Quarterly, 7* (4), 18–23.

34. Thurman, H. (1979). *With head and heart.* New York: Harcourt Brace Jovanovich.

35. Thurman (1979), p. 7.

36. Thurman (1979), p. 226.

37. Thurman (1979), p. 8.

38. Coles, R. (1993). Introduction. In G. Nabhan & S. Trimble (Eds.), *The geography of childhood: Why children need wild places* (pp. xxiii–xxiv). Boston: Beacon Press.

39. Kotlowitz, A. (1991). *There are no children here* (p. 7). New York: Anchor.

40. Crain, W. (2005). *Theories of development: Concepts and applications* (5th ed., Chap. 3). Upper Saddle River, NJ: Prentice Hall.

41. Wilson (1993).

42. Pearce (1977).

43. Cobb (1959).

44. Crain (2003), pp. 47–51.

45. Foulkes, D. (1999). *Children's dreaming and the development of consciousness.* Cambridge, MA: Harvard University Press; see also Crain (2003), pp. 49–51.

46. Sobel (1979), p. 211.

47. Moore & Wong (1997).

48. Russell, H. (2001). *Ten-minute field trips* (3rd ed.). Arlington, VA: National Science Teachers Press.

49. Lieberman, G., & Hoody, L. (1998). *Closing the achievement gap: Using the environment as an integrated context for learning.* Poway, CA: Science Wizards.

50. Hart (1979), p. 242; Francis (1986).

51. Hart (1979); Moore (1986).

52. Moore (1986), p. 243.

53. Learning through Landscapes Trust, Third floor, Southside Offices, the Law Court, Winchester, Hampshire SO23 9DL, UK. See especially Adams, E. *Learning through Landscapes: Final report (1990).* For additional ideas on designing nature areas, see Hart, R. (1997). *Children's participation.* New York: UNICEF.

54. Crain (2003), pp. 27–29, 63.

55. For examples of the sweeping effects of real estate development, see Louv, R. (2005). *Last child in the woods: Saving our children from nature-deficit disorder,* p. 30. Chapel Hill, NC: Algonquin Books.

ANY GIVEN SATURDAY

David Reed

The daily commute to my work location, as an administrator for the Gilbert Public School District in Gilbert, Arizona, is generally no different from the commute of any other district employee. Most educators arrive at school between 6:30 and 7:30 AM Monday through Friday to begin their daily routine within one of the fastest-growing districts in one of the fastest-growing communities in the United States. What is unique to my administrative position is that my trek to school each week includes six mornings, and has for nearly nine school years. As administrator of the district Saturday School Programs, I make the trip to Greenfield Junior High School thirty Saturdays each school year.

The Gilbert Saturday School Program has grown from a single program with a staff of 2, serving 5 secondary schools and, on average, 25 students per week to a program that includes 5 subprograms, serves 12 secondary schools, supports more than 150 students each week, and employs 7 and 10 part-time and regular staff. All staff members are paid on an hourly stipend basis, extended beyond their regular district contract. The program, initially a 100 percent financial loss, now generates enough income to offset program costs and has even helped to fund expansion of its own services. Once a program considered purely negative encompassing remediation and discipline, the Saturday School now entails a wide array of programs that focus on remediation, credit recovery, discipline, and ethical behavior reinforcement.

The Gilbert Public School District has doubled in size in the past 10 years and is expected to nearly double again in the next 10. Currently consisting of 36 schools, including 23 elementary, 6 junior high, 4 high school, and 3 alternative campuses, the student population has grown from ten thousand students in 1994 to a current student population of more than ten thousand high school students and a total of over thirty-five thousand students in K–12. Now consisting of over 18,000 students in grades 6–12, any of these students may be joining me, assigned or voluntarily, during the scheduled four hours on any given Saturday!

THE SATURDAY RESPONSIBILITY CENTER

The Saturday responsibility center, or "breakfast club" as it is affectionately known, was the foundation of the Saturday school programs and the main motivator to the development of the program as it appears today. "Saturday detention," as it was labeled in its original state back in 1996, when I first started monitoring the program as detention teacher, was developed to assist secondary school administrators with an out-of-school discipline option in lieu of an in-school or out-of-school suspension. The primary infractions that earn students an assignment to Saturday morning with the breakfast club generally center on responsibility; thus the reasoning for the transition of the label to "responsibility center." The disciplinary infractions might include excessive tardiness, ditching, or for junior high students, excessive lack of responsibility with regard to the PRIDE (Personal Responsibility in Daily Effort) program. The PRIDE program is a responsibility program that requires each student to carry a planner during the school day. The student will get a "yes" stamp from each teacher in their schedule when they have their materials, their homework finished, and they arrive to class and are in their seat on time. If any one of these areas of responsibility is not completed, the student receives a "no" stamp and is scheduled for ninth hour that day. This extra period of the day is a 30-minute study hall period after the regular school day. If a student is given five or more ninth hours in a month, they are scheduled for a trip to the Saturday Responsibility Center. Within the standard progressive discipline system, the responsibility center might be utilized somewhere between an assignment between in-school options such as community service, lunch detention, or in-school suspension and other out-of-school options that are administered during the regular school week.

The responsibility center is a four-hour study hall that meets from 8:00 AM to 12:00 noon. All Gilbert School District polices and procedures are enforced, including the district dress code. No hats, headphones, sleeping, or talking. Students must sit up, with feet on the floor, and remain engaged in a learning activity, or at least appear to be. If the student fails to bring something to do, the student can call for a delivery or books for reading are provided. Students who arrive late are signed in at the time they arrive. If a student is signed in late they are reminded that there is no guarantee that their time will count and it is up to the assigning school administrator to give the student full credit for the time or not. It is always amazing to me that whenever a student is late I will quip at them, "let me guess, you're here today for tardiness." That accusation usually gets a smile from the student and to my knowledge, to date, I haven't been wrong yet. The students are given one warning about sleeping, dress code, or other behavior infractions. If nonconforming behavior continues, they are reassigned to an isolated seat in the cafeteria. If that or other inappropriate behavior continues beyond this point, they are referred to the Saturday School Administrator, me. At that point, I have a personal

conference with the student. The student is allowed to return to the responsibility center if I am convinced that they are sincere in the efforts to follow the teacher's direction and the program rules. Referral to my level does not occur regularly, as after nine years of supervising the program, word has gotten out and the students know my level of tolerance, especially on Saturdays. I may have to deal with fewer than ten students in this manner during the entire school year. It was related to me recently that some high school students are choosing to do in-school suspension for the day rather than attend the Saturday responsibility center. The majority of the time, I am successful in returning the student to the center and no further action is required. Some will just admit they can't make it because of lack of sleep the night before. I explain to them that, as the Saturday Administrator, I do not control their destiny. If they do not complete the requirements of their assigned Saturday discipline, I just refer them back to their assigning administrator and that administrator will exercise whatever follow-up discipline they deem fit, depending on the circumstance surrounding the referral and the student's past discipline record.

The responsibility center will average 40 students per weekend and, in recent years, has been utilized more by the middle schools. The number from each school varies and is usually dependent on where the responsibility center option fits on the administration's progressive discipline ladder. Some schools have more internal discipline measures than others. One administrator will use the responsibility center at the first infraction and others will use it as the second or third.

SATURDAY REMEDIATION AND CREDIT RECOVERY

The Saturday credit recovery classes were the next programs to be implemented in the Saturday School. Started in the fall of 1997 as a service to the junior high students who were enrolled in the district secondary alternative school, the program quickly expanded to the three traditional district junior highs. The program grew quickly and initially supported more than 100 students in the spring of 1998. Since the district was already paying staff on Saturday for detention, it made sense to provide students the opportunity to recover credit on Saturday as well. The key to this idea was that we would charge tuition for the service just like the junior high credit recovery summer school. The funds generated from the tuition for the Saturday classes enabled the Saturday programs to be in the black the first year. A program that had been costing the district a few thousand dollars a year to provide was supporting itself to the point of expansion. Students were generally referred to the alternative school due to excessive credit deficiency, and because Gilbert School District policy requires students to pass all core academics to be promoted to high school, the need for these ongoing credit recovery courses had become obvious.[1] The credit recovery program enabled junior high students, especially eighth-graders, the opportunity to be remediated and recover their credit deficiencies before summer school. This allowed them to graduate and attend promotion with their fellow classmates or reduce summer school needs if they continued to fail additional course during their spring eighth-grade semester. The other interesting result is that students who take advantage of the Saturday credit recovery classes in the spring generally perform better in their regular classes as well. During the spring of 2003, all the seventh-grade students who failed first semester math and enrolled in the spring 2003 Saturday credit recovery classes passed their seventh-grade second semester math class. As a group, the students averaged nearly a 1.5-point increase in their overall math grade point average. Interestingly, these same

students, who were not required to attend summer school 2003 because they made up first semester and passed their spring math class, lost a whole grade point in their average gain by the end of their fall 2003 eighth-grade semester. Is this a plug for ongoing remediation? It is certainly something to be looked at carefully as the Saturday program grows. The seventh-grade group from spring 2004 has been tracked since they completed their Saturday school session. A total of 43 seventh-grade students attended spring 2004 math classes. Of that group, 42 were issued passing grades in their spring 2004 regular seventh-grade, second-semester math classes. Of this group, 38 attended a regular Gilbert public junior high first-semester eighth grade and received a final semester grade in the fall of 2004. Of those 38 students, 37 passed their eighth-grade, first-semester math classes. To further emphasize the possible affects of ongoing and immediate remediation, this group's math grade point average increased from zero in the fall of their seventh-grade year to a 1.8 at the conclusion of their fall eighth-grade school year. These students will continue to be tracked through the second semester of eighth grade. Tracking will include review of their scores on the standardized AIMS (Arizona Instrument to Measure Standards) test, scheduled for spring of the eighth-grade year.

A drop-in secondary math tutoring was added to the Saturday school program in the spring of 1999. The math-tutoring lab is available to students 27 Saturdays per school year. This program is funded from the junior high credit recovery tuition thus; there is no charge to parents for the tutoring program. The math-tutoring lab is staffed by one district high school math teacher during the first and third quarters of the school year and, due to increased usage as the semester winds down, is staffed by two of these math professionals during the second and fourth quarters of the school year. During the year the tutoring staff is representative of each high school and is scheduled quarterly on a rotating basis. Each teacher generally works up to nine weeks at a time. The majority of the math tutoring staff has worked with the program consistently for the entire duration of the program's existence. Predominantly, the students who utilize the program are seventh- through twelfth-graders, requiring the staff to be prepared for students at various grades and levels of competency. These levels can range from basic facts that a student has not mastered: multiplication, fractions, place value, and order of operations, up to and through calculus. The math-tutoring lab will accommodate elementary grades, but it is requested that the parent remain with the student if they are of elementary age. The program currently supports nearly forty students weekly. The students who take advantage of the program are not always failing or in danger of failing. Many are high achieving students, even honors level, who enjoy the opportunity to get help in a structured environment, without distractions, and in a more concentrated fashion. Students are required to bring work they wish to get assistance with and their textbook. Unfortunately, some parents will abuse the service by using it as a babysitting service. If the teacher identifies a student who is disruptive, loitering, or unwilling to stay active, they are referred to the administrator and asked to call for a ride or they are escorted to the responsibility center. In most cases, once the responsibility center becomes the option, the students amazingly find academic work to do or secure a ride. As the responsibility center is a supervised study hall, it works as a perfect assignment option. Because of the structure of the school, students who are just hanging out, whether inside or out, are identified quickly and asked to call home or are assigned to a room for supervision. There is a sign-in log or attendance roster in all rooms, so full accountability of attendance is documented.

Because of growing numbers in the lab and the diversity of learning levels, the need to accommodate lower-level students without exhausting the tutors, whose expertise was in demand by the higher-level students, became a priority. In the past, teachers would bring with them several higher-level students, who were seeking service hours as part of their school course work, to assist with lower-level learners. This strategy has worked well for all participants, especially those aspiring to pursue math education as a career. Most of the high school math clubs require service hours for their students, so high-level math students are recruited to assist in the lab as well. Nonetheless, the need for additional tutoring staff support became essential to providing a high-quality remediation experience.

In the fall of 2002, a partnership was developed with the local community colleges in the Phoenix-metro East Valley to help solve the staffing problem. Initially started with Rio Salado Community College's postbaccalaureate program, the partnership has now expanded to four local community colleges and includes Mesa Community College, Red Mountain Community College, and Chandler/Gilbert Community College. Again, this has been a huge success for all stakeholders. The college students needed to perform practicum hours for their required courses and the majority had full-time careers while transitioning into public education. The service learning coordinator for Rio Salado was frustrated because she was responsible for placing students and could not find opportunities outside of the traditional school day. The Saturday School was the perfect answer for their needs. Education students could do their classroom observation practicum hours in the junior high remediation/recovery classes and their tutoring service hours could be completed in the math-tutoring lab or one-on-one with students who were extremely low in the remediation/recovery classes. These community college students provided more than 400 free hours of tutoring to the Saturday School Program in the spring of 2003. These students continue to provide hundreds of hours of tutoring service each semester. Many of these students have repeatedly lauded their experiences at the Saturday School.

SATURDAY JUNIOR HIGH "CHARACTER COUNTS!" PROGRAM

At the beginning of the 2000 school year, the Gilbert School District was awarded a grant from the state of Arizona to implement "Character Counts!" throughout the district's schools. The Character Counts! Program is sponsored by the Josephson Institute of Ethics.[2] It encompasses six pillars of character, which include trustworthiness, respect, responsibility, fairness, caring, and citizenship. During the fall of 2000, a character education class was developed. Introduced and developed in lieu of the out-of-school suspension option, the program focuses on the ethical philosophies contained within the pillars of Character Counts! This program was developed and implemented for use as an additional discipline alternative for junior high administrators. At that time, the district contained four junior high schools with an enrollment of nearly 5,000 seventh- and eighth-grade students. Each junior high school was allotted five participants per week in the program. If a school were not using their full allotment of available slots, the Saturday School Program Administrator would work with the other junior high schools, generally with more students and higher usage based on their discipline philosophy, to reallocate the extra slots.

The first classes were held during the spring, 2001, semester. Students were referred for three Saturdays—12 hours—of character training in response to disciplinary infractions at their school. The infractions were generally of a suspendable nature and included such behaviors as theft, lying, cheating, forgery, ditching, truancy, disrespect to students or staff, and various types of harassment.[3] The students are referred for three Saturdays at four hours each. The facilitator of the classes, a Gilbert District certified teacher and a Character Counts! certified teacher, initially were paid for services by the grant funds. The grant having expired, expenses are now covered by the tuition income from Saturday School credit recovery classes.

The facilitator focuses on two of the six pillars each Saturday. Because the referrals are on a rotational basis, the students in the classes are at various stages of the program process. The improvement of attitude and behavior exhibited by the majority of the students during the three weeks is obvious and amazing. Once the student completes the three Saturdays and 12 hours of instruction, they receive a certificate of completion and the discipline issue that sent them to the training is considered a closed matter for the student. If the student has no further discipline problems, the issue never surfaces again. If a student misses a week, due to what the assigning administrator considers to be a legitimate reason, if reassigned, the student must wait for the pillars they miss to come around again.

The administrators can also use the Character Counts! program to reduce consequences for a more severe incident such as fighting or possession of prescription or nonprescription drugs. Fighting will generally require a 10-day suspension and drugs will require from 5 to 10 days, depending on the circumstances.[4] Many students caught in these situations just make extremely bad decisions, and unfortunately, sometimes so do parents. Under the discipline policy, there are minimums for various offenses. Even though 5 to 7 suspension days may be warranted for carrying an aspirin or an inhaler, the administrator can use the Character Counts! program to reduce the number of days the student is out of school and many times can use an in-school suspension for the remaining days. Many students will get 3 to 5 days of in- or out-of-school suspension and Saturday Character Counts!, thus reducing the time the student is out of school. By the spring of 2002, a fifth junior high had been opened and total junior high student enrollment was approaching 6,000 students. High demand for slots in the program reached the point that offering a second class became necessary and was implemented in the spring of 2002. The dual classes—taught by teachers of different gender, with two different styles—allowed students with particular behavioral needs to be placed with the teacher who would afford him or her the best experience.

Initial data accumulated during the 2001–03 school years on the impact of the character program reflected an 87 percent drop in repeat disciplinary problems by the students who attended the Saturday training. Students who were given out-of-school suspension showed a much higher rate of repeat offenses, 65 percent, and the offenses were generally of a higher level than for those who attended the character training on Saturday. During the spring 2004 semester, 133 junior high students completed the program during the 15 Saturdays the classes met. An exit survey was administered to both students and parents. Of the 133 students who finished the course, 59 percent of the students and 48 percent of the parents responded that attending the program had helped the student. In response to whether the course would cause them to make personal changes, 67 percent of the students responded yes. When asked if they would approach the situation that sent them to the class differently, 80 percent responded yes. The responses to the overall impression of the course experience reflected that 62 percent of the students and 75 percent of the parents rated the experience as good to excellent. Again, follow-up disciplinary

data have shown a substantial drop in repeat referrals, with 65 percent of the students referred not having an additional disciplinary write-up since their completion of the course. This is compared to 55 percent of the students receiving in- or out-of-school suspension but not attending Character Counts! having repeat discipline referral issues. Again, generally these repeat offenses were of a more severe behavior. The most impressive statistic is that fewer than 5 percent of the eighth-grade students who attended and completed Character Counts! ended up being referred to an alternative school placement, whereas nearly 10 percent of those eighth-grade students issued in- or out-of-school suspensions eventually were referred to the alternative school site because of bad behavior or poor grades.

CONCLUSIONS

As the consistent and ever-impending pressure of standardized testing and the mandates laid down by the No Child Left Behind Act motivate the entire U.S. public education system to reevaluate its educational processes, the pressure on remediation and credit recovery programs to be accountable has hit hard as well.[5] The Band-Aid approach to moving students through the system will no longer do, at least not in the Gilbert Public School District. During the past three years, as full administrator of the Saturday School Programs and in unison and with direct support and guidance by the district curriculum director and district superintendency, we have reevaluated the overall purpose, process, and expected results of the district remediation/credit recovery programs for middle school students. As this is one of the primary missions of the Saturday School and the program that generates the income that supports the entire program, the need to establish quality, rigor, and validity has become increasingly essential.

A major addition to the Saturday reme- diation/credit recovery curriculum will be the implementation of an assessment tool for all students registered in the program. This assessment process was initially ad- ministered in the math credit recovery classes. Started in the spring of 2003, the assessment process is intended to identify critical deficiencies that the students may have in the math objectives necessary to perform the higher level operations now required in middle school and eventually high school math. The assessment process includes both qualitative and quantitative data. In conjunction with the numerical as- sessment tool, the students are asked to write a reflective narrative expressing their feeling toward math, their experiences, and their perceived reasons for requiring the remediation class, and what they hope to accomplish during the class. The stu- dents are then asked to write another re- flective narrative at the conclusion of the math remediation course. It is important that the students' attitude toward the aca- demic discipline they are being remedi- ated in be assessed as well as their academic gain. It is strongly perceived that many of these students fail classes, espe- cially math, not because of ability, but be- cause of their attitude toward the course and their assumed inability to master the objectives. It is believed that in many in- stances, this negative attitude is inherited from the parents or other close social con- tacts the student may encounter. The num- ber of times I have sat in a parent meeting to discuss a struggling student and a state- ment such as " I couldn't do math either" comes out of the parent's mouth tends to reinforce this speculation about attitude and academic success. If the parent consis- tently justifies lack of success or failure to the student, the educator's job begins to appear insurmountable.

Does immediate and ongoing remedia- tion assist students in recovering objectives not previously mastered by students? This is one of the questions that the Saturday

School Program hopes to answer. Initial re- search shows that, on average, students who attend spring Saturday School to make up failed math classes from the pre- vious fall semester not only recover the math deficiency they enrolled with, but on average increase their math grade as a group by 1.5 grade points during the se- mester they are attending the Saturday School. Other benefits seemed to emanate from their participation in the remediation program. None of the students who fin- ished the semester in their traditional jun- ior high school failed their regular math while attending Saturday School, and not one was required to attend summer school to make up credit deficiencies. An unfortu- nate statistic that became apparent later was that the same group dropped a whole grade point, on average, during their fall eighth-grade semester and one-third failed math during their next semester of junior high. Thus, just six months from the time they finished the Saturday remediation course and passed their second semester seventh-grade math course, the entire group's math performance dropped sub- stantially. Initially it would seem that on- going remediation for struggling students is essential in supporting and maintaining gains realized during the semester the stu- dent attended Saturday remediation. To test this hypothesis, a sample from the group of seventh- and eighth-grade stu- dents attending Saturday math during spring, 2005, will be granted free tuition to summer remediation courses. This group will then be compared to a sample who at- tended Saturday School but didn't attend summer school, and also compared to the group who required spring, 2005, Satur- day School but chose to recover this credit in summer 2005 instead. Did waiting for summer credit recovery have a negative effect on their spring 2005 math class? Will it have a negative effect of their fall, 2005, math classes? We shall see.

The Town of Gilbert is considered to be one of the fastest-growing, most affluent communities in the United States. This affluence generates high expectations for Gilbert Public Schools and the students who attend the 36 schools in the district. These high expectations motivate the foundations that generate interest in and the need for such programs as the Saturday School. Because of this affluence, the Gilbert parents are able and more than willing to subsidize the cost of their students' need for these remediation services. It would be inferred by many outsiders that these remediation services are required as a result of inadequacy within the Gilbert School District's elementary education system, but it is necessitated more by the high transience rate of the Gilbert population. The Gilbert School District enrolls thousands of new students per school year, many in their late elementary- to middle-school years, bringing previous academic deficiencies when the arrive. Because of the district's "no pass, no graduate" policy, many of these students get caught in the middle.[6] The need for ongoing remediation services is essential to ensure that these incoming students have the opportunity to move on to high school with the skills to be successful at the expected level, especially when the students are assessed as academically competent by the standardized tests and just need to remediate deficiencies generally caused by inconsistent enrollment in school due to numerous reasons. These reasons might include excessive absence due to illness, moving back and forth between custodial parents, and many of the other newly diagnosed problems plaguing our students today including social anxiety and depression.[7] These inherited test scores are one of the many reasons that standardized testing will be difficult to use as an accountability tool for students, teachers, schools, and districts.[8] Regardless, the accountability is impending and a genuine concern for the Gilbert school community. Remediation and credit recovery of these students is and will continue to be a genuine concern and a high priority for this district.

Another factor contributing to the necessity for expansion of remediation and credit recovery programs is the migration of students from the state of Arizona's myriad charter school options and home schools to the traditional district public schools. Arizona leads the nation in the charter school movement, now funding hundreds of K–12 schools statewide to the tune of millions of dollars annually.[9] The number of students migrating from state-funded charter schools and non–state-funded private and home schools to the traditional public secondary schools are enormous and growing each year. Initial research in the Gilbert District reflects that a large portion of the students who leave their traditional elementary school for a charter school return to the traditional public school during their secondary school years. Unfortunately, many of these students are low in academic and social skills and require extensive academic and disciplinary remediation services to recover their academic deficiencies and enable to be socially successful in the traditional school environment. There are 57 public charter schools within 10 miles of the center of the Gilbert community. The majority of these charter schools, 38, only serve K–6 or K–8, requiring parents to transfer their student to the local district school in middle school or high school.[10] Many homeschool parents find it very difficult to continue to support the homeschool effort once the student reaches the higher academic levels, especially in mathematics and the sciences. Again, this is when the public school district, especially a highly successful one, is most vulnerable to what would appear to be a slight flaw in the public education system. By law, the students live within the district and the parents have the right to attend the local district public school at any time.[11] Again, this is when the district also tends to inherit academic deficiencies they had no prior influence on. If the student had attended Gilbert Public Schools during their entire elementary school experience, would it have made an impact on their current academic abilities? How many students identified as "special-needs" after their transfer to the traditional public school might not have required these accommodation services if they had been in the traditional model at the onset? Last, how many high school students return to the nontraditional public charter school after entering high school because they do not qualify for special-needs services, but do not have the academic or social skills to foster a successful experience in the traditional public high school? We'll never know for those showing up today—but for a study for the future, one would think so.

Other programs developed within the Saturday School Program that directly support the effort to meet the needs of all students and the demands of No Child Left Behind include grant programs for those students who exhibit financial need when they are required to make up failed classes, and English Language Learners (ELL) tutoring services for second-language students. The Saturday Programs were also expanded to include sixth-grade students for the tutoring and Character Counts! It has been recommended that a Saturday Center for Success be developed for high school students requiring credit recovery for graduation requirements. The services of the Saturday School are always available to district students working through distance learning or correspondence. The district now allows 3 of their 21 graduation credits to be attained in this manner; thus the need for in-school tutoring support services is increasing rapidly.[12] These services are especially beneficial for special needs students who are attaining graduation credits online or through correspondence and require or are entitled to support accommodation services outlined with their Individual Education Plan (IEP) as outlined in IDEA '97.[13] The Saturday tu-

toring is extremely favorable to parents of students working through distance learning who are not well motivated or managing their time appropriately. Again, the program serves as a positive reinforcement and discipline for frustrated parents at the same time.

Full tuition grants are rarely given and must be recommended by a school or district administrator. It has been determined over many years of remediation and recovery management that students and parents who have not invested something in the recovery process tend to take minimal responsibility and exhibit little ownership in the process. Unfortunately this lack of ownership by the parent tends to affect the student's motivation and performance during the remediation/recovery process. This lack of motivation generally is exhibited through poor performance, disruptive behavior, and excessive absenteeism. The issue of charging tuition for the credit recovery courses becomes especially prevalent when a student moves in from out-of-state with graduation deficiencies and the previous school district had no policy mandating that the students must make up the classes. I have found out, personally, that the junior high graduation policy varies widely between districts and states. Many districts, even some bordering the Gilbert District, do not require junior high students to make up their academic deficiencies before promotion to high school. This issue is frustrating to new Gilbert district parents and students, and I have been the brunt of much of this frustration over the years. Fortunately for Gilbert schools, the prevailing attitude of incoming parents is frustration not with the Gilbert District, but with the student's previous district, as most parents fully agree with and understand the intent of the policy. The Gilbert District's junior high promotion policy makes credit recovery additionally complicated when students must recover more than one class.[14] Some students must make up as many as an entire semester's worth of credit deficiencies. This can run into hundreds of dollars in tuition for the parent. Some parents may feel a financial hardship. Some do not feel they should be required to pay. Many times it is very difficult to make the parent understand how school funding is managed and justified. Numerous times a parent will refuse to pay in an effort to set an example for and make a point to the student. "If I have to pay for the classes, I'll just hold him back another year."

Obviously, this statement, implied action, and subversive and somewhat misguided motivation by the parent bring up another major issue for the student and the school. What makes a student a good candidate for retention? Does failing five classes during the semester automatically qualify them for alternative placement? An immediate justifiable argument is that excessive failure does not automatically make a student a good candidate for retention. The detriments to a student's mental health, social reaction, and self-esteem have been researched extensively. It has been proven that, generally, retention at the secondary level, especially middle school, results in less-than-positive outcomes for the student both academically and socially. Should the parent have the sole decision on retention of their students? Recently, a parent decided to retain his seventh-grade student because the parent felt that another year of maturity and growth would give his son a better chance at a football scholarship after high school. The student had better than average grades. Similar to decisions for special-needs students during an IEP meeting, a decision to retain should be a decision made by a qualified team of educators, the parents, and other professionals who are unbiased and have the student's best interest at heart.[15]

In addition, what makes a student a good candidate for placement in an alternative school? These schools are designed for the sole purpose of credit acceleration and recovery. Should five failed classes result in direct referral to an accelerated alternative program? Many parents shy away from these schools because of the stigma that is attached to them. "Isn't that where all the bad kids go?" Unfortunately this can be a valid concern for parents of students who may have had problems in transition to junior high, medical problems, or became trapped in the shuffling-between-custodial-parents game that dominates our society today. Based on personal experience, these schools provide a credible acceleration or social alternative experience to these students trapped in unusual situations, but unfortunately, they also tend to house the district discipline problems including those referred for long-term suspension.

The development of tutoring for ELL was created out of a dual program need by both the district and the community colleges.[16] One of the courses required for community college education programs included ELL. To give future teachers the opportunity to work with this group, the ELL tutoring lab was created. The lab supported students in grades as low as grade 5 and up through grade 12 and required the parent to remain on-site with the student during the tutoring session. It was felt that this requirement would enhance parent involvement and possibly even help them with their English language skills in an indirect way.

The ability to provide satisfactory remediation services for the special-needs group—including students qualifying for special education, students requiring accommodations under Section 504 of the Rehabilitation Act of 1973, and ELLs (English Language Learners)—has always been a major challenge for the Saturday School Program.[17] These students are not exempt from the district's no pass, no promotion policy, which makes necessary the development of programs and curriculum to satisfy the needs of these students in their effort to maintain their graduation eligibility in the same timely manner as the regular education students. Special needs students also have the option of being given a pass/fail grade instead of the standard letter grade. If a special needs student is failing a course after a certain point in the semester, should this option automatically take affect? This provision could be written into the student's IEP and implemented at a time that the IEP team determines it would be appropriate.[18]

One practice that some district schools have used to support a seventh-grade student's effort in their credit recovery is to add the deficiency into the student's eighth-grade schedule in place of their elective class. Placement of a student in an eighth-grade academic core schedule in conjunction with a seventh-grade academic core deficiency appears to be a contradiction in common sense, especially when the student had one to two options to make up the course in a remediation program outside of their school schedule.

The addition of sixth-grade students in the Saturday Character Counts! program was a direct result of requests by the district elementary administrators. During the process of implementing this program during the past three years, many of the junior high assistant principals have become elementary administrators. While serving in the position of junior high assistant principal, they acted as the primary referral source to Saturday School for their students. During this time, the administrators quickly realized the benefit of using the Character Counts! program in lieu of suspension for their junior high students. Once they assumed the position of elementary principal, the need for this type of intervention became evident, particularly for sixth-graders. Referral of these sixth-grade students was piloted in the spring of 2004 and deemed a highly successful way to intervene with older elementary students exhibiting excessive disruptive behavior including bullying, harassment, and disrespect to staff and other students. It was decided to continue the inclusion of fifth- and sixth-grade students in the Sat-

urday Character Counts! during the fall of 2004, with follow-up research on the program's effect on these students during junior high transition.

The Saturday Center for Success would enable high school students requiring recovery of required graduation credits another opportunity to do so. The program would be open only to students needing to make up required academic graduation credits that the student previously failed. Similar to all other district out-of-schedule credit recovery options, these courses would be offered on a tuition basis. A major controversy that has developed out of this proposal centers on the issue of required seat time to justify credit. Should a student be required to accomplish the 90 hours of seat time originally required for the academic credit? If a student is issued a grade of F, then they must have attended, at minimum, the 80 days required by law before being dropped for nonattendance. If the student had been dropped for nonattendance, the grade would be recorded as a WF on the student's transcript. It is being proposed that the students be given an assessment based on the course objectives to determine their current level of proficiency. The students would then be remediated on the objectives not mastered according to the assessment. Under this proposed format, the amount of seat hours required to recover the needed academic credit would vary based on the results of the student's preassessment. The acceptance of this method is deemed favorable, but the type of grade the student earns then becomes an issue. Should the class now be considered pass/fail?

Recently, the district hearing officer began assigning Character Counts! as a behavior contract stipulation for junior high students suspended under zero-tolerance policies. Generally, these hearings result from major infractions such as drug possession, weapons, or racial harassment, and have a direct impact on the status of the student's educational placement after serving their 10-day suspension.[19] The hearing officer now makes attendance at Character Counts! a stipulation of the student's behavior contract requirements. Also, again just recently, the district has partnered with Banner Health to provide anger management and drug awareness services to high school students suspended and sent to the hearing officer for infractions related to these services. These counseling services will be added to the Saturday School Program in the fall of 2005.

During the past eight years, the Gilbert School District's Saturday School Program has grown from a one-room detention, costing the district thousands per year, to a fully functional program that supports itself financially and provides numerous remediation and credit recovery programs for thousands of secondary students. The need to justify these services and track their effects on students' academic and behavior performance is inevitable and essential to ensure continued growth, success, and validity of the programs. The Gilbert School District is expected to add another 15 schools and 15,000 students during the next few years. The assessment tools being implemented at this time will help ensure the best possible remediation/recovery services for students who seek them during their Gilbert Public School career.

NOTES

1. Gilbert Public Schools District Policy I-7275 IKEAA. *Junior high promotion requirements*. (2004, March 4). Retrieved June 1, 2004, from http://gpsaccess.gilbert.k12.az.us/policy Manual.nsf/wPolicies/B28773F9EBC91DBF 07256BE2006C77A7? OpenDocument.

2. Josephson Institute of Ethics. *Character counts!*, Los Angeles, CA 90045. Retrieved June 1, 2004, from http://charactercounts.org.

3. Gilbert Public Schools District Policy J-4600, JK. *Student discipline*. (2000, July 13). Retrieved June 1, 2004, from http://gpsaccess.gilbert. k12.az.us/policyManual.nsf/wPolicies/ 98854A7D5993D52A07256BE2006C7C18?Open Document.

4. Gilbert Public Schools District Policy J-4600 (2000).

5. U.S. Department of Education. *No Child Left Behind*. (2002, January 8). Retrieved May 28, 2004, from http://www.ed.gov/nclb/landing.jhtml.

6. Gilbert Public School District Policy J-1400, JG. *Assignment of students to classes and grade levels*. (2000, July 13). Retrieved June 1, 2004, from http://gpsaccess.gilbert.k12.az.us/policy Manual.nsf/wPolicies/D6160F4FBAD9F93B 07256BE2006C79B4?OpenDocument.

7. *Individuals with Disabilities Education Act*. (1997, June 4). Retrieved May 28, 2004, from http://www.ed.gov/offices/OSERS/Policy/ IDEA/index.html.

8. National Research Council. (1999). *High stakes: Testing for tracking promotion and graduation* (J. Heubert & R. Hauser, Eds.). Washington, DC: National Academy Press.

9. Arizona Department of Education. *Arizona charter school list*. Retrieved June 1, 2004, from http://www.ade.state.az.us.

10. Arizona Department of Education (2004).

11. Gilbert Public School District Policy j-0650. *Student admissions*. (2003, December 4). Retrieved June 1, 2004, from http://gpsaccess.gilbert. k12.az.us/policyManual.nsf/wPolicies/ FDEA8A3A9A1F796507256BE2006C7902? OpenDocument.

12. Gilbert Public Schools District Policy I-7350 IKF. *Graduation requirements*. (2004, June 17). Retrieved June 1, 2004, from http://gpsaccess. gilbert.k12.az.us/policyManual.nsf/wPolicies/ 49D6687094521C1707256BE2006C77AF?Open Document.

13. *Individuals with Disabilities Education Act* (1997).

14. Gilbert Public Schools District Policies: I-7200, IKE. *Promotion and retention of students*. Retrieved June 1, 2004, from http://gpsaccess. gilbert.k12.az.us/policyManual.nsf/wPolicies/ D097E617810054C407256BE2006C7744? OpenDocument and I-7275, IKEAA, *Promotion and retention of junior high students*. Retrieved June 1, 2004, from http://gpsaccess.gilbert.k12. az.us/policyManual.nsf/wPolicies/B28773 F9EBC91DBF07256BE2006C77A7?Open Document.

15. *Individuals with Disabilities Education Act* (1997).

16. Gilbert Public Schools District Policy I-2931. *Bilingual instruction/English as a second language*. (2000, July 13).

17. Gilbert Public Schools District Policy I-2931 (2000); *Individuals with Disabilities Education Act* (1997).

18. *Individuals with Disabilities Education Act* (1997).

19. Gilbert Public Schools District Policy J-4600 (2000).

PURPLE LEAVES AND CHARLEY HORSES: THE DICHOTOMOUS DEFINITION OF URBAN EDUCATION

Tricia Kress

Everything is subjective. I learned that early on when I told my brother that the leaves on a tree were purple, and he responded with, "No they're not; they're burgundy, dummy." It never occurred to him that something as standard as the color of autumn leaves could be subjective unless you were color-blind, but I knew to just keep my mouth shut about it—unless I wanted the word "dummy" to be followed by a charley horse. And so it was, whenever we had differing opinions, somehow it would always end in "dummy" or charley horse until I learned that he was bigger, I would never win, and charley horses really hurt.

Twenty years later, I find us having essentially the same argument, but we're discussing politics, not fall leaves. My brother is the conservative of the family, and I suppose, in comparison with my parents, who are liberal, I am a radical. Now that we're older, he refrains from calling me dummy (though I'm sure sometimes he wants to), and he's abandoned the charley horse treatment, but the result is still the same. I know when to keep my mouth shut so I can avoid his wrath. As far as he's concerned, something either is or isn't— there is no in-between. Whereas, I have come to understand that what's burgundy for one could well be purple for another.

As Varela states, "Reality is not a given: it is perceiver-dependent, not because the perceiver 'constructs' it as he or she pleases,

but because what *counts* as a relevant world is inseparable from the structure of the perceiver."[1] It is this awareness of subjectivity that makes the question "What is urban education?" particularly challenging for me. Who am I to say what it is or isn't? To be quite honest, I'm not sure that I've yet gained enough knowledge to offer a comprehensive answer to that. I know what it might be to some though not to others, and I'm not even sure what it is to me sometimes, because every time I pick up another book, I learn something else, and suddenly the words "urban education" take on yet a whole new meaning. What I am certain of is this: "Urban education" means something different to everyone based on their gender, race, sexual orientation, nationality, culture, socioeconomic status, age, or profession. In every definition, it is a juxtaposition of positive intentions and negative outcomes. At times I find it a bit confusing myself, so perhaps I'll just lay out a few of these dichotomous classifications to illustrate what I mean.

LIBERATING AND OPPRESSIVE

For those who choose to or understand how to play the game, urban education can be used as a means to further themselves. By graduating from school with good grades and good test scores, students can enter college and (supposedly) get a good job when they graduate. They can become enlightened to the workings of society outside of what they see in their own neighborhoods. Students can create from it a forum for resistance against government and being marginalized if they remain in school and make demands for an education that addresses the lived realities they experience every day. In this respect, "[t]eaching and learning are profoundly political practices. They are political at every moment of the circuit: in the conditions of production (Who produces knowledge? For whom?), in the knowledges and knowledge forms themselves (Knowledge according to what agenda? Useful for what?), their publication, circulation, and accessibility, their professional popular uses, and their impacts on daily life." [2]

But the students who are unaware of underlying political currents and future consequences will find that school can also be a place where authority figures will try to snuff out their individuality or weed them out and prevent them from receiving further education, thus denying them room for class mobility or societal reform through educational empowerment. And because education is usually seen as a forum for equal opportunity, not achieving in school becomes "the consequences of individual choice or personal inadequacies, not the normal outgrowths of our [sic] institutions. The problem, clearly, is to fix up the people, not to change the [sic] structures which regulate their lives." [3] So those who are ignorant to or resistant toward the inner workings of the game of education are oppressed by it rather than empowered by it.

MULTICULTURAL AND DISCRIMINATORY

Because urban areas often have diverse populations, when looking at school dynamics, public education systems within urban areas seem to be very diverse as well. There are children from many nationalities, cultures, and ethnic backgrounds.

In an effort to address multicultural interests, teachers are required to integrate into their curriculum units that provide information on various historical and cultural issues from varying perspectives. Often teachers are given texts that are considered "multicultural" and required to teach them to their classes.

However, that a city has a diverse population does not imply that all its schools will have diverse populations. Because students are zoned to schools by the area in which they live, students from the same areas will attend the same schools. And since residential areas are usually separated by socioeconomic status, children from poor areas are zoned for the same schools, just as students from wealthier areas are zoned for the same schools. Primarily minorities often populate many of the poorer zones within urban areas; thus, minorities are often zoned within the same schools; this creates (regardless of intention) segregation within the schools and, quite often, very unequal learning environments and resources. [4]

In New York City a majority of teachers in public schools are white. This in itself is problematic because it shows that our society is not necessarily multicultural after all; and because many of these teachers aren't of color, their understanding of what multicultural means, and what it means for a child of color to be part of the larger society, might be very different from that of their students. While teachers may be required to incorporate multicultural texts into their curricula, it is often common for white middle class folks to ignore issues of race under the guise that we are all created equal, so therefore, they "don't see" difference in their students. However, by ignoring diversity in general, teachers are ignoring the diverse bodies that are in the room as well as their diverse needs. Rather than just going through the motions of assigning "multicultural" texts, educators need to create a space where students can bring their own experiences and diverse knowledges to the foreground and then to think critically about them. As Lisa Delpit says:

[T]he best solutions will arise from the acceptance that alternative worldviews exist—that there are valid alternative means to any end, as well as valid alternative ends in themselves. We all interpret behaviors, information, and situations through our own cultural lenses; these lenses operate involuntarily, below the level of conscious awareness, making it seem that our view is simply 'the way it is.' Learning to interpret across cultures demands reflecting on our own experiences, analyzing our own culture, examining and comparing varying perspectives. We must consciously and voluntarily make our cultural lenses apparent.[5]

Without this type of reflection and critical consciousness, urban schools can never truly be spaces of diversity, democracy, and liberation. In a standardized curriculum such as we have now in New York City, students' histories, experiences, knowledges, and languages must be checked at the door, or removed, in order for the curriculum to be taught. They must become "raceless," "classless," "sexless," "voiceless," and invisible. "Despite the rhetoric of American education, [a packaged curriculum] does not teach children to be independent, but rather to be dependent on external sources for direction, for truth, for meaning. It trains children both to seek meaning solely from the text and to seek truth outside of their own good sense."[6] It decontextualizes students and teachers and undermines the diversity that students and teachers bring with them to the classroom. To oppose this, teachers need to find a means to "celebrate, not merely tolerate, diversity in our classrooms. Not only should teachers and students who share group membership delight in their own cultural and linguistic history, but all teachers must revel in the diversity of their students and that of the world outside the classroom community."[7]

A CHARITY CASE AND AN ENTREPRENEURIAL FORUM

Our government, our politicians, and our large corporations have made a point of pushing for the funding of public education. It has been accepted into our culture that all children should have an equal opportunity to be educated. For this reason, whereas property taxes are a major source of school funding, the government draws money from other sources as well. In addition, politicians often use education funding as a political platform. This is always a hot debate topic, and it seems that most politicians who are in the spotlight have something to say about the need for more funding for schools. Major corporations get in on the action too. Many donate products to schools and some even donate funds.

However, this, too, is a double-edged sword. Charity is not always just charitable; it is often used for personal gain. Although the government does allocate funds, those who run our nation expect to see certain measures met in return. This is where the push for standards originates. Nothing can be accomplished without money, and once money is involved, suddenly we're looking at a business, not just a social service. Like any business, there must be a way to measure productivity. The powers that be use standardized testing to do this. Administrators and politicians feel the need to verify that money is being appropriately managed, but standardized testing is not necessarily an accurate representation of accomplishment for all students in all schools. Standardized testing and packaged curricula have also become a major moneymaking business.

Furthermore, education is a powerful political topic and can often be used for leverage. Politicians will push for higher standards in education to gain public favor by showing the public that they are working toward what is best for our children and our society. The problem here, again, is the idea that standards are an accurate measure of productivity. These politicians may not have the slightest inkling of what's best for our children. The new policy being administered by New York Mayor Bloomberg is a great example of that. By unifying schools, their curricula, and classroom practices, he is punishing schools that have low performance rates on standardized tests. As a businessman, clearly he is thinking of schools as businesses and students and teachers as workers. How can you get workers to be more productive? Find a formula that works and then apply it to all your workers uniformly. The current trends of one-size-fits-all curricula can be terribly problematic. "To provide schooling for everyone's children that reflects liberal, middle-class values and aspirations is to ensure the maintenance of the status quo, to ensure that power—the culture of power–remains in the hands of those who already have it."[8] What develops is an ugly and self-perpetuating cycle. Parents, teachers, and students don't necessarily like what is happening with the standardized curriculum movement, but if it has to happen, then they want their children to be prepared, so they will perform well on high-staked tests. In this case, they not only accept the instruction and materials that are provided, they eventually begin to demand them.

This type of mentality is rather unsettling because in schools we're dealing with the development of people. By pushing standards and uniformity, we almost seem to be trying to manufacture productive citizens, much as a factory would try to build cars on an assembly line. Yet, it's been proven time and again that workers who feel they're appreciated and active participants in their companies are more productive because they are more eager to work. In a curriculum that does not leave room for student contribution, "[s]tudents become 'fact collec-

tors,' not knowledge workers who can conduct research and interpret data. Intelligence is defined in a narrow way that excludes those qualities that make individuals agents of positive social change. The use of such a limited definition may leave students with unique characteristics unrewarded and unaware of their potential achievements."[9] So what our mayor has done is reward schools with higher performance rates by allowing them more freedom with curriculum and classroom practice, thus offering a source of incentive and confidence. Teachers and students within these schools might wind up excelling even more than they were, thereby causing standards to rise; whereas schools without this incentive might still improve, but perhaps not as much as they have the potential to. Not to mention, when standards rise, suddenly, these "troubled" schools' accomplishments are not nearly as profound. By mandating a uniform curriculum in this way, the mayor has created an even greater slope on an already unequal playing field. In a situation such as this, the only winners are those who were already excelling in school, and the test makers and publishing houses that profit from the books and test materials purchased by the city.

As far as corporations are concerned, although it is true that they are doing a public service by donating materials and money to schools, education is also a huge industry. There is a lot of money to be made within the schools. For example, if a corporation donates computers or software to a school, that corporation in return will receive a tax write-off and free advertising. We see this with Apple computers. By donating Apple computers to schools, children and teachers learn to use these machines but not PCs, and are thus inclined to want an Apple as their personal computer. For the Apple Corporation, this is an attempt to secure a corner of the Microsoft-dominated technology market. We see similar occurrences with software manufacturers. Schools may receive funding and teacher training to implement computer software packets, but often the software is of little value other than for supplemental use or enrichment to lessons already covered in class; teacher training is often insufficient, and the software winds up being used as nothing other than a motivational tool. Yet the manufacturer still makes a profit and earns renown because its software is being "used" in more classrooms. For example, in the 1980s when computers were first being introduced into schools, Apple Corporation was seeking a 200 percent tax write-off for donating computers to schools. "While schools struggled with the pros and cons of Apple's gift, the deals seemed [for Apple] to be [made] in heaven . . . The giveaway, which put no more than 1.4 computers into each eligible school—was generating additional sales to both schools and parents."[10] Are teachers, students, and parents appreciative of donations made by corporations? Of course, but at the same time, this is not driven by mere generosity; there is a tremendous potential for corporate gain.

HOPELESS AND HOPE ITSELF

Public school systems seem to be a pariah of U.S. society. They are an albatross around the nation's big, ugly neck, and those who are in charge of educational reform around the nation often seem to be inflicting more damage than good. Test scores, productivity, and self-confidence in a majority of schools are so low that it's no wonder many people blame our urban schools and teachers for many of our society's ills. With all the horror stories on the news about violence; physical and sexual abuse in the schools; unsafe buildings and neglect; and teachers who seemingly have little knowledge of subject matter, much less a knowledge of how to

get kids to engage in that subject matter, it sometimes seems that the school administrators should just pack it all in and start anew.

Maybe school reform isn't the answer. Maybe upheaval would be a better option—destroy the system and start from the ground up. Sometimes it seems that there is no viable solution to our educational woes. When we live in a society that tends to revel in the sensational—especially the negative and surface-level sensational—it's easy to lose sight of where the real problems lay. And in a time when everything seems to be both instantly disposable and simultaneously at our disposal, it's easy to fall into the "throw it out and start anew" mentality. Yet it's this very mentality that keeps people from seeing just how essential our educational system is. I'm sure your average citizen doesn't realize just how long we've had problems with education, and how yesterday's problems have such a critical influence on what happens today. People often treat problems in education as if they are new and thus quickly treatable, but we won't really know the results of our efforts toward reform until the children in the middle of these contemporary reforms are adults. After all, we're only now seeing the results of the education reforms of the 1980s and 1990s. These problems in education are so ingrained that it will take decades to see change.

At the same time, urban education, public education, is our hope to create a better future. By educating teachers and students about some of the inner workings of our society, we can lead children to ask questions about what they have been told is true. From there, people within our society may learn how to demand information, knowledge, power, and ultimately a more democratic and just society. People may begin to understand that what they see on TV or what they read is not always the end-all, be-all truth—that maybe there is no one definition of truth but rather multiple truths. Maybe I am being a bit too optimistic because even though you can see outside the box and think outside the box, it doesn't mean that you can really get out of it—at least not yet.

Returning to the analogy of my relationship with my brother, I distinctly remember one of his favorite childhood torments (other than calling me "dummy" and giving me a charley horse, that is). I was a very tiny child, and my brother loved to lock me inside of things—kitchen cabinets, hall closets, sleeping bags; you name it, I was locked inside it. He always had a good chuckle over it, but it was particularly scary for me. Sometimes when I was locked in a hall closet or a cabinet with his back against the door, I'd sit quietly in the dark and wait for what seemed like forever, and when I felt like his attention was starting to wander, I'd throw my body against the door and push him hard enough so I'd get a glimpse of my freedom when the door budged about an inch open. Then he'd firmly dig in his heels and slam the door on me again, and we'd go through this process until he got bored or until I screamed in such panic that I actually frightened him enough to let me out. As I got older and bigger, I began to realize that eventually I could push hard enough to get out, or even better, I learned to outsmart him so as not to get locked up in the first place.

Unfortunately, changing large bureaucratic systems—like pushing my way out of the locked closet—is a very slow process. We cannot expect to present reforms and have them immediately implemented. Still, we must be patient, aggressive, and supportive of reforms that include educators in creating nurturing learning environments for their diverse student populations. Looking back on that childhood image now, it is actually comical to me, but it wasn't funny then. If I really try to remember how it felt at the time, I can still conjure up the terror of claustrophobia. By using my brother as an analogy, I do not intend to trivialize our educa-

tional problems, nor do I mean to create a villain of him. Yet I can't help but make a connection between the two issues. For me, being involved in urban education is very much like being in that hall closet. I sometimes feel like teachers, students, and families are so closed in by all the forces pushing from the outside, but every now and then there is a glimpse of what it means to be on the other side of the door; I know that at some point we'll all get out. It's that little glimpse that gives me hope—I hang on, anticipating that with patience and persistence maybe we will be able to conquer the dominant, and when we finally push the door open we can comment on the purple leaves without fear of "dummy" or a charley horse.

NOTES

1. Varela, F. (1999). *Ethical know-how: Action, wisdom, and cognition* (p. 13). Stanford, CA: Stanford University Press.

2. Johnson, as quoted in Giroux, H. (2000). *Stealing innocence: Corporate culture's war on children* (pp. 3–4). New York: Palgrave.

3. Bowles, S., & Gintis, H. (1976). *Schooling in capitalist America: Educational reform and the contradictions of economic life* (p. 26). New York: Basic Books, Inc.

4. Dreier, P., Mollenkopf, J., & Swanstrom, T. (2001). *Place matters: Metro-politics for the twenty-first century.* Lawrence: University Press of Kansas.

5. Delpit, L. (1995). *Other people's children: Cultural conflict in the classroom* (p. 151). New York: The New Press.

6. Delpit (1995), p.102.

7. Delpit (1995), p. 67.

8. Delpit (1995), p. 28.

9. Kincheloe, J. (2001). *Getting beyond the facts: Teaching social studies/social sciences in the twenty-first century* (2nd ed., p. 50). New York: Peter Lang.

10. Oppenheimer, T. (2003). *The flickering mind: The false promise of technology in the classroom and how learning can be saved* (p. 35). New York: Random House.

EXPLORING URBAN LANDSCAPES: A POSTMODERN APPROACH TO LEARNING

Priya Parmar and Shorna Broussard

Tell me, and I will forget.
Show me, and I may remember.
Involve me, and I will understand.

—Confucius

Why do most adolescents dislike school or find it boring and/or meaningless? The answer seems obvious but is often ignored in the age of increased standardization and high-stakes testing. Teachers who decontextualize learning tend to view students as objects who learn through rote memorization and teacher-directed activities by which learning is reduced to specialized, fragmented parts. Therefore, students' knowledge is measured and assessed by standard, objective, and quantified methods. As a result, much of the teacher's role is reduced to routine and mechanical work, a role that may even be considered as having low status. This mechanized role teachers play reflects what is known as a traditional modernist positivist approach to education. Teachers are reduced to mere "technicians" whose sole purpose is to transmit or deposit information to the presumed empty receptacle of the student. This approach values the covering of content through the use of textbooks, which ultimately leads to passiveness and adherence among both students and teachers.[1]

The modernist positivist view does not allow students to develop a critical consciousness, nor does it allow them to challenge or question the traditional canons. Rather, modernists view knowledge as fixed, operating within a banking system or technocratic view of education. Consequently, critical scholars have helped develop and draw upon what is known as a postmodern critique of Western European modernism.[2]

Critical postmodernism rejects the notion that students are simply empty vessels waiting to be filled. Students already come to school with valuable experiences and knowledge that should be heard and addressed. Simply listening and attempting to understand and include students' voice, experiences, and knowledge into daily instruction will help teachers build collaborative, dialogic relationships with their students. Teachers are then more apt to consider alternative, critical pedagogies as valid and valuable knowledge because of its direct correlation to students' lives. Critical postmodernism is concerned with awareness of self, others, and the environment in which one and others live (the larger social context). Therefore, education should expand beyond the traditional textbooks and classroom walls and extend to outside, environmental, and community involvement. Critical postmodernism strives to empower teachers and students by contextualizing learning, validating subjugated voices and knowledge, and allowing for the critical examination and challenging of traditional, modernist methodologies. This inclusive pedagogy is taken one step further by advocating social activism in order to create change.[3] Contextualizing environmental, outdoor education programs is empowering because students' personal lives and historics become the primary sources of their learning

A critical postmodern approach to teaching leads to an empowering, emancipating, democratic classroom where the voices of all students are heard and legitimized. Postmodern educators, as suggested in this research study, can use experiential, outdoor urban education designs to create a new consciousness that help youth become aware of environmental issues relating to natural resource sustainability.

CASE STUDY ON EFFECTIVENESS OF URBAN OUTDOOR EDUCATION

There has been a considerable amount of research into the effectiveness of outdoor learning experiences, as these types of environmental education programs have been shown to provide an empowering opportunity for youth to develop critical thinking skills that critique and challenge traditional canons; bring their knowledge and experiences into the classroom; build strength of character; enhance human relationships; increase environmental knowledge; and foster environmental connections. To be informed, critical citizens, youth need to think about the centrality of environmental issues to their lives and how the environment affects their communities. Too often, youth—especially those living in urban areas—have little understanding of issues that relate to the sustainability of their communities and the broader natural environment. Youth must be knowledgeable and aware of these issues in order to make informed decisions relating to resource sustainability.

Because today's youth are the future stewards of the earth's precious natural resources, efforts should be made to engage them in environmental education. A tremendous need exists to involve urban youth in addressing issues that relate to their communities, lifestyles, and natural environment—especially since today we

place unprecedented demands on forests for wood products and environmental, recreational, and aesthetic benefits. If we are to sustain these forests that enhance regional quality of life, we must engage all citizens, and foster an awareness of the realities of forests and forestry so that individual decisions collectively bode well for our forests and consequently our future.

This research evaluated how effective three increasing levels of urban environmental educational programming were on urban youths' attitudes and knowledge about the environment, specifically the forested environment. Many scholars have argued that urban environments represent ideal settings for urban environmental education and can lead to appreciation of cities' greenspaces.[4] Additionally, hands-on, outdoor, interactive experiences are very effective ways to help youth learn about issues relating to the environment and empower them to become more engaged with the natural environment.[5]

In designing a successful urban-focused environmental education project, we incorporated five key elements. First, we utilized the urban environment, as it is a comfortable, practical, and ideal place for environmental education to take place. It is for these reasons that an urban forestry education component (Cobbs Creek) was included in the educational program. Cobbs Creek served not only as a forestry education component, but also as an introductory procedure to help students (1) become more familiar with being outdoors and examining trees, and (2) address any fears or discomforts associated with learning in a forested environment. The Cobbs Creek educational component was also the bridge between the classroom exercises and the trip to the rural forest that is sometimes quite foreboding in the mind of young city dwellers. Cobbs Creek is unique in that it is the largest urban park in the United States, with many riparian areas, creeks, and trees to examine. It is also a place that was familiar to the students, many of whom visited the park regularly, thus making classroom instruction contextual and meaningful.

Second, we also know from previous research that the school system is a center of student activity and a good avenue into the urban environment.[6] It is for this reason that public schools in the Philadelphia School District were targeted. Because it has been shown that many attitudes are formed by the time a student reaches high school, younger, more impressionable middle-school-aged students were selected to participate in this study.[7] The science class context was chosen because the students were developing literacy and critical thinking skills in science that encouraged the students' opinions and experiences when new material was introduced. The ultimate goal was for students to make their own informed decisions about the content being analyzed. Also, at the middle-school level, students were still learning, evaluating, and determining how communities managed shared resources such as air, water, land, and forests. A science-based forestry education program using a postmodern paradigm fit well with the existing curriculum dealing with space, earth, and all its resources.

Two outdoor educational components were used in this study: urban outdoor education and suburban field demonstrations. An indoor educational component using the Project Learning Tree Curriculum was also included as an initial venture for the students into the area of environmental education. Project Learning Tree (PLT) is a widely used forestry-based environmental education curriculum that has been found to be effective in increasing knowledge and changing attitudes, particularly in second- to eighth-grade children. An activity from the PLT curriculum was used as part of the indoor education. Because reinforcement is more likely to enhance attitude changes and knowledge gains, three cumulative educational components were used, each building upon the knowledge gained previously while introducing new topics at the same time.

Educational programs need to be evaluated to demonstrate effectiveness, yet allow enough room for educators to choose among alternative pedagogies that suit their individual classrooms and student needs. It is thus crucial that attitude and behavior research be applied in the design of educational programs. This will provide support for their effectiveness as empowering approaches for environmental education programming.

Last, some students may tend to perform and behave differently when a guest is present. This is known as the Hawthorne effect.[8] To determine whether the students performed better on the questionnaires simply because there was a speaker and not because of the educational program, we included a placebo group as well. These students received a college preparation talk, and we did not cover any topics that would produce any knowledge or attitude gain for the measures in this study. For comparison, a control group was also included. This group received no educational program.

URBAN ENVIRONMENTS

It is widely believed that environmental concerns are important to Caucasian, economically privileged people, and that people of color, especially in inner cities, have little interest in such matters. But in fact, research has consistently shown that there is little evidence of a black–white environmental concern gap, and differences between the races are actually very small.[9] Researchers such as Kahn have suggested that children's diverse and rich appreciation of nature, and their moral responsiveness to its preservation, are not suppressed by the serious constraints of living in an economically impoverished inner city.[10]

With the majority of the U.S. population residing in urban areas, urban residents make the decisions that affect the nation and the management of its natural resources. Too often, youth, especially those living in urban areas, have little understanding of environmental issues that affect the sustainability of their communities. Because Philadelphia is the fifth largest U.S. city and houses 15 percent of Pennsylvania's population, it was an ideal city on which to focus an environmental education effort informed by a critical postmodern approach to learning. The educational program was carried out in the West Philadelphia area, which is 72 percent black, 24 percent white, and 1 percent Hispanic (1990 Census). Female-headed households with children younger then 18 and without husbands present comprise 6.2 percent of Philadelphia households (2000 Census). For the entire city, 59 percent of the youths (age 8–18) are minority and 25 percent are below poverty level. For single mothers with children, 35 percent of those families are below poverty level (2000 Census). These striking statistics relating to family structure, poverty, and other contributing social and economic factors in Philadelphia demonstrate the challenges that many children face growing up in the inner city. The critical postmodern approach used in this environmental education program acknowledges the social and economic complexities involved, and recognizes the political implications of using a reductionist, positivist approach informed by modernism. Despite the ominous social and economic concerns, inner-city youth have strong perceptions about environmental issues and care about the environment and conservation.

DISCOVERING THE ENVIRONMENT: CASE STUDY OF PHILADELPHIA MIDDLE-SCHOOL STUDENTS

This case study aimed to foster a sense of forest stewardship in urban youths; promote critical thinking skills by critiquing traditional texts; increase students' knowledge levels in the area of forest management and timber harvesting; effect positive attitude changes toward forest management; increase student participation by validating personal experiences, voices, and subjugated knowledges; and promote social activism in local communities. We designed a three-stage educational program aimed at helping urban youth learn about forestry and forest management. We compared three types of forestry education delivery methods: indoor education, outdoor education in an urban environment, and outdoor education at a demonstration forest. Central to the research project was fostering a forest stewardship ethic with urban youth and measuring the success of various educational methods in reaching this essential audience.[11]

The goal was to compare the educational gains and attitudinal changes after each of the three cumulative educational activities to determine their effectiveness. The first educational program was an indoor classroom session consisting of a slide presentation on the history of Pennsylvania's forests and a Project Learning Tree activity. The second educational activity was an outdoor urban forestry activity at Cobbs Creek in Philadelphia. The third treatment was a guided tour of the French Creek Forest Stewardship Demonstration Area in Reading. The classroom activities covered the topics of forest history, natural forest processes, silviculture, threats to forest sustainability, importance of trees, and tree facts. The second education component was an outdoor urban forestry activity at Cobbs Creek in Philadelphia. Cobbs Creek is part of the 8,700-acre Fairmount Park, which is the largest urban landscaped park in the United States. The Cobbs Creek activities included tree measurement and forest ecology, and a reinforcement of topics presented in the classroom. The students worked in pairs to measure tree diameter, height, and crown cover. Students also identified the trees that they measured. Back in the classroom, the students recorded all the data and created a graph of the tree characteristics for the section of Cobbs Creek that we visited. These urban forestry exercises were aimed at helping students make the link to an important natural resource in their community while further illustrating the role that forests play in their everyday lives. Teachers were encouraged to contextualize learning by using students' past experiences at Cobbs Creek as part of instruction. Students, as well, were encouraged to share their experiences at Cobbs Creek, and critique, question, and address any concerns regarding the content presented to them. Activities at French Creek centered on timber harvesting and how harvesting affects forest sustainability and how it is used as a management tool. Areas of forest facts and ecology were also studied, critiqued, and challenged. Students' previous experiences and knowledge were also encouraged during learning activities at both locations. Data about student attitudes and knowledge about forestry were obtained by administering a questionnaire to the students before and after the activities.

Three middle schools in the Philadelphia School District participated. One teacher was chosen from each of the schools on the basis of his or her school involvement, motivation, and willingness to participate in the study. Each teacher had two of his or her classes participate in the research project. In addition, one control or placebo classroom was used in each school. The experimental groups were given flexibility when implementing instruction and students were allowed to critique, challenge, and question traditional approaches to learning about science and the environment. We wanted to employ this design to demonstrate the effectiveness of this pedagogy compared to traditional techniques employed by instructors in the control and placebo classrooms. The

selected design is classified as a nonequivalent control group design.[12] The non-random effects were controlled by randomly and equally distributing treatments across all classes. There were also control groups at two schools and a placebo group at one school. This experimental design minimized the testing effect by assuring that each student only took the survey twice. A total of 182 students took part in this study, with 71 students being assigned to the control and placebo groups while 111 students were randomly assigned to three experimental treatment groups.

EFFECTIVENESS OF OUTDOOR EDUCATION

In terms of knowledge gain, the outdoor treatments education components resulted in significant gain for sixth-, seventh-, and eighth-graders when compared to the control and placebo groups. However, for the eighth-graders, both the indoor classroom instruction and outdoor instruction caused the students to exhibit significant gains in critical thinking skills and content knowledge. While the educational effectiveness varied for the sixth- and seventh-graders, the students in the outdoor treatment groups consistently learned more about forestry than the control/placebo group. These results support the body of literature that claims people learn better if alternative pedagogies are allowed. Contextualizing learning, critically analyzing and challenging texts, validating subjugated knowledges, and fostering dialogic, collaborative relationships between student and teacher reflect the alternative pedagogies used in this environmental education program. Although outdoor education is the mode of choice, especially for natural resources education, the classroom treatment worked for the eighth-grade students. Studies have also shown that while outdoor experiences produce knowledge gain, indoor experiences can also be effective,[13] as this study has shown. The ideal combination would incorporate both indoor and out-door sessions. Indoor sessions are useful for orientation and introductory exercises, or when outdoor experiences are not possible. While outdoor education has unique benefits that cannot be realized indoors, indoor instruction should not be discounted either.

URBAN SCHOOLS AS AN AVENUE FOR ENVIRONMENTAL EDUCATION

Because schools can be effective avenues for environmental education, they should continue to be utilized. A critical postmodern approach of an environmental education program can easily be incorporated into the already existing curriculum, while as the same time meeting current science education standards simply by allowing critical analysis and challenging of texts as well as including students' voices and experiences during instruction. We used the Project Learning Tree curricula, which has activities classified by grade level, subject in school, indoor or outdoor, and time required. Many of the materials used in the PLT are readily available in the school, and the activities were planned in fifty-minute sessions, just as classes are. Teachers were encouraged to expand or "manipulate" the learning activities in order to meet individual needs of their students. Students were encouraged to draw upon their own previous experiences and knowledge when introduced to new concepts. For this project, the first two treatments required no additional resources from the teachers and could easily be done again at a later date with any class as long as learning was contextual and student inquiry was welcomed. We gave the teachers complete copies of the activities and other educational resources so that they could do the activity on their own. The trip to the French Creek Demonstration Forest did require buses and travel time, but school districts can provide funds for off-campus field trips. For this project, the Pennsylva-nia Department of Education provided funding for the travel. Penn State, in partnership with state and federal forestry and natural resource agencies, established seven Forest Stewardship Demonstration Areas across Pennsylvania to encourage responsible forest resource management through education. These seven demonstration forests are available for use by educators. Additionally, Penn State established several educational programs for urban youth environmental education, working through local community groups and focusing on empowering teachers.[14]

EFFECTIVENESS OF FRENCH CREEK DEMONSTRATION FOREST

The Forest Stewardship Demonstration Area was a valuable educational tool that contributed to youths' knowledge and understanding of forest ecology and silviculture concepts beyond that achieved by an indoor experience alone. The field demonstration provided youth an opportunity to familiarize themselves with alternative timber harvesting practices and evaluate or reevaluate their views of these practices. Only after experiencing the timber harvesting demonstrations did the students adopt attitudes in favor of sustainably managing forests. They felt that if done properly, harvesting trees is necessary and is sometimes useful for the residual trees. Also, after experimenting at French Creek, they believed that harvesting trees does not result in permanent destruction of forests and that trees do indeed grow back. All grades experienced this attitude change. However, seeing the demonstration forest did not change the sixth-graders' anti-timber harvesting attitude. These youngsters possessed a dichotomous attitude where they were against harvesting, but at the same time believed that cutting trees in certain situations is acceptable.

Before the students toured the demonstration forest, their low knowledge about forestry was positively correlated with an attitude against timber harvesting. However, after seeing at French Creek the various ways a forest can be managed, the students who learned about forestry did not possess negative attitudes toward cutting trees and agreed that harvesting is necessary at times. These students also believed that harvesting trees does not result in permanent destruction of the forest and that the trees grow back.

CONCLUSIONS

The results demonstrated that although knowledge of forestry can be gained from classroom or urban forestry activities, the only way that attitudes change is by actually experiencing the direct results of managing forests. With all the competing negative images of timber harvesting that are portrayed by the media, a critical postmodern approach critiquing such images and misrepresentations should be one of the goals of any natural resource education program. These negative images translate into opposition against the forest industry that often manifests itself in unsound policies. Youth should be given the opportunity to critically analyze and challenge traditional assumptions so that when they need to make decisions on managing our shared resources, they can do so in an informed fashion. Therefore, if a goal is to open and/or expand upon youths' perceptions and attitudes about forestry, then exposing them to alternative pedagogies that foster critical analysis of texts, include students' experiences and knowledge, and encourage hands-on, interactive, experiential approaches to learning, is the most effective way.

This educational program was designed to foster critical thinking skills informed by critical postmodernism in hopes of creating informed, empowered young citizens with a proper knowledge base to guide future decisions. As a result of the program, the youth learned more about the environment, shed their negative views about forestry, and adopted attitudes in favor of managing our natural environmental and resources sustainability. Based on these findings, it can be concluded that classroom exercises that involve and validate student voices, experiences, and knowledge, and incorporate urban forestry activities and demonstration forests, which promote experiential learning, are valuable and empowering components of an educational program that contribute to critical, informed citizenry, participant knowledge gain, and attitude change in the area of environmental education.

NOTES

We thank the teachers and students of the Philadelphia School District for their participation in this program. For generous financial and intellectual support, we also thank Larry Nielsen and Stephen Jones (formerly of Penn State University), and the Pennsylvania Department of Education.

1. Parmar, P. (2002). *KRS-ONE going against the grain: A critical study of rap music as a postmodern text.* Doctoral dissertation, The Pennsylvania State University, University Park, PA.

2. Kincheloe, J., Slattery, P., & Steinberg, S. (2000). *Contextualizing teaching: Introduction to education and educational foundations.* New York: Addison Wesley Longman.

3. Kincheloe, Slattery, & Steinberg (2000).

4. Kahn, P. Jr., & Friedman, B. (1995). Environmental views and values of children in an inner-city black community. *Child Development,* 66 (2), 1403–1417; Lutz, D. (1995). Eco-ed grows in Brooklyn. *EPA Journal,* 21 (2), 16–17.

5. Bowman, M., & Shepard, C. (1985). Introducing minorities to natural resource career opportunities. *Ohio Journal of Science,* 85 (2), 29–33.

6. Running Grass. (1994). Towards a multicultural education. *Multicultural Education,* 2 (1), 4–6.

7. Knapp, C. (1972). Attitudes and values in environmental education. *Journal of Environmental Education,* 4 (2), 26–29.

8. Franke, R., & Kaul, J. (1970). The Hawthorne experiments: First statistical interpretation. *American Sociological Review, 43,* 623–643.

9. Jones, R., & Carter, L. (1994). Concern for the environment among black Americans: An assessment of common assumptions. *Social Science Quarterly, 75* (3), 560–579; Mohai, P. (1990). Black environmentalism. *Social Science Quarterly, 71,* 744–765; Mohai, P., & Bryant, B. (1998). Is there a "race effect" on the concern for environmental quality? *Public Opinion Quarterly, 62* (4), 475–505.

10. Kahn & Friedman (1995).

11. Broussard, S., Jones, S., Nielsen, L., & Flanagan, C. (2001). Forest stewardship education: Fostering positive attitudes in urban youth. *Journal of Forestry, 99* (1), 37–42.

12. Campbell, D., & Stanley, J. (1963). *Experimental and quasi-experimental designs for research.* Boston: Houghton Mifflin Co.

13. Janus, H. (1984). The effect of environmental education instruction on children's attitudes toward the environment. Science Education, *66* (5), 33–36.

14. Broussard, S., & Jones, S. (2001). Extension, communities, and schools: Results of a collaborative forestry education project in Philadelphia. *Journal of Extension, 39* (3) [online journal].

Power and Urban Education

GLOBAL CAPITALISM AND URBAN EDUCATION

David Baronov

With the exception of the few remaining foreign-controlled lands such as Iraq and Puerto Rico, virtually all public education programs around the world are shaped by decisions taken at the national, state, and local levels. The role of global capitalism in shaping urban education is, therefore, perhaps not immediately evident. Indeed, global capitalism alone provides us with a far from complete understanding of urban education in the United States today. At best, it describes a set of compelling circumstances to which national, state, and local decision makers must respond. Ultimately, the state of urban education is the product of an ongoing political process in which various stakeholders consult, petition, and/or protest before the appropriate public officials. As such, it is largely the case that local decisions and activism continue to shape urban education. At the same time, the forces of global capitalism establish important limitations regarding the options available to those who set urban education policy in the United States.

THE NATURE OF CONTEMPORARY GLOBAL CAPITALISM

"Globalization" has emerged as the watchword of the new millennium. There is a common belief that we are today experiencing greater movement across the globe (by people, ideas, diseases, etc.) and greater articulation between far-flung social and economic processes (Chinese prison labor and Wal-Mart shoppers in Fargo, North Dakota). This points, internationally, to a growing economic interdependence. Globalization represents the most visible face of global capitalism. Its ideological and material forms advance the interests of global capitalism and, therefore, the term globalization can provide a useful shorthand when discussing the contemporary period of global capitalism. Two major developments have set the pace for this current era of globalization.

On the one hand, with the end of Cold War, the United States rose to a position of unchallenged global prominence, achieving hegemonic influence in the financial, industrial, and military realms. This permits the establishment of neoliberal policies and institutions that promote global trade and investment, such as the World Trade Organization, and allows U.S. officials to undermine those initiatives deemed counter to their interests, such as the Kyoto Agreement on global warming. On the other hand, the current era of globalization is associated with a series of advances in technology, communication, and transportation that have dramatically reduced the costs of locating production overseas and facilitated international financial transactions. This constitutes the technical and material infrastructure that undergirds a web of interlocking networks, which integrate disparate social and economic activities from around the world.

Thus, at the most general level, globalization refers to a set of policy decisions referred to as neoliberalism and a set of economic and material forces, such as technological innovation. In combination, these neoliberal policies and economic and material forces have unleashed an extraordinary transformation of people's lives around the world. Given the range of popular interpretations, it is helpful to try to capture some key features of globalization that mark it as a historically unique, contemporary phenomenon. The current era of globalization is characterized by five developments within global capitalism:

- Greater global trade
- Greater foreign direct investment by multinational corporations
- Greater economic regionalism
- Greater integration of international finance
- Greater role of "services" within global trade

Greater Global Trade

Beginning in the 1970s, there have been dramatic increases in global trade. The Japanese electronics industry and French automakers sought to enter U.S. markets, for instance, while U.S. farmers moved to expand agricultural exports. Most trade agreements at this time involved bilateral arrangements between individual nations or small groups of nations. The groundwork was being prepared, however, for the larger trade pacts of the 1990s. Global agreements (the World Trade Organization) and regional agreements (NAFTA, MERCOSUR) created international net-works of global trade that have exponentially expanded the movement of goods and services around the world.[1]

The result of greater global trade has been multifaceted. On the one hand, the world has witnessed increasing economic interdependence between nations and between regions. Today, the industrial policies of one nation can have far-reaching consequences for other nations next door or halfway around the world. At the same time, this expanded contact between wealthy and poor nations has led to an increasing influence of Western culture in non-Western societies. Movies, music, and fast food are major exports from wealthy nations to poor.[2] A sense of despair and resentment by many has resulted—with the attacks on the Pentagon and the World Trade Center representing the most extreme manifestations. Lastly, increased global migration has followed from greater global trade. Along with the movement of goods and services, people have been on the move. This mass movement of humanity has primarily flowed from poor nations to wealthy nations in search of jobs and opportunities.[3]

Greater Foreign Direct Investment by Multinational Corporations

By the mid-1980s, the phenomenon of foreign direct investment was reaching new heights. Multinational corporations sought to move offshore and set up production and distribution plants across the globe. Today, multinational corporations—such as IBM, Nestlé, and Renault—have moved production facilities to low-wage nations in an effort to produce goods more cheaply. China, for example, has been a major winner in this move by corporations to directly invest in poorer nations for the production of goods (and increasingly services) that will primarily be sold to consumers in wealthy nations. The workforce in wealthy countries can scarcely compete with the cost of Chinese prison labor.

Greater foreign investment has resulted in dwindling employment prospects and decreasing unionization in the wealthy nations alongside deteriorating environmental conditions and labor rights in poor nations. The deindustrialization of the traditional heartland of manufacturing in many wealthy nations over the past decades has been accompanied by a patchwork of production plants (export production zones) in poor nations.[4] The movement of industrial jobs from the northeast region of the United States to cheap assembly plants along the Mexican/U.S. border is an example. This signals the so-called "race to the bottom" in which poor nations compete with one another to provide favorable investment conditions, such as low pay, antiunion policies, and lax environmental standards.[5]

Greater Economic Regionalism

In light of global trade agreements, a greater economic regionalism has emerged. The Cold War inspired a number of strategic regional pacts that coordinated military assets and defense policies between nations. The new regional pacts emphasize economic cooperation. These regional agreements promote eliminating trade barriers (by lowering tariffs), stabilizing currency exchanges, and regulating the movement of people between nations.[6] Examples of such regional pacts are the European Community and NAFTA. These agreements are designed to bind nations as regional partners in a strategic alliance that purportedly strengthens each nation's bargaining power in the global economy more effectively than an individual nation could muster on its own. For example, the United States continues to nervously eye the European Community as it strengthens its alliance and builds its leverage vis-à-vis the United States.

The result of greater economic regionalism has been to place greater emphasis on a nation's geopolitical location on the world map as a factor in its development.

As a consequence, an unfortunate location can greatly impede a nation's participation in the global economy—as is the case for many African and Latin American nations. Regionalism also tends to pressure those nations with progressive environmental or labor laws to come into conformity with others in the geographic alliance.[7] It is argued by many, as a consequence, that state actors have less and less influence in setting national policy.[8] This is why many who oppose aspects of globalization focus their protest on regional and global meetings (such as meetings of the European Union or the World Economic Forum), replacing past strategies that targeted national capitols.

Greater Integration of International Finance

International finance is a complex and highly profitable arena for wealthy global investors. The major activities associated with international finance are foreign exchange trading and foreign investment. Foreign exchange trading involves the buying and selling of national currencies. This is a highly speculative venture in which investors attempt to anticipate fluctuations in the value of different nations' currencies. Foreign investment involves the effort of wealthy individuals and companies to find profitable investment opportunities around the world. Advances in communication technology have greatly facilitated the rapid movement of such investments, allowing instantaneous shifts of enormous sums, at times, with highly damaging effect.[9] Driving this rapid growth within international finance are trade agreements that deregulate national financial markets alongside the expansion of assets held in mutual funds and pension funds in the 1990s (especially in the U.S.) in search of greater profit.

A result of the greater integration of international finance has been to radically accelerate the movement of investors' money around the world. Consequently, the impact of these investments, as seen in the 1997 Asian Crisis, has been significantly enhanced.[10] Given the degree of financial speculation in international currencies and other high-risk investment instruments, financial markets have grown increasingly volatile and are marked by considerable instability. Investors' interests in short-term profit do not coincide with a company's interest in building long-term value. As a result, investor speculative activity rather than publicly debated priorities or national industrial policies, tend to shape economic development patterns.[11] The power of the financial marketplace over democratic institutions is a very real concern.

Greater Role of "Services" within Global Trade

One of the most important developments within the global economy over the past decade has been the increasing role of services as a commodity in global trade. The category of services represents a wide-ranging set of activities that support economic transactions and productive activities. This includes everything from the work of a bank vice president to that of a filing clerk. Traditionally, activities tied to services have been the most difficult tasks to move overseas. Given modern communication and computer technologies, many routine service tasks, such as data entry, medical billing, customer services via telephone, and computer programming, have been increasingly relocated to low-wage nations.[12] Typically, the only service jobs remaining in wealthy nations are those requiring direct contact with the customer—such as retail sales, restaurant work, or auto repair. These jobs typically do not pay well.

The result of this greater role of services within global trade has been a major shift of routine service activities from high-wage wealthy nations to low-wage poor nations. Just as those workers from wealthy nations who lost jobs due to deindustrialization were being retrained for service industry jobs, those jobs have been increasingly outsourced to poor nations. The service jobs that remain in the wealthy nations are generally in high-paying occupations (lawyers, professors, financial consultants) or low-paying occupations (hospital orderlies, K–12 educators, fast-food workers), with a dwindling middle stratum.[13] The service jobs that go to poor nations carry the same threat as manufacturing jobs of further relocation if the host nation does not maintain conditions that are favorable to investors. As with foreign direct investment, the greater role of services within global trade primarily provides flexibility for investors to increase their profits by chasing after the cheapest labor force available within the global economy, pitting one poor nation against another.

URBAN REALITIES IN THE ERA OF GLOBALIZATION

Over the past thirty years, these forces of globalization have radically reshaped the entire socioeconomic topography of the United States. In this period, the gap between the wealthy and the poor has widened. Ethnic/racial segregation has increased and tens of thousands of manufacturing jobs have left the United States, while the remaining living-wage jobs have migrated from cities to the suburbs. Today, growing populations of disenfranchised and impoverished ethnic/racial minorities find themselves concentrated in large urban areas. The impact of these trends on cities in the United States has been profound and points to major challenges regarding policy options for those striving to improve urban education. Of particular concern are three developments stemming from globalization with direct consequences for urban education policy:

- Global migration from rural to urban areas and from poor to wealthy nations
- Transformation of the U.S. economy (alongside deindustrialization)
- Social and economic polarization within the United States.

Global Migration from Rural to Urban Areas and from Poor to Wealthy Nations

The processes of globalization have contributed to two major migration patterns. First, there has been a massive movement of people from rural to urban areas. As a result, growing rings of poverty and despair have surrounded major cities of the world, such as São Paulo, Bombay, and Johannesburg.[14] Today, great masses of displaced agricultural communities have taken refuge in urban centers teeming with shantytowns. Second, the movement of people from poor to wealthy nations has continued at a strong pace.[15] The dream of a better life remains a potent motivator among the world's poor. As a result, those who can, migrate from poor to wealthy nations. Invariably, the world's poor must take the lowest paying and least desirable jobs when they arrive. This entails either seasonal agricultural work, which tends to keep workers constantly on the move or, more typically, low-wage jobs in the urban-based service industry.

Given this pattern, most immigrants in the United States tend to disproportionately settle in urban areas and, consequently, urban school systems are increasingly asked to assist students both with their academic needs as well as their cultural adjustment to U.S. society. In addition, given the proximity of the United States to Latin America and due to changes in U.S. immigration policy in 1965, Latino/-a and Asian immigrants are especially prominent among these newcomers. While contributing to an exciting and vibrant multicultural learning environment, additional resources and time are required to meet bilingual needs and to facilitate adjustment.

Beyond differences tied to ethnicity and language, however, a large number of urban immigrant families represent displaced agrarian families. Thus, many students' families operate within the cultural norms of a rural household. Often the parents have little or no formal education and there is little in their backgrounds to orient either the students or their parents regarding the expectations and norms of the U.S. educational system—such as study habits or peer interaction. Compounding these cultural issues, many of these students reside in areas of significant poverty, which often requires both parents to work double shifts.

Transformation of the U.S. Economy

One of the central roles for any K–12 educational system is to prepare students to be responsible citizens and productive members of society. This entails, in part, developing a skilled workforce for the national economy.[16] However, given the pace of U.S. deindustrialization over the past few decades, and the accompanying occupational shifts, it is no longer clear what skills to emphasize or even what social role education plays in contemporary society. For example, preparing a workforce for the future was much easier during an era of onerous yet steady manufacturing jobs when employers' fortunes were tied to local community development. In light of the expanded role of low-wage, unstable jobs in the U.S. economy, it is difficult to tell students that working hard in school will reliably result in a set of employable skills and abilities.[17] The reality is that, as part of a global workforce, a student's future is one of uncertainty and change.

The urban/suburban divide is further exacerbated by these developments. The movement of wealthy whites from urban areas to the outer suburbs over the past few decades has accelerated the movement of jobs and resources away from the urban poor. Both the loss of urban manufacturing jobs along with the growth of exclusive, wealthy suburbs have hurt urban educational systems by shrinking the tax base and by moving living-wage jobs to the suburbs. As a result, the poorest of the poor remain concentrated in large urban school districts that feature a stark socioeconomic homogeneity and depleted and fragmented communities.[18]

This picture is further complicated by government policies designed to deter poor youth from illicit behavior in an era of great uncertainty and dismal job prospects. In 2002, the number of African Americans in prison exceeded 800,000. A labyrinth of anticrime measures targeting the urban poor—including curfews, three-strikes legislation, zero-tolerance drug laws, and antigang units with sweeping powers—are in force in urban areas across the country.[19] Urban educators must work with students whose daily lives involve interaction with punitive police tactics in their neighborhoods. The disruptive and dispiriting impact of these policies on students (and their families and friends) is a further obstacle for urban educators to overcome.

Social and Economic Polarization within the United States

The reason that urban education has fallen as a public priority is largely tied to the enormous gap between the wealthy and the poor in the United States. By the late 1990s, the poorest twenty percent of U.S. families had an average income of $14,620, while the wealthiest twenty percent of families had an average income ten times this amount, $145,990.[20] Today, the interests of the wealthy in the United States are tied more closely to the interests of the wealthy classes in other nations than to the interests of the poor in their own nation. Global trade and finance link their fortunes. One result of this wealth gap has been the concentration of the poor in large urban school districts. Thus, if the interests of the wealthy and the poor in

the United States do not coincide, it is not clear why, beyond philanthropy, the wealthy would have any concern for improving impoverished urban schools. Increasingly, the world of the wealthy and the world of the poor are separate and decidedly unequal.[21]

Along with the increasing gap between the wealthy and poor there has been an increasing segregation of U.S. ethnic/racial minorities. Ethnic/racial segregation in the United States today is of historic proportions.[22] Meanwhile, ethnic/racial minorities represent a majority (or plurality) of students in large urban educational systems across the country. The resource disparity between urban and suburban schools reflects this pattern. The predominantly white professional class has migrated to the suburbs, and a predictable shift of political power from urban machine politics to suburban soccer moms has accompanied them.[23] So long as their situation can be successfully sectioned off and kept from view, it is doubtful that non-minorities in the United States will act to improve urban schools.

URBAN EDUCATION IN THE CONTEXT OF GLOBAL CAPITALISM

It is impossible to provide any intelligible analysis of urban education absent an understanding of the profound social transformation across urban communities in light of global capitalism over the past three decades. The primary challenges presented by global capitalism for urban education today are:

- Increasing concentrations of poverty
- Hypersegregation of ethnic/racial minorities
- Disinvestment in urban areas and dwindling economic opportunities
- Repressive anticrime tactics directed at urban youth
- Concentration of political and economic power in the suburbs
- Educational aspirations of Asian and Latino/-a immigrant students with diverse cultural roots

The impact of globalization notwithstanding, an erroneous general consensus predominates among official U.S. policy makers that the major problems of urban education can be traced to any number of microlevel conditions—for instance, broken families, sexual promiscuity among teens, the drug epidemic, and teen violence. As a result, most urban education reforms downplay the influence of globalization and emphasize policies that address superficial, surface-level conditions. Ironically, these policies tend to be consistent with the same neoliberal, market-based solutions that provide the ideological underpinnings for globalization.

Pedro Noguera has written eloquently about this persistent gap between the chronic socioeconomic conditions confronting urban public schools and the inappropriate and inadequate policy responses.

Urban public schools frequently serve as important social welfare institutions. With meager resources, they attempt to address at least some of the nutritional and health needs of poor children. They do so because those charged with educating poor children generally recognize that it is impossible to serve their academic needs without simultaneously addressing their basic need for health and safety. For this reason, those who castigate and disparage urban public schools without offering viable solutions for improving or replacing them jeopardize the interests of those who depend on them . . . Most of the popular educational reforms enacted by states and federal government (e.g., standards and accountability through high-stakes testing, charter schools, etc.) fail to address the severe social and economic conditions in urban areas that invariably affect the quality and character of public schools.[24]

Neoliberal Reforms

In the context of the current era of globalization, neoliberal policies represent efforts by governments to create a uniform global system for economic investment. Differences between nations' laws and policies are reduced. This has resulted in deregulating financial institutions, lowering tax rates, minimizing environmental standards, and eliminating labor laws. These neoliberal policies have their counterpart in policies designed to transform urban education. In fact, proponents of neoliberal education reforms argue that precisely because today we must compete in a competitive global environment, it is imperative, from the perspective of quality control, that we develop schools that produce students with a common and predictable set of skills and abilities. To gauge progress in this regard, it is vital that student learning be measurable. This requires standardized testing. It is further suggested that student learning outcomes can be made more consistent and uniform by developing homogeneous teaching practices and by demanding specific teacher certification requirements. Neoliberal ideologues advocate education reform in three areas.

- Standardized testing and curricula
- Teacher certification
- Focus on the three R's over extracurricular activities

Today, the movement for standardized student testing and standardized curricula is in full swing. The George W. Bush Administration's No Child Left Behind program is just one manifestation of this larger phenomenon.[25] The stated purpose of standardized testing is to create a measurable set of uniform criteria by which to compare students and schools, with the ultimate goal of minimizing differences in achievement.[26] A further benefit is greater control over each school's measures of success and its curricula. Today, testing students' retention and recitation of facts gleaned from rudimentary lesson plans is the primary measure of success. Alternative learning outcomes, such as creative problem solving, are less easily captured through standardized tests. Additionally, given the importance of these test scores for determining school rankings, whoever controls these tests controls the curricula to prepare for the test. The result is greater uniformity and standardization of the curricula. This goal of standardized learning outcomes is consistent with the aim of greater standardization and uniformity promoted by the stewards of global capitalism.

The current emphasis on teacher certification is a further example of a neoliberal policy advancing standardization through quality control measures. Teacher certification is held out as a method for guaranteeing minimal standards for teachers entering the classroom. The assumption is that the decline in urban school performance is tied, to a significant degree, to teacher incompetence. Certainly it is far simpler to rectify alleged teacher shortcomings than to directly address the rapidly deteriorating socioeconomic conditions that confront urban education today. The emphasis on teacher certification provides an opportunity to downplay the social environment as a factor explaining poorly performing schools as well as a venue for ensuring greater uniformity across the teaching pool.[27] This uniformity concerns both the knowledge of one's subject matter as well as teachers' values and attitudes. Fostering narrowly construed values and attitudes about the challenges of education facilitates efforts to downplay the role of globalization as a consideration within the learning process.

Alongside standardized testing and curricula and teacher certification, has been the perennial, national call for a return to the so-called three R's and an elimination of extracurricular activities.[28] The crude ideology that reduces K–12 education to a mere training ground for tomorrow's global workforce is most fully exposed by this emphasis on the "essentials" of education (reading, writing, math) rather than the "frills" such as art and music. Ironically, proponents of preparing a global workforce see no contradiction in cutting back on opportunities to study foreign languages, comparative religion, cultural anthropology, international politics, and so on. At the same time, those pushing for lesson plans that emphasize reading, writing, and math tend to prefer a rather narrow approach to these subjects that discourages creative problem solving and emphasizes rudimentary, rule-based understanding.[29] This further advances the agenda of generating standardized learning outcomes designed to produce students prepared to join a homogeneous and interchangeable global workforce.

Market-Based Reforms

Along with promoting neoliberal policies, advocates of globalization have actively championed the role of market-based solutions to social problems. Third World poverty and underdevelopment are attributed to government restrictions on free trade.[30] It is argued that creating free markets will lead to a more efficient allocation of resources, which will attract foreign investment and spur economic development. The magic of the competitive marketplace, it is argued, should replace government-directed social engineering in these poor countries. By analogy, many education reformers believe that the best solution to poorly performing urban schools is to introduce market-based reforms. Advocates of market-based solutions contend that once schools are forced to compete with one another, educational improvement will follow.[31] Magnet schools and privatization (charter schools, school voucher programs, outsourcing administrative services) are the primary examples of market-based reforms.

The basic purpose of magnet schools is to foster competition between schools within the public school system by developing a specialization in a particular academic field (math and science) or a pedagogical style ("open" classrooms).[32] A common criticism of magnet school programs is that they tend to marginalize those schools that are less successful within a district and that this disproportionately impacts students from the poorest areas. Roslyn Mickelson recounts developments in Charlotte's magnet school program in the early 1990s.

Soon after the [Charlotte school] district replaced its mandatory desegregation plan with a voluntary one built around choice among magnet schools, it became apparent to many parents and other citizens that there were gross inequalities in resources available in magnets, newer schools, and older schools primarily in the urban core. They noted that the magnet strategy for reform left many schools in dire need of attention and additional resources. In the view of some critics, these inequities exacerbated existing race and class disparities in opportunities to learn. People complained that the magnet program, rather than addressing educational inequality, was exacerbating it by draining funds that could be spent for all schools.[33]

The cornerstone of market-based urban school reform is privatization—the process whereby private corporations receive contracts to provide services traditionally delivered by government. In the field of urban education reform there are three primary forms of privatization: (1) Charter schools are privately established and administered schools supported with public funds. Proponents of charter schools argue that this structure permits greater freedom for school administrators to experiment with innovative approaches.[34] (2) School choice provides publicly funded vouchers for students to attend private schools. As with charter schools, it is argued that allowing students to choose between attending public or private school will pressure public schools to improve.[35] (3) Outsourcing the administration of schools to private companies involves hiring private firms—such as Education Alternative, Inc. or the Edison Project—to actually run an individual

school or potentially an entire school district. The rationale for outsourcing such services is that corporate leaders can bring efficiencies and best practices from the bottom-line world of business to public education.

The basic premise for each of these reforms is that the educational process is basically a commodity and that a school is, therefore, analogous to a company in the business of providing a service.[36] Teachers are service providers and students are their clients. It follows that, given their expertise in the field of effectively and efficiently providing services, businessmen and women should serve as the leaders for education reform. Because free markets and competition shape the guiding ideology of the U.S. business class, these are the strategies they emphasize for public school reform. Magnet schools, charter schools, school vouchers, and outsourcing are all designed to promote competition between schools and to spur innovation and improvement. This fits conveniently with the tenets of global capitalism, which advocate the broad privatization of traditional government functions so that the number of collective goods can be cut to a minimum.[37] Any restrictions on private enterprise (such as government-provided medical care) are considered obstacles to progress through free market competition. In this respect, public education systems represent a major target for the ideologues of globalization. If the superiority of privately run school systems can be demonstrated, this would mark a significant step in the dismantling of public education systems in the United States and around the world.

CONCLUSION

It remains the case that national, state, and local officials are most directly responsible for shaping urban education policy. At the same time, the forces of global capitalism today impose certain limitations on the options available to these officials. Greater global trade has increased economic interdependence internationally over the past few decades, as the movement of people, goods, and services has multiplied exponentially. The capacity of companies and industries to move production facilities to low-wage labor zones has created a fierce competition between wealthy and poor nations for these jobs. Regional trade agreements, such as NAFTA, have reduced trade barriers between nations and tied the interests of nations to others in their region. The deregulation of financial markets and currency exchanges has allowed investors to rapidly move their money and shift resources around the world at unprecedented rates. The ability to move service jobs to low-wage zones permits multinational corporations to realize significant profits and contributes to a race to the bottom among nations with low-wage zones.

These global changes have contributed to a host of growing challenges that face urban education today. The gap separating the wealthy and the poor has led to an increasing concentration of poverty, while ethnic/racial disparities have created a pattern of hypersegregation that gathers poor nonwhites in large urban areas ringed by wealthy, white suburbs. The expansion of suburbs alongside disinvestment in urban areas has left few viable economic opportunities for those remaining in cities. An array of repressive anticrime policies has been established to monitor and sanction the growing population of discouraged and marginalized urban youth. The concentration of political and economic power in the suburbs has reduced both the clout and the resources available to urban school districts. The contemporary pattern of U.S. immigration attracts many Asian and Latino/-a families to urban centers, where both their cultural adaptation as well as

their high educational aspirations must be accommodated.

The major policy responses to these challenges for urban education over the past two decades have typically emphasized neoliberal and market-based reforms. The neoliberal approach is consistent with the ideals of globalization that promote standardization and uniformity across all international transactions. Standardized testing and curricula, teacher certification requirements, and an emphasis on the three R's are all designed to enhance quality control within education and to create uniform student learning outcomes that produce students with a common set of interchangeable skills. Market-based reforms also reflect globalization's ideological influence. Fostering competition between schools (through magnet schools or school vouchers) and cultivating service-oriented, bottom-line, business practices (through privatization of school administration) are designed to improve urban education by pressuring schools to adopt the practices of others, while turning teachers into service providers and students into clients. The ultimate goal of neoliberal and market-based reforms is to transform urban public education into an efficient, privately managed, service-based industry with predictable and uniform student learning outcomes that generate homogenous, interchangeable students.

NOTES

1. NAFTA and MERCOSUR refer, respectively, to the North American Free Trade Agreement among Mexico, the United States, and Canada, and to *El Mercado Común del Sur* (The Common Market of the South) among Argentina, Brazil, Uruguay, and Paraguay; Gilpin, R. (2002). *Global political economy: Understanding the international economic order.* Princeton, NJ: Princeton University Press.

2. Abrahamson, M. (2004). Global cities. New York: Oxford University Press.

3. Sassen, S. (1988). The mobility of labor and capital: A study in international investment and labor flow. Cambridge: Cambridge University Press.

4. Falk, R. (1999). Predatory capitalism: A critique. Cambridge, UK: Polity Press.

5. Reich, R. (1991). The work of nations: Capitalism in the 21st century. New York: A.A. Knopf.

6. Mittleman, J. (2000). The globalization syndrome: Transformation and resistance. Princeton, NJ: Princeton University Press.

7. Mittleman (2000).

8. Kuttner, R. (2000). The role of governments in the global economy. In W. Hutton & A. Giddens (Eds.), Global capitalism (pp. 147–163). New York: The New Press.

9. Soros, G. (2000). The new global financial architecture. In W. Hutton & A. Giddens (Eds.), Global capitalism (pp. 86–93). New York: The New Press.

10. Falk (1999).

11. Gilpin (2002).

12. Sassen (1988); Braverman, H. (1975). Labor and monopoly capital: The degradation of work in the 20th century. New York: Monthly Review Press.

13. Reich (1999); Ray, C., & Mickelson, R. (1993). Restructured students for restructured work: The economy, school reform and noncollege-bound youth. Sociology of Education, 66, 1–23.

14. Falk (1999); Sassen (1988).

15. Falk (1999).

16. Bowles, S., & Gintis, H. (1976). Schooling in capitalist America: Educational reform and the contradictions of economic life. London: Routledge & K. Paul.

17. Wilson, J. (1996). When work disappears: The world of the new urban poor. New York: Random House; Anyon, J. (1997). Ghetto schooling: A political economy of urban education reform. New York: Teacher's College Press.

18. Kozol, J. (1991). Savage inequalities: Children in America's schools. New York: Crown Publishers; Massey, D., & Denton, N. (1993). American apartheid: Segregation and the making of the underclass. Cambridge, MA: Harvard University Press.

19. Wilson (1996).

20. Bernstein, J., Boushey, H., McNichol, E., & Zahradnik, R. (2002). Pulling apart: A state-by-state analysis of income trends. Washington, DC: Center on Budget and Policy Priorities.

21. Reich (1991).

22. Massey & Denton (1993); Fossey, R. (2003). School desegregation is over in the inner cities: What do we do now? In L. Mirón & E. St. John (Eds.), Reinterpreting urban school reform: Have urban schools failed, or has the reform movement failed urban schools (pp. 15–32). Albany, NY: SUNY Press.

23. Wilson (1996).

24. Noguera, P. (2003). City schools and the American dream: Reclaiming the promise of public education (p. 6). New York: Teachers College Press.

25. Mickelson, R. (2000). Corporations and classrooms: A critical examination of the business agenda for urban school reform. In K. McClafferty, C. Torres, & T. Mitchell (Eds.), Challenges of urban education: Sociological perspectives for the next century (pp. 127–174). Albany, NY: SUNY Press; Noguera (2003).

26. Noguera (2003).

27. Anyon (1997).

28. Firestone, W., Goertz, M., & Natriello, G. (1997). From cashbox to classroom: The struggle for fiscal reform and educational change in New Jersey. New York: Teachers College Press.

29. Firestone, Goertz, & Natriello (1997).

30. Abrahamson (2004).

31. Noguera (2003); Cookson, P. (1994). School choice: The struggle for soul of American education. New Haven: Yale University Press; Henig, J. (1994). Rethinking school choice: Limits of the market metaphor. Princeton, NJ: Princeton University Press; Rasell, E., & Rothstein, R. (1993). School choice: Examining the evidence. Washington DC: Economic Policy Institute.

32. Mickelson (2000).

33. Mickelson (2000), p. 134.

34. Rasell & Rothstein (1993).

35. Cookson (1994); Ridenour, C., & St. John, E. (2003). Private scholarships and school choice: Innovation or class reproduction. In L. Mirón & E. St. John (Eds.), Reinterpreting urban school reform: Have urban schools failed, or has the reform movement failed urban schools (pp. 177–208). Albany, NY: SUNY Press.

36. Henig (1994).

37. Kuttner, R. (1997). Everything for sale: The virtues and limits of markets. New York: Alfred Knopf; Falk (1999).

TOWARD AN ANTICOLONIAL EDUCATION

Mostafa Mouhie Eddine and Rebecca Sánchez

Under the green umbrella of capitalism, the West has been committing the worst atrocities known to humankind. From colonialism, slavery, genocide, and class and gender oppression, to appropriation, the West has been adamant about its agenda: profit. The education system, as a part of the colonial capitalist structure, perpetuates the hierarchical structure of oppression. The purpose of this piece is threefold. First, we will discuss capitalism and its colonial schema; second, we will accentuate the historical role of education in maintaining the colonial structures; and third, we will entertain the anticolonial discursive paradigm that banks on indigenous knowledge in order to create borderlands of resistance.

CAPITALISM AND COLONIALISM

Colonization begins with a forced entry; as in the conquest of the Americas and Algeria. After contact, the colonizing powers try zealously to undermine and sabotage the cultural values of the natives. These acts are performed by a minority, elite, ruling class that embodies the core: the spring of power. The core's position is further reinforced by racist ideologies that blame the natives for their own misery, savagery, and oppression. In this context, conquest is legitimized via "ridiculing" the "otherness" of the natives.[1]

The conqueror is driven by a capitalist agenda to acquire land, natural resources, cheap labor, and new markets. This is what Karl Marx described as primitive accumulation of capital.[2] Said magnifies the rapid rate at which Europe conquered the rest of the world in the following: "Consider that in 1800, Western powers claimed 55 percent but actually held approximately 35 percent

of the earth's surface, and by 1878 the proportion was 67 percent, a rate of 83,000 square miles per year. By 1914, the annual rate has risen to an astonishing 240,000 square miles, and Europe held a grand total of roughly 85 percent of the earth as colonies, protectorates, dependencies, dominions, and commonwealths."[3]

In retrospect, the West needed raw material to support its growing economies. Africa, Asia, and the Americas were the fertile grounds for colonialism. In the United States, for example, the cotton industry thrived because the natives were displaced from their lands, and the slaves provided cheap labor in the South. The cotton industry accounted for 58 percent of the dollar value of all American exports.[4] The exploitations of the natives and the slaves were legitimized via the act of "othering."[5] The savage, the heathen, and the uncivilized needed the religious creeds, the values, and the language of the white master in order to be delivered from their own ignorance.

COLONIALISM IN THE UNITED STATES

The first Anglo-Saxon settlers in North America had developed a sense of cultural superiority during their conquest of Ireland. The English considered the Irish as savages whose salvation rested on assimilating to the Anglo way of life.[6] The feeling by the English and their belief in their own cultural superiority gave them *la carte blanche* to expropriate the lands of Native Americans, a source of raw material, and to enslave African Americans, a source of free labor. The Constitution of the United States further reinforced the superiority of the Anglo-Saxon. In fact, Benjamin Franklin, one of the Founding Fathers, argued that the English were the "principled body of white people" who should populate North America and that land, Native American lands, should be cleared for the principled race.[7] In addition, the Constitution, through the Naturalization Act of 1790, denied the right of citizenship to Native Americans because they were considered domestic foreigners.[8] African Americans, under the Constitution, were property whose job was to ensure that enough cotton was produced in order to keep the capitalist troglodytes up north happy.[9] In essence, the Declaration of Independence locked the natives, the slaves, and people of color to a "legalized" position of subordination. We will now analyze the role of education in maintaining colonialism.

EDUCATION AND ITS TREATMENT OF THE OTHER

The education system in the United States is colonialist in its nature, because it was built on Anglo-Saxon ideals. From its inception, the school system advocated Anglo-Saxon uniformity framed under a national culture, which excluded all the others, even the new European immigrants.[10] In the early period of the nineteenth century, for instance, Noah Webster, who is referred to as the Schoolmaster of the Americas, worked relentlessly to standardize an American version of the dictionary of the English language, an American version of the Bible, and an American spelling book.[11] Webster is one of the first American scholars who succeeded in his attempt to create a national Anglo-American culture, a norm which still beats at the heart of this country. The "culture of wars" at the university level is a lingering part of the debates about what national culture is and what type of knowledge is valued.[12]

It is vital to note that some pockets in the academia are succeeding in decentralizing the Anglo-Saxon core, which has reigned for the last 300 years. Levine in *The Opening of the American Mind* documents the culture of wars and shows the progress that has been gained throughout the last century at the university level.[13] The Anglo-Saxon canon is the colonial ideological force that excludes all the others. This exclusive canon will not reign for long though, as we are seeing a counter hegemonic discourse in the areas of women's studies, Chicana studies, African- American studies, and indigenous studies. The core of the Anglo culture is being challenged and the voices of the others are gaining strength. In order to engage in this further, the manner in which education has historically worked to maintain the colonial agenda of capitalism must be described.

The early settlers in the thirteen colonies were perplexed with how to deal with Native Americans. They could not kill them all. The answer to the "Indian problem" resulted in the mission of assimilation. It was the only way to salvage the natives' souls and deliver them from anguish.[14] In 1766, Samson Occom, an Anglican missionary, went to England to raise money to educate the Indians. His plea was received with much more consideration and sympathy in England than in the New World. He raised more than 11,000 pounds to later found Dartmouth College. Wheelock wrote,

I have turned out forty Indians who were good readers, writers, and instructed in the principles of Christian religion . . . Well behaved while with me . . . by contact with the vices of their tribes, not more than half preserved their characters unstained. The rest were sunk into as low, savage, and brutish way of living as they were before and many of the most promise have fallen lowest.[15]

The early attempts to assimilate the natives went in vain. One hundred years later, Lieutenant Richard Henry Pratt landed support from the community in Carlisle, Pennsylvania, and Congress to open up a boarding school whose motto was "to kill the Indian and save the man." Native children were taken from their nations and stripped from every element of their cultures. They were soaked and baptized in the new culture.[16] They could not speak their languages, and they were forced into domestication in accordance with Anglo-American values. The Carlisle Institute prepared Native American girls to become maids and servants. As for Native American boys, they were trained to fulfill menial jobs. Education for the natives meant assimilation and producing a class of obedient workers who filled the lower strata of the job market.[17] The outing system, a training program, helped native students to become apprenticed in positions of servitude. Education for the natives created a pool of a workforce that was exploited by capital greed.[18]

The Carlisle mission, along with the missions of other boarding schools, was not much different from the schools established for the free slaves. Contrary to popular beliefs, the slaves were very keen on obtaining education, even under the harshest conditions of slavery. Slaves were cruelly punished if caught reading and teaching others how to read. Anderson documented the history of black education in the South between 1860 and 1935.[19] He found that freed slaves started their own schools with little help from the government. The southern planters opposed and placed many obstacles to hinder the education of the freed slaves, yet they were unable to stop the freed slaves' desire and anguish for learning. Many African Americans believed that education would lead to true emancipation. Alas, the capitalist system had a different agenda for the freed slaves. Once again, under the green umbrella of profit, Southern and Northern whites supported the establishment of the Hampton and Tuskegee Institutes. These two schools focused on teaching manual labor and on producing a workforce that would satisfy the lower echelon of the job market. *Plessey v. Fergusson* (1896) cemented separation and made it legal. African Americans were institutionally denied access to equal education and were therefore rendered to the margins.

The Industrial Revolution, at the turn of the century, created a massive working class. Schools became an avenue through which the ideals of industrialism and Americanization were to be practiced. Immigrants and their children needed to be domesticated and apprenticed into the factory mentality. Schools were about what Peter McLaren and Henry Giroux call the avenues through which capitalist social relations and ideologies were reinforced.[20] In short, schools were a site of class reproduction. In his critique of modernism and postmodernism, Doll provides a historical litany that students were in fact objectified into automatons for the capitalist engines. "Our schools are in a sense, factories in which the raw material (children) is to be shaped and fashioned into products to meet the various demands of life."[21]

Education has always been a champion of the agendas of the elite classes. Schools are not only about reproducing colonialism, but also indoctrinate the oppressed into believing in the myths of meritocracy—a bourgeois idea that relegates the oppressed to the position of the periphery and shifts the blame to those who are exploited and oppressed.[22] In the case of the United States, the oppressed are further divided through the color lines and gender lines.[23] The capitalist system injected the white working class with psychological wages, indoctrinated them in the myth of meritocracy and in the allegory of education, separated them from the others, and displaced them when their skills were no longer needed. The working class, a marginal group along with the rest of the oppressed, is just another property, a by-product of colonialism.

Under the veil of profit, capitalism will go to bed with anybody. The bottom line is green. The mighty dollar is mightier than class, race, gender, sexuality, and ability. Sadly, we still fall prey to the politics of compartmentalization and separation. This form of disciplined pedagogy tends to essentialize a particular form of oppression at the expense of other forms of domination.[24] The anticolonial discursive calls into question the nature of power dynamics of oppression with a critical gaze without losing sight of the authority and the passion of experience.[25]

In these times of "post-," the passion and the authority of experience have become appropriated by capital. Now corporations such as Benetton are banking on human suffering throughout the world. Giroux in *Disturbing Pleasures* exposes the new commodity of capital: the consumption of social change.[26] Capital has caught up with the notion of fluidity and multiple subjectivities only to expose human affliction for the sake of manifold revenue. Under the multioppressive regime, race, gender, class, ability, and sexuality become multiple sites of profit. It is no longer customary to physically enslave and colonize; capital has found multiple ways to bank on the exotic other. Jonathan Rutherford as quoted in hooks, argues that

Paradoxically, capital has fallen in love with difference: advertisement thrives on selling us things that will enhance our uniqueness and individuality. It is no longer about keeping up with the Joneses; it's about being different from them. From world music to exotic holidays in Third World locations, ethnic TV dinners to Peruvian hats, cultural difference sells.[27]

Ironically, the exotic other still endures the savage inequalities and inequities of a school system that rewards property value over human principles. In New York, as described by Kozol, those who live in affluent neighborhoods (high property values) merit the right to a superior education.[28] The poor who live in the ghetto—the majority of this segment of the population being people of color—have no right to quality education. Race, class, and many forms of oppression do matter.[29]

ANTICOLONIAL INDIGENOUS KNOWLEDGE

The European conquest and colonization of much of the world was multifaceted and included but was not limited to forced labor, economic disruptions, genocide, and territorial appropriation. One of the most salient features of colonialism however, and the one of concern here, was the authoring of the colonized into Western narrative structures.[30] This form of narrative represents the colonial agenda. It is the formal narrative that becomes commonsensical, which is studied in school, and that society values.[31] In retrospect, official knowledge is the manifestation of the colonial structure that still insists on dominating most of the world.[32] At this juncture, however, we will call into presence the power of indigenous knowledge in creating liberatory borderlands that counter the Eurocentric view of the world. Such a knowledge base offers an alternative theoretical and pedagogical perspective that has the power to impact the oppressed and the marginalized in our schools.

The anticolonial discursive juxtaposes the situations of the oppressed through the power dynamics that are inherent to the colonial structures. It is pivotal to distinguish here between positivistic and deterministic dialogues that see colonial theory as locked in binaries and the fluidity of the anticolonial discursive.[33] The relationship between the center and the periphery, the colonizer and the colonized, the oppressor and the oppressed, are some of the examples of this positivist paradigm. In an attempt to move beyond this limiting scope, we choose to ascribe to the anticolonial discursive, not as a fixed theory, but as a theory in the making. It is fluid, hybrid, and contextual. This paradigm calls into question the power dynamics that subjugate and render the oppressed to the positions of subordination. Fluidity of the anticolonial discursive has to be understood under the guise of autonomy and the passion of experience.[34] There is nothing "post" about postcolonialism. Oppression is real, not fluid, yet individuals have the multiple subjectivities to combat the oppressive regime. One cannot ascribe to nihilism and despair. Racism, sexism, class oppression, heterosexism, and many forms of oppression are real and not imagined. Toni Morrison, for example, speaks eloquently to the symbolic worth of race: "Race has become metaphorical—a way of referring to distinguishing forces, events, classes, and expressions of social decay and economic division far more threatening to the body politic than biological 'race' ever was."[35] Race is woven in the very fabric of the United States.

As significant as race is, it has to be understood in relation to other forms of oppression. The anticolonial discursive looks at the dynamics of power structures with a critical gaze. Class, gender, and sexual orientation are looked at as sites of struggles, sites of marginality, and sites for possibilities to build alliances—a common zone of resistance.[36] In essence, common resistance alters the hegemonic discourse, by creating a third space,[37] a borderland—*una cultura Mestiza*—that transcends the boundaries of the Anglo-Saxon norms, and that plays by different rules.[38]

Borderlands are spaces in the margins inhabited by those who are the subjects of oppression, yet Anzaldua refuses to surrender and redefines the meaning of marginality.[39] Her story, along with the stories of other Chicanas and Chicanos, is transforming the peripheries and altering the colonial central structures of the United States. Along these lines, Delgado proposes that knowledge and reality are socially constructed, that indigenous knowledge provides members of a group with a catalyst for psychic self-preservation, and that exchanging knowledge helps people to overcome ethnocentrism.[40] In the case of the United States,

Eurocentrism is the discourse that needs to be overcome.

Marginality is a position defined by the center locking and determining the fate of the oppressed. This position robs individuals from their agencies. hooks redefined marginality:

Understanding marginality as a position and a place of resistance is crucial for oppressed, exploited, colonized people. If we only view the margin as a sign of marking despair, a deep nihilism penetrates in a destructive way the very ground of our being.[41]

Borderlands need to be expanded to accommodate the oppressed. Borderlands are created every day through alliance building, through counter storytelling, and through revitalizing the cultural, indigenous founts of knowledge.[42] Borderlands are about forming communities within the margins. Trueba speaks about resistance and defiance in the case of Latinos/as in facing discrimination, oppression, and exclusion: The common experience of oppression, rejection, and exclusion is redefined, reinterpreted, and used constructively to gain political power and collective recognition.[43] It is precisely the feelings of exclusion and oppression that create the need for developing the new ethnicities, a new kinship system, a new set of personal relationships, almost a new larger family where we can all protect each other.[44] Trueba's entreaty, in our perspective, is calling for the oppressed—the inhabitants of the borderlands—to dialogue, to form a system of affinity, and to form new sets of dialogical identities that redefine marginality and colonialism.

Anticolonial discursive is about the emancipatory process framed in the proclamation of the past, the present, and a vision for the future through conscious dialogue, alliance building, and through banking on indigenous knowledge. It is context bound and milieu specific. As importantly, decolonization is fluid and not fixed. Decolonization is not an intellectual act in the Western sense. It is a way of life through which the subject deprecates the forces of exploitation and subjugation, and claims the voices of the peasants, the working class, the natives, and all the displaced others. Decolonization is about denouncing the exploitative practices of the capitalist regime. At its nucleus is the disentanglement of the bourgeois class and its ideals. Decolonization is part of what Paulo Freire refers to as "*Conscientizacion*."[45] Anticolonial education juxtaposes the realities of the oppressed and offers them a myriad of possibilities. This outcome can only be reached through conscious dialogue. It is with conscious love that we can begin to understand ourselves and our connectedness to the others. Neocolonialism is breathing under the protection of capitalism in our poor communities and in the so-called Third World countries. We, as loving and mindful human beings, need to decolonize our minds; decolonize our spaces; and form alliances to speak, to name, and to act. It is in this context that the colonized have a myriad of emancipatory possibilities that the colonizing other never envisioned. Along these lines, Paulo Freire speaks:

No matter where the oppressed are found, the act of love is commitment to their cause—the cause of liberation. And this commitment, because it is loving, is dialogical. As an act of bravery, love cannot be sentimental: as an act of freedom, it must not serve as a pretext for manipulation. It must generate other acts of freedom; otherwise, it is not love. Only by abolishing the situation of oppression is it possible to restore the love which that situation made impossible. If I do not love the world, if I do not love people I can not enter into dialogue.[46]

Armed with love, we dare to question that which separates the intellectual from the authentic and seeks to monopolize knowledge. We are humbly reminded that to engage in any kind of dialogue, one has to engage in the postdisciplinary "conversations" that strive to transform rather than

conform.[47] Love is not sentimental. It is driven by an agenda to abolish oppression, to teach for emancipation, and to decolonize. Love for the human cause unites more than separates. It is the kind of love that flows in the midst of the harshest oppressive regimes to speak against atrocities and human sufferings. It is the kind of love that has no precincts regardless of where oppression exists. Love raises global consciousness. James Baldwin, an African-American freedom fighter and an intellectual who struggled to link his work to his world, dared to transcend the imposed colonial borders. He eloquently highlights and articulates global consciousness in the following:

Any real commitment to black freedom in this country will have the effect of reordering our priorities, and altering our commitments, so that, for horrendous examples, we would be supporting black freedom fighters in South Africa and Angola, and would not be allied with Portugal, would be closer to Cuba than we are to Spain, would be supporting Arab nations instead of Israel, and would never have felt compelled to follow the French into Southeast Asia.[48]

Anticolonial discursive encompasses teaching for freedom. This act of freedom is a way of life that sees education as instrumental to the cause of the oppressor, yet turns desolation into a flare that ignites and illuminates a path of resistance, a path of defiance, and a road that refuses to become a casualty of despondency. In the spirit of emancipation, Gordon Bennett describes his work in the following:

If I were to choose a single word to describe my art practice it would be the word question. If I were to choose a single word to describe my underlying drive it would be freedom. This should not be regarded as a heroic proclamation. Freedom is a practice. It is a way of thinking in other ways to those we have been accustomed to. Freedom is never assumed by laws and institutions that are intended to guarantee it. To be free is to be able to question the way the power is exercised, disputing claims to domination.[49]

NOTES

1. Said, E. (1993). *Culture and imperialism.* New York: Vantage Books. Said, E. (1979). *Orientalism.* New York: Vintage Book.

2. Miles, R. (1987). *Capitalism and unfree labor: Anomaly or necessity.* New York: Tavistock Publication.

3. Said, E. (1993), p. 8.

4. Takaki, R. (1993). *A different mirror: A history of multicultural America.* Boston: Little Brown and Company.

5. Said, E. (1979). *Orientalism.* New York: Vintage Books.

6. Takaki (1993).

7. Takaki (1993).

8. Takaki (1993).

9. King, J. (2000). *Race.* Mahwah, NJ: Lawrence Erlbaum Associates, Inc.

10. Takaki (1993); Macedo, D. (2002). The colonialism of the English-only movement. *Education Research, 29* (3), 15–24; Said (1993).

11. Spring, J. (2001). *Deculturalization and the struggle for equality.* New York: McGraw-Hill.

12. Levine, W. (1997). *The opening of the American mind.* Boston: Beacon Press.

13. Levine (1997).

14. Reyhner, J., & Eder, J. (1992). *A history of Indian education* (Jon Reyhner and Jeanne).

15. Reyhner & Eder (1992), p. 92.

16. Reyhner & Eder (1992).

17. Lomawaima, T. (1993). Domesticity in the federal Indian schools: The power of authority over mind and body. *American Ethnologist, 20* (2), 227–240.

18. Adams, W. (1995). *Education for extinction: American Indians and the boarding school experience.* Lawrence: University Press of Kansas.

19. Anderson, J. (1988). *The education of blacks in the South, 1860–1935.* Chapel Hill, NC: University of North Carolina Press.

20. Giroux, H. (1994). *Disturbing pleasures: Learning popular culture.* New York: Routledge.

21. Doll, W. (1993). *A postmodern perspective on curriculum.* New York: Teachers College Press, p. 47.

22. Freire, P. (1970). *Pedagogy of the oppressed.* New York: Continuum.

23. Du Bois, W. (1961). *The souls of black folk.* New York: Fawcett Publication, Inc. hooks, b. (1994). *Teaching to transgress.* New York: Routledge.

24. Dimitriadis, C. (2001). *Reading & teaching the postcolonial: From Baldwin to Basquiat and beyond.* New York: Teachers College Press.

25. hooks, b. (1994). *Teaching to transgress.* New York: Routledge.

26. Giroux (1994).

27. hooks (1994), p. 17.

28. Kozol, J. (1991). *Savage inequalities: Children in America's schools.* New York: Crown Publications.

29. hooks (1994); West, C. (1993). *Race matters.* Boston: Beacon Press.

30. Gutierrez, J. (2001). *Critical race narratives.* New York: New York University Press; Said (1993); Said (1979).

31. Wertsch, J. (1998). *Mind as action.* New York: Oxford.

32. Gutierrez (2001).

33. Alireza, D. (2001). The power of social theory: The anticolonial discursive framework. *Journal of Education Thought, 35* (3), 297–323.

34. hooks (1994).

35. Morrison, T. (1992). *Playing in the dark: Whiteness in the literacy imagination.* Cambridge, MA: Harvard University Press, p. 63.

36. Alireza (2001).

37. Pulido, L. (2001). To arrive is to begin: Benjamin Saenz's Carry Me Like Water and the Pilgrimage of Origin in the Borderlands. *STLC, 25* (1), 306–315.

38. Anzaldua, G. (1987). *Borderlands, the new mestiza = la frontera.* San Francisco: Spinsters/ Aunt Lute.

39. Anzaldua (1987).

40. Delgado Bernal, B. (1998). Using a Chicana feminist epistemology in educational research. *Harvard Educational Review, 68* (4), 555–582.

41. hooks, b. (1990). *Yearning.* New York: Routledge, p. 150.

42. Moll, L., & Diaz, S. (1987). Change as the goal of education research. *Anthropology & Education Quarterly, 18* (4), 287–299.

43. Trueba, E. (1999). *Latinos unidos: From cultural diversity to politics of solidarity.* Lanham, MD: Rowman and Littlefield Publishers.

44. Trueba (1999).

45. Freire, P. (1996). *Pedagogy of hope.* New York: Continuum.

46. Dimitriadis (2001), pp. 70–71.

47. Dimitriadis (2001), p. 41.

48. Dimitriadis (2001), p. 34.

49. Dimitriadis (2001), p. 34.

EDUCATION IN A GLOBALIZED SOCIETY: OVER FIVE CENTURIES, THE COLONIAL STRUGGLE CONTINUES

Joseph Carroll-Miranda

AN INTRODUCTION TO THE INTRODUCTION

Urban cities like New York have unique characteristics that can be described as a *tecnópolis.*[1] Tecnópolises are the materialization of an urban-geographical segment of a technocratic society. As such, urban cities have the distinction that their economies and modes of production are seriously dependent on and mediated with information and communication technologies (ICT). The fusion of technology in all of the daily facets of the urban center's life creates a virtual cyborgzation of day-to-day praxis mediated via ICT.[2] In other words, information and communication technologies have historically restructured both the economy and internal dynamics of the urban center.[3] According to authors like Manuel Castells and Peter Hall, the tecnópolis condition is usually present in the urban centers of striving First World economies. New York City, known by many as the economic capital of the world, lives up to its name in this sense. The urban is transmutating into the techno-urban. In doing so, education becomes an institution that foments the constitution of the urban-techno subject. In other words, tecnópolis is the urban architecture of a Cyborg-State, and the cyborg condition reflects its citizen subjectivities. The cyborgzation of urban education policies, methodology, and curriculum is the main focus of this text.

In this general context, education has a similar fate. The urban scenarios of New York City's tecnópolis condition are rather mind-boggling. Not only are myriad cutting-edge policies, curricula, methodologies, and pedagogical praxes nurtured, produced, and given birth to within this global economy mecca, but they also become international standards of ideal education and international policy. The United Nations Educational, Scientific, and Cultural Organization (UNESCO) has a physical location in the tecnópolis of New York City. This organization plays a crucial role in the ways education policy is created, adopted, and implemented in developing countries. As such, the educational system of numerous countries will adopt the recommendations, suggestions, and expert knowledge produced within this international body.

Capitalist and modernist educational models have been the critique of the vast works of Paulo Freire, bell hooks, Stanley Aranowitz, Henry Giroux, Peter McLaren, Michael Apple, Joe Kincheloe, Shirley Steinberg, and Donaldo Macedo, as well as countless other critical pedagogues. Their works have given me a unique analytical perspective on the purpose of educational policy within urban centers in the United States and other parts of the world.

Interestingly enough, with an acquired critical pedagogue lens, UNESCO policies will become a center unit of analysis within this chapter. In addition, the type of education adopted internationally has the desired outcome of creating a myriad of tecnópolises worldwide. Better still, developing countries need to shift their traditional urban centers into cutting-edge tecnópolises, which ideally can function as peers in the global economy. To what extent this global tecnópolis phenomenon is truth or fallacy will be the task of the subsequent pages. Nonetheless, urban education tecnópolises such as New York City have the historical conjuncture of dictating international urban education policies, methodologies, curriculum, and models of pedagogy.

INTRODUCTION

Global capitalism, characterized by Antonio Negri and Michael Hardt as an empire,[4] has a specific agenda of expanding and consolidating its influence and dominion to the farthest corners of the world. Such characteristics of global capital are known by some as imperialism, neocolonialism, neoliberalism, hegemony, or just simply oppression and exploitation.[5] The empire uses various tactics ranging from military might to more "subtle" forms of domination via education and psychology.[6]

GLOBALIZATION AND NEOCOLONIALISM

Contemporary informatics makes the post-modern global order logistically workable just as modern technologies made modern states possible. Modern states, as well as modern science, the machine age, modern war and European Imperialism all developed simultaneously in a messy, bloody conversation and confrontation. This is all the more sobering when we realize that today we are in the midst of a similar conversation, as technoscience and politics make another staggering transition.

—*H. Gray and S. Mentor*[7]

The foregoing epigraph is an excellent pretext for the following discussion. Postmodern literature calls for the end of universalistic or grand narrative/meta-narrative overgeneralizing concepts.[8] As a result of our "postmodern" condition in the field of political economy, there is not a general consensus as to what globalization is. There is a common thread that refers to globalization as the extant transnational political and economical social order.[9] Other scholars ascribe to the belief that globalization is an ongoing historical process of over 500 years spearheaded by European westward, eastward, and southward expansions.[10] This European expansion constituted a colonial era where there was not a corner of the world that was not a victim of European colonialism and imperialism. Although particularly after World War II, there was a process of decolonization; many political, economical, and psychological influences and dependencies prevailed in these "liberated" colonies. In this context, globalization is an ongoing process of imperialism that materialized centuries of colonialism worldwide. Through time, colonialism metamorphosed into complex relationships of global networks that materialized the extant era of neocolonialism.[11] Postcolonial theory is an extreme fertile ground of theories that helps us to understand the myriad extant neocolonial relationships throughout the world. Via postcolonialism, scholars engage in a process of knowledge construction where the multiple influences, relationships, dynamics, and psyche characteristic of imperial and colonial conditions are perpetuated by ex-colonial states, policies, structures, and subjectivities.[12]

The understanding of neocolonial relationships is crucial to fully understand the social, political, cultural, and psychological effects of globalization. The abstract concept of globalization is perhaps even more significant than its rote definition. This chapter will focus on the following two main areas: (1) information and communication technologies (ITC) and flexible mode of production and (2) international structures and policies.

INFORMATION AND COMMUNICATION TECHNOLOGIES AND FLEXIBLE MODE OF PRODUCTION

In the context of "advanced" capitalism, like a retro virus, capitalism has the obligation to expand, self-perpetuate, or die. Capitalist expansion must consolidate its domain worldwide. Such consolidation is what Italian sociologist Toni Negri denominates as the empire. This empire materializes itself via the combination of the creation and dissemination of information and communication technologies, intertwined with centuries of bloody relationships of imperialism and colonialism that paved and continues to pave the way for the current social and political "stability" that guarantees this empire survives by any means.[13] The concept of empire will be used throughout this chapter to engulf the historical process of global capital and its pertinent political, economical, cultural, and psychological hegemonic projects of domination.

According to Spanish sociologist Manuel Castells, we live in the information age.[14] The information age is the extant sociohistorical reality in which our economies are mediated and interwoven with ICT. Information and communication technologies are defined as all those pieces of technologies that process, analyze, and host information (i.e., computers, routers, bridges, TCP/IP, servers, computers, UNIX, LINUX, etc.). In fact, according to Castells, information has become a commodity.[15] As such, wealth and surplus value are accumulated via the mode of information. This is why "advanced" capitalism is inherently mediated through ICTs. The means of production, nowadays, are dependent on both technology and information. Without ICTs, globalization would not be possible and the empire would be a sci-fi story instead of a reality.

Political economists concur that ICTs are the driving force that permitted the possibility of an ever increasingly fast global economical system.[16] The speeds of global capital transactions are only possible via ICTs. The vast networks of information interconnected via cellular, satellite, and microwave services permit what is called a flexible mode of production. Learning from the devastating effects of the overproduction crisis of 1929, capitalism avoids at all

cost overproducing any product. In the context of globalization, corporations have adopted the policy of producing only what they can sell. For example, the Dell Computer Corporation does not make a computer unless it has already been sold. Dell production tactics are known as a flexible mode of production.[17] A flexible mode of production is characterized by multiple strategic geographical points of production integrated via information/communication technologies. For instance, Dell has multiple plants all over the world. In the different parts of the world, they produce different parts of a Dell computer. The casing could be built in China, the motherboards in Taiwan, and the transistors' parts in Mexico, while the administrative operations are conducted in the United States. Via information technologies, the U.S. administrative center coordinates the production of parts all over the world in such an integrated fashion that there is no overproduction of parts. This is what political economists call flexible mode of production. Dell does not produce computers for the 6.7-billion-world population. Doing so would be corporate suicide. Instead, they target the 500–800 million people worldwide who can afford to buy the products, and base their production on these more realistic numbers.

Another fundamental characteristic of ICTs and flexible mode of production is what Dickens refers to as time and space compression.[18] Time and space compression is the interwoven relationship between ICTs and flexible mode of production. In fact, flexible mode of production is economically viable due to time and space compression. The vast networks of ICTs create a historical phenomenon where notions of time and space are compressed.[19] Corporations can access and disseminate information vital to their success. Because of time and space compression, Dell Corporation can communicate, in various forms, to all of their assembly plants worldwide. At the stroke of a key, they can find out and decide how many parts need to be purchased, produced, and sold simultaneously. This is only possible through the materialization of vast networks of ICTs that are currently the lifeline of the information age and global capitalism.[20]

INTERNATIONAL STRUCTURES AND POLICIES

Toni Negri's empire is more than mere combinations of ICTs and economists' preference of a particular mode of production. The empire is a hybrid culmination of political, economical, cultural, and psychological historical processes. During and predominantly after World War II, there was a proliferation of international institutions. The United Nations (UN), International Monetary Fund (IMF), World Bank (WB), General Agreement of Trade and Tariffs (GATT), and North Atlantic Treaty Organization (NATO) were all created in less than a decade.[21] These organizations, among others, spearheaded the political and economical agenda of globalization. The creation of an international/transnational government and economical system became the agenda of all these international bodies, in their own particular way.

The WB, IMF, WTO, and GATT were and are the economical policy makers. The economic policies created by these international institutions benefit a transnational economical elite. The ways the policies are articulated creates a neocolonial condition known as economical dependency. The economic model of dependency has been the modus operandi for developing countries. The economical dependency model consists of multiple laws, structures, and policies that shape and mold a developing country's future. For instance, a developing country needs external investments, international loans, and a way to design a prosperous economy. To secure this financial backing, they need to both consult with and gain approval from the International Monetary Fund and the World Bank. The IMF and WB will give a developing country the resources and infrastructure it needs, as long as their recommendations are followed. So for example, if Ecuador needs the resources and infrastructure for better roads and transportation systems, both the IMF and WB will tell them where, how, and with what to build the roads. But if Ecuador wants to conserve its mountains and the IMF and WB believe it's cheaper and better to blow them up, Ecuador has to blow up the mountains to build the road. Also, if Ecuador wishes to stimulate the local economy by using Ecuadorian building material, but the IMF and WB believe they need to use U.S. or European construction material, they must submit to the IMF's and WB's will. The policies of economical development are geared and articulated to maintain a "subtle" dominance over countries that have been historically stripped of their wealth and resources via their colonial past.[22] Through the models of economical dependency, the colonies become neocolonies.

The emergence of the World Trade Organization and treaties such as the North American Free Trade Agreement (NAFTA), Asian Pacific Economic Cooperation (APEC), and *Mercado Común del Sur* (MERCOSUR), have accentuated the politics of economical dependencies. These international bodies articulate, implement, and materialize the way geographical regions will produce what is in function of the global economy. So, for instance, any country that wishes to enhance its agricultural industry is forced to submit itself to the will of these multiple international institutions. For instance, the northern African country of Somalia was the victim of an extreme famine that "needed" military intervention.[23] At the time, Somalia was undergoing some economical restructuring. Part of that restructuring affected its agricultural industry. Ironically, the country that was victim of a serious famine produced more than fifty percent of all the peanuts consumed by European countries.[24] As part of Somalia's strategy to insert itself in the global economy, it was forced to transform its agricultural industry into producing only peanuts. Lands that previously fed the Somalian people stopped producing multiple crops and had to just produce peanuts for exportation purposes only. All of this food is produced, but leaves the country.

Somalia is an extreme case, but multiple countries in Latin America, and all over the world, are instructed by the IMF, WB, WTO, and GATT to produce certain kinds of crops. For instance, Brazil provides soy and wood, Ecuador produces bananas, Ghana produces pineapple, China manufactures plastics, Haiti produces Disney paraphernalia and major league baseballs, Taiwan and Hong Kong produce electronic parts, and so on. The products that multiple countries produce are determined by the IMF, WB, WTO, GATT, NAFTA, APEC, MERCOSUR, and their respective treaties, models of economical development, funding, infrastructures, and policies.[25]

The empire's tactics of economic dependency models for developing countries are a continuation of colonial rule in postcolonial ways, materializing neocolonization worldwide. In the following sections, we will examine what globalization and the empire have to do with education and colonialism, postcolonialism, and neocolonialism.

THE U.N. DECADE OF LITERACY: A "SUBTLE" FORM OF NEOCOLONIALISM

A Sociohistorical Pretext

Toni Negri's empire is characterized by political economists as a point in human history where absolute poverty is at an unprecedented high.[26] Absolute poverty is the lack of even the most basic living conditions, which include at least one meal per day, a house or shelter in which to live, running water, electricity, and access to health care and education.[27] In the empire of the twenty-first century, the rich are getting richer and the poor are getting poorer. As you read this chapter, one percent of the world's population controls ninety percent of its wealth.[28] In times where there appears not to be enough wealth for everybody, conglomerates of elite capitalists have at least $1 trillion of speculative capital. This means there is a trillion dollars floating in ICT networks, waiting to be invested in a viable moneymaking scheme. The accumulation of wealth is such that if the conglomerate of elite capitalists wanted to invest in the enrichment of the human race, they could give $1,000 to each of the 6.7 billion inhabitants of the planet and still have billions of dollars left to invest in their moneymaking schemes. This accumulation of wealth and the heightening of poverty is truly a historical precedent never seen before.[29]

The empire needs to do something about these figures. It cannot maintain itself under such extreme conditions of global injustices. According to many scholars, a continuation of wealth accumulation without serious redistribution will cause an economical recession that will make the stock market crash look like a walk in the park. Multiple capitalist magnates, such as the Rockefellers, Carnegies, Bilderbergs, and Rothschilds, recognize this possibility. As such they have put time, money, and effort into creating some of the international institutions like the UN, WTO, WB, IMF, Council of Foreign Relations, and Trilateral Commission, among others.[30] In doing so, their economical empires perpetuate themselves. Furthermore, these international institutions are intertwined to create, disseminate, and implement models and policies of economic development, education, foreign aid, diplomatic treaties and negotiations, and humanitarian aid. In fact, it is the task of a division of the U.N.—the United Nations Educational, Cultural, and Scientific Organization (UNESCO)—to minimize and eliminate the reality of absolute poverty and deal with issues that greatly affect developing countries.

Education and Colonization

Historically, education has been a crucial tool to implement and perpetuate colonial and imperial relations of dominance.[31] According to Spring, education was the tool that, to a greater or lesser extent, "transformed" Native American culture to bring it into harmony with the emerging nation of the United States. Under the pretext of civilizing the savage natives, they dramatically altered their worldview from a collective one to a more individualistic one.[32] Furthermore, they instilled the importance and necessity of private property, using the land resources for purposes other than hunting, gathering, and performing religious ceremonies and pilgrimages to places that were considered sacred.[33] Education has been used in more "modern" times to "educate" the colonial natives about the virtues of liberal capitalist society. According to Carnoy, education has been used as a form of cultural imperialism. Educational programs in colonial and postcolonial India, Africa, and Latin America were the means to instill and guarantee that the capitalist system is perpetuated via a capitalist culture that will guarantee a capitalist society.[34] Values that are not in tune with the capitalist logic are deemed barbaric, uncivilized, and uneducated.[35] In the twenty-first century, Negri's empire is doing the same things. Under the guise of Gramcy's notion of hegemony, "modern" models and projects of global education are attempting to do the same thing.

Education for All

One of the few international institutions that has "aggressively" tried to deal with the issues and problems arising from global poverty is UNESCO. The lack of education, particularly literacy, is a big concern among developing and developed countries. For example, the U.N. published the *United Nations Literacy Decade: Education for All Plan of Action*, which states:

Literacy is not only an indispensable tool for lifelong education and learning but is also an essential requisite for citizenship and human and social development. The right of every individual to education, as recognized in the Universal Declaration of Human Rights, is strongly rooted in the right to literacy. Major efforts have been devoted to literacy over the last fifty years both through remedial and preventive measures.[36]

Under the agenda of the literacy decade, the U.N., via UNESCO, has the arduous task of eliminating illiteracy worldwide by 2012–2015. One of the sections of the *Literacy for All* document states,

Literacy for All has to address the literacy needs of the individual as well as the family, literacy in the workplace and in the community, as well as in society and in the nation, in tune with the goals of economic, social and cultural development of all people in all countries.[37]

As the reader can appreciate this quote, we can analyze how the literacy agenda has as a guiding light the global empire. According to the vision, literacy has to address the needs of illiterate populations worldwide "in tune with the goals of economic social and cultural development of all people in all countries."[38] In tune to what goals? Who defines them? What kind of development? Who dictates such development? Under the extant conditions of the empire, it appears to be the case that the transnational elite is the one doing all of the defining of both the pertinent goals and models of development. In other words, UNESCO's education for

all is to summit the global illiterate population into the global economical, social,
and cultural system of the empire.
Although the literacy for all agenda is
neither inherently good nor bad, and is
paradoxically an undeniable necessity,
the wording is highly problematic. The
discourse, implicit within the wording,
looks like, feels like, and tastes like neocolonial and cultural imperialist tactics to
expand the empire's sphere of influence
and domination.

The apparent definition of literacy is
used rather loosely. In none of the U.N. documents reviewed was there a clear definition of literacy. They use literacy
depending on their discursive needs. In the
Literacy for All document, literacy is acquiring basic reading and writing skills. Paradoxically, the document suggests that the
traditional definition of literacy is viewed
as limited. For instance, "literacy policies
and programs today require going beyond
the limited view of literacy that has dominated in the past. Literacy for all requires
a renewed vision of literacy."[39] Renewed
visions of literacy include "updated" applications such as media literacy and information communication technology literacy,
which can be broken down into computer
literacy and network literacy, among others.[40] In this context, literacy, education,
and ICT are interwoven in a broad international agenda of education in relation to
global economy, politics, and culture.

ICTs, THE EMPIRE, AND NEOCOLONIZATION

In the rapidly changing world of today's knowledge society, with the progressive use of newer
and innovative technological means of communication, literacy requirements continue to
expand regularly. In order to survive in today's
globalized world, it has become necessary for
all people to learn new *literacies* and develop the
ability to locate, evaluate, and effectively use
information in multiple manners.[41]

—UNESCO

The empire has a concrete agenda to
expand its influence and dominance
worldwide. The implementation of the
empire's agenda is disseminated via international institutions such as the U.N.,
WTO, WB, IMF, and treaties such as
NAFTA, MERCOSUR, APEC, and GATT,
among others. Informational and communications technologies, educational agendas of multiple literacies, and economic
development are currently interwoven at
both macroeconomic and microsocial levels. The macroeconomic structures of
dependency combined with cultural imperialist education are consolidating the
empire's reach to the farthest corners of the
globe. The U.N.-implemented *Education for
All* program is not necessarily interested in
educating for the love of knowledge. In
fact, it believes that the poorest and most
underdeveloped countries do not have the
capability to produce knowledge like First
World countries can. The UNESCO general
report of May 2001, states:

Poor countries—and poor people—differ from
rich ones not only because they have less capital but also because they have less knowledge.
Knowledge is often complex and costly to create and disseminate, and that is why much of it
is created in industrialized countries. Developing countries can acquire knowledge from
external sources as well as create their own.
The success of the development experience in
Asia relative to Africa and Latin America is
due in part to the ability of East Asian countries to acquire and apply knowledge.[42]

According to the U.N. report, East Asia
has been relatively more successful than
Africa and Latin America because it has
both acquired and applied knowledge that
is relevant only within the context of global capital. The knowledge acquired and
applied by East Asia goes hand in hand
with the empire's neocolonial consolidation of power and dominance. If Africa
and Latin America are not as successful, it
is because either they do not acquire the
proper knowledge or they apply it in the
wrong ways. But who defines what is cor-

rect knowledge creation, acquisition, and proper application?

The U.N. report exposes that there are two kinds of knowledge: "(A) technical or 'know-how' knowledge; and (B) knowledge about attributes. Knowledge about attributes 'illuminates every economic transaction, revealing preferences, giving clarity to exchanges.'"[43] Furthermore, "the lack of such knowledge results in imperfect markets, the collapse of markets or, worse still, the absence of markets, all of which are detrimental to development and hurt the poor."[44]

In the empire context, certain forms of knowledge are privileged, particularly those in tune with global capital. For example,

Knowledge and information are incorporated into goods and services. Knowledge and information are sources of wealth creation and value added in their own right. As their amount and value increase, there is a proportionate decrease in the amount and value of other inputs such as labour, capital, materials etc. The concentration of knowledge and information-intensive industries in the industrialized countries contributes significantly to the development and technology gap between industrialized and developing countries.[45]

The impending necessity of creating knowledge and cultures that benefit and enrich global capital has propelled the United Nations to create an ICT task force. Similar to UNESCO's *Education for All* agenda, the ICT task force has the mandate to minimize and eliminate the global digital divide. According to the U.N.'s ICT task force document, they: "plan to use information and communications technologies to combat poverty."[46] Therefore, the ICT task force is looking for ways to create policies, educational programs, and efficient economic models. In their document, they state that there is a need to:

(a) forge strategic partnerships between the United Nations system, private industry, trusts and foundations, donor governments, program countries, and other relevant international actors; (b) develop innovative modalities for strengthening the ICT capacity of develop-

ing countries; (c) pool the experiences of both developed and developing countries in introducing and promoting ICT for development; and (d) mobilize resources supported by voluntary contributions.[47]

It is interesting to note that part of their partnerships with private sectors include information and communication magnates such as Cisco (they produce servers, hubs, bridges, and routers that serve as the nuts and bolts of the ICT networks) and Microsoft (a corporation that has an extant monopoly with software such as Office, Internet Explorer, Outlook, and Publisher, among others).[48]

The knowledge and information that are embedded within the vast ICT networks of global capital that are a source of accumulation of wealth will be considered as gold. Apparently this is the type of knowledge that needs to be taught via the *Education for All* and *Literacy Decade* programs of the United Nations. The development, creation, and dissemination of knowledge embedded within global capital are a form of neocolonization. Neocolonial dominance is asserted culturally and psychologically, via educational programs that legitimate certain knowledge as the only way for countries, citizens, communities, and individuals to insert themselves effectively in the global economy. Welcome to what George Bush, Sr., vehemently boasted of in his presidential term of 1988–92 as the New World Order.

FINAL THOUGHTS

Not everything the United Nation does is a form of neocolonization. The *Education for All* and *Literacy Decade* programs have been used as examples of instances where policies, construction of certain knowledges, legitimacy of certain knowledges, and the embedded nature of education and literacy with global capital, serve as instances of neocolonization. Neocolonization occurs when the education is only in relation to the global economy.

Some documents examined in this chapter (i.e., *Education for All*, *Literacy Decade*, and ICT task force) tie education agendas with neoliberal projects of economic, political, social, cultural, and psychological processes that facilitate the empire of global capital. The educational, literacy, and ICT programs serve as tools of neocolonization as long as they continue to privilege, validate, and legitimize knowledge in relation to global capital.

Historically, any geographical region that has defied the global capital empire has met stiff resistance and repression.[49] We have the current examples of both the Zapatistas in Mexico and the Ogoni in Nigeria. Both cultures have defied global capital. The Zapatistas are resisting being once again stripped from their land by oil companies and the Ogonis are both claiming their lands back and demanding reparations for serious environmental contamination due to oil extraction by Shell Oil Corporation. Both of them have suffered harsh repression in the forms of public executions, torture, and imprisonment, while simultaneously, any alternative non-economy-dependent model of economical development proposed has been systematically turned down.[50]

There is always reason for hope and empowerment. Global education programs and ICT dissemination have the potential to force the empire to reexamine its hegemonic ways.[51] The current macroeconomic structures are characterized by their policies of trickle-down economics. For instance, the fact that multiple anti-WTO manifestations have challenged the oppressive nature of such institutions at their meetings in Seattle; Washington, DC; Prague; and Cancun, to name a few, proves there is discontent among world citizens.[52] In the organization of such anti-WTO protests, ICTs were an integral organizational component.[53] In such context, extant neocolonial experiences and structures can be redefined in a global system of social justice.[54] The task falls upon those who are involved in the various programs of education, literacy, and ICT dissemination. If literacy is imparted within critical literacy models, education is based on practices of critical pedagogy geared toward emancipation, and ICT dissemination is nurtured to excel in its potential emancipatory possibilities, then we are faced with a conundrum of a global utopia. If, on the other hand, the current policies of economical, political, military, cultural, social, and psychological domination remain in place, then the global capital elite will continue to profit from their sophisticated structures, tactics, and policies of hegemonic neocolonization. In this gloomy social historical reality, educators, educational institutions, educational policies, and education advocates have the arduous task of becoming beacons of light in the struggle for education for all who ascribe to beliefs of social justice, solidarity, and emancipation as the driving force of all educational activity.[55]

NOTES

1. Castells, M., & Hall, P. (1994). *Las tecnópolis del mundo: La formación de los complejos industriales del siglo xxi*. Madrid: Alianza Editorial.

2. Hables, G. (Ed.). (1995). *The cyborg handbook*. New York & London: Routledge.

3. Castells, M. (1995). *La ciudad informacional: Tecnologías de la información, reestructuración económica y el proceso urbano-regional*. Madrid: Alianza Editorial.

4. Hardt, M., & Negri, A. (2000). *El imperio*. Madrid: Paidos y Sociedad 95.

5. Dickens, P. (1998). *The global shift: Transforming the world economy*. New York: The Guilford Press; Hoogvelt, A. (1998). *Globalization and the post-colonial world: The new political economy of the globe*. Baltimore: John Hopkins University Press; Horton, R. (1998). *Globalization and the nation state*. New York: St. Martin's Press; Carnoy, M. (1988). *Educación como imperialismo cultural*. Mexico: S.XXI; Klowby, J. (1997). *Inequity, power and development: The task of political sociology*. Atlantic Highlands, NJ: Humanities Press.

6. Hardt & Negri (2000).

7. Gray, H., & Mentor, S. (1995). The cyborg body politics: Version 1. In G. Hables (Ed.), *The cyborg handbook*. New York & London: Routledge.

8. Sarup, M. (1996). *Identity, culture and identity and the postmodern world*. Athens: The University of Georgia Press.

9. Dickens (1998); Horton (1998).

10. Klowby (1997); Robinson (1997), *Promoting poliarchy*, Atlantic Highlands, NJ: Humanities Press.

11. Hoogvelt, A. (1998). *Globalization and the post-colonial world: The new political economy of the globe*. Baltimore: John Hopkins University Press.

12. Ashcroft, B., Griffiths, G., & Tiffin, H. (1995). *Postcolonial study reader*. London: Routledge.

13. Hardt & Negri (2000).

14. Castells, M. (1998). *La era de la información: Economía, sociedad y cultura Vol. III fin del milenio*. Madrid: Alianza Editorial.

15. Castells, M. (2000). *The information age: Economy, society and culture: Vol. I. The rise of the network society*. Australia: Blackwell Publishing.

16. Please read the works of Dickens (1998); Klowby (1997); Horton (1998); and Castells (1998).

17. For a more detailed account on flexible mode of production, please look at Dickens (1998).

18. Dickens (1998).

19. Dickens (1998).

20. Castells (2000).

21. Hardt & Negri (2000).

22. Hoogvelt (1998).

23. Chomsky, N. (1998). *Deterring democracy*. New York: Hill and Wang.

24. Robinson (1997).

25. Stiglitz, J. (2003). *Globalization and its discontents*. New York: W.W. Norton.

26. Klowby (1997).

27. Klowby (1997).

28. Klowby (1997).

29. Klowby (1997).

30. Still, W. (1990). *New world order*. Lafayette, LA: Huntington House Publisher; Perloff, J. (1988). *The shadows of power: The council on foreign relations and the American decline*. Appleton, WI: Western Islands Publishers.

31. Carnoy, M. (1988). *La educación como imperialismo culutral*. S.XXI Mexico.

32. Spring, J. (2000). *Deculturalization and education*. New York: Houghton Mifflin.

33. Spring (2000).

34. Carnoy (1998).

35. Carnoy (1998).

36. UNESCO. (2002). *United Nations literacy decade: education for all: plan of action*. New York: United Nations Educational, Scientific and Cultural Organization.

37. UNESCO (2002).

38. UNESCO (2002).

39. UNESCO (2002).

40. Tyner, K. (1998). *Literacy in the digital world: Teaching and learning in the age of information*. Mahwah, NJ: Laurence Erlbaum Assoc.

41. UNESCO (2002).

42. UNESCO. (2001a). *The role of the United Nations in promoting development, particularly with respect to access to and transfer of knowledge and technology, especially information and communication technologies, inter alia, through partnerships with relevant stakeholders, including the private sector: Report of the Secretary General of the Economical and Social Council*. New York: United Nations Educational, Scientific and Cultural Organization.

43. UNESCO. (2001b). *Plan to use information & communications technologies to combat poverty*. New York: United Nations Educational, Scientific and Cultural Organization.

44. UNESCO (2001b).

45. UNESCO. (2001c). *Literacy for all: A United Nations literacy decade*. New York: United Nations Educational, Scientific and Cultural Organization.

46. UNESCO (2001b).

47. UNESCO (2001b).

48. UNESCO (2001b).

49. Blum, W. (1995). *Killing hope: U.S. military and CIA interventions since WW II*. Monroe, ME: Common Courage Press; Chomsky (1996).

50. Castells, M. (2004). *The information age: Economy, society and culture: Vol. II. The power of identity*. Australia: Blackwell Publishing; Stiglitz (2003).

51. Welton, N., & Wolf, L. (2002). *Global uprising: Confronting the tyrannies of the 21st century: Stories from a new generation of activists*. Canada: New Society Publishers; Castells (2004).

52. Welton & Wolf (2002); Castells (2004).

53. Vegh, S. (2003). Classifying forms of online activism: The case of cyberprotests against the world. In M. Mccaughey & M. Ayers (Eds.), *Cyberactivism: Online activism in theory and practice*. London: Routledge.

54. Welton, N., & Wolf, L. (2002).

55. See Freire, P. (1998). *Teachers as cultural workers: Letters to those who dare to teach*. New York: Westview Press; Freire, P. (1998). *Education for critical consciousness*. New York: Continuum Publishing Company; Freire, P. (1996).

Pedagogy of the oppressed. New York: Continuum Publishing Company; Aranowitz, S.
(2001). *The last good job in America: Work and*

education in the global technoculture. New York:
Rowman & Littlefield Publishers, Inc.

UNIVERSITIES, REGIONAL POLICY, AND THE KNOWLEDGE ECONOMY

Michael A. Peters and Tim May

THE NEW ECONOMY?

In the West, educational policy has given way to talk of the knowledge economy under the sway of world policy organizations like the Organisation for Economic Co-operation and Development (OECD) and the World Bank. The terms "knowledge economy" and "knowledge capitalism" emerged in the mid-1990s to become national policy templates for many Western governments and developing economies. The government of the United Kingdom (U.K.), for example, has pronounced the end of the comprehensive school, based on a "one-size-fits-all" welfare state ideology, and signaled a shift to a fully consumer-driven system of public services in health and education, based on the market ideology of choice and diversity. This shift to the "social market" is underwritten and accompanied by an emphasis on national competitiveness within the global economy and the way in which the "new economy" demands new levels of flexible skilled knowledge workers. This chapter examines the discourse of the knowledge economy and education as an "industry of the future" that can promote regional development, with the attendant emphasis on public–private partnerships and the cultural reconstruction of city entrepreneurial cultures and clustering of knowledge capital activities.

Digitalization, speed, and compression are the forces at work that have trans-formed the global economy and now have begun to affect every aspect of knowledge production—its organization, storage, retrieval, and transmission. The knowledge economy has certainly arrived, although this does not mean the end of the business cycle, as many early advocates of the new economy maintained. But it does signal structural economic shifts and new sources of growth in some Western economies (e.g., U.S., Finland) that delivered both low unemployment and low inflation due to increased productivity. Although it is clear that investment in ICT (Information and Communications Technology) and ICT-driven productivity growth has led to a higher growth path, there is a risk of exaggerating the growth potential due to ICT investment alone. Yet as a recent OECD report put it:

It would be wrong to conclude that there was nothing exceptional about the recent U.S. experience, that the new economy was in fact a myth. Some of the arguments posited by new economy sceptics are of course true: the effect of ICT may be no greater than other important inventions of the past, like electricity generation and the internal combustion engine. Moreover, far greater productivity surges were recorded in previous decades, not least in the period before the 1970s.[1]

Nevertheless, the evidence suggests that something new is taking place in the structure of OECD economies. The report continues by maintaining that ICT has facilitated productivity-enhancing changes in the firm, in both new and traditional industries, but only when accompanied with greater skills and changes in the organisation of work. Consequently, policies that engage ICT, human capital, innovation and entrepreneurship in the growth process, alongside fundamental policies to control inflation and instil competition, while controlling public finances are likely to bear the most fruit over the longer term.[2]

Crucially, the report investigates and recommends a set of relationships and policies that harness ICT, human capital, innovation, and business creation, focusing on the wider diffusion of ICT and the role of education and training policies in meeting today's skill requirements.

Clearly, the Internet economy is becoming an integral part of the global economy, creating jobs, increasing productivity, and transforming companies and institutions. Employment in the Internet economy is growing faster than in the traditional economy. In the U.S. economy alone, the Internet generated an estimated $830 billion in revenues in 2000, which represented a 58 percent increase over 1989.[3] J. Bradford DeLong, former deputy assistant secretary for economic policy in the U.S. Department of the Treasury, depicts the "new economy," asserting it is both a knowledge and an innovation knowledge where clusters of innovation, based on new technologies and new business models, succeed each other. He maintains it is likely to continue for an extended time, and its consequences are pervasive. He provides an analytical overview of the digital economy, which conveys how different it is from the market economy of orthodox economics. He likens the digital economy to the enclosure of the common lands in early modern Britain, which paved the way for the agricultural and industrial revolutions. Digital commodities, he maintains, do not behave like standard goods and services of economic theory: They are nonrivalrous, barely excludable,

and not transparent. The store of music track is not diminished when one downloads a track from the Internet; it is difficult, if not impossible, to restrict distribution of goods that can be reproduced with no or little cost, and a consumer does not know how good software is before purchase or indeed how its successor versions will perform in the future.

It is important to recognize that the knowledge economy is both classical and new. Danny Quah of the London School of Economics indicates that the economic importance of knowledge can be found in examples where deployment of machines boosted economic performance such as in the Industrial Revolution. By contrast, he talks of the "weightless economy" "where the economic significance of knowledge achieves its greatest contemporary resonance" and suggests it comprises four main elements:

1. Information and communications technology (ICT), the Internet.
2. Intellectual assets: Not only patents and copyrights but also, more broadly, name brands, trademarks, advertising, financial and consulting services, and education.
3. Electronic libraries and databases: including new media, video entertainment, and broadcasting.
4. Biotechnology: carbon-based libraries and databases, pharmaceuticals.

Elsewhere he argues:

Digital goods are bitstrings, sequences of 0s and 1s, which have economic value. They are distinguished from other goods by five characteristics: digital goods are nonrival, infinitely expansible, discrete, aspatial, and recombinant.[4]

Quah has been influential in suggesting that knowledge concentrations spontaneously emerge in space, even when physical distance and transportation costs are irrelevant. The dynamics of spatial distributions manifest themselves in convergent clusters. This is an important feature, especially given the development of the economy first in Silicon Valley.

In *Getting the Measure of the New Economy*, Diane Coyle and Danny Quah note the 11 percent productivity gap between the U.K. and Germany, and the 45 percent productivity gap with the United States (1999 base year), while at the same time acknowledging the considerable impact of ICT on the economy.[5] They demonstrate on the basis of evidence from the United States that those businesses responding the quickest to ICT developments are driving forward the rest of the economy. At the same time, they maintain that technology takes time to filter through and set up the cascade effects that are evident in change organizational and business practices. They acknowledge that after the dot-com bubble burst, confidence in the new economy has waned, yet they remain optimistic about long-term technology-led economic growth based on the processing power of the microchip, which encompasses well-known developments like the Internet and developments in information and communications technologies with gene technology, nanotechnology, robotics, and advanced materials. They write:

Advocates of the notion of the new economy cited supporting factors uniquely combined in the U.S. economy, particularly minimal government, high levels of competition, encouragement of entrepreneurship, and access to venture capital. What gave the theory bite, though, was the vision that the widespread diffusion of technology had permanently changed the way economies had worked for the better.[6]

They also develop a set of indicators to measure the changes to the deep structure of the economy brought about by technology.

CLUSTERING EFFECTS OF NEW ICT-DRIVEN ECONOMY ACTIVITY

One of the most significant features of these economic changes is the way in which against expectations a sort of geographical clustering of new economic activity appears to have taken place. This clustering even applies to the boarder accounts of its development and spread. The Silicon Valley view of the e-conomy maintains that the center-periphery model with development spreading from the West Coast, south of Palo Alto, forced the development of a single international market that is dominated by U.S. multinationals. By contrast, the pluri-view suggests that Internet leading-edge use and e-commerce centers are beginning to emerge in Europe and Asia, and as new technologies emerge, along with different uses, business models, and legal frameworks, they will challenge the early dominance of U.S. policy and the international market. If there are different local configurations of market demand and distinct trajectories of development and separate national e-conomies, then they are most likely to emerge around fundamental empirical criteria such as distinct technologies and applications; locally differentiated market structures; different business models; perhaps, distinct structures of comparative advantage; and culturally different legal and policy frameworks.

The alleged aspatial character of digital goods seems to fly in the face of empirical evidence. Given their "weightlessness," digital goods are theorized to spread easily across the globe without favoring particular locations, yet empirical analysis reveals exactly the opposite—that the production of digital goods like other goods becomes geographically concentrated. In fact, as Quah argues, "the geographical clustering of computer software and digital media production, academic and commercial R & D, and financial services, among other digital goods, is likely tighter than for ordinary goods and services."[7] He argues further that the aspatiality of digital goods does not imply that space no longer matters; indeed, only transportation costs no longer matter, and others factors normally associated with geography take on a heightened importance.

He indicates that embodied human capital clusters geographically because communication of tacit knowledge is most efficient in close proximity. In other words, "synchronous face-to-face interactions matter for transmitting (nonbitstring) knowledge."[8] On this understanding, sometimes learning is considered the core of a theory of clustering, focusing on the existence, the internal organization, and boundaries of the cluster.[9]

The major theoretical question is, why has industry clustering reappeared in advanced economies when it had all but disappeared in the mid-twentieth century? Phillip Cooke suggests that the "knowledge economy" consists of fragments and runs against conventional economic analysis that assumes individualistic competition within an ordered economic equilibrium.[10] By contrast, with the knowledge economy he points to *disequilibrium* or economic and social imbalance, *collaborative* economic action as the basis of modern capitalism, and the *systemic* nature of strategic competitiveness of groups' actions based on consensus rather than individual opportunism. Against the status of the lonely Nietzschean heroic individual and entrepreneur characterized by Schumpeter, Cooke suggests the sources of innovation lie in networks of social relationships, that is, *knowledge networks*. He argues:

clusters are crucial to economic imbalance . . . they rest upon collaboration of a generally non-market-destroying type that is simply essential for modern economic organization, and . . . clusters have systemic organizational characteristics that go against much economic orthodoxy.[11]

Such an analysis then directly leads to an emphasis on "the geographical dimension of learning, knowledge transfer, collaboration and the exploitation of the spillovers." Cooke concurs with Quah that "proximity in a cluster offers the opportunity for tacit knowledge exchange or 'treacherous' learning that may be hindered in large firms by 'group think' and corporate culture."[12]

Government policy has changed to accent and foster the geographical cluster of new economic activity. It is clear that that Labour government sees the "knowledge-driven economy" as key to the U.K.'s competitive success. The strategy behind the adoption of this concept is to promote high-tech venture capital "clusters" in the regions. In part, the U.K. strategy is strongly influenced by Michael Porter's work on the role of clusters in forging U.S. innovativeness and competitiveness.[13] Regional development agencies (RDAs) in Britain are encouraged to develop "cluster" policies based on knowledge industries.

For instance, the *White Paper on Enterprise, Skills, and Innovation* (2001) emphasizes the role of universities in the regional development of clusters in the knowledge economy:

The role of our universities in the economy is crucial. They are powerful drivers of innovation and change in science and technology, the arts, humanities, design and other creative disciplines. They produce people with knowledge and skills; they generate new knowledge and import it from diverse sources; and they apply knowledge in a range of environments. They are also the seedbed for new industries, products and services and are at the hub of business networks and industrial clusters of the knowledge economy.[14]

The examples can be developed further. The U.K. Office of Sciences and Technology emphasizes the importance of "knowledge transfer."

Within a modern, knowledge-driven economy, knowledge transfer is about transferring good ideas, research results and skills between universities, other research organisations, business and the wider community to enable innovative new products and services to be developed.[15]

This kind of emphasis can be clearly seen in OST's Higher Education Innovation Fund (HEIF):

We have now established the Higher Education Innovation Fund (HEIF), which together with the existing Higher Education Reach Out to Business and the Community fund (HEROBC), is worth £140 million over three years, to further build on universities' potential to act as drivers of growth in the knowledge economy. HEIF provides special funding to enable HEIs to respond to the needs of business, through both the continuing development of capacity in universities to interact with business and the community (building on HEROBC), and large, strategic, collaborative projects to strengthen university-business partnerships.[16]

More broadly, the U.K. government's economic strategy can be seen as being based on investment in science, engineering, and technology. In the recent White Paper, *Investing in Innovation: A Strategy for Science, Engineering and Technology,* the focus is on the twin strategies of renewing the physical and human capital, which underpins research and investing in capacity to exploit the burgeoning opportunities of new science.[17] In this strategy, universities are encouraged to link with business to create value for the regional and national economy where Regional Development Agencies play an enhanced role in developing knowledge transfer programs.

The regional development role of knowledge industries has received increasing attention in the United States and by the European Union (EU). CEOs for Cities, for example, an organization that explores best practices in urban economic development and proposes new strategic frameworks on emerging trends, recently partnered with the Initiative for a Competitive Inner City (ICIC) to develop a national study of the impact of higher education on urban economies. The study introduces a strategic impact framework and features case studies and best practices in university partnerships, including studies of both Virginia Commonwealth University (VCU) in Richmond, and Columbia University in New York City. The report begins:

Unleashing the local economic development capacity of these institutions (colleges and universities) should be a national priority. While ambitious, it is an agenda that does not require massive new funding or heroic changes in day-to-day operations of colleges and universities, city government or community groups.[18]

The Lisbon European Council set the "bold and ambitious" ten-year goal of making the EU the most dynamic, competitive, sustainable knowledge-based economy in the world. Yet the transition to the knowledge-based economy has been slow, and there is now recognition that spending on higher education needs to be strengthened. The argument is made that the European ability to produce, diffuse, and use knowledge effectively relies heavily on its capacity to produce highly educated people for its firms to be engaged in a continuing process of innovation. Yet lifelong learning is still not a reality for most Europeans citizens. It is now recognized that the European innovation systems have not been successful in exploiting the new techno-economic paradigm rooted in information technology that is reflected in the European paradox of a strong science base but weak innovation performance. As Lundvall and Borras argue: "A major policy objective of innovation policy must be to contribute to the learning capability of firms, knowledge institutions and people and to promote innovation and adaptation."[19] They point to "human resource development, new forms of firm organisation, network formation, new role for knowledge intensive business services and for universities as the key elements in speeding up the catching-up within this paradigm." A new regional policy focusing increasingly on the role of universities and of higher education more generally, first recognized in the Bologne agreement, has begun to theorize these economic imperatives in new spatialized knowledge networks. The role of universities in regional development has gone beyond the study of technology transfer and direct employment effects of spin-off companies and the establishment of science parks to embrace the wider ethos of the enhancement of human and social capital within a region, including emphasis on student recruitment and regional placement policies, university professional development programs for local managers based on local research, the development of research networks that serve as a basis for embedding the local businesses in the global economy, and a more research- and information-sensitive negotiation of the local/global interface.

UNIVERSITIES: THE MANCHESTER KNOWLEDGE CAPITAL INITIATIVE

In the North West of the United Kingdom, this policy context is reflected in several recent developments. The North West Universities Association (NWUA) was formed in 1999 and works increasingly closely with the North West Development Agency (NWDA) and other regional partners. In 2001, the North West established England's first science council, bringing together representatives from industry, regional agencies, and the universities to lobby on behalf of the region and advise and launch the Regional Science Strategy.[20] This was subsequently published in 2002 and sets forward cluster-based actions in five priority areas (biotechnology, environmental technologies, chemicals, aerospace, and nuclear energy) to link universities better with industry and regional partners. The model is one of "excellence with relevance."

Many RDAs are now devolving the implementation of aspects of regional strategies to subregional bodies, recognizing that some issues are better tackled at a lower spatial scale. At the same time, local authorities are collaborating with neighbors and partners to "upscale" their cities and tackle joint issues through a cross-boundary approach. The movement also now includes health authorities, universities, LEAs, skills agencies, charities, and the police who are active in their own city-regional partnerships. In a number of cases, the private sector is giving the lead to city-regional thinking, particularly in the arena of economic and planning policy.[21] In the Greater Manchester context, we see the development of the Greater Manchester subregional strategy, led by the Association of Greater Manchester Authorities (AGMA), launched on June 20, 2003. An essential element of this strategy focuses on enhancing the subregional core and building on the university assets concentrated therein.[22]

With this background in mind, the vision of Manchester: Knowledge Capital (KC) is

to create an internationally acclaimed "Knowledge Capital" within the Greater Manchester conurbation, which will position Manchester, branded as the Knowledge Capital, at the heart of the Knowledge Economy, significantly contributing to the economic growth of the nation and the North West region leading to a healthier city/region with a vibrant, safe and attractive environment in which to live, work and play, for people of all ages, social and cultural backgrounds.[23]

This initiative can be seen in the context of two major changes that are fundamentally reshaping our society, economy, and the institutions and practices of modern life: the development of the knowledge economy and changing notions of scale. These two factors have led to increasing attention being given to the role of universities in driving local and regional economies, reflected in a wealth of new policies being developed at international, national, regional, and subregional scales. These policies raise many challenges for universities and for their localities and a number of different responses, as international and national comparisons indicate. In this context, KC represents a much needed and valuable opportunity for the universities to position themselves at the heart of the city-region's response to the global knowledge economy.

From the forty interviews and documentary work conducted in the four universities (Manchester, MUU, Salford, and UMIST) with senior managers and those individuals who were considered key to successful implementation of KC, we can see the extent to which understandings remain aspirational at a variety of levels across the universities. Relatively speaking, the most well developed attempts at clarifying the meaning of KC are provided, not surprisingly, by those who are championing and driving the process for the universities. Overall, these are a small number of individuals in senior management positions. Here we see an explicit identification of a role; that is, creating the conditions that will enable its development. The role of senior managers is to create not only a vision, but also an infrastructure that will function without too much top-down planning to provide support and incentives.

Yet a clear aim of KC and one given by central government is that the universities should act in collaboration with each other and with other agencies for the benefit of the city-region. This was both implicit and explicit in many of the interviews. In particular, one senior manager spoke of a great strength of the city of Manchester being a "mutual trust between the key players." This is matched with the view of one senior manager in Manchester City Council who said that KC provided a context in which: "We construct the new HEI sector in such a way that it interfaces very effectively and coherently with a significantly wider world [than has been historically the case]." Many of these interviewees—while unpacking, or alternatively trying hard to populate, the notion of KC—also sought clarification as to its geographical focus. Some took it to concentrate on the North West of England, others Greater Manchester, some Manchester, but all with a degree of uncertainty. The idea of "capital" itself was also a source of ambiguity, with ideas of human capital and innovation mixing with those of cultural and physical capital and Manchester seeking to place itself more securely as

the "capital" of the North West. Importantly, what we see here are differences in aspiration and interpretation according to the remit of the individual interviewed. Those further up the hierarchy tended to be supportive of the idea in terms of its potential, while those with a concern for implementation and its implications for practice tended to be more uncertain. This belief came from an experience of so many "next big thing" initiatives that produced more work without tangible benefit. It also came from the institutional incentives that were available for engagement at different levels. As one interviewee put it, in relation to practices surrounding international research excellence (of which they were a part), KC should be about

achieving some sort of culture shift within the institution . . . the notion that you can only be taken seriously if you go to conferences in North America or Munich or whatever and that anything where you dirty your hands on things local, I mean, by definition is seen as trivial . . . the international and the local can readily co-exist together . . . [the University needs] levers to pull locally and to ensure that this might happen and all of the incentives and reward structures still tend to reinforce the argument.[24]

Incentivization and reward within the different institutions and how they relate to practice is clearly a major issue and one that has not been adequately considered in relation to the developmental potential of KC.

Two issues, in particular, then become important: (1) to develop the conditions that facilitate activities; and (2) for those activities to feed into KC in order that it moves from concept to action. What is required for this process is a set of practices that would populate the concept. As one person put it, it cannot just be about:

museums and office blocks and such like in the centre, but actually focus on regeneration through knowledge applied to entrepreneurial activities . . . that seems to me to be an excellent extension and the next stage after we've physically transformed the city into something worth living in . . . then we've got to jump start some entrepreneurial activity or it will be another Sheffield Centre for Popular Culture![25]

There were also differences between the institutions in terms of how they approach the potential of Knowledge Capital. Thus, those associated with UMIST/Victoria tended to see the development of KC as one of "added value." In other words, it was concerned with repackaging and exploiting existing opportunities for institutional benefit and that of the city as a whole, in terms of the location of the university and its relations with key stakeholders. This concerned the development of relations of mutuality with the city council and other organizations in providing a context and environment for attracting staff, finance, investment, and facilities to Manchester. It would also provide further evidence of an "innovative milieu" through the development of incubation facilities (for the exploitation of knowledge), infrastructure (physical and human), and other visible signs of activity (e.g., cultural in relation to art galleries, theatres, and museums). To this extent, the development of KC is part of the overall strategy of the "Project Unity" merger in seeking to counterbalance the "Golden Triangle" of Oxford, Cambridge, and London and become a "Harvard of the North" and part of an extended "Golden Diamond."

Such international aspirations should be seen against a change in recent years in which both institutions have moved a long way from being seen as "in" but not "of" the region. It was emphasized that the shift toward an internationally focused and renowned institution was not incompatible with a local and engaged focus, as it was a contributor to the "well-being" of an area. The development of Victoria as a world-class research university was illustrated by developments in biomedical research (a £40 million complex for biomedical research relates to what was described as a "biomedical corridor" in Oxford Road) and growing relationships between medical facilities, the National Health Service (NHS), pharmaceutical companies, and spin-out enterprises. Victoria's focus was in positioning itself as an international first-class, science-based research university able to attract the brightest students, leading-edge academics, and develop the facilities that match these aspirations to particular developments. The associations that exist between academics within Greater Manchester and the North West region temper the international dimension of activities in some departments (e.g., biomedical science and collaborative links with Liverpool). In addition, the level of activity may not directly relate to the locality, but that is not to suggest it does not have local implications. For instance, in terms of the opportunities presented by the merger for new centers of research excellence, this person spoke about a centre for climate change:

The atmospheric physicists know all about modelling of the climate and atmosphere etc, making connections with the earth sciences, setting up a more environmentally orientated physics and earth sciences school . . . the merger is an opportunity to reconfigure into these new knowledge lumps . . . so in that sense there's tremendous opportunity for rearranging some of the intellectual furniture, and I would have thought that presents opportunities for new research directions focused on spin off and entrepreneurial activities.[26]

Allowing such possibilities to flourish over time, as opposed to imposing a vision upon sets of practices, is precisely how some of the most advantageous developments may take place. In addition, while there are international aspirations, there are also different levels of engagement within Victoria and UMIST. Planning and Landscape and Architecture, for example, have worked on KC design projects and possess a long tradition of working with local communities in terms of outreach, widening participation, and issues associated with multiculturalism.

KC at MMU tended not to be seen as a repackaging of existing processes, but as a means of continually cultivating relationships between the university and the region around a number of strategic themes in which they were investing their energies and resources. These areas of activity were: Network for Enterprise; Innovation in Art and Design; Regeneration; Sport and Physical Activity; Clothing, Design and Technology; and Aviation, Transport and Environment.

KC was regarded as enhancing those areas of activity, as well as being transformative; in the process it brought greater recognition to the university in terms of its overall identity. This has been prevalent in terms of creativity and culture, for example, art, design, fashion, and sport. MMU was regarded as having a strong vocational base with a regional focus. The university possessed clear areas of research excellence (seven four-star departments and one five-star department in the latest research assessment exercise [RAE]), but was seen as having a focus on widening participation through outreach activities, through enterprise in local schools, through the large number of teachers who are trained in the institution, through continuing professional development, and via such initiatives as the Community Entrepreneurship Scheme. Problem solving and innovation with local businesses led in interviews to an emphasis upon practical engagement. For example, in terms of fashion, MMU deals with developments and ideas for clothes that sell at retail, not clothing that ranks as high fashion. Thinking about this emphasis in terms of seeking to welcome people into universities who wouldn't otherwise come in, this person noted in respect to the Manchester Fashion Network that there was an opportunity to enhance recognition through KC. Overall, it was viewed as an important means of providing coordination and coherence to a wide variety of activities that saw the university seeking to reach out to people who wouldn't normally engage with higher education.

This latter aspiration is shared with Salford in which one senior manager viewed KC as an "infrastructure of possibilities." Here academics and the institutions could form relationships of knowledge creation, production, and sharing for multiple beneficiaries. KC was an aspiration to create a structure within which people can move and be creative. There was also the sense generally that KC related to aspirations in terms of the mixed aims at Salford of teaching, research, and enterprise. The flow of knowledge and the movement of people within a defined area was key to this notion.

Salford was seen to have notable pockets of research excellence (e.g., in Information Systems, the Built Environment, European Studies and Urban Regeneration, Media, Art and Design, and Public Health, as well as in training in Professions Allied to Medicine). Its reputation in these areas was seen in terms of its distinctive strengths in addressing business, industrial, and commercial interests in, for example, the design and deployment of "enabling technologies" through working in partnership. This ethos was linked to the potential seen in KC. An emphasis was also placed on widening access and participation via a number of initiatives, with the aim of raising young people's aspirations. Mentoring was, for example, one program of work mentioned, while the relationship between skills and student was seen to be accommodated within Salford. Overall, therefore, KC was seen as enhancing existing agendas in teaching, enterprise, and research, all of which were driven by the idea of being an "engaged" university working in partnership with a variety of stakeholders.

All this takes place against a background of change in which understanding differences between institutions, as well as similarities among them, is required. At the launch of the Higher Education Funding Council for England's (HEFCE) draft strategic plan,[27] Sir Howard Newby was quoted as saying that individual universities "must build upon their own chosen areas of strength, and work in collaboration with other providers, so that the sector as a whole continues to deliver all that is required of it in the increasingly competitive global marketplace."

Complementarity, on the basis of an understanding of distinctiveness, was seen as crucial to the development of KC by all those interviewed. This is not to suggest there is no competition between the universities as they seek to differentiate their niche markets and convey a particular identity to an outside audience. That means recognizing the distinctive strengths of each institution.

In terms of further engagement and making the universities meaningful to citizens, a large number of deprived wards surround Manchester. As one person put it: "We have a huge mountain to climb in terms of raising the aspirations of local people . . . young people." Spatially speaking, this also relates to a tension between what is seen as the "urban core." KC might be very successful, for example, in attracting a larger pool of knowledge workers. Some of these may stay in the "center," but there are no schools and so where will they go if they have, or want children? In this sense, how will this community benefit those who already exist in areas such as East Manchester, Hulme, and Moss Side? How are these latter groups to benefit from KC?

New urban and regional education futures have recently become the basis for both the knowledge economy and also dreams of the renewal of the postindustrial city. This movement that depends upon a reconceptualization of regional development has the prospect of emphasizing the university as a local source of research, expertise, and innovation, and providing a knowledge base for local industries to thrive in the global economy. Perhaps, more important, it holds the promise of rearticulating the links between the university and the communities it serves to enhance civic traditions and thickening democracy.

NOTES

1. OECD. (2001). *The new economy: Beyond the hype.* http://www.oecd.org/dataoecd/2/26/2380634.pdf.

2. Quah, D. (2001). *Economic growth: Measurement.* LSE Economics Department. Retrieved June 4, 2005, from http://econ.lse.ac.U.K./~dquah/p/0108iesbs.pdf.

3. See The Internet Economy Indicators at http://www.internetindicators.com/execsummry.html.

4. Quah, D. (2002). *Digital goods and the new economy.* Centre for Economic Performance, LSE. Retrieved September 3, 2004, from http://cep.lse.ac.U.K./pubs/download/dp0563.pdf.

5. Coyle, D., & Quah, D. (2002). *Getting the measure of the new economy.* http://www.theworkfoundation.com/pdf/New_Economy.pdf.

6. Coyle & Quah (2002).

7. Quah (2002).

8. Quah (2002).

9. Maskell, P. (2001). *Growth and territorial configuration of economic activity.* Retrieved September 3, 2004, from http://www.druid.dk/conferences/nw/paper1/maskell.pdf.

10. Cooke, P. (2002). *Knowledge economies: Clusters, learning and cooperative advantage.* London: Routledge.

11. Cooke (2002), p. 2.

12. Cooke (2002), p. 3.

13. Porter, M. (1999). *The microeconomic foundations of competitiveness and the role of clusters.* http://www.cit.ms/archive/gov_conf_2001/porter/exe_briefing.pdf.

14. *Opportunity for all in a world of change: A White Paper on Enterprise, Skills and Innovation.* http://www.dti.gov.U.K./opportunityforall/.

15. U.K. Office of Science and Technology (OST) on "Knowledge Transfer." http://www.ost.gov.U.K./enterprise/knowledge/index.htm.

16. OST on "Knowledge Transfer."

17. U.K. Office of Science and Technology (OST). (2002). *Investing in innovation: A strategy for*

science, engineering and technology. Available at www.ost.gov.uk/policy/science_strategy.pdf.

18. Joint Study by Initiative for a Competitive Inner City and CEOs for Cities (2002). *Leveraging colleges and universities for urban economic revitalization: An action agenda.* HYPERLINK "http://www.ceosforcities.org/research/2002/leveraging_colleges/"http://www.ceosforcities.org/research/2002/leveraging_colleges/.

19. Lundvall, B-A., & Borras, S. (1998). *Innovation policy in the globalising learning economy.* http://www.cordis.lu/tser/src/sumfinal.htm.

20. NWDA. (2002). *Science strategy England's northwest.* Warrington: North West Development Agency.

21. Centre for Sustainable Urban and Regional Futures (SURF). (2003). *Evaluating urban futures: Enhancing quality and improving effectiveness.* SURF: University of Salford. www.surf.salford.ac.U.K.

22. AGMA. (2002). http://www.agma.gov.U.K./agma/FinalVersionStrategy.pdf.

23. AGMA. (2002). http://www.manchester knowledge.com/knowledge.html.

24. Centre for Sustainable Urban and Regional Futures (SURF). (2003, May). *Knowledge capital from conception to action.* SURF: University of Salford.www.surf.salford.ac.U.K.

25. SURF (2003, May).

26. SURF (2003, May).

27. HEFCE's draft strategic plan (2003–08). http://www.hefce.ac.U.K./News/hefce/2003/stratplan.asp.

THE INDIVIDUAL VERSUS THE COLLECTIVE IN A TIME OF GLOBALIZATION: EDUCATIONAL IMPLICATIONS

Judith J. Slater

Institutions are produced as a response to and consequence of humanly produced perceptions of need. These perceptions are transformed into actions that are "taken for granted as reality by the ordinary members of society in the subjective meaningful conduct of their lives."[1] This real world and its enactment as action supercede the theoretical, and this plays out in a field that is collectively bargained for by rules that are internal and compromised as the situation warrants. Individuals navigate and persist in light of the collective nature of the institutions that they find themselves a part of. They balance their own perceptions with those of the collective even when they may be at odds with the prevailing notions and forms of acceptable behavior. Although individual behavior is situated within the context of the objective history of the collective, it is also influenced by the power and control of that society and by the relationships that society has with the rest of the world.

Globalization has confounded this perception of balance. It is no longer a question of the individual and the community, but the individual situated within a series of communities that are linked to global currents. This cumulative process of interacting and communication is greatly accelerated today and is evidenced by the interconnectedness of the world through finance, capital, and regulatory institutions. Historically periods of consolidation and innovation have been followed by reform of politics, society, and institutions that require restrictions in conflict with democratic ideals.[2] Today there are questions about universal freedom and equality of education in a globalized context. These questions are pressing as necessary conditions for human welfare and individual rights in globalized economies. The plethora of articles about globalization and its affects on people worldwide, on the economic and social, political, educational, and personal, point out that the movement today does not necessarily take into account human development. It is the larger collective that is paramount in decisions and individual voice and individual benefit is secondary. The future of human development and its sustainability is being shaped by conflicting trends of globalization and cultural and individual identity. Societies are evolving, transforming cultures, creating wealth, poverty, and innovation, and at the same time imposing and instilling loss of control and involvement for individuals.

An example of local response to this loss of control is the spiraling of rhetoric that escalates beyond reason, as when there is talk of war.[3] The parallel for education is the standards and accountability movement, whose stakes keep going up in the form of the rhetoric of competition and superiority worldwide. This is accompanied by threats of retaliation that move beyond reasonable expectations for success. There seems to be a snowball effect that there is too much invested in the rhetoric to stop, so more and more effort is expended in a process that is never profitable. Yet, further sanctions are put in place in the guise of compliance with an acceptable position of dogmatism. This is typical of hierarchical societies but less so of communal environments that might suggest to back off and wait so that the cost is not unrealistic to the goal unless judgment, conscious thinking, and mutual agreement are the means to achieve a solution to the problem.

The premise of this essay is that critical commentary is necessary at this time with regard to the effects of globalization on the individual and whether the practical effects of communal thinking locally, nationally, and globally can lead to enhancement of the moral and practical realities fostered upon education today. This premise that there be global consideration to this situation is clarified with what globalization is meant to signify unity and integration of purpose and goal seeking, but it has polarized rather than united.[4] It has dismantled a safety net enveloping the poor, as the regulatory system of protectionism has been taken apart in the name of promoting exports. In British Columbia, the lumberyards sit idle and the workers are jobless, as Japan stockpiled all the lumber it could in the past decade and now the one market has closed. Meanwhile, there has been a ripple effect on the economy, as the large proportion of lumber workers are unable to buy services offered by the rest of this fragile system. And this is in a developed nation! What of poor nations whose workers do not profit from globalization and are being left out of the loop? The most evident effect of globalization is the spikes and valleys that come from connecting economies of each country without placing control mechanisms from the state on the commerce.[5] Other examples exist such as the assemblage of parts of cars in Mexico without the transference of the technology to produce their own. Without technology transfer and the closing of markets to imports, little filters down to sustain growth and the poor remain an underclass that is unskilled.

[T]he poor suffer when America is the supermarket of the world, even at bargain prices. There is plenty of food for the world, and even many countries with severe malnutrition are food exporters. The problem is that people cannot afford it. Three-quarters of the world's poor are rural. If they are forced off their land by subsidized grain imports, they starve.[6]

The solution is import substitution, to close markets and develop domestic ability to produce their own products for the populace. Globalization needs to be a tool to provide food, health, housing, and education to those that need it for development.[7]

Education quantity in a global environment was thought to mean an investment in human capital that brought rewards to a population, and that there were real advantages to the accumulation of human capital by an individual. Today there is a view that educational payoff is to advance a skilled labor force to be competitive in a global market. Yet, variance in enrollment and quantity of education and its return seem more relevant than when the focus is on quality and real opportunity in terms of outcome. Therefore, questions of gender, race, and socioeconomic group impinge on the value of education to achieve economic advantage.[8]

Some call for a rethinking of relativistic morality in light of new interconnections requiring collaboration, networks, and global capitalistic intermingling that bring closer larger issues of poverty, war, famine, and disease.[9] One major role of education is to transmit the moral code to the population. But globalization issues question whether this can remain parochial. No longer can we turn our backs on poorer nations because now there is information and access. As in local communities, each life affects all others and all lives are now internationally created. This constrains us as well as offering opportunities to reexamine what it means to be connected to and respond to others. While this need has been responded to by cross-boarder government collaboration in legal, policing, and military confabulations, it has had less of an effect on our parochial view of what it means to work together and to use education to create what Dewey refers to as community. Moral codes of conduct are part of the purposes of schooling, and the certainty of being governed legally in accordance with known rules (rules of law) is a mission of schools.[10] Yet, in light of globalization, government and the equilibrating mechanisms of the global market influence the applications as they affect education and the community. Globalization fragments

politics as it integrates markets. It also influences democratic practices by its enactment. A society of human freedom expects the certainty of being governed in accordance with known rules and laws. But industrialization led to a reduction of class conflict through the process of law. And what about a common rule of law applicable to all nations? It doesn't exist; therefore, rules are established that limit individual rights, and these rules may not be sustainable in the long run since the rules seem to benefit the few. The idea that communal norms will be established in this time of globalization that support the accumulation of human capital without more structural, hierarchical restrictions is unlikely.[11] Cooperative systems cannot evolve when there is lack of transparency in governance, established cultures, and lack of common rules of law and justice. Individuals follow the rules of law when it is in their best interests to do so. The conditions of doing so are that the other citizens do so as well. These conditions are not evident in this phase of globalization at any level of analysis.

How then is education made responsive to the global human context? How should the individual act in such a tenuous complex environment?

John Dewey notes that what is valued is temporal. What values guide acceptable behavior are tempered with other values when certain political, economic, or community mores are advanced as more correct at a particular moment in time.[12] All these influences are imbued with materialistic, or scientific (in pragmatist terms), conditions of usefulness at particular moments in history. It is not just situational; it is temporal in the sense that certain positions are perpetuated long after they have outlived their usefulness—or are they continued by the privileged to control the masses? Soros proposes, "Reality is affected by the beliefs of participants in the market."[13] The values are understood and accepted as a possibility of action, given certain circumstances and certain conditions that allow them to be acted upon.

What is judged best and how that judgment is made for a particular circumstance is based, we believe, on criteria. There are criteria for best skating routine at the Olympics, and opinions are formed by learned judgments, and the public accepts those opinions as truth. "Human beings have a yen for hierarchies; even if the most important aspects of our lives don't easily lend themselves to ranking, we feel compelled to try it anyway." Critics are "writers paid . . . to deliver scientifically unfalsifiable opinions."[14] Yet, the prize, the goal, is relativistic and relational, even though it is expected to be more definitive, like scores on a test, representing truth through the actions of the bearer. But real life in a complex world involves choices and those choices are made by individuals with a particular taste and point of view beyond the standard or code of behavior, beyond their actions, and ingrained in their beliefs and values, whether honorable or not. Although we rely on experts to give us expectations of behavior as it is supposed to be, it becomes a popular vote of morality that sets the standard. Critics, prize judges, and the marketplace are all involved in the celebration of those choices.

Questions of a priori theories about behavior are equally damaging. Dewey[15] says that tastes are not cultivated, that liking is liking, that enjoyment—in one's own life and in one's own decisions in action—cannot be regulated by having rules of conduct and morals delegated and mandated as rules and laws of behavior. We cannot rely on definite truth about behaviors, but instead upon the conditions of use at the moment in the real world. And we have the ability then to take action or not in each circumstance, as we make up our mind and influence others to do the same and to act in one way or another. Caleb Carr's book *The Lessons of Terror* cites Vattel's Law from the 1758

book, *The Law of Nations*, describing how to determine whether a war is just. The Law states that one needs to assess how the sides are fighting as well as what they are fighting for. "Just causes can be betrayed by unjust behavior on the battlefield, like killing civilians or prisoners or employing disproportionate force to attain an objective."[16] Good causes can be undermined by bad means, such as terrorism. The paradox is that you are more likely to win when both sides exercise restraint, when the battle is fought directly without the intervention of civilians. In *Killing Time*, Carr further notes that there is an inherent philosophical and ethical superiority of the United States termed moral exceptionalism.[17] It is the rationalization of action so you can live with yourself. Great crimes are committed in the name of moral exceptionalism in order to reach a position of unchallengeable power. When power is one sided, terror may pay off better. Power is the issue, and for our purposes the critical question is whose power makes the decisions of what behavior is moral and just. The strong must understand the weak and their subservient position to the conditions of the crisis. Restraint of those who hold the power is strength, according to Carr, and a precondition for victory.[18] The ideal is only useful if it fits into the reality of the moment. Sometimes less than the ideal is the best compromise for all concerned.

There is a further problem using old notions of behavior based on custom or institutional prescriptions concerning behavior. "[U]sing old standards to meet new conditions" without modification produces disruption in human life.[19] This is either fought back against as the old attitudes prevail, or they cause a change in orientation to what constitutes appropriate behavior. Hopefully, eventually these changes cause buy-ins to change beliefs and values that propel the behaviors in the environments under question. If not, we regulate and limit either the new or old behaviors until they conform to the ethic of behavior that has been adopted or perpetuated at the moment. Who regulates the transformation or the maintenance? Who has that responsibility in schools, in government, in economics, in global issues of access and control, that are guided by strict codes of conduct that are in turn promulgated as beliefs of indoctrination?

Rather, common interest, that of forsaking one's own interest for that of others, giving up our chance to be the only winner for the good of another winning, is the best position.[20] An example is that of the lottery to enter the country. The more people who apply to be part of the pool, the less of a chance the individual has to win a spot. Cooperation implies that fewer people apply, even precisely a maximum according to the number of openings, so that all get in this time. Subsequently, if this is done each time, it ensures entrance for everyone. Rather, there is competition to take advantage of opportunities, almost by chance, as individualistic interests are served at the expense of the community best interests.

What motivates human thinking that causes this decision making to be so individualistic at the expense of community? Can cooperation develop in a world where everyone is governed by his or her own self-interest?[21] Traits needed for cooperation include the following: niceness (never initiating competition), forgiveness (returning to cooperation after a lapse into individualistic behavior), provocability (if the opponent competes, react to the opponent and retaliate), and transparency (let the opponent know that you will give back what they give, which can lengthen the goal-seeking behavior of each).

For liberal democracy to work in a time of globalization and to sustain the liberal ideal in civic life, sustainable public investment in education is needed to facilitate and foster cultural diversity and responsible citizenry. This promotes the public good if coupled with mutual respect among citizens, mutual trust that the state acts in ways that are legitimized as necessary and not merely imposition of interests that do not share the public trust, and transparency in the actions of the state to make available the information necessary to make wise decisions. Of course, there is little to show that these three conditions are being met. There is a modicum of civic participation, and information disclosure is mired in opacity and disclosed only under threat of reprisal by other government agencies (such as the recent disclosures of pre-September 11 events by the government). The resulting culture is infused with a form of international taste in products, worldview, materialism, and virtual interchanges of commodity consciousness.[22] Capital flows are nontraditionally moved as are the trade in knowledge and information across borderless economies. To navigate the new waters of this boundaryless realm, there have to be civil minimums demanded from government. There has to be an unregulated flow of information that is free and does not coincide with civil interests and economic support of government. People are the first order, not economics or politics or long-term solutions, but individual accessibility and entrepreneurial advantage. There is little concern for the nation and for ideology as pragmatic self-interest holds sway.

Personal rights, through the vehicle of human rights, means a new normative framework for those who fall outside of the traditional national citizenship categories. This undermines the traditional notion of citizenship and civic training as a requirement for participation in political and social life.[23] This means that new processes must be established that can transform social action for economics, politics, and education. For education, Torres cites higher use fees, privatization, decentralization, and problems in quality as challenges faced by this new focus on personal rights, and that mass schooling as it is being transformed is only responding to the development of the cultural framework existing today, as it has in the past. Schooling is the

ceremonial induction into modern society, as an extended initiation rite that symbolically transforms unformed children into enhanced individuals authorized to participate in the modern economy, polity, and society, and it does so by definition.[24]

The state is therefore the modernizer as it reasserts itself and modernizes with current legitimization (material, capital, and technical know-how). It does this to externally survive in the globalization process. It faces problems when those signals are in conflict with the communities it serves.

Modern school reform has taken on social, political, and economic capital, and the rhetoric fueling the practices are driven by declining competitiveness in a global economy. His argument is that this type of reform is completely ahistorical, as evidenced by each new wave repeating the criticism, and the solutions, of old. The problem is that the residue of school reform remains as new ideas are implemented, layering on each other so that success and failure are murky in terms of cause and effect. Yet, economic utility driving schools is the effect of the global perspective of competition, and failure to enact real change comes as a result of "economic reality, not educational reasoning and moral principle."[25]

Where then does the individual fit in this global scheme? In an analysis of citizenship, at the first level are notions of identity and right; second is politics of identity, multiculturalism, and emerging membership in the community is multiple and spans boundaries of state, nation, and locality with the ensuing demands of association at each level; third is the internationalization of democracy worldwide and the system of attainment that is separate from that of nations and states.[26] In all, territorial boundaries are no longer relevant to the discussion, as societies are defined by multiple connections and networks that are political, social, economic entities that are evolving constantly.

If education is viewed under the notion of instrumental rationality (a Weberian notion of purposeful instrumental action), then there are certain expectations of behavior that can be predicted for the success of an individual or organization's goal. There are empirical predictions made to rational behaviors, and control of expectation is purposely formulated based on evidence and truthfulness,[27] but this does not take into account real-life situations and pragmatic determinations that are not transparent in origin. There is instability between democracy and capitalism, and the expectations of schools to strengthen society. This is not realistic or rational in a globalized world where the nature of democracy is changing. And this is the Deweyan promise—that democracy will change and be altered by circumstance as the community changes. But, if there is persistence in doing business the way it has always been done, then successful mediation between the individual and the collective, using education as a vehicle to provide knowledge and skills to facilitate that gap, will not be fulfilled.

In moving toward cooperation, Von Neumann's principle of rationality holds that you have to know the opponent can be as smart as you are and that each wants to profit as much as possible and that each will play the bargaining game optimally.[28] But you can't play without full information because you can't prepare for the negotiation without full disclosure. Such is the Weberian notion of rationality of values (which is a philosophic question) and rationality of means or method of decision making.[29] This is a pragmatic position that each person will promote his or her own pure interest depending on how advantageous the game is, and there is the assumption that the opponent does likewise. The rationality leads to diverse strategies. One's fate is bound to the other person's while each pursues his or her own future. Mutual defection creates a common optimum. Each person is forced to figure out the subjective value of a situation, and since there is no absolute correct decision, and complex choices affect the whole physical psyche, a lot of what goes on is intuitive based on feedback from participating.

EQUILIBRIUM

John Nash developed game theory and the notion of equilibrium. Starting with the accepted position of Adam Smith, the way people interact with each other was thought to be controlled by an invisible hand, by unseen forces that guided them as they do in competitive markets creating a natural equilibrium of price and value in capitalistic environments.[30] Nash proved this false by positing the theory of equilibrium to explain how, through compromise, many players sharing or hiding information can form coalitions and act the way ordinary people do in negotiations. Personal interest and gain are fundamental forces of such negotiation, and an individual's actions are of worth and matter. It is not a divine force, but just people interacting in space, distance, time, and relationships; therefore, behavior is not predictable. Attempts at systematizing and regulating what is not about to be regulated is relevant to our discussion, because the enactment of behaviors is a human interaction that exists as a thought in time and space and cannot precisely be described. Instead we can only enumerate the restriction we place on the behaviors that do not comply with the construct. On the one hand, we try to provide order in the messiness of life in relationships and in beliefs and values that form our identity. On the other hand, we get frustrated because it is hard to systematize and be

certain about that which is chaotic. That is the problem of transmission of morals or values in education that would prepare for global participation.

For Nash, selfish competitors create order from a competitive struggle, and selfish self-interest results in the most people losing. The classic example is the Prisoner's Dilemma. Two men are arrested as suspects in a major crime, but they arrest them for a minor one. They are separated and interrogated. They are given a choice: to confess the major crime and implicate the other, or to remain silent. If both remain silent, each gets one year in prison for the minor crime. If one confesses and the other does not, the other gets five years and the confessor is set free. If both confess, each prisoner gets three years. If both parties pursue their own interests, the outcome is far worse than if they both cooperate. The cooperative option here is for both to remain silent, while the noncompetitive option is to confess and both will be worse off. The dilemma is all about cooperation and the necessity and frequent near-impossibility of acting only in your own self-interest. The noncooperative strategy is competition whereas cooperation means that you give something up.

Because there are potential mutual gains, Nash's outcome results from an unspecified process of negotiation or strategizing by individual bargainers each acting in his or her own interests. The cooperative solution cuts through the details, so it is useful for predictive purposes about how people will act in the future.[31] Within schools we deal with the present rather than negotiate for positions in the future. We concentrate on the playing of the game to win, rather than to position ourselves for a less conflictual future. The current strategies used in schools set up winners and losers, restrictive positions that require enforcing punitive measures over and over again if the rules of conduct are broken. There is no resolution, only tacit collusion to change behaviors.

For Nash, everyone has to learn to play better, form coalitions, see what others do, and determine what is best for all. This is true especially in a time of globalization.

Decisions about behavior are strategic reactions to lived variables. Equilibrium is reached when each individual's behavior results in a similar reaction by all others. The best response of all players is to create equilibrium in accordance with each other and their community. You have to understand what is at stake and that if you persist only in your position the community will not respond as a collective. This strategy used in social conflict situations produces results that are consistent preferences represented by their utility and allows behaviors to become predictable over time. The rules of the game for the equilibrium, or strategies and player preferences of individuals and of institutions, exhibit four elements that can be used to analyze all situations of social conflict and cooperation. First, participants jointly determine the outcome in which each tries to obtain the outcome most favorable to them. Second, you have to know the other's position and have complete information about their preferences and possible strategies. Third, the players must be rational and base their actions on rational theory. This is important and part of the reason you cannot negotiate with irrational terrorists. Fourth, if not one player can profit, the best response is to do nothing. Bargaining is important because it leads to a unique solution that has each individual determining what it is worth to be able to participate in the bargaining. Behaviors are the result of open lines of communication, reduction of fixed threats of win-lose strategies, and being able to view the situation from the other person's perspective. Dogmatic demands and threats do not work to produce stability over time. Equilibrium is reached only from that which is negotiated as uncertainty of outcome is reduced. This process of equilibrium striving can be a gauge to determine the level of cooperation that will be achieved as a result of the negotiation. The robustness of the solution is its durability and utility long term, because it is an outcome of a social process of working together to form solutions and predictions of future behavior.[32] Thus, the individual forsakes their own interest for the good of the collective if they are better off than they would be in their present circumstance. No one gets exactly what they want as an optimum, but the compromise position, that of equilibrium, benefits all in ways that the community is better off.

SOLUTION SEEKING

Here is the position I would like to offer. To come to terms with a global communal ethic means to get people to give up their own faith in their personal capacity and capability to see the other's point of view. To persist in the behaviors that mimic others, to have faith that others will act in ways consistent with our own beliefs or values, will not occur unless we understand the other person's beliefs and values, unless we persist in finding creative solutions while understanding the human sensibility to take in cues for what is real and what is perceived, and we can then choose to accommodate or not.[33] Behaviors are choice driven, pragmatic, and based on their perceptions. It is personal or socially inspired, selfish or self-serving, or aimed toward Kant's Other, but it is theirs alone. A shared humanity and socially constructed authenticity is the best offering to understand the other. Personal authenticity is not enough since it requires confirmation from outside and exists only in relationship to others. Instead, there is a compromise solution, an equilibrium that is situational and appropriate for the moment that can be reached through compromise.

Our response to globalization and our response to terrorism are tied to identity formation. Responses are products of a collective point of view and interpretation of the other. Of course, we can transfer causes and make them our own, but the socially constructed reality of the habitus of everyday life limits the possibilities for action,[34] because the status of culture serves to censor information received and limits our ability to determine the truth. Goodness is imperfect, subject to exaggeration and abuse, but it is a reality that is strived for, but personally interpreted and acted upon.[35] Collective belief can be in the unbelievable, as in the Arthur Miller play *The Crucible*,[36] when evidence is rejected because of a purposeful falsity that feeds on faith. False beliefs, embedded socially constructed ones, are the hardest to change, especially if they are not true today but were true in the past. It is our job as curriculum workers to point out the falsities of theory and practice and to find strength in positions that are less dogmatic but yet respond to the global realities of our times. Civic education's effects are debatable in imparting to American students proper attitudes and dispositions concerning tolerance or love of country. Although the responsibility for civic education is delegated to public schooling, it is ineffective at best, especially in uncertain times as when there is threat of war and when civic education is focused on patriotism (as led to such exclusionary and restrictive behavior as the internment of Americans of Japanese ancestry after the bombing of Pearl Harbor and restrictions on teaching the German language in schools in 1917). The problem Murphy discloses is not in the content but in the ability of teaching attitudes,[37] which is best acquired, according to Dewey and others, through active participation in public life, by actively participating in the decision-making process and in the pursuit of knowledge to make informed decisions. Murphy suggests instead that we teach academic or intellectual virtues in the pursuit of truth rather than separate instruction in

civic virtues. It must be grounded in the reality of the moment, in the pragmatic facts that drive decisions made to participate in a collective process that maximizes the use of that information for the benefit of the community. Those decisions must be tied to real efforts of participation and praxis so that the collective is better off in practice than it was before.

I am suggesting an awareness that there need not always be winners and losers in the negotiation of the behaviors that we find acceptable and appropriate, and that the compromise benefits everyone when rationally constructed and honestly played out. There are spirals in the relativistic game of community behaviors. At the core are the personal values and beliefs we have about ourselves. The next level outward is the environment and community in which we live. The level after that is the politically defined nationhood that we are a part of, and finally there is the realm of global relativism. As you move outward in the spiral, beliefs become more abstract. Inner-spiral choices are based on our identification and beliefs and values as individual interpretations of rules and restrictions. But outer-level beliefs are abstract representations that have less well-defined behavioral norms. They represent abstracts such as freedom, democracy, nationalism, truth, and beauty, issues of life, community, place, and time. These abstracts are increasingly interconnected in the global village. They represent orientations and choices made based on personal beliefs and identifications. If decisions to act are based on an understanding and empathy for the other's point of view, they can lead to authentic actions that are best for the larger international community.

In an age where there are potentially conflicts between individual, national, and international interests, globalization plays an important part in successfully reducing tensions by connecting people and places in environments that are peaceful and tolerant and solution seeking. Although education is a major factor in aiding this process of skill acquisition and resource utility, it also serves as a breeding ground for the preparation for economic independence for each participating region. Education is not able to find solutions alone without changes in practices that advance the notions of world citizenry and mutual problem solving that are beyond practices of domination and exploitation. Achieving equilibrium in changing times is hard work and needs to be shared by all agencies that participate in the game.

Curriculum workers are faced with the task of making sense of the translation of these, and we work in the "in-between,"[38] which makes our burden more difficult. That in-between represents the real work to be done in this area. The in-between for community occurs between the rule makers and the students, between the nation and the school systems, and between this nation and others who share a common interest and a common fate. It is the nebulous area that can influence the idea of belonging to a larger community and to the world. To benefit from that desired position, the students have to internalize a state of being where their core beliefs and values have an inclination to be associated with and connected to the larger community. They have to gain strategies and skills to keep them playing the game of community for them to achieve an internally housed sense that they want to belong. To maximize the potential of the association, cooperative equilibrium is the means. Selfish behaviors must be seen as destructive to the chance of building this community and it is only by recognizing this that culture moves forward.

NOTES

1. Berger, P., & Luckman, T. (1967). *The social construction of reality: A treatise in the sociology of knowledge.* New York: Random House.

2. Sirageldin, I. (2002). *Sustainable human development in the twenty-first century: An evolutionary perspective.* Unpublished position paper.

3. Merő, L. (1998). *Moral calculations: Game theory, logic, and human frailty.* New York: Springer-Verlag.

4. Rosenberg, T. (2002, August 18). The free trade fix. *New York Times Magazine*, pp. 28–33, 50, and 74–75.

5. Rosenberg (2002), p. 31.

6. Rosenberg (2002), p. 50.

7. Rosenberg (2002), p. 75.

8. Sirageldin (2002).

9. Sassen, S. (2002, January 18). Globalization after September 11. *The Chronicle of Higher Education*, pp. B11–B12.

10. Sirageldin (2002).

11. Sirageldin (2002).

12. Dewey, J. (1929/1960). *The quest for certainty.* New York: Capricorn Books.

13. Gottlieb, A. (2002, March 3). Who wants to be a millionaire? *New York Times Book Review*, p. 11.

14. Miller, L. (2002, February 4). Who's to judge? *New York Times Magazine*, pp. 9–10.

15. Dewey (1929/1960).

16. Ignatieff, M. (2002, February 17). Barbarians at the gates. *New York Times Book Review*, p. 8.

17. Carr, C. (2000). *Killing time.* New York: Warner Books.

18. Ignatieff, Barbarians at the gates.

19. Dewey (1929/1960), p. 273.

20. Merő (1998).

21. Merő (1998).

22. Torres, C. (2002). Globalization, education, and citizenship: Solidarity versus markets? *American Educational Research Journal, 39* (2), 363–378.

23. Torres (2002).

24. Torres (2002).

25. Goodlad, J. (2002). Kudzu, rabbits, and school reform. *Phi Delta Kappan, 84* (1), 16–23.

26. Torres (2002).

27. Torres (2002).

28. Merő (1998).

29. Merő (1998).

30. Rockmore, D. (2002, January 25). Exploiting a beautiful mind. *The Chronicle of Higher Education*, pp. B18–B19.

31. Dixit, A. *John Nash—Founder of modern game theory.* Retrieved January 25, 2000, from: www.princeton.edu/~dixitak/home/nashenco.pdf.

32. van Damme, E. *John Nash and the analysis of rational behavior.* Retrieved January 25, 2000, from: www.kub.nl/~few5/center/staff/vdamme/nashap.pdf.

33. Ruddick, L. (2001, November 23). The near enemy of the humanities is professionalism. *The Chronicle of Higher Education,* pp. B7–B9.

34. Bourdieu, P. (1993). *The field of cultural production.* New York: Columbia University Press.

35. Merullo, R. (2002, September 13). A skeptical appreciation of the value of goodness. *The Chronicle of Higher Education,* p. B20.

36. Miller, A. (1995). The crucible. In C. Bigsby (Ed.), *The portable Arthur Miller* (pp. 132–258). New York: Penguin Books.

37. Murphy, J. (2002, September 15). Good students and good citizens. *The New York Times,* p. WK15.

38. Arendt, H. (1958). *The human condition.* Chicago: University of Chicago Press.

SCHOOL FINANCE IN URBAN AMERICA

Lynne A. Weikart

A sea change in financing our schools is under way. It follows the changes in education itself: standards-based reform, accountability, and marketization. As these momentous movements shape our schools, so too are the ways we finance our schools changing—from the traditional local property tax to far greater state support and increased private funding.

The study of school finance focuses on how public schools are funded to educate 48 million students in the United States and examines the degrees of equity and adequacy in that funding. As an increasing number of states adopt standards based education reform that seeks to thrust students to greater achievement levels, school and district officials face many challenges in order to meet these standards. Clearly, in order to meet states' standards, sufficient resources must be provided to all schools. On average, school districts receive funding from three major sources: federal (7%), state (50%) and locality (43%). Because the states are providing half of all funding, it is unrealistic to think that the demand for higher standards will be met unless states provide adequate funding.

URBAN PROBLEM

Our cities have a large proportion of public school students. Over 31 percent of all students attend school in 226 large school districts among the 16,000 school districts in America. This translates into 31 percent of all students being educated in just 1.5 percent of school districts.[1]

Financing schools in our cities is particularly challenging because the school population is so needy. Eligibility for the free or reduced-price lunch program provides a proxy measure of low-income family status.

The hundred largest school districts had a disproportionate percentage of students eligible for the free and reduced-price lunch program relative to all public school districts. Among schools that reported free and reduced-price lunch eligibility, 54 percent of students in the 100 largest school districts were eligible, compared with 40 percent of students in all districts.[2] The Council of the Great City Schools, which tracks 62 of the largest cities, found that 70 percent of the students qualified for free or reduced-price lunch eligibility.[3]

There is another type of neediness. Students who speak a language other than

English are more costly to educate. Nationwide 10.4 percent of the U.S. population is foreign-born, which is the highest percentage since 1930, and the proportion in cities is 16 percent.[4] In cities an average of 21 percent of the students are English language learners compared with the national average of approximately 5 percent. The percentage can be as high as 58 percent in Miami-Dade County.[5]

An excellent tool for measuring neediness is the *Targeting Index* for state funding of major city school districts across the country. "This index shows the degree to which each urban school district receives state funding commensurate with that city's share of the state's poor school children."[6] The higher the index, the better the funding relative to poverty. The average for all 61 major cities was .62. In other words, these cities received about 62 percent of the state funding "they would otherwise acquire if the State distributed all of its K-12 education revenues on the basis of poverty alone."[7] New York City's target index was .54, similar to Baltimore, Chicago, and Cleveland.

The cities confront higher standards at a time when they can least afford to meet such standards. Urban district and school officials create and implement urban educational policy within a very difficult environment—less spending than the average spending in the country. In 2000, current expenditures per pupil were $6,911 in the United States and jurisdications, higher than the $6,000 in the 100 largest school districts.[8]

The last decade has witnessed greater investment in the cities, although the size of the city is a determining factor. In constant dollars, total expenditures (including capital) over time rose 25 percent from 1991–92 to 2000–01, from $6,950 to $8,500, but the patterns differ based on the size of city. The highest total expenditures were in big cities ($9,450) and in the urban fringes of large cities ($9,150). "Expenditures per student in midsize cities ($8,580)

and in rural areas ($8,420) were below average, while those in urban fringes of midsize cities ($7,900), small towns ($7,700), and large towns ($7,530) were the lowest."[9] Of course, much of this relates to the variations in costs of living in different parts of the country. However, enrollment grew much faster in the urban fringes of large cities—over 115 percent—far greater than the 12 percent in large cities and 21.7 percent in midsize cities.[10] Families continued to settle in the suburbs.

Cities faced particular challenges because their tax base had been so eroded by the middle-class flight to the suburbs, leaving the cities with fewer resources to educate the poorest students. As minorities have entered urban school systems, whites have left. As schools struggle with increased educational standards, city school students have become increasingly minority. The Council of the Great City Schools is a coalition of 62 of the nation's largest urban public school systems. In these 62 cities 15.0 percent of the nation's public school students were enrolled in school year 2001–2002. More significantly, "76.9 percent of students in the Great City Schools in 2001–2002 were African American, Hispanic, Asian American or other students of color, compared with about 37.9 percent nationwide."[11]

Students in urban schools score lower in both math and reading tests than state and national averages. How much lower depends on the city, the state, and the test.[12] Urban schools face difficult problems, although that does not mean they are any less efficient than other schools. Studies demonstrate that urban schools spend proportionately less on administration and employ fewer administrative staff relative to teachers than either suburban or rural schools. Urban school systems actually devote a smaller share of current expenditures to administration, almost 15 percent less than rural districts.[13] It is not reassuring that schools with higher percentages of poor and minority students in the inner cities experience more teacher absenteeism.[14]

These trends did not happen overnight.

In the years between 1910 and 1970, more than 6.5 million African Americans migrated to urban areas. In 1990, approximately 83 percent of the African-American population lived in metropolitan centers . . . As a result, 40 percent of all African Americans are concentrated in only 11 central cities.[15]

Race and ethnicity cannot be ignored when discussing the financing of urban schools. This trend of African-American flight to the cities continues, but has changed directions in the last ten years; African Americans are moving back to the South but to the cities.

The South scored net gains of black migrants from all three of the other regions of the U.S. during the late 1990s, reversing a 35-year trend. Southern metropolitan areas, particularly Atlanta, led the way in attracting black migrants in the late 1990s. In contrast, the major metropolitan areas of New York, Chicago, Los Angeles, and San Francisco experienced the greatest out-migration of blacks during the same period.[16]

This massive movement out of the cities would not have been possible without federal policies such as tax deductions for homeowners. "[F]ederal sponsorship of secondary mortgage markets, and also the mortgage guarantee programs operated by the Federal Housing Administration subsidized and protected the suburbs."[17] Add to that the federal policy of massive highway construction, and it is understandable how suburbs and their schools flourished after World War II. Schools in the suburbs, regardless of racial makeup, often have more resources, and students score higher on achievement tests.[18] For example, in the largest urban system in the country, New York City, the 1997–98 per pupil expenditure was $8,171 while the surrounding suburbs had far higher expenditures, $12,467 in Nassau and $12,749 in Westchester.[19] However, sub-

urbs are not immune to problems. Myron Orfield has pointed out that 40 percent of the suburbs are at risk fiscally.[20]

HISTORY OF FINANCING SCHOOLS

In America's early history, towns and counties used local property taxes to support their local schools. Many states required towns to do so. Gradually, in the late nineteenth and early twentieth centuries, a system of common schooling was fashioned throughout the country with the states providing some subsidies.[21] The major source of revenue remained the property tax. This dependence upon property tax meant that some school districts received a vast amount of financial support because their location was a wealthier suburb. Other school districts were not so lucky: Their towns and suburbs were poor, and they could not provide adequate funding.

When hard times hit beginning in the 1930s, city services were left to decay. And with the dependency upon the property tax, the schools suffered. Business leaders fought any tax increases. The decline in financing urban schools began in the 1930s. An interesting example is Newark, New Jersey, where spending for schools decreased beginning in the 1930s. By the 1960s, with more African Americans moving into the city and whites moving to the suburbs, financial support further eroded.[22]

The second stage of school finance began in 1970 when John Coons and Stephen Sugarman at Northwestern University Law School wrote *Private Wealth and Public Schools*, and argued for wealth neutrality; that is, given the Equal Protection Clause of the Constitution, states should not allow district spending to be related to district wealth.[23] Wealth neutrality grew out of the widespread belief in equal educational opportunity. It is no surprise that these ideas began to flourish during the civil rights struggle of the 1960s. During this time, Arthur Wise, a graduate student at the University of Chicago, wrote his dissertation on applying equal protection theory to school finance. A year later, in 1977, California courts in *Serrano v. Priest* agreed with Wise and Coons and held that the California education finance system violated the Equal Protection Clause. California relied too heavily on local property taxes, which were by definition inequitable across the state. The consequence of such a practice meant that the wealthy suburbs had highly financed schools while the inner cities were poorly financed.

Two years later in *San Antonio Independent School District v. Rodriguez*, the U.S. Supreme Court in 1973 ruled that the federal government was not responsible for education; rather, it was a state responsibility. That was the beginning. There were many court cases in many states all struggling over the issue of equity in resource allocation. Many of the attorneys and analysts involved in these court cases had been trained in universities that had received funding from James Kelly at the Ford Foundation. The Foundation had set out to force the states to deal with educational inequities. As of 1999, 43 out of 50 states "had faced legal challenges in state court alleging that the school finance system violated the state constitution's education and/or equal protection clauses; 20 states lost these challenges and were ordered to reform the education finance system."[24] These reforms often concentrated upon spending equity and wealth neutrality.

Equity can have many meanings. Berne and Stiefel (1984) summarized several concepts of equity and alternative ways to measure them.[25] Their major distinctions were horizontal and vertical equity. Horizontal equity specifies that "equally situated children should be treated equally."[26] Many court cases used horizontal equity when considering inputs because this is by definition equal opportunity. Vertical equity also came into prominence; that is, "differently situated children should be treated differently."[27]

Vertical equity is an appealing concept because it takes into consideration differences among pupils and also outcomes. Title 1 of the No Child Left Behind Act (NCLB) is based on vertical equity. Although there is basic agreement that some children may need more resources, there remains little agreement about how to measure this.

What has been the result of thirty years of court cases based upon equity of resources? Most studies agree that wealthy districts continue to spend more per pupil on education than poor districts. However, has there at least been improvement in spending equity or wealth neutrality? Studies differ. One proclaimed that court ordered reform resulted in "fundamentally restructuring school finance and generating more equitable distribution of resources."[28] However, in a more recent study, Hoxby argued "equalization efforts have often left poor districts worse off than before."[29] In general, thirty years of school finance reform has been disappointing.

California is an excellent example of the limits of emphasizing equity. The decision in *Serrano v. Priest* in 1977 was successful in achieving greater spending parity among California school districts.

While equally distributed, California education revenues became enmeshed in a downward spiral of defense department cutbacks and other economic setbacks . . . The outcome was ever lower per pupil spending levels relative to the national averages.[30]

There was greater equity, but less spending regardless of location—city, suburb, small town, or rural area.

Metzler explained Hoxby's findings through an examination of state funding approaches. He maintained that the "distribution of education resources is primarily a function of the distribution of political power in the state."[31] Such a distribution is usually an "inequitable equilibrium" which, regardless of court decisions, will eventually return to its state of inequitable equilibrium.

According to Metzler, the solution was really a political one: "If we were truly interested in a permanent shift of resources to a more equitable one, we would change the political equilibrium that exists in most states or rely on courts to impose solutions on resistant legislatures."[32]

CURRENT STRUGGLES

As school finance reformers confronted thirty years of mixed results in attempting to obtain equity, the reformers began to grapple with increased educational standards. Such a demand meant that the reformers could use the movement toward standards-based education reform as a path to gaining increased resources for underfunded schools. Hence, we arrive at adequacy, a third stage of educational finance. As the country has shifted toward standards-based education reform, the policy debate has shifted from a concern for equity in educational resources to ensuring that students have adequate resources to enable them to attain the higher educational standards.

Adequacy refers to "the cost and implementation structure needed to reach high minimum levels of student achievement in low-income schools."[33] The definition of adequacy begins with the idea of adequate performance by students. How much and what kinds of resources are needed to obtain that adequate performance? And that is an answer only the courts can provide. There have been a series of court cases based upon adequacy of resources rather than equity of resources. Several states—Alabama, Mississippi, New Hampshire, North Carolina, Ohio, Vermont, Wyoming, and New York—are examining practical definitions of adequacy for their education finance systems. In these discussions, adequacy is "increasingly being defined by the outcomes produced by school inputs, not by the inputs alone."[34] In essence, if students are not reaching expected standards, students are most likely attending schools with insufficient resources.

To determine adequate funding levels, policy judgments must be made about the level of attainment for students and the resource levels required for schools to succeed in their students' attaining the required levels.[35] *Pauley v. Kelley* (1979), heard in the West Virginia Supreme Court, was one of the earliest adequacy cases. The court listed a series of competencies that each child should obtain, and the legislature had to fund schools that could develop these capacities. The competencies delineated by the court were literacy, basic mathematics, knowledge of government, knowledge of the student's environment, work-training and advanced academic training, recreation, creative arts, and ethics.[36] Other court cases were similar.

Using adequacy as the measure of educational resources was established as a distinct theory in school finance litigation in 1989 when the Kentucky Supreme Court found that "the entire Kentucky system of education violated the mandates of the state constitution, and ordered the state to overhaul the entire system of education to bring it into compliance."[37] The Court emphasized how little funding the state provided for education. Adequacy became a powerful tool to force states to increase funds to schools. Using theories of adequacy rather than equity has made a difference. The plaintiffs have won about two-thirds of litigation based on adequacy; whereas plaintiffs have won only one-third of the cases based on equity.[38]

Pursuing adequacy rather than equity has changed the rules. Pursuing equity in school finance formulas does not necessarily lead to greater state control. But adequacy almost always increases state participation in the life of schools since it is the state that sets the standards of attainment. Similarly, pursuing equity does not focus attention on outcomes, just the inputs of resources. Adequacy focuses attention on the outcomes, particularly low performance of students. In addition, local control will suffer under adequacy since the individual schools and their districts are now being held to state standards. Adequacy of resources is now widely used in the state courts, and only time will tell the outcome. Clearly, the emphasis upon adequacy has meant more centralization of decision-making at the state level.

In the recent past, state policymakers were in the enviable position of being able to simultaneously increase education spending and cut taxes. From 1996 to 2001, per-student expenditures for K–12 education increased by $1,741, more than 30.6 percent. This increase was 13.6 percent above inflation (or $773 per student). That ended in 2001 with the nationwide recession. In March, 2001, the National Conference of State Legislatures (NCSL) reported that 19 states had either made cuts in their FY01 budgets or were on the verge of doing so.[39] Of the states making cuts, only one—Alabama—was forced to make actual cuts in education spending. In fact, most states were looking at education spending increases for FY02, albeit at a slower rate than in previous years.[40] All of this changed with the terrorist attacks on September 11, 2001. Significant slowdowns in spending at the state and local level have occurred. Certainly the current fiscal downturn in the states has meant that the states cut back significantly in spending in general and for education. It remains unclear how long this downturn will continue and how deep it will be.

CHALLENGES IN FINANCING URBAN SCHOOLS

The first challenge in financing urban schools is that the emphasis on adequacy of resources combined with the demand for higher educational standards has resulted in closer examination at the school level rather than the district level. Although much as been written about equity and adequacy of funding school districts, little has been written about the equity and adequacy resource issues of individual schools within a district. Research on ways districts allocate funds to the schools is miniscule. As pressures mount on students to achieve higher standards, pressures on how school officials allocate their dollars to ensure that students succeed dramatically expand. The research in how schools are financed and how schools allocate dollars has just begun. A common assumption is that in order for students to meet increased educational standards, the schools must have a better understanding of how their dollars are spent than schools currently have in a traditional top down system.[41]

A few cities—namely, Victoria, Australia, and Edmonton, Canada, and cities countrywide in England—have implemented school-based financing systems. A good example is Edmonton, where the assumption has been made that schools are in a much better position to decide how to allocate dollars.[42] States within the United States are not as interested in school-based finance or budgeting. The movement is curtailed by the demand of district officials for uniform policies that drastically reduces any decision-making at the school level. Providing more decision-making to school officials is hard to realize in the United States where states are heavily involved in dictating educational standards, curriculum, and accountability systems, and districts, under these increased pressures, dictate to the local schools.

The issue of equity and adequacy of resources within the districts has been examined at the state level, but not comparatively across the country. (See the work of the Education Finance Research Consortium in New York and the Public Policy Institute of California.)

The second challenge is to understand the impact of race and ethnicity upon the cities' schools. In cities, school district officials have moved toward centralization: New York, Chicago, and Los Angeles all have strong superintendents who seek to dictate ways schools will organize themoclves and spend their dollars. Part of this centralization can be traced to minority children being the majorities in urban school districts. As whites retreated to the suburbs, minority children were left in the cities. The attempts to integrate the schools ended when it was clear that not enough white students existed for purposes of integration. Parents in suburban and more white districts have enormous say about their schools, not so the cities.

The only path toward integration would be a regional plan, and the Supreme Court's refusal to back metropolitan busing ended that.[43] There is an enormous task at hand: improving city schools, which have fewer resources and poorer students than the surrounding suburbs. The racial exclusivity of the suburbs is a reality that is difficult to overcome.

The third challenge is citizens' unwillingness to support further taxation. Since the local property tax is the most significant source of revenue for local schools, the success of that tax lies in the hands of the voting public in those school districts. In the case of California, voters agreed to freeze the property tax resulting in heavy cuts across school districts. Across the nation, voters can say no to school budgets by voting no on property tax increases.

With globalization, cities face increased competition in attracting corporations. The result is that corporations are demanding tax relief (tax abatements) to remain in the cities or to bring new business to the cities. For example, business tax relief has cost the Toledo School District about $13.7 million a year, which is about 14 percent of its revenues.[44] Illinois estimated that school districts' share of property tax from corporations had decreased from 50 to 44 percent in the last decade.[45] This decrease in educational tax bases comes at a time when states play a more central role in education.

Court cases have made local schools more dependent upon state fiscal support. In the case of several states (Ohio, New Hampshire, and Wyoming) where the low-wealth school districts won their legal challenges, it has meant a switch from local property taxes to a statewide tax structure.[46] Other states (Maryland and Oregon, for example) have tried to move to an adequacy-based funding formula without the pressure of being sued. The increasing shift to a more state-controlled school funding system has put further pressure on ever-shrinking state budgets. As the states play a larger financial role, they also play a greater regulatory and governance role. The extreme is Philadelphia School District, which was taken over by the state in December, 2001, for its poor performance. Pennsylvania, ranking significantly below the state average in financing education, moved immediately toward privatization of Philadelphia's public schools.

This is the fourth challenge—how to deal with the disinvestment in public education and the concomitant marketization of education, which may have dramatic effect on funding for public education. The conceptual framework supporting marketization is that competition inherent in market-based systems will result in greater efficiency and higher achievement with little or no increase in cost.[47] Such a movement is intertwined with capitalist globalization.

The movement toward private schools has been going on for some time. Many whites deserted public schools in the south after the Supreme Court decision of *Brown v. Board of Education* because whites fled the threat of integration and set up their own white schools. Concomitant with that movement was another movement—the fundamentalist Christians setting up their own schools. Once the whites abandoned the schools, funding for the minority students remaining behind was sharply curtailed. Now the abandonment of the public schools has moved to the North.

Both vouchers and charter schools encourage students to leave the traditional public schools. This includes the most ambitious black and Hispanic families.

Charter schools are usually publicly funded. However, charter schools almost always receive funding from the local public school district, which results in the public schools receiving fewer funds. By 2000, more than 1,400 charter schools were operating in 27 states and were educating more than 200,000 students, which is almost 1 percent of the school population. In Arizona, 4 percent of the students are enrolled in charter schools.[48] It is difficult to predict the future of charter schools; however, they have grown quickly, and low-income parents have responded positively to the idea of school choice.

The first state-funded voucher program established for disadvantaged students was in Milwaukee, Wisconsin, in 1989. It then spread to Cleveland, Ohio, and Florida, which became the first state to enact a statewide voucher program in 1999. Given the legal issues around the use of public funds for religious purposes, it is unclear how successful voucher programs will be.

CONCLUSION

It is too soon to say what impact adequacy will have on urban schools. An emerging trend is that state courts—when dealing with issues of adequacy of educational resources—are ordering legislatures to fix the problem, and that more court cases are being won by the plaintiffs. In Kentucky this order included revamping the entire system, and the Kentucky court's action has had a ripple effect across the country. Adequacy will bring the states to center stage. More state involvement need not result in urban investment. States could define adequacy as the bare minimum and invest even less in our urban schools. Yet, by the late 1990s, the states increased their investment. Throughout the country, the states' share of resources outpaced the funding provide on the local level.[49]

As the states increase their investment, the tax structure for education can shift from the property tax, a local stable tax, to state taxes, such as sales and income taxes, which are not as stable. This could indeed create problems for schools in general and urban schools in particular. Wealthier suburbs could resolve any financial issues leaving urban school systems to face declining state revenues. It is too soon to tell the results of the most recent turn in litigation.

NOTES

1. Fuhrman, S. (2004). *Urban educational challenges: Is reform the answer?* Retrieved June 15, 2005, from http://www.urbanedjournal.org/archive/Issue%201/FeatureArticles/article0004.html.

2. National Center of Educational Statistics. (2002a). *The Condition of education 2002.* Retrieved June 16, 2005, from http://nces.ed.gov/programs/coe/2002/section1/indicator03.asp.

3. Council of the Great City Schools. (2000). *Adequate state financing of urban schools: An analysis of state funding of the NYC public schools.* Washington, DC: Author.

4. Ellen, I., O'Regan, K., Schwartz, A., & Stiefel. L. (2001). *Immigrant children and urban schools: Evidence from NYC on segregation and its consequences for schooling.* (Working Paper #2001-20). New York: Robert F. Wagner Graduate School of Public Service, New York University.

5. Council of the Great City Schools (2000).

6. Council of the Great City Schools (2000).

7. Council of the Great City Schools (2000).

8. National Center of Educational Statistics. (2002b). Characteristics of the 100 largest public elementary and secondary school districts 2001–2002. Retrieved June 16, 2005, from http://nces.ed.gov/pubs2003/100_largest/discussion.asp#4.

9. National Center of Educational Statistics. (2004). *The Condition of education 2004. Public elementary and secondary education, indicator 25.* Retrieved June 15, 2005, from http://nces.ed.gov/programs/coe/2004/pdf/35_2004.pdf.

10. National Center of Educational Statistics. (2004).

11. Council of the Great City Schools. (2004, March). *Beating the odds IV: A city-by-city analysis of student performance and achievement gap on state*

assessments, results from 2002–2003 school year. Retrieved June 16, 2005, from http://www.cgcs.org/reports/beat_the_oddsIV.html.

12. Fuhrman (2004).

13. Ballou, D. (1998). *The condition of urban school finance: Efficient resource allocation in urban schools.* Retrieved June 16, 2005, from http://nces.ed.gov/pubs98/finance/98217-4.asp.

14. Ballou (1998).

15. Henig, J., Hula, R., Orr, M., & Pedescleaux, D. (1999). *The color of school reform: Race, politics, and the challenge of urban education.* Princeton, NJ: Princeton University Press.

16. Frey, W. (2004, May). The new great migration: Black Americans' return to the South, 1965–2000. Retrieved from http://www.brookings.edu/urban/publications/20040524_frey.htm.

17. Katznelson, I., & Weir, M. (1985). *Schooling for all: Class, race, and the decline of the democratic ideal* (p. 217). New York: Basic Books.

18. Guerrier, M. (2004). *High-need African-American and Latino students doing better in suburban districts* (p. 6). New York: Educational Priorities Panel.

19. Council of the Great City Schools (2004).

20. Orfield. M. (2002). *American metropolitics: The new suburban reality.* Washington, DC: The Brookings Institution.

21. Guthrie, J., & Rothstein, R. (2001). A new millennium and a likely new era of education finance. In S. Chaikind & W. Fowler (Eds.). *Education finance in the new millennium, American Education Finance Association 2001 Yearbook* (p. 100). Larchmont, NY: Eye on Education.

22. Anyon. J. (1997). *Ghetto schooling: A political economy of urban education reform.* New York: Teachers College Press.

23. Coons, J., & Sugarman, S. (1970). *Private wealth and public schools.* Boston, MA: Harvard University Press.

24. Metzler, J. (2003). Studies in judicial remedies and public engagement. In *Inequitable equilibrium: School finance in the United States* (p. 5). New York: Campaign for Fiscal Equity.

25. Berne, R., & Stiefel, L. (1984). *The measurement of equity in school finance.* Baltimore: John Hopkins University Press.

26. Berne, R., & Stiefel, L. (1999). Concepts of school finance equity: 1970 to the present. In H. Ladd, R. Chalk, & J. Hansen (Eds.), *Equity and adequacy in school finance* (p. 19). Washington, DC: National Academy Press.

27. Berne & Stiefel (1999), p. 20.

28. Evans, W., Murray, S., & Schwab, R. (1999). The impact of court-mandated school finance reform. In H. Ladd, R. Chalk, and J. Hansen (Eds.), *Equity and adequacy in education finance: Issues and perspectives* (p. 72). Washington, DC: National Academy Press.

29. Hoxby, C. (2001). All school finance equalizations are not created equal. *Quarterly Journal of Economics,* 1189–1190.

30. DeMoss, K., & Wong, K. (2004). *Money, politics, and law: Intersections & conflicts in the provision of educational opportunity* (2004 Yearbook of the American Education Finance Association, p. 5). Larchmont, NY: Eye on Education.

31. Metzler (2003), p. 5.

32. Metzler (2003), p. 46.

33. Clune, W. (2005). Available at http://www.wcer.wisc.edu/people/pi.php?sid=105.

34. Guthrie, J., & Rothstein, R. (2000). Enabling adequacy to achieve reality. In H. Ladd, R. Chalk & J. Hansen (Eds.), *Equity, and adequacy in Education Finance: Issues and Perspectives* (p. 215). Washington, DC: National Academy Press.

35. Guthrie & Rothstein (2001), p. 104.

36. Guthrie & Rothstein (2001), p. 105.

37. Minorini, P., & Sugarman, S. (1999). Educational adequacy and the courts. In H. Ladd, R. Chalk & J. Hansen (Eds.), *Equity, and adequacy in Education Finance: Issues and Perspectives* (p. 195). Washington, DC: National Academy Press.

38. Education Commission of the States. 2004. Retrieved from http://www.ecs.org/ecsmain.asp?page=/html/issues.asp.

39. National Conference of State Legislatures (2001). Web site.

40. Education Commission of the States (2004). Retrieved June 17, 2005, from http://www.ecs.org/ecsmain.asp?page=/html/issues.asp.

41. Goertz, M., & Odden, A. American Educational Finance Association. (1999). *School-based financing* (p. 159). Thousand Oaks, CA: Corwin Press.

42. Caldwell, B., & Spinks, J. (1992). *Leading the self-managed school.* London: Falmer Press.

43. Katznelson & Weir (1985), p. 206.

44. Tomsho. R. (2001, July 18). Public interests: In Toledo, a tension between school funds and business breaks—Hefty tax abatements keep firms in town but drain education coffers, too—Moldy walls, aging boilers. *Wall Street Journal,* p. A1.

45. Tomsho (2001).

46. Education Commission of the States (2004).

47. Rossmiller, R. (2001). Funding in the new millennium. In S. Chaikind & W. Fowler (Eds.), *Education finance in the new millennium, American Education Finance Association 2001 Yearbook* (p. 12). Larchmont, NY: Eye on Education.

48. Rossmiller (2001), p. 29.

49. Fowler, W. Jr., and Chaikind, S. (2001). Conclusion. In S. Chaikind & W. Fowler (Eds.), *Education finance in the new millennium, American Education Finance Association 2001 Yearbook* (p. 193). Larchmont, NY: Eye on Education.

Language and Urban Education

EVALUATING PROGRAMS FOR ENGLISH LANGUAGE LEARNERS: POSSIBILITIES FOR BILITERACY IN URBAN SCHOOL DISTRICTS IN CALIFORNIA

Karen Cadiero-Kaplan and Alberto M. Ochoa

By 2030, English Language Learners (ELLs) will represent 70 percent of the total student population in the United States.[1] This is becoming a reality in the urban communities of Southern California, as these areas account for more than 57 percent of the ELL enrollment in the state.[2] An analysis of demographic characteristics of California K–12 students indicates that since 1985, there has been an increase of more than 100 percent in the number of ELLs.[3] Presently, there are more than 1.6 million students whose first language is not English. It is estimated that these numbers will increase to 3 million students by 2010, with more than 80 percent of students coming from Spanish-speaking backgrounds and attending schools in urban areas.[4]

At the same time that the K–12 student population is growing more linguistically diverse, present policy and programming in schools is marginalizing students whose first language is not English. In large part this occurs by failing to nurture each student's native language and culture as part of their educational development;[5] doing so would require a commitment toward equity and excellence for ethnolinguistically diverse students. To incorporate such values, schools must have a pluralistic vision—one inclusive of language and culture, where high-quality educational materials are available to all, and where human and financial resources are utilized to promote academic achievement and high biliteracy standards (i.e., attainment of academic proficiency in two languages) for all students, with authentic accountability systems across all levels. This requires a public policy commitment to high-quality education that includes community responsibility as a part of the process.[6]

This chapter will highlight two urban school districts committed to a multilingual pluralistic vision for schools. We will articulate the self-evaluation process that administrators, teachers, parents, and university professors engaged in to determine each district's potential to work toward equity and excellence in programming for ethnolinguistically diverse students.

In the process of engaging such ideals, we also recognize that schools are stratified institutions. As such, they provide education programs that can be depicted as "high-status," where knowledge yields social and economic control for its members, or "low-status," where education relegates students to a second-class citizenship both within the K–12 public school system and in the larger society.[7] Further, we acknowledge that urban schools approach bilingual programming in one of two ways: either through a compensatory or high-quality education model. According to Brisk, a *compensatory education* policy focuses on the choice of language, where the policy makers determine which language of instruction will be utilized.[8] Within this model the overriding goal of education is to "teach students English as quickly as possible."[9] Because "English is viewed as the only means for acquisition of knowledge, students' fluency in English is the essential condition to receiving an education."[10] This latter view is most prevalent today in many urban schools. Conversely, a *high-quality education* model focuses on a student's right to a good education with the goal being "to educate students to their highest potential" where English is only a part of the educational goal. In a high-quality model, "bilingual learners access knowledge not only through English but through their native languages."[11] Within this model there is a recognition and value for the varied cultural experiences and knowledge of students, goals the two districts we work with have as part of their mission statements.

EVALUATION FOCUS

The challenge for urban schools serving large numbers of ELLs is to have strategies to evaluate their language and academic programs. These strategies, which we will outline, have the potential to raise the status of the academic success of urban students through high-quality educational models that value the language and culture of ELLs. The questions driving these projects were:

- What are the present services being provided to ELLs in the La Vista Elementary (LVESD) and Dulce Union High (DUHSD) School Districts to support biliteracy development?
- What instructional services are in place in the LVESD and DUHSD that have the potential to develop biliteracy competence?

An action research approach was used in the examination of these two questions, involving a team from each school district and guided by an observational instrument designed to collect data on eight program components.

This chapter focuses on the process utilized by the LVESD and DUHSD in the evaluation of their programs for ELLs, on what they learned, and on next steps. In this section we provide background data and definitions regarding bilingual programming, district demographics, and the politics and pedagogy that spurred the project, along with key research regarding policy and programming issues.

Defining Bilingual Education

Because the focus of this project is bilingual education, it is important to note the varying models and goals of bilingual education. The first model considered, the *early-exit transitional bilingual program*, is the most common, where children are taught in their native language in addition to English, with the goal of mainstreaming students into an English-only curriculum within two to three years without further native language instruction. Second, *maintenance bilingual* or *late-exit* programs help students maintain and preserve their native language as they acquire English. They are taught in both languages, from four to six years, with the goal of acquiring English (L2) and the ability to maintain fluency in their native or primary language (L1) in the process.[12] Third are *developmental* or *enrichment bilingual* programs, where academic proficiency in both the student's primary language and English is the goal. This occurs in dual-language immersion models, where both non-English speakers and monolingual English speakers participate in learning both social and academic language in two languages simultaneously for a period of at least six years; the goal of these programs is full biliteracy. For this project, biliteracy is defined as the development of academic proficiency in the primary language (L1), simultaneous with the development of language and academic proficiency in English (L2), resulting in academic biliteracy in both the L1 and L2 by the fifth and sixth-grade levels. Academic proficiency is ongoing at the junior and high school levels, enabling students to take rigorous biliteracy courses under the core requirements for entry into the California university system. Research indicates that success with bilingual education occurs when language minority children use their native or heritage language in the school as a medium of instruction. The overriding goal of such programs is the development of full bilingualism, linguistically and academically.[13] All of these models were present to some degree in the LVES and DUHS districts; also key are the bilingual teachers, who work most directly with this population.

Bilingual teachers are linguistically and academically proficient in English and another language. In the case of the schools addressed in our context, the language is Spanish. In addition, these teachers are trained to teach core subject areas (i.e., science and math) in both English and Spanish, and are trained in teaching English language development (ELD) with the ability to implement bilingual teaching strategies to address the linguistic, cultural, and academic development of ELLs.[14]

Student Population: Demographics and National Achievement Trends

The participating school districts currently have 40 elementary schools and 27 middle and high schools. By 2004, LVESD had become the largest urban elementary school district in California, serving more than 25,000 students, including 8,890 ELL students. The DUHSD district comprises of eight middle schools, two junior high schools, ten senior high schools, and seven adult education programs. The high school district serves more than 38,000 students, including approximately 9,400 ELL students (or 25%), with the majority having Spanish as their first language. The district demographic data in Table 2 indicate the top four language populations for the both districts from 1997 to 2002, with Spanish speakers making up the majority of students receiving services for ELD and bilingual education, with an average increase of 448 students per year at the high school level; these data are similar for the elementary district.

Academic rigor in California urban schools is lacking for ethnically and linguistically diverse students. In 1997, Latino/-a students represented 7.5 percent of Advanced Placement (AP) math students and 6.7 percent of AP science students, whereas 8.2 percent of AP math students and 8.5 percent of AP science students were black. In the same year, white students represented 72.4 percent of AP math students and 72.8 percent of AP science students.[15]

The National Center for Education Statistics (NCES 2001) reports on the status of dropouts from 1972 to 1999 of 16- to 24-year-olds by race and ethnicity across the country. In 1999, Latino/-a and Hispanic students accounted for 37.7 percent of all dropouts. This is reflected in Table 3, Dropout Rates by Race and Ethnicity, which presents a persistent and disproportional dropout rate for Latino/-a and Hispanic students, the majority population both of these urban school districts serve.

Since the early 1970s the percentage of underachieving Latino/-a and low-income students has changed very little. It has been found that more than 75 percent of

Table 2.
LVESD- and DUHSD-Wide Language Census 1997–2002 Comparison

School District	1997	1998	1999	2000	2001	2002
LCESD LEP Population by Native Language	7067	7327	7409	7718	8438	8898
Spanish	6505	6794	6918	7240	7851	8251
Philippino	133	125	77	75	122	174
Japanese	131	115	135	140	127	138
Korean	128	113	117	121	165	121
DUHSD LEP Population by Native Language	**6349**	**6975**	**7288**	**7773**	**7699**	**9925**
Spanish	5858	6459	6821	7227	7499	9437
Philippino	240	254	247	243	222	249
Japanese	71	65	57	64	54	42
Korean	30	37	32	50	66	55

Source: CBEDS R-30 DATA Quest Language Census 1997–2002.

Table 3.
Dropout Rates by Race and Ethnicity

Year	Total Rate for All Groups	White	Black/African American	Latino/-a Hispanic
1972	14.6	12.3	21.3	34.3
1975	13.9	11.4	22.9	29.2
1978	14.2	11.9	20.2	33.3
1981	13.9	11.4	18.4	33.2
1984	13.1	11.0	15.5	29.8
1987	12.7	10.4	14.1	28.6
1990	12.1	9.0	13.2	32.4
1993	11.0	7.9	13.6	27.5
1996	11.1	7.3	13.0	29.4
1999	11.2	7.3	12.6	28.6

Source: National Center for Educational Statistics. (2001). The condition of education 2001. Washington, DC: U.S. Department of Education, Table 23-1.

Latino students are generally under-achieving by the third grade[16] and the achievement gap remains constant in middle and high school. In addition, there is an absence of data and accountability for assessing and developing the skills of these students to provide them access to the core curriculum and courses that yield access to the systems of higher education. The absence of a systemic school accountability process to determine instructional and school program effectiveness allows schools to perpetuate educational expectations that justify low achievement and student disempowerment,[17] which are concerns for LVESD and DUHSD.

Policy Context

Due to the demographics, achievement trends, and language needs of the student populations these districts serve, they along with us had a strong interest in evaluating their educational programming for ELLs after the passage of California's Proposition 227, which abruptly changed the way bilingual programs were maintained; that is, rather than the "default option" for the education of ELLs in the schools being a bilingual program, the "conventional option" for these students became structured English immersion (SEI), a program lasting normally one year in which students are taught "overwhelmingly" in English.[18] This language policy is subtractive, or compensatory, in nature because the goal is to have students speak English as rapidly as possible without native language instructional support or development.[19] Thus, Proposition 227 shifted the responsibility of bilingual instruction from schools providing such instruction based on their existing programs to parents having to request a bilingual program as an alternative to SEI. This program model contradicts key research findings on second language acquisition that indicate, first, it takes six to seven years to fully acquire a second language, and second, students best acquire English when they are fluent in reading and writing in the their L1 and maintain support for L1 as they acquire and learn English in appropriate bilingual programs or programs that provide L1 support in literacy with a combination of English as a second language (ESL) and English language development (ELD) classes, and sheltered or specially designed academic instruction in English (SDAIE) classes for contextualized content area instruction in English.[20]

So, although Proposition 227 was intended to restrict schools' offerings of bilingual programming, with the support of parents and school communities, it is possible for urban schools to provide language-rich and academically rigorous programs that promote biliteracy.

EVALUATION PROCESSES

In both the LVESD and the DUHSD, we worked with a team of concerned administrators, teachers, and parents to plan the approach to undertake each district's program curriculum audit, named the Post-Proposition 227 Curriculum Audit. The evaluation project began with LVESD in August, 2000, and followed with DUHSD in August, 2001. Both curriculum audits utilized the same model and processes described below. It is important to note that the LVESD first approached us, and what was supposed to be a one-year evaluation/audit continued for two years. During the first year of the LVESD, project administrators from the DUHSD approached and invited us to work with them for the same purpose; since the LVESD is a feeder district to the DUHSD, it also served to inform articulation across districts. Thus, both evaluation projects were initiated by concerned stakeholders from the school districts, with the shared purpose of assessing how well they were achieving the goals of their district's vision or mission statement. The mission statements share the goals of developing

- Students who are high-achieving innovative thinkers
- Learning that is connected to the student's culture and experiences
- Multiliterate students with multicultural perspectives
- Strength in diversity
- Student-based decision making
- Parental voice
- Learning linked to the world outside the classroom

These goals support the bilingual policy of both urban districts with an aim to provide equitable academic experiences for students who have a home language other than English and to implement flexible, student-centered courses of study that prepare students for the global, multilingual society of the twenty-first century.

Methodology

For each district, the curriculum audit process was conducted over a one-year period, beginning in August and ending in July of the following year. This process was conducted twice for the LVESD and once for the DUHSD because of the level of funding available.

Due to the impact of Proposition 227, other districts with bilingual programs across the state were also concerned and so audits began to be conducted at both state and local levels. However, this project was unlike other Post-227 reviews, in that rather than going in from the outside as "researchers" or "policy makers" looking in on programs, we started from inside, the districts and schools worked collaboratively with key stakeholders.[21] This was not a mandated process but rather, a proactive review to assess strengths and needs in serving ELL students. As outside consultants, we worked with each district's curriculum audit team, made up of at least ten members, including school principals, the bilingual director, and concerned teachers and parents. The audit teams met to formulate the research processes, instruments, and procedures. School site visits were scheduled and teachers surveyed at the selected school sites. The main procedures outlined in Table 4, Curriculum Audit Process, reflect the procedure each district went through.

School Identification

It was apparent at the outset that it would not be possible to evaluate all schools in either district, given the limited resources both financial and human. As a result, of the 37 schools in the LVESD, 12 schools were visited during the first year of the audit and 11 in the second year. For DUHSD, 8 schools of the 27 in the district were selected for site vis-

its during spring of 2002. The criteria used to determine which schools were to be included were socioeconomic status (SES), number of ELL students, and feeder school patterns both across districts and within the DUHSD. The schools were selected based on low to high enrollment of ELLs, low to high SES; in addition, middle/junior high schools were selected based on their respective feeder high schools. The researchers along with each district's curriculum audit committee visited each school site for two days. During each visit the team observed classrooms, met with students, teachers, parents, and the school advisory team for bilingual and ELD services. The number of committee members to visit any one school site ranged from at least four to no more than eight and always included a university researcher, administrator, teacher, and parent participant.

Instruments, Field Testing, and Data Gathering

The data gathered provide an overview of trends in how these school districts addressed the educational needs of ELL students across a continuum of eight key areas of educational programming: Program Approaches, Value for Learners, Expectations for Learners, Instructional Goals, Literacy Orientation, Resources, Accountability and Assessment, Parent Involvement/Engagement.

These eight dimensions of programming are derived from the research literature on policy and programming of ELLs,[22] and were used to develop an observational instrument that was utilized by the visiting team to collect data.

- *Program Design and Approaches*. This dimension examined the multiple programs presently utilized or engaged to service ELLs within classrooms and schools.
- *Value for Learners*. This area examined views of ELLs in relation to school policy and program and by concerned stakeholders (i.e., teachers, administrators, parents, and students).

Table 4.
Curriculum Audit Process

Task	Purpose	Outcome	Timeline
Establish process for curriculum audit design and school coordination	Involve district bilingual committee and coordinate with schools' schedules and school staff; develop review process	Design, plan, and establish process for post-227 curriculum audit with rubrics and timelines	August–October
Design post-227 curriculum audit study approach	Curriculum 227 audit committee meetings to conceptualize focus	Committee discussion of design, conceptualization, and formulation of study approach	November
Review existing school data	Identify schools with low and high critical mass of students and existing ELL academic trends	Identification of schools, school profiles by ELL student, and academic achievement trends in selected academic areas	December
Identify schools to be visited	Calendar of schools to be visited in academic year	Set appointment dates and send letters to sites as to purpose of visit	January
Adaptation and field test of instrument/rubrics	Identify eight areas of curriculum audit and operationalize each area	Adaptation and field testing of instrument for data collection & analysis	February–March
School visits	Visit school sites—two days by team of 5 to 8 members including parents, teachers, administrator	Observations, interviews, teacher surveys, and data collection by school, N = 23 elementary N = 8 secondary	March–April
Analysis of data	Identify patterns based on services, approaches, and depth of services to ELL children	Findings reviewed by committee for reporting to district administration & school board; development of school profiles using observations, interviews, and data on each of the selected schools	May & June
Report of findings to school board	Findings of service, approaches, depth of services to ELL children Reviewed by committee for report to district administration school board	Report on findings based on services, approaches, depth of services to ELL students	July

- *Expectations for Learners.* This area identified and examined the expectations of students as defined by the stakeholders, policy, and programs.
- *Instructional Goals.* This area identified and examined the goal of instruction and learning, along with expectations related to academic development in L1 and L2.
- *Literacy Orientation.* This area examined the type of literacy promoted among stakeholders. Areas examined included the value that is placed on literacy and recognition for various forms of literacy and language learning.
- *Curriculum Resources.* This area examined the financial and human resources allocated or dedicated to programming and curricula for ELLs.

- *Instructional Accountability and Assessment.* This area examined the accountability of not only student achievement and success, but program implementation and fiscal allocation of resources.
- *Parent Involvement and Engagement.* This area identified and examined how parents are valued and involved in school activities and degree of collaboration between home and school.

To validate the eight constructs of the evaluation, the instrument was field tested in two comparable schools not involved in the study. Observations of each of the eight areas were collected at the two school sites visited, data analyzed and discussed, and a rubric was developed to assess the level of evidence and consistency across sites.

The rubric, with a rating scale of 1 to 5, was used to identify the perceptions of the visiting team in each of the eight areas of observation.[23] A score of 5 indicated that the team found exceptional evidence and consistency with regard to the area under observation (e.g., Program Design and Approaches). A score of 1 indicated that the team found low evidence and consistency. For each of the eight dimensions, the visiting team identified guiding questions to operationalize its findings. (For example, relative to the Program Design and Approaches dimension, it was inquired of ELD academic staff, "Are the particular teachers who are assigned to teach the most knowledgeable and experienced?")

The data gathering per school site consisted of a minimum of one set of two-day visits. Before each school site visit, the visiting team was provided with data and characteristics of the school and how the school acknowledged and recognized ELL students as part of the school community. The visits yielded many notes and observations. At the end of each two-day visit, members of the respective committees met to discuss their individual ratings. Consensus was derived for each rating across the eight dimensions. Notes were recorded; for each rating, a report was drafted and

sent to the school site and each committee member for their input. The input was incorporated into the data and the final school site report was shared.

School site interviews involved the school principal and members of the leadership team. These interviews focused on understanding the organizational climate of the school and on the type of programs and services to ELLs. Interviews with parents and teachers took the form of focus groups, each group consisting of three to ten participants. The focus of teacher and parent interviews consisted of ascertaining the intensity and consistency of services to ELLs with regard to school expectations, program design, curriculum materials, literacy development, professional development, and school support. Parent interviews focused on their access to information, involvement with the school site, and type and quality of parental engagement. Notes from all interviews and focus groups were taken and summarized, then correlated with observations, surveys, and school data in reporting the findings.[24]

OVERALL FINDINGS AND RECOMMENDATIONS

The following is a synthesis of the results derived from the observational and survey data collected from both school districts. These results reflect the trends the committee identified across the 23 elementary schools and 8 middle and high schools. Along with the findings in each area are general recommendations that are aligned with the eight components of schooling assessed. Any significant differences between the LVESD and DUHSD are noted where they might have differed.

Program Design and Approaches

Across all the schools, it was found that at least adequate ELD programming was offered and provided to ELLs. However, all the school programs for ELLs varied from structured English immersion (SEI) to early and late exit bilingual transitional models.

In addition, both elementary and secondary schools that did not have a clearly articulated bilingual or ELD program did not provide the necessary academic rigor to ELL students to assure their academic development. Although all schools visited met legal ELL compliance under the guidelines of Proposition 227, the majority of schools did not offer a comprehensive academic or cognitively demanding curriculum to ELLs that promotes biliteracy. There were of course exceptions to this, as there were several elementary schools with late exit or dual language immersion programs that ran counter to this finding and did provide key examples of programming that fostered academic literacy in both Spanish and English.

To address these concerns we recommended greater academic rigor in ELD and across school programs. As a result of these recommendations both districts have begun to reassess the rigor of their ELD and academic programming. For example, DUHSD approved the granting of a high school biliteracy diploma that meets the standards set by the district for college entrance. To date, more than 100 students in the district have received this honor.

Value for Learners

It was found that all school sites articulated a value for and understanding of biliteracy for all of their students. It was noted that the majority of administrators, teachers, and staff value their students' language and culture as resources and assets, but many schools did not demonstrate the value as an academic outcome. It was recommended that the schools and district make it a priority to promote and articulate an agenda that makes clear the value of biliteracy to lifelong social, economic, and educational goals. In addition, a biliteracy agenda and policy for DUHSD needs to be articulated so all schools have the opportunity to establish additive biliteracy programs.

Expectations for Learners

In this area, all school sites focused on high achievement in reading and math for their students. However, the expectation for the majority of ELLs, especially at the 4th- to 12th-grade levels, is to transition to English. Therefore, although all schools are working and demonstrating educational processes that align state standards with school curriculum, the curriculum alignment for ELLs in many bilingual and most SEI settings was not evident. To address this concern it was recommended that schools continue to increase the academic rigor of ELLs and programs by establishing a cognitively demanding curriculum, one that promotes academic status equalization for their ELL students and fosters expectations for high achievement in reading and math in Spanish and English.

Instructional Goals

It was agreed that all school sites had teachers with knowledge of SDAIE instructional strategies. Yet, evidence of SDAIE strategies being utilized across classrooms and programs was inconsistent. At the elementary schools the quality of ELD and the use of ELD standards were found to be lacking consistency and intensity. At the middle- and high-school levels, there was inconsistent articulation of ELD and/or bilingual programs as an academic department. This addresses the need to value the professional rigor of ELD and bilingual programs as equal to other academic departments. For example, at some school sites ELD was part of the English department, whereas at others it was part of a content-specific academic department.

Literacy Orientation

The overall literacy orientation of the majority of 4th- to 12th-grade levels was English reading and writing. For example, most school sites had more than one English literacy intervention program. At the elementary level they included Project RESULTS, GLAD, use of accelerated reading programs and phonics in English, WriteSource, Open Court, and INTO English. At the middle-high school sites they included Accelerated Reader, Project WRITE, Corrective Reading, and several other commercial programs. Although these are important components, native language development or Spanish interventions were nonexistent or limited to no more than one or two programs. This sets up a priority on developing English readers and writers, rather than developing biliterate individuals.

Our recommendations are for more programs that focus on academic rigor in L1 and L2 and to promote and implement more curriculum programs/interventions that focus on Spanish literacy development.

Resources and Curriculum: L1 (Spanish) and L2 (English)

When examining resources for curriculum in L1 and English, it was found that the school sites had varying qualities of L1 textbooks and resources for academic development (e.g., computer software and reference materials). The quantity and quality of L1 materials varied from high to low in the schools. In this area, most school sites lacked quality curriculum subject matter resources in L1. For English, all school sites have and use district-recommended ELD curriculum texts and resources; all school sites provided quality curriculum subject matter resources in English that match the basic college requirements, but lacked the same resources in Spanish.

It was recommended that the district provide greater equity in the quantity and quality of L1 textbooks and resources for the academic development and support of ELL students' access to and comprehension of core subject matter. At a minimum, the district should provide for the acquisition of L1 books and reference resources in all school libraries.

Resources: Professional Development

It was determined that teachers at all school sites have received ongoing and appropriate support for ELD professional development. However, the teacher focus groups and survey data indicated that a significant number of teachers were not aware of how bilingual students were placed. At the same time, most teachers agreed that for ELLs the degree of proficiency in both their L1 and English is positively related to academic achievement. Positively, we found that school sites provided time and space for department meetings; we recommended this time as an opportunity for dialogue and articulation of ELL placement and services.

Both districts agreed to continue to provide training for teachers in the use of SDAIE strategies, as well as to develop the professional capacity of teachers to provide ELD and core curriculum instruction to ELL students.

Instructional and Fiscal Accountability and Assessment

It was observed that K–6 and 7–8 school sites had weak articulation across programs, and although grades 7–8 and 9–12 school sites had stronger academic articulation, it was generally perceived as not strong across districts. The use of multiple measures was evident with a strong focus on standardized tests including the SAT-9 (Stanford Academic Test), STAR (Standardized Testing and Reporting), and CAHSEE (California High School Exit Exam), all of which serve as strong academic indicators in English. In some instances, a Spanish equivalent to the SAT-9, the SABE (Spanish Assessment of Basic Education), was utilized as a measure for Spanish-literate students. In terms of ELD, all schools utilized the state-mandated CELDT exam (California English Language Development Test). This assessment, along with other classroom authentic assessments, determines a student's level of English proficiency and placement. Although all assessment measures provided rich data on student progress and achievement, schools lacked a consistent systematic way of utilizing the data for informing instructional processes and program articulation.

To ensure greater equity in assessment for ELL students, we recommended the need for districts to promote and monitor all assessment systems, including classroom-based assessment measures and outcomes. In addition, schools should take more time to develop K–6, 7–8, and 9–12 curriculum articulation. It is imperative that urban school communities implement accountability systems that address the prevention of early underachievement and provide its youth with the core curriculum that prepares them for a multilingual world that is based on an information economy. In the area of fiscal accountability, school data indicated adequate evidence of necessary resources that need to be more adequately allocated to service ELL students.

Parent Involvement

All schools visited provided minimal to adequate support services to Latino/-a parents and students. All school sites had parent committees that discussed ELL issues and held meetings from two to eight times a year. Parents had access to information across all sites, but the quality and accuracy of information provided varied. It was observed that all school sites were searching for ways to better connect with the parent community in general.

Parent involvement was the lowest rated area of these projects. Schools, for the most part, did not provide parents with the depth and insights as to what is necessary for their children to have access to a rigorous curriculum. We recommend ongoing training for parents on home-school collaboration, including supporting processes in educating parents on how to navigate the school system.

Research on parent involvement speaks to the importance of their inclusion in the school community to raise student achievement, however, as this study found few schools actively involve parents.[25] To truly involve parents in the school community, parent activities and practices need to match the culture and schedules of parents, not the school system.

CONCLUSIONS AND IMPLICATIONS

The results of these curriculum audits provide insights as to what is possible when stakeholders and researchers focus on examining urban school practices that align with core goals and concepts of the mission and policies districts set forth. The findings of these curriculum audits address more generally the educational crisis of our ELL students who are negotiating two languages and two cultures. The ELL student population presently faces many obstacles to achieve educational equity and excellence. The findings revealed that although the school district has the capacity, including credentialed personnel, value, and intent to provide pedagogically sound programs to ELLs, schools services lacked the educational consistency and academic rigor to provide equal educational access. Although Spanish/English biliteracy programs in both school districts is a goal, it is not a reality. No school allocated more than 5 percent of its courses to an academic biliteracy approach. Although both LVESD and DUHSD had adequate and consistent ELD programs, few schools incorporated ELD and academic instruction in the primary language toward a viable academic biliteracy program.

This project suggests that four major policies need to be implemented at the elementary to high school levels to shift the paradigm from remediation, or compensatory, to one of quality or academic empowerment with a goal of access to higher education for ethnolinguistically diverse students. First, action research curriculum audits need to be instituted involving all stakeholder groups in the school district in order to be informed about the quality, consistency, and depth of educational practice being provided to ELLs. Second, there is a need for a *language policy* that is supportive of additive language programs that have multiliteracy as an educational outcome and world standard for all students. Third, there must be *accountability* of school programs and services that ensures equal opportunity to the core curriculum and uses multiple measures to assess the language and academic development for our nations ethnolinguistically diverse students. Last, there must be high academic standards that promote biliteracy, including courses that are rigorous and aligned to the core curriculum necessary for access to our nations college and university systems. Thus, if we truly believe in equal educational opportunity, it is imperative that educators begin preparing our ELL learners for fundamental biliteracy communication, along with computational and problem-solving skills that are necessary to have access to higher education and the world of work in the informational and technological society of the twenty-first century.

Our present global economy calls for multiliteracy standards, not monolingualism. To achieve this goal, the findings of this type of action research curriculum audit will need to be duplicated in other urban schools. This approach, however, requires researchers, educators, and policy makers to examine the wide variety of urban settings that are made up of ethnolinguistic communities that bring more than seventy languages and cultures to our schools every day. The rich diversity of languages they bring should not be viewed as deficits or obstacles to be diminished, denied, or overcome, but as national treasures, assets to be nurtured and developed to their highest potential. We must work toward the status equalization of languages in not just schools, but also in the nation, for biliteracy can only enrich cross-cultural

understanding for our children, their families, and our world.

NOTES

1. Garcia, E. (2001). *Hispanic education in the United States: Raices y alas.* New York: Rowan & Littlefield.

2. California Consortium for Teacher Development. (1997). *Teacher education and credentialing for student diversity: The case in California.* Santa Cruz: University of California, Santa Cruz.

3. California Basic Educational Data Systems (CBEDS). (2001). Sacramento, CA: California Department of Education. An annual collection of basic student and staff data; including student enrollment, numbers of graduates and dropouts, course enrollment figures, and enrollment in alternative, gifted, and talented education. Retrieved from http://www.cde.ca.gov/ds/sd/cb/.

4. U.S. Department of Commerce. (2000, March). *Current population survey: The Hispanic population in the United States, population characteristics.* Washington, DC: U.S. Bureau of the Census.

5. Tollefson, J. (2000). Policy and ideology in the spread of English. In J. Hall & W. Eggington (Eds.), *The sociopolitics of English language teaching.* Buffalo, New York: Multilingual Matters.

6. Kozol, J. (1991). *Savage inequalities: Children in America's schools.* New York: Harper Perennial; Macedo, D., & Bartolome, L. (1999). *Dancing with bigotry.* New York: St. Martin's Press; McCaleb, S. (1994). *Building communities of learners: A collaboration among teachers, students, families, and community.* New York: St. Martin's Press.

7. Barrera, M. (1988). *Beyond Aztlan: Ethnic autonomy in comparative perspective.* Notre Dame, IN: University of Notre Dame Press; Darder, A. (1995). *Culture and difference: Critical perspectives.* Westport, CT: Bergin & Garvey; Espinosa, R., & Ochoa, A. (1992). *The educational attainment of California youth: A public equity crisis.* San Diego, CA: San Diego State University; Kitchen, D. (1990). *Educational tracking.* Unpublished. San Diego State University, San Diego, CA, and Claremont Graduate School, Claremont, CA; Oakes, J. (1985). *Keeping track: How schools structure inequality.* New Haven, CT: Yale University Press; Ochoa, A. (1995). Language policy and social implica-

tions for addressing the bicultural immigrant experience in the United States. In A. Darder (Ed.), *Culture and difference: Critical perspectives.* Westport, CT: Bergin & Garvey.

8. Brisk, M. (1998). *Bilingual education: From compensatory to quality schooling.* Mahwah, NJ: Lawrence Erlbaum Associates.

9. Brisk (1998).

10. Brisk (1998), p. xviii.

11. Brisk (1998), p. xix.

12. Baker, C. (2001). *Foundations of bilingual education and bilingualism.* Clevedon Avon, England: Multilingual Matters.

13. Baker (2001).

14. Baker (2001).

15. Latino Educational Summit. (2001). *Educational summit report 2003.* San Diego, CA: San Diego County Office of Education.

16. Garcia (2001); Orfield, G., & Yun, J. (1999). *Resegregation in American schools.* The Civil Rights Project. Boston, MA: Harvard University.

17. Espinosa & Ochoa (1992).

18. Kerper-Mora, J. *Proposition 227's second anniversary: Triumph or travesty?* Retrieved December, 2000, from: http://coe.sdsu.edu/people/jmora/Prop227/227YearTwo.htm.

19. Baker (2001).

20. Baker (2001); Cummins, J. (1994). Primary language instruction and the education of language minority students. In C. Leyba (Ed.), *Schooling and language minority students: A theoretical framework* (pp. 3–49). Los Angeles, CA:

Evaluation Dissemination and Assessment Center, California State University, Los Angeles.

21. Elliot, J. (1991). *Action research for educational change.* Philadelphia: Open University Press; Noffke, S., & Stevenson, R. (Eds.). (1995). *Educational action research: Becoming practically critical.* New York: Teachers College Columbia.

22. Cummins (1994); August, D., & Hakuta, K. (Eds.). (1997). *Improving schooling for language minority children: Research agenda.* Washington, DC: National Academy Press; Kelly, U. (1997). *Schooling desire: Literacy, cultural politics, and pedagogy.* New York: Routledge.

23. Ochoa, A., & Cadiero-Kaplan, K. (2004). Towards promoting biliteracy and academic achievement: Educational programs for high school Latino English language learners. *The High School Journal, 87* (3), 27–43.

24. Ochoa & Cadiero-Kaplan (2004).

25. Nuñez, R. (1994). *Schools, parent,s and empowerment: An ethnographic study of Mexican-American-origin parents' participation in their children's education.* Unpublished doctoral dissertation, San Diego State University, San Diego, CA and Claremont Graduate School, Claremont, CA; Olivos, E. (2003). *Dialectical tensions, contradictions, and resistance: A study of the relationship between Latino parents and the public school system within a socioeconomic structure of dominance.* Unpublished doctoral dissertation, San Diego State University, San Diego, CA and Claremont Graduate School, Claremont, CA.

BILINGUAL-BICULTURAL LITERACY PEDAGOGIES AND THE POLITICS OF PROJECT HEAD START

Ronald L. Mize, Silverio Haro, Claudia Huiza, Anthony Navarrete, Patricia Rivas-McCrae, and Alfonso Rodriguez

San Diego, the seventh largest metropolitan city in the United States according to the 2000 U.S. Census, is home to a population that is becoming increasingly immigrant and nonwhite. Although whites currently constitute 55 percent of the population (the only major metropolitan city in California that has retained a majority-majority population in spite of the statewide trend toward majority-minority status), Latinos/-as comprise more than one-fourth of the total population (27%).[1] According to the San Diego Unified School District, school-aged children are now majority-minority and overwhelmingly Latino/-a—41 percent, compared to the second largest group, whites, who constitute 26 percent.[2] By the end of this decade, it is expected that Latinos/-as will constitute the outright majority of students in the city. The San Diego economy is increasingly bimodal, a city of haves and have-nots. Even though the city is on the U.S.-Mexico border, the lived experiences of Latinos/-as do not necessarily benefit from a proximity to Mexico. Latinos/-as are at the bottom of every social, economic, health, and education indicator of well-being.

Project Head Start, initiated as one facet of the 1960s War on Poverty, is the last-standing poverty relief program in the face of what is often deemed by scholars as the current War on the Poor.[3] It was initially introduced in San Diego to serve the economically disadvantaged from African-American inner-city neighborhoods and Mexican-American *barrios*. Yet, Project Head Start in San Diego has attempted to respond to the changing demographics of the city. This entry is based upon data collected from a training program funded, under the auspices of a Hispanic Serving Higher Education Institution partnership grant, by the Administration on Children, Youth, and Families and administered at California State University–San Marcos. An exploration of our cultural pedagogy training program is based on the testimony of the Head Start teachers who began the first early childhood classrooms in San Diego to the recent inductees into the *kulturkampf* (culture wars) of contemporary urban San Diego. In particular, the training program we administered assisted teachers in developing and in many ways legitimating pedagogical practices that focus on early literacy efforts for bilingual/bicultural students. We introduce mural making by introducing Head Start teachers to the muralists of Chicano Park, Mexican and Chicano musical styles by local musicians, culturally relevant bilingual children's literature, Chicano history, Chicano and Mexican culture, and many other aspects in the hope of bridging the home culture/school culture divide that places so many Latino/-a

students at a serious disadvantage at such an early age.

This project, highly aware of the cultural politics of promoting a positive view of Chicano/-a culture, is situated in the larger political forces that attempt to impede its full actualization. On one front, the overall conservative attack on education[4] has found a new federal target for elimination as witnessed by the current attempts at dismantling Head Start at the highest levels. On another but closely related front, the attack on bilingual education in the aftermath of California Proposition 227 has led to the influx of English-only immersion programs while seriously undercutting the mission of Head Start aimed at educating preschool children in both their home language and English. As racialized minorities take on a numerical majority in urban San Diego, it is the aim of this chapter to both detail the current attacks on immigrants, language rights, and cultural pluralism, as well as document the substantial progress made by Latina *soldaderas-maestras* (soldier-teachers) who succeed in imparting culturally relevant and linguistically appropriate knowledge formation to early learners.

After a delineation of the social demographics that relate to the San Diego Head Start population, a historical periodization of Head Start will show how the federal program has had to alter its aims, missions, and directions to ensure continued funding. A brief discussion of the neoconservative attack on education programs such as Head Start will be coupled with the California propositions that have directly impacted the Latino/-a population in San Diego. Our training program on bicultural/bilingual cultural competencies will demonstrate how we view our work, and the work of Head Start teachers in San Diego, as attempts at stemming the tide of anti-Latino/-a, anti-immigrant activities. These attempts will be demonstrated through the examples of various teachers, center directors, family social workers, and parents associated with Head Start.

THE SOCIODEMOGRAPHICS OF URBAN SAN DIEGO

Nationwide, Latinos/-as are the fastest growing group at a rate of 9.8 percent in the past two years. Estimates published on the *USA Today* Census Web site project the Latino/-a population to exceed 114 million by 2060—a figure that represents nearly 40 percent of the current U.S. total population.[5] In California, Latinos/-as are the largest minority group in the state (a nationwide trend as well) and according to the 2000 Census comprise 32.4 percent of the population. If demographic trends continue, the Latino/-a population will be the largest single group in the state within the next few decades.

Even though whites constitute 60 percent of the total California state population, in the major cities, they constitute less than one-half of the population. In Los Angeles; San Francisco; Orange County; and larger cities in the Central and Imperial Valleys such as Fresno, Modesto, Sacramento, Brawley, and El Centro, whites do not constitute the majority of the population. San Diego is the last major California city that is still majority-majority, but current Asian and Latino/-a growth rates demonstrate that by the end of the decade, San Diego, too, will join the ranks of majority-minority cities.

In addition to ethnic and racial stratification, San Diego also demonstrates many of the features of a bimodal class structure (an erasure of the middle class and a metropolis that is increasingly divided between the haves and have-nots). In San Diego, the increasingly bimodal class structure is evidenced with a median per capita personal income (MSA) in 2001 of $33,883 for Latinos/-as (compared to whites' median income of $65,000). With a median home sale price of $230,000, the ability to achieve a comfortable standard of living is restricted to those at the top ranks of the income spectrum. Statewide, the Latino/-a population has the highest rate of those living in poverty (more than 20%) and children constitute 42 percent of the state's poor. In San Diego, the current population has 82,509 children under the age of 5. This represents 7 percent of the total population and all children represent 27 percent of total population.[6] The vast majority of those children are nonwhite and/or immigrant.

Data from the San Diego Unified School District (which covers the city of San Diego) show that Latinos/-as constitute 41 percent of the student population and, by the end of the decade, will constitute more than 50 percent of the student base. The second largest group, whites, only constitutes 26 percent of the total student population. If one looks at the entire county of San Diego, one will find that whites and Latinos/-as constitute an equal percentage of students (both at 39.8%). Nearly 60 percent of San Diego Unified students qualify for free or reduced school lunches.

Other educational and health and indicators show Latinos/-as are consistently ranked at the bottom of nearly all well-being measures. Native Americans and African Americans tend to drop out of San Diego high schools at the highest rate, but Latinos/-as also drop out at a rate much higher than the overall average, ranking third in terms of most dropouts. In standardized examinations, Latinos/-as in San Diego rank drastically lower then all other groups in percentage of scores at or above the 50th national percentile rank in reading on the Stanford-9 Test. From 1998 to 2000, only 24 percent of San Diego Latino/-a third-graders scored at or above the national ranking whereas overall, 50 percent of all students and 70 percent of white students scored at or above the national average. Latinos/-as had the highest rate of teenage pregnancy in San Diego County at a rate of 64.4 per 1,000 females age 15–17. Latino/-a children ranked last in terms of percentage covered by any form of health insurance. One-fourth of all Latino/-a children go without health coverage in San Diego. Coupling these statistics with the highest rates of poverty and lowest median income, Latinos/-as are finding themselves at the bottom of the socioeconomic ladder and suffering the consequences. Considering the fact that poverty is concentrated within the youngest age groups, one of the few resources still available to poor Latino/-a children is Head Start.

A BRIEF HISTORY OF HEAD START

Head Start was designed as a poverty relief measure enacted among the War on Poverty policies of the Lyndon Baines Johnson administration. Aimed at preschool-aged children, Head Start is a means-tested program designed to address poverty, particularly in racialized communities, in both urban and rural locales. Head Start was enacted in 1963 to ensure low-income students would be given not just a fair start, but a head start, in a pre-K comprehensive program that included academic, social, nutritional, health, and family support services. President Johnson, in his speech, "To Fulfill These Rights," encapsulates the rationale for Head Start and other antipoverty programs. He stated:

You do not take a person who, for years, has been hobbled by chains and liberate him, bring him up to the starting line of a race and then say, 'You are free to compete with all the others,' and still justly believe that you have been completely fair. Thus it is not enough just to open the gates of opportunity. All our citizens must have the ability to walk through those gates.[7]

So in many ways, Head Start became the first line of attack in the War on Poverty. Yet, Project Head Start was hampered from the beginning by two interrelated factors: (1) a reliance upon the deficit model of education as defining black cul-

ture, and (2) the overall racist climate of the day. Sociologist Stephen Steinberg has noted that the remainder of Johnson's speech was based on Daniel Patrick Moynihan's delineation of the cultural deficit model and many of the programs derived from this liberal approach assumed that cultural and familial deficiencies had to be overcome before economic and racial equality could be attained.[8] Historical sociologist Jill Quadagno has demonstrated in *The Color of Welfare* how the measures within the War on Poverty amounted to half-hearted attempts at remedying socioeconomic inequalities due to the prevalence of racism in shaping the political debate.[9]

The first phase of Project Head Start was the "community empowerment" phase (1965–80) that sought to bypass state and local governments in the funding process and provide federal funds directly to community action groups that served the underserved populations of the United States. Many Southern politicians viewed this as a federal government attempt at instituting programs and providing funding for poor African Americans to thwart their locally controlled systems of racial segregation and unequal access to public services. But the origins of Head Start in predominately Latino/-a areas such as the Southwest meant that this national program with a black-white binary focus would be regionalized and localized to the communities in which it would be deployed. Most of the scholarly literature on Head Start tends to be focused on race as a black-white issue, but Head Start is beginning to acknowledge the relevance of Latinos/-as and Native Americans as a crucial component of Project Head Start. At the national level, this bureaucratic recognition has certainly come before a full scholarly awareness of the special issues that Latino/-a children face in their social, emotional, linguistic, and cognitive development.

As Head Start at the federal level moved away from community empowerment and thus many community action groups became much more bureaucratized, the issue of cultural awareness was supplanted by calls for "school readiness." This second phase, which really defined Head Start in the 1990s but can trace its origins throughout the 1980s as well, came precisely at the time when Head Start was becoming much more diverse in its student base. It was a time also marked by the beginning of the outright dismantlement of the safety net and minimal welfare state that developed out of the New Deal and Great Society programs. The outright war on the poor that began with the Reagan administration required Head Start to redesign itself into a politically salient language and focus. School readiness became the vehicle for keeping Head Start off the chopping block. Given this confluence of factors, it probably was no surprise that when the Department of Health and Human Services implemented the Head Start Family and Child Experiences Survey in 2000, it reported program weakness in the area of cultural awareness for 75 percent of the national Head Start-surveyed sites.

The current phase of "accountability" is in some ways a logical extension of school readiness and the implicitly anticommunity empowerment aspect of a narrow focus on academics rather than a whole child approach. The current political situation of neoconservatism means that Project Head Start will be even further underfunded and greater cultural awareness will be replaced by "universal" early literacy programs that assume one language, one culture, one ethnicity. Amid the current debates about the Bush administration lying to secure a free pass to declare war on Iraq, the FCC deregulation debacle, corporate fraud scandals, the constitutional amendment to "protect marriage," and cutting funds from Temporary Assistance for Needy Families (TANF) to support a "marriage enrichment program," a person would most likely have

missed a very quietly "debated" reauthorization bill (HR 2210) that passed 217 to 216 just after 1 AM EST on Friday, July 25, 2003. Yet the reauthorization bill, approved by the House over the objection of 11 Republicans voting with the Democrats (with two Democrats not voting), might have led to the complete dismantlement of Head Start, if the bill had made it through the Senate.

The Senate never called the bill for a vote, and Head Start has been operating without a reauthorization act through the time of writing. In September 2005, the House approved H.R. 2123, the School Readiness Act, without block grants and with temporary suspension of the National Reporting System. Chipping away at the foundation of Head Start, rather than fully dismantling it, seems to be the current strategy in Congress. Recently introduced in Head Start legislation are language that emphasizes English proficiency for LEP students, more coordination with LEAs (public school districts), and greater autonomy for religious organizations to make employment decisions based on religious principles (seen by some as discrimination on the basis of religion). At the time of writing, the Senate has not set a date to vote on its version of the School Readiness Act.

The initial reason that Head Start bypassed state governments to fund community action programs (including nonprofit religious organizations) was because states had historically denied services to their poor, particularly their minority poor. Head Start was created specifically to bypass racist and segregationist Southern states that would ensure that funds targeted to help poor children out of poverty would never find their way into aggrieved communities. The Bush administration-sponsored bill is in fact pushing to turn back the clock 40 years in how Head Start is funded. The Title 2 provision would allow eight state governments to apply for the block-granting of

Head Start (i.e., allow funds to be controlled and disbursed by the states, not directly by the federal government to local governments).

But the larger issue is the impetus in Head Start reauthorization for an even larger bureaucratic shift that will most likely take away that which is most effective. The Bush plan calls for moving Head Start out of the Department of Health and Human Services (DHHS) and into the Department of Education. The call is a result of forcing Head Start into a school-readiness model. Rather than treating Head Start children from the "whole child" approach, the exclusive focus will be on early literacy and some mathematical awareness (i.e., academic preparation). Much of what constitutes Head Start as a provider of comprehensive family services will be reduced to pre-K academic preparation.

Currently, the DHHS Web site has published a research report on how Head Start is "failing," with suggestions for "improving Head Start."[10] Not coincidentally, every deficiency cited fits perfectly with each recommendation in the Bush plan for Head Start. The report, titled "Strengthening Head Start: What the Evidence Shows," relies upon carefully selected case studies and measures to support the rationale for the creation of the report: "The President's Plan will strengthen Head Start and enable coordination of early childhood systems" (actual title of report Section VI). With the results preordained, the report consists of evidence that supports the Bush plan for universal literacy pedagogical approaches (all children learn one way via one language—English—and the one "American" culture as defined by cultural conservatives such as William J. Bennett and Lynne Cheney).

CONSERVATIVE ATTACK ON EDUCATION

Apple has very aptly elucidated the current conservative attack on U.S. educa-

tion.[11] Whether it be a call for school vouchers and homeschooling, the imposition of state or federal standards on educational outcomes, right-wing religious assaults on curricula, or the aim of turning education into vocational-technical training for business, Apple identifies each group within the conservative restoration that is attempting to control the educational process according to its goals and ideologies. His delineation of the right-wing agenda articulates with the Bush plan for Head Start—the emphasis on outcomes based on federal mandates for testing, the notion that early literacy equals English-only literacy, one universal pedagogical method for English language acquisition, and holding teachers accountable while ignoring the fact that Head Start has not been fully funded for more than 20 years. In fact, more children qualify for Head Start than can be accepted by centers, and the pay for most Head Start teaching staff with dependents is so low, they qualify for Head Start.

These restrictive measures are compounded in states like California that have publicly expressed particularly anti-immigrant and anti-Latino/-a stances. The voter initiatives in recent California elections certainly attest to the racialized climate of urban education. California Proposition 63 in 1986 was designed to make English the "official language of the state." It was followed by Proposition 227 in 1998, the so-called Save Our Children initiative, which required the placement of "limited English proficiency" students in English-only classrooms (so-called immersion programs) after one year of English as a second language (ESL) instruction. Coupling these propositions with those that deny public services to immigrants (Proposition 187) and ending affirmative action in state hiring and school admittance decisions (Proposition 209), cultural critic George Lipsitz calls "California in the 1990s the human rights equivalent of Mississippi in the 1960s."[12] Within Head Start guidelines, it quite clearly states that students are to be taught in their home language as well as English. The architects of Head Start realized quite early what researchers on bilingual education are now coming to realize as a social fact—non-English speaking students learn English better when their home language skills are enhanced concomitantly.

BILINGUAL/BICULTURAL EARLY LITERACY TRAINING

Recent research on bilingual education can be viewed in some ways as an attempt at transcending a political debate steeped in an ideological debate on assimilation versus cultural pluralism into a vehicle for understanding how language acquisition impacts learning. In our training program with Head Start teachers, we introduce several popular myths about language diversity and the best data available on why bilingual-bicultural pedagogical approaches tend to best facilitate learning for initial non-English speakers.[13] The four major popular myths we discuss are (1) the predominance of English is threatened, (2) English literacy is the only literacy that matters, (3) English illiteracy is high because language minorities do not want to learn English, and (4) the best way to promote English literacy is through English-only instruction.

To counter the myth that the predominance of English is under attack, we cite that according to Census data, in 1990 only 13.8 percent of the population spoke a language other than English. Whereas in 1910, 23 percent of the U.S. population age 10 and older did not speak English. We show how the United States has always been a multilingual nation from its inception. We discuss the early role of the German language in many Midwestern states and the fact that the original California State Constitution was in English and Spanish and provisions were made in that Constitution to make the state's official documents available in both languages.

To counter the second myth that English literacy is the only literacy worth knowing, we refer to research conducted on cohorts of students in San Diego Unified School District.[14] Portes and Rumbaut find that among Latino/-a and Asian students, those most likely to score highly on predictors of high school success were those with bilingual abilities. As expected, limited English proficiency students were likely to drop out and have lower grade point averages (GPAs), but students with English-only proficiency were more likely to drop out and have lower GPAs than their bilingual counterparts. All too often, literacy itself is often assumed to be the same as English literacy. Current Head Start documents on early literacy have universally subscribed to this fallacy. It is also assumed that lack of English literacy is seen as being a sign of low intelligence. Yet, we find in the current global labor market that bilingual and multilingual abilities have become highly marketable job skills.

The third myth is that English illiteracy is high because language minorities are not eager to learn English. On the day that California Proposition 63 passed, more than 40,000 adults were on waiting lists for ESL classes in Los Angeles alone. During our extensive work with Head Start teachers and parents over the past four years, the single most requested adult education program was English instruction courses of study.

Finally, the myth that the best way to promote English literacy is through English-only programs has been countered by recent research that finds that second language learners benefit from the continued development of their first language. In Feliciano's Census-based study of Asians and Latino/-as, she finds:

bilingual students are less likely to drop out than English-only speakers, students in bilingual households are less likely to drop out than those in English-dominant or English-limited households, and students in immigrant households are less likely to drop out than those in nonimmigrant households. These findings suggest that those who enjoy the greatest educational success are not those who have abandoned their ethnic cultures and are most acculturated. Rather, bicultural youths who can draw resources from both the immigrant community and mainstream society are best situated to enjoy educational success.[15]

As we move toward a multilingual world, we challenge Head Start teachers in San Diego to recognize the difference between literacy and English literacy, stress attitudes and curricula that support positive examples of biculturalism as well as bilingualism, encourage staff development in the areas of cultural proficiencies necessary for the local pre-K population, and emphasize the benefits of multilingual knowledge for all children.

HEAD START AND LATINO/-A EMPOWERMENT

In the face of this political maelstrom are Head Start families, teachers, directors, and family social workers who are creating genuine and long-lasting changes for Latino/-a children. In San Diego County, approximately 56 percent of Head Start enrollees are Latino/-a. Overall, when Head Start programs work well in reaching their Latino/-a clientele, they hold minicelebrations for *Cinco de Mayo*, Mexican Independence Day (*16 de Septiembre*), and *El Dia de los Muertos*; make art projects for Mother's Day; and seek parental input in deciding other events to celebrate. Some teachers complain that they cannot celebrate the *Dias de los Santos* because of the strictly enforced separation between church and state. Other teachers find ways to incorporate holy days of significance to Mexican culture into their curriculum in creative ways. Through the illustration of a few Latino/-a Head Start parents, teachers and family social workers, their positive impact can be evidenced.

When we initially started our research with Latino/-a families, we found that generally they wanted to go unnoticed, will go out of their way to not disturb or even call attention to themselves, and reluctantly will speak to any stranger who approaches them. Even though our research group is Latino/-a and bilingual/bicultural, rarely did Head Start parents give information about themselves unless we described ourselves as affiliated with Head Start. From this, we posit that Head Start has made an important headway into their people's lives, by first of all posing no obvious threat to them.

We found that, for the most part, parents are interested in their children's education and they tend to their children as much as their budget will allow. The families we have worked with, who are currently struggling with their undocumented status, are extremely hard workers and ingenious at finding ways of honestly making a living. One such parent, Don Francisco, has a seven-year-old child who was, at the time we met him, in his last months of the Head Start program. He formerly worked in the fields, but hurt his back, so he was unemployed and had to devise a way to make ends meet. He rents a room in a house with at least two other families and now drives a van picking up people from home and taking them to their *mandado* (grocery shopping) or work. He clears about $800 to $1000 per month and with this he supports his partner and his son. He has a case pending due to the nature of his injury at the job.

Head Start teachers often get the help of Head Start parents, as part of the program is for the parents to donate time and spend time with the children in the classroom. The families we interviewed rarely have any type of health insurance, and they generally do not visit a doctor until they are extremely ill, because they cannot afford it. They will take their family across the border to Tijuana, if at all possible, or to an herbalist before tapping into Medicaid or community health clinics.[16] These impediments on life chances make the efforts and triumphs of individual teachers in Head Start all that more powerful.

Ms. Evelia Alcaraz[17] is certainly the mainstay and memory of Head Start in San Diego. Although she makes her classrooms accessible and open to all, her passing on and celebration of Mexican culture is the hallmark of her center. The only female originator of San Diego's renowned Taco Shop Poets, Ms. Evelia has raised her children, some of her grandchildren, and thousands of Head Start children while working as a teacher and center director for San Diego Head Start since the first program was introduced to the city in 1965.

Ms. Marie Alianza is newer to Head Start, but her dedication to Head Start families is evidenced by her working with a Sudanese family in an exclusively Mexican Head Start center. Her goal is not only to make the family feel welcome, but find ways to express Sudanese culture to all of the children. In some ways, she is ensuring a lesson learned from the early days of Head Start in San Diego. When Latinos/-as were the numerical minority in several Head Start centers, some African-American teachers made sure that families would feel welcomed and their cultural and linguistic traits would be fostered as a community project.

This notion of Head Start as a community of helpers is demonstrated in the efforts of three family social workers–(FSWs)—Toni Marquez, Connie Valdez, and Dora Hernandez—who arranged for an undocumented family to move into one of their homes in San Diego while an FSW moved her entire family to their second home in Tijuana. Families cannot qualify for Head Start if they cannot prove a permanent place of residence and because this family was living in a hotel, this was the sacrifice made to ensure high-quality Head Start for children, regardless of their parents' citizenship status.

CONCLUSION

There are certain structural features of Head Start that facilitate empowerment. Parental involvement and authoritative decision making by parent councils, the presence of community action organizations even through all the changes, the requirement that children be taught in their home language, and a commitment to promote from within make Head Start an organization with a potential for alleviating poverty. The barriers are many and most employees of Head Start, if they have children, often qualify for Head Start themselves. But it is most often the teachers and staff, those who unfortunately often go unnamed and unrecognized, who commit themselves and their children to the Project and make Head Start the positive force for social change in the lives of Latino/-as and poor folks, in general, particularly in urban San Diego.

Specific Head Start centers have been able to create an entire, fully enveloping environment that both affirms cultural expression and provides a high-quality standard of living. Two public housing projects, El Mercado Apartments in Barrio Logan and San Marcos III Head Start and city housing project, aim at reaching Mexican immigrants in the central city and migrant/seasonal farm workers in North County of San Diego, respectively. Located adjacent to Chicano Park, Mercado Head Start is the community center of a unique housing project that relies on traditional Mexican architecture and colors to bring a vibrant feeling to the most economically depressed community in San Diego. The public space of Chicano Park makes for a wonderfully integrated fusion of culture, art, and living for its low-income residents. In our training programs, we work with Chicano Park muralist Mario Torero throughout San Diego to help Head Start teachers think about including mural making and their local communities into their curricula. The San Marcos Head Start, operated by the Mexican-American Anti-Poverty Advisory Committee (MAAC), a Chicano advocacy group, represents a partnership with the city of San Marcos to provide high-quality housing and Head Start facilities in a community that is not particularly receptive to the needs of its Latino/-a farm worker residents. Both centers understand that childhood development does not exist in a vacuum, and that proper housing, nutrition, medicine, bridging to kindergarten, economic options outside of seasonal and temporary employment, and adult education (from ESL and job training to higher education preparation)—all in a culturally relevant and affirming environment—make Head Start work in the manner it was intended (to improve life chances by attending to the whole needs of pre-K children by addressing both their individual and environmental disadvantages). Bridging the homeschool culture divide will never be a one-sided process that requires a serious state commitment (from the local to national) to again put the whole needs of the child at the forefront of socially relevant programs.

NOTES

Funding for this research and training comes from the Department of Health and Human Services, Administration on Children, Youth and Families (Grant 90-YP-0003) to California State University San Marcos (CSUSM). Ronald L. Mize, PhD, main Principal Investigator and Assistant Professor, Department of Development Sociology and Latino Studies Program, Cornell University; Silverio Haro, Co-Principal Investigator CSUSM; Claudia Huiza, CPhil, University of California San Diego; Anthony Navarrete, CPhil, University of California San Diego; Patricia Rivas-McCrae, CSUSM; Alfonso Rodriguez, PhD, In-Kind Co-Principal Investigator and Director of Training, Research, and Evaluation, Neighborhood House Association Head Start Program of San Diego County. Dr. Rodriguez has been involved in research and training in Head Start for the past 24 years. Please direct all inquiries to Ronald L. Mize, Department of Development Sociology, Warren Hall, Cornell University, Ithaca, NY 14853-7801; phone (607) 255-2024; e-mail: rlm65@cornell.edu.

1. San Diego Association of Governments (SANDAG). Demographics and Other Data. Retrieved November 20, 2005, from http://www.sandag.org/resources/demographics_and_other_data/demographics/census/pdfs/profiles_may02.pdf.

2. San Diego Unified School District (SDUSD). Ed-Data Profiles and Reports 2004 Data. Retrieved November 20, 2005, from http://www.ed-data.k12.ca.us/.

3. Ehrenreich, B. (2002). *Nickeled and dimed: On (not) getting by in America.* New York: Metropolitan Books; Gans, H. (1996). *The war against the poor: The underclass and anti-poverty policy.* New York: Basic Books; Sidel, R. (1998). *Keeping women and children last: America's war on the poor.* New York: Penguin Books.

4. Apple, M. (2000). *Official knowledge: Democratic education in a conservative age* (2nd ed.). New York: Routledge; Apple, M. (2001). *Educating the "right way": Markets, standards, God, and inequality.* New York: Routledge.

5. *USA Today.* Census 2000 Website. Retrieved November 20, 2005, from http://www.usatoday.com/news/nation/census/front.htm.

6. SANDAG. SANDAG Data Warehouse. Retrieved November 20, 2005, from http://www.sandag.org.

7. Steinberg, S. (1997). The liberal retreat from race during the post-civil rights era. In W. Lubiano (Ed.), *The house that race built: Black Americans, U.S. terrain* (pp. 13–47). New York: Pantheon Books.

8. Steinberg (1997).

9. Quadagno, J. (1994). *The color of welfare: How racism undermined the war on poverty.* New York: Oxford University Press.

10. U.S. Department of Health and Human Services (DHHS). Official Web site of Head Start Bureau. Retrieved November 20, 2005, from http://www.acf.hhs.gov/programs/hsb/; DHHS, Strengthening Head Start: What the evidence shows. Retrieved November 20, 2005, from http://aspe.hhs.gov/hsp/Strengthen HeadStart03/index.htm.

11. Apple (2000); Apple (2001).

12. Lipsitz, G. (1998). *The possessive investment in whiteness: How white people profit from identity politics* (p. xviii). Philadelphia: Temple University Press.

13. Crawford, J. (2000). At war with diversity: U.S. language policy in an age of anxiety. *Bilingual education and bilingualism* (Vol. 25). New

York: Multilingual Matters; Feliciano, C. (2001). The benefits of biculturalism: Exposure to immigrant culture and dropping out of school among Asian and Latino/-a youths. *Social Science Quarterly, 82* (4), 865–879; Krashen, S. (1997). *Under attack: The case against bilingual education.* New York: Language Education Association; Krashen, S. (1999). *Condemned without a trial: Bogus arguments against bilingual education.* New York: Heinemann; Portes, A., & Rumbaut, R. (1996). *Immigrant America.* Berkeley: University of California Press; Tse, L. (2001). *Why don't they learn English: Separating fact from fallacy in the U.S. language debate.* Language and Literacy Series. New York: Teachers College Press; Valdes, G. (2001). Learning and not learning English: Latino/-a students in American schools. *Multicultural Education* (Vol. 9). New York: Teachers College Press.

14. Portes & Rumbaut (1996), pp. 201–207.

15. Feliciano (2001).

16. Specific data can be found in Seid, M., Castañeda, D., Mize, R., Zivkovic, M., & Varni, J. (2003). Crossing the border for health care: Access and primary care characteristics for young children of Latino/-a farm workers along the U.S.-Mexico border. *Ambulatory Pediatrics, 3* (3), 121–130.

17. Head Start teacher profiles can also be found in Mize, R., Haro, S., Huiza, C., Navarrete, A., Rivas-McCrae, P., & Rodriguez, A. (Publication forthcoming March, 2006). Latinas and Project Head Start. In V. Ruiz & V. Sanchez Korrol (Eds.), *Latinas in the United States: A historical encyclopedia.* Bloomington: University of Indiana Press.

Cultural Studies and Urban Education

HOLLYWOOD'S DEPICTION OF URBAN SCHOOLS: DOCUMENTARY OR FICTION?

Amanda M. Rudolph

Nearly everyone in America has seen a fictionalized representation of the nation's public school system. Schools, teachers, and students are represented in movies, plays, situation comedies, TV dramas, commercials, books, and music. In any entertainment genre one can find a fictional depiction of students, teachers, or schools. As Americans are bombarded with these images, their impressions and ideas of urban schools and schools in general are shaped and molded. For the Mid-western stay-at-home mom, her only exposure to urbanicity may be through these types of experiences. It is important for educators to look at the representations of schools and analyze the messages that are being sent to the American population.

Fictional representations of schools and students are abundant. For this chapter, only representations of urban schools will be addressed. And to narrow down the field to a manageable topic, only dramatic films will be discussed. The school film genre encompasses dramas, thrillers, comedic spoofs,

dark comedies, and many more. Interestingly, it is the drama that repeatedly depicts urban students and schools. James Trier, faculty member at University of North Carolina at Chapel Hill, suggests that, in contrast to urban school movies, movies about suburban students tend to be comedies such as *Ferris Bueller's Day Off* and *American Pie*.[1] Hollywood has repeatedly produced and distributed dramatic films that portray urban schools: *Stand and Deliver, Lean on Me, Dangerous Minds,* and *187*. Evidently, there is something about the dramatic urban school movie formula that leads to successful films. The popularity and continued production of such films raises the following several questions:

1. Why are these movies so successful?
2. What messages or ideas are these movies conveying to viewers?
3. What are the implications of such messages for educators?

This chapter will address these issues and offer suggestions for educators.

Bulman's research on school-based films lists twenty films that depict urban schools.[2] Obviously all these films cannot be dealt with in great detail in this discussion. For the purposes of this chapter, three films will be used as examples of urban school movies: *Lean on Me*,[3] *Dangerous Minds*,[4] and *187*.[5] These films offer a diverse sample of the types of urban movies included on Bulman's list. An overview of the plot and story of the films will be provided. The discussion will then address the common characteristics of the films and will compare those to the actual demographics of urban schools. Finally, implications based on the comparisons will be explored for the general population and educators.

OVERVIEW OF EXAMPLE FILMS DEPICTING URBAN SCHOOLS

The three movies chosen as examples of films depicting urban schooling are *Lean on Me*, *Dangerous Minds*, and *187*. Each of these films contains similar representations of urban students and teachers; each film is also unique in its depiction of the school system. A brief synopsis of each film follows.

Lean on Me

Lean on Me tells the story of Joe Clark, a black educator in New Jersey, who is offered the job of principal in the worst school in the city of Paterson. The film begins with a background scene from 1967. Joe Clark is an engaging and enthusiastic but rogue teacher. His class is disrupted when a coworker enters and informs him that the union is meeting without them. Clark bursts into the meeting and learns that he has been transferred to another school as a condition to pay raises for the rest of the faculty. The film then cuts to the present, 1987, and East Side High School. The school is shown with excessive graffiti and trash in the halls. The majority of the students are

black and Hispanic. In these few minutes of film set to rap music, students are fighting each other, vandalizing the school, selling drugs, assaulting teachers, and carrying guns. The film then cuts to the mayor of the town talking with the superintendent about East Side's test scores. On last year's standardized test, East Side had a 38 percent pass rate. To avoid a takeover of the school by the state, this year's pass rate must be 75 percent. The person chosen for the job is Joe Clark, currently an elementary school principal. After much debate, Clark takes the job.

Joe Clark takes over East Side High School. On his first day, he reassigns teachers and expels 300 students who are drug dealers and problem students. Immediately his administration ignites controversy in the community. He continues to implement standards of zero tolerance and drastic measures such as locking the doors with chains so drug dealers cannot get into the school. Eventually, these tactics get him arrested but win over the students of the school. In the final scene of the movie, students have gathered to protest his arrest and possible dismissal by the school board. In the very last moment of the movie, the vice principal runs through the crowd with a letter for Clark; it is the news that East Side has a pass rate above 75 percent. Clark saved East Side High, the students, and his job.[6]

Dangerous Minds

In the opening scenes of *Dangerous Minds*, which are filmed in black and white and set to rap music, the audience sees a run-down neighborhood covered with graffiti and filled with black and Hispanic youths waiting for the bus. Around the children are drug dealers and homeless people. The students board the bus and as the bus approaches the school the film fades into color. At the school, veteran teacher Hal Griffith introduces Louanne Johnson to the school principal. Johnson is looking for a place to finish her student teaching and the vice principal hires her as a full-time teacher for the Academy class. The principal explains the Academy classes are filled with "special kids."[7] Johnson will start work the next day.

Johnson's first day in class ends with her leaving frustrated and ready to quit. The class full of Hispanic and black students hardly acknowledge her, and when they do, it is only to harass her. Her mentor Griffith tells her, "All you gotta' do is get their attention."[8] Overnight, Johnson reads several texts on discipline, including *Assertive Discipline* by Lee Canter, and laughs off the suggestions. The next day Johnson arrives at school dressed in jeans, boots, and a leather jacket. She begins class by writing, "I am a U.S. Marine" on the board and asks the students if they know karate. She succeeds in getting their attention. Her tactics are not ignored by the administration; the principal reprimands her for allowing fighting in class and demands she follow the established curriculum. She continues to engage the students by offering candy for correct answers, trips to theme parks for reading poetry, and dinner for research. The one student who will not participate, Emilio, finally connects to her after she breaks up a fight and gets personally involved with students by conducting home visits. A drug dealer threatens Emilio and Johnson brings him to her home to hide. During the night she convinces him to talk to the principal about the situation. In the morning, she learns the principal turned Emilio away because he did not knock on the door. Later, she is given the news of Emilio's murder. Overwhelmed by everything she has experienced this year, Johnson decides to quit. The students come together and convince her to stay. She has changed their lives for the better and hers as well.[9]

187

The beginning of *187* provides the background for the rest of the film. The opening of the film show a run-down Bronx high school filled with trash. Students are mostly Hispanic and black. In classrooms, students respond to teachers' questions with cursing and vulgarities. Trevor Garfield is a science teacher who seems to be reaching his students. During class, he opens a textbook to find "187" written along with his name on all the pages. He informs the principal that "187" is the police code for murder and he takes the graffiti as a serious threat since he has failed this particular student. The principal tells him not to worry. On the way back to class Garfield is stabbed several times by the student in the hall.

The film picks up 15 months later. Garfield has moved to Los Angeles and is working as a substitute teacher. The film shows the school at which Garfield will be working. The school has a police officer with a metal detector wand at the entrance. There is graffiti on the walls and desks. The entire school has chain link fence around it. Several classrooms are housed in portable buildings that do not have air conditioning. Garfield begins the day teaching and looks for chalk in the teacher's desk only to find a gun. Dave Childress, teacher, enters and informs Garfield he is in the wrong classroom and shows him the correct class. Garfield is taking over a pregnant teacher's class. The previous week the teacher was cornered by several young Hispanic males and in self-defense kicked one of the students. She is on leave pending an investigation of her assault on a student. The administration is scared of any type of lawsuit from any student. The same students, Benny and Cesar, threaten and bully Garfield as well as the computer teacher, Ellen Henry. Childress and Henry befriend Garfield. After Henry confides in Garfield about her fear of Benny, Benny disappears. During class, Garfield accuses Cesar of stealing his pocket watch. A few days later, Cesar is shot with a syringe of drugs and wakes up with his finger missing. Luckily, the finger is mailed to the hospital and reat-tached. Cesar is convinced Garfield is responsible and tells the police who are not convinced. Benny's body is found by the L.A. Police Department and Henry becomes suspicious of Garfield after find-ing rosary beads in Garfield's house that look like Benny's. Meanwhile, Garfield has been tutoring a young Hispanic girl, Rita, in the school library and once at his home. The school board becomes con-cerned with Garfield's behavior with the girl and decides not to ask him back next year in order to avoid any legal problems. Cesar rallies his friends and they break into Garfield's house to confront him. Garfield admits he killed Benny and cut off Cesar's finger. Inspired by the movie *Deer Hunter*, Cesar loads a gun with one bullet and spins the chamber. He insists Garfield shoot himself. Garfield pulls the trigger and nothing happens. Garfield and Cesar argue about machismo and fear. Garfield bullies Cesar into playing a dan-gerous game of Russian roulette. After several rounds and much arguing, Garfield screams he will take Cesar's turn because he is willing to die to show Cesar how stupid he is. He fires the gun, killing himself. Cesar is outraged and angry that he did not take his turn; he fires the gun, killing himself. The friends flee. The final scene of the movie shows Rita reading an essay at graduation about Garfield's posi-tive influence on her life.[10]

It is interesting to note that *Lean on Me* and *Dangerous Minds* are advertised as being based on true events. *187* ends with an addendum that the movie was written by a teacher. All three films claim a con-nection to reality, but the Hollywood per-spective also influences all three.

DISCUSSION OF COMMON CHARACTERISTICS IN FILMS

These films all share some common characteristics about the representations of urban schools and issues that are repre-sented in the stories. These characteristics can be broken down into two main catego-ries: demographic facts and Hollywood influences. The demographic facts can be compared to educational statistics to determine if the film representation of the schools is realistic. Hollywood influences are issues and ideas in the films that are enhanced or highlighted to create dra-matic tension; these influences may or may not represent a realistic picture of schools.

Common Demographics Facts in Urban School Films

In the films *Lean on Me*, *Dangerous Minds*, and *187*, there are several common-alities based on demographics. According to Bulman, the urban student is character-ized as being from "lower- and working-class homes" and "are often nonwhite."[11] He also states that these students are part of a violent school system and "behave poorly in the classroom, and express a great deal of frustration with the formal structure of the school."[12] Each film depicts these very concepts by portraying an urban high school with: a majority pop-ulation of Hispanic and black students, a majority population of poor students, run-down and graffiti-covered buildings, and extreme violence.

Representation of Ethnicity

All three of the example films show urban schools with a student population comprised of almost exclusively Hispanic and black students. *Lean on Me* contains a scene that shows Clark addressing the entire student body. He asks the white stu-dents to stand and a small group rises. Clark states that these are his white kids and if they had anywhere else to go they would have already left the school.[13] In *Dangerous Minds*, Johnson's students are mainly Hispanic students with a few white and black students. Interestingly, all the student roles integral to the plot are Hispanic or black.[14] *187* depicts a high school almost completely Hispanic. Of the student characters, only one is white.[15] In 2000, 38.7 percent of the entire enrolled K–12 student population in America were minorities.[16] In another report, 36.7 percent of schools that enrolled 900 or more students reported a minority population of more than 75 percent of the total student population.[17] Overall, minority students make up almost 40 percent of the student population. According to the U.S. Department of Education, minorities may comprise the majority of the student population in *some* larger schools. By no means are all large schools solely composed of Hispanic and black students, as Hollywood films may lead the audience to believe.

Representation of Poverty

The three example films also show a great number of students as poor students. In *Lean on Me* and *187,* the students' homes are shown as run-down and crowded apartments and trailers.[18] In *Dangerous Minds*, Emilio tells Johnson that he fights because he is poor and from a broken home. In fact, he asks her if she hasn't "seen all the movies" implying that the films offer poverty and divorce as causes for violence.[19] The U.S. Department of Education reports that 15.8 percent of all students enrolled in an urban area school are considered to be living in poverty.[20] In a central city of a large metropolitan statistical area, 24.4 percent of students are living in poverty.[21] Up to one-fourth of a school population could be poor based on the statistics, but in the films of Hollywood the majority of the students are depicted as living in poverty.

Representation of Facilities

Of the three movies, *187* depicts the worst facilities for school buildings. The movie shows a school campus surrounded by chain link fences, classes meeting in portable buildings with no air conditioning, and graffiti and trash.[22] The facilities

in *Lean on Me* are not much better; the school is covered in graffiti and trash.[23] *Dangerous Minds* is set in a run-down older school.[24] According to the U.S. Department of Education, 45 percent of all central city schools have portable buildings compared to 44 percent in urban fringe/large towns and 29 percent in rural/small towns.[25] The percentage of schools with at least one building feature rated as less than adequate is 56 percent for central city, 44 percent for urban fringe/large town, and 52 percent for rural/small town schools.[26] Comparatively, higher percentages of central city schools report plans to make building improvements in the next two years.[27] Based on the statistics, it seems that most school systems in America are in need of updating and repairs. Interestingly, it is more urban schools that report initiating these repairs in the near future. The representation that schools are forced to use portable buildings may be accurate, but it is not a problem exclusive to urban schools.

Representation of Violence

All of the example movies contain extreme acts of violence. Both *Lean on Me* and *Dangerous Minds* include fights between students that are ended with teacher intervention.[28] *187* shows a student stabbing a teacher repeatedly with a large nail.[29] Also, all three movies show guns at school as well as some type of sexual harassment. The U.S. Department of Education reports that 17 percent of city schools reported serious violent crimes, with 5 percent reporting rape or other sexual battery and 10 percent reporting physical attacks or fights with weapons.[30] These percentages were higher than urban fringe (11%, 4%, and 6%), town (5%, 1%, and 3%), and rural (8%, 2%, and 5%) schools. The percentages of schools reporting less serious or nonviolent crimes were higher for the urban fringe and town schools than for the central city schools.[31]

Although the percentage of city schools reporting serious crimes is higher than the other types of schools, the percentage is still relatively low compared to the numerous representations of violence in urban school films.

Hollywood Influences in Urban School Films

Hollywood has added issues and ideas in the urban school films that make for a more dramatic film. Two major ideas are repeated in the urban school genre: the heroic individual teacher and the domineering bureaucratic administration. Each of these films centers on a single teacher who goes against the system to help his or her students. The films also show the administration as oppositional to the heroic teacher. These two concepts have an impact on the representations of urban schools.

Teacher as Hero

In *Lean on Me* and *Dangerous Minds*, the protagonist is an individual educator (teacher or principal) who fights the system as a lone revolutionist. Principal Joe Clark carries a bat to school and locks the children in while dominating and intimidating the faculty.[32] Johnson discards the canon of research on classroom management to implement her own token economy as she also disregards the developed curriculum for what she considers more engaging.[33] These representations of teachers are common in urban school films. In his research, Bulman discusses the idea of the individual reformationist.

This lone figure is able to ignore the cynicism of veteran teachers, escape the iron cage of the school bureaucracy, and speak directly to the hearts and minds of these troubled youth who are, by the end of the film, transformed from apathetic working-class and poor students into studious and sincere students with middle-class aspirations.[34] Bulman continues, saying that these teachers can succeed without: teacher training, smaller class sizes, a supportive staff, strong leadership, parental participation, technological tools, corporate partnership, school restructuring, a higher salary, a longer school day, vouchers, or more financial resources. All they need to bring to the classroom is discipline, tough love, high expectations, and . . . common sense about individual achievement and personal responsibility.[35]

The idea that a single teacher can change a class is not troublesome; it is the idea that *only* an untrained or rogue educator can make those changes that is disconcerting. The message from Hollywood is clear. Educated and veteran teachers and educators are not successful in their jobs.

Administration as Antihero

In the three example films, the administration fails or hinders the progress of the teacher and/or principal. Principal Joe Clark is given edicts from the superintendent that undermine his decisions. Eventually, the school board questions his strategies as well.[36] In *Dangerous Minds*, Johnson is told to stick to the curriculum and is reprimanded for teaching karate. In a later scene, the principal asks Johnson if she took the students on a field trip as a reward for schoolwork. She replies that the trip to the theme park was a spontaneous decision and she paid for the students because she was so moved by the invitation.[37] She resorts to lying to the administration in order to continue her teaching practices. The most outlandish example of an inept administration is in *187*. Garfield tells his principal he has been mortally threatened and the principal says he will fine the student for writing in the textbook.[38] In his film research, Bulman also discusses the administration.

The teachers and staff are generally shown as uncaring, incompetent, and ineffective educators. These characters represent what many Americans believe to be typical of the urban public school "crisis"—a selfish, inept, wasteful, and uncaring bureaucracy. These are schools with no soul—just troubled students, failed educational methods, burned-out school personnel, too many arcane rules, and too much paperwork.[39] Obviously, the message is that the faculty and administration cannot work together to educate the urban student. The administrative bureaucracy has grown so large it has become completely ineffective.

All of these representations in the urban school film have an impact on the audiences of the movies. The representation of ethnicity, poverty, facilities, and violence color the way the public views urban schools. The Hollywood spin on the heroic teacher and the villainous administration will also influence the public's opinion of urban schools. And some of those audience members will be educators and administrators. What are they learning from these and other films?

IMPLICATIONS FOR THE AUDIENCE

The implications for the audiences of these films are wide ranging. First, the general public will view these movies and come away with skewed and dramatized ideas about the urban school. These ideas may shape the way the average citizen votes or supports legislation. Second, educators will see these films and their impressions of urban schools based on the films could impact their pedagogy and educational philosophy.

The General Public

As discussed earlier, the typical urban school film may not be an accurate representation of urban schools. The movies are usually dealing with Hispanic and black students from poverty level homes attending run-down and violent schools. The statistics reflect a somewhat tamer picture of the urban school. So what is the general audience member learning from these movies?

Unfortunately, the urban school movie helps to maintain the stereotypes of minority groups and the urban school. Bulman concludes his research, saying that by simplifying the many problems of urban public education and turning inner-city students and public-school teachers into caricatures of their respective social classes, Hollywood is doing nothing but reflecting middle-class anxiety about the problems of inner-city schools and the naive hope that such problems need not a substantial political commitment from all members of society, but merely the individual moral conversion of the poor students.[40] The movies offer a quick fix to many of society's issues. An individual teacher with enough courage and gumption can reduce school violence, drug use, apathy, and crime. If the general public buys into the fiction of the teacher-hero, the real problems of education will not be addressed.

The Future Educator

The implications for future educators are unique and interesting. It is an oversight to dismiss the urban school movie as insignificant in the preservice teacher's education. In the past few years I have watched many students use clips from these movies in lessons and presentations as examples of good teaching. I have also seen teacher educators ask for reviews of movies about education as assignments. The use of these movies in the curriculum can be an effective means for discussion; the danger is not to discuss the films critically. Trier reports that in his preservice teacher classes, students "admitted that their own images of inner city schools were probably derived from having watched such films."[41] If the preservice teacher is basing his or her ideas of urban education solely on these films, he or she is getting an inaccurate picture of urban education.

Teacher educators need to address the issues raised in the urban school film in a critical manner. Trier uses the "videocompilations" of school films to spark discussion about schools and schooling. His students made realistic evaluations of the films.[42]

Most students observed that all school films were unrealistic to some degree, and sometimes they were unrealistic in absurd ways, but students also explained that analyzing the discrepancies between the cinematic representation and their own experiences in schools was valuable and productive.[43] Even though the urban school film offers a fantastic representation of schools and students, it also offers an opportunity to analyze and discuss those representations.

CONCLUSION

In conclusion, the urban school genre usually creates movies that are mostly unrealistic representations of urban schools, urban teachers, and urban students. If our future educators and our teacher educators do not challenge these stereotypes, they will only be perpetuated. To address and solve the real issues of urban schools, it is necessary to discuss why Hollywood continues to portray the urban school in such a way. The urban school film genre began in 1955 with *Blackboard Jungle* and shows no signs of disappearing anytime soon. For the sake of the urban student, these films must be viewed and discussed. Without knowing what Hollywood and the movie-going public perceive as the reality of the urban school, how can urban schools and teachers and students grow and improve?

NOTES

1. Toppo, G. (2003, April 24). A "cinematic smear" of school life. *USA Today*, p. 10D. Retrieved May 20, 2004, from the Academic Search Premier database, http://search.epnet.com/login.aspx?direct=true&db=aph&an=J0E110849704003.

2. Bulman, R. (2002). Teachers in the 'hood: Hollywood's middle-class fantasy. *The Urban Review, 34* (3), 251–276.

3. Avildsen, J. (Director). (1989). *Lean on me* [Motion picture]. United States: Warner Brothers.

4. Smith, J. (Director). (1995). *Dangerous minds* [Motion picture]. United States: Hollywood Pictures.

5. Reynolds, K. (Director). (1997). *187* [Motion picture]. United States: Icon Production.

6. Avildsen (1989).

7. Smith (1995).

8. Smith (1995).

9. Smith (1995).

10. Reynolds (1997).

11. Bulman (2002), p. 257.

12. Bulman (2002), p. 257.

13. Avildsen (1989).

14. Smith (1995).

15. Reynolds (1997).

16. U.S. Department of Education. (2003). *The condition of education 2003* (NCES 2003-067). Washington, DC: U.S. Government Printing Office, p. 125.

17. U.S. Department of Education (2003), p. 150.

18. Avildsen (1989); Reynolds (1997).

19. Smith (1995).

20. U.S. Department of Education (2003), p. 97.

21. U.S. Department of Education (2003), p. 97.

22. Reynolds (1997).

23. Avildsen (1989).

24. Smith (1995).

25. U.S. Department of Education. (2002). *Digest of educational statistics 2002* (p. 126). Washington, DC: U.S. Government Printing Office. Retrieved May 30, 2004 from National Center for Educational Statistics Web Site: http://nces.ed.gov/programs/digest/d02.

26. U.S. Department of Education (2002), p. 126.

27. U.S. Department of Education (2002).

28. Avildsen (2003); Smith (1995).

29. Reynolds (1997).

30. U.S. Department of Education (2002), p. 168.

31. U.S. Department of Education (2002), p. 169.

32. Avildsen (2003).

33. Smith (1995).

34. Bulman (2002), p. 262.

35. Bulman (2002), p. 262.

36. Avildsen (1989).

37. Smith (1995).

38. Reynolds (1997).

39. Bulman (2002), p. 260–261.

40. Bulman (2002), p. 273–274.

41. Trier, J. (2001). The cinematic representation of the personal and professional lives of teachers. *Teacher Education Quarterly, 28* (3), 128.

42. Trier, J. (2003). School film "videocompilations" as pedagogical texts in preservice education. *Journal of Curriculum Theorizing, 19* (1), 125–147. Retrieved May 30, 2204 from First

Search database, http://newfirstsearch.oclc.org/images/WSPL/wsppdf1/HTML/07253/AXT37/4FT.HTM.

43. Trier (2003), p. 10.

THE REVOLUTIONARY PRAXIS OF PUNKORE STREET PEDAGOGY

Joseph Carroll-Miranda and Curry Malott

Nearly everyone knows of Robin Hood, the hero of Sherwood Forest who stole from the rich to give to the poor. The story perseveres because it speaks to enduring conditions of inequality and injustice, and equally enduring fantasies of righteous rebellion. This myth of the social bandit is part of our cultural heritage.[1]

—*Eric Hobsbawm*

This chapter is about youth resistance, written from the old-school, bi-classed (working- and middle-), multiethnic, and multicultured perspectives of the authors—a west-coast SK8punk of British, German, and Irish descent, and a Puerto Rican undergrounder. While recognizing the importance of other subcultures (such as hip-hop for example), we focus on PunKore scenes—the multiple communities that evolve around punk, hard-core, and other forms of rockish underground culture. Our personal experience and knowledge of Punkore scenes span our twenty years' participation in them.

The arguments herein primarily deal with the progressive aspects of PunKore's specific street pedagogical practices (as we understand and know them) that have changed lives and rendered PunKore part of a potentially revolutionary force capable of dismantling the social relationships that lead to what Glenn Rikowski refers to as "the capitalization of humanity."[2] What follows is, first, a discussion of youth resistance as it relates to the capitalization of humanity. Next, we will outline what we think have been and continue to be the essence of the most revolutionary

aspects of PunKore pedagogy. Finally, we will outline what the pedagogical practices of these PunKore scenes of human resistance mean for us in terms of our lived praxis.

EMERGENCE OF THE PUNKORE SCENE

Subcultures are cultural resistance. The question is where does this resistance lead?

—*S. Duncombe (Ed.)*
Cultural Resistance Reader

Michael Neary argues that "the Modern condition of 'youth' was invented in 1948, as part of the Employment and Training Act of 1948" in order to lure more young people into British training programs designed to produce a workforce conducive to the capitalist imperative.[3] According to Neary, "the status of youth does not refer to any young person, but is a status attributed to the young working class based entirely on their capacity to become the commodity of labor power: to exist as abstract labor."[4] Similar patterns abound in the United States, and throughout the capitalized world, as capitalist education seeks to instill in youth a commitment to capitalism, and a naturalized desire to sell one's labor power in the market for a wage, that is, to become capital.[5]

This drive to capitalize humanity, of course, is threatened and challenged by what Glenn Rikoski describes as "our capacity for reflexivity, to attain awareness of the existence and practical application of processes of the production of ourselves as labor-power."[6] It is therefore not surprising that there exists a long and continuing history of human resistance to the capitalization of humanity, that at its best is marked by a taking back of one's labor power to fight capital through the combined strategies of direct action in the workplace, as well as a refusal to work and live as capital, informed by the creation of oppositional, yet always complex and contradictory, cultural practices such as PunKore scenes.

The generations born in postwar Britain were largely disenfranchised by the status quo as jobs became less available, wages fell, and racism and other forms of divisiveness rose. Those postwar youth who understood that the extant government and economic system would never alleviate the human suffering engendered by capitalism, took their struggle to the streets through the creation of subcultures based on the refusal to participate in traditional society. As a result, countercultural manifestations have been informed by both progressive and reactionary motivations. Beginning in the 1950s and the 1960s, many progressive youth began to create their own culture.

It was within this context of working-class disempowerment and rising racism that the youth-based countercultures in Britain (and the U.S.) emerged. At their most radical and potentially revolutionary moments, the mods, Rude Boys, and skinheads challenged British society to guarantee what was promised and expected as a minimum of social stability and recognition by, among other things, fighting racism. At their worst, they terrorized

innocent people and strengthened capital by further limiting workers' ability to come together as exploited labor in struggle against the divisive tendencies of capital.

Urban street riots, depicted in the film *Quadrophrenia* as an expression of youthful rage against government and the capitalist system, were common in the United Kingdom during the 1960s.[7] Hebdige expands on this general social discontent, arguing that "the MOD was determined to compensate for his relatively low position in the daytime status—stakes over which he had no control, by exercising complete dominion over his private estate—his appearance and choice of leisure pursuits."[8] Although a necessary first step and thus a place of departure, it is not enough to take control of one's leisure time. As many ethnographers of student resistance underscore, resistance does not tend to be motivated by concrete critiques of capital and social injustices in general, or by a conscious desire to work for social justice. Rather, resistance tends to be motivated by an intuitive, reflexive response to oppressive and dehumanizing educational and social systems and relationships.[9]

We concur with Hill et al. that the complete loss of faith in the system to live up to its democratic promises is what sparked the countercultures of the 1960s and 1970s, and paved the way for the late 1970s, early 1980s PunKore scenes.[10] For example, we could not commence to talk about punk or a hard-core scene if it were not for the influence of the United Kingdom's mods, Rude Boys, skinheads, and street punks.[11] The cultural and musical revolution that these countercultures sparked are being felt to this day.[12]

The skinhead counterculture, whose roots stem not from fascism, but from the Jamaica-based African Rude Boys, is a working-class youth phenomenon, which emerged in the United Kingdom in the late 1960s. As a counterculture, they challenged the industrial and postindustrial economic conditions of workers' exploitation, motivated by their general disenchantment with Britain's social and political order. George Marshall,[13] an original skin from the late '60s, in his book *Spirit of '69: A Skinhead Bible*, gives us an historical overview of how the skinhead counterculture emerged. Skinheads are a fusional metamorphosis of the mods and the Rude Boys.[14]

While the mods emerged as a predominantly white countercultural phenomenon of the early '60s, the Rude Boys, on the other hand, grew from Jamaican immigrants in southern neighborhoods such as Brixton. The Rude Boys were known as one of the roughest and toughest street cultures in the postwar United Kingdom.[15] The potentially revolutionary militancy of the Rude Boys influenced some in Britain's white working class to the extent that they started their own version, the skinheads, reflected by their passion to be tough enough to resist anything, while simultaneously enjoying the music of rock-steady, ska, and reggae. However, it is important to note that fascist skinheads rarely praise the African roots of their culture. In bands like Symarip, The Specials, and Madness, the interconnectivity between skinheads and the Rude Boy 2tone counterculture is reflected.[16] Within this scene are strong currents of racial harmony and of healing the hatred of racism predominating in those and these times. In fact, the precursors of reggae, rock steady, and ska are commonly referred to in PunKore scenes as "Skinhead Reggae."[17]

In its more progressive and potentially revolutionary countercultural moments, the skinheads produced a working-class culture of resistance, expressed in lyrics from "The Business," "The Oppressed," "Stiff Little Fingers," "Angelic Upstarts," "Sham 69," "The Blitz," "Cock Sparrow," and countless others. The skinhead music of the early to mid-'70s is referred to as "Oi,"[18] also known as "street punk" by others in the PunKore scene. Regardless of the name, Oi and street punk lyrics, both pro-

gressive and reactionary, continue to give us series of documented oral histories, experiences of street life, and beliefs shared by the working class, the lumpen proletariat, and even the middle class. For example, these 1978 lyrics from "Sham 69":

Hey little rich boy. Take a good look at me.
Hey little rich boy. Take a good look at me.
Why should I let it worry me?
I'll never believe you're better than me.

Although it is true that PunKore scenes (like other subcultures or cultures in general) can at times be sexist, racist, and homophobic and support the labor/capital relationship, these traits are not inherent within the scene. They are indicative of the larger society from which the scene emerged. Those in PunKore scenes, like everyone else in society, suffer at various levels of intensity from the counterrevolutionary illnesses of white supremacy, sexism, homophobia, and the idea that capitalism is humankind's only choice. The progressive role of the subculture is therefore to heal people while simultaneously creating the foundations for revolutionary change. For example, according to Kathleen Hanna,[19] lead singer of the popular underground street punk band Bikini Kill, self-healing can and does occur within PunKore scenes. In the Riot Grrrl Manifesto, a document informing the actions of an entire music-oriented, subcultural movement, Hanna states:

We hate capitalism in all forms and see our main goal as sharing information and staying alive, instead of making profits or being cool according to traditional standards . . . Because self-defeating behaviors (like fucking boys without condoms, drinking to excess, ignoring true-soul girlfriends, or belittling ourselves and other girls) would not be so easy if we lived in communities where we felt loved and wanted and valued.[20]

From this quote we see how one participant views the possibilities of a PunKore pedagogy as both the reality and the potential of a self-healing community. Through the self-healing praxis and street pedagogy, members of the PunKore scene engage in Freire's concept of *"conscientiza-ción."*[21] To facilitate and advance this discussion, we look to recent academic works on pedagogies of revolution.

THE TEMPORARY AUTONOMOUS ZONE (TAZ) AND REVOLUTIONARY PEDAGOGY OF PUNKORE SCENES

In fact I have deliberately refrained from defining the TAZ- I circle around the subject, firing off exploratory beams. In the end the TAZ is almost self-explanatory. If the phrase became current it would be understood without difficulty . . . understood in action.[22]

—Hakim Bey

Rikowski argues that Peter McLaren has been leading the struggle to rekindle the revolutionary potency of critical pedagogy by "reclaiming [it] for the urgent task of increasing our awareness of our social condition, as a first step in changing it."[23] What is more, McLaren stresses the point that awareness by itself is not sufficient. That is, what is needed is a commitment to social justice giving way to a transformation of consciousness to action.[24] As we will attempt to demonstrate below, McLaren's pedagogy of revolution can help not only to advance our PunKore pedagogies, but also shares common characteristics with the PunKore scenes' revolutionary pedagogy of the late '70s and early '80s and its continuing legacy of independent resistance.

However, youth countercultures have been co-opted, and thus need to be reclaimed and revitalized for the purpose of social justice. That is, the results of corporate advertisers and marketers taking out the social message of punk rock and turning it into a new style can currently be purchased and consumed in the form of clothing as well as watered-down music. Nevertheless, because of the independent

nature of progressive PunKore scenes, much of it has retained its potentially revolutionary aspects. An important difference of focus between the revolutionary pedagogy outlined by McLaren and the one outlined below is music, and its unique ability to mobilize people across space and time. The unique experience created through music is referred to by Hakim Bey as a temporary autonomous zone (TAZ), whether progressive or reactionary.[25] We will explain this phenomenon in subsequent paragraphs.

Echoing Bey's concept of the TAZ, Everyman and Jamison argue that the music generated by particular movements can inspire to action future generations who live under similar conditions.[26] The current popular underground group, the Dropkick Murphys, an Irish skinhead band out of Boston, for example, not only adorn their album sleeves with the anti-racist quotes of Martin Luther King, but have also done covers of labor songs from the Industrial Workers of the World (IWW). Their 1998 "Which Side Are You On?" and their 2003 cover of Woody Guthrie's "Gonna' Be a Blackout Tonight" are two examples. These songs exemplify the Murphys' message of working-class solidarity and struggle. In "Which Side Are You On?" the lyric, "My daddy was a miner, and I'm a miner's son, I'll stick with the union until every battle's won," is representative of the attention the Dropkick Murphys pay to forging bonds between PunKore rockers and members of the working class such as police officers and construction workers. On their 2002 "Live on St. Patrick's Day" album, lead singer Al Barr introduces a song about "good cops who don't abuse their power who are just protectin' our sorry asses because in the punk world everybody writes songs about hatin' cops, and some of 'em are fuckin' good shits, and they're here tonight. This one's called John Law." In this potentially revolutionary pedagogical performance, the Murphys led the struggle to create a space where working-class youth and working-class police officers could come together. This is reminiscent of how the IWW, with the tactic of music and slogan of "one big union" attempted to show the interconnectedness of the entire working class.

What does a PunKore revolutionary pedagogy look like? At its best, it is a pedagogy of community, of coming together to heal wounds and organize against oppression. It is a pedagogy of emotion, of venting one's frustration, and of expressing oneself through the rhythm of the music—but most important, it is a pedagogy of possibility, and a celebration of the collective creative potential realized through the discoveries made when engaged in a DIY (Do It Yourself) praxis in the midst of a TAZ. In 1991, Jesse—aka "J," of Operation Ivy—highlighted the potentialities of a revolutionary PunKore pedagogy as follows:

Music is an indirect force for change because it provides an anchor against human tragedy. In this sense, it works toward a reconciled world. It can also be the direct experience of change. At certain points during some shows, the reconciled world is already here, at least in that second, at that place. Operation Ivy was very lucky to have experienced this. Those seconds reveal that the momentum that drives a subculture is more important then any particular band. The momentum is made of all the people who stay interested, and keep their sense of urgency and hope.

Jesse's comments reflect the materialization of a progressive TAZ, spaces created out of, and for, collective struggle. These zones are the lifeline of what we consider to be the PunKore scene and the focus of the potentially revolutionary PunKore pedagogy. As "J" eloquently articulates, "at certain points during shows the reconciled world is already here at least in that second, at that place." This goes to the heart of Bey's notion of the TAZ.[27] It has been our experience that in PunKore scenes a mood, energy, feeling, emotion—hence, a reality—is created. Many times, this temporarily created reality shows us that we can live, interact, and establish human relationships, tactics, and a DIY praxis that defies global-capitalist hegemony.

The PunKore scenes that create TAZs become the foundation from which a countercultural praxis emerges and counterhegemonic identities are formed. Defiant and revolutionary ideas and praxis become and are a way of life. As a Sk8terpunker and an undergrounder, we have experienced how the TAZ serves as a breeding ground for a revolutionary pedagogy defying oppressive conditions of both global capital and cultural/social relations. As veterans of the PunKore scenes we have seen a TAZ second expanding to minutes, minutes to hours, hours to days, days to weeks, weeks to months and sometimes months to years.

For example, in 1999 and 2000, the UNAM (National Autonomous University of México) was paralyzed in a student strike that lasted more than a year. The strike was a reaction to and protest of President Carlos Salinas de Gortari's neoliberal policies in all facets of Mexican life. Under direction of the World Bank and International Monetary Fund, Salinas was responsible for the privatization, deregulation, and liberalization of formally public institutions and corporations. This paved the way for adoption of the North American Free Trade Agreement, which has opened the economic floodgates of the U.S./Mexico border and allowed the wealth created by the Mexican working class to flow North, against gravity. As a result, Mexican poverty and suffering have skyrocketed.

During the strike, the image of punk anarchist Zapatistas was used to discredit the validity of the students' claims. Nevertheless, through the strike, UNAM students created a TAZ that evoked memories of the Paris communes and revolts of 1968. However, the UNAM students' turn-of-the-century uprising lasted much longer than had the protest of the summer of 1968. In this TAZ, UNAM students got a taste of communal freedom that, owing to its collective solidarity, lasted more than a year.

Music, arts, and theater were the soul of the UNAM students' struggle. Close to the one-year anniversary of the strike, the students reaffirmed their vows against neoliberalism and demanded free, high-quality education for all at a music festival that lasted more than one day. The internationally known revolutionary band, Rage Against the Machine, participated in a solidarity concert called "The Battle of Mexico City." Money raised at the concert was given to the striking students of UNAM.

The anecdote of the UNAM strike, among countless others, has been a source of inspiration that translates into aspirations of creating a liberating TAZ where oppressive relationships of global capital and social/cultural praxis are deconstructed, destroyed, altered and mutated into a different way of life freed from the constraints of the past. Experiencing and striving to forge the TAZ through our PunKore pedagogy of revolution has convinced us we can live in a different way. That is, through participating in the construction and maintenance of a TAZ were participants have the opportunity to simultaneously become aware of their social position and act to change it through an ethics of social justice.

In these spaces of resistance (progressive TAZs) constructed by the vibes, lyrical content, and overall message of the band(s) dominating a scene or particular show, and the consciousness and actions of the audience the acts attract, which, in most motivated cities, occur almost every night, participants are in a unique position to channel the constant flow of collective energy. Through the revolutionary, counterhegemonic PunKore pedagogy, despite the omnipresent existence of the counter-revolutionary, hegemonic pedagogy of the white supremacist, sexist, homophobic, glorifier of the working class PunKore,

this energy is converted into a social movement for social justice, thereby making strides in reconciling the internal contradictions of the counter-revolutionary. The counterrevolutionary PunKore participants' sexism and glorification of manual labor work against their own class interests and against the counterhegemonic potential of the scene.

In his reflections and analysis of "the scene," Steven Blush highlights the "messiness" of any democratic movement for social justice.[28] That is, because not every participant was motivated by the same drive against oppression, or haunted by the self-destruction of despair, it has continued to form and re-form around its internal contradictions responding to both larger social structures, and the participants society creates and is created by. As a result, potentially revolutionary PunKore scenes tend to not only transmit "thought-provoking lyrics," but are also backed up by a "fuck-you attitude." This combination, at its best, not only encourages deeper understandings of one's social position as it relates to larger social structures, but also challenges participants to take action as advocated by such critical pedagogues as McLaren.[29]

For example, in the late 1980s and early 1990s, lead singer Raybeez of the New York City hard-core group, Warzone, emerged as one of the main organizers protesting policies that created the gentrification of less affluent sectors of the city. Through live musical performances and squatting in buildings targeted for demolition, Raybeez and other activists achieved success in halting rent increases. Punks, skinheads, hardcore kids, and others in the PunKore scene took the streets in protest. However, owing to multiple factors related to the power of capital, and in the wake of Raybeez's death, over time, the rents did increase, and Warzone's mobilization was temporarily halted. These examples point to the power of music as a mobilizing force in the creation of a revolutionary pedagogy.

Like Guevara and Freire, revolutionary PunKore bands and "the scene" make the potentially revolutionary PunKore scene what it is, as demonstrated in the above quotes, and play important roles in constructing progressive TAZs. That is, the punkore scene, in its nascent days especially, served an important uniting function for those disaffected youth who were unaware of the existence of others like themselves.

PunKore scenes can also practice a pedagogy of hatred, by uncritically supporting their internalized ideas, values, and beliefs transmitted through the cultural institutions controlled by the ruling class such as the mass media, education, and the state. Sometimes PunKore scenes can teach sexism, racism, and homophobia, and can even support the labor-capital relation through the celebration of manual labor. We are neither glorifying nor demonizing the PunKore scene. We merely recognize its historic role, in a specific time and space—characterized as a TAZ—where revolution is created, planned, and lived in multiple facets of our day-to-day lives. For a full discussion of the hegemonic and counterhegemonic tendencies of punk rock, see Malott and Peña.[30] In the last section we will demonstrate how we live the PunKore pedagogy, described above, through our own praxis as SK8punk and undergrounder academics.

THE PRAXIS OF ONE SK8PUNK

I was a maintenance man, a line cook, I worked in the factories I went to school, I hated it, I got my Cs and Ds. We rode our skates, we smoked our weed, we chilled with the fuckin' jonesers . . . We used our punk rock skating, and built a fuckin' crew . . . The time is now, the place is here, what do you stand for? . . . Will we fuckin' buckle, under all this pressure? Or do we have the skills, to commit a radical gesture?

—*Curry Malott*

I sing these lyrics from my song, "Jonez Boyz," as an old-school, West Coast, SK8punk, and member of the band, Ajogún, in Las Cruces, New Mexico, situated in the U.S./Mexican borderlands, at PunKore shows at local underground music stores, parties, and clubs. Las Cruces is situated within a relatively small urban county of approximately 100,000 people, over thirty percent of whom live below the official poverty line.

My role is therefore to attempt to engage people, through my music, in conversations concerning our social situation. I draw on my own experiences and perspectives as examples and points of departure. Driving this point home and using the space not only in the songs, but also between the songs, the band members (including the co-lead vocalist and coauthor of this chapter) and I let the audience know about our various campaigns such as our Cop Watch activities. We accompany this with the distribution of fliers describing the rights people have in interactions with the police.

As a group that is part of the local progressive PunKore scene, we frequently play shows with out-of-town bands on tour. It is not uncommon for bands with similar political bent to express their joy at knowing of other bands engaged in fighting the good fight. Other bands and fans in general who like our vibe mention not only our music, but our lyrics as well. Perhaps it's because it's easier to express feelings about lyrics than about music that folks always mention how enthused they are that our lyrics—be they mine or the other singers,' and often transmitted in Spanish—have substance and generate debate.

Folks unfamiliar with the skateboard scene—a scene fused with punk rock in its most underground moments—assume that it is just another sport, the youthful pastime of "juveniles," and that I, a 32-year-old PhD, need to "grow up." Skateboarding, however, is not a mere "sport." It is a way of life, and true, die-hard skaters, those who are in it for "the duration," create progressive TAZs that can last a lifetime. This attitude does not, however, invoke a pedagogy of violence as much as it declares a pedagogy of "let me create my own reality and my own life, and I won't bother you." When I was in high school, my crew, the Jonez Boyz, through the creation of our own TAZ, hooked up with other crews, creating larger, better connected networks of solidarity. Through this pedagogy of love and brother- and sisterhood, and existing on the margins of society, ways of living, previously unlived, were formed. Our DIY pedagogy coupled with a praxis of communal living materialized through some of the skaters I used to ride with, including Marc "Red" Scott from Portland, Oregon, and Mark "Munk" Hubbard from Seattle, Washington.

These guys and their crews took the DIY philosophy to a level none of us ever thought possible through the construction of an anti-park skate park, "Burnside," in Portland, Oregon under the Burnside Bridge.[31] Red, whose father was a carpenter, and his crew started constructing banks under the Burnside Bridge in 1990 without permission from the city—they just went for it. In the 2003 documentary, *Northwest*, Red describes how he and his friends started building bowls and quarter-pipes out of cement under the Burnside Bridge, regardless of what anybody said.[32] Red describes how through this process they met "some allies along the way who said 'leave these guys alone, they're not hurting anybody.'" As a result, the city eventually granted them permission to keep what turned into the pirated Burnside Skate Park. Red and his crew learned to build world-class skate parks, and have since been commissioned to build city parks throughout the Northwest and all over the world.

Through his pedagogy, Munk humbly takes on not only the DIY philosophy of punk, but—despite his pro-skater status—is also open to working with anyone interested in participating in the scene, which is similar to the pedagogy of Ché Guevara described by McLaren.[33] This potentially revolutionary pedagogy is in stark contrast to other professional skaters and park designers who practice a much more elitist pedagogy of exclusion, working with only those deemed sufficiently experienced and committed. Within Munk's SK8punk pedagogy, which I, myself, practice in the Southwest, a potentially revolutionary force exists with the potential to transform not only our immediate lives within the capitalist system, as many skaters have, but also to completely uproot and transform the labor-capital relation through a DIY pedagogy of community building, humility, and courage practiced on a large scale. What follows is the complementary pedagogical praxis of revolution emerging out of Puerto Rico.

THE PRAXIS OF ONE UNDERGROUNDER

The TAZ is like an uprising which does not engage directly with the State, a guerilla operation which liberates an area (of land, of time, of imagination) and then dissolves itself to reform elsewhere/elsewhen, before the State can crush it.[34]

—*Hakim Bey*

Born in the revolutionary struggle within Puerto Rico, I was introduced to a world where dreams were a concrete way of materializing revolutions. This belief was inculcated shortly but surely through the Latin American struggle folk songs of Aires Bucaneros, Roy Brown, Silvio Rodriguez, Pablo Milanes, Mercedes Sosa, Victor Jara, and Intillimani, among others. Through "Trova," a sense of pride, emancipation, self-determination, and sensibility to all forms of oppression became what are known as my pillars of an undergrounder subjectivity. I stress underground, for in her experience as a radical student in the 1960s, my mother and her comrades had to live a semiclandestine life. The FBI, CIA, and local government tactics of repression were a day-to-day reality that resulted in the political persecution, torture, and assassination of many in the struggle. Through the underground community and mutual solidarity, many managed to survive.

In my teen years I was introduced to the world of underground punk, hard–core, and OI musical scenes. Raw and aggressive music perfectly complemented my rage against the U.S. empire and its historic role in killing anything that came in its way of consolidating hegemonic control. It was in this progressive PunKore scene where I would discuss the nationalist and socialist movements of liberation for Puerto Rico. While drinking and hanging out, we aspired and plotted to create emancipatory TAZs through our multiple shows as a source of instigating, breeding, and materializing revolution. Shows of the PunKore scenes were instances where our revolutionary tendencies bloomed, for they had a fertile and concrete community, space, and time to grow in. For us, revolutionary TAZs were and are a way of life. We felt free so we became free.

Later I embarked upon higher education and brought my PunKore praxis with me. In fact, many of my friends in the PunKore scene were also students at the University of Puerto Rico. The PunKore scene was not only in the streets but in the university as well. There I got involved in multiple student movements that engaged in a Latin American style of revolutionary praxis. For us, the TAZ, created via the PunKore scene, was the lifeline of our revolution. It would have been practically impossible to mobilize thousands of students to paralyze the university without multiple musical concerts and rallies. TAZ, via music and theater, broke barriers of apathy facilitating the bloom of various movements against multiple forms of injustices. We dealt with all kinds of issues: imperialism, decolonization, capitalism, racism, homophobia, and xenophobia, among other forms of oppression.

As an undergrounder I've lived the phenomenon that any form of underground music creates a space where revolutionary tactics and life help materialize in counter cultures and counter hegemonic forces. For me it has been vital to any form of resistance against oppressive conditions. Music is the soul of the revolution without it I think its dead.

Music as a form of organizing is not inherently the property of the Latin American struggle. Here in the United States, it has been used on a constant basis throughout its history. Music massified and mobilized revolutions. Some of the most recent examples have been tours with Rage Against the Machine. Their tours they rallied the cause for clemency and immediate release of both Leonard Peltier and Mumia Abu-Jamal, while simultaneously shining light on the Zapatista struggle. Other musical groups such as Ozomatli are always to be found in Chicana/-o and borderland issues.

Music in an underground fashion was and is a key element in helping organize the massive mobilizations against the oppressive nature of the World Trade Organization and other transnational capitalist elite organizations in Seattle, Prague, and elsewhere. It is in this fashion that the authors of this chapter engage in consciously creating temporary autonomous zones of liberation where the praxis of the PunKore scenes' pedagogy helps create a community that addresses the eradication of oppression, however it may manifest itself.

Currently I work in multiple community efforts with my colleague, TAZ-mate, and coauthor of this chapter. From staffing literature tables, to free speech activism, Cop Watch, *migra* watch, the *Ni una Más* campaign to stop the assassination of *maquiladora* workers in Ciudad Juarez, to anti-war protests and theater of the oppressed workshops, we have been seriously involved in borderland politics and resistance. Our DIY TAZ-making praxis materialized in creating a PunKore band in the borderland scene known as Ajogún.

CONCLUSION

PunKore represents part of the world's working- and middle-class response to an increasingly unjust world. It represents one youth subculture out of many, which, if united with all countercultures beyond all boundaries, possesses a revolutionary potential capable of smashing the relationships that oppress us, and building new ones that allow us to develop our collective creative capacities in the humanization of not only the world, but our selves. Our vision of PunKore resonates particularly well with the pedagogies of previous revolutionary struggles. Translating into English some words of Ernesto Ché Guevara, our revolutionary TAZ-creating praxis strives to create a community and alternative way of life where we all "feel that indignation against any form of oppression against anyone in the world becomes and is the most beautiful quality of a revolutionary." We want to "be realists and do the impossible."

To all undergrounders worldwide who are creating TAZ/counterhegemonic communities, *hasta la victoria siempre*.

NOTES

This chapter is based on the article by Curry Malott and Joseph Carroll-Miranda, "PunKore Scenes as Revolutionary Street Pedagogy," published in *JCEPS* 1 (2) and located online at http://www.jceps.com/index.php?pageID=article&articleID=13.

1. Hobsbawm, E. (2002). Primitive rebels. In S. Duncombe (Ed.), *Cultural resistance reader*. London: Verso.
2. Rikowski, G. (2002). Education, capital, and the transhuman. In D. Hill, P. McLaren, and G. Rikowski (Eds.), *Marxism against post-*

modernism in educational theory. New York: Lexington Books.
3. Neary, M. (2002). Youth, training, and the politics of "cool." In D. Hill, P. McLaren, and G. Rikowski (Eds.), *Marxism against postmodernism in educational theory*. New York: Lexington Books.
4. Neary (2002).
5. McLaren, P. (2000). *Che Guevara, Paulo Freire, and the pedagogy of revolution*. New York: Rowman & Littlefield; McLaren, P. (2000). Reconsidering Marx in post-Marxist times: A requiem for postmodernism? *Educational Researcher*, 25–33; McLaren, P. & Farahmand-pur, R. (2002). Breaking signifying chains: A Marxist position on postmodernism. In D. Hill, P. McLaren, and G. Rikowski (Eds.), *Marxism against postmodernism in educational theory*. New York: Lexington Books; Ross, W. (2000). Diverting democracy: The curriculum standards movement and social studies education. In D. Hursh & W. Ross (Eds.), *Democratic social education: Social studies for social change*. New York: Falmer Press.
6. Rikowski (2002).
7. Hebdige, D. (2002). The meaning of MOD. In S. Duncombe. (Ed.), *Cultural resistance reader*. London: Verso.
8. Hebdige (2002).
9. Willis, P. (1977). *Learning to labour: How working-class kids get working-class jobs*. Westmead, England: Saxon House; MacLeod, J. (1987). *Ain't no makin' it: Leveled aspirations in a low-income neighborhood*. Boulder, CO: Westview; Weis, L. (1990). *Working-class without work: High school students in a deindustrializing economy*. New York: Routledge.
10. Hill, D., Sanders, M., & Hankin, T. (2002). Marxism, class analysis, and postmodernism. In D. Hill, P. McLaren, and G. Rikowski (Eds.), *Marxism against postmodernism in educational theory*. New York: Lexington Books.
11. Hobsbawm (2002); Hebdige (2002); Clarke, J. (2002). The skinheads and the magical recovery of community. In S. Duncombe. (Ed.), *Cultural resistance reader*. London: Verso.
12. Hanna, K. (2002). Interview in *Punk Planet*. In S. Duncombe (Ed.), *Cultural resistance reader*. London: Verso.
13. Marshall, G. (1991). *Spirit of '69: A skinhead Bible*. U.K.: STP Publishing.
14. Marshall (1991).
15. Marshall (1991).

16. Symarip (1991). *Skinhead Moonstomp*. Trojan Records, 10786-20564 [CD].

17. Marshall (1991).

18. Marshall (1991).

19. Hanna (2002).

20. Hanna (2002).

21. Freire, P. (1998). *Pedagogy of freedom*. Lanham, MD: Rowman & Littlefield.

22. Bey, H. (2002). TAZ: The temporary autonomous zone. In S. Duncombe (Ed.), *Cultural resistance reader*. London: Verso.

23. Rikowski (2002).

24. Rikowski (2002).

25. Bey (2002).

26. Eyerman, R. & Jamison, A. (1998). *Music and social movements: Mobilizing traditions in the twentieth century*. Cambridge, England: Cambridge University Press.

27. Bey (2002).

28. Blush, S. (2001). *American hardcore: A tribal history*. Los Angeles: Feral House.

29. McLaren, P. (2002). Marxist revolutionary praxis: A curriculum of transgression. *Journal of Critical Inquiry into Curriculum and Instruction*, 3 (3), 36–41.

30. Malott, C. & Peña, M. (in press). *Punk rocker's revolution: Pedagogy of gender, race, and class*. New York: Peter Lang.

31. Borden, L. (2001). *Skateboarding, space and the city: Architecture and the body*. New York: Berg.

32. Nichols, B., and Charnoski, R. (Producer and Director). (2003). *Northwest* [Film]. New York: Charnoski Productions and Flexifilm.

33. McLaren (2000).

34. Bey (2002).

CIVIL RIGHT, NOBLE CAUSE, AND TROJAN HORSE: NEWS PORTRAYALS OF VOUCHERS AND URBAN EDUCATION

Eric Haas

If you are an African-American child going to an urban school, a voucher will protect your right to a quality education. If Americans want to help improve the education of poor, inner-city students, then they should give them vouchers to go to the school of their choice. Government bureaucracies have caused urban school to be failures. Private business and the marketplace will make them excellent.

The sentences above are some of the latest language about urban education in the news. Linking vouchers with urban education continues the rhetoric that government is the problem, whereas private business and marketplace practices are the solution. Further combining vouchers and urban education with a civil right to education extends the reach of this rhetoric. Private business and the marketplace, once the opponent of civil rights, are now presented as their protector. This expansion of the logic of the education marketplace will likely have a profound effect on urban schools.

THE LANGUAGE OF EDUCATION POLICY IN THE NEWSPAPER MATTERS

How an urban education policy is framed—what parts of our identity, values, and hopes it evokes through the language used to promote it—determines in part how it is enacted or defeated. This chapter examines how proponents of vouchers are linking them with inner-city schools and civil rights to gain acceptance of pilot programs throughout the country. Understanding the assumptions, ambiguities, and contradictions of this language can give educators, researchers, and policy makers insight into the development of public opinion and policy on urban education.

The language examined is taken from newspaper articles that concern vouchers and urban schools. Newspaper articles are examined because the news media both reflect and shape the terms of education policy debates.[1] In other words, the manner in which vouchers and urban education are presented together in newspapers is evidence of how the relationship between the two is viewed by the news media, the policy advocates presented in the news articles, and the policy makers and the public who read them.[2]

THE IMPORTANCE OF POLICY LANGUAGE

Terms such as "urban education," "voucher," and "civil rights" do not have intrinsic, universal meanings. Instead, what they mean can differ by person and context and over time.[3] How "urban education," "voucher," and "civil rights" are understood depend on the language used to describe them, on past and current events, and on the knowledge, experience, and values of readers. For example, policy language that links the terms "vouchers" and "urban education" with civil rights will likely create a different meaning for those terms than language that links "vouchers" and "urban education" with religious freedom. The meanings of these collections of terms will also differ and change depending on past and current events that involve vouchers, urban education, and a host of other social happenings, including the success or failure of other voucher programs, higher or lower test scores in urban schools, legal gains or setbacks in affirmative action cases and, say, concerns about terrorists using vouchers to run anti-American schools. How much weight policy makers and the public attribute to any of these events often depends on the extent and character of their coverage in the news.[4]

The meaning of an urban education policy in a newspaper piece will also depend on who is reading it. The ideas, emotions, and experiences that a reader brings to the piece will interact with what the news piece states explicitly, what it leaves ambiguous, and what it leaves out.[5] A news piece that links vouchers and urban education may evoke feelings in some readers that this education policy will be a threat to stable, high-achieving schools. Adding language about the use of vouchers to protect the civil right to a quality education for urban students may ease tensions by evoking an egalitarian purpose.[6] Similarly, parents who think of marketplace exploitation when they read about voucher proposals may be more supportive when vouchers are presented as a means to protect the right to quality education set down in *Brown v. Board of Education*.[7]

To uncover the layers of possible meaning associated with linking vouchers, urban education, and civil rights, it is important to examine three aspects of the newspaper pieces: (1) the education policy language itself; (2) references to other language and ideas in the education policy language; and (3) the larger context of events that surround vouchers and urban education.[8] There is not sufficient space for an extensive analysis here; however, select examples of news articles are scrutinized for the link among vouchers, urban education, and civil rights. Specifically examined is how the right to quality education is perceived.

THE LANGUAGE ITSELF

Examining news pieces that report on vouchers and urban education demonstrates some patterns in how the two are linked. Proponents link them in two main ways. First, proponents emphasize quality education for urban students as a civil right, and advocate vouchers as the best means to meet the legal obligation to provide it. Second, they emphasize quality urban education as a moral imperative—but not a legal obligation—and vouchers as the best way to meet it. In the latter, providing vouchers to inner-city students is made equivalent to a noble cause. Both characterize the purpose and process of education in business language.

Newspaper articles also include voucher opponents who contend that vouchers are a Trojan horse. They will bring high promises, but they will deliver low-quality education that will eventually end public education. Newspaper articles generally reference voucher opponents to present the possible failures of voucher programs without offering alternative public school reforms. Thus, voucher opponents indirectly affirm the purpose and process of education in business terms. Examples of each of these presentations are examined below.

Vouchers as a Civil Right

Voucher proponents who link them with urban education present vouchers as a more effective way to protect the civil right to a quality education. They are, the proponents contend, better than the current government-managed urban public schools. As such, vouchers are presented as the best, and possibly only, means to fulfill the hard-won civil right to equal educational opportunity set forth in *Brown v. Board of Education*. This presentation of voucher programs follows a general pattern: (1) the terrible state of all urban schools is noted; (2) the failure of urban schools is linked to government bureaucracy or teachers unions; (3) the civil right to a quality education is evoked as the foundational impetus for reform; and (4) marketplace and business-oriented reforms are presented as the best or only way to protect this civil right.

An opinion piece written by Jeff Jacoby and published in the *Boston Globe* is a representative example. The premise of Jacoby's piece, titled "Vouchers and Equal Education," is that a marketplace reform is needed to achieve the educational quality

called for in *Brown v. Board of Education*.[9] Jacoby's argument includes the four elements listed above.

The article states repeatedly that public schools are in terrible shape. For example, Jacoby states that overall public schools are "nothing to boast about" and that "few are crummier than the dreadful urban public schools."[10] He backs his conclusion with the chilling statistic, "the average black high school senior today is less competent in reading, math, and history than the average white eighth-grader."[11] Although some would argue that Jacoby's condemnation of urban education is overly simplistic and broad,[12] he presents them as well-accepted truths in no need of further support.[13]

Jacoby places the blame for the sad state of urban schools in two places: the government bureaucracy that manages them and the deficiencies of poor, black culture. He calls government management of public schools the "Soviet model" and a "monopoly . . . [that] wastes money, performs indifferently, and doesn't care much if its customers— American mothers and fathers—are satisfied."[14] Urban public schools, he asserts, are "inferior" because they are a "one-size-fits-all product of sclerotic government bureaucracies."[15] Jacoby also blames poor student performance on the bad culture of black families. Poor, black students would do better, he contends, if their families had higher expectations, worked harder, and watched less television. Again, Jacoby presents his condemnations as accepted truths, although others do disagree.[16]

Jacoby reminds the reader that *Brown v. Board of Education* held that the U.S. Constitution requires that all students must be given an equal opportunity to receive a quality education. Jacoby claims that, despite soaring per-pupil spending and the hiring of a large number of additional teachers, the promise of *Brown* "is still a mirage."[17] *Brown* set forth a legal mandate that the government management of public schools has not, and cannot, meet.

Jacoby's solution is the marketplace management of public schools in the form of vouchers.

By now it is obvious that spending even more money and hiring even more teachers isn't going to bring about the equality that *Brown* called for. Neither will shifting students around on the basis of skin color, as decades of forced busing certainly proved. So maybe it's time to try a really radical reform: choice. . . For two generations we have claimed that educational equality is a constitutional right. The way to finally make good on that claim is to offer a voucher of equal value to the parents of every child—letting the funding follow the student, no matter who runs the school. Putting power in the hands of parents is the real key to equality—and the key to excellence, too.[18]

Jacoby presents simplistic, and likely false, dichotomies that contrast effective and ineffective schools as equivalent to public versus marketplace management. One might agree with Jacoby that more money and more teachers alone will not bring about equal educational opportunity for urban students without reaching his conclusion that the only solution is vouchers. Other changes that would likely contribute to more effective urban schools, such as better, more affordable health care and a living wage for all U.S. citizens, including urban residents, are not discussed in Jacoby's article.[19]

In sum, Jacoby argues that the right to a quality education created by the U.S. Constitution and the Supreme Court can only be protected by private enterprise and market competition. Through the marketplace, competition alone will produce equality by making all schools excellent. Government bureaucracy, in contrast, can only produce educational haves and have-nots.

Other newspaper pieces similarly link vouchers, urban schools, and civil rights. For example, the *New York Times* published a news analysis of the George W. Bush Administration's plan to give vouchers to parents of students in "failing" Title I schools.[20] In this article, titled "Adding a Financial Threat to Familiar Promises on Education," the *New York Times* quotes William Taylor, now of a group called the Citizens' Commission on Civil Rights, who presents President Bush as a maverick who will use vouchers to protect the rights of disadvantaged minorities in the spirit of 1960s civil rights activism:

"But," he [William Taylor] added, "the whole history of civil rights enforcement has been that when the government shows it's serious, the recipients of government money will comply and the kids will get the services they need."

In seeking to flex the punitive muscle of federal education law—specifically the 36-year-old $8 billion Title I program, which aids the nation's poorest and lowest-achieving students—Mr. Bush is allying himself most closely with President Lyndon B. Johnson, who withheld money from Southern school districts that refused to embrace desegregation, said Mr. Taylor, the director of the United States Commission on Civil Rights in the Johnson Administration.[21]

According to Taylor, vouchers are the successor to the civil rights movement because they punish the government bureaucrats who refuse to offer quality education to the nation's poor.

The importance of this shift in language lies in its attempt to change the perception of the relationship between two contradictory forces in U.S. society: civil rights and private enterprise. For centuries, U.S. private businesses regularly violated the civil rights of people of color.[22] Only recently have the Civil Rights Act of 1964 and numerous protests limited (but not ended) discrimination by private businesses. More fundamental is the contention that education in a capitalist society is inherently discriminatory.[23] A capitalist marketplace operates through competition based on the threat and promise of differential accumulation. Under the logic of the education marketplace, a school would make itself more successful by the ability to develop within its students the knowledge and talent to give them an economic advantage over graduates of other schools.

Education policy language that links equal educational opportunity with marketplace competition becomes an Orwellian proposition: Hierarchy is equality.

One way to soften this contradiction is to present vouchers as a noble gesture rather than as the protector of a legal right. In this presentation of education policy, proponents present vouchers as a noble cause through which society can assist less fortunate students who attend urban schools. The structure of noble cause logic uses language similar to the four elements contained in the language of vouchers as a civil right.

Vouchers as a Noble Cause

One example of this noble cause language is a news analysis of the education policy debate in the *New York Times*, titled "Education Plan by Bush Shows New Consensus."[24] First, it states that urban schools are in a terrible state. Urban education is described as the "the plight of poor, minority children in inner-city schools" and as being inflicted with "plagues of illiteracy and high dropout rates."[25] Second, the problems of urban education are loosely attributed to "experimental curriculums and individual portfolios" as well as to "people with a direct interest in the status quo" and "the power of the teachers' unions."[26] Then, the solutions are drawn exclusively from the language of business and the marketplace: "competition, accountability and a focus on fundamentals" including vouchers.[27]

In noble cause language, compassion is the fundamental impetus for school reform and it is grounded in legislation, not the U.S. Constitution. Noble cause language shifts society's relationship to urban education from a legal obligation individually enforceable as a U.S. Constitutional right to a moral obligation that is compelling, but individually unenforceable, absent legislation. The difference is subtle, but significant. U.S. Constitutional rights are grounded in one's humanity and citizenship and are thus inalienable. These rights are the closest U.S. society has to unalterable human rights. Rights derived from legislation, on the other hand, are grounded in the will of the political majority. They are inherently impermanent and they change as the political majority modifies them over time. Thus, no legislation ever needs to be enacted or continued. Vouchers and other business-model changes are linked to a desire, but not a constitutional obligation, to assist the less fortunate that continues from President Johnson's Great Society legislation. The *New York Times* article includes this description of the history preceding the current federal voucher debate:

> To be sure, the education debate has always emphasized the disadvantaged, particularly at the federal level. From the desegregation of schools in the 1950s to the Great Society programs of the 1960s, the bulk of federal attention and money has focused on the needy.[28]

The current push for federal education vouchers is presented as the latest descendent of the civil rights move\ment. Yet, by describing the students as "needy" rather than "entitled," this language shifts education away from a legal right and more toward neighborly assistance.

Continuing in this theme, the article links a better urban education and vouchers to the need for a more educated labor force, the desire for educational equity, and the altruistic push to "help":

> With corporate leaders dissatisfied about the quality of the labor pool helping steer the discussion, talk from years past about experimental curriculums and individual portfolios has been overshadowed by a bottom-line approach stressing basic skills, tests and accountability— all aimed at the neediest students in impoverished urban districts.
>
> "The whole discussion is an equity discussion," said Diane Ravitch, the education historian. "The tenor of the discussion is: Do charter schools help poor kids? Do vouchers help poor kids? Is state testing good or bad for poor kids? How can we design a system that increases equity?"[29]

This article equates equity with business and the marketplace in two ways. Business and the marketplace are both the management process and the primary goals of education. Quality education for all concerns making urban students more prepared for the workforce. The best way to achieve that is for schools to be managed like businesses. That the aim of urban education might also include contesting and transforming society and the workforce is not considered.[30]

The language of vouchers as a noble cause also softens some of the contradictions inherent in presenting them as a means to protect civil rights. While invoking the marketplace as the primary means of providing for the right to quality education, vouchers are also presented as help rather than as the only means to a quality education. The implication appears to be that they would only be implemented when they would be an improvement over government-run public schools. That this may be inherently impossible or unlikely is not addressed. Despite these likely contradictions, the mere expansion of voucher language to include urban education and civil rights has important policy implications.

REFERENCES TO BUSINESS LANGUAGE AND IDEAS

When voucher supporters present vouchers as a means to fulfill the promises of *Brown* and Title I,[31] they present a subtle but important shift in the relationship between individuals and society. Civil rights language that emerged out of the 1960s was based on the concept of entitlement to fundamental rights based on common humanity and shared citizenship.[32] This language placed a large responsibility on society to ensure a level playing field, even going so far as having the government, not just protect civil rights, but also take active steps to eliminate past civil rights abuses and current inequalities in education through such programs as Title I, busing, and affirmative action. These programs and policies were intended, at least in part, to use the power of the government to meet the obligations of society to treat all its citizens justly, something not always done between private individuals and by private business. The enactment of the Civil Rights Act of 1964 put the U.S. government in its role as a protector of civil rights at odds with the business community.[33]

Presenting vouchers—a program based on marketplace mechanisms—as the best means to advance civil rights redefines the right to a quality education away from a right of citizenship to something akin to a property right that must be exercised by a responsible consumer. In this language, the citizen-consumer's use of free enterprise—buying the service of education from the best school and leaving schools that do not provide good service—becomes the means to ensure one's civil rights. Thus, the citizen-consumer alone is responsible for "exercising" the right to a quality education. The government's responsibility extends only to protecting the free exchange of educational goods and services. In this framing, the government is an enabler of individual rights, but does not guarantee them. It has no direct responsibility for the individual, nor for creating a just society.

Jacoby's piece in the *Boston Globe* supports his call for vouchers by directly blaming the problems of urban education on the poor parental choices of minority parents and on bad government. Responsible consumers are the only solution. According to Jacoby, the quality of education would improve for poor, urban, minority students if education were treated more like "food or clothing or health care—where the market generates lots of options and parents are free to choose among them."[34] By this logic, a student's civil right to quality education is limited only by a parent's injudicious use of their voucher. Civil rights violations result only from bad individual choices, not unjust societal choices. The role of government, then, is to get out of the way. The business logic of property rights applied to civil rights is subtly supported by the presentation of urban educational problems as resulting from poor individual choices, as something akin to natural causes, or as simply existing of unknown cause. The concept that society as a whole might have a role in urban education problems, either directly or through related issues like unequal health care and employment opportunities, is denied or ignored. Government, therefore, has no direct responsibility to correct them.

The Wilgoren piece in the *New York Times* describes high dropout rates and illiteracy as "inner-city plagues."[35] Linking urban educational problems with the plague invites readers to view them not only as widespread and horrific, but also as unavoidable natural occurrences. Readers are not invited to see high dropout rates and illiteracy as societal creations. How differently might a reader perceive urban education problems if the *New York Times* were to present the illiterate student and the student who drops out of school as "cursed"—afflicted by something placed on one person by another?

Wilgoren also presents the problems in urban education as existing without cause. Inner-city students are described simply as "needy" and urban schools as "impoverished."[36] No cause is given. No actor or action caused the impoverishment or the neediness. They just seem to be that way. The reader is not invited to view society as being responsible.

The power of the language of any policy is that with repeated use over time, it can push out other policy options and limit what is considered in the public debate. Thus, as the language of voucher policies and their underlying business logic are repeated in the news, they become more commonplace, and eventually become the dominant language of reform. Vouchers, along with the business and marketplace logic that supports them, become the accepted commonsense start of the education reform debate. At this point even opponents of using vouchers to improve urban schools begin to contest them in business language.

Vouchers as a Trojan Horse

Critics of vouchers as the means to bettering urban schools predominantly use a version of the business language used by voucher proponents. Their contrary language is simply that vouchers do not work. Voucher critics do not question the business model of education, only whether vouchers will achieve the competitive equity that voucher proponents contend they will.

Consider a news article in the *New York Times* that described the Senate debate that ultimately defeated the Bush voucher proposal in his No Child Left Behind legislation.[37] In this article, titled, "Senate Rejects Tuition Aid, A Key to Bush Education Plan," opponents of vouchers for low-income city students present them as a Trojan horse sent to undermine public schools. The article does not explain why government-managed urban public schools are considered worth saving nor does it present an alternative vision of how the government might better advance civil rights than can the marketplace.

Republicans contend that publicly financed vouchers are an innovative way to give children in dead-end schools a better education and to force public schools to improve. Democrats who say the approach offers only false hope to children argue that vouchers are a threat to public schools, which will see some money steered to private schools.

"It sounds so good," said Senator Hillary Rodham Clinton, Democrat of New York, "but it has a number of serious flaws that doom it. Experiments have demonstrated absolutely no evidence that vouchers help improve student achievement.

"Secondly, we know that vouchers do not help the students who need the help the most. They do nothing to help improve public schools. Vouchers only further segregate and stratify our public schools."[38]

According to the Democrats referenced in this article, one should support government-managed public schools only because vouchers and the marketplace would perform even worse. There is no discussion of why public schools could be an important societal institution in and of themselves.

Similar language is used in a lengthy piece in the *New York Times* about New Zealand's experience with school vouchers.[39] In "A Cautionary Tale from New Zealand," professor of public policy Helen Ladd and her husband, Edward Fiske, an education consultant and former education editor of the *New York Times*, describe the failure of vouchers to improve "troubled urban schools" in New Zealand as a lesson for U.S. education policy.[40] They state that the New Zealand government's refusal to intervene to assist troubled urban schools, as called for under the theory of the educational marketplace, led to increased racial and economic segregation in schools. The result was that schools in middle- and upper-middle-income communities often improved, while schools with poor populations spiraled downward. To combat this, the New Zealand government eventually changed course and began to directly assist the troubled schools. It provided additional money for school health clinics and new equipment, and to buy out underperforming staff.

In this article, Fiske and Ladd criticize the logic of the education marketplace in property right language, but do not explicitly embrace the language of education as an entitlement right. Fiske and Ladd describe how the government had to take a direct role in providing quality education beyond the promoting and protecting

marketplace. They conclude that vouchers and individual choice of school alone do not work for poor, urban students.

Still, Fiske and Ladd do not make clear the fundamental motivation behind the New Zealand government's decision to intervene. Did it intervene because it needed to temporarily correct this new program of marketplace management? Or did the New Zealand government intervene because it saw an active and mutual obligation between individuals and society that is best protected and advanced through government? In other words, was the New Zealand government fixing or replacing marketplace management? The news piece does not say.

In addition, Fiske and Ladd are unclear about the purpose of schooling. In their news article, Fiske and Ladd discuss "success in school" and indicate that schools can be "successful," but they do not define what these terms mean.[41] To help interpret these terms, as well as the government's intention in intervening on behalf of urban schools, it is best to consider them in light of the pervasive use of business practices and goals in education and other government activities.

THE LARGER CONTEXT

Two trends in U.S. society appear especially relevant to interpreting the language of urban education policy: the application of marketplace principles to an ever-growing share of society and the expansion of "equity" to mean all of U.S. education, rather than segments within it. The pervasiveness of these concepts makes their extension to education more likely.

Over the last twenty years, outsourcing government activities to private businesses has steadily increased.[42] The military is emblematic of the privatization of government activities. In Operation Iraqi Freedom, for example, private contractors prepare soldiers' meals, provide Internet services, and interrogate prisoners.[43]

The education marketplace has similarly expanded. Schools outsource their janitorial and food services. Vouchers, charter schools, tuition tax credits, and private educational management organizations like Edison Schools, Inc., have increased significantly in the last twenty years.[44] School districts sell public building space to soft drink manufacturers and other advertisers to raise funds for school programs.[45] International corporations like pharmaceutical giant GlaxoSmithKline provide free curricula and lesson plans to schools.[46]

Business leaders and business language increasingly set the education agenda. Since the Reagan Administration published "A Nation at Risk,"[47] the education debate has been inundated with notions of how schools can prepare students to be better workers and make the nation more economically competitive in the global marketplace. Referring to the need to maintain the "once unchallenged preeminence [of the United States] in commerce, industry, science, and technological innovation,"[48] "A Nation at Risk" considers other educational activities to be distracting and harmful:

Our society and its educational institutions seem to have lost sight of the basic purposes of schooling, and of the high expectations and disciplined effort needed to attain them. . . . That we have compromised this commitment is, upon reflection, hardly surprising, given the multitude of often conflicting demands we have placed on our Nation's schools and colleges. They are routinely called on to provide solutions to personal, social, and political problems that the home and other institutions either will not or cannot resolve. We must understand that these demands on our schools and colleges often exact an educational cost as well as a financial one.[49]

Business leaders, in turn, have taken an active role in shaping state and federal education policy. Describing and orienting education according to the needs and pri-orities of business and the marketplace are now common in the language and activities both outside and within the education community.[50]

"A Nation at Risk" also began to reshape the meaning of equity. Dating to the civil rights movement, education equity has concerned disparities within the U.S. educational system. Among these were the lack of funding and resources for urban schools. When "A Nation at Risk" condemned the entire U.S. educational system as failing to produce a competitive workforce, it specifically shifted the debate away from equalizing disparate funding, resources, and social conditions among school districts. Rather, it cast all school districts as burdened with problems affecting the nation's economic well-being:

All, regardless of race or class or economic status, are entitled to a fair chance and to the tools for developing their individual powers of mind and spirit to the utmost. This promise means that all children by virtue of their own efforts, competently guided, can hope to attain the mature and informed judgment needed to secure gainful employment, and to manage their own lives, thereby serving not only their own interests but also the progress of society itself.[51]

To support this statement, "A Nation at Risk" presented statistics on the failure of U.S. education as a whole. It did not separate out the high test scores of wealthy, white suburban students from the low test scores of poor, minority, urban students.[52] It presented equity as making U.S. students equal to students from competitor nations rather than setting as a goal the equalization of educational opportunities among poor urban students and their well-to-do suburban counterparts.

A Little of Both Leaves a Business Message

Some news pieces attempt to find a middle ground between proponents and opponents of vouchers for urban public schools. They draw bits from both camps—managerial innovation from the voucher proponents and more money and support for all schools from the voucher opponents. This mix of language, however, still presents a mostly pro-business model or property right view of education. It places the fulfillment of a right to quality education almost completely on the individual and only slightly on society. Further, it leaves unsaid the purpose of education, which in the current educational climate, makes it likely to be interpreted as economic competitiveness alone.

Take, for example, an opinion piece in the *Washington Post* by Professor Paul Hill of the University of Washington's Center on Reinventing Public Education.[53] In "Aha! School Choice Can Work in D.C.," Hill argues that a properly designed voucher system could go a long way toward providing quality education to impoverished children in poor-performing public schools, many of which are urban schools. One of the obvious requirements—which Hill lists in his "Well duh!" category—is that all schools should receive equal per-pupil spending. He writes:

In a public school setting, equal per-pupil spending—whether a child attends a traditional public school, charter school, magnet program or other option [like vouchers]—is critical to give families, particularly poor ones, not just alternatives but good alternatives to failing local schools.[54]

This type of equality—equal spending power—presents a property right, business model approach to education. All that is necessary for good education is parents acting as good consumers. Society is assumed to have achieved a level playing field and thus there is no obligation to go beyond the notion of "same as equal."

To the extent that poor, urban schools were to receive more from society in the language of a communal obligation to student learning, it comes in the form of bonuses to attract teachers to the most difficult schools. Hill puts it this way: "A few creative incentives could work wonders: By using extra grant money to offer bonuses, school districts could lure excellent teachers to tough classrooms."[55]

Of further interest is the lack of specificity about what vouchers would improve in schools. Hill describes the improvement as "higher achievement" and "quality of academics"—but what do these terms mean? Do they mean making students better quality laborers as called for in "A Nation at Risk"? Or do they mean active citizens and reflective thinkers who also challenge and transform the status quo? Hill leaves these terms for the reader to interpret. Given the strong influence of the business community and the prevalence of business language in the current language of education generally and within discussions of vouchers specifically, it is more likely that readers will interpret ambiguous terms like "higher achievement" to mean the development of students as more globally competitive workers than as well-rounded, critical citizens.

CONCLUSION

Language matters in education policy. When newspapers and voucher supporters present vouchers as the best means to enhance urban students' civil right to equal educational opportunity, they extend the logic of the marketplace to the very core of the nation's social structure. Education is a property right. Civil rights are a property right. Government efforts to equalize social inequalities only make the situation worse. Equality through competition is no longer contradictory; it becomes common sense.

NOTES

1. van Dijk, T. (2000). Critical discourse analysis. In D. Schiffrin, D. Tannen, & H. Hamilton (Eds.), *The handbook of discourse analysis.* Oxford: Blackwell; Fairclough, N. (1995). *Critical discourse analysis: The critical study of language.* Harlow, UK: Longman; Herman, E. &

Chomsky, N. (1988). *Manufacturing consent: The political economy of the mass media.* New York: Pantheon; Kingdon, J. (1984). *Agendas, alternatives, and public policy.* Boston: Little, Brown.

2. Fairclough, N. (1995). *Media discourse.* London: Arnold; Lawrence, R. (2000). *The politics of force: Media and the construction of police brutality.* Berkeley, CA: University of California Press.

3. Ball, S. (1994). *Education reform: A critical and post-structural approach.* Buckingham, UK: Open University Press; Ball, S. (2002). *Class strategies and the education market: The middle classes and social advantage.* London: Routledge-Falmer; Fairclough, *Critical discourse analysis*; Smith, M. (2004). *Political spectacle and the fate of American schools.* New York: RoutledgeFalmer.

4. Lawrence (2000).

5. Fairclough. *Critical discourse analysis*; Foucault, M. (1980). *Power/knowledge: Selected interviews and other writings 1972–1977.* New York: Pantheon Books; Rosenblatt, L. (1994). The transactional theory of reading and writing. In R. Ruddell, M. Ruddell, & H. Singer (Eds.), *Theoretical models* and processes of reading (4th ed.). Newark, DE: International Reading.

6. See, e.g., Wilgoren, J. (2001, January 23). Education plan by Bush shows new consensus. *New York Times.* p. A1.

7. *Brown v. Board of Education,* 347 U.S. 483 (1954).

8. Fairclough. *Media discourse*; Fairclough. *Critical discourse analysis.*

9. Jacoby, J. (2004, May 30). Vouchers and equal education. *Boston Globe* p. D11.

10. Jacoby (2004).

11. Jacoby (2004).

12. Berliner, D., & Biddle, B. (1995). *The manufactured crisis: Myths, fraud, and the attack on America's public schools.* Reading, MA: Addison-Wesley; Meier, D. (1995). *The power of their ideas: Lessons for America from a small school in Harlem.* Boston: Beacon Press.

13. van Dijk (2000).

14. Jacoby (2004).

15. Jacoby (2004).

16. See, e.g., Ayers, W., & Ford, P. (1996). *City kids, city teachers: A* view from the front row. New York: New Press; Bracey, G. (2003). *What you should know about the war against America's public schools.* Boston: Allyn and Bacon.

17. Jacoby (2004).

18. Jacoby (2004).

19. Berliner & Biddle. *The manufactured crisis*; Rothstein, R. (2004). *Class and schools: Using social, economic, and educational reform to close the black-white achievement gap.* Washington, DC: Economic Policy Institute.

20. Steinberg, J. (2001, January 26). Adding a financial threat to familiar promises on education. *New York Times.* p. A17.

21. Steinberg (2001, January 26).

22. See, e.g., Zinn, H. (1980). *A people's history of the United States.* New York: Harper and Row.

23. See, e.g., Ball. *Class strategies*; Dale, R. (1989). *The state and education policy.* Oxford, UK: Oxford University Press.

24. Wilgoren (2001, January 23).

25. Wilgoren (2001, January 23).

26. Wilgoren (2001, January 23).

27. Wilgoren (2001, January 23).

28. Wilgoren (2001, January 23).

29. Wilgoren (2001, January 23).

30. See, e.g., Ayers, W., Hunt, J., & Quinn, T. (1998). *Teaching for social justice: A democracy and education reader.* New York: Teachers College Press.

31. The Elementary and Secondary Education Act, renamed the No Child Left Behind Act, 20 U.S.C. §§101–9601 (2002).

32. See, e.g., Campbell, C. (1997). *Civil rights chronicle: Letters from the South.* Jackson, MS: University of Mississippi Press.

33. Civil Rights Act of 1964, 42 U.S.C. §2000a et seq. (1964).

34. Jacoby (2004).

35. Wilgoren (2001, January 23).

36. Wilgoren (2001, January 23).

37. Alvarez, L. (2001, June 13). Senate rejects tuition aid, a key to Bush education plan. *New York Times.* p. A26.

38. Alvarez (2001, June 13).

39. Fiske, E., & Ladd, H. (2000, August 6). A cautionary tale from New Zealand. *New York Times: Education Life Supplement.* p. 34.

40. Fiske & Ladd (2000, August 6), p. 34.

41. Fiske & Ladd (2000, August 6), p. 34.

42. Savas, E. (2000). *Privatization and public-private partnerships.* New York: Chatham House.

43. Council on Foreign Relations. Iraq: military outsourcing. http://www.cfr.org/background/background_iraq_outsourcing.php; Singer, P. (2003). *Corporate warriors: The rise of the privatized military industry.* Ithaca, NY: Cornell University Press.

44. Bracey (2003).

45. Molnar, A. (1996). *Giving kids the business: The commercialization of America's schools.* New York: Westview Press; Saltman, K. (2000). *Col-*

lateral damage: Corporatizing public schools—A threat to democracy. Lanham, MD. Rowman and Littlefield.

46. GlaxoSmithKline. Dedicated to science education. http://www.gsk.com/education/11_19 years.htm.

47. National Commission on Excellence in Education. (1983). *A nation at risk.* Washington, DC: Government Printing Office. http://www.ed.gov/pubs/NatAtRisk/risk.html.

48. National Commission on Excellence in Education. *A nation at risk,* p. 1.

49. National Commission on Excellence in Education. *A nation at risk,* pp. 3–4.

50. Anderson, G. (2001). Disciplining leaders: A critical discourse analysis of the ISLLC National Examination and Performance Standards in Educational Administration. *Int. J. Leadership in Education* 4 No. 3: pp. 199–216; Mulderrig, J. (2003). Consuming education: A critical discourse analysis of social actors in new Labour's education policy. *Journal for Critical Education Policy Studies* 1 No. 1. www.jceps.com/?pageID=article&articleID=2.

51. National Commission on Excellence in Education. *A nation at risk,* p. 11.

52. Berliner & Biddle (1995).

53. Hill, P. (2003, September 21). Aha! School choice can work in DC; Vouchers can't cure a crippled system, but they're a start. *Washington Post.* p. B1.

54. Hill (2003, September 21), p. B5.

55. Hill (2003, September 21), p. B5.

Research and Urban Education

UTILIZING *CARIÑO* IN THE DEVELOPMENT OF RESEARCH METHODOLOGIES

Jeffrey M. R. Duncan-Andrade

My mother ends her e-mails with the words *con cariño*. Cariño is often translated as *caring*, *affection*, or *love*, but much is lost in this translation. Cariño is more a concept than a word. It is the foundation of relationships among the poor and working classes—often the only thing left to give, in families raising children on substandard wages. Angela Valenzuela describes cariño in the context of schooling as *authentic caring*, a concept distinctly different from what she calls *aesthetic caring*. She explains that schools serving poor and working-class Latino/-a children often fail to develop reciprocal relationships whereby children are authentically cared for and, in turn, open themselves up to care about school. Drawing from the literature on caring in schools,[1] Valenzuela argues that "schools are structured around an *aesthetic* caring whose essence lies in 'an attention to things and ideas.'"[2] This leads to a culture of false caring, one where the most powerful members of the relationship define themselves as caring despite the fact that the recipients of their so-called caring do not perceive it as such. Ultimately, aesthetic caring results in pragmatic relationships between school officials and students, straining the teaching and learning process.

Not far removed from the practice of aesthetic caring is the technocratic jargon of educational discourse that encourages an "impersonal and objective language, including such terms as goals, strategies, and standardized curricula, that is used in decisions made by one group for another."[3] This discourse is largely shaped by education research agendas that view authentic caring as an afterthought. At their worst, these agendas promote scientific objectivity that frowns upon overt discussions of caring in an effort to mirror more traditional forms of research.

This chapter analyzes recent federal legislation that promotes traditional scientific research models in education. Emerging from this analysis is a call for educational researchers to blaze a new path in social science research—one that foregrounds the ethic of cariño while maintaining the rigor of established scientific research. Examples of education research agendas grounded in cariño are included to demonstrate the viability for future growth in this direction.

WHAT IS EDUCATIONAL RESEARCH?

The debate over what constitutes legitimate education research has been heavily influenced by the federal No Child Left Behind Act (NCLB). Shortly after NCLB was signed into law in January, 2002, the George W. Bush administration enacted the Education Sciences Reform Act of 2002. This act, in turn, established the Federal Institute of Education Sciences, which aims to transform education "into an evidence-based field in which decision makers routinely seek out the best available research and data before adopting programs or practices that will affect significant numbers of students"[4]

According to the Institute's guidebook on effective educational intervention, *Identifying and Implementing Educational Practices Supported by Rigorous Evidence: A User-Friendly Guide* (2003), practitioners can use research that is supported by "strong" or "possible" evidence of effectiveness to improve their schools.[5] A study can boast of strong evidence of effectiveness if its research is backed by quality (well-designed and implemented randomized controlled trials) and quantity (effectiveness in two or more similar school/classroom settings) evidence. If not supported by strong indicators of effectiveness, research backed by possible evidence of effectiveness may also be considered worthy of implementation. Possibly effective studies are defined as studies that show some promise using randomly controlled trials and/or using comparison-group studies with "very closely matched" focal groups. The Federal Institute of Education Sciences rubric asserts that educational researchers aiming to place their studies in either of these two categories should align their methodologies more closely with "the fields of medicine and welfare policy [which] show that practice guided by rigorous evidence can produce remarkable advances."[6] Inherent in this logic is the belief that research's "gold standard," based on random controlled trials, can elucidate what works in schools.[7]

At first glance, it is difficult to disagree with these ideas because educational research has long been considered pseudo-science and has produced little evidence to refute such critiques. Further, our tenuous position in the research community gives cause for looking long and hard at our methodologies and claims they produce. We should have consensus in the educational research community to use and expect rigorous evidence gathering and analysis as a precursor to our research based conclusions. We should also expect, as in medical and social welfare research communities, that our work produces meaningful and documented change in our spheres of influence.

On the surface, NCLB's direction for educational research seems logical and in the best interest of schools and the research community. Upon deeper examination, however, this direction for educational research steers us down a dangerous road, one that Emerson forewarns us to avoid:

There is a time in every man's education when he arrives at the conviction that envy is ignorance; that imitation is suicide; that he must take himself for better, for worse, as his portion; that though the wide universe is full of good, no kernel of nourishing corn can come to him but through his toil bestowed on that plot of ground which is given to him to till.[8]

The road that we, as educational researchers, must hoe is not the same as that of the other disciplines. The ground bestowed on us begs a different kind of nourishment than is required of other fields. Like the field of education itself, educational research should be grounded in authentically caring relationships, a culture of cariño.

A Brief Overview of Traditional Educational Research Paradigms

Burkhardt and Schoenfeld propose improving education research to make it more useful, more influential, and better-funded enterprise.[9] Their analysis of traditions in education research are worth exploring at length to paint a broad picture of the field. Burkhardt and Schoenfeld categorize education research paradigms under three main headings: humanities, science, and engineering.

Citing the Higher Education Research Funding Council for England and Wales, they describe the humanities process as:

[O]riginal investigation undertaken in order to gain knowledge and understanding; scholarship; the invention and generation of ideas . . . where these lead to new or substantially improved insights.[10]

Without empirical data to back these ideas and inventions, the humanities paradigm, despite being "the oldest tradition in education," rarely produces much more than "critical commentary."[11]

The science approach, although noted as having a hotly contested definition, is described as:

[F]ocused on the development of better insight; of improved knowledge and understanding of "how the world works" through the analysis of phenomena; and the building of models that explain them.[12]

Unlike the humanities design, the science approach uses empirical testing to investigate identifiable problems. This difference is cited as being imperative for the legitimization of the research findings. The shortcoming of this approach is that it does not produce practical solutions to the problems that it investigates.

For Burkhardt and Schoenfeld, the engineering approach is considered the best research method because it relies on empirical testing aimed at producing a practical impact. They again draw from the Higher Education Research Funding Council's definition:

[I]t [the engineering approach] can be described as "the use of existing knowledge in experimental development to produce new or substantially improved materials, devices, products, and processes, including design and construction."[13]

While reflecting the best practices of the humanities and science approaches (strong theoretical grounding and empirical testing), the engineering approach has the primary purpose of producing tools and processes that address the local problem. Although touted as the best of the three approaches, the engineering model does not produce solutions that can be easily implemented for large-scale change.[14]

TWO PROBLEMS WITH CONVENTIONAL EDUCATION RESEARCH

Burkhardt and Schoenfeld's summation of the main education research traditions is thorough and useful to the degree that it gives us a sense of where mainstream education research has been and where it is headed. They make important points: There is a need for more empirical studies that produce educational tools supported by documented and sustained change in schools; and educational research must produce more bang for the buck, and the way to do that is to produce research methodologies that link research and practice.[15]

Absent from this discussion and from many of the mainstream critiques on the state of educational research are two of the most significant problems facing educational research communities: (1) the continued effort to model educational research on other research-based fields, and (2) the absence of a prioritization of an ethic of authentic caring in educational research. Before discussing the first of these problems, it is important to revisit Emerson's sense that "imitation is suicide." Emerson explains that we cannot produce meaningful work except by hoeing the road we are given. For educational research this is not the road of medicine, social work, physics, or any of the other so-called respected research fields. The protocols of educational research laid out by the Bush administration's Department of Education (DOE) miss the mark with their suggestions that education should follow the lead of social welfare and medicine in their efforts to produce meaningful research. The consistent failure of educational research to produce meaningful local or national change, particularly in the urban communities of color that are most often studied and least served, is not for a lack of methodological rigor. The Department of Education's insistence on closer adherence to the protocols and products of science-based research (empirical testing, scaleable product development) is tantamount to professional suicide. This is not to say that educational research should altogether abandon the use of scientific methods. Instead, it is a critique of the field's identity crisis, one that cannot be solved by attempting to replicate the efforts of other research fields. We should continue to develop and demand rigorous research methodologies in our field, but not with an eye toward "lab-to-engineering-to-marketing linkages" typical of "the drug companies, Bell Labs, Xerox PARC and IBM."[16] Our field should not seek to legitimate itself through more efficient contribution to a market driven enterprise. Education research should not attempt to generate scaleable products for sale at market. We are a field that is charged with caring for and educating young people. We have never found a way to reconcile this purpose with our sense of research agendas and methodologies of inquiry. The resulting effect has been a professional identity crisis, one that has the field of education occupying the margins of academia and the research community, beholden to funding sources shallow enough to ensure that education research agendas remain complicit with a field that is defined for us rather than by us. The time has come for the educational research community to come of age; to heed Emerson's advice that for better, for worse, we can only be fulfilled when we foreground our portion on that which makes our field unique, an ethic of authentic caring.

In order to ground our work in an ethic of caring, we must ask ourselves two key questions: (1) What does authentic caring look like in educational research; and (2) What is the difference between authentic caring and aesthetic caring in a research agenda?

BREAKING THE MOLD: PUTTING CARIÑO FIRST IN EDUCATION RESEARCH AGENDAS

Authentic Caring in Educational Research

Education is a unique enterprise, one that is a far cry from controlled laboratories or county general hospitals. Educators interact with their students almost every day for nine months each year. The frequency of interactions between teachers and students significantly differentiates education interventions from the other enterprises that conventional thinking suggests are worth modeling ourselves after. The traditional educational discourse and research methodology, which focuses on things and ideas rather than people and material conditions, has largely resulted in an educational research paradigm that seeks to find the "one best system."[17] For poor and working-class children in particular, this effort to create cookie-cutter reform models has meant decades of educational stagnation and their resultant socioeconomic marginalization.

Some researchers are rethinking educational research by emphasizing reciprocal relationships with schools, leading to deeper commitments for researchers to the school's and community's welfare. These educational researchers understand that each school's unique set of stakeholders and material conditions requires a research methodology that recognizes these differences. Rather than aiming to develop a model that can be laid on top of any school, this educational research approach focuses on forming relationships that pay attention to the special needs of a particular school. This focus on relationships translates into a greater emphasis on producing real change in the schools where the research is taking place.

INTERVENTION FOR EMANCIPATORY CHANGE

An approach to educational research that emphasizes cariño has also been called action research and described as an intervention for "emancipatory change":[18]

In stark contrast to "policy studies," whose aim is to provide "useful," expert knowledge for institutional planning, the core of critical action research involves its participatory and communally discursive structure and the cycle of action and reflection it initiates. The knowledge enabled through such reflexive and shared study leads not to bureaucratic directives, but, more important, to the possibility for emancipatory change.[19]

The value of this type of critical research is its focus on empowering individuals as agents of meaningful, sustainable change. The direct aim of this type of research agenda is to positively impact the material conditions of those involved with the study; it is an approach to research that gives more than it receives. By focusing more directly on improving the immediate circumstances, it de-emphasizes the traditional method of searching for empirical truths that can be implemented on a large scale. Instead, it seeks to democratize the tools of research and knowledge creation.[20] This way, when researchers leave, they leave behind a sense of hope and promise, one that is directly tied to the individual actors' sense of themselves as capable change agents. Beyond a heightened awareness of the capacity to change, this kind of research also leaves behind a set of tools that can be used and reused to continually improve the conditions most in need of attention. This is unique, because traditional research methods leave these tools in the hands of the researchers; so when the researcher leaves, so do the tools to research and, to a large extent, so does the sense of agency.

Research agendas that are committed to collaboration with participants as colleagues rather than subjects can result in richer studies. This approach reduces dependency based colonial models of knowledge production that have historically reproduced the status quo. By inserting multiple voices into the conversation, the process of identifying problems and researching solutions becomes more democratic. As well, this research program provides a grounded, structured form for individual and structural reflexivity that can serve as a mechanism for ongoing feedback and adaptation as new and different issues arise that need the attention of research. Perhaps most important, it recognizes the complexity of each individual set of conditions and encourages a sensibility of local agency and control for developing solutions for local problems. This is not to say that sites cannot learn from the research of others; this is not a subtractive model or a zero sum game. Instead, this is an additive model of educational research, which suggests that sweeping policy amendments will not be sufficient to bring about the local attention to change that is necessary in institutions like schools. What is necessary is a combination of progressive policy and more attention to localized research that allows for broad policies to be locally efficacious and relevant.

CARING RESEARCH METHODS IN PRACTICE

The Diversity Project

A growing group of researchers are employing the strategies of an action-oriented research methodology. One such example is the work in the San Francisco Bay Area of the Berkeley High School-based Diversity Project. Between 1996 and 2000, under the direction of former UC-Berkeley Professor Pedro Noguera, the project was a collaborative effort that included more than thirty teachers, students, parents, school board members, and university researchers.[21] As Noguera describes it:

We purposefully created a team including the various constituencies that make up the school because we wanted to ensure that our work would not contribute to further polarization. Our plan was to use findings generated from our research to guide and influence changes at the school.[22]

The project was initiated by a parent at Berkeley High School (BHS) with the aim of addressing persistent issues of racial inequality and disparate achievement for black and Latino/-a students. The logic behind using research to address this issue resided in the belief that the inquiry process itself could shed new light on ways to approach an issue that had become normalized at the school. For Noguera, this sort of collaborative research held the potential to do more than "document patterns of racial disparity," it stood to "bring about a change in student outcomes" by changing "the way in which people thought about racial patterns at the school."[23]

Four years later, the Diversity Project has not solved the issues of educational inequality at BHS, and no scaleable policy panacea has emerged from the data analysis. What has changed at BHS is the way that the least powerful groups participate in the direction of the school. Spurred on by the project's research, black and Latino/-a parents have become increasingly more organized around issues of educational opportunity. One organization, Parents of Children of African Descent (PCAD), used the project's research that showed high rates of failure in ninth-grade math to create a new course that supported these students. Their program proved largely successful and has worked to disrupt these previously accepted patterns of failure.[24]

The greatest strength of this approach to educational research is its tendency to create long-lasting collaborations because of its emphasis on developing caring relationships. This extended relationship shows a commitment to people rather than ideas and implies a stick-to-itiveness that is necessary for addressing the more complex problems of a school; this is particularly important when working to deconstruct problems that have been left unchallenged for decades. The other outcome of these types of extended collaborative research relationships is the democratization of the process. The sharing of the leadership responsibilities and the process has allowed BHS to continue the work long after the researchers are gone.[25]

THE LAAMP PROJECT

Another example of action-oriented research is the Los Angeles Annenberg Metropolitan Project (LAAMP). As a collaboration between UCLA's Institute for Democracy, Education, and Access (IDEA), and a local school district, LAAMP brought together a group of researchers to address a set of issues similar to those being addressed by Berkeley's Diversity Project. In an effort to address persistent rates of academic marginalization for black and Latino/-a students at Pacific Beach High School and districtwide, a group of university researchers, district-level officials, school officials, teachers, parents, and students collaborated on a multi-year research and equity project.

LAAMP situated its research methodology inside a framework that aimed to produce meaningful change while engaging in research that documented the process of school reform. Beginning in 1995, this work set up a series of inquiry groups as a way to start dialogue around issues of equity and access in the district, which was faced with the challenge of disrupting a bimodal school system. In effect, this meant addressing the fact that white and Asian students were finding high levels of success in the same school where high numbers of black and Latino/-a students were failing. Despite being inside the same school wall, this set of bimodel outcomes had become normalized across the district. Ultimately, the inquiry groups brought together parents, students, administrators, and school staff to discuss this pressing problem through a set of shared readings, and then used those discussions to conceive of ways to disrupt the issues of inequality. These inquiry groups were guided by "critical friends"—researchers and faculty from IDEA who helped give the participants a language for confronting these issues in productive ways.[26] As one elementary school teacher described it:

Inquiry has allowed me to reflect on my teaching practices with a group of teachers with whom I typically would not have the opportunity to sit and talk. . . . Topics of discussion centered around our school's two "essential questions": (1) "What can I do to ensure that the inequitable pattern of student achievement no longer exists?" and (2) "What can I do to ensure that there is student and parent voice in my classroom?"[27]

At the high school, the decision was made to also include students in the inquiry groups, further emphasizing the commitment to democratic participation in the school improvement efforts sparked by the project. To allow for more extended conversations, the project also researched the use of inquiry retreats; these were off-campus retreats where inquiry participants were able to dialogue and problem solve for lengthy periods of time.

Feeling like the project needed to have a more immediate impact on student learning, a classroom-based component was added in year three of the project. Beginning in 1997, a group of the university researchers from LAAMP partnered with a social studies teacher at Pacific Beach High School and began the Futures Project. From 1997–2001, the Futures Project gave year-round academic and social support to a cohort of 30 black, Latino/-a and Southeast Asian students from their 9th- through 12th-grade years.

By all predictive measures (i.e., standardized tests, socioeconomic status, race, and course enrollment), Futures students had mediocre prospects for completing high school, qualifying for entry into a four-year college, and successfully engaging in curricula leading to a baccalaureate degree.[28]

By providing students with additional support from the university research team, including access to summer research apprenticeship seminars at UCLA, this group of students was empowered to research and "challenge unjust policies and practices" that limit access for black, Latino/-a and other nonwhite student groups.[29] Over the course of the four years, the success of these students became a powerful counter-narrative, stimulating important conversations about the possibilities for groups that had traditionally failed at Pacific Beach High School. By the end of the four years, 29 of the 30 Futures participants graduated from high school, and 25 of them gained acceptance to four-year universities.[30]

By 2002, both LAAMP and Futures were finished. The research that came out of these projects continues to influence state and national academic and policy circles. Equally as important, this research continued to impact the Pacific School District, most particularly Pacific Beach High School, long after the researchers left. The work that resulted from the employment of this caring research methodology created school and community cultures more attentive to issues of equity.

Like the work at Berkeley, participants are quick to say that plenty of work remains to be done in the district. However, they also point out that the research helped to develop mechanisms for public reporting and a language of social justice that has continued on in the work of progressive-minded students, teachers, and community based organizations.

INDIVIDUAL RESEARCHER AGENCY

To this point, I have described university-based research projects that have brought to bear a variety of resources on school sites. However, I would suggest that individual researchers can also positively impact schools by employing a research methodology that privileges cariño. My own work in an Oakland, California, high school is an example of the impact that one researcher can have with a research agenda focused on addressing a school problem while they are researching it.

From 1997–2001, I directed and researched the efficacy of a sports-based academic and social support program called the Lady Wildcat Basketball Program (LWBP). As a way of investigating the role of youth culture in the academic and social development of urban youth, I designed and implemented a year-round basketball program that provided its thirty participants with continual academic and social support. The research model focused on working collaboratively with the high school participants, parents, teachers, university undergraduate tutors, community members, and community organizations to develop a college going culture to counter the rampant academic failure in Oakland schools.

Using traditional qualitative research tools, the research documented the progress of the program through attention to four focal students; three of the focal students started the program as ninth-graders in summer of 1997, and the other began as a ninth-grader in 1998. With the research as the backdrop, the LWBP became the most successful in the city, producing: back-to-back-to-back league championships, a top-ten state ranking and a 100 percent graduation and college admissions rate for its four-year participants.[31]

The overwhelming success of the program led to the creation of a set of expectations programwide. Parent and student participants came to expect that the young people would receive year-round social and academic support that would facilitate their matriculation to a college or university. A powerful counter-narrative to the school's grade point average of 1.6 for black students, college attendance became matter-of-fact for LWBP participants and its 75 percent black participants. For the students, the program became a site of intervention in their academic and personal lives that rivaled the most supportive of family structures:

Sandra: For me, it's been like my family. If I have problems or anything I know who to go to. I never really worry anymore about getting stuck . . . you know about not being able to get through things because I know people here can help me and that they want to help me.

Lizette: This isn't really like a team to me. It's more like a family. We do everything together . . . eat, study, travel, play . . . everything . . . even cry. We've come so far in the last four years that no one can really understand us. People say all the time to us that they wish they had friends like we have in this program. They ask me how we do it. I tell them we work hard at it (laughing).[32]

Many parents felt much the same as their children about the impact of the program on participants' academic and social lives:

Monica: I've seen my daughter's sense of herself and responsibility to others grow. In this program she has been provided with a second family . . . a group at school that I like her to spend time with. A real good group of friends that guide her right.

Linda: She (Mika) has a place she feels she belongs. Academically she has never done better. She has friendships and seems to feel comfortable with herself. She seems more accessible than many teens—less rebellious and angry. The attention to team building has developed this.[33]

The impact of the LWBP ultimately began to reverberate throughout the athletic department at the school. With the continuous combination of academic and athletic success, the athletic director and assistant principal began asking the other athletic programs to implement similar academic support programs for their participants. The boys' basketball program in particular invested heavily in the academic support model of the LWBP and found increasing academic stability and growth for its participants.

In addition to a shift in the institutional culture of athletic participation, the program acted as a conduit for several of the university undergraduate tutors to enter coaching and teaching in urban schools. Several student participants also began pursuing university degrees and activities that will allow them to return to urban communities as teachers and community organizers.

The LWBP did not produce schoolwide change, and for some its success was at the price of a unilateral focus on the program rather than on a more rounded high school experience. Other critics lamented that the program bred a closed-door community, inaccessible to those who lacked athletic potential or desire. There is much to be learned from these critiques; however, the successes of the program stand, nonetheless, as testament to the potential of action-based educational research to create caring projects that have immediate and lasting positive impacts on those involved in the research. Although it is helpful to have the resources of a project the size of the Diversity or Futures Projects, the LWBP shows that individual researchers can also implement effective educational action research.

Implications for
Educational Research Agenda

Valenzuela's articulation of the concept of cariño, or caring,[34] as a central tenant of good teaching seems to have shot wide of many education researchers working in poor and nonwhite urban schools. Too often, these research agendas take no responsibility for improving the quality of services at research sites and have even less commitment to improving the lives of the subjects that reside there. The challenge to the educational research community is to rethink the merits of business as usual research agendas, now disguised under more progressive and convoluted titles such as No Child Left Behind. This calls for educational researchers to develop lines of questioning and data collection methods that foreground a sense of cariño rather than striving to simplify data acquisition.

NOTES

1. Gilligan, C. (1982). *In a different voice*. Cambridge, MA: Harvard University Press; Noddings, N. (1992). *The challenge to care in schools: An alternative approach to education*. New York: Teachers College Press; Prillaman, R., & Eaker, D. (1994). *The tapestry of caring: Education as nurturance*. Norwood, NJ: Ablex.

2. Valenzuela, A. (1999). *Subtractive schooling: U.S.-Mexican youth and the politics of caring* (p. 22). New York: SUNY Press.

3. Valenzuela (1999), p. 22.

4. U.S. Department of Education. (2005). About the *Institute of Education Sciences*. *Retrieved November 23, 2005, from Federal Department of Education Web site*: http://www.ed.gov/about/offices/list/ies/index.html.

5. Coalition for Evidence-Based Policy. (2002). *Identifying and implementing educational practices supported by rigorous evidence* (pp. 1–28). Washington, DC: U.S. Department of Education.

6. Coalition for Evidence-Based Policy (2002), p. iv.

7. Coalition for Evidence-Based Policy (2002), p. iii.

8. Emerson, R. (1841). *Self-Reliance*. Retrieved July 20, 2005 from http://www.emersoncentral.com/selfreliance.htm.

9. Burkhardt, H., & Schoenfeld, A. (2003). Improving education research: Toward a more useful, more influential, and better-funded enterprise. *Educational Researcher, 32* (9), 3–14.

10. Burkhardt & Schoenfeld (2003), p. 5.

11. Burkhardt & Schoenfeld (2003), p. 5.

12. Burkhardt & Schoenfeld (2003), p. 5.

13. Burkhardt & Schoenfeld (2003), p. 5.

14. Burkhardt & Schoenfeld (2003).

15. Burkhardt & Schoenfeld (2003).

16. Burkhardt & Schoenfeld (2003), p. 5.

17. Tyack, D. (1974). *The one best system: A history of American urban education*. Cambridge, MA: Harvard University Press.

18. Kincheloe, J., & McLaren, P. (1998). Rethinking critical qualitative research. In N. Denzin & Y. Lincoln (Eds.), *Handbook of research on qualitative research* (pp. 260–299).Thousand Oaks, CA: Sage.

19. McLaren, P., & Giarelli, J. (1995). Introduction: Critical theory and educational research. (1995). In

P. McLaren & J. Giarelli (Eds.), *Critical Theory and Educational Research*. New York: SUNY Press.

20. Nader, L.(1999). *Up the anthropologist— Perspectives gained from studying up*. In D. Hymes (Ed.), *Reinventing anthropology* Ann Arbor: University of Michigan Press.

21. Noguera, P. (2004). *City schools and the American dream*. New York: Teachers College Press.

22. Noguera (2004), p. 67.

23. Noguera (2004), p. 67.

24. Noguera (2004), p. 80.

25. Noguera (2004).

26. Oakes, J., & Lipton, M. (2003). *Teaching to change the world*. 2nd edition. Boston: McGraw Hill.

27. Oakes & Lipton (2003), p. 385.

28. Collatos, A., et al. (2004). Critical sociology in K–16 early intervention: Remaking Latino pathways to higher education. *Journal of Hispanic Higher Education*, 3 (2), p. 165.

29. Collatos et al. (2004).

30. Collatos et al. (2004).

31. Duncan-Andrade, J. (under contract). *What urban schools can learn from a successful sports program: Ballin', best friends, and breakin' cycles*. New York: Peter Lang.

32. Duncan-Andrade (under contract).

33. Duncan-Andrade (under contract).

34. Valenzuela (1999).

TANGLING THE KNOT WHILE LOOSENING THE STRINGS: EXAMINING THE LIMITS AND POSSIBILITIES OF URBAN EDUCATION FOR AFRICAN-AMERICAN MALES

Anthony L. Brown and Keffrelyn D. Brown

Since the early twentieth century, educators have focused on the challenges associated with schooling in large, metropolitan settings. Whether this discussion targeted "city" or "urban" schools, such work sought to untangle the difficulties associated with providing effective schooling for all students. Both historically and in the contemporary context, one method used to accomplish this task is to identify and target specific students most likely to experience problems within the urban school environment. Although numerous categories have emerged over the last century to define and name these students (e.g., problem student, incorrigible, backward, culturally deprived, at-risk), this process relies upon a standard of normality in which certain children and adolescents (as well as families and communities) become positioned as normal, while others are seen as at worst, deviant or as at best, different from this imagined norm. Though

these efforts are intended to correct or change the social conditions related to urban schooling, they often lead to the creation of normalizing discourses that both create and constrain the possibilities of thought and action by ascribing fixed, essentialized meanings about particular students.

The purpose of this chapter is to examine how normalizing discourses operate within and limit the possibilities of urban education research and practice, particularly in relation to African-American male students who since the 1980s have been positioned as both a problem and as at-risk. Drawing from the insights of Michel Foucault's analytics of power, the first part of this chapter outlines a conceptual framework for understanding the idea of normalizing discourse. The second part of the chapter examines how urban education research normalizes the African-American male student as both a problem and as at-risk. The chapter concludes by considering the implications of normalizing discourse on future urban education research and practice.

POWER AND DISCOURSES OF NORMALITY

In *The History of Sexuality: An Introduction*, Michel Foucault advances a conception of power that acknowledges its integral relationship with discourse, or the rules and ways of thinking and speaking. Here, discourse serves as a tool whereby societal knowledge, coupled with power relations, emerge and make possible the creation of subject positions (individual/group identity) as well as the concomitant ways of thinking and acting associated with those created subjects. Normalization, or the process in which people, things, behaviors, and ways of thinking and being become positioned as fixed and knowable is one manifestation of Foucault's analytics of power.[1]

The form of power discussed by Foucault is not located in a central or sovereign location, rather it manifests in multiple relations deployed in complex, often strategic societal networks that guide the possibilities of conduct and outcome.[2] Power has a productive quality in that it allows for "active, material practice in constructing the world."[3] One productive aspect of power is how it operates in the constitution of subjects, or the way in which people understand and become defined by others, as well as themselves. Foucault is concerned with how beings come to life—that is, how they become constituted as living, breathing entities with essentialized characteristics. This process is situated in a historical understanding of how a person becomes first categorized as an individual, marked by and attached to his or her own individuality, who then later embodies a self that is imposed by a law of truth that he or she is bound to recognize and acknowledge.[4]

That both the subject and others recognize and understand the subject through specific societal markers is a fundamental aspect of productive power relations that make normalizing discourses possible.

Within education research, discourses of normalization generally refer to how particular individuals or groups of students become positioned and understood by themselves and others, with a particular focus on marking those values and beliefs that differentiate between the normal and the abnormal.[5] While these works typically bound the research inquiry within the confines of schools and/or classrooms, the processes and knowledge that inform the construction of subjects circulates across sites outside of the conveniently bounded school or classroom space. Often in education research what constitutes normal becomes juxtaposed against what is considered abnormal or deviant. Within these educational settings it is assumed that understanding normalcy and deviance relies on relational thinking, as one cannot understand what is abnormal or deviant without first having a notion of what is normal.

In this chapter, the idea of normalizing discourse moves in a somewhat different direction from the way it is typically discussed in education research. Rather than focusing on the relational way in which some people and things get positioned as normal or abnormal, this chapter considers how normalizing discourses constitute particular subject positions (e.g., good teacher; bad parent; African-American males),[6] as well as how these positions become recognized as fixed, knowable, and fully understandable. These entities become fixed, or essentialized in relation to how they are discussed, recognized, and understood by others, often through: (1) populational reasoning that uses statistics to divide, classify, and understand the characteristics of groups,[7] and (2) the use of narratives, or what Homi Bhabha refers to as the "same old stories" told about these entities.[8] Normalizing discourses generally operate as unquestioned knowledge within a society and are presented in ways that assume common understanding over time and across wide groups of people.[9] In urban education research and practice, African-American males are often situated within normalizing discourses.

POWER, DISCOURSE, AND THE AFRICAN-AMERICAN MALE SUBJECT

Since the 1960s, urban education research has examined the challenges faced by African-American students. The 1980s ushered in a somewhat new concern: understanding and meeting the unique educational needs of African-American male students. For example, since this time there have been numerous books,[10] Congressional hearings,[11] and peer-reviewed articles focused on the African-American male student.[12] In addition, academic journals have devoted special volumes to the examination of black male students. In autumn, 1994, *The Journal of Negro Education* published a special volume, titled "Pedagogical and Contextual Issues Affecting African American Males in School and Society." In 2003, the *Urban Education* journal devoted two special volumes (July and September) on the challenges facing African-American male students.

How, then, does one go about examining the issues facing the black male in educational contexts? How is the African-American male subject constructed and understood across educational discourse? From what knowledge base does this work draw? Both sociological and educational research about African-American males has helped to construct a normalizing discourse about African-American male students. Throughout the early and mid-twentieth century, social science research explored three central themes that inform education discourses on the black male including their: (1) presumed lack of fathers and proper male role models,[13] (2)

(maladaptive) cultural adaptations in response to the larger social context,[14] and (3) material conditions in relation to other groups within the U.S. society (e.g., poverty, education).[15] Whereas this research suggested who the African-American male was and how he behaved,[16] it also made it possible to construct particular interventions fashioned specifically for this student, by explaining the condition or crisis he faced.

The following sections investigate how urban education research uses normalizing discourses by situating the black male student as an essentialized, fully knowable subject and then draws from this knowledge when developing unique interventions to meet his academic needs. This dual relationship does not have to occur in the context of any one piece of research to be considered a normalizing discourse and consequently is not presented in this paper in such a manner. In the discussion that follows, the authors present examples of the discourses deployed in urban education research that help to create the black male subject and later, how these same discourses get picked up by others when promoting specific educational interventions for these individuals. The first section explores how the African-American male subject is constituted through urban education research. The second section examines how these discourses get deployed in educational interventions for black male students.

CREATING THE AFRICAN-AMERICAN MALE SUBJECT

This process of creating the black male subject is often accomplished through the use of three types of rationales. On the basis of African-American males' presumed social status, identity construction, linguistic discourses, and styles of learning, these rationales are later used to justify the use of unique/alternative programs and curriculum and pedagogical strategies for these students. These rationales are. (1) statistical rationales, (2) behavioral rationales, and (3) cultural rationales.

When discussing the African-American male in research, authors typically use statistical evidence to illustrate the dire social conditions facing black males in the United States. This literature points to increased rates of homicide, homelessness, poor health (e.g., HIV/AIDS, drug addiction), incarceration and unemployment among African-American men.[17] In the specific case of urban education research, this strategy is employed to show the adverse circumstances faced by the African-American males in school, pointing to statistics that suggest black male students have high suspension, expulsion, and drop-out rates,[18] as well as disproportionately high placement in special education classes,[19] as well as high levels of illiteracy and academic underachievement.[20] This statistical strategy, although not unique to research on African-American males, is usually found in the opening sections of published work on this subject as a way to set up the relevance of the topic of study.[21]

Urban education research also draws on psychological rationales to explain the unique compensatory adaptations made by African-American males. Several scholars assert that African-American males have developed behavioral patterns to compensate for their psychological deficits, including, self-doubt, alienation, low self-esteem and distorted self-image.[22] Some researchers identify the following behaviors as characteristic of the urban African-American distorted male image: the "make one" image (i.e., fathering a child), "player of women" image (i.e., womanizing), and "take one" image (i.e., being tough or machismo).[23] James Patton argues that these behaviors are indicative of contemporary "nonfunctional" definitions of socialization and manhood.[24] Richard Majors and Jane Billson define these behaviors as *compulsive masculinity,* or typical black male masculine values that are reflected through "rigid prescrip-

tions for toughness, sexual promiscuity, manipulation, thrill-seeking, and a willingness to use violence to resolve interpersonal conflict."[25] Consequently, researchers claim that the African-American male establishes an African-American male behavioral and cultural norm that is antithetical and oppositional to mainstream models of behavior and interaction.[26] When this discourse is situated within a school context, researchers claim that African-American males form an *oppositional identity* or *cultural aversion* to learning that results in persistent levels of intellectual disengagement and academic underachievement. For example, Pedro Noguera highlights the need for policy interventions that address the problematic educational experiences of African-American males:

Institutionally, this may require programmatic interventions aimed at buffering and offsetting the various risks to which black males are particularly vulnerable. However, to be effective such initiatives must also involve efforts to counter and transform cultural patterns and what Ogbu (1987) has called the "oppositional identities" adopted by black males that undermine the importance they attach to education.[27]

Here, Noguera illustrates one common premise of education interventions for black males—the belief that such undertakings must specifically combat and reverse the problematic, self-imposed behaviors of these children and youth.

Cultural rationales focus on the cultural and linguistic differences of African-American males, suggesting that teachers implement pedagogical practices that build off these differences. What separates a cultural rationale from a psychological rationale is the specific attention given to speech, language, and discourse to explain the distinctiveness of African-American male students. Much of this work is premised on previous scholarship that suggests the African-American community has acquired unique and distinct discourse practices.

Several scholars have argued that schools need to understand the acculturated experiences of African-American children and implement strategies conducive to their unique linguistic discourse.[28] For example Peter Murrell points out that:

Discourse practices and the communicative features within the African American community, particularly the powerful oral traditions, can serve an important role in the educative process.[29]

This perspective suggests that through the use of African-American discourse practices teachers can promote conceptual learning in literacy. Since the 1960s, researchers have examined the verbal games and exchanges that occur between African-American males such as "jonin'" and "playing the dozens."[30] "Jonin'" and "playing the dozens" are rapid-fire, playful verbal contests between African-American males in which the goal is to develop clever metaphors that signify elements of truth, myth, and hyperbole. While stating that he does not condone the negative aspects these communication styles often employ, Jawanza Kunjufu adds, "[I]f we want to save black boys, we must transfer their cultural strengths into the classroom experience."[31] Accomplishing this, however, is not an easy task.

It is not uncommon for urban education research to show how culturally specific forms of communication between African-American male students is both unrecognized and underutilized in the traditional school setting. For example, when discussing African-American students generally and black males in particular, Peter Murrell points out that "teacher preparation programs lack access to pedagogical expertise drawn from the culture, language, and history of African Americans."[32] Murrell suggests that this lack of specific cultural knowledge about the black male places this student at a severe learning disadvantage. In addition, when drawing from his research with preadolescent African-American males, Jabari Mahiri suggests the

need for "approaches that schools can take to better reflect and accommodate the unique ways that literate behaviors and literacy skills are developed and practiced in a communicative style that is culturally based," because "the language uses . . . observed among the boys [African-American males in the study] are strikingly different from the passive transmission model of learning that is commonly employed in mainstream school literacy efforts."[33] The research from Murrell and Mahari imply that in order to close any potential cultural gap or incongruence between African-American male students and school knowledge, teachers need to scaffold instruction in relation to the *specific* ways that black American males communicate.[34]

In relation to the above statistical, psychological, and cultural rationales, who then is the African-American male? How do these discourses constitute his subjectivity? While statistical rationales drawn from census data render the black male as at-risk and endangered, these discourses also situate him as a problem that requires urgent and immediate intervention. Psychological rationales suggest that because of his social reality, the black male possesses a distorted and abnormal sense of self. Finally, cultural rationales position the African-American male as verbally gifted, poetic, and metaphorically clever. These gifts emerge in relation to the everyday realities and experiences faced by black males, as well as the cultural legacy of the larger African-American community.

EDUCATION INTERVENTIONS FOR THE AFRICAN-AMERICAN MALE

Recognizing the material challenges facing African-American males as a result of centuries of discrimination, political violence, and oppression, as well as the perennial struggle for equitable education opportunities in the United States, researchers during the 1980s began to develop education interventions specifically for these students. That these interventions relied upon existing perspectives on what constituted the African-American male is evident in the solutions they offered. As a result of the statistical, psychological, and cultural rationales advanced in urban education research on black males, the education community is given a normalizing frame to see, talk about, and—ultimately—act on this subject. The next section examines some of the popular interventions proposed for African-American male students.

Education interventions proposed for African-American males have been situated both within and outside of the school context, and many of the statistical, psychological, and cultural rationales outlined previously justify the kinds of interventions offered. When discussing general education interventions proposed for African-American males, Noguera points out:

[T]he common theme underlying each of these initiatives is an assumption that the needs of black males can best be served through efforts specifically targeted at them, even if those efforts require isolating black males in order to apply the intervention.[35]

One intervention for African-American males that has received considerable attention is the creation of rites of passage and mentor programs.

The goal of rites of passage and mentor programs is to provide guidance for black males as they transition into manhood. Rites of passage programs utilize similar Afro-centric principles and pedagogies to develop the appropriate behaviors of African-American males. These programs are designed to combat the unhealthy behaviors of African-American males— such as drug abuse, violence, and gang activity.[36] These programs also assume that when students are provided pedagogies that speak to their concerns, their self-confidence and pride increases, thus leading to heightened levels of academic success.[37] Mentoring programs, on the other hand, often vary across settings. For example, the 100 Black Men mentor program expands the traditional one-on-one mentoring by utilizing groups to facilitate their mentees' goals.[38] Other mentor programs, such as Project 2000, arose out of the belief that black boys needed more extensive opportunities to work directly with black male adults in school settings. About these programs, Spencer Holland states, "[T]he primary objective of the program is to provide positive adult male role models, particularly African-American men, in the daily life of African-American boys."[39]

In terms of classroom strategies, one of the earliest attempts in the mid-1980s to address the expressive discourse or learning style of African-American males came from the observations of Jawanza Kunjufu. From these observations, Kunjufu found that African-American males possess a unique style of expression when playing the dozens that could be transferred to the classroom. He asserts that through these activities, black males possess the following linguistic strengths: (1) quick thinking skills, (2) rhythmic understanding, (3) expansive vocabulary, and (4) public speaking potential. Kunjufu also emphasizes the need for teachers to understand the various expressive patterns of African-American boys, but further suggests that educators need to channel these strengths into more positive academic activities, such as spelling bees, spelling through rhyming and debates.[40] Likewise, Janice Hale-Benson argues that black males possess unique learning styles that should be accounted for when trying to improve academic achievement. She argues that teachers and schools must acknowledge that black males and black children have unique cultural orientations that are generally people-oriented, feeling-oriented, and non-verbal.[41]

Murrell also focuses on the unique discourses of African-American males. He argues that teachers who acquire more knowledge of African-American male cultural expression can more effectively address these students' educational concerns. Murrell asserts that *responsive teaching* identifies the specific speech activities that promote the development of African-American males, as well as assist in their academic achievement. According to Murrell, these speech activities "frame the discourse" within which African-American males routinely operate. These include: (1) a question-posing, teacher-challenging approach; (2) a preference for request-for-information teacher inquiries; (3) an eagerness to show off the information they possess; (4) a penchant for extended application; and (5) a preference for "getting over" rather than admitting ignorance.[42]

Relating discourse with athletics, Mahiri found that the linguistic discourse of African-American males could also be identified in sports activities such as basketball. Mahiri argues that when African-American males play basketball, they convey a set of complex literacy discourses that requires them to manipulate discrete elements of text. He calls these ways of communicating as the *discourse of basketball*, which refers to specific language terms, cognitive images, and interactional modes of speech associated with the game of basketball. For Mahiri the discourse of basketball takes place on and off the basketball court and involves topics, discussions, literacy, and analysis of several elements of the game, such as actual play, college and professional statistics, and the detailed and analytical literacy used to understand basketball video games. Mahiri goes on to suggest that because basketball has high motivational value for black boys, incorporating the discourse of basketball into classroom pedagogy will motivate these students to engage in literacy learning and improve their overall academic achievement.[43]

Another common intervention for black males is the development of African-American male immersion schools.[44] The development of all-male academies is premised on three core beliefs about the black male: (1) they have no adequate role models, (2) they live in absent-father homes, and (3) they suffer from feelings of inadequacy and low self-esteem and consequently engage in compensatory masculine behaviors. To address these concerns, all-male academies ideally would hire black male teachers who would act as role models. In addition, these schools would provide alternative curricular programs that combat and challenge the maladaptive student behavior. Although in recent discussions, immersion schools have received less attention because of legal constraints, education researchers and practitioners have continued to discuss the need for gender-specific education for African-American males.[45]

As the previous section illustrates, intervention arguments for African-American males are generally guided by a fixed conceptual reasoning about the cultural and psychological contexts of these individuals' lives. While it is for certain that many African-American males share these contexts, across educational literature it is common to find interventions that position African-American males as a homogeneous group. To this extent, we suggest that rationales used to explain the social and educational lives of black boys, coupled with arguments made for intervening on them, unintentionally help to reproduce a normalizing discourse that fastens in place how one can conceptualize and act on behalf of African-American male students.

CONCLUSION

The previous discussion illustrates how normalizing discourses operate in urban education research focused on African-American male students. Normalizing discourses help construct a particular subject—in this case the African-American male—in a way that frames the possible ways of looking at, understanding, and ultimately intervening on his behalf. Returning to Foucault's analytics of power, normalizing discourse is a power relationship that relies on the circulation of multiple discourses and relationships (e.g., social science research, urban education research, social and material realities, and cultural-historical practices) that converge and make possible the creation of people, things, and ways of thinking and being. Concerning power, Foucault states:

[It] must be understood in the first instance as the multiplicity of force relations immanent in the sphere in which they operate and which constitute their own organization; as the process which, through ceaseless struggles and confrontations, transforms, strengthens, or reverses them; as the support which these force relations find in one another; and lastly, as the strategies in which they take effect, whose general design or institutional crystallization is embodied in the state apparatus, in the formulation of the law, in the various social hegemonies.[46]

Here, "[p]ower is everywhere; not because it embraces everything, but because it comes from everywhere."[47] This suggests that power relations are necessary and inevitable, as Foucault argues, "[a] society without power relations can only be an abstraction."[48]

Power relations become evident in the research and intervention process undertaken by social scientists and educators who, both in the past and present, attempt to address the adverse material conditions facing the African-American male. While it is clear that, given the sociopolitical circumstances facing this subject, such work seemed (and perhaps, continues to seem) necessary, this work relies on past historical and empirical discourses that tend to position the African-American male as essentially endangered and in crisis. And while for the most part, there has been a shift away from positioning the black male as innately deviant, culturally deprived, and responsible for his own condition, discourses about his subjectivity fashion him as fundamentally at-risk and culturally homogenous even when theorizing about him from a cultural difference perspective

(e.g., culturally distinct patterns of behavior) or through a structural analysis (e.g., addressing material realities created by institutional practices).

The concerns raised in this chapter are not novel. During the early twentieth century, black scholar Alain Locke challenged intellectual perspectives that essentialized what constituted African Americans, as well as how to best meet their educational needs. This prominent African-American thinker took a lead in questioning the then popular belief that race and culture were innately determined. Locke's insistence that "race operates as tradition, as preferred traits and values" indicates some agreement with the belief that social reality helps to shape African-American culture and behavior. However, Locke's concern that cultural explanations for behavior might lead to essentializing discourses that overly determine the constituted black subject is implied in his comments about these intellectual explanations.[49] Locke cautions in this regard, "[b]ut a school of thought or art or social theory that lays claim to totalitarian rectitude must, I think, be challenged."[50]

Challenging potential normalizing discourses is a necessary activity in any society concerned with the effects of power relations. Since power relations are inevitable in society but do not possess any predetermined, specific configuration, the impetus for interrogating existing relations of power through "analysis, elaboration, and bringing into question"[51] how these relationships operate becomes the task of its citizens. In the case of urban education research, this chapter has tried to question the role normalizing discourses play in creating a seemingly static, knowable African-American male subject who requires a particular kind of education intervention. What this work points to are the unintended consequences that emerge when trying to change and address the material, everyday realities facing black men and boys. Since the

1990s, urban education theorists have illuminated the potential unintended effects of normalizing discourse on African-American males in urban education research.[52] These authors suggest the need to move beyond perspectives that essentialize or offer generalized prescriptions for how to work with these individuals. Additionally, normalizing discourses also make it difficult to address the challenges facing black males who do not fall within the typical, or "same old stories"[53] told and understood about them as a collective group. James Earl Davis states:

Not all Black boys are the same. This simple point is not an obvious one given most of the discussions about the so-called Black boy problem in American schools. But where are the high-achieving African-American boys? It is apparent from the national conversation on troubled boyhood that the inclusion of high-achieving Black boys' experiences muddles the discussion . . . Racism, stereotypes, lower expectations, and pervasive peer and popular culture define the "other" boyhood crisis that many Black boys face daily.[54]

Additionally, Garrett Duncan suggests the need to listen more closely to the voices of African-American males to note the differences in their experiences and behaviors, even when these students appear to come from similar backgrounds.[55] Such an approach would help researchers, policy makers, and school personnel move away from simple, unquestioned perceptions of what it means to be black and male in U.S. schools and society.

Indeed, the proverbial tangled knot that researchers, policy makers, and educators attempt to untangle when addressing the material conditions and educational challenges faced by African-American males becomes more twisted and harder to unravel when normalizing discourses are taken into account. While this dilemma does not and should not debilitate the work of those concerned with the plight of African-American males, it does promise to make educational research and practice a more difficult, and clearly a less certain, task.

NOTES

1. Foucault, M. (1990). *The history of sexuality: An introduction*. New York: Vintage.

2. Foucault, M. (1983). Afterword: The subject of power. In H. Dreyfus & P. Rabinow (Eds.), *Michel Foucault: Beyond structuralism and hermeneutics* (2nd ed., pp. 208–226). Chicago: University of Chicago Press.

3. Popkewitz, T. (2000). Globalization/ regionalization, knowledge, and the educational practices: Some notes on comparative strategies for educational research. In T. Popkewitz (Ed.), *Educational knowledge: Changing relationships between the state, civil society, and the educational community* (p. 16). New York: State University of New York Press.

4. Foucault (1983).

5. Ferguson, A. (2001). *Bad boys: Public schools in the making of masculinity*. Ann Arbor: University of Michigan Press; Goldstein, R. (2004). Who are our urban students and what makes them so "different"? In S. Steinberg & J. Kincheloe (Eds.), *19 urban questions: Teaching in the city* (pp. 41–51). New York: Peter Lang; Marsh, M. (2003). *The social fashioning of teacher identities*. New York: Peter Lang; Perry, P. (2002). *Shades of white: White kids and racial identities in high school*. Durham, NC: Duke University Press; Popkewitz, T. (1998). *Struggling for the soul: The politics of schooling and the construction of the teacher*. New York: Teachers College Press.

6. Hacking, I. (2002). *Historical ontology*. Cambridge, MA: Harvard University Press; Marsh (2003); Popkewitz (1998).

7. Popkewitz (1998).

8. Bhabha, H. (1994). *The location of culture*. London: Routledge.

9. Perry (2002).

10. Brown, M., & Davis, J. (2000). *Black sons to mothers: Compliments, critiques, and challenges for cultural workers in education*. New York: Peter Lang; Gibbs, J. (1988). *Young, black and male in America: An endangered species*. New York: Auburn House; Polite, V., & Davis, J. (1999). *African-American males in school and society: Practices & policies for effective education*. New York: Teachers College Press.

11. United States Commission on Civil Rights. (1991, March 19). *The crisis of the young African*

American male in the inner cities: Congressional Report 1.2: AF 8/v. 1.v. 2. Washington, DC: Government Printing Office.

12. Garibaldi, A. (1992). Educating and motivating the African-American male to succeed. *Journal of Negro Education, 61* (1), 4–11; Leake, D., & Leake, B. (1992). Islands of hope: Milwaukee's African American immersion schools. *Journal of Negro Education, 61* (1), 24–29.

13. Frazier, E. (1940). The Negro family and Negro youth, *Journal of Negro Education, 9* (3), 290–299.

14. Clark, K. (1965). *Dark ghetto: Dilemmas of social power.* New York: Harper & Row.

15. Moynihan, P. (1967). The Negro family: The case for national action. In R. Rainwater & W. Yancey (Eds.), *The Moynihan report and the politics of controversy* (pp. 47–132). Cambridge, MA: M.I.T.

16. Kelley, R. (1994). *Yo' mama's dysfunctional! Fighting the culture wars in America.* Boston: Beacon.

17. Gibbs (1988); Lee, C. *Empowering black males.* Available from http://www.ericfacility.net.

18. Lee (1991); Majors, R. (2001). *Educating our black children: New approaches.* New York: Routledge; Murrell, P. (1994). In search of responsive teaching for African American males: An investigation of students' experiences of middle school mathematics curriculum. *Journal of Negro Education, 63* (4), 556–569.

19. Murrell, P. (1993). Afrocentric immersion: Academic and personal development of African American males in public schools. In T. Perry & J. Fraser (Eds.), *Freedom's plow: Teaching in the multicultural classroom* (pp. 231–259). New York: Routledge; Murrell, 1994.

20. Slaughter-Defoe, D., & Richards, H. (1995). Literacy for empowerment: The case of black males. In V. Gadsen & D. Wagner (Eds.), *Literacy among African American youth: Issues in learning, teaching, and schooling* (pp. 125–147). Cresskill, NJ: Hampton; Holland, S. (1996). Project 2000: An educational mentoring and academic support model for inner-city African American boys. *Journal of Negro Education, 65* (3), 315–321; Lee, (1991); Reed, R. (1988). Education and achievement of young black males. In J. Gibbs (Ed.), *Young black, and male in America: An endangered species* (pp. 37–93). Westport, CT: Greenwood.

21. Holland (1996); Mahiri, J. (1994a). African American males and learning: What dis-

courses in sports offer schooling. *Anthropology & Education Quarterly, 25* (3), 364–375; Murrell (1993).

22. Majors, R., & Billson, J. (1992). *Cool pose: The dilemmas of black manhood in America.* New York: Touchtone; Patton, J. (1995). The education of African American males: Frameworks for developing authenticity. *Journal of African American Men, 1* (1), 5–26; White, J., & Cone, J. (1999). *Black man emerging: Facing the past and seizing the future in America.* New York: Routledge.

23. Patton (1995); Oliver, W. (1989). Black males and social problems: Prevention through Afrocentric socialization. *Journal of Black Studies, 20* (1), 15–39.

24. Patton (1995).

25. Majors & Billson (1992), p. 34.

26. Majors & Billson (1992); Noguera, P. (2003). The trouble with black boys: The role and influence of environmental and cultural factors on the academic performance of African American males. *Urban Education, 38* (4), 431–459; Patton (1995).

27. Noguera (2003), p. 437.

28. Kunjufu, J. (1986). *Countering the conspiracy to destroy black boys* (Vol. 2). Chicago: African American Images; Mahiri, J. (1994b). Discourses in sports: Language and literacy features of preadolescent African American males in a youth basketball program. *Journal of Negro Education, 60* (3), 364–375.

29. Murrell (1993), p. 247.

30. Kochman, T. (1967). Rapping in the ghetto. In L. Rainwater (Ed.), *Soul* (pp. 51–76). New York: Aldine; Liebow, E. (1967). *Tally's corner: A study of Negro streetcorner men.* Boston: Little, Brown and Company.

31. Kunjufu (1986), p. 16.

32. Murrell (1994), p. 556.

33. Mahiri (1994a), p. 306.

34. Murrell (1994); Mahiri (1994a).

35. Noguera, P. (1996). Responding to the crisis confronting California's black male youth: Providing support without furthering marginalization. *Journal of Negro Education, 65* (2), 221.

36. Alford, K., McKenry, P., & Gavazzi, S. (2001). Enhancing achievement in adolescent black males: The rites of passage link. In R. Majors (Ed.), *Educating our black children: New directions and radical approaches* (pp. 141–156). New York: Falmer Routledge.

37. Fashola, O. (2003). Developing the talents of African American male students during non-

school hours. *Urban Education, 38* (4), 390–430; Watts, R., & Jagers, R. (Eds.). (1997). *Manhood development in urban American communities.* New York: Hayworth; Warfield-Coppock, N. (1992). The rites of passage movement: A resurgence of African-centered practices for socializing African American youth. *Journal of Negro Education, 61* (4), 471–482.

38. Dortch, T. (2000). *The miracles of mentoring: How to encourage and lead future generations.* New York: Doubleday/Broadway Books.

39. Holland (2000), p. 317.

40. Kunjufu (1986).

41. Hale-Benson, J. (1986). *Black children: Their roots, culture, and learning styles* (2nd ed.). Baltimore, MD: John Hopkins.

42. Murrell (1994).

43. Mahiri (1994b).

44. Leake & Leake (1992).

45. Cooper, R., & Jordan, W. (2003). Cultural issues in comprehensive school reform. *Urban Education, 38* (4), 380–397.

46. Foucault (1990), pp. 92–93.

47. Foucault (1990), p. 93.

48. Foucault (1983), pp. 222–223.

49. Locke, A. (1968). *The new negro.* New York: Athneum.

50. Locke, A. (1989). Who and what is "Negro"? In L. Harris (Ed.), *The philosophy of Alain Locke: Harlem Renaissance and beyond* (p. 211). Philadelphia: Temple University.

51. Foucault (1983).

52. Davis, J. (2003). Early schooling and academic achievement of African American males. *Urban Education, 38* (5), 515–537; Duncan, G. (2002). Beyond love: A critical race ethnography of the schooling of adolescent males. *Equity & Excellence, 35* (2), 131–143; Gordon, E.T., Gordon, E.W., & Nembhard, J. Social science literature concerning African American men. *Journal of Negro Education, 63* (4), 508–531; Noguera (1996).

53. Bhabha (1994).

54. Davis (2003).

55. Duncan (2002).

MULTISITED ETHNOGRAPHIC APPROACHES IN URBAN EDUCATION TODAY

Greg Dimitriadis and Lois Weis

CULTURE AND EDUCATION

Studying out-of-school culture is nothing new. A long and venerable history of work in the "anthropology of education" contextualizes the practice of education in specific cultural sites and settings.[1] Formal schooling is seen as one tool of socialization, one way culture is transmitted from generation to generation. But, as Spindler and others point out, it is not the only such tool. Older and younger people engage in multiple practices of enculturation—for example, through storytelling or dinner table talk—that have critical educative implications. This work has been largely comparative. George and Louise Spindler, for example, studied several different Native American groups in the United States, highlighting the "cultural variations that mark education in every society in relationship to every other."[2] Much of this work has been concerned with uncovering cultural mismatches between home and school settings. The goal, here, is to help educators in "overcoming defenses by bringing unconscious motivations, assumptions, orientations to conscious awareness,"[3] ultimately helping to eliminate racial bias in education through radical contextualization and cultural sensitivity.

Such work relies, of course, on specific ideas or theories about culture itself—namely, that culture is a bounded object of study and can be understood as such; in other words, that it is discrete and can be contained. Yet, notions of cultural containment belie the contemporary reality of migration, mediation, and complex cultural transactions so much a part of the quotidian for many youth in the United States and beyond. Culture—as so much work in globalization has made clear—is interconnected, in transit, the result of various often unequally situated and disjunctive flows and trajectories.[4] As Eisenhart argues, these new tensions around culture have helped to muddle debates around ethnographic methodology.[5] If culture can no longer be contained in discrete sites and settings, the traditional tools of qualitative inquiry need re-thinking.

Multisited ethnography offers a key response to this muddling that Eisenhart highlights.[6] Doing multisited ethnography, according to George Marcus, means "tracing and describing the connections and relationships among sites previously thought incommensurate."[7] The multisited ethnographer must, in any project, "keep in view and mind two or more ethnographically conceived sites juxtaposed."[8] By way of direction, Marcus offers the diction: "follow the people," "follow the thing," "follow the metaphor," "follow the plot, story, or allegory," "follow the life or biography," and "follow the conflict."[9] All imply different starting points for tracing connections across and between different sites—individual biographies, objects, and/ or stories. As he notes,

Multisited research is designed around chains, paths, threads, conjunctions, or juxtapositions of locations in which the ethnographer establishes some form of literal physical presence, with an explicit, posited logic of association or connection among sites that in fact defines the argument of the ethnography.[10]

In other words, the researcher defines a question and then draws links intuitively across different, tangible sites. This has resulted in ethnographic work in anthropology that has followed the same population across locations, as in, say, nurses traveling between India and the United States, or software developers from Ire-

land engaging in work for companies in the United States.[11] In education, it has meant studies like Eisenhart and Finkel's *Women's Science*,[12] which looked at the multiple sites (e.g., alternative high schools, classes, and local activist groups) where women learn to become scientists.

Yet, multisited ethnography is not simply "a set of *methods* that are very specifically prescriptive for the conduct of fieldwork."[13] It has also challenged us to re-think our *research imaginary* more broadly, implying a kind of self-reflexivity about how particular ethnographic sites are imagined, how objects are delimited. Marcus argues, in fact, that multisited ethnographies can be constructed around a single, strategically selected locale. Such ethnographies treat "the system as background," although they try not to lose sight of the fact that "it is integrally constitutive of cultural life within the bounded subject matter."[14] As a key example of this kind of reconfigured multisited ethnography, Marcus offers the well-known school ethnography, *Learning to Labor*. Although the primary site for this research is a single school, Willis juxtaposes and explores (largely through self-report data) a small group of working-class lads, as well as working-class conformist youth across sites including school, the shop floor, home, the dance hall and local bars. All sites are put into dialogue with one another in order to explain how class structures are reproduced and validated through and in everyday cultural practices. Willis makes every effort to explain larger issues of class through his rich ethnographic description of young people—though, as Marcus points out, without similar immersion in multiple sites, Willis risks reproducing "canned visions of capitalism," a point we will return to toward the end of this chapter.[15]

In sum, multisited ethnographic work—even work focused on a single, strategically selected locale—has challenged us to re-think fundamentally our research imaginary in school research in ways that push the borders of the home-school nexus. Here, we interrogate two sites that resonate deeply in contemporary ethnographic research in education—community-based learning sites and popular cultural texts. We call attention to the new critical energies at work in the sites and the particular challenges they offer contemporary education researchers. Both are sites where young people's lives are being explored in ways that look beyond simple home–school binaries. Both also reflect our own particular research agendas.[16] As such, we explore them both for their own unique potential as well as the ways in which they are illustrative of a larger set of issues, hoping to wedge open discussion and broader theoretical concerns. We begin with a look at community-based organizations and safe spaces.

COMMUNITY-BASED LEARNING SETTINGS AND SAFE SPACES

Shirley Brice Heath's *Ways with Words* is, of course, a germinal text in the area of home/school connections.[17] Here, Heath looks at home language practices across three differently situated communities, noting which kinds of practices prepare students in what kinds of ways for success or failure in school. Different students possess different kinds of literacy skills, rooted in home practices that are differentially valued or validated in school. Focused on the variable nature of literacy, this work opens up a range of questions and concerns related to language, learning practices, and specific institutions, including cross-case comparisons between and across dominant and non-dominant learning settings.

Heath and her colleagues have extended this work over the past several years to focus on what they call community-based organizations (CBOs), highlighting the ways in which community is the "third area beyond school and family" for school

researchers.[18] Focusing on the organizations young people identified as most successful, and deploying what they call "guerilla ethnographers," Heath and McLaughlin spent five years looking at sixty different organizations, gathering data from 24,000 youth in predominantly low-income and marginalized community settings across the country.[19] This research serves to establish the critical importance of these sites as well as identify key characteristics of the most successful such organizations,[20] stressing the key notion that CBOs are not bureaucratic institutions, as (typically) are schools, but emergent and unpredictable ones. Such institutions draw on the strengths of particular young people, working with particular adults, on specific tasks, with real risks and real consequences in specific settings. CBOs typically offer young people the opportunity to work through real-world activities that demand their full participation. As Heath notes:

Community organizations that create positive learning environments exhibit these same features. Work takes place within a "temporal arc," with phases that move from planning and preparation for the task ahead; to practice and deliberation along with ample trial-and-error learning, to final intensive readiness for production or performance; and, ultimately, to a culminating presentation of the work that has gone before.[21]

Community-based organizations may include arts-based activities, such as theater, dance, and music,[22] as well as sports-based activities, such as gymnastics, baseball, and basketball.[23] For example, while putting on a drama to raise money for a trip, young people have to decide (among other things) who will design the costumes; who will design the sets; who will act, write, advertise, and manage the finances; and so forth. These activities unfold under the guiding hand of older, better skilled community workers, or "wizards,"[24] individuals who see young people as resources to be employed, not problems to be managed.[25]

By way of example, Heath looked at the everyday talk of a coach (Victor Cage) and his community center based basketball team (the Dynamos) as they worked through their season. Here the coach modeled conditional "what if" phrases as they worked to co-create a set of flexible rules and strategies to accomplish specific tasks. This kind of work depends on "carrying distributed knowledge, shared skills, and discourse patterns through a project over a period of time."[26] As Heath notes, the team internalized a set of rules that they were able to adapt flexibly when the coach transgressed them. Ultimately, the team created a "sense of place with a keen notion of the role of rules and ways of planning and talking about relations between rule setting and rule breaking."[27]

This work has been marked by a split between school and nonschool settings. According to Heath, schools often prefigure relevant curricula based on simple notions of identity, assuming, for example, that young people desire activities defined by adults as ethnically or culturally relevant. According to Heath and McLaughlin, CBOs thrive on the complex, already existing social networks of young people—on their ability to mobilize specific sets of personal resources to deal with concrete concerns and challenges. Lived identities in these organizations, as Heath and McLaughlin argue, are "complex, and embedded in achievement, responsibility, and . . . immediate support network[s][28] in ways that exceed the easy delineation of (multi)cultural borders and boundaries." There is nothing predicable or stable about the ways ethnicity and identity play out in these organizations, nor do these organizations make a priori assumptions about young people and culture.[29]

Community organizations, particularly those in which the arts are intensely integrated, generate unexpected contexts and collaborations that often add up to some outcomes that are tough to achieve elsewhere, blurring lines of racial and ethnic division and crossing linguistic barriers.[30]

For the most part, then, Heath and her colleagues have not situated their research in schools. One gets the sense—with only occasional exceptions[31]—that schools are a vestige of another era and that for disenfranchised youth, in particular, the most interesting and important kind of education is happening outside of school. They sum up with the observation, "Schools are experienced as hostile and demeaning environments where neither inner-city youth nor their interests are taken seriously."[32] Furthermore, schools are no longer training youth for the kinds of flexible problem-solving activities that are so necessary for job readiness in the information age. Such work, again, is happening in community-based organizations.

Although less focused on skills, similar ideas have been developed by Michelle Fine, Lois Weis, and colleagues on safe spaces.[33] Not marked by the same split between in-school and out-of-school settings, Fine and Weis' work has focused on the imaginative resources young people use to carve out spaces for themselves in different settings, both inside and outside of school. Young people, they argue, carve these safe spaces in a variety of sites—in school and out of school—creating "counterpublics," to use Nancy Fraser's term, ironically out of the very exclusionary practices of the public sphere.

These spaces are not just a set of geographical/spatial arrangements but, rather, theoretical, analytical, and spatial displacements—a crack, a fissure, a fleeting or sustained set of commitments. Individual dreams, collective work, and critical thoughts are smuggled in and reimagined.[34]

Refusing the school–non-school binary, these authors explore how young people take up public spaces[35] and how within the context of great poverty and the dismantling of the public safety net, they carve out private ones.

By way of example, the authors juxtapose two sites: Molly Olga, a neighborhood arts center in Buffalo, and an Orisha spiritual community in New York City.[36] In the first site, a diverse group of participants meet in an urban community to work under the tutelage of its director, Molly Bethel. Molly Olga's poly-vocal feel encourages people who do not normally interact with each other—from poor black youth to white upper-middle-class housewives—to discuss common concerns. It is a thriving "community of difference" constituted through aesthetic practice. In the second example, the authors highlight the micro-moves of a "self-consciously heterogeneous spiritual community" in New York City as participants invent and reinvent religious practices of the African and Cuban Diaspora, making them relevant for broad groups of urban dwellers. In both cases, the authors highlight "spaces in which 'difference' signals interest, engagement, commitment, and opportunity" that look beyond the "walls of school."[37]

Additional work focuses more specifically on school culture. Weis and Fine, for example, juxtapose the powerful day-to-day work within two in-school sites—an abstinence-based sex education program and a de-tracked and racially integrated World Literature class—both located in Northeastern urban schools.[38] In the first example, the authors demonstrate how the program participants stretch beyond the official intent of the program (abstinence only) to "traverse a variety of subjects regarding race, gender, sexuality, and men." Under the guidance of the program's leader, Doris Carbonell-Medina, this weekly meeting becomes a safe space for these young women as they discuss salient issues in honest and personally meaningful ways. In the second example, the authors show how a World Literature class can be a powerful space in which to engage questions of identity and difference. They write:

Students have learned to engage in this space, for 45 minutes a day, with power, "difference," and a capacity to re-vision. Some with delight

and some still disturbed, they know that everyone will get the chance to speak and be heard."[39]

The authors go to great lengths to trace the discourse as it evolves over a year-long period as students discuss books like *Of Mice and Men*, *Two Old Women*, and *La Llorana*:

Rather than assuming a priori parameters, work on community-based organizations and "safe spaces" raises important questions as to where "education" is happening today. Juxtaposing in-school and out-of-school sites, this work powerfully reframes contemporary educational questions and agendas. For Heath, McLaughlin, and colleagues, this has meant an elaborated discussion of what kinds of "skills" are fostered in these sites, and how these skills translate across the kinds of tasks most associated with our contemporary information age. For Weis, Fine, and colleagues, this has meant looking at how a variety of young people "homestead," or claim authentic and meaningful spaces and identities within a variety of sites, both in school and out of school. This work intentionally de-centers the home–school binary in educational research, evoking the myriad of ways in which "community" is a "third area" of study.[40]

POPULAR CULTURE

Further pushing the question of contemporary out-of-school curricula, recent research has stretched well beyond the home–school binary in its growing focus on popular cultures and technologies. Paralleling research on alternative learning sites, this work has challenged our assumptions about what counts as educational curricula or texts for young people. Indeed, as a range of scholars have argued, popular culture increasingly offers a terrain upon which young people are navigating their lives and meeting their everyday needs and concerns.[41] These cultural texts are proliferating in complex ways in and through video, film, television, and music technologies, as well as computers and the internet—all of which have increasingly complex relationships to and with each other.

Recent work on popular culture and education has looked at how young people have used these texts in practice or performance.[42] David Buckingham and Julian Sefton-Green, for example, have treated media literacy as a kind of symbolic social action. Their work has explored how young people mobilize popular texts as discursive resources in particular and meaningful ways, using them to negotiate senses of self and community. In *Cultural Studies Goes to School*,[43] the authors offer several case studies of young people using the media to create personally relevant texts—from magazines to photographs to popular music—as they "author" their lives, so to speak. They write,

In adopting 'critical' positions in discourse, in staking out their tastes and identities, and in intervening directly in popular cultural forms, these [youth] are actively defining themselves in relation to wider social, cultural, and ideological forces.[44]

This is a less defensive approach than are many current media literacy approaches.[45] In fact, Buckingham has noted that this kind of work often invites problematic kinds of pleasures from students.[46] Even these—perhaps especially these—must be understood if we are to engage with the lives of young people in authentic ways.

Sefton-Green extends this work, focusing on the relationship between popular media culture, the arts, and the internet.[47] In *Young People, Creativity and New Technologies*, Sefton-Green gathers recent theoretical and empirical work "to describe the opportunities digital technologies offer for communicating, disseminating and making culture as well as acting as a vehicle for personal and collective self-expression."[48] Among other topics, contributors discuss multimedia memoirs, self-produced CD-ROMs, on-line school scrapbooks, and personal Web pages. These new and creative uses of information technology are

part of a broader redefinition of youth culture that has implications for all manner of educational practice—from the classroom to the dance floor and beyond.[49]

More recently, scholars in education have moved toward less prefigured, ethnographic approaches that look at the ways young people construct identities through popular culture and their implications for school life.[50] For example, Dimitriadis's recent work looks at how young people construct notions of self, history, and place through their uses of hip-hop texts, focusing on how these young people use these texts in concert with—and in counter-distinction to—school texts. For example, Dimitriadis looked at the ways in which two teenagers constructed notions of a Southern tradition through their use of Southern rap texts; how young people constructed notions of history through viewing the film *Panther*, a film they connected to hip-hop culture more broadly; and how young people constructed powerful senses of self through talk about the life and death of icon Tupac Shakur. All are examples of popular culture's reach and power. He writes, "We see popular culture more and more, providing the narratives that young people are drawing on to deal with the issues and the concerns most pressing in their lives." He shows, "These investments played out in often unpredictable ways."[51]

Dolby and Yon have developed similar ethnographic projects in the field of education, though both have looked to settings outside the United States. Dolby,[52] in a particularly fascinating study, looks at how young people at a high school in South Africa (Fernwood High) negotiate ideas about race in the aftermath of apartheid. Here, music and fashion became ways to carve out ideas about being white, black, and colored, at a moment when a priori racial categories are called into question. These popular symbols circulated and were ascribed different meanings at different times. Rave music, for example, "is understood specifically as 'white' music. A colored student who listens to rave would be ostracized by her or his classmates, and seen as a threat to 'colored' identity."[53] In sum, she argues:

"Race" at Fernwood reinvents itself (as it does constantly) as a site of identification that takes its meaning, in large part, from affect and affective investments. Students are invested in the emotions of desire that surround consumptive practices, particularly the practices of global youth culture.[54]

Yon, in turn, looked at a multiethnic high school in Toronto (Maple Heights), focusing on the ways in which young people negotiate their day-to-day identities. Yon offers portraits of different young people and the creation of complicated identities through their investments in popular culture. He writes:

Many of the signs and symbols of the popular cultures of these youth, like dress codes and musical tastes, are racialized. This means that the signifiers of race can also change with the changing signs of culture and identity, and what it means to be a certain race is different from one context to the next.[55]

He offers several examples of young people constructing notions of self through popular culture. These include a Canadian-born black, a white youth who identifies with black culture, as well as a black immigrant from the Caribbean—all of whom use popular culture to negotiate and stake out particular senses of self.

In sum, Dimitriadis, Dolby, and Yon make it clear that we cannot understand young people's identities in predictable ways. More and more, as this work makes clear, we must ask ourselves what kinds of curricula—broadly defined—young people draw on to understand, explain, and live through the world around them. This is messy terrain, one that extends beyond a priori notions about identity often privileged by educators. As these authors make clear, the multiple uses to which popular culture is put challenge and belie easy

notions of cultural identification. Young people in the United States and around the world are elaborating complex kinds of social and cultural identifications through music like hip-hop and techno in ways that challenge predictive notions about texts, practices, and identities. "The global context of popular culture," Dolby writes, is critical for "the marking of racialized borders, and for their subsequent displacement and rearrangement."[56]

NEW DIRECTIONS

As this research demonstrates, and as anthropologists have long noted, education takes place both within and beyond the boundaries of school. Today though, education is an increasingly emergent phenomenon, unfolding across numerous sites and settings with and in between multiple texts. It is the "in-between"—the moving back and forth between sites and texts—that increasingly defines our children's lives and cultural landscapes and must, therefore, define our research agenda.

Yet, multisited work in education has not, for the most part, explored these sites, literal or otherwise, as existing in dynamic interrelation to other sites in specific and particular ways. While we have many studies of single sites, we do not have a sense of how these sites are enmeshed in particular ways in complex webs of relationships for their participants. We have one kind of mapping here; one where sites take on meaning in the context of other isolated sites as well as self-report data on the backstage knowledge of participants. Missing, it seems, are more relational kinds of studies—studies that, for example to return to Marcus, "follow the people," "follow the biographies," or "follow the story" in complex and inevitably unpredictable ways.

Indeed, while Heath and McLaughlin have suggested looking away from traditional schools and focusing only on CBOs, there seems a danger of reifying these sites as objects of study. Just as *Learning to Labor* often reproduced canned ideas about capitalism, we are perhaps in danger here of reproducing clichés about what happens in schools if we rely only on participants' self-report data about these sites. Instead of turning away from the study of schools, we suggest figuring out, in particular and situated ways, the relationship *between* multiple sites—schools, community centers, job sites, and so forth—and the skills they encourage and enable for young people. This means actually doing the research cross-site in a way that we have not done before. Additionally, while Weis and Fine have included in-school and out-of-school sites in their work, there is a parallel danger of focusing on single-sited studies in isolation from one another, as Weis and Fine tend to do. While these authors have taken great pains to show internal dynamism around identity within these sites, we have little sense of how participants live their lives *across* and *between* sites. If identity is always an emergent construction, we need to understand more clearly how these identities play out in relation to and with each other in the space of the "in between."

Like work on CBOs and safe spaces, work on popular culture and education has overwhelmingly been single-sited. For example, studies by Dimitriadis, Dolby, and Yon focus on single settings—a community center and two high schools, respectively.[57] In each case we gain a clear picture of a particular educational site and a specific group of young people. In each of these cases, we are asked to expand our notion of education—where it happens and with what texts. Yet, we get little sense of how different sites—understood on their own terms—invite the working across that we discuss here. For example, while Dimitriadis talks about his participants' experiences in traditional schools, he relies largely on self-reported data rather than entering the school site first hand. In turn,

neither Dolby nor Yon look at young people's uses of these texts in ways that extend beyond school settings. Missing, it seems, is research that follows individuals and groups as they traverse a wide range of texts in different settings, and perhaps at different times of their life.

Re-engaging with the power and limitations of the work discussed throughout, we offer here a beginning set of imagined possibilities for engaging in the kind of ethnographic work discussed above. Ethnographies that recognize and take seriously into account the many sites of education can help to work against naturalized frames, categories and theories in education—offering an important advance in our thinking about youth and schooling. Indeed, we must be responsible for the questions we ask and stretch beyond the taken-for-granted categories and assumptions. There is no neutral terrain here. How we frame problems and objects of study can very well reproduce unfair power relationships in our work. With multisited ethnography, we can both denaturalize our object of study and conduct powerful work in the field—a twin imperative for our continued relevancy. We ask you, the reader, to imagine with us what such work might look like and invite continued discussion. Our list below, then, for imagined possibilities, is meant only as a beginning.

1. We begin by calling for more studies of different groups in ostensibly the same space. In other words, it is critically important that we understand how teen men and women appropriate an array of popular cultural texts and/or programs, for example. This project must be stretched to involve teen men and women of different races, ethnicities, sexualities and/or social class—all the time, following Heath, Dimitriadis, McCarthy, and others, questioning our a priori assumptions here. Understanding how different groups across and within race, for example, make meaning of texts or programs is an important project. We know from our own work that there is

no one African-American, for example, appropriation of a text. Rather, different groups *within* any given category, work, texts vary differently. This needs to be built within a new research imaginary.

2. As noted throughout, we would also encourage more studies of youth across spaces such as community centers and popular culture, as well as school, family, and so forth. Often we go into one such site, while ignoring all others, or rely upon self-reported data as to individual/group behavior in sites other than the one in which we are physically immersed. We have engaged in such single-site studies ourselves (Dimitriadis in community centers and with popular culture; Weis in community centers and schools) and understand full well the difficulties of following youth through varying zones of action. Nevertheless we would suggest that we must begin to do this work. This might involve a team of researchers, perhaps one person in the school, one in the families, and so forth. Again we understand full well the difficulties of establishing rapport and trust, even for one person, much less a team of people. But we would argue that we must begin to think along these lines in order to explore the range of action in youth's lives and urge others to join with us as we pursue these ideas.

These two suggestions are grounded largely in the above discussion. It is important to note, however, that multisited work has an important temporal and regional component, as well. As George Marcus notes, it gives us important ways to understand the often disjunctive and uneven distribution of social, cultural, and material imperatives.[58] Suggestions (3) through (5) offer ways to push further the important implications of multisited ethnography, in ways we have not yet discussed.

3. As we indicated throughout, we see great possibilities in "following the people" or "following the individual" across sites and texts. Most ethnographic studies, however, are inevitably done at a single point in time at a single site. While we learn a great deal from such studies, what we do not know is what happens to them after they leave these specific locations. Culturalist theoretical challenges, although important, do not enable us to probe the linkages between actual school experiences as explored by ethnographers, and life chances and choices in other sites. Thus, multisited work in education could powerfully be conducted over time as well as space. We have some examples of follow-up studies, such as Jay MacLeod's *Ain't No Makin' It*, Claire Wallace's *For Richer, For Poorer*, and Paul Willis' *Learning to Labor*. These studies, however, tend to be short-term follow-ups. Willis, for example, followed his subjects only briefly into the work force. Although we certainly understand why investigators do not engage in long-term follow-up studies, such studies would go a long way toward unpacking the ways in which individuals and/or groups move through different spaces. It is only through such long-term follow-ups that we can begin to understand the interlocking connections between and among race, social class, gender, schooling and the new economy, engaging theoretical debates in this area and going far beyond what we know to date. Lois Weis begins such long-term work in *Class Reunion: The Remaking of the American White Working Class* (2004), her 15-year follow-up of white working-class students who originally appear in *Working Class Without Work: High School Students in a De-industrializing Economy* (1990). We all for many more such studies across social class and race/ethnicity.[59]

4. Stretching further we would like to see increased studies of groups similar in race, class, and gender across geographic sites within the United States. Michelle Fine and Lois Weis, for example, map experiences and practices since leaving high school among African-American, Latino/Latina, and white men and women in the urban Northeast.[60] Based on their data, Fine and Weis come to conclusions regarding the economy, body politic, and the state. Yet, as Peter McLaren reminds us, Los Angeles is a wholly different space, no doubt producing different scenarios.[61] And Atlanta has

a far more thriving economy than the Northeast, where Lois and Michelle worked, as well as a different kind of racial history. Asking the same kinds of questions in varying geographic contexts within the United States will go a long way toward understanding the relationships between the state and economy and the ways in which individuals and/or groups forge their lives.

5. Along the lines outlined above, we must also begin to situate our studies globally. Groups can be studied between and among countries such as the United States, Australia, and England, for example, and more time needs to be taken contextualizing what we find within the global economy and meaning systems. In addition, we can usefully explore concepts like race, for example, by focusing carefully on groups within different national contexts. Nadine Dolby, for one, has begun this work in South Africa, and we would encourage others to pursue her agenda.[62]

FINAL (FOR NOW) THOUGHTS

The above demand a different set of understandings as to what constitutes what we call "the research imaginary" in education, how we contextualize and understand what we envision as education, and how we think students get it. Indeed, if we accept a notion of education that implies only traditional school sites and curricula, our work potentially ignores a variety of important complexities in young people's lives—how education happens outside of school; what students bring to the school; and how this intersects with what school offers. At worst, if we uncritically accept a priori parameters for what education is, we are in danger of simply reproducing the same set of questions, problems, and issues we have inherited. As Jan Nespor writes in *Tangled up in School*,

When groups and processes are analytically detached from each other . . . it becomes easy to slide into the bleak loops of contemporary educational debate. . . . The debate becomes less

simple, but more constructive, when we focus on dense interconnections among various actors and processes.[63]

We have, we argue, an imperative to reimagine our object of study—one that forces us to re-engage with the lives of youth on fresh terrain, simultaneously challenging predictable notions of culture and identity. This demands cross-site and cross-space collaborative work in forms that we have not previously engaged— 2004 is a very different space for all of us than thirty years ago. We invite this conversation to continue as we all imagine what research around these issues might look like in the next decade.

NOTES

1. Spindler, G. (Ed.). (2000). *Fifty years of anthropology and education: 1950–2000*. Mahwah, NJ: Erlbaum.

2. Spindler (2000), p. 30–31.

3. Spindler (2000), p. 30.

4. Appadurai, A. (1996). *Modernity at large: Cultural dimensions of globalizations*. Minneapolis, MN: University of Minneapolis Press; Massey, D. (1994). *Space, place, and gender*. Minneapolis: University of Minneapolis Press.

5. Eisenhart, M. (2001). Educational ethnography past, present, and future: Ideas to think with. *Educational Researcher, 30* (8), 16–27.

6. Burawoy, M., et al. (2000). *Global ethnography*. Berkeley: University of California Press; Marcus, G. (1986). Contemporary problems of ethnography in the modern world system. In J. Clifford & G. Marcus (Eds.), *Writing culture: The poetics and politics of ethnography* (pp. 165–193). Berkeley: University of California Press; Marcus, G. (1998). *Ethnography through thick and thin*. Princeton, NJ: Princeton University Press.

7. Marcus (1998), p. 14.

8. Marcus (1998), p. 14.

9. Marcus (1998), pp. 90–95.

10. Marcus (1998), p. 90.

11. Burawoy et al. (2000).

12. Eisenhart, M., & Finkel, E. (1998). *Women's science: Learning and succeeding from the margins*. Chicago: University of Chicago Press.

13. Eisenhart & Finkel (1998), p. 6.

14. Marcus (1998), p. 172.

15. Marcus (1998), p. 45.

16. Dimitriadis, G. (2001). *Performing identity/performing culture: Hip hop as text, pedagogy, and lived practice*. New York: Peter Lang; Dimitriadis, G., & McCarthy, C. (2001). *Reading and teaching the postcolonial: From Baldwin to Basquiat and Beyond*. New York: Teachers College Press; Dimitriadis, G., & Weis, L. (2001). Imagining possibilities with and for contemporary youth: (Re)writing and (Re)visioning education today. *Qualitative Research, 1* (2), 223–240; Fine, M., & Weis, L. (1998). *The unknown city: Lives of poor and working-class young adults*. Boston: Beacon Press; Weis, L., & Fine, M. (2001). Extraordinary conversations in public schools. *International Journal of Qualitative Studies in Education, 14* (4), 497–524.

17. Heath, S. (1983). *Ways with words: Language, life, and work in communities and classrooms*. Cambridge: Cambridge University Press.

18. Heath, S. (2001). Three's not a crowd: Plans, roles, and focus in the arts. *Educational Researcher, 30* (7), 10–17.

19. Heath, S., & McLaughlin, M. (Eds.). (1993). *Identity and inner-city youth: Beyond ethnicity and gender*. New York: Teachers College Press.

20. McLaughlin, M., Irby, M., & Langman, J. (1994). *Urban sanctuaries: Neighborhood organizations in the lives and futures of inner-city youth*. San Francisco: Jossey-Bass.

21. Heath (2001), p. 12.

22. Ball, A., & Heath, S. (1993). Dances of identity: Finding an ethnic self in the arts. In S. Heath & M. McLaughlin (Eds.), *Identity and inner-city youth: Beyond ethnicity and gender* (pp. 69–93). New York: Teachers College Press.

23. Heath, S. (1991). Inner-city life to literature: Drama in language learning. *TESOL Quarterly, 27* (2), 177–192; Mahiri, J. (1998). *Shooting for excellence: African American and youth culture in new century schools*. Urbana, IL: National Counsel of Teachers of Education.

24. McLaughlin, Irby, & Langman (1994).

25. Dimitriadis & Weis (2001).

26. Heath, S. (1996). Ruling places: Adaptation in development by inner-city youth. In R. Jessor, A. Colby, & R. Schweder (Eds.), *Ethnography and human development: Context and meaning in social inquiry* (pp. 225–251). Chicago: University of Chicago Press.

27. Heath (1996), p. 246.

28. Heath & McLaughlin (Eds.) (1993), p. 32.

29. Heath & McLaughlin (Eds.) (1993), p. 20.

30. Heath (2001), p. 16.

31. Heath & McLaughlin (Eds.) (1993).

32. McLaughlin, M., & Irby, M. (1994). Urban sanctuaries: Neighborhood organizations that keep hope alive. *Phi Delta Kappan, 76* (4), 305.

33. Dimitriadis & Weis, 2001; Fine & Weis, 1998; Hall, J. (2001). *Canal town youth: Community organization and the development of adolescent identity*. Albany: SUNY Press; Weiler, J. (2000). *Codes and contradictions: Race, gender identity, and schooling*. Albany: SUNY Press; Weis & Fine, 2001.

34. Fine, M., Weis, L., Centrie, C., & Roberts, R. (2000). Educating beyond the borders of schooling. *Anthropology & Education Quarterly, 31* (2), 132.

35. Kelly, G. (1997). *From Vietnam to America: A chronicle of the Vietnamese immigration to the United States*. Boulder, CO: Westview Press.

36. Fine, Weis, Centrie, & Roberts (2000).

37. Fine, Weis, Centrie, & Roberts (2000), p. 149.

38. Weis & Fine (2001).

39. Weis & Fine (2001).

40. Heath (2001), p. 15.

41. Dimitriadis (2001).

42. Buckingham, D. (1993). *Children talking television: The making of television literacy*. London: The Falmer Press; Buckingham, D. (1996). *Moving images: Understanding children's emotional responses to television*. Manchester, England: Manchester University Press; Buckingham, D. (Ed.). (1998). *Teaching popular culture: Beyond radical pedagogy*. London: UCL Press; Buckingham, D., & Sefton-Green, J. (1995). *Cultural studies goes to school: Reading and teaching popular media*. London: Taylor & Francis; Tobin, J. (2000). *Good guys don't wear hats: Children's talk about the media*. New York: Teachers College Press.

43. Buckingham & Sefton-Green (1995).

44. Buckingham & Sefton-Green (1995), p. 82.

45. Brunner, C., & Tally, W. (1999). *The new media literacy handbook: An educator's guide to bringing new media into the classroom*. New York: Doubleday.

46. D. Buckingham (Ed.) (1998).

47. Sefton-Green, J. (Ed.). (1998). *Digital diversions: Youth culture in the age of multimedia*. New York: Routledge; Sefton-Green, J. (Ed.). (1999). *Young people, creativity and new technologies*. New York: Routledge.

48. Sefton-Green (Ed.) (1999), p. 1.

49. Sefton-Green (Ed.) (1998).

50. Dimitriadis, 2001; Dolby, N. (2001). *Constructing race: Youth, identity, and popular culture*

in South Africa. Albany: SUNY Press.; Yon, D. (2000). *Elusive culture: Schooling, race, and identity in global times.* Albany: SUNY Press.

51. Dimitriadis (2001), p. 120.

52. Dolby, N. (2000). Changing selves: Multicultural education and the challenge of new identities. *Teachers College Record, 102* (5), 898–912; Dolby (2001).

53. Dolby (2000), p. 206.

54. Dolby (2000), p. 203.

55. Dolby (2000), p. 71.

56. Dolby (2001), p. 9.

57. Dimitriadis (2001); Dolby (2001); Yon (2000).

58. Marcus (1998).

59. Weis, L. (1990). *Working class without work: High school students in a de-industrializing economy.* New York: Routledge; Weis (2004). *Class reunion: The remaking of the American white working class.* New York: Routledge.

60. Fine & Weis (1998).

61. McLaren, P. (1997). *Revolutionary multiculturalism: Pedagogies of dissent for the new millennium.* Boulder, CO: Westview Press.

62. Dolby (2001).

63. Nespor, J. (1997). *Tangled up in school.* Mahwah, NJ: Erlbaum.

OBJECTIVITY IN EDUCATIONAL RESEARCH: THE QUEST FOR CERTAINTY BETWEEN THE 1950S AND 1970S

Greg Wiggan

BACKGROUND: MAPPING THE SOCIAL LANDSCAPE

After World War II, there was a growing belief in the desirability of social equality. This belief was advocated by African Americans who fought in the war, hoping that white Americans would reward them for their patriotism by granting them civil rights and equality. During the war, school segregation continued to belie the basic premise of equality in public education.[1] As late as 1951, most states had laws that permitted separate education for black and white children. However, the 1954 *Brown v. Board of Education* case transformed American history. In the case, the National Association for the Advancement of Colored People (NAACP) represented Linda Brown, a black student who was forced to attend school several miles from her home because coeducation of black and white children was prohibited. The Supreme Court ruled that separate education was inherently unequal; therefore, public schools had to be desegregated.[2] The NAACP's victory in *Brown v. Board of Education* was the turning point in the struggle for civil rights. The victory reassured advocates of equality and civil rights that their activism could effect social change.[3]

Although it was met with great resistance, the ruling in *Brown v. Board of Education* brought hopes of transforming public schools as well as the social and economic landscape. However, fifty years after *Brown v. Board of Education*, today's public schools are still segregated; and more importantly, the issue of inequality continues to be a concern not only in schools, but also in the social and economic system. For some, the idea of improving school equity means that students are simply bused to schools in other neighborhoods. While that might be a noble goal, yet it does little to improve the racialized structure of public education and the cycle of school failure. Rather than providing a quality education to all children regardless of their race or social class (like the victory in *Brown v. Board of Education* was supposed to accomplish), the current system forces the poor as well as black and brown parents to chase after the carrot (quality schools) on a stick (neighborhoods) that is always in sight, but they are never able to catch up to it.

OBJECTIVITY ENTHRONED

After the *Brown* case, there was an enormous growth in public school expenditure and programs aimed at addressing social inequality. There was an eagerness on the part of policy makers to base institutional reform on objective (empirical) research. This led to an influx of social science researchers attempting to investigate social and educational inequality for the purpose of creating social change. The involvement of members of the academy in research aimed at policy making perpetuated a noble dream of objectivity in school research.[4] By objectivity, I am referring to the presumption that social phenomenon can be perceived independent of experience. In other words, it is the belief that the truth about a phenomenon can be known if subjectivity is avoided. Objectivity emphasizes empirical methods of investigation, focusing less on personal accounts and more on quantifiable measures. Research was not only being produced as scholarship, but also for policy recommendations. As a result, questions of objectivity and legitimate scholarship became more central in educational discourse.

As the policy implications of school research grew, the government became one of the major sources of funding for educational research, and it favored policy-oriented studies that were quantitatively based.[5] The government reified quantitative research as the standard for school and policy evaluation.[6] Because the primary goal of government supported research was policy making, it had to be uniform and objective so that decisions could be made based on empirical data.[7] During this time, the prevailing notion was that government resources were better used to fund quantitative rather than qualitative research,

because the former involved less researcher bias and subjectivity, which were believed to be inherent in qualitative studies. Qualitative research was viewed as being open-ended and flexible; therefore, it was unable to reveal the facts about student achievement and school inequality issues. In addition, qualitative research was not as generalizable, which limited its utility in public policy areas. Hence, quantitative studies were not only viewed as being most reliable, but were ultimately enthroned as the standard for school research.

The emphasis on quantitative research presumed a form of direct realism, supposing that researchers could perceive social phenomenon free of intermediary subjectivity.[8] Due to the demand for objectivity, what qualitative research could reveal about personal experience and enlightenment was regarded as inferior to the knowledge provided by systematic and quantifiable measurements, which was being called objective.[9] This approach to objectivity was somewhat of a naïve way of viewing social phenomenon, which undermined personal accounts and led to extremism in educational research.

REPOSITIONING FOR OBJECTIVITY

In 1963, the founding of the American journal *Sociology of Education* marked the formal recognition of the growing prestige of the discipline.[10] Although there was a previous attempt to unite sociology and education, namely in 1927 with the *American Journal of Educational Sociology*, the journal reflected less sociological principles and more general concerns about education. During this time, most educational sociologists were in schools of education rather than sociology departments. Due to the low esteem that was generally associated with educational researchers, there were barriers concerning the respectability of the discipline.[11] Schools of education were generally viewed as sites where practitioners were trained, rather than places of rigorous academic studies for serious intellectuals.[12] The consensus was that schools of education lacked an academic discipline and offered low-level university curriculum.[13]

As a result of the lack of esteem assigned to schools of education, educational sociologists attempted to enhance the image of their field. More educational sociologists worked out of sociology departments, as opposed to schools of education. Furthermore, rather than referring to themselves as educational sociologists, they called themselves sociologists of education and attempted to prove that their work warranted scholarly merit.

In 1964 the U.S. Congress passed the Civil Rights Act, and it directed the Commissioner of Education to study inequality of educational opportunity among racial groups. This was intended to be a two-year study sponsored by the government. Furthermore, the findings of this study, documenting what the problems were in public schools, were to be presented to the President and Congress. James Coleman, a professor of sociology at Johns Hopkins University, headed the committee on education. The study began promptly, and in 1966 the report, titled *Equality of Educational Opportunity*, was published by the Government Printing Office.[14] The report examined material differences between school districts, comparing such things as school and class size, student background, teacher training, learning facilities, and student expenditure. In the report, Coleman found that the characteristics of school districts were not significantly related to school achievement as much as were the problems in students' families and communities.[15] Coleman's study marked the beginning of large quantitative research aimed at providing overreaching generalizations about public education.

After the Coleman report, Blau and Duncan's study, *The American Occupational Structure*, became one of the most influential works in education. The authors' work reinforced the belief that objectivity could be attained in research. This study was intended to examine education and occupation mobility. The authors proposed that the occupational structure is the basis of the stratification system in contemporary industrial societies.[16] Sampling 20,700 males between ages 20 and 64 and applying multivariate analysis, they found that the impact of educational factors was the single largest contributor to one's life chances. Blau and Duncan developed a statistical model to predict how much education contributed to individual occupational attainment. This research had a profound influence on the future of educational research.[17] Like the Coleman report, this study was used to make broad generalizations about schools. Although Blau and Duncan excluded minorities from their sample, their study was heralded as objective scholarship with wide implications for educational policy.

Similarly, in 1969 a study published by Arthur Jensen drew much attention. Jensen argued that educational and social policies should be based on the premise that the intellect of minorities, particularly African Americans, was genetically inferior to Caucasians.[18] Jensen posited that educational attainment was linked to genetic determinants, which were quantifiable, but could not be mediated through social programs. Although Jensen's study was quantitative, his research was racially charged, and may have cast doubt on the belief that quantitative research was more objective than qualitative inquiry. However, his work drew an enormous amount of attention. And similarly, more recent scholars arguing for racial and or genetic deficiency continue to receive applause (see Herrnstein and Murray's *Bell Curve* and Lynn and Vanhanen's *IQ and the Wealth of Nations*).

By the 1970s, other studies contributed to the practice of objectivity in educational research. In 1972, Christopher

Jencks et al. published *Inequality: A Reassessment of the Effect of Family and Schooling in America*. Like the other studies before it, these researchers exemplified the new way of doing objectivity in educational research. The new way of doing research not only entailed quantitative data, but also the use of large samples aimed at making generalizations for public policy.[19] Support for this study came from a number of sources including the United States Office of Education and the Massachusetts State Department of Education.[20] This study was aimed at informing neighborhood and school decision-making processes.[21]

Jencks et al. argued that the growing belief that social equality could be achieved through educational equality was problematic. During the 1960s, a popular way of viewing school failure was to examine the inequality in financial resources available to minority students, as well as the differential treatment they received in schools.[22] Jencks et al. postulated that reform strategies focusing on education were not only inadequate, but also misguided. Education reformers were devoting their efforts to addressing the War on Poverty by providing resources to create equity in schools. However, the authors questioned the effectiveness of this approach.

According to Jencks et al., equalizing the resources and the time spent in school would not be sufficient to reduce economic difference in students' homes. They argued that there was no evidence that school reform could substantially reduce social inequality or differential school performance. Rather, they proposed that these differences could be understood in terms of students' family characteristics.[23] In addition, they argued that a realistic solution to inequality would be to redistribute wealth and create more equity in parents' income.[24]

In 1974 Raymond Boudon produced a study titled *Education, Opportunity, and Social Inequality*. In the same tradition as its precursors, this study was a quantitative investigation, which was funded in part by the U.S. Office of Education. The main question in this study was whether rates of occupational or social mobility across generations were altered by improvements in education. Using a quantitative model, Boudon concluded that stratification was the principal factor responsible for inequality of educational and social opportunities. In addition, he argued that reduction in economic disparities would have the greatest impact on educational and social inequalities.[25]

Like the other studies, Boudon's work reflected the belief that quantitative work provided more precise descriptions of social phenomenon. Sponsors of educational research were interested in scholarship that could inform public policy or legitimatize their decision making process. Only the most rigorous work could receive consideration for funding, because the scholarship would be used as the scapegoat for policymakers engaging in public debates and political processes.

By the mid-1970s, the sociology of education literature was filled with quantitative works of objectivity. However, in the late 1970s scholars began to recognize that the literature was lacking personal accounts and interpretations from participants' viewpoints. With the growing influence of symbolic interactionism, ethnomethodology, phenomenology, and other interpretive perspectives that challenged objectivity and positivistic claims, education research would soon reflect more interpretive perspectives. There was a resurgence of qualitative inquiry in the school achievement debate when researchers like John Ogbu, Ray Rist, and August Hollingshead published major interpretive works in the field. Finally, the sociology of education literature regained some balance between quantitative and qualitative studies, as some of the clout surrounding the earlier perspective was challenged and influenced by interpretive frameworks.

CONCLUSION

Between the 1950s and 1970s, the problem of objectivity was one of the most fundamental challenges that faced the social sciences.[26] Researchers struggled to understand how biases could be avoided in social research. During this time, there was a demand for educational researchers to produce policy-oriented studies. These studies where supposed to be objective, where objectivity was being equated with quantitative, empirical investigation. As a result, a series of studies were conducted with the aim of objectivity. These studies, however, scarcely relied on the personal accounts of individuals, while privileging statistical modeling used to predict future outcomes. The perception was that quantitative studies were less biased and therefore more objective. Furthermore, these studies seemingly allowed for broad generalizations and public policy perspectives.

Although quantitative and qualitative research are different in terms of the way they inform our understanding of social phenomenon, they are both important methods of investigation.[27] However, while researchers were pursuing objectivity, they failed to embrace the value of interpretive research. The noble dream of objectivity was reinforced by the governments' sponsorship of quantitative studies. As research was conducted, policy was created and implemented, and in some cases it failed to produce desired outcomes. Soon it was evident that objectivity in educational research was like nailing jelly to the wall.[28] Therefore, the only meaning that objectivity could have was doing rigorous research by documenting and supporting one's arguments and making explicit the values premises underlying one's research.

For today's educational researcher, the issues of low student achievement and school failure reemerge as social problems in the field of education. While researchers generally use social and genetic perspectives (student opposi-

tional identity, social class and/or culture of poverty, and biological models) to explain school achievement and school failure issues, there are important areas that still need to be addressed. These specific issues have to do with the examination of students' beliefs about the quality of their education, as well as investigating the educational progress students believe is necessary to improve school achievement.

While much attention has been given to survey research, students' perspectives need to be understood more precisely so that intervention programs can be developed more effectively. Rather than simply producing scholarship to serve the interest of political parties or agencies, researchers must maintain the integrity of their work. Furthermore, individual experiences must be taken more seriously if we are to improve our understanding of social phenomenon.

NOTES

1. Tyack, D. (1967). *Turning points in American educational history* (p. 274). Waltham, MA: Blaisdell Publishing.

2. Tyack (1967), pp. 274, 304–308.

3. Karenga, M. (1993). *Introduction to black studies* (2nd ed., p. 168). Los Angeles: University of Sankore Press.

4. Karenga (1993); Karabel, J., & Halsey, A. (1977). *Power and ideology in education* (p. 5). New York: Oxford University Press; Novick, P. (1988). *That noble dream: The "objectivity question" and the American historical profession* (pp. 1–17). Cambridge: Cambridge University Press.

5. Karabel & Halsey (1977), pp. 5–6; McCartney, P. (1971). *Effect of financial support on growth of sociological specialties* (pp. 395–406). In E. Tiryakian (Ed.), *The phenomenon of sociology.* New York: Appleton Century-Crofts.

6. Dresch, S. (1975). A critique of planning models for postsecondary education: Current feasibility, potential relevance, and a prospectus for further research. *Journal of Higher Education, 46* (3), 245–286; Sussmann, L. (1967). Educational research programs of the Office of Educa-

tion: An interview with Dr. R. Louis Bright, associate commissioner for research, *Sociology of Education*, 40 (2), 158–169; Brown, F. (1975). Assessment and evaluation of urban schools. *Journal of Negro Education*, 44 (3), 377–384.

7. Eisner, E. (1994). *The educational imagination of the design and evaluation of school* (3rd ed., p. 215). New York: Macmillan.

8. Pojman, L. (2001). What can we know? An introduction to the theory of knowledge (2nd ed., pp. 64–79, 343). Belmont, CA: Wadsworth.

9. Saha, L., & Zubrzycki, J. (1997). Classical sociological theories of education. In L. Saha (Ed.), *International encyclopedia of the sociology of education* (pp. 241–246). Canberra, Australia: Pergamon.

10. Karabel & Halsey (1977), p. 3.

11. Karabel & Halsey (1977), pp. 3–4.

12. Bartky, J. (1955). The school of education and the university, *Journal of Higher Education*, 26 (5), 254–260.

13. Bartky (1955), p. 255.

14. Kent, J. (1968). The Coleman report: Opening Pandora's box. *Phi Delta Kappan*, 49, 242–245.

15. Coleman, J. (1966). *Equality of educational opportunity* (pp. 316–317). Washington, DC: U.S. Government Printing Office.

16. Blau, P., & Duncan, O. (1967). *The American occupational structure* (p. vii). New York: John Wiley & Sons.

17. Bennett deMarrais, K., & LeCompte, M. (1995). *The way schools work: A sociological analysis of education* (p. 183). White Plains, NY: Longman Publishers.

18. Jensen, A. (1969). How much can we boost IQ and scholastic achievement? *Harvard Educational Review*, 39 (1), 1–23.

19. Coleman, J. (1973). Review of the book *Inequality: A reassessment of the effect of family and schooling in America* by C. Jencks, M. Smith, H. Acland, M. Bane, D. Cohen, H. Gintis, B. Heyns, and S. Michelson, *American Journal of Sociology*, 78 (6), 1523–1544.

20. Jencks et al. (p. vi).

21. Cain, G. (1974). Socioeconomic background and achievement. *American Journal of Sociology*, 79 (6), 1497–1509.

22. Bennett deMarrais & LeCompte (1995), p. 237.

23. Jencks et al. (1972), p. 8.

24. Jencks et al. (1972), pp. 253–265.

25. Boudon, R. (1974). *Education, opportunity and social inequality: Changing prospects in Western society* (pp. 193–201). New York: John Wiley & Sons.

26. Myrdal, G. (1969). *Objectivity in social research: The 1967 Wimmer lecture* (pp. 3–5). New York: Random House.

27. Eisner (1994), pp. 235.

28. Novick (1988), pp. 1–17.

Aesthetics and Urban Education

IN THE MIDDLE: AN ARTIST/RESEARCHER EXPERIENCES URBAN REFORM

Joanne Kilgour Dowdy

INTRODUCTION

The black female community activists who founded schools in the late nineteenth century and twentieth century saw their commitment to the education of women as the means to improve the condition of all blacks. Their shared philosophy was based on three tenets: (1) the moral superiority of women; (2) the view that the black woman was entirely responsible for the development of all blacks; and (3) the expectation that black women would attend to the needs of their (black) sisters.[1] Publications such as Anna Julia Cooper's book, *A Voice from the South*,[2] in which she wrote on womanhood, and her 1899 presentations at the Hampton Negro Conference, are testimonials to the concern that educated black women expressed at the time regarding moral development in girls and women in their urban American communities.

These "club women," as the progressive black women have been referred to, were important to the transformation of the image of black women after abolition in 1865. They were determined to erase the stereotype of black women as licentious because of their historic subjugation to white slave masters.[3] Giddings also describes the development of the "cult of true womanhood" as it was translated from the white community by black club women who worked to change the material and moral conditions of the post-slavery black community.[4] Mary McLeod Bethune, an educator and activist, claimed that black women "recognized the importance of uplifting [their] people through social, civic, and religious activities."[5] Mary Church Terrell, educator and writer, declared war on immorality and low socioeconomic status among blacks by insisting that the more intelligent and influential blacks had a responsibility to "uplift those beneath them."[6] Nannie Burroughs, school principal and activist, spoke and wrote about the "respectability" of the working-class woman, encouraging club women who were involved in social uplift programs to find the "ordinary, common-sense, spirit-filled, everyday woman" and involve her in the movement for racial uplift.[7]

The abolition of slavery led to a demand for improved educational resources. It was in this national environment of re-envision-ing the future of black people that the women leaders began organizing schools that gave children the experiences that enabled them to carry out work beyond menial tasks. Reading, writing, and arith-metic were foundation courses for all blacks enrolled as beginning students, regardless of age and former experience. Through their activism, these female community leaders managed to mobilize forces that trans-formed the post-slavery population. Com-munity activity in the minds of these "club sisters" represented a hands-on approach to changing the conditions created by the forces of racism, sexism, and classism.

THE UNIVERSITY FELLOW

The work of the University Fellow, or "inspector"—the person responsible for the least well-served African-American students in Middle School—was to ensure that students who were failing classes would receive the academic support needed to improve their performance. I had the privilege of serving as a present-day University Fellow, and the five-week drama/writing/workshop I implemented allowed me to work with teachers commit-ted to enhancing their teaching philosophy so that all their students would have a bet-ter chance of succeeding.

In my job as a University Fellow, between 1997 and 1999, I investigated problems and then actuated solutions that would lead to more successes. I provided an opportunity for all the children to focus on improving their writing skills through experiences with the dramatic arts. This was a space in which I could make practi-cal inroads into the teachers' pedagogy and advance the agenda of the urban reform initiative. Like my black sisters of the nineteenth-century club movement, I made sure that a group of urban black children experienced success in main-stream literacy. School improvement that was aimed at one group of students, the

least well-served, allowed other partici-pants in the class to benefit from this new, drama-based pedagogy.

The teachers' belief in the potential of students was most evident in the attitude of a white, male colleague who imple-mented the drama/writing workshop in his eighth-grade classroom. Mr. Grady worked as a co-learner with the students and was willing to admit that he was growing in expertise as the class pro-ceeded. His resistance to fear and lack of confidence among the students encour-aged an atmosphere of cooperation and adventure in the children. He demon-strated his commitment to students' learn-ing by doing rather than by listening to him lecture or by completing written exer-cises in their notebooks.

THE URBAN ATLANTA COALITION COMPACT

In the tradition of the club women of the post-slavery era, the Urban Atlanta Coali-tion Compact (UACC) was created to serve the least successful African-Ameri-can students in seven public schools of metropolitan Atlanta from 1997 to 2001. At each of these schools a University Fel-low (UF) was the liaison between Sher-man State University and the school. The UF's duties included: (1) creating a school profile based on interviews with a broad representation of students, faculty, sup-port staff, and parents; (2) facilitating com-munication between the director of the UACC and the leaders of the Action Team, a school-based teacher group; and (3) working in individual classrooms as the need for her expertise arose. For example, as a language arts specialist, I was expected to provide classroom support for the faculty in that unit. An important responsibility of the UF was to relay infor-mation efficiently between the individual school and the university as planning for school activities and other UACC business was conducted. The UF worked with the

Action Team to promote the implementation of the reform initiatives that had been created to improve the education of the least well-served African-American students in the urban school.[8]

In my role as University Fellow at Middle School, the only middle school in the Urban Atlanta Coalition Compact, I implemented several key elements for successful involvement in urban education by the faculty and students. These benchmarks are described in Delpit's "Ten Factors Essential to Success in Urban Classrooms." (See Table 5.)

In one eighth-grade classroom I, as the UF, along with a group of teachers from the language arts faculty, implemented a drama initiative. This project developed into a five-week unit of drama exercises and writing activities that supported the development of the writing skills of low-achieving students in two classes. In two other classes we introduced a unit where students worked to collect and translate the slang terms and idioms from their home language into standard English versions. The point of the exercise was, first, to create a space in the classroom where students felt free to bring in their home language and celebrate it. Secondly, we wanted to build a bridge to standard English so that students could feel comfortable going back and forth from one form of the language to another, enriched by the knowledge that they had more than one mode of communication available to them. We also implemented a nine-week poetry and performance workshop.[9] The Action Team also supported a plan for training teachers in anti-racism techniques, and in an individualized academic program for students who had been retained at Middle School in the year that the UACC reform initiative arrived at the urban school.

Middle School represented a microcosm of the city in which it was situated. Even though 80 percent of the teachers and staff at Middle School voted to become involved with the UACC, I still feel that my presence in the school generated a cautious attitude among the faculty. This perceived reservation made me feel like a club woman of the nineteenth century, an "inspector" of the least well-served urban students. The high percentage of children from lower economic neighborhoods, and the way in which the faculty were developing measures to ensure the success of the failing African Americans in their charge, were only two of the hot issues that I had to negotiate over the first year.

Table 5.
Dr. Lisa Delpit: Ten Factors Essential to Success in Urban Classrooms

1. Do not teach less content to poor, urban children, but understand their brilliance and teach more!
2. Whatever methodology or instructional program is used, demand critical thinking.
3. Assure that all children gain access to "basic skills," the conventions and strategies that are essential to success in American education.
4. Provide the emotional ego strength to challenge racist societal views of the competence and worthiness of the children and their families.
5. Recognize and build on strengths.
6. Use familiar metaphors and experiences from the children's world to connect what they already know to school knowledge.
7. Create a sense of family and caring.
8. Monitor and assess needs and then address them with a wealth of diverse strategies.
9. Honor and respect the children's home culture(s).
10. Foster a sense of children's connection to community to something greater than themselves.

My job as the UF led me to ask questions about students who were not performing at grade level in reading and writing, involving me in situations that pitted my sense of moral responsibility against the "conventions" of the white-dominated parent association. In the presence of this powerful group of professionals, it was difficult to feel comfortable in the school. My feeling of being an interrupter of the school culture, or inspector of the premises where black children were being educated according to white middle-class values,[10] can best be explained through some of the comments that I documented during the initial self-study that the school did in 1998. The quotes from teachers, parents, and staff members that stand out to me after seven years include: "Even though this [black] kid may have a 'B' average and the white kid has a 'B' average, more time is spent with the white one" (staff); and "There are [teachers] who are victims of their training and think that the issue with the African-American child is impenetrable" (parent). From the staff I heard: "Looks like almost two schools, white school here, black school there"; and "There is a lack of understanding of the different cultures that we have here, primarily lack of understanding between the black and white cultures." The strongest comment came from a mother who protested that "The school should not "discount me as a black parent 'cause I'm just as concerned about my child. I will not allow [them] to bring down . . . his self-esteem."

THE MIDDLE SCHOOL DRAMA WORKSHOP

Middle School is part of a small municipal school cluster. There are seven elementary schools, one middle school, and one high school in this urban environment. The elementary schools have traditionally housed populations of children of the same racial background. When the students arrive at Middle School it is usually the first time that they encounter children of a different racial background in their classrooms. There is also a wide range in the economic levels of the children from the black and white majority neighborhoods. These differences in racial and economic status create an undercurrent of tension in the school. Interviews with black and white students conducted by a research team did reveal several instances where teachers of both races gave unstintingly to the black children who graduated to Middle School from a predominantly black elementary school.[11]

Middle School has 622 students, of whom 55 percent are black, 41 percent are white, 1 percent are Latino, and 3 percent are multiracial and international. Of the total, 39 percent are eligible for free or reduced-fee lunches.[12] The divide between the social backgrounds of the black and white children may be partly explained by the fact that many of the black children live in public housing, while the white children live in middle-class homes. Both of these groups live within easy reach of the school and can be seen walking, cycling, traveling in school buses, or being driven by their parents and guardians.

In my role as University Fellow I had worked on UACC, the urban school reform project, at Middle School for a few weeks before the drama/writing workshop was launched in October, 1997. The teachers who were interested in doing drama in the reform project were in the language arts classrooms. We formed a small study group and began meeting at off-hours in order to try out exercises that teachers would later do in their classrooms. This kinesthetic approach to teaching became an opportunity to see teachers from another perspective.[13] They were not only interested in student success in the traditional curriculum, but also wanted to see their charges come into their own and take pride in their heritage as black people with a history of achieve ment in the sciences and arts. The dramatists were club women and men in their own right. They created the acting workshop to improve the chances of reaching those students not being served by traditional classroom pedagogy.

The Philosophy behind the Drama/ Writing Workshop

It was important for me to get into a classroom during my first month's work at Middle School, to collaborate with a teacher, and to make a difference in the individual lives of the urban students. Teachers, especially those engaged in the drama group, had to demonstrate their commitment to the philosophy of high expectations for the least well-served African-American students in order to realize the practical phase of the reform agenda. As an acknowledged black club woman working at the end of the twentieth century, I was impatient to see children who had been suffering under the restraints of the desk/pencil/paper traditional mode of teaching move over to an experiential way of learning. I knew that the children who learned best by being active during the lesson, as well as the teachers in the drama group, were ready for engagement through UACC-inspired teaching.

One teacher in the language arts faculty had a need to learn new methods of literacy instruction. Mr. Grady, a white, male teacher, wanted to engage the failing students in his class so that they could succeed at the level he believed was necessary for passing the state-mandated test at the end of the school year. He first described these children to me as the ones who had "free lunch" and those who came from "bad neighborhoods." At a later point in our discussion, he admitted that he did not know what kind of music the children enjoyed, if they did any leisure reading, or whether they attended church with their parents or extended family. Our first discussion gave me a good idea about the kind of work that was necessary to build a solid community feeling in Mr. Grady's classroom.

During my second discussion with Mr. Grady, in his planning period, I decided to introduce him to some principles of drama for the language arts classroom. When Mr. Grady invited me to mentor him in his language arts classes, I was able to demonstrate some of the drama activities that could be included in a writing workshop. In collaboration with Mr. Grady and the urban students in his eighth-grade class, I developed a series of lessons that helped students explore writing from an actor's perspective. The progressive steps facilitated the students' ability to identify the characters in a piece of writing, turn the story into a script, and then to demonstrate their understanding of the characters through the performance of an improvised dramatic work. Mr. Grady was encouraged to videotape the student improvisations and use the recordings as texts that the students could review, discuss, write about, and reflect on as they developed their writing skills.

Because I believe, along with others, that we all participate in "play-acting" from early childhood to well into our mature years,[14] I worked with Mr. Grady to create a classroom that was highly responsive to dramatic experiments. Encouraging students to improvise lines based on the text that they were reading, to come up with dialogue based on character descriptions that the writer had offered in the novel, or to feed off of each other in small scenes that were based on some pivotal event in a story, all led them to experience excitement and to invest in the drama and writing exercises. This new enthusiasm for the drama/writing class also led Mr. Grady to change the look of his classroom by bringing in a couch from his home and setting up reading corners where students could relax with a book, or write when they felt inspired after a dramatic exercise.

Coaxing people to act "as if" allows them the opportunity to reveal their feelings, to commit to the project at hand, and to experience the support of a group as they develop their creative responses to a poem or other text.[15] With these ideas in mind, I provided exercises that I had garnered from my acting training at the Julliard School. Students were asked to write letters in character, to talk as characters in particular attitudes (anger, sadness, distress), or to mime scenes that would show their characters' attitudes.

The levels of actor training explored gave students a chance to find their own space for engagement—i.e., the kinds of experiences that they were willing to "act out" in public. The topics covered in the drama improvisation workshops included, among others: friendship, loneliness, racism, domestic abuse, women's rights, parent/children relationships, and love. The wide range of emotions evoked through this kind of dramatic exploration enabled the students to find words and actions to show the attitudes that they wanted to demonstrate. The students got to decide which emotions to deal with under the given circumstances of their mood, experience, and interest at the time of the training.

The drama/writing workshop also gave me an opportunity to "operationalize" Delpit's Ten Factors Essential to Success in Urban Classrooms. During the time we worked in the UACC, Dr. Delpit had repeatedly referred to our "marching orders," which included such imperatives as: develop content-rich classes; encourage critical thinking; use "basic skills" as a fact of formal education; allow students to develop the "ego strength to challenge racist societal views" of their potential; build on strengths; use children's home language to build a bridge to formal school English; create a family atmosphere in the school; address diverse needs and attend to them with various strategies; honor the children's home culture; and develop a sense of connectedness to the community so that children can perceive themselves as more than individuals.

Details of the Drama/Writing Workshop

Mr. Grady and I agreed on a list of guidelines at the start of the collaboration. I also met with the language arts teacher before he began each step in his drama/writing workshop. We decided to follow the lead of the students once we introduced them to the principles of character analysis and improvisation of dramatic scenes based on scene study. Mr. Grady also used dramatic principles based on his own experience with the drama group, which he met with in the early-morning sessions that I organized for teachers in the building. His first objective with the eighth-grade class was to get the students interested in performing scenes based on the literature they read from the syllabus. From that step we shaped the drama/writing unit for student success by asking the students to rewrite scenes they had read after thinking about the beginning, middle and end of each scene. Mr. Grady did not tell the students how to fill the scenes with content since he trusted that their imaginations would suffice. Also, when some students showed a greater inclination to direct scenes that were written in class, or run the video camera when scenes were being recorded, Mr. Grady assigned student director roles that would use these talents.

One of the exercises that evolved from working with student responses to the written text and their development of scripted scenes from these stories was the mask exercise. Mr. Grady had students read a portion of a novel and choose characters that were interesting to them. Each student would look for all the characteristics of the personality he or she chose as the writer described them, and then create a written composite of that person. After the details of the characters' lives and abilities were established, the students were encouraged to create masks with papier-mâché. The art teacher was enlisted to provide materials and support while the students constructed their masks and later decorated them to show the outstanding personality traits that the novel described for their characters' lives. This activity led to scenes between characters in mask, an extensive writing response to the work of creating the masks, and then writing as if the students were the characters themselves. All of the performance products were videotaped by the students.

Lessons Learned

Multiple Ways of Knowing

There are many ways of "knowing" and expressing our experience. Harste reminds us that different symbol systems used for communication among human beings represent ways we "make and share meaning."[16] It is this incentive to find various expressions and connect with the journey of human experience that guided Middle School students' efforts to "hear" the voice of characters. To challenge Mr. Grady's class, we needed to expand "ways of knowing" for both Mr. Grady and his students. Through drama, art, video production, and language communication, we encouraged the students to analyze written texts for more successful learning inside and outside the classroom.[17]

Mr. Grady began using different aspects of his training that formerly he had found neither time, interest, support, nor enthusiasm to use in the language arts classroom. For example, he was able to share a large jazz music collection with the students when they began to read literature that mentioned certain musicians. This music contributed to the atmosphere that Mr. Grady used to create an inviting classroom where the urban students felt welcomed and appreciated. He also demonstrated his fondness for acting

when he dramatized characters and explained the ways in which he identified with certain stories that he read in class. Mr. Grady began writing every morning before the class began, and was able to tell students about his struggle with certain aspects of his creativity as the semester progressed. He found himself being challenged to commit his imagination and emotion to the creation of characters. Mr. Grady also displayed his artistic taste when he decided to bring in a sofa and carpet to recreate the classroom. I imagine that the students felt their teacher had suddenly become more "human," less an authority figure and more a "club" member who supported children's learning in the way that a club woman would do. By bringing his sincere interest in writing, acting, video production and reading to the task of teaching urban students, Mr. Grady enhanced his potential for success as a teacher.

Realizing the Urban Reform Agenda

Clearly, the expectations in relation to the students and teachers in Middle School's classrooms that the UACC urban reform agenda had primed me to have were realized in this drama/writing workshop. It was no accident that some male students, mostly black, began to participate in the project. Before the UACC they may have felt invisible in the classroom with their white teacher, Mr. Grady. They may have had a similar experience to the graduate students who described themselves as "noises in the attic" within the white academic environment of higher education.[18] Or, the urban students might have identified with Carter Woodson's description of the "mis-education of the Negro" and what it was like to feel ill-fitted as a black person in a Eurocentric culture.[19]

The drama/writing project ensured that all the students were invited to bring their experiences and creativity to the language arts classroom. In Mr. Grady's class, they participated as artists of equal status. This urban classroom valued the students' culture and used their experiences as a bridge to new knowledge through the use of their home community's languages and experiences.[20] The use of each student's home language in describing and performing the characters in the readings created space for the different cultures to co-exist in Middle School.

Critical thinking was also a necessary part of the journey to performing the characters. The students had to ask questions of the writer, the story, themselves, and their classmates in order to construct realistic personae for their dramatic improvisations and literary products. Individual learners showed their life experiences and needs as students, which allowed Mr. Grady, and myself, to learn more about students and to respond on a more personal basis to them as artists. A family atmosphere developed in the classroom as a result of the kind of listening students did for performances created around literary characters. Quiet students found ways to show their emotional life, and outgoing students developed ways to use words to help them paint their intimate realities. Previously retiring students found voices to communicate through their contributions as designers of sets, rehearsal directors, or video-camera operators. A climate based on mutual respect for each other's work became the norm in the writing workshop.

More important for the student participants and for Mr. Grady, high expectations of performances in the drama/writing workshop became the natural order of business. These changes were captured in our videotapes of the classes when students performed their written creations. The video presentations allowed the students, Mr. Grady, and myself to appreciate the growth of students in the many dimensions that the drama/writing workshop facilitated. The students had evolved in their willingness and ability to be physically involved in character representations and more com-

fortable with the idea of sharing their life experiences through the writing and performance of their creations.

The drama/writing workshop made it possible for this University Fellow to find a practical way to put the UACC urban reform agenda to work. As a modern-day club woman and artist/researcher, I fortunately found it impossible to avoid the call for social uplift at Middle School. I was compelled to be a community organizer on behalf of the least well-served children, and to enlist Mr. Grady in the effort to make success possible for all his charges. More importantly, we were both motivated to take action in the language arts classroom, and to implement teaching methods that would improve chances of success among the least well-served African-American students. In the service of the legacy of the club women, we achieved many of the marching orders Dr. Delpit gave us to assure the improvement of the education of the children. By introducing a kinesthetic approach to teaching the urban middle-school students,[21] I encouraged Mr. Grady to find ways to ensure that his students could creatively demonstrate their understanding of life.

CONCLUSION

Teachers who embrace multiple ways of knowing and encourage students to participate in activities leading to new ways of communicating develop a philosophy of teaching that informs all their experiences. Consequently, the ten factors that Delpit advances to promote successful classrooms for urban children become a challenge that teachers can meet effectively. By encouraging this kind of pedagogy, the artist/researcher creates a space where positive attitudes facilitate creative learning.

This article represents the concerted effort to review the plans, methods and successes that resulted when Mr. Grady and I developed a common "language" to facilitate the arts-based pedagogy in the middle-school urban classroom. Students video-taped doing their dramatic scenes demonstrated their understanding of the steps that led them to identify with and perform their characters using the text from novels or their original scripts. The individual performances videotaped so that the students and Mr. Grady could review and appreciate the work. Mr. Grady was pleased enough with the student work to show an excerpt of the videotape with students in masks to his graduate colleagues at the university where he was studying literacy methods for middle school. Mr. Grady also wrote a term paper, and later presented a workshop for teachers, based on his research on kinesthetic learning principles and the need for students to be physically engaged in what they study in classrooms.

Throughout this country's history, most blacks have lived near or below the poverty line,[22] and this disadvantage is exacerbated by other factors in the educational environment of black children. We must, therefore, salute the success of any classroom initiative that increases the learning potential of the least well-served students in our urban schools. Since most black children live with a single parent, usually a mother, it is imperative to provide schooling that will enhance the children's chances of overcoming the effects of straitened economic and social circumstances. Also, the students must have positive role models who are black, female, and literate. As the artist/researcher working with Mr. Grady, I was able to provide this example.

As a researcher/teacher/artist, I claim my heritage from the order of black women community workers who include Mary McLeod Bethune, Frances Ellen Watkins Harper, Fannie Barrier Williams, Anna Julia Cooper, Fannie Jackson Coppin, Sarah J. Early, and Hallie Q. Brown.[23] The acknowledgement of my ancestors as I worked with Mr. Grady and his students as a University Fellow in the Urban Coalition

Compact ensured my alertness to opportunities to create successful experiences in that eighth-grade urban classroom. I became aware of the importance of my role as "inspector," and determined to play that role well. I am glad that I adopted this title for myself after realizing that my arrival at Middle School was a signal to the staff and teachers of the school that those children least well-served were my wards. It is equally important to me that, as a club woman, that I grew in knowledge about how I could facilitate reform in an urban middle school. It was a revolutionary experience for me, for Mr. Grady, and for his students when we held hands as collaborators. This experience is a testimony to the improvements that a few committed people can make in the service of African-American students.

NOTES

1. Perkins, L. (1980). Black women and the philosophy of "race uplift" prior to emancipation. Working paper, National Institute of Education (ED). Washington: ERIC Document Reproduction Service No. ED 221 444.

2. Cooper, A. (1892). *A voice from the South.* Xenia, Ohio: Aldine Printing House.

3. Batker, C. (1998). Love me like I like to be: The sexual politics of Hurston's *Their eyes were watching God;* the classic blues, and the black women's club movement. *African American Review, 32* (2), pp. 199–213.

4. Giddings, P. (1984). *When and where I enter: The impact of black women on race and sex in America.* New York: Bantam Books.

5. Lerner, G. (Ed.). (1973). *Black women in white America: A documentary history.* New York: Random House.

6. Higginbotham, E. (1993). *Righteous discontent: The women's movement in the black Baptist church: 1880–1920,* p. 206. Cambridge, MA: Harvard University Press.

7. Higginbotham (1993), p. 208.

8. Obidah, J. (1999). First-year documentation and evaluation report of the Urban Atlanta Coalition Compact. Atlanta: Georgia State University, Alonzo A. Crim Center for Educational Excellence.

9. Dowdy, J. (2002). Ovuh Dyuh. In L. Delpit & J. Dowdy (Eds.), *The skin that we speak: Thoughts on language and culture in the classroom*, pp. 3–14. New York: The New Press.

10. Delpit, L. (1995). *Other people's children: Cultural conflict in the classroom*. New York: New Press.

11. Meyers, B., Dowdy, J. & Paterson, P. (2000). Finding the missing voices: Perspectives of the least visible families and their willingness and capacity for school involvement. *Current Issues in Middle Level Education, 7* (2), pp. 59–79.

12. (1999–2000). Georgia Public Education Report Card.

13. Dowdy, J. (1999). Becoming the poem: How poetry can facilitate working across differences in a classroom. *The Change Agent. Adult Education for Social Justice: News, Issues, and Ideas*. New England, MA: Literacy Resource Center.

14. Lederer, H. (1981). The play's the thing: The use of theater in language teaching. *Studies in Language Learning, 3*, pp. 35–41.

15. King, N. (1981). From literature to drama to life. In N. McCaslin (Ed.), *Children and Drama*, pp. 164–177. New York: Longman Inc.

16. Harste, J. (1994). Visions of literacy. *Indiana Media Journal, 17* (1), pp. 27–32.

17. Short, K., Harste, J. & Burke, C. (1996). *Creating classrooms for authors and inquirers*. Portsmouth, NH: Heineman.

18. Dowdy, J., Givens, G., Murillo Jr., E., Shenoy, D. & Villenas, S. (2000). Noises in the attic: The legacy of expectations in the academy. *International Journal of Qualitative Studies in Education 13* (5), pp. 429–446.

19. Woodson, C. (1994). *The mis-education of the negro*. Newport News, Virginia: United Brothers and Sisters Graphics and Printing.

20. Delpit, L. (2002). No kinda sense. In L. Delpit & J. Dowdy (Eds.), *The skin that we speak: Thoughts on language and culture in the classroom*, pp. 31–48. New York: The New Press; Baker, J. (2002). Trilingualism. In L. Delpit & J. Dowdy (Eds.), *The skin that we speak: Thoughts on language and culture in the classroom*, pp. 49–62. New York: The New Press.

21. Gardner, H. (1983). *Frames of Mind*. New York: Basic Books; Barbe, W. & Milone, M. (1980, January). Modality. *Instructor*, pp. 44–49; Reiff, J. (1992). *Learning styles: What research says to the teacher*. Washington: National Education Association.

22. Farley, R. (1997). Racial trends and differences in the United States 30 years after the civil rights decade. *Social Science Research 26*, pp. 235–262.

23. Robinson, L. France Ellen Watkins Harper. Retrieved from http://www.africana.com/Articles/tt_289.htm.

AESTHETICS AND URBAN EDUCATION: URBAN LEARNERS' AFFIRMATION AND TRANSFORMATION THROUGH ARTS AND HUMAN DEVELOPMENT EDUCATION

Kent Seidel with Imelda Castañeda-Emenaker

The purpose of art is to lay bare the questions that have been concealed by the answers.

—*James Baldwin, author*

The term "aesthetic" is most commonly associated with the discussion of beauty, often related to the meaning and value of an artistic effort. The word comes from the ancient Greek meaning "sense perception" and "to perceive." We will use the term "aesthetics" instead of arts, humanities, or liberal arts because our discussion will address several dimensions of aesthetic perception in education and urban communities. We will (1) address the current status of the arts in education and the community; (2) look at some of the theories underlying the transformative potential of the arts and aesthetic experience; and (3) discuss ways in which the arts and humanities can transform both education and community so that both are more successful.

In the deepest sense, we suggest that the arts and humanities can work together with education to alter how urban communities are perceived by their residents, neighbors, and visitors. Urban centers are too often viewed through a lens of deficits, focusing on high poverty, decay, and the migration of the wealthier, predominately white population to the suburban fringes. Yet urban areas remain our centers of civilization, with great resources to counter the deficits. An aesthetic focus has the potential to change perceptions of our urban core, in ways more profound than merely improving appearance with well-placed art, although that is a part of it.

Echoing the sentiments about urban settings, the arts have most frequently been brought to education to address deficits–to reach students that are outside the mainstream; to validate "other," minority cultures and help "at-risk" students find a place in school; to provide alternatives for learning "core subjects" to students who do not learn well via "traditional" approaches. Research provides evidence that the arts *are* effective in doing these things, even where deficit thinking was the motivator. Why, then, are we not educating all students with the arts, especially in our "at-risk, high-need" urban communities? We suggest that the arts are most effective when they truly transform the teaching and learning process, giving both voice and perceptive insight to all members of the learning community. This is a difficult transformation, however, and one that tends to unsettle the status quo.

Some scholars (e.g., Goodwin, Hilliard, Ladson-Billings) suggest that things will not change educationally for at-risk youth until we look at our own beliefs about and choices of interaction with these children. The same may be true for our urban communities, and we offer a theoretical line of reasoning for thinking transformationally about urban communities and education–using the arts and humanities not to fix what is wrong, but to embrace what can be right. It is a subtle, but incredibly important, difference in perception.

THE ARTS IN EDUCATION AND THE COMMUNITY

There is nothing worse than a sharp image of a fuzzy concept.

—Ansel Adams, photographer

In recent decades, arts advocates have been vocal regarding the importance of the arts as an integral, substantive part of the education of every individual. Although the research has many challenges ahead, there is strong evidence of the value of education that incorporates a strong arts element. Such education may occur in a traditional public school, or it may take place less formally within a healthy learning community. We also encourage the reader to consider a broad spectrum of artistic endeavors—not only classical traditions in dance, literature, music, theatre, and visual arts, but also arts rooted in folk, family, street and community which have not yet found their way into the established academy; not just museums, symphonies, and theatres, but any community collective committed to creative effort.

Each of the arts education examples highlighted in this chapter emphasizes a strong community connection as central to its success. This brings to the fore a concern, however: if the arts are to have a positive impact on our schools and communities, they must be present in our schools and communities. In reviewing the research, one finds many assertions that the arts are disproportionately leaving urban areas. Fortunately, a close look at the evidence suggests hope.

AESTHETIC OPPORTUNITIES: WEAK, POLARIZED, BUT POSSIBLE

Most schools still offer some music and visual arts instruction, and urban centers still boast a plethora of diverse arts opportunities, even if these are often burdened by resource limitations. The 1999 National Center for Education Statistics survey of U.S. public schools found that nearly all elementary schools (94 percent nationally, 96 percent in city locales, defined as "a large or mid-sized central city of a Metropolitan Statistical Area")[1] offer music instruction, and 87 percent offer visual arts (85 percent in cities). Fewer offered dance (20 percent, 23 percent in cities) or theatre (19 percent, 22 percent in cities).[2] At the secondary level, 90 percent of schools offered music (same for cities) and 93 percent (96 percent cities) offered visual arts instruction. Again, dance and theatre lag behind, with dance in 14 percent of schools nationally (but in 22 percent of city schools) and theatre offered in 48 percent of schools (50 percent of city schools).[3] There is a discrepancy for schools with a high percentage of students in poverty (75 percent or more qualified for free or reduced-price lunches), but it is fairly negligible with the exception of elementary music (88 percent offering instruction, vs. 94 percent nationally); elementary visual arts (79 percent vs. 87 percent); and secondary level visual arts (85 percent vs. 93 percent) and theatre (36 percent vs. 48 percent).

The true difference in arts instruction for many urban schools, which tend to have a higher percentage of poor and minority student populations, is in the *quality* of instruction and in the students' individual likelihood of participation in the arts that are offered. The report finds that elementary schools with the lowest minority enrollments and schools with the lowest poverty concentration were more likely to have dedicated rooms, special equipment, district curriculum guides for music and visual arts, and input from arts specialists on staff hiring, curriculum, and allocation of arts funds.[4] At the secondary level, schools with the lowest minority enrollments and schools with the lowest poverty concentration were much more likely to receive outside funding for music programs, to have two or more full-time visual arts teachers, and to have a dedicated space with special equipment for visual arts.[5] Combine these differences with the likelihood that students must have time, support, and resources for after- or before-school arts participation, and that they must stay in school to participate, and it is not surprising that arts education is becoming more polarized.

This polarization is not trivial if one considers creative expression, education, and the participation in community that attends these endeavors to be important human rights. The 1997 National Assessment of Educational Progress found evidence of polarization among groups of students as well, with "white and Asian students" attaining higher average scores than "black or Hispanic students."[6]

The NAEP study also found that higher levels of parental education were associated with higher levels of student performance for music, visual arts, and theatre. Education levels are also directly associated with adult participation in the arts. According to the National Endowment for the Arts,[7] there is a significant difference and direct correlation between level of education and arts participation and attendance. The differences are not as extreme overall for income level differences, however, except for the lowest income bracket and for certain art forms.

The polarization that we see among populations that are privileged and educated and those who are less so creates a difficult dichotomy for our urban centers in particular. The majority of large arts and humanities institutions are in urban sites. Museums are natural partners for education, with 88 percent providing K-12 educational programming, usually based on local and state curriculum standards.[8] There are only 75 dance companies with annual budgets of $1 million or more, but all are in major urban centers. Cities also have numerous community and "fringe" venues. Chicago, for example, has "at least 258 dance-making entities," and Washington, DC has 186 dance-making entities, predominately "culturally-specific" (41 percent) or modern dance (30 percent) in nature.[9]

Unfortunately there is often a disconnection, or at best a lack of mutual awareness, among these resources. As we discuss later, these entities participate in different aesthetic communities, so a disconnect is not surprising. However, if urban communities hope to tap the power of aesthetics in education and renewal, the trend data indicate that their many arts, community, and school entities must connect. This connection is perhaps the only commonality among every arts education success story that we have found in urban settings.

HUMANIZING OUR CENTERS OF CIVILIZATION

All our knowledge has its origins in our perceptions.

—*Leonardo da Vinci*

In this section we discuss cognitive aspects of creativity and the role of education in our society, considering each with regard to the relationship of the individual with the community. The interaction of creativity and education, and the power of expression that they can give to members of the learning community (both in-school and at-large), are an important concept underlying why the arts can be so effective in transforming lives and schools. The connection of creativity, education, and community is particularly crucial for our

urban areas, as these places have the diversity, human concentration, and variety of resources to succeed as strong centers of healthy civilization.

CREATIVITY AND THE ACADEMY

Mihalyi Csikszentmihalyi, arguably the leading scholar on creativity, notes that very little separates humans from other animals. One finds in the animal kingdom communication, communities and social structures, divisions of labor, nurturing families, ability to learn, and tool use. What one does not find, at least so far, is the ability to create a long-term record of these things, and to build upon them over time. It is this ability to pass knowledge and skills from one to another and from generation to generation which produces what Csikszentmihalyi calls "big-C creativity," as well as education, the arts, and historical record. "Big-C creativity" refers to artistic and scientific efforts that build upon prior knowledge to advance the field, as opposed to the personal, "small-C creative" activities that we may pursue to enrich our lives–painting a picture, decorating a house, and the like.

Creativity (and, we will argue, artistic expressions of creativity in particular) and education are inextricable, and both rely on their interaction with a community of peers to flourish. For clarity, we will call this aesthetic community of peers the "academy."

Creativity . . . is a process by which a symbolic domain in the culture is changed. New songs, new ideas, new machines are what creativity is about. But because these changes do not happen automatically as in biological evolution, it is necessary to consider the price we must pay for creativity to occur. It takes effort to change traditions. For example, a musician must learn the musical tradition, the notation system, the way instruments are played before she can think of writing a new song; before an inventor can improve on airplane design he has to learn physics, aerodynamics, and why birds don't fall out of the sky.[10]

The individual learns from the traditions of the past and from those around her; her work is reviewed by her colleagues in the academy; that which is deemed worthy of attention will move beyond the academy to gain societal value and acceptance and, in so doing, will become part of the record for future creators. This reiterative process engages individuals with many communities, present, past, and future. It can be argued that no creative or aesthetic progress can ever be made without these communities, and the interaction requires education, whether formal or informal. Even the most radical and rebellious work gains some part of its identity from the community and preceding bodies of work. Note, too, that the process of working with an academy of creative peers is similar regardless of the aesthetic endeavor. What varies is the relationship of the various academies with society at large and with each other. An example from music: there is a formal classical tradition that may come to mind immediately as "The Academy"—an entire system resulting in orchestras, operas and symphonies, and traditional music education. But one also finds an academy of aesthetic peers among street rappers, church choirs, and coffee-shop musicians. Hip-hop and rap are an example of an academy that has radically changed in its recognition by society.

In recent decades, the field of education has attempted to define the disciplinary traditions that will provide the best educational background for our youth. Standards for "what every child should know and be able to do" have been created for nearly every subject taught in the schools, including the arts. Discussion of these standards is beyond the purview of this chapter; but the notion of a discipline of learning shaped by an academy, and traditions that will ground students in cognitive representations of the world, is important. Howard Gardner identifies a shift in thinking about thinking that is certainly key to educators:

The key notion of the cognitive revolution is "mental representation." Cognitive psychologists believe that individuals have ideas, images, and various "languages" in their mind-brain; these representations are real and important, and are susceptible to study by scientists and to change by educators. . . .

The simple shift to representations brought about a revolution in thinking about the two earlier strands of psychology. No longer did one focus simply on behaviors. Indeed, one might almost think of behaviors as being epiphenomena (that is, as being the shadows of our determining mental representations).[11]

Echoing the broadest sense of the aesthetic, Gardner equates these mental representations of the world to disciplines of study, lenses that shape how one interprets the world and how one creates new knowledge. He suggests the importance of teaching students to think like a scientist, an artist, an historian—in other words, to master the skills, knowledge, and traditions of thought that will provide learners with access to the academy, which will in turn provide them with the ability to create.

The discipline traditions focus attention in particular ways, and attention is the key to both creativity and education, according to Csikszentmihalyi. "If we want to learn anything we must pay attention to the information to be learned. And attention is a limited resource."[12] Attention provides both impetus and possibility for the creative effort to succeed. We can process only so much information at any given time, and our cognitive processes have evolved to provide us with remarkable capacity for "chunking" and organizing information in contextual ways.[13] The disciplines help with this. One might argue that the ability to focus attention is the essential core skill of education.

If creativity and education make us unique as humans, then creative expression and education—the connection to the communities of the past, present, and future—are not a privilege or a frill, but a most basic human right. The arts and humanities in particular are records of cultures and of individuals within those cultures. Just as "history belongs to the winners," so cultures and individuals become important or marginalized as their aesthetic voice is included or excluded from society's "attentional record." Selection of the curriculum and the inclusion or exclusion of the voices attended to (or not) by the school will in turn affect the attention of the community and the status of the many creative academies within society at large. The arts can transform education not because they "reach" a student and assimilate him or her into the majority culture, but because they *connect* students (and adults) to the knowledge and traditions of the larger community in a way that also encourages participation and expression of individual voices.

SEEING WITH INTELLIGENT EYES, HEARING ABSENT VOICES

Education is the ability to listen to almost anything without losing your temper or your self-confidence.

—Robert Frost

Urban communities are diverse communities, and to be healthy they must find ways to embrace that diversity as a strength. The arts have great potential to foster the interaction of the individual and the group. They educate by giving voice to the individual while respecting and embracing diversity of expression and ideas. By learning to bring both experience and reflection to our seeing, we can honor community as well as the creations of other cultures.

The Intelligent Eye: Understanding "Other"

The arts and humanities are a way for educators to reach students different from themselves, and can bring communities together by fostering understanding of multiple cultures. One cannot become the "other," but one can gain a reasonably good—and respectful—understanding of

the other by learning to see reflectively through the arts. David Perkins puts it this way:

Experiential intelligence . . . specializes in the quick take. It thrives on the expected. It honors the predictable over the adventurous, and the simple over the subtle. . . . Reflective intelligence refers to the knowledge, skills, and attitudes that contribute to mental self-management. . . . At the broadest level, this controlling role of reflective intelligence can be viewed as a matter of dispositions—to give looking time, to look broadly and adventurously, to look clearly and deeply, and to look in an organized fashion.[14]

To foster community, we must move from defining others using experiential intelligence, to understanding others—and ourselves—using reflective intelligence. Aesthetic artifacts are an effective subject for reflective intelligence. The artistic record of an individual and, collectively, of a culture, lend incredible insight into history, beliefs, values, and present and future potential. Reflective seeing also encourages us to define ourselves as individuals, instead of defining ourselves through rejection of others who do not, experientially, seem like us. Stereotypes come from the "quick take" of experiential intelligence, using a pattern of assumptions about culture and group to simplistically classify individuals. Aesthetic activities can teach us to think beyond the quick take of cultural background, as Maxine Greene describes:

Cultural background surely plays a part in shaping identity; but it does not determine identity. It may well create differences that must be honored; it may occasion styles and orientations that must be understood; it may give rise to tastes, values, even prejudices that must be taken into account.[15]

Finding Voice

For both education and community transformation, the aesthetic affirmation of the individual voice may be the most effective way to ensure participation in the learning community. For many students, participation in the group is more or less assured. They are not absent from the status quo or the expectations of student achievement. Even if they do not value education or school, they understand that by participating they will be better suited to take their place in a community that they already "own." Marginalized students are a different story. They must see the real possibility of reward from education by seeing how their voices contribute to society. This is the territory, unsettling to some, to which the transformational aesthetic takes us. By noticing the previously silent, we affirm the potential of the individual to be a force in the creative academy, and to change the academy's relationship with society's attentional record. This is a way to have a voice that might actually be heard. Maxine Greene again:

To help the diverse students we know articulate their stories is not only to help them pursue the meanings of their lives—to find out *how* things are happening and to keep posing questions about the why. It is to move them to learn the new things, to reach out for the proficiencies and capacities, the craft required to be fully participant in this society, and to do so without losing the consciousness of who they are.[16]

This is not merely an issue of motivating students by somehow connecting the curriculum with their life experiences; this is about offering them the real possibility of reward from education by helping them to see how their voices exist within, and contribute to, society. Our students' voices can either be implied by their absence, or included as valuable contributors to our definitions of student achievement.

The reiterative process of artistic creation, "big-C Creativity" and its interplay with academies and society, when considered with the concept of reflective intelligence, presents something of a paradox. Artistic efforts *must* be about the individual or individuals who create; they can be inspired by the "other," but cannot be "other." However, it is learning to see and understand the creative efforts of others that enables us each to

know something of substance about community members who are unlike us. In so doing, we all join the community.

To illustrate the individual's role in the aesthetic process, consider "protest theatre" such as that of Brecht, Boal, and recent South African artists. These artists focus on drawing attention to the creative work in order to cause those outside of it—the spectators, or "spect-actors," as Boal calls them—to question the status quo. They do not seek to arouse empathy, a sense of "belonging with" the actors, but rather a distancing that will foster introspection and analysis. These artists understand that their voice must always be interpreted by others through their own experiences. Here is Brecht instructing actors:

The actor must play the incidents as historical ones. Historical incidents are unique transitory incidents associated with particular periods. The conduct of the persons involved in them is not fixed and "universally human"; it includes elements that have been or may be overtaken by the course of history, and is subject to criticism from the immediately following period's point of view. The conduct of those born before us is alienated from us by an incessant evolution.[17]

Consciously bringing aesthetic voice to all members of the urban community has potential to help each member find and express his or her voice. As records of our sense perceptions, the arts and humanities allow ideas to take concrete form, providing an important artifact of the community's transformation and reminding individuals of their parts in it.

TRANSFORMING OUR PERCEPTIONS: THE AESTHETIC URBAN LEARNING COMMUNITY

Too much sanity may be madness. And maddest of all, to see life as it is and not as it should be!

—*Miguel de Cervantes*

In this section we look at the research record of the effects of arts education, and discuss how the aesthetic can, indeed must, move beyond the school walls to embrace and transform the community. In doing so, we define urban education broadly to mean the education of all members of the urban community. As school entities, we are almost uniquely suited to the task of mitigating the "mass-market" forces of policy—those that are concerned about preparing workers, maintaining current rules, reinforcing historical power structures. We are in a unique position to help our students and community members engage in learning and creating. Of all pursuits, the arts and humanities may lend themselves best to lifelong learning. They are able to include adults and youth on equal footing, learning and doing side-by-side.

Urban communities are often faced with challenging educational tasks, possessing disproportionate numbers of disadvantaged students, greater extremes of poverty, and greater strains on available resources than their suburban counterparts. We noted above that the arts have most frequently been incorporated to address such problems. Consider that of 62 studies summarized in the *Critical Links* report,[18] nearly all that address inner-city study sites and/or urban issues do so from the perspective of using the arts to address learning or social problems in these settings. That the arts are effective in addressing problems within the schools is to be celebrated, but we urge mindfulness so that we do not limit our understanding of the aesthetic dimension of education to that of a prescription for student and school deficits.

Transforming Academic and Social Development

There is already much evidence of a definitive correlation, if not a proven causal connection, between arts participation and factors key to academic and social development. We do not feel it necessary to make a strong distinction between the two here. Should the arts be a causal factor in success

for young people, the implications are fairly obvious regarding the inclusion of arts for all students. But correlations as strong as those identified in numerous studies indicate that there is at least a relationship of privilege between the aesthetic dimension and success in life. It is this relationship that is relevant to our discussion, and it is a relationship surely worth further study.

Time and again, research shows a strong correlation between academic success and arts participation, especially in the areas of mathematics and language. For example, math, verbal, and composite SAT scores are strongly correlated with increased participation in arts classes.[19] A comparative study of thousands of students in the National Educational Longitudinal Survey (NELS) showed that students (in general and those in low socio-economic status subgroups) with consistent high levels of involvement in music in middle- and high-school years had significantly higher levels of mathematics proficiency by grade 12. In addition, sustained involvement in theatre was associated with gains in reading proficiency, self concept and motivation, and higher levels of empathy and tolerance for others.[20] Although it may be hypothesized that students with strong verbal and math skills tend to self-select into arts classes, there are independent studies that support causal links between theatre and music in particular and learning verbal and mathematics skills, respectively.[21] Certain social and developmental benefits are found consistently in the research as well. For example, a case study project involving 2,269 11th-year students found that arts classes resulted in enjoyment, learning about social and cultural issues, development of creativity and thinking skills, enriched expressive skills, self confidence, and social development.[22] These types of benefits appear throughout the literature.

Many artists and educators cite the open-ended, risk-taking nature of the arts as key to developing students' personal and academic abilities. Veteran arts educator Jessica Hoffman Davis discusses the value of failure:

Arts encounters with mistake making, with facing and building on what's wrong, have tremendous implications for learning in other disciplines. But they are uniquely accessed in the safety of arts classrooms where, perhaps ironically, risk taking and failure may fruitfully abound. Safe from the hard edges of right and wrong answers, safe from agendas that exclude multiple perspectives, safe from assessments that are sure of themselves, arts classrooms provide opportunities for students to explore the messy uncertain realities that preoccupy their lived lives within and beyond the world of school.[23]

Such perspectives on engaging the world and learning are consistent with research on creativity and cognitive science.

Transforming Teaching and Learning

Inclusion of the arts and humanities in substantive ways puts students and teachers into interactive roles different from what one might expect to find in the traditional American classroom. These interactions lead to the transformation of the teaching and learning process, which seems to be essential for the benefits to students to reliably occur. Some examples of these noted changes in practice include:

- Being more student-focused, with teachers acting as coaches and facilitators of learning[24]
- Expanded teaching strategies, emphasizing risk taking, revision, and improvement; and inquiry-based and hands-on approaches that let students engage problems and test their own solutions[25]
- Finding options for assessing students progress and gaining new insights into student learning that teachers may otherwise have overlooked[26]
- More collaboration among teachers, and by teachers with the community and community arts resources[27]
- Valuing young people and placing them in positions of high expectation and responsibility in collaboration with adults[28]

The transformation of the relationship between learner and teacher cannot be emphasized strongly enough. Not only does it change the way a student works at learning, it provides life role models. In a study of 811 high school students, the proportion of minority students identifying a music teacher as a role model was significantly larger than for any other discipline—36 percent as opposed to 28 percent of English teachers, 11 percent of elementary teachers, 7 percent of physical education/sports teachers, and 1 percent of principals.[29]

Transforming the Connection of School to the World

There is also consistent evidence that the arts connect the educational effort to the "real world" and to the community in powerful ways. The *Champions of Change* report notes that "The arts experiences described in the research show remarkable consistency with the evolving workplace. Ideas are what matter, and the ability to generate ideas, to bring ideas to life and to communicate them is what matters to workplace success."[30] Evaluators of the "Transforming Education Through the Arts Challenge" found that teachers were exposed to, and learned to work with, a wide variety of community and arts resources.[31]

Transforming the Urban Site into an Aesthetic Learning Community

Artists and scholars suggest that a transformation can occur by giving the arts and humanities an active role in the education of all members of the urban community. According to Seana Lowe, several elements are needed for art to serve as an effective tool for community development, such as: (1) a "safe and fun" mood, coming together for the purpose of "artistic and community-building processes," and (2) "shared goals of community building and art."[32] The artist is a key catalyst, and Lowe compares the process to ritual:

Community art can affect personal and social transformation if utilized as a model for ritual interaction because of the combined influence of ritual and art. Ritual is a unique type of social interaction that serves as a context for possible change, and art uniquely inspires openings in imagination and need fulfillment.

Supported by the transformative influence of the artist's role, ritual has the capacity to recreate social frameworks by engaging human sentiment, and the symbols it produces can create social facts.[33]

In their introduction to the special issue of *Education and Urban Society* focusing on art education, Debra Holloway and Beth Krensky note that:

Transformative art education that provides students with opportunities to develop voice and make positive changes in their lives is rare, yet it does exist in schools and community centers in urban settings throughout the United States. . . . There are particular art education pedagogies that promote social responsibility, including community-based, feminist, moral/ethical, critical, and multicultural art education.[34]

It is interesting to note that the particular approaches cited by Holloway and Krensky have in common a conscious effort to make the voice of a marginalized academy heard within the larger society. The interplay of our creative academies is something of an intellectual evolution, but it does not need to be a competitive survival of the fittest. Unlike biological evolution, which may threaten the individual in service of the greater good of the species, creative evolution values and validates the individual voice. If we hope to make schools work for all children in our communities, we must move beyond the quick take to use our reflective intelligence to see each individual and his or her potential to contribute to the intellectual and creative evolution. This is an enormous challenge to each person in the community, but our urban centers in particular must rise to meet it. By including a true aesthetic dimension throughout our urban schools and communities, we will be better able to educate all our children effectively and strengthen our centers of civilization.

EXAMPLES OF PROJECTS THAT USE THE ARTS TO IMPROVE URBAN COMMUNITIES AND EDUCATION

Project ACE: Arts in Community Education—Milwaukee, Wisconsin

Arts in Community Education (ACE) brings learning through music into the classroom every day for Milwaukee children. The program integrates the arts with all subject areas in grades K–5, and supports school curricula in music and arts in grades 6–8. It serves more than 7,500 students and their parents. More than 400 teachers and professional musicians have been involved with the program. ACE was recognized by the Wisconsin Department of Public Instruction as a powerful enhancement of young people's education.[35]

CAPE: Chicago Arts Partnerships in Education—Illinois

The Chicago Arts Partnerships in Education brings together 37 schools, 53 professional arts organizations, and 27 community organizations. Evaluation indicated the value of the partnerships, demonstrated by the success of the collaboration of artists, schools, and the larger community. Six years into the project, teachers were fully integrating the arts into their subjects. Classroom and school climate improved, and students made significant gains in achievement as measured by Illinois standardized tests, the Iowa Test of Basic Skills, and subject and grade-level assessments. CAPE has been replicated across nine cities in the United States, Canada, and England.[36]

Art in the Market Project—Cincinnati, Ohio

Art in the Market is a partnership of the Community Design Center at the University of Cincinnati with two other organizations—the Citizen's Committee on Youth and Impact Over-the-Rhine—designed to serve at-risk youth aged 14–18 in Cincinnati's inner-city "Over-the-Rhine" community. Findlay Market, located in Over-the-Rhine, has been the site of Art in the Market projects since 1996. More than 200 youths have participated. The art products from the project are considered a welcome addition in the Over-the-Rhine community, and participants reported a greater willingness to work in their community. Representatives of the community, market vendors, the advisory council, parents, and the Art in the Market staff were all pleased with the results of the project.[37]

Pudding and Puppets: Using Accessible Art to Promote Family Literacy—Louisville, Kentucky

Using materials as varied as cookies with instant-pudding icing and paper bags transformed into puppets, arts educators from the Speed Museum work with recently arrived refugee children and their parents to promote family literacy. The emphasis is on having fun and finding simple, affordable ways to build literacy into everyday activities. The family literacy program of Catholic Charities Migration and Refugee Services serves multiple refugee communities, but most recently has welcomed a large number of Somali Bantu families. With little or no formal education experience and no English language skills, these parents face incredible challenges as they endeavor to support their children's schooling. Arts-based family literacy programs such as this partnership offer examples of the ways in which parents can encourage learning and the exploration of ideas. Other recent projects at the resettlement center have used photography and indigenous fiber arts to encourage self-expression and community involvement among recently arrived refugee families.

Rainier Vista Arts Program—Seattle, Washington

This year-round Arts Program for the young residents of the Rainier Vista public housing community is a partnership of the Seattle Housing Authority and the Chil-

dren's Museum of Seattle. The program focuses on the arts of specific cultures and brings in guest artists, actors, musicians, and dancers to instruct the children and develop exhibits and performances. The afterschool program offers hands-on experience in the visual, performing, and literary arts supplemented with field trips to museums, libraries, cultural institutions, galleries, and artists' studios. In the summer program, students are provided with breakfast and lunch and participate in discipline-specific classes. The program has been cited by the U.S. Department of Housing and Urban Development as a model for public housing communities.[38]

The 52nd Street Project—New York City

"The purpose of the 52nd Street Project is to give every child the experience of success through writing and performing his or her own plays. Economically disadvantaged children from the Hell's Kitchen neighborhood of New York City are paired with professional theater artists to create, mount, and perform original theater pieces. Workshops take place in local community centers and theaters, as well as out-of-town retreats. The 52nd Street Project has written a practical guide to teaching theater arts to children."[39]

The Partnership for Arts, Culture, and Education—Dallas, Texas

The Partnership for Arts, Culture, and Education (PACE) brings more than fifty arts and cultural organizations together to facilitate arts and cultural programming for students. In a four-year assessment project, PACE found that integrating community-based arts and cultural enrichment into the core curriculum improved student achievement. Their study found significant differences in academic achievement in language arts as measured by standardized state-mandated tests. Teachers collaborated to align core subjects through thematic units that served as the basis for selecting community arts experiences for the students.[40]

NOTES

1. U.S. Department of Education, National Center for Education Statistics (NCES). *Elementary School Arts Education Survey: Fall 1999*, p. A-14. Washington, DC: U.S. Government Printing Office.

2. U.S. Department of Education, NCES (1999).

3. U.S. Department of Education, NCES (1999).

4. U.S. Department of Education, NCES (1999), p. 89.

5. U.S. Department of Education, NCES (1999), p. 89.

6. U.S. Department of Education, Office of Educational Research and Improvement. (1999). The *NAEP 1997 arts report card*, p. 142. Washington, DC: U.S. Government Printing Office.

7. Nichols, B. (2003). *Demographic characteristics of arts attendance, 2002*. Research Division Note #82. Washington, DC: National Endowment for the Arts.

8. American Association of Museums. (2003). *Museums working in the public interest*. Retrieved December 10, 2004, from http://www.aam-us.org/resources/general/publicinterest.cfm.

9. DanceUSA. (2004). *Facts and Figures*. Retrieved November 12, 2004, from http://www.danceusa.org.

10. Csikszentmihalyi, M. (1996). *Creativity: Flow and the psychology of discovery and invention*, p. 8. New York: HarperCollins.

11. Gardner, H. (1999). *The disciplined mind: What all students should understand*, p. 67. New York: Simon & Schuster.

12. Csikszentmihalyi, *Creativity: flow and the psychology of discovery and invention*, p. 8.

13. Bransford, J., Brown, A., & Cocking, R. (Eds.), (2000). *How people learn: Brain, mind, experience, and school (Expanded Edition)*. Washington, DC: National Academy Press.

14. Perkins, D. (1994). *The intelligent eye: Learning to think by looking at art*, p. 82. Santa Monica, CA: The J. Paul Getty Trust.

15. Greene, M. (1995). *Releasing the imagination: Essays on education, the arts, and social change*, p. 163. San Francisco: Jossey-Bass.

16. Greene (1995), p. 5.

17. Brecht, B. (1967). A short description of a new technique of acting which produces an alienation effect. In S. Clayes (Ed.), *Drama and Discussion*, p. 322. New York: Meredith Publishing Co.

18. Deasy, R. (Ed.). (2002). *Critical links. Learning in the arts and student academic and social development*. Washington, DC: Arts Education Partnership.

19. Deasy (2002), p. 96.

20. Catterall, J., Chapleau, R., & Iwanaga, J. (1999). Involvement in the arts and human development: General involvement and intensive involvement in music and theater arts, p. 2. In E. Fiske (Ed.), (1999). *Champions of change: The impact of arts on learning*. Washington, DC: Arts Education Partnership and the President's Committee on the Arts and Humanities.

21. Kase-Polisini, J. (Ed.). (1985). *Creative drama in a developmental context*. New York: University Press of America; Deasy (2002); Fiske (1999); Podlozny (2000). Strengthening verbal skills through the use of classroom drama: A clear link, pp. 239–276. *The Journal of Aesthetic Education*, 34 (3–4); Welch, N. (Ed.). (1995). *Schools, communities, and the arts: A research compendium*. Washington: National Endowment for the Arts.

22. Deasy (2002), p. 76.

23. Davis, J. (2003, October 8). In defense of failure. *Education Week*.

24. Horowitz, R. (2004). *Summary of large-scale arts partnership evaluations*, p. 22. Washington: Arts Education Partnership.

25. Horowitz (2004), pp. 22–24; Seidel, K. (1995). *Leaders' theatre: A case study of how high school students develop leadership skills through participation in theatre*. Unpublished doctoral dissertation, University of Cincinnati, OH; Fiske (1999), pp. ix–x.

26. Horowitz (2004); Weitz, J. (1996). *Coming up taller: Arts and humanities programs for children and youth at risk*. Washington: President's Committee on the Arts and Humanities.

27. Horowitz (2004), pp. 23–24; Seidel (1995); Fiske (1999); Castañeda, I., & Zorn, D. (2001). *AAAE Arts Connections longitudinal study: A technical report*. Cincinnati, OH: University of Cincinnati Evaluation Services Center.

28. Seidel (1995); Fiske (1999); Weitz (1996); McLaughlin, M. (2001). Community counts. *Educational Leadership*, 58 (7), pp. 14–18.

29. Hamann, D., & Walker, L. (1993). Music teachers as role models for African American students. *Journal of Research in Music Education*, 41.

30. Fiske (1999), p. x.

31. Killeen, D., Frechtling, J., & Perone, D. (2002). *Transforming education through the arts challenge, final evaluation report.* Columbus, OH: The National Arts Education Consortium, Ohio State University. Available online at http://www.aep-arts.org.

32. Lowe, S. (2001). The art of community transformation. *Education and Urban Society, 33* (4), p. 468.

33. Lewis, A. (1980). The ritual process and community development. *Community Development Journal, 15* (3).

34. Holloway, D., & Krensky, B. (Eds.), (2001). The arts, urban education, and social change, p. 359. *Education and Urban Society, 33* (4).

35. Milwaukee Symphony, Education programs. (2004). Retrieved from http://www.milwaukeesymphony.org.

36. Catterall, J., & Waldorf, L. Chicago arts partnership in education: Summary evaluation. In Fiske (1999), pp. 38–62

37. *Evaluation reports on the Art in the Market Project prepared for the community design center.* (2000, 2001, 2002, 2003). Cincinnati, OH: University of Cincinnati Evaluation Services Center.

38. Weitz (1996), p. 69.

39. Weitz (1996), p. 86.

40. Tunks, J. (1997). Evaluation Report: *The partnership assessment project: Changing the face of American education.* Dallas, TX: Partnership for Arts, Culture, and Education.

AESTHETIC CONSCIOUSNESS AND DANCE CURRICULUM: LIBERATION POSSIBILITIES FOR INNER-CITY SCHOOLS

Donald Blumenfeld-Jones

In this chapter I explore how teaching modern expressionist dance to inner-city school children might be part of a liberation educational practice. In the context of teaching the arts, "liberation" means: people developing an "aesthetic consciousness" which provides the ability to come to grips with the emotional and physical constituents of their realities in ways that allow them to more consciously experience those realities (which are often, in the midst of living them, opaque to understanding). Through such encounters they may be able to think of new ways to be in those realities that lead to a greater range of possible lives they might lead, lives that would not be merely a pursuit of individual happiness but understood as ensconced within a communal context of responsibility for each other. In the specific case of teaching dance, liberation could take place through students creating their own dances out of the material of their own lives as the vehicle for developing aesthetic consciousness.

I will explore this liberation possibility in a number of steps. First, I will develop the concept of "aesthetic consciousness" in real-world social contexts related to what it means to be a cultured person and a person with taste, developing an awareness of the relation between aesthetics, class, and race. Second, I will connect these ideas to identity politics, laying out the terrain of modern dance possibilities as species of identity politics. I will do this for one particular population, African-American children. Last, I will describe a project I enacted in an African-American public inner-city middle school in Durham, North Carolina. Through these steps I will try to show how a certain form of identity politics provides the possibility for what I term an "authenticating" aesthetic practice, in which lies the aforementioned experiential possibilities. While the specific focus is on an African-American inner-city project, I hope the reader will be able to read "outward" to other contexts by considering how the discussion resonates with her/his experience and/or thinking.

AESTHETICS, LIVING AESTHETICALLY, AND SOCIAL CLASS/RACE

I will begin by clarifying what I mean by "aesthetics." The word derives from the Greek and means "sense perception or sensation" and is, in philosophy, "the study of what is immediately pleasing to our visual or auditory perception or to our imagination" as well as "the study of the nature of beauty." More conventionally, it is usually associated with the arts and is the study of "taste and criticism in the creative and performing arts."[1] The basic aesthetics questions are "What is beauty?" and "What is imagination and how does it function?" and, for the arts, the subquestions are, for instance, "How do the arts deal with beauty?", "What is art?", and "What are the criteria for assessing the quality of a specific work of art?" The art questions, and their answers, are designed to help viewers of art understand art and for artists to ground their practices in an intelligible understanding of what they are trying to accomplish. The answers to these questions have, of course, varied over the centuries according to differing social and political contexts.[2]

The questions of beauty and sensation, however, are not restricted to the arts. For instance, the degree to which people attend to their likes and dislikes in personal style in the areas of clothing, housing, furnishings, food, and so on, and attend to ways of being with others,[3] to that extent they are concerned with beauty, sensation, and sensual awareness, and can be said to be "living aesthetically." Conventionally, people today make their aesthetic choices with a consumerist consciousness, connecting beauty and sensation with buying the right food, clothing, makeup, movies, music, books, and so forth, in order to feel as if they are living the beautiful life, leading to improving their chances at success in life. Such consumerism is not confined to any one social class. For each social class people are known by what they wear, where they live, what vehicle they drive, what kind of food they eat, what kind of entertainment they consume, and they establish public identities in terms of how particular goods bestow particular social status, connecting them to a particular community. In all of this, aesthetics is at work.

"Beauty," the fundamental aesthetic concern, informs the above-mentioned choices. When people choose to dress in a certain way, that choice is meant to convey beauty to others (and to make themselves feel beautiful as well), not in any conventional sense of "beauty" but in the sense that their particular community would see as "beautiful." However, people do not, generally, construe their choices for becoming beautiful with aesthetics. Rather, as I have already noted, they construe aesthetics and art to be synonymous. In this synonymity, art is not merely "art" but, is, rather, high art,[4] which represents real beauty and is part of what Raymond Williams termed the "selective tradition."[5] This "real art" is consumed by those who occupy the power centers of society, as they attend symphonies, the theater, museums, and so forth, filling their lives with socially sanctioned beauty. It is not necessarily the case that they always like "high art," but it is with "high art" that they are most associated. It is the wealthy who pay millions for a Van Gogh painting; who attend charity functions for the opera and symphony; who pay large sums to attend symphony, opera, and theatrical productions; and who attend museum and gallery openings. These individuals subscribe to the aesthetic of the selective tradition and have access to and, supposedly, appreciation for it. Such subscription sanctions them as cultured and, in turn, as natural wielders of social power. On the other side of culture is Gans's "popular culture" designation. This tacitly references people who value country-western music, television game shows, soap operas, MTV, hip-hop culture, rock and roll, and the like, and who purchase paintings of dogs playing cards, of bucolic fields, of clowns, and of doe-eyed children, and enjoy painted velvet paintings. Such people tend to be members of the middle and working classes. People who claim enjoyment of country-western music, television game shows, and so forth, do not identify their interests in these objects as an interest in "the arts," and they do not subscribe to the value of aesthetics in their lives, for while they may enjoy their own form of beauty, it is not beauty in the aesthetics sense. This tinges their interests with a distinctly déclassé flavor, even to them. The distinction between what is really art (really beautiful) and what is neither art nor beautiful is based on a class definition of art and beauty. Pierre Bourdieu's *Distinction*[6] explicitly laid out this terrain as he explored the different social classes' view of what it means to have "good taste" and ably showed the social structures that resulted in the working-class membership viewing itself as having no aesthetic taste but enjoying its lack since the "having of social taste" was onerous. Nevertheless, it should be understood, in my thinking, that the working class in that study and the working class, the working poor, and the lower middle class do not lack aesthetics but possess, rather, a certain view of the value and meaning of aesthetics cultivated throughout society such that their hegemonized consciousness labels their taste as invalid or illegitimate as they subscribe to the inferiority of their own taste. The selective tradition that performs this labeling is found in school rules and curricula, which maintain and nurture the high/low culture distinction and are used to distribute valued school goods (students who appreciate high art are more likely to receive better teaching and better curricula), which, in turn, are used to distribute social goods. The elite class, who most benefits from such thinking, and whose representatives (school administrators and faculty) administer this thinking, view popular culture as dangerous and in need of being eliminated from school experience. In this way, the selective tradition is not only the most valued tradition but, also, the only tradition of real value.

Getting more specific about the relation between aesthetic living, popular culture, and danger, African-American children who live in or around the official poverty line in urban settings clearly have very specific aesthetics in terms of clothing and music, which are obviously important to them (given the percentage of their income they spend on such things). This communal popular culture aesthetic has been seen by society outside their communities as representing social danger (although this "ghetto" culture has become increasingly popular with middle-class white youth, to the dismay and fear of their parents). The hip-hop aesthetic is exemplary of this and the ways in which schools deal with this culture informs us of the meanings ascribed to the aesthetic by those outside of it. Succinctly, the hip-hop aesthetic is associated, by the larger society, with criminality and with encouraging anti-authority attitudes and is seen to lack social propriety and the ability to help young people succeed in life. This translates, in schools, into the banning of baseball caps worn turned to the side and the banning of certain other clothing.

An excellent example of this occurred recently in a Scottsdale, Arizona, school where an outstanding African-American student, Marlon Morgan (nominated for Youth of the Year by his local Boys and Girls Club, longtime Boys and Girls Club volunteer, editor of the school newspaper sports section, and fine student), was arrested on campus for wearing his hat sideways after refusing an order by campus security guards to turn it forward and then refusing to go to the assistant principal's office. Marlon pointed out that other youths (white) were wearing their hats sideways and weren't being asked to change. He was subsequently jailed for disorderly conduct, insubordination to police, and trespassing (he was eating lunch in his school cafeteria), and was suspended from school for three days. When he protested his differential treatment, the school and district officials replied that wearing his hat in that way was a sign of disrespect for authority (he broke the school dress code) and of being a gangbanger. (This despite much evidence to the contrary.) The National Association for the Advancement of Colored People (NAACP) became involved and his mother protested, eventually getting his suspension shortened to one day. Then, at the end of the school year a picture appeared in the student newspaper with Marlon and another African-American student who was wearing his hat sideways. The school administration seized all the newspapers and ordered the newspaper staff (including Marlon, the incoming sports editor for 2004–05) to tear the picture out of all the copies. They would have done the same for the yearbook (from which the picture was taken) if it hadn't been too costly to produce new yearbooks.[7]

We may ask why the administration of the school was so adamant in its policy and why the policy existed in the first place. Clearly they had labeled an aesthetic choice "subversive and dangerous," and even though an upstanding citizen of their school was wearing the clothing, he was accused of potentially provoking violence and danger. Obviously the school administration and school district (which are beholden, through the governing board membership and the most powerful voices speaking out at board meetings, to the power elites in the community) believe in the power of an aesthetic to be resonant with a deep consciousness that pervades all actions. Marlon was seen to be potentially violent and dangerous even though he had never shown signs of such behavior. Thus, his community's aesthetic was banned from the school (even though others, wearing hats in the same fashion, were not harassed). Beyond this specific set of incidents, while school people continue to condemn the hip-hop aesthetic (the school has

maintained its dress code policies), they also fail to make "proper" aesthetics a central part of the curriculum. In the present environment of high-stakes testing, the arts are usually the first programs to be eliminated from schools. Aesthetics is clearly seen as a frill for inner-city children living in or near poverty, too rarified to be useful to people living in difficult economic, service-poor settings with lack of access to social resources. These children need to pass the basic academic testing program before money can be devoted to the arts in the schools. In short, the community's aesthetics are kept out of the school, but aesthetics of any kind is also not present in the curriculum.

In the face of these kinds of issues and arguments around aesthetics for inner-city children, how can we address developing an "aesthetic consciousness" in an urban setting? One obvious answer is to break down the barriers between the students' everyday lives and school life. In this case, allow hip-hop culture to be in the schools, acknowledging it as a legitimate form of aesthetic life. Use it as one base for developing art and art "appreciation." Open up the canon to critique. In these ways, the community's culture becomes the basis for curriculum rather than being adjunct or ignored. Another approach focuses not on popular culture but on using the making of art to explore the sensual aspects of life as markers of meaning in terms of how we are living our present lives. Rather than inculcate people with the knowledge of what is valued and what is not (a focus on high art), people make art in order to discover the life and beauty in their lives. Through such a mode of education, art might become critically useful and not just "a document of barbarity,"[8] institutionalizing the privilege of some on the backs of the massive others. Larger issues of life can be explored, which can, even, critique how art is bought and sold by those with the wealth and power. My task is, now, to develop this reasoning for liberation education through a more concrete and detailed discussion of, first, the relation between identity politics and possible dance resources and, then, through describing and discussing my particular project within the middle school.

DANCE AND THE AFRICAN-AMERICAN COMMUNITY: THE VARIETY WITHIN IDENTITY POLITICS

What are the possible dance resources that would be available for use in the school in which I taught? While some of the resources I will discuss were, in fact, not available to the students, because they exist in the world, they might have been available and are, therefore, pertinent to the discussion. One point should be made about "identity politics" as a guide to curriculum thinking. Such politics already exist through the above-mentioned "selective tradition" that informs the school curriculum, a tradition redolent with white privilege. "African-American" is the racially marked condition of unmarked "whiteness" (to borrow the discourse analysis in which being unmarked is the power position), and curriculum decisions are already made with whiteness tacitly in mind. To focus on African-American dance artists, as such, is to honor a tradition in the dance art absent from school life (except for the first species of identity politics dance art which I shall discuss) but which has a great deal to offer. Ironically, in thinking of identity politics and dance, African-American dance artists are no more monolithic than white dance artists, and the variety tells us that identity politics is not a neat and easily bounded term. Thus, even though some African-American artists do not choose to make art in reference to their racial/ethnic identity, they are yet marked by their status by others (reviewers, audiences, funding agencies). There is no escaping race in the United States.

One of the resources directly available to the children in this Southern city was a local dance company, headed by Chuck Davis, a dancer who had lived in New York City prior to moving to Durham, North Carolina, originally through the auspices of the American Dance Festival before he decided to take up permanent residence there and create a dance company. Mr. Davis had, for many years, taught for the National Endowment for the Arts through their "Dancers in Schools" program and was very experienced working with young people in schools. The company he established in Durham focused on performing dances of Africa and on teaching these dances in workshops and through outreach work into schools. He represented that segment of the African-American community who want to vivify the ancestry of today's African Americans, strengthening the individual's sense of valuable self, by focusing on who they were, as various peoples, prior to their imprisonment in Africa and subsequent enslavement within the United States. Various projects of Henry Louis Gates, Jr., (his TV series touring Africa and his *Encyclopedia Africana*) are other examples of this movement. Mr. Davis's company represented the only specifically African-American dance resource available to the community. I would argue that such dance fits easily, as an adjunct, occasional experience, within school settings because it is sufficiently exotic and distant from everyday life, that it poses no danger of altering that everyday life.

A second dance approach to African-American experience is exemplified in the work of Katherine Dunham. This approach to aesthetics and the African-American community has a strong anthropological cast (Dunham holds a PhD in anthropology), as the works that are produced are highly influenced by anthropological study of various black cultures, with a special focus on Haitian culture. Her study of the movement of these cultures was mixed with ballet and modern dance to produce a distinctive approach to movement that became known as the Katherine Dunham technique. This technique was rendered choreographically into spectacular theater, which Ms. Dunham characterized as "revues." She did not intend to reproduce "authenticity" in Davis's way, so much as communicate about culture through her art. She also differs from Davis in that at the time she was choreographing for and touring with her company (in the 1940s, '50s, and '60s), her dance was celebrated for its sensuality and aliveness but also, sometimes, branded as lascivious and teetering on the brink of obscenity. Although she became world-renowned and celebrated, her sensual work was seen as dangerous in its frank portrayal of such sensuality. As with Davis's heritage approach, Dunham invigorated a positive identity through making aesthetically legitimate the sensual life.[9]

Moving away from a heritage perspective, the focus shifts to celebrating the strength and vitality of African-American culture here in the United States. This is exemplified by the work of Alvin Ailey, who thematically explored "cultural" aspects of African-American life through such signature works as *Cry* (dealing with a black woman's grief), *Revelations* (dealing with the Southern experience, postemancipation), and solo studies of various great African-American musicians; and in the work of Donald McKayle, who choreographed numerous works based on street life in the African-American community. Ailey derived his movement vocabulary and dance technique from Lester Horton, a white maverick choreographer working in Los Angeles rather than New York City, who was the first choreographer to thoroughly integrate a dance company. With Horton's presence, identity politics presents a useful (something positive is achieved through it) but complex concept.

A fourth possible position takes a more or less race/ethnicity neutral stance

toward dance and is exemplified by such artists as Bebe Miller and Bill T. Jones, both of whom may or may not explore what it means to be African American. Their focus is on their life experience in many guises, and they do not draw upon anthropological understandings as a base or upon culturally explicit forms. Rather, they function from a more or less "pure" modern dance base, as they are more interested in movement, music, and humanness than in speaking directly to people through conventionally legible forms (such as gospel music or dances about prostitutes in the community or the character of a jazz musician, and so forth). For instance, according to a 1999 *Dance Magazine* review of Bebe Miller:

[Miller] may be creating a new genre of dance: black urban flamenco. . . . From the get-go, Miller directs provocative questions toward the audience. She slyly asks if anyone is looking for the gay dancers on the stage, and she wonders aloud how many times the conversation shifts toward the fact that the company director is an African-American woman. Her troupe, composed of people of many colors, could be a microcosm of New York City—and she addresses her choreography toward the crazy quilt of city living.[10]

This reviewer reflects Miller's simultaneous awareness of her racial status, her questioning of any racial categories through her pastiche of references (black, urban, flamenco), and her direct acknowledgment of the salience of race in this society. She does not, as with Chuck Davis, Katherine Dunham, and Alvin Ailey, actively embrace her African heritage or African-American heritage, but she is more critical than they. In a similar example of postmodern pastiche, Bill T. Jones acknowledges publicly the influence of his Buddhist beliefs on his work. Jones has adopted the "postmodern" dance practice, drawing from ballet, a variety of modern dance vocabularies, and everyday movements, put together in idiosyncratic ways that reflect his individuality rather than his consciousness as an African-American choreographer. And yet, Jones has explored the issue of being African American in his choreography, particularly in his evening-length dance, "Last Supper at Uncle Tom's Cabin/The Promised Land." He has also been deeply involved, artistically, with the AIDS epidemic and homosexuality as issues. He creates work that is explicitly "political" in these regards, but that is rarely explicitly African American in theme. Nevertheless, Jones, as with Miller, is usually viewed as an African-American choreographer, rather than just a choreographer.

I will now turn to describing the project I enacted in the context of the above possibilities.

A MODERN DANCE PROJECT FOR THE MIDDLE SCHOOL

The program that I designed and produced was sponsored by the National Endowment for the Arts during the fall of 1981. It lasted six weeks and took place in a middle school in the eastern part of town, which was populated almost exclusively by African Americans. The school was nearly entirely African American although the faculty was predominantly white. Under the terms of this grant, my responsibility was to teach dance to the entire school. I had all morning every day of school, and I had each class (sixth, seventh, and eighth grades) for approximately forty minutes twice a week. I also arranged to have a special group on Fridays who would volunteer to have an extra class. In this extra class the students would create choreography that would be presented at a school assembly at the end of the six weeks. This arrangement was not part of the original grant (which had been secured by someone else), but was central to my version of the project. I

wanted young people to experience the fullness of bringing something from imagination to concrete fulfillment, including performing what they created. This full experience could provide a vision of their potentials as people and dancers and, potentially, act as a vehicle for liberation education. In order to show why this project had liberatory characteristics, I need to describe what I do when I teach dance.

My work comes out of the German Expressionist tradition developed by Mary Wigman in the first part of the twentieth century and carried on by Hanya Holm and Alwin Nikolais (at whose school I studied, including studying with Holm), and Phyllis Lamhut, with whom I studied and in whose company I danced for seven years. The gist of the German Expressionist approach is a focus upon the essence of an idea or event expressed in movement, exploring and revealing the inner state which that idea and/or event produces. The movement that is created is not obviously connected with the idea or event. For example, to make a dance dealing with poverty, one might not costume that dance in ragged clothing or portray hunger in obvious ways. Rather, movement stimulated by cultivating the inner state of "poverty" and "hunger" would become the movement for the dance; the artist is being expressive but not representational. The dance becomes "authentic" in the sense that a more direct human connection is made between inner states and ideas/events than between the idea/event and its external correlates.

In the Expressionist tradition, the dancer/choreographer discovers the authenticity of inner states through cultivating the pure movement potentials of her/his body. Rather than teach to an already established movement vocabulary (ballet, conventional modern dance forms, folkloric style of dances, such as Chuck Davis's work), the dancer/choreographer is taught about the potential for any movement the dancer/

choreographer might wish to make. The teaching focuses on coming to know, experientially, the movement potentials for various body parts (legs, arms, fingers, toes, face, upper body, middle torso, and lower body), how movement occupies space (close to the ground, normal level, moving into the air, and attending to how moving in directions feels), how movement occupies time (slow motion, fast motion, and time as pure duration or how long it takes to perform a movement), and about the body as sculptural shape. As these abilities to know one's moving body are developed, attention is turned to cultivating an understanding of inner states, beginning with more obvious ones related to the emotions, but, eventually, branching out into ideas and events as also having inner state responses that can be made into choreography. It is in this regard that the German Expressionist tradition provides potential for liberation. Once the dancer/choreographer comes to understand abstraction and the process of extracting essences from an experience, s/he has the ability to submit her/his daily life experience to the same process, developing new awareness of life circumstances, including the pain associated with that life. This pain, experienced in this way, might lead the person to seek the sources of the pain and do something about them, perhaps even through sharing the dances with others who can begin to connect with those life experiences. In this way, dance might contribute to social change.

Returning to the project, I worked with the children in this middle school with the basic abstract vocabulary curriculum set out above. My idea was to help them develop a sense of themselves as moving beings who felt and who could, in turn, manifest feelings into movement and organize the movements to express certain states of affairs. For the Friday group, we focused specifically on choreography built around the four "concepts" of body motion, space, time, and shape. Although this may seem purely abstract and disconnected from their daily lives, the "content" of the inner states they explored as they created these so-called abstract dances inevitably expressed their daily lives because whatever movements emerged from their bodies was a direct expression of that life. I did not have time to pursue this connection because the grant ran out and the school wouldn't have considered making this project part of their regular curriculum. However, it was clear to me that they were expressing their daily lives in the kind of energies they employed in their movement explorations as well as in the kinds of movement they chose, albeit abstractly conceptualized and performed. Although they had never seen dance like this (only break dancing and dancing on television), they took to it immediately and strongly. It attracted their sense of inner self and the freedom to create outside of the constraints of commercialized movement vocabulary and brought to them the opportunity to think anew and in ways that amazed them (as they communicated to me). In this I was participating most strongly in the tradition exemplified by Miller and Jones.

The most important "outcome" of this six-week workshop for the school was the final performance of the Friday group. Both the school people (students, teachers, administration, staff) and the young people themselves were overwhelmingly enthused by the final performance. They saw something in themselves of which they had no previous idea; it emanated from a place that was genuine and energized. It was, in fact, so energized that the Friday group asked me if I would approach the school administration about doing the performance again at a local elementary school. I agreed, approached the administration of the school, and secured their permission to do this performance, which we subsequently did two weeks later. This interval required more visits to the school, in order to rehearse for the performance as well as accompanying the students as the "artistic director" of the event to the school and teaching them, in so functioning, what it meant to perform for a public. When we performed at the elementary school, the middle schoolers were again greeted with great enthusiasm and pride by the students, faculty, and administration of that school.

What made this project significant from the point of view of developing an aesthetic consciousness that might be liberating? One way to conceptualize the program is to see it as what Lowe refers to as using the arts to "ameliorate social problems and to promote healthy communities. In particular, . . . to address social issues, . . . a recognition of the power of art to effect individual and social change and its ability to compel changes in individual identity, . . . to develop and express collective identity, to build community, and to address community problems."[11] For a time both the participants in the special workshop designed to produce the performance (which, as I have stated, had not been part of the original project) and the school people not involved in the Friday group began to structure an identity, that was particularly identity-building as African-American young people capable of something new, different, and authentic to themselves as people. The school became a place that could potentially develop an identity through art, and the students were celebrated for the skilled performance of their own movement. In these ways, individual change occurred and collective identity was fostered.

The project was, to some degree, "radical" in that the faculty didn't believe that these children were capable of a high level of professional investment in serious creation, and I was able to show them that they were wrong about these young people. Some teachers, when they brought their classes to study with me for a class period, either ignored what we

were doing by leaving for the class time or stayed and ignored what we were doing. One teacher, in particular, actively attempted to undermine my work with the young people by doing exactly what I asked her not to do: yell at the young people when they were "misbehaving" in her eyes (I didn't see their activity as "misbehavior" but as exuberance that held motional potential and could be channeled into dancing) and stating out loud that this program was a waste of these children's time. With this same teacher, when during one class one young man was becoming very aggressive with another student and I intervened and was attacked, she did nothing but watch. Thus, in general the faculty of the school was not very supportive of the project. So, although we did not enact critically social work of an explicit political type during the six weeks, we moved from a state of near total resistance by some children and faculty, tepid response by others, and active enthusiasm by some, to a place where the project was acknowledged as a great, albeit surprising (except to me) success. A new vision of these children's future was forwarded. To this degree, the work might be characterized as "radical."

In the end, the project was only potentially liberating in that there was no opportunity to pursue it further. However, we can see the potentials for such liberation in the way in which the project was carried out. First, I did not impose a foreign vocabulary upon the students (ballet, modern dance of one sort or another). Rather, I began with the basic facts about all human movement, no matter what its origin or meanings. All human movement is involved with body motion, space, time, and shape. We didn't study a school of dance, but rather a way of dancing. Second, the movements came from the students. As with most liberation-oriented curriculum initiatives, this is crucial: The material for the curriculum can only relate directly to the lives of the students if the lives of the students are at the center of the curriculum. Third, a process for exploring was offered (the German Expressionist tradition), which did not allow for the students to simply bring in prepackaged versions of human movement (in the form of that present-day popular dance), but to explore movement itself as movement. In so doing, break dancing, for instance, might come in but it would be subjected to motional exploration, as would any other movement. It would not be accepted as privileged movement to be learned and well executed if one were to consider oneself a dancer. Fourth, anyone could participate and skill was centered not around athletic ability to perform movement but on dedication to exploration of any movement. This democratized a potentially elitist practice (only those with great, innate physical skill would ordinarily be allowed to participate and perform). Fifth—and this is where the undeveloped potential lies—had we been able to stay together for a long time, I would have taught toward the students exploring their daily lives in a more explicit manner, but with abstraction/essence/expression at the heart of the exploration. In this way, they might have been able to develop dance that, when viewed as well as experienced by them, might have engaged others in conversations about their experiences of the dancing that would lead toward consideration of new ways of living in their community. Additionally, we would have worked to see every movement they made in their daily lives as having aesthetic potential. This is a species of aesthetic consciousness that transforms daily living into a daily creative act. Further, as they became sensitized to movement, they could view movements that they see in a new critical light through an aesthetic analytic lens. Last, in all this, their status as African Americans would be featured, in that the material for their dances would be directly related to deep inner states of being

structured through their lives as African Americans living in the United States. It is this approach to dance, replete with aesthetic consciousness, that I believe holds the greatest opportunity for what I have termed "authenticating" personal and social liberation education through the arts.

NOTES

1. Mautner, T. (Ed.). *Dictionary of philosophy* (p. 8). New York and London: Penguin Books.

2. Wolff, J. (1981). *The social production of art.* New York: St. Martin's Press; Eagleton, T. (1990), *The ideology of the aesthetic.* Oxford, UK: Basil Blackwell.

3. Goffman, E. (1959). *The presentation of self in everyday life.* Garden City, NY: Doubleday.

4. Gans, H. (1974). Popular culture and high culture; an analysis and evaluation of taste. New York: Basic Books.

5. Williams, R. Base and superstructure in Marxist cultural theory. *New Left Review, 82,* 3–16.

6. Bourdieu, P. (1984). Distinction: A social critique of the judgement of taste. Richard Nice, Trans. London: Routledge & Kegan Paul.

7. Bittner, E. (2004, March 13). Sideways ballcap lands Scottsdale teenager in jail. *Arizona Republic*; Bittner, E. (2004, May 20). Saguaro's cap controversy won't die. *Arizona Republic*; Ryman, A., & Bittner, E. (2004, March 16). District will investigate handling of hat incident. *Arizona Republic.*

8. Benjamin, W. (1986). Theses on the philosophy of history. In H. Adams and L. Searle (Eds.), *Critical theory since 1965* (p. 682). Tallahassee: University of Florida Press.

9. Dunham, K., Biography of Katherine Dunham. Retrieved from the John F. Kennedy Center for the Performing Arts Web site: http://www.kennedy-center.org/calendar/index.cfm?fuseaction=showIndividual&entitY_id=3721&source_type=A; Harman, T. (1974). *African rhythm—American dance: A biography of Katherine Dunham.* New York: Knopf.

10. Carman, J. (1999, August). Bebe Miller Company, the Joyce Theater, a review. *Dance Magazine.* Retrieved from http://articles.findarticles.com/p/articles/mim1083/is_8_73/ai_55292594.

11. Lowe, S. (2001, August). The art of community transformation. *Education and Urban Society, 22* (4), 457.

CREATING CONNECTIONS, SHAPING COMMUNITY: ARTISTS/TEACHERS IN URBAN CONTEXTS (URBAN GYPSIES)

Gene Diaz

Artists are people who live across and among various contexts. For the most part, they are multiple-jobbers who engage in work other than their artistic production to pay their bills and meet expenses. They inhabit many worlds, yet they are part of a discursive community that frequently brings them together at meetings and forums, concerts, exhibits, performances, and in some cases, schools and universities.[1] Through the art they create and the collaborative processes they generate, artists create connections that grow across neighborhoods, between communities and cultures, and within and across generations. As the gypsies of urban culture, they travel among us, leaving their creative work of collaborative art building as a kind of glue that holds our sometimes fractured and fragile communities together, fostering continuity and solidarity.

Those artists who are also educators, those that hold school contracts, and those that work as itinerant teachers across schools and districts, or within community arts organizations or galleries, frequently move across the borders and boundaries of their particular neighborhoods and geographic locations when they travel to work. The urban landscape requires this of many of us, since we don't live where we work. Unique to teaching artists, however, is the work that they do in bringing their home along with them. Their home is the art that they inhabit—the incredibly complex array of artifacts, materials, and urban detritus that inhabits the back part of teaching artists' cars or their ever-present backpacks, and the creative impulses they, themselves, exhibit and encourage in their students.

Teaching artists make connections between their art form and all areas of their lives, from their work in schools to their political views and to aspects of other people's lives, students most often. In the inaugural issue of the *Teaching Artist Journal*, Eric Booth suggests that as teaching artists engage people in creating meaning through art, they also create connections between their art experiences and their and others' lives. "They artistically engage participants as meaning makers. Phillip Ying suggests that a good subtitle for the *Teaching Artist Journal* might have been *Art that Connects*."[2]

Debra Holloway and Beth Kensky, as guest editors of *Education and Urban Society* in a special issue in 2001, focused on the importance of arts education in and outside of schools in urban contexts. They suggest that "an increasing number of art educators and educational researchers have found that the arts' effect on personal development influences the social context and has profound implications for social change."[3] Seeing the arts as a vehicle for "communicating ideas, revealing symbols, forging connections, and helping to prepare individuals for social interaction," they support claims that the arts have the power to transform the community and the social context within which the creator and the works exist.

Not all artists are teachers, and not all artists should be in schools. The success of the urban teaching or community artist depends upon their ability to bring people along on their journey of discovery; this journey requires creative exploration and expression of engagement in risk-taking and imagination. Like the contemporary gypsies of Spain or Rumania, these urban gypsies maintain traditions that have evolved over the years of their participation in their respective cultures. For artist/teachers, these traditions combine a sense of commitment to the communities we live in and the people who are our neighbors with a sense of dedication to art-making as social agency. At a forum for community artists in New Orleans years ago in which a panel of successful artists and arts critics spoke to the rag-tag audience of multiple-jobbing artists, one of the questions to the group was, "Why do you make art?" The response from a younger member of the group standing near the rear of the alternative gallery space on Magazine Street was: "Because I can't NOT do it!" I ask the question, "What is it about what we do, that we can't NOT do it?"

This chapter looks at teaching artists and community artists—urban gypsies— in two cities as they create connections, shape community, and build culture. With examples from New Orleans and Philadelphia, the stories come from the perspective of the artists working in schools and communities.

NEW ORLEANS

Arts Connection is a staff development program designed to provide comprehensive discipline-based arts education to students and their teachers in dance, theater, and visual art in the elementary schools of the New Orleans Public School (NOPS) system. Through ongoing collaborative artist/teacher and classroom teacher partnerships, students receive thematic integrated, interdisciplinary lessons focused on arts history, production, aesthetics, and critical analysis. In 1998 I conducted an evaluation of the program based in ethnographic research methods. Many of the artist/teachers were my colleagues in another summer arts program in nearby Metairie known as Country Day Creative Arts.

Arts Connection emerged as an outgrowth of the Cultural Resources Program through the commitment and dedication of the then cultural arts coordinator in New Orleans, Shirley Trusty-Corey. From writing funding requests for the performing arts, Trusty-Corey moved into writing grants for artist residencies for visual artists. These residencies provided space in the schools and the time for students and artists to work collaboratively. Although artist residencies today are common practice, at that time, in the early 1980s, they were relatively new and untried. Trusty-Corey told me, "I certainly had the concept of artists being residents at schools before there was funding sources that one could tap into, that were called artists-in-residence programs."

The concept that was evolving through these efforts was that of providing students with educational experiences that honored a sense of creativity and aesthetics. Trusty-Corey believed that, despite the existence of a few art and music classes, aesthetic experiences were missing in schools at that time. Certainly theater and creative dramatics were not available to students, and dance. "Heaven forbid!" she exclaimed in mock horror. Itinerant music teachers, like so many traveling troubadours, made the rounds of as many schools as their time and budget permitted. But a coherent, organized arts program was needed to provide students with the challenging experiences of creative expression and to provide a rigorous, consistent curriculum for the arts. This was the goal of *Arts Connection*.

As Trusty-Corey saw that there was a lack of value placed on the arts in education and a lack of resources to sustain a program, her mission became clear. She would develop a program that used the arts resources available in the community and connect them with schools that had a need and a vision. As a problem solver by nature, she found the solution in forming a connection between the artists in the community and the students in the schools. Not all artists are educators; in fact, very few are able to meet the requirements of becoming an artist/teacher. Perhaps recognizing this fact is the most important insight that Trusty-Corey brought to the beginnings of *Arts Connection*.

As classroom teachers participated in the program, they repeatedly emphasized the changes in their practices, their ways of thinking about specific topics, and their development as individuals as a result of working with the artist/teachers. These changes were attributed to the use of discipline-based arts education (DBAE) activities led by the artist/teachers of *Arts Connection*. By definition, DBAE activities must incorporate four elements into the lessons: art production, art history, aesthetics, and art criticism. While each lesson offers a different balance of these elements, together they form a consistent basis for the projects that evolve through a continuous interdisciplinary collaboration between the artist/teachers and the classroom teachers.

The teaching methods and practices that are employed in presenting the program in the schools are based in experiential learning, or learning by doing, and on constructivist learning principles. Constructivist principles are based in the notion that students will construct their own knowledge as they participate in learning activities and are exposed to situations to which they bring their own life experiences. Constructivist classrooms reflect the principle that teachers do not act as knowledge purveyors but as facilitators of learning. Some of the practices employed by artist/teachers in this program include creative expression through art projects and performances, collaborative elaboration of group projects and productions, individual research and analysis, and assisted performance and production. These practices are congruent with the stated aims of the program and offer students opportunities to take responsibility for their own learning experiences.

Because of the structured format of the school day, leaving little unscheduled time available, teachers and artist/teachers find limited opportunities for sharing experiences with one another. Generally, while the artist/teacher is preparing for an art lesson, the teacher is in the classroom with the students. Other than the initial planning session at the beginning of the semester, many artist/teachers have little time for discussing follow-ups with the classroom teacher. The biannual workshops, however, provide more direct interaction between them, although there is not a specific method currently used for them to offer suggestions for each other. The "Regular Classroom Teacher's Survey," which teachers fill out at the end of their time with the program, incorporates questions with answers on a Likert scale, which provides only a glimpse at what the teacher is thinking.

The lessons and activities the artist/teachers bring into the classrooms and the schools in the program are specifically designed by practicing artists, and as such would generally not be activities that could be developed by a nonspecialist classroom teacher alone. However, many teachers found that working side-by-side with an artist enabled them to perceive their students differently, observe the world around them in a new way, and embellish their own work with new visions. It is unlikely that teachers will become artists or arts educators through their involvement of a semester or a year in the program, but it is not unlikely that they will become more aesthetic educators, more creative explorers, and more active learners.

Throughout *Arts Connection* are examples of students and teachers connecting with their own culture through activities that focus on their cultural heritage, their specific environment, and their personal lives. In a predominately African-American population of students, there are many visual arts activities based on the Harlem

Renaissance artists and writers; dance and theater pieces based in the historically significant Underground Railroad; murals of important black historical figures; and studies of the architecture of African peoples. Many activities involve students going out and looking at their neighborhoods, their school communities, and their families. This focus brings to the students, and the teachers, an increased awareness of and sense of responsibility for their own communities and cultures, and the world around them.[4]

It is through this sense of responsibility that students, and teachers, become empowered to make their own choices. Whether writing a script, designing a mural, or developing a dance, students make critical decisions based in creative choices. These decision-making processes and creative endeavors are learning experiences that can transfer to other areas of their lives, both inside and outside of schools. Whereas academic subjects traditionally are based in "getting it right," artistic expression is based in "getting it." Students and teachers relish the ability to succeed through the creative activities in the arts offered through *Arts Connection*. Because they are not pressured to "get it right," the traditional trappings of learning do not constrain the creative experience, suggesting to the casual observer that what they are doing is "just fun." In the words of one artist/teacher:

I really find it a unique experience for the kids. And the thing I've always liked about it is that it's taught in a way that all the kids can feel somehow successful, and be learning without realizing they're learning.

Not only are they learning, but research also indicates that artistic cultural enrichment programs such as *Arts Connection* make a difference in student achievement in other areas. The Partnership Assessment Program, a four-year assessment study by the Texas-based Partnership for Arts, Culture and Education (PACE) found that ele-

mentary students in socioeconomically deprived settings, such as the students in many of New Orleans's public schools, benefit academically from exposure to community arts and cultural programming.[5]

There is not enough art in our schools to avail all students of the opportunities for dreaming a future full of possibilities, a future complete with opportunities, and a future, in the words of student April Green, "where there would be no very hopeless people." Art is not a luxury item partaken of during times of prosperity, but an essential component of quality education, without which our students might never gain the dispositions which both Elliot Eisner and James Catterall propose as a particularly important set of outcomes for arts education: the abilities to imagine possibilities, explore ambiguity, and recognize multiple perspectives.[6] Without the arts how can our students contribute to forming a more equitable society, a more just and peaceful world, and their own sense of hope?

Arts Connection offers one example of the connections made across communities by teaching artists. It represents the fostering of what Maxine Greene would call a humane community. In schools where students with the stigma of "lower socioeconomic class" frequently become recipients of mindless training or treatment programs from well-intentioned educators and policy makers, this program considers students and teachers alike to be "capable of imagining, of choosing, and of acting from their own vantage points on perceived possibilities."[7] The teaching artists in this program encourage teachers to explore possibilities for learning through and in the arts, and create yet another connection across this diverse city.

PHILADELPHIA

Center in the Park, a nonprofit community center in Northwest Philadelphia, focuses on the needs of older people by offering academic, leisure, health, and life enrichment courses and activities. The programs are meant to expand the ambitions, capabilities, and creative capacities of older adults.[8] In 1997 several of the visual art course instructors noticed that the elders, predominantly African American, told stories to each other and to the instructors as they created clay sculptures and elaborate paintings. Their stories centered around their experiences of growing up in a severely racialized city, and focused on themes such as: a sense of community; the value of education and persistence; the importance of family lessons and advice; the pain of experiencing prejudice and discrimination; and their hopeful visions for the future.

Together with John Broomhall, the executive director of the Pennsylvania Alliance for Arts Education (PAAE), these artists conceived of a project in which these stories could come alive, through the arts, for children in elementary schools in the area to foster cultural continuity and forge intergenerational understanding. The elders agreed to participate in this project and offered their narratives in order to establish a cultural continuum through the sensitive application of their content to arts activities and lessons. In the words of African-American novelist Paule Marshall:

An oppressed people cannot overcome their oppressors and take control of their lives until they have a clear and truthful picture of all that has gone before, until they begin to use their history creatively.[9]

As an artist/teacher and ethnographer, I was called on to gather the stories that would inform the project. I arranged to meet with the participants in two focus group interview sessions, and subsequently transcribe, sort, and edit the narratives of the elders. I then met with the artists who were working in the schools to discuss the outcome of the group storytelling.

Focus group interviews were specifically indicated for this project because of the emphasis expressed in the project proposal on maintaining and continuing cultural integrity. The research process itself presents an opportunity to explicitly contribute to cultural continuity by respecting the nature of storytelling as a culturally specific activity. Storytelling is a uniquely social practice in which people share their experiences with others for multiple purposes: informing, influencing, effecting change, and sharing communal values. Within the African-American Diaspora, storytelling has traditionally been the specific work of the female members of the community, and has been identified with bonding and folk culture.[10] Thus, conducting focus groups in which a number of members sit and tell stories to one another is in itself an example of fostering cultural continuity.

The narrators in the focus groups participated in an openly friendly discussion that lacked any sense of suspicion or uneasiness. In a group of their peers, they exchanged their tales of growing up and growing old in the pre-Civil Rights era in Philadelphia. They remembered events together, recalled similar incidents in their lives, and corroborated beliefs and values exemplified in the stories. The "Oh, yeahs" and "Um-hmms" peppered throughout the tape recordings of the stories reveal a connection between the narrators' lives deeper than the common meeting place or their current life circumstances. The stories consisted of personal anecdotes, personal reflections, and observations of events or situations in the lives of the narrators, their families, and communities. Those selected and transcribed for the project were representative of the larger group of stories. The criteria for selection of the stories included in the project consisted of the following: They were appropriate for young children; they represented values and beliefs of the culture; they contained detailed description and visual imagery; they reflected the characters of the narrators.

A major aspect of traditional African and African-American cultures is the belief in the continuity of the culture from the ancestors to the descendants. A disintegration of community results when members leave and make no commitment to their culture and its continuity. Thus, traditions such as storytelling can be used to revitalize communities through a recreation of a cultural continuum. In the contemporary urban culture of America's inner-city communities, the fragmentation of daily life disrupts this continuity and leaves little space and time for the practice of traditional methods for maintaining community. This project sought to reopen that space, and revitalize the practice of traditional oral literature in the African-American community in the Germantown area of Philadelphia.

The purpose and function of stories in folktales is to initiate and to instruct; women speak of power and the responsibility to pass on to future generations the stories of their experiences.[11] In the words of Sadie Delany, an African-American centenarian, "Young people need to know their family history, and it's the responsibility of old folks like us to tell them."[12] The stories included in this project represented part of an effort to make the connection between the lives of the elders of the Germantown community and the lives of children in the neighboring elementary schools. As such they are representative not just of this community, but also of the African-American culture born of the struggle to maintain dignity and respect in a society that classified African Americans as second-class citizens. Many of the narrators told of their own or their parents' journeys from the segregated South, yet their focus is not on bitterness derived from discrimination, but on the lessons they learned along the way. They told of the values instilled in them through the support and encouragement of their fami-

lies and communities—values such as integrity, responsibility, cleanliness, persistence, and compassion. They told of the participation of the community, the church, and the schools in forming their ability to overcome the difficulties of poverty and prejudice and "live a good life." Like the Delany sisters, they confirm that "We didn't have one penny—not one penny—when we were growing up, but we had a blessed childhood."[13]

After I compiled the stories and the project directors made the connection to one of the neighborhood schools, we were invited, along with the storytellers themselves, to visit during a school faculty meeting. We were an interesting mix as we arrived at the school library that day, white and black, old and young, professionals and working class, yet we shared the purpose of creating a sense of connection through the arts. As the teachers questioned us about the project, the storytellers dropped into their stories once again, with a visible effect on the teachers gathered in the room. Tentatively at first, and more emphatically as the discussion progressed, the teachers invited the storytellers to become part of the school, to participate in classes, to visit with their students. While they were delighted with the offer of the participation with the artist/teachers and their work with the stories, they were passionate about having the seniors of their community become active participants in their school. The connection was made. The gypsies created magic in this community.

COMMUNITIES OF POSSIBILITY

For the most part we think of community as a place where people reside, or as a group of people who hold a common connection and share a workspace or a purpose for being together. Yet Maxine Greene suggests that in thinking about community, we emphasize process words—words such as making, creating, connecting, weaving, saying. Community is not a mandate, but an achievement we make together.

Community cannot be produced simply through rational formulation, nor through edict. Like freedom, it has to be achieved by persons offered the space in which to discover what they recognize together and appreciate in common; they have to find ways to make intersubjective sense. Again, it ought to be a space infused by the kind of imaginative awareness that enables those involved to imagine alternative possibilities for their own becoming and their group's becoming. Community is not a question of which social contracts are the most reasonable for individuals to enter. It is a question of what might contribute to the pursuit of shared goals: what ways of being together, of attaining mutuality, of reaching toward some common world.[14]

In the case of *Arts Connection*, the shared goals are for students to imagine, and create with their teachers, their own futures, their common world. As with the students, artists, and teachers in the *Center in the Park* project, community comes through connecting their futures with their pasts; learning from the imaginative resilience of the elders who suffered and persevered in their quest for equality. Students learn to imagine alternative possibilities as they actively engage, actively say, create, weave, and build in the projects the teaching artists connect with their lives.

Alternatives to undemocratic schooling and the fractured landscapes described in Karel Rose and Joe Kincheloe's book *Art, Culture, and Education* take shape in many cities across the United States. Those of us who, like Kincheloe, are aware of the transformative effects of the arts are indeed compelled to "use it for most socially just purposes and to connect it to the project of promoting more tantalizing modes of being human."[15] We design learning activities such as those Rose describes in her Arts and Society class for Lesley University, in which teachers become artists who make critical choices about curriculum instead of relying on the manufacturers of textbooks

to determine what is of most worth for students to learn in our schools. We create theatre projects in which teachers engage with students and principals in a dialogue about democratic schools. Democratic schools, where children are "encouraged to study and investigate as a process of discovering the truth for themselves," as Noam Chomsky suggests, can still be found in a few imaginative alternative contexts.[16]

In Durham, North Carolina, in the innovative program *Literacy through Photography*, in which local artists and writers collaborate with teachers in now 14 schools, student photography becomes the catalyst for investigations of self, community, family, and dreams. The artist-in-residence program has four goals: (1) to give students and teachers the opportunity to interact with artists; (2) to give artists the opportunity to develop projects within an educational context; (3) to increase the students' range of visual literacy and written capabilities; and (4) to create models for other Durham public schools.[17]

In Boston, Massachusetts, two collaborations supported by the National Arts and Learning Collaborative have focused on transforming the Marshall School, a community school in Southeastern Boston, into one where the teachers and students actively engage in artistic and aesthetic teaching. Creative arts educators from Lesley University have created professional development workshops for participating teachers; and students from a nearby private arts school offer arts-based afterschool activities with students from the Marshall School.

These few examples of the possibilities to foster connections and create community through the participation of artists in schools and communities illustrate the transformative nature of the arts in our urban environments. Lowe offers additional evidence in her analysis of community art to form "common ties of solidarity and collective identity among participants."[18] The arts are about quality— quality of education and quality of life.

Although many educators make claims about the effects of art experience on academic achievement, such as the above-mentioned PACE assessment, we need not lose sight of the underlying experience. As they move among us, these urban gypsies, the artist teachers, make cultural connections that improve the quality of life and learning for our students and our communities.

NOTES

Pseudonyms have been used for the school and the district throughout the analysis of this project—most commonly, "Pacific Beach High School" and "Pacific Beach School District." Other references are to "James Madison High School."

1. Diaz, G. (1998). *Making connections*. New Orleans Public Schools; Becker, H. (1982). *Art worlds*. Berkeley, CA: University of California Press.

2. Booth, E. (2003). Seeking definition: What is a teaching artist? *Teaching Artist Journal, 1* (1), 7.

3. Holloway, D., & Krensky, B. (2001). Introduction: The arts, urban education, and social change. *Education and Urban Society, 33* (4), 355.

4. Diaz, G. (1998). *Making connections*. New Orleans Public Schools.

5. Tunks, J. (1998). Integrating community arts programming into the curriculum: A case study in Texas. Arts Education Policy Review, *98* (3), 21–27.

6. Eisner, E. (1998, January). Does experience in the arts boost academic achievement? *Art Education*; Catterall, J. (1997, September). Does experience in the arts boost academic achievement? A response to Eisner. Review draft.

7. Greene, M. (1995). *Releasing the imagination: Essays on education, the arts, and social change*. San Francisco: Jossey-Bass, Inc.

8. *Center in the Park*. Retrieved June 10, 2004, from http://www.volunteersolutions.org/volunteerway/org/215646.html.

9. Cited in Wilentz, G. (1992). *Binding cultures*. Bloomington: Indiana University Press.

10. Wilentz, G. (1992). *Binding cultures*. Bloomington: Indiana University Press.

11. Wilentz (1992).

12. Delany, S. (1994). *The Delany sisters' book of everyday wisdom*. New York: Kodansha International.

13. Delany (1994), p. 3.

14. Greene (1995), p. 39.

15. Rose, K., & Kincheloe, J. (2003). *Art, culture, and education: Artful teaching in a fractured landscape* (p. 11). New York: Peter Lang.

16. Chomsky, N. (2000). *Chomsky on MisEducation*. Lanham, MD: Rowman & Littlefield Publishers, Inc.

17. Dixon, D., & Ungemah, L. (1998). *Artists in the classroom: Ten collaborative projects*. Durham, NC: The Center for Documentary Studies at Duke University.

18. Lowe, S. (2001). The art of community transformation. *Education and Urban Society, 33* (4), 457–471.

URBAN ART MUSEUMS AND THE EDUCATION OF TEACHERS AND STUDENTS

Victoria Ramirez

A dedication on the façade of the large, metropolitan art museum where I work, carved in stone, reads, "Erected for the People, By the People, and for Use of the People." Although written more than 100 years ago, this commitment still holds true today, as museums around the country increasingly consider themselves to be institutions that place the needs and interests of their audience at the core of what they do.

But is this commitment unusual? Historically, and perhaps by reputation, museums have not placed such importance on their audience and have not established a place for the people.

It [a community] erects these buildings and collects their contents as it now builds a cathedral. These things reflect and establish a superior cultural status, while their segregation from the common life reflects the fact that they are not part of native and spontaneous culture. They are a kind of counterpart of a holier-than-thou attitude, exhibited not toward persons as such but toward the interests and occupations that absorb most of the community's time and energy.[1]

In 1934, John Dewey observed that museums, by nature of their institutional goals, were not erected for the people, but for and by certain people, a select part of society that defined museums simply as houses of objects. Museums, collections, and their activities were primarily driven by a mission to collect, preserve, and exhibit objects. Prior to the 1960s, consideration of who walks through the museum doors and encouragement of museum participation "by the people" was not a primary goal of many museums.[2]

Museums are changing and are increasingly reconsidering ways to improve the accessibility of their institution as a place of learning for people of diverse backgrounds and levels of understanding of art. Museums are seeking ways to develop deeper relationships with diverse audiences and encourage their participation in museum activities. In 2003, the Urban Network published a book describing how they brought together urban museums from cities throughout the country and explored the ways in which different institutions are developing strategies that "attract, serve, and engage diverse audiences."[3] Focusing on their individual metropolitan communities, this initiative developed goals that sought to cultivate a museum audience that better reflected the demographics of their urban environment and implement a concentrated effort that increased museum participation by people

traditionally underserved by the museum. This focus on museum audience is forward-thinking, as museums strive for change during a time when their communities are quickly changing and becoming more diverse. Keenly recognizing the decades that "popular culture existed outside the walls of most museums,"[4] museums directors are no longer content with institutions that house dusty relics of the past. Institutional goals and interests are evolving and through collecting practices, exhibitions, and educational programming initiatives, museums are demonstrating a committed desire to be institutions that are as vibrant and diverse as the communities they serve.

Audience-focused initiatives must be a museumwide commitment. While education departments are establishing programs and opportunities that seek to bring diverse audiences to the museum, collecting habits and exhibition schedules must also reflect this commitment to better engage the community in museum activities. In this regard, museums are considering their audiences and potential audiences when acquiring a work of art and during the development of their exhibitions. Taking note to feature works of art by more diverse artists and different types of exhibitions in their galleries, today's museum professionals recognize the importance of their visitors making a connection with what they encounter in the galleries. Works by local artists, theme-based exhibitions relevant to the community, and more innovative programming have become an important part of the museum's primary mission. Dispelling Dewey's 1934 vision of museums as "holier-than-thou cathedrals," the museum today is making efforts to appeal to greater and less-traditional audiences. These changes particularly affect schools and students, as the opportunity for their engagement with the museum becomes richer, more diverse, and ultimately more meaningful.

The focus of this chapter is limited to the experience of students and teachers in the museum and their experience as viewers making meaning of what they see. Thus, the term "visitor" implies student and/or teacher. Also, although not specified, the examples shared are the experiences of a large urban museum whose initiatives are efforts that place value and importance on the urban communities in which they live. Specifically, this chapter examines the museum as a place of learning and discovery through vignettes based on three aspects of the museum: the collection, the exhibition, and the educational program. Collecting habits of museums once followed the tastes and interests of the patrons and donors. Now, more museums are taking the visitor and their audience into consideration when acquiring works of art, and collecting, for example, works by local or regional artists. Art that may spark a conversation about a communal or pertinent issue or offer an opportunity for visitors to see themselves in the museum is becoming increasingly commonplace in the galleries.

The same can be said for museum exhibitions. No longer necessarily only about highlighting certain artists or time periods, exhibition schedules now feature theme-based shows that present works of art focused on a particular issue, concept, or idea. In this sense, the exhibition is not simply presented to the visitor for their passive enjoyment, but is displayed in the gallery to empower the visitor to begin a dialogue about the art and make meaning of what they see. The exhibition is not a separate entity, but in some ways reflects or speaks to the community. Art by student artists or exhibitions that are a by-product of a museum/school collaboration, for example, are also becoming important components of a museum's mission, as they open a dialogue between the museum and community and, maybe even more importantly, open a dialogue among the community.

At the heart of the educational mission of most museums is the interpretation of the works of art. Most museums, regardless of size or nature of collection, offer organized staff- or volunteer-led tours of their galleries as one of their primary opportunities for visitors to engage with the art. But museums are forming new approaches to their tour opportunities, especially for school tours, and are emphasizing the importance of students making meaning of art for themselves. In an attempt to erase the attitude that museum experiences are a tangential part of students' education, organized tours are becoming more student-centered in their approach and are focused more than ever on providing students with an individual experience with art. In this regard, educators recognize and capitalize on the difference between learning in a museum and a classroom, and structure more museum experiences that are self-directed in nature.[5]

SPEAKING TO THE COMMUNITY: THE MUSEUM COLLECTION

A few years ago I was leading a group of third-graders around the museum and we stopped at a display containing a group of Greek vases. The students, who had already studied ancient Greece in their classroom, immediately recognized the objects, so we were able to discuss how the objects were used, why certain images were painted on the surface, and the size and shape of the different vessels. I felt the students were really examining the works in critical ways when a young boy asked, "Where's the real one?" With that one question my whole perspective on museums and visitors' experience with objects changed, as I realized that for many who come to the museum there is still a sense of disbelief that they are actually engaging with the *real* thing. For many museum visitors, both adults and the young boy looking at the Greek vase, there is a disconnect from what they are seeing and that they are in the presence of the actual work of art—the real work that was touched by the artist's hands, buried for hundreds of years, or created in a distant place.

After I did my best to explain to the student that they were indeed in the presence of the actual object, our tour of Greek art continued and the students slowly began to see the museum as a place filled with "real things." A new sense of awe and excitement permeated the group. For the rest of our tour, the students were rethinking their definition of the museum, the works of art, and the purpose of their field trip. The students' comments were now reflective and made me think not only about the works of art and the museum, but the ways in which other visitors engage with what they see. These students were not only experiencing art, but were also considering the museum as a construct within which the experience takes place.

The students on my tour were thinking about Greek art within the context of understanding how the museum visitor makes meaning of works of art as individual objects within the construct of the museum. While these students were making meaning of what they were seeing based on their previous experiences and knowledge, they were subscribing to the idea of museums and art as an independent experience. Dewey writes about the intersection of previous experience and an experience with art when he emphasizes the importance of not viewing that experience "as qualitatively apart from the rest of life. Instead, we need to see it as a refinement, a clarification, and an intensification of those qualities of every experience."[6]

Falk and Dierking developed a construct with which to describe such a museum experience, the Contextual Model of Learning. Considering the museum as a unique learning environment, this approach describes learning as embedded in a series of contexts that occur in the physical and sociocultural world. Taking into consideration the museum as an effective force on one's experience, Falk and Dierking include four types of contexts in their model: the personal, sociocultural, the physical, and time, and posit that learning is the process of the interactions between these contexts.[7] The four contexts take into account not only the work of art itself, but the museum as an environment that shapes and influences one's experience with that work of art. Also important in this model is the viewer and what they bring to the museum experience and what they take away with them. The visit is structured by the museum, as the design of the building, layout of the galleries, and presentation of the work influences the experience with art. For the students studying Greek art, their own previous understandings, their interaction with the other students, and the museum environment all combined to shape their experience and understanding of the Greek vase. My open-ended questions may have prompted my group to think about what they were looking at, but their responses were based on their own understanding of what they were seeing and the understandings of others in the group. The experience with the work of art is couched within the context and environment of the museum. Falk and Dierking's Contextual Model of Learning helps define and describe the uniqueness of learning in a museum environment by emphasizing the uniqueness of the environment. Carol Duncan articulates the relationship between visitor and museum by defining the museum as more than a house of objects or architectural structure. She describes the museum as a space that is "marked off and culturally designated as reserved for a special quality of attention—in this case, for contemplation and learning."[8]

Works of art that speak to the needs, concerns, or interests of their visitor or shape and reflect their urban community can challenge one's ideas and opinions and help museum audiences see themselves in the art. Art that engages the viewer on multiple levels, such as an installation work, provides visitors with a unique opportunity to actually become a part of a work and engage with it in ways that cannot be replicated outside the gallery setting. In a Deweyan sense, installation art may be the definitive art experience, as the experience itself often requires some physical participation from the visitor, as they are invited to physically interact with the work by walking into or around the piece. To further engage the viewer, an installation artist may incorporate sound, scent, and even tactile materials, resulting in a multisensory work that participates in a dialogue with the viewer.

Installation art can offer students and teachers some of the most memorable and powerful gallery experiences. While leading a tour of an exhibition of work by African-American artists, I had the opportunity to introduce a group of high school educators to several installation works of art. Engaging with one of the works, I found the usual group chatter lessened as the teachers quietly walked through, read, or were enveloped by the experience. One specific work, an installation by artist Vicki Meek, prompted a variety of responses from my teacher group and generated the most dialogue of all the works in the gallery.

Created in 1992, *The Crying Room: A Memorial to the Ancestors* is a mixed-media installation by artist Vicki Meek. Exhibited in a small gallery, the work combines sight, sound, smell, and an interactive component as visitors are provided with pencils and small slips of paper on which to write an "offering." These offerings are then pinned to one of the walls of the installation. The visitor enters the space, dimly lit in red and white lights, and immediately hears a chanting voice and soft music. A mound of sand, lava rock, and a long trough of cowry shells are arranged on the floor. Candles line the black walls, which contain writing in stark white lettering and an African Yoruba design. The wall reads: "400 years of slavery, 15 million enslaved, 30 million died." Also on the wall, arranged in the shape of Gothic church windows, are tiny coffin-like unopened sardine cans, adorned with the name and age of a deceased individual.

In her installations and assemblages, Meek analyzes major aspects of African-American history. *The Crying Room: A Memorial to the Ancestors* is a powerful commemorative statement, a celebration of the survival of the human spirit in the face of adversity. But Meek is not creating the work alone. In this piece, she includes an opportunity for visitors to participate by providing paper and pencils on the back wall where one can write an "offering." Reflecting on this work and my tour for the high school educators, I found myself intrigued by how each teacher made sense of Vicki Meek's work and contributed to the wall of "offerings." While some hesitated and simply read the slips of paper contributed by others, other teachers carefully composed personal messages or responses to existing messages. As the offerings were not really organized on the wall in any particular fashion, some visitors responded to one another with their messages through the placement of their paper within the wall of other offerings. As was intended by the artist, the teachers were participating in the work by taking part in a written and a silent dialogue with both themselves and others who chose to leave their comments.

The participatory component of the piece represents the community, as visitors express their ideas, thoughts, and opinions through their offerings. One does not have to include an offering to participate in the dialogue, as visitors—such as the teachers on my tour—can read the wall of offerings and silently participate. Offerings on the wall are in many different languages and are written to deceased relatives, friends, and even pets. Messages were written by young and old—

"freedom" in young-handed letters; "Where is the love?" and "Viva Venezuela" in more elegant script. Because the offerings are anonymous, many visitors feel more comfortable expressing themselves. One visitor wrote: "Dear Ms Art, The light shines in this work like a beacon of hope wrapped around my future." In this work not only are visitors having an experience with the art, but an opportunity to share with the community. One can visit the installation alone, as I have many times, and be a part of the community just by reading the offerings. For the high school teachers on my tour, the museum visit was no longer confined to the participants in the group, but included the community who had previously left offerings. The museum was part of a community and the group was part of that community outside the museum doors.

With works of art such as the Vicki Meek installation, the museum has redefined itself as a communal place for dialogue and a public forum where people can come together to create new knowledge and think about their world in new ways. The museum is a living and breathing, dynamic place where different ideas and perspectives are reflected and expressed. Speaking to our senses and requiring our participation through writings on slips of paper, the Meek installation emphasizes the importance of our experience being connected to something outside of ourselves.

Instead of signifying being shut up within one's own private feelings and sensations, experience signifies active and alert commerce with the world; at its height it signifies complete interpenetration of self and the world of objects and events.[9]

In this respect, experience within the museum involves more than just our own selves and our past experiences, but is an exchange between the art, the artist, other visitors, and the museum itself. Thus experience is not a purely cognitive, insular interaction, but it involves all of our connectors to the world—our senses. According to Dewey, the senses are our greatest connections to that which is outside of our private selves; sight, sound, smell, touch, and taste are entryways to our inner selves. Experience in a museum setting requires the alertness of our entire body, as we are not passively viewing works of art as mere spectators, but we are part of the experience as we maneuver ourselves through the museum. Body, museum, and experience are intertwined in the way Falk and Dierking's Social Contextual Model takes into consideration the components that define an experience with art in a museum. Dewey describes this interaction as a "rhythm" which takes place between viewer and surroundings.[10] With a developing rhythm, the viewer builds a relationship with the art and the museum just like the third-grade students discovered the realness of the Greek art and the teachers engaged with *The Crying Room*. Both of these groups engaged in a rhythm of understanding between themselves and the art. But, experience does not happen instantaneously. It unfolds over time in a flow of understanding about an object, situation, or place. Art is a part of life and the intersection of art and life is the experience. Dewey defines great art not as those works that have specific indefinable qualities, but those works that, throughout time, can be valued and experienced in new ways by different people.[11] Art is an imaginative and emotional experience, and the most meaningful art and aesthetic experiences can only take place with the *real* work of art.

The ideas of Dewey, Falk, and Dierking prompt me to reconsider the museum experience of my third-grade tour group, who had been studying ancient Greece in their classroom. The students visited the museum with an understanding of the context of Greek vessels, but did not truly understand the function of the museum until one brave boy asked where the real Greek vase was located. After that realization, the students' interaction with the art and experience in the museum changed. Each student's excitement played off of one another as they saw new works of art and imagined the life of that work and other visitors coming to the museum with the same sense of wonder and excitement as they had that day. The same can be said about the high school teachers' interaction with the Meek installation. The physical and emotional experience of the art combined with the interaction of writing or reading the "offerings" resulted in a complex conversation between the teachers and the work. For both of these examples, the visit to the museum and the experience with the art was not a passive activity, but one that, consciously or not, prompted the students and teachers to begin to think about themselves, their community, and the world in a new way. Art, and their experience with the museum, is not a segregated activity but a part of life.

MUSEUM EXHIBITIONS: A REFLECTION OF THE COMMUNITY

For many visitors, especially students, *experiencing* the museum can be especially challenging as they tend to have either negative perceptions of the museum or they feel that the museum is not a place where they can see or discover themselves. A look at an in-gallery visitor comment book provides an opportunity for visitors to anonymously speak to the museum and express their thoughts and opinions about their experience. "This is boring" is written too frequently in several museum visitor comment books. In another example, to further emphasize the disconnect between the museum and their student visitors, Therese Quinn of the Art Institute of Chicago developed a museum class in which local high school students visited various museums throughout Chicago and reflected on their impressions and experiences. The overall consensus of the high school students was that museums are "boring" and the collections "stale." In Quinn's experience, the stu-

dents expressed a disconnect between themselves and the museums by explaining that they could not see why they should visit them in the first place.[12]

Experiences such as Quinn's reveal that if museums truly want to be places where students can see themselves and if they want to create experiences for schools in their community, they must consider their visitors in what they do—including the creation and presentation of exhibitions. There are a variety of different types of museum exhibitions. Some are more academic in nature, speaking more to the field than the average museum visitor. Others are more sweeping views that provide the visitor with a broader look at a topic—a selection of masterpieces or highlights from a collection, for example. But exhibitions can also demonstrate a commitment to their audience by presenting works that speak to or reflect the needs and interests of their specific community.

As museums seek to become institutions more like the community of which they are a part, the types of exhibitions they host are changing. More and more museums are devoting specific galleries or spaces to student work. My own institution has an almost ten-year relationship with a local high school photography teacher who creates an assignment for his students that culminates in an annual exhibition of student work at the museum. The students are assigned to walk their neighborhood streets and photograph the people and places that define their community. The images created are personal statements that reveal the students' perceptions and the physical features and spirit that define their neighborhood. Students are instructed to shoot dozens of images and choose the strongest photographs they feel best reflect their vision. The images chosen are submitted to the museum for consideration in the final exhibition, which consists of approximately thirty photographs. The exhibition is titled *Eye on Third Ward*, a reference to the part of the city where the images were taken.

Eye on Third Ward is a look at a community through the eyes of high school students. The most popular subject matter of the work is family, neighbors, and friends, followed by photographs of homes, buildings, and various city landmarks. As individual photographs, these images speak to issues of hope, poverty, and the people that comprise the community. As a collective exhibition, they offer a look at one of the oldest historically African-American neighborhoods in the city through the eyes of students who call it home.

An integral part of the exhibition is the opening reception, which invites friends, family, and the media to the museum to meet the student artists and celebrate the exhibition. Unlike opening receptions offered for other museum exhibitions, this event attracts more families and is typically held on a Sunday afternoon to accommodate the after-church crowd. The celebration attracts upward of 300 people who typically do not visit the museum. But for this event the museum is a part of the community, and the community can see themselves in a new way—through the eyes of the students.

There is a sense of pride in the exhibition, and students feel empowered to talk about their photographs. Museum visitors recognize community landmarks, popular stores, and even people from the neighborhood. But, the museum benefits equally from the collaboration by recognizing that it is when students and communities see themselves in the art that they find the most meaning in both the art and the museum. Erasing the reputation Dewey spoke of in 1934 of the museum as an isolated institution that simply collects and preserves objects, the museum is striving to be a vital part of the community. Through exhibitions such as *Eye on Third Ward*, students have the opportunity to discover works of art in the museum and, most importantly, see the connection between art and their lives.

Visitor responses from the in-gallery comment book emphasize the importance for the community making connections to the art in the gallery. Consisting of mostly comments of praise, some visitors contribute their opinions, others scribble drawings, and some pages of the book include actual dialogue where visitors are responding to the comments of others. Interestingly, messages in comment books in galleries with student art tend to speak more of the artists than of the work itself. Comments include: "Children are our future artists;" "Love the children's work;" and "This place is s-o-o-o boring, except for this kid art." Other comments include actual sketches appearing to be from the hands of children. Here, the child viewer is relating to the student art by creating their own sketch, as if to say, "These students are artists, and I am one too." The students are inspired by the art, and they interact with it by creating work of their own. Adult comments also express support for student work in the museum and ask for more student art in more museum galleries. Comments include: "Better than the pieces in the rest of the museum" and "Life is always more refreshing when seen through the eyes of others." One visitor even commented, "It was nice to see a good exhibit in such a white museum."

The number of comments in the comment books and the time visitors take to include their thoughts indicates that visitors are positively responding to the work and respond favorably to the museum presenting exhibitions of student work. But for museums in urban environments, community-based initiatives, such as *Eye on Third Ward*, demonstrate their commitment to the place in which they live. Urban environments such as the one in which I am situated are marked with a dense population of diverse people who desire and seek experiences that connect their community. In this sense, it is the urban museum's obligation to offer such opportunities for its community.

For museums to truly connect and expand their audience, including community-based exhibitions in their schedule is a critical step. Museum visitors need the opportunity to see themselves in the museum and make connections between their lives and art. Our compartmentalized classrooms separate the arts from other disciplines so much so that it is challenging for students to see how integrated and tightly woven art is to our everyday lives as people. Advocates, such as Maxine Greene, write of the importance of the arts in a public school education as a means for reshaping imagination and "developing a dialogue to becoming more wide-awake to the world."[13] Greene clarifies her position by challenging teachers to encourage learners to "name their own worlds."[14] Art and the museum can help students find and develop their own voice that will shape and define their own worlds.

For the students, whether their work is featured in the exhibition or not, it is their experience with student-based exhibitions that can yield some of the most powerful museum experiences. Seeing artists just like themselves and thinking about the work within the context of the museum can empower students to believe they have a voice and that their opinions, thoughts, and ideas have value. Offering students an opportunity to engage with other student work can be reflective and prompt them to organize and articulate their ideas and consider what and why they think of the world the way that they do.[15]

Engaging with art made by other students provides another context for students to create and engage in dialogue about their own thoughts, concerns, interests, and motivations. This interaction allows students to make meaning of their world and provides educators an opportunity to understand how surroundings affect the ways in which students construct knowledge, make meaning, and come to an understanding about what is around them.[16] For *Eye on Third Ward*, sometimes students visiting the exhibition enter the gallery and do not initially realize they are looking at photographs made by their contemporaries. This realization prompts another look and intrigues them enough to look at each work and see what the student photographers have to say. Museums can learn from these experiences and develop a better sense of how these discoveries are made and how future museum programs, resources, and experiences can be crafted so they are more meaningful for the student.

EDUCATIONAL PROGRAMMING: MAKING THE MUSEUM ONE'S OWN

Most students visit the museum as part of a field trip experience. Typically lasting about one hour, the field trip is usually led by a volunteer docent or museum educator who has a predetermined plan for the students' visit. Carefully mapping the travel routes through the museum and choosing the works of art for focus, the field trip experience is literally a prescribed lesson plan in the museum. The tour leader knows what the tour will cover and which works of art the students will see before ever meeting the group. The ideas of social interaction and group learning and discovery are secondary, as students need to quickly assimilate to their new environment, meet their new museum teacher, and participate in the experience that has already been structured for them.

But some museums are changing and have initiated a new type of tour called Open Space in which the students take the lead in creating their own experience by determining which works of art are discussed on their museum visit. Based on an approach more typically utilized in business meetings, Open Space allows the participants to guide the activities and goals of the activity with the help of a museum facilitator. In the Open Space tour approach, the museum docent or tour leader does not predetermine the focus works of art, but allows the students to browse the gallery at their leisure and choose the works for discussion. Students are prompted by the facilitator to consider which works of art strike them or which intrigue them. The student leads their own experience with the art, as they choose the works of interest to them individually and as a group. Falk and Dierking define this personal context as one's "reservoir of knowledge, attitudes, and experience, influenced by the physical characteristics of the museum."[17]

Questions are raised, and discussions are sparked by the students' own curiosities and interests. This approach is particularly successful, as museums are better able to craft a more meaningful and memorable experience for students. Utilizing the Open Space approach also respects the students as individuals with thoughts, ideas, experiences, and opinions. In this approach, students and their chaperones are discovering the work together—by asking questions, making connections, and coming to a better understanding of what art meant to them and their lives. The Open Space tour emphasizes discussion and participation and thus the museum visit is social, emphasizing the importance of group learning.

With Open Space, art becomes an object requiring discussion and discovery. During the tour, the docent or tour leader does not stand next to the work of art being discussed while the rest of the group look at the work. Instead the entire group walks around the gallery together. In this format, no one person has a better relationship or understanding of any work of art. Each work belongs to everyone equally. This approach also emphasizes the importance of Falk and Dierking's Contextual Model of Learning, where the physical space of the museum is factored into the experience; as students are encouraged to pursue their own interests, they are making sense of the museum as a construct.[18] Museums as non-traditional learning environments offer the opportunity for students to openly discuss and reflect outside the confines of the classroom. Studies by museums and universities, including one by Bank Street College in New York City, have examined student field trip experiences and discovered that visits in which students could exercise choice and personalize the experience were some of the most effective and remembered experiences. The docent, or museum educator, learns as well by gaining a sense of which works of art the students are interested in, and what makes them question, curious, or speaks to them. In a Freirean sense, the student, tour guide, and chaperones are learning and discovering the works of art in the galleries together. All are encouraged to share their ideas, interests, and opinions and thus the visitors are not reduced to objects who have been alienated from their own decision making.[19] With Open Space, the students are in control, and their experience is shaped by their own decision making.

In my experience, at the start of a museum tour when I have asked students what they expect to see and discover during their museum visit, I have heard "we are going to see a bunch of old stuff" and "art is only made by dead people." Given these beginnings, the question remains, "How do you meaningfully contextualize this work for students and dispel the myth that art is for and about someone else?" Open Space allows meaningful connections to be made with works of art by building on the social aspects of the experience and allowing students to discover on their own and at their own pace. Students who are talking amongst themselves about art or those who wander off because another work of art has caught their eye are not told to be quiet or join the group, but rather this type of interaction between student and the art is welcomed and encouraged.

Museums are social institutions. Experiences are social. By promoting social engagement in the galleries, the experiences are more meaningful and are memorable for the students. Open Space tours advocate this type of learning and interaction and place the role of "tour guide" in the hands of the student.

CONCLUSION

Once again I consider Dewey's 1934 description of a museum and its collection as an institution that "reflect(s) and establish(es) a superior culture."[20] But I believe through collections, exhibitions, and educational programming opportunities, museums are slowly changing their attitudes and practices and doing what they can to erase that reputation. Museums are playing an increasingly important role in their communities, and more and more audiences are engaging with art and viewing their local museum as a place "Erected for the People, By the People, and for Use of the People."

NOTES

1. Dewey, J. (1934). *Art as experience* (p. 9). New York: Perigee Books.

2. Alexander, E. (1993). *Museums in motion.* Nashville: American Association for State and Local History.

3. Amdur Sptiz, J., & Thom, M. (2003). *Urban network: Museums embracing communities* (p. 3). Chicago: The Field Museum.

4. Amdur Sptiz & Thom (2003), p. 11.

5. Falk, J., & Dierking, L. (1992). *The museum experience.* Washington, DC: Whalesback Books.

6. Jackson, P. (1998). *John Dewey and the lessons of art* (p. 8). New Haven: Yale University Press.

7. Falk, J., & Dierking, L. (2000). *Learning from museums.* New York: AltaMira Press.

8. Duncan, C. (1995). *Civilizing rituals: Inside public art museums* (p. 10). New York: Routledge.

9. Dewey (1934), p. 19.

10. Dewey (1934).

11. Dewey (1934).

12. Quinn, T. (2001). Where we can see ourselves? *Rethinking Schools, 16* (2).

13. Greene, M. (1995). *Releasing the imagination.* San Francisco: Jossey-Bass.

14. Greene (1995), p. 11.

15. Greene (1995).

16. Kincheloe, J., Steinberg, S., Rodriguez, N., & Chennault, R. (1998). *White reign: Deploying whiteness in America.* New York: St. Martin's Press.

17. Falk & Dierking (1992), p. 25.

18. Falk & Dierking (2000).

19. Freire, P. (1970). *Pedagogy of the oppressed.* New York: Continuum.

20. Dewey (1934).

THE ARTS IN URBAN EDUCATION

Merryl Goldberg

To live, we hope; To hope, we dream; To dream, we imagine our improved future. To imagine, we act; We make constant our effort to realize our dream. To realize our dream, we improvise our realities.

Improvisation is ancient and modern; It is arts; It is philosophy; It is life. To live, we improvise.

—Xin Li
The Tao of Life Stories[1]

This chapter discusses the improvisations of several individuals as they enact projects and programs in the arts in urban school settings. It is about people who are dedicated teachers, community members, artists, principals, and parents who have a dual role of warrior, fighting for what they perceive is an excellent education for their children. It is about finding ways to realize what is possible while working within large systems that all too often are more of a barrier than an opening.

By federal law, a comprehensive and equitable schooling for all children includes an education in and through the arts. In this chapter I raise issues specific to urban schools in California, such as English language learners mainstreamed throughout classes and how the arts open important learning opportunities. I look at how schools within urban settings can subvert the system to include the arts as central to the curriculum despite top-down directives to teach only to reading and math, and how arts-rich school environments can bring diverse groups within the community together.

Artists and arts institutions working with schools and school districts have a unique and important role in subverting the system. As Judith Hill writes:

We have a rich and deep presence in the public schools, and we work with classroom teachers and students daily, yet we are also free of the many strictures and structures that commandeer public school life. We mediate our students' lives by creating intentionally educative experiences rather than by executing somebody else's ideas of what and how to teach; the power of the curriculum and the nature of instruction is in our hands. . . . It is our own educational ideals and our school partners to whom we must hold ourselves accountable. This makes for delicious dangers and opportunities.[2]

Although Hill was discussing urban education and the arts in general, her point is right on the money for our situation in southern California. My work in California is in several districts where the arts play a significant part in the culture of schools through partnerships with artists and arts institutions. Although I have worked in and with schools for more than ten years now, I am continually amazed to witness kids' and teachers' sense of purpose, inten-

sity, and motivation as they work in and through the arts. Children are not only capable of amazingly creative and complex undertakings, but such undertakings come to them naturally. They are eager to take risks and work toward a goal. One look at any one of the settings I will describe in this chapter is a reminder of what an opportunity we all have to believe in kids and their often amazing ability to understand their world through arts.

Through the arts, children can dream, hope, imagine, escape, reflect, try on a new identity, or make visible an identity that they had hidden. In the urban settings where I work, we find children with very limited English skills confidently exploring Newton's physics through mime. We find a student who is completely alienated to science until his teacher discovers that enabling him to draw during class completely opens him to the world of science. We find students, who, "against all odds" have an inner urge to express themselves, not necessarily thinking of what they do as art.[3] We find children with hidden talents—kept hidden until the opportunity and encouragement of a particular teacher embraced them.

Children in urban settings often lack the financial means of their counterparts in suburban settings, and thus have had less opportunity to have their artistic talents "discovered" through an afterschool art program or by an art teacher. However, children in urban settings are no less creative and artistic than those in more wealthy districts. In some instances, the lack of formal arts activities gives rise to the blossoming of creativity. As well, urban landscapes are often glorious canvases of artwork and performing arts. For example, in San Diego we have Chicano Park, an important and historical park with mural after mural depicting Chicano culture. To embrace the creative urge in children and encourage it in urban settings is a fundamentally humane way to support our collective future.

IT IS THE LAW

All children are entitled to an equitable and comprehensive education and that education includes the arts as a core academic subject. Under the No Child Left Behind Act, all four arts disciplines—music, visual arts, dance, and theater—are defined as "core academic subjects" on equal footing with math, science, language arts, and social studies. In addition, there are national standards in arts education to guide the K–12 curriculum, and here in California we have a mandate in the visual and performing arts, with a framework that spans all four disciplines and all grades, pre-kindergarten through grade 12.

I would also like to shatter two myths about the arts and their role in education as a way to contextualize the discussion in this chapter.

Myth Number 1: The arts are not economically important. They do not hold the promise of a good job.

Education in the arts prepares the U.S. workforce for jobs in the robust arts industry, as well as in numerous other industries. For example, California alone has 89,710 arts-related businesses, including jobs related to animation, movies, television production, lighting technicians, recording artists, gallery owners, and so on. According to the 2004-updated study, *The Arts: A Competitive Advantage for California II*, these businesses employ 516,054 individuals (California Arts Council). That is more people than all the students and faculty currently enrolled throughout the entire California State University system. These jobs do not take into account all the individuals who work in arts-related jobs outside of arts businesses, such as Web masters, brochure designers, self-employed local artists, and arts teachers in schools. Nor do they account for the artistic skills essential to fields such as architecture.

Sadly, many of the arts jobs in California go to individuals from outside the state and even outside the country because our students are inadequately trained for arts work. For example, although individuals can learn computer techniques quickly for jobs that rely on computer animation, these techniques cannot make up for the lack of arts training needed to create the original artwork or storyboards.

Myth Number 2: The arts are nice—but they are far less important than a child's ability to read and write and do arithmetic.

Research has shown (and continues to show) that schools in which the arts are present have higher test scores in all areas; more motivation and participation among students, teachers, and parents; and more success among exceptional students, gifted and talented learners, and English language learners.[4] High school students who have taken arts classes consistently score higher on the SAT.[5] Further, the arts teach students important lessons in discipline, perseverance, creativity, and risk taking. These skills are becoming more and more prevalent in a transforming workforce where employment in areas that demand imagination and creativity are seeing great gains.[6]

Every parent wishes for the best education for their children. Most would agree that an education that includes the arts, science labs, up-to-date technology, and well-trained teachers and staff is what all children deserve. Unfortunately, in urban education, school budgets rarely can begin to provide even a small piece of the ideal. Systemwide decision making often makes it challenging to fund the arts, even in the best of circumstances, and those individuals who believe in the arts need to find ways to circumvent the system in order to succeed.

Obviously, one way to change the system would be to change the reality of the budget. Although school districts within suburban locations can raise funds to support an excellent education through their tax base and the establishment of educational foundations, urban schools are often lacking in this area. Thus, schools wanting to include the arts often need to find a way to circumvent the challenge of the budget by changing their status to have more autonomy from the system, partnering with arts institutions, writing for grants, or independently raising funds for projects.

The more realistic potential for systematic change would be to lobby at the local and state political level for general funding for the arts. For example, a community outside of Boston recently voted to override a tax cap for school funding so that art and music teachers could be restored to school funding. Unfortunately, despite the glimmers of hope, such as with the previous example, arts programming whether in the public schools or in the general public (museums, concert halls, etc.) has been under attack for quite some time. Some would argue that the arts have little purpose in education, maybe even in society. This is not the case historically or culturally if we look around the globe. The arts were so important to the Greeks, for example, that they were indistinguishable from basic activities associated with the pursuit of truth or beauty.

In many cultures, the arts have been inseparable from everyday activity, and do not even have names associated with specific acts (such as singing or visual art). However, when the arts were first introduced to public school education, they had specific purposes. Music was first introduced into the public schools in an urban setting—Boston, 1838—to promote hymn singing. Boston was also home to the first drawing program, which was introduced as a result of the Industrial Drawing Act of 1870 (adopted by legislators, composed and signed by manufacturers). The Industrial Drawing Act was designed to introduce drawing to children for the purpose of training individuals for work related to design in manufacturing.

Arts remained a significant aspect of an integrated curriculum within schools until the 1950s when, in direct response to events surrounding the launching of Sputnik, discipline-based study became the norm. The purpose of a new discipline-based education with special emphasis on science and mathematics was intended as a method to create a cadre of citizens who could effectively compete with the Soviets, especially in science.

Arts educators joined the discipline-specific frenzy of the late fifties and moved forward with curriculum that focused on the study of arts for their own sake. By that I mean study of great works or art, or studying the technique involved in creating art. Individuals associated with the Getty Foundation in the late 1970s and 1980s broadened the definition of discipline-based education in the arts to include the study of historical and aesthetic contexts. Many people bought into this discipline-based arts education, and for good reason; it was thorough and very well thought out. It was adopted as a basis for many arts education programs, including the California Frameworks for elementary education. It was challenged in terms of what some perceived as a narrow Western focus, and to the Getty Foundation's credit, they expanded their focus and materials to become more multicultural. However, as education budgets dwindled, the fight for arts became tougher and tougher.

By the 1980s another challenge to U.S. education emerged: the education of an increasingly multilingual and multicultural student body in the context of a society immersed in technology. In response to these challenges, several theories emerged and blossomed onto the education scene, including Howard Gardner's theory of Multiple Intelligences. Gardner's theory had a tremendous impact on education, broadening teachers' views on how to teach and reach students. Soon after, the arts started playing another role, an additional one to the discipline-based roles outlined by Getty. The arts began to play an important role in interdisciplinary learning, providing learners with strategies to express subject matter through arts-based methods. For example, students learning about metamorphosis might dramatize the life cycle of a butterfly to understand it, or draw from nature as a method to study ecology. Often this is referred to as "learning through the arts."[7] In the 1997 California Department of Education publication of *Artswork*, "Literacy in and through the arts," was recognized as a core principle. Art was deemed as not only a discipline to be studied, but as a guiding force for the study of other subjects.

THE CHALLENGE OF ARTS EDUCATION IN URBAN SETTINGS

Education in the arts has challenges in most settings, and some more specific to urban settings. To frame these challenges, I discuss two urban school districts in southern California, each with its own unique set of circumstances: Escondido Elementary School District (about 45 miles north of San Diego), and San Diego City Schools. I also touch upon a charter school for the arts in Oakland to provide an example of what is possible for children who wish to pursue a career in the arts.

Community involvement and creating partnerships can be key to success in building capacity to support arts in urban schools. In my examples, the community plays a significant role in the success of a program, as does the presence of artists in schools representing arts institutions. By community I mean the local community including parents, artists, politicians, and donors, as well as the school community itself comprised of the children, teachers, staff, and administration. By artists, I am referring to professional artists of many backgrounds and cultures working in classrooms as part of their daily experience.

SUAVE

Escondido, California, is roughly 45 miles north of the border with Tijuana, Mexico. It is a moderate-sized city of approximately 133,000 with a significant Mexican-American population. Many of the children entering the elementary schools are native Spanish speakers, and in some schools the majority of the population are English language learners. Since 1994, a program called SUAVE (*Socios Unidos para Artes Via Educación* [transl. United Community for Arts in Education]) has been part of the school district's professional development. It is a relatively poor district in terms of funding. At the time of this writing, they are forming a foundation to begin finding outside funds to supplement their budget.

SUAVE came into existence to serve several needs of the local community. In 1993, a newly built (and city-owned) Center for the Arts needed to create an educational program in order to fulfill its agreed-upon mission. Funding for new schools was delayed in an agreement that the arts center would provide arts education for tax-sharing partners. I was new to the area at the time, having been hired as faculty at Cal State–San Marcos in the neighboring city, which was part of the tax-sharing partnership. At that time, budgets were fairly robust, and the school districts, arts center, and university were able to create ideal programs. In that culture, we were able to build a partnership, share costs, and implement a joint program.

I developed SUAVE in collaboration with several local teachers, principals, and community members. In choosing where to begin the program (within the tax-sharing partnership), we identified three principals who were not only inclined toward the arts, but had either backgrounds in the arts or professional associations with the arts. The original principals were thrilled to pilot the program. Thus, we began with grassroots support and built community buy-in. The principals set the tone for their teachers, and we were off to an exciting beginning.

I realized rather quickly that even though budgets were decent in the early nineties, arts specialists were absent from the district. Classroom teachers were responsible for arts education if the children were to receive any training in the arts at all. However, most teachers, having grown up in California, were themselves not trained in the arts, having gone through schooling with very little arts education due to Proposition 13, which dramatically changed the funding for public education in the late 1970s. The classroom teachers, although interested in the arts, did not feel at all competent to teach the arts. I decided on another approach—the teaching through the arts approach. In other words, train teachers to use the arts to teach content: using drama to enact the life cycles of insects, creating puppets to act out periods of history, using dance to understand mathematical concepts such as complex patterning, and using visual arts to study nature.

This technique of learning through the arts by pairing professional artists with classroom teachers brings life to classrooms, and students began to shine in significant ways. Teachers have expanded their methods of reaching their students. One teacher put it this way:[8]

Until (the artist) started having us do movement to poems and things like that I hadn't thought of doing a social studies lesson this way. We teach about the land bridge, people coming across the land bridge to North America and becoming Native Americans. So I took a section of the playground . . . [and] had them act out the whole thing. And we slowly crossed the land bridge and moved down toward North America and then down to South America. We were chasing herds of animals and some of the kids were the mammoths. As we moved toward the equator we noticed it was getting warmer. I know that they are going to remember that. It wasn't just the two-page spread in the social studies book with a picture . . . of an Eskimo or whatever in furs and a bunch of words. . . . They acted it out, they moved, they walked, I talked to them the whole time.

Another significant impact of the program was its effectiveness in gaining skills to help English language learners succeed:

When working in dual language instruction, [teaching through the arts] made it very visual and concrete for the kids. Kids have benefited from it, bilingual kids learning a second language—I mean it is just so visual, so tangible for them to acquire and have access to the curriculum that it has made such a big difference in the way I teach. Everything is so tangible across the curriculum. I mean they can understand; they can see it, they can feel it, they can act it, they can say it.

In a three-year research project sponsored by the Spencer and MacArthur Foundations, SUAVE's success and limitations were looked at very closely. In documenting and analyzing curriculum jointly developed by teacher/artist pairs, my team found the arts often are used in interesting ways, including as a tool for assessing student learning, and as an effective tool for reaching English language learners.[9]

The discovery of the potential of the arts in reaching English language learners became a significant highlight of the program over the last ten years. So much so, that the program became a recipient of a Department of Education Model Arts Grant (No Child Left Behind Act) to look specifically at the impact of the arts in teaching English language learners. The role of arts within the district began shifting from an arts education and professional development emphasis to the arts' role in teaching students English.

As a surprising side result to our studies, we found that teachers, after having been trained in using the arts in the ways that artists use the arts, have become more interested in the arts in and of themselves as important disciplines in their own rights. Teachers have taken art classes, are attending more performances, and are in effect, introducing discipline-based arts education into their classrooms. In other words, the teachers themselves are finding an importance or purposefulness of arts as a discrete subject on their own, and are incorporating the study of arts into their curriculum. Thus, although it may be a backdoor approach to invigorating arts education, learning through the arts is important as an educational strategy, and also creates a stage for the discipline of arts to be studied.

Often, artists in residence are left to their own devices. In the SUAVE program, artists meet weekly and have formed a strong community. In our "coaches' meetings" we discuss what is going on in classrooms, and brainstorm effective ways to reach teachers and support them in their efforts to teach curriculum through the arts. Classroom teachers know we meet every week and will on occasion attend the coaches' meeting, or send along questions or ideas to share. A typical coaches' meeting entails coaches bringing challenges to the table, such as, "one of my fourth-grade teachers wants to focus on division and movement; do you have any ideas on what I could do?"

Another significant aspect of the program is writing for grants to support teachers and artists to attend workshops together. We have been successful in this arena, and teachers and artists have been able to learn side by side on trips to India to study puppetry, to Mexico to study fandango, and in mini workshops held at the Center for the Arts, Escondido, with visiting artists such as Marcel Marceau, Bella Lewitsky, Ballet Hispanico, Missoula Children's Theater, and the Shakespeare Company.

At the time of this writing, the state of the school district's budget is about as dismal as ever. Even though the program is jointly funded by the university, arts center, and grants, the district was to provide its share, which came to $50,000 (a reduction from its contributions of the past). However, the program went on the cut list for the district. Not surprisingly, and due to the grassroots formation of the program and community buy-in, numerous parents, teachers, artists, and community arts organizations began to protest. While the district did not come up with the funds, a private foundation

dedicated to improving the lives and education of Latino families stepped up to the plate to fill in the gap. Hence the program continues in full force for at least another year while the district tries to find the money for the future.

Several school board members as well as the superintendent have publicly stated support for the SUAVE program; however, when push comes to shove, they have relied on the generosity of the community. Fortunately, the community has been able to come through and support the children. This is not always the case. This is especially difficult in urban settings unless the city has a dedicated community donor or individuals who will consistently come forward for children.

FREESE ELEMENTARY

Like many big school districts, a challenge for any individual school is to work within the district and still hang on to some autonomy. Individual schools have less freedom in larger districts than in small districts, because decisions such as whether or not to hire arts specialists, are made at the district level and not at the school site level. In smaller school districts, there is more freedom site to site— and in middle-class and wealthier communities, school sites in collaboration with PTAs often can raise enough money to hire arts specialists.

In San Diego City Schools, a vibrant special educator took another approach to arts education. Freese Elementary is a city school in southeast San Diego. The neighborhood has changed over time—in the past it was a primarily African-American community and has evolved to a community that is roughly one-third African American, one-third Latino, and one-third Filipino. It is a poor neighborhood, and San Diego City Schools, like most city schools is California, is a poorly funded district. For the last several years it has been run from a top-down administration. However, at the time of this publication, a new administration is in charge and it is hoped that change will be in the air. Even more than Escondido, schools within the San Diego City Schools have very little autonomy.

Freese Elementary took another approach, and a very successful one. They applied for magnet status to become a culture and arts school. They were granted that status, which provided them the freedom to set up curriculum differently from the mandated math and reading blocks at all other schools. Mary Pat Hutt, the special education teacher now in charge of arts coordination at Freese, began networking like crazy with the arts institutions in San Diego. Unabashedly, she would call the opera, museums, symphony, playhouses, and pull on the heartstrings of whomever she could at each institution and ask for tickets for her kids who had never experienced live performances. She was so successful that the school attracted more than thirty arts partners; won grants from a number of agencies, including National Geographic; and has a teaching staff that is quite stable (not so common for city schools). Family nights are arts-centered and bring families from the community together.

Hutt, her principal, and teachers—like those individuals involved in SUAVE—have taken a decidedly grassroots approach to their school in the midst of a system that is top-down. The students are brought into curriculum decisions and given "release time" to discuss and critique projects and programs at their school. Their input is part of the decision-making process at the school. All artists who work in the schools also engage in reflective thinking concerning their work at the school. A sense of ownership in learning is created and valued.

OAKLAND ACADEMY OF THE ARTS— A CHARTER SCHOOL

I would like to briefly mention another important way to provide arts experiences to children in urban settings by briefly highlighting the Oakland Arts Academy. Jerry Brown, the mayor of Oakland (at the time of this writing), decided to embark on opening a charter high school for the arts with its mission being pre-professional training in the arts within a college-preparatory curriculum. This is an approach to education that directly benefits children who wish to pursue an arts career. Charter schools are public schools that receive the same funding as other schools, but have autonomy when it comes to decision making and approaches to the curriculum. The charter school is a way to "work the system" rather than subvert it, to achieve an arts education goal.

The Oakland Academy of the Arts became a reality in 2002 under the direction of Loni Berry, when it opened its doors at the Alice Arts Center with 100 ninth-graders. The school was created to provide an opportunity for teens talented in the arts to receive a college-preparatory education with training in the arts. The school attracted many more students than could be admitted. Admittance was by audition. Students attending this school begin their studies at 8:30 AM and conclude at 5:30 PM. Often they stay even later to rehearse shows or put up a gallery of original artwork. Students have access to formal dance classes, animation, arts, music, theater, and arts technology.

They have a community of teachers, arts and non-arts, who work together and coordinate the curriculum across disciplines. Teachers have created a "windows" approach to the curriculum, whereby a period and culture in history, such as Leningrad, 1914, becomes a window through which each teacher and his or her students approach their discipline. Several windows are approached each semester. Even in its infancy (the school will serve 400 students by 2005), the school is achieving the highest test scores in the district, has a 97 percent attendance rate, and is a vibrant school full of inspirational and motivated kids.

THE ARTS AND RISK TAKING

Significant in all of these examples is an attention to taking risks, to working outside of systems, working within systems, and working despite systems. It is not so surprising that risk taking would be a significant factor in the success of arts in urban settings.

The *American Heritage Dictionary* defines risk as "the possibility of suffering harm or loss, danger."[10] Artists, however, are drawn to risk, and more often than not, risk is defined as perceiving or exploring the possible. One SUAVE artist put it this way: "Attempting something beyond the realm of what is known to the person taking the risk." Another put it this way: "That which calls to be . . . a journeyer into the unknown."

Shirley Brice Heath,[11] in describing arts-based afterschool programs, writes this of risk:

Risk heightens learning at effective youth-based organizations. While public rhetoric laments the fate of 'at-risk youth,' our research reveals how youth depend on certain kinds of risk for development. Rather than live at its mercy, youth in arts organizations use the predictability of risks in the arts to intensify the quality of their interactions, products, performances.

Risk taking within teaching has been identified as a positive and essential ingredient for successful teacher learning and growth.[12] It requires individuals to engage in uncertain behaviors with a potential for negative consequences.[13]

Part of my interest in risk is in uncovering the positive role of risk taking in teaching and learning, not only for teachers, but also for students. Risk taking is familiar to the artists as it underlies the nature of artistry. In describing "risk," the artists of the SUAVE program have offered the following definitions:[14]

- Trying something new without certainty of the results
- Attempting something beyond the realm of what is known to the person taking the risk

- Reveal, ignite, shape, know, kindle
- That which calls to be, to be accomplished and seems beyond usually connected with fear and failing, or exhilaration to jump and dive in and try

When asked about their definition of themselves as artists, it was no surprise to uncover that risk also defined their view of themselves as artists. For example, an artist is:

- One who takes risks in society to speak their truth through the media of dance, visual arts, performance, and poetry.
- One who ardently "arts," a way of being, seeing, and hearing—using all the senses to perceive dreams and realities.
- Someone who takes risks at making people feel and see their own lives.
- A creator, transformer, innovator, and interpreter; a person who colors life, redefines and recreates reality, crosses established boundaries, speaks universal languages, and reaches the soul

Rather than focus on prevention and detention for "at-risk" youth, the organizations Heath examined urge creativity and invention with young people as "competent risk-takers across a range of media and situations" (p. 21). She continues, "The high risk embedded in the performances and exhibitions of these organizations creates an atmosphere in which students know how to solicit support, challenge themselves and others, and share work and resources whenever possible. Critique, as an *improvisational* and reciprocal process, amplifies practice gained during project planning. . ." (p. 26) [italics added].

COMING FULL CIRCLE

To live, we hope;
To hope, we dream;
To dream, we imagine our improved future.
To imagine, we act;
We make constant our effort to realize our dream.
To realize our dream, we improvise our realities.[15]

—*Xin Li*

The programs and individuals I have described and discussed in this chapter are improvisers, dreamers, and risk-takers. The teachers, artists, parents, and administrators involved with SUAVE, Freese Elementary, and the Oakland Academy for the Arts have worked relentlessly to bring arts into the lives of the children in their community. They are ardent arts activists in addition to their roles as teachers, artists in the schools, administrators, or parents. They have realized their dreams into realities. The realities do not come without their price of constant advocacy and continual action toward attaining public support. The community of artists, teachers, parents, students, and administrators described in this chapter know how to work in and through systems, and ultimately, how to subvert systems through attaining grants, speaking at school board meetings, creating status within schools that provide for more autonomy, such as magnet or charter school status. They realize dreams through constant and dedicated effort—and more often than not, go to bed completely exhausted.

The challenge and creativity of working inside and outside of the urban school systems is possible, if not exhilarating. Efforts to integrate the arts into urban education often provide the opening that can uncover children's arts talents. The potential and talents of children who engage in the arts is limitless. Their improved futures are no doubt enhanced by the folks who are willing to improvise school realities and create the opportunity to dream.

NOTES

1. Li, X. (2002). *The Tao of life stories: Chinese language, poetry, and culture in education*. New York: Peter Lang Publishers.

2. Hill, J. (2004). What is urban education in an age of standardization and scripted learning? In S. Steinberg & J. Kincheloe (Eds.), *19 urban questions: Teaching in the city* (p. 124). New York: Peter Lang Publishers.

3. Rubin, S. (2004). *Art against the odds: From slave quilts to prison paintings*. New York: Crown Publishers.

4. Goldberg, M. (2001). *Arts and learning: An integrated approach to teaching and learning in multicultural and multilingual settings*, 2nd edition. New York: Addison Wesley/Longman; Goldberg, M. (2004). *Teaching English language learners through the arts: A SUAVE experience*. New York: Pearson/Allyn and Bacon.

5. Catterall, J., Chapleau, R., & Iwanaga, J. (1999). Involvement in the arts and human development: General involvement and intensive involvement in music and theater arts. In *Champion of change: The impact of the arts on learning*. The Arts Education Partnership and the President's Committee on the Arts and Humanities.

6. Cox, W., Alm, R., & Holmes, N. (2004, May 13). Where the jobs are [Op-Chart]. *New York Times Op-Ed*.

7. Goldberg (2001); Gallas, K. (1994). *The languages of learning: How children talk, write, dance, draw, and sing their understanding of the world*. New York: Teachers College Press.

8. Goldberg (2004).

9. Goldberg (2004).

10. *American Heritage Dictionary* (second college edition, p. 1065). (1985). Boston: Houghton Mifflin Company.

11. Heath, S. (1999). Imaginative actuality: Learning in the arts during nonschool hours (p. 27). In *Champion of change: The impact of the arts learning*. The Arts Education Partnership and the President's Committee on the Arts and Humanities.

12. Cohen, D., & Barnes, C. (1993). Conclusion: A new pedagogy for policy. In D. Cohen, M. McLaughlin, & J. Talbert (Eds.), *Teaching for understanding: Challenges for policy and practice* (pp. 240–275). San Francisco: Jossey-Bass Publishers; Darling-Hammond, L., & McLaughlin, M. (1996). Policies that support professional development in an era of reform. In M. McLaughlin & I. Oberman (Eds.), *Teacher learning: New policies, new practices* (pp. 202–218). New York: Teachers College Press; Fullan, M., & Miles, M. (1996). Getting reform right: What works and what doesn't. *Phi Delta Kappan, 7* (10), 744–752; Fullan, M., & Miles, M. (1996). Getting reform right: What works and what doesn't. *Phi Delta Kappan, 7* (10), 744–752.

13. Fullan, M. (1995). The limits and the potential of professional development. In T.

Cuckoy & M. Huberman (Eds.), *Professional development in education: New paradigms and practices*. New York: Teachers College Press.

14. Goldberg (2004).
15. Li (2002).

CITIES: CONTESTED AESTHETIC SPACES

Karel Rose

My father had a boundless, indiscriminate love for New York City. One of his favorite songs was "East Side, West Side." I remember his body swaying and singing the words as if they were a hymn, a paean to his birthplace. Since he never went beyond the sixth grade in school, the streets were his teachers. The city was an extension of his body. It was in his strong muscular arms and his heavily calloused hands. He was permanently anchored to the rhythms, the sights, sound, and smells of uptown and downtown. He had an ever-expanding collection of postcards: Grand Central Terminal, the Flatiron Building, the Washington Market, The Empire State Building. My favorite was the one of a crowded street on the lower east side, an exotic place that gave me a new version of my world. The picture showed people of different ethnicities selling brooms, pickles, wooden bowls, and shoes. A young girl peddled strawberries. I could just about hear the foreign-accented street cries and smell the knishes. The people wore the clothes from the pushcarts.

My father did hard labor in the city every night. He would deliver newspapers, tying them up and then hoisting them onto his truck. I can still see the metal ring that he wore on his pinky finger for cutting the heavy rope that bound the stacks of papers. I used to beg to be taken along but that never came to be. I wanted to experience the city at night, see it go to sleep and awaken with the dawn. The windshield of the truck would be my lens. I wanted to be the first to read tomorrow's headlines.

When my father's coworkers would have a beer at my house, they would tell me that he was always smiling, engaged everyone in conversation, eager to hear their stories. He told me about the Italian newspaper dealer on the corner of Delancey and Essex Streets who gave him comic books for the "kids," his nightly coffee break with the black truck driver from Alabama to whom he loaned money and the Asian hunchback who serviced his truck. When he became a foreman, he hired workers who differed as much in appearance as they did in cultural commitments. This was his urban pool. They were all his friends. He didn't seem to see the diversity, and if he did, it only enriched his life. My father's response to difference contradicted the negative conceptions about the "other," which I learned from my silk-stocking school and an assortment of friends and relatives. When I got older and unpacked my metaphoric suitcase, I gladly discarded many of these attitudes. I am grateful that my father's generous perceptions of people and his embrace of difference prevailed.

My father's love of the city extended to places where he never went. When he was in his seventies, I took him to the Metropolitan Opera House for a performance of "Madame Butterfly." The story resonated for him and he was completely comfortable with the crowds and the glamour. He had amassed a wealth of information from living and working in the city. Although his experiences outdistanced his ability to reflect on them, they made his life rich.

As a white woman teaching at The City University of New York, a working-class uni-

versity, I often reflect back upon my early years with my father and try to analyze why those boundary crossings came so easily to him. Out of necessity and a genuine impulse of care, he never put up walls or feared difference. I slowly learned to appreciate his multiple versions of the world. I am deeply connected to those memories, reinventing them and changing myself in the process. As all children should, I now have the freedom to honor his memory in my own way, if only in the default mode. My father's version of "East Side, West Side" has embellished my own understandings and desires to continually cross my own borders. What better place than a large, diverse city for this teacher to challenge her preconceptions and work for social justice.

In this chapter, I want to explore how urban teachers can heighten their artistic and moral sensibilities through more profound emotional and intellectual engagements with the city that surrounds them. One of my major objectives is to heighten awareness of the many aesthetic opportunities that suffuse city life and wedge cracks in the safe of narrow-mindedness and parochialism. Building on issues Joe Kincheloe and I raise in our book, *Art, Culture and Education*,[1] I want to continue to explore the relationships between teaching and aesthetic experience. The following list of questions drives this chapter:

- How does the discourse of art help us to analyze teaching?
- How are teaching and art hermeneutical activities?
- How do context, cultural climate, time, and place influence teaching and art?
- How does aesthetic experience conflate with knowing?
- How do urban ceremonies, rituals, and events raise questions that connect to the discourses of art and teaching?

Some more difficult questions:

- How might experiences with the arts assist students and teachers to engage with critical social issues?
- How are the arts catalysts for social change?

PRIVATE AND PUBLIC WORLDS

My life prepares me for my life. As a teacher and writer, my private and public worlds merge. I cannot easily separate teaching from traveling, a good play from a good class, dancing at a wedding from choreographing a class presentation. Similarly, curriculum and pedagogy are conflated as is education and democracy. I'm not sure that I agree with those Buddhists who speak about the distinction between being and doing. The preparation of teachers, from my perspective, is all about developing independent, empowered thinkers who do not live their own lives in discrete curriculum areas. I fantasize that on Saturday nights, over a glass of wine, my students will have grand conversations and argue passionately about the issues that we discussed in Wednesday's philosophy class. I want them to connect their private worlds to the compelling concerns of our time. They need to confront what enrages them. Is it homelessness, racism, child abuse, poverty, war? The synergy with others will come when it connects to their own humanity.

The rich artistic and often chaotic world of urban life helps to reframe crucial issues. A reflective classroom can be the scrim, the mediation center, or the place where the intellectual and artistic merge and where concerns can be safely negotiated. In an earlier book, I noted that the artistic tone, however, is not moral; it is ironic. The artist in control of the art form maintains an aesthetic distance, struggling between his or her own passions and the subject matter.[2] The things of art stand away from the world and invite perception. The frame is real.[3] But the frame may be enlarged to include even those things that cannot be placed between the covers of a book, a gilt frame, or on a stage. Sometimes, it remains the task of the perceiver to imagine the framing and personally discover the aesthetic moments. Although greeted with mixed emotions,

"The Gates Project," in which Christo and Jeanne-Claude created a blaze of saffron fabric throughout Central Park for 16 days, was an opportunity for people to create their own framing and rely upon their own definitions of art.

TEACHERS AS ARTISTS

Teachers who do not have a rich background in the arts may not always acknowledge the many informal aesthetic encounters in their lives. Mimicking the way they were taught, they create spatial and temporal boundaries that organize knowledge into discrete boxes. This reification of old epistemologies with their convenient categories may be initially comforting, but too often this compartmentalization provides a false sense of finality and discourages creative thinking. Deferring completion, retaining the element of surprise and focusing on the process that Picasso has described as "a sum of destructions" heightens interest and mitigates against boredom.[4] Just as a good Scrabble player finds a way to build new words from old ones, so the artful teacher improvises and revises the extant categories. No version is final. Teaching is a constant negotiation among the students, the content, and the teacher. At its best, it is an articulate, informed argument.

Curricular and pedagogy are enlivened when the multiple languages and conceits of the arts are celebrated. Color, rhythm, texture, form, image, and improvisation are not bound to individual disciplines but inform perception across curricular boundaries. The arts are not just clarifiers for something else but significant ways of knowing unto themselves. Pasting the "Battle Hymn of the Republic" onto the study of the Civil War illuminates neither the history nor the music. Each must stand alone and be appreciated for its particular attributes; each way of knowing contributes to understanding the other but on its own terms.

Joe Kincheloe argues that US society is not generally aware of the relationships connecting art, politics, culture, and education. I agree. One of the goals of teacher education should be to highlight these connections. Teachers need both art and didactic texts to address these complex interactions. Aesthetic experience is a way of knowing that articulates feeling facts. For it is the safe remove of art in its address to the emotions that inspires concern, invites questions, and democratizes the classroom. A cry of pain aesthetically rendered may be more persuasive than the essay, but it has limitations. Resistance may occur if there is an emotional unwillingness to confront that which illuminates life in a painful way. The reciprocal relationship between aesthetics and thinking, the rigorousness and intellectual content of the arts, and the concept of multiple intelligences as mutually reinforcing thought processes provide considerable support for educators.[5]

THE CITY AS AESTHETIC LABORATORY

The artistry of the city may elude us as we rush to catch the bus and dodge the cars. But the crowds, the first snowfall, the textures, the changing reflections, and the tender human street encounters are worthy of notice. A keen observer, a determined voyeur raises many hermeneutical questions. Teachers wandering the city in search of the artful will ask: "What is art?" Who decides?" "Does location count?" Variants of these questions continue to haunt teachers when they reflect on their pedagogy, the prescribed curricula, and standardized testing. It may be a tenuous situation to encourage students to interpret, criticize, and interact with controversial issues. Urban teachers often feel that they are in the eye of a hurricane and need support. Acknowledging the uniqueness of each voice is what John Dewey meant when he implored us not to create a rift between art and ordinary experience.

Democracy is perhaps the most compelling argument when students are encouraged to be rigorous questioners.

"High Art: Low Art" was a course that Joe Kincheloe and I designed. We were determined to help our students recognize art as an agent for social change. It would be necessary to expose them to the social complexities and fallout when aesthetic expression crosses traditional boundaries. Not wishing to "throw the baby out with the bath water," we acknowledged that all art enriches lives, but the focus in our class would be the role of transgressive art in a democracy. Throughout history, the distinction between high and low art has been carefully monitored except for a few spurts when art forms from different domains nourished each other. Think about the way Negro spirituals and jazz infuse contemporary music and opera.

Urban teachers—all teachers—need to know that there is not one single story. The aesthetic perspectives of feminists, non-Westerners, and outsiders are critical to our understanding of contemporary issues. Their voices belong in our classrooms and teachers as the storytellers of the culture need to present and transform these stories for their students. The arts challenge our intellect and our deepest emotions and as a result are significant catalysts for social change. The issue is not only about standards or which art has most value (all art has value) or appreciating art on its own terms, but it is also the recognition that aesthetic experiences foster intellectual consciousness of significant social issues. Historically, great artists have expressed their deep concern for social issues, hoping that their work might have political impact. Centuries ago, Breugel and Goya, among others, did so before their time was ready to accept their ideas. Today, with greater freedom, many contemporary artists create their own "Sensation," when they address the social crises of the day in their works, seeking not necessarily to beautify the world but to reflect it. The 2000 Brooklyn Museum "Sensation" exhibit became the final subject of our course.

Our class used the city as aesthetic laboratory. We wandered the city streets, visited museums, and interviewed artists, curators, and community people. There was heated discussion about what art should do for people. How did culture determine preferences? Should art be beautiful, consoling, disturbing, truthful? It may not be necessary to respond to these dichotomies. There are serious problems attending art's selective value. There is a need to acknowledge people's dependence on cultural frameworks and the admissibility of a simultaneous plurality of truths and realities for all.[6] For almost as long as there has been art, there has been iconoclasm and "art rage." Why the concern? All artworks aspire to be arguments for arguments' sake.[7] Aesthetic experiences foster engagement by speaking to our emotions. That may be why some view the arts as dangerous whereas others appreciate the aroused feelings that connect us to the world. Teachers need to be aware of this complicated schism and openly explore with their students ideas about what is beautiful. The urban setting raises many social and political questions; the context is often artful, the process is often artful, the product may not be "beautiful."

DIVERSITY IN AN AESTHETIC CONTEXT

Cities are ecotones, environmental edges that teem with diversity. Given their size, imposing order, and constant movement, cities can be liberating or constricting, thrilling or terrifying. The museums, the concert halls, those grand and imposing institutions, formally and cautiously honor diversity and influence our artistic perceptions. But aesthetic preferences have a way of "outing." They come outdoors, making visible an ecotone that often escapes the imprimateur of the museum.

It is 8:30 AM on a summer day in New York City. The city is already awake. A hand truck laden with clothes is pushed by an immigrant man. A Calvin Klein commercial shoot halts as an ambulance with sirens blaring races down the street. Everyone is an original. Skin tone, hairstyle, jewelry, age, and ethnicity change even before I turn the corner. Hats piled high on the corner wagon are reminiscent of the children's book, Caps for Sale. *The colors stir up their own exquisite sensations. There are music, hawkers screaming incomprehensibly, people talking into their cell phones. Max Beerbohm said that a quiet city is a contradiction in terms. The smell of hot dogs, a Proustian moment, reminds me of my youth. I realize that I didn't have breakfast but the walk is its own sensual feast. I'm satisfied, not hungry.*

My walk bears eloquent testimony to what Rachel Carson called the "lifelong durability of the sense of wonder."[8] I am completely engaged; I can't stop looking. I feel pleasure and satisfaction. What is artistically good is whatever articulates and presents feeling to our understanding.[9] But not being in a museum or gallery, no one but me has decided that I am having an aesthetic experience. What freedom! I simultaneously read many visual languages; the group waiting on line at the Social Security Office, the skinny models rushing to work, the mother carrying a baby and clutching the hand of a crying toddler. I get to Times Square. The billboards scream their seductions. The news of another tragedy appears on the marquis of a building. I need a vocabulary to write about these visual experiences. So will my students. The languages of the arts will work. We'll speak of shape, color, texture, plot, form, design, and balance. We'll interchange languages as we choreograph the visual and write poetry about urban sounds. The diversity resides not only in the people. The buildings, the open spaces, the fruit stands, the billboards, all speak to differences. I know now what Diane Ackerman means when she revels in synesthesia, the stimulation of one sense stimulating the other. The senses correspond to each other; a sound can be translated through perfume and a perfume through vision.[10] It is all so seamless; the sensory blending never ends.

On a summer weekend, fairs and festivals are everywhere. Ethnic groups from around the world accustomed to a rich street life bring their culture outside. At these urban rituals, everyone shares the same space. The exuberance is infectious. I see a large group surrounding a street singer. He and the audience sway to the music. In Street Theater, no fourth wall separates actors from audience; we are all part of the play. I must not separate myself either. I know that I am getting ready for tomorrow's class. They, too, must experience the wonder and beauty of the streets and carefully observe:

- *The commonplace (a woman in a babushka peeling potatoes)*
- *The contradictions (a display of African masks juxtaposed against an art deco building)*
- *The close-up wonder of the ordinary (an Asian woman's long black hair shining in the sun.)*

Cities are the stews of the world. Exotic foods are constantly being added to the pot as recently transplanted people try to make sense of their new world. They write their stories, visually depict their longings on canvases and the walls of buildings. They newcomers open stores and perform their music and rituals out of doors. As if by spontaneous combustion, street graphics appear and the streets become a giant storyboard. I help my students to read the world by taking a walk in the city. I ask them to "read" the architecture that frames our private and public spaces. What do they tell about the values of the architect? About the powers that financed the buildings? Why do buildings such as the White House, Big Ben, and Eiffel Tower become synonymous with the city itself? The Forum (Pompeii), the Brandenburg Gate (Berlin), the Parthenon (Athens), and the World Trade Center (New York) are drenched with symbolic meaning. These structures overwhelm us as a flood of emotions and ideas link the concrete and the abstract. Teachers need to clarify the relationships between abstract thinking and tangible forms. Learning to read between the words, the signs, and the objects is a skill that needs practice. Symbolic and abstract thinking encourage students to extend their range beyond the anecdotal, escape their particular frame of reference, and see beyond the materialism that suffuses them.

Students at The City University of New York understand diversity. Many have scaled unfamiliar walls, discarded metaphoric clothes from their suitcases, and broken the mold by being the first in their families to go to college. But like all of us, their boundaries always need revision. A walk in the city will help. There's a white father with his Asian son, a West Indian woman wheeling a sleeping white baby, two men holding hands, a young woman with her much older lover sipping wine at an outdoor café, and a man in a motorized wheelchair zigzagging through the crowd. It's a tableau that I want to freeze. I will show my students the work of the Ashcan School artists, Reginald Marsh and John Sloan, who, striving to counter social injustice, depicted workers in the city. Joseph Stella spent many nights under the Brooklyn Bridge before he painted his eponymous work. The bridge for him was the place where you faced nature, diversity, and the many wonders of the city. Today, there is general agreement that the Brooklyn Bridge is one of the classic and most beautiful walks in the world.

DISLOCATION AND OUTSIDERNESS

People who migrate within their own country or across international borders yearn for a better life. Some are disappointed and exchange their old chains for new shackles. They adjust in different ways: Some live in ghettos to maintain a sense of security and others reach out to new frontiers. In the United States, it is very difficult for people of color. Black Americans, in particular, have been denied access whether in the north or the south to the detriment of their quality of life. Jacob Lawrence painted his "Great Migration" series poignantly showing the conflicts, struggles, and outsiderness of black Americans in their own country. Fortunately, for him, "Out of the struggle came a kind of power and even beauty."[11] The arts, for some, are a means of making sense of a hostile and often lonely world.

My students spent time at "Crossing the Boulevard,"[12] an exhibit at the Queens Museum of Art in 2003, by documentary artists Warren Lehrer and Judith Sloan. The exhibit is an example of how the arts enable newcomers to respond to the dislocations they feel between their country of origin and their new home. The artists interviewed hundreds of people in Queens, a New York City borough where 138 different languages are spoken— probably the most ethnically diverse locality in the United States. The exhibition includes striking photographs, stories both in text and on audio, and original music. It is a testimony to people from around the world who have recreated their artistic roots to relieve the sense of outsiderness. A group of Nigerian women who started a church sang prayer songs. A Nepalese man honoring the Charya Buddhist tradition told his story in dance. A woman from Kabul wrote about the cosmopolitan city that she left and the mother she hasn't seen in 22 years. An Egyptian man proudly exclaimed that he was the first to start a café on the block. The arts granted professors, students, film makers, members of the Falun Gong, factory workers, dishwashers, security guards, and lawyers a means of expression to balance the world of their forebears with the realities of life in New York City. This richness just outside the walls of urban schools and universities just waits to be discovered.

The students returned to class connected to the ways in which the arts through multiple symbol systems can dispel dislocation and open doors to insiderness. Words, music, movement, and theater illuminated our understanding of complex concepts. The stories resonated as we looked at difference, rather than sameness, and inspired connections rather than dislocations. How instructive for teachers who have to take a curriculum and transform it into another symbol system. Truth and beauty, artfulness and interpretation are not limited to what is already between the covers of published books or on the walls of museums. It begins with personal experience and the awareness that philosopher-kings live in our own backyards. The search for authenticity, so gracefully revealed at the Queens exhibition, was empowering. Reinvention of the self is a life's work for all of us. The great thinkers who preceded and who live with us are better accessed when we acknowledge our own understandings.

PRAXIS FOR SOCIAL JUSTICE

The deep chasm between social classes, the unfair treatment of racial minorities, and the continuing marginalization of women demand and inspire aesthetic responses. The power of the arts to alter perceptions for good and noble reasons cannot be assumed. The arts may be used to support brutal repression as in Nazi Germany or the development of justice, equality, and democracy. Tyrants and saviors have recognized the power of the aesthetic for reaching the emotions and concentrating attention. The arts have been labeled filthy, ugly, sick, and dangerous. Why else burn books; outlaw "degenerate" art; or censor adult films, plays, and exhibitions? From the educator's perspective, the capacity of the arts to speak to both the emotions and the intellect is a powerful pedagogical tool for praxis in social justice. Teachers always search for ways to prepare students for the unfamiliar and extend their reservoir of experiences. The "safe remove" of the art work helps students integrate powerful contradictory and disturbing feelings and imagine themselves in another's world. They stumble on discoveries. In the classroom, the exchange of ideas increases and students not only show up but are in the moment. As the terms that define outsider/insider art become blurred and art that addresses social issues is more visible in mainstream venues, new ways of thinking emerge. The need to confront inequality and domination is the work of many artists and provides direction to hospitable teachers who want to find new ways to question the canon and prescriptive "truths." Artists raise moral questions about what the world should and could be like. What follows are some examples of public art in urban areas and discussion of some sad cities that rigorously and critically ask us to examine issues of social justice.

PUBLIC ART

The artist is Judy Baca who designed "World Wall: A Vision of the Future Without Fear." This 210-foot mural in seven parts, first displayed in Los Angeles, addresses the contemporary issues of global importance: war, peace, and interdependence. Executed with the support of ethnic scholars, multicultural neighborhood youth, and hundreds of local support staff, the process was as important as the product. Different parts of this mural are now touring the world. Baca has produced more than 73 murals in almost every ethnic community in Los Angeles that address the needs of different groups. A video of her work has been produced by PBS and is part of the Annenberg series, "A World of Art."

On Avenue C in Manhattan, Hispanics have painted a large mural whose large letters read "Loisada," the Hispanic phonetic spelling of "Lower East Side."

Sue Coe, the activist artist, designs such public art as murals or billboards that encourage social action. Her themes address AIDS, animal rights, and workers. In Chicago and in Pittsfield, Massachusetts, billboards featured horrific images of animals being slaughtered.

SHRINES AND HOMAGE TO THE DEAD

Public mourning may take the form of makeshift shrines. Sacred spaces spontaneously spring up providing clues about the dead and the living. The deaths at Columbine High School, for example, called forth their own responses. The small and the grandiose, side by side, assumed their own idiosyncratic aesthetic as people mourned the deaths and their own disbelief. Transformations of private grief into public statements are seen in cities and towns in response to world events, the death of revered individuals, or outrage at injustice. Whether mourning ethnic cleansing in Bosnia, starvation in Somalia, the deaths in the Iraq War, the stoning of Islamic women, or the abusive death of a child, shrines are statements. Heightening consciousness of the issues behind the tragedies, they may encourage praxis. Whether people mourn Martin Luther King or Jimi Hendrix, they are marking their support for the person as well as for their belief systems.

NINE/ELEVEN

Nine/eleven was a watershed. After 9/11, the memorials spoke not only to the dead but also to the political issues that burst into flame on that fateful day. The deluge of patriotic responses was everywhere in evidence across America. There were trucks covered with dozens of flags, buildings and artifacts painted with the Stars and Stripes. Commemorative murals were all over honoring the firefighters, police, and others who bravely responded to the tragedy. One Harlem mural showed the Statue of Liberty crying blood. A photograph by Robert Rauschenberg also depicted a solemn Statue of Liberty cradling the Twin Towers in her arms. But there were also "flag" clothing, toys, backpacks, and "We're Proud to Be American" bumper stickers. The conflation of commodification and patriotism is a slippery slope, for this was a difficult time to question patriotism. But there were displays that raised issues about U.S. policies on billboards, door fronts, and walls, and in stenciled statements around the country. Barry Dawson's keen photographic eye captured many of the varied responses at this time.[13]

SAD CITIES

Sometimes cities make aesthetic statements without consciously meaning to do so. Their cry of pain resonates with us and although the scene is not beautiful (who said art has to be beautiful?), they remind us that we are all part of the music.

Not all cities can hide their warts. They literally wash their laundry in public. Without calling for social action, their very existence cries out for response. Poverty and racism, the roots of urban deprivation abound. It is hard to forget the images of the squatter settlements outside Johannesburg or the tents in the cemeteries of New Delhi. The necessity for a life lived on the streets is a given in the sad cities. Colorful as the daily functions of washing, shaving, and hair cutting may be for the tourist, they are not so for the residents. Commercial enterprises such as dyeing fabrics or baking tortillas, which may seem exotic, exist out of necessity. Means of transportation may provide local color, but they are lessons in ingenuity and the remnants of a past that remains a necessity in the present. In Cuzco, Luxor, and Lahore, as in hundreds of other places around the world, carts and bicycles pulled by people as well as animals are the reminders of the daily struggle to survive.

Ghettos, in most large cities, are often sad places reminding us of the pervasive discrimination and economic deprivation. In some cases, a former president may decide to make a statement and buy an office in a ghetto, but the world outside remains a grim place. There are the street people, many who are homeless, neglected children, and the unemployed just waiting for something to happen. The garbage-littered streets, junked cars, and ramshackle housing testify to the misery. Most often the schools in the ghettos reflect the absence of social responsibility.

Despite many signs of social decay, racism, the growing gaps between rich and poor, and environmental destruction, there is much hope. Jane Jacobs, the author of the great American classic *The Death and Life of Great American Cities*, identifies in her new but discouraging book *Dark Age Ahead* the promise of higher education for changing the world.[14] The tragedies that are reflected in sad cities and ghettos may mirror our own feelings about being disconnected from a more complete life. But in these lost places, we see courage, the willingness to work through the darker side, and the terrors of annihilation. As educators, we have to teach hope even when we, ourselves, may feel hopeless.

THESIS

A thesis belongs at the beginning. Because many of the ideas that follow have already been expressed in this chapter, I beg your indulgence for this transgression. I believe:

- The arts possess an exceptional capacity to inspire concern through the release of energy and passion.
- The "safe remove" of art helps us to integrate powerful contradictory and disturbing feelings, as we see ourselves in others' experiences, and increases our capacity for caring.
- Art encourages the imagination, and all learning requires imaginative thinking.

- Art can exist for its own sake. It can also exist for social praxis without compromising the artistic process.
- Both teachers and artists bring new forms into existence.

EPILOGUE

I wish my father could have read this chapter. We could communicate about something that bridged our differences. Telling our story and thinking about our thoughts in another context is a beginning. This is the meaning of reflection and the purpose of this chapter. I know that I'll keep looking at those old postcards of New York City.

NOTES

1. Rose, K., & Kincheloe, J. (2003). *Art, culture and education: Artful teaching in a fractured landscape*. New York: Peter Lang.

2. Rose, K. (1971). *A gift of the spirit*. New York: Holt, Rinehart & Winston.

3. Grumet, M. (1988). Where the line is drawn. In *Bitter milk*. Amherst, MA: University of Massachusetts Press.

4. Bruner, J. (1973). *Beyond the information given: Studies in the psychology of knowing*. New York: Norton.

5. Stewart, M. (1997). *Thinking through aesthetics*. Worcester, MA: Davis; Gardner, H. (1983). *Frames of mind*. New York: Basic Books.

6. Dissanayake, E. (1988). *What is art for?* Seattle: University of Washington Press.

7. Smith, R. (2003, May 13). Why attack art? *New York Times*, p. E1.

8. Carson, R. (1956). *The sense of wonder*. New York: Harper & Row.

9. Langer, S. (1956). *Problems of art*. New York: Scribners.

10. Ackerman, D. (1990). *A natural history of the senses*. New York: Vintage Books.

11. Lawrence, J. (1995). *The great migration: An American story*. New York: HarperCollins.

12. Lehrer, W., & Sloan, J. (2003). *Crossing the boulevard: Strangers, neighbors, and aliens in a new America*. New York: Norton.

13. Dawson, B. (2003). *Street graphics*. New York: Thames & Hudson.

14. Jacobs, J. (2004). *Dark age ahead*. New York: Random House.

Education Policy and Urban Education

SYSTEM-TO-SYSTEM PARTNERSHIP AS A REFORM STRATEGY FOR URBAN SCHOOLS

Marleen C. Pugach, Linda Post, Christine Anderson,
Robert Lehmann, and Daniel J. Donder

Partnerships for reforming urban schools are often short-lived, dependent on a single strong leader in one or more of the partner organizations, and involve only a small number of targeted schools. As such, partnerships tend not to be successful in achieving *systemic* reform in urban schools. Many stakeholders and constituencies within urban communities are committed to improving education in their public schools and make significant contributions to this end. Often, however, these represent only limited partnerships—between one business and one school, between one agency and a small number of schools, between a university's teacher education program and one or two specific schools, or short-term grants to a several schools. Individual schools may get a boost—and much needed additional resources—by partnering, for example, with a university as a professional development school, with a health organization to install a school-based clinic, or with a Boys and Girls Club

of YMCA to provide after-school programming. Partnerships like these certainly may be critical to the success of the individual schools that are fortunate enough to participate. But taken together, such efforts do not have the cumulative effect of addressing the full scale of challenges that exist within urban school districts as a whole.

The challenges facing urban schools are systemic, and although each individual school must certainly engage in its own improvement, reforming urban education school by school will simply not get the job done when individual schools exist within a larger educational system that itself requires reform. Done in isolation, small-scale partnership efforts do not span the central players and constituencies that are fundamental to the operation of the schools. Therefore, they cannot hope to have a sustained effect on closing the persistent achievement gap. To attain success in reform and to close the achievement gap that continues to challenge urban schools, it will take a carefully coordinated effort on the part of the community as a whole, a partnership that engages education, community and business leaders, and marshals a collective commitment to the public schools. Partnerships have the potential to support widespread, systemic reform if the partnership itself is designed and implemented as a rigorous reform strategy that is squarely focused on improving the quality of teaching and learning for children and youth in urban schools.

The Milwaukee Partnership Academy (MPA) represents a sustained attempt to reform urban schools by engaging multiple education, community, and business partners in a *system-to-system* reform. It is based on the belief that improving the quality of teaching and learning in the Milwaukee Public Schools (MPS) is the joint business of the universities and colleges, the public schools, and the community at large. These stakeholders must join together to form a serious, long-term, action-oriented partnership—and be willing to support change within and across the partner organizations that all make up the system that currently is failing urban schools—for serious reform to have a chance of succeeding.[1] The stakes for the economic and social well-being of the community and its current and future citizens are the foundation for the sense of urgency that should drive institutions and organizations within urban communities to join together to plan and implement coordinated, aligned initiatives that are needed to improve the educational experience and success of students in all urban schools—not only to those in a few schools.

WHO ARE THE PARTNERS AND WHAT ARE THE PARTNERSHIP'S PRIORITIES?

The MPA is an urban P–16 council made up of three interrelated groups that form its governing structure: (1) the Executive Partners, (2) the Partners, which represent wide community constituencies, and (3) the Implementation Team, which is the action arm of the MPA. These three groups interact on a regular basis. The partnership's priorities are set by the Executive Partners and are carried out by an Executive Director.

The Executive Partners

The ten-member Executive Partners group is made up of leaders of major organizations within the community. They include:

1. The Chancellor of the University of Wisconsin-Milwaukee
2. The Superintendent of the Milwaukee Public Schools
3. The Executive Director of the Milwaukee Teachers' Education Association, the local teachers' union
4. The President of the MPS Board of School Directors
5. The President of the Milwaukee Area Technical College (MATC)
6. The President of the Milwaukee Metropolitan Association of Commerce, the local chamber of commerce
7. The Chair of the Education Committee of the Greater Milwaukee Committee, a group of business leaders
8. The President of the Private Industry Council
9. The Mayor of the City of Milwaukee
10. The President the Helen Bader Foundation, a local foundation with historical ties to the education community.

Once a month the Executive Partners meet to discuss the MPA's progress and to make decisions regarding the policies and priorities of the partnership. An additional meeting that is held quarterly is a meeting of the full group of partners from across the community. One of the members of the Executive Partners group leads the quarterly meeting, which is a public, two-hour meeting of the full MPA.

These leaders command attention, control resources, and hold power in their organizations and in the community, and their presence is fundamental to the joint commitment to institutionalize, stabilize, and sustain the partnership and, thus, provide stability to education reform in Milwaukee's urban schools. The visible participation of high level leaders—they do not send representatives to meetings but rather have made a commitment to attend themselves—provides credibility to the importance of the MPA. The culture of the partnership has created the expectation that the leaders of these organizations are present at each meeting themselves, with no substitutes, to work together on the goal of improving education in the community.

To focus its work, the Executive Partners identify a set of priorities that address the overall mission of the partnership, namely, to ensure that every child is on grade level in reading, writing, and mathematics. These priorities are essential to the work of the MPA because they provide a common understanding of where and how resources and efforts are to be aligned. In this way, they can begin to counteract the cycle that typically prevails in urban schools, namely, generating and then discarding new, often unrelated, initiatives every year. These priorities are revisited each summer, not to change direction, but rather to fine-tune the work and to respond to conditions that may have changed and that affect their implementation. The current MPA priorities include:

1. Districtwide implementation of a comprehensive literacy and mathematics framework
2. Tutoring and family literacy
3. Teacher and principal quality (with an emphasis on coaching and embedded professional development)
4. Research and evaluation
5. Skunkworks (a group that thinks "out of the box" about educational issues)
6. Community partners (to align the work of informal educational agencies and foundations with the MPA)

The MPA Partners

Participation in the MPA exists laterally across the community, and vertically within partner organizations through its extensive group of Partners. Partners include broad representation from the metropolitan community. Leaders from the public library, the YMCA, the museum, and the zoo, for example, participate regularly in the MPA. Membership also includes the deans of the School of Education, College of Letters and Sciences, and Peck School of the Arts at UWM, as well as the Chairperson of the Department of Curriculum and Instruction. The broad range of affiliates extends as well to the local foundation and donor community, private colleges and universities, as well as to the ongoing, consistent presence of government officials—for example, the state Superintendent of Public Instruction, who regularly attends each meeting with staff.

These quarterly Partner meetings serve an important public function for the partnership. It is here that the Executive Partners report on their work, workgroups report on their progress, and the input of community stakeholders is solicited on MPA initiatives. These meetings provide ongoing momentum for the work of the partnership at the community level. In addition, they function to create a common understanding of the activities that are being implemented to address the priorities and to align the language and concepts that undergird the collective efforts of the partners. Quarterly meetings begin with a report from the superintendent of schools and from the partnership's Executive Director. Discussions about critical issues in the district and the community take place. Each meeting is an important opportunity both to honor accomplishments and to refocus and recommit the partnership to its goal of improving the quality of education for the children of Milwaukee. Ultimately, the dialogue is focused on the well-being of the children of the community, and there is a high level of awareness that collective leadership across the full complement of partners is unique and, as such, provides a unique and unusual opportunity to make a difference for the entire local urban community.

The Implementation Team

Partnerships that are serious about reforming urban education cannot merely meet to discuss the issues. The Implementation Team is the action arm of the MPA and is charged with creating and carrying out action plans to support the MPA's priorities. This team was appointed in 2001 and includes multiple representatives from the partner organizations. The Executive Director of the MPA chairs the team, sets the agenda, and keeps the work of the group on track. For each priority there is a workgroup that reports to the full Implementation Team, which meets on a biweekly basis. The Implementation Team's workgroups extend participation to include any interested stakeholders, and it is not uncommon for the Executive Director to get calls from individuals who wish to participate; participation is entirely voluntary.

From an initial schedule of weekly meetings for two full years (2001–03), the team now meets one half-day per week on a biweekly basis, 12 months of the year. The full team meets for two hours, during which workgroups report on their progress. This helps to avoid duplication of effort and also enables workgroups to combine their meetings and short-term goals appropriately. This is followed by a two-hour meeting of each of the workgroups (although some workgroups meet on a different schedule). Periodically representatives of specific programs that are relevant to the workgroups make brief presentations to the team.

The Implementation Team is commonly referred to as the place where the "real work" of the MPA gets done. The goal of its work is to keep focused on the critical priorities of the partnership and resist having efforts be diffused across a broad range of unrelated initiatives. This team keeps it focus on aligning initiatives, realigning resources for the priorities, garnering new resources in an aligned manner, and streamlining the work of the schools—in short, to change the way "business is done" within and across the partners to improve the quality of teaching and learning. If the Executive Partners are thought of as having responsibility to work "on the system," the Implementation Team has the responsibility of working "in the systems," that is, in the various systems within each of the partner organizations themselves.

Key related activities of the district flow through the Implementation Team for ongoing direction and feedback. Early in its first year, this team directly addressed the long-standing skepticism of local teachers that any initiative could be sustained over time or that enough people in charge had the big picture in mind. As the team planned for introducing the priorities, the question of how to gain the teachers' "buy in" and the seriousness of purpose were central considerations. The direct participation of the teachers union in all levels of the partnership helped ensure that from the outset of the partnership, there was a shared understanding of the teachers' concerns and how to address them. The existence of the partnership as a whole, and the Implementation Team in particular, have begun to permeate the vocabulary of all partners and it is becoming common knowledge that if one wishes to interact with senior people from the partner organizations regularly, every other Monday afternoon, which is when the team meets, is the time and place to find them.

Although there are official voting members of this team representing the principal organizations in the partnership, the work that has been accomplished to date has been accomplished by consensus. Membership on the Implementation Team remains constant and includes representatives from the district, the local public university, the community college, the teachers' union (including its president), parents, community organizations, and two representatives from the five private colleges and universities in the area. The three university and college representatives are all senior faculty members who carry a high degree of status on campus. Leaders of the major departments in the school district, including the Director of Teaching and Learning, the Chief Academic Officer, the Director of Assessment and Accountability, and the Director of Leadership Support, are part of the district's membership. Stability of membership is required because this team must deal with complex issues that challenge the status quo directly; this requires a high degree of trust among members.

The Implementation Team is a labor-intensive effort, which has become a critical source of brainstorming, action, and consensus building around the work of the partnership. This team is evidence of an important principle of the partnership—namely, that it takes *both* senior-level leadership on a communitywide basis and leadership at the level of those who take daily action to be successful in achieving system-wide change. Implementation Team members are asked to participate in the quarterly MPA Partner meetings, and several do; workgroup chairs must be present to report on the progress of their group's goals. A substantial portion of the agenda for the quarterly meetings evolves directly from the work of the Implementation Team, and the agenda for the team is directed by the decisions of the Executive Committee.

HOW DOES AN URBAN PARTNERSHIP ALIGN ITS WORK?

The MPA provides the Milwaukee community with a broad-based infrastructure to promote sustained engagement in aligning the educational efforts of all partners to produce a shared educational framework within which to improve student learning. Unlike the situation in many other urban communities, the infrastructure provided by the MPA creates a local policy environment that is focused on mobilizing the various strengths and resources of the urban community toward collaborative and shared responsibility in ensuring student success in the Milwaukee Public Schools. It provides a structure for the regular presence of leaders from various constituencies to demonstrate their commitment to education in the community, with a common interest in the quality of learning for Milwaukee's youth and a commitment to shared responsibility to provide stability and sustainability in reforming education.

The MPA not only allows multiple stakeholders and key constituents to come together to make the changes that will ensure student success in the educational system, but by providing shared identity and visibility to this collaborative relationship, it has also compelled a more consistent commitment and greater accountability on the part of all the partners. The breadth and range of this constantly growing partnership indicates an increasing public awareness that reforming urban education is a collective responsibility and that this change must be systemic. As such, all participating partners realize their role in contributing to a collective vision of school success, and consider how their organization may need to change to maximize its contribution to local educational reform. How resources and activities are aligned is central to this effort. With the concept of alignment firmly established, local leaders look toward deliberately creating opportunities for alignment across the regular range of activities, requirements, and resources that exist both within the school district and across the partners, and consider new ways of thinking about their own organization's commitment to the education community.

One important example of alignment relates to one of the strategic priorities of the MPA—*teacher and principal quality*. The ongoing professional development of teachers is a critical component in reaching the goal of having all children on grade level in reading, writing, and mathematics. Like the other priorities of the MPA, the teacher and principal quality priority has as one of its goals the coordination and alignment of resources to improve the district's capacity to offer high quality professional development opportunities that are squarely focused on the goals of the district. Typically, especially in a decentralized system of schools, principals and teacher committees seek professional development opportunities wherever they can. Many high-quality opportunities for professional development are offered across several departments of the district, but as is the case in many large urban districts, they have not been well aligned. The development of the MPA has provided an entity that can shape, broker, align, assess, and evaluate professional development opportunities for teachers in MPS to help improve classroom practice specifically for urban schools. Working in a highly coordinated fashion through the Implementation Team, the ongoing development of teachers is seen as a community-wide responsibility in Milwaukee; which is a fundamental assumption of the MPA itself.

Related to professional development is the role of the local institutions of higher education, the relationship of their goals to the priorities of the MPA, and reforms needed within these institutions. As state requirements for teacher education shift, the intersection of those changes with the goals of the partnership has become extended territory for discussions about alignment. For example, when the state shifted to a standards-based approach to initial teacher certification and a career ladder for moving to permanent licensure,

the MPA viewed this as an opportunity to create—with these institutions, the district, and the teachers union—a conceptual framework for what those standards mean, specifically for teachers in urban schools, that would guide the career-long professional development of MPS teachers as they move from initial to permanent status. This document, *Characteristics of a High-Performing Urban Classroom*, provides a common language for dialogue about instruction in several critical areas. A final example of alignment as regards teacher and principal quality is the development of a comprehensive induction system for new teachers, which is aligned to the new state career ladder.

Another area in which the MPA is building a commitment to alignment is through grant writing. Partners seek grants to support the priorities of the MPA and work across institutions within the partnership to develop proposals. Grants are seen as opportunities to support various aspects of the MPA priorities and these priorities shape how grants are written and which partners are included. As grants are being prepared, progress is reported out to both the Implementation Team and at quarterly MPA meetings. As the MPA has grown in stature in the community, grant writers from various institutions, not limited to Milwaukee, are increasingly interested in drawing on the partnership as part of the rationale for their proposals. To ensure alignment, individuals or groups that wish to submit a grant that references the MPA as part of the rationale must present the proposal to the Implementation Team. The Research and Evaluation Workgroup co-chairs review the proposal and bring it to the full Implementation Team for approval; only then will the grant writers receive a letter of support from the MPA. In addition, those who staff the grant in question must contribute directly to the work of the MPA. If this has not occurred before the grant is written, it becomes a condition of MPA approval that participation in the MPA take place. In addition, the Director of the Division of Assessment and Accountability often receives grant proposals directly and, if they are related to the priorities of the MPA, brings those to the Implementation Team for approval as well. These are all efforts to align the work to the priorities of the MPA, maximize resources, widen the scope of participation in the community, and reshape the view and practice of research from an individual to a collective purpose. This requires changes—especially for the colleges and universities—in the way grant writing is conducted. The regular meetings of the Implementation Team assure that grant writers have frequent, easy access to the MPA to support grant preparation in a timely manner. Further, the MPA has worked with local donors to provide direct support to strategic organizational strategies, for example, to support school-based leadership teams, known locally as Learning Teams, as the agents of organizational change in the schools.

A third example is the concerted effort to increase the number of school nurses in MPS. The number is markedly low in Milwaukee, compared to the rest of the state, which directly affects the ability of the children in MPS to focus on their studies. This effort began at the district superintendent's office. The partnership became a focal point for this effort by educating the partners about this problem and by bringing together the deans of nursing and education from area institutions to support the effort and to rethink their preparation programs in relationship to the schools.

Alignment, focus, and keeping on message continue to be critical to the success of this partnership. The process of shaping the actions of the partners around the priorities and goals of the partnership—as a mutual and reciprocal activity—is never a completed task, but requires constant attention if the alignment process is to result in the level and scope of improvements that are needed.

BUILDING TRUST ACROSS LARGE URBAN BUREAUCRACIES

Whether it is entering into a joint business venture, embarking on a long-term personal relationship, or developing a complex partnership with multiple organizations, the concept of trust building is essential if there is to be meaningful involvement and mutual benefit. In many ways, the first two examples cited are far easier to develop and sustain than the latter. Individuals seeking to join resources and expertise in a business climate usually have had previous knowledge of each other's work and experience in a professional environment that helps them decide whether or not entering into a working partnership is in their mutual interests. And certainly those who are making decisions concerning life partnerships often have developed close relationships that start with an opening of self and continue by nurturing an ongoing commitment.

Organizational partnerships, on the other hand, often begin with certain stressors already in place and are faced with the challenges of not only overcoming past histories, but also reversing relationships that may have been founded on diametrically opposed philosophies. For example, in a complex structure such as the Milwaukee Partnership Academy, partners who are firmly planted on opposite sides of the school voucher issue work together in concert around a framework for improving Milwaukee Public Schools. One has to ask how organizations that are so polarized ideologically on such a fundamental level can even be at the same table, let alone develop and sustain a trusting relationship. The answer, although quite basic in theory, is far more complex in practice. The fact is that, unlike business partners or married couples who enter into long-term relationships from a base that may already be strong, with the desire to make it even better, organizational partnerships are often begun in an environment that may be less than ideal, but may risk even further peril without systemic change. In other words, all parties must believe it is in their individual and collective best interests to work together for the greater good.

The real challenge then is to get the parties to realize that, if there is to be an end product that is beneficial to all, they must set aside their personal agendas and trust that others will do the same. This should not require a compromise of values or an expectation that others should cede their fundamental beliefs in an effort to make the partnership work. To do so would most assuredly guarantee failure. Rather, the partners must develop a level of trust that says, "This is where we stand when it comes to this issue. We understand that while we are both working toward a common goal, we can respectfully disagree on this issue and trust that neither party will use its influence to try to leverage the other partners in this area." This can only work if several key pieces are in play.

First, issues about which disagreement exists cannot be so fundamentally opposed to the very reason for the partnership that parties cannot function within their common agenda. Given the voucher example previously cited, both the teachers union and the chamber of commerce can stand solidly on opposite sides of this issue. As long as their common agenda recognizes that a strong public school system benefits the entire community, they can work together through the MPA to improve student achievement within Milwaukee Public Schools and continue to support their positions on vouchers outside of the partnership. This relationship can only work if there is a level of trust between partners that is open and honest about issues of disagreement, and if the partners remain true to their commitment to the common goal of improving education for all of Milwaukee's students.

A second important aspect in the success of such an arrangement is the role of the other partners in helping strengthen relationships between parties, especially in instances where day-to-day operations can put a strain on the partnership. Several examples may clarify this point. During a time of intense collective bargaining between the union and the district, for example, it is imperative that the other partners are sensitive to this dynamic and keep both parties focused on the bigger picture. Similarly, when staffing concerns arise between the university and the district's human resources department, the other partners need to be sensitive to such potential problems and refocus energy toward the larger goal. Approaching problems as an expected part of the process enables the partners to address them less as crises or adversarial events and more as barriers that require the best thinking of all of the partners, as well as timely interventions and solutions. A strong partnership can actually enhance these working relationships and help to mitigate otherwise damaging situations.

The third, and probably most important, component to a successful partnership is that the reason for its very existence has to be of such significance that the partners would be negatively impacted if the partnership were to dissolve. In other words, the stakes must be so high for the success of the partnership that each of the parties must commit to a positive outcome—because failure is not a viable option for the students in MPS and for the community. This last point emphasizes the necessity for a relationship among all partners built on trust. As trust builds across the partners, honest feedback and criticism can take place relative to all of the partners. Each partner serves as a friendly critic of the others in a context of trust and a shared focus. Each partner must be daring enough to bring to its constituency the work of the partnership, and each must honor the trust that the other partners place in it. To do otherwise could destroy the partnership.

SUSTAINING THE PARTNERSHIP FOR LONG-TERM EFFECTIVENESS

This then leads us to a brief discussion on sustainability. For any partnership to be effective it must stand the test of time. There are most certainly no guarantees to the longevity of any relationship, even those that are founded on mutual respect and understanding, borne out by the high divorce rate and equally high number of business failures reported in this country every year. Several tenets in establishing organizational partnerships can help to maintain the relationship. Especially important is the realization that, although strong individuals are necessary to any working relationship, particularly in the establishment phase, solid structures are far more important.

Most assuredly, with time, individuals will come and go, but if the partnership is to sustain and grow, it must be able to withstand such mobility, and consequently structures must be in place early on to make this happen. This partnership has sustained three major leadership changes—the local superintendent, the chancellor of the local university, and the teachers union—indicating that it is becoming institutionalized as a way of approaching educational reform in Milwaukee's urban community and in its urban schools. During these transitions, key leaders—both formally and behind the scenes—worked assiduously to communicate the goals and benefits of the partnership to the new leaders. As the MPA is increasingly established as a force in the community, its visibility, existence, and success can create the expectation that new leaders will sustain active participation.

Another key factor in the sustainability of organizational partnerships is the development of mechanisms to deal with surfacing problems, as well as intermittent crises, quickly and effectively. At the outset, the partners need to identify individuals who are given the authority to make decisions for their respective organizations, and this group needs to meet on a regular basis to identify and address issues as they arise. Trust is strengthened and nourished with each successful resolution to such situations, and as trust grows, the chances of sustaining the partnership increase. And probably the single most important factor in the success of any partnership is communication. Structures need to be in place not only for a regular sharing of ideas and concerns, but also for periodic retreats of a more substantive nature that allow for midcourse assessment and directional adjustments.

In terms of meeting the challenges facing urban schools, there is perhaps no single reform effort that holds such promise as the forming and forging of such partnerships. Because the potential is so great and the desired outcomes equally promising, the risks of such endeavors are certainly worth exploring. If the parties are so inclined, however, they must be willing to travel outside of their normal operational comfort zone and be willing to place their organizational trust in each other and, more importantly, in the newly formed entity that is the partnership.

HOW CAN SYSTEMIC PARTNERSHIPS BENEFIT URBAN SCHOOLS?

What are the specific benefits that can accrue to urban schools within a systemic urban partnership? What results have been attained thus far?

Urban partnerships uncover the complexity within the array of institutions and organizations that are responsible for P-16 education. Each education partner learns the complexity of each other's institutions and bureaucracies and provides a realistic understanding regarding how business gets done—and how business needs to change to better support the schools.

Further, the partnership provides a structure within which all of the local area institutions that prepare teachers come together regularly to discuss relevant issues, raise concerns, and interact collectively with school district personnel. This occurs through the regular structures of the partnership. It also takes place through a new local organization, the Metropolitan Milwaukee Area Deans of Education, which is convened by the Dean of the School of Education at the University of Wisconsin-Milwaukee and includes all the education deans from the local public and private institutions as well as the Executive Director of the MPA. Because the partnership's priorities—and not the priorities of any individual institution of higher education—drive the MPA, each institution has to rethink its relationship to the district and how best to contribute to it. For example, this is the group that convened the joint meeting of the deans of nursing and education to address the shortage of school nurses in the district.

Next, there is a joint sense of accountability across partner institutions, which shifts the conversation from blaming the school district in an isolated fashion for problems and challenges to a conversation based on joint responsibility for its improvement. The structure and membership of the MPA enable the tone of local discourse about education to be a discourse of mutual learning and action across education and economic forces and institutions within the community.

The partnership also enables regular discussions to take place regarding teachers' content preparation by having school district and partnership personnel interact with deans and faculty in the arts and sciences on a regular basis. The resources of the institutions of higher education are not limited to education departments, but extend campus-wide as a way of beginning to rethink the relationship between the academic disciplines, the preparation of teachers, and the school district's curriculum. Further, the relationship between academic preparation at the community college and the four-year institutions is also facilitated through the partnership.

Finally, because the partnership is committed to using evidence to drive its work, data regarding the academic performance of students are being looked at and disaggregated in new ways. For example, a new reporting structure instituted in the first set of priorities provided data on individual students, classroom progress, and school-wide progress in a formal report that was never before available. This also enabled a discussion of how data are collected and what data are needed. These data were never before collected, with the result that district teachers, administrators, and families were not well informed about student progress.

In terms of student learning, the MPA is starting to see the results of its work in improved student achievement in the elementary grades that has been sustained over a three-year period, although challenges still exist at the secondary level. The comprehensive literacy and mathematics frameworks have resulted in a sustained commitment to job-embedded professional development in each local school site. School-based learning teams that require the membership of teacher leaders in literacy (literacy coaches) and mathematics (mathematics teacher leaders), as well as the building principal, have been developed and implemented to take responsibility for creating professional learning communities in each school and to use local evidence to inform its decision making. A coaching model for principals and teachers sustains the focus on teacher development. These early accomplishments enable the partnership to renew its commitment to sustaining its work for long-term gains—rather than changing course because the gains are not broad enough or deep enough in the short term, which is typically how urban districts have functioned in the past.

CONCLUSION

Why are systemic partnerships so crucial to the improvement of urban schools? The various institutional bureaucracies that affect education are larger, more numerous, and perhaps more intractable in urban communities. Often they cloud the issues rather than clarify them. Through its structure of distributed and shared leadership, the MPA not only allows its members to cut across institutional and organizational boundaries to work collaboratively toward improving the quality of urban education, but also lets the partners engage with each other to envision and plan for education reform without being limited as much as usual by existing bureaucratic governance structures. The mission of the MPA—shared responsibility and accountability for student success—is echoed by other P-16 councils across the nation. By joining together, the entire community takes responsibility for the education of its students and serves as a counterweight to the long-standing practice of blaming either the school district or the teachers union for the problems that exist.

What is unique and groundbreaking about the MPA is the manner in which the partners have embraced the challenge of aligning efforts to improving the education of all children through better preparation, recruitment, and retention of teachers in an urban setting. The MPA presents a bold move on the part of various institutions and organizations in Milwaukee. It is not the "initiative of the week." Rather, this work represents a collective commitment to accept the challenge that improvement means staying the course, while also maintaining a sense of urgency as a driving force to improve the education—and the future—of students in urban schools.

NOTES

The authors would like to acknowledge each of their colleagues who work on and contribute to the Milwaukee Partnership Academy, as well as Nancy Zimpher and Kenneth Howey, who were instrumental in establishing the partnership and supporting it in its early years.

1. Pugach, M., Post, L., & Thurman, A. (2006). All-university engagement in education reform: The Milwaukee partnership academy. In S. Percy, N. Zimpher, & M. Brukhardt (Eds.), *Creating a new kind of university*. Bolton, MA: Anker Publishing.

DIVERSITY AND SECURITY CHALLENGES FOR URBAN SCHOOL PLANNING AND CHANGE

Carol A. Mullen

What are some of the major challenges in preparing teachers for their future roles as leaders of urban schools? Specifically, what roles do security and diversity play in relation to one another as educational reform goals? This chapter addresses these two questions.

The potential impact of terrorism attacks on schools has necessitated a new role for leadership teams at the school and district level. Although learning how to deal with terrorism has become central to U.S. foreign policy, transference has only just begun: Principals and superintendents have been called upon to guide action for preventing catastrophe and simultaneously to promote the health of school populations. In this picture health has two central meanings—safety and inclusion—and involves crisis awareness and diversity awareness.

CLIMATE OF CRISIS AND UNCERTAINTY

The responsibility for security will need to be shaped in accordance with cultural diversity goals and a democratic commitment to safe and inclusive schools. Importantly, although efforts to counter escalated violence can create safer schools, goals of diversity and democracy have yet to be mindfully integrated as part of this vision.

Violence prevention at the school community level is a timely topic for both scholarship and practice, which researchers and practitioners have only begun to address. Leaders engaged in planning (bio)terrorism prevention have before them the challenge to promote diversity and security consciousness in crisis emergency preparedness. Any planning that addresses making schools safe without taking into account diversity issues will create an unbalanced coordination effort, even unintentionally permitting racial acts. As recognized by the co-editors of this publication, "The crisis atmosphere and the uncertainty of the continuity of urban educational governance structures make it difficult for urban school administrators and teachers to focus on long term projects."[1] The climate of crisis in America tends to thwart long-term planning within its urban schools, which ironically diverts attention away from the responsibility of forging communities out of ethically and economically diverse cultures that are free of "hidden interpersonal violence (bullying, harassment, and sexual violence)."[2]

School principal teams face the challenge of guiding action at all K–12 levels in order to demonstrate the cultural awareness and problem-solving required for developing emergency preparedness and response systems consistent with expectations for homeland security. Although efforts to counter the threat of new forms of violence can create safer schools, the national goals of diversity and democracy cannot be sacrificed in the process. Indeed, with the tightening of security, the country has been witnessing an escalation in the scapegoating of particular ethnic groups.[3] The protection of schools through emergency preparedness therefore demands vigilance against racial profiling.

Stories about racially motivated acts have abounded since 9/11/2001. For example, a Middle-Eastern university student experienced blatant mistreatment by national authorities. Handcuffed and detained after he registered, as required, by the U.S. Citizenship and Immigration Services (USCIS) for having aroused suspicion, he was later discovered to have been "guilty" only of registering for less than a full load of courses that semester—a course load that his advisor had approved.[4] It appears that even when communities of color access what K.S. Berry refers to as "institutionalized sites of whiteness," that "signs of racial superiority and cultural hegemony" remain hidden, obscuring "the violence of power and privilege."[5] Once triggered, racially motivated assaults guised as security, protection, and patriotism rise with grave consequences for schools and society.

School leaders need to learn to deal productively with what on the surface appears to be a contradiction between emergency prevention and diversity awareness. This requires more than sensitivity to the complex issues involved, perhaps even the recognition of a new leadership disposition expressed as a whole-community attitude that envisions stakeholder groups as collaborators in fostering safety, tolerance, and inclusion while vigilantly monitoring inhumane incidents.

PIVOTAL TERMS AND DEFINITIONS

Key definitions herein include *diversity awareness*, which refers to the capacity of school leaders to demonstrate "democratic fairness and justice" in identifying and changing "systemic racism" as well as the "inequitable treatment of children of color in our schools."[6]

Next, the term *rationalized racism* may be original: it denotes the opposite of social justice, meaning those values and behaviors that violate the fundamental premise of democracy and the right of every citizen to be treated equally in all public spheres, including schools.

Racial profiling, which is pervasive in society and ranges from employment and promotion contexts to policing and arrests,[7] underscores the escalated stereotyping of outsiders, internationals, and persons of color as potential sources of threat within the context of violence prevention.

Finally, *terrorism* means repressing or domineering by means of panic and fear. And *bioterrorism* is "the intentional use of infectious biological agents, or germs, to cause illness."[8] The author will use "(bio)terrorism" throughout this chapter to represent both terms.

TRENDS IN THE RELEVANT LITERATURE

This section spans terrorism and policy, school safety trends in the literature, and leadership standards for school administrators.

Terrorism and Learning

Terrorism and learning how to deal with inherent perpetual threats at the national and global level have become central to U.S. foreign policy. However, this transference has yet to occur locally, at the organizational level of schools and universities.[9] At this time, curriculum remains almost unaffected while major universities throughout the country conduct "national security research" that addresses "the federal government's homeland security priorities." For example, the state of Florida recently awarded $5 million to the University of South Florida to build a Center for Biodefense.[10]

Given that the nation's security concerns have changed so dramatically since the tragedy of 9/11 and the war with Iraq, schools are being called upon to think and act differently. Activism is needed at the action-oriented preventive level, as well as at the more abstract level of conceptualizing violence (e.g., terrorism, (bio)terrorism, and war) and its potential impact on schools. Specialized types of curricula have begun emerging to help children and adolescents understand racially-sensitive issues resulting from terrorism, particularly that of "wrongful attribution," and also to help them process powerful feelings of fear, hatred, and anger.[11]

Innovative programs that comprehensively address the issue of building skills and awareness in diversity–security planning have sporadically appeared. The Texas School Safety Center claims to prepare school administrators to address cultural sensitivity in developing more secure school environments.[12] A significant challenge for leadership teams and university educators is to resist avoiding diversity–security planning while engaged in the process of crisis prevention and change. A surface approach to whole-school change would separate diversity from security awareness-building or simply pay homage to the former. As a solution, diversity training can be carried out simultaneously with emergency planning to reinforce their interrelatedness in achieving safer schools. However, beyond sketchy programmatic descriptions, an understanding of this change process has yet to be illuminated in the literature.

In some educational and societal circles it appears that commitment to social justice has been reinvigorated. On the other hand, some curriculum theorists and policy analysts have described what they see as a "new security regime" coming to life, one that is "dangerous" and that goes beyond the attempt to protect U.S. citizens in order to promote "a new political order."[13] The vigilant activity of the FBI has apparently "increased at colleges and universities since the 9/11 attacks and the passage of the USA Patriot Act in 2001."[14] This act gives the FBI and other national and state authorities the freedom to conduct surveillance and intelligence work without hindrance, in effect suspending the civil rights of students and faculty at college campuses.[15] International students and faculty have been targeted during such campaigns, and some have been subject to detainment and imprisonment, even where terrorist connections have been alleged but not proven. It becomes obvious, then, why emergency procedures must not be developed and enforced independent of a school's diversity mission.

In the following section I describe a master's-level course that I taught in my role as university professor, in which an anonymous FBI agent and sheriff participated as guest lecturers. These individuals were identified by class members as knowledgeable community-based partners. The group of practicing K–12 teachers and aspiring school leaders had interacted with the guest lecturers in their respective K–12 school settings, and had recommended them as potential speakers.

On a related topic, the threat of terrorism for school communities throughout our nation occupies a space between reality and fantasy, or between the here-and-now and the imagined future. Given that acts of violence within school environments typically involve explosives and weaponry brought onto campuses by students,[16] the attention terrorism receives in school planning is understandably less immediate. Also, the threat experienced by schools is typically from students and

employees, members of the internal population, rather than from outside forces.[17] Having established the source of most threats launched against U.S. schools, it is also believed by some that schools increasingly constitute soft targets that could attract terrorist attacks.[18]

Children and schools represent national icons that may be in preeminent danger, much like renowned buildings, as demonstrated by 9/11. As Kenneth S. Trump, president of National School Safety and Security Services, claims, "Al Qaeda has reportedly made a direct threat to kill one million of America's children…and schools and school buses with children aboard have been victims of terrorist violence abroad."[19] According to safety and legal specialists, schools must be more protected than ever, as they house innocent citizens and signify the future.

The American Red Cross warns that institutions should prepare for the unthinkable. Under the Homeland Security Advisory System, Code Orange (high threat condition) dictates that school leaders become "alert to suspicious activity and report it to proper authorities" and "review emergency plans," as well as "discuss children's fears concerning possible terrorist attacks." Code Red (severe threat condition) means that such vigilant activities are to be escalated; also, lessons are to be taught on fear and terrorism with mental health counselors available on site.[20]

School Safety Trends in the Literature

Procedural information has rapidly become increasingly available for facilitating the development of whole-school coordination plans and safer contexts for learning. These articles and news updates pertaining to security and terrorism precautions, accessible via the Internet, tend to emphasize the value of particular interventions. Among the most popular elements are student-run, anti-violence organizations; ongoing communication with local experts in emergency operating systems;

partnerships with mental health services, emergency personnel, and other agencies; regular whole-school drills that include and extend beyond bomb threats; security improvement through surveillance measures and increased awareness; and student-staff assemblies that focus on resolving conflict and identifying violent behaviors.[21]

Another literature base emphasizes that emergency plans be developed on site by administrators, teachers, and other partners in order to satisfy the needs of particular situations and entire schools. Context supercedes the value of adopting templates developed by others, as "no single strategy" or set of change strategies fits all school contexts.[22] However, school teams may find available templates useful as starting points for creating and enforcing their own security plans.

In contrast, few research-based case studies have been published that provide living accounts of emergency preparedness, especially from the school practitioner's perspective. In one such account, a teacher leader in Florida explores unresolved questions concerning violence prevention.[23] For this case investigation, a lockdown drill is the basis of the featured scenario. Author P.E. Llewellyn deconstructs this event from the reactions of the assistant principals and principals involved, real "actors" whom she interviewed in her quest to learn to what extent her own district was safety-conscious. However, Llewellyn does not raise the issue of diversity, and particularly of racial awareness.

In another case study, a principal's story about change illustrates a local school process—in Israel. Chen Schechter's narrative features a principal, a former military leader, who successfully led a communal process during a crisis after conducting a self-study assessment of violence. Both personal and cultural levels of instability at the school were investigated, and key stakeholders participated in shared decision making and action. "Process-orientation learning, as opposed to a quick-fix orientation," was modeled, despite the pressure from faculty to rush the change process.[24]

LEADERSHIP STANDARDS FOR SCHOOL ADMINISTRATORS

Professors in leadership studies are currently expected to follow Educational Leadership Constituent Council (ELCC) standards for developing and teaching courses. However, meeting the ELCC standards implies a certain readiness that is not easily conceptualized, taught, or measured by school leaders, university researchers, and policymakers. Only one mention of safety appears in the ELCC standards: "Develop and administer policies that provide a safe school environment and promote student health and welfare."[25] While one could counter that emergency (e.g., bioterrorism) preparation is an example of this standard, this position overlooks contextual issues and how dramatically the world is changing. Instead, the standards give the impression that issues of safety are what they have always been for schools, a myth that promotes complacency or even denial.[26] Managerial-oriented principals (such as those envisioned by the ELCC standards) protect the status quo instead of forging productive change, which some view as endangering the health of schools.[27]

The teaching of the university curriculum that this chaper reports involved risk. A course that deals with (bio)terrorism planning may not be in keeping with the standards or indicators governing those aspects of leadership that a faculty member is supposed to teach. With the adoption of national standards by which to judge university preparation programs that are accredited by the National Council for Accreditation of Teacher Education (NCATE), unresolved issues are evident.

EMPIRICAL CASE STUDY CONTEXT

This empirical case study uses as data the emergency preparation reports that a group of school practitioners collaboratively wrote.[28] The six coauthored case studies were compiled as a course book, and references throughout this chapter will be made to the compilation of student papers that were published internally as a course book.[29] As will be revealed, the treatment of diversity awareness, rationalized racism, and racial profiling was out of step with the expectations for the assignment, and the expectations themselves were less explicit than they should have been. These outcomes serve to emphasize just how difficult it seems to be, even for experienced educators, to integrate emergency preparation with diversity awareness for today's urban schools.[30]

The exercise in diversity–security awareness-building was launched with a challenge put to the teacher group to think "out of the box." On the one hand, individuals were to learn about the impact of biological, chemical, and nuclear terrorism on schools while generating possibilities for aiding prevention and facilitating coordination responsibility. On the other hand, they were to integrate diversity awareness and balance the overall agenda by finding ways to support a new climate of school reform: "Violence prevention and humanitarian values must go hand-in-hand."

Participant Profile and Pedagogical Innovation

A group of 25 master's degree students in an educational leadership program at the University of South Florida, a doctoral, research-extensive institution, participated in a course titled Case Studies in School Administration. The class included only five males, two African Americans, and one Latina. As is typical of this particular graduate context, the majority were U.S. white female students, ranging from 30 to 55 years of age. All were K–12 teachers at the elementary, middle, and high school levels. Four had assumed the dual role of acting assistant principal, and most aspired to be building administrators.

The author had been redesigning the course for increased relevance and contemporary appeal over a five-year period. The spring, 2003, semester in question was no exception and, in fact, represented a culminating effort. The student evaluations portrayed it as a high-risk, cutting-edge experiment in diversity–security preparedness that was timely and important for administrators and teachers alike.

BIOTERRORISM REPORTS

(Bio)terrorism Project Guidelines

The students' crisis management case studies–part fiction, part factual–contained stories and research illustrating the threat of (bio)terrorism and preparedness at the local school-district-community level. Because this topic is new for most students, especially as related to school community awareness and preparation, the goal for the assignment was to gather information from as many sources as possible (e.g., published reports, Internet sites, and experts). This public health issue was presented as one that should concern everyone, not just emergency personnel, policymakers, and media journalists. In an effort to think collectively about the emerging role of leadership as related to crisis prevention and community participation, information about terrorism and bioterrorism was discussed. Guest speakers shared specialized knowledge. Additionally, documented accounts of racial profiling and its recent escalation in the lives of students across the country were also furnished.[31]

The level of discussion was in concert with the pedagogical goal of shedding light on the current realities of what I referred to as rationalized racism at all levels of the educational system. The thought-provoking constructs of "cultural hegemony" and "white privilege"[32] were not used during the discourse. The serious time constraints imposed by the nontraditional academic calendar of eight sessions meant that accessibility was essential, so stories of racism had priority—particularly those documented following 9/11.

The objectives for class members were to explore the issues of (bio)terrorism and racism that confront school leadership today by writing case studies, and to express creativity. The syllabus identified the case study components to be incorporated into the report, ranging from scenario development to planning to tentative solutions. The written instructions were as follows:

Write a case study in (bio)terrorism preparedness that fits your school context(s) and that includes the key stakeholders involved (e.g., superintendent, principal, lead teacher, parent, student, expert, community agency). This is not an isolated problem, but rather one that grows out of the new national standards for violence prevention and expectations for consciousness-raising. Develop a specific scenario and examples that fit this context (e.g., anthrax and contagious disease [e.g., smallpox] threats).

Questions for consideration in your report include:

1. Do you know how to best educate your faculty and school about terrorism and biochemical prevention?
2. Specifically, do you know how and what data to gather and analyze, in order to promote awareness about protection, survival, and future concerns?

   - As examples, do you know which agencies can help with increasing awareness, and do you know their specific areas of expertise and functions (e.g., public health and community medical care centers)?
   - Do you know what you can do to protect yourself and your school relative to different kinds of attack, such as one involving a biochemical agent?
   - Finally, if relevant, identify the most likely biochemical agents and their properties and effects, as well as the treatments for infectious and/or contaminating agents.

In your case study, provide preventive guidelines or coordination plans for bioterrorism attacks. Specify any staff or school training that may be needed, *identify tensions and deep cultural issues* [emphasis added], and keep recommendations or solutions open. Involve key agencies and stakeholders in the assessment of the problem, and interview knowledgeable leaders and specialists in the state and/or at your school and county. Locate and incorporate relevant sources (at least 10) in your report.

Case Study Results: Overview

A comprehensive, analytical reading of the six case studies, yielding five major themes, will now be briefly discussed. In all instances, the case studies reflect the assignment components, with one consistent and significant omission: implications for monitoring racial profiling and increasing diversity awareness. This language, although not specified in the syllabus, was used and illustrated in the class during all meetings. The reports introduced creative elements, including appropriate uses of humor in the development of scenarios and characters (e.g., Dr. Spores, a hospital physician). In no specific order, the case writers developed these six scenarios:

1. Anthrax scare and contamination via flower delivery to a school.
2. A school's exposure to smallpox and the threat of contagious disease.
3. Dispersal of lethal gases from small airplanes flying over a school.
4. Radiological attack on a school via a missile launch into a nuclear power plant.
5. Takeover of the local nuclear power plant in the vicinity of a school.
6. Invasion of a school through contamination of its water supply.

Thematic Patterns in the Reports

Identifying high-risk, (bio)terrorist targets. The writers identified areas within schools as well as markers surrounding them as potentially high-risk terrorist targets.

These included widespread exposure to anthrax through an everyday delivery of flowers to the school office. Similarly, another group constructed a building-level terrorism attack through the spread of smallpox, in the innocuous form of a kindergarten boy who had gone on a cruise on an infected ship. A third case featured the deliberate and widespread contamination of a school's water supply, originating from its own food service facilities. Other cases staged terrorism targets in the immediate communities, but with direct effects on particular schools in the area, through such methods as an air strike using a nearby airport landing strip and a missile launch at a nuclear power plant, as well as the hostile takeover of a nuclear plant.

The imaginary scenarios described had realistic dimensions. Notably, one of the class members' schools was situated directly beside an airplane landing strip, and two others were within a few miles of a nuclear power plant.

Locating the necessary resources. All the emergency prevention reports highlighted resources where (bio)terrorism had erupted within the school communities. The students viewed expert advice, clear procedures, reports, and school funding as indispensable resources for emergency planning. Funding from state and federal governments was recommended to obtain expert consultation and cover the costs of staff training and bioterrorism crisis management. Existing publications from knowledgeable sources were thought essential for educating teachers on how to enhance school security, and so guidelines were incorporated from practical reports.[33]

The case studies encouraged ongoing research for local emergency and other officials to stay current, and stressed the need to update school emergency policies and available expertise. Being able to readily access the necessary information at one's school was highlighted. Some groups believed that a critical resource

was information that had already been memorized by staff concerning procedures to be followed for every conceivable emergency, and even names and phone numbers of key agencies.

Given that official plans for addressing (bio)terrorism were not yet underway in any of the students' actual K–12 schools, one significant resource was the insight shared by local agencies and state experts in the class I taught. To this end, updates were incorporated into the reports to reflect surveillance tips (e.g., maintaining highly visible, well-lit school buildings so that intruders and objects cannot be concealed) from the FBI agent, county sheriff, and other guest speakers.

Partnering with external agencies. Class member reports recognized partnership development as a solution for resolving the relative isolation, complacency, and even deficiencies of schools. One case study portrayed the local emergency ward of a hospital as an avenue for both immediate treatment and a sustained relationship. Better relations with one's own school district personnel and board members were also generally perceived as valuable. Also, reports maintained that any specialist at the school, district, or community level involved in crisis management, such as supervisors and coordinators, should become immediate allies in the coordination of emergency plans at the building level.

All groups saw the necessity for creating and sustaining new unions with existing agencies. These included law enforcement and public health, as well as disease, poison control, and bioterrorism alert centers. Even school weather stations were mentioned in one report, in which the student writers hypothesized that schools across the nation could help save lives in the event of a chemical or biological attack by participating in a national weather monitoring network.

These results fit with the National Public Health Leadership Institute's recommendation that critical relationships be built and reinforced at the school level, beyond skills-based training that prepares leaders for emergencies and bioterrorism.[34] Developing multi-institutional partnerships that link schools, universities, and businesses, particularly in impoverished urban and rural areas of the country, can bring strength and power to each school entity.

Developing a preventive plan for bioterrorism. Every group's case study offered a preventive emergency plan for their schools and school districts; however, the execution of this process seemed to suggest that two somewhat different approaches involving grassroots engagement had been used, probably unwittingly.

For example, in "The Delivery: A Case Study in Bioterrorism Preparedness," the emergency coordination planning process was portrayed as a community partnership endeavor. However, it was the district officials who created the context for input from stakeholder representatives, such as medical experts and law enforcement as well as university and government specialists. It seems disconcerting, even disempowering, that the writers, who are teachers, did not include school representatives—persons like themselves—in their own district planning scenarios. Lines of power and authority are covert bureaucratic structures throughout this case study, even at the point where school personnel finally enter the scene–as recipients of the school district's crisis prevention training for onsite implementation. Here, at the school level, the two components emphasized were: (1) notification of the district supervisor, and (2) containment, following the directions provided, of the bioterrorism agent. Thus, the expectation in this overview of who assumes leadership and who follows seems self-evident, or not subject to question and the opportunity for transformation.

A second approach, representing the middle ground, is reflected in "Case Study: The Cruise to Smallpox, a Week of More than Sun Exposure." Here, the local school context is understood as having agency in the development of coordination plans. However, the role of the school, and specifically that of teachers and administrators, is not actually stated per se. For example, the sentences in this section of the report were constructed with the presumed referents of school, teacher, and administrator, as in "planned coordination with the county and local government emergency management agencies." It can probably be assumed from this semantic construction that some group at the school site is fulfilling the action; however, the nouns are not provided and so must be inferred.

None of the case studies provided a view of teachers and administrators grappling with change together, or of one group channeling genuine support to the other to do so. One explanation might be that class members seemed unaware of the status of the emergency plans in their own schools and district. Anticipating this possibility, the instructor recommended that the groups interview knowledgeable leaders in the state. From this encounter with others, the writers typically learned that, as one group wrote, "All schools in our Florida county have evacuation plans for inclement weather, bomb threats, etc., but no official plans to specifically address terrorism."[35]

Coping with the effects of (bio)terrorism. Although coping with the effects of (bio)terrorism was the least developed theme across the case studies, it nevertheless provided a convergent point of reflection on a critical topic. Several reports mentioned post-traumatic stress syndrome and the various agencies that are prepared to assist with trauma disorder at the school level.[36] The student writers saw the need for preventive care in this context as a rationale for school leaders to develop partnerships with outside agencies.

For all groups, the theme of coping was an outgrowth of the coordination plans they had developed. They emphasized strong bonds with students, families, faculty, government workers, and community agencies. Another recommendation aimed at emotions management and school preparation involved the ongoing training of staff at all educational levels in the acceptance of this new reality. One group strongly suggested that local communities sponsor Neighborhood Watch groups to look out not only for suspicious persons but also for "possible terrorists." This recommendation did not include a reflection on the consequences for racial profiling. Finally, school evacuation drills related to terrorism and bioterrorism threats were endorsed, with support for involving community emergency officials in rehearsals.

DISCUSSION AND REFLECTION

Analysis of the crisis management case studies suggests that, although the master's class experienced a breakthrough in crisis planning, the students insufficiently considered democratic concerns. Related to this, a critical reading of the papers highlights the limited imagined roles of teachers in urban schools. The case studies generally define teachers and even building leaders as passive recipients of orders, not as empowered decision makers. It was disturbing to learn the extent to which dynamics of bureaucratic control were not only implicitly communicated but also presumed to be the natural order and self-evident. These were presented as narrative ideas and actions that supported the plots described rather than as sources of critique. The change agentry of school persons was contingent on the permission granted by school districts, in accordance with decisions endorsed from the top down.

Beyond this experienced K–12 group there appears to be a reified, paternalistic view of school and central administration for many teachers.[37] This "follower mentality" probably reinforces an unconscious acceptance of one's lesser role in the hierarchy, consequently harnessing opportunities for change. One of the new conceptual frames of the master's course features critical philosophical introspection as applied to the worldviews of educators. Teachers who aspire to lead schools may find it empowering to have a profound understanding of the worldview they embody and, where necessary, alternatives that offer not transitory substitutes but a higher threshold for democratic participation.

Reflection on the pedagogical experiment itself brought to light the need for explicit writing direction and reinforcement. School practitioners may require oral and verbal support in order to confront the difficult topic of rationalized racism and its effects on emergency planning, particularly involving (bio)terrorism and the fears this ignites. They also need time for reflection and experimentation, as well as opportunities for collaboration and critique. School practitioners are not alone in the need to collectively bring cultural sensitivity to the forefront of institutional reform. Professors and policymakers also may find it crucial to grapple with more profound understandings of cultural diversity, teacher empowerment, and crisis planning in urban education.

The case-study exercise discussed above provides only a beginning step in this direction; the small sample used (of one group at a single university) makes it difficult to know what can be generalized. However, the questions raised and the results shared should have relevance for anyone inspired to enact social justice agendas where power inequities and personal truths are acknowledged. Also, the broader issues of balancing concerns regarding the appropriate responses to the threats of terrorism are, undoubtedly, of wide interest.

The revised syllabus for this course now expands upon and deepens the original statement, "identify tensions and deep cultural issues." The new instructions for case studies guide the writers to probe relevant issues in readings on racism, diversity, and learning. The groups have since built into their school scenarios and coordination plans practical ideas related to racial interrogation, social justice, and tolerance. Greater balance has been afforded, but the security issue still tends to overshadow the diversity issue, and their interrelationship is not as well understood as it could be. By continuing their own research, these students can return to their workplaces with new possibilities for developing guidelines for healthy school communities that manifest democracy as a condition of security. The effort to produce a more fully-awakened consciousness through emergency planning, whether at the university or school level, necessitates deliberate intervention. Peter N. Stearns, a university provost, claims that any such attempt at transformation is a form of "culture management" where cultural factors are intentionally altered in order to bring about changes in human and social behavior.[38]

Finally, the extent to which crises in terrorism have been manufactured in the United States is not addressed here, but is nonetheless a recognized debate. Legislative mandates involving safety and liability issues for schools have spawned marketers in the form of consulting firms that target crisis preparedness training.[39] Such coalescing realities make it difficult to ascertain how much emergency school responsiveness is rational and authentic apart from media capitalists' own motives. Terrorism cannot escape scrutiny, then, as a marketing and media extravaganza that strategically garners material for both profit and headlines. In their book, *Kinderculture: The Corporate Construction of Childhood*, Steinberg and Kincheloe explore myriad ways in which corporate America shapes childhood identity through a supersaturated, media-frenzied world.[40] This version of reality exhumes the subtext of terrorism and questions the political forces behind the creation of high-scrutiny institutions that promote collective fear and restrict human freedom.

POSTSCRIPT

The road to leadership necessitates a steep climb in today's postmodern urban context. Activism forces change through the confrontation of profound contradictions not only in our immediate environments, but also within our own learning and leading. Through deliberate intervention and reflective inquiry, practitioners can imagine anew while questioning what is taken for granted, and can thereby enact change.

NOTES

In accordance with the University of South Florida's rule 6C4-10.109.B-6, the author confirms that the opinions stated in this publication are her own.

The author, a university professor, is grateful to her graduate students for their participation in this pedagogical experiment, and for their permission to quote from their materials without attribution. The author presented an earlier version of this chapter at the 2003 annual meeting of the University Council for Educational Administration, Portland, OR, and has published a more detailed version in Chapter 10 of her book, *Fire and ice: Igniting and channeling passion in new qualitative researchers* (New York: Peter Lang).

1. Kincheloe, J., Anderson, P., Rose, K., Griffith, D., & Hayes, K. (2003). *Prospectus: Urban education: An encyclopedia*, p. 2. Westport, CT: Greenwood Publishing Group.

2. Lucas, P. (2003, March). Being down: Challenging violence in urban schools. *Teachers College Record, 105* (1), pp. 1–3. Retrieved May 8, 2005, from http://www.tcrecord.org/PrintContent. asp? ContentID=10909.

3. Hoover, E. (2003, April 11). Closing the gates: A student under suspicion. Special report. *Chronicle of Higher Education, 49* (31), p. A12.

4. Hoover (2003).

5. Berry, K. (2002). Color me white: Dismantling white privilege with young students.

Taboo: Journal of Culture and Education, 6 (10), pp. 85–96.

6. Skrla, L., Scheurich, J., Johnson, Jr., J., & Koschoreck, J. (2001). Accountability for equity: Can state policy leverage social justice? *International Journal of Leadership in Education, 4* (3), pp. 237–260.

7. Hoover (2003).

8. Connecticut Department of Public Health. (2003, February). Bioterriorism preparedness fact sheet, pp. 1-4. Retrieved March 10, 2005, from http://www.dph.state.ct.us/Agency_News/FCT_bioterror.

9. National School Safety and Security Services. (2001). Terrorism & school safety: School safety issues related to the terrorist attacks on the United States, pp. 1–8. Retrieved June 15, 2005, from http://www.schoolsecurity.org/resources/nasro_survey_2002.html.

10. Borrego, A. (2003, April 11). The money scramble: Colleges rush to capitalize on the government's push for homeland security. Special report. *Chronicle of Higher Education, 49* (31), p. A22.

11. Jolly, E., Malloy, S., & Felt, M. (2001). Beyond blame: Reacting to the terrorist attack. A curriculum for middle and high school students, pp. 1–25. Newton, MA: Education Development Center. Retrieved July 3, 2005, from http://www.edc.org/spotlight/schools/beyondblame.htm.

12. Texas School Safety Center (2003). Resources online. Retrieved July 18, 2005, from http://www.txssc.swt.edu/resources.htm.

13. Rizvi, F. (2003). Democracy and education after September 11. *Globalisation, Societies and Education, 1* (1), pp. 25–40.

14. Arnone, M. (2003, April 11). Watchful eyes: The FBI steps up its work on campuses, spurring fear and anger among many academics. Special report. *Chronicle of Higher Education, 49* (31), p. A14.

15. Arnone (2003).

16. Sheriff (anonymous), guest lecture. (2003, March).

17. FBI agent (anonymous), guest lecture. (2003, March).

18. FBI agent (anonymous), guest lecture. (2003, March).

19. Trump, K. (2002, July). The impact of terrorism on school safety planning. *School Planning & Management*, pp. 22–26.

20. American Red Cross. (2003, February). Homeland security advisory system recommendations. Retrieved March 1, 2005, from http://www.tallytown.com/redcross/hsas.

21. Della-Giustina, D., Kerr, S., & Georgevich, D. (2000). Terrorism & violence in our schools. *Professional Safety, 45* (3), pp. 16–21.

22. Fullan, M. (1999). *Change forces: The sequel.* London: Sage.

23. Llewellyn, P. (2004, Spring). Will I be ready as an administrator for school emergencies? *International Journal of Educational Reform, 13* (2), pp. 118–125.

24. Schechter, C. (2002, April-June). Marching in the land of uncertainty: Transforming school culture through communal deliberative process. *International Journal of Leadership in Education, 5* (2), pp. 105–128.

25. Educational Leadership Constituent Council (ELCC). (2002). Educational Leadership Constituent Standards. Arlington, VA: National Policy Board for Educational Administration. Retrieved May 18, 2005, from http://www.npbea.org.

26. Mullen, C. (2003). (Bio)terrorism prevention and rationalized racism: Contradictions in homeland security for schools. Paper presented November 23, 2003, at the annual meeting of the University Council for Educational Administration, Portland, OR.

27. Riehl, C. (2000). The principal's role in creating inclusive schools for diverse students: A review of normative, empirical, and critical literature on the practice of educational administration. *Review of Educational Research, 70* (1), pp. 55–81.

28. Mullen, C. (2005). *Fire and ice: Igniting and channeling passion in new qualitative researchers.* New York: Peter Lang.

29. Mullen, C. (2003, April). *Top secret! School crisis management case studies.* Internally published as Case Studies in School Administration at the University of South Florida, Tampa, FL.

30. Mullen (2005).

31. Hoover (2003, April).

32. Berry (2002).

33. Federal Emergency Management Agency. (n.d.). Emergency management guide for business and industry. Retrieved from http://www.fema.gov/library/biz2.shtm. U.S. Department of Justice. (2001, September). OVC handbook for coping after terrorism. Retrieved June 8, 2005, from http://www.ojp.usdoj.gov/ovc/publications/infores/cat_hndbk.

34. National Public Health Leadership Institute. (2003, April). Public health grand rounds,

bioterrorism revisited—Leadership lessons learned?! pp. 1–4. Retrieved July 19, 2005, from http://www.phli.org/.

35. Mullen (2003, April), p. 7. Interview with unnamed county director of transportation.

36. American Red Cross. (2003, February.) Homeland security advisory system recommendations. Retrieved June 13, 2005, from http://www.tallytown.com/redcross/hsas.

37. Mullen, C. (2002). Teacher activism in education reform. *Teacher Development, 6* (1), pp. 1–128.

38. Stearns, P. (2003, May 2). Expanding the agenda of cultural research, pp. B7–B9. *Chronicle of Higher Education, 49* (34).

39. National Policy Board for Educational Administration. (2002). *Instructions to implement standards for advanced programs in educational leadership.* Arlington, VA: NPBEA.

40. Steinberg, S., & Kincheloe, J. (1997). *Kinderculture: The corporate construction of childhood.* Boulder, CO: Westview Press.

Bibliography

AAM/American Association of Museums. (2003). *Museums working in the public interest.* Retrieved May 27, 2004, from http://www.aam-us.org/resources/general/publicinterest.cfm.

Adams, W. (1995). Education for extinction: American Indians and the boarding school *experience.* Lawrence: University Press of Kansas.

Alexander, C., & Langer, E. (Eds.). (1990). Higher stages of human development: Perspectives on adult growth. New York: Oxford.

Anderson, J. (1988). *The education of blacks in the south, 1860–1935.* Chapel Hill: University of North Carolina Press.

Anderson, P., & Summerfield, J. (2004). In S. Steinberg & J. Kincheloe (Eds.). *19 urban questions: Teaching in the city.* New York: Peter Lang.

Anzaldúa, G. (1987). *Borderlands: The new mestiza = La frontera* (1st ed.). San Francisco: Spinsters/Aunt Lute.

Appadurai, A. (1996). *Modernity at large: Cultural dimensions of globalization.* Minneapolis: University of Minnesota Press.

Apple, M. (1993). The politics of official knowledge: Does a national curriculum make sense? *Teachers College Record, 95* (2), 222–241.

————. (1996). *Cultural politics and education.* New York: Teachers College Press.

————. (1996). Dominance and dependency: Situating *The Bell Curve* within the conservative restoration. In J. Kincheloe, S. Steinberg, & A. Gresson (Eds.), *Measured lies: The bell curve examined.* New York: St. Martin's Press.

————. (1999). Power, meaning, and identity: Essays in critical educational studies. New York: Peter Lang.

Aptheker, H. (1989). *The literary legacy of W.E.B. DuBois.* New York: Kraus International.

Arguelles, L. (2002). How do we live, learn and die: A teacher and some of her students meditate and walk on an engaged Buddhist path. In J. Miller & Y. Nakagawa (Eds.), *Nurturing our wholeness: Perspectives on spirituality in education* (pp. 285–303). Brandon, VT: Foundation for Educational Renewal.

Ark, T. (2002). The case for small high schools. *Educational Leadership, 59* (5), 55–59.

Aronowitz, S., & Giroux, H. (1993). *Education still under siege* (2nd ed.). Westport, CT: Bergan & Garvey.

Arrien, A. (2001). The way of the teacher: Principles of deep engagement. In L. Lantieri (Ed.), *Schools with spirit: Nurturing the inner lives of children and teachers* (pp. 148–157). Boston: Beacon Press.

Asgharzadeh, A., & Sefa Dei, G. (2001). The power of social theory: The anticolonial discursive framework. *Journal of Education Thought, 35* (3), 297–323.

Associated Press. (2003). *White teachers fleeing black schools!* Monday, January 13, 2003: CNN.com/education. Retrieved July 7, 2004, from http://www.cnn.com/2003/EDUCATION/01/13/resegregation. teachers.ap/.

Aveling, N. (2002). Student teachers' resistance to exploring racism: Reflections on "doing" border pedagogy. *Asia-Pacific Journal of Teacher Education, 30* (2), 119–130.

Ayers, W. (2000). Simple justice: Thinking about teaching and learning, equity and the fight for small schools. In W. Akers, M. Klonsky, & G. Lyon (Eds.), *A simple justice: The challenge of small schools.* New York: Teachers College Press.

Babb, F. (1989). *Between the field and the cooking pot: The political economy of marketwomen in Peru.* Austin: University of Texas Press.

Ball, A., & Heath, S. (1993). Dances of identity: Finding an ethnic self in the arts. In S. Heath & M. McLaughlin (Eds.), *Identity and inner-city youth: Beyond ethnicity and gender* (pp. 69–93). New York: Teachers College Press.

Bamburg, J. (1994). *Raising expectations to improve student learning.* Retrieved March, 2003, from http://www.ncrel.org/sdrs/areas/issues/educatrs/leadrshp/ie0bam.htm.

Bartky, J. (1955). The school of education and the university. *Journal of Higher Education, 26* (5), 254–260.

Bennett de Marrais, K., & LeCompte, M. (1995). *The way schools work: A sociological analysis of education.* White Plains, NY: Longman.

Bey, H. (2002). TAZ: The temporary autonomous zone. In S. Duncombe (Ed.), *Cultural resistance reader.* London: Verso.

Beyer, L., & Apple, M. (1998). *The curriculum: Problems, politics, and possibilities.* Albany: State University of New York Press.

Blau, P., & Dudley, O. (1967). *The American occupational structure.* New York: John Wiley & Sons.

Bloom, S. (1997). *Creating sanctuary: Toward the evolution of sane societies.* New York: Routledge.

Blush, S. (2001). *American hardcore: A tribal history.* Los Angeles, CA: Feral House.

Bodeau, D. (1999). *Metabeings and individuals: Aids and obstacles to growth.* Retrieved March, 2003, from http://www.gurus.com/dugdeb/essays/metabeings.html.

Borden, L. (2001). *Skateboarding, space, and the city: Architecture and the body.* New York: Berg.

Boudon, R. (1974). *Education, opportunity, and social inequality: Changing prospects in Western society.* New York: John Wiley & Sons.

Bourdieu, P., & Passeron, J. (1977). *Reproduction in education, society and culture.* London: Sage.

Bransford, J., Brown, A., & Cocking, R. (Eds.). (2000). *How people learn: Brain, mind, experience, and school (expanded edition).* Washington, DC: National Academy Press.

Brecht, B. (1964). A short description of a new technique of acting which produces an alienation effect. In *Brecht on Theatre.* John Willet, Trans. New York: Hill and Wang (pp. 136–147).

Brown, F. (1975). Assessment and evaluation of urban schools. *Journal of Negro Education,* (3), 377–384.

Brown, P. (2002, March 24). Latest way to cut grade school stress: Yoga. *New York Times,* p. 33.

Brown, R. (2002). Taming our emotions: Tibetan Buddhism and teacher education. In J. Miller & Y. Nakagawa (Eds.), *Nurturing our wholeness: Perspectives on spirituality in education* (pp. 3–12). Brandon, VT: Foundation for Educational Renewal.

Brown, W. (1995). *States of injury: Power and freedom in late modernity.* Princeton, NJ: Princeton University Press.

Bruner, J. (1996). *The culture of education.* Cambridge, MA: Harvard University Press.

Brunner, C., & Tally, W. (1999). *The new media literacy handbook: An educator's guide to bringing new media into the classroom.* New York: Doubleday.

Buckingham, D. (1993). *Children talking television: The making of television literacy.* London: Falmer Press.

————. (1996). *Moving images: Understanding children's emotional responses to television.* Manchester, UK: Manchester University Press.

———— (Ed.). (1998). *Teaching popular culture: Beyond radical pedagogy.* London: UCL Press.

————, & Sefton-Green, J. (1995). *Cultural studies goes to school: Reading and teaching popular media.* London: Taylor & Francis.

Bullock, H. (1967). *A history of negro education in the south: From 1619 to the present.* Cambridge, MA: Harvard University Press.

Burack, C. (1999, September). Returning meditation to education. *Tikkun.* Retrieved August 18, 2002, from http://www.findarticles.com/cf_)/m1548/5_14/56065507.

Burawoy, M., Blum, J., George, S., Gille, Z., Gowan, T., Haney, L., et al. (2000). *Global ethnography.* Berkeley: University of California Press.

Busch, C. (2003, July/August). It's cool to be grounded. *Yoga Journal,* 94–99, 154–156.

Bush, G.W. (2001, January 29). *No child left behind.* U.S. Department of Education. Retrieved February 18, 2002, from http://www.ed.gov/inits/nclb/index.html.

Bynoe, Y. (2004). *Stand & deliver: Political activism, leadership, and hip hop culture* (p. 158). New York: Soft Skull Press.

Cain, G. (1974). Socioeconomic background and achievement. *American Journal of Sociology, 79* (6), 1497–1509.

Callinicos, A. (1993). *Race and class.* London: Bookmarks.

Carvan, M., Nolen, A., & Yinger, R. (2002). *Power through partnership: The urban network for the improvement of teacher education.* Retrieved March, 2003, from http://www.urbannetworks.net/documents/tacte%20article,%20final%20revision%201-14-02.pdf.

Castañeda, I., & Zorn, D. (2001). *AAAE Arts Connections longitudinal study: A technical report.* Cincinnati, OH: University of Cincinnati Evaluation Services Center.

————, Zorn, D., Ray, G., Pangallo, M., Geresy, S., & Taylor, G. (2002). *An in-depth study to document how the arts make a difference in student learning.* Paper presented at the annual meeting of the American Educational Research Association, New Orleans, April 2002.

Catterall, J., Chapleau, R., & Iwanaga, J. (1999). Involvement in the arts and human development: General involvement and intensive involvement in music and theater arts. In E. Fiske (Ed.), *Champions of change* (pp. 1–18). Washington, DC: Arts Education Partnership.

————, & Waldorf, L. (1999). Chicago Arts Partnership in Education: Summary evaluation. In E. Fiske (Ed.), *Champions of change* (pp. 38–62). Washington, DC: Arts Education Partnership.

Chizhik, E. (2003). Reflecting on the challenges of preparing suburban teachers for urban schools. *Education and Urban Society, 35* (4), 443–461.

Chomsky, N. (2000). *Chomsky on miseducation.* New York: Rowman & Littlefield.

Churchill, W. (1996). *From a native son.* Boston: South End.

Clarke, J. (2002). The skinheads and the magical recovery of community. In Duncombe, S. (Ed.), *Cultural resistance reader.* London: Verso.

Cochran-Smith, M. (1995). Uncertain allies: Understanding the boundaries of race and teaching. *Harvard Educational Review, 65* (4), 541–570.

Coleman, J. (1966). *Equality of educational opportunity.* Washington, DC: U.S. Government Printing Office.

————. (1973). Review of *Inequality: A reassessment of the effect of family and schooling in America* by C. Jencks, M. Smith, H. Acland, M. Bane, D. Cohen, H. Gintis, et al. *American Journal of Sociology, 78* (6), 1523–1544.

————, et al. (1966). *Equality of educational opportunity.* U.S. Dept. of Health, Education, and Welfare, Office of Education. Washington, DC: U.S. Government Printing Office.

Cross, J. (1998). *Informal politics: Street vendors and the state in Mexico City.* Stanford, CA: Stanford University Press.

Crowell, S. (n.d.). *Case studies.* Center for Contemplative Mind. Retrieved May 30, 2004, from http://www. contemplativemind.org/resources/pubs/case_studies.pdf.

Csikszentmihalyi, M. (1996). *Creativity: Flow and the psychology of discovery and invention.* New York: HarperCollins.

Cuello, J. (1999). *Reconstructing the paradigm for teaching and learning at the university: Lessons from the field of an urban campus.* Retrieved March, 2003, from http://www.culma.wayne.edu/obs/reconstructing.htm.

DanceUSA. (2004). *Facts and figures.* Retrieved May 27, 2004, from http://www.danceusa.org.

Darling-Hammond, L. (1997). *The right to learn: A blueprint for creating schools that work.* San Franscisco: Jossey-Bass.

———, Ancess, J., & Ort, S. (2002). Reinventing high school: Outcomes of the coalition campus schools project. *American Educational Research Journal, 39* (3), 639–673.

Daspit, T. (2000). Rap pedagogies: "Bring(ing) the noise" of "knowledge born on the microphone" to radical education. In T. Daspit & J. Weaver (Eds.), *Popular culture and critical pedagogy: Reading, constructing, connecting.* New York: Falmer Press.

Deasy, R. (Ed.). (2002). *Critical links: Learning in the arts and student academic and social development.* Washington, DC: Arts Education Partnership.

DeChillo, S. (2002, December 14). Stretch. Pose. Rest. It's kindergarten yoga. *New York Times,* B1.

Delgado Bernal, D. (1998). Using a Chicana feminist epistemology in educational research. *Harvard Educational Review, 68* (4), 555–582.

Delpit, L. (1988). The silenced dialogue: Power and pedagogy in educating other people's children. *Harvard Educational Review, 58* (3), 280–298.

Denzin, N., & Lincoln, Y. (Eds.). (2000). *Handbook of qualitative research.* Thousand Oaks, CA: Sage.

De Soto, H. (1989). *The other path of development: The invisible revolution in the third world.* New York: Harper and Row.

Dewey, J. (1916). *Democracy and education.* New York: Free Press.

Dignard, L., & Havet, J. (1995). *Women in micro- and small-scale enterprise development.* Boulder, CO: Westview Press.

Dimitriadis, G. (2001). *Performing identity/performing culture: Hip hop as text, pedagogy, and lived practice.* New York: Peter Lang.

———, & McCarthy, C. (2001). *Reading and teaching the postcolonial: From Baldwin to Basquiat and beyond.* New York: Teachers College Press.

———, & Weis, L. (2001). Imagining possibilities with and for contemporary youth: (Re)writing and (re)visioning education today. *Qualitative Research, 1* (2), 223–240.

Dolby, N. (2000). Changing selves: Multicultural education and the challenge of new identities. *Teachers College Record, 102* (5), 898–912.

———. (2001). *Constructing race: Youth, identity, and popular culture in South Africa.* Albany: SUNY Press.

Doll, W. (1993). *A postmodern perspective on curriculum.* New York: Teachers College Press.

Dresch, S. (1975). A critique of planning models for postsecondary education: Current feasibility, potential relevance, and a prospectus for further research. *Journal of Higher Education, 46* (3), 245–286.

Dropkick Murphys. (2000). *Sing loud, sing proud* [CD]. Los Angeles: Hellcat Records.

Du Bois, W. (1920). Latin. *Crisis Magazine, 20* (3), 120.

———. (1961). *The souls of black folk.* Greenwich, CT: Fawcett Publications.

———. (1973). *The education of black people: Ten critiques, 1906–1960.* New York: Monthly Review Press.

⸻. (1986). *The souls of black folk.* New York: First Vintage Books/The Library of America Edition.

⸻. (1992). *Black reconstruction in America 1860–1880* (p. 184). New York: Free Press.

⸻. (1996). *The Philadelphia negro* (p. 388). Philadelphia: University of Pennsylvania Press.

⸻. (2002). *Dusk of dawn: An essay toward an autobiography of a race concept.* Piscataway, NJ: Transaction Publishers.

Duneier, M. (1999). *Sidewalk.* New York: Farrar, Strauss, & Giroux.

Edward, S. (1979). *Orientalism.* New York: Vintage Books.

⸻. (1993). *Culture and imperialism.* New York: Vintage Books.

Eisenhart, M. (2001). Educational ethnography past, present, and future: Ideas to think with. *Educational Researcher, 30* (8), 16–27.

⸻, & Finkel, E. (1998). *Women's science: Learning and succeeding from the margins.* Chicago: University of Chicago Press.

Eisner, E. (1994). *The educational imagination of the design and evaluation of school* (3rd ed.). New York: Macmillan.

Ellsworth, E. (1989). Why doesn't this feel empowering? Working through the repressive myths of critical pedagogy. *Harvard Education Review, 59* (3), 297–324.

Elmore, R. (1997). *Education policy and practice in the aftermath of TIMSS.* Retrieved March, 2003, from http://www.enc.org/TIMSS/addtools/pubs/symp/cd163/cd163.htm.

Evans, P., & Timberlake, M. (1980). Dependence, inequality, and the growth of tertiary: A comparative analysis of less developed countries. *American Sociological Review, 45,* 532–552.

Eyerman, R., & Jamison, A. (1998). *Music and social movements: Mobilizing traditions in the twentieth century.* Cambridge, UK: Cambridge University Press.

Fanon, F. (1991). *The wretched of the earth* (C. Farrington, Trans.). New York: Grove Press.

Fenwick, T. (2000). *Experiential learning in adult education: A comparative framework.* Retrieved March, 2003, from http://www.ualberta.ca/~tfenwick/ext/aeq.htm.

Fine, M. (2000). A small price to pay for justice. In W. Akers, M. Klonsky, & G. Lyon (Eds.), *A simple justice: The challenge of small schools.* New York: Teachers College Press.

⸻, & Weis, L. (1998). *The unknown city: Lives of poor and working-class young adults.* Boston: Beacon Press.

⸻, Centrie, C., & Roberts, R. (2000). Educating beyond the borders of schooling. *Anthropology & Education Quarterly, 31* (2), 131–151.

Fischer, N. (1998, Fall). Teaching meditation to young people. *Turning Wheel: Journal of the Buddhist Peace Fellowship,* 29–31.

Fiske, E. (Ed.). (1999). *Champions of change: The impact of the arts on learning.* Washington, DC: Arts Education Partnership and the President's Committee on the Arts and Humanities.

Fontana, D., & Slack, I. (1997). *Teaching meditation to children: Simple steps to relaxation and well-being.* London: Thorsons/HarperCollins.

Forbes, D. (2004). *Boyz 2 Buddhas: Counseling urban high school male athletes in the zone.* New York: Peter Lang.

⸻. (2004). What is the role of counseling in urban schools? In S. Steinberg & J. Kincheloe (Eds.), *Nineteen urban questions: Teaching in the city* (pp. 69–83). New York: Peter Lang.

Fordham, S. (1996) *Blacked out: Dilemmas of race, identity, and success at capital high.* Chicago: University of Chicago Press.

Frankenberg, R. (1993). *White women, race matters; the social construction of whiteness.* Minneapolis: University of Minnesota Press.

Frechtling, J., Killeen, D., & Perone, D. (2002). *Transforming education through the arts challenge*. Final evaluation report. Rockville, MD: Westat.

Freire, P. (1970). *Pedagogy of the oppressed*. New York: Continuum.

———. (1996). *Pedagogy of hope*. New York: Continuum.

———. (1996). *Pedagogy of the oppressed*. New York: Continuum.

———. (1998). *Pedagogy of freedom*. Lanham, MD: Rowman & Littlefield.

———. (1998). *Teacher as cultural workers: Letters to those who dare to teach*. Boulder, CO: Westview Press.

Fuhrman, S. (2002). *Urban education: Is reform the answer?* Retrieved March, 2003, from http://www.urbanedjournal.org/archive/issue%201/featurearticles/article0004.html.

Fukuyama, M., & Sevig, T. (1999). *Integrating spirituality into multicultural counseling*. Thousand Oaks, CA: Sage.

Gallagher, C. (1995). White reconstruction in the university. *Socialist Review, 94* (1 & 2), 165–187.

Garbarino, J. (2000). *Lost boys: Why our sons turn violent and how we can save them*. New York: Anchor.

Gardner, H. (1999). *The disciplined mind: What all students should understand*. New York: Simon & Schuster.

Gardner, P., Ritblatt, S., & Beatty, J. (2000). Academic achievement and parental involvement as a function of high school size. *The High School Journal, 83* (2), 21–27.

Gay, G., & Howard, T. (2000). Multicultural teacher education for the 21st century. *The Teacher Educator, 36* (Pt. 1), 1–16.

Geertz, C. (1963). *Peddlers and princes, social change and economic modernization in two Indonesian towns*. Chicago: University of Chicago Press.

Geneva, G. (2000). *Culturally responsive teaching*. New York: Teachers College Press.

Getz, A., & Gordhamer, S. (n.d.). *Interview on mindfulness and violent youth*. Retrieved November 4, 2003, from http://www.youthhorizons.org/interview/James/html.

Gilmore, P., & Glatthorn, A. (Eds.). (1982). *Children in and out of school: Ethnography and education*. Washington, DC: Center for Applied Linguistics.

Gilroy, P. (1993). *The black Atlantic: Modernity and double consciousness*. Cambridge, MA: Harvard University Press.

Giroux, H. (1994). *Disturbing pleasures: Learning popular culture*. New York: Routledge.

———. (1997). Rewriting the discourse of racial identity: Towards a pedagogy and politics of whiteness. *Harvard Educational Review, 67* (2), 285–320.

———, & McLaren, P. (1986). Teacher education and the politics of engagement: The case for democratic schooling. *Harvard Educational Review, 56* (2), 213–238.

Glazer, S. (1999). Conclusion: The heart of learning. In S. Glazer (Ed.), *The heart of learning: Spirituality in education* (pp. 247–250). New York: Tarcher.

Glickman, C. (2003). *Holding sacred ground: Courageous leadership for democratic schools*. San Francisco: Jossey-Bass.

Goodwin, L. (Ed.). (1997). *Assessment for equity and inclusion: Embracing all our children*. New York: Routledge.

Greene, M. (1995). *Releasing the imagination: Essays on education, the arts, and social change*. San Francisco: Jossey-Bass.

Gursky, D. (2002). Recruiting minority teachers. [Electronic version]. *American Teacher, 86* (February), 28–34. Retrieved July 8, 2004, from http://www.aft.org/pubsreports/american_teacher/feb02/feature.html.

Gutierrez, J. (2001). *Critical race narratives*. New York: New York University Press.

Haberman, M. (2002). *Achieving "high quality" in the selection, preparation, and retention of teachers*. EducationNews.org. Retrieved March, 2003, from http://www.educationnews.org.

———. (2004). *Urban education: The state of urban schooling at the start of the twenty-first century.* EducationNews.org. Retrieved March, 2003, from http://www.education news.org.

Halford, J. (1996). *Urban education: Policies of promise.* Retrieved March, 2003, from http://www.ascd.org/publications/infobrief/issue5.html.

Hall, J. (2001). *Canal town youth: Community organization and the development of adolescent identity.* Albany: SUNY Press.

Hall, P. (1999). The effects of meditation on the academic performance of African American college students. *Journal of Black Studies, 29* (3), 408–415.

Hamann, D., & Walker, L. (1993). Music teachers as role models for African-American students. *Journal of Research in Music Education, 41* (Winter), 303–314.

Hampel, R. (2002). Historical perspectives on small schools. *Phi Delta Kappan, 83* (5), 357–363.

Hanna, K. (2002). Interview in punk planet. In S. Duncombe (Ed.), *Cultural resistance reader.* London: Verso.

Hanrahan, M. (1998). *A legitimate place for intuition and other a-logical processes in research and hence in reports of research.* Paper Presented at 1998 Conference of Australian Association of Research in Education. Retrieved March, 2003, from http://www.aare.edu.au/98pap/han98331.htm.

Harding, S. (1998). *Is science multicultural? Postcolonialisms, feminisms, and epistemologies.* Bloomington: Indiana University Press.

Harland, J., Kinder, K., Lord, P., Stott, A., Schagen, I., & Haynes, J. (2000). *Arts education in secondary schools: Effects and effectiveness.* Berkshire, UK: National Foundation for Educational Research.

Harrison, F. (1991). Women in Jamaica's urban informal economy. In Mohanty, C., Russo, A., & Torres, L. (Eds.), *Third world women and the politics of feminism* (pp. 173–196). Bloomington: Indiana University Press.

Hart, T. (n.d.). *Case studies.* Center for Contemplative Mind. Retrieved May 30, 2004, from http://www.contemplativemind.org/resources/pubs/case_studies.pdf.

Heath, S. (1983). *Ways with words: Language, life, and work in communities and classrooms.* Cambridge, UK: Cambridge University Press.

———. (1991). Inner-city life to literature: Drama in language learning. *TESOL Quarterly, 27* (2), 177–192.

———. (1996). Ruling places: Adaptation in development by inner-city youth. In R. Jessor, A. Colby, & R. Schweder (Eds.), *Ethnography and human development: Context and meaning in social inquiry* (pp. 225–251). Chicago: University of Chicago Press.

———. (1999). Imaginative actuality: Learning in the arts during the nonschool hours. In E. Fiske (Ed.), *Champions of change* (pp. 19–34). Washington, DC: Arts Education Partnership.

———. (2001). Three's not a crowd: Plans, roles, and focus in the arts. *Educational Researcher, 30* (7), 10–17.

———, & McLaughlin, M. (Eds.). (1993). *Identity and inner-city youth: Beyond ethnicity and gender.* New York: Teachers College Press.

———, & McLaughlin, M. (1994). The best of both worlds: Connecting community schools and community youth organizations for all-day, all-year learning. *Educational Administration Quarterly, 30* (3), 278–300.

Hebdige, D. (2002). The meaning of MOD. In S. Duncombe (Ed.), *Cultural resistance reader.* London: Verso.

Helms J. (1990). *Black and white racial identity: Theory and research in counseling.* New York: Greenwood.

Henke, S. (2000). *Representations of secondary urban education: Infusing cultural studies into teacher education.* Unpublished doctoral dissertation, Miami University.

Herrnstein, R., & Murray, C. (1994). *The bell curve: Intelligence and class structure in America*. New York: Free Press.

Hess, A. (2000). Who leads small schools? Teacher leadership in the midst of democratic governance. In W. Akers, M. Klonsky, & G. Lyon (Eds.), *A simple justice: the challenge of small schools*. New York: Teachers College Press.

Hill, D., Sanders, M., & Hankin, T. (2002). Marxism, class analysis and postmodern-ism. In D. Hill, P. McLaren, & G. Rikowski (Eds.), *Marxism against postmodernism in educational theory*. New York: Lexington Books.

Hill, P., & Celio, M. (1998). *Fixing urban schools*. Washington, DC: Brookings Institute.

Hilliard, A., III. (1997). Language, culture, and the assessment of African American children. In L. Goodwin (Ed.), *Assessment for equity and inclusion: Embracing all our children*. New York: Routledge.

Hobsbawm, E. (2002). Primitive rebels. In S. Duncombe (Ed.), *Cultural resistance reader*. London: Verso.

Hodgkinson, H. (2002). Demographics in teacher education: An overview. *Journal of Teacher Education, 53* (2), 102–105.

Hoffman Davis, J. (2003, October 8). In defense of failure. *Education Week, 23* (6), pp. 28, 30.

Hollingshead, A. (1949). *Elmtown's youth: The impact of social classes on adolescents*. New York: John Wiley & Sons.

———. (1975). *Elmtown's youth and Elmtown revisited*. New York: John Wiley & Sons.

Holloway, D., & Krensky, B. (Eds.). (2001). The arts, urban education, and social change [Special issue]. *Education and Urban Society, 33* (4).

hooks, b. (1990). *Black looks*. New York: Routledge.

———. (1990). *Yearning*. New York: Routledge.

———. (1994). *Teaching to transgress: Education as the freedom of practice*. New York: Routledge.

Horn, R. (2000). *Teacher talk: A postformal inquiry into educational change*. New York: Peter Lang.

Horowitz, R. (2004). *Summary of large-scale arts partnership evaluations*. Washington, DC: Arts Education Partnership.

Howard, G. (1999). *We can't teach what we don't know*. New York: Teachers College Press.

Hudis, P. (2000). Can capital be controlled? *The Journal of Marxist-Humanism?* Retrieved April 20, 2001, from http://www.newsandletters.org/Issues/2000/April/4.00_essay.htm.

Hung, D., Bopry, J., Looi, K., & Koh, T. (2005). Situated cognition and beyond: Martin Heidegger on transformations in being and identity. In J. Kincheloe & R. Horn (Eds.), *Educational psychology: An encyclopedia*. Westport, CT: Greenwood.

Hurley, D. (2003). *Developing students as change agents: Urban education and reform*. Retrieved March, 2003, from http://www.eastern.edu/publications/emme/2003 spring/hurley.html.

Intrator, S. (2002). *Stories of the courage to teach: Honoring the teacher's heart*. San Francisco: Jossey-Bass.

Irvine, J. (1991). *Black students and school failure*. New York: Praeger.

Itzigohn, J. (2000). *Developing, poverty: The state, labor market deregulation, and the informal economy in Costa Rica and the Dominican Republic*. University Park: University of Pennsylvania Press.

Jacobs, J. (2004). *Dark age ahead*. New York: Random House.

James, J. (1997). *Transcending the talented tenth: Black leaders and American intellectuals*. New York: Routledge.

Jensen, A. (1969). How much can we boost IQ and scholastic achievement? *Harvard Educational Review, 39* (1), 1–23.

Joel, S. (2000). *Deculturation and the struggle for euality.* Burr Ridge, IL: McGraw-Hill High Education Press.

Johnson, J. (2002). Will parents and teachers get on the bandwagon to reduce school size? *Phi Delta Kappan, 83* (5), 353–356.

Jones, R. (2001, January/April). The liberatory education of the talented tenth: Critical consciousness and the continuing black humanization project. *The Negro Educational Review, 52* (1/2) 3–18.

Kabat-Zinn, J. (1994). *Wherever you go there you are: Mindfulness meditation in everyday life* (p. 21). New York: Hyperion.

Karabel, J., & Halsey, A. (1977). *Power and ideology in education.* New York: Oxford University Press.

Karenga, M. (1993). *Introduction to black studies* (2nd ed.). Los Angeles: University of Sankore Press.

Kase-Polisini, J. (Ed.). (1985). *Creative drama in a developmental context.* New York: University Press of America.

Kegan, R. (1994). *In over our heads: The mental demands of modern life.* Cambridge, MA: Harvard University Press.

Kelley, G. (1997). *From Vietnam to America: A chronicle of the Vietnamese immigration of the United States.* Boulder, CO: Westview Press.

Kent, J. (1968). The Coleman report: Opening Pandora's box. *Phi Delta Kappan, 49,* 242–245.

Kessler, R. (n.d.). *The teaching presence.* The PassageWays Institute. Retrieved September 25, 2002, from http://www.mediatorsfoundation.org/isel/articles. html.

————. (2000). *The soul of education: Helping students find connection, compassion, and character at school.* Alexandria, VA: ASCD.

Kincheloe, J. (1995). *Toil and trouble: Good work, smart workers, and the integration of academic and vocational education.* New York: Peter Lang.

————. (2003). Critical ontology: Visions of selfhood and curriculum. *JCT: Journal of Curriculum Theorizing, 19* (1), 47–64.

————. (2005). *Classroom teaching: An introduction.* New York: Peter Lang.

————. (2005). *Critical constructivism.* New York: Peter Lang.

Kincheloe, J., & Steinberg, S. (1993). A tentative description of post-formal thinking: The critical confrontation with cognitive theory. *Harvard Educational Review, 63* (3), 296–320.

————. (1997). *Changing multiculturalism.* Buckingham: Open University Press.

————. (1998). Addressing the crisis of whiteness: Reconfiguring white identity in pedagogy of whiteness. In J. Kinchloe, S. Steinberg, N. Rodriguez, & R. Chennault (Eds.), *White reign: Deploying whiteness in America* (pp. 3–29). New York: St. Martin's Griffin.

————, & Gresson, A. (Eds.). (1996). *Measured lies: The bell curve examined.* New York: St. Martin's Press.

————, & Hinchey, P. (1999). *The postformal reader: Cognition and education.* New York: Falmer Press.

————, & Villaverde, L. (Eds.). (1999). *Rethinking intelligence: Confronting psychological assumptions about teaching and learning.* New York: Routledge.

Kindlon, D., & Thompson, M. (2000). *Raising Cain: Protecting the emotional life of boys.* New York: Ballantine.

King, J. (1994). Dysconscious racism: Ideology, identity, and the miseducation of teachers. In L. Stone (Ed.), *The education feminism reader* (pp. 336–348). New York: Routledge.

————. (2000). *Race.* Mahwah, NJ: Lawrence Erlbaum Associates.

Kinnucan-Welsch, K. (2005). Reconsidering teacher professional development through constructivist principles. In J. Kincheloe & R. Horn (Eds.), *Educational psychology: An encyclopedia*. Westport, CT: Greenwood.

Klonsky, M. (2000). Grounded insights. In W. Akers, M. Klonsky, & G. Lyon (Eds.), *A simple justice: The challenge of small schools*. New York: Teachers College Press.

Klonsky, S. (2000). Art, with algebra, guards the gate. In W. Akers, M. Klonsky, & G. Lyon (Eds.), *A simple justice: The challenge of small schools*. New York: Teachers College Press.

———, & Klonsky, M. (1999). In Chicago: Countering anonymity through small schools. *Educational Leadership, 57* (1), 38–41.

Kozol, J. (1991). *Savage inequalities: Children in America's schools* (1st ed.). New York: Crown.

Krishnamurti, J. (2000). *On education*. Chennai, India: Krishnamurti Foundation India.

Ladson-Billings, G. (1994/1997). *The dreamkeepers: Successful teachers of African-American children* (1st and 2nd eds.). San Francisco: Jossey-Bass.

———, & Tate, W. (1995, Fall). Toward a critical race theory of education. *Teachers College Record, 97* (1), 47–68.

———. (2000). Fighting for our lives: Preparing teachers to teach African American students. *Journal of Teacher Education, 51* (3), 206–214.

Lantieri, L. (2001). A vision of schools with spirit. In L. Lantieri (Ed.), *Schools with spirit: Nurturing the inner lives of children and teachers* (pp. 7–20). Boston: Beacon.

Latham, A., Gitomer, D., & Ziome, R. (1999). What the tests tell us about new teachers. [Electronic version]. *Educational Leadership, 56*, 23–26.

Lavine-Rasky, C. (2000). Framing whiteness: Working through the tensions in introducing whiteness to educators. *Race, Ethnicity and Education, 3* (3), 271–292.

Lee, E., Menkart, D., & Okazawa-Rey, M. (Eds) (1999). Beyond heroes and holidays: A practical guide to K–12 anti-racist, multicultural education and staff development. Washington, DC: Network of Educators on the Americas.

Leonardo, Z. (2004). Race. In J. Kincheloe & D. Weil (Eds.), *Critical thinking and learning: An encyclopedia for parents and teachers*. Westport, CT: Greenwood.

Lepani, B. (1998). *Information literacy: The challenge of the digital age*. Retrieved March, 2003, from http://www.acal. edu.au/lepani.htm.

Lesko, N., & Bloom, L. (1998). Close encounters: Truth, experience and interpretation. *Curriculum Studies, 30* (4), 375–395.

———, & Bloom, N. (2000). The haunting of multicultural epistemology and pedagogy. In R. Mahalingam & C. McCarthy (Eds.), *Multicultural curriculum: New directions for social theory, practice and policy* (pp. 242–260). New York: Routledge.

Lester, J. (1971). *The seventh son: The thought and writings of W.E.B. DuBois* (Vol. II). New York: Vintage Books.

Levant, R. (1995). Toward the reconstruction of masculinity. In R. Levant. & W. Pollack (Eds.), *A new psychology of man* (pp. 229–251). New York: Basic.

Levine, W. (1996). *The opening of the American mind*. Boston: Beacon Press.

Levine-Rasky, C. (2000). Framing whiteness: Working through the tensions in introducing whiteness to educators. *Race, Ethnicity and Education, 3* (3), 271–292.

Levinson, B., & Holland, D. (1996). The cultural production of the educated person: An introduction. In B. Levinson, D. Foley, & D. Holland (Eds.), *The cultural production of the educated person: Critical ethnographies of schooling and local practices* (pp. 1–31). Albany: SUNY Press.

Lewis, A. (1954, May). *Economic development with unlimited supplies of labour, 22* (2), 139–191. The Manchester School of Economics and Social Studies.

———. (1980). The ritual process and community development. *Community Development Journal, 15* (3), 190–199.

Lewis, D. (1993). *W.E.B. DuBois: Biography of a race, 1868–1919.* New York: Henry Holt.

Lindsey L. (2000). *Sociology: Social life and social issues.* Upper Saddle River, NJ: Prentice Hall.

Loevinger, J., & Wessler, R. (1970). *Measuring ego development* (Vols. 1 & 2). San Francisco: Jossey-Bass.

Lomawaima, T. (1993). Domesticity in the federal indian schools: The power of authority over mind and body. *American Ethnologist, 20* (2), 227–240.

London, B., & Smith, D. (1988). Urban bias, dependence, and economic stagnation in non-core nations. *American Sociological Review, 53* (3), 454–463.

Lowe, S. (2001). The art of community transformation. *Education and Urban Society, 33* (4), 457–471.

Lyon, G. (2000). When *jamas* is enough: Creating a school for a community (a conversation with Tamara Witzl). In W. Akers, M. Klonsky, & G. Lyon (Eds.), *A simple justice: The challenge of small schools.* New York: Teachers College Press.

Macedo, D. (2002). The colonialism of the English only movement. *Education Research, 29* (3), 15–24.

MacLeod, J. (1987). *Ain't no makin' it: Leveled aspirations in a low-income neighborhood.* Boulder, CO: Westview Press.

———. (1995). *Ain't no makin' it: Aspirations and attainment in a low-income neighborhood.* Boulder, CO: Westview Press.

Madison, G. (1988). *The hermeneutics of postmodernity: Figures and themes.* Bloomington: Indiana University Press.

Mahiri, J. (1998). *Shooting for excellence: African American and youth culture in new century schools.* Urbana, IL: National Council of Teachers of English.

Malaki, A. (1996). *Development patterns in the commonwealth Caribbean: Jamaica and Trinidad and Tobago.* Institute of Latin American Studies. Stockholm: Almqvist & Wiksell International.

Malewski, E. (2001). Administration–Administrative leadership and public consciousness: Discourse matters in the struggle for new standards. In J. Kincheloe & D. Weil (Eds.), *Standards and schooling in the United States: An encyclopedia* (3 vols.). Santa Barbara, CA: ABC-Clio.

Mahalingham, R., & McCarthy, C. (2000). *Multicultural curriculum: New directions for social theory, practice and policy.* New York: Routledge.

Malott, C., & Peña, M. (2004). *Punk rocker's revolution: Pedagogy of gender, race and class.* New York: Peter Lang.

Marcus, G. (1986). Contemporary problems of ethnography in the modern world system. In J. Clifford & G. Marcus (Eds.), *Writing culture: The poetics and politics of ethnography* (pp. 165–193). Berkeley: University of California Press.

———. (1998). *Ethnography through thick and thin.* Princeton, NJ: Princeton University Press.

Marger, M. (2000). *Race and ethnic relations.* Belmont, CA: Wadsworth.

Marshall G. (1991). *Spirit of '69: A skinhead bible.* London: STP Publishing.

Massey, D. (1994). *Space, place, and gender.* Minneapolis: University of Minneapolis Press.

Mattera, P. (1985). *Off the books.* New York: St. Martin's Press.

May, T. (1993). *Between genealogy and epistemology: Psychology, politics, and knowledge in the thought of Michel Foucault.* University Park: Pennsylvania State University Press.

McCarthy, C. (1998). Living with anxiety: Race and the renarration of public life. In J. Kincheloe, S. Steinberg, N. Rodrigues, & R. Chennault (Eds.), *White reign: Deploying whiteness in America* (pp. 329–341). New York: St. Martin's Press.

McCartney, J. (1971). Effect of financial support on growth of sociological specialties. In E. Tiryakian (Ed.), *The phenomenon of sociology.* (pp. 395–406). New York: Appleton Century-Crofts.

McCoy, K. (1997). White noise—The sound of epidemic: Reading/writing a climate of intelligibility around the "crisis" of difference. *Qualitative Studies in Education, 10* (3), 333–347.

McDermott, P., & Rothenberg, J. (2000). Why urban parents resist involvement in their children's elementary education. *The Qualitative Report, 5* (3/4). Retrieved March, 2003, from http://www.nova.edu/ssss/qr/qr5-3/mcdermott.html.

McIntyre, A. (1997). Making meaning of whiteness: Exploring racial identity with white teachers. Albany: State University of New York Press.

———. (2002). Exploring whiteness and multicultural education with prospective teacher. *Curriculum Inquiry, 32* (1), 31–49.

McLaren, P. (1994). *Life in school: An introduction to critical pedagogy in the foundation of education.* White Plains, NY: Longman.

———. (1997). Decentering whiteness: In search of a revolutionary multiculturalism. In *Multicultural education, 1* (5), 12–15.

———. (1997). *Revolutionary multiculturalism: Pedagogies of dissent for the new millennium.* Boulder, CO: Westview Press.

———. (1997). Unthinking whiteness, rethinking democracy: Or farewell to the blonde beast; toward a revolutionary multiculturalism. *Educational Foundations, 11* (2), 5–39.

———. (2000). *Che Guevara, Paulo Freire, and the pedagogy of revolution.* New York: Rowman & Littlefield.

———. (2002). *Life in schools: An introduction to critical pedagogy in the foundations of education* (4th ed.). Boston: Allyn & Bacon.

———. (2002). Marxist revolutionary praxis: A curriculum of transgression. *Journal of Critical Inquiry into Curriculum and Instruction, 3* (3), 36–41.

———, & Farahmandpur, R. (2005). *Teaching against global capitalism and the new imperialism: A critical pedagogy.* New York: Rowman & Littlefield.

———, & Farahmandpur, R. (2002). Breaking signifying chains: A Marxist position on postmodernism. In D. Hill, P. McLaren, & G. Rikowski (Eds.), *Marxism against postmodernism in educational theory.* New York: Lexington Books.

———, & Giroux, H. (1997). *Writing from the margins: Geographies of identity and power.* Boulder, CO: Westview Press.

McLaughlin, M. (2001). Community counts. *Educational Leadership, 58* (7), 14–18.

———, & Irby, M. (1994). Urban sanctuaries: Neighborhood organizations that keep hope alive. *Phi Delta Kappan, 76* (4), 300–304.

———, Irby, M., & Langman, J. (1994). *Urban sanctuaries: Neighborhood organizations in the lives and futures of inner-city youth.* San Francisco: Jossey-Bass.

MDRC (Manpower Demonstration Research Corporation) for the Council of the Great City Schools. (2002). *Foundations for success: Case studies of how urban school systems improve student achievement.* Retrieved March, 2003, from http://www.cgcs.rg/reports/foundations.html.

Meditation benefits abound for schoolchildren, study finds. (2003, January 21). Medical College of Georgia. Retrieved July 26, 2003, from http://www.mcg.edu/news/2003.

Meier, D. (2002). Just let us be: The genesis of a small public school. *Educational Leadership, 59* (5), 76–79.

———. (2000). The crisis of relationships. In W. Akers, M. Klonsky, & G. Lyon (Eds.), *A simple justice: The challenge of small schools.* New York: Teachers College Press.

———, & Schwartz, P. (1995). Central Park East Secondary School: The hard part is making it happen. In M. Apple & J. Beane (Eds.), *Democratic education.* Alexandria, VA: Association for Supervision and Curriculum Development.

Michie, G. (2005). *See you when we get there: Teaching for change in urban schools.* New York: Teachers College Press.

Miles, R. (1987). *Capitalism and unfree labor: Anomaly or necessity?* New York: Tavistock.

Miller, J. (1994). *The contemplative practitioner: Meditation in education and the professions.* Westport, CT: Bergin & Garvey.

Miller, R. (1997). *What are schools for? Holistic education in American culture.* Brandon, VT: Holistic Education Press.

Milwaukee Symphony. (2004). *Education programs.* Retrieved May 12, 2004, from http://www.milwaukeesymphony.org.

Miron, L. (2004). How do we locate resistance in urban schools. In S. Steinberg & J. Kincheloe (Eds.), *19 urban questions: Teaching in the city.* New York: Peter Lang.

Moll, L., & Diaz, S. (1987). Change as the goal of education research. *Anthropology & _Education Quarterly, 18* (4), 287–299.

Moore, J. (2003). *Booker T. Washington, W.E.B. DuBois, and the struggle for racial uplift.* Wilmington, DE: Scholarly Resources.

Morgan, H. (1995). *Historical perspectives on the education of black children.* Westport, CT: Praeger.

Morrell, E. (2003). Legitimate peripheral participation as professional development: Lessons from a summer research seminar. *Teacher Education Quarterly.* Retrieved March, 2003, from http://www.findarticles.com/p/articles/mi_qa3960/is_200304/ai_ n9166599.

Morrison, T. (1992). *Playing in the dark: Whiteness in the literacy imagination.* Cambridge, MA: Harvard University Press.

Morrow, R., & Torres, C. (1995). *Social theory and education: A critique of theories of social and cultural reproduction.* Albany: State University of New York Press.

National Commission on Excellence in Education. (1983). *A nation at risk: The imperative for educational reform.* Washington, DC: Government Printing Office.

National Council for Accreditation of Teacher Education (NCATE). (2002). *Professional standards for the accreditation of schools, colleges and departments of education,* Washington, DC: NCATE.

Nations, C. (2005). Allowing children to make sense of our world: Accepting and embracing constructivist/engaged learning approaches to teaching and learning. In J. Kincheloe & R. Horn (Eds.), *Educational psychology: An encyclopedia.* Westport, CT: Greenwood.

Neary, M. (2002). Youth, training and the politics of "cool." In D. Hill, P. McLaren, & G. Rikowski (Eds.), *Marxism against postmodernism in educational theory.* New York: Lexington Books.

Nespor, J. (1997). *Tangled up in school.* Mahwah, NJ: Lawrence Erlbaum Associates.

Ng, J. (2003). Multicultural education in teacher training programs and its implications on preparedness for effective work in urban settings. In G. Lopez & L. Parker (Eds.), *Interrogating racism in qualitative research methodology.* New York: Peter Lang.

Nichols, B. (2003). *Demographic characteristics of arts attendance, 2002.* Research division note #82, July 2003. Washington, DC: National Endowment for the Arts.

———, & Charnoski, R. (Producer & Director). (2003). *Northwest* [Film]. New York: Charnoski Productions and Flexifilm.

Nieto, S. (1992). *Affirming diversity: The sociopolitical context of multicultural education.* New York: Longman.

———. (2003). *What keeps teachers going?* New York: Teachers College Press.

Nietzsche, F. (1996). *On the genealogy of morals a polemic: By way of clarification and supplement to my last book, Beyond good and evil.* Oxford: Oxford University Press.

Noddings, N. (2005). *The challenge to care in schools: An alternative approach to education* (2nd ed.). New York: Teachers College Press.

Norris, N. (1998). Curriculum evaluation revisited. *Cambridge Journal of Education, 28* (2), 207–219.

Novick, M. (1995). *White lies/white power: The fight against white supremacy and reactionary violence.* Monroe, ME: Common Courage Press.

Novick, P. (1988). *That noble dream: The "objectivity question" and the American historical profession.* Cambridge, UK: Cambridge University Press.

Ogbu, J. (1978). *Minority education and caste: The American system in cross cultural perspective.* San Diego: Academic Press.

O'Reilley, M. (1998). *Radical presence: Teaching as contemplative practice.* Portsmouth, NH: Boynton-Cook/Heinemann.

O'Sullivan, E. (1999). *Transformative learning: Educational vision for the twenty-first century.* New York: Zed.

Owen, D., & Doerr, M. (1999). *None of the above: The truth behind the SATs.* Lanham, MD: Rowman & Littlefield.

Palmer, P. (1998). *The courage to teach: Exploring the inner landscape of a teacher's life.* San Francisco: Jossey-Bass.

Perkins, D. (1994). *The intelligent eye: Learning to think by looking at art.* Santa Monica, CA: J. Paul Getty Trust.

———. (1995). *Outsmarting IQ: The emerging science of learnable intelligence.* New York: The Free Press.

Peterson, B. (1995). La escuela frantney: A journey toward democracy. In M. Apple & J. Beane (Eds.), *Democratic education.* Alexandria, VA: Association for Supervision and Curriculum Development.

Peterson, K. (1994). *Building collaborative cultures: Seeking ways to reshape urban schools.* Retrieved March, 2003, from http://www.ncrel.org.sdrs/areas/issues/educatrs/leadrship/le0pet. htm.

Pickering, J. (1999). The self is a semiotic process. *Journal of Consciousness Studies, 6* (4), 31–47.

Pipher, M. (1994). *Reviving Ophelia: Saving the selves of adolescent girls.* New York: Grosset/Putnam.

Podlozny, A. (2000). Strengthening verbal skills through the use of classroom drama: A clear link. *The Journal of Aesthetic Education, 34* (3–4): 239–276.

Pojman, L. (2001). *What can we know? An introduction to the theory of knowledge* (2nd ed.). Belmont, CA: Wadsworth.

Portes, A., Castells, M., & Benton, L. (1989). *The informal economy: Studies in advanced and less developed countries.* Baltimore, MD: Johns Hopkins University Press.

Prawat, R. (2000, August). The two faces of Deweyan pragmatism: Inductionism versus social constructivism. *Teachers College Record, 102* (4).

Pulido, L. (2001, Winter). To arrive is to begin: Benjamin Saenz's Carry me like water and the pilgrimage of origin in the borderlands. *Studies in Twentieth Century Literature, 25* (1), Special issue on Literature and Popular Culture of the U.S.-Mexican Border.

Purpel, D. (1989). *The moral and spiritual crisis in education: A curriculum for justice and compassion in education.* Granby, MA: Bergin & Garvey.

Quartz, K., Olsen, B. & Duncan-Andrade, J. (2003). *The fragility of urban teaching: A longitudinal study of career development and activism.* Retrieved March, 2003, from http:// www.idea.gseis.ucla. edu/publications/utec/reports/pdf.

Rakowski, C. (1994). *Contrapunto: The informal sector debate in Latin American perspectives.* New York: State University Press of New York.

Reddock, R. (1994). *Women, labor, and politics in Trinidad and Tobago.* London: Zed Books.

Reed, A., Jr. (1997). *W.E.B. Du Bois and American political thought* (p. 53). New York: Oxford University Press.

Reyhner, J. & Eder, J. (1989). A history of Indian Education. Billings, MT: Eastern Montana College Publication.

Rikowski, G. (2002). Education, capital and the transhuman. In D. Hill, P. McLaren, & G. Rikowski (Eds.), *Marxism against postmodernism in educational theory.* New York: Lexington Books.

Rist, R. (1970). Student social class and teacher expectations: The self-fulfilling prophecy in ghetto education. *Harvard Educational Review, 70* (3), 257–265.

Rockefeller, S. (1994). *Meditation, social change, and undergraduate education* (p. 4). The Contemplative Mind in Society Meeting of the Working Group. Retrieved September 20, 2000, from http://www.contemplativemind.org/Rockefellerpaper.htm.

Roman, L. (1993). White is a color! White defensivenss, postmodernism, and anti-racist pedagogy. In C. McCarthy & W. Crinchlow (Eds.), *Race, identity and representation in education.* New York: Routledge.

Rose, K. (2005). Philosophy matters for teachers. In J. Kincheloe (Ed.), *Classroom teaching: An introduction.* New York: Peter Lang.

———, & Kincheloe, J. (2003). *Art, culture, and education: Artful teaching in a fractured landscape.* New York: Peter Lang.

Ross, W. (2000). Diverting democracy: The curriculum standards movement and social studies education. In D. Hursh & W. Ross (Eds.), *Democratic social education: Social studies for social change* (pp. 43–63). New York: Falmer Press.

Rozman, D. (1994). *Meditating with children: The art of concentration and centering.* Boulder Creek, CA: Planetary.

Safa, H. (1995). Economic restructuring and gender subordination. In M. Smith & J. Feagin. (Eds.), *The capitalist city: Global restructuring and community politics* (pp. 252–274). New York: Basil Blackwell.

Saha, L., & Zubrzycki, J. (1997). Classical sociological theories of education. In L. Saha (Ed.), *International encyclopedia of the sociology of education.* Canberra, Australia: Pergamon.

Sanyal, B. (1991). Organizing the self-employed: The politics of the urban informal sector. *International Labor Review, 130,* 39–56.

Scheler, M. (1961). *Ressentiment* (W.W. Holdheim, Trans.). New York: Schocken Books.

Schick, C. (2000). By "virtue of being white": Resistance in anti-racist pedagogy. *Race, ethnicity and education, 3* (1), 84–102.

Schubert, W. (2000). John Dewey as a philosophical basis for small schools. In W. Akers, M. Klonsky, & G. Lyon (Eds.), *A simple justice: The challenge of small schools.* New York: Teachers College Press.

Schugurensky, D. (2000). *Citizenship learning and democratic engagement: Political capital revisited.* Retrieved November, 2004, from http://www.edst.educ.ubc.ca/aerc/2000/schugurenskyd1-final.PDF.

Sefton-Green, J. (Ed.). (1998). *Digital diversions: Youth culture in the age of multimedia.* New York: Routledge.

———. (1999). *Young people, creativity, and new technologies.* New York: Routledge.

Seidel, K. (1995). *Leaders' theatre: A case study of how high school students develop leadership skills through participation in theatre.* Unpublished doctoral dissertation, University of Cincinnati, Cincinnati, OH.

Shor, I. (1992). *Empowering education: Critical teaching for social change.* Chicago: University of Chicago Press.

Shujaa, M. (Ed.). (2001). *Beyond desegregation: The politics of quality in African-American schooling.* Thousand Oaks, CA: Corwin Press.

Simmer-Brown, J. (1999). Commitment and openness: A contemplative approach to pluralism. In S. Glazer (Ed.), *The heart of learning: Spirituality in education* (pp. 97–112). New York: Tarcher.

Sink, M. (2003, February 8). Yoga in Aspen public schools draws opposition. *New York Times,* p. 36.

Skinhead Reggae. (1999). On a Trojan box set (60768-02892). [CD]. London: Trojan Records.

Sleeter, C. (1993). How white teachers construct race. In C. McCarthy & W. Crinchlow (Eds.), *Race, identity and representation in education.* New York: Routledge.

————. (1996). *Multicultural education as social activism.* Albany: State University of New York Press.

————, & McLaren, P. (Eds.). (1995). *Multicultural education, critical pedagogy, and the politics of difference.* Albany: State University of New York Press.

Smith, D. (1996). *Third world cities in global perspective: The political economy of uneven urbanization.* Boulder, CO: Westview Press.

Smith, L. (1999). *Decolonizing methodologies: Research and indigenous peoples.* Dunedin, NZ: University of Otago Press.

Soja, E. (1989). *Postmodern geographies.* London & New York: Verso.

Soloman, R. (1990). Nietzsche, postmodernism, and resentment. In C. Koelb (Ed.), *Nietzsche as a postmodernist: Essays pro and contra* (pp. 267–293). Albany: State University of New York Press.

Sparks, D. (2003, Spring). Interview with Peter Block: The answer to "when?" is "now." *Journal of Staff Development, 24* (2), pp. 52–55. Retrieved May 30, 2004, from http://www.nsdc.org/library/publications/jsd/block242.cfm.

————. (2003, Summer). Honor the human heart: Schools have a responsibility to nurture those who work in them. Interview with Parker Palmer. *Journal of Staff Development, 24* (3), pp. 49–53. Retrieved October 17, 2003, from http://www.nsdc.org/library/publications/jsd/palmer243.html.

Spindler, G. (Ed.). (2000). *Fifty years of anthropology and education: 1950–2000.* Mahwah, NJ: Lawrence Erlbaum Associates.

Spirituality in leadership. (2002, September). *School Administrator.* Retrieved September 20, 2002, from http://www.aasa.org/publications/sa/2002_09.

Steinberg, S. (2001). *Multi/intercultural conversations: A reader.* New York: Peter Lang.

————, Kincheloe, J., & Hinchey, P. (1999). *The post-formal reader: Cognition and education.* New York: Falmer.

Stern, D. (2000). Practicing social justice in the high school classroom. In W. Akers, M. Klonsky, & G. Lyon (Eds.), *A simple justice: The challenge of small schools.* New York: Teachers College Press.

Sunker, H. (1994). Pedagogy and politics: Heydorn's survival through education and its challenge to contemporary theories of education (bildung). In S. Miedema, G. Bieste, & W. Wardekke (Eds.), *The politics of human science.* Brussels, Belgium: VUB Press.

Sussmann, L. (1967). Educational research programs of the office of education: An interview with Dr. R. Louis Bright, Associate Commissioner for Research. *Sociology of Education, 40* (2), 158–169.

Symarip. (1991). On *Skinhead moonstomp: The Album.* [CD]. London: Trojan Records, 10786-20564.

Takaki, R. (1993). *A different mirror: A history of multicultural America.* Boston: Little, Brown.

Tatum, B. (1997). *Why are all the black kids sitting together in the cafeteria? and other conversations about race.* New York: Basic Books.

Taylor, E. (2005). Transformative learning: Developing a critical worldview. In J. Kincheloe & R. Horn (Eds.), *Educational psychology: An encyclopedia.* Westport, CT: Greenwood.

Terman, M. (1923). *Intelligence tests and school reorganization.* New York. World Book.

Testing teacher candidates: The role of licensure tests in improving teacher quality. (n.d.). Retrieved May 30, 2004, from http://books.nap.edu/catalog/10090.html.

Thayer-Bacon, B. (2000). *Transforming critical thinking: Thinking constructively.* New York: Teachers College Press.

————. (2003). *Relational "(e)pistemologies."* New York: Peter Lang.

Thorndike, L. (1920). *Intelligence and its uses.* New York. Harper.

Timberlake, M., & Kentor, J. (1983). Economic dependence, overurban-ization, and economic growth: A study of less developed countries. *The Sociological Quarterly, 24,* 489–507.

Tobin, J. (2000). *"Good guys don't wear hats". Children's talk about the media.* New York: Teachers College Press.

Tripp, A. (1997). Changing the rules: The politics of liberalization and the urban informal economy in Tanzania. Berkeley, Los Angeles, & London: University of California Press.

Trueba, E. (1999). *Latinos unidos: From cultural diversity to politics of solidarity.* Lanham, MD: Rowman & Littlefield.

Tunks, J. (1997). *The partnership assessment project: Changing the face of American education.* Evaluation report. Dallas, TX: Partnership for Arts, Culture, & Education.

University of Cincinnati Evaluation Services Center. (2000, 2001, 2002, 2003). *Evaluation reports on the art in the market project prepared for the Community Design Center.* Cincinnati, OH: Author.

Urban Teacher Collaborative, The. (2000). *Urban teacher challenge report, council of the great city schools.* Retrieved January 22, 2003, from http://www.cgcs.org.

U.S. Department of Education, National Center for Education Statistics. (1999). *Elementary school arts education survey: Fall 1999.* Fast Response Survey System. FRSS 67. Washington, DC: National Center for Education Statistics.

U.S. Department of Education, National Center for Education Statistics. (1999). *Secondary school arts education survey: Fall 1999.* Fast Response Survey System. FRSS 67. Washington, DC: National Center for Education Statistics.

U.S. Department of Education, Office of Educational Research and Improvement. (1999). *The NAEP 1997 arts report card.* Washington, DC: National Center for Education Statistics.

USSR (Urban Schools Symposium Report). (1998). *Relationship, commun-ity, and positive reframing: Addressing the needs.* Retrieved March, 2003, from http://www.inclusiveschools.org/procsho.htm.

Vaughn, K., & Winner, E. (2000). SAT scores of students who study the arts: What we can and cannot conclude about the association. *The Journal of Aesthetic Education, 34* (3–4), 77–89.

Wallace, C. (1987). *For richer, for poorer.* New York: Tavistock.

Wang, M., & Kovach, J. (1996). Bridging the achievement gap in urban schools: Reducing educational segregation and advancing resilience-promoting strategies. In B. Weil, D. (2001). World class standards? Whose world, which economic classes, and what standards? In J. Kincheloe & D. Weil (Eds.), *Standards and schooling in the United States: An encyclopedia.* (3 vols.). Santa Barbara, CA: ABC-Clio.

Wasley, P., & Lear, R. (2001). Small schools, real gains. *Educational Leadership, 58* (6), 22–27.

Watkins, W. (2001). *The white architects of black education: Ideology and power in America, 1865–1954.* New York: Teachers College Press.

Weiler, J. (2000). *Codes and contradictions: Race, gender identity, and schooling.* Albany: SUNY Press.

Weiner, L. (1993). *Preparing teachers for urban schools: Lessons from thirty years of school reform.* New York: Teacher College Press.

———. (1999). *Urban teaching: The essentials.* New York: Teachers College Press.

Weis, L. (1990). *Working-class without work: High school students in a de-industrializing economy.* New York: Routledge.

———, & Fine, M. (Eds.). (2000). *Construction sites: Excavating race, class, and gender among urban youth.* New York: Teachers College Press.

———, & Fine, M. (2001). Extraordinary conversations in public schools. *International Journal of Qualitative Studies in Education, 14* (4), 497–524.

Weitz, J. (1996). *Coming up taller: Arts and humanities programs for children and youth at risk.* Washington, DC: President's Committee on the Arts and Humanities.

Welch, N. (Ed.). (1995). *Schools, communities, and the arts: A research compendium.* Washington, DC: National Endowment for the Arts.

Werner, C. (1999). *A change is gonna come: Music, race & the soul of America.* New York: Penguin.

Wertsch, J. (1998). *Mind as action.* New York: Oxford.

West, C. (1993). *Race matters.* Boston: Beacon Press.

Wilber, K. (1998). *The marriage of sense and soul: Integrating science and religion.* New York: Broadway.

Wilber, K. (2000). *Integral psychology: Consciousness, spirit, psychology, therapy.* Boston: Shambhala.

Willis, P. (1976). *Learning to labor: How working class kids get working class jobs.* New York: Columbia University Press.

———. (1977). *Learning to labour: How working-class kids get working-class jobs.* Westmead, England: Saxon House.

Winant, H. (1997). Whiteness and contemporary U.S. racial politics. In M. Fine, L. Weis, L. Powell, & L. Wong (Eds.). *Off white: Readings on race, power, and society* (pp. 40–56). New York: Routledge.

Yasin, S. (1999). The supply and demand of elementary and secondary school teachers in the United States. *ERIC Digest.* [Electronic version]. Washington, DC: ERIC Clearinghouse on Teaching and Teacher Education. Retrieved June, 2004, from http://www.ericdigests.org/2000-3/demand.htm.

Yon, D. (2000). *Elusive culture: Schooling, race, and identity in global times.* Albany: SUNY Press.

Young, M., & Rosick, J. (2000). Interrogating whiteness. *Educational Researcher, 29* (2) 39–44.

Zajonc, A. (2003, Winter). Spirituality in higher education: Overcoming the divide. *Liberal Education, 89* (1), 50–58. Retrieved November 21, 2005, from http://www.findarticles.com/p/articles/mi_m0NKR/is_1_89/ai_99907663.

Zeichner, K. (1996). Closing the achievement gap: Opportunity to learn, standards and assessment. In B. Williams (Ed.), *Closing the achievement gap: A vision for changing beliefs and practices.* Alexandria, VA: Association for Supervision and Curriculum Development.

Zellner, W. (1995). *Countercultures: A sociological analysis.* New York: St. Martin's Press.

Index

About the Contributors

CHRISTINE ANDERSON is currently serving as the Executive Director of the Milwaukee Partnership Academy (MPA). The purpose of the MPA is to enhance the quality of teaching and learning in the Milwaukee Public Schools (MPS). The 2003 Wisconsin PK-16 Leadership Council awarded Dr. Anderson and the MPA a "Program of Distinction" award as an urban initiative that clearly represents the best of educational collaboration by bringing together a diverse group of leaders from the area public schools, public and private postsecondary education sectors, the local education association and school board, as well as industry and business. She has worked in MPS since 1974 in various capacities—as a classroom teacher, drug resource coordinator, human relations specialist, and teacher-leader of the Home and Hospital Instruction Program. She has received many teaching awards including a Kohl Fellowship, MPS High School Teacher of the Year in 1990, and most recently, the National High School Association Wisconsin Educator of the Year, 1998–1999. From 1979 to 1982, she served as president of the Milwaukee Teachers' Education Association. Her area of emphasis has always been developing teacher-leaders and embedding professional development at schools. She has chaired professional development teams that include work on teacher emeritus and mentoring programs, developing Goals for 2000, and the development of a teacher center. She has presented at numerous conferences and has been recognized by *Milwaukee Magazine* as an educator who will influence education in Milwaukee. Dr. Anderson received a PhD from the University of Wisconsin-Milwaukee in 1990 in Urban Education with a minor in Industrial and Labor Relations. In 2006, the U.S. Postal Service named Dr. Anderson a "Woman putting a Stamp on Metro Milwaukee in Education."

PHILIP M. ANDERSON is Professor of Urban Education and Executive Officer of the PhD Program in Urban Education at the Graduate Center of the City University of New York and Professor of Secondary Education and Youth Services at Queens College/CUNY. He has produced numerous publications on the teaching of literary reading, the English curriculum, cultural theories and schooling, teacher preparation, and curriculum theory and praxis.

MARY M. ATWATER is a professor in the Science Education Department at the University of Georgia. With her strong physical science background, she has designed and conducted professional development activities for urban elementary and middle school teachers that focused on enhancing both science content knowledge and pedagogical content knowledge. In addition, she has been very active in developing standards for teachers of early adolescents with the National Board of Professional Teaching Standards. Her research focuses on the socio-cultural-political factors that influence science teaching and learning.

DAVID BARONOV is Associate Professor and Chair of the Sociology Department at St. John Fisher College in Rochester, New York. He has recently published *Conceptual Foundations of Social Research Methods* (2004, Paradigm). In addition, he has published numerous chapters and articles in *Radical Pedagogy, Caribbean Studies, Socialism and Democracy,* and *The Discourse of Sociological Practice.*

LINDA B. BENBOW is a PhD candidate (ABD) in the Sociology Department at the Graduate School and University Center, CUNY, and has fulfilled the requirements for the Women's Certificate Program. She teaches as a full-time lecturer in the Sociology and Black Studies Departments at the State University of New York at New Paltz. Her areas of concentration are organizational effectiveness, race and ethnicity, women and work, and stratification. Linda's in-progress dissertation, near completion, is an ethnographic study of diversity in the workplace entitled *Race, Class, and Gender in a Federal Bureaucracy: The Paradoxes of Diversity.* She has developed and taught the following: Introduction to Sociology, Social Inequality, Sociology of Children, Contemporary Social Issues in the Black Community, Black and Latino Leadership, and Social Problems. Linda has cotaught an introduction to women's studies course, Women: Images and Realities.

GRACE BENIGNO is a doctoral student in the Department of Curriculum and Instruction at the University of Maryland at College Park with a research interest in mathematics education.

DONALD BLUMENFELD-JONES is the Lincoln Associate Professor for Ethics and Education at Arizona State University. He specializes in arts-based education research, ethics and classroom discipline, hermeneutics, and critical social theory and curriculum. He has published in such journals as the *Journal of Curriculum Theorizing, Educational Theory, Journal of Thought, Journal of Qualitative Studies in Education,* and *Qualitative Inquiry.* He also has numerous book chapters dealing with dance curriculum, ethics and curriculum, and arts-based education research. Prior to his academic career, he danced professionally for twenty years, studying, performing, and choreographing modern dance in New York City. He has performed, choreographed, and taught throughout the United States and Canada.

THOMAS BRIGNALL III received his PhD in Sociology from Western Michigan University. He currently teaches at Tennessee Technical University in the Department of Sociology and Political Sciences. His research interests are currently in education inequality, race relations, political movements, pop culture, and the social implications of the Internet. His primary teaching interests are in sociological theory, race/class/gender, mass media, technology and society, and music in social movements.

SHORNA BROUSSARD is currently an Assistant Professor in the Department of Forestry and Natural Resources at Purdue University. Dr. Broussard has an extensive background in educational program evaluation, a field of study that focuses on evaluating the process and outcomes of educational strategies. Prior work has included a national program evaluation of Natural Resource Extension programs, environmental education curriculum development and evaluation with urban youth, and innovative program design and development to reach underserved audiences. Dr. Broussard is the Communications and Educations Editor of the *Journal of Forestry* and her published works include papers in the *Journals of Forestry Extension* and several book chapters in *Conserving Biodiversity in Agricultural Landscapes (2004).*

ANTHONY L. BROWN is a doctoral candidate in the Department of Curriculum & Instruction at the University of Wisconsin-Madison. A former elementary school teacher and school administrator, his research interests include teacher pedagogy, multicultural education, and the educational history of African Americans. His current research examines the social and academic interactions between African-American male teachers and African-American male students.

KEFFRELYN D. BROWN is a doctoral candidate in the Department of Curriculum and Instruction at the University of Wisconsin-Madison. She has worked as an elementary and middle school teacher, as well as a school administrator and curriculum consultant/writer. Her current research focuses on how multiple educational sites conceptualize the ideas of risk and academic achievement.

PATRICIA BURDELL is an Associate Professor in the Teacher Education and Professional Department at Central Michigan University in Mount Pleasant Michigan. She taught middle school and high school for twenty years in Lansing, Michigan, prior to obtaining her doctorate in curriculum and instruction from the University of Wisconsin at Madison in 1993. Her interests are in the critical analysis of the curriculum of adolescents and young adults in secondary schools; reflective engagement in teacher education curriculum and practice; and issues related to the use of personal narrative as a methodology in educational literature.

MALCOLM B. BUTLER is a former middle school and high school mathematics and science teacher. Dr. Butler is currently an Assistant Professor in the Science Education Department at the University of Georgia. Prior to the University of Georgia, he spent time on the faculty at Texas A&M University-Corpus Christi. He also spent two years as a Mathematics and Science Program Specialist with the Southeast Eisenhower Regional Consortium for Mathematics and Science Education. In this capacity, Dr. Butler spent part of his time providing technical assistant and professional development to rural and urban communities across the southeastern United States.

SHIRLEY BYNUM is a Program Specialist for Career-Technical Education in Winston-Salem/Forsyth County Schools, Winston-Salem, NC. Dr. Bynum is responsible for curriculum, current research, and safety issues in the program areas of Business and Marketing Education, Career Management, Family and Consumer Sciences, and Health Occupations. Dr. Bynum earned her doctorate in curriculum and teaching with a curriculum specialist license, and a postbaccalaureate certificate from the Women's Studies Program at the University of North Carolina, Greensboro. Her research interests include black spiritual women, outreach ministries, power of relationships, and curriculum.

KAREN CADIERO-KAPLAN is Associate Professor in the Policy Studies in Language and Cross Cultural Department in the College of Education at San Diego State University. She has published articles in the areas of critical literacy, language policy, and critical issues of technology in K–12 classrooms. She recently published a book, *The Literacy Curriculum and Bilingual Education: A Critical Examination,* with a focus on research on literacy curriculum and programming in schools.

JOSEPH CARROLL-MIRANDA was born and raised in San Juan, Puerto Rico. He was and is seriously involved in student movements and student government for more than a decade in Puerto Rico, Latin America, and with Global Youth. Joseph earned his BA from the University of Puerto Rico in 1998. In addition, he earned his MA in Curriculum and Instruction from New Mexico State University. Currently he is a semester short of the ABD designation for a doctorate in Curriculum and Instruction, focusing on Learning Technologies with a minor in Critical Pedagogy.

RONNIE CASELLA is Associate Professor of Educational Foundations and Secondary Education at Central Connecticut State University. His research interests include violence and conflict resolution, urban education, and globalization. He is the author of *"Being Down": Challenging Violence in Urban Schools* and *At Zero Tolerance: Punishment, Prevention, and School Violence* and of articles that have appeared in *The Urban Review,*

Teachers College Record, Urban Education, Anthropology and Education Quarterly, and other journals. He is on the Advisory Committee for the Safe Schools and Communities Coalition of the Governor's Prevention Partnership for Connecticut and has worked closely with various community and peace groups.

IMELDA CASTAÑEDA-EMENAKER earned her doctoral degree in educational foundations from the University of Cincinnati. Dr. Castañeda-Emenaker is a researcher, evaluation specialist, teacher, and experienced administrator. Her areas of interest and research are in multicultural issues, alternative education, and integrated curriculum. As an Asian, Dr. Castañeda-Emenaker brings her multicultural perspectives into her various endeavors. She is currently working as consultant and evaluator for seven alternative schools in different counties of Ohio. In the area of integrated curriculum, Dr. Castañeda-Emenaker had been involved with the evaluation of an arts integrated curriculum program in Greater Cincinnati for six years. She wrote articles, technical reports, and presented papers in professional conferences along the areas of multicultural issues, alternative education, and integrated curriculum. Her administrative experience includes managing a college, directing outreach programs and service learning, and administering a restaurant school for street children in the Philippines. Dr. Castañeda-Emenaker is currently a research associate, evaluation specialist, and adjunct professor at the University of Cincinnati.

LESLEY COIA is an Associate Professor and the Director of Teacher Education Programs at Agnes Scott College. She taught English (7–12) in London and East Anglia, and English as a Foreign Language for Kursverksamheten, the extramural department of Stockholm University in Sweden. She received her PhD in Philosophy of Education from the University of London Institute of Education. Her research interests include self-study practices in teacher education, feminist philosophy, and autoethnography. Her work has been published in *The National Reading Conference Yearbook, Perspectives on Urban Education,* and *The Encyclopaedia of Life Writing.*

WILLIAM CRAIN is Professor of Psychology at The City College of New York and the editor of the journal *Encounter: Education for Meaning and Social Justice.*

MYRON H. DEMBO is the Stephen Crocker Professor in Education in the Rossier School of Education at the University of Southern California. He is a fellow in the American Psychological Association and an associate editor of the *Elementary School Journal* and *Journal of College Reading and Learning.Behavior.* Professor Dembo specializes in the areas of learning and motivation with a focus on teaching students how to become more self-regulated learners. He has written three books and more than 75 research articles on the teaching-learning process. His educational psychology textbook, *Applying Educational Psychology,* is now in its fifth edition. His most recent book is *Motivation and Learning Strategies for College Success: A Self-Management Approach* (2nd ed.).

GENE DIAZ is a visual artist and educational ethnographer who teaches courses in curriculum theory, arts-based research, and critical ethnography at Lesley University. A Fulbright Scholar in Medellin, Colombia, in 2002, she collaborated with Zayda Sierra in teaching and research at the Universidad de Antioquia. In 2004 she coedited, with Martha McKenna, *Teaching for Aesthetic Experience,* based on the work of Maxine Greene, published by Peter Lang.

ANNE DICHELE is an Associate Professor of Reading and Language Arts at Quinnipiac University, Hamden, Connecticut, in the Master of Arts in Teaching Program, Division of Education. Dr. Dichele was previously a Reading Consultant for the Boston School system and an elementary school teacher.

GREG DIMITRIADIS is an Associate Professor in the Department of Educational Leadership and Policy at the University at Buffalo, SUNY.

DANIEL J. DONDER is currently principal of Riverside University High School in the Milwaukee Public Schools. He is former Director of Strategic Planning and Community Outreach for the Milwaukee Public Schools. He served as the district's external point of contact with community groups, businesses, and government entities and serves as the communication link between the superintendent and other administrators, city and county offices, and schools. He provides collaborative leadership with the partners of the Milwaukee Partnership Academy. Dr. Donder received a PhD in 1984 at the University of Illinois at Urbana-Champaign with an emphasis on special education and school administration. He has worked in many educational settings with the Milwaukee Public Schools: as a special education teacher, special education supervisor, middle school principal, and high school principal. A strong advocate for special education needs, he has presented at national conferences and published research-based articles and chapters pertaining to education of students with severe handicaps in regular education settings and articles pertaining to proactive administrative strategies to ensure the success of students with disabilities in regular education classrooms. He has also presented at national conferences pertaining to social justice issues and the critical need for students to enroll and pass algebra as a gate-keeper for high school graduation and opportunities for success in post high school. He is an arts advocate and promoted the arts as principal at Lincoln Middle School of the Arts and Milwaukee High School of the Arts and has also presented at national conferences illustrating the relationship of students' involvement in arts and the positive relationship to academic achievement. Dr. Donder is currently an active participant in professional organizations pertaining to middle level education and numerous boards of directors for local arts organizations. In addition, he has been the recipient of local awards for educational leadership.

JOANNE KILGOUR DOWDY is an Associate Professor at Kent State University, Ohio. A graduate of Juilliard School in the theatre division, Dr. Dowdy continues to use her drama training to prepare teachers for the literacy classroom and as a performer who facilitates writing development through interactive workshops. Her major research interests include documenting the experiences of black women involved in education from adult basic literacy to higher education. Her first book is a volume coedited with Dr. Lisa Delpit, titled The Skin that We Speak: Thoughts on Language and Culture in the Classroom (The New Press). Her second book, GED Stories: Black Women & Their Struggle for Social Equity, is published by Peter Lang.

TIBBI DUBOYS earned a Bachelor's degree in Classics at Brooklyn College, a Master's degree in Counseling and Guidance at Hunter College, and a PhD in Counselor Education at Fordham University. Prior to joining the faculty in the School of Education at Brooklyn College, she taught third, fourth, and sixth grades in public schools in Brooklyn. She found Social Studies least focused upon in elementary schools, and brought to the college her interest in teacher's interpretations of the social science disciplines. She has often spoken publicly about the Holocaust, and has published in this area as well. She is interested in the ways in which oppression has influenced and affected the lives of children. She is completing a book about Holocaust education, and is planning another. She is an Associate Professor in the School of Education at Brooklyn College of the City University of New York.

JEFFREY M. R. DUNCAN-ANDRADE is Assistant Professor of Raza Studies and Education Administration and Interdisciplinary Studies, and Co-Director of the Educational Equity Initiative at San Francisco State University's Cesar Chavez Institute. Duncan-Andrade's research interests and publications span the areas of urban school-

ing and curriculum change, urban teacher retention and development, critical pedagogy, and cultural and ethnic studies. He is currently completing a co-authored book
on effective uses of critical pedagogy in the secondary classroom and a book on the
role of youth culture in the culture of schools and the classroom.

MOSTAFA MOUHIE EDDINE was born and raised in Casa Blanca, Morocco. He
received his undergraduate degree in psychology and a master's in education at University of Massachusetts, Amherst. He is currently working on his PhD in curriculum
and instruction with a major in critical pedagogy and a minor in teaching English as a
second language from New Mexico State University.

GUSTAVO E. FISCHMAN is an assistant professor in the Division of Curriculum and
Instruction at Arizona State University. His research interests are in the areas of
comparative and international education, gender studies, and qualitative studies in
education. Dr. Fischman is the author of two books and several articles on Latin
American education, teacher education, cultural studies and education, and gender
issues in education. He is associate editor of the online journals Reseñas Educativas/
Education Review and Archivos Analíticos de Políticas Educativas/Education Policy
Analysis Archives.

DAVID FORBES teaches school counseling in the School of Education, Brooklyn
College/CUNY. He is the author of *Boyz 2 Buddhas: Counseling Urban High School Male
Athletes in the Zone* (2004, Peter Lang) and *False Fixes: The Cultural Politics of Drugs,
Alcohol, and Addictive Relations* (1994, SUNY Press). He worked in a school-based sub-
stance abuse prevention program in Brooklyn and practices meditation and yoga.

LUIS ARMANDO GANDIN earned a PhD at the University of Wisconsin-Madison
and is Professor of Sociology of Education in the School of Education of the Federal
University of Rio Grande do Sul in Porto Alegre, Brazil. His research interests are in
the areas of critical analysis of educational policy, curriculum theory, and education
for transformation. Dr. Gandin has published three books, collaborated on chapters in
books, and written articles in academic journals in Brazil, Australia, Portugal, the
United States, and the United Kingdom. He is editor of the journal Currículo sem
Fronteiras (http://www.curriculosemfronteiras.org), a free-access, peer-reviewed
academic journal, with many articles available both in Portuguese and in English.

HOLLYCE C. GILES is Associate Professor in the School of Education at Brooklyn
College, City University of New York. Dr. Giles has served as Education Advisor with
the Industrial Areas Foundation, and is currently a Senior Research Fellow with the
Public Education Association, and is currently a Senior Research Fellow at the Institute for Education and Social Policy at New York University. Her research and publications focus on the social and psychological dimensions of community organizing
initiatives to reform schools. She holds a Master of Divinity degree from Union Theolog-
ical Seminary and a PhD in Counseling Psychology from Teachers College, Columbia
University, and is a psychologist in private practice.

MARIE GIRONDA is a 31-year-veteran English Honors and Advanced Placement
teacher in a magnet high school in the same district where coauthor John Pascarella
teaches. She is a PhD candidate in modern history and literature at Drew University in
Madison, New Jersey.

MERRYL GOLDBERG is a Professor of Visual and Performing Arts at California State
University San Marcos (CSUSM), where she teaches courses on arts and learning, and
music. She is also Founder and Director of Center ARTES (Art, Research, Teaching,
Education, and Schools) at CSUSM, an organization whose mission is to restore arts
education to schools and communities in California. She also oversees the Arts and
Lectures Series for the university. Merryl is a professional saxophonist and recording

artist. She toured internationally for 13 years with the Klezmer Conservatory Band, and has recorded more than a dozen CDs with Vanguard Records, Rounder Records, and other labels. Her publications include the books *Teaching English Language Learners through the Arts: A SUAVE Experience* (2004, Allyn & Bacon), *Integrating the Arts: An Approach to An Integrated Approach to Teaching and Learning in Multicultural and Multilingual Settings*, 3rd edition (2006, Allyn & Bacon), and *Arts as Education* (1992, Harvard Educational Review), as well as articles and book chapters on learning through the arts. She is the recipient of Spencer, John D. and Catherine T. MacArthur, and Fulbright-Hays Foundations grants relating to her work with arts in the schools. Her program, SUAVE, is the recipient of the U.S. Department of Education Model Arts grant and numerous California Arts Council and California Department of Education grants. Merryl lives in southern California with her daughter, Liana Cai Goldberg.

MORDECHAI GORDON is an Associate Professor of Education in the Division of Education at Quinnipiac University, Hamden, Connecticut. He is the editor of *Hannah Arendt and Education: Renewing our Common World* (2002, Westview Press) and author of numerous articles in journals such as *Educational Theory* and *Encounter: Education for Meaning and Social Justice*.

MERIDITH GOULD has more than 15 years' experience working with inner-city youth. She is a diversity, conflict resolution, violence prevention, leadership, communication, and anger-management trainer. She has worked for many nonprofit and public policy organizations as a program associate, consultant, lobbyist, and researcher. She is an adjunct professor at Spelman College, Emory University, and Southern Polytechnical College in Atlanta, Georgia, while completing her dissertation. She has designed and conducted numerous trainings for youth and educators. Meridith earned a BA in sociology with a concentration in racial and ethnic relations, an MS in dispute resolution, and is ABD with a PhD in conflict analysis and resolution.

ERIC HAAS is a lawyer and Assistant Professor of Education Policy at the University of Connecticut. His research interests include education law and media presentations of education issues.

SILVERIO HARO teaches part-time for California State University at San Marcos and Palomar College. His experience focuses on issues of equity and access, with special attention to attrition and persistence among university students, precollegiate programming for underrepresented groups, and leadership development and capacity-building among minority-based community organizations. His areas of research include campus climate assessment, aspects of institutional quality within higher education, and educational outcomes assessment.

KECIA HAYES is currently a PhD candidate and MAGNET Scholar at the CUNY Graduate Center. Her research focuses on how social policies and practices impact the educational experiences of children and parents of color in urban communities. kecia's dissertation examines the educational experiences of court-involved youth. She has taught graduate courses at the International Center for Cooperation and Conflict Resolution of Teachers College, Columbia University, and was an educational consultant with the NYU School of Education Metropolitan Center, as well as the Center for Social and Emotional Education. She is a founding Trustee of Harlem Episcopal School. kecia has provided research assistance for *The Colors of Excellence: Hiring and Keeping Teachers of Color in Independent Schools* by editors Pearl Rock Kane and Alfonso J. Orsini, coauthored a chapter in *19 Urban Questions: Teaching in the City* by editors Shirley Steinberg and Joe Kincheloe, and is an editor of two forthcoming texts *Metropedagogy: Power, Justice, and the Urban Classroom* from Sense Publishers, and *City Kids: Understanding, Appreciating, and Teaching Them* from Peter Lang Publishing.

FRANCES HELYAR is a doctoral student in Urban Education and Leadership at City University of New York. She is also a broadcaster, an elementary school teacher, and a substitute teacher.

RAYMOND A. HORN, JR., is a retired public school educator and Assistant Professor of Education and Director of the Interdisciplinary Doctor of Education Program for Educational Leaders at Saint Joseph's University. Dr. Horn has numerous publications in the fields of educational leadership, teacher education, and curriculum studies. His most recent books are *Understanding Educational Reform: A Reference Handbook* and *Standards Primer*. Dr. Horn's research interests include critical theory, cultural studies, and educational change and reform.

CLAUDIA HUIZA holds a BA in Spanish and English and American Literature and a Master's degree in Comparative Literature from the University of California at San Diego (UCSD). She is ABD in Literature and Cultural Studies at UCSD. She teaches at National University, American Intercontinental University, and Kaplan University.

CHANNELLE JAMES is a lecturer at the University of North Carolina at Greensboro in the Department of Business Administration. Dr. James teaches undergraduate courses in business administration and works primarily with freshmen business majors. Dr. James earned her doctorate in curriculum and teaching/cultural studies and a postbaccalaureate certificate in Women's Studies at the University of North Carolina at Greenboro. Her research areas include diversity, cultural studies, and ethics and justice in business practices.

GAETANE JEAN-MARIE is an Assistant Professor at Florida International University, Department of Educational Leadership and Policy Studies. Dr. Jean-Marie teaches graduate courses in leadership and education, and school personnel management in the Educational Leadership/Administration program area. Dr. Jean-Marie earned her doctorate in curriculum and teaching/cultural studies with a postbaccalaureate certificate from the Women's Studies Program at the University of North Carolina, Greensboro. Her research interests include women and educational leadership, urban school reform, and issues of equity and social justice.

KAREN EMBRY JENLINK is Dean of the School of Education at St. Edward's University in Austin, Texas. She currently serves as associate editor of *Teacher Education and Practice* and recently published her second book, *Portraits of Teacher Preparation: Learning to Teach in a Changing America*. Her research focuses on teacher preparation, urban education, teacher identity, and leadership.

PATRICK M. JENLINK is a Professor of Doctoral Studies in the Department of Secondary Education and Educational Leadership, as well as the Director of the Educational Research Center at Stephen F. Austin State University in Nacogdoches, Texas. Currently, his teaching emphasis in doctoral studies includes courses in ethics and philosophy of leadership, critical studies in politics and policy, and dynamics of change. Dr. Jenlink's research interests include politics of identity, social systems design and change, cultural-historical activity theory, democratic education and leadership, and postmodern inquiry methods. He has authored numerous articles, guest-edited journals, authored or coauthored numerous chapters in books, and edited or coedited several books. Currently he serves as editor of *Teacher Education & Practice* and as coeditor of *Scholar-Practitioner Quarterly*. His most recent books are *Dialogue as a Collective Means of Communication* (Kluwer Publishing) and *Portraits of Teacher Preparation: Learning to Teach in a Changing America* (Rowman & Littlefield, 2005). Dr. Jenlink's current book projects include the coedited *Scholar-Practitioner Leadership: A Post-formal Inquiry* (forthcoming from Peter Lang) and *Developing Scholar-Practitioner Leaders: The Empowerment of Educators* (forthcoming from Falmer Press).

MARINA KARIDES is an Assistant Professor at Florida Atlantic University. She has conducted research on street vendors in the The Republic of Trinidad and Tobago and The Republic of Cyprus. She is currently working on a book about Port of Spain street vendors, globalization, and the construction of space.

JOE L. KINCHELOE holds the Canada Research Chair in Education at McGill University in Montreal. He is the author of numerous books and articles about pedagogy, research, education and social justice, issues of cognition and cultural context, and educational reform.

TRICIA KRESS is a third-year doctoral student in the Urban Education Department at The Graduate Center of the City University of New York and she is a doctoral fellow sponsored by The Discovery Institute at The College of Staten Island, CUNY. She began working with educational technology in 1994 when she designed *The Magic Rabbit*, an interactive CD-ROM combining silent video with text to help demonstrate English verb tense changes to ASL (American Sign Language) students. In 1998 she began working as an adjunct professor teaching composition and college writing for the English Department at The College of Staten Island and Kean University. Two years later, she returned to her roots and began teaching Computers for Teachers and Computers for Teachers on Sabbatical. Currently, she is involved with The Discovery Institute's Curriculum Writing Workshops for in-service teachers, and has organized a group of teachers to write lessons specifically geared to incorporating computers into the New York City public high school English curriculum.

ROBERT LEHMANN is past president of the Milwaukee Teachers' Education Association, an organization that represents more than 8,000 educators in the Milwaukee Public Schools system. He began his teaching career with MPS in 1972 and has taught English and reading at both the middle and the high school levels. Prior to assuming his duties as MTEA president in 2001, Mr. Lehmann was coordinator of the MPS/MTEA TEAM Program, a nationally acclaimed peer review program that the union and district developed jointly in 1996. He returned to this position in 2005, following his presidency. His leadership vision is founded on the belief that public education unions must be lead partners in shaping educational improvement.

TONDRA L. LODER is currently an Assistant Professor in the Educational Foundations Program in the School of Education at the University of Alabama at Birmingham. Her research examines the influence of social change and public policy on the lives of urban educators and urban education from the theoretical and methodological perspectives of the life course and life history.

MARVIN LYNN is an Assistant Professor of Minority and Urban Education in the Department of Curriculum and Instruction at the University of Maryland at College Park. His research explores race, urban schooling, and the work and lives of black male teachers. His work has been influential in expanding the discourse on critical race theory and education. Among several articles published in this area, his article "Toward a Critical Pedagogy" has been widely used in a number of disciplines to help draw important links between race and teaching. He has published articles in *Urban Education*, *Review of Research in Education*, *Educational Philosophy and Theory*, and others. This year, his articles will appear in such journals as *Teachers College Record*, *Qualitative Studies in Education*, and *Educational Theory*. He is cofounder and director of the Minority and Urban Education program in the Department of Curriculum and Instruction at the University of Maryland.

CURRY MALOTT is professor of education in a number of colleges and universities throughout New York City and the state. His research interests include the social studies, Marxism, and the counterhegemonic reality and potential of countercultural formations as spaces of resistance. Included in his list of publications is the recently published book, *Punk Rocker's Revolution: A Pedagogy of Race, Class, and Gender* (2004). Malott continues to ride his skateboard and produce music under the banner of what he calls "the Punk Army."

TIM MAY earned degrees at the London School of Economics and Political Science (1985) and Universities of Surrey (1986) and Plymouth (1990). Tim has authored, co-authored, and edited books on social theory, methodology, methods and philosophy of social science, organizational transformation, and thinking sociologically. He is series editor of *Issues in Society* (McGraw-Hill/Open University Press) and Director of the Centre for Sustainable Urban and Regional Futures (www.surf.salford.ac.uk), where he conducts research into urban policy, universities and regionalization, science policy, knowledge production and transfer, and economic and social development.

COLLEEN MITCHELL is an MA student in the Department of Urban Planning at the University of Maryland at College Park.

RONALD L. MIZE is currently Assistant Professor of Latino Studies and Development Sociology at Cornell University. He was the main Principal Investigator, from 2000 to 2004, for the CSU-San Marcos-San Diego Head Start Higher Education Partnership, funded by the DHHS-Administration on Children Youth and Families. He previously taught sociology, ethnic studies, and history at the University of Saint Francis-Fort Wayne, CSU-San Marcos, University of California–San Diego, Southwestern College, Colorado State University, and University of Wisconsin–Rock County. His research focuses on the historical and contemporary lived experiences of Chicano/a and Mexican immigrant communities. He has published in *Latino Studies Journal, Cleveland State Law Review, Ambulatory Pediatrics, Contemporary Sociology, Rural Sociology,* and several encyclopedias.

CAROL A. MULLEN is Associate Professor of leadership studies at the University of South Florida. Her fields of research include mentorship and diversity, and she supervises the Writers in Training (WITs), a thriving doctoral cohort. Dr. Mullen has published more than 130 journal articles and book chapters and, as guest editor, 11 special issues of academic journals. This award-winning qualitative researcher has also published nine books, most recently *A Graduate Student Guide* (2006, Rowman & Littlefield), as well as *Climbing the Himalayas of School Leadership* (2004, ScarecrowEducation), as well as *Fire and Ice* and *The Mentorship Primer* (2005, Peter Lang). Dr. Mullen is editor of the refereed international journal *Mentoring & Tutoring* (Carfax Publishing/Taylor & Francis Group).

ANTHONY NAVARRETE is a doctoral candidate in Literature at the University of California at San Diego (UCSD). He was program manager for the California State University–San Marcos Head Start program between 2000 and 2004. He currently teaches in the writing program at UCSD.

ALBERTO M. OCHOA is Professor and Chair of the Department of Policy Studies in Language and Cross-Cultural Education in the College of Education at San Diego State University. Since 1975, he has worked with more than sixty school districts, providing technical assistance in the areas of language policy and assessment, bilingual instructional programs, curriculum programming, staff development, community development, organizational development and school climate, program management, and monitoring and evaluation. His research interests include public equity, school desegregation, language policy, critical pedagogy, student achievement, and parental leadership.

EDWARD M. OLIVOS is an Assistant Professor in the Division of Teacher Education at California State University–Dominguez Hills. He has published in the areas of critical literacy, parent participation, critical pedagogy, and biliteracy issues of K–12 classrooms. He taught elementary school in bicultural communities for more than ten years in San Diego.

CYNTHIA ONORE is a Professor in the Department of Curriculum and Teaching at Montclair State University in New Jersey. During her tenure as Director of the Center of Pedagogy at Montclair State, Dr. Onore created the Urban Teaching Academy, a program designed to recruit, prepare, and support teachers for New Jersey's urban schools. A former high school English teacher in Newark and New York City, Dr. Onore was founding director of teacher education at The New School University. She has also been a faculty member in English Education at The City College of New York and Teachers College. Her research interests include urban teacher education, professional development for school leadership and change, and collaboration in teacher education.

GLORIA PARK is a doctoral student in the Department of Curriculum and Instruction at the University of Maryland at College Park, with a research interest in teaching English as a second language.

PRIYA PARMAR is an Assistant Professor of Adolescence Education at Brooklyn College-CUNY. Professor Parmar's scholarly interests include critical and multiple literacies, multicultural education, youth and hip-hop culture, and other contemporary issues in the field of cultural studies in which economic, political, and social justice issues are addressed. Professor Parmar's published scholarly works include "Critical Thinking and Rap Music: The Critical Pedagogy of KRS-One" in *The Encyclopedia of Critical Thinking* (2004, Greenwood) and *Encyclopedia of Contemporary Youth Culture*, coedited with Shirley Steinberg and Birgit Richard (Greenwood Publishing, 2005). Her forthcoming book, *Rapping Against the Grain: The Pedagogy of an Urban Griot: KRS-One*, will be published by Sense Publishers in 2006.

JOHN PASCARELLA is a first-year English teacher at a magnet high school in an inner-city community in northern New Jersey and a part-time PhD candidate in Urban Education at The City University of New York Graduate Center. He is also a published writer and assistant editor of *Taboo: The Journal of Culture and Education.*

MICHAEL A. PETERS is Professor of Education at the University of Illinois at Urbana-Champaign and Adjunct Professor at the Faculty of Education, the University of Auckland (New Zealand), and School of Communication Studies at the Auckland University of Technology. He has research interests in educational theory and policy and in contemporary philosophy. He has published more than thirty books in these fields, including *Poststructuralism and Educational Research* (2004); *Critical Theory and the Human Condition* (2003); *Futures of Critical Theory* (2004); *Poststructuralism, Marxism and Neoliberalism: Between Theory and Politics* (2001); *Nietzsche's Legacy for Education: Past and Present Values,* (2001); *Wittgenstein: Philosophy, Postmodernism, Pedagogy* (1999) with James Marshall; *Poststructuralism, Politics and Education* (1996); *Curriculum in the Postmodern Condition* (2000), and *Education and the Postmodern Condition* (1995).

LINDA POST is Chairperson and Associate Professor in the Department of Curriculum and Instruction at the University of Wisconsin-Milwaukee. As such, she provides leadership in all teacher education programs and has worked extensively in the area of selection and retention of teachers for children in urban poverty. Over the past six years, Dr. Post has been in a leadership role in the development of alternative certification programs nationally. Her Metropolitan Multicultural Teacher Education Program is regarded as a model of excellence by the National Association for Alternative Certification. She has been a resource in the development and implementation of the Milwaukee Teacher Education Center. Dr. Post is currently the Director of the Urban

Network to Improve Teacher Education (UNITE) and also serves as the Great Cities Universities (GCU) team leader for the Milwaukee Partnership Academy (MPA) at UW-Milwaukee.

MARLEEN C. PUGACH is Professor of Teacher Education in the Department of Curriculum and Instruction at the University of Wisconsin-Milwaukee and Director of the Collaborative Teacher Education Program for Urban Communities. She earned her PhD at the University of Illinois at Urbana-Champaign in 1983. Her scholarly interests include the preparation of teachers for urban schools, school-university partnerships, and building collaborative relationships between the preparation of special and general education teachers. Dr. Pugach has authored and coauthored numerous articles and book chapters on special education and teacher education. She is coauthor of *Collaborative Practitioners, Collaborative Schools*, and coeditor of *Teacher Education in Transition* and *Curriculum Trends, Special Education, and Reform*. She is a member of the American Educational Research Association (AERA) and is chapter author for AERA's Panel on Research in Teacher Education. Dr. Pugach was the principal investigator of the PT3 *Technology and Urban Teaching Grant* and is currently coprincipal investigator of the Carnegie Corporation Teachers for a New Era project, both at the University of Wisconsin-Milwaukee. In February, 1998, she received the Margaret Lindsey Award from the American Association of Colleges for Teacher Education for her contributions to research in teacher education.

VICTORIA RAMIREZ is the School Programs Manager at the Museum of Fine Arts, Houston, where she manages museum and school collaborations including the development of teacher programming and curriculum materials. She is also pursuing her doctoral degree in social education at the University of Houston. She has a master of arts in museum education from the George Washington University and a bachelor's degree in art history from the University of Maryland.

DAVID REED is an Administrator of Distance Learning, Saturday School Programs, and Secondary Summer School for the Gilbert Public School District in Gilbert, Arizona. He earned his Bachelor of Science degree in Occupational Education from Southern Illinois University, a Master of Education degree in Curriculum and Instruction from Arizona State University, and is currently a PhD student in Educational Leadership and Policy Studies in the College of Education at Arizona State University.

PATRICIA RIVAS-McCRAE studied Latin American Studies at San Diego State University. Inspired by her work with Head Start, she is working toward a degree in Early Education. Upon completion of the CSU-San Marcos Head Start grant, she returned to San Diego Hospice and Palliative Care, where she worked with the HIV/AIDS Case Management Program.

ALFONSO RODRIGUEZ is In-Kind Co-Principal Investigator and Director of Training, Research, and Evaluation for Neighborhood House Association Head Start Program of San Diego County. Dr. Rodriguez has been involved with research and training in Head Start for the past 24 years.

JILL ROGERS graduated from a dual degree program at Columbia University's Law School and Teachers College in May 2004. During 2003, she was a coordinator of Legal Outreach's Summer Law Institute where she taught eighth-graders about the law and being a lawyer. Before moving to New York she became a certified teacher while at Northwestern University, and taught high school English briefly at the Latin School of Chicago. She thanks L'Tanya Evans, Daniel Rubin, Sara Schwebel, Julia Heaton, Jane Spinak, Douglas Rogers, and Nancy Rogers for their help with this book's chapter, "Tolerance with Children: A Critique of Zero Tolerance in School Discipline."

KAREL ROSE is Professor of Education and Women's Studies at the City University of New York. (CUNY) (Brooklyn College) and is a member of the doctoral faculty at the CUNY Graduate Center. She has worked with teachers at all levels in the United States and abroad, and lectures widely on women's issues. Dr. Rose's publications include books on literacy and African-American literature, and articles on feminism, writing, the arts, and teacher education. Her most recent book, the coauthored publication *Arts, Culture and Education: Artful Teaching in a Fractured Landscape*, was published in 2003. Dr. Rose's primary research interests are the arts and social issues and university faculty development. She was honored by Brooklyn College with the Teacher of Excellence Award and in 2005 received the Tow Award for Distinguished Teaching.

WOLFF-MICHAEL ROTH is Lansdowne Professor of Applied Cognitive Science at the University of Victoria, Canada. His research interests are broad and focus on knowing and learning across contexts of human social life (formal education, workplace, mundane life) and across the lifespan. Together with Ken Tobin, he has conducted extensive research on teaching in urban schools in Philadelphia. Roth has published 16 books and more than 300 articles and chapters. His recent publications include *Rethinking Scientific Literacy* (2004), *Toward an Anthropology of Graphing* (2003), *Being and Becoming in the Classroom* (2002), and *Talking Science: Language and Learning in Science Classrooms* (2005).

AMANDA M. RUDOLPH earned her PhD in Curriculum and Instruction with an emphasis in arts education from the University of Arkansas. She is currently an Assistant Professor at Stephen F. Austin State University in Nacogdoches, Texas.

ROBERT RUEDA is a Professor in the area of Educational Psychology at the Rossier School of Education at the University of Southern California. His research has focused on the sociocultural basis of learning as mediated by instruction, with a focus on reading and literacy in English learners, students in at-risk conditions, and students with mild learning handicaps. He has most recently been affiliated with two major national research centers, CREDE (Center for Excellence, Diversity, and Education at the University of California at Santa Cruz) and CIERA (Center for the Improvement of Early Reading Achievement at the University of Michigan), and serves on the Advisory Board of CRESST (Center for Research on Evaluation, Standards, and Student Testing at the University of California at Los Angeles). His most recent work has focused on how paraeducators mediate instruction and provide cultural scaffolding to English learners and on issues of reading engagement among inner-city immigrant students in a central city community. He has consulted with a variety of professional, educational, and government organizations, has spoken at a wide range of professional meetings, and has published widely in the previously mentioned areas. He served as a panel member on the National Academy of Science Report on the Overrepresentation of Minority Students in Special Education and is currently serving as a member of the National Literacy Panel (SRI International and Center for Applied Linguistics) looking at issues in early reading with English language learners.

REBECCA SÁNCHEZ is a doctoral student in the Department of Curriculum and Instruction at New Mexico State University. Her specialization area is critical pedagogy and her minor area is linguistics. Her research interests are in critical teacher development, democratic education, and critical theory. Rebecca is the coordinator of a project that aims to recruit, retain, and fund teachers returning to the university for MA-level degrees in bilingual education and as Teachers of English to Speakers of Other Languages (TESOL).

RUPAM SARAN is an elementary school teacher with the New York City Department of Education. Ms. Saran is a migrant from India and a doctoral student at The Graduate Center, City University of New York. Her research is on Asian-Indian students and the complexities of positive stereotyping. She is on the math committee for professional development of early childhood teachers. Rupam Saran is a recipient of the CUNY Writing Fellowship dissertation award for the 2005–06 academic year.

ROSLYN ABT SCHINDLER is Associate Professor and deputized Chair in the Department of Interdisciplinary Studies in the College of Liberal Arts and Sciences at Wayne State University (Detroit, Michigan). She publishes in the fields of interdisciplinary studies, adult learning, and Holocaust Studies, and is past president of the Association for Integrative Studies. She is coeditor, with Joachim Dyck, Martin Herman, and Marvin Schindler, of the two-volume *Festschrift, University Governance and Humanistic Scholarship: Studies in Honor of Diether Haenicke* (2002).

KENT SEIDEL is Assistant Professor with the Educational Administration and Urban Education Leadership graduate programs at the University of Cincinnati (Ohio) and serves as Executive Director for the Alliance for Curriculum Reform, a collaborative project of more than 20 national education organizations. He holds a PhD in Education Research and Theatre Education. Dr. Seidel was editor and contributing author for *Assessing Student Learning: A Practical Guide* (2000). He has also written on program evaluation and student assessment for the National Association of Secondary School Principals and the Association for Supervision and Curriculum Development, and has a book in publication on the use of student achievement data in school improvement. He has written on performing arts research for the *New Handbook of Research on Music Teaching & Learning* and contributed articles to *Arts Education Policy Review* and the national journal *Teaching Theatre*. Dr. Seidel has consulted on development of arts education standards and assessments for six states and several urban districts, as well as numerous schools and community arts organizations. He was one of 25 National Steering Committee members overseeing the development of the National Assessment of Educational Progress exams for the arts and one of six authors of the *National Standards for Arts Education* in theatre.

JUDITH J. SLATER is Professor of Education at Florida International University where she teaches courses in curriculum theory, evaluation, and organizational culture. She is the author of Anatomy of a Collaboration and Acts of Alignment, and is coeditor of The Freirean Legacy: Educating for Social Justice, Pedagogy of Place and the forthcoming Teen Life in Asia.

ANTHONY TADDUNI served as an AmeriCorps member in Atlanta Public Schools for two years, where he trained inner-city students in peer mediation and engaged students in enrichment programming focusing on human rights, diversity, leadership, and community service. He is a member of the Atlanta chapter of the National Coalition Building Institute (NCBI). Anthony also serves on the steering committee for Southern Truth and Reconciliation (STAR), a nonprofit agency that aims to aid communities in addressing histories of racial and ethnic violence through community education and community-building events. He is a graduate of Emory University.

MONICA TAYLOR is currently an Assistant Professor in the Department of Curriculum and Teaching in the College of Education and Human Services at Montclair State University in Montclair, New Jersey. She received her doctorate at the University of Arizona in Language, Reading, and Culture. Her research interests include autobiography as a reflective tool for teachers, self study, feminist pedagogy, teaching for social justice, new literacies and adolescent culture, and professional development school partnerships.

DEIDRE ANN TYLER is an Associate Professor of Sociology at Salt Lake Community College and an Adjunct Assistant Professor of Sociology at the University of Utah. Her areas of interest include education, black families, and gender. She is a motivational speaker and the author of *A Woman's Guide to Setting Boundaries*.

LYNNE A. WEIKART entered academia as an Associate Professor of Public Adminis- tration at Baruch College School of Public Affairs after a dintinguished career in New York State and City government. Specializing in urban budgeting and finance, Dr. Weikart has delivered lectures and presentations on urban issues at New York's Non- profit Connection, Progressive Urban Agenda for the New Millennium, and Interna- tional Center for Advanced Studies and at numerous conferences. Dr. Weikart was also Executive Director of City Project, a nonprofit fiscal think tank that advocates equity and social justice in the allocation of government resources. She is the author of several articles on urban budgeting and finance issues.

LOIS WEIS is Distinguished Professor of Sociology of Education at the University at Buffalo, State University of New York. She is author or coauthor of numerous books pertaining to race, social class, gender, and schooling in the United States. Her most recent books include *Class Reunion: The Remaking of an American White Working Middle Class* (Routledge, 2004); *Working Method: Research and Social Justice* (with Michelle Fine, Routledge, 2004); *Silenced Voices and Extraordinary Conversations: Re-Imagining Schools* (Teachers College Press, 2003), and *Beyond Black and White: New Faces and Voices in U.S. Schools* (State University of New York Press, 1997, with Maxine Seller). Her newest collection, *Beyond Silenced Voices: Class, Race, and Gender in United States Schools,* was released by SUNY Press in 2005. Dr. Weis sits on numerous editorial boards and is editor of the *Power, Social Identity, and Education* book series with SUNY Press.

JEN WEISS is a doctoral candidate in Urban Education at the City University of New York Graduate Center. She is Founder of Urban Word NYC, an afterschool program for teenagers based in New York City, and the coauthor of *Brave New Voices: Teaching Spoken Word Poetry* (2001, Heinemann). Recipient of the Graduate Center Dissertation Research Grant (2006–2007), she researches urban youth, literacy, and surveillance.

GREG WIGGAN is an Assistant Professor of Sociology at Salem College in North Carolina. His research interests include student achievement and educational policy studies in urban communities or in an urban sociological context. He is also interested in racial and ethnic relations and the racialization of the social class system. An addi- tional principal concern is imperialism and globalization in developing countries. He is interested in the role of the World Trade Organization, the International Monetary Fund, and the World Bank in creating public policies in developing countries.

A. DEE WILLIAMS is a doctoral student in the Department of Curriculum and Instruction at the University of Maryland at College Park, with a research interest in urban teacher education.